BUSINESS ANALYTICS
Communicating with Numbers

The McGraw-Hill Series in Operations and Decision Sciences

SUPPLY CHAIN MANAGEMENT

Bowersox, Closs, Cooper, and Bowersox
Supply Chain Logistics Management
Fifth Edition

Johnson
Purchasing and Supply Management
Sixteenth Edition

Simchi-Levi, Kaminsky, and Simchi-Levi
Designing and Managing the Supply Chain: Concepts, Strategies, Case Studies
Third Edition

Stock and Manrodt
Supply Chain Management

PROJECT MANAGEMENT

Larson
Project Management: The Managerial Process
Eighth Edition

SERVICE OPERATIONS MANAGEMENT

Bordoloi, Fitzsimmons, and Fitzsimmons
Service Management: Operations, Strategy, Information Technology
Ninth Edition

MANAGEMENT SCIENCE

Hillier and Hillier
Introduction to Management Science: A Modeling and Case Studies Approach with Spreadsheets
Sixth Edition

BUSINESS RESEARCH METHODS

Schindler
Business Research Methods
Thirteenth Edition

BUSINESS FORECASTING

Keating and Wilson
Forecasting and Predictive Analytics
Seventh Edition

BUSINESS SYSTEMS DYNAMICS

Sterman
Business Dynamics: Systems Thinking and Modeling for a Complex World

OPERATIONS MANAGEMENT

Cachon and Terwiesch
Matching Supply with Demand: An Introduction to Operations Management
Fourth Edition

Cachon and Terwiesch
Operations Management
Second Edition

Jacobs and Chase
Operations and Supply Chain Management
Sixteenth Edition

Jacobs and Chase
Operations and Supply Chain Management: The Core
Fifth Edition

Schroeder and Goldstein
Operations Management in the Supply Chain: Decisions and Cases
Eighth Edition

Stevenson
Operations Management
Fourteenth Edition

Swink, Melnyk, and Hartley
Managing Operations Across the Supply Chain
Fourth Edition

BUSINESS STATISTICS

Bowerman, Drougas, Duckworth, Froelich, Hummel, Moninger, and Schur
Business Statistics and Analytics in Practice
Ninth Edition

Doane and Seward
Applied Statistics in Business and Economics
Sixth Edition

Doane and Seward
Essential Statistics in Business and Economics
Third Edition

Jaggia and Kelly
Business Statistics: Communicating with Numbers
Third Edition

Jaggia and Kelly
Essentials of Business Statistics: Communicating with Numbers
Second Edition

Lind, Marchal, and Wathen
Basic Statistics for Business and Economics
Ninth Edition

Lind, Marchal, and Wathen
Statistical Techniques in Business and Economics
Eighteenth Edition

McGuckian
Connect Master: Business Statistics

BUSINESS ANALYTICS

Communicating with Numbers

Sanjiv Jaggia
California Polytechnic State University

Kevin Lertwachara
California Polytechnic State University

Alison Kelly
Suffolk University

Leida Chen
California Polytechnic State University

Mc Graw Hill

BUSINESS ANALYTICS

This book is printed on acid-free paper.

1 2 3 4 5 6 7 8 9 LWI 24 23 22 21 20

ISBN 978-1-260-57601-6
MHID 1-260-57601-9

Cover Image: *People head logo Nietz_studio/Shutterstock*

mheducation.com/highered

Dedicated to our families

ABOUT THE AUTHORS

Sanjiv Jaggia

Courtesy Sanjiv Jaggia

Sanjiv Jaggia is a professor of economics and finance at California Polytechnic State University in San Luis Obispo. Dr. Jaggia holds a Ph.D. from Indiana University and is a Chartered Financial Analyst (CFA®). He enjoys research in statistics and econometrics applied to a wide range of business disciplines. Dr. Jaggia has published several papers in leading academic journals and has co-authored two successful textbooks in business statistics. His ability to communicate in the classroom has been acknowledged by several teaching awards. Dr. Jaggia resides in San Luis Obispo with his wife and daughter. In his spare time, he enjoys cooking, hiking, and listening to a wide range of music.

Alison Kelly

Courtesy Alison Kelly

Alison Kelly is a professor of economics at Suffolk University in Boston. Dr. Kelly holds a Ph.D. from Boston College and is a Chartered Financial Analyst (CFA®). Dr. Kelly has published in a wide variety of academic journals and has co-authored two successful textbooks in business statistics. Her courses in applied statistics and econometrics are well received by students as well as working professionals. Dr. Kelly resides in Hamilton, Massachusetts, with her husband, daughter, and son. In her spare time, she enjoys exercising and gardening.

Kevin Lertwachara

Teresa Cameron/Frank Gonzales/ California Polytechnic State University

Kevin Lertwachara is a professor of information systems at California Polytechnic State University in San Luis Obispo. Dr. Lertwachara holds a Ph.D. in Operations and Information Management from the University of Connecticut. Dr. Lertwachara's research focuses on technology-based innovation, electronic commerce, health care informatics, and business analytics and his work has been published in scholarly books and leading academic journals. He teaches business analytics at both the undergraduate and graduate levels and has received several teaching awards. Dr. Lertwachara resides in the central coast of California with his wife and three sons. In his spare time, he coaches his sons' soccer and futsal teams.

Leida Chen

Courtesy of Leida Chen

Leida Chen is a professor of information systems at California Polytechnic State University in San Luis Obispo. Dr. Chen earned a Ph.D. in Management Information Systems from University of Memphis. His research and consulting interests are in the areas of business analytics, technology diffusion, and global information systems. Dr. Chen has published over 50 research articles in leading information systems journals, over 30 articles and book chapters in national and international conference proceedings and edited books, and a book on mobile application development. He teaches business analytics at both the undergraduate and graduate levels. In his spare time, Dr. Chen enjoys hiking, painting, and traveling with his wife and son to interesting places around the world.

FROM THE AUTHORS

Data and analytics capabilities have made a leap forward in recent years and have changed the way businesses make decisions. The explosion in the field is partly due to the growing availability of vast amounts of data, improved computational power, and the development of sophisticated algorithms. More than ever, colleges and universities need a curriculum that emphasizes business analytics, and companies need data-savvy professionals who can turn data into insights and action. To meet these needs, business colleges have been scrambling to include business analytics courses in their undergraduate curriculum. At the graduate level, these courses are fast becoming a requirement in MBA programs and in specialized masters and certificate programs in business analytics.

We wrote *Business Analytics: Communicating with Numbers* from the ground up to prepare students to understand, manage, and visualize the data; apply the appropriate analysis tools; and communicate the findings and their relevance. Unlike other texts that simply repackage traditional statistics and operations research topics, our text seamlessly threads the topics of data wrangling, descriptive analytics, predictive analytics, and prescriptive analytics into a cohesive whole.

Experiential learning opportunities have been proven effective in teaching applied and complex subjects such as business analytics. In this text, we provide a holistic analytics process, including dealing with real-life data that are not necessarily 'clean' and/or 'small'. Similarly, we stress the importance of effectively communicating findings by including features such as a synopsis (a short writing sample) and a sample report (a longer writing sample) in every chapter. These features help students develop skills in articulating the business value of analytics by communicating insights gained from a nontechnical standpoint.

The text's comprehensive coverage of all relevant business analytics topics gives instructors the flexibility to select the topics that best align with their course objectives. All chapters are designed to be modular, making it easy for instructors to include only the key chapters, or sections within a chapter, they intend to cover. For example, the text can be adapted for an introductory course covering data wrangling (Chapter 2), data visualization (Chapter 3), summary measures (Chapter 3), statistical theories (Chapters 4 and 5), and regression analysis (Chapters 6 and 7), or an advanced business analytics course focusing on predictive (Chapters 8, 9, 10, 11, and 12) and prescriptive modeling (Chapter 13).

In this text, we have chosen Excel with Analytic Solver (an Excel add-in) and R as the software packages due to their accessibility, ease of use, and powerful features for demonstrating analytics concepts and performing analytics on real-world data. In most chapters, the instructor can select to cover either Excel or R (or both) based on the course objectives and the technical background of the students. These software packages can be accessible to students through university computer labs, educational licenses, and free, open-source licenses. For this edition, all examples and exercise problems are solved using the latest versions of the software as of writing, namely, Microsoft Office Professional 2016, Analytic Solver 2019, and R version 3.5.3. We recommend that the same versions of the software be used in order to replicate the results presented in the text. When new versions of the software packages are released in the future, we plan to incorporate any substantial changes in future editions of the text or provide updates online if the differences are relatively minor.

Sanjiv Jaggia
Alison Kelly
Kevin Lertwachara
Leida Chen

Business Analytics: Communicating with Numbers

Reviewer Quotes

"I love everything I see! I love the application demonstrated through the case study in each chapter, and I like the use of Excel and Solver, specifically. . . I also love the case study and examples to help students apply the material."

Kristin Pettey, Southwestern College – Kansas

"I can't agree with the approach. . . to data analytics more. I have been looking for a textbook like this."

Jahyun Goo, Florida Atlantic University

"End of chapter material is excellent ("Writing with Big Data"). . ."

Kevin Brown, Asbury University

"I strongly applaud that this text offers a holistic approach to data analysis and places the emphasis on communicating with data. The Big Data and Data Mining sections seem promising with coverage of topics of the latest models and methods."

Hao Chen, UW Platteville

"The TOC includes all the major areas needed for a foundational level of knowledge and the added value of teaching how to communicate with the information garnered will make a strong textbook."

Roman Rabinovich, Boston University

Unique Key Features

The pedagogy of *Business Analytics* includes popular features from our *Business Statistics* texts along with new features pertaining to business analytics. Countless reviewers have added their feedback and direction to ensure we have built a product that we believe addresses the needs of the market.

Holistic Approach to Data Analytics

Business analytics is a very broad topic consisting of statistics, computer science, and management information systems with a wide variety of applications in business areas including marketing, HR management, economics, accounting, and finance.

The text offers a holistic approach to business analytics, combining qualitative reasoning with quantitative tools to identify key business problems and translate analytics into decisions that improve business performance.

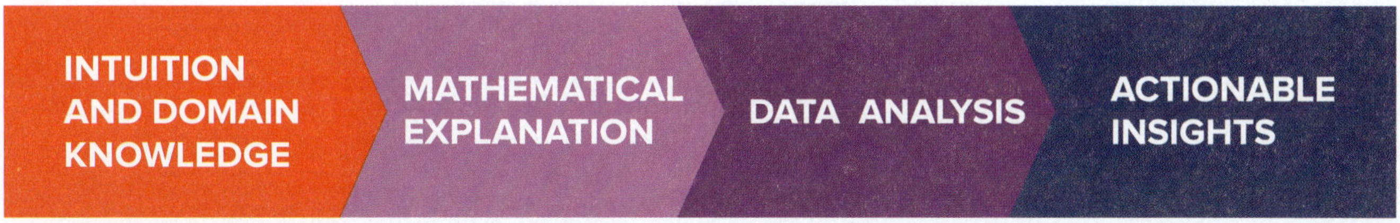

Integrated Introductory Case

Each chapter opens with a real-life case study that forms the basis for several examples within the chapter. The questions included in the examples create a roadmap for mastering the most important learning outcomes within the chapter. A synopsis of each chapter's introductory case is presented once the questions pertaining to the case have been answered.

INTRODUCTORY CASE

24/7 Fitness Center Annual Membership

24/7 Fitness Center is a high-end full-service gym and recruits its members through advertisements and monthly open house events. Each open house attendee is given a tour and a one-day pass. Potential members register for the open house event by answering a few questions about themselves and their exercise routine. The fitness center staff places a follow-up phone call with the potential member and sends information to open house attendees by mail in the hopes of signing the potential member up for an annual membership.

Janet Williams, a manager at 24/7 Fitness Center, wants to develop a data-driven strategy for selecting which new open house attendees to contact. She has compiled information from 1,000 past open house attendees in the Gym_Data worksheet of the ***Gym*** data file. The data include whether or not the attendee purchases a club membership (Enroll equals 1 if purchase, 0 otherwise), the age and the annual income of the attendee, and the average number of hours that the attendee exercises per week. Janet also collects the age, income, and number of hours spent on weekly exercise from 23 new open house attendees and maintains a separate worksheet called Gym_Score in the ***Gym*** data file. Because these are new open house attendees, there is no enrollment information on this worksheet. A portion of the two worksheets is shown in Table 9.1.

TABLE 9.1 24/7 Fitness Data

a. The *Gym_Data* Worksheet

Enroll	Age	Income	Hours
1	26	18000	14
0	43	13000	9
⋮	⋮	⋮	⋮
0	48	67000	18

b. The *Gym_Score* Worksheet

Age	Income	Hours
22	33000	5
23	65000	9
⋮	⋮	⋮
51	88000	6

Janet would like to use the data to accomplish the following tasks.

1. Develop a data-driven classification model for predicting whether or not a potential member will purchase a gym membership.
2. Identify which of the 23 new open house attendees are likely to purchase a gym membership.

A synopsis of this case is provided in Section 9.2.

SYNOPSIS OF INTRODUCTORY CASE

Gyms and exercise facilities usually have a high turnover rate among their members. Like other gyms, 24/7 Fitness Center relies on recruiting new members on a regular basis in order to sustain its business and financial well-being. Completely familiar with data analytics techniques, Janet Williams, a manager at 24/7 Fitness Center, uses the KNN method to analyze data from the gym's past open house. She wants to gain a better insight into which attendees are likely to purchase a gym membership after attending this event.

Overall, Janet finds that the KNN analysis provides reasonably high accuracy in predicting whether or not potential gym members will purchase a membership. The accuracy, sensitivity, and specificity rates from the test data set are well above 80%. More importantly, the KNN analysis identifies individual open house attendees who are likely to purchase a gym membership. For example, the analysis results indicate that open house attendees who are 50 years or older with a relatively high annual income and those in the same age group who spend at least nine hours on weekly exercise are more likely to enroll after attending the open house. With these types of actionable insights, Janet decides to train her staff to regularly analyze the monthly open house data in order to help 24/7 Fitness Center grow its membership base.

Writing with Big Data

A distinctive feature of *Business Analytics* is access to select big data sets with relevance to numerous applications to which students can relate. In most chapters, we have a designated section where we use these big data sets to help introduce problems, formulate possible solutions, and communicate the findings, based on the concepts introduced in the chapter. Using a sample report, our intent is to show students how to articulate the business value of analytics by communicating insights gained from a nontechnical standpoint.

5.4 WRITING WITH DATA

Ariel Skelley/Blend Images LLC

When using big data, we typically do not construct confidence intervals or perform hypothesis tests. Why is this the case? It turns out that if the sample size is sufficiently large, there is little difference in the estimates of $\overline{X}$ or the estimates of $\overline{P}$ generated by different random samples.

Recall that we use $se(\overline{X}) = \frac{s}{\sqrt{n}}$ to gauge the variability in $\overline{X}$ and $se(\overline{P}) = \sqrt{\frac{\overline{p}(1-\overline{p})}{n}}$ to gauge the variability in $\overline{P}$. In both cases, the variability depends on the size of the sample on which the value of the estimator is based. If the sample size is sufficiently large, then the variability virtually disappears, or, equivalently, $se(\overline{X})$ and $se(\overline{P})$ approach zero. Thus, with big data, it is not very meaningful to construct confidence intervals for the population mean or the population proportion because the margin of error also approaches zero; under these circumstances, when estimating μ or p, it is sufficient to use the estimate of the relevant point estimator.

Recall too that when testing the population mean, the value of the test statistic is calculated as $t_{df} = (\overline{x} - \mu_0)/(s/\sqrt{n})$; and when testing the population proportion, the value of the test statistic is calculated as $z = (\overline{p} - p_0)/(\sqrt{\overline{p}(1-\overline{p})/n})$. With big data, the value of the respective test statistic increases, leading to a small *p*-value, and thus rejection of the null hypothesis in virtually any scenario.

Thus, if the sample size is sufficiently large, statistical inference is not very useful. In this Writing with Data section, we focus on a case study where the sample size is relatively small.

Case Study

According to a 2018 paper released by the Economic Policy Institute, a nonprofit, nonpartisan think tank in Washington, D.C., income inequality continues to grow in the United States. Over the years, the rich have become richer while working-class wages have stagnated. A local Latino politician has been vocal regarding his concern about the welfare of Latinx. In various speeches, he has stated that the mean salary of Latinx households in his county has fallen below the 2017 mean of approximately $50,000. He has also stated that the proportion of Latinx households making less than $30,000 has risen above the 2017 level of 20%. Both of his statements are based on income data for 36 Latinx households in the county. A portion of the data is shown in Table 5.6.

TABLE 5.6 Latinx Household Income (in $1,000s)

FILE *Latinx_Income*

Income
23
63
⋮
47

Sample Report—Income Inequality in the United States

One of the hotly debated topics in the United States is that of growing income inequality. This trend, which has picked up post Great Recession, is a reversal of what was seen during and after the Great Depression, where the gap between rich and poor narrowed. Market forces such as increased trade and technological advances have made highly skilled and well-educated workers more productive, thus increasing their pay. Institutional forces, such as deregulation, the decline of unions, and the stagnation of the minimum wage, have contributed to income inequality. Arguably, this income inequality has been felt by minorities, especially African Americans and Latinxs, because a very high proportion of both groups is working class.

A sample of 36 Latinx households resulted in a mean household income of $47,278 with a standard deviation of $19,524. The sample mean is below the 2017 level of $50,000. In addition, eight Latinx households, or approximately 22%, make less than $30,000. Based on these results, a politician concludes that current market conditions continue to negatively impact the welfare of Latinxs. However, it is essential to provide statistically significant evidence to substantiate these claims. Toward this end, formal tests of hypotheses regarding the population mean and the population proportion are conducted. The results of the tests are summarized in Table 5.7.

TABLE 5.7 Test Statistic Values and *p*-Values for Hypothesis Tests

Hypotheses	Test Statistic Value	*p*-value
$H_0: \mu \geq 50$ $H_A: \mu < 50$	$t_{35} = \frac{47.278 - 50}{19.524/\sqrt{36}} = -0.837$	0.204
$H_0: p \leq 0.20$ $H_A: p > 0.20$	$z = \frac{0.222 - 0.20}{\sqrt{\frac{(0.20)(0.80)}{36}}} = 0.333$	0.369

When testing whether the mean income of Latinx households has fallen below the 2017 level of $50,000, a test statistic value of −0.837 is obtained. Given a *p*-value of 0.204, the null hypothesis regarding the population mean, specified in Table 5.7, cannot be rejected at any reasonable level of significance. Similarly, given a *p*-value of 0.369, the null hypothesis regarding the population proportion cannot be rejected. Therefore, sample evidence does not support the claims that the mean income of Latinx households has fallen below $50,000 or that the proportion of Latinx households making less than $30,000 has risen above 20%. Perhaps the politician's remarks were based on a cursory look at the sample statistics and not on a thorough statistical analysis.

Suggested Case Studies

Report 5.1 FILE ***Fidelity_Returns.*** The accompanying data are the annual returns for two mutual funds offered by the investment giant Fidelity for the years 2001–2017. The Fidelity Select Automotive mutual fund invests primarily in companies engaged in the manufacturing, marketing, or sales of automobiles, trucks, specialty vehicles, parts, tires, and related services. The Fidelity Gold mutual fund invests primarily in companies engaged in exploration, mining, processing, or dealing in gold and, to a lesser degree, in other precious metals and minerals. In a report, use the sample information to

- Calculate descriptive statistics to compare the returns of the mutual funds
- Assess reward by constructing and interpreting 95% confidence intervals for the population mean return. What assumption did you make when constructing the confidence intervals?

Report 5.2 FILE ***Field_Choice.*** A 2018 Pew Research Center survey finds that more than half of Americans (52%) believe that young people do not pursue a degree in science, technology,

Emphasis on Data Mining

Data mining is one of the most sought-after skills that employers want college graduates to have. It leverages large data sets and computer power to build predictive models that support decision making. In addition to two comprehensive chapters devoted to linear and logistic regression models, and a chapter on business forecasting, the text includes four exclusive chapters on data mining. These include detailed analysis of both supervised and unsupervised learning, covering relevant topics such as principle component analysis, *k*-nearest neighbors, naïve Bayes, classification and regression trees, ensemble trees, hierarchical and *k*-means clustering, and association rules. Each chapter offers relatable real-world problems, conceptual explanations, and easy-to-follow computer instructions. There are over 200 exercises in these four exclusive chapters.

FIGURE 8.5 The cumulative lift chart

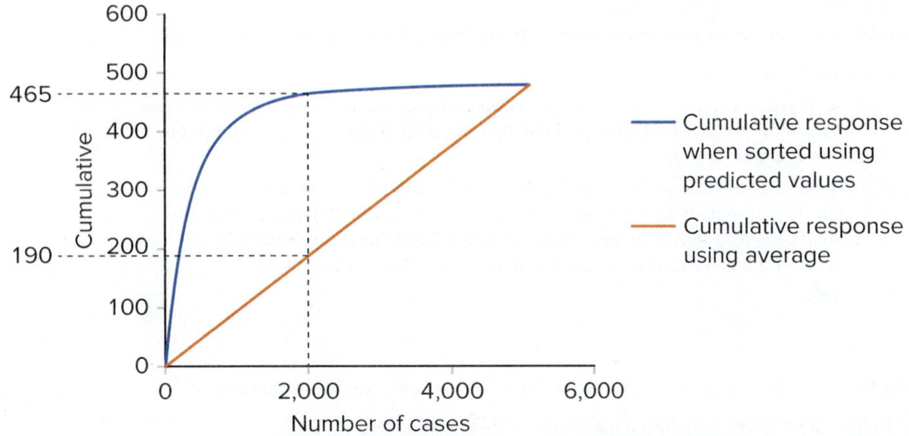

Four Chapters on Data Mining

- Introduction to Data Mining
- Supervised Data Mining: *k*-Nearest Neighbors and Naïve Bayes
- Supervised Data Mining: Decision Trees
- Unsupervised Data Mining

TABLE 8.14 Prediction Performance Measures

Performance Measure	Model 1	Model 2
RMSE	171.3489	174.1758
ME	11.2530	12.0480
MAD	115.1650	117.9920
MPE	−2.05%	−2.08%
MAPE	15.51%	15.95%

FIGURE 10.1 A simplified decision tree

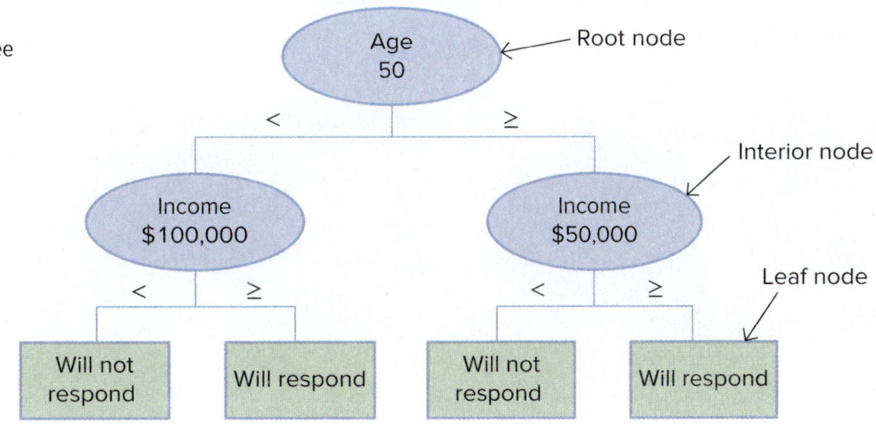

Computer Software

The text includes hands-on tutorials and problem-solving examples featuring Microsoft Excel, Analytic Solver (an Excel add-in software for data mining analysis), as well as R (a powerful software that merges the convenience of statistical packages with the power of coding).

Throughout the text, students learn to use the software to solve real-world problems and to reinforce the concepts discussed in the chapters. Students will also learn how to visualize and communicate with data using charts and infographics featured in the software.

Estimating a Linear Regression Model with Excel or R

Using Excel

In order to obtain the regression output in Table 6.2 using Excel, we follow these steps.

FILE *College*

A. Open the ***College*** data file.

B. Choose **Data > Data Analysis > Regression** from the menu. (Recall from Chapter 3 that if you do not see the **Data Analysis** option under **Data**, you must add in the **Analysis Toolpak** option.)

C. See Figure 6.3. In the *Regression* dialog box, click on the box next to *Input Y Range*, and then select the data for Earnings. Click on the box next to *Input X Range*, and then *simultaneously* select the data for Cost, Grad, Debt, and City. Select *Labels* because we are using Earnings, Cost, Grad, Debt, and City as headings.

D. Click **OK**.

Using R

In order to obtain the regression output in Table 6.2 using R, we follow these steps.

A. Import the ***College*** data into a data frame (table) and label it myData.

B. By default, R will report the regression output using scientific notation. We opt to turn this option off using the following command:

```
> options(scipen=999)
```

In order to turn scientific notation back on, we would enter options(scipen=0) at the prompt.

C. Use the **lm** function to create a linear model, which we label Multiple. Note that we use the '+' sign to add predictor variables, even if we believe that a negative relationship may exist between the response variable and the predictor variables. You will not see output after you implement this step.

```
> Multiple <- lm(Earnings ~ Cost + Grad + Debt + City, data = myData)
```

D. Use the **summary** function to view the summary regression output. Figure 6.4 shows the R regression output. We have put the intercept and the slope coefficients in boldface. As expected, these values are identical to the ones obtained using Excel.

```
> summary(Multiple)
```

Exercises and McGraw-Hill's Connect®

Every chapter contains dozens of applied examples from all walks of life, including business, economics, sports, health, housing, the environment, polling, psychology, and more.

We also know the importance of ancillaries—like the Instructor's Solution Manual (ISM)—and the technology component, specifically Connect. As we write *Business Analytics,* we are simultaneously developing these components with the hope of making them seamless with the text itself.

We know from experience that these components cannot be developed in isolation. For example, we review every Connect exercise as well as evaluate rounding rules and revise tolerance levels. Given the extremely positive feedback from users of our *Business Statistics* texts, we follow the same approach with *Business Analytics.*

Exercise 3.25

A researcher at a marketing firm examines whether the age of a consumer matters when buying athletic clothing. Her initial feeling is that Brand A attracts a younger customer, whereas the more established companies (Brands B and C) draw an older clientele. For 600 recent purchases of athletic clothing, she collects data on a customer's age (Age equals 1 if the customer is under 35, 0 otherwise) and the brand name of the athletic clothing (A, B, or C). A portion of the data is shown in the accompanying table.

Purchase	Age	Brand
1	1	A
2	1	C
⋮	⋮	⋮
600	0	B

Click here for the Excel Data File

a-1. Construct a contingency table that cross-classifies the data by Age and Brand. Provide the frequencies in the accompanying table.

	Brand		
Age	**A**	**B**	**C**
≥ 35 years old (0)	54	72	78
< 35 years old (1)	174	132	90

Exercise 9.13

Daniel Lara, a human resources manager at a large tech consulting firm has been reading about using analytics to predict the success of new employees. With the fast-changing nature of the tech industry, some employees have had difficulties staying current in their field and have missed the opportunity to be promoted into a management position. Daniel is particularly interested in whether or not a new employee is likely to be promoted into a management role after 10 years with the company. He gathers information about 300 current employees who have worked for the firm for at least 10 years. The information was based on the job application that the employees provided when they originally applied for a job at the firm. For each employee, the following variables are listed: Promoted (1 if promoted within 10 years, 0 otherwise), GPA (college GPA at graduation), Sports (number of athletic activities during college), and Leadership (number of leadership roles in student organizations). A portion of the ***HR_Data*** worksheet is shown in the accompanying table.

Promoted	GPA	Sports	Leadership
0	3.28	0	[illegible]
1	3.93	6	[illegible]
⋮		⋮	
0	3.54	5	0

Exercise 3.25

Click here for the Excel Data File : *HR_Data*

Click here for the Excel Data File: *HR_Score*

a-1. Use the HR_Data worksheet to help Daniel perform KNN analysis to determine the optimal *k* between 1 and 10. Partition the data set randomly into 50% training, 30% validation, and 20% test and use 12345 as the default random seed. Use 0.5 as the cutoff value for this analysis. Enter the optimal *k* in the box below:

Optimal k	8

McGraw Hill connect®

FOR INSTRUCTORS

You're in the driver's seat.

Want to build your own course? No problem. Prefer to use our turnkey, prebuilt course? Easy. Want to make changes throughout the semester? Sure. And you'll save time with Connect's auto-grading too.

65% Less Time Grading

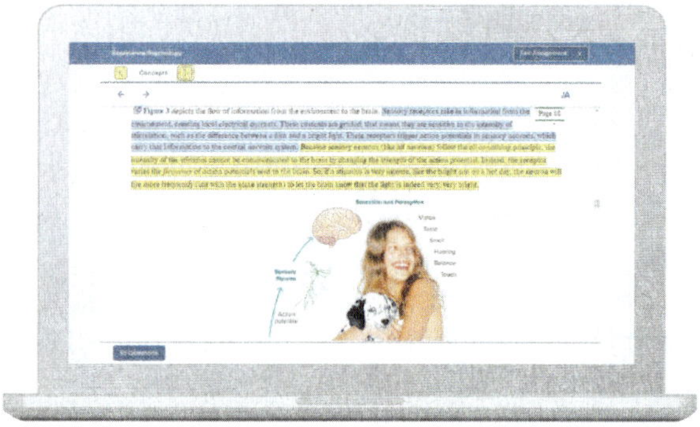

Laptop: McGraw-Hill; Woman/dog: George Doyle/Getty Images

They'll thank you for it.

Adaptive study resources like SmartBook® 2.0 help your students be better prepared in less time. You can transform your class time from dull definitions to dynamic debates. Find out more about the powerful personalized learning experience available in SmartBook 2.0 at **www.mheducation.com/highered/connect/smartbook**

Make it simple, make it affordable.

Connect makes it easy with seamless integration using any of the major Learning Management Systems—Blackboard®, Canvas, and D2L, among others—to let you organize your course in one convenient location. Give your students access to digital materials at a discount with our inclusive access program. Ask your McGraw-Hill representative for more information.

Padlock: Jobalou/Getty Images

Solutions for your challenges.

A product isn't a solution. Real solutions are affordable, reliable, and come with training and ongoing support when you need it and how you want it. Our Customer Experience Group can also help you troubleshoot tech problems—although Connect's 99% uptime means you might not need to call them. See for yourself at **status.mheducation.com**

Checkmark: Jobalou/Getty Images

SUPPORT AT every step

FOR STUDENTS

Effective, efficient studying.

Connect helps you be more productive with your study time and get better grades using tools like SmartBook 2.0, which highlights key concepts and creates a personalized study plan. Connect sets you up for success, so you walk into class with confidence and walk out with better grades.

Study anytime, anywhere.

Download the free ReadAnywhere app and access your online eBook or SmartBook 2.0 assignments when it's convenient, even if you're offline. And since the app automatically syncs with your eBook and SmartBook 2.0 assignments in Connect, all of your work is available every time you open it. Find out more at **www.mheducation.com/readanywhere**

> ***"I really liked this app—it made it easy to study when you don't have your text-book in front of you."***
>
> - Jordan Cunningham,
> Eastern Washington University

Calendar: owattaphotos/Getty Images

No surprises.

The Connect Calendar and Reports tools keep you on track with the work you need to get done and your assignment scores. Life gets busy; Connect tools help you keep learning through it all.

Learning for everyone.

McGraw-Hill works directly with Accessibility Services Departments and faculty to meet the learning needs of all students. Please contact your Accessibility Services office and ask them to email accessibility@mheducation.com, or visit **www.mheducation.com/about/accessibility** for more information.

Top: Jenner Images/Getty Images, Left: Hero Images/Getty Images, Right: Hero Images/Getty Images

Resources for Instructors and Students

Instructor Library

The Connect Instructor Library is your repository for additional resources to improve student engagement in and out of class. You can select and use any asset that enhances your course. The Connect Instructor Library includes:

- Instructor's Manual
- Instructor's Solutions Manual
- Test Bank
- Data Sets
- PowerPoint Presentations
- Digital Image Library

R Package

R is a powerful software that merges the convenience of statistical packages with the power of coding. It is open source as well as cross-platform compatible and gives students the flexibility to work with large data sets using a wide range of analytics techniques. The software is continuously evolving to include packages that support new analytical methods. In addition, students can access rich online resources and tap into the expertise of a worldwide community of R users. In Appendix C, we introduce some fundamental features of R and also provide instructions on how to obtain solutions for many solved examples in the text.

As with other texts that use R, differences between software versions are likely to result in minor inconsistencies in analytics outcomes in algorithm-rich Chapters 9, 10, 11, and parts of Chapter 12. In these chapters, the solved examples and exercise problems are based on R version 3.5.3 on Microsoft Windows. Even though there will be newer versions of R when you prepare to download it, we highly recommend that you download R version 3.5.3 in order to replicate the results presented in the text.

Analytic Solver

The Excel-based user interface of Analytic Solver reduces the learning curve for students allowing them to focus on problem solving rather than trying to learn a new software package. The solved examples and exercise problems are based on Analytic Solver 2019. Newer versions of Analytic Solver will likely produce the same analysis results but may have a slightly different user interface. For consistency, we recommend that you use Analytic Solver 2019 with this text.

Analytic Solver can be used with Microsoft Excel for Windows (as an add-in), or "in the cloud" at **AnalyticSolver.com** using any device (PC, Mac, tablet) with a web browser. It offers comprehensive features for prescriptive analytics (optimization, simulation, decision analysis) and predictive analytics (forecasting, data mining, text mining). Its optimization features are upward compatible from the standard Solver in Excel. If interested in having students get low-cost academic access for class use, instructors should send an email to support@solver.com to get their course code and receive student pricing and access information as well as their own access information.

Student Resources

Students have access to data files, tutorials, and detailed progress reporting within Connect. Key textbook resources can also be accessed through the Additional Student Resources page: **www.mhhe.com/JaggiaBA1e**.

McGraw-Hill Customer Care Contact Information

At McGraw-Hill, we understand that getting the most from new technology can be challenging. That's why our services don't stop after you purchase our products. You can e-mail our product specialists 24 hours a day to get product training online. Or you can search our knowledge bank of frequently asked questions on our support website.

For customer support, call 800-331-5094 or visit **www.mhhe.com/support**. One of our technical support analysts will be able to assist you in a timely fashion.

ACKNOWLEDGMENTS

We would like to thank the following instructors for their feedback and careful reviews during the development process:

Sung K. Ahn, Washington State University
Triss Ashton, Tarleton State University
Anteneh Ayanso, Brock University
Matthew Bailey, Bucknell University
Palash Beram Saint Louis University
Matthew Brenn, University of Akron
Paul Brooks, Virginia Commonwealth University
Kevin Brown, Asbury University
Kevin Caskey, SUNY New Paltz
Paolo Catasti, Virginia Commonwealth University
Michael Cervetti, University of Memphis
Jimmy Chen, Bucknell University
Jen-Yi Chen, Cleveland State University
Rex Cheung, San Francisco State University
Alan Chow, University of South Alabama,
Matthew Dean, University of Southern Maine
Alisa DiSalvo, St. Mary's University Twin Cities
Mark Dobeck, Cleveland State University
Joan Donohue, University of South Carolina
Kathy Enget, University at Albany- SUNY
Kathryn Ernstberger, Indiana University Southeast
Robertas Gabrys, University of Southern California
Ridvan Gedik, University of New Haven
Roger Grinde, University of New Hampshire
Thomas Groleau, Carthage College
Babita Gupta, California State University Monterey Bay
Serina Al Haddad, Rollins College
Dan Harpool, University of Arkansas Little Rock
Fady Harfoush, Loyola University Chicago
Paul Holmes, Ashland University
Ping-Hung Hsieh, Oregon State University
Kuang-Chung Hsu, University of Central Oklahoma
Jason Imbrogno, University of Northern Alabama
Marina Johnson, Montclair State University
Jerzy Kamburowski, University of Toledo
Reza Kheirandish, Clayton State University
Esther Klein, St. Francis College
Bharat Kolluri, University of Hartford
Mohammad Merhi, Indiana University
Jacob Miller, Southern Utah University
Sinjini Mitra, California State University Fullerton
Kyle Moninger, Bowling Green State University
Rex Moody, Angelo State University
Ebrahim Mortaz, Pace University
Kristin Pettey, Southwestern College
Daniel Power, University of Northern Iowa
Zbigniew Przasnyski, Loyola Marymount University
Sharma Pillutla, Towson University
Roman Rabinovich, Boston University
Michael Ratajczyk, Saint Mary's College
R. Christopher L. Riley, Delta State University
Leslie Rush, University of Hawaii West Oahu
Avijit Sarkar, University of Redlands
Dmitriy Shaltayev, Christopher Newport University
Mike Shurden, Lander University
Pearl Steinbuch, Boston University
Alicia Strandberg, Villanova University School of Business
David Taylor, Sacred Heart University
Stan Taylor, California State University Sacramento
Pablo Trejo, Miami Dade College
Nikhil Varaiya, San Diego State University
Timothy Vaughan, University of Wisconsin Eau Claire
Fen Wang, Central Washington University
Kanghyun Yoon, University of Central Oklahoma
John Yu, Saint Joseph's University
Oliver Yi, San Jose State University
Liang Xu, Slippery Rock University of Pennsylvania
Yong Xu, Ferris State University
Jay Zagorsky, Boston University

We are grateful for the assistance of the following people who helped us develop and review the assessment content and additional resources:

Anteneh Ayanso, Brock University
John Draper, The Ohio State University
Alex Firsov, Oracle Corporation
Stephanie Henry, Workday, Inc.
Phuong Lam (Rose) Hoang, California Polytechnic State University
Eric Lee Kambestad, California Polytechnic State University
Vincent Mastuntano, Suffolk University
Corey Pang, California Polytechnic State University
Kristen Pettey, Southwestern College
Matthew Spector, California Polytechnic State University
Wendi Sun, Rockland Trust
Zhaowei (Justin) Wang, Citizens Financial Group
Brie Winkles, University of West Alabama

In addition, special thanks to the wonderful and supportive team at McGraw-Hill: Ryan McAndrews, Product Developer; Thomas Finn, Content Development Editor; Noelle Bathurst, Portfolio Manager; Harper Christopher, Executive Marketing Manager; Sarah Thomas, Market Development Manager; Pat Frederickson, Core Content Project Manager; Jamie Koch, Assessment Content Project Manager; Egzon Shaqiri, Designer; Chuck Synovec, Portfolio Director; Natalie King, Marketing Director; Kevin Moran, Director of Digital Content; and Tim Vertovec, Managing Director.

BRIEF CONTENTS

CONTENTS

BUSINESS ANALYTICS
Communicating with Numbers

1 Introduction to Business Analytics

LEARNING OBJECTIVES

After reading this chapter, you should be able to:

- LO **1.1** **Explain the importance of business analytics.**
- LO **1.2** **Explain the various types of data.**
- LO **1.3** **Describe variables and types of measurement scales.**
- LO **1.4** **Describe different data sources and file formats.**

At every moment, data are being generated at an increasing velocity from countless sources in an overwhelming volume. In just about any contemporary human activity, the analysis of large amounts of data, under the umbrella of business or data analytics, helps us make better decisions. Managers, consumers, bankers, sports enthusiasts, politicians, and medical professionals are increasingly turning to data to boost a company's revenue, deepen customer engagement, find better options on consumer products, prevent threats and fraud, assess riskiness of loans, succeed in sports and elections, provide better diagnoses and cures for diseases, and so on. In the broadest sense, business analytics involves the methodology of extracting information and knowledge from data for which an important first step is to understand data and data types.

In this chapter, we will provide an overview and real-world examples of business analytics. We will also describe various types of data and measurement scales of variables that will later help us choose appropriate techniques for analyzing data. Finally, we will discuss how we can take advantage of data sources that are publicly available and review some standard formats that people use to store and disseminate data.

©CampPhoto/iStock/Getty Images

INTRODUCTORY CASE

Vacation in Belize

After graduating from a university in southern California, Emily Hernandez is excited to go on a vacation in Belize with her friends. There are different airlines that offer flights from southern California to Belize City. Emily prefers a direct flight from Los Angeles but is also worried about staying within her budget. Other, less expensive, options would mean making one or even two additional stops en route to Belize City. Once arriving at Belize City, she plans to take a sea ferry to one of the resort hotels on Ambergris Caye Island. Purchasing a vacation package from one of these hotels would be most cost effective, but Emily wants to make sure that the hotel she chooses has all the amenities she wants, such as an early check-in option, a complimentary breakfast, recreational activities, and sightseeing services. She also wants to make sure that the hotel is reputable and has good customer reviews.

Emily starts researching her options for flights and hotels by searching for deals on the Internet. She has organized and kept meticulous records of the information she has found so that she can compare all the options. She would like to use this information to:

1. Find a flight that is convenient as well as affordable.
2. Choose a reputable hotel that is priced under $200 per night.

A synopsis of this case is provided at the end of Section 1.2.

LO 1.1

1.1 OVERVIEW OF BUSINESS ANALYTICS

Explain the importance of business analytics.

Data and analytics capabilities have made a leap forward in recent years and have changed the way businesses make decisions. In the broadest sense, business analytics (also referred to as data analytics) involves the methodology of extracting information and knowledge from data that improves a company's bottom-line and enhances consumer experience. At the core, business analytics benefits companies by developing better marketing strategies, deepening customer engagement, enhancing efficiency in procurement, uncovering ways to reduce expenses, identifying emerging market trends, mitigating risk and fraud, etc. The explosion in the field is partly due to the growing availability of vast amounts of data, improved computational power, and the development of sophisticated algorithms. More than ever, colleges and universities need a curriculum that emphasizes business analytics, and companies need data-savvy professionals who can turn data into insights and action.

Business analytics is a broad topic, encompassing statistics, computer science, and information systems with a wide variety of applications in marketing, human resource management, economics, finance, health, sports, politics, etc. Unlike data science that is focused on advanced computer algorithms to develop applications for end users, business analytics tends to focus more on the analysis of the available data.

Raw data do not offer much value or insights. With the advancement of data and analytics capabilities, capturing a large amount of data or implementing complex statistical models has been simplified. However, in order to extract value from data, we need to be able to understand the business context, ask the right questions from the data, identify appropriate analysis models, and communicate information into verbal and written language. It is important to note that numerical results are not very useful unless they are accompanied with clearly stated actionable business insights.

BUSINESS ANALYTICS

Business analytics combines qualitative reasoning with quantitative tools to identify key business problems and translate data analysis into decisions that improve business performance.

There are different types of analytics techniques designed to extract value from data that can be grouped into three broad categories: descriptive analytics, predictive analytics, and prescriptive analytics.

- **Descriptive analytics** refers to gathering, organizing, tabulating, and visualizing data to summarize '*what has happened?*' Examples of descriptive analytics include financial reports, public health statistics, enrollment at universities, student report cards, and crime rates across regions and time. The descriptive information can also be presented in a number of formats including written reports, tables, graphs, and maps.
- **Predictive analytics** refers to using historical data to predict '*what could happen in the future?*' Analytical models help identify associations between variables, and these associations are used to estimate the likelihood of a specific outcome. Examples of predictive analytics include identifying customers who are most likely to respond to specific marketing campaigns, admitted students who are likely to enroll, credit card transactions that are likely to be fraudulent, or the incidence of crime at certain regions and times.
- **Prescriptive analytics** refers to using optimization and simulation algorithms to provide advice on '*what should we do?*' It explores several possible actions and suggests a course of action. Examples include providing advice on scheduling employees' work hours and supply level in order to meet customer demand, selecting a mix of products to manufacture, choosing an investment portfolio to meet a financial goal, or targeting marketing campaigns to specific customer groups on a limited budget.

These three categories of analytics serve different functions in the problem-solving process. Descriptive analytics is often referred to as **business intelligence (BI)**, which provides organizations and their users with the ability to access and manipulate data interactively through reports, dashboards, applications, and visualization tools. BI uses past data integrated from multiple sources to inform decision making and identify problems and solutions. Most BI questions can be solved using complex queries of the enterprise databases. For example, a typical BI question for an online music streaming company would be, "During the first quarter of 2020, how many country songs recommended by the music service were skipped by a U.S.-based female listener within five seconds of playing?" The answer to this question can be found by querying and summarizing historical data and is useful for making decisions related to the effectiveness of the music recommendation system of the company.

Predictive and prescriptive analytics, on the other hand, are commonly considered advanced predictions. They focus on building predictive and prescriptive models that help organizations understand what might happen in the future. Advanced prediction problems are solved using statistics and data mining techniques. For the online music streaming company example, an advanced prediction question would be, "What are the key factors that influence a U.S.-based female listener's music choice?" The answer to this question cannot be directly found in the enterprise databases and requires complex learning and analysis of the relevant historical data.

The three categories of business analytics can also be viewed according to the level of sophistication and business values they offer. For many people, using predictive analytics to predict the future is more valuable than simply summarizing data and describing what happened in the past. In addition, predictive techniques tend to require more complex modeling and analysis tools than most descriptive techniques. Likewise, using prescriptive techniques to provide actionable recommendations could be more valuable than predicting a number of possible outcomes in the future. Turning data-driven recommendations into action also requires thoughtful consideration and organizational commitment beyond developing descriptive and predictive analytical models.

Figure 1.1 categorizes business analytics into three stages of development based on its value and the level of organizational commitment to data-driven decision making. Most chapters of this text can also be grouped within each of the three analytics categories as shown in Figure 1.1.

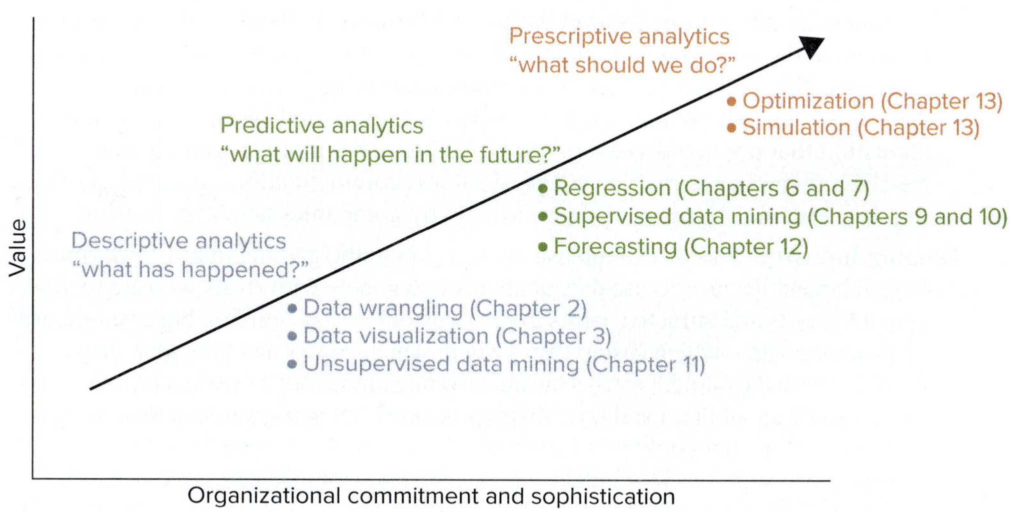

FIGURE 1.1 Three stages of business analytics

In addition to the chapters presented in Figure 1.1, Chapters 1 (Introduction to Business Analytics), 4 (Probability and Probability Distributions), 5 (Statistical Inference), and 8 (Introduction to Data Mining) cover prerequisite knowledge to the other topics in the text. Regardless of the analysis techniques we use, the overall goal of analytics is to improve business decision making. Essential to this goal is the ability to communicate the insights and value of data. Throughout the text, students will not only learn to conduct data analysis but also to tell an impactful story conveyed in written form to those who may not know detailed statistical and computational methods.

Important Business Analytics Applications

Data and analytics permeate our daily lives. We are often unaware of the impact that analytics has on even the most mundane activities, such as buying clothes, saving for retirement, checking e-mails, interacting on social media, and watching a TV show. We will now highlight some of the important applications of business analytics.

Fashion Retailers. Traditional businesses ranging from apparel companies to food retailers invest heavily in data and analytics technologies in order to remain competitive and profitable. Once acclaimed as the company that "dictated how America dressed" by *The New York Times,* the Gap, Inc., experienced disappointing sales in recent years as the fast fashion industry got increasingly crowded with major international competitors, such as Zara, H&M, and Uniqlo, entering the U.S. market. To turn the company around, Art Peck, Gap's CEO, revolutionized the company by using insights gained from transactional and customer databases as well as social media data. Instead of relying solely on the vision of creative directors, Gap uses predictive analytics to help determine the next season's assortment of products. Peck also encouraged his employees to use big data to inform a wide range of decision making, including identifying loyal customers, matching products to customers, enhancing customer satisfaction, and managing product rebuys. As the result of these changes, the company is now able to combine the trends identified in data with real-time store sales to quickly bring more relevant products to market.

Online Subscription. Netflix, one of the largest content-streaming companies, transformed the entertainment industry with its innovative business model. One of the engines that propelled its success was a sophisticated analytics tool called CineMatch, a recommendation system for movies and TV shows. CineMatch was so crucial to Netflix's ability to sustain and grow its customer base that the company launched a one million dollar competition challenging the contestants to improve the CineMatch recommendation algorithm. Netflix provided the contestants with a data set of over 100 million user ratings given to about 20,000 movies. The winning team, BellKor's Pragmatic Chaos, developed an algorithm that predicted viewers' movie ratings 10% more accurately than Netflix's own algorithm. Nowadays, similar recommendation systems based on big data and analytics are used pervasively by companies across industries.

Gaming Industry. Faced with intense competition in the gaming industry, Harrah's Entertainment decided to use data analytics to compete with rivals who are touting opulent resorts and attractive perks to their customers. By building huge warehouses of customer data—which casino they visited, which games and how long they played, where they dined, etc.—Harrah customized visitors' experiences based on what it knew about them and turned "promiscuous" customers into "monogamous" customers who would only go to Harrah's. Analytics also helped drive Harrah's operating decisions, such as hotel room pricing and slot machine placement. The analytics efforts paid off financially. Adjusted earnings per share increased fivefold within seven years. Improved profits generated from its data-driven decision making allowed Harrah's to invest in facility upgrades and global expansion.

Sports. Sports analytics uses data on players' statistics and other sports-related information to drive decision making. Long before the analytics buzz, the

Oakland Athletics baseball team, referred to as the A's, used analytics to build a playoff-bound team. (The A's approach to the game was also depicted in the movie *Moneyball.*) Traditionally, professional baseball recruiters relied heavily on subjective measures, such as body type, speed, and projected confidence for scouting players. Recognizing this shortcoming, the A's took advantage of sabermetrics, which is an application of statistical analysis to baseball, to assess hidden worth in undervalued players. The model was built on the premise that a team with a high on-base percentage was likely to score more runs and, therefore, win more games. The A's drafted and traded for players that fit this system, not necessarily requiring them to fit the body type and other subjective features that dictated the decisions of other clubs. Despite being one of the poorest-funded teams in Major League Baseball, the A's were able to pick talented players cheaply, making them one of the most successful franchises in 2002 and 2003. This success has since revolutionized all major professional sports, with each team having its own analytics department or an analytics expert.

Healthcare. Big data and analytics are also increasingly used in the medical field. By analyzing 46 billion data points on over 200,000 adult patients, Google's artificial intelligence system has developed a model for predicting hospital visit outcomes and final diagnoses. Google's system claims to be able to predict patient death 24 to 48 hours before existing hospital models can, allowing life-saving procedures to be administered. Another example of big data in medicine is the Cancer Moonshot program, sponsored by the U.S. National Cancer Institute, with an ambitious goal of developing a cure for cancer. The program provides medical researchers with access to a vast amount of cancer patient data. By analyzing biopsy reports, treatment plans, and recovery rates of patients, researchers are able to study trends in how certain cancer proteins interact with different treatments and recommend the most promising treatment plan for the individual patient.

These examples show that analytics is taking a radical approach to improving organizations' decision-making abilities. The data-driven approach is replacing and complementing the traditional decision-making process that relies heavily on a few experts and their subjective judgment. This has led to more accurate, often overlooked, and unexpected findings, which have morphed into competitive advantages with the help of the right domain expertise.

While the promise of big data analytics is exciting, organizations cannot neglect the greater responsibilities that come with this newly acquired power. As we capitalize on the data collected from our customers and constituents, we must realize that there are enormous risks involved in using these data, especially in the forms of data security and privacy. Many stories of data breach and misuse serve as chilling reminders of these risks. For example, in 2018, Marriott International disclosed a massive data breach that affected up to 500 million guests. Private data accessed by the hackers included names, addresses, phone numbers, e-mail addresses, passport numbers, and encrypted credit card details. Breaches like this can lead to identity theft and/or financial fraud. In another example, Cambridge Analytica, a political data firm hired by President Donald Trump's 2016 election campaign, harvested private information from over 50 million Facebook profiles to create personality models for voters, which were later used to create digital ads to influence voter behaviors. Facebook has since tightened its policies on third-party access to user profiles, but the incident created enormous backlash against the social media company. As these cases illustrate, analytics must be conducted in a responsible and ethical way.

The diverse nature of analytics applications requires deep understanding of data and data types. In the remaining part of this chapter, we will describe the various types of data and measurement scales that help us choose appropriate techniques for analyzing data. We will also discuss how we can take advantage of data sources that are publicly available, and review some standard formats that people use to store and disseminate data.

LO 1.2

1.2 TYPES OF DATA

Explain the various types of data.

Every day, consumers and businesses use many kinds of data from various sources to help make decisions. An important first step for making decisions is to find the right data and prepare it for the analysis. In general, **data** are compilations of facts, figures, or other contents, both numerical and nonnumerical. Data of all types and formats are generated from multiple sources. Insights from all of these data can enable businesses to make better decisions, such as deepening customer engagement, optimizing operations, preventing threats and fraud, and capitalizing on new sources of revenue. We often find a large amount of data at our disposal. However, we also derive insights from relatively small data sets, such as from consumer focus groups, marketing surveys, or reports from government agencies.

Data that have been organized, analyzed, and processed in a meaningful and purposeful way become **information**. We use a blend of data, contextual information, experience, and intuition to derive **knowledge** that can be applied and put into action in specific situations.

> **DATA, INFORMATION, AND KNOWLEDGE**
>
> Data are compilations of facts, figures, or other contents, both numerical and nonnumerical. Information is a set of data that are organized and processed in a meaningful and purposeful way. Knowledge is derived from a blend of data, contextual information, experience, and intuition.

In the introductory case, Emily is looking for flights from Los Angeles International Airport (LAX) to Belize City (BZE), as well as hotels in Belize. An online search on Orbitz.com yields a total of 1,420 combinations of flight schedules. She also finds information on 19 hotels that are within her budget. Figure 1.2 shows a portion of the airfare and hotel information that Emily finds on the Internet.

Before we analyze the information that Emily has gathered, it is important to understand different types of data. In this section, we focus on the various data categorizations.

Sample and Population Data

There are several ways to categorize data depending on how they are collected, their format, and specific values they represent. In most instances, it is not feasible to collect data that comprise the **population** of all elements of interest. Therefore, a subset of data—a **sample**—is used for the analysis. Traditional statistical techniques use sample information to draw conclusions about the population.

> **POPULATION VERSUS SAMPLE**
>
> A population consists of all observations or items of interest in an analysis. A sample is a subset of the population. We examine sample data to make inferences about the population.

It is generally not feasible to obtain population data due to prohibitive costs and/or practicality. We rely on sampling because we are unable to use population data for two main reasons.

- **Obtaining information on the entire population is expensive.** Suppose we are interested in the average lifespan of a Duracell AAA battery. It would be incredibly expensive to test each battery. And moreover, in the end, all batteries would be dead and the answer to the original question would be useless.

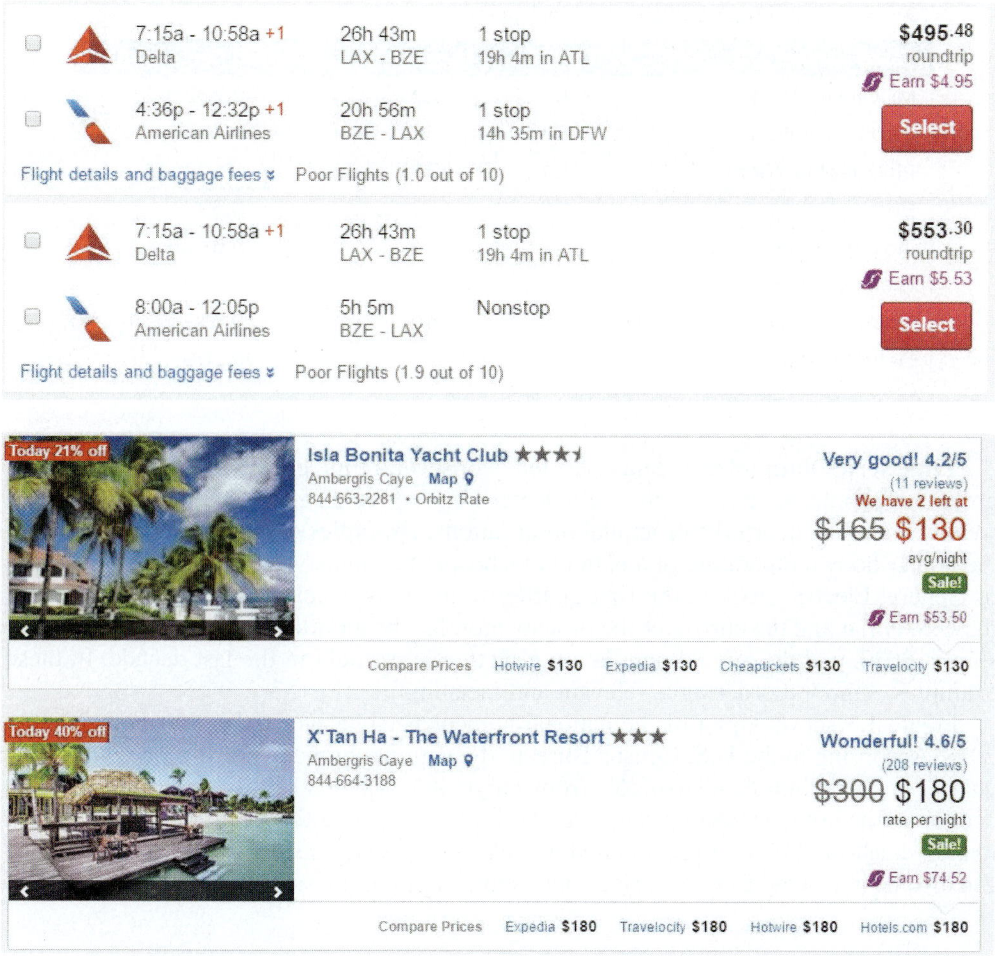

FIGURE 1.2 Screen shot of airfare and hotel search results from Orbitz.com
Source: Orbitz.com

- **It is impossible to examine every member of the population.** Consider how the monthly unemployment rate in the United States is calculated by the Bureau of Labor Statistics (BLS). Is it reasonable to assume that the the BLS contacts each individual in the labor force, and asks whether or not he or she is employed? Given that there are over 160 million individuals in the labor force, this task would be impossible to complete in 30 days. Instead, the BLS conducts a monthly sample survey of about 60,000 households to measure the extent of unemployment in the United States.

In the introductory case, Emily is working with sample data. The population would have consisted of all the airlines and hotels, some of which may not even have shown up in an online search.

Cross-Sectional and Time Series Data

Sample data are generally collected in one of two ways. **Cross-sectional data** refer to data collected by recording a characteristic of many subjects at the same point in time, or without regard to differences in time. Subjects might include individuals, households, firms, industries, regions, and countries. The National Basketball Association (NBA) data presented in Table 1.1 is an example of cross-sectional data because it displays the team standings at the end of the 2018–2019 season. The eight teams may not have ended the season precisely on the same day and time, but the differences in time are of no relevance in this example. Other examples of cross-sectional data include the recorded grades of students in a class, the sale prices of single-family homes sold last month, the current price of gasoline in different cities in the United States, and the starting salaries of recent business graduates from the University of Connecticut.

TABLE 1.1 2018–2019 NBA Eastern Conference

Team name	Wins	Losses	Winning percentage
Milwaukee Bucks	60	22	0.732
Toronto Raptors*	58	24	0.707
Philadephia 76ers	51	31	0.622
Boston Celtics	49	33	0.598
Indiana Pacers	48	34	0.585
Brooklyn Nets	42	40	0.512
Orlando Magic	42	40	0.512
Detroit Pistons	41	41	0.500

*The Toronto Raptors won their first NBA title during the 2018-2019 season.

Time series data refer to data collected over several time periods focusing on certain groups of people, specific events, or objects. Time series data can include hourly, daily, weekly, monthly, quarterly, or annual observations. Examples of time series data include the hourly body temperature of a patient in a hospital's intensive care unit, the daily price of General Electric stock in the first quarter of 2020, the weekly exchange rate between the U.S. dollar and the euro over the past six months, the monthly sales of cars at a dealership in 2020, and the annual population growth rate of India in the last decade. In these examples, temporal ordering is relevant and meaningful.

Figure 1.3 shows a plot of the national homeownership rate in the U.S. from 2000 to 2018. According to the U.S. Census Bureau, the national homeownership rate in the first quarter of 2016 plummeted to 63.6% from a high of 69.4% in 2004. An explanation for the decline in the homeownership rate is the stricter lending practices caused by the housing market crash in 2007 that precipitated a banking crisis and deep recession. This decline can also be attributed to home prices outpacing wages in the sample period.

FIGURE 1.3
Homeownership Rate (in %) in the U.S. from 2000 through 2018
Source: Federal Reserve Bank of St. Louis

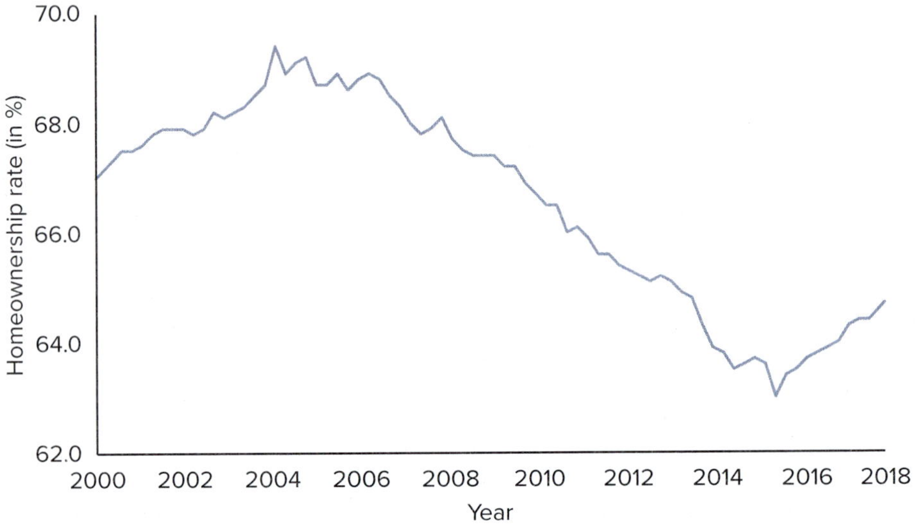

Structured and Unstructured Data

When you think of data, the first image that probably pops in your head is lots of numbers and perhaps some charts and graphs. In reality, data can come in multiple forms. For example, information exchange in social networking websites such as Facebook, LinkedIn, and Twitter also constitute data. In order to better understand the various forms of data, we make a distinction between structured and unstructured data.

Generally, **structured data** reside in a predefined, row-column format. We use spreadsheet or database applications (see Section 2.1) to enter, store, query, and analyze structured data. Examples of structured data include numbers, dates, and groups of words and numbers, typically stored in a tabular format. Structured data often consist of numerical information that is objective and is not open to interpretation.

Point-of-sale and financial data are examples of structured data and are usually designed to capture a business process or transaction. Examples include the sale of retail products, money transfer between bank accounts, and the student enrollment in a university course. When individual consumers buy products from a retail store, each transaction is captured into a record of structured data.

Consider the sales invoice shown in Figure 1.4. Whenever a customer places an order like this, there is a predefined set of data to be collected, such as the transaction date, shipping address, and the units of product being purchased. Even though a receipt or an invoice may not always be presented in rows and columns, the predefined structure allows businesses and organizations to translate the data on the document into a row-column format. As we will see in Example 1.1, the flight information collected for the introductory case may not fit precisely in a tabular format, but because of the structured nature of the data, it can easily be summarized into rows and columns.

Tranquility Home and Garden

8 Harmony Drive

San Francisco, CA 94126

Phone: (415) SOL-SAVE

Date: July 1, 2020

Invoice number: A9239145-W

Customer Name: Kevin Lau
Account Number: KL0927

Street Address: 123 Solstice Circle
City: San Francisco

State/Province: California
Postal Code: 94126

Telephone: (415) 234-4550

Product code	Product description	Units ordered	Price per unit	Extended Price
421-L	8W LED light bulbs	27	$7.59	$204.93
389-P	Chlorine removing shower filter	6	$19.99	$119.94
682-K	Compostable cutlery (box sets)	5	$14.99	$74.95

Total amount: $399.82
Sales Tax: $31.99
Shipping fee: $6.99
Grand total: $438.80

FIGURE 1.4 A sample invoice from a retail transaction

At one time, due to the high cost and performance limitations of storing and processing data, companies and organizations relied mostly on structured data, which could be effectively managed with spreadsheet and database applications. For decades, they relied on this type of data to run their businesses and operations. Today, with the advent of the digital age, most experts agree that only about 20% of all data used in business decisions are structured data. The remaining 80% are unstructured.

Unlike structured data, **unstructured data** (or unmodeled data) do not conform to a predefined, row-column format. They tend to be textual (e.g., written reports, e-mail messages, doctor's notes, or open-ended survey responses) or have multimedia contents (e.g., photographs, videos, and audio data). Even though these data may have some-implied structure (e.g., a report title, e-mail's subject line, or a time stamp on a photograph), they are still considered unstructured as they do not conform to a row-column model required in most database systems. Social media data such as Twitter, YouTube, Facebook, and blogs are examples of unstructured data.

Both structured and unstructured data can be either **human-generated** or **machine-generated**. For structured data, human-generated data include information on price, income, retail sales, age, gender, etc., whereas machine-generated data include information from manufacturing sensors (rotations per minute), speed cameras (miles per hour), web server logs (number of visitors), etc. For unstructured data, human-generated data include texts of internal e-mails, social media data, presentations, mobile phone conversations, and text message data, and so on, whereas machine-generated data include satellite images, meteorological data, surveillance video data, traffic camera images, and others. In this text, we focus on structured data. Text analytics and other sophisticated tools to analyze unstructured data are beyond the scope of this text.

Big Data

Nowadays, businesses and organizations generate and gather more and more data at an increasing pace. The term **big data** is a catch-phrase, meaning a massive volume of both structured and unstructured data that are extremely difficult to manage, process, and analyze using traditional data-processing tools. Despite the challenges, big data present great opportunities to gain knowledge and business intelligence with potential game-changing impacts on company revenues, competitive advantage, and organizational efficiency. More formally, a widely accepted definition of big data is "high-volume, high-velocity and/or high-variety information assets that demand cost-effective, innovative forms of information processing that enable enhanced insight, decision making, and process automation" (www.gartner.com). The three characteristics (the three Vs) of big data are:

- **Volume**: An immense amount of data is compiled from a single source or a wide range of sources, including business transactions, household and personal devices, manufacturing equipment, social media, and other online portals.
- **Velocity**: In addition to volume, data from a variety of sources get generated at a rapid speed. Managing these data streams can become a critical issue for many organizations.
- **Variety**: Data also come in all types, forms, and granularity, both structured and unstructured. These data may include numbers, text, and figures as well as audio, video, e-mails, and other multimedia elements.

In addition to the three defining characteristics of big data, we also need to pay close attention to the veracity of the data and the business value that they can generate. **Veracity** refers to the credibility and quality of data. One must verify the reliability and accuracy of the data content prior to relying on the data to make decisions. This becomes increasingly challenging with the rapid growth of data volume fueled by social media and automatic data collection. **Value** derived from big data is perhaps the most important aspect of any analytics initiative. Having a plethora of data does not guarantee that useful insights or measurable improvements will be generated. Organizations must develop a methodical plan for formulating business questions, curating the right data, and unlocking the hidden potential in big data.

Big data, however, do not necessarily imply complete (population) data. Take, for example, the analysis of all Facebook users. It certainly involves big data, but if we consider all Internet users in the world, Facebook users are only a very large sample. There are many Internet users who do not use Facebook, so the data on Facebook do not represent the population. Even if we define the population as pertaining to those who use online social media, Facebook is still one of many social media portals that consumers use. And because different social media are used for different purposes, data collected from these sites may very well reflect different populations of Internet users; this distinction is especially important from a strategic business standpoint. Therefore, Facebook data are simply a very large sample.

In addition, we may choose not to use big data in its entirety even when they are available. Sometimes it is just inconvenient to analyze a very large data set as it is computationally burdensome, even with a modern, high-capacity computer system. Other times, the additional benefits of working with big data may not justify the associated costs. In sum, we often choose to work with a small data set, which in a sense is a sample drawn from big data.

STRUCTURED, UNSTRUCTURED, AND BIG DATA

Structured data are data that reside in a predefined, row-column format, while unstructured data do not conform to a predefined, row-column format. Big data is a term used to describe a massive volume of both structured and unstructured data that are extremely difficult to manage, process, and analyze using traditional data-processing tools. Big data, however, do not necessary imply complete (population) data.

EXAMPLE 1.1

In the introductory case, Emily is looking for roundtrip flight schedules offered by different airlines from Los Angeles, California, to Belize City. Once arriving at Belize City, she plans to purchase a vacation package from one of the resort hotels on Ambergris Caye Island. She has compiled information on flight schedules and hotel options from search results on Orbitz.com. Her initial search yields 1,420 flight schedules and 19 hotels. In its current format, Emily is overwhelmed by the amount of data and knows that she needs to refine her search. She would like to focus on flights that are convenient (short duration) and relatively inexpensive. For hotels, she would like an affordable hotel (priced under $200 per night) with good reviews (above-average review on a 5-point scale). Given Emily's preferences, summarize the online information in tabular form.

SOLUTION:

We first search for roundtrip flight schedules where priority is given to short flight times and low prices. Even though the flight information is not in a perfect row-column configuration, the structured nature of the data allows us to summarize the information in a tabular format. The four most relevant options are presented in Panel A of Table 1.2. Given these options, it seems that the American/Delta choice might be the best for her. Similarly, once we refine the search to include only hotels that fall within her budget of under $200 per night and have an average consumer rating above 4 on a 5-point scale, the number of hotel options declines from 19 to five. These five options are presented in Panel B of Table 1.2. In this case, her

TABLE 1.2 Tabular Format of Flight Search and Hotel Results

Panel A. Flight Search Results

		Los Angeles to Belize City			Belize City to Los Angeles		
Airlines	Price	Departure time	Duration	Number of stops	Departure time	Duration	Number of stops
Delta/American	$495.48	7:15am	26h 43m	1	4:36pm	20h 56m	1
Delta/American	$553.30	7:15am	26h 43m	1	8:00am	5h 5m	0
United/Delta	$929.91	6:55am	6h 58m	1	10:30am	5h 2m	0
American/Delta	$632.91	7:00am	7h 41m	1	10:30am	5h 2m	0

Panel B. Hotel Results

Hotel under $200	Average Rating	Number of Reviews	Price per night
Isla Bonita Yacht Club	4.2	11	$130
X'Tan Ha – The Waterfront	4.6	208	$180
Mata Rocks Resort	4.2	212	$165
Costa Blu	4.5	8	$165
Blue Tang Inn	4.2	26	$179

choice of hotel is not clear-cut. The hotel with the highest rating is also the most expensive (X'Tan Ha – The Waterfront), while the least expensive hotel has the lowest rating (Isla Bonita Yacht Club) and the rating is based on only 11 reviews. Emily will now base her final hotel choice on online reviews. These reviews constitute unstructured data that do not conform to a row-column format.

SYNOPSIS OF INTRODUCTORY CASE

David Schulz Photography/Shutterstock

Emily Hernandez is excited to go on vacation in Belize with her friends. She decides to search on Orbitz.com for flights that are convenient as well as affordable. She also wants to find a reputable hotel in Ambergris Caye Island that is priced under \$200 per night. Although she finds 1,420 options for the flight, she focuses on morning flights with priority given to lower prices and shorter flight times.

There are four airline options that she finds suitable. With a price of \$495.48, the Delta/American option is the cheapest, but the flight time is over 20 hours each way. The United/Delta option offers the shortest flight times; however, it comes with a price tag of \$929.91. Emily decides on the American/Delta option, which seems most reasonable with a price of \$632.91, a flight time of under eight hours to Belize, and only five hours on the return. In regard to hotels, Bonita Yacht Club offers the cheapest price of \$130, but it comes with a relatively low rating of 4.2.

In addition, Emily is concerned about the credibility of the rating as it is based on only 11 reviews. Although not the cheapest, Emily decides to go with X'Tan Ha – The Waterfront. It has the highest rating of 4.6 and the price still falls within her budget of under \$200. In these reviews, Emily consistently finds key phrases such as "great location," "clean room," "comfortable bed," and "helpful staff." Finally, the pictures that guests have posted are consistent with the images published by the resort on its website.

EXERCISES 1.2

Applications

1. A few years ago, it came as a surprise when Apple's iPhone 4 was found to have a problem. Users complained of weak reception, and sometimes even dropped calls, when they cradled the phone in their hands in a particular way. A survey at a local store found that 2% of iPhone 4 users experienced this reception problem.
   a. Describe the relevant population.
   b. Is 2% associated with the population or the sample?
2. Many people regard video games as an obsession for youngsters, but, in fact, the average age of a video game player is 35 years old. Is the value 35 likely the actual or the estimated average age of the population? Explain.
3. An accounting professor wants to know the average GPA of the students enrolled in her class. She looks up information on Blackboard about the students enrolled in her class and computes the average GPA as 3.29. Describe the relevant population.
4. Recent college graduates with an engineering degree continue to earn high salaries. An online search revealed that the average annual salary for an entry-level position in engineering is \$65,000.
   a. What is the relevant population?
   b. Do you think the average salary of \$65,000 is computed from the population? Explain.
5. Research suggests that depression significantly increases the risk of developing dementia later in life. Suppose that in a study involving 949 elderly persons, it was found that 22% of those who had depression went on to develop dementia, compared to only 17% of those who did not have depression.
   a. Describe the relevant population and the sample.
   b. Are the numbers 22% and 17% associated with the population or a sample?
6. Go to www.zillow.com and find the sale price of 20 single-family homes sold in Las Vegas, Nevada, in the last 30 days. Structure

the data in a tabular format and include the sale price, the number of bedrooms, the square footage, and the age of the house. Do these data represent cross-sectional or time series data?

7. Go to www.finance.yahoo.com to get the current stock quote for Home Depot (ticker symbol = HD). Use the ticker symbol to search for historical prices and create a table that includes the monthly adjusted close price of Home Depot stock for the last 12 months. Do these data represent cross-sectional or time series data?
8. Go to the *New York Times* website at www.nytimes.com and review the front page. Would you consider the data on the page to be structured or unstructured? Explain.
9. Conduct an online search to compare small hybrid vehicles (e.g., Toyota Prius, Ford Fusion, Chevrolet Volt) on price, fuel economy, and other specifications. Do you consider the search results structured or unstructured data? Explain.
10. Find Under Armour's annual revenue from the past 10 years. Are the data considered structured or unstructured? Explain. Are they cross-sectional or time series data?
11. Ask 20 of your friends about their online social media usage, specifically whether or not they use Facebook, Instagram, and Snapchat; how often they use each social media portal; and their overall satisfaction of each of these portals. Create a table that presents this information. Are the data considered structured or unstructured? Are they cross-sectional or time series data?
12. Ask 20 of your friends whether they live in a dormitory, a rental unit, or other form of accommodation. Also find out their approximate monthly lodging expenses. Create a table that uses this information. Are the data considered structured or unstructured? Are they cross-sectional or time series data?
13. Go to the U.S. Census Bureau website at www.census.gov and search for the most recent median household income for Alabama, Arizona, California, Florida, Georgia, Indiana, Iowa, Maine, Massachusetts, Minnesota, Mississippi, New Mexico, North Dakota, and Washington. Do these data represent cross-sectional or time series data? Comment on the regional differences in income.

1.3 VARIABLES AND SCALES OF MEASUREMENT

LO 1.3

Describe variables and types of measurement scales.

For business analytics, we invariably focus on people, firms, or events with particular characteristics. When a characteristic of interest differs in kind or degree among various observations (records), then the characteristic can be termed a **variable**. Marital status and income are examples of variables because a person's marital status and income vary from person to person. Variables are further classified as either **categorical** (qualitative) or **numerical** (quantitative). The observations of a categorical variable represent categories, whereas the observations of a numerical variable represent meaningful numbers. For example, marital status is a categorical variable, whereas income is a numerical variable.

For a categorical variable, we use labels or names to identify the distinguishing characteristic of each observation. For instance, a university may identify each student's status as either at the undergraduate or the graduate level, where the education level is a categorical variable representing two categories. Categorical variables can also be defined by more than two categories. Examples include marital status (single, married, widowed, divorced, separated), IT firm (hardware, software, cloud), and course grade (A, B, C, D, F). It is important to note that categories are often converted into numerical codes for purposes of data processing, which we will discuss in Chapter 2.

For a numerical variable, we use numbers to identify the distinguishing characteristic of each observation. Numerical variables, in turn, are either discrete or continuous. A **discrete variable** assumes a countable number of values. Consider the number of children in a family or the number of points scored in a basketball game. We may observe values such as 3 children in a family or 90 points being scored in a basketball game, but we will not observe 1.3 children or 92.5 scored points. The values that a discrete variable assumes need not be whole numbers. For example, the price of a stock for a particular firm is a discrete variable. The stock price may take on a value of $20.37 or $20.38, but it cannot take on a value between these two points. A **continuous variable** is characterized by uncountable values within an interval. Weight, height, time, and investment return are all examples of continuous variables. For example, an unlimited number of values occur between the weights of 100 and 101 pounds, such as 100.3, 100.625, 100.8342, and so on. In practice, however, continuous variables are often measured in discrete values. We may report a newborn's weight (a continuous variable) in discrete terms as 6 pounds 10 ounces and another newborn's weight in similar discrete terms as 6 pounds 11 ounces.

CATEGORICAL AND NUMERICAL VARIABLES

A variable is a general characteristic being observed on a set of people, objects, or events, where each observation varies in kind or degree.

- The observations of a categorical variable assume names or labels.
- The observations of a numerical variable assume meaningful numerical values. A numerical variable can be further categorized as either discrete or continuous. A discrete variable assumes a countable number of values, whereas a continuous variable is characterized by uncountable values.

EXAMPLE 1.2

In the introductory case, Emily has conducted an online search on airfares and hotels for her planned vacation to Ambergris Caye Island. She has summarized the information in Table 1.2. What types of variables are included in the airfare and hotel data?

SOLUTION:

Airlines and hotels are categorical variables because the observations—the names—are merely labels. On the other hand, the roundtrip price, the average rating, the number of reviews, and the price per night are numerical variables because the observations are all meaningful numbers. Note that the roundtrip price, the number of reviews, and the price per night represent discrete variables because they can only assume a countable number of values. The average rating is continuous because it is characterized by uncountable values within the 0 to 5 interval. The date and time variables are considered numerical; however, if we were to consider the days of the week (e.g., Monday, Tuesday, etc.) in the flight schedules, then the variable days would be considered a categorical variable.

The Measurement Scales

In order to choose the appropriate techniques for summarizing and analyzing variables, we need to distinguish between the different measurement scales. The data for any variable can be classified into one of four major measurement scales: nominal, ordinal, interval, or ratio. Nominal and ordinal scales are used for categorical variables, whereas interval and ratio scales are used for numerical variables. We discuss these scales in ascending order of sophistication.

The **nominal scale** represents the least sophisticated level of measurement. If we are presented with nominal data, all we can do is categorize or group the data. The values in the data set differ merely by name or label. Table 1.3 lists the 30 large, publicly-owned companies that comprise the Dow Jones Industrial Average (DJIA). The DJIA is a stock market index that shows how these U.S.-based companies have traded during a standard trading session in the stock market. Table 1.3 also indicates where stocks of these companies are traded: on either the National Association of Securities Dealers Automated Quotations (Nasdaq) or the New York Stock Exchange (NYSE). These data are classified as nominal scale because we are simply able to group or categorize them. Specifically, only five stocks are traded on the Nasdaq, whereas the remaining 25 are traded on the NYSE.

Often, we substitute numbers for the particular categorical characteristic or trait that we are grouping. For instance, we might use the number 0 to show that a company's stock is traded on the Nasdaq and the number 1 to show that a company's stock is traded on the NYSE. One reason why we do this is for ease of exposition; always referring to the National Association of Securities Dealers Automated Quotations, or even the Nasdaq, can be awkward and unwieldy.

TABLE 1.3 Companies of the DJIA and Exchange Where Stock is Traded

Company	Exchange	Company	Exchange
3M (MMM)	NYSE	Johnson & Johnson (JNJ)	NYSE
American Express (AXP)	NYSE	JPMorgan Chase (JPM)	NYSE
Apple (AAPL)	Nasdaq	McDonald's (MCD)	NYSE
Boeing (BA)	NYSE	Merck (MRK)	NYSE
Caterpillar (CAT)	NYSE	Microsoft (MFST)	Nasdaq
Chevron (CVX)	NYSE	Nike (NKE)	NYSE
Cisco (CSCO)	Nasdaq	Pfizer (PFE)	NYSE
Coca-Cola (KO)	NYSE	Procter & Gamble (PG)	NYSE
Disney (DIS)	NYSE	Travelers (TRV)	NYSE
DowDupont (DWDP)	NYSE	United Health (UNH)	NYSE
ExxonMobil (XOM)	NYSE	United Technologies (UTX)	NYSE
Goldman Sachs (GS)	NYSE	Verizon (VZ)	NYSE
Home Depot (HD)	NYSE	Visa (V)	NYSE
IBM (IBM)	NYSE	Wal-Mart (WMT)	NYSE
Intel (INTC)	Nasdaq	Walgreen (WBA)	Nasdaq

Source: https://money.cnn.com/data/dow30/; information retrieved on February 16, 2019

Compared to the nominal scale, the **ordinal scale** reflects a stronger level of measurement. With ordinal data, we are able to both categorize and rank the data with respect to some characteristic or trait. The weakness with ordinal data is that we cannot interpret the difference between the ranked values because the actual numbers used are arbitrary. For example, in the introductory case, Emily looks at hotel reviews where consumers are asked to classify the service at a particular hotel as excellent (5 stars), very good (4 stars), good (3 stars), fair (2 stars), or poor (1 star). We summarize the categories and their respective ratings in Table 1.4.

TABLE 1.4 Hotel Survey Categories with Ratings

Category	Rating
Excellent	5
Very good	4
Good	3
Fair	2
Poor	1

In Table 1.4, the value attached to excellent (5 stars) is higher than the value attached to good (3 stars), indicating that the response of excellent is preferred to good. However, we can easily redefine the ratings, as we show in Table 1.5.

TABLE 1.5 Hotel Survey Categories with Redefined Ratings

Category	Rating
Excellent	100
Very good	80
Good	70
Fair	50
Poor	40

In Table 1.5, excellent still receives a higher value than good, but now the difference between the two categories is 30 points (100 – 70), as compared to a difference of 2 points (5 – 3) when we use the first classification. In other words, differences between categories are meaningless with ordinal data. (We also should note that we could reverse the ordering so that, for instance, excellent equals 40 and poor equals 100; this renumbering would not change the nature of the data.)

As mentioned earlier, observations of a categorical variable are typically expressed in words but are coded into numbers for purposes of data processing. When summarizing the results of a categorical variable, we typically count the number of observations that fall into each category or calculate the percentage of observations that fall into each category. However, with a categorical variable, we are unable to perform meaningful arithmetic operations, such as addition and subtraction.

With data that is measured on the **interval scale**, we are able to categorize and rank the data as well as find meaningful differences between observations. The Fahrenheit scale for temperatures is an example of interval-scaled data. Not only is 60 degrees Fahrenheit hotter than 50 degrees Fahrenheit, the same difference of 10 degrees also exists between 90 and 80 degrees Fahrenheit.

The main drawback of interval-scaled data is that the value of zero is arbitrarily chosen; the zero point of interval-scaled data does not reflect a complete absence of what is being measured. No specific meaning is attached to 0 degrees Fahrenheit other than to say it is 10 degrees colder than 10 degrees Fahrenheit. With an arbitrary zero point, meaningful ratios cannot be constructed. For instance, it is senseless to say that 80 degrees is twice as hot as 40 degrees; in other words, the ratio 80/40 has no meaning.

The **ratio scale** represents the strongest level of measurement. The ratio scale has all the characteristics of the interval scale as well as a true zero point, which allows us to interpret the ratios between observations. The ratio scale is used in many business applications. Variables such as sales, profits, and inventory levels are expressed on the ratio scale. A meaningful zero point allows us to state, for example, that profits for firm A are double those of firm B. Variables such as weight, time, and distance are also measured on a ratio scale because zero is meaningful.

Unlike nominal- and ordinal-scaled variables (categorical variables), arithmetic operations are valid on interval- and ratio-scaled variables (numerical variables). In later chapters, we will calculate summary measures, such as the mean, the median, and the variance, for numerical variables; we cannot calculate these measures if the variable is categorical in nature.

MEASUREMENT SCALES

The observations for any variable can be classified into one of four major measurement scales: nominal, ordinal, interval, or ratio.

- Nominal: Observations differ merely by name or label.
- Ordinal: Observations can be categorized and ranked; however, differences between the ranked observations are meaningless.
- Interval: Observations can be categorized and ranked, and differences between observations are meaningful. The main drawback of the interval scale is that the value of zero is arbitrarily chosen.
- Ratio: Observations have all the characteristics of interval-scaled data as well as a true zero point; thus, meaningful ratios can be calculated.

Nominal and ordinal scales are used for categorical variables, whereas interval and ratio scales are used for numerical variables.

EXAMPLE 1.3

FILE *Tween_Survey*

The owner of a ski resort two hours outside Boston, Massachusetts, is interested in serving the needs of the "tween" population (children aged 8 to 12 years old). He believes that tween spending power has grown over the past few years, and he wants their skiing experience to be memorable so that they want to return. At the end of last year's ski season, he asked 20 tweens the following four questions.

- Q1. On your car drive to the resort, which music streaming service was playing?
- Q2. On a scale of 1 to 4, rate the quality of the food at the resort (where 1 is poor, 2 is fair, 3 is good, and 4 is excellent).
- Q3. Presently, the main dining area closes at 3:00 pm. What time do you think it should close?
- Q4. How much of your own money did you spend at the lodge today?

A portion of their responses is shown in Table 1.6. Identify the scale of measurement for each variable used in the survey. Given the tween responses, provide suggestions to the owner for improvement.

TABLE 1.6 Tween Responses to Resort Survey

Tween	Music Streaming	Food Quality	Closing Time	Own Money Spent ($)
1	Apple Music	4	5:00 pm	20
2	Pandora	2	5:00 pm	10
⋮	⋮	⋮	⋮	⋮
20	Spotify	2	4:30 pm	10

SOLUTION:

- Q1. Responses for music streaming service are nominal because the observations differ merely in label. Twelve of the 20 tweens, or 60%, listened to Spotify. If the resort wishes to contact tweens using this means, then it may want to direct its advertising dollars to this streaming service.
- Q2. Food quality responses are on an ordinal scale because we can both categorize and rank the observations. Eleven of the 20 tweens, or 55%, felt that the food quality was, at best, fair. Perhaps a more extensive survey that focuses solely on food quality would reveal the reason for their apparent dissatisfaction.
- Q3. Closing time responses are on an interval scale. We can say that 3:30 pm is 30 minutes later than 3:00 pm, and 6:00 pm is 30 minutes later than 5:30 pm; that is, differences between observations are meaningful. The closing time responses, however, have no apparent zero point. We could arbitrarily define the zero point at 12:00 am, but ratios are still meaningless. In other words, it makes no sense to form the ratio 6:00 pm/3:00 pm and conclude that 6:00 pm is twice as long a time period as 3:00 pm. A review of the closing time responses shows that the vast majority (19 out of 20) would like the dining area to remain open later.
- Q4. The tweens' responses with respect to their own money spent at the resort are on a ratio scale. We can categorize and rank observations as well as calculate meaningful differences. Moreover, because there is a natural zero point, valid ratios can also be calculated. Seventeen of the 20 tweens spent their own money at the lodge. It does appear that the discretionary spending of this age group is significant. The owner would be wise to cater to some of their preferences.

EXERCISES 1.3

Applications

14. Which of the following variables are categorical and which are numerical? If the variable is numerical, then specify whether the variable is discrete or continuous.
    a. Points scored in a football game.
    b. Racial composition of a high school classroom.
    c. Heights of 15-year-olds.
15. Which of the following variables are categorical and which are numerical? If the variable is numerical, then specify whether the variable is discrete or continuous.
    a. Colors of cars in a mall parking lot.
    b. Time it takes each student to complete a final exam.
    c. The number of patrons who frequent a restaurant.
16. In each of the following scenarios, define the type of measurement scale.
    a. A kindergarten teacher marks whether each student is a boy or a girl.
    b. A ski resort records the daily temperature during the month of January.
    c. A restaurant surveys its customers about the quality of its waiting staff on a scale of 1 to 4, where 1 is poor and 4 is excellent.
17. In each of the following scenarios, define the type of measurement scale.
    a. An investor collects data on the weekly closing price of gold throughout the year.
    b. An analyst assigns a sample of bond issues to one of the following credit ratings, given in descending order of credit quality (increasing probability of default): AAA, AA, BBB, BB, CC, D.
    c. The dean of the business school at a local university categorizes students by major (i.e., accounting, finance, marketing, etc.) to help in determining class offerings in the future.
18. In each of the following scenarios, define the type of measurement scale.
    a. A meteorologist records the amount of monthly rainfall over the past year.
    b. A sociologist notes the birth year of 50 individuals.
    c. An investor monitors the daily stock price of BP following the 2010 oil disaster in the Gulf of Mexico.
19. FILE ***Major.*** A professor records the majors of her 30 students. A portion of the data is shown in the accompanying table.

Student	Major
1	Accounting
2	Management
⋮	⋮
30	Economics

    a. What is the measurement scale of these data?
    b. Summarize the results in tabular form.
    c. What information can be extracted from the data?
20. FILE ***DOW.*** The accompanying table shows a portion of the 30 companies that comprise the Dow Jones Industrial Average (DJIA). For each company, the data set lists the year that it joined the DJIA, its industry, and its stock price (in $) as of February 15, 2019.

Company	Year	Industry	Price
3M (MMM)	1976	Health Care	208.9
American Express (AXP)	1982	Finance	107.4
⋮	⋮	⋮	⋮
Walgreen (WBA)	2018	Health Care	73.43

    a. What is the measurement scale of the Industry variable?
    b. What is the measurement scale of the Year variable? What are the strengths of this type of measurement scale? What are its weaknesses?
    c. What is the measurement scale of the Price variable? What are the strengths of this type of measurement scale?

LO 1.4

Describe different data sources and file formats.

1.4 DATA SOURCES AND FILE FORMATS

At every moment, data are being generated at an increasing velocity from countless sources in an overwhelming volume. Many experts believe that 90% of the data in the world today was created in the last two years alone. Not surprisingly, businesses continue to grapple with how to best ingest, understand, and operationalize large volumes of data.

We access much of the data in this text by simply using a search engine like Google. These search engines direct us to data-providing sites. For instance, searching for economic data leads you to the Bureau of Economic Analysis (http://bea.gov), the Bureau of Labor Statistics (http://www.bls.gov), the Federal Reserve Economic Data (https://research.stlouisfed.org), and the U.S. Census Bureau (http://www.census.gov). These websites provide data on inflation, unemployment, gross domestic product (GDP), and much more, including useful international data. Similarly, excellent world development indicator data are available at http://data.worldbank.org.

The *Wall Street Journal*, *The New York Times*, *USA Today*, *The Economist*, *Business Week*, *Forbes*, and *Fortune* are all reputable publications that provide all sorts of data. We would like to point out that all of these data sources represent only a small portion of publicly available data. In this text, we have compiled a number of big data sets, based on online data sources, that are integrated throughout the text.

Structured data have been used extensively for many years and are often found in tabular formats. As people work more and more in collaboration with one another, a need usually arises for an ability to exchange information between different parties. Formatting data in an agreed-upon or standardized manner is important for allowing other people to understand the data contained in a file. There are many standards for file formats. For example, a text file can be organized into rows and columns to store in a table. Two common layouts for simple text files are a fixed-width format and a delimited format. In addition to text files, we can use a markup language to provide a structure to data. Three widely used markup languages are eXtensible Markup Language (XML), HyperText Markup Language (HTML), and JavaScript Object Notation (JSON). We now provide an overview of these formats and markup languages.

Fixed-Width Format

In a data file with a **fixed-width format** (or fixed-length format), each column starts and ends at the same place in every row. The actual data are stored as plain text characters in a digital file. Consider the information in Table 1.7. It shows the first name, telephone number, and annual salary for three individuals.

TABLE 1.7 Sample Data for Format Illustration

Name	Telephone	Salary
Rich	419-528-0915	160000
Benjamin	203-991-3608	93000
Eduardo	618-345-1278	187000

The information in Table 1.7 can be organized into a fixed-width format as shown in Figure 1.5. The first, second, and third columns of Figure 1.5 are defined to have column widths of 8, 12, and 7 characters, respectively. Every observation or record has the exact same column widths. The fixed-width file has the simplicity of design where specific data can be found at the exact same location for every record. This can help speed up record search when the data set is very large. Furthermore, because only raw data are stored, fixed-width files tend to be significantly smaller in size compared to other data formats such as XML that include data labels and tags. However, the number of characters of each column (the column width) needs to be predetermined. In Figure 1.5, the Name column is predefined to have at most 8 characters; any names with more than 8 characters will be truncated. Finally, at times, the columns seem to run into each other. For these reasons, other formats are more popular.

FIGURE 1.5 A fixed-width file format

```
Name    Telephone   Salary
Rich    419-528-0915160000
Benjamin203-991-3608 93000
Eduardo 618-345-1278187000
```

Delimited Format

Another widely used file format to store tabular data is a **delimited format**. In Figure 1.6, we show the information in Table 1.7 in a delimited format, where each piece of data is separated by a comma.

FIGURE 1.6 A comma-separated value (csv) file format

```
Name,Telephone,Salary
Rich,419-528-0915,160000
Benjamin,203-991-3608,93000
Eduardo,618-345-1278,187000
```

In a delimited format, a comma is called a delimiter, and the file is called a comma-delimited or comma-separated value (csv) file. Sometimes, other characters such as semicolons are used as delimiters. In a delimited file, each piece of data can contain as many characters as applicable. For example, unlike the fixed-width file shown in Figure 1.5, a comma-separated value file does not limit a person's name to only eight characters.

Fixed-width and delimited files usually include plain text data that can be opened in most text editing software such as Microsoft Word and Notepad in Microsoft Windows, TextEdit in Mac, and online tools such as Google Docs.

eXtensible Markup Language

The **eXtensible Markup Language (XML)** is a simple language for representing structured data. XML is one of the most widely used formats for sharing structured information between computer programs, between people, and between computers and people. It uses markup tags to define the structure of data. Using the information from Table 1.7, Figure 1.7 shows an example of data coded in XML format.

FIGURE 1.7 An XML file format

```
<Data>
<Person>
     <Name>Rich</Name>
     <Telephone>419-528-915</Telephone>
     <Salary>160000</Salary>
</Person>
<Person>
     <Name>Benjamin</Name>
     <Telephone>203-991-608</Telephone>
     <Salary>93000</Salary>
</Person>
<Person>
     <Name>Eduardo</Name>
     <Telephone>618-345-278</Telephone>
     <Salary>187000</Salary>
</Person>
</Data>
```

Each piece of data is usually enclosed in a pair of 'tags' that follow specific XML syntax. For example, a telephone number starts with an opening tag (<Telephone>) and ends with a closing tag (</Telephone>). The XML code is case-sensitive; therefore, <Telephone> and <telephone> would indicate two different pieces of information. The tags in Figure 1.7 are not based on any predefined standard. The XML language allows each user to define his or her own tags and document structure, but XML tag names should generally be self-explanatory. The XML file format is designed to support readability. This makes the XML file format especially suitable for transporting data between computer applications without losing the meanings of the data. However, due to the additional labels and tags, XML data files tend to be much larger in size than fixed-width and delimited data files that contain the same data, making data download and parsing more time-consuming and computationally intensive.

HyperText Markup Language

Like XML, the **HyperText Markup Language (HTML)** is a mark-up language that uses tags to define its data in web pages. The key distinction between XML and HTML is that XML tells us or computer applications what the data are, whereas HTML tells the web browser how to display the data. Using the information from Table 1.7, Figure 1.8 shows an example of data coded in HTML.

FIGURE 1.8 An HTML file format

```
<table>
  <tr>
    <th>Name</th>
    <th>Telephone</th>
    <th>Salary</th>
  </tr>
  <tr>
    <td>Rich</td>
    <td>419-528-0915</td>
    <td>160000</td>
  </tr>
  <tr>
    <td>Benjamin</td>
    <td>203-991-3608</td>
    <td>93000</td>
  </tr>
  <tr>
    <td>Eduardo</td>
    <td>618-345-1278</td>
    <td>187000</td>
  </tr>
</table>
```

Tags such as <table> are used to provide structure for textual data, such as headings, paragraphs, and tables. In Figure 1.8, the opening <table> and closing </table> tags indicate the beginning and completion of a table. Unlike XML where users can define their own markup tags, HTML tags conform to standards maintained by organizations such as the World Wide Web Consortium (W3C). Web browsers such as Google Chrome and Safari are designed to interpret the HTML code that follows these standards. For example, the tag <th> is understood by web browsers as a table heading. In our example, there are three columns and headings (i.e., Name, Telephone, and Salary). The <tr> tag, on the other hand, defines a row, and the <td> tag defines each cell within a row. Unlike XML, HTML is case-insensitive.

JavaScript Object Notation

The **JavaScript Object Notation (JSON)** has become a popular alternative to XML in recent years as open data sharing has grown in popularity. JSON is a standard for transmitting human-readable data in compact files. Originally a subset of the JavaScript syntax, JSON is currently a data standard supported by a wide range of modern programming languages such as C, Java, and Python. Using the information from Table 1.7, Figure 1.9 shows an example of data coded in JSON format.

FIGURE 1.9 A JSON file format


```
{
  "Person":     [
     {
       "Name": "Rich",
       "Telephone": "419-528-0915",
       "Salary": "160000"
     },
     {
       "Name": "Benjamin",
       "Telephone": "203-991-3608",
       "Salary": "93000"
     },
     {
       "Name": "Eduardo",
       "Telephone": "618-345-1278",
       "Salary": "187000"
     }
          ]
}
```


The JSON format is self-explanatory just as the XML format is, but it offers several advantages over the XML format. First, the JSON format is not as verbose as the XML format, making data files smaller in size. The difference in size is especially noticeable for very large data sets. Second, the JSON format supports a wide range of data types not readily available in the XML format. Finally, parsing JSON data files is faster and less resource intensive. For these reasons, the JSON format has become a widely adopted standard for open data sharing.

DATA FILE FORMATS AND MARKUP LANGUAGES

There are many standards for data file formats. Two common layouts for simple text files are the fixed-width format and the delimited format.

- With a fixed-width format, each column has a fixed width and starts and ends at the same place in every row.
- With a delimited format, each column is separated by a delimiter such as a comma. Each column can contain as many characters as applicable.

Markup languages also provide a structure to data. Three widely used languages are the eXtensible Markup Language (XML), the HyperText Markup Language (HTML), and the JavaScript Object Notation (JSON).

- XML is a simple text-based markup language for representing structured data. It uses user-defined markup tags to specify the structure of data.
- HTML is a simple text-based markup language for displaying content in web browsers.
- JSON is a standard for transmitting human-readable data in compact files.

EXERCISES 1.4

Applications

21. A used car salesperson recently sold two Mercedes, three Toyota, six Ford, and four Hyundai sedans. He wants to record the sales data.
    a. Organize the data into a fixed-width format (eight characters for brand name and four characters for the number of cars sold).
    b. Organize the data in a delimited format.
    c. Code the data in XML format.
    d. Code the data in HTML table format.
    e. Code the data in JSON format.
22. Last year, Oracle hired three finance majors from the local university. Robert Schneider started with a salary of $56,000, Chun Zhang with $52,000, Sunil Banerjee with $58,000, and Linda Jones with $60,000. Oracle wants to record the hiring data.
    a. Organize the data into a fixed-width format (10 characters for first name, 10 characters for last name, and six characters for salary).
    b. Organize the data in a delimited format.
    c. Code the data in XML format.
    d. Code the data in HTML table format.
    e. Code the data in JSON format.
23. The following table lists the population, in millions, in India and China, the two most populous countries in the world, for the years 2013 through 2017.

Year	India	China
2013	1278.56	1357.38
2014	1293.86	1364.27
2015	1309.05	1371.22
2016	1324.17	1378.67
2017	1339.18	1386.40

    a. Organize the data into a fixed-width format (four characters for Year, eight characters for India, and eight characters for China).
    b. Organize the data in a delimited format.
24. The following table lists the top five countries in the world in terms of their happiness index on a 10-point scale, and their corresponding GDP per capita as reported by the United Nations in 2017.

Country	Happiness	GDP
Finland	7.769	45670
Denmark	7.600	57533
Norway	7.544	75295
Iceland	7.494	73060
Netherlands	7.488	48754

    a. Organize the data into a fixed-width format (11 characters for Country, 10 characters for Happiness, and six characters for GDP).
    b. Organize the data in a delimited format.
25. The following three students were honored at a local high school for securing admissions to prestigious universities.

Name	University
Bridget	Yale
Minori	Stanford
Matthew	Harvard

    a. Organize the data into a fixed-width format (10 characters for Name and 10 characters for University).
    b. Organize the data in a delimited format.
    c. Code the data in XML format.
    d. Code the data in HTML table format.
    e. Code the data in JSON format.
26. According to *Forbes,* Michael Trout of the Los Angeles Angels, with earnings of $39 million, was the highest-paid player in baseball in 2019. Bryce Harper of the Philadelphia Phillies ranked second at $36.5 million. The Boston Red Sox pitcher David Price was baseball's third-highest-paid player at $32 million.
    a. Code the data on the player name, baseball team, and salary in the XML format.
    b. Repeat part a using the HTML table format.
    c. Repeat part a using the JSON format.
27. According to *U.S. News and World Report,* a statistician was the best business profession in 2019 with 12,600 projected jobs and a median salary of $84,060. A mathematician was the second-best profession with 900 projected jobs and a median salary of $103,010. Interestingly, both of these career paths are related to data analytics.
    a. Code the information on the profession, projected jobs, and median salary in XML format.
    b. Repeat part a using the HTML table format.
    c. Repeat part a using the JSON format.

1.5 WRITING WITH BIG DATA

As mentioned at the beginning of this chapter, data are not very useful unless they are converted into insightful information that is clearly articulated in written or verbal language. As such, an important aspect of business analytics is to communicate with numbers rather than focus on number crunching. In this and subsequent chapters, we include a sample report based on observations and analysis of data to convey the information in written form. These reports are intended for a nontechnical audience who may not be familiar with the details of the statistical and computational methods. Consider the following case study and accompanying report based on music popularity data.

Case Study

Since 1940, the *Billboard* magazine has published a variety of weekly music popularity charts. Today, the magazine uses a combination of sales volume, airplay on radio, digital downloads, and online streams in order to determine the chart rankings. One of the most highly watched *Billboard* charts is the Hot 100, which provides a weekly ranking of the top 100 music singles. Each entry on the Hot 100 chart lists the current rank, last week's rank, highest position, and the number of weeks the song has been on the chart. Other *Billboard* charts rank music by genre such as Pop, Rock, R&B, and Latin or rank the popularity of music albums and artists.

Maya Alexander is a reporter for her university's newspaper, *The Campus Gazette*. She wants to launch a new Film & Music column that will include commentary, summarized data, and statistics on music popularity. In an effort to convince her editor to give her this assignment, Maya researches and evaluates what *The Campus Gazette* might be able to use from the *Billboard* website (http://www.billboard.com).

Sample Report—Billboard Charts

Music is an integral part of campus life. A new Film & Music column in *The Campus Gazette* is likely to be very popular among the campus audience. The *Billboard* website publishes weekly data on music popularity charts ranging from the top 100 singles (Hot 100) to digital sales by music genre. We can summarize these numerical data for music genres that are most popular among college students and publish them in the new Film & Music column. The popularity charts on the *Billboard* website are coded in the HTML data format and can be easily imported into a table. For example, the Hot 100 chart shown in Figure 1.10 coded as an HTML table can be readily downloaded into a table in a text document.

FIGURE 1.10 *Billboard*'s Hot 100 Chart

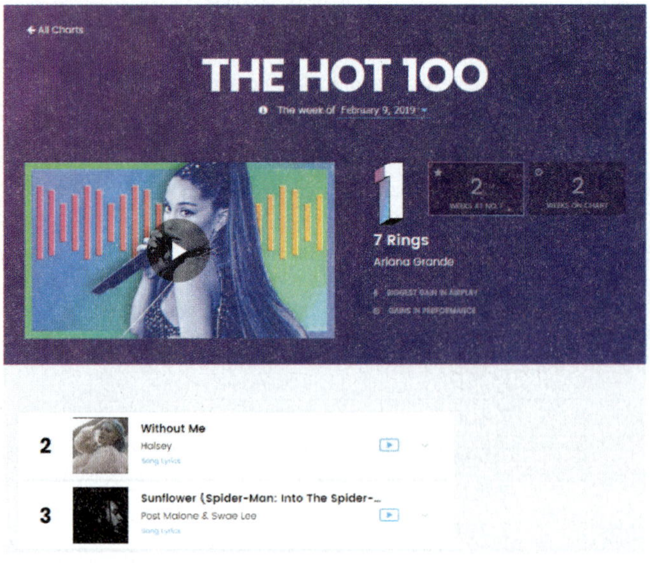

Source: Billboard.com

Our readers may also be interested in following the top music singles by genre. For example, Table 1.8 is an example of a summary table listing the top five singles in Country, Pop, and Rock, which is easily compiled from three different *Billboard* charts. This summary table can be complemented with written commentaries based on information provided by the popularity charts such as the highest chart position and the number of weeks on the chart for each song.

TABLE 1.8 Top Five Hot Singles by Music Genre

	Country		Pop		Rock	
Rank	Song	Artist	Song	Artist	Song	Artist
1	Tequila	Dan + Shay	Without Me	Halsey	High Hopes	Panic! At the Disco
2	Speechless	Dan + Shay	Thank U, Next	Ariana Grande	Natural	Imagine Dragons
3	Meant To Be	Bebe Rexha	High Hopes	Panic! At the Disco	Broken	lovelytheband
4	Beautiful Crazy	Luke Combs	East Side	benny blanco	Bad Liar	Imagine Dragons
5	Girl Like You	Jason Aldean	Sunflower	Post Malone	Harmony Hall	Vampire Weekend

According to the most recent sales and market performance, the *Billboard* website also organizes songs and albums into categories such as 'Gains in Performance,' 'Biggest Gain in Streams,' and 'Biggest Gain in Digital Sales.' These songs and albums have not yet reached the top 5 positions, but their rankings are quickly moving up on the popularity charts. *The Campus Gazette* can establish itself as a music trendsetter on campus by introducing our readers to these up-and-coming songs and albums in a new Film & Music column. Figure 1.11 shows an example of an up-and-coming single on the Hot 100 chart. Similar to the popularity charts, these music categories are formatted using the HTML standard on the *Billboard* website and can be readily imported into a text document. We can create commentaries on selected songs and albums from these lists to introduce up-and-coming music to our readers.

FIGURE 1.11 Up-and-coming music on *Billboard* charts

Source: Billboard.com

Suggested Case Studies

As you have learned throughout the chapter, data from an endless number of online sources such as corporations, nonprofit organizations, and government agencies are available for us to explore and investigate. The following are some suggestions using online, publicly available data.

Report 1.1. Finland is the happiest country in the world, according to the 2018 Happiness Index Report by the United Nation (http://www.worldhappiness.report). In fact, several Scandinavian countries have consistently held the top spots among the 156 countries included in the annual Happiness Index Report in the past several years. Visit the Happiness Index website, explore, and write a report based on the current data provided on the website.

Report 1.2. Millions of tourists visit Yosemite National Park in California each year. Stunning waterfalls, giant redwood trees, and spectacular granite rock formations are among the main attractions at the iconic park. However, the winding roads leading to the Yosemite Valley may be closed occasionally due to severe weather conditions. Visit a weather forecast website such as http://www.weather.com and explore the weather data around Yosemite Park. Write a report to advise a tourist planning a visit.

2 Data Management and Wrangling

LEARNING OBJECTIVES

After reading this chapter, you should be able to:

LO **2.1** Describe the key concepts related to data management.

LO **2.2** Inspect and explore data.

LO **2.3** Apply data preparation techniques to handle missing values and to subset data.

LO **2.4** Transform numerical variables.

LO **2.5** Transform categorical variables.

Data wrangling is the process of retrieving, cleansing, integrating, transforming, and enriching data to support analytics. It is often considered one of the most critical and time-consuming steps in an analytics project. In this chapter, we focus on four key tasks during the data wrangling process: data management, data inspection, data preparation, and data transformation.

We first provide an overview of data management. Although data management is primarily the responsibility of the information technology group, understanding the relevant concepts, data structure, and data retrieval technologies is essential to the success of analytics professionals. After obtaining relevant data, most analytics professionals spend a considerable amount of time inspecting, cleaning, and preparing the data for subsequent analysis. These tasks often involve counting and sorting relevant variables to review basic information and potential data quality issues. For data preparation, we discuss two commonly used techniques: handling missing values and subsetting data. We then examine two strategies for handling missing values: omission and imputation. Finally, we focus on data transformation techniques for both numerical and categorical variables. For numerical variables, common data transformation techniques include binning, creating new variables, and rescaling. For categorical variables, common data transformation techniques include reducing categories, creating dummy variables, and creating category scores.

©Yuliia Mazurkevych/Shutterstoick

INTRODUCTORY CASE

Gaining Insights into Retail Customer Data

Organic Food Superstore is an online grocery store that specializes in providing organic food products to health-conscious consumers. The company offers a membership-based service that ships fresh ingredients for a wide range of chef-designed meals to its members' homes. Catherine Hill is a marketing manager at Organic Food Superstore. She has been assigned to market the company's new line of Asian-inspired meals. Research has shown that the most likely customers for healthy ethnic cuisines are college-educated millennials (born between 1982 and 2000).

In order to spend the company's marketing dollars efficiently, Catherine wants to focus on this target demographic when designing the marketing campaign. With the help of the information technology (IT) group, Catherine has acquired a representative sample that includes each customer's identification number (CustID), sex (Sex), race (Race), birthdate (BirthDate), whether the customer has a college degree (College), household size (HouseholdSize), zip code (ZipCode), annual income (Income), total spending in 2017 (Spending2017), total spending in 2018 (Spending2018), total number of orders during the past 24 months (NumOfOrders), number of days since the last order (DaysSinceLast), the customer's rating on the last purchase (Satisfaction), and the channel through which the customer was originally acquired (Channel). Table 2.1 shows a portion of the data set.

FILE *Customers*

TABLE 2.1 A Sample of Organic Food Superstore Customers

CustID	Sex	Race	BirthDate	...	Channel
1530016	Female	Black	12/16/1986	...	SM
1531136	Male	White	5/9/1993	...	TV
⋮	⋮	⋮	⋮	⋮	⋮
1579979	Male	White	7/5/1999	...	SM

Catherine will use the Customers data set to:

1. Identify Organic Food Superstore's college-educated millennial customers.
2. Compare the profiles of female and male college-educated millennial customers.

A synopsis of this case is provided at the end of Section 2.3.

LO 2.1

2.1 DATA MANAGEMENT

Describe the key concepts related to data management.

Data wrangling is the process of retrieving, cleansing, integrating, transforming, and enriching data to support subsequent data analysis. This valuable process focuses on transforming the raw data into a format that is more appropriate and easier to analyze. The objectives of data wrangling include improving data quality, reducing the time and effort required to perform analytics, and helping reveal the true intelligence in the data.

Data wrangling is an essential part of business analytics. As mentioned in Chapter 1, the increasing volume and variety of data compel organizations to spend a large amount of time and resources in garnering, cleaning, and organizing data before performing any analysis. As the amount of data grows, the need and difficulties involving data wrangling increase. In practice, the inability to clean and organize big data is among the primary barriers preventing organizations from taking full advantage of business analytics. Analytics professionals can no longer rely solely on the corporate IT department for data retrieval and preparation. According to interviews and expert estimates, analytics professionals spend from 50–80% of their time in the mundane task of collecting and preparing unruly data, before analytics can be applied (*The New York Times*, August 17, 2014).

As such, analytics professionals have to become more self-reliant and possess the necessary skills for data wrangling as well as performing data analysis. This practice allows organizations to address business problems much more quickly and make better-informed decisions. At the same time, the self-service model requires analytics professionals to have a broader skill set than just statistical and data mining techniques.

> **DATA WRANGLING**
>
> Data wrangling is the process of retrieving, cleansing, integrating, transforming, and enriching data to support subsequent data analysis.

We first provide an overview of **data management**. In a very broad sense, data management is a process that an organization uses to acquire, organize, store, manipulate, and distribute data. Organizations today have a plethora of data created and stored using different, often incompatible, technologies. For the past few decades, most organizations have adopted the database approach for storing and managing data. This has tremendously improved the efficiency and effectiveness of the data management process and ultimately the quality of data. A **database** is a collection of data logically organized to enable easy retrieval, management, and distribution of data.

The most common type of database used in organizations today is the **relational database**. A relational database consists of one or more logically related data files, often called tables or relations. Each table is a two-dimensional grid that consists of rows (also called records or tuples) and columns (also called fields or attributes). A column (e.g., sex of a customer, price of a product, etc.) contains a characteristic of a physical object (e.g., products or places), an event (e.g., business transactions), or a person (e.g., customers, students). A collection of related fields makes up a record, which represents an object, event, or person. A software application for defining, manipulating, and managing data in databases is called a **database management system** (DBMS). Popular DBMS packages include Oracle, IBM DB2, SQL Server, MySQL, and Microsoft Access.

> **DATA MANAGEMENT**
>
> Data management is the process that an organization uses to acquire, organize, store, manipulate, and distribute data.
>
> The most common type of database (a collection of data) is the relational database. A relational database consists of one or more logically related data files, where each data file is a two-dimensional grid that consists of rows and columns.

Data Modeling: The Entity-Relationship Diagram

To understand how and where data can be extracted, one needs to understand the structure of the data, also known as the data model. **Data modeling** is the process of defining the structure of a database. Relational databases are modeled in a way to offer great flexibility and ease of data retrieval.

An **entity-relationship diagram (ERD)** is a graphical representation used to model the structure of the data. An **entity** is a generalized category to represent persons, places, things, or events about which we want to store data in a database table. A single occurrence of an entity is called an **instance**. In most situations, an instance is represented as a record in a database table. For example, Claire Johnson is an instance of a CUSTOMER entity, and organic oatmeal is an instance of a PRODUCT entity. Each entity has specific characteristics called attributes or fields, which are represented as columns in a database table. Customers' last names and product descriptions are examples of attributes in a database table.

Entity Relationships

Two entities can have a one-to-one (1:1), one-to-many (1:M), or many-to-many (M:N) **relationship** with each other that represents certain business facts or rules. A 1:1 relationship is less common than the other two types. In a business setting, we might use a 1:1 relationship to describe a situation where each department can have only one manager, and each manager can only manage one department. Recall Organic Food Superstore from the introductory case; Figure 2.1 shows an ERD for the store that illustrates examples of 1:M and M:N relationships. The diagram shows three entities: CUSTOMER, ORDER, and PRODUCT. The relationship between CUSTOMER and ORDER entities is 1:M because one customer can place many orders over time, but each order can only belong to one customer. The relationship between ORDER and PRODUCT is M:N because an order can contain many products and the same product can appear in many orders.

In Figure 2.1, each entity is represented in a rectangular-shaped box in which attributes of the entity are listed. For each entity, there is a special type of attribute called **primary key** (PK), which is an attribute that uniquely identifies each instance of the entity. For example, Customer_ID is the primary key for the CUSTOMER entity because each customer would have a unique ID number. Because the primary key attribute uniquely identifies each instance of the entity, it is often used to create a data structure called an index for fast data retrieval and searches.

Some entities (e.g., ORDER) have another special type of attribute called **foreign key** (FK). A foreign key is defined as a primary key of a related entity. Because Customer_ID is the primary key of the CUSTOMER entity, which shares a relationship with the ORDER entity, it is considered a foreign key in the ORDER entity. A pair of the primary and foreign keys is used to establish the 1:M relationship between two entities. By matching the values in the Customer_ID fields of the CUSTOMER and ORDER entities, we can quickly find out which customer placed which order.

FIGURE 2.1 Example of an entity relationship diagram

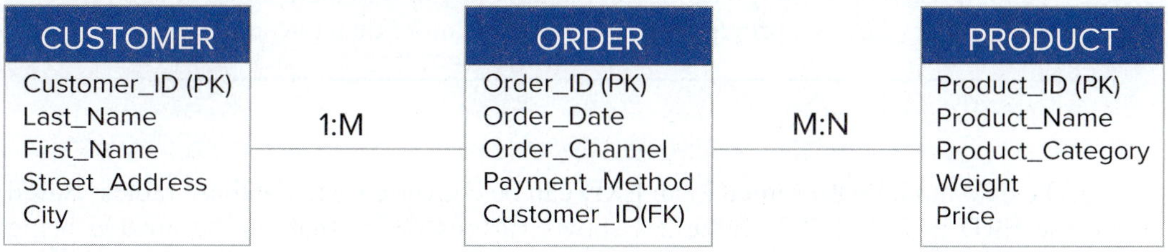

The ERD in Figure 2.1 is not yet complete as it is missing the ordered products and purchase quantities in the ORDER entity. Storing these data in the ORDER entity is not appropriate as one does not know in advance how many products are going to be in each order, therefore making it impossible to create the correct number of attributes. To resolve this issue, we simply create an intermediate entity, ORDER_DETAIL, between the ORDER and PRODUCT entities, as shown in Figure 2.2. As a result, the M:N relationship is decomposed into two 1:M relationships. An order has many detailed line items, but each line item can only belong to one order. While a product may appear in many orders and order lines, an order line can only contain one product.

FIGURE 2.2 An expanded entity relationship diagram

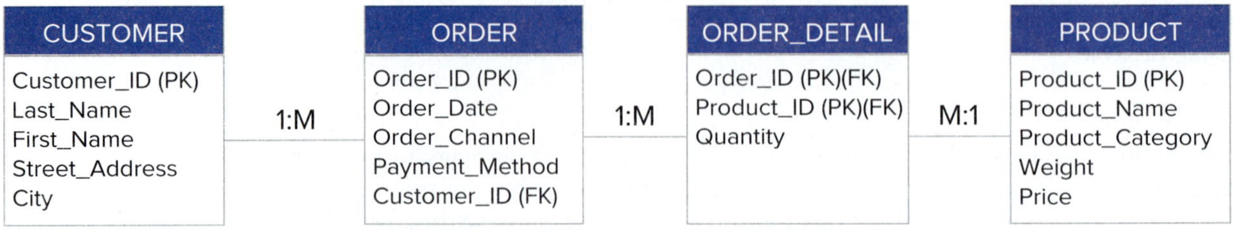

In the ORDER_DETAIL entity, two attributes, Order_ID and Product_ID, together create a unique identifier for each instance. In this situation, Order_ID and Product_ID are referred to as a **composite primary key**, which is a primary key that consists of more than one attribute. We use a composite primary key when none of the individual attributes alone can uniquely identify each instance of the entity. For example, neither Order_ID nor Product_ID alone can uniquely identify each line item of an order, but a combination of them can uniquely identify each line item. Because both Order_ID and Product_ID are primary keys of other entities related to ORDER_DETAIL, they also serve as foreign keys. By matching the primary and foreign key pair, the system can quickly find out which order contains a line item for a particular product.

THE ENTITY-RELATIONSHIP DIAGRAM (ERD)

An entity-relationship diagram (ERD) is a schematic used to illustrate the structure of the data.

- An entity is a generalized category to represent persons, places, things, or events.
- A relationship between entities represents certain business facts or rules. The types of relationships include one-to-one (1:1), one-to-many (1:M), and many-to-many (M:N).
- A primary key is an attribute that uniquely identifies each instance of an entity, whereas a foreign key is the primary key of a related entity. A composite primary key is a primary key that contains more than one attribute.

The data model represented in an ERD can be converted into database tables. Based on the ERD in Figure 2.2, Table 2.2 shows various tables that can be created using Organic Food Superstore sample data. Can you find out which customer placed an order for organic sweet potato on October 15, 2018? Did this customer order any other products? By matching the primary and foreign keys of the CUSTOMER, ORDER,

ORDER_DETAIL, and PRODUCT tables, we can establish relationships among these tables. With these relationships, we can extract useful information from multiple tables. For example, using his customer ID (i.e., 1531136), we learn that James Anderson was the customer who placed an order on October 15, 2018, using his mobile phone and paying for the order with his PayPal account. In addition, we can also see that he purchased organic sweet potato and organic oatmeal.

TABLE 2.2 Database Tables for Organic Food Superstore

a) CUSTOMER table

Customer_ID	Last_Name	First_Name	Street_Address	City	. . .
1530016	Johnson	Claire	532 Main Street	Los Angeles	. . .
1531136	Anderson	James	1322 Cary Street	Los Angeles	. . .
⋮	⋮	⋮	⋮	⋮	⋮
1532160	Smith	Terry	663 Johnson Ave.	Los Angeles	. . .

b) ORDER table

Order_ID	Order_Date	Order_Channel	Payment_Method	. . .	Customer_ID
1484001	09/12/2018	Web	Credit/Debit Card	. . .	1530016
1484212	3/24/2018	Web	Credit/Debit Card	. . .	1530016
⋮	⋮	⋮	⋮	⋮	⋮
1482141	10/15/2018	Mobile	Paypal	. . .	1531136

c) ORDER_DETAIL table

Order_ID	Product_ID	Quantity
1484001	4378	1
1482141	4305	1
⋮	⋮	⋮
1482141	4330	2

d) PRODUCT table

Product_ID	Product_Name	Product_Category	Weight	Price	. . .
4305	Organic Oatmeal	Cereals	2	2.49	. . .
4330	Organic Sweet Potato	Produce	1	1.39	. . .
⋮	⋮	⋮	⋮	⋮	⋮
4378	Gluten-Free Bread	Bakery	1.5	6.99	. . .

Data Retrieval in the Database Environment

Once data are stored in a relational database, we can retrieve them using database queries. The most popular query language used today is **Structured Query Language (SQL)**. SQL is a language for manipulating data in a relational database using relatively simple and intuitive commands. While a comprehensive discussion of SQL is beyond the scope of this text, we briefly demonstrate how simple SQL statements can be used to retrieve data from a database.

The basic structure of a SQL statement is relatively simple and usually consists of three keywords: Select, From, and Where. The Select keyword is followed by the names of attributes we want to retrieve. The From keyword specifies the tables from which to retrieve the data. We usually want to retrieve data based on selection criteria specified in the Where clause. The following SQL statement retrieves first and last names of the customers who live in Los Angles from the CUSTOMER table.

Select Last_Name, First_Name

From CUSTOMER

Where City = "Los Angeles"

While simple queries like the previous one are useful, we often need to compile data from multiple tables and apply more than one selection criteria. For example, we may want to retrieve the customer names, order IDs, and order quantities of organic sweet potato purchases on October 15, 2018. The following SQL query returns this information.

Select CUSTOMER.Last_Name, CUSTOMER.First_Name, ORDER.Order_ID, ORDER_DETAIL.Quantity

From CUSTOMER, ORDER, ORDER_DETAIL, PRODUCT

Where PRODUCT.Product_Name = "Organic Sweet Potato"

and ORDER.Order_Date = "10/15/2018"
and CUSTOMER.Customer_ID = ORDER.Customer_ID
and ORDER.Order_ID = ORDER_DETAIL.Order_ID
and ORDER_DETAIL.Product_ID = PRODUCT.Product_ID

Because the Select clause specifies the attributes to retrieve and these attributes may come from different tables, we use the *table_name.attribute_name* format to tell the DBMS from which table the attributes are retrieved (e.g., *CUSTOMER.Last_Name* refers to the last name attribute in the CUSTOMER table). The From clause lists all the tables that have the attributes to be retrieved and the attributes used in the selection criteria. The Where clause lists multiple conditions and links them using the "and" keyword. The last three conditions match the values of the primary and foreign key pairs based on the relationships depicted in Figure 2.2.

STRUCTURED QUERY LANGUAGE (SQL)

In a relational database, data can be retrieved using Structured Query Language (SQL) statements, whose basic structure consists of the Select, From, and Where keywords. SQL statements specify the attributes, tables, and criteria the retrieved data must meet.

While the SQL commands in the previous two examples provide the flexibility for data retrieval, many modern DBMS packages such as Microsoft Access, Oracle, and SQL Server offer a graphical interface option where the user constructs a database query by dragging and dropping the query components (e.g., fields, tables, conditions, etc.) into a form. The DBMS then translates user selections into SQL statements to retrieve data.

Data Warehouse and Data Mart

Although the relational database environment provides businesses with an efficient and effective way to manage data, the proliferation of isolated databases maintained by different business departments makes it difficult to analyze data across departments and business units. This phenomenon has also given rise to data redundancy and inconsistency. As a result, many organizations have developed an enterprise data warehouse, which offers an integrated, accurate "single version of truth" to support decision making.

An enterprise data warehouse or **data warehouse** is a central repository of data from multiple departments within an organization. One of its primary purposes is to support managerial decision making, and, therefore, data in a data warehouse are usually organized around subjects such as sales, customers, or products that are relevant to business decision making. In order to integrate data from different databases generated by various business departments, an extraction, transformation, and load (ETL) process is undertaken to retrieve, reconcile, and transform data into a consistent format, and then load the final data into a data warehouse. A data warehouse provides a historical and comprehensive view of the entire organization.

As you can imagine, the volume of the data in a data warehouse can become very large very quickly. While a data warehouse integrates data across the entire organization, a **data mart** is a small-scale data warehouse or a subset of the enterprise data warehouse that focuses on one particular subject or decision area. For example, a data mart can be designed to support the marketing department for analyzing customer behaviors, and it contains only the data relevant to such analyses.

The structure of a data mart conforms to a multidimensional data model called a **star schema**, which is a specialized relational database model. Figure 2.3 displays the star schema for Organic Food Superstore. In the star schema, there are two types of tables: dimension and fact tables. The **dimension table** describes business dimensions of interest such as customer, product, location, and time. The **fact table** contains facts about the business operation, often in a quantitative format.

> **DATA WAREHOUSE AND DATA MART**
>
> A data warehouse is a central repository of data from multiple departments within an organization to support managerial decision making. Analytics professionals tend to acquire data from data marts, which are small-scale data warehouses that only contain data that are relevant to certain subjects or decision areas. Data in a data mart are organized using a multidimensional data model called a star schema, which includes dimension and fact tables.

Each of the dimension tables has a 1:M relationship with the fact table. Hence, the primary keys of the dimension tables are also the foreign keys in the fact table. At the same time, the combination of the primary keys of the dimension tables forms the composite primary key of the fact table. The fact table is usually depicted at the center surrounded by multiple dimension tables forming the shape of a star. In reality, it is not uncommon to see multiple fact tables sharing relationships with a group of dimension tables in a data mart.

One of the key advantages of the star schema is its ability to "slice and dice" data based on different dimensions. For example, in the data model shown in Figure 2.3, sales data can be retrieved based on who the customer is; which product or product category is involved; the year, quarter, or month of the order; where the customer lives; or through which channel the order was submitted simply by matching the primary keys of the dimension tables with the foreign keys of the fact table.

In recent years, new forms of databases to support big data have emerged. The most notable is the NoSQL or "Not Only SQL" database. The NoSQL database is a nonrelational database that supports the storage of a wide range of data types including structured, semi-structured, and unstructured data. It also offers the flexibility, performance, and scalability needed to handle extremely high volumes of data. Analytics professionals will likely see NoSQL databases implemented alongside relational databases to support organizations' data needs in today's environment.

FIGURE 2.3 Star schema of a data mart for Organic Food Superstore

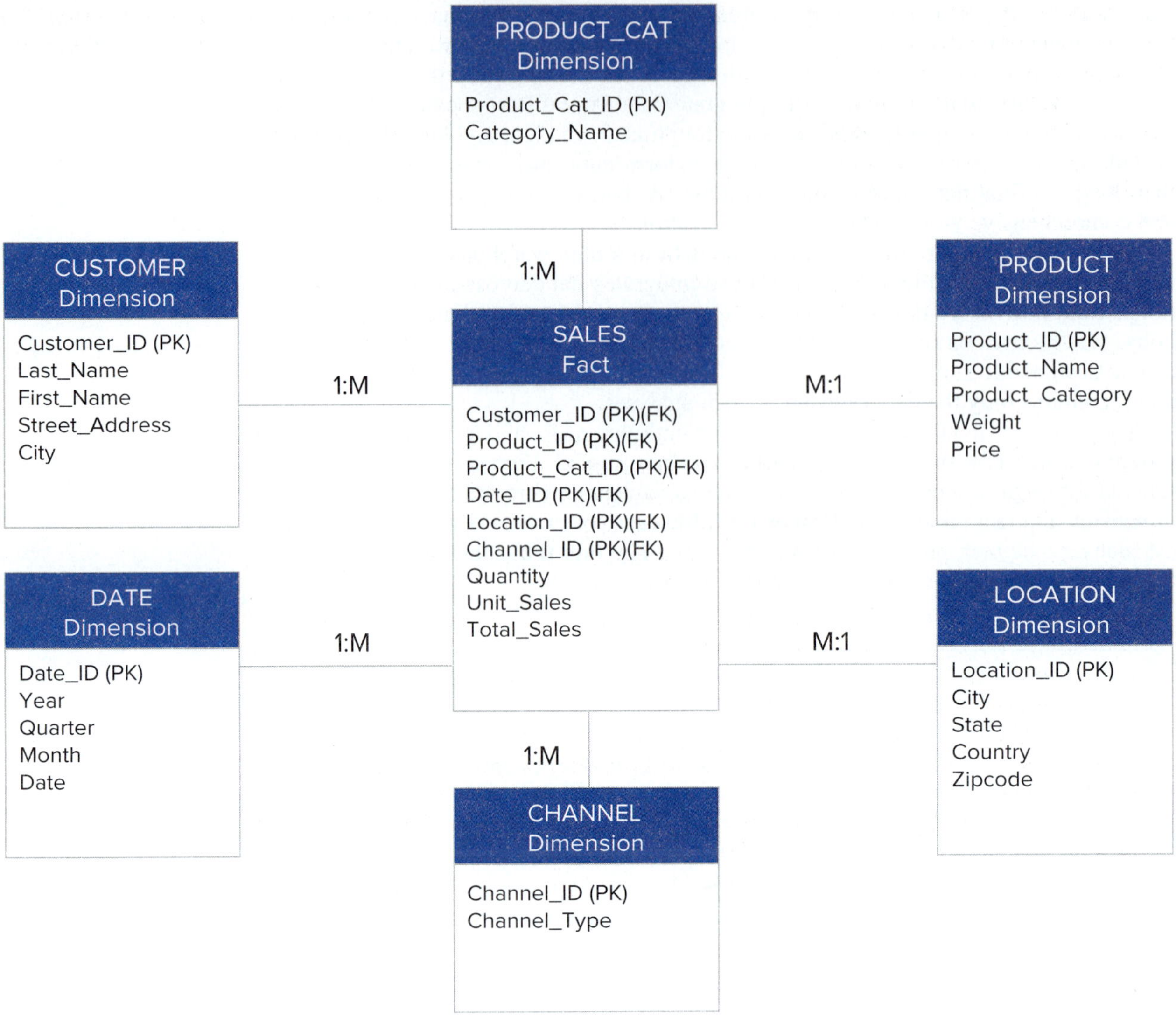

Exercises 2.1

Applications

1. Which of the following statements correctly describe the data wrangling process? Select all that apply. Explain if incorrect.
   a. Data wrangling is the process of retrieving, cleansing, integrating, transforming, and enriching data.
   b. Data wrangling is the process of defining and modeling the structure of a database to represent real-world events.
   c. The objectives of data wrangling include improving data quality and reducing the time and effort required to perform analytics.
   d. Data wrangling focuses on transforming the raw data into a format that is more appropriate and easier to analyze.
2. Which of the following statements about entity-relationship diagrams (ERDs) are correct? Select all that apply. Explain if incorrect.
   a. An entity usually represents persons, places, things, or events about which we want to store data.
   b. A foreign key is an attribute that uniquely identifies each instance of the entity.
   c. A composite key is a key that consists of more than one attribute.
   d. A relationship between entities represents certain business facts or rules.
3. Which of the following statements correctly identify and describe the key elements of a relational database? Select all that apply. Explain if incorrect.

a. A table in a relational database is a two-dimensional grid that contains actual data.
b. A field or a column represents a characteristic of a physical object, an event, or a person.
c. A relational database includes software tools for advanced data visualization.
d. A tuple or a record in a table represents a physical object, an event, or a person.

4. Which of the following statements best describes what a foreign key is? Select all that apply. Explain if incorrect.
   a. It is an attribute that uniquely identifies each instance of the entity.
   b. It is a primary key that consists of multiple attributes.
   c. It is the primary key of a related database table.
   d. It is a single occurrence of an entity.
5. Which type of relationship–one-to-one (1:1), one-to-many (1:M), or many-to-many (M:N)–do the following business rules describe?
   a. One manager can supervise multiple employees, and one employee may report to multiple managers.
   b. A business department has multiple employees, but each employee can be assigned to only one department.
   c. A company can have only one CEO, and each CEO can work for only one company.
   d. An academic adviser can work with multiple students, while each student is assigned to only one adviser.
   e. A golf course offers a membership to many members, and a golfer can potentially sign up for a membership at multiple golf courses.
   f. A soccer team consists of multiple players, while an individual player can play for only one team at a time.
6. Which of the following statements correctly describe benefits of Structured Query Language (SQL)? Select all that apply. Explain if incorrect.
   a. SQL can be used to manipulate structured, semi-structured, and unstructured data.
   b. SQL commands allow users to select data based on multiple selection criteria.
   c. SQL can be used to compile data from multiple tables.
   d. SQL commands are relatively simple and intuitive.
7. Which of the following statements about data warehouses and data marts are correct? Select all that apply. Explain if incorrect.
   a. A data warehouse is a subset of the enterprise database that focuses on one particular subject or decision area.
   b. The dimension table describes business dimensions of interest, such as customer, product, location, and time, while the fact table contains facts about the business operation.
   c. A star schema represents a multidimensional data model.
   d. A data warehouse is the central repository of data from multiple departments within a business enterprise to support managerial decision making.

2.2 DATA INSPECTION

LO 2.2

Inspect and explore data.

Once the raw data are extracted from the database, data warehouse, or data mart, we usually review and inspect the data set to assess data quality and relevant information for subsequent analysis. In addition to visually reviewing data, counting and sorting are among the very first tasks most data analysts perform to gain a better understanding and insights into the data. Counting and sorting data help us verify that the data set is complete or that it may have missing values, especially for important variables. Sorting data also allows us to review the range of values for each variable. We can sort data based on a single variable or multiple variables.

In Example 2.1, we demonstrate how to use counting and sorting features in Excel and R to inspect and gain insights into the data. While these features also allow us to detect missing values, we discuss the treatment of missing values in Section 2.3.

EXAMPLE 2.1

FILE *Gig*

BalanceGig is a company that matches independent workers for short-term engagements with businesses in the construction, automotive, and high-tech industries. The 'gig' employees work only for a short period of time, often on a particular project or a specific task. A manager at BalanceGig extracts the employee data from their most recent work engagement, including the hourly wage (HourlyWage), the client's industry (Industry), and the employee's job classification (Job). A portion of the *Gig* data set is shown in Table 2.3.

TABLE 2.3 Gig Employee Data

EmployeeID	HourlyWage	Industry	Job
1	32.81	Construction	Analyst
2	46	Automotive	Engineer
⋮	⋮	⋮	⋮
604	26.09	Construction	Other

The manager suspects that data about the gig employees are sometimes incomplete, perhaps due to the short engagement and the transient nature of the employees. She would like to find the number of missing observations for the HourlyWage, Industry, and Job variables. In addition, she would like information on the number of employees who (1) worked in the automotive industry, (2) earned more than \$30 per hour, and (3) worked in the automotive industry and earned more than \$30 per hour. Finally, the manager would like to know the hourly wage of the lowest- and the highest-paid employees at the company as a whole and the hourly wage of the lowest- and the highest-paid accountants who worked in the automotive and the tech industries.

Use counting and sorting functions in Excel and R to find the relevant information requested by the manager, and then summarize the results.

Important: Due to different fonts and type settings, copying and pasting Excel or R functions from this text directly into Excel or R may cause errors. When such errors occur, you may need to replace special characters such as quotation marks and parentheses or delete extra spaces in the functions.

SOLUTION:

Using Excel

a. Open the *Gig* data file. Note that the employee data are currently sorted by their employee ID in column A. Scroll to the end of the data set and note that the last record is in row 605. With the column heading in row 1, the data set has a total of 604 records.

b. We use two Excel functions, **COUNT** and **COUNTA**, to inspect the number of values in each column. The **COUNT** function counts the number of cells that contain numeric values and, therefore, can only apply to the EmployeeID and HourlyWage variables. The **COUNTA** function counts the number of cells that are not empty and is applicable to all four variables. Because HourlyWage is a numerical variable, we can enter either =COUNT(B2:B605) or =COUNTA(B2:B605) in an empty cell to count the number of values for HourlyWage. We get 604 values, implying that there are no missing values. Similarly, we enter =COUNTA(C2:C605) and =COUNTA(D2:D605) in empty cells to count the number of values for the Industry (column C) and Job (column D) variables. Because these two variables are non-numerical, we use **COUNTA** instead of **COUNT**. Verify that the number of records for Industry and Job are 594 and 588, respectively, indicating that there are 10 and 16 blank or missing values, respectively, in these two variables.

c. To count the number of employees in each industry, we use the **COUNTIF** function. Entering =COUNTIF(C2:C605,"=Automotive") in an empty cell will show that 190 of the 604 employees worked in the automotive industry. Similarly, entering =COUNTIF(B2:B605,">30") in an empty cell will show that 536 employees earned more than \$30 per hour. Note that the first parameter in the **COUNTIF** function is the range of cells to be counted, and the second parameter specifies the selection criterion. Other logical operators such as >=, <, <=, and <> (not equal to) can also be used in the **COUNTIF** function.

d. To count the number of employees with multiple selection criteria, we use the **COUNTIFS** function. For example, entering =COUNTIFS(C2:C605, "=Automotive", B2:B605,">30") in an empty cell will show that 181 employees worked in the automotive industry and earned more than $30 per hour. Additional data ranges and selection criteria can be added in corresponding pairs. The >=, <, <=, and <> operators can also be used in the **COUNTIFS** function.

e. To sort all employees by their hourly wage, highlight cells A1 through D605. From the menu, click **Data > Sort** (in the Sort & Filter group). Make sure that the *My data has headers* checkbox is checked. Select HourlyWage for the *Sort by* option and choose the *Smallest to Largest* (or ascending) order. Click **OK**.

At the top of the sorted list, verify that there are three employees with the lowest hourly wage of $24.28. To sort data in descending order, repeat step e but choose the *Largest to Smallest* (or descending) order. Verify that the highest hourly wage is $51.00.

f. To sort the data based on multiple variables, again highlight cells A1:D605 and go to **Data > Sort**. Choose Industry in the *Sort by* option and the *A to Z* (or ascending) order. Click the *Add Level* button and choose Job in the *Then by* option and the *A to Z* order. Click the *Add Level* button again and choose HourlyWage in the second *Then by* option and the *Smallest to Largest* order. Click **OK**. We see that the lowest- and the highest-paid accountants who worked in the automotive industry made $28.74 and $49.32 per hour, respectively.

Similarly, sorting the data by industry in descending order (*Z to A*) and then by job classification and hourly wage in ascending order reveals that the lowest- and the highest-paid accountants in the Tech industry made $36.13 and $49.49 per hour, respectively.

g. To resort the data set to its original order, again highlight cells A1:D605 and go to **Data > Sort**. Select each of the *Then by* rows and click the *Delete Level* button. Choose EmployeeID in the *Sort by* option and the *Smallest to Largest* order.

Using R

Before following all R instructions, make sure that you have read Appendix C ("Getting Started with R"). We assume that you have downloaded R and RStudio and that you know how to import an Excel file. Throughout the text, our goal is to provide the simplest way to obtain the relevant output. We denote all function names in **boldface** and all options within a function in *italics*.

a. Import the ***Gig*** data file into a data frame (table) and label it myData. Keep in mind that the R language is case sensitive.

b. We use the **dim** function in R to count the number of observations and variables. Verify that the R output shows 604 observations and four variables. Enter:

```
> dim(myData)
```

c. Two common functions to display a portion of data are **head** and **View**. The **head** function displays the first few observations in the data set, and the **View** function (case sensitive) displays a spreadsheet-style data viewer where the user can scroll through rows and columns. Verify that the first employee in the data set is an analyst who worked in the construction industry and made $32.81 per hour. Enter:

```
> head(myData)
> View(myData)
```

d. R stores missing values as *NA*, and we use the **is.na** function to identify the observations with missing values. R labels observations with missing values as "True" and observations without missing values as "False." In order to inspect the Industry variable for missing values, enter:

```
> is.na(myData$Industry)
```

e. For a large data set, having to look through all observations is inconvenient. Alternately, we can use the **which** function together with the **is.na** function to identify "which" observations contain missing values. The following command identifies 10 observations by row number as having a missing value in the Industry variable. Verify that the first observation with a missing Industry value is in row 24. Enter:

```
> which (is.na(myData$Industry))
```

f. To inspect the 24th observation, we specify row 24 in the myData data frame. Enter:

```
> myData[24,]
```

Note that there are two elements within the square bracket, separated by a comma. The first element identifies a row number (also called row index), and the second element after the comma identifies a column number (also called column index). Leaving the second element blank will display all columns. To inspect an observation in row 24 and column 3, we enter `myData[24, 3]`. In a small data set, we can also review the missing values by scrolling to the specific rows and columns in the data viewer produced by the **View** function. As mentioned earlier, the treatment of missing values is discussed in Section 2.3.

g. To identify and count the number of employees with multiple selection criteria, we use the **which** and **length** functions. In the following command, we identify which employees worked in the automotive industry with the **which** function and count the number of these employees using the **length** function. The double equal sign (==), also called equality operator, is used to check whether the industry is automotive. In R, text characters such as 'Automotive' are enclosed in quotation marks. Enter:

```
> length(which(myData$Industry=='Automotive'))
```

We can also use the >, >=, <, <=, and != (not equal to) operators in the selection criteria. For example, using the following command, we can determine the number of employees who earn more than $30 per hour. Enter:

```
> length(which(myData$HourlyWage > 30))
```

Note that there are 190 employees in the automotive industry and there are 536 employees who earn more than $30 per hour.

h. To count how many employees worked in a particular industry and earned more than a particular wage, we use the **and** operator (&). The following command shows that 181 employees worked in the automotive industry and earned more than $30 per hour. Enter:

```
> length(which(myData$Industry=='Automotive' & myData$HourlyWage >
30))
```

i. We use the **order** function to sort the observations of a variable. In order to sort the HourlyWage variable and store the order data set in a new data frame called sortedData1, enter:

```
> sortedData1 <- myData[order(myData$HourlyWage),]
> View(sortedData1)
```

The **View** function shows that the lowest and highest hourly wages are \$24.28 and \$51.00, respectively. By default, the sorting is performed in ascending order. To sort in descending order, enter:

```
> sortedData1 <- myData[order(myData$HourlyWage, decreasing =
TRUE),]
```

j. To sort data by multiple variables, we specify the variables in the **order** function. The following command sorts the data by industry, job classification, and hourly wage, all in ascending order, and stores the ordered data in a data frame called sortedData2. Enter:

```
> sortedData2 <- myData[order(myData$Industry, myData$Job,
myData$HourlyWage),]
> View(sortedData2)
```

The **View** function shows that the lowest-paid accountant who worked in the automotive industry made \$28.74 per hour.

k. To sort the data by industry and job classification in ascending order and then by hourly wage in descending order, we insert a minus sign in front of the hourly wage variable. Verify that the highest-paid accountant in the automotive industry made \$49.32 per hour. Enter:

```
> sortedData3 <- myData[order(myData$Industry, myData$Job,
-myData$HourlyWage),]
> View(sortedData3)
```

l. The industry and job classification variables are non-numerical. As a result, to sort the data by industry in descending order and then by job classification and hourly wage in ascending order, we use the **xtfrm** function with the minus sign in front of the Industry variable. Enter:

```
> sortedData4 <- myData[order(-xtfrm(myData$Industry), myData$Job,
myData$HourlyWage),]
> View(sortedData4)
```

The **View** function reveals that the lowest- and the highest-paid accountants in the technology industry made \$36.13 and \$49.49 per hour, respectively.

m. To sort the data by industry, job, and hourly wage, all in descending order, we use the *decreasing* option in the **order** function. Verify that the highest-paid sales representative in the technology industry made \$48.87. Enter:

```
> sortedData5 <- myData[order(myData$Industry, myData$Job,
myData$HourlyWage, decreasing = TRUE),]
> View(sortedData5)
```

n. To export the sorted data from step m as a comma-separated value file, we use the **write.csv** function. Verify that the exported file is in the default folder (e.g., My Document on Microsoft Windows). Other data frames in R can be exported using a similar statement. Enter:

```
> write.csv(sortedData5,"sortedData5.csv")
```

Summary

- There are a total of 604 records in the data set. There are no missing values in the HourlyWage variable. The Industry and Job variables have 10 and 16 missing values, respectively.
- 190 employees worked in the automotive industry, 536 employees earned more than \$30 per hour, and 181 employees worked in the automotive industry and earned more than \$30 per hour.

- The lowest and the highest hourly wages in the data set are $24.28 and $51.00, respectively. The three employees who had the lowest hourly wage of $24.28 all worked in the construction industry and were hired as Engineer, Sales Rep, and Accountant, respectively. Interestingly, the employee with the highest hourly wage of $51.00 also worked in the construction industry in a job type classified as Other.
- The lowest- and the highest-paid accountants who worked in the automotive industry made $28.74 and $49.32 per hour, respectively. In the technology industry, the lowest- and the highest-paid accountants made $36.13 and $49.49 per hour, respectively. Note that the lowest hourly wage for an accountant is considerably higher in the technology industry compared to the automotive industry ($36.13 > $28.74).

There are many ways to count and sort data to obtain useful insights. To gain further insights, students are encouraged to experiment with the ***Gig*** data using different combinations of counting and sorting options than the ones used in Example 2.1.

EXERCISES 2.2

Mechanics

8. **FILE** ***Exercise_2.8.*** The accompanying data set contains two numerical variables, x_1 and x_2.
   a. For x_2, how many of the observations are equal to 2?
   b. Sort x_1 and then x_2, both in ascending order. After the variables have been sorted, what is the first observation for x_1 and x_2?
   c. Sort x_1 and then x_2, both in descending order. After the variables have been sorted, what is the first observation for x_1 and x_2?
   d. Sort x_1 in ascending order and x_2 in descending order. After the variables have been sorted, what is the first observation for x_1 and x_2?
   e. How many missing values are there in x_1 and x_2?
9. **FILE** ***Exercise_2.9.*** The accompanying data set contains three numerical variables, x_1, x_2, and x_3.
   a. For x_1, how many of the observations are greater than 30?
   b. Sort x_1, x_2, and then x_3 all in ascending order. After the variables have been sorted, what is the first observation for x_1, x_2, and x_3?
   c. Sort x_1 and x_2 in descending order and x_3 in ascending order. After the variables have been sorted, what is the first observation for x_1, x_2, and x_3?
   d. How many missing values are there in x_1, x_2, and x_3?
10. **FILE** ***Exercise_2.10.*** The accompanying data set contains three numerical variables, x_1, x_2, and x_3, and one categorical variable, x_4.
   a. For x_4, how many of the observations are less than three?
   b. Sort x_1, x_2, x_3, and then x_4 all in ascending order. After the variables have been sorted, what is the first observation for x_1, x_2, x_3, and x_4?
   c. Sort x_1, x_2, x_3, and then x_4 all in descending order. After the variables have been sorted, what is the first observation for x_1, x_2, x_3, and x_4?
   d. How many missing values are there in x_1, x_2, x_3, and x_4?
   e. How many observations are there in each category in x_4?

Applications

11. **FILE** ***SAT***. The following table lists a portion of the average writing and math SAT scores for the 50 states as well as the District of Columbia, Puerto Rico, and the U.S. Virgin Islands for the year 2017 as reported by the College Board.

State	Writing	Math
Alabama	595	571
Alaska	562	544
⋮	⋮	⋮
Wyoming	633	635

   a. Sort the data by writing scores in descending order. Which state has the highest average writing score? What is the average math score of that state?
   b. Sort the data by math scores in ascending order. Which state has the lowest average math score? What is the average writing score of that state?
   c. How many states reported an average math score higher than 600?
   d. How many states reported an average writing score lower than 550?
12. **FILE** ***Fitness.*** A social science study conducts a survey of 418 individuals about how often they exercise, marital status, and annual income. A portion of the ***Fitness*** data is shown in the accompanying table.

ID	Exercise	Married	Income
1	Always	Yes	106299
2	Sometimes	Yes	86570
⋮	⋮	⋮	⋮
418	Often	No	92690

a. Sort the data by annual income. Of the 10 highest income earners, how many of them are married and always exercise?
b. Sort the data by marital status and exercise both in descending order. How many of the individuals who are married and exercise sometimes earn more than $110,000 per year?
c. How many missing values are there in each variable?
d. How many individuals are married and unmarried?
e. How many married individuals always exercise? How many unmarried individuals never exercise?

13. **FILE** ***Spend***. A company conducts a consumer survey with questions about home ownership (OwnHome: Yes/No), car ownership (OwnCar: Yes/No), annual household spending on food (Food), and annual household spending on travel (Travel). A portion of the data is shown in the accompanying table.

ID	OwnHome	OwnCar	Food	Travel
1	Yes	Yes	5472.43	827.4
2	No	Yes	9130.73	863.55
⋮	⋮	⋮	⋮	⋮
500	No	No	6205.97	3667.5

a. Sort the data by home ownership, car ownership, and the travel spending all in descending order. How much did the first customer on the ordered list spend on food?
b. Sort the data only by the travel spending amount in descending order. Of the 10 customers who spend the most on traveling, how many of them are homeowners? How many of them are both homeowners and car owners?
c. How many missing values are there in each variable?
d. How many customers are homeowners?
e. How many customers are homeowners but do not own a car?

14. **FILE** ***Demographics.*** The accompanying table shows a portion of data that shows an individual's income (Income in $1,000s), age, sex (F = female, M = male), and marital status (Married; Y = yes, N = no).

Individual	Income	Age	Sex	Married
1	87	46	F	Y
2	97	52	M	Y
⋮	⋮	⋮	⋮	⋮
890	69	44	F	N

a. Count the number of males and females in the data.
b. What percentages of males and females are married?
c. Of the 10 individuals with the highest income, how many are married males.
d. What are the highest and the lowest incomes of males and females?
e. What are the highest and lowest incomes of married and unmarried males?

15. **FILE** ***Admission.*** College admission is a competitive process where, among other things, the SAT and high school GPA scores of students are evaluated to make an admission decision. The accompanying data set contains the admission decision (Decision; Admit/Deny), SAT score, Female (Yes/No), and high school GPA (HSGPA) for 1,230 students. A portion of the data is shown in the accompanying table.

Student	Decision	SAT	Female	HSGPA
1	Deny	873	No	2.57
2	Deny	861	Yes	2.65
⋮	⋮	⋮	⋮	⋮
1230	Admit	1410	No	4.28

a. Count the number of male and female students.
b. What percentages of male and female students are admitted?
c. Of the 10 students with the highest HSGPA, how many are males?
d. Of the 10 students with the lowest SAT, how many are females?
e. What are the highest and the lowest SAT scores of admitted male and female students?

2.3 DATA PREPARATION

LO 2.3

Apply data preparation techniques to handle missing values and to subset data.

Once we have inspected and explored data, we can start the data preparation process. In this section, we examine two important data preparation techniques: handling missing values and subsetting data. As mentioned in Section 2.2, there may be missing values in the key variables that are crucial for subsequent analysis. Moreover, most data analysis projects focus only on a portion (subset) of the data, rather than the entire data set; or sometimes the objective of the analysis is to compare two subgroups of the data.

Handling Missing Values

Missing values are a common data quality problem found in data sets both large and small. This issue can lead to significant reduction in the number of usable observations and biases in analysis results. For example, in a data set with 20 variables, if 5% of the values, spread randomly across the observations and variables, are missing, then potentially only $(1 - 0.05)^{20} = 0.3585$, or 35.85% of the observations, would be complete and usable. Understanding why the values are missing is the first step in the treatment of missing values.

Sometimes data are missing because the respondents decline to provide the information due to its sensitive nature (e.g., race, sexual orientation, economic status, etc.). In these cases, missing values are usually not distributed randomly across observations but tend to concentrate within one or more subgroups. For example, research has shown that male respondents often skip questions related to depression in a survey.

In other cases, data values are missing because some of the items do not apply to every respondent. For instance, patients who are still in the hospital do not have values in the discharge date column. Missing values can also be caused by human errors, sloppy data collection, and equipment failures.

Because missing values are often unavoidable in real life, it is important to learn how to handle observations with missing values. There are two common strategies for dealing with missing values: **omission** and **imputation**. The omission strategy, also called complete-case analysis, recommends that observations with missing values be excluded from the analysis. This approach is appropriate when the amount of missing values is small or missing values are concentrated in a small number of observations. Otherwise, it can lead to severe loss of data, as illustrated earlier.

The imputation strategy replaces missing values with some reasonable imputed values. The most commonly used imputation strategy for numerical variables is the simple mean imputation where the missing values are replaced with the mean (average) values across relevant observations. For example, if the annual household income for an observation is missing, we replace the missing value with the mean household income across all observations or across a homogenous group (e.g., households with the same zip code).

Simple mean imputation is easy to implement and allows observations with missing values to be included in the analysis without adding more variability to the data set. However, if a large number of missing values need to be imputed, simple mean imputation will likely distort the relationships among variables, leading to biased results. For example, the total square footage of a house tends to have a positive relationship with the value of the house. If a data set contains many missing total square footage values and these missing values are replaced with mean total square footage of the rest of the houses in the data set, then the relationship between total square footage and house value will likely be distorted. More advanced imputation techniques such as regression mean imputation that better preserve the relationships among variables can be used in these cases. Advanced imputation techniques are beyond the scope of this text.

In the case of categorical variables, the most frequent category is often used as the imputed value. For instance, if some values of sex are missing in a data set, we might replace these missing values with the predominant sex category among the rest of the observations. For categorical variables, an "Unknown" category may be created to signify missing values. This approach is especially useful if the data are missing for a reason; the fact that the values are missing for these observations may suggest certain patterns and relationships in the data.

In addition to the omission and imputation strategies, other approaches may be considered when handling missing values. If the variable that has many missing values is deemed unimportant or can be represented using a proxy variable that does not have missing values, the variable may be excluded from the analysis. Finally, some analytics techniques such as decision trees (discussed in Chapter 10) are robust and can be applied to data sets even with the inclusion of missing values.

HANDLING MISSING VALUES

There are two common strategies for dealing with missing values.

- The omission strategy recommends that observations with missing values be excluded from subsequent analysis.
- The imputation strategy recommends that the missing values be replaced with some reasonable imputed values. For numerical variables, it is common to use mean imputation. For categorical variables, it is common to impute the most predominant category.

In Example 2.2, we demonstrate how to handle missing values with the omission and imputation strategies using Excel with Analytic Solver and R.

EXAMPLE 2.2

Sarah Johnson, the manager of a local restaurant, has conducted a survey to gauge customers' perception about the eatery. Each customer rated the restaurant on its ambience, cleanliness, service, and food using a scale of 1 (lowest) to 7 (highest). Table 2.4 displays a portion of the survey data.

FILE *Restaurant_Reviews*

TABLE 2.4 Restaurant Reviews

RecordNum	Ambience	Cleanliness	Service	Food
1	4	5	6	4
2	6	6		6
⋮	⋮	⋮	⋮	⋮
150	3	5	6	7

Sarah notices that there are a number of missing values in the survey. Use the ***Restaurant_Reviews*** data to first detect the missing values. Then use both omission and imputation strategies to handle the missing values.

SOLUTION:

Using Excel with Analytic Solver

a. Open the ***Restaurant_Reviews*** data file.

b. We use the Conditional Formatting feature in Excel to detect missing values. Select the data range B2:D151. Choose **Home > Conditional Formatting > New Rule. . .**. Select *Format only cells that contain* as the rule type. Select *Format only cells with: Blanks* as the rule description. Click on the *Format* button. Select the *Fill* tab and pick the color red. Click **OK**. Click **OK** again. Now the cells with missing values are highlighted in red.

c. Here, we use the **COUNTBLANK** function to detect the number of missing values for each observation. Create a new column with the column heading "# of Missing Values" in column F. Enter the formula =COUNTBLANK(B2:E2) in cell F2. Fill the range F3:F151 with the formula in F2. This formula shows "0" in the result for the observations without missing values. For the observations with missing values, the formula shows the number of variables with missing values. Verify that observations 2, 13, 26, and 100 each has one missing value, and observation 134 has two missing values.

d. To count the total number of missing values in the entire data set, enter the formula =SUM(F2:F151) in cell F152. The result shows that there is a total of six missing values.

e. To identify variables with missing values, enter the formula =COUNTBLANK(B2:B151) in cell B152. Fill the range C152:E152 with the formula in B152. The result shows that the Ambience (column B), Cleanliness (column C), and Food (column E) variables each has one missing value, and the Service variable (column D) has three missing values.

f. We start with the omission strategy to handle missing values. Choose **Data Mining > Transform > Missing Data Handling**. Select data range $B$1:$E$151. Check the box *Variable names in the first row*. Select Ambience, Cleanliness, Service, and Food by holding the Ctrl button. Choose *Delete record* as the treatment. Click on the *Apply to selected variable(s)* button. Click **OK**. A new worksheet *Imputation* is created and shows a transformed data table with the observations with missing values deleted. A part of the *Imputation* worksheet is displayed in Figure 2.4. The results show that 5 observations were deleted due to missing values, leaving 145 complete observations in the final data set. The transformed data set is ready for data analysis.

FIGURE 2.4 Omission strategy results

Imputer Parameters					
Variable	RecordNum	Ambience	Cleanliness	Service	Food
Reduction Type	NONE	DELETE RECORD	DELETE RECORD	DELETE RECORD	DELETE RECORD
# Records Treated	0	1	1	3	1
Missing Value Code					
# Output Records	145				
# Records Deleted	5				

g. We now use the simple mean imputation strategy to handle the missing values. Return to the *Restaurant_Reviews* worksheet. Choose **Data Mining > Transform > Missing Data Handling**. Select data range $B$1:$E$151. Check the box *Variable names in the first row*. Select Ambience, Cleanliness, Service, and Food by holding the Ctrl button. Choose *Mean* as the treatment. Click on the *Apply to selected variable(s)* button. Another new worksheet called *Imputation1* is created and shows all 150 observations. Figure 2.5 displays part of the *Imputation1* worksheet. The results show that the mean values were used to replace the missing values and that all 150 observations are retained. Verify that the service ratings for observations 2, 100, and 134 are now 5.97, which is the mean rating. Again, the transformed data set is ready for data analysis.

FIGURE 2.5 Imputation strategy results

Imputer Parameters					
Variable	RecordNum	Ambience	Cleanliness	Service	Food
Reduction Type	NONE	MEAN	MEAN	MEAN	MEAN
# Records Treated	0	1	1	3	1
Missing Value Code					
# Output Records	150				
# Records Deleted	0				

Using R

a. Import the ***Restaurant_Reviews*** data into a data frame (table) and label it myData.

b. To detect missing values in a data set, we use the **is.na** function. Recall from Example 2.1 that missing values are labelled as *NA* in R, and the **is.na** function returns TRUE if a missing value is detected and FALSE otherwise. Enter:

```
> is.na(myData)
```

Figure 2.6 displays a portion of the output, where we have highlighted the missing values. The service rating for observation 2 and cleanliness rating for observation 13 are labeled TRUE because they are missing. The rest of the values are labeled FALSE because they are not missing.

```
        RecordNum Ambience Cleanliness Service  Food
 [1,]     FALSE    FALSE       FALSE   FALSE FALSE
 [2,]     FALSE    FALSE       FALSE    TRUE FALSE
 [3,]     FALSE    FALSE       FALSE   FALSE FALSE
 [4,]     FALSE    FALSE       FALSE   FALSE FALSE
 [5,]     FALSE    FALSE       FALSE   FALSE FALSE
 [6,]     FALSE    FALSE       FALSE   FALSE FALSE
 [7,]     FALSE    FALSE       FALSE   FALSE FALSE
 [8,]     FALSE    FALSE       FALSE   FALSE FALSE
 [9,]     FALSE    FALSE       FALSE   FALSE FALSE
[10,]     FALSE    FALSE       FALSE   FALSE FALSE
[11,]     FALSE    FALSE       FALSE   FALSE FALSE
[12,]     FALSE    FALSE       FALSE   FALSE FALSE
[13,]     FALSE    FALSE        TRUE   FALSE FALSE
[14,]     FALSE    FALSE       FALSE   FALSE FALSE
[15,]     FALSE    FALSE       FALSE   FALSE FALSE
```

FIGURE 2.6 R output for detecting missing values

To detect missing values, say, in the Service variable, we enter:

```
> is.na(myData$Service)
```

c. If we have a large data set, using the **is.na** function to detect missing values can be cumbersome. Alternatively, we can use the **complete.cases** function to identify the rows in the data frame or cases that are complete. Recall that leaving the second element, after the comma, blank will display all columns. Enter:

```
> myData[complete.cases(myData), ]
```

d. Because our data are mostly complete, listing all the complete cases may not be convenient. Instead, we can use the *not* operator (**!** character) with the **complete.cases** function to identify observations with missing values. The **!** character in front of the **complete.cases** function identifies individual rows that are not complete (or cases with missing values). Enter:

```
> myData[!complete.cases(myData), ]
```

Figure 2.7 shows observations 2, 13, 26, 100, and 134 have missing values.

```
  RecordNum Ambience Cleanliness Service Food
1         2        6           6      NA    6
2        13        6          NA       7    5
3        26        6           7       5   NA
4       100        6           6      NA    3
5       134       NA           5      NA    6
```

FIGURE 2.7 Observations with missing values

e. To implement the omission strategy, we use the **na.omit** function to remove observations with missing values and store the resulting data set in the omissionData data frame. The **View** function displays the updated data. Enter:

```
> omissionData <- na.omit(myData)
> View(omissionData)
```

R creates a new data frame, omissionData, that contains 145 complete cases. Verify that there are no missing values in the new data set. This data set is ready for data analysis.

f. To implement the simple mean imputation strategy, we start with the original data frame, **myData**. We then calculate the average value using the **mean** function. The option **na.rm = TRUE** ignores the missing values when calculating the average values. In order to compute the average values for the Ambience and Service variables, enter:

```
> ambienceMean <- mean(myData$Ambience, na.rm = TRUE)
> serviceMean <- mean(myData$Service, na.rm = TRUE)
```

Verify that the means for the Ambience and Service variables are 4.42953 and 5.965986, respectively.

g. To impute the missing values in the Ambience and Service variables, we again use the **is.na** function to identify the missing values and replace them with the means calculated in step f. Enter:

```
> myData$Ambience[is.na(myData$Ambience)] <- ambienceMean
> myData$Service[is.na(myData$Service)] <- serviceMean
```

Students are encouraged to calculate the mean and impute missing values in the Cleanliness and Food variables and inspect the resulting data set to make sure that the missing values have been replaced by the average ratings. The resulting data set is then ready for data analysis.

Another important data preparation task involves the treatment of extremely small or large values, referred to as outliers. It is noteworthy that in the presence of outliers, it is preferred to use the median instead of the mean to impute missing values. Both Analytic Solver and R allow easy imputation with the median computed by using the **MEDIAN(*data range*)** function in Excel or the **median** function in R. Refer to Chapter 3 for a detailed discussion on outliers and the median.

Subsetting

The process of extracting portions of a data set that are relevant to the analysis is called **subsetting**. It is commonly used to pre-process the data prior to analysis. For example, a multinational company has sales data for its global operations, and it creates a subset of sales data by country and performs analysis accordingly. For time series data, which are data indexed in time order, we may choose to create subsets of recent observations and observations from the distant past in order to analyze them separately. Subsetting can also be used to eliminate unwanted data such as observations that contain missing values, low-quality data, or outliers. Sometimes, subsetting involves excluding variables instead of observations. For example, we might remove variables that are irrelevant to the problem, variables that contain redundant information (e.g., property value and property tax or employee's age and experience), or variables with excessive amounts of missing values.

SUBSETTING

Subsetting is the process of extracting parts of a data set that is of interest to the analytics professional.

Subsetting can also be performed as part of descriptive analytics that helps reveal insights in the data. For example, by subsetting student records into groups with various academic performance levels, we may be able to identify high-achieving students and relevant attributes that contribute to their success. Similarly, by comparing subsets of medical records with different treatment results, we may identify potential contributing factors of success in a treatment.

Table 2.5 shows important summary measures from two subsets of medical records of tuberculosis treatments administered in a developing country. Here, subsets 1 and 2 represent successful and unsuccessful treatments, respectively.

TABLE 2.5 Summary Data of Tuberculosis Treatment

Summary Measures	Successful Treatments	Unsuccessful Treatments
% of Male Patients	64.3%	12.7%
Average Education Level	3.8	2.1
% of Patients with Good Incomes	92.7%	28.1%

Note that the sex, education level (1: lowest; 5: highest), and income of the patients differ considerably between the two subsets. Not surprisingly, male patients, especially those with higher education and income levels, have better success with tuberculosis treatment than female patients with lower education and income levels. This simple analysis highlights the importance of contributing factors in tuberculosis control efforts.

In Example 2.3, we demonstrate how to use subsetting functions in Excel and R to select or exclude variables and/or observations from the original data set.

EXAMPLE 2.3

FILE *Customers*

In the introductory case, Catherine Hill wants to gain a better understanding of Organic Food Superstore's customers who are college-educated millennials, born between 1982 and 2000. She feels that sex, household size, income, total spending in 2018, total number of orders in the past 24 months, and channel through which the customer was acquired are useful for her to create a profile of these customers. Use Excel and R to first identify college-educated millenial customers in the ***Customers*** data file. Then, create subsets of female and male college-educated millenial customers. The synopsis that follows this example provides a summary of the results.

SOLUTION:

Using Excel

a. Open the ***Customers*** data file.
b. We first filter the data set to include only college-educated millennials. Select the data range A1:N201. From the menu choose **Home > Sort & Filter > Filter**. The column headings (A1:N1) will turn into drop-down boxes.
c. Click on the drop-down box in E1 (College). Uncheck *(Select all)*, then check the box next to *Yes*. Click **OK**. This step shows only those customers who have a college degree (Yes) by hiding those who don't (No) in the data set.
d. Click on the drop-down box in D1 (BirthDate). Select **Date filters > Between**. See Figure 2.8. In the *Custom AutoFilter* dialog box, enter "1/1/1982" next to the *is after or equal to* box or select the date from the calendar object. Select *And* and enter "12/31/1999" next to the *is before or equal to* box or select the date from the calendar object. Click **OK**. The data set now only displays college-educated millennials who were born between 1982 and 2000.

FIGURE 2.8 Excel's AutoFilter dialog box

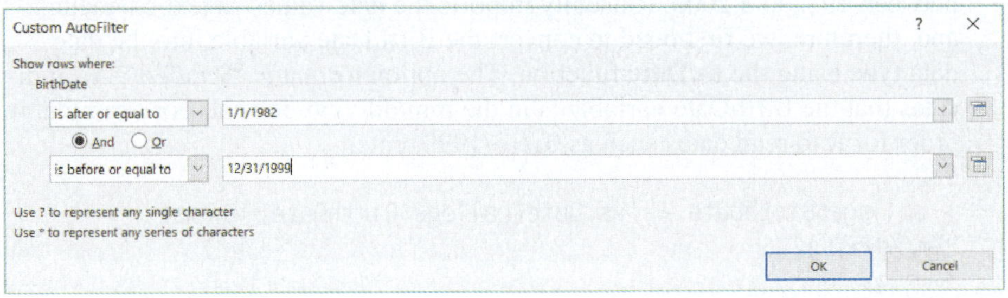

e. Select the entire filtered data that are left in the worksheet. Copy and paste the filtered data to a new worksheet. Verify that the new worksheet contains 59 observations of college-educated millennials. Rename the new worksheet as *College-Educated Millennials*.

f. We now exclude the variables that are not relevant to the current analysis. In the *College-Educated Millennials* worksheet, select cell A1 (CustID). From the menu choose **Home > Delete > Delete Sheet Columns** to remove the CustID column. Repeat this step for the Race, BirthDate, College, ZipCode, Spending2017, DaysSinceLast, and Satisfaction columns from the data set.

g. To subset the college-educated millennials data by sex, select column A. From the menu choose **Home > Sort & Filter > Sort A to Z.** If prompted, select *Expand the selection* in the *Sort Warning* dialog box and click *Sort*. The observations are now sorted by sex in alphabetic order. The female customer records are followed by male customer records.

h. Create two new worksheets and assign the worksheet names *Female* and *Male*. Copy and paste the female and male customer records, including the column headings, to the new *Female* and *Male* worksheets, respectively. Table 2.6 shows a portion of the results.

TABLE 2.6 College-Educated Millennial Customers

a) Female College-Educated Millennials

Sex	HouseholdSize	Income	Spending2018	NumOfOrders	Channel
Female	5	53000	241	3	SM
Female	3	84000	153	2	Web
⋮	⋮	⋮	⋮	⋮	⋮
Female	1	52000	586	13	Referral

b) Male College-Educated Millennials

Sex	HouseholdSize	Income	Spending2018	NumOfOrders	Channel
Male	5	94000	843	12	TV
Male	1	97000	1028	17	Web
⋮	⋮	⋮	⋮	⋮	⋮
Male	5	102000	926	10	SM

Using R

a. Import the ***Customers*** data into a data frame (table) and label it myData.

b. To select college-educated millennials, we first select all customers with a college degree. Recall that the double equal sign (==) is used to check whether the College value is "Yes." Enter:

```
> college <- myData[myData$College=='Yes', ]
```

c. We now use the Birthdate variable to select the millennials who were born between 1982 and 2000. R usually imports the date values as text characters, and, therefore, we first need to convert the BirthDate variable into the date data type using the **as.Date** function. The option format = "%m/%d/%Y" indicates that the BirthDate variable is in the mm/dd/yyyy format. For example, in order for R to read dates such as 01/13/1990, enter:

```
> college$BirthDate <- as.Date(college$BirthDate, format =
"%m/%d/%Y")
```

Other common date formats include "%Y-%m-%d", "%b %d, %Y", and "%B %d, %Y" that will read dates specified as 1990-01-13, Jan 13, 1990, and January 13, 1990, respectively.

d. We also use the **as.Date** function to specify the cutoff dates, January 1, 1982, and December 31, 1999, before using them as selection criteria for selecting the millennials in our data. Enter:

```
> cutoffdate1 <- as.Date("01/01/1982", format = "%m/%d/%Y")
> cutoffdate2 <- as.Date("12/31/1999", format = "%m/%d/%Y")
> millenials <- college[college$BirthDate >= cutoffdate1 &
college$BirthDate <= cutoffdate2, ]
```

Verify that the millennials data frame contains 59 college-educated millennials.

e. To include only the Sex, HouseholdSize, Income, Spending2018, NumOfOrders, and Channel variables in the millenials data frame, we specify the column indices of these variables using the **c** function. Enter:

```
> subset1 <- millenials[ , c(2,6,8,10,11,14)]
```

Alternately, we can create a new data frame by specifying the names of the variables to include. Enter:

```
> subset2 <- millenials[ , c("Sex", "HouseholdSize", "Income",
"Spending2018", "NumOfOrders", "Channel")]
```

Note that subset1 and subset2 data are identical.

f. R imports non-numerical variables such as Sex and Channel as text characters. Before further subsetting and examining the data, we convert Sex and Channel into categorical variables (called factors in R) by using the **as.factor** function. Enter:

```
> subset1$Sex <- as.factor(subset1$Sex)
> subset1$Channel <- as.factor(subset1$Channel)
```

To verify that the Channel variable has been converted into a factor or a categorical variable, enter:

```
> is.factor(subset1$Channel)
```

This command returns TRUE if the variable is a factor, and FALSE otherwise.

g. To create two subsets of data based on Sex, we use the **split** function. Enter:

```
> sex <- split(subset1, subset1$Sex)
```

The sex data frame contains two subsets: Female and Male. We can now access and view the Female and Male subsets. Enter:

```
> sex$Female
> sex$Male
> View(sex$Female)
> View(sex$Male)
```

Verify that there are 21 female college-educated millennials and 38 male college-educated millennials. Your results should be similar to Table 2.6.

h. In some situations, we might simply want to subset data based on data ranges. For example, we use the following statement to subset data to include observations 1 to 50 and observations 101 to 200. Enter:

```
> dataRanges <- myData[c(1:50, 101:200),]
```

SYNOPSIS OF INTRODUCTORY CASE

hbpictures/Shutterstock

Catherine Hill has been assigned to help market Organic Food Superstore's new line of Asian-inspired meals. In order to understand the potential target market for this product, Catherine subsetted the data that contain a representative sample of the company's customers to include only college-educated millennials. She also partitioned the data set into two subsets based on sex to compare the profiles of female and male college-educated millennials.

The differences between the female and male customers have given Catherine some ideas for the marketing campaign that she is about to design. For example, the data show that an overwhelming portion of the male customers were acquired through social media ads, while female customers tend to be enticed by web ads or referrals. She plans to design and run a series of social media ads about the new product line with content that targets male customers. For female customers, Catherine wants to focus her marketing efforts on web banner ads and the company's referral program.

Furthermore, as the male customers seem to place more frequent but smaller orders than female customers do, Catherine plans to work with her marketing team to develop some cross-sell and upsell strategies that target male customers. Given the fact that the company's male college-educated millennial customers tend to be high-income earners, Catherine is confident that with the right message and product offerings, her marketing team will be able to develop strategies for increasing the total spending of these customers.

EXERCISES 2.3

Mechanics

16. The following table contains three variables and five observations with some missing values.

x_1	x_2	x_3
248	3.5	
124	3.8	55
150		74
196	4.5	32
	6.2	63

a. Handle the missing values using the omission strategy. How many observations remain in the data set and have complete cases?

b. Handle the missing values using the simple mean imputation strategy. How many missing values are replaced? What are the means of x_1, x_2, and x_3?

17. FILE ***Exercise_2.17***. The accompanying data set contains four variables, x_1, x_2, x_3, and x_4.

a. Subset the data set to include only observations that have a date on or after May 1, 1975, for x_3. How many observations are in the subset data?

b. Split the data set based on the binary values for x_4. What are the average values for x_1 for the two subsets?

18. FILE ***Exercise_2.18.*** The accompanying data set contains five variables, x_1, x_2, x_3, x_4, and x_5.

a. Subset the data set to include only x_2, x_3, and x_4. How many missing values are there in the three remaining variables?

b. Remove all observations that have "Own" as the value for x_2 and have values lower than 150 for x_3. How many observations remain in the data set? What are the average values for x_3 and x_4?

19. FILE ***Exercise_2.19***. The accompanying data set contains five variables, x_1, x_2, x_3, x_4, and x_5. There are missing values in the data set.

a. Which variables have missing values?

b. Which observations have missing values?

c. How many missing values are in the data set?

d. Handle the missing values using the omission strategy. How many observations remain in the data set and have complete cases?

20. FILE ***Exercise_2.20***. The accompanying data set contains five variables, x_1, x_2, x_3, x_4, and x_5. There are missing values in the data set. Handle the missing values using the simple mean imputation strategy for numerical variables and the predominant category strategy for categorical variables.

a. How many missing values are there for each variable?

b. What are the values for imputing missing values in x_1, x_2, x_3, x_4, and x_5?

21. **FILE** ***Exercise_2.21***. The accompanying data set contains five variables, x_1, x_2, x_3, x_4, and x_5.
   a. Are there missing values for x_1? If so, impute the missing values using the mean value of x_1. After imputation, what is the mean of x_1?
   b. Are there missing values for x_2? If so, impute the missing values using the mean value of x_2. After imputation, what is the mean of x_2?
   c. If there are missing values in x_4, impute the missing values using the median value of x_4. (Hint: Use the **MEDIAN(*data range*)** function in Excel or the **median** function in R.) After imputation, what is the median of x_4?

22. **FILE** ***Exercise_2.22***. The accompanying data set contains five variables, x_1, x_2, x_3, x_4, and x_5. There are missing values in the data set.
   a. Which variables have missing values?
   b. Which observations have missing values?
   c. How many missing values are in the data set?
   d. Handle the missing values using the omission strategy. How many observations remain in the data set and have complete cases?

23. **FILE** ***Exercise_2.23***. The accompanying data set contains four variables, x_1, x_2, x_3, and x_4. There are missing values in the data set.
   a. Subset the data set to include only x_1, x_2, and x_3.
   b. Which variables have missing values?
   c. Which observations have missing values?
   d. How many missing values are in the data set?
   e. Handle the missing values using the omission strategy. How many observations remain in the data set and have complete cases?
   f. Split the data set based on the categories of x_2. How many observations are in each subset?

24. **FILE** ***Exercise_2.24***. The accompanying data set contains seven variables, x_1, x_2, x_3, x_4, x_5, x_6, and x_7. There are missing values in the data set.
   a. Remove variables x_2, x_6, and x_7 from the data set. Which of the remaining variables have missing values?
   b. Which observations have missing values?
   c. How many missing values are in the data set?
   d. If there are missing values in x_1, replace the missing values with "Unknown." How many missing values were replaced?
   e. Handle the missing values for numerical variables using the imputation strategy. If there are missing values in x_3, impute the missing values using the mean value of x_3. If there are missing values in x_4, impute the missing values using the median value of x_4. If there are missing values in x_5, impute the missing values using the mean value of x_5. What are the average values of x_3, x_4, and x_5 after imputation?
   f. Remove observations that have the value "F" for x_1 and values lower than 1,020 for x_4. How many observations remain in the data set?

Applications

25. **FILE** ***Population.*** The US Census Bureau records the population for the 50 states each year. The accompanying table shows a portion of these data for the years 2010 to 2018.

State	2010	2011	...	2018
Alabama	4,785,448	4,798,834	...	4,887,871
Alaska	713,906	722,038	...	737,438
⋮	⋮	⋮	⋮	⋮
Wyoming	564,483	567,224	...	577,737

   a. Create two subsets of the state population data: one with 2018 population great than or equal to 5 million and one with 2018 population less than 5 million. How many observations are in each subset?
   b. In the subset of states with 5 million or more people, remove the states with over 10 million people. How many states were removed?

26. **FILE** ***Travel_Plan.*** Jerry Stevenson is the manager of a travel agency. He wants to build a model that can predict whether or not a customer will travel within the next year. He has compiled a data set that contains the following variables: whether the individual has a college degree (College), whether the individual has a credit card (CreditCard), annual household spending on food (FoodSpend in $), annual income (Income in $), and whether the customer has plans to travel within the next year (TravelPlan, 1 = have travel plans; 0 = do not have travel plans). A portion of the ***Travel_Plan*** data is shown in the accompanying table.

College	CreditCard	FoodSpend	Income	TravelPlan
Yes	No	1706.89	49412	1
No	No	2892.9	55416	0
⋮	⋮	⋮	⋮	⋮
No	Yes	2617	50900	0

   a. Are there any missing values in the data set? If there are, which variables have missing values? How many missing values are there in the data set?
   b. Use the omission strategy to handle missing values. How many observations are removed due to missing values?

27. **FILE** ***Travel_Plan.*** Refer to the previous exercise for a description of the problem and data set.
   a. Based on his past experience, Jerry knows that whether the individual has a credit card or not has nothing to do with his or her travel plans and would like to remove this variable. Remove the variable CreditCard from the data set.

b. In order to better understand his customers with high incomes, Jerry wants to create a subset of the data that only includes customers with annual incomes higher than $75,000 and who plan to travel within the next year. Subset the data to build the list of customers who meet these criteria. How many observations are in this subset?
c. Return to the original data set. Use the imputation strategy to handle missing values. If there are missing values for the FoodSpend variable, impute the missing values using the mean of the variable. If there are missing values for the Income variable, impute the missing values using the median of the variable. What are the average values of FoodSpend and Income after imputation?

28. **FILE** ***Football_Players.*** Denise Lau is an avid football fan and religiously follows every game of the National Football League. During the 2017 season, she meticulously keeps a record of how each quarterback has played throughout the season. Denise is making a presentation at the local NFL fan club about these quarterbacks. The accompanying table shows a portion of the data that Denise has recorded, with the following variables: the player's name (Player), team's name (Team), completed passes (Comp), attempted passes (Att), completion percentage (Pct), total yards thrown (Yds), average yards per attempt (Avg), yards thrown per game (Yds/G), number of touch downs (TD), and number of interceptions (Int).

Player	Team	Comp	. . .	Int
Aaron Rodgers	GB	154	. . .	6
Alex Smith	KC	341	. . .	5
⋮	⋮	⋮	⋮	⋮
Tyrod Taylor	BUF	263	. . .	4

a. Are there any missing values in the data set? If there are, which variables have missing values? Which observations have missing values? How many missing values are there in the data set?
b. Use the omission strategy to handle missing values. How many observations are removed due to missing values?

29. **FILE** ***Football_Players.*** Refer to the previous exercise for a description of the data set. Denise feels that, for her presentation, it would remove some biases if the player names and team names are suppressed. Remove these variables from the data set.
a. Denise also wants to remove outlier cases where the players have less than five touchdowns or more than 20 interceptions. Remove these observations from the data set. How many observations were removed from the data?
b. Return to the original data set. Use the imputation strategy to handle missing values. If there are missing values for Comp, Att, Pct, Yds, Avg, or Yds/G, impute the missing values using the mean of the variable. If there are missing values for TD or Int, impute the missing values using the median of the variable. What are the average values of Comp, Att, Pct, Yds, Avg, and Yds/G after imputation?

30. **FILE** ***Salaries.*** Ian Stevens is a human resource analyst working for the city of Seattle. He is performing a compensation analysis of city employees. The accompanying data set contains three variables: Department, Job Title, and Hourly Rate (in $). A few hourly rates are missing in the data.

Department	Job Title	Hourly Rate
Public Utilities	Res&Eval Asst	32.81
Sustainability & Environ Dept	StratAdvsr3,Exempt	62.27
⋮	⋮	⋮
Public Utilities	Capital Prjts Coord, Asst	42.71

a. Split the data set into a number of subsets based on Department. How many subsets are created?
b. Which subset contains missing values? How many missing values are in that data set?
c. Use the imputation strategy to replace the missing values with the mean of the variable. What is the average hourly rate for each subset?

31. **FILE** ***Stocks.*** Investors usually consider a variety of information to make investment decisions. The accompanying table displays a sample of large publicly traded corporations and their financial information. Relevant information includes stock price (Price), dividend as a percentage of share price (Dividend), price to earnings ratio (PE), earnings per share (EPS), book value, lowest and highest share prices within the past 52 weeks (52 wk low and 52 wk high), market value of the company's shares (Market cap), and earnings before interest, taxes, depreciation, and amortization (EBITDA in $ billions).

Name	Price	Dividend	. . .	EBITDA
3M	189.09	2.48	. . .	8.70
Abbott Lab	45.00	2.34	. . .	4.59
⋮	⋮	⋮	⋮	⋮
Zoetis	53.07	0.79	. . .	1.70

a. As the price to earnings ratio is often considered a better assessment of stock valuation than stock price or earnings per share alone, the financial analyst would like to remove Price and EPS from the data set. Remove these variables from the data set.
b. The financial analyst is most interested in companies with a higher book value than market cap. Remove all

observations that have a lower book value than market cap. How many observations are left in the data set?

32. FILE ***Stocks.*** Refer to the previous exercise for a description of the problem and data set. The financial analyst wants to find out if there are any missing values in the data set.
    a. Are there any missing values in the data set? If there are, which variables have missing values? Which observations have missing values? How many missing values are there in the data set?
    b. Use the omission strategy to handle missing values. How many observations are removed due to missing values?
    c. Return to the original data set. If there are missing values for Price, Dividend, Book Value, 52 wk low, or 52 wk high, replace the missing value with "M," which stands for "Missing." If there are missing values for PE, EPS, Market cap, or EBITDA, use the imputation strategy to replace the missing values with the median of the variable. What are the imputed values for the variables with missing data?

33. FILE ***Longitudinal_Partial.*** The accompanying table contains a portion of data from the National Longitudinal Survey (NLS), which follows over 12,000 individuals in the United States over time. Variables in this analysis include the following information on individuals: Urban (1 if lives in urban area, 0 otherwise), Siblings (number of siblings), White (1 if white, 0 otherwise), Christian (1 if Christian, 0 otherwise), FamilySize, Height, Weight (in pounds), and Income (in $).

Urban	Siblings	White	. . .	Income
1	8	1	. . .	0
1	1	1	. . .	40000
⋮	⋮	⋮	⋮	⋮
1	2	1	. . .	43000

    a. Remove Height and Weight from the data set.
    b. Subset the data to create two data sets, one that includes observations who live in an urban area and have incomes over $40,000 and one that includes the rest of the observations.

34. FILE ***Longitudinal_Partial.*** Refer to the previous exercise for a description of the data set.
    a. Are there any missing values in the data set? If there are, which variables have missing values? Which observations have missing values? How many missing values are there in the data set?
    b. Use the omission strategy to handle missing values. How many observations are removed due to missing values?
    c. Return to the original data set. If there are missing values for Height or Weight, use the imputation strategy to replace the missing values with the mean of the variable. If there are missing values for Siblings, FamilySiz, or Income, replace the missing values with the median of the variable. What are the imputed values of the variables with missing data?

2.4 TRANSFORMING NUMERICAL DATA

LO 2.4

Transform numerical variables.

Data transformation is the data conversion process from one format or structure to another. It is performed to meet the requirements of statistical and data mining techniques used for the analysis. Examples of transforming numerical data include transforming an individual's date of birth to age, combining height and weight to create body mass index, calculating percentages, or converting values to natural logarithms. Sometimes it makes sense to group a vast range of numerical values into a small number of "bins." For example, we might want to arrange numerical ages into age intervals such as 20 to 39, 40 to 59, and 60 to 80, or convert dates into seasons such as fall, winter, spring, and summer.

> **DATA TRANSFORMATION**
> Data transformation is the data conversion process from one format or structure to another.

In this section, we describe techniques for transforming numerical variables into categorical values (or binning) and mathematical transformations of numerical variables. Section 2.5 explores techniques for transforming categorical variables.

Binning

Binning is the process of transforming numerical variables into categorical variables by grouping the numerical values into a small number of groups or bins. It is important that the bins are consecutive and nonoverlapping so that each numerical value falls into one, and only one, bin. For example, we might want to transform income values into three groups: below $50,000, between $50,000 and $100,000, and above $100,000. The three income groups can be labeled as "low," "medium," and "high" or "1," "2," and "3." Binning can be an effective way to reduce noise in the data if we believe that all observations in the same bin tend to behave the same way. For example, the transformation of the income values into three groups makes sense when we are more interested in a person's earning power (low, medium, or high) rather than the actual income value.

> **BINNING**
>
> Binning is a common data transformation technique that converts numerical variables into categorical variables by grouping the numerical values into a small number of bins.

As noted above, binning reduces the noise in the data often due to minor observation errors. For example, with binning, outliers in the data (e.g., individuals with extremely high income, perhaps recorded incorrectly) will be part of the last bin and, therefore, will not distort subsequent data analysis. Binning is also useful in categorizing observations and meeting the categorical data requirements of some data mining analytics techniques such as naïve Bayes (discussed in Chapter 9).

In addition to binning numerical values according to user-defined boundaries, bins are also often created to have equal intervals. For example, we can create bins that represent an interval of 10 degrees in temperature or 10 years in age. We can also create bins of equal counts, where individual bins have the same number of observations. For example, by binning a class of 200 students into 10 equal-size groups based on their grades, we can find out the relative academic standing of the students. Students in the bin with the highest grades represent the top 10% of the class.

In Example 2.4, we demonstrate how to use Analytic Solver and R to create bins with equal counts, equal intervals, and user-defined intervals.

EXAMPLE 2.4

FILE
Customers

In order to better understand her customers, Catherine Hill would like to perform the RFM analysis, a popular marketing technique used to identify high-value customers. RFM stands for recency, frequency, and monetary. The RFM ratings can be created from the DaysSinceLast (recency), NumOfOrders (frequency), and Spending2018 (monetary) variables.

Following the 80/20 business rule (i.e., 80% of your business comes from 20% of your best customers), for each of the three RFM variables, Catherine would like to bin customers into five equal-size groups, with 20% of the customers included in each group. Each group is also assigned a score from 1 to 5, with 5 being the highest. Customers with the RFM rating of 555 are considered the most valuable customers to the company.

In addition to the RFM binning, Catherine would like to bin the Income variable into five equal intervals. Finally, she would like to start a tiered membership status where different services and rewards are offered to customers depending on how much they spent in 2018. She would like to assign the bronze membership status to customers who spent less than $250, silver membership status to those who spent $250 or more but less than $1,000, and the gold membership status to those who spent $1,000 or more.

Use Analytic Solver and R to bin variables according to Catherine's specifications. Summarize the results.

SOLUTION:

Using Analytic Solver

a. Open the ***Customers*** data file.

b. To create the recency score, we need to first transform the variable DaysSinceLast to reverse the order of the data because the fewer the number of days since the last purchase, the greater is the recency score. Create a new column with the column heading DaysSinceLastReverse in column O. Enter the formula =L2*(−1) in cell O2. Verify that the value of cell O2 is −101. Fill the range O3:O201 with the formula in O2.

c. Choose **Data Mining > Transform > Transform Continuous Data > Bin**. Select data range $A$1:$O$201. Check the box *Variable names in the first row*.

d. Select DaysSinceLastReverse from the variable list. Change *#bins for variable* to 5. Choose *Equal count* for the *Bins to be made with* option. Choose *Rank of the bin* for the *Value in the binned variable is* option. Specify both the *start* and *interval* values to be 1. Click on the *Apply to Selected Variable* button. Repeat this step for NumOfOrders and Spending2018. Click on the *Finish* button.

   Two new worksheets, *Bin_Output* and *Bin_Transform*, are created. The *Bin_Output* worksheet shows the summary information such as the number of observations in each bin. The *Bin_Transform* worksheet displays the scores for each RFM parameter for the renamed variables, Binned_DaysSinceLastReverse, Binned_NumOfOrders, and Binned_Spending2018. Verify that the values of the first customer for Binned_DaysSinceLastReverse, Binned_NumOfOrders, and Binned_Spending2018 are 4, 1, and 1, respectively.

e. To create the RFM score for each customer, we create a new column with the column heading RFM in cell S12 in the *Bin_Transform* worksheet. Enter =CONCATENATE(R13, N13, M13) in cell S13. The **CONCATENATE** function merges multiple text values into one cell. Recall that cells R13, N13, and M13 represent the recency, frequency, and monetary indices, respectively, for the first customer. This formula creates a 3-digit RFM score for the first customer; verify that the first customer has an RFM score of 411. Fill the range S14:S212 with the formula in S13.

f. We now copy and paste the RFM values in the data range S12:S212 in the *Bin_Transform* worksheet to the data range P1:P201 in the ***Customers*** data file. To ensure that you paste the values, and not the formula, use the *Paste Special . . .* option and choose *Values*.

g. We now bin the Income variable into 5 groups with equal intervals. With the ***Customers*** worksheet active, choose **Data Mining > Transform > Transform Continuous Data > Bin**. Select data range $A$1:$P$201. Check the box *Variable names in the first row*. Select Income from the variable list. Change *#bins for variable* to 5. Choose *Equal interval* for the *Bins to be made with* option. Choose *Rank of the bin* for the *Value in the binned variable is* option. Specify both the start and interval values to be 1. Click *Apply to Selected Variable* and *Finish*.

h. Two new worksheets, *Bin_Output1* and *Bin_Transform1*, are created. The *Bin_Output1* worksheet shows summary information such as the ranges of each bin. The *Bin_Transform1* worksheet shows the data set with the new column, Binned_Income, displaying the customer's income category. Verify that the first customer is in the income category 1. Copy the Binned_Income column in the data range L12:L212 in the *Bin_Transform1* worksheet and paste it in the data range Q1:Q201 in the ***Customers*** worksheet using the *Paste Special . . .* option and choosing *Values*.

i. Make sure the ***Customers*** worksheet is active. To assign customers to the tiered membership system that Catherine designed, we have to first define tiered membership. In order to describe the range of spending for each membership tier, enter the values from Table 2.7 in cells S1:T4.

TABLE 2.7 Lookup Table

Column S	Column T
Spending	Membership
0	Bronze
250	Silver
1000	Gold

j. Add the column heading "Membership_Tier" in cell R1. We use the **VLOOKUP** function to bin the spending values into user-defined categories, or membership tiers in this example. The **VLOOKUP** function has four parameters: (1) the lookup value (a member's spending in 2018 in column J); (2) a lookup or reference table (ranges of spending and corresponding membership tiers in cells S2:T4, without the column headings); (3) column number in the lookup table that contains the output (the output, Bronze, Silver, or Gold, is in the second column in the lookup table); and (4) whether we want to look up a value within a range (TRUE) or find an exact match (FALSE).

Enter =VLOOKUP(J2, $S$2:$T$4, 2, TRUE) in cell R2. This function assigns the first customer to a membership tier according to the spending in 2018. Note that the dollar signs in $S$2:$T$4 ensure that when the formula is copied to another cell in column R the references to cells S2:T4 remain unchanged. Fill the range R3:R201 with the formula in R2 to assign a membership tier to each customer. Verify that the membership tier for the first customer is Bronze.

Using R

a. Import the ***Customers*** data into a data frame and label it myData.

b. To create the recency score, we first transform the variable DaysSinceLast to reverse the order of the data because the fewer the number of days since the last purchase, the greater is the recency score. Create a new variable called DaysSinceLastReverse by multiplying DaysSinceLast by −1. We use the **as.numeric** function to ensure that the DaysSinceLastReverse variable is a numerical type. Enter:

```
> myData$DaysSinceLastReverse <- as.numeric(myData$DaysSinceLast
* -1)
```

c. We now create five equal-sized bins for DaysSinceLastReverse (recency), NumOfOrders (frequency), and Spending2018 (monetary). As the bins represent the 20%, 40%, 60%, 80%, and 100% quantiles, we first use the **quantile** function to find the range for each bin and store and then view the ranges in an object called recencyBins. Enter:

```
> recencyBins <- quantile(myData$DaysSinceLastReverse,
probs=seq(0, 1, by=0.20))
> recencyBins
```

Figure 2.9 shows the ranges for the five equal-sized bins.

FIGURE 2.9 Ranges for the recency bins

```
    0%    20%    40%    60%    80%   100%
-360.0 -294.2 -218.4 -146.8  -76.0   -6.0
```

We repeat similar commands for the number of orders (frequencyBins) and the Spending2018 (monetaryBins) variables. Enter:

```
> frequencyBins <- quantile(myData$NumOfOrders, probs=seq(0, 1,
by=0.20))
> monetaryBins <- quantile(myData$Spending2018, probs=seq(0, 1,
by=0.20))
```

Note that if we were to create 10 equal-sized bins, we would change the *probs* option to `probs=seq(0, 1, by=0.10)`.

d. We use the **cut** function to bin the data. The *breaks* option of the **cut** function specifies the ranges of the bins created in step c. The *labels* option assigns a label to each bin. The right=FALSE option ensures that the intervals are closed on the left and open on the right. The include.lowest=TRUE option must be used along with the right=FALSE option so that the largest value is included in the last bin. Enter:

```
> myData$Recency <- cut(myData$DaysSinceLastReverse,
breaks=recencyBins,labels=c("1", "2", "3", "4", "5"), include.
lowest=TRUE, right=FALSE)
> myData$Frequency <- cut(myData$NumOfOrders, breaks=frequencyBins,
labels=c("1", "2", "3", "4", "5"), include.lowest=TRUE, right=FALSE)
> myData$Monetary <- cut(myData$Spending2018, breaks=monetaryBins,
labels=c("1", "2", "3", "4", "5"), include.lowest=TRUE, right=FALSE)
```

The prior commands assign numbers 1 to 5 to the equal-sized bins for the three RFM variables. The RFM indices are stored in three new variables, Recency, Frequency, and Monetary. If we were to create and assign labels to 10 equal-sized bins, we would use `labels=c("1", "2", "3", "4", "5", "6", "7", "8", "9", "10")`. Other labels can also be assigned to the bins as appropriate.

e. To create the RFM score, we combine the three RFM indices using the **paste** function, and then use the **head** function to view the first few observations. Enter:

```
> myData$RFM <- paste(myData$Recency, myData$Frequency,
myData$Monetary)
> head(myData$RFM)
```

Verify that the first observation of the RFM variable is 411.

f. We now bin the Income variable into 5 groups with equal intervals using the **cut** function. The *breaks* option specifies 5 bins with equal intervals. We assign numbers 1 (lowest) to 5 (highest) to the bins and then use the **head** function to view the first few observations. Enter:

```
> myData$BinnedIncome <- cut(myData$Income, breaks=5, labels=
c("1", "2", "3", "4", "5"), include.lowest=TRUE, right=FALSE)
> head(myData$BinnedIncome)
```

Verify that the first observation of the BinnedIncome variable is 1. To create a different number of bins, change the **breaks** value (e.g., `breaks = 3` will create three bins).

g. We use the **levels** and **cut** functions to display the ranges of the 5 intervals created in step f. Enter:

```
> levels(cut(myData$Income, breaks=5))
```

Verify that the first interval is (3.09e+04,5.82e+04] or from $30,900 up to, and including, $58,200.

h. To find out the number of observations that belong to each bin, use the **table** function. Enter:

```
> table(myData$BinnedIncome)
```

Verify that the first bin, or the lowest income category, has 67 customers.

i. To create the membership tiers or user-defined bins proposed by Catherine, we again use the **cut** function. Recall that customers who spent less than $250 are assigned to the Bronze membership, those who spent $250 or more but less than $1,000 receive the Silver membership, and those who spent $1,000 or more receive the Gold membership. We use the *breaks* option to specify user-defined ranges. The Inf keyword assigns any values above $1,000 to the last bin. We then use the **head** and **View** functions to view the output in various formats. Enter:

```
> myData$MembershipTier <- cut(myData$Spending2018, breaks =
c(0, 250, 1000, Inf),labels = c("Bronze", "Silver", "Gold"))
> head(myData$MembershipTier)
> View(myData)
```

Verify that the membership tier for the first customer is Bronze.

Summary

Table 2.8 shows a portion of the ***Customers*** data that now includes variables that have been binned according to Catherine's specifications. The first customer has an RFM score of 411, which suggests that this customer purchased from Organic Food Superstore quite recently but made very few purchases and spent very little money during the past year. Not surprisingly, this customer also has the least desirable bronze membership. In addition, in terms of income, the majority of customers belong to the first three bins; only nine customers have income in the two highest income groups.

It is important to note that the binning algorithm is implemented differently in R and Analytic Solver. In this example, we obtain an identical result in both software, but in other cases, R and Analytic Solver may yield different binning results.

TABLE 2.8 Customers Data with Binned Variables

CustID	. . .	RFM	Binned Income	Membership Tier
1530016	. . .	411	1	Bronze
1531136	. . .	244	3	Silver
⋮	⋮	⋮	⋮	⋮
1579979	. . .	434	3	Silver

Students are encouraged to experiment with other binning options with the ***Customers*** data. For example, experiment with binning Income into two categories, High and Low, or redesign the membership program with four or five tiers. There are many real-life applications where numerical variables should be converted into categories, and the number of categories should be determined appropriately according to the context of the analysis. For example, to convert students' exam scores into categories, we might use two bins (Pass and Fail) or five bins (A, B, C, D, and F grades).

Mathematical Transformations

As discussed earlier, data transformation is an important step in bringing out the information in the data set, which can then be used for further data analysis. In addition to binning, another common approach is to create new variables through mathematical transformations of existing variables. For example, to analyze diabetes risk, doctors and dieticians often focus on body mass index (BMI), which is calculated as weight in kilograms divided by squared height in meters, rather than focusing on either weight or height alone. Similarly, in order to analyze trend, we often transform raw data values into percentages.

Sometimes data on variables such as income, firm size, and house prices are highly skewed; skewness is discussed in Section 3.4 of Chapter 3. For example, according to a Federal Reserve report, the richest 1% of families in the U.S. controlled 38.6% of the country's wealth in 2016 (*CNN*, September 27, 2017). The extremely high (or low) values of skewed variables significantly inflate (or deflate) the average for the entire data set, making it difficult to detect meaningful relationships with skewed variables. A popular mathematical transformation that reduces skewness in data is the natural logarithm transformation. Another transformation to reduce data skewness is the square root transformation.

Another common data transformation involves calendar dates. Statistical software usually stores date values as numbers. For example, in R, date objects are stored as the number of days since January 1, 1970, using negative numbers for earlier dates. For example, January 31, 1970, has a value of 30, and December 15, 1969, has a value of −17. Excel implements a similar approach to store date values but uses a reference value of 1 for January 1, 1900. Transformation of date values is often performed to help bring useful information out of the data. A retail company might convert customers' birthdates into ages in order to examine the differences in purchase behaviors across age groups. Similarly, by subtracting the airplane ticket booking date from the actual travel date, an airline carrier can identify last-minute travelers, who may behave very differently from early planners.

Sometimes transforming date values into seasons helps enrich the data set by creating relevant variables to support subsequent analyses. For example, by extracting and focusing on the months in which gym members first joined the health club, we may find that members who joined during the summer months are more interested in the aquatic exercise programs, whereas those who joined during the winter months are more interested in the strength-training programs. This insight can help fitness clubs adjust their marketing strategies based on seasonality.

Example 2.5 demonstrates how to use Excel and R to perform the following mathematical transformations: (1) compute the percentage difference between two values, (2) perform a logarithm transformation, and (3) extract information from date values.

EXAMPLE 2.5

After a closer review of her customers, Catherine Hill feels that the difference and the percentage difference between a customer's 2017 and 2018 spending may be more useful to understanding the customer's spending patterns than the yearly spending values. Therefore, Catherine wants to generate two new variables that capture the year-to-year difference and the percentage difference in spending. She also notices that the income variable is highly skewed, with most customers' incomes falling between $40,000 and $100,000, with only a few very-high-income earners. She has been advised to transform the income variable into natural logarithms, which will reduce the skewness of the data.

FILE *Customers*

Catherine would also like to convert customer birthdates into ages as of January 1, 2019, for exploring differences in purchase behaviors of customers across age groups. Finally, she would like to create a new variable that captures the birth month of the customers so that seasonal products can be marketed to these customers during their birth month.

Use Excel and R to transform variables according to Catherine's specifications.

SOLUTION:

Using Excel

a. Open the ***Customer*** data file.

b. Create the column heading SpendingDiff in cell O1. Enter the formula =J2 - I2 in cell O2. Verify that the resulting value in cell O2 is −46. Fill the range O3:O201 with the formula in O2.

c. Create the column heading PctSpendingDiff in cell P1. Enter the formula = (J2 – I2)/I2 in cell P2. In the drop-down menu of the Home menu tab, change from *General* to *Percentage* (%). Verify that the value in cell P2 is −16.03%. Fill the range P3:P201 with the formula in P2.

d. Create the column heading IncomeLn in cell R1. The **LN** function provides a natural logarithm transformation. Enter the formula =LN(H2) in cell R2. Verify that the value in cell R2 is 10.8780. Fill the range R3:R201 with the formula in R2.

e. Create the column heading Age in cell S1. The **YEARFRAC** function calculates the difference in years between two dates, and the **INT** function displays only the integer portion of the value and discards the decimal places. Enter the formula =INT(YEARFRAC(D2, "01-01-2019")) in cell S2. Verify that the customer's age as of January 1, 2019, is 32 years. Fill the range S3:S201 with the formula in S2.

f. Create the column heading BirthMonth in cell T1. The **MONTH** function extracts the month element from a date value. Enter the formula =MONTH(D2) in cell T2. Verify that the value in cell T2 is 12. Fill the range T3:T201 with the formula in T2.

Table 2.9 shows a portion of the data that includes the five transformed variables. Other useful Excel functions related to date values include **DAY**, **YEAR**, **WEEKDAY**, **TODAY**, and **NOW**. The **DAY** and **YEAR** functions extract the date and the year elements, respectively. The **WEEKDAY** function identifies the weekday as an integer value from 1 to 7 (1 for Sunday and 7 for Saturday). Finally, =TODAY() and =NOW() return the values of the current date and current time, respectively.

TABLE 2.9 Five Transformed Variables

CustID	. . .	SpendingDiff	PctSpendingDiff	IncomeLn	Age	BirthMonth
1530016	. . .	−46	−16.03%	10.8780	32	12
1531136	. . .	−384	−31.30%	11.4511	25	5
⋮	⋮	⋮	⋮	⋮	⋮	⋮
1579979	. . .	−154	−14.26%	11.5327	19	7

Using R

a. Import the ***Customer*** data into a data frame (table) and label it myData.

b. We find the spending difference, and then use the **head** function to view the first few observations. Enter:

```
> myData$SpendingDiff <- myData$Spending2018 - myData$Spending2017
> head(myData$SpendingDiff)
```

Verify that the first observation of the SpendingDiff variable is −46.

c. We create the percentage spending difference and round it to two decimal places using the **round** function. We then place the "%" sign using the **paste** function and use the **head** function to view the first few observations. Enter:

```
> myData$PctSpendingDiff <- round((myData$SpendingDiff /
myData$Spending2017)*100, digits = 2)
> myData$PctSpendingDiff <- paste(myData$PctSpendingDiff, "%")
> head(myData$PctSpendingDiff)
```

Verify that the first observation of the PctSpendingDiff variable is −16.03%.

d. We use the **log** function for the natural logarithm transformation, and then use the **head** function to view the first few observations. Enter:

```
> myData$IncomeLn <- log(myData$Income)
> head(myData$IncomeLn)
```

Verify that the first observation of the IncomeLn variable is 10.87805. The IncomeLn values are slightly different from those in Table 2.9 because Table 2.9 is formatted to show only four decimal places. For the base 10 logarithm transformation, use the **log10** function in place of the **log** function.

e. To calculate a customer's age as of January 1, 2019, we first need to convert the Birthdate variable into the data values and create a new variable for the January 1, 2019, date. Enter:

```
> myData$BirthDate <- as.Date(myData$BirthDate, format = "%m/%d/%Y")
> endDate <- as.Date("01/01/2019", format = "%m/%d/%Y")
```

f. We use the **difftime** function to find out the number of days between the customer's birthdate and January 1, 2019. By dividing the difference in days by 365.25, we account for the leap years (by using 365.25 instead of 365) and obtain the difference in years. We use the **as.numeric** function to ensure that the Age variable has a numerical type. Finally, we use the **floor** function to remove the decimal places so that the age of a customer is an integer and the **head** function to view the first few observations. Enter:

```
> myData$Age <- difftime(endDate, myData$BirthDate)/365.25
> myData$Age <- as.numeric(myData$Age)
> myData$Age <- floor(myData$Age)
> head(myData$Age)
```

Verify that the first customer's age as of January 1, 2019, is 32 years.

g. We use the **months** function to extract the month name from the Birthdate variable, the **match** function to convert month names (January to December) to numbers (1 to 12), and the **head** function to view the first few observations. Enter:

```
> myData$BirthMonth <- months(myData$BirthDate)
> myData$BirthMonth <- match(myData$BirthMonth, month.name)
> head(myData$BirthMonth)
```

Verify that the first customer's birthday is in month 12 (December).

h. We use the **View** function to display a spreadsheet-style data. The output should be consistent with Table 2.9. Enter:

```
> View(myData)
```

Other useful date-related functions include **weekdays** and **format**. The **weekdays** function returns the day of the week; for example > `weekdays(as.Date("2000-12-25"))` returns "Monday". The **format** function returns the specified element of a date value; for example, > `format(as.Date("2000-12-25"), "%Y")` returns the year element "2000". Besides the "%Y" parameter, "%d" and "%m" specify the date and month elements. The `Sys.Date()` and `Sys.time()` functions return the current date and time values, respectively.

Another common transformation for numerical data is rescaling, which is performed when the variables in a data set are measured using different scales. For example, annual income measured in dollars typically ranges from thousands to millions, whereas the number of children typically contains values in low single digits. The variability in measurement scales can place undue influence on larger-scale variables, resulting in inaccurate outcomes. Therefore, it is commonplace to rescale the data using either standardization or normalization, especially in data mining techniques; a detailed discussion on such transformations can be found in Chapter 8.

EXERCISES 2.4

Mechanics

35. FILE ***Exercise_2.35.*** The accompanying data contains three variables and six observations.

x_1	x_2	x_3
248	3.5	78
124	3.8	55
210	1.6	66
150	4.8	74
196	4.5	32
234	6.2	63

a. Bin the values of x_1 into two equal-size groups. Label the groups with numbers 1 (lower values) and 2 (higher values). What is the average value of x_1 for group 1? (Hint: Sort the data by group number before calculating the average.)

b. Bin the values of x_2 into three equal interval groups. Label the groups with numbers 1 (lowest values) to 3 (highest values). How many observations are assigned to group 1?

c. Bin the values of x_3 into the following two groups: ≤ 50 and > 50. Label the groups with numbers 1 (lower values) and 2 (higher values). How many observations are assigned to group 2?

36. FILE ***Exercise_2.36.*** The accompanying data set contains three variables, x_1, x_2, and x_3.

a. Bin the values of x_1 into three equal-size groups. Label the groups with numbers 1 (lowest values) to 3 (highest values). How many observations are assigned to group 1?

b. Bin the values of x_2 into three equal-interval groups. Label the groups with numbers 1 (lowest values) to 3 (highest values). How many observations are assigned to group 2?

c. Bin the values of x_3 into the following three groups: $< 50{,}000$, between 50,000 and 100,000, and $> 100{,}000$. Label the groups with numbers 1 (lowest values) to 3 (highest values). How many observations are assigned to group 1?

37. FILE ***Exercise_2.37.*** The accompanying data set contains three variables, x_1, x_2, and x_3.

a. Bin the values of x_1 into three equal-size groups. Label the groups with "low" (lowest values), "medium," and "high" (highest values). How many observations are assigned to group medium?

b. Bin the values of x_2 into three equal-interval groups. Label the groups with "low" (lowest values), "medium," and "high" (highest values). How many observations are assigned to group high?

c. Bin the values of x_3 into the following three groups: < 20, between 20 and 30, and > 30. Label the groups with "low" (lowest values), "medium," and "high" (highest values). How many observations are assigned to group low?

38. FILE ***Exercise_2.38.*** The accompanying data set contains three variables, x_1, x_2, and x_3.

a. Bin the values of x_1, x_2, and x_3 into five equal-size groups. Label the groups with numbers 1 (lowest) to 5 (highest).

b. Combine the group labels of x_1, x_2, and x_3 to create a score like the RFM score described in Example 2.4. How many observations have the score "431"? How many observations have the score "222"?

39. The following table contains two variables and five observations.

x_1	x_2
248	350
124	148
150	130
196	145
240	180

a. Create a new variable called "Sum" that contains the sum of the values of x_1 and x_2 for each observation. What is the average value of Sum?

b. Create a new variable called "Difference" that contains the absolute difference between the values of x_1 and x_2 for each observation. What is the average value of Difference?

40. **FILE** ***Exercise_2.40.*** The accompanying data set contains three variables, x_1, x_2, and x_3.

   a. Create a new variable called "Difference" that contains the difference between the values of x_1 and x_2 for each observation (i.e., $x_2 - x_1$). What is the average difference?

   b. Create a new variable called "PercentDifference" that contains the percent difference between the values of x_1 and x_2 for each observation (i.e., $(x_2 - x_1)/x_1$). What is the average percent difference?

   c. Create a new variable called "Log" that contains the natural logarithms for x_3. What is the average logarithm value?

41. **FILE** ***Exercise_2.41.*** The accompanying data set contains three variables, x_1, x_2, and x_3.

   a. Create a new variable called "Difference" that contains the difference between the values of x_1 and x_2 for each observation (i.e., $x_2 - x_1$). What is the average difference?

   b. Create a new variable called "PercentDifference" that contains the percent difference between the values of x_1 and x_2 for each observation (i.e., $(x_2 - x_1)/x_1$). What is the average percent difference?

   c. Create a new variable called "Log" that contains the natural logarithms for x_3. Bin the logarithm values into five equal-interval groups. Label the groups using numbers 1 (lowest values) to 5 (highest values). How many observations are in group 2?

42. **FILE** ***Exercise_2.42.*** The accompanying data set contains two variables, *Date1* and *Date2*.

   a. Create a new variable called "DifferenceInYear" that contains the difference between *Date1* and *Date2* in year for each observation. What is the average difference in year? (Hint: Use the YEARFRAC function if you are using Excel to complete this problem.)

   b. Create a new variable called "Month" that contains the month values extracted from *Date1*. What is the average month value?

   c. Bin the month values in four equal-interval groups. Label the groups using numbers 1 (lowest values) to four (highest values). Which group has the highest number of observations?

Application

43. **FILE** ***Population.*** The U.S. Census Bureau records the population for the 50 states each year. The accompanying table shows a portion of these data for the years 2010 to 2018.

State	2010	2011	...	2018
Alabama	4,785,448	4,798,834	...	4,887,871
Alaska	713,906	722,038	...	737,438
⋮	⋮	⋮	⋮	⋮
Wyoming	564,483	567,224	...	577,737

   a. Bin the 2017 population values into four equal-size groups. Label the groups using numbers 1 (lowest values) to 4 (highest values). How many states are assigned to group 4?

   b. Bin the 2018 population values into four equal-interval groups. Label the groups using numbers 1 (lowest values) to 4 (highest values). How many states are assigned to group 2? Compare the groups in parts a and b. Which states are in higher groups for the 2018 population than for the 2017 population?

   c. Bin the 2018 population values into the following three groups: < 1,000,000, between 1,000,000 and 5,000,000, and > 5,000,000. Label the groups using numbers 1 (lowest values) to 3 (highest values). How many observations are assigned to group 2?

44. **FILE** ***Population.*** Refer to the previous exercise for a description of the data set.

   a. Create a new variable called "Difference" that contains the difference between the 2018 population and the 2017 population for each state (i.e., 2018 population - 2017 population). What is the average difference?

   b. Create a new variable called "PercentDifference" that contains the percent difference between the 2017 and 2018 population values for the states (i.e., (2018 population - 2017 population)/2017 population). What is the average percent difference?

   c. Create a new variable called "Log" that contains the natural logarithms for the 2018 population values for the states. Bin the logarithm values into five equal-interval groups. Label the groups using numbers 1 (lowest values) to 5 (highest values). How many observations are in group 2?

   d. Create a new variable called "SquareRoot" that contains the square root of the 2018 population values for the states. Bin the square root values into five equal-interval groups. Label the groups using numbers 1 (lowest values) to 5 (highest values). How many observations are in group 2?

   e. Compare the groups in parts c and d. Are the groupings the same or different?

45. **FILE** ***Credit_Cards.*** Greg Metcalf works for a national credit card company, and he is performing a customer value analysis on a subset of credit card customers. In order to perform the RFM analysis on the customers, Greg has compiled a data set that contains the dates of the last transaction (LastTransactionDate), total number of transactions in the past two years (Frequency), and total spending during the past two years (Spending). A portion of the data set is shown in the accompanying table.

LastTransactionDate	Frequency	Spending
5/20/2017	407	41903
8/16/2018	454	35918
⋮	⋮	⋮
8/14/2017	49	27918

a. Greg wants to calculate the number of days between January 1, 2019, and the last transaction date. Create a new variable "DaysSinceLast" that contains the number of days since the last transaction. (Hint: Use the DATEDIF function if you are using Excel to complete this problem.) What is the average number of days since the last purchase for all the customers?
b. Create the RFM scores for each customer. How many customers have an RFM score of 555? What is their average spending?
c. Create a new variable called "LogSpending" that contains the natural logarithms for the total spending during the past two years. Bin the logarithm values into five equal-interval groups. Label the groups using numbers 1 (lowest values) to 5 (highest values). How many observations are in group 2?
d. Create a new variable called "AverageOrderSize" that contains the average spending per order. This is calculated by dividing total spending (Spending) by total number of transactions (Frequency) in the past two years. Bin the values of AverageOrderSize into five equal-interval groups. Label the groups using numbers 1 (lowest values) to 5 (highest values). How many observations are in group 2?
e. Compare the groups in parts c and d. Are the groupings the same or different?

46. **FILE** ***Game_Players.*** TurboX is a online video game company that makes three types of video games: action, role play, and sports. It is interested in understanding its millennial customers. By combining the data from its customer database and a customer survey, TurboX compiled a data set that has the following variables: the player's satisfaction with the online game purchase experience (Satisfaction), the enjoyment level of the game played (Enjoyment), whether the player will recommend the game to others (Recommend), which type of game the player played (Type), total spending on games last year (SpendingLastYear), total spending on games this year (SpendingThisYear), and the date of birth of the player (BirthDate).

Satisfaction	Enjoyment	Recommend	...	BirthDate
Satisfied	High	Neutral	...	7/30/1992
Very Satisfied	High	Will	...	10/17/1984
⋮	⋮	⋮	⋮	⋮
Neutral	High	Will	...	8/11/1988

a. Bin the total spending on games last year into four equal-size groups. Label the groups using numbers 1 (lowest values) to 4 (highest values). How many customers are assigned to group 4?
b. Bin the total spending on games this year into four equal-interval groups. Label the groups using numbers 1 (lowest values) to 4 (highest values). How many customers are assigned to group 3?
c. Bin the total spending on games this year into the following three groups: < 250, between 250 and 500, and > 500. Label the groups using numbers 1 (lowest values) to 3 (highest values). How many observations are assigned to group 2?
d. Create a new variable called "Difference" that contains the difference between this year's and last year's spending on games for the players (i.e., SpendingThisYear - SpendingLastYear). What is the average difference?
e. Create a new variable called "PercentDifference" that contains the percent difference between this year's and last year's spending on games for the players (i.e., (SpendingThisYear - SpendingLastYear)/SpendingLastYear). What is the average percent difference?
f. Create a new variable "Age" that contains the players' ages as of January 1, 2019. What is the average age of the players?
g. Create a new variable "BirthMonth" that contains the players' birth month extracted from their dates of birth. Which month is the most frequent birth month?

47. **FILE** ***Engineers.*** Erin Thomas, an HR manager of an engineering firm, wants to perform an analysis on the data about the company's engineers. The variables included in the data are date of birth (BirthDate), personality type according to the Myers-Briggs Personality assessment (Personality), annual salary (Salary), level of the position (Level), and number of professional certificates achieved (Certificates). The accompanying table shows a portion of the data set.

BirthDate	Personality	Salary	Level	Certificates
7/31/1973	Explorer	48000	Engineer I	0
8/29/1967	Diplomat	44000	Engineer I	5
⋮	⋮	⋮	⋮	⋮
6/9/1972	Explorer	76000	Engineer II	4

a. Create a new variable "Age" that contains the engineers' ages as of January 1, 2019. What is the average age of the engineers?
b. Bin the age values into three equal-size groups. Label the groups using numbers 1 (lowest age values) to 3 (highest age values). How many observations are in group 3?
c. Bin the annual salary values into four equal interval groups. Label the groups using numbers 1 (lowest salary values) to 4 (highest salary values). How many engineers are assigned to group 4?
d. Bin the number of professional certificates achieved into the following three groups: < 2, between 2 and 4, and over 4. Label the groups "Low," "Medium," and "High." How many engineers are in the "High" group?

48. **FILE** ***Patients.*** Jerry Stevenson is the manager of a medical clinic in Scottsdale, AZ. He wants to analyze patient data to identify high-risk patients for cardiovascular diseases. From medical literature, he learned that the risk of cardiovascular diseases is influenced by a patient's age, body mass index (BMI), amount of exercise, race, and education level. Jerry has compiled a data set with the following variables for his clinic's patients: race (Race), education level (Education), body weight in kilograms (Weight), height in meters (Height), date of birth (BirthDate), and number of minutes of exercise per week (Exercise). The accompanying table shows a portion of the data set.

Race	Education	Weight	Height	BirthDate	Exercise
Non-Hispanic White	College	57	1.58	3/1/1982	138
Non-Hispanic Black	HS	80	1.71	2/14/1960	249
⋮	⋮	⋮	⋮	⋮	⋮
American Indian	Graduate	50	1.69	7/11/1992	264

a. Create a new variable called "BMI" that contains the body mass index of the patients. BMI is calculated as weight in kilograms/(height in meters)^2. What is the average BMI of the patients?

b. Create a new variable "Age" that contains the patients' ages as of January 1, 2019. What is the average age of the patients?

c. Bin the patients' ages into five equal-size groups. Label the groups using numbers 1 (youngest) to 5 (oldest). How many patients are in group 4?

d. Bin the patients' total minutes of exercise per week into five equal-size groups. Label the groups using number 1 (highest values) to 5 (lowest values). How many patients are in group 5?

e. Bin the patients' BMI into five equal-size groups. Label the groups using numbers 1 (lowest values) to 5 (highest values). How many patients are in group 1?

f. Create a risk score for each patient by concatenating the group numbers obtained in parts c, d, and e. How many patients are in the risk group of 555?

2.5 TRANSFORMING CATEGORICAL DATA

LO 2.5

Transform categorical variables.

As discussed in Chapter 1, we use labels or names to identify the distinguishing characteristics of a categorical variable. For instance, a firm may identify each customer as either a male or a female. Here, the sex of a customer is a categorical variable representing two categories. Categorical variables can also be defined by more than two categories. Examples include marital status (single, married, widowed, divorced, separated) and the performance of a manager (excellent, good, fair, poor). Recall that we use nominal and ordinal measurement scales to represent categorical variables. In the above examples, the measurement scales for marital status and performance of a manager are nominal and ordinal, respectively.

While categorical variables are known to represent less sophisticated levels of measurement, they are often the most important variables in the analysis. For example, the sex of a customer may contain the most useful information on the customer's spending behavior. Categorical data do, however, present unique challenges in data wrangling. As many analysis techniques are limited in their abilities to handle categorical data directly, steps to simplify or transform categorical data into numerical formats are often performed prior to analysis. In this section, we discuss three common approaches for transforming categorical data: category reduction, dummy variables, and category scores.

Category Reduction

Sometimes nominal or ordinal variables come with too many categories. This presents a number of potential problems. First, variables with too many categories pull down model performance because, unlike a single parameter of a numerical variable, several parameters associated with the categories of a categorical variable must be analyzed. Second, if a variable has some categories that rarely occur, it is difficult to capture the impact of these categories accurately. In addition, a relatively small sample may not contain any observations in certain categories, creating errors when the analytical model is later applied to a larger data set with observations in all categories. Third, if one category clearly dominates in terms of occurrence, the categorical variable will fail to make a positive impact because modeling success is dependent on being able to differentiate among the observations.

An effective strategy for dealing with these issues is category reduction, where we collapse some of the categories to create fewer nonoverlapping categories. Determining the appropriate number of categories often depends on the data, context, and disciplinary norms, but there are a few general guidelines.

The first guideline states that categories with very few observations may be combined to create the "Other" category. For example, in a data set that contains the demographic data about potential customers, if many zip code categories only have a few observations, it is recommended that an "Other" category be created for these observations. The rationale behind this approach is that a critical mass can be created for this "Other" category to help reveal patterns and relationships in data.

Another guideline states that categories with a similar impact may be combined. For example, when studying public transportation ridership patterns, one tends to find that the ridership levels remain relatively stable during the weekdays and then change drastically for the weekends. Therefore, we may combine data from Monday through Friday into the "Weekdays" category and Saturday and Sunday into the "Weekends" category to simplify data from seven to only two categories.

Example 2.6 demonstrates how to use Excel with Analytic Solver and R for category reduction.

EXAMPLE 2.6

FILE *Customers*

After gaining some insights from the ***Customers*** data set, Catherine would like to analyze race. However, in its current form, the data set would limit her ability to do a meaningful analysis given the large number of categories of the race variable; plus some categories have very few observations. As a result, she needs to perform a series of data transformations to prepare the data for subsequent analysis. Use Excel with Analytic Solver and R to create a new category called Other that represents the two least-frequent categories.

SOLUTION:

Using Excel with Analytic Solver

a. Open the ***Customers*** data file.

b. Choose **Data Mining > Transform > Transform Categorical Data > Reduce Categories**. See Figure 2.10. In the *Reduce Categories* dialog box, select data range $A$1:$N$201. Check the box *First row contains headers*. Select Race from the *Category variable* drop-down box. Once the variable is selected, Analytic Solver presents the frequency for each race category from the most frequent to the least frequent.

In order to combine the two least-frequent categories, we select the *By frequency* option and set *Limit number of categories to* option to 5. Analytic Solver will automatically combine the 5th and 6th least-frequent categories into one category. Click *Apply*. Click **OK**. A new worksheet, *Category_Reduction*, is created with a new column, Reduced_Race. Numeric coding is used to represent the categories, with 1 representing the most frequent category and 5 representing the least frequent category. If you compare the list to the original data, you will see that both American Indian and Pacific Islander have been combined into the new category 5.

c. Copy the Reduced_Race column in cells F28:F228 and paste the values (use the *Paste Special . . .* option and choose *Values*) to cells O1:O201 in the ***Customers*** worksheet.

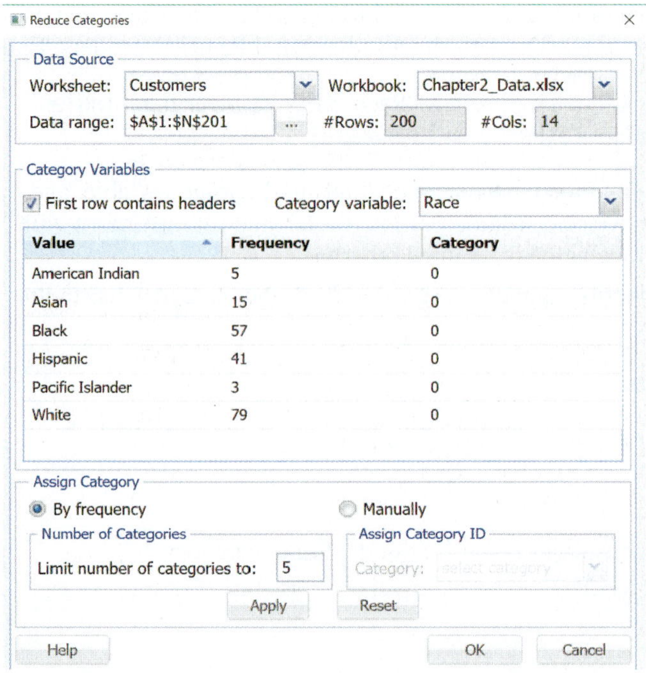

FIGURE 2.10 Analytic Solver's dialog box for Reduce Categories

d. To retain the category names instead of recoding them into numbers, we use the **IF** function. An **IF** statement has the following structure: =IF(*a logical test resulting in TRUE or FALSE, result if the logical test is TRUE, result if the logical test is FALSE*). Because there are five categories in the New_Race variable, we need to use multiple **IF** statements, or nested IFs, to change the numbers into category names. Figure 2.11 provides an illustration of how the IF function works in this example. In the ***Customers*** worksheet, enter the column heading NewRace in cell P1. In Cell P2, enter the formula =IF(O2=1, "White", IF(O2=2, "Black", IF(O2=3, "Hispanic", IF(O2=4, "Asian", "Other")))) in cell P2. Fill the range P3:P201 with the formula in P2. Verify that the 19th observation represents the first customer in the Other category.

FIGURE 2.11 Illustration of Excel's IF function

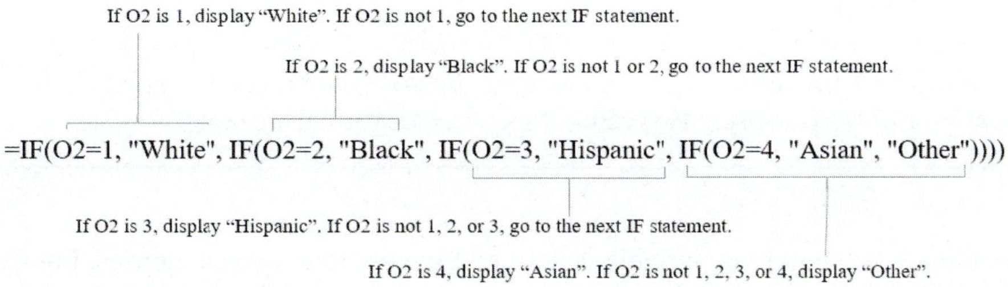

Using R

a. Import the ***Customers*** data into a data frame (table) and label it myData.

b. First, we inspect the frequency of each Race category to identify the two least-frequent categories. Enter:

```
> table(myData$Race)
```

The table shows that American Indians and Pacific Islanders are the two least-frequent categories with only five and three observations, respectively.

c. We use the **ifelse** function to create a new variable called NewRace that uses the Other category to represent American Indians and Pacific Islanders. Enter:

```
> myData$NewRace <- ifelse(myData$Race %in% c("American Indian",
"Pacific Islander"), "Other", myData$Race)
```

Note that the **ifelse** function evaluates the values in the Race variable, and if the value is either American Indian or Pacific Islander, it replaces it with Other; the original race value is retained otherwise.

d. We use the **table** function again to verify that the Other category has eight observations. Enter:

```
> table(myData$NewRace)
```

e. We use the **View** function to display spreadsheet-style data. Enter:

```
> View(myData)
```

Verify that the 19th customer is the first in the Other category.

Dummy Variables

In many analytical models, such as regression models discussed in later chapters, categorical variables must first be converted into numerical variables. For other models, dealing with numerical data is often easier than categorical data because it avoids the complexities of the semantics pertaining to each category of the variable. A **dummy variable**, also referred to as an indicator or a binary variable, is commonly used to describe two categories of a variable. It assumes a value of 1 for one of the categories and 0 for the other category, referred to as the reference or the benchmark category. For example, we can define a dummy variable to categorize a person's sex using 1 for male and 0 for female, using females as the reference category. Dummy variables do not suggest any ranking of the categories and, therefore, without any loss of generality, we can define 1 for female and 0 for male, using males as the reference category. All interpretation of the results is made in relation to the reference category.

A DUMMY VARIABLE

A dummy variable, also referred to as an indicator or a binary variable, takes on values of 1 or 0 to describe two categories of a categorical variable.

Oftentimes, a categorical variable is defined by more than two categories. For example, the mode of transportation used to commute may be described by three categories: Public Transportation, Driving Alone, and Car Pooling. Given k categories of a variable, the general rule is to create $k - 1$ dummy variables, using the last category as reference. For the mode-of-transportation example, we need to define only two dummy variables. Suppose we define two dummy variables d_1 and d_2, where d_1 equals 1 for Public Transportation, 0 otherwise, and d_2 equals 1 for Driving Alone, 0 otherwise. Here, Car Pooling, the reference category, is indicated when $d_1 = d_2 = 0$. Therefore, adding the third dummy variable for Car Pooling would create information redundancy; certain analytical models cannot even be estimated with k dummy variables.

Example 2.7 shows how to create dummy variables using Analytic Solver and R.

EXAMPLE 2.7

FILE
Customers

For the new Asian-inspired meal kits, Catherine feels that understanding the channels through which customers were acquired is important to predict customers' future behaviors. In order to include the Channel variable in her predictive model, Catherine needs to convert the Channel categories into dummy variables. Because web banner ads are probably the most common marketing tools used by Organic Food Superstore, she plans to use the Web channel as the reference category and assess the effects of other channels in relation to the Web channel. Use Excel with Analytic Solver and R to create the relevant dummy variables for the Channel variable.

SOLUTION:

Using Excel with Analytic Solver

a. Open the ***Customers*** data file.

b. Choose **Data Mining > Transform > Transform Categorical Data > Create Dummies**. Select data range $A$1:$N$201 and check the box *First row contains headers*. Select Channel from the *Variables* list. Click on the arrow to send it to the *Variables to be factored* box. Click **OK**. A new worksheet, *Encoding*, is created. Four dummy variables, Channel_Referral, Channel_SM, Channel_TV, and Channel_Web, have been created.

c. Because we use Web channel as the reference category, we will copy the dummy variables except Channel_Web to the ***Customers*** worksheet. Copy the dummy variables from cells Q24:S224 in the *Encoding* worksheet and paste the values (use the *Paste Special . . .* option and choose *Values*) to cells O1:Q201 in the ***Customers*** worksheet. Verify that the dummy variable values for the first observation are 0, 1, and 0, respectively.

Using R

a. Import the ***Customers*** data into a data frame (table) and label it myData.

b. We use the **ifelse** function to create a dummy variable for individual categories in the Channel variable. The **ifelse** function evaluates the categories in the Channel variable, and, for example, if the category is Referral, then the function assigns a 1 to the new Channel_Referral variable, and 0 otherwise. Two other dummy variables, Channel_SM and Channel_TV, are created similarly. Note that we leave out the last channel, Web, as it is a reference category. Enter:

```
> myData$Channel_Referral <- ifelse(myData$Channel == "Referral",
1, 0)
> myData$Channel_SM <- ifelse(myData$Channel == "SM", 1, 0)
> myData$Channel_TV <- ifelse(myData$Channel == "TV", 1, 0)
```

c. We use the **View** function to display spreadsheet-style data. Enter:

```
> View(myData)
```

Verify that the dummy variable values for the first observation are 0, 1, and 0, respectively.

There are packages in R, such as dummy, dummies, and fastDummies, that help create dummy variables. Students are encouraged to explore and experiment with these other options.

Category Scores

Finally, another common transformation of categorical variables is to create category scores. This approach is most appropriate if the data are ordinal and have natural, ordered categories. For example, in customer satisfaction surveys, we often use ordinal scales, such as very dissatisfied, somewhat dissatisfied, neutral, somewhat satisfied, and very satisfied, to indicate the level of satisfaction. While the satisfaction variable is categorical, the categories are ordered. In such cases, we can recode the categories numerically using numbers 1 through 5, with 1 being very dissatisfied and 5 being very satisfied. This transformation allows the categorical variable to be treated as a numerical variable in certain analytical models. With this transformation, we need not convert a categorical variable into several dummy variables or to reduce its categories. For an effective transformation, however, we assume equal increments between the category scores, which may not be appropriate in certain situations.

Example 2.8 shows how to convert a categorical variable into category scores using Excel and R.

EXAMPLE 2.8

FILE
Customers

For the new Asian-inspired meal kits, Catherine wants to pay attention to customer satisfaction. As the customer satisfaction ratings represent ordinal data, she wants to convert them to category scores ranging from 1 (Very Dissatisfied) to 5 (Very Satisfied) to make the variable more readily usable in predictive models. Use Excel and R to create category scores for the Satisfaction variable.

SOLUTION:

Using Excel

a. Open the ***Customers*** data file.

b. Enter the column heading Satisfaction_Score in cell O1. Enter the formula =IF(M2="Very Satisfied", 5, IF(M2="Somewhat Satisfied", 4, IF(M2="Neutral", 3, IF(M2="Somewhat Dissatisfied", 2, 1)))) in cell O2. Fill the range O3:O201 with the formula in O2. The scores are now ordered based on the degree to which the customer is satisfied with Organic Food Superstore's service. See Example 2.6 for further information on the nested IF statement. Verify that the first four satisfaction scores are 1, 3, 5, and 1, respectively.

Analytic Solver provides an option to create category scores (**Data Mining > Transform > Transform Categorical Data > Create Category Scores**). However, it is not appropriate for our application because it assigns numerical scores to the categories based on their order of appearance. For example, a satisfaction score of Very Dissatisfied is assigned number 1 as it is the first to appear in the data. If Neutral was the first observation, then that would have been assigned number 1.

Using R

a. Import the ***Customers*** data into a data frame (table) and label it myData.

b. We use the **ifelse** function, in a nested format, to create category scores for the Satisfaction variable. Enter:

```
> myData$Satisfaction_Score <- ifelse(myData$Satisfaction ==
"Very Dissatisfied", 1, ifelse(myData$Satisfaction == "Somewhat
Dissatisfied", 2, ifelse(myData$Satisfaction == "Neutral", 3,
ifelse(myData$Satisfaction == "Somewhat Satisfied", 4, 5))))
```

Note that the **ifelse** function evaluates the values in the Satisfaction variable, and if the value is Very Dissatisfied, the function assigns a 1 to the new

Satisfaction_Score variable. Because it is a nested format, if the value is not Very Dissatisfied but is Somewhat Dissatisfied, the function assigns a 2, and so on. If the values in the Satisfaction variable are none of the first four scores, the function assigns 5 to the Satisfaction_Score variable.

c. We use the **View** function to display spreadsheet-style data. Enter:

```
> View(myData)
```

Verify that the first four satisfaction scores are 1, 3, 5, and 1, respectively.

EXERCISES 2.5

Mechanics

49. The following table has three variables and six observations.

Sex	Income	Decision
Female	95000	Approve
Male	65000	Approve
Female	55000	Need More Information
Male	72000	Reject
Male	58000	Approve
Male	102000	Approve

a. Convert Sex into dummy variables. Use the most frequent category as the reference category. Which category is the reference category?

b. Transform Decision into dummy variables. Use the most frequent category as the reference category. Which category is the reference category?

c. Transform the Decision values into category scores where Approve = 1, Reject = 2, and Need More Information = 3. How many observations have a category score of 2?

50. **FILE** ***Exercise_2.50.*** The accompanying data set contains three variables, x_1, x_2, and x_3.

a. The variable x_1 contains 6 categories ranging from "A" to "F." Reduce the number of categories to five by combining the two least-frequent categories. Name the new category "Other." How many observations are in the "Other" category?

b. The variable x_2 contains six categories ranging from "A" to "F." This variable is ordinal, meaning that the categories are ordered. "A" represents the lowest level, whereas "F" represents the highest level. Replace the category names with category scores ranging from 1 (lowest) to 6 (highest). What is the average category score for x_2?

c. The variable x_3 contains four unordered categories. To facilitate subsequent analyses, we need to convert x_3 into dummy variables. How many dummy variables should be created? Create the dummy variables using Category1 as the reference category.

51. **FILE** ***Exercise_2.51.*** The accompanying data set contains two variables, Birthdate and LoanDecision.

a. LoanDecision contains three unordered categories. To facilitate subsequent analyses, we need to convert LoanDecision into dummy variables. How many dummy variables should be created? Create the dummy variables using "Need more information" as the reference category.

b. Create a new variable based on LoanDecision. The new variable should have only two categories: "Approve" and "Not approve." The "Not approve" category combines the "Reject" and "Need more information" categories. How many observations are in the "Not approve" category?

52. **FILE** ***Exercise_2.52.*** The accompanying data set contains two variables, x_1 and x_2.

a. The variable x_1 contains three categories ranging from "Low" to "High." Convert the category names into category scores (i.e., 1 = "Low", 2 = "Medium", and 3 = "High"). How many observations have a category score of 3?

b. Reduce the number of categories in x_2 by combining the three least-frequent categories. Name the new category "Other". How many observations are in the "Other" category?

c. Convert the new x_2 into dummy variables. How many dummy variables should be created? Create the dummy variables using the "Other" category as the reference category.

53. **FILE** ***Exercise_2.53.*** The accompanying data set contains three variables, x_1, x_2, and x_3.

a. The variable x_1 contains 3 categories: S, M, and L. Convert the category names into category scores (i.e., S = 1, M = 2, and L = 3). How many observations have a category score of 3?

b. Transform x_2 into an appropriate number of dummy variables. How many dummy variables should be created?

c. The variable x_3 contains four categories: A, B, C, and D. Reduce the number of categories by combining the two least-frequent categories into a new category E. How many observations are in the E category?

Applications

54. **FILE** ***Home_Loan.*** Consider the following portion of data that includes information about home loan applications. Variables on each application include the application number (Application), whether the application is conventional or subsidized by the federal housing administration (LoanType), whether the property is a single-family or multifamily home (PropertyType), and whether the application is for a first-time purchase or refinancing (Purpose).

Application	LoanType	PropertyType	Purpose
1	Conventional	Single-family	Purchase
2	Conventional	Multi-family	Refinancing
⋮	⋮	⋮	⋮
103	Federal Housing	Single-family	Purchase

a. Are the variables LoanType, PropertyType, and Purpose nominal or ordinal data? Why?

b. Which categories are the most frequent categories for LoanType, PropertyType, and Purpose?

c. To facilitate subsequent analyses, transform LoanType, PropertyType, and Purpose into dummy variables. Use the most frequent categories of the variables as the reference categories. Which categories of LoanType, PropertyType, and Purpose are the reference categories? How many dummy variables are created in total?

55. **FILE** ***Shipment.*** A manager of a local package delivery store believes that too many of the packages were damaged or lost. She extracts a sample of 75 packages with the following variables: the package number (Package), the status of the package (Status: Delivered, Damaged, or Lost), the delivery type (Delivery: Standard, Express, or Same day), and the size of the package (Size: S, M, L, and XL). A portion of the data is shown in the accompanying table.

Package	Status	Delivery	Size
1	Delivered	Standard	XL
2	Damaged	Express	S
⋮	⋮	⋮	⋮
75	Lost	Same day	M

a. Transform the Delivery variable into dummy variables. Use the most frequent category as the reference category. How many dummy variables should be created? Which category of Delivery is the reference category?

b. Combine the two least frequent categories in the Size variable into a new category called Other. How many observations are there in the new category?

c. Replace the category names in the Status variable with scores 1 (Lost), 2 (Damaged), or 3 (Delivered). What is the average status score of the 75 packages?

56. **FILE** ***Technician.*** After each thunderstorm, a technician is assigned to do a check on cellular towers in his or her service area. For each visit, the technician records in a database the tower number (Tower), the unit model (Model: A or B), and the extent of the damage to the unit (Damage: None, Minor, Partial, Severe, and Total for a total loss). A portion of the data is shown in the accompanying table.

Tower	Model	Damage
1	A	Minor
2	A	None
⋮	⋮	⋮
98	B	Partial

a. Transform the Model variable into dummy variables. How many dummy variables should be created?

b. Transform the Damage variable into categorical scores ranging from 4 (Total) to 3 (Severe), 2 (Partial), 1 (Minor), and 0 (None). What is the average damage score of the cell towers?

57. **FILE** ***Game_Players.*** Refer to Exercise 2.46 for a description of the problem and data set.

a. The variable Satisfaction contains five ordered categories: Very Dissatisfied, Dissatisfied, Neutral, Satisfied, and Very Satisfied. Replace the category names with scores ranging from 1 (Very Dissatisfied) to 5 (Very Satisfied). What is the average satisfaction score of the players?

b. The variable Enjoyment contains five ordered categories: Very Low, Low, Neutral, High, and Very High. Replace the category names with scores ranging from 1 (Very Low) to 5 (Very High). What is the average enjoyment score of the players?

c. The variable Recommend contains five ordered categories: Definitely Will Not, Will Not, Neutral, Will, and Definitely Will. Replace the category names with scores ranging from 1 (Definitely Will Not) to 5 (Definitely Will). What is the average recommendation score of the players?

d. The variable Type contains three unordered game categories: Action, Role Play, and Sports. To facilitate subsequent analyses, transform Type into dummy variables. Use the least frequent category as the reference category. Which category is the reference category? How many dummy variables should be created?

58. **FILE** ***Engineers.*** Refer to Exercise 2.47 for a description of the problem and data set.

a. The variable Personality contains four unordered personality types: Analyst, Diplomat, Explorer, and Sentinel. To facilitate subsequent analyses, Erin needs to convert this variable into dummy variables. How many dummy variables should be created? Create the dummy variables using Analyst type as the reference category. How many observations are in the reference category?

b. The variable Level contains three ordered position levels: Engineer I (lowest), Engineer II, and Senior Engineer (highest). Replace the level names with scores ranging from 1 (lowest) to 3 (highest). What is the average level score of the engineers?

59. FILE ***Patients.*** Refer to Exercise 2.48 for a description of the problem and data set.

a. The variable Race contains five unordered categories: American Indian, Asian/Pacific Islander, Hispanic, Non-Hispanic Black, and Non-Hispanic White. Reduce the number of categories to four by combining the two least frequent categories. Name the new category "Other." How many observations are in the "Other" category?

b. Transform the Race variable with the new categories into dummy variables. Use the most frequent race category in the data as the reference category. Which category is the reference category? How many dummy variables should be created?

c. The variable Education contains four ordered categories: HS (lowest educational attainment level), Some College, College, and Graduate (highest educational attainment level). Replace the category names with category scores ranging from 1 (lowest) to 4 (highest). What is the average category score for Education?

2.6 WRITING WITH BIG DATA

FILE
TechSales_Reps

Case Study

Cassius Weatherby is a human resources manager at a major technology firm that produces software and hardware products. He would like to analyze the net promoter score (NPS) of sales professionals at the company. The NPS measures customer satisfaction and loyalty by asking customers how likely they are to recommend the company to others on a scale of 0 (unlikely) to 10 (very likely). This measure is an especially important indicator for the company's software business as a large percentage of the sales leads come from customer referrals. Cassius wants to identify relevant factors that are linked with the NPS that a sales professional receives. These insights can help the company make better hiring decisions and develop a more effective training program.

With the help of the company's IT group, a data set with over 20,000 records of sales professionals is extracted from the enterprise data warehouse. The relevant variables include the product line to which the sales professional is assigned, age, sex, the number of years with the company, whether the sales professional has a college degree, personality type based on the Myers-Briggs Personality assessment, the number of professional certificates acquired, the average score from the 360-degree annual evaluation, base salary, and the average NPS received. Cassius is tasked with inspecting and reviewing the data and preparing a report for the company's top management team.

Sample Report—Evaluation of Net Promoter Scores

The net promoter score (NPS) is a key indicator of customer satisfaction and loyalty. It measures how likely a customer would recommend a product or company to others. Because our software line for business relies heavily on customer referrals to generate sales leads, the NPS that our sales professionals receive is a key indicator of our company's future success.

dizain/Shutterstock

From a total of about 20,000 records of sales professionals, we select only the sales professionals in the software product group and divide them into two categories: those with an average NPS below nine and those with an average NPS of nine or ten. When a customer gives a sales professional an NPS of nine or ten, the customer is considered "enthusiastically loyal," meaning that they are very likely to continue purchasing from us and refer their colleagues to our company. Based on the NPS categorization, we then divide the sales professionals into two categories: those with zero to three professional certificates and those with four or more professional certificates. Table 2.10 shows the results. Of the 12,130 sales professionals in the software product group, we find that 65.57% have earned less than 4 professional certificates, whereas 34.43% have earned four or more. However, there appears to be a link between those with 4 or more professional certificates and NPS values. For those who received an NPS of nine or ten, we find that 62.60% have earned at least four professional certificates. Similarly, for those who received an NPS of below nine, we find that 73.00% earned less than four professional certificates.

Although this might simply suggest that high-achieving employees tend to be self-motivated to earn professional certificates, we also believe that sales professionals with sufficient technical knowledge can effectively communicate and assist their customers in finding technology solutions, which will lead to increased customer satisfaction and loyalty. Our training and development program must place a greater emphasis on helping the employees earn relevant certifications and acquire necessary technical knowledge.

TABLE 2.10 Sales Professionals by the Number of Certificates and NPS Value

Number of certificates	Full Sample (n = 12,130)	NPS < 9 (n = 9,598)	NPS ≥ 9 (n = 2,532)
0 to 3	65.57%	73.00%	37.40%
4 or more	34.43%	27.00%	62.60%

Based on NPS categorization, we then divide the sales professionals into categories based on personality type. Table 2.11 shows the results. In addition to professional certification, we find that personality types are linked with NPS values. Among the four personality types, Diplomats and Explorers account for 72.69% of all the sales professionals in the software group. However, when we divide the employees based on the NPS values, these two personality types account for 91.63% of the group with an average NPS of nine or ten, whereas they account for only 67.69% for the below nine NPS group.

TABLE 2.11 Sales Professionals by Personality Type and NPS Value

Myers-Briggs Personality Type	Full Sample (n = 12,130)	NPS < 9 (n = 9,598)	NPS ≥ 9 (n = 2,532)
Analyst	12.13%	14.47%	3.24%
Diplomat	35.62%	33.07%	45.30%
Explorer	37.07%	34.62%	46.33%
Sentinel	15.19%	17.84%	5.13%

We also examined NPS variations by other variables such as age, sex, education attainment, sales, and commission but did not find considerable differences in NPS categorization. Other variables such as salary and the tenure of the employee with the company are not included in our initial analysis.

Based on the insights from this analysis, we request that the company appoint an analytics task force to conduct a more comprehensive analysis of sales professionals. We strongly suggest that the analysis focus on professional certification and personality, among relevant factors for determining the NPS value. At a minimum, two goals of the task force should include making recommendations on (1) a redesign of our training and development program to focus on helping employees acquire relevant professional certificates and (2) the efficacy of using personality types as part of the hiring decision.

Suggested Case Studies

Data wrangling is a crucial step in any data analytics project. The data inspection, preparation, and transformation techniques discussed in this chapter can be applied to many data sets. Here are some suggestions using the big data that accompanies this text.

Report 2.1 **FILE** ***CA_Crash***. Subset the data set based on the location, day of the week, type of collision, and lighting condition. Compare these subsets of data to find interesting patterns. Can you identify any links between crash fatality and the aforementioned variables? Are there any missing values? Which strategy should you use to handle the missing values? Because many of the variables are categorical, you should consider transforming them into dummy variables prior to the analysis.

Report 2.2 **FILE** ***House_Price***. Subset the data based on variables, such as number of bedrooms, number of bathrooms, home square footage, lot square footage, and age of the house. Which variables can be removed when predicting house prices? Are there any variables that display a skewed distribution? If there are, perform logarithm transformations for these variables. Would it make sense to transform some of the numeric values into categorical values using the binning strategy? Is equal size or equal interval binning strategy more appropriate in these situations?

Report 2.3 **FILE** ***Longitudinal_Survey***. Subset the data based on age, sex, or race. Are there any missing values in the data? Which strategy should you use to handle the missing values? Consider if any new variables can be created using the existing variables. Explore the opportunities of transforming numeric variables through binning and transforming categorical variables by creating dummy variables.

Report 2.4 **FILE** ***Mortgage_Approval***. Consider whether data distribution skewness exists in some of the numeric variables, and if it does, determine how to transform the data into a less skewed distribution. Does it make sense to reduce the number of categories for some variables? Perform data subsetting and use simple summary measures such as averages and frequency counts to find out if any differences exist across subsets.

3 Data Visualization and Summary Measures

LEARNING OBJECTIVES

After reading this chapter, you should be able to:

LO **3.1** Visualize categorical and numerical variables.

LO **3.2** Construct and interpret a contingency table and a stacked bar chart.

LO **3.3** Construct and interpret a scatterplot.

LO **3.4** Construct and interpret a scatterplot with a categorical variable, a bubble plot, a line chart, and a heat map.

LO **3.5** Calculate and interpret summary measures.

LO **3.6** Use boxplots and *z*-scores to identify outliers.

People often have difficulty processing information provided by data in its raw form. In this chapter, we present several tabular and graphical tools as well as summary measures that help us organize and present data. We first summarize a single variable by constructing a frequency distribution. A frequency distribution is a tabular method for condensing and summarizing data. For a visual representation of a frequency distribution, we construct a bar chart for a categorical variable and a histogram for a numerical variable.

We then examine the relationship between two variables by constructing a contingency table and a stacked column chart for categorical variables, and by constructing a scatterplot for numerical variables. We also discuss additional data visualizations including a scatterplot with a categorical variable, a bubble plot, a line chart, and a heat map.

Next, we focus on summary measures. These measures provide precise, objectively determined values that are easy to calculate, interpret, and compare with one another. Finally, we examine boxplots and *z*-scores, which are two common ways for detecting outliers.

©Tzido Sun/Shutterstock

INTRODUCTORY CASE

Investment Decision

Dorothy Brennan works as a financial advisor at a large investment firm. She meets with an inexperienced investor who has some questions regarding two approaches to mutual fund investing: growth investing versus value investing. The investor has heard that growth funds invest in companies whose stock prices are expected to grow at a faster rate, relative to the overall stock market. Value funds, on the other hand, invest in companies whose stock prices are below their true worth. The investor has also heard that the main component of investment return is through capital appreciation in growth funds and through dividend income in value funds.

The investor shows Dorothy the annual return data for Fidelity's Growth Index mutual fund (Growth) and Fidelity's Value Index mutual fund (Value). Table 3.1 shows a portion of the annual returns (in %) for these two mutual funds from 1984 to 2018.

TABLE 3.1 Annual Returns (in %) for Growth and Value

Year	Growth	Value
1984	−4.53	−17.34
1985	36.76	15.67
⋮	⋮	⋮
2018	−5.5	−8.59

FILE *Growth_Value*

It is difficult for the investor to draw any conclusions from the data in its present form. In addition to clarifying the style differences in growth investing versus value investing, Dorothy will use the sample information to:

1. Calculate and interpret the typical return for these two mutual funds.
2. Calculate and interpret the investment risk for these two mutual funds.
3. Determine which mutual fund provides the greater return relative to risk.

A synopsis of this case is provided at the end of Section 3.4.

LO 3.1

3.1 METHODS TO VISUALIZE CATEGORICAL AND NUMERICAL VARIABLES

Visualize categorical and numerical variables.

In this section, we present several tabular and graphical tools that help us organize and present data concerning a single variable. We examine common ways to summarize both a categorical variable as well as a numerical variable.

Methods to Visualize a Categorical Variable

Recall from Chapter 1 that a categorical variable consists of observations that represent labels or names. For example, participants in a survey are often asked to indicate their gender or race, or provide ratings of a product. When presented with a categorical variable, it is often useful to summarize the data with a frequency distribution and/or a bar chart. We first discuss the construction of a frequency distribution. Consider the following example.

A Frequency Distribution for a Categorical Variable

Suppose the Human Resources department of a large technology company maintains relevant personnel information regarding each employee's personality type based on the Myers-Briggs assessment. The Myers-Briggs assessment breaks down personality types into four categories:

- Analyst: An analyst tends to be open-minded and strong-willed. He/she likes to work independently and usually approaches things from a very practical perspective.
- Diplomat: A diplomat cares about people and tends to have a lot of empathy toward others.
- Explorer: An explorer tends to be very good at making quick, rational decisions in difficult situations.
- Sentinel: A sentinel likes stability, order, and security, and tends to be hard working and meticulous.

Table 3.2 shows a portion of the Myers-Briggs assessment results for 1,000 employees. The Myers-Briggs variable is a categorical variable that is of nominal scale, and the observations in Table 3.2 merely represent labels. Data presented in this format—that is, in raw form—are very difficult to interpret. Converting the raw data into a **frequency distribution** is often a first step in making the data more manageable and easier to assess.

FILE
Myers_Briggs

TABLE 3.2 Myers-Briggs Assessment Results

Employee	Myers-Briggs Assessment
1	Diplomat
2	Diplomat
⋮	⋮
1000	Explorer

As shown in Table 3.3, the categories of the variable form the first column of a frequency distribution. We then record the number of employees that fall into each category. We can readily see from Table 3.3 that the Explorer personality type occurs with the most frequency, while the Analyst personality type occurs with the least frequency. In some applications, especially when comparing data sets of differing sizes, our needs may be better served by focusing on the relative frequency for each category rather than its frequency. The relative frequency for each category is calculated by dividing the frequency by the sample size. We can easily convert relative frequencies into percentages by multiplying by 100. Table 3.3 shows that 40.4% of the employees fall into the Explorer personality type.

TABLE 3.3 Frequency Distribution for the Myers-Briggs Variable

Personality Type	Frequency	Relative Frequency
Analyst	116	0.116
Diplomat	324	0.324
Explorer	404	0.404
Sentinel	156	0.156

USING A FREQUENCY DISTRIBUTION TO DISPLAY A CATEGORICAL VARIABLE

A frequency distribution for a categorical variable groups the data into categories and records the number of observations that fall into each category. The relative frequency for each category equals the proportion of observations in each category.

A Bar Chart

Next, we show a graphical representation of a frequency distribution. We first construct a vertical **bar chart**, sometimes referred to as a column chart. The height of each bar is equal to the frequency or the relative frequency of the corresponding category. Figure 3.1 shows the bar chart for the Myers-Briggs variable.

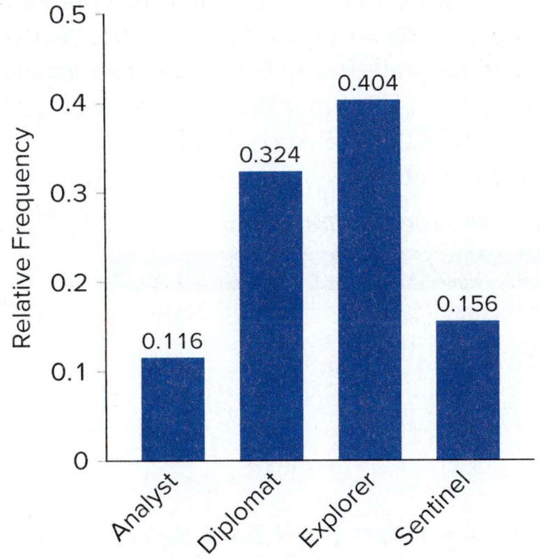

FIGURE 3.1 Bar chart for the Myers-Briggs variable

USING A BAR CHART TO DISPLAY A CATEGORICAL VARIABLE

A bar chart depicts the frequency or the relative frequency for each category of the categorical variable as a series of horizontal or vertical bars, the lengths of which are proportional to the values that are to be depicted.

EXAMPLE 3.1

FILE *Transit_Survey*

Recently, an urban university conducted a transportation survey as part of its commitment to reduce its carbon footprint and comply with the federal Clean Air Act. The survey was distributed to students, faculty, and staff members in order to learn the patterns of their daily commute. One of the questions asked: During a typical school week, how do you commute from home to school. Possible responses included Drive_Alone, Public_Transit, Bicycle, Walk, and Other. Six hundred people responded to the survey. Table 3.4 shows a portion of the survey results.

TABLE 3.4 ***Transit_Survey*** **Data**

Respondent	Mode of Transportation
1	Bicycle
2	Public_Transit
⋮	⋮
600	Walk

Construct a frequency distribution and a bar chart using Excel and R, and summarize the results.

Important: Due to different fonts and type settings, copying and pasting Excel or R functions from this text directly into Excel or R may cause errors. When such errors occur, you may need to replace special characters such as quotation marks and parentheses or delete extra spaces in the functions.

SOLUTION:

Using Excel

a. Open the ***Transit_Survey*** data file.

b. Enter the column headings Mode of Transportation and Number of Respondents in cells D1 and E1, respectively. Enter the column heading Drive_Alone in cell D2. Enter the formula =COUNTIF(A2:A601, "Drive_Alone") in cell E2. Enter the column heading Public_Transit in cell D3. Enter the formula =COUNTIF(A2:A601, "Public_Transit") in cell E3. Enter the column heading Bicycle in cell D4. Enter the formula =COUNTIF(A2:A601, "Bicycle") in cell E4. Enter the column heading Walk in cell D5. Enter the formula =COUNTIF(A2:A601, "Walk") in cell E5. Enter the column heading Other in cell D6. Enter the formula =COUNTIF(A2:A601, "Other") in cell E6. Table 3.5 shows the frequency distribution.

TABLE 3.5 Frequency Distribution for ***Transit_Survey***

Mode of Transportation	Number of Respondents
Drive_Alone	57
Public_Transit	273
Bicycle	111
Walk	141
Other	18

c. Select cells D2:E6. Choose **Insert > Insert Bar Chart**. Select the option on the top left side. (If you are having trouble finding this option after selecting **Insert**, look for the horizontal bars above **Charts**.) Figure 3.2 shows the bar

FIGURE 3.2 Bar chart for ***Transit_Survey***

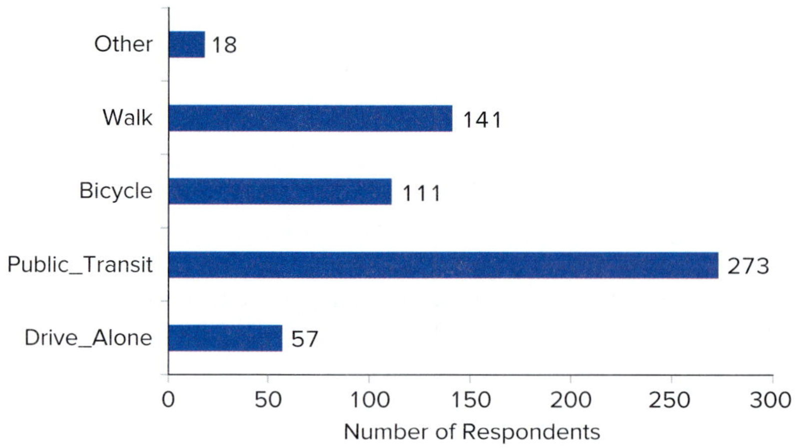

chart. Note that in this instance we have constructed a horizontal bar chart. If you wish to construct a vertical bar chart, then you would choose **Insert > Column Chart**.

d. Formatting (regarding axis titles, gridlines, etc.) can be done by selecting the '+' sign at the top right of the chart or by selecting **Add Chart Elements** from the menu. Check the box next to *Data Labels* in the *Chart Elements* pop-up box to display frequencies in the bar chart (or the column chart).

Using R

As mentioned in Chapter 2, before following all R instructions, make sure that you have read Appendix C ("Getting Started with R"). We assume that you have downloaded R and RStudio, and that you know how to import an Excel file. Throughout the text, our goal is to provide the simplest way to obtain the relevant output. We denote all function names in **boldface** and all options within a function in *italics*. It is important to keep in mind that R is case sensitive.

a. Import the ***Transit_Survey*** data into a data frame (table) and label it myData.

b. We use the **table** function to create a frequency distribution labeled Frequency. As outlined in Appendix C, we typically identify a variable within a data frame using the expression $var, where var denotes the variable name. Here, we need to enclose the variable name with single quotations because the variable name, Mode of Transportation, consists of more than one word. If you retype Frequency, you will see that the resulting frequency distribution is not very attractive. For this reason, we use the **View** function to create a more appealing frequency distribution. Recall from Chapter 2 that the **View** function creates a spreadsheet-style data viewer. Enter:

```
> Frequency <- table(myData$'Mode of Transportation')
> Frequency
> View(Frequency)
```

The only difference in the frequency distribution that R produces compared to the one that appears in Table 3.5 is that the category names are arranged in alphabetical order.

c. We use the **barplot** function to construct a bar chart. R offers a number of options for formatting. Here, we use *main* to add a title, *xlab* to provide a label for the x-axis, *horiz* to indicate a horizontal bar chart, *col* to define color, *xlim* to extend the horizontal axis units from 0 to 300, *las* = 1 to display the category names perpendicular to the y-axis, and *cex.names* to reduce the font size of the category names so that they are not truncated. Finally, we use the **abline** function to insert the y-axis.

```
> barplot(Frequency,main="Bar Chart for Transit Survey",
xlab="Number of Respondents", horiz=TRUE, col="blue",
xlim=c(0,300), las=1, cex.names=0.5)
> abline(v=0)
```

There are a few differences in the bar chart that R produces compared to the one that appears in Figure 3.2, but these differences are cosmetic.

Summary

Table 3.5 and Figure 3.2 reveal that the most common commuting mode at this urban university is public transportation. Walking and riding a bicycle are the next most common commuting modes. These results are not surprising for a university that is located in a city.

Methods to Visualize a Numerical Variable

With a numerical variable, each observation represents a meaningful amount or count. The number of patents held by pharmaceutical firms (count) and household incomes (amount) are examples of numerical variables. Although different in nature from a categorical variable, we still use a frequency distribution to summarize a numerical variable.

A Frequency Distribution for a Numerical Variable

When we constructed a frequency distribution for a categorical variable, the raw data could be categorized in a well-defined way; we simply counted the number of observations in each category. For a numerical variable, instead of categories, we construct a series of intervals (sometimes called classes). We must make certain decisions about the number of intervals, as well as the width of each interval. When making these decisions, we consider the following guidelines.

- *Intervals are mutually exclusive.* For example, suppose the first two intervals of a frequency distribution are defined as $300 < x \leq 400$ and $400 < x \leq 500$, where x is the value of an observation. If $x = 400$, then it would fall into the first interval. In other words, intervals do not overlap, and each observation falls into one, and only one, interval.
- *The total number of intervals in a frequency distribution usually ranges from 5 to 20.* Smaller data sets tend to have fewer intervals than larger data sets. Recall that the goal of constructing a frequency distribution is to summarize the data in a form that accurately depicts the group as a whole. If we have too many intervals, then this advantage of the frequency distribution is lost. Similarly, if the frequency distribution has too few classes, then considerable accuracy and detail are lost.
- *Intervals are exhaustive.* The total number of intervals covers the entire sample (or population).
- *Interval limits are easy to recognize and interpret.* For example, the intervals $-10 < x \leq 0$, $0 < x \leq 10$, etc. are preferred to the intervals $-8 < x \leq 2$, $2 < x \leq 12$, etc. Also, as a starting point for approximating the width of each interval, we often use the formula: (largest observation – smallest observation)/(number of intervals).

USING A FREQUENCY DISTRIBUTION TO DISPLAY A NUMERICAL VARIABLE

For a numerical variable, a frequency distribution groups data into intervals and records the number of observations that falls into each interval. The relative frequency for each interval equals the proportion of observations in each interval.

The Growth variable from the introductory case is a numerical variable because the data reflect annual returns (in %) for Fidelity's Growth Index mutual fund from 1984 to 2018. Here we will create a frequency distribution with six intervals. The minimum and maximum observations for the Growth variable are −40.9 and 79.48, respectively. (Obtaining summary measures will be discussed in Section 3.4.) Using the approximation formula to find the width of each interval, we calculate $(79.48 - (-40.9))/6 = 20.0633$. However, intervals with a width of 20.0633 would not have limits that are easily recognizable. For this reason, we will define the lower limit of the first interval as −50 and have each interval be of width 25 that is, $-50 < x \leq -25$, $-25 < x \leq 0$, etc., where x is the annual return.

As shown in Table 3.6, the data are more manageable using a frequency distribution, but some detail is lost because we no longer see the actual observations. From the frequency distribution, we can now readily observe that the most likely return for the Growth variable is between 0% and 25%; there were 17 observations in this interval.

We also note that no observations fall between 50% and 75%, and only one observation falls between 75% and 100%; we will see later that this observation is called an outlier. Summing the values in the frequency column shows that the sample size (or n) is 35. The relative frequency for each interval is again calculated by dividing the frequency by the sample size. As before, a relative frequency can be converted into a percentage by multiplying by 100. The third column of Table 3.6 shows that 48.57% of the returns for the Growth variable fell between 0% and 25%.

TABLE 3.6 Frequency Distribution for Growth

Interval (in %)	Frequency	Relative Frequency
$-50 < x \leq -25$	3	0.0857
$-25 < x \leq 0$	5	0.1429
$0 < x \leq 25$	17	0.4857
$25 < x \leq 50$	9	0.2571
$50 < x \leq 75$	0	0
$75 < x \leq 100$	1	0.0286

A Histogram

Next, we show a graphical representation of a frequency distribution. For numerical data, a **histogram** is essentially the counterpart to the vertical bar chart that we use for categorical data.

When constructing a histogram, we typically mark off the interval limits along the horizontal axis. The height of each bar represents either the frequency or the relative frequency for each interval. No gaps appear between the interval limits.

> **USING A HISTOGRAM TO DISPLAY A NUMERICAL VARIABLE**
>
> A histogram is a series of rectangles where the width and height of each rectangle represent the interval width and frequency (or relative frequency) of the respective interval.

Figure 3.3 shows a histogram for the frequency distribution shown in Table 3.6. The advantage of a visual display is that we can quickly see where most of the observations tend to cluster, as well as the spread and shape of the data. From Figure 3.3 we can see that annual returns for the Growth variable ranged from −50% to 100%. Annual returns from 0% to 25% were the most likely, whereas annual returns over 50% were very unlikely.

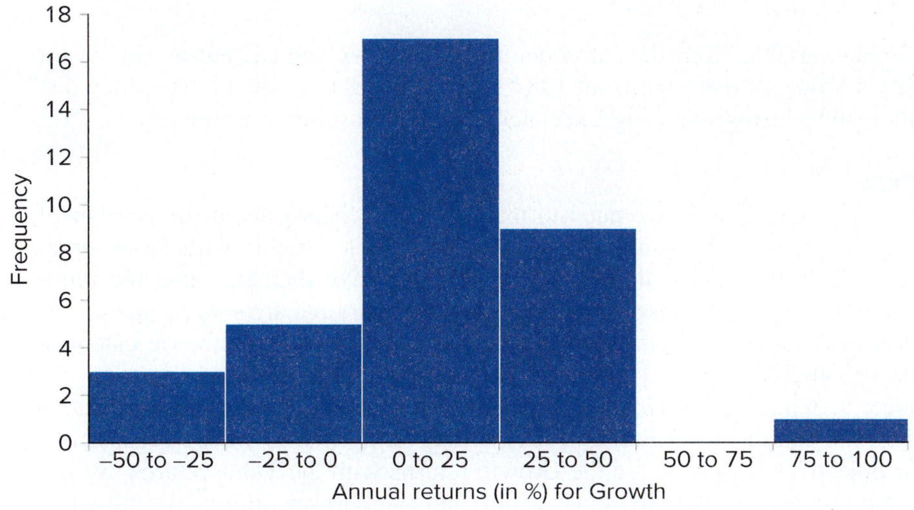

FIGURE 3.3 Histogram for the annual returns (in %) for Growth

A histogram also provides information on the shape of the distribution. In general, the shape of most distributions can be categorized as either symmetric or skewed. A symmetric distribution is one that is a mirror image of itself on both sides of its center. That is, the location of values below the center correspond to those above the center. As we will see in Chapter 4, the smoothed histogram for many data sets approximates a bell-shaped curve, which is indicative of the well-known normal distribution. Figure 3.4(a) shows a histogram with a symmetric distribution. If the edges were smoothed, this histogram would look somewhat bell-shaped.

If the distribution is not symmetric, then it is either positively skewed or negatively skewed. Figure 3.4(b) shows a histogram with a positively skewed, or skewed to the right, distribution. The long tail that extends to the right reflects the presence of a small number of relatively large values. Figure 3.4 (c) shows a histogram with a negatively skewed, or skewed to the left, distribution because it has a long tail extending off to the left. Data with a negatively skewed distribution have a small number of relatively small values.

The histogram for the Growth variable in Figure 3.3 shows that it is not a symmetric distribution; however, it is harder to discern whether it is positively skewed or negatively skewed. It turns out that the distribution is slightly positively skewed. We are able to make this conclusion by examining the skewness coefficient for the Growth variable. As we will see in Section 3.4, the skewness coefficient is a summary measure that is routinely provided in Excel output.

FIGURE 3.4 Histograms with differing shapes

(a) Symmetric distribution (b) Positively skewed distribution (c) Negatively skewed distribution

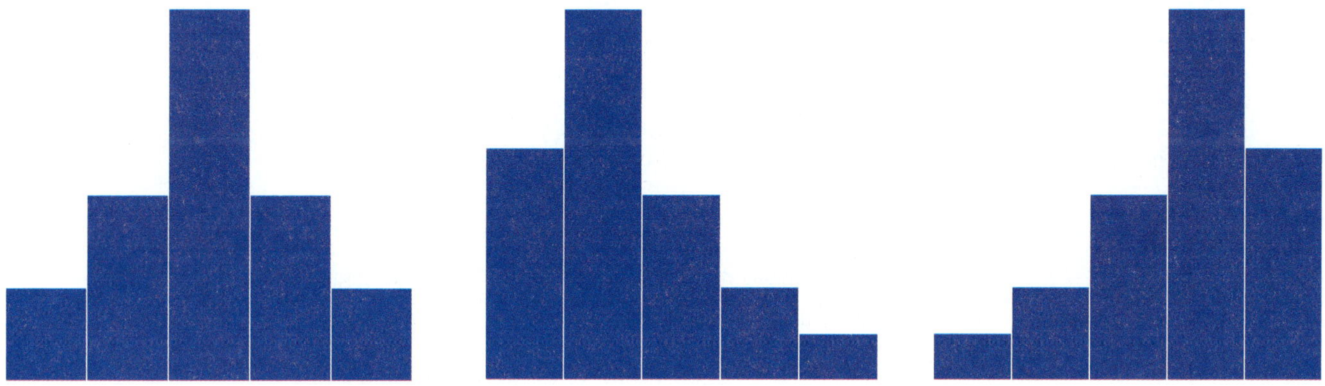

EXAMPLE 3.2

FILE *Growth_Value*

The Value variable from the introductory case shows annual returns (in %) for Fidelity's Value mutual fund from 1984 through 2018. Construct a frequency distribution and a histogram using Excel and R, and then summarize the results.

SOLUTION:

Before using Excel or R, we need to make some decisions about the number of intervals, as well as the width of each interval. For a variable with 35 observations, it would be reasonable to use five intervals. We then find that the minimum and the maximum observations for the Value variable are −46.52 and 44.08, respectively. Using the formula to approximate the interval width, we calculate (44.08 −(−46.52))/5 = 18.12. It would be perfectly acceptable to construct, for instance, a frequency distribution with five intervals where each interval has a width of 20, and the lower limit of the first interval is −50. However, because one of our objectives is to compare the Growth returns with the Value returns, we use the same number of intervals, same width, and same lower limit as we did when we constructed the frequency distribution for Growth; that is, we use six intervals, each with a width of 25, and the first interval has a lower limit of −50.

Using Excel

a. Open the ***Growth_Value*** data file.

b. In cell E1 enter the heading Interval Limits, and in cells E2 through E7 enter the upper limit of each interval, so −25, 0, 25, 50, 75, and 100. The reason for these entries will be explained shortly.

c. From the menu choose **Data** > **Data Analysis** > **Histogram** > **OK**. (Note: If you do not see the **Data Analysis** option under **Data**, you must add in the **Analysis Toolpak** option. From the menu choose **File** > **Options** > **Add-Ins** and choose *Go* at the bottom of the dialog box. Select **Analysis Toolpak** and then click **OK**. If you have installed this option properly, you should now see **Data Analysis** under **Data**.)

d. See Figure 3.5. In the *Histogram* dialog box, next to *Input Range*, select the Value observations. Excel uses the term "bins" for the interval limits. If we leave the *Bin Range* box empty, Excel creates evenly distributed intervals using the minimum and maximum values of the data as end points. This approach is rarely satisfactory. In order to construct a histogram that is more informative, we use the upper limits of each class as the bin values. Next to *Bin Range*, we select cells E1:E7 (the Interval Limits observations). (We check the *Labels* box because we have included the names Value and Interval Limits as part of the selection.) Under *Output Options,* select *Output Range* and enter cell G1 and then select **Chart Output**. Click **OK**.

FIGURE 3.5 Excel's dialog box for a histogram

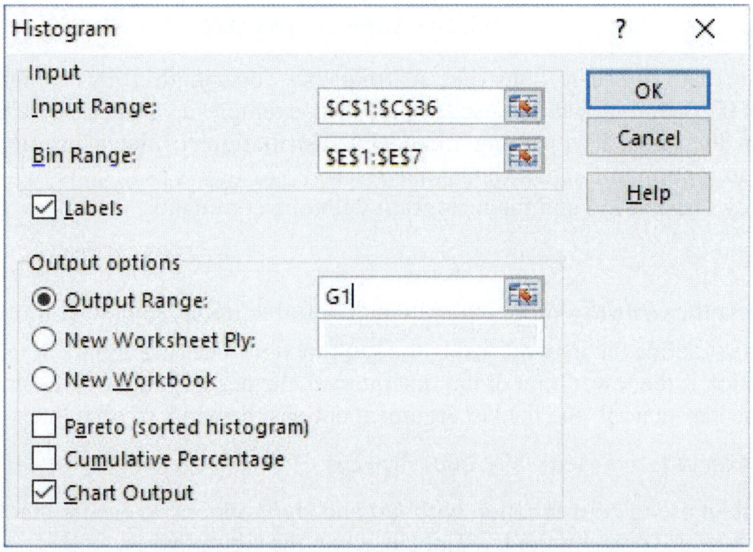

Table 3.7 shows the frequency distribution for Value. In the event that the given interval limits do not include all the data points, Excel automatically adds another interval labeled "More" to the resulting frequency distribution and histogram. Because we observe zero observations in this interval, we delete this interval for expositional purposes. Also, it is important to note that Excel defines its intervals by including the value of the upper class limit for each interval. For example, if the value −25 appeared in the data, Excel would have accounted for this observation in the first interval.

In order to calculate the relative frequency for each interval, we go to cell I2 and enter =H2/35. We then select cell I2 and drag down to cell I7, and from the menu we choose **Home > Fill > Down**. The third column of Table 3.7 shows the relative frequencies for each interval.

TABLE 3.7 Frequency Distribution for Value

Interval (in %)	Frequency	Relative Frequency
$-50 < x \leq -25$	1	0.0286
$-25 < x \leq 0$	7	0.2000
$0 < x \leq 25$	21	0.6000
$25 < x \leq 50$	6	0.1714
$50 < x \leq 75$	0	0.0000
$75 < x \leq 100$	0	0.0000

e. Because Excel leaves spaces between the rectangles in the histogram, we right-click on any of the rectangles, choose **Format Data Series**, change the *Gap Width* to 0, and then choose **Close**. Formatting (regarding axis titles, grid-lines, etc.) can be done by selecting **Format > Add Chart Element** from the menu. Figure 3.6 shows the histogram for Value.

FIGURE 3.6 Histogram for the annual returns (in %) for Value

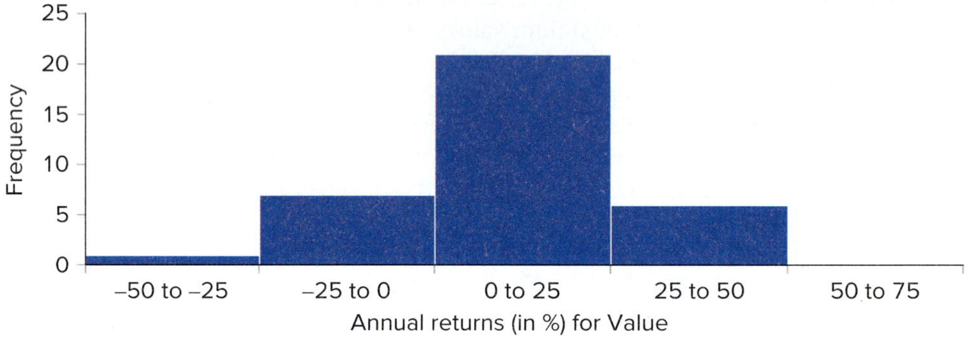

Note that you can construct a frequency distribution by using Excel's COUNTIF function that we used in the last example as well as in Chapter 2. You can then use the resulting frequency distribution to plot a histogram. The Histogram option in Excel's Data Analysis Toolpak allows us to construct both the frequency distribution and the histogram with one command.

Using R

a. Import the ***Growth_Value*** data into a data frame (table) and label it myData.

b. We first define the intervals using the **seq** function. The first argument in the function is the lower limit of the first interval, the next argument is the upper limit of the last interval, and the last argument defines the width of each interval. Enter:

```
> intervals <- seq(-50, 100, by=25)
```

c. We then use the **cut** function with *left* and *right* options to ensure that the intervals are open on the left and closed on the right; that is, $-50 < x \leq -25$, $-25 < x \leq 0$, etc. Enter:

```
> value.cut <- cut(myData$Value, intervals, left=FALSE, right=TRUE)
```

d. We use the **table** function to create a frequency distribution labeled value.freq. If you retype value.freq, you will see that the resulting frequency distribution is not very attractive. For these reasons, we use the **View** function to create a more appealing frequency distribution. Enter:

```
> value.freq <- table(value.cut)
> value.freq
> View(value.freq)
```

The frequency distribution that R produces should be comparable to Table 3.7.

e. We use the **hist** function to construct a histogram. We define the *breaks* option using the intervals that we defined in step b. Again, we set the *right* option equal to TRUE so that the intervals are right-closed (implying left-opened). As when constructing a bar chart, R offers a number of options for formatting. Here, we use *main* to add a title, *xlab* to provide a label for the x-axis, and *col* to define color. Enter:

```
> hist(myData$Value, breaks=intervals, right=TRUE, main="Histogram
for the annual returns (in %) for the Value Fund", xlab="Annual
Returns (in %) for Value", col="blue")
```

The histogram that R produces should be comparable to Figure 3.6.

Summary

From Table 3.7, we see that the range of annual returns for Value is between −50% and 50%. The range for Value is narrower than the one for Growth. Similar to Growth, the most likely return is in the 0% to 25% interval because the most observations (21) fall in this interval. Unlike Growth, none of the observations is greater than 50%. From Figure 3.6, we see that the distribution of Value is not symmetric; it is negatively skewed with a tail running off to the left.

Cautionary Comments When Constructing or Interpreting Charts or Graphs

As with many of the analytical methods that we examine throughout this text, the possibility exists for unintentional, as well as purposeful, distortions of graphical information. As a careful researcher, you should follow these basic guidelines:

- The simplest graph should be used for a given set of data. Strive for clarity and avoid unnecessary adornments.
- Axes should be clearly marked with the numbers of their respective scales; each axis should be labeled.
- When creating a bar chart or a histogram, each bar/rectangle should be of the same width. Differing widths create distortions.
- The vertical axis should not be given a very high value as an upper limit. In these instances, the data may appear compressed so that an increase (or decrease) of the data is not as apparent as it perhaps should be. For example, Figure 3.7(a) plots the daily price for a barrel of crude oil for the first quarter of the year. Due to

FILE *Crude_Oil*

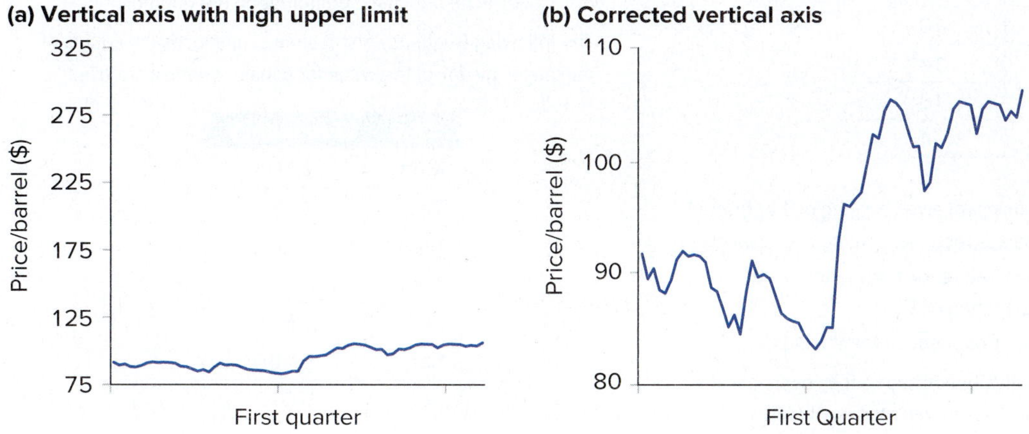

FIGURE 3.7 Misleading vertical axis: unreasonably high upper limit

Middle East unrest, the price of crude oil rose from a low of \$83.13 per barrel to a high of \$106.19 per barrel, or approximately 28% $\left(= \frac{106.19 - 83.13}{83.13}\right)$. However, because Figure 3.7(a) uses a high value as an upper limit on the vertical axis (\$325), the rise in price appears dampened. Figure 3.7(b) shows a vertical axis with an upper limit of \$110; this value better reflects the upper limit observed during this time period.

FILE *Stockprice*

- The vertical axis should not be stretched so that an increase (or decrease) of the data appears more pronounced than warranted. For example, Figure 3.8(a) charts the daily closing stock price of a large retailer for the week of April 4. It is true that the stock price declined over the week from a high of \$60.15 to a low of \$59.46; this amounts to a \$0.69 decrease, or an approximate 1% decline. However, because the vertical axis is stretched, the drop in stock price appears more dramatic. Figure 3.8(b) shows a vertical axis that has not been stretched.

FIGURE 3.8 Misleading scale on vertical axis: stretched scale

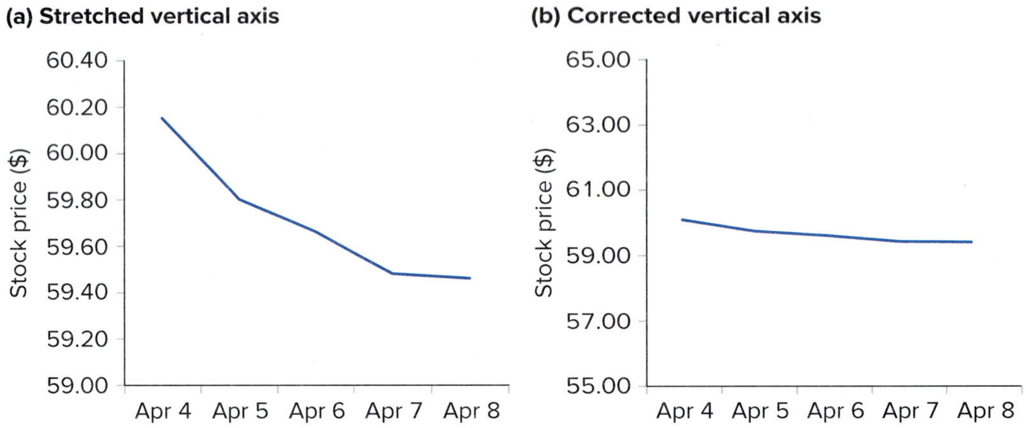

EXERCISES 3.1

Applications

1. Fifty pro-football rookies were rated on a scale of 1 to 5, based on performance at a training camp as well as on past performance. A ranking of 1 indicated a poor prospect, whereas a ranking of 5 indicated an excellent prospect. The following frequency distribution was constructed.

Rating	Frequency
1	4
2	10
3	14
4	18
5	4

   a. How many of the rookies received a rating of 4 or better? How many of the rookies received a rating of 2 or worse?
   b. Construct the relative frequency distribution. What proportion received a rating of 5?
   c. Construct a bar chart. Comment on the findings.

2. The following frequency distribution shows the counts of sales of men's shirts at an online retailer over the weekend.

Size	Frequency
Small	80
Medium	175
Large	210
X-Large	115

   a. Construct the relative frequency distribution. What proportion of sales were for a medium-sized shirt?
   b. Construct a bar chart. Comment on the findings.

3. The following frequency distribution summarizes the counts of purchases by day of the week for a major domestic retailer.

Day	Frequency
Mon	2,504
Tue	2,880
Wed	3,402
Thur	3,566
Fri	4,576
Sat	5,550
Sun	5,022

a. Construct the relative frequency distribution. What proportion of the purchases occurred on Wednesday?
b. Construct a bar chart using relative frequencies. Comment on the findings.

4. In 2018, the U.S. Census Bureau provided the following frequency distribution for the number of people (in 1,000s) who live below the poverty level by region.

Region	Number of People
Northeast	6,373
Midwest	7,647
South	16,609
West	9,069

a. Construct the relative frequency distribution. What proportion of people who live below the poverty level live in the Midwest?
b. Construct a bar chart. Comment on the findings.

5. A recent poll of 3,057 individuals asked: "What's the longest vacation you plan to take this summer?" The following relative frequency distribution summarizes the results.

Response	Relative Frequency
A few days	0.21
A few long weekends	0.18
One week	0.36
Two weeks	0.25

a. Construct the frequency distribution. How many people are going to take a one-week vacation this summer?
b. Construct a bar chart. Comment on the findings.

6. FILE ***Dining.*** A local restaurant is committed to providing its patrons with the best dining experience possible. On a recent survey, the restaurant asked patrons to rate the quality of their entrées. The responses ranged from 1 to 5, where 1 indicated a disappointing entrée and 5 indicated an exceptional entrée. A portion of the 200 responses is as follows:

Response	Rating
1	3
2	5
⋮	⋮
200	4

a. Construct the frequency distribution that summarizes the results from the survey. Which rating appeared with the most frequency?
b. Construct a bar chart. Are the patrons generally satisfied with the quality of their entrées? Explain.

7. FILE ***Health.*** Patients at North Shore Family Practice are required to fill out a questionnaire that gives the doctor an overall idea of each patient's health. The first question is: "In general, what is the quality of your health?" The patient chooses Excellent, Good, Fair, or Poor. A portion of the 150 responses is as follows:

Response	Quality
1	Fair
2	Good
⋮	⋮
150	Good

a. Construct the frequency distribution that summarizes the results from the questionnaire. What is the most common response to the questionnaire?
b. Construct a bar chart. How would you characterize the health of patients at this medical practice? Explain.

8. FILE ***Millennials.*** A 2014 Religious Landscape Study by the Pew Research Center found that 35% of Millennials (Americans born between 1981 and 1996) identified themselves as not religious. A researcher wonders if this finding is consistent today. She surveys 600 Millennials and asks them to rate their faith. Possible responses were Strongly Religious, Somewhat Religious, Slightly Religious, and Not Religious. A portion of the 600 responses is as follows:

Response	Faith
1	Slightly Religious
2	Slightly Religious
⋮	⋮
600	Somewhat Religious

a. Construct the frequency distribution that summarizes the results from the survey. What is the most common response to the survey?
b. Construct a bar chart. Do the researcher's results appear consistent with those found by the Pew Research Center? Explain.

9. A researcher conducts a mileage economy test involving 80 cars. The frequency distribution describing average miles per gallon (mpg) appears in the following table.

Average mpg	Frequency
$15 \leq x < 20$	15
$20 \leq x < 25$	30
$25 \leq x < 30$	15
$30 \leq x < 35$	10
$35 \leq x < 40$	7
$40 \leq x < 45$	3

a. Construct the relative frequency distribution. What proportion of the cars got at least 20 mpg but less than 25 mpg? What proportion of the cars got less than 35 mpg? What proportion of the cars got 35 mpg or more?
b. Construct a histogram. Comment on the shape of the distribution.

10. Consider the following relative frequency distribution that summarizes the returns (in %) for 500 small cap stocks.

Return (%)	Relative Frequency
$-20 \le x < -10$	0.04
$-10 \le x < 0$	0.25
$0 \le x < 10$	0.42
$10 \le x < 20$	0.25
$20 \le x < 30$	0.04

a. Construct the frequency distribution. How many of the stocks had a return of at least 10% but less than 20%?

b. Construct a histogram. Comment on the shape of the distribution.

11. The manager at a water park constructed the following frequency distribution to summarize attendance in July and August.

Attendance	Frequency
$1{,}000 \le x < 1{,}250$	5
$1{,}250 \le x < 1{,}500$	6
$1{,}500 \le x < 1{,}750$	10
$1{,}750 \le x < 2{,}000$	20
$2{,}000 \le x < 2{,}250$	15
$2{,}250 \le x < 2{,}500$	4

a. Construct the relative frequency distribution. What proportion of the time was attendance at least 1,750 but less than 2,000? What proportion of the time was attendance less than 1,750? What proportion of the time was attendance 1,750 or more?

b. Construct a histogram. Comment on the shape of the distribution.

12. Fifty cities provided information on vacancy rates (in %) in local apartments in the following frequency distribution.

Vacancy Rate (%)	Relative Frequency
$0 \le x < 3$	0.10
$3 \le x < 6$	0.20
$6 \le x < 9$	0.40
$9 \le x < 12$	0.20
$12 \le x < 15$	0.10

a. Construct the frequency distribution. How many of the cities had a vacancy rate of at least 6% but less than 9%? How many of the cities had a vacancy rate of at least 9%?

b. Construct a histogram. Comment on the shape of the distribution.

13. The following relative frequency histogram summarizes the median household income for the 50 states as reported by the U.S. Census Bureau in 2010.

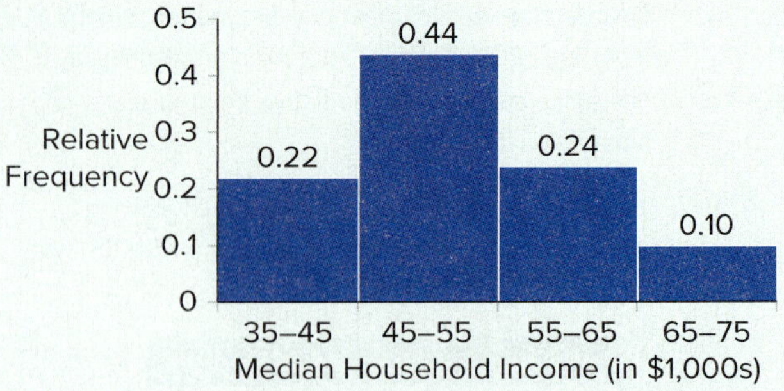

a. Is the distribution symmetric? If not, is it positively or negatively skewed?

b. What percentage of the states had median household income between $45,000 and $55,000?

c. What percentage of the states had median household income between $35,000 and $55,000?

14. The following histogram summarizes Apple Inc.'s monthly stock price for the years 2014 through 2018.

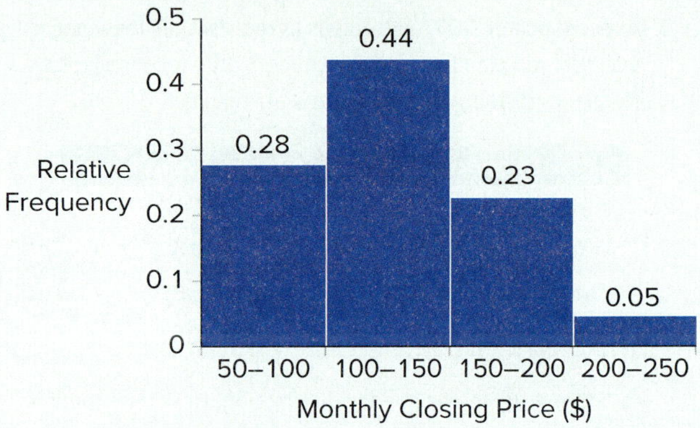

a. Is the distribution symmetric? If not, is it positively or negatively skewed?

b. Over this five-year period, approximate the minimum monthly stock price and the maximum monthly stock price.

c. Over this five-year period, which interval had the highest relative frequency?

15. The following histogram summarizes the salaries (in $100,000s) for the 30 highest-paid portfolio managers at a large investment firm over the past year.

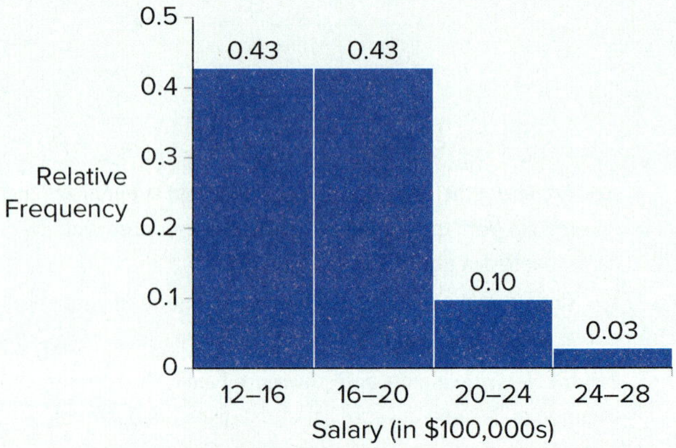

a. Is the distribution symmetric? If not, is it positively or negatively skewed?

b. How many of the portfolio managers earned between $2,000,000 and $2,400,000?

c. Approximately how many of the portfolio managers earned between $1,200,000 and $2,000,000?

16. **FILE** ***Prime.*** Amazon Prime is a $119-per-year service that gives the company's customers free two-day shipping and discounted rates on overnight delivery. Prime customers also get other perks, such as free e-books. The accompanying table shows a portion of the annual expenditures (in $) for 100 Prime customers.

Customer	Expenditures
1	1272
2	1089
⋮	⋮
100	1389

a. Construct the frequency distribution for Expenditures. Use six intervals with widths of $400 < x \leq 700$; $700 < x \leq 1{,}000$; etc. How many customers spent between $701 and $1,000?

b. How many customers spent $1,300 or less? How many customers spent more than $1,300?

17. **FILE** ***Census.*** The following table lists a portion of median house values (in $) for the 50 states as reported by the U.S. Census Bureau in 2010.

State	House Value
Alabama	117600
Alaska	229100
⋮	⋮
Wyoming	174000

a. Construct the frequency distribution and the histogram for the median house values. Use six intervals with widths of $0 < x \leq 100{,}000$; $100{,}000 < x \leq 200{,}000$; etc. Which interval had the highest frequency? How many of the states had median house values of $300,000 or less?

b. Is the distribution symmetric? If not, is it positively or negatively skewed?

18. **FILE** ***DJIA_2019.*** The accompanying table shows a portion of the daily price index for the Dow Jones Industrial Average (DJIA) for the first half of 2019.

Day	DJIA
January 1, 2019	23346
January 2, 2019	22686
⋮	⋮
June 28, 2019	26600

a. Construct the frequency distribution and the histogram for the DJIA. Use five intervals with widths of $22{,}000 < x \leq 23{,}000$; $23{,}000 < x \leq 24{,}000$; etc. On how many days during the first half of 2019 was the DJIA more than 26,000?

b. Is the distribution symmetric? If not, is it positively or negatively skewed?

19. **FILE** ***Gas_2019.*** The following table lists a portion of the average price (in $) for a gallon of gas for the 50 states and the District of Columbia as reported by AAA Gas Prices on January 2, 2019.

State	Price
Alabama	1.94
Alaska	3.06
⋮	⋮
Wyoming	2.59

a. Construct the frequency distribution and the histogram for the average price of gas. Use six intervals with widths of $1.70 < x \leq 2.00$; $2.00 < x \leq 2.30$; etc. Which interval had the highest frequency? How many of the states had average gas prices greater than $2.60?

b. Is the distribution symmetric? If not, is it positively or negatively skewed?

20. The accompanying figure plots the monthly stock price of a large construction company from July 2017 through March 2019. The stock has experienced tremendous growth over this time period, almost tripling in price. Does the figure reflect this growth? If not, why not?

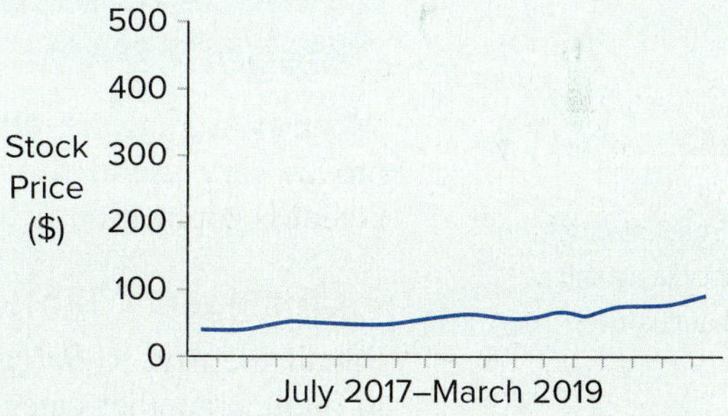

21. Annual sales at a small pharmaceutical firm have been rather stagnant over the most recent five-year period, exhibiting only 1.2% growth over this time frame. A research analyst prepares the accompanying graph for inclusion in a sales report.

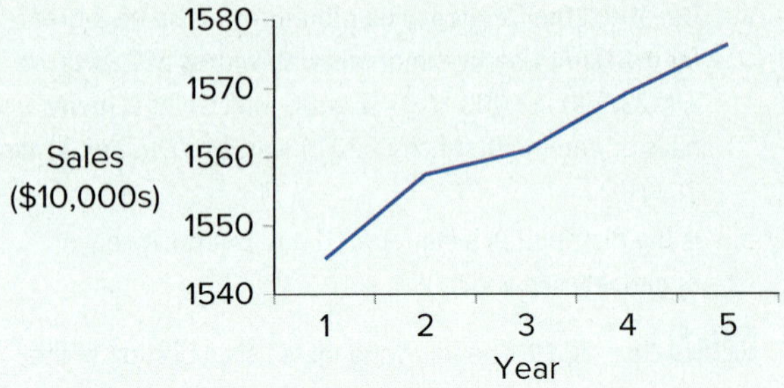

Does this graph accurately reflect what has happened to sales over the last five years? If not, why not?

3.2 METHODS TO VISUALIZE THE RELATIONSHIP BETWEEN TWO VARIABLES

All of the tabular and graphical tools presented thus far have focused on describing one variable. However, in many instances we are interested in the relationship between two variables. People in virtually every discipline examine how one variable may systematically influence another variable. Consider, for instance, how

- Incomes vary with education.
- Sales vary with advertising expenditures.
- Stock prices vary with corporate profits.
- Crop yields vary with the use of fertilizer.
- Cholesterol levels vary with dietary intake.
- Employee absences vary with work shift.

We first introduce contingency tables and stacked column charts, two common tabular and graphical methods that help us summarize the relationship between two categorical variables. Then we show a scatterplot, which is a common graphical method that allows us to determine whether two numerical variables are related in some systematic way.

Methods to Visualize the Relationship between Two Categorical Variables

LO 3.2

Construct and interpret a contingency table and a stacked bar chart.

When examining the relationship between two categorical variables, a **contingency table** proves very useful. Contingency tables are widely used in marketing as well as other business applications. Consider the following example.

A Contingency Table

Recall the ***Myers_Briggs*** data set discussed in Section 3.1. If we expand the data set to include another categorical variable, say one's sex, it would allow us to examine the relationship between personality type and one's sex. Perhaps we are interested in whether certain personality types are more prevalent among males versus females. Table 3.8 shows a portion of the expanded data set, ***Myers_Briggs2***.

FILE
Myers_Briggs2

TABLE 3.8 Expanded Myers-Briggs Assessment Results

Employee	Myers-Briggs Assessment	Sex
1	Diplomat	Female
2	Diplomat	Female
⋮	⋮	⋮
1000	Explorer	Male

A contingency table that shows the frequencies for personality type and sex is displayed in Table 3.9. As you can see, 55 female employees fall into the Analyst personality type whereas 61 male employees fall into this personality type.

TABLE 3.9 Contingency Table for Expanded Myers-Brigg Example

	Analyst	Diplomat	Explorer	Sentinel
Female	55	164	194	79
Male	61	160	210	77

USING A CONTINGENCY TABLE TO DISPLAY TWO CATEGORICAL VARIABLES

A contingency table shows the frequencies for two categorical variables, x and y, where each cell represents a mutually exclusive combination of the pair of x and y values.

A Stacked Column Chart

The information in a contingency table can be shown graphically using a **stacked column chart**. A stacked column chart is an advanced version of the column chart that we discussed in Section 3.1. It is designed to visualize more than one categorical variable, plus it allows for the comparison of composition within each category.

Figure 3.9 shows the stacked column chart for personality type and sex. Each column in the chart represents all the employees of a personality type, and the two segments in each column represent female employees and male employees. As the chart shows, no discernable differences in personality type can be found depending on whether an employee is female or male.

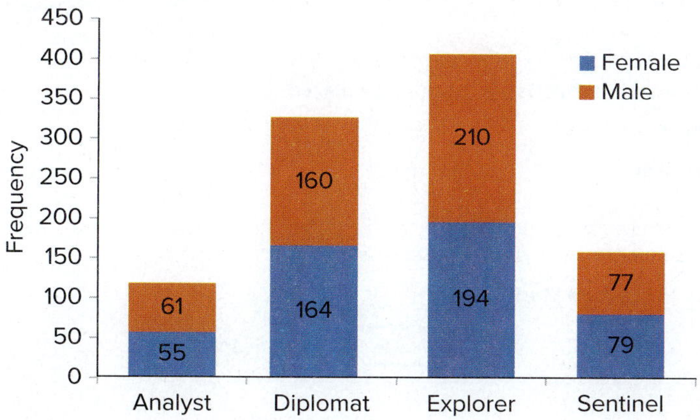

FIGURE 3.9 A stacked column chart for personality type and sex

In order to illustrate the construction of a contingency table and a stacked column chart, consider the following example.

EXAMPLE 3.3

An online retailer recently sent e-mails to customers that included a promotional discount. The retailer wonders whether there is any relationship between a customer's location in the U.S. (Midwest, Northeast, South, or West) and whether the customer made a purchase with the discount (yes or no). Table 3.10 shows a portion of the results from 600 e-mail accounts.

FILE *Promotion*

TABLE 3.10 Location and Purchase Survey Responses

Email	Location	Purchase
1	West	yes
2	Northeast	yes
⋮	⋮	⋮
600	South	no

Construct a contingency table and a stacked column chart using Excel and R, and then summarize the results.

SOLUTION:

Using Excel

a. Open the ***Promotion*** data file.

b. Click anywhere on the data (we choose cell A5). From the menu, select **Insert > Pivot Table**. Figure 3.10 shows the *Create PivotTable* dialog box. Because we clicked on the data before creating a pivot table, the default option in *Select a table or range* should already be populated. We choose to place the pivot table in the existing worksheet beginning in cell E1. Check the box next to the *Add this data to the Data Model* option. Then click **OK**.

FIGURE 3.10 Excel's Create PivotTable Dialog Box

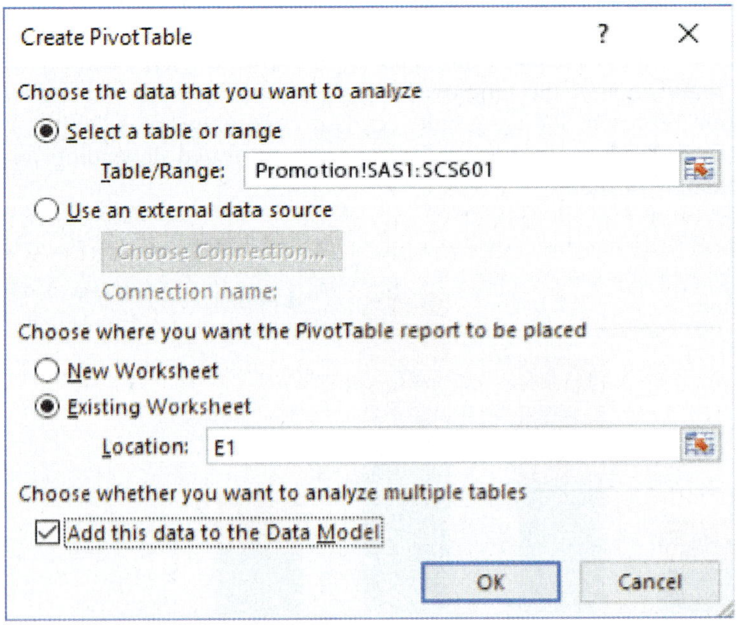

c. A menu will appear on the right side of the screen called *PivotTable Fields*. In the top of this menu you will see all of the variables in our data set. In the bottom part of the menu, there is a grid with four fields: Filters, Rows, Columns, and Values; see Figure 3.11. Drag the Location variable to the Rows field. Drag the Purchase variable to the Columns field. Drag the Email variable to the Values field. If the Email variable in the Values field is not presented as a count (for example, it may be presented as a sum), you will need to change it. Click the arrow below the Values field and select *Value Field Settings*. In the dialog box, select the *Summarize value field by* tab, and then, in the drop-down menu, select *Count*. Click **OK**.

FIGURE 3.11 Excel's Pivot Table Fields

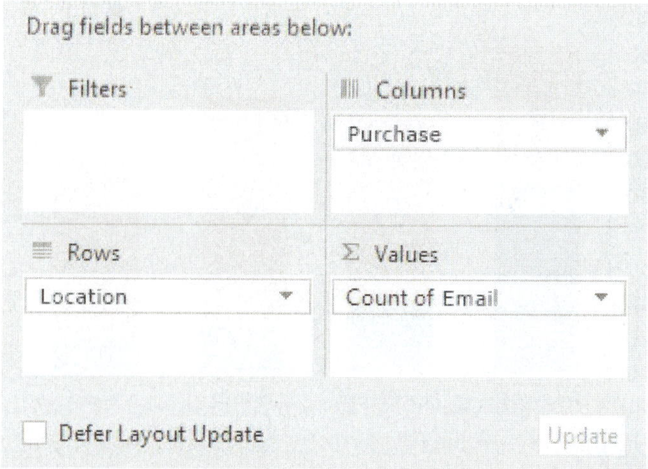

The resulting contingency table should be similar to Table 3.11.

TABLE 3.11 Contingency Table for the Location and Purchase Example

	Purchase		
Location	**No**	**Yes**	Total
Midwest	107	77	**184**
Northeast	41	102	**143**
South	24	130	**154**
West	18	101	**119**
Total	**190**	**410**	**600**

Sometimes it is preferable to convert counts to percentages, as shown in Table 3.12. In order to make this change, go back to the *Value Field Settings* dialog box, select the *Show values as* tab, and in the drop-down menu select *% of Grand Total*.

TABLE 3.12 Percent Table for the Location and Purchase Example

	Purchase		
Location	**No**	**Yes**	Total
Midwest	17.83%	12.83%	**30.67%**
Northeast	6.83%	17.00%	**23.83%**
South	4.00%	21.67%	**25.67%**
West	3.00%	16.83%	**19.83%**
Total	**31.67%**	**68.33%**	**100.00%**

d. We now illustrate how to create a stacked column chart using the contingency table. Make sure that the contingency table shows counts as in Table 3.11. Select the cells E2:G6. Choose **Insert > Insert Column or Bar Chart > Stacked Column**.

e. Formatting (regarding axis titles, gridlines, etc.) can be done by selecting the '+' sign at the top right of the chart or by selecting **Add Chart Elements** from the menu. Check the box next to *Data Labels* in the *Chart Elements* pop-up box to display frequencies in the column chart. The resulting stacked column chart is shown in Figure 3.12.

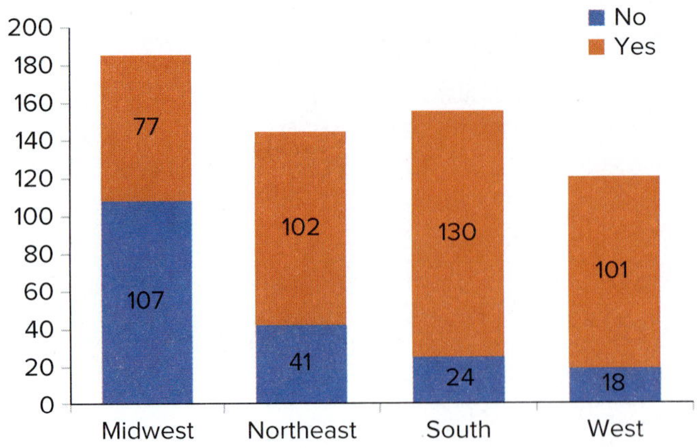

FIGURE 3.12 A stacked column chart for the Location and Purchase example

Using R

a. Import the ***Promotion*** data into a data frame (table) and label it myData.

b. In order to create a contingency table, labeled as myTable, we use the **table**(*row, column*) function and specify the *row* and *column* variables. If you retype myTable, you will see a contingency table that resembles Table 3.11. If we use the **prop.table** function, then R returns cell proportions that, when converted to percentages, are the same as those that appear in Table 3.12. Enter:

```
> myTable <- table(myData$Location, myData$Purchase)
> myTable
> prop.table(myTable)
```

c. To create a stacked column chart similar to Figure 3.12, we need to first create a contingency table with the Purchase variable in rows and the Location variable in columns. Enter:

```
> myNewTable <- table(myData$Purchase, myData$Location)
```

d. We use the **barplot** function to construct a column chart. As we saw when constructing a bar chart and a histogram, R offers a number of options for formatting. Here we use *main* to add a title; *col* to define colors for the segments of the columns; *legend* to create a legend; *xlab* and *ylab* to provide labels for the x-axis and y-axis, respectively; and *ylim* to extend the vertical axis units from 0 to 200. Enter:

```
> barplot(myNewTable, main="Location and Purchase",
col=c('blue','red'), legend=rownames(myNewTable), xlab='Location',
ylab='Count', ylim = c(0,200))
```

The resulting stacked column chart should look similar to Figure 3.12.

Summary

Compared to Table 3.10 with just raw data, Table 3.11, Table 3.12, and Figure 3.12 present the results of the location and purchase example in a much more informative format. We can readily see that of the 600 e-mail recipients, 410 of them made a purchase using the promotional discount. With a 68.33% positive response rate, this marketing strategy seemed successful. However, there do appear to be some differences depending on location. Recipients residing in the South and West were a lot more likely to make a purchase (130 out of 154 and 101 out of 119, respectively) compared to those residing in the Midwest (77 out of 184). It would be wise for the retailer to examine if there are other traits that the customers in the South and West share (age, gender, etc.). That way, in the next marketing campaign, the e-mails can be even more targeted.

> **USING A STACKED COLUMN CHART TO DISPLAY TWO CATEGORICAL VARIABLES**
>
> A stacked column chart is designed to visualize more than one categorical variable. It allows for the comparison of composition within each category.

A Method to Visualize the Relationship between Two Numerical Variables

LO 3.3

Construct and interpret a scatterplot.

When examining the relationship between two numerical variables, a **scatterplot** is a simple, yet useful, graphical tool. Each point in a scatterplot represents a paired observation for the two variables. When constructing a scatterplot, we generally refer to one of the variables as x and represent it on the horizontal axis (x-axis) and the other variable as y and represent it on the vertical axis (y-axis). We then plot each pairing: (x_1, y_1), (x_2, y_2), and so on. Once the data are plotted, the graph may reveal that

- A linear relationship exists between the two variables;
- A nonlinear relationship exists between the two variables; or
- No relationship exists between the two variables.

For example, Figure 3.13(a) shows points on a scatterplot clustered together along a line with a negative slope; we infer that the two variables have a negative linear relationship. Figure 3.13(b) depicts a positive nonlinear relationship; as x increases, y tends to increase at an increasing rate. The points in Figure 3.13(c) are scattered with no apparent pattern; thus, there is no relationship between the two variables.

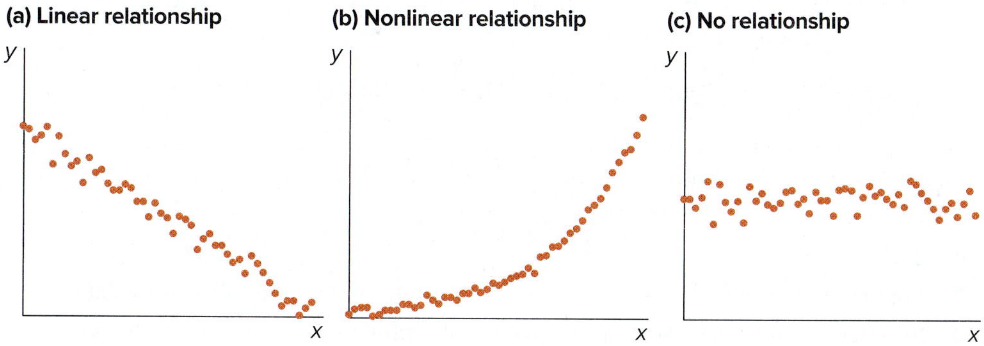

FIGURE 3.13 Scatterplots depicting various relationships between two variables

> **USING A SCATTERPLOT TO DISPLAY THE RELATIONSHIP BETWEEN TWO NUMERICAL VARIABLES**
>
> A scatterplot is a graphical tool that helps in determining whether or not two numerical variables are related in some systematic way. Each point in a scatterplot represents a paired observation for the two variables.

In order to illustrate a scatterplot, consider the following example.

EXAMPLE 3.4

Recall the ***Growth_Value*** data set that contains annual returns for Fidelity's Growth and Value mutual funds from 1984 to 2018. Construct a scatterplot of Value against Growth using Excel and R, and then summarize the results.

FILE
Growth_Value

SOLUTION:

Using Excel

a. Open the ***Growth_Value*** data file.

b. When constructing a scatterplot, Excel places the variable that appears in the first column on the x-axis and the variable that appears in the second column on the y-axis. Because we want Growth to be on the x-axis and Value on the y-axis, we do not need to rearrange the order of the columns. We simultaneously select the observations for the Growth and Value variables and choose **Insert > Insert Scatter or Bubble Chart > Scatter**. (If you are having trouble finding this option, look for the graph with data points above **Charts**.) The resulting scatterplot should be similar to Figure 3.14.

c. Formatting (regarding axis titles, gridlines, etc.) can be done by selecting **Format > Add Chart Element** from the menu.

FIGURE 3.14 A scatterplot of Value against Growth

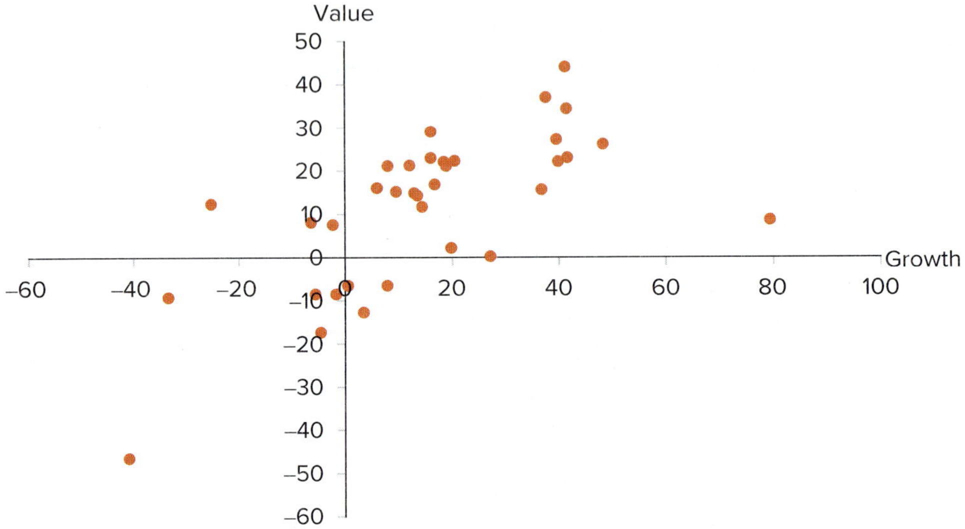

Using R

a. Import the ***Growth_Value*** data into a data frame (table) and label it myData.

b. In order to construct a scatterplot, we use the **plot(***y~x*, . . .**)** function. As we saw when constructing a bar chart and a histogram, R offers a number of options for formatting. Here, we use *main* to add a title; *xlab* and *ylab* to provide labels for the x-axis and the y-axis, respectively; *col* to define color; and *pch* to choose the marker for the data points—in particular, *pch* = 16 displays filled circles as data markers. Enter:

```
> plot(myData$Value~myData$Growth, main="Scatterplot of Value
against Growth", xlab="Growth", ylab="Value", col="chocolate",
pch=16)
```

The resulting scatterplot should be similar to Figure 3.14.

Summary

From Figure 3.14, we can infer that there is a positive relationship between Value and Growth; that is, as the annual return for Value increases, the annual return for Growth tends to increase as well.

EXERCISES 3.2

Applications

22. **FILE** ***Bar.*** At a local bar in a small Midwestern town, beer and wine are the only two alcoholic options. The manager conducts a survey on the bar's customers over the past weekend. Customers are asked to identify their sex (defined as male or female) and their drink choice (beer, wine, or soft drink). A portion of the responses is shown in the accompanying table.

Customer	Sex	Drink Choice
1	male	beer
2	male	beer
⋮	⋮	⋮
270	female	soft drink

a. Construct a contingency table that cross-classifies the data by Sex and Drink Choice. How many of the customers were male? How many of the customers drank wine?

b. Given that a customer is male, what is the likelihood that he drank beer? Given that a customer is female, what is the likelihood that she drank beer?

c. Construct a stacked column chart. Comment on the findings.

23. **FILE** ***Friends.*** It has been generally believed that it is not feasible for men and women to be just friends. Others argue that this belief may not be true anymore because gone are the days when men worked and women stayed at home and the only way they could get together was for romance (www.npr.org, November 12, 2016). A researcher conducts a survey on 186 students. The students are asked their sex (male or female) and if it is feasible for men and women to be just friends (yes or no). A portion of the responses is shown in the accompanying table.

Student	Sex	Feasible
1	female	yes
2	female	yes
⋮	⋮	⋮
186	male	no

a. Construct a contingency table that cross-classifies the data by Sex and Feasible. How many of the students were female? How many of the students felt that it was feasible for men and women to be just friends?

b. What is the likelihood that a male student feels that men and women can be just friends? What is the likelihood that a female student feels that men and women can be just friends?

c. Construct a stacked column chart. Do male and female students feel the same or differently about this topic? Explain.

24. **FILE** ***Shift.*** Metalworks, a supplier of fabricated industrial parts, wonders if there is any connection between when a component is constructed (Shift is equal to 1, 2, or 3) and whether or not it is defective (Defective is equal to Yes if the component is defective, No otherwise). The supplier collects data on the construction of 300 components. A portion of the data is shown in the accompanying table.

Component	Shift	Defective
1	1	No
2	1	Yes
⋮	⋮	⋮
300	3	No

a. Construct a contingency table that cross-classifies the data by shift and whether or not the component is defective. How many components constructed during Shift 1 were defective? How many components constructed during Shift 2 were not defective?

b. Given that the component was defective, what is the likelihood that it was constructed during Shift 2? Given that the component was defective, what is the likelihood that it was constructed during Shift 3? Does there seem to be any connection between when a component is constructed and whether or not it is defective? Explain.

c. Construct a stacked column chart. Are the defect rates consistent across all shifts? Explain.

25. **FILE** ***Athletic.*** A researcher at a marketing firm examines whether the age of a consumer matters when buying athletic clothing. Her initial feeling is that Brand A attracts a younger customer, whereas the more established companies (Brands B and C) draw an older clientele. For 600 recent purchases of athletic clothing, she collects data on a customer's age (Age equals 1 if the customer is under 35, 0 otherwise) and the brand name of the athletic clothing (A, B, or C). A portion of the data is shown in the accompanying table.

Purchase	Age	Brand
1	1	A
2	1	A
⋮	⋮	⋮
600	0	C

a. Construct a contingency table that cross-classifies the data by Age and Brand. How many of the purchases were for Brand A? How many of the purchases were from customers under 35 years old?

b. Given that the purchase was made by a customer under 35 years old, what is the likelihood that the customer purchased Brand A? Brand B? Brand C? Do the data seem to support the researcher's belief? Explain.

c. Construct a stacked column chart. Does there appear to be a relationship between the age of the customer and the brand purchased?

26. **FILE** ***Study.*** A report suggests that business majors spend the least amount of time on course work compared to all other college students (*The Washington Post*, January 28, 2017). A provost of a university conducts a survey on 270 students. Students are asked their major (business or nonbusiness) and if they study hard (yes or no), where study hard is defined as spending at least 20 hours per week on course work. A portion of the responses is shown in the accompanying table.

Student	Major	Study Hard
1	business	yes
2	business	yes
⋮	⋮	⋮
270	nonbusiness	no

a. Construct a contingency table that cross-classifies the data by Major and Study Hard. How many of the students are business majors? How many of the students study hard?

b. Given that the student is a business major, what is the likelihood that the student studies hard? Given that the student is a nonbusiness major, what is the likelihood that the student studies hard? Do the data seem to support the findings in the report? Explain.

c. Construct a stacked column chart. Comment on the findings.

27. **FILE** ***Test_Scores.*** The accompanying table shows a portion of midterm and final grades for 32 students. Construct a scatterplot of Final against Midterm. Describe the relationship.

Final	Midterm
86	78
94	97
⋮	⋮
91	47

28. **FILE** ***Life_Obesity.*** The accompanying table shows a portion of life expectancies (in years) and obesity rates (in %) for the 50 states and the District of Columbia. Construct a scatterplot of Life Expectancy against Obesity. Describe the relationship.

State	Life Expectancy	Obesity
Alabama	75.4	36.3
Alaska	78.3	34.2
⋮	⋮	⋮
Wyoming	78.3	28.8

29. **FILE** ***Consumption.*** The accompanying table shows a portion of quarterly data for average U.S. annual consumption (Consumption in \$) and disposable income (Income in \$) for the years 2000–2016. Construct a scatterplot of Consumption against Income. Describe the relationship.

Date	Consumption	Income
Q1, 2000	28634	31192
Q2, 2000	28837	31438
⋮	⋮	⋮
Q4, 2016	35987	39254

30. **FILE** ***Return.*** In order to diversify risk, investors are often encouraged to invest in assets whose returns have either a negative relationship or no relationship. The accompanying table shows a portion of the annual return data (in %) on two assets. Construct a scatterplot of Return B against Return A. In order to diversify risk, would the investor be wise to include both of these assets in her portfolio? Explain.

Return A	Return B
−20	2
−5	0
⋮	⋮
10	2

31. **FILE** ***Healthy_Living.*** Healthy living has always been an important goal for any society. Most would agree that a diet that is rich in fruits and vegetables (FV) and regular exercise have a positive effect on health, while smoking has a negative effect on health. The accompanying table shows a portion of the percentage of these variables observed in various states in the United States.

State	Health	FV	Exercise	Smoking
AK	88.7	23.3	60.6	14.6
AL	78.3	20.3	41.0	16.4
⋮	⋮	⋮	⋮	⋮
WY	87.5	23.3	57.2	15.2

a. Construct a scatterplot of Health against Exercise. Describe the relationship.

b. Construct a scatterplot of Health against Smoking. Describe the relationship.

32. **FILE** ***Car_Price.*** The accompanying table shows a portion of data consisting of the price, the age, and the mileage for 20 used sedans.

Price	Age	Mileage
13590	6	61485
13775	6	54344
⋮	⋮	⋮
11988	8	42408

a. Construct a scatterplot of Price against Age. Describe the relationship.

b. Construct a scatterplot of Price against Mileage. Describe the relationship.

3.3 OTHER DATA VISUALIZATION METHODS

LO 3.4

Construct and interpret a scatterplot with a categorical variable, a bubble plot, a line chart, and a heat map.

In Section 3.2, we constructed a scatterplot that was used to visualize the relationship between two numerical variables. Here, we extend our discussion of a scatterplot by incorporating a categorical variable. We also present three additional visualization methods: bubble plots, line charts, and heat maps.

A Scatterplot with a Categorical Variable

Recall that we use a scatterplot to display the relationship between two numerical variables. For example, if we plot property value against square footage, then we anticipate a positive relationship between these two variables; that is, the bigger the house, the more it is worth. If we have a third variable in the data set, say the property type (a single-family home, a condominium, etc.), we can incorporate this categorical variable within the scatterplot by using different colors or symbols. This allows us to see if the relationship between property value and square footage differs across different property types. This plot is referred to as a **scatterplot with a categorical variable**.

We illustrate the use of a scatterplot with a categorical variable in Example 3.5.

EXAMPLE 3.5

FILE *Birth_Life*

The ***Birth_Life*** data file contains information on the following variables for 10 countries in 2010: country name (Country Name), life expectancy (Life Exp in years), birth rate (Birth Rate in percent), GNI per capita (GNI in $), and level of development (Development). A portion of the ***Birth_Life*** data set is shown in Table 3.13.

TABLE 3.13 A Portion of the ***Birth_Life*** Data Set

Country Name	Life Exp	Birth Rate	GNI	Development
Congo, Dem. Rep.	50.00	45.96	130	Developing
India	62.59	26.46	440	Developing
⋮	⋮	⋮	⋮	⋮
Japan	81.08	9.40	36230	Developed

Use Excel and R to construct a scatterplot of birth rate against life expectancy that also incorporates the Development variable (categorical). Summarize the results.

SOLUTION:

Using Excel

a. Open the ***Birth_Life*** data file.

b. In order to create a scatterplot that incorporates a categorical variable, the categorical variable should be sorted by category. Here, the Development variable is already sorted; that is, the first six countries are developing countries and the remaining four countries are developed countries. Select **Insert > Insert Scatter or Bubble Chart > Scatter**. This creates a placeholder for the scatterplot in the worksheet.

c. Select **Design > Select Data**. In the *Select Data Source* dialog box, click the *Add* button. This opens the *Edit Series* dialog box for you to select the data for the x-axis and the y-axis of the scatterplot. Enter "Developing" as the *Series name*, select cells B2 through B7 as the *Series X values,* and select cells C2 through C7 as the *Series Y values*. Click **OK** in the *Edit Series* dialog box. This plots birth rate against life expectancy for the six developing countries.

d. Click *Add* to open the *Edit Series* dialog box. Enter "Developed" as the *Series name*, select cells B8 through B11 as the *Series X values*, and select cells C8 through C11 as the *Series Y values*. Click **OK** in the *Edit Series* dialog box. This plots birth rate against life expectancy for the four developed countries. Click **OK** in the *Select Data Source* dialog box.

e. Formatting (regarding axis titles, gridlines, etc.) can be done by selecting **Format > Add Chart Element** from the menu. The resulting scatterplot should be similar to Figure 3.15.

FIGURE 3.15 A scatterplot of birth rate against life expectancy

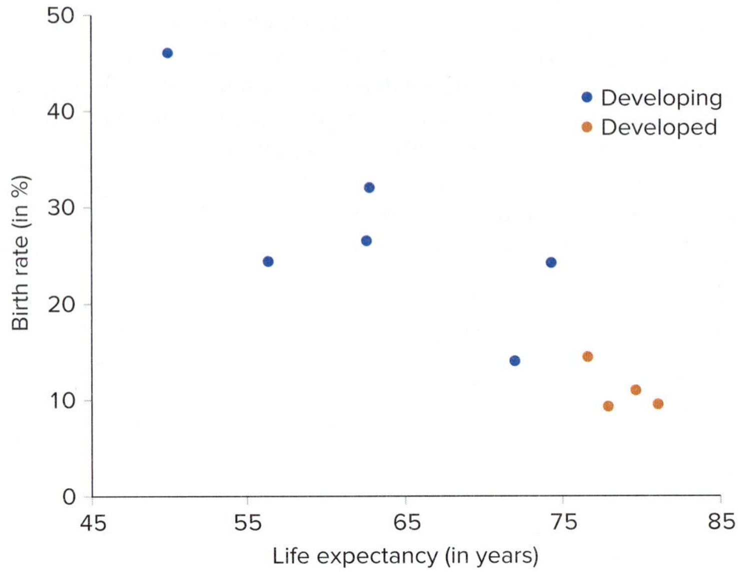

Using R

a. Import the ***Birth_Life*** data into a data frame (table) and label it myData.

b. To create a scatterplot that incorporates the Development variable, we use the **plot** function. Here we use the options *main* to add a title; *col* to define colors for the segments of the columns; *xlab* and *ylab* to provide labels for the x-axis and y-axis, respectively; *pch* to define the shape of the marker; and *col* to define the color of the marker. The shapes and colors of the markers are based on the categories of the Development variable. Enter:

```
> plot(myData$'Birth Rate'~myData$'Life Exp', main="Scatterplot
of Birth Rate against Life Expectancy", xlab = "Life
Expectancy (in years)", ylab = "Birth Rate (in %)", pch=16,
col=ifelse(myData$Development == "Developing", 20, 26))
```

c. We add a legend on the right side of the scatterplot using the **legend** function. Enter:

```
> legend("right", legend=c("Developing", "Developed"), pch=16,
col=c(20, 26))
```

The resulting scatterplot should be similar to Figure 3.15.

Summary

From Figure 3.15, we see a negative linear relationship between birth rate and life expectancy. That is, countries with lower birth rates tend to have higher life expectancies. This relationship holds true for both developing and developed countries. We also see that, in general, developed countries have lower birth rates and higher life expectancies as compared to developing countries.

A Bubble Plot

A **bubble plot** shows the relationship between three numerical variables. In a bubble plot, the third numerical variable is represented by the size of the bubble. For instance, a bubble plot may plot a college student's study time against screen time and use the size of the bubble to represent the student's GPA. This bubble plot would help us understand the relationships between study time, screen time, and academic performance.

We illustrate the use of a bubble plot in Example 3.6.

EXAMPLE 3.6

FILE
Birth_Life

Revisit the ***Birth_Life*** data from Example 3.5. Use Excel and R to construct a bubble plot of birth rate against life expectancy that uses the GNI variable for the size of the bubbles. Summarize the results.

SOLUTION:

Using Excel

a. Open the ***Birth_Life*** data file.

b. Select **Insert > Insert Scatter or Bubble Chart > Bubble**. This creates a placeholder for the plot in the worksheet.

c. Select **Design > Select Data**. In the *Select Data Source* dialog box, click the *Add* button. This opens the *Edit Series* dialog box for you to select the variables for the x-axis, the y-axis, and the bubble size. Select cells B2 through B11 as the *Series X values*, select cells C2 through C11 as the *Series Y values*, and select cells D2 through D11 as the *Series bubble size*. Click **OK** in the *Edit Series* dialog box. Click **OK** in the *Select Data Source* dialog box.

d. Formatting (regarding axis titles, gridlines, etc.) can be done by selecting **Format > Add Chart Element** from the menu. The resulting bubble plot should be similar to Figure 3.16.

FIGURE 3.16 A bubble plot of birth rate, life expectancy, and GNI

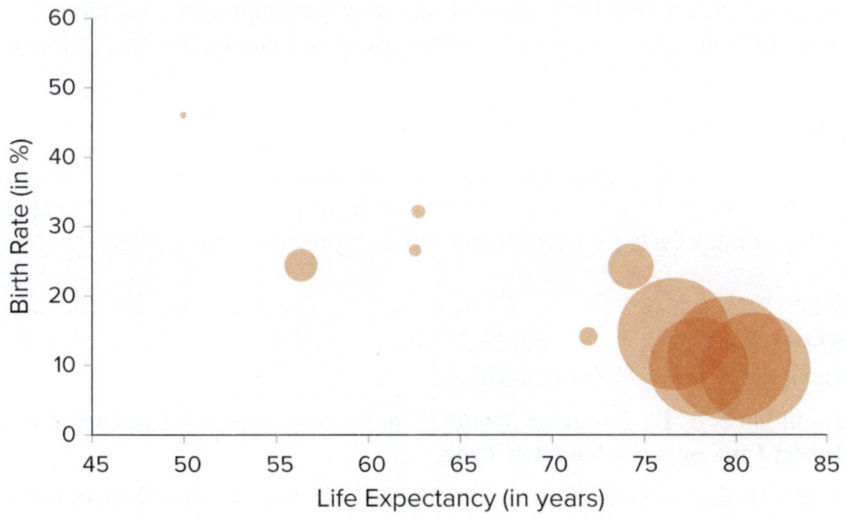

Using R

a. Import the ***Birth_Life*** data into a data frame (table) and label it myData.

b. We first create an empty plot by using the **plot** function (with the appropriate *x* and *y* variables) and the option *type* = *"n"*, which means no plotting. Enter:

```
> plot(myData$'Birth Rate'~myData$'Life Exp', type="n")
```

c. We then use the **symbols** function to plot the bubbles representing the observations. We use the options *circles*, *inches*, and *bg* to specify the radii, sizes, and color of the bubbles, respectively. The bubbles are sized based on the values of the GNI of the countries. As in Example 3.5, we also use the options *main*, *xlab*, and *ylab*. Enter:

```
> symbols(myData$'Birth Rate'~myData$'Life Exp',
circles=myData$GNI, inches = 0.5, bg = 'blue', main="A bubble plot
of birth rate, life expectancy, and GNI", xlab = "Life Expectancy
(in years)", ylab = "Birth Rate (in %)")
```

The resulting bubble plot should be similar to Figure 3.16.

Summary

From Figure 3.16 we see that a country's birth rate and its average life expectancy display a negative linear relationship. We also see that countries with low birth rates and high life expectancies have higher GNI per capita, which is indicative of developed countries.

A Line Chart

A **line chart** displays a numerical variable as a series of data points connected by a line. A line chart is especially useful for tracking changes or trends over time. For example, using a line chart that plots the sales of Samsung's smartphones over time, we can easily tell whether the sales follow an upward, a downward, or a steady trend. It is also easy for us to identify any major changes that happened in the past on a line chart. For example, due to a major product recall, Samsung experienced a significant drop in sales in late 2016. We can easily identify the event from the line chart because the data point for that year would dip dramatically.

When multiple lines are plotted in the same chart, we can compare these observations on one or more dimensions. For example, if we simultaneously plot the historical sales of Apple's iPhones alongside those of Samsung's smartphones, we would be able to compare the trends and the rates of change of the two companies. We may even detect interesting patterns such as whether a drop in the sales of Samsung's smartphones coincides with a surge in the sales of iPhones. In order to illustrate the use of line charts, consider Example 3.7.

EXAMPLE 3.7

FILE
Growth_Value

Recall the introductory case where data are provided on the annual returns (in %) for Fidelity's Growth and Value mutual funds from 1984 to 2018. Use Excel and R to construct line charts for Growth and Value. Summarize the results.

SOLUTION:

Using Excel

a. Open the ***Growth_Value*** data file.

b. Highlight cells B1 through C36 and then, from the menu, select **Insert > Insert Line or Area Chart > Line**.

c. Select **Design > Select Data** and click the *Edit* button under *Horizontal (Category) Axis Labels*. In the *Axis Labels* dialog box, highlight cells A2 through A34 in the *Axis label range* box. Click **OK**. The years appear in the line plot. Due to space limitations, Excel only displays the even number years along the horizontal axis.

d. Formatting (regarding axis titles, gridlines, etc.) can be done by selecting **Format > Add Chart Element** from the menu. The resulting line chart should be similar to Figure 3.17.

FIGURE 3.17 A line chart for the Growth and Value mutual funds

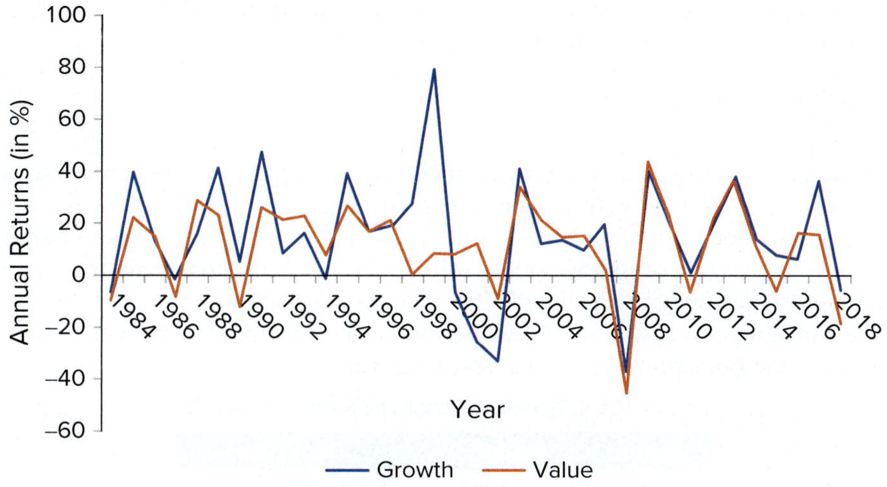

Using R

a. Import the ***Growth_Value*** data into a data frame (table) and label it myData.

b. We first use the **plot** function to create a line chart for the Growth variable. Here we use the options; *col* to define the color of the marker; *type* to define the type of plot where "l" means line; and *ylim* to provide limits on the y-axis. As in Example 3.5, we also use the options *main*, *xlab*, and *ylab*. Enter:

```
> plot(myData$Growth~myData$Year, main="A line chart for the
Growth and Value mutual funds", xlab="Year", ylab="Annual Returns",
col = "blue", type = "l", ylim = c(-100, 100) )
```

c. We then add a red line for the Value mutual fund using the **lines** function. Enter:

```
> lines(myData$Value~myData$Year, col="red", type = "l")
```

d. We add a legend at the bottom of the chart using the **legend** function. The *lty* =1 option specifies that the legend is based on the two solid lines. Enter:

```
> legend("bottom", legend=c("Growth", "Value"), col=c("blue",
"red"), lty=1)
```

The resulting line chart should be similar to Figure 3.17.

Summary

The line chart in Figure 3.17 compares the annual returns of Fidelity's Growth and Value mutual funds over a period of 35 years. In general, both funds tend to move in the same direction. However, during the dot-com bubble that occurred roughly between 1995 and 2000, the technology-heavy Growth fund shows dramatically higher returns as compared to the Value fund, which tends to favor traditional companies. The subsequent burst of the dot-com bubble shows a reversal of that trend.

A Heat Map

A **heat map** is an important visualization tool that uses color or color intensity to display relationships between variables. Heat maps are especially useful to identify combinations of the categorical variables that have economic significance. There are a number of ways to display a heat map, but they all share one thing in common—they use color to communicate the relationships between the variables that would be harder to understand by simply inspecting the raw data. For example, we can use a heat map to show which products are the best-or worst-selling products at various stores or show the most- or least-frequently downloaded music genres across various music streaming platforms. Example 3.8 illustrates the use of a heat map.

EXAMPLE 3.8

FILE *Bookstores*

A national bookstore chain is trying to understand customer preferences at various store locations. The marketing department has acquired a list of 500 of the most recent transactions from four of its stores. The data set includes the record number (Record), which one of its four stores sold the book (BookStore), and the type of book sold (BookType). The marketing department wants to visualize the data using a heat map to help it understand customer preferences at different stores. A portion of the ***Bookstores*** data set is shown in Table 3.14.

TABLE 3.14 Transaction Results for Bookstore Example

Record	BookStore	BookType
1	Store2	Biography
2	Store2	Children book
⋮	⋮	⋮
500	Store4	Romance

Use Excel and R to construct a heat map to visualize the sales of various types of books at different stores. Summarize the results.

SOLUTION:

Using Excel

a. Open the ***Bookstores*** data file.

b. Before we can create a heat map, we need to first construct a contingency table that summarizes each type of book sold as a percentage of all books sold at each store. Click anywhere on the data (we choose cell A5). From the menu, select **Insert > Pivot Table**. The option in *Select a table or range* should already be populated with the data range A1:C501. Place the PivotTable report in the existing worksheet beginning in cell E1.

c. In *PivotTable Fields*, drag the BookStore and BookType variables to the Rows and Columns fields, respectively. Drag Record to the Values field. Click the arrow below Values and select *Value Field Settings*. In order to read the Record variable as a count, click the arrow below the Values tab and select *Value Field Settings*. In the dialog box, select the *Summarize value field by* tab, and then in the drop-down menu select *Count*. In the *Show values as* tab, we choose *% of Row* down menu. Click **OK**. You should see a contingency table starting in cell E1.

d. Select the data range F3:K6. From the menu, select **Home > Conditional Formatting > Color Scales > Green – Yellow – Red Color Scale.**

The resulting heat map should be similar to Figure 3.18. Excel's color scale works in descending order of magnitude; that is, for the green-yellow-red color scale, green denotes the larger values, yellow denotes the median values, and red denotes the smaller values. We advise you to experiment with different color scales in Excel to see how the heat map changes.

FIGURE 3.18 Excel's heat map for the bookstore example

Row Labels	Biography	Children book	Romance	Sci-fi	Self help	Travel guide	Grand Total
Store1	17.78%	17.78%	16.30%	18.52%	9.63%	20.00%	100.00%
Store2	13.04%	20.00%	25.22%	14.78%	14.78%	12.17%	100.00%
Store3	20.55%	15.75%	8.90%	19.18%	15.75%	19.86%	100.00%
Store4	17.31%	14.42%	20.19%	20.19%	14.42%	13.46%	100.00%
Grand Total	**17.40%**	**17.00%**	**17.00%**	**18.20%**	**13.60%**	**16.80%**	**100.00%**

Using R

a. Import the ***Bookstores*** data into a data frame (table) and label it myData.

b. We first use the **table** function to create a contingency table, labeled myTable, that summarizes the number of each type of book sold at each store. We then use the **rowSums** function to retrieve the total number of books sold at each store and divide the values in the contingency table by those numbers to get a modified contingency table that summarizes each type of book sold as a percentage of all books sold at each store. Enter:

```
> myTable <-table(myData$BookStore, myData$BookType)
> myTable <- myTable/rowSums(myTable)
```

c. In order to construct a heat map in R, the data must be converted into a data matrix, which is a two-dimensional data structure whose columns must have the same data type and length. We use the **as.matrix** function to make this conversion and label the data matrix as myData.matrix. Enter:

```
> myData.matrix <- as.matrix(myTable)
```

d. We use the **heatmap** function to construct the heat map. We choose the *heat.color* pallet with 256 colors using *col* = *heat.colors*(256). By default, the color pallet uses warm colors (e.g., orange and red) to show smaller values and cool colors (e.g., yellow and white) to show larger values. We use the *scale* = *"none"* option to ensure that the data are not standardized when used to plot the heat map. Finally, we use *Rowv* = *NA* and *Colv* = *NA* to suppress a tree-like diagram called a dendrogram. A dendrogram will be discussed later in Chapter 11. Enter:

```
> heatmap(myData.matrix, col = heat.colors(256), scale = "none",
Rowv= NA, Colv = NA)
```

The resulting heat map is shown in Figure 3.19(a).

e. Alternatively, we can specify our own colors so that less-popular book genres have cooler colors and the more-popular genres have warmer colors. Because the most popular book genre accounts for 25.22% of the book sales at the store, we create a vector, myBreaks, that contains numbers from 0 (0%) to 0.30 (30%) with increments of 0.05 (5%). The color assigned to each number interval is stored in the vector myCol. For example, if the book genre accounts for 0% to 5% of the book sales at the store, the color blue will be assigned to that genre; alternatively, if the book genre accounts for 25% to 30% of the book sales at the store, a warm red color, coded "red3" will be assigned. We then assign our own color key using *col* and *breaks* for the new heat map. Enter:

```
> myBreaks <- c(0, 0.05, 0.10, 0.15, 0.20, 0.25, 0.30)
> myCol <- c("blue", "green", "yellow", "orange1", "red1",
"red3")
> heatmap(myData.matrix, col = myCol, breaks = myBreaks, scale =
"none", Rowv = NA, Colv = NA)
```

The resulting heat map is shown in Figure 3.19(b); the colors may appear different from what you see on your computer screen.

FIGURE 3.19 R's heat maps for the bookstore example

Summary

The heat maps in Figures 3.18 and 3.19 reveal that customers' book preferences do differ across different store locations. For example, romance fictions are the most popular books sold at Store2 but the least popular at Store3. Self-help books are the least popular books at Store1. The management can use this information to make decisions about how many copies of each type of book to stock at each store.

ADDITIONAL GRAPHICAL DISPLAYS

The following graphical displays are additional ways to visualize relationships between variables that would be harder to understand by simply inspecting the raw data.

- A scatterplot with a categorical variable shows the relationship between two numerical variables and a categorical variable in a two-dimensional graph. The categorical variable is typically represented by different colors for each category.
- A bubble plot shows the relationship between three numerical variables in a two-dimensional graph. The third numerical variable is represented by the size of the bubble.
- A line chart shows a numerical variable as a series of data points connected by a line. It is especially useful for tracking changes or trends over time.
- A heat map uses color or color intensity to display relationships between variables. Heat maps are especially useful for identifying combinations of the categorical variables that have economic significance.

Options for Advanced Visualizations

In addition to the data visualizations discussed in this chapter, advanced software tools for constructing sophisticated, aesthetically pleasing, and interactive visualizations are available. Two popular advanced visualization tools include the ggplot2 package in R and Tableau.

The ggplot2 package is one of the most popular graphic packages in R for producing elegant, publication-quality graphics. The package is created based on a set of concepts called the Grammar of Graphics, which breaks up graphs into data, aesthetics (e.g., color and size), and geometric (e.g., lines and shapes) components.

Tableau is a stand-alone data visualization software that has gained tremendous popularity for its attractive output, versatility, and ease of use. One of the key features of Tableau is its ability to extract data from a wide range of sources from Excel files on a personal computer to Oracle databases on a cloud, computing platform. The product is designed to allow users with little technical experience to develop attractive visualizations interactively and to drill down the data for business insights. Users can easily switch between different visualizations to select the most compelling graphs for their storytelling. In addition, Tableau allows users to create interactive dashboards, which can display real-time data, to support business decision making.

Detailed discussion of the ggplot2 package in R and/or Tableau is outside of the scope of this text.

EXERCISES 3.3

Applications

33. **FILE** ***InternetStocks.*** A financial analyst wants to compare the performance of the stocks of two Internet companies, Amazon (AMZN) and Google (GOOG). She records the average closing prices of the two stocks for the years 2010 through 2016. A portion of the data is shown in the accompanying table. Construct a line chart that shows the movements of the two stocks over time using two lines each with a unique color. Describe the overall trend of price movement for the two stocks. Which stock shows the greater trajectory of price appreciation?

Year	AMZN	GOOG
2010	180.00	593.97
2011	173.10	645.90
⋮	⋮	⋮
2016	749.86	771.82

34. **FILE** ***India_China.*** It is believed that India will overtake China to become the world's most populous nation much sooner than previously thought (*CNN*, June 19, 2019). The accompanying data file, compiled by the World Bank, contains the population data, in millions, for India and China from 1960 to 2017. Construct a line chart that shows the changes in the two countries' populations over time using two lines each with a unique color. Describe the overall trend of population growth in the two countries. Which country shows the faster population growth during the past 40 years?

Year	India	China
1960	449.48	667.07
1961	458.49	660.33
⋮	⋮	⋮
2017	1339.18	1386.40

35. **FILE** ***HighSchool_SAT.*** The accompanying table shows a portion of the average SAT math score (Math), the average SAT writing score (Writing), the number of test takers (Test Taker), and whether the school is a private or public school (Type) for 25 high schools in a major metropolitan area.

School	Math	Writing	Test Taker	Type
1	456	423	228	Public
2	437	393	475	Public
⋮	⋮	⋮	⋮	⋮
25	592	592	127	Private

a. Construct a bubble plot that shows the math score on the x-axis, the writing score on the y-axis, and the number of test takers as the size of the bubble. Do math score and writing score show a linear, nonlinear, or no relationship? If the relationship is a linear relationship, is it a positive or negative relationship? Do math score and the size of the school (using the number of test takers as a proxy) show a linear, nonlinear, or no relationship?

b. Construct a scatterplot that shows the math score on the x-axis and the writing score on the y-axis. Use different colors or symbols to show whether the high school is a private or public school. Describe the relationships between math score, writing score, and school type. Does the relationship between math score and writing score hold true for both private and public schools?

36. **FILE** ***Car_Price.*** The accompanying table shows a portion of data consisting of the selling price, the age, and the mileage for 20 used sedans.

Price	Age	Mileage
13590	6	61485
13775	6	54344
⋮	⋮	⋮
11988	8	42408

a. Construct a bubble plot that shows price on the x-axis, age on the y-axis, and mileage as the sizes of the bubbles. Describe the relationships between price, age, and mileage of these used sedans.

b. Convert Mileage into a categorical variable, Mileage_Category, by assigning all cars with less than 50,000 miles to the "Low_Mileage" category and the rest to the "High_Mileage" category. How many cars are in the "High_Mileage" category?

c. Construct a scatterplot using Price, Age, and Mileage_Category. Use different colors or symbols to show cars that belong to the different mileage categories. Describe the relationships between price, age, and mileage of these used sedans. Does the relationship between price and age hold true for both mileage categories?

37. **FILE** ***TShirts.*** A company that sells unisex t-shirts is interested in finding out the color and size of its best-selling t-shirt. The accompanying data file contains the size, color, and quantity of t-shirts that were ordered during the last 1,000 transactions. A portion of the data is shown in the accompanying table.

Transaction	Quantity	Size	Color
1	1	XL	Purple
2	3	M	Blue
⋮	⋮	⋮	⋮
1000	1	S	Red

a. Construct a contingency table that shows the total quantity sold for each color and size combination. How many size M red t-shirts were sold? How many size XL purple t-shirts were sold?

b. Construct a heat map that displays colors or color intensity based on the total quantity sold. Which two color and size combinations are the most popular ones? Which two are the least popular ones?

38. **FILE** ***Crime_Analysis.*** The local police department is performing a crime analysis to find out which crimes are most likely to occur at which locations. The accompanying data file contains the types of crimes (CrimeType) that occurred at various locations (Location) in the city over the past five years. A portion of the data is shown in the accompanying table.

Record	CrimeType	Location
1	Narcotics	Street
2	Assault	Residence
⋮	⋮	⋮
10385	Burglary	Residence

a. Construct a contingency table that shows the frequencies for CrimeType and Location combinations. How many of the crimes were for burglary and happened in a residence?

b. Construct a heat map that displays colors or color intensity based on the frequencies. Which three crime type and location combinations are the most frequent ones?

LO 3.5

3.4 SUMMARY MEASURES

Calculate and interpret summary measures.

In addition to tables and graphs, we can also use numerical descriptive measures to extract meaningful information from data. These measures provide precise, objectively determined values that are easy to calculate, interpret, and compare with one another.

We first calculate several measures of central location, which attempt to find a typical or central value for the data. We then examine measures of dispersion and measures of shape. Measures of dispersion gauge the underlying variability of the data. Measures of shape reveal whether or not the distribution is symmetric and whether the tails of the distribution are more or less extreme than the normal distribution. Finally, we discuss measures of association, which show whether two numerical variables have a linear relationship.

Measures of Central Location

The term *central location* relates to the way numerical data tend to cluster around some middle or central value. Measures of central location attempt to find a typical or central value that describes the data. Examples include finding a typical value that describes the return on an investment, the number of defects in a production process, the salary of a business graduate, the rental price in a neighborhood, the number of customers at a local convenience store, and so on. We discuss the three most widely used measures of central location: the mean, the median, and the mode. We also discuss a percentile, which is technically a measure of location (though not necessarily central location); however, it is also used as a measure of relative position because it is so easy to interpret.

The Mean

The **arithmetic mean** is the primary measure of central location. Generally, we refer to the arithmetic mean as simply the **mean** or the **average**. In order to calculate the mean of a variable, we simply add up all the observations and divide by the number of observations. The only thing that differs between a population mean and a sample mean is the notation. The population mean is referred to as μ, where μ is the Greek letter mu (pronounced as "mew"). For observations $x_1, x_2, \ldots, x_N$, the population mean is calculated as $\frac{\Sigma x_i}{N}$, where N is the number of observations in the population. The sample mean is referred to as $\bar{x}$ (pronounced x-bar). For observations $x_1, x_2, \ldots, x_n$, the sample mean is calculated as $\frac{\Sigma x_i}{n}$, where n is the number of observations in the sample. We refer to the population mean as a **parameter** and the sample mean as a **statistic**. Because the population mean is generally unknown, we often use the sample mean to estimate the population mean.

The Median

The mean is used extensively in data analysis. However, it can give a misleading description of the center of the distribution in the presence of extremely small or large observations, also referred to as **outliers**. Because the mean can be affected by outliers, we often also calculate the **median** as a measure of central location. The median is the middle value of a data set; that is, an equal number of observations lie above and below the median. After arranging the data in ascending order (smallest to largest), we calculate the median as (1) the middle value if the number of observations is odd or (2) the average of the two middle values if the number of observations is even.

Many government publications and other data sources publish both the mean and the median in order to accurately portray a variable's typical value. If the mean and the median differ significantly, then it is likely that the variable contains outliers. For instance, in 2017 the U.S. Census Bureau determined that the median income for American households was \$61,372; however, the mean income was \$86,220. It is well documented that a small number of households in the United States have income that is considerably higher than the typical American household income. As a result, these top-earning households influence the mean by pushing its value significantly above the value of the median.

The Mode

The **mode** of a variable is the observation that occurs most frequently. A variable can have more than one mode, or even no mode. If a variable has one mode, then we say it is unimodal. If it has two modes, then it is common to call it bimodal. If two or more modes exist, then the variable is multimodal. Generally, the mode's usefulness as a measure of central location tends to diminish for a variable with more than three modes. If we want to summarize a categorical variable, then the mode is the only meaningful measure of central location.

MEASURES OF CENTRAL LOCATION

- The mean is the most commonly used measure of central location. The population mean is denoted as μ, and the sample mean is denoted as $\bar{x}$. One weakness of the mean is that it is unduly influenced by outliers.
- The median is the middle observation of a variable; that is, it divides the variable in half. The median is especially useful when outliers are present.
- The mode is the most frequently occurring observation of a variable. A variable may have no mode or more than one mode. The mode is the only meaningful measure of central location for a categorical variable.

FILE
Growth_Value

EXAMPLE 3.9

Using Excel and R, calculate the mean and the median for the Growth and the Value variables from the introductory case. Summarize the results.

SOLUTION:

Using Excel

I. Excel's Formula Option Excel provides built-in formulas for virtually every summary measure that we may need. To illustrate, we follow these steps to calculate the mean and the median for the Growth variable.

a. Open the ***Growth_Value*** data file.

b. Enter =AVERAGE(B2:B36). Verify that the output is 15.1074.

c. To calculate the median, enter =MEDIAN(B2:B36). Verify that the output is 14.44.

If we want to calculate the mean return for the Value variable, and because the data occupy cells C2 through C36 on the spreadsheet, we enter =AVERAGE(C2:C36). Because the Growth and Value variables each contains 35 unique observations and no duplicates, it is not practical to compute the mode. For other variables, we enter =MODE(array) to calculate the mode, where the notation array specifies the range of cells to be included in the calculation. When introducing new functions later in this chapter and other chapters, we will follow this format. The first and second columns of Table 3.15 show various descriptive measures and

TABLE 3.15 Descriptive Measures and Corresponding Function Names in Excel and R

Descriptive Measure	Excel	R
Location		
Mean	=AVERAGE(array)	mean(df$var)[a]
Median	=MEDIAN(array)	median(df$var)
Mode	=MODE(array)	NA[b]
Minimum	=MIN(array)	min(df$var)
Maximum	=MAX(array)	max(df$var)
Percentile	=PERCENTILE.INC(array, p)[c]	quantile(df$var, p)[c]
Multiple measures	*NA*	summary(df)
Dispersion		
Range	=MAX(array)-MIN(array)	range(df$var)[d]
Mean Absolute Deviation	=AVEDEV(array)	mad(df$var)[e]
Sample Variance	=VAR.S(array)	var(df$var)
Sample Standard Deviation	=STDEV.S(array)	sd(df$var)
Shape		
Skewness	=SKEW(array)	NA
Kurtosis	=KURT(array)	NA
Association		
Sample Covariance	=COVARIANCE.S(array1,array2)	cov(df)
Correlation	=CORREL(array1,array2)	cor(df)

[a] The notation *df* refers to the data frame or file and the notation *var* refers to the variable name. The variable name should be specified in single quotations if it consists of more than one word or if it is a number.

[b] *NA* denotes that a simple function is not readily available.

[c] The parameter p takes on a value between 0 and 1.

[d] The **range** function in R returns the minimum and maximum values, so the range can be calculated by taking the difference between the two values.

[e] The **mad** function calculates the median absolute deviation, rather than the mean absolute deviation. Alternatively, we can install the 'lsr' package in R and use the **aad** function, which computes the mean absolute deviation.

corresponding function names in Excel. We will refer back to Table 3.15 on a few occasions in this chapter.

II. Excel's Data Analysis Toolpak Option Another way to obtain summary measures is to use Excel's Data Analysis Toolpak option. One advantage of this option is that it provides numerous summary measures using a single command. Again, we illustrate this option using the data from the introductory case.

a. Open the ***Growth_Value*** data file.
b. From the menu, choose **Data > Data Analysis > Descriptive Statistics > OK**. (Note: As mentioned in Section 3.1, if you do not see **Data Analysis** under **Data**, you must add in the **Analysis Toolpak** option.)
c. See Figure 3.20. In the *Descriptive Statistics* dialog box, click on the box next to *Input Range*, then select the data and the headings for the Growth and Value variables. Select the options *Labels in First Row* and *Summary Statistics*. Select *Output Range* and enter cell E1. Then click **OK**.

FIGURE 3.20 Excel's Descriptive Statistics dialog box

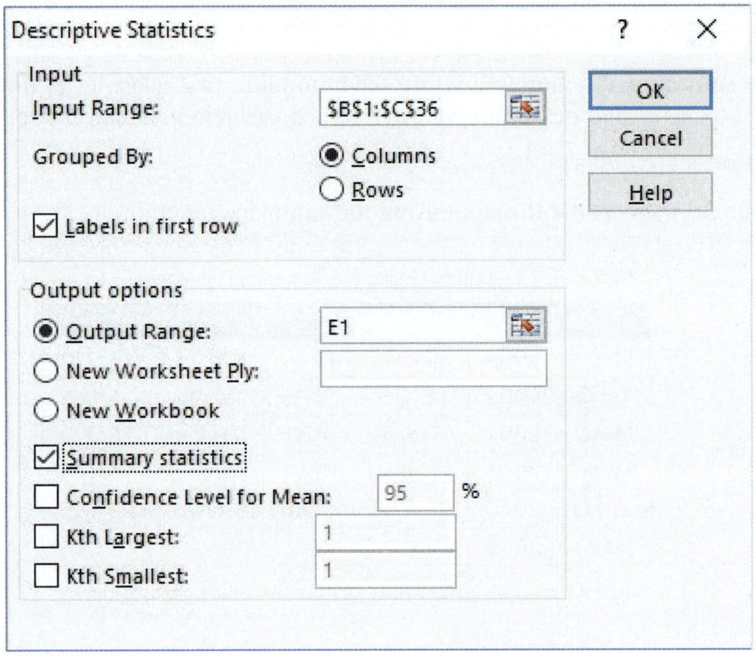

d. Table 3.16 presents the Excel output. If the output is difficult to read, highlight the output and choose **Home > Format > Column > Autofit Selection**. As noted earlier, Excel provides numerous summary measures; we have put the measures of central location in boldface. Note that Excel reports the mode as #N/A, which means no value appears more than once.

Using R

Like Excel, R has many built-in formulas or functions. In R, we denote all function names in **boldface** and all options within a function in *italics*. The first and third columns of Table 3.15 show various descriptive measures and corresponding function names in R.

a. Import the ***Growth_Value*** data into a data frame (table) and label it myData.
b. The **mean** function will return the mean for a specified variable in a data frame. In order to find the mean for the Growth variable, enter:

```
> mean(myData$Growth)
```

And R returns: 15.10743.

TABLE 3.16 Excel's Output Using the Data Analysis Toolpak

Growth		Value	
Mean	**15.10742857**	**Mean**	**11.44457143**
Standard Error	4.026783239	Standard Error	3.028998513
Median	**14.44**	**Median**	**15.09**
Mode	**#N/A**	**Mode**	**#N/A**
Standard Deviation	23.82277091	Standard Deviation	17.91979686
Sample Variance	567.5244138	Sample Variance	321.1191197
Kurtosis	1.064454138	Kurtosis	1.893804308
Skewness	0.02988603	Skewness	−1.007368283
Range	120.38	Range	90.6
Minimum	−40.9	Minimum	−46.52
Maximum	79.48	Maximum	44.08
Sum	528.76	Sum	400.56
Count	35	Count	35

c. The **summary** function will return the minimum, first quartile, median, mean, third quartile, and maximum values for each variable in a data frame. Enter:

```
> summary(myData)
```

Table 3.17 shows the R output using the summary function.

TABLE 3.17 R Output Using the **summary** Function

Year*	Growth	Value
Min. :1984	Min. :−40.90	Min. :−46.520
1st Qu. :1992	1st Qu. : 2.13	1st Qu. : 1.195
Median :2001	Median : 14.44	Median : 15.090
Mean :2001	Mean : 15.11	Mean : 11.445
3rd Qu. :2010	3rd Qu. : 32.00	3rd Qu. : 22.185
Max. :2018	Max. : 79.48	Max. : 44.080

*Note that in this example, the summary statistics for the variable Year are not useful.

Summary

From Tables 3.16 and 3.17 we see that the average return for the Growth mutual fund is greater than the average return for the Value mutual fund, 15.11% > 11.445%. Interestingly, however, the median return for the Value mutual fund is greater than the median return for the Growth fund, 15.09% > 14.44%. This example illustrates why it is useful to examine both the mean and the median when summarizing central location, especially when outliers may be present. Neither variable has a mode.

A Percentile

Recall that the median is the middle observation of a variable; that is, half of the observations fall below this observation and half fall above it. The median is also called the 50th percentile. In many instances, we are interested in a **percentile** other than the 50th percentile. In general, the pth percentile divides a variable into two parts:

- Approximately p percent of the observations are less than the pth percentile.
- Approximately $(100 - p)$ percent of the observations are greater than the pth percentile.

A percentile is technically a measure of location; however, it is also used as a measure of relative position because it is so easy to interpret. For example, suppose you obtained a raw score of 650 on the math portion of the SAT, where scores range from 200 to 800. It may not be readily apparent how you did relative to other students that took the same test. However, if you know that the raw score corresponds to the 75th percentile, then you know that approximately 75% of students had scores lower than your score and approximately 25% of students had scores higher than your score.

Earlier, we found that the median or the 50th percentile for the Growth mutual fund was 14.44%. When we calculate the 25th, the 50th, and the 75th percentiles for a variable, we have effectively divided the data into four equal parts, or quarters. Thus, the 25th percentile is also referred to as the first quartile (Q1), the 50th percentile is referred to as the second quartile (Q2), and the 75th percentile is referred to as the third quartile (Q3).

Software packages, like Excel and R, use different algorithms to calculate percentiles. However, with larger sample sizes, the differences, if any, tend to be negligible. When calculating the *p*th percentile in Excel, we can use the PERCENTILE.INC function. The corresponding command in R is the **quantile** function. These functions are summarized in Table 3.15. However, when we use the **summary** function in R, all quartiles are reported.

> **A PERCENTILE**
>
> In general, the *p*th percentile divides a variable into two parts:
>
> - Approximately *p* percent of the observations are less than the *p*th percentile.
> - Approximately $(100 - p)$ percent of the observations are greater than the *p*th percentile.

EXAMPLE 3.10

Using Table 3.17, interpret the first and the third quartiles for the Growth variable from the introductory case.

SOLUTION:

The first quartile for the Growth variable is 2.13%. Approximately 25% of the returns are less than 2.13%, and approximately 75% of the returns are greater than 2.13%. The third quartile for the Growth variable is 32.00%. Approximately 75% of the returns are less than 32.00%, and approximately 25% of the returns are greater than 32.00%.

Measures of Dispersion

While measures of central location reflect the typical or central value of a variable, they fail to describe the underlying dispersion of the variable. We now discuss several measures of dispersion that gauge the variability of a data set. Each measure is a numerical value that equals zero if all observations are identical and increases as the observations become more diverse.

The Range

The **range** is the simplest measure of dispersion; it is the difference between the maximum and the minimum observations of a variable. The range is not considered a good measure of dispersion because it focuses solely on the extreme observations and ignores every other observation of a variable.

The Interquartile Range

The **interquartile range** (IQR) is the difference between the third quartile and the first quartile, or, equivalently, IQR = Q3 − Q1. We can think of IQR as the range of the middle 50% of the observations of the variable. Even though IQR does not depend on the extreme observations, it does not incorporate all the observations.

The Mean Absolute Deviation

As a starting point, a good measure of dispersion should consider differences of all observations from the mean (or the median when outliers are present). However, if we simply average all differences from the mean, the positives and the negatives will cancel out, even though they both contribute to dispersion, and the resulting average will equal zero. The **mean absolute deviation** (MAD) is an average of the absolute differences between the observations and the mean. For sample observations $x_1, x_2, \ldots, x_n$, the sample MAD is calculated as $\frac{\sum|x_i - \bar{x}|}{n}$. If we have access to population data, then we simply substitute the population mean μ for the sample mean $\bar{x}$ and the population size N for the sample size n.

The Variance and the Standard Deviation

The **variance** and the **standard deviation** are the two most widely used measures of dispersion. Instead of calculating the average of the absolute differences from the mean, as in MAD, we calculate the average of the squared differences from the mean. The squaring of differences from the mean emphasizes larger differences more than smaller ones; MAD weighs large and small differences equally.

The formula for the variance differs depending on whether we have a sample or a population. The sample variance, denoted as s^2, is calculated as $\frac{\sum(x_i - \bar{x})^2}{n-1}$; whereas the population variance, denoted as the Greek letter sigma squared σ^2, is calculated as $\frac{\sum(x_i - \mu)^2}{N}$. Also, whatever the units of the variable, the variance has squared units. In order to return to the original units of measurement, we take the positive square root of s^2 or σ^2, which gives us either the sample standard deviation s or the population standard deviation σ.

Table 3.15 shows the function names for various measures of dispersion in Excel and R. Recall too that Excel's Descriptive Statistics option using the Data Analysis Toolpak provides many summary measures using a single command. For measures of dispersion, Excel's Descriptive Statistics option treats the data as a sample and calculates the sample variance and the sample standard deviation. These values for the Growth and the Value mutual funds are shown in Table 3.16.

MEASURES OF DISPERSION

Measures of dispersion can be summarized as follows.

- The range is the difference between the maximum and the minimum observations. The main weakness of the range is that is ignores all observations except the extremes.
- The interquartile range (IQR) is the difference between the third quartile and the first quartile. The measure does not rely on the extreme observations; however, it does not incorporate all observations.
- The mean absolute deviation (MAD) is an average of the absolute differences between the observations and the mean.
- The variance is an average of the squared differences between the observations and the mean. The standard deviation is the positive square root of the variance.

An Application Using the Mean and the Standard Deviation—The Sharpe Ratio

In general, investments with higher returns also carry higher risk. Investments include financial assets such as stocks, bonds, and mutual funds. The average return represents an investor's reward, whereas variance, or, equivalently, standard deviation, corresponds to risk.

Nobel Laureate William Sharpe developed what he originally called the "reward-to-variability" ratio. However, academics and finance professionals prefer to call it the Sharpe ratio. The Sharpe ratio is often calculated as $\frac{\bar{x}_i - R_f}{s_i}$, where $\bar{x}_i$ is the mean return for investment i, R_f is the mean return for a risk-free asset such as a Treasury bill (T-bill), and s_i is the standard deviation for investment i. The numerator of the Sharpe ratio measures the extra reward that investors receive for the added risk taken—this difference is often called excess return. The higher the Sharpe ratio, the better the investment compensates its investors for risk.

EXAMPLE 3.11

Use the information in Table 3.18 to

a. Compare the risk of investing in Growth versus Value using the standard deviation.

b. Calculate and interpret the Sharpe ratios for Growth and Value. Assume that the return on a 1-year T-bill is 2%.

SOLUTION:

a. Because the standard deviation of Growth is greater than the standard deviation of Value, 23.8228 > 17.9198, Growth is considered riskier than Value.

b. Given that the return on a 1-year T-bill is 2%, $R_f = 2$. Plugging in the values of the relevant means and standard deviations into the Sharpe ratio yields:

$$\text{Sharpe ratio for Growth: } \frac{\bar{x}_i - R_f}{s_i} = \frac{15.1074 - 2}{23.8228} = 0.5502$$

$$\text{Sharpe ratio for Value: } \frac{\bar{x}_i - R_f}{s_i} = \frac{11.4446 - 2}{17.9198} = 0.5270$$

We had earlier shown that the Growth mutual fund had a higher return, which is good, along with a higher standard deviation, which is bad. We can use the Sharpe ratio to make a valid comparison between the funds. The Growth mutual fund provides a higher Sharpe ratio than the Value mutual fund (0.5502 > 0.5270); therefore, the Growth mutual fund offered more reward per unit of risk.

Measures of Shape

In this section, we examine measures of shape, namely, the skewness coefficient and the kurtosis coefficient.

The Skewness Coefficient

Recall from Section 3.1 that a symmetric distribution is one that is a mirror image of itself on both sides of its center. The skewness coefficient measures the degree to which a distribution is not symmetric about its mean. A common way to calculate the **skewness coefficient** is $\frac{n}{(n-1)(n-2)}\sum\left(\frac{x_i - \bar{x}}{s}\right)^3$. When we use Excel's Descriptive Statistics option in its Analysis Toolpak, this is the formula that is applied. R also calculates the skewness coefficient, but it requires the use of a package and the output differs slightly depending on the package that is used.

A symmetric distribution has a skewness coefficient of zero. Thus, the normal distribution has a skewness coefficient of zero. A positively skewed distribution has a positive skewness coefficient, whereas a negatively skewed distribution has a negative skewness coefficient. If two return distributions are the same except for skewness (for example, they have the same mean and standard deviation), investors would prefer the distribution with positive skewness because that distribution implies a greater probability of extremely large gains.

The Kurtosis Coefficient

The **kurtosis coefficient** is a summary measure that tells us whether the tails of the distribution are more or less extreme than the normal distribution. A distribution that has tails that are more extreme than the normal distribution is leptokurtic (*lepto* from the Greek word for slender). A return distribution is often leptokurtic, which means that its tails are longer than the normal distribution—implying the existence of outliers. If a return distribution is in fact leptokurtic, but we assume that it is normally distributed in statistical models, then we will underestimate the likelihood of very bad or very good returns. A platykurtic (*platy* from the Greek word for broad) distribution is one that has shorter tails, or tails that are less extreme, than the normal distribution.

The kurtosis coefficient of a normal distribution is 3.0. A common way to calculate the kurtosis coefficient is $\frac{n}{(n-1)(n-2)(n-3)}\sum\left(\frac{x_i-\bar{x}}{s}\right)^4$. Many statistical packages report **excess kurtosis**, which is calculated as the kurtosis coefficient minus 3. Thus, a normal distribution has excess kurtosis equal to zero. Excel calculates excess kurtosis when we use the Descriptive Statistics option in its Analysis Toolpak. R also calculates the kurtosis coefficient, but again, it requires the use of a package and the output varies depending on the package that is used.

MEASURES OF SHAPE

Measures of shape can be summarized as follows.

- The skewness coefficient measures the degree to which a distribution is not symmetric about its mean. A symmetric distribution has a skewness coefficient of 0. A positively (negatively) skewed distribution has a positive (negative) skewness coefficient.
- The kurtosis coefficient measures whether the tails of a distribution are more or less extreme than the normal distribution. Because the normal distribution has a kurtosis coefficient of 3, it is common to calculate the excess kurtosis of a distribution as the kurtosis coefficient minus 3.

EXAMPLE 3.12

Interpret the skewness and the kurtosis coefficients in Table 3.16 for the Growth and Value variables from the introductory case.

SOLUTION: The skewness coefficient and the (excess) kurtosis coefficient for Growth are 0.0299 and 1.06, respectively. These values imply that the return distribution for Growth is positively skewed, and the distribution has longer tails than the normal distribution. With a skewness coefficient of −1.0074 and a (excess) kurtosis coefficient of 1.8938, the return distribution for Value is negatively skewed, and it too has longer tails than the normal distribution.

Measures of Association

In Section 3.2 we used a scatterplot to visually assess whether two numerical variables had some type of systematic relationship. Here, we present two numerical measures of association that quantify the direction and strength of the linear relationship between two variables, x and y. It is important to point out that these measures are not appropriate when the underlying relationship between the variables is nonlinear.

The Covariance

An objective numerical measure that reveals the direction of the linear relationship between two variables is called the **covariance**. Like variance, the formula for the covariance depends on whether we have a sample or a population. The sample covariance, denoted as s_{xy}, is calculated as $\frac{\Sigma(x_i - \bar{x})(y_i - \bar{y})}{n-1}$. The population covariance, denoted as σ_{xy}, is calculated as $\frac{\Sigma(x_i - \mu_x)(y_i - \mu_y)}{N}$.

The value of the covariance can be negative, positive, or 0.

- If the covariance is negative, then x and y have a negative linear relationship.
- If the covariance is positive, then x and y have a positive linear relationship.
- If the covariance is zero, then x and y have no linear relationship.

The covariance is difficult to interpret because it is sensitive to the units of measurement. That is, the covariance between two variables might be 100 and the covariance between two other variables might be 100,000, yet all we can conclude is that both sets of variables have a positive linear relationship. We cannot comment on the strength of the relationships.

The Correlation Coefficient

An easier measure to interpret is the **correlation coefficient**. It describes both the direction and the strength of the linear relationship between x and y. The sample correlation coefficient, denoted as r_{xy}, is calculated as $\frac{s_{xy}}{s_x s_y}$, where s_{xy} denotes the sample covariance and s_x and s_y denote the sample standard deviations of the variables x and y, respectively. The population correlation coefficient, denoted as ρ_{xy} (the Greek letter rho), is calculated as $\frac{\sigma_{xy}}{\sigma_x \sigma_y}$, where σ_{xy} denotes the population covariance and σ_x and σ_y denote the population standard deviations. The correlation coefficient is unit-free because the units in the numerator cancel with those in the denominator. The value of the correlation coefficient falls between -1 and 1.

- If the correlation coefficient equals -1, then x and y have a perfect negative linear relationship.
- If the correlation coefficient equals 0, then x and y are not linearly related.
- If the correlation coefficient equals 1, then x and y have a perfect positive linear relationship.

Other values for the correlation coefficient must be interpreted with reference to -1, 0, or 1. For instance, a correlation coefficient equal to -0.80 indicates a strong negative relationship, whereas a correlation coefficient equal to 0.12 indicates a weak positive relationship. Table 3.15 shows the function names for the covariance and the correlation coefficient in Excel and R.

> **MEASURES OF ASSOCIATION**
>
> Measures of association can be summarized as follows.
>
> - The covariance between two variables x and y indicates whether they have a negative linear relationship, a positive linear relationship, or no linear relationship.
> - The correlation coefficient between two variables x and y indicates the direction and the strength of the linear relationship.

EXAMPLE 3.13

FILE
Growth_Value

Using Excel and R, calculate the correlation coefficient between the Growth and the Value variables from the introductory case. Then summarize the results.

SOLUTION:

Using Excel

a. Open the ***Growth_Value*** data file.

b. Note that the data for the Growth variable are in cells B2 through B36 (array1) and the data for the Value variable are in cells C2 through C36 (array2). We enter =CORREL(B2:B36, C2:C36), and Excel returns 0.6572.

Using R

a. Import the ***Growth_Value*** data into a data frame (table) and label it myData.

b. The **cor** function will return a matrix that lists the correlation coefficient for each pairing of variables in the data frame. Enter:

```
> cor(myData)
```

And R returns:

	Year	Growth	Value
Year	1.00000000	−0.08071914	−0.07909256
Growth	−0.08071914	1.00000000	**0.65719566**
Value	−0.07909256	**0.65719566**	1.00000000

We are interested in the correlation coefficient between Growth and Value, which appears twice in this matrix (see boldface values). We also see the value 1 along the diagonal of the matrix, which measures the correlation between each variable and itself. The correlation coefficient between Year and Growth and the correlation coefficient between Year and Value are meaningless in this application.

Summary

The correlation coefficient between Growth and Value of 0.6572 indicates that the variables have a moderate positive linear relationship. In other words, on average, when one fund's return is above its mean, the other fund's return tends to be above its mean, and vice versa. In order to diversify risk, an investor is often advised to invest in assets (such as stocks, bonds, and mutual funds) whose returns are not strongly correlated. If asset returns do not have a strong positive correlation, then if one investment does poorly, the other may still do well.

SYNOPSIS OF INTRODUCTORY CASE

Growth investing and value investing are two fundamental styles in stock and mutual fund investing. Proponents of growth investing believe that companies that are growing faster than their peers are trendsetters and will be able to maintain their superior growth. By investing in the stocks of these companies, they expect their investment to grow at a rate faster than the overall stock market. By comparison, value investors focus on the stocks of companies that are trading at a discount relative to the overall market or a specific sector. Investors of value stocks believe that these stocks are undervalued and that their price will increase once their true value is recognized by

Ingram Publishing/Getty Images

other investors. The debate between growth and value investing is age-old, and which style dominates depends on the sample period used for the analysis.

An analysis of annual return data for Fidelity's Growth and Value mutual funds for the years 1984 through 2018 provides important information for an investor trying to determine whether to invest in a growth mutual fund, a value mutual fund, or both types of mutual funds. Over this period, the mean return for the Growth fund of 15.11% is greater than the mean return for the Value fund of 11.44%. While the mean return typically represents the reward of investing, it does not incorporate the risk of investing. Standard deviation tends to be the most common measure of risk with financial data. Because the standard deviation for the Growth fund (23.82%) is greater than the standard deviation for the Value fund (17.92%), the Growth fund is likelier to have returns farther above and below its mean. Finally, given a risk-free rate of 2%, the Sharpe ratio for the Growth fund is 0.5502, compared to that for the Value fund of 0.5270, indicating that the Growth fund provides more reward per unit of risk. Assuming that the behavior of these returns will continue, the investor will favor investing in Growth over Value. A commonly used disclaimer, however, states that past performance is no guarantee of future results. Because the two styles often complement each other, it might be advisable for the investor to add diversity to his portfolio by using them together.

EXERCISES 3.4

Applications

39. **FILE** ***Corporations.*** Monthly stock prices (in $) for Corporation A and Corporation B are collected for five years. A portion of the data is shown in the accompanying table.

Date	A	B
1/1/2014	47.95	65.59
2/1/2014	52.95	65.61
⋮	⋮	⋮
12/1/2018	66.09	92.64

a. Calculate the mean and the standard deviation for each corporation's stock price.

b. Which corporation had the higher average stock price over the time period? Which corporation's stock price had greater dispersion as measured by the standard deviation?

40. **FILE** ***HD_Lowe's.*** Annual revenues (in $ millions) for Home Depot and Lowe's Corporation are collected for 13 years. A portion of the data is shown in the accompanying table.

Year	HD	Lowe's
2006	77019	43243
2007	79022	46927
⋮	⋮	⋮
2018	100904	68619

a. For each company, calculate the mean and the median revenues for this time period. Which company had higher average revenues?

b. For each company, calculate the variance and the standard deviation for this time period. Which company's revenues had more dispersion as measured by the standard deviation?

41. **FILE** ***Prime.*** The accompanying table shows a portion of the annual expenditures (in $) for 100 Amazon Prime customers.

Customer	Expenditures
1	1272
2	1089
⋮	⋮
100	1389

a. Find the mean and the median of annual expenditures.

b. Calculate and interpret the first quartile and the third quartile for annual expenditures. [Note: If you are using Excel, use the PERCENTILE.INC function to calculate a percentile.]

42. **FILE** ***Gas_2019.*** The following table lists a portion of the average price (in $) for a gallon of gas for the 50 states and the District of Columbia as reported by AAA Gas Prices on January 2, 2019.

State	Price
Alaska	3.06
Alabama	1.94
⋮	⋮
Wyoming	2.59

a. Find the mean and the median for gas price.

b. Calculate and interpret the first quartile and the third quartile for gas price. [Note: If you are using Excel, use the PERCENTILE.INC function to calculate a percentile.]

c. Calculate the sample variance and the sample standard deviation.

43. **FILE** ***Rent.*** The following table shows a portion of the monthly rent and square footage for 40 rentals in a large college town.

House	Rent	Sqft
1	645	500
2	675	648
⋮	⋮	⋮
40	2400	2700

a. Calculate the mean and the standard deviation for monthly rent.

b. Calculate the mean and the standard deviation for square footage.

44. Refer to the previous exercise for a description of the data.

a. The skewness and (excess) kurtosis coefficients for monthly rent are 1.0198 and 0.4790, respectively. Interpret these values.

b. The skewness and (excess) kurtosis coefficients for square footage are 3.0573 and 12.3484, respectively. Interpret these values.

45. **FILE** ***Highway.*** Many environmental groups and politicians are suggesting a return to the federal 55-mile-per-hour (mph) speed limit on America's highways. They argue that not only will a lower national speed limit reduce greenhouse emissions, it will also increase traffic safety. A researcher believes that a lower speed limit will not increase traffic safety because he feels that traffic safety is based on the variability of the speeds with which people are driving, rather than the average speed. The researcher gathers the speeds of 40 cars from a highway with a speed limit of 55 mph (Highway 1) and the speeds of 40 cars from a highway with a speed limit of 65 mph (Highway 2). A portion of the data is shown in the accompanying table.

Car	Highway 1	Highway 2
1	60	70
2	55	65
⋮	⋮	⋮
40	52	65

a. Calculate the mean and the median for each highway.

b. Calculate the standard deviation for each highway.

c. Do the data support the researcher's belief? Explain.

46. **FILE** ***Firms.*** Monthly stock prices (in $) for Firm A and Firm B are collected for five years. A portion of the data is shown in the accompanying table.

Date	A	B
1/1/2014	63.85	75.56
2/1/2014	66.04	78.68
⋮	⋮	⋮
12/1/2018	89.98	126.38

a. Calculate the mean, the variance, and the standard deviation for each firm's stock price.

b. Which firm had the higher average stock price over the time period?

c. Which firm's stock price had greater dispersion as measured by the standard deviation?

47. **FILE** ***Country.*** The accompanying table shows a portion of the annual returns (in %) for a mutual fund focusing on investments in Latin America and a mutual fund focusing on investments in Canada from 1994 through 2018.

Year	Latin America	Canada
1994	−23.17	−11.98
1995	−16.46	19.39
⋮	⋮	⋮
2018	−10.37	−14.29

a. Which fund had the higher reward over this time period? Explain.

b. Which fund was riskier over this time period? Explain.

c. Given a risk-free rate of 2%, which fund has the higher Sharpe ratio? What does this ratio imply?

48. Refer to the previous exercise for a description of the data.

a. The skewness and (excess) kurtosis coefficients for the Latin America fund are 0.3215 and −0.7026, respectively. Interpret these values.

b. The skewness and (excess) kurtosis coefficients for the Canada fund are −0.2531 and 0.0118, respectively. Interpret these values.

49. **FILE** ***Tech_Energy.*** The accompanying table shows a portion of the annual returns (in %) for a technology mutual fund and an energy mutual fund from 1982 through 2018.

Year	Technology	Energy
1982	56.32	−12.16
1983	52.47	20.27
⋮	⋮	⋮
2018	−8.79	−24.92

a. Which fund had the higher average return?

b. Which fund was riskier over this time period?

c. Given a risk-free rate of 2%, which fund had the higher Sharpe ratio? What does this ratio imply?

50. **FILE** ***Test_Scores.*** The accompanying data file shows midterm and final grades for 32 students. Calculate and interpret the correlation coefficient.

51. **FILE** ***Life_Obesity.*** The accompanying data file shows life expectancies (in years) and obesity rates (in %) for the 50 states and the District of Columbia. Calculate and interpret the correlation coefficient.

52. FILE ***Happiness_Age.*** Many attempts have been made to relate happiness with various factors. A 2018 study in the *Journal of Happiness* relates happiness with age and finds that holding everything else constant, people are least happy when they are in their mid-40s. The accompanying data file shows a respondent's age and his/her perception of well-being on a scale from 0 to 100.

a. Calculate and interpret the correlation coefficient between age and happiness.

b. Construct a scatterplot to point out a flaw with the correlation analysis in part a.

3.5 DETECTING OUTLIERS

LO 3.6

Use boxplots and z-scores to identify outliers

Extremely large or small observations for a variable are referred to as outliers, which can unduly influence summary statistics, such as the mean or the standard deviation. In a small sample, the impact of outliers is particularly pronounced. Sometimes, outliers may just be due to random variations, in which case the relevant observations should remain in the data set. Alternatively, outliers may indicate bad data due to incorrectly recorded observations or incorrectly included observations in the data set. In such cases, the relevant observations should be corrected or simply deleted from the data set. However, there are no universally agreed upon methods for treating outliers. Various approaches are used across different disciplines and applications.

In any event, it is important to be able to identify potential outliers so that one can take corrective actions, if needed. In this section, we first construct a boxplot, which is an effective tool for identifying outliers. A series of boxplots are also useful when comparing similar information for a variable gathered at another place or time. Another method for detecting outliers is to use z-scores.

A Boxplot

A common way to quickly summarize a variable is to use a five-number summary. A five-number summary shows the minimum value, the quartiles (Q1, Q2, and Q3), and the maximum value of the variable. A **boxplot**, also referred to as a box-and-whisker plot, is a convenient way to graphically display the five-number summary of a variable. In general, a boxplot is constructed as follows:

- Plot the five-number summary values in ascending order on the horizontal axis.
- Draw a box encompassing the first and third quartiles.
- Draw a dashed vertical line in the box at the median.
- Calculate the interquartile range (IQR). Recall that IQR = Q3 − Q1. Draw a line ("whisker") that extends from Q1 to the minimum value that is not farther than 1.5 × IQR from Q1. Similarly, draw a line that extends from Q3 to the maximum value that is not farther than 1.5 × IQR from Q3.
- Use an asterisk (or other symbol) to indicate observations that are farther than 1.5 × IQR from the box. These observations are considered outliers.

Consider the boxplot in Figure 3.21. The left whisker extends from Q1 to the minimum value (Min) because Min is not farther than 1.5 × IQR from Q1. The right whisker, on the other hand, does not extend from Q3 to the maximum value because there is an observation that is farther than 1.5 × IQR from Q3. The asterisk indicates that this observation is considered an outlier.

A boxplot is also used to informally gauge the shape of the distribution. Symmetry is implied if the median is in the center of the box and the left and right whiskers are equidistant from their respective quartiles. If the median is left of center and the right whisker is longer than the left whisker, then the distribution is positively skewed.

Similarly, if the median is right of center and the left whisker is longer than the right whisker, then the distribution is negatively skewed. If outliers exist, we need to include them when comparing the lengths of the left and right whiskers.

From Figure 3.21, we note that the median is located to the left of center and that an outlier exists on the right side. Here the right whisker is longer than the left whisker, and if the outlier is included, then the right whisker becomes even longer. This indicates that the underlying distribution is positively skewed.

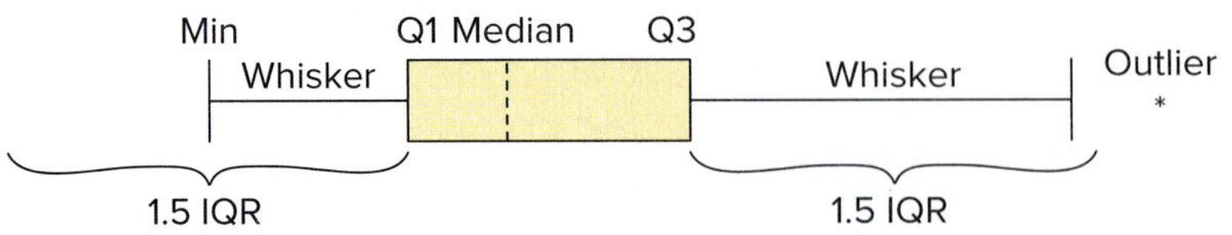

FIGURE 3.21 An example of a boxplot

Unfortunately, Excel does not provide a simple and straightforward way to construct a boxplot; however, R does. Consider the following example.

FILE
Growth_Value

EXAMPLE 3.14

Use R to construct a boxplot for the Growth and Value variables from the introductory case. Interpret the results.

SOLUTION:

Using R

a. Import the ***Growth_Value*** data into a data frame (table) and label it myData.

b. We use the **boxplot** function. For options within the function, we use *main* to provide a title, *xlab* to label the x-axis, *names* to label each variable, *horizontal* to construct a horizontal boxplot (as opposed to a vertical boxplot), and *col* to give color to the IQR portion. Enter:

```
> boxplot(myData$Growth, myData$Value, main= "Boxplots for Growth
and Value", xlab="Annual Returns, 1984-2018 (in percent)", names
=c("Growth","Value"), horizontal = TRUE, col="gold")
```

Figure 3.22 shows the output that R returns.

FIGURE 3.22 Boxplots for Growth and Value

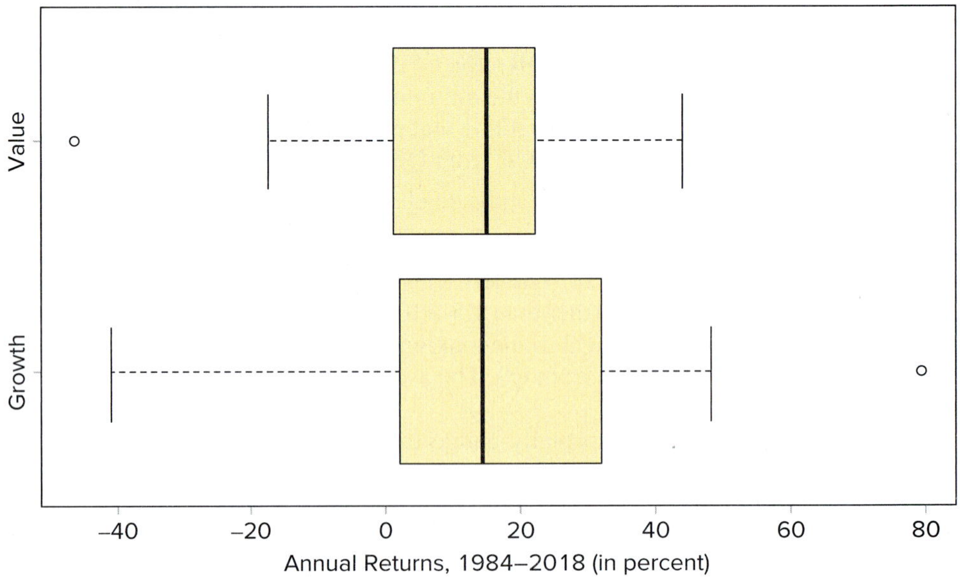

c. To treat outliers, we use the *out* parameter in the **boxplot** function to extract and store their values in a new data frame (table). Enter:

```
> outliersGrowth <- boxplot(myData$Growth)$out
> outliersValue <- boxplot(myData$Value)$out
```

Verify that there is one outlier (79.48) for the Growth variable and one outlier (−46.52) for the Value variable.

d. One approach to treat outliers in R is to replace them with NAs, which represent missing values. The **%in%** operator is for value matching, and we use it here to find the outliers in the Growth and Value variables. We then use the **ifelse** function to replace the outliers with NAs and store updated data in two new variables, newGrowth and newValue. Enter:

```
> myData$newGrowth <- ifelse(myData$Growth %in% outliersGrowth,
NA, myData$Growth)
> myData$newValue <- ifelse(myData$Value %in% outliersValue, NA,
myData$Value)
```

Verify that the newGrowth observation for year 1999 and the newValue observation for year 2008 are now NAs. Note: With outliers replaced with NAs, we have the option to implement the omission and the imputation strategies for treatment of missing values described in Section 2.4.

e. Once the outliers are replaced with NAs, we can recalculate summary measures. We use the **summary** function to compare the means of the original variables with outliers and the new variables without outliers. Enter:

```
> summary(myData)
```

Verify that the means of the newGrowth and newValue variables are 13.210 and 13.149, respectively, and that they are different from the means of the original Growth and Value variables.

Summary

The median returns for the two mutual funds are indicated by the bold and wider vertical lines in Figure 3.22. As we already found, the median returns for the two funds are similar (15.09% for Value versus 14.44% for Growth). However, Value has an outlier on the left-hand side, as indicated by the circle, while Growth has an outlier on the right-hand side.

For Value, the outlier on the left-hand side coupled with a median that falls to the right of center in the IQR box suggests that this distribution is negatively skewed. This is consistent with the negative skewness coefficient that was calculated for this variable in Section 3.4.

On the other hand, Growth has an outlier on the right-hand side with a median that falls to the left of center in the IQR box. The distribution of Growth is positively skewed. Again, this is consistent with the positive skewness coefficient that was calculated for this variable in Section 3.4.

z-Scores

The mean and the standard deviation are the most extensively used measures of central location and dispersion, respectively. Unlike the mean, it is not easy to interpret the standard deviation intuitively. All we can say is that a low value for the standard deviation indicates that the observations are close to the mean, while a high value for the standard deviation indicates that the observations are more dispersed from the mean.

We will first use the empirical rule to make precise statements regarding the percentage of observations that fall within a specified number of standard deviations from the mean.

We then compute a z-score that measures the relative location of an observation and indicates whether it is an outlier.

The Empirical Rule

If the observations are drawn from a relatively symmetric and bell-shaped distribution—perhaps determined by an inspection of its histogram—then we can make precise statements about the percentage of observations that fall within certain intervals. Symmetry and bell-shaped are characteristics of the normal distribution, a topic that we discuss in more detail in Chapter 4. The normal distribution is often used as an approximation for many real-world applications. Given a sample mean $\bar{x}$, a sample standard deviation s, and a relatively symmetric and bell-shaped distribution, the **empirical rule** states that

- Approximately 68% of all observations fall in the interval $\bar{x} \pm s$,
- Approximately 95% of all observations fall in the interval $\bar{x} \pm 2s$, and
- Almost all observations fall in the interval $\bar{x} \pm 3s$.

Figure 3.23 illustrates the empirical rule.

FIGURE 3.23 Graphical representation of the empirical rule

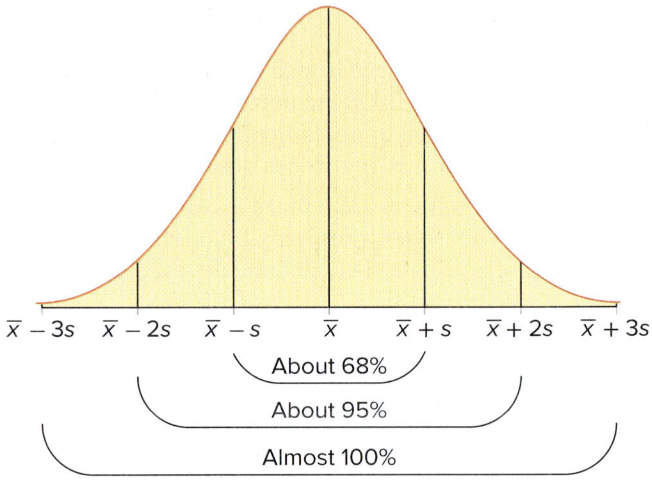

EXAMPLE 3.15

A large lecture class has 280 students. The professor has announced that the mean score on an exam is 74 with a standard deviation of 8. The distribution of scores is bell-shaped.

a. Approximately how many students scored within 58 and 90?

b. Approximately how many students scored more than 90?

SOLUTION:

a. The score 58 is two standard deviations below the mean ($\bar{x} - 2s = 74 - (2 \times 8) = 58$), while the score 90 is two standard deviations above the mean ($\bar{x} + 2s = 74 + (2 \times 8) = 90$). For a bell-shaped distribution, the empirical rule states that approximately 95% of the observations fall within two standard deviations of the mean. Therefore, about 95% of 280 students, or $0.95 \times 280 = 266$ students, scored within 58 and 90.

b. We know that the score 90 is two standard deviations above the mean. Because approximately 95% of the observations fall within two standard deviations of the mean, we can infer that 5% of the observations fall outside the interval. Therefore, given the symmetry of the distribution, about half of 5%, or 2.5%, of 280 students scored above 90. Equivalently, about seven students (0.025×280), scored above 90 on the exam. If the professor uses a cutoff score above 90 for an A, then only seven students in the class are expected to get an A.

Calculating *z*-Scores

It is often instructive to use the mean and the standard deviation to find the relative location of an observation. Suppose a student gets a score of 90 on her accounting exam and a score of 90 on her marketing exam. While the student's scores are identical in both classes, her relative position in these classes may be quite different. What if the mean score was different in the classes? Even with the same mean scores, what if the standard deviation was different in the classes? Both the mean and the standard deviation are needed to find the relative position of this student in both classes.

We use the **z-score** to find the relative position of an observation by dividing the difference of the observation from the mean by the standard deviation, or, equivalently, $z = \frac{x - \bar{x}}{s}$. A z-score is a unitless measure. It measures the distance of an observation from the mean in terms of standard deviations. For example, a z-score of two implies that the observation is two standard deviations above the mean. Similarly, a z-score of -1.5 implies that the observation is 1.5 standard deviations below the mean.

Converting observations into z-scores is also called **standardizing** the observations. Standardization is a common technique used in data analytics when dealing with variables measured using different scales. We will revisit this topic in Chapter 8 to discuss the use of standardization techniques in data mining.

EXAMPLE 3.16

The mean and the standard deviation of scores on an accounting exam are 74 and eight, respectively. The mean and the standard deviation of scores on a marketing exam are 78 and 10, respectively. Find the z-scores for a student who scores 90 in both classes.

SOLUTION: The z-score in the accounting class is $z = \frac{90 - 74}{8} = 2$. Similarly, the z-score in the marketing class is $z = \frac{90 - 78}{10} = 1.2$. Therefore, the student has fared relatively better in accounting because she is two standard deviations above the mean, as compared to marketing, where she is only 1.2 standard deviations above the mean.

If the distribution of a variable is relatively symmetric and bell-shaped, we can also use z-scores to detect outliers. Because almost all observations fall within three standard deviations of the mean, it is common to treat an observation as an outlier if its z-score is more than 3 or less than -3. Such observations must be reviewed to determine if they should remain in the data set.

EXAMPLE 3.17

Table 3.18 shows the minimum and maximum observations as well as the means and standard deviations for the Growth and Value variables from the introductory case. Calculate the z-scores for the minimum and the maximum observations for each variable. Are the results consistent with the boxplots constructed in Figure 3.22? Explain.

TABLE 3.18 Summary Statistics for the Growth and Value Variables (in %)

Fund	Minimum	Maximum	Mean	Standard Deviation
Growth	−40.90	79.48	15.1074	23.8228
Value	−46.52	44.08	11.4446	17.9198

SOLUTION: For Growth, the z-scores for the minimum and the maximum observations are:

$$\text{Minimum: } z = \frac{-40.90 - 15.1074}{23.8228} = -2.3510$$

$$\text{Maximum: } z = \frac{79.48 - 15.1074}{23.8228} = 2.7021$$

For Value, the z-scores for the minimum and the maximum observations are:

$$\text{Minimum: } z = \frac{-46.92 - 11.4446}{17.9198} = -3.2347$$

$$\text{Maximum: } z = \frac{44.08 - 11.4446}{17.9198} = 1.8212$$

For Growth, because the absolute value of both z-scores is less than 3, it would suggest that there are no outliers for the Growth variable. However, the boxplot in Figure 3.22 indicates that there is an outlier. How do we resolve this apparent inconsistency? Remember that z-scores are reliable indicators of outliers when the distribution is relatively bell-shaped and symmetric. Because the boxplot indicates that the Growth variable is positively skewed, we are better served identifying outliers in this case with a boxplot. For Value, the minimum observation is identified as an outlier in the boxplot as well as by its z-score with a value of −3.2347.

IDENTIFYING OUTLIERS

- A boxplot is a convenient way to graphically display the five-number summary of a variable. If outliers are present, then they are indicated as asterisks (or another symbol) that are farther than 1.5 × IQR from the box.
- The z-score measures the relative position of an observation within a distribution and is calculated as $z = \frac{x - \bar{x}}{s}$. If the distribution of a variable is relatively symmetric and bell-shaped, then it is common to treat an observation as an outlier if its z-score is more than 3 or less than −3.

EXERCISES 3.5

Applications

53. Consider the following boxplot.

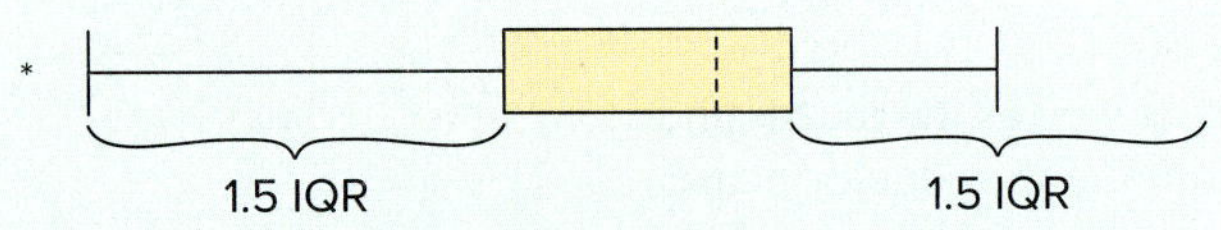

a. Does the boxplot indicate possible outliers in the data?

b. Comment on the skewness of the underlying distribution.

54. Consider the following boxplot.

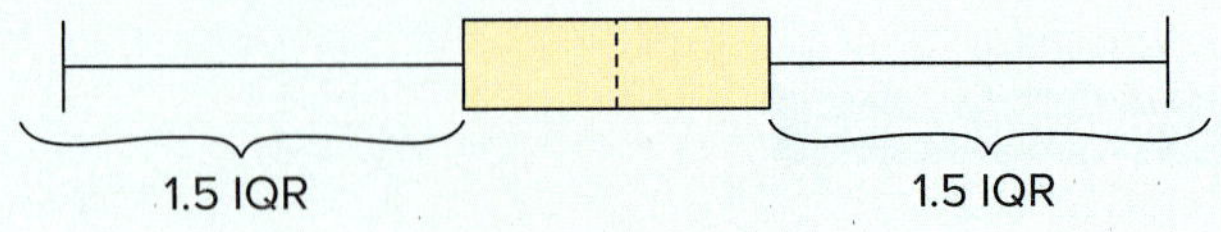

a. Does the boxplot indicate possible outliers in the data?

b. Comment on the skewness of the underlying distribution.

55. Consider the following five-point summary for a variable that was obtained using 200 observations.

Min	Q1	Median	Q3	Max
34	54	66	78	98

a. Interpret Q1 and Q3.

b. Calculate the interquartile range. Determine whether any outliers exist.

c. Is the distribution symmetric? If not, comment on its skewness.

56. Consider the following five-point summary for a variable that was obtained using 500 observations.

Min	Q1	Median	Q3	Max
125	200	300	550	1300

a. Interpret Q1 and Q3.
b. Calculate the interquartile range. Determine whether any outliers exist.
c. Is the distribution symmetric? If not, comment on its skewness.

57. A sample of the salaries of assistant professors on the business faculty at a local university revealed a mean income of $100,000 with a standard deviation of $10,000. Assume that salaries follow a bell-shaped distribution. Use the empirical rule to answer the following questions.
a. Approximately what percentage of the salaries fall between $90,000 and $110,000?
b. Approximately what percentage of the salaries fall between $80,000 and $120,000?
c. Approximately what percentage of the salaries are greater than $120,000?

58. It is often assumed that IQ scores follow a bell-shaped distribution with a mean of 100 and a standard deviation of 16. Use the empirical rule to answer the following questions.
a. Approximately what percentage of scores are between 84 and 116?
b. Approximately what percentage of scores are less than 68?
c. Approximately what percentage of scores are more than 116?

59. The historical returns on a portfolio had an average return of 8% and a standard deviation of 6%. Assume returns on the portfolio follow a bell-shaped distribution. Use the empirical rule to answer the following questions.
a. Approximately what percentage of returns were between 2% and 14%?
b. Approximately what percentage of returns were greater than 14%?
c. Approximately what percentage of returns were below −4%?

60. On average, an American professional football game lasts about three hours, even though the ball is actually in play only 11 minutes. Assume that game times follow a bell-shaped distribution and that the standard deviation is 0.4 hour. Use the empirical rule to answer the following questions.
a. Approximately what percentage of games last between 2.2 hours and 3.8 hours?
b. Approximately what percentage of games last longer than 3.4 hours?
c. Approximately what percentage of games last less than 2.2 hours?

61. **FILE** ***Prime.*** The accompanying data file shows the annual expenditures (Expenditures in $) for 100 Amazon Prime customers.
a. Construct a boxplot for the Expenditures variable. Does the boxplot suggest that outliers exist?
b. Use *z*-scores to determine if there are any outliers for the Expenditures variable. Are your results consistent with part a? Explain why or why not.

62. **FILE** ***Debt.*** The accompanying data file shows the average monthly debt payments (Debt in $) for residents of 26 metropolitan areas.
a. Construct a boxplot for the Debt variable. Does the boxplot suggest that outliers exist?
b. Use *z*-scores to determine if there are any outliers for the Debt variable. Are your results consistent with part a? Explain why or why not.

63. **FILE** ***Gas_2019.*** The accompanying data file shows the average price of gas (Price in $ per gallon) for the 50 states during January 2019.
a. Construct a boxplot for the Price variable. Does the boxplot suggest that outliers exist?
b. Use *z*-scores to determine if there are any outliers for the Price variable. Are your results consistent with part a? Explain why or why not.
c. Use the information from the boxplot to replace outliers with NAs. What is the mean of the average price of gas without the outliers?

64. **FILE** ***Tech_Energy.*** The accompanying data file shows the annual return (in %) for Fidelity's Technology and Energy mutual funds from 1982 through 2018.
a. Construct a boxplot for the Technology variable. Does the boxplot suggest that outliers exist?
b. Use *z*-scores to determine if there are any outliers for the Technology variable. Are your results consistent with part a? Explain why or why not.
c. Construct a boxplot for the Energy variable. Does the boxplot suggest that outliers exist?
d. Use *z*-scores to determine if there are any outliers for the Energy variable. Are your results consistent with part c? Explain why or why not.
e. Use the information from the two boxplots to replace outliers with NAs. What are the new averages for the Technology and Energy variables?

3.6 WRITING WITH BIG DATA

When confronted with a very large data set, a necessary first step for any analysis is to convert the raw data into a more meaningful form. Tabular and graphical methods as well as summary measures prove very useful. Consider the following big data case.

Case Study

FILE
House_Price

An investor currently owns real estate in the college town of Blacksburg, Virginia—home to the Virginia Tech Hokies. He would like to expand his holdings by purchasing similar rental property in either Athens, Georgia, or Chapel Hill, North Carolina. As a preliminary step, he would like information on house prices in these two areas. He is interested in properties that have at least two bedrooms and that are listed for less than $1,000,000. The following report will summarize previous sales that have satisfied these criteria.

Sample Report – Investing in College Town Real Estate

kali9/Getty Images

There are a number of reasons why you might consider investing in a rental property near a university. First, there's a large pool of renters, including students, faculty, and staff. Second, because many universities are unable to house their students beyond freshman year, students offer a steady stream of rental demand. Finally, university towns tend to be filled with restaurants, shopping, and nightlife. All of these factors can make it easier for you to market your property.

The following report examines house prices in Athens, Georgia—home to the University of Georgia Bulldogs—and Chapel Hill, North Carolina—home to the University of North Carolina Tar Heels. The sample consists of 293 house sales in Athens and 351 house sales in Chapel Hill. In addition, all houses in the sample had at least two bedrooms and sold for less than $1,000,000. Table 3.19 provides the most relevant summary measures for the analysis.

TABLE 3.19 Summary Measures for House Prices (in $) in Athens and Chapel Hill

Summary Measure	Athens, GA	Chapel Hill, NC
Mean	219,671	429,152
Median	177,500	395,000
Minimum	41,125	105,000
Maximum	910,000	950,000
Standard deviation	147,648	186,762
Coefficient of variation	0.67	0.44
Number of houses	293	351

The average house price in Athens is $219,671, as opposed to $429,152 in Chapel Hill, a difference of almost $210,000. In Athens, the median house price is $177,500, suggesting that half of the house prices are below this value and half are above this value. The corresponding value in Chapel Hill is $395,000. The difference in medians between these two cities is close to $218,000. In both cities, the median is quite a bit less than the mean, which implies that outliers, some extremely high house prices in this case, are likely present.

While the mean and the median represent where house prices tend to cluster, they do not relay information about the variability in house prices. Generally, standard deviation is used as a measure of variability. The standard deviation for house prices in Chapel Hill is greater than the standard deviation for house prices in Athens ($186,762 > $147,648), suggesting that, compared to Athens, house prices in Chapel Hill are more dispersed from the mean.

Table 3.20 shows the relative frequency distribution for the house prices in both cities. The relative frequency distribution reinforces the findings from the summary measures, that is, house prices in Athens are more affordable than houses in Chapel Hill. In Athens, 51% of the prices fell in the range \$100,000 to \$200,000, but only 9% of the prices in Chapel Hill fell in this range. Moreover, 91% of houses in Athens versus only 51% of houses in Chapel Hill sold for less than \$400,000.

TABLE 3.20 Frequency Distribution for House Prices in Athens and Chapel Hill

Interval (in \$)	Athens, GA	Chapel Hill, NC
$0 < x \leq 100{,}000$	0.11	0.00
$100{,}000 < x \leq 200{,}000$	0.51	0.09
$200{,}000 < x \leq 300{,}000$	0.19	0.17
$300{,}000 < x \leq 400{,}000$	0.10	0.25
$400{,}000 < x \leq 500{,}000$	0.03	0.17
$500{,}000 < x \leq 600{,}000$	0.03	0.14
$600{,}000 < x \leq 700{,}000$	0.02	0.07
$700{,}000 < x \leq 800{,}000$	0.00	0.07
$800{,}000 < x \leq 900{,}000$	0.01	0.03
$900{,}000 < x \leq 1{,}000{,}000$	0.00	0.01

Finally, Figure 3.24 shows the boxplots of house prices for each city. The boxplots reveal two more major points with respect to house prices in these two cities:

- In each boxplot, the median is off-center within the box, being located to the left of center.
- In each boxplot, there are outliers on the right side. However, there are far fewer outliers in the Chapel Hill distribution as compared to the Athens distribution.

These two observations suggest that both distributions are positively skewed. This implies that the bulk of the house prices falls in the lower end of the distribution, and there are relatively few very-high-priced houses.

FIGURE 3.24 Boxplots of house prices in Athens, Georgia, and Chapel Hill, North Carolina

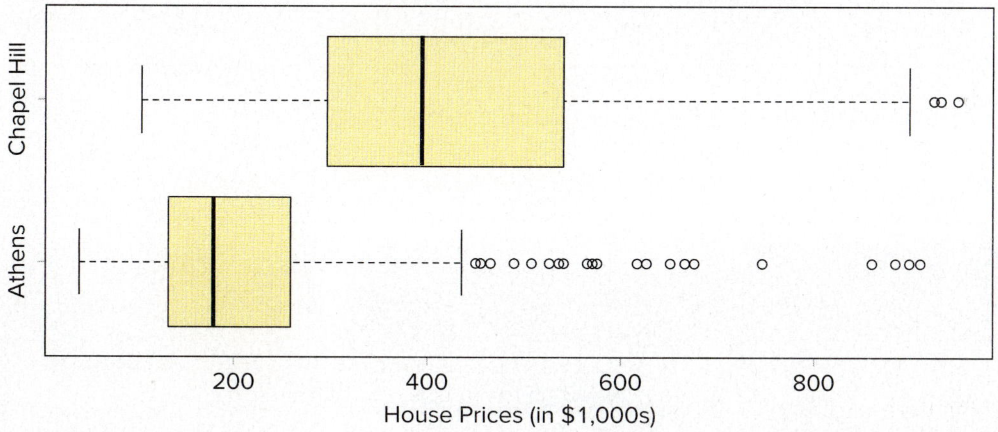

This report summarizes house prices in Athens, Georgia, and Chapel Hill, North Carolina. On average, houses in Chapel Hill are almost twice as expensive as those in Athens. Moreover, if outliers are removed from the analysis, house prices in Athens are less variable than house prices in Chapel Hill. However, before any investor purchases property in either city, many other factors should be considered, such as the strength of the rental market and average income in each city.

Suggested Case Studies

Tabular and graphical methods as well as summary measures prove very useful when analyzing the big data that accompanies this text. Here are some suggestions.

Report 3.1 FILE ***House_Price.*** Perform a similar analysis to the one conducted in this section, but choose two other college towns.

Report 3.2 FILE ***College_Admissions.*** Use tabular and graphical methods as well as summary measures to examine the SAT scores of those students who were admitted to the School of Business & Economics versus those students who were admitted to the School of Arts & Letters.

Report 3.3 FILE ***Longitudinal_Survey.*** Use tabular and graphical methods as well as summary measures to examine the weight of a respondent depending on whether or not the respondent is an outgoing or a shy individual.

Report 3.4 FILE ***TechSales_Reps.*** Use tabular and graphical methods as well as summary measures to examine the salaries of sales representatives depending on their personality types and gender in the software and hardware groups.

4 Probability and Probability Distributions

LEARNING OBJECTIVES

After reading this chapter, you should be able to:

LO **4.1** **Describe probability concepts and the rules of probability.**

LO **4.2** **Apply the total probability rule and Bayes' theorem.**

LO **4.3** **Describe a discrete random variable and its probability distribution.**

LO **4.4** **Calculate probabilities for binomial and Poisson distributions.**

LO **4.5** **Describe the normal distribution and calculate its associated probabilities.**

Every day we make choices about issues in the presence of uncertainty. By figuring out the chances of various events, we are better prepared to make the more desirable choices. For example, given the weather forecast, we determine whether we should wear a jacket or carry an umbrella. Similarly, retailers tweak their sales force in anticipation of an increase or decrease in shoppers, and the Federal Reserve adjusts interest rates based on its anticipation of growth and inflation. This chapter presents the essential probability tools needed to frame and address many real-world issues involving uncertainty.

We extend our discussion about probability by introducing the concept of a random variable. A random variable summarizes the results of an experiment in terms of numerical values and can be classified as discrete or continuous depending on the range of values that it assumes. A discrete random variable assumes a countable number of distinct values, whereas a continuous random variable is characterized by uncountable values. Finally, we discuss two widely used discrete probability distributions, namely the binomial and the Poisson distributions. We also discuss the normal distribution, which is the most extensively used continuous probability distribution and is the cornerstone of statistical inference.

INTRODUCTORY CASE

Linking Support for Legalizing Marijuana with Age Group

Support for marijuana legalization in the United States has grown remarkably over the past few decades. In 1969, when the question was first presented, only 12% of Americans were in favor of its legalization. This support increased to over 25% by the late 1970s. While support was stagnant from 1981 to 1997, the turn of the century brought a renewed interest in its legalization, with the percentage of Americans in favor exceeding 30% by 2000 and 40% by 2009.

Alexis Lewis works for a drug policy institute that focuses on science, health, and human rights. She is analyzing the demographic breakdown of marijuana supporters. Using results from a Pew Research Center survey conducted from August 23-September 2, 2016, she has found that support for marijuana legalization varies considerably depending on a person's age group. Alexis compiles information on support based on age group, as shown in Table 4.1.

TABLE 4.1 Percentage Support for Legalizing Marijuana by Age Group

Age Group	Support
Millennial (18–35)	71%
Generation X (36–51)	57
Baby Boomer (52–70)	56
Silent (71–88)	33

Alexis understands that an important factor determining the fate of marijuana legalization concerns each age group's ability to sway the vote. For adults eligible to vote, she breaks down each age group's voting power. The Millennial, Generation X, Baby Boomer, and Silent generations account for 31%, 25%, 31%, and 13% of the voting population, respectively. She would like to use the data to accomplish the following tasks.

1. Calculate and interpret relevant conditional, unconditional, and joint probabilities.
2. Calculate and interpret the probability of all Americans who support the legalization of marijuana.

A synopsis of this case is provided in Section 4.2.

LO 4.1

Describe probability concepts and the rules of probability.

4.1 PROBABILITY CONCEPTS AND PROBABILITY RULES

We are better prepared to deal with uncertainty if we know the probabilities that describe which events are likely and which are unlikely. A **probability** is a numerical value that measures the likelihood that an event occurs. This value is between zero and one, where a value of zero indicates *impossible* events and a value of one indicates *definite* events. In order to define an event and assign the appropriate probability to it, it is useful to first establish some terminology and impose some structure on the situation.

An **experiment** is a process that leads to one of several possible outcomes. The diversity of the outcomes of an experiment is due to the uncertainty of the real world. When changing a branding strategy, it is uncertain if the profits will go up or down. You can think of this as an experiment because the actual outcome will be determined only over time. Other examples of an experiment include the extent of fraudulent credit card transactions, the sale of a new product, and the letter grade in a course.

A **sample space**, denoted by S, of an experiment contains all possible outcomes of the experiment. For example, suppose the sample space representing the letter grade in a course is given by $S = \{A, B, C, D, F\}$. The sample space for an experiment need not be unique. For example, in the above experiment, we can also define the sample space with just P (pass) and F (fail) outcomes; that is, $S = \{P, F\}$. Note that if the teacher also gives out an I (incomplete) grade, then neither of the sample spaces defined above is valid because they do not contain all possible outcomes of the experiment.

Events

An **event** is a subset of the sample space. A simple event consists of just one of the possible outcomes of an experiment. Getting an A in a course is an example of a simple event. An event may also contain several outcomes of an experiment. For example, we can define an event as getting a passing grade in a course; this event is formed by the subset of outcomes A, B, C, and D.

Events are considered **exhaustive** if they include all outcomes in the sample space. In the grade-distribution example, the events of getting grades A and B are not exhaustive events because they do not include many feasible grades in the sample space. However, the events P and F, defined as "pass" and "fail," respectively, are exhaustive.

Another important probability concept concerns **mutually exclusive** events. For two mutually exclusive events, the occurrence of one event precludes the occurrence of the other. Going back to the grade-distribution example, while the events of getting grades A and B are not exhaustive, they are mutually exclusive because you cannot possibly get an A as well as a B in the same course. Grades P and F, on the other hand, are both mutually exclusive and exhaustive.

EXPERIMENTS AND EVENTS

- An experiment is a process that leads to one of several possible outcomes. A sample space, denoted S, of an experiment contains all possible outcomes of the experiment.
- An event is any subset of outcomes of the experiment. It is called a simple event if it contains a single outcome.
- Events are exhaustive if all possible outcomes of an experiment belong to the events. Events are mutually exclusive if they do not share any common outcome of an experiment.

For any experiment, we can define events based on one or more outcomes of the experiment and also combine events to form new events. The **union** of two events, denoted

$A \cup B$, is the event consisting of all outcomes in A or B. A useful way to illustrate these concepts is through the use of a Venn diagram. Figure 4.1 shows a Venn diagram where the rectangle represents the sample space S and the two circles represent events A and B. The union $A \cup B$ is the portion in the Venn diagram that is included in either A or B.

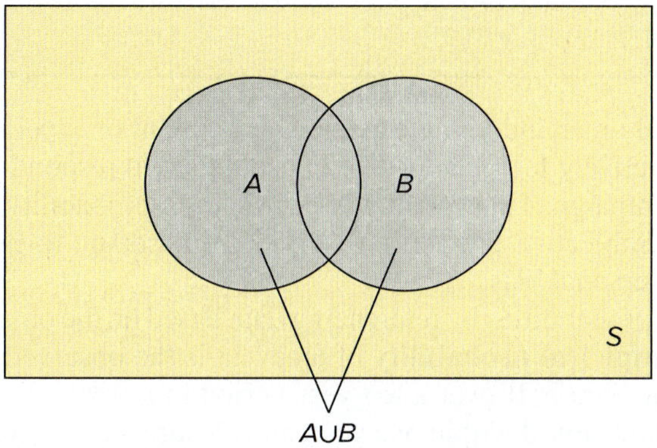

FIGURE 4.1
The union of two events, $A \cup B$

The **intersection** of two events, denoted $A \cap B$, is the event consisting of all outcomes in A and B. Figure 4.2 depicts the intersection of two events A and B. The intersection $A \cap B$ is the portion in the Venn diagram that is included in both A and B.

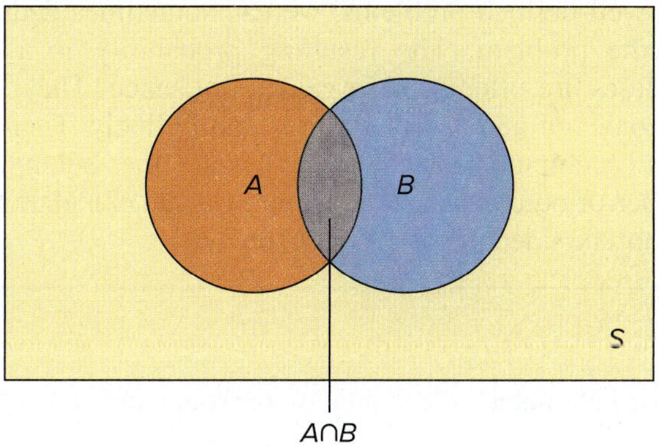

FIGURE 4.2
The intersection of two events, $A \cap B$

The **complement** of event A, denoted A^c, is the event consisting of all outcomes in the sample space S that are not in A.

> **COMBINING EVENTS**
>
> - The union of two events, denoted $A \cup B$, is the event consisting of all outcomes in A or B.
> - The intersection of two events, denoted $A \cap B$, is the event consisting of all outcomes in A and B.
> - The complement of event A, denoted A^c, is the event consisting of all outcomes in the sample space S that are not in A.

Assigning Probabilities

Now that we have described a valid sample space and the various ways in which we can define events from that sample space, we are ready to assign probabilities. When we arrive at a probability, we generally are able to categorize the probability as a subjective probability, an empirical probability, or a classical probability. Regardless of the method used, there are two defining properties of probability.

THE TWO DEFINING PROPERTIES OF PROBABILITY

1. The probability of any event A is a value between 0 and 1; that is, $0 \leq P(A) \leq 1$.
2. The sum of the probabilities of any list of mutually exclusive and exhaustive events equals 1.

The **subjective probability** is based on an individual's personal judgment or experience. For example, a manager may instinctively feel that 14% of consumers will respond positively to the firm's social media campaign. This personal assessment of probability does not explicitly reference any data. Subjective probabilities differ from person to person and may contain a high degree of personal bias.

In many instances, we calculate probabilities by referencing data based on the observed outcomes of an experiment. The **empirical probability** of an event is the observed relative frequency with which an event occurs. If over a ten year period in a particular city, 152 restaurants out of 180 opened and closed within one year, and closure within a year is our benchmark for failure, we can determine the empirical probability of restaurant failures for that city as $152/180 = 0.84$. It is important to note that the empirical probability is reliable if the experiment is run a very large number of times. In the above example, it may be misleading to report a failure rate of 0.40 based on 2 out of 5 restaurants opening and closing within one year.

In a more narrow range of well-defined problems, we can sometimes deduce probabilities by reasoning about the problem. The resulting probability is a **classical probability**. Classical probabilities are often used in games of chance. They are based on the assumption that all outcomes of an experiment are equally likely. Therefore, the classical probability of an event is computed as the number of outcomes belonging to the event divided by the total number of outcomes. For example, we can calculate the probability of rolling a two with a fair six-sided die as $1/6 = 0.1667$.

CATEGORIZING PROBABILITIES

- A subjective probability is calculated by drawing on personal and subjective judgment.
- An empirical probability is calculated as a relative frequency of occurrence.
- A classical probability is based on logical analysis rather than on observation or personal judgment.

Since empirical and classical probabilities generally do not vary from person to person, they are often grouped as objective probabilities.

Rules of Probability

We will now present various rules used to combine probabilities of events.

The **complement rule** follows from one of the defining properties of probability: The sum of probabilities assigned to simple events in a sample space must equal one. Therefore, for an event A and its complement A^c, we get $P(A) + P(A^c) = 1$. Rearranging this equation, we obtain the complement rule.

THE COMPLEMENT RULE

The complement of an event A is derived as $P(A^c) = 1 - P(A)$.

The complement rule is quite straightforward and rather simple, but it is widely used and powerful.

EXAMPLE 4.1

A manager at Moksha Yoga Center believes that 37% of female and 30% of male open house attendees she contacts will purchase a membership.

a. What is the probability that a randomly selected female contacted by the manager will not purchase a membership?

b. What is the probability that a randomly selected male contacted by the manager will not purchase a membership?

SOLUTION:

a. Let's define A as the event that a randomly selected female contacted by the manager will purchase a membership; thus, $P(A) = 0.37$. In this problem, we are interested in the complement of A. So $P(A^c) = 1 - P(A) = 1 - 0.37 = 0.63$.

b. Similarly, we define B as the event that a randomly selected male contacted by the manager will purchase a membership, so $P(B) = 0.30$. Thus, $P(B^c) = 1 - P(B) = 1 - 0.30 = 0.70$.

The **addition rule** allows us to find the probability of the union of two events. Suppose we want to find the probability that either A occurs or B occurs, so in probability terms, $P(A \cup B)$. Recall from Figure 4.1 that the union, $A \cup B$, is the portion in the Venn diagram that is included in event A or event B, whereas the intersection, $A \cap B$, is the portion in the Venn diagram that is included in both A and B.

If we try to obtain $P(A \cup B)$ by simply summing $P(A)$ with $P(B)$, then we overstate the probability because we double-count the probability of the intersection of A and B, $P(A \cap B)$. It is common to refer to $P(A \cap B)$ as the **joint probability** of events A and B. When implementing the addition rule, we sum $P(A)$ and $P(B)$ and then subtract $P(A \cap B)$ from this sum.

THE ADDITION RULE

The probability that event A or event B occurs is derived as

$$P(A \cup B) = P(A) + P(B) - P(A \cap B).$$

EXAMPLE 4.2

Anthony feels that he has a 75% chance of getting an A in Statistics and a 55% chance of getting an A in Managerial Economics. He also believes he has a 40% chance of getting an A in both classes.

a. What is the probability that he gets an A in at least one of these courses?

b. What is the probability that he does not get an A in either of these courses?

SOLUTION:

a. Let $P(A_S)$ correspond to the probability of getting an A in Statistics and $P(A_M)$ correspond to the probability of getting an A in Managerial Economics. Thus, $P(A_S) = 0.75$ and $P(A_M) = 0.55$. In addition, the joint probability that Anthony gets an A in both classes, $P(A_S \cap A_M) = 0.40$. In order to find the probability that he receives an A in at least one of these courses, we calculate:

$$P(A_S \cup A_M) = P(A_S) + P(A_M) - P(A_S \cap A_M) = 0.75 + 0.55 - 0.40 = 0.90.$$

b. The probability that he does not receive an A in either of these two courses is actually the complement of the union of the two events; that is, $P((A_S \cup A_M)^c)$. We calculated the union in part a, so using the complement rule we have

$$P((A_S \cup A_M)^c) = 1 - P(A_S \cup A_M) = 1 - 0.90 = 0.10.$$

An alternative expression that correctly captures the required probability is $P((A_S \cup A_M)^c) = P(A_S^c \cap A_M^c)$. A common mistake is to calculate the probability as $P((A_S \cap A_M)^c) = 1 - P(A_S \cap A_M) = 1 - 0.40 = 0.60$, which simply indicates that there is a 60% chance that Anthony will not get an A in both courses. This is clearly not the required probability that Anthony does not get an A in either course.

Note that for mutually exclusive events A and B, the joint probability is zero; that is, $P(A \cap B) = 0$. We need not concern ourselves with double-counting, and, therefore, the probability of the union is simply the sum of the two probabilities.

In business applications, the probability of interest is often a **conditional probability**. Examples include the probability that a customer will make an online purchase conditional on receiving an e-mail with a discount offer; the probability of making a six-figure salary conditional on getting an MBA; and the probability that sales will improve conditional on the firm launching a new innovative product.

Let's use an example to illustrate the concept of conditional probability. Suppose the probability that a recent business college graduate finds a suitable job is 0.80. The probability of finding a suitable job is 0.90 if the recent business college graduate has prior work experience. Here, the probability of an event is conditional on the occurrence of another event. If A represents "finding a job" and B represents "prior work experience," then $P(A) = 0.80$ and the conditional probability is denoted as $P(A \mid B) = 0.90$. In this example, the probability of finding a suitable job increases from 0.80 to 0.90 when conditioned on prior work experience. In general, the conditional probability, $P(A \mid B)$, is greater than the **unconditional probability**, $P(A)$, if B exerts a positive influence on A. Similarly, $P(A \mid B)$ is less than $P(A)$ when B exerts a negative influence on A. Finally, if B exerts no influence on A, then $P(A \mid B)$ equals $P(A)$. It is common to refer to "unconditional probability" simply as "probability."

We rely on the Venn diagram in Figure 4.2 to explain the conditional probability. Because $P(A \mid B)$ represents the probability of A conditional on B (B has occurred), the original sample space S reduces to B. The conditional probability $P(A \mid B)$ is based on the portion of A that is included in B. It is derived as the ratio of the probability of the intersection of A and B to the probability of B.

CONDITIONAL PROBABILITY

The probability that A occurs given that B has occurred is derived as $P(A \mid B) = \frac{P(A \cap B)}{P(B)}$.

EXAMPLE 4.3

Economic globalization is defined as the integration of national economies into the international economy through trade, foreign direct investment, capital flows, migration, and the spread of technology. Although globalization is generally viewed favorably, it also increases the vulnerability of a country to economic conditions of other countries. An economist predicts a 60% chance that country A will perform poorly and a 25% chance that country B will perform poorly. There is also a 16% chance that both countries will perform poorly.

a. What is the probability that country A performs poorly given that country B performs poorly?

b. What is the probability that country B performs poorly given that country A performs poorly?

c. Interpret your findings.

SOLUTION:

We first write down the available information in probability terms. Defining A as "country A performing poorly" and B as "country B performing poorly," we have the following information: $P(A) = 0.60$, $P(B) = 0.25$, and $P(A \cap B) = 0.16$.

a. $P(A \mid B) = \dfrac{P(A \cap B)}{P(B)} = \dfrac{0.16}{0.25} = 0.64$

b. $P(B \mid A) = \dfrac{P(A \cap B)}{P(A)} = \dfrac{0.16}{0.60} = 0.27$

c. It appears that globalization has definitely made these countries vulnerable to the economic woes of the other country. The probability that country A performs poorly increases from 60% to 64% when country B has performed poorly. Similarly, the probability that country B performs poorly increases from 25% to 27% when conditioned on country A performing poorly.

In some situations, we are interested in finding the joint probability $P(A \cap B)$. Using the conditional probability formula $P(A \mid B) = \frac{P(A \cap B)}{P(B)}$, we can easily derive $P(A \cap B) = P(A \mid B)P(B)$. Because we calculate the product of two probabilities to find $P(A \cap B)$, we refer to it as the **multiplication rule** for probabilities.

THE MULTIPLICATION RULE

The joint probability of events A and B is derived as $P(A \cap B) = P(A \mid B)P(B)$.

EXAMPLE 4.4

A manager believes that 14% of consumers will respond positively to the firm's social media campaign. Also, 24% of those who respond positively will become loyal customers. Find the probability that the next recipient of their social media campaign will react positively and will become a loyal customer.

SOLUTION:

Let the event R represent a consumer who responds positively to a social media campaign and the event L represent a loyal customer. Therefore, $P(R) = 0.14$ and $P(L \mid R) = 0.24$. We calculate the probability that the next recipient of a social media campaign will react positively and become a loyal customer as $P(R \cap L) = P(L \mid R)P(R) = 0.24 \times 0.14 = 0.0336$.

Of particular interest to researchers is whether or not two events influence one another. Two events are **independent** if the occurrence of one event does not affect the probability of the occurrence of the other event. Similarly, events are considered **dependent** if the occurrence of one is related to the probability of the occurrence of the other. We generally test for the independence of two events by comparing the conditional probability of one event, for instance $P(A \mid B)$, to the probability, $P(A)$. If these two probabilities are the same, we say that the two events, A and B, are independent; if the probabilities differ, the two events are dependent.

INDEPENDENT VERSUS DEPENDENT EVENTS

Two events, A and B, are independent if $P(A \mid B) = P(A)$ or, equivalently, $P(A \cap B) = P(A \mid B)P(B) = P(A)P(B)$. Otherwise, the events are dependent.

EXAMPLE 4.5

Suppose that for a given year there is a 2% chance that your desktop computer will crash and a 6% chance that your laptop computer will crash. Moreover, there is a 0.12% chance that both computers will crash. Is the reliability of the two computers independent of each other?

SOLUTION:

Let event D represent the outcome that your desktop crashes and event L represent the outcome that your laptop crashes. Therefore, $P(D) = 0.02$, $P(L) = 0.06$, and $P(D \cap L) = 0.0012$. The reliability of the two computers is independent because

$$P(D \mid L) = \frac{P(D \cap L)}{P(L)} = \frac{0.0012}{0.06} = 0.02 = P(D).$$

In other words, if your laptop crashes, it does not alter the probability that your desktop also crashes. Equivalently, we show that the events are independent because $P(D \cap L) = P(D)P(L) = 0.0012$.

EXERCISES 4.1

Applications

1. Consider the following scenarios to determine if the mentioned combination of attributes represents a union or an intersection.
   a. A marketing firm is looking for a candidate with a business degree and at least five years of work experience.
   b. A family has decided to purchase Toyota or Honda.
2. You apply for a position at two firms. Let event A represent the outcome of getting an offer from the first firm and event B represent the outcome of getting an offer from the second firm.
   a. Explain why events A and B are not exhaustive.
   b. Explain why events A and B are not mutually exclusive.
3. The probabilities that stock A will rise in price is 0.40 and that stock B will rise in price is 0.60. Further, if stock B rises in price, the probability that stock A will also rise in price is 0.50.
   a. What is the probability that at least one of the stocks will rise in price?
   b. Are events A and B mutually exclusive? Explain.
   c. Are events A and B independent? Explain.
4. Fraud detection has become an indispensable tool for banks and credit card companies to combat fraudulent credit card transactions. A fraud detection firm raises an alarm on 5% of all transactions and on 80% of fraudulent transactions. What is the probability that the transaction is fraudulent if the firm does not raise an alarm? Assume that 1% of all transactions are fraudulent.
5. Dr. Miriam Johnson has been teaching accounting for over 20 years. From her experience, she knows that 60% of her students do homework regularly. Moreover, 95% of the students who do their homework regularly pass the course. She also knows that 85% of her students pass the course.
   a. What is the probability that a student will do homework regularly and also pass the course?
   b. What is the probability that a student will neither do homework regularly nor pass the course?
   c. Are the events “pass the course” and “do homework regularly” mutually exclusive? Explain.
   d. Are the events “pass the course” and “do homework regularly” independent? Explain.
6. Mike Danes has been delayed in going to the annual sales event at one of his favorite apparel stores. His friend has just texted him that there are only 20 shirts left, of which eight are in size M, 10 in size L, and two in size XL. Also nine of the shirts are white, five are blue, and the remaining are of mixed

colors. Mike is interested in getting a white or a blue shirt in size L. Define the events A = Getting a white or a blue shirt and B = Getting a shirt in size L.

a. Find $P(A)$, $P(A^c)$, and $P(B)$.

b. Are the events A and B mutually exclusive? Explain.

c. Would you describe Mike's preference by the events $A \cup B$ or $A \cap B$?

7. An analyst estimates that the probability of default on a seven-year AA-rated bond is 0.06, while that on a seven-year A-rated bond is 0.13. The probability that they will both default is 0.04.

a. What is the probability that at least one of the bonds defaults?

b. What is the probability that neither the seven-year AA-rated bond nor the seven-year A-rated bond defaults?

c. Given that the seven-year AA-rated bond defaults, what is the probability that the seven-year A-rated bond also defaults?

8. A manufacturing firm just received a shipment of 20 assembly parts, of slightly varied sizes, from a vendor. The manager knows that there are only 15 parts in the shipment that would be suitable. He examines these parts one at a time.

a. Find the probability that the first part is suitable.

b. If the first part is suitable, find the probability that the second part is also suitable.

c. If the first part is suitable, find the probability that the second part is not suitable.

9. Apple products have become a household name in America, with the average household owning 2.6 Apple products (*CNBC*, October 10, 2017). Suppose that in the Midwest, the likelihood of owning an Apple product is 61% for households with kids and 48% for households without kids. Suppose there are 1,200 households in a representative community, of which 820 are with kids and the rest are without kids.

a. Are the events "household with kids" and "household without kids" mutually exclusive and exhaustive? Explain.

b. What is the probability that a household is without kids?

c. What is the probability that a household is with kids and owns an Apple product?

d. What is the probability that a household is without kids and does not own an Apple product?

10. As part of the 2010 financial overhaul, bank regulators are renewing efforts to require Wall Street executives to cut back on bonuses (*The Wall Street Journal*, March 5, 2019). It is known that 10 out of 15 members of the board of directors of a company are in favor of the bonus. Suppose two members were randomly selected by the media.

a. What is the probability that both of them were in favor of the bonus?

b. What is the probability that neither of them was in favor of the bonus?

11. Christine Wong has asked Dave and Mike to help her move into a new apartment on Sunday morning. She has asked them both, in case one of them does not show up. From past experience, Christine knows that there is a 40% chance that Dave will not show up and a 30% chance that Mike will not show up. Dave and Mike do not know each other and their decisions can be assumed to be independent.

a. What is the probability that both Dave and Mike will show up?

b. What is the probability that at least one of them will show up?

c. What is the probability that neither Dave nor Mike will show up?

12. It is reported that 85% of Asian, 78% of white, 70% of Hispanic, and 38% of black children have two parents at home. Suppose there are 500 students in a representative school, of which 280 are white, 50 are Asian, 100 are Hispanic, and 70 are black.

a. Are the events "Asian" and "black" mutually exclusive and exhaustive? Explain.

b. What is the probability that a child is not white?

c. What is the probability that a child is white and has both parents at home?

d. What is the probability that a child is Asian and does not have both parents at home?

13. Surgery for a painful, common back condition often results in significantly reduced back pain and better physical function than treatment with drugs and physical therapy. A researcher followed 803 patients, of whom 398 ended up getting surgery. After two years, of those who had surgery, 63% said they had a major improvement in their condition, compared with 29% among those who received nonsurgical treatment.

a. What is the probability that a patient had surgery? What is the probability that a patient did not have surgery?

b. What is the probability that a patient had surgery and experienced a major improvement in his or her condition?

c. What is the probability that a patient received nonsurgical treatment and experienced a major improvement in his or her condition?

14. Despite the availability of several modes of transportation, including metro and ride-booking services, most people in the Washington, D.C., area continue to drive their own cars to get around (*The Washington Post*, June 6, 2019). According to a survey, 62% of area adults use their own cars daily. Suppose only 38% of the area's adults under 35 use their own cars daily. It is known that 43% of the area's adults are under 35.

a. What is the probability that a Washington, D.C., area adult is under 35 and uses his/her own car daily?

b. If a Washington, D.C., area adult uses his/her own car daily, what is the probability that he/she is under 35?

4.2 THE TOTAL PROBABILITY RULE AND BAYES' THEOREM

In this section, we present two important rules in probability theory: the total probability rule and Bayes' theorem. The **total probability rule** is a useful tool for breaking the computation of a probability into distinct cases. **Bayes' theorem** uses this rule to update the probability of an event that has been affected by a new piece of evidence.

The Total Probability Rule and Bayes' Theorem

LO 4.2

Apply the total probability rule and Bayes' theorem.

Often in business the probability of an event is not readily apparent from the given information. The total probability rule expresses the probability of an event in terms of joint or conditional probabilities. Let $P(A)$ denote the probability of an event of interest. We can express $P(A)$ as the sum of probabilities of the intersections of A with some mutually exclusive and exhaustive events corresponding to an experiment. For instance, consider event B and its complement B^c. Figure 4.3 shows the sample space partitioned into these two mutually exclusive and exhaustive events. The circle, representing event A, consists entirely of its intersections with B and B^c. According to the total probability rule, $P(A)$ equals the sum of $P(A \cap B)$ and $P(A \cap B^c)$.

FIGURE 4.3
The total probability rule:
$P(A) = P(A \cap B) + P(A \cap B^c)$

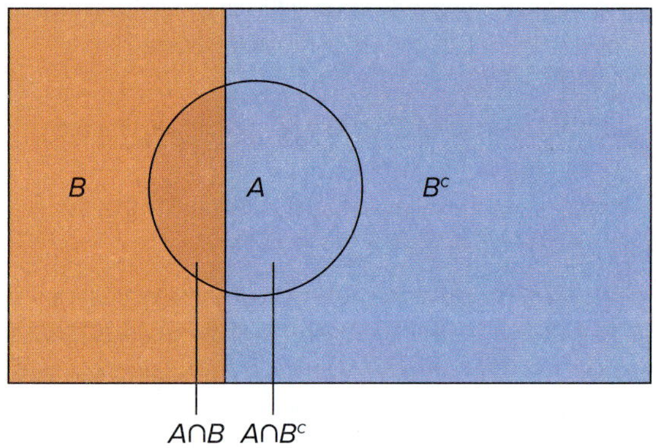

Oftentimes the joint probabilities needed to compute the total probability are not explicitly specified. Therefore, we use the multiplication rule to derive these probabilities from the conditional probabilities as $P(A \cap B) = P(A \mid B)P(B)$ and $P(A \cap B^c) = P(A \mid B^c)P(B^c)$.

The total probability rule is also needed to derive Bayes' theorem. Bayes' theorem is a procedure for updating probabilities based on new information. The original probability is an unconditional probability called a **prior probability**, in the sense that it reflects only what we know now before the arrival of any new information. On the basis of new information, we update the prior probability to arrive at a conditional probability called a **posterior probability**.

Suppose we know that 99% of the individuals who take a lie detector test tell the truth. Therefore, the prior probability of telling the truth is 0.99. Suppose an individual takes the lie detector test and the results indicate that the individual lied. Bayes' theorem updates a prior probability to compute a posterior probability, which in the above example is essentially a conditional probability based on the information that the lie detector has detected a lie.

Let $P(B)$ denote the prior probability and $P(B \mid A)$ the posterior probability. Note that the posterior probability is conditional on event A, representing new information. Recall the conditional probability formula from Section 4.1:

$$P(B \mid A) = \frac{P(A \cap B)}{P(A)}.$$

In some instances, we may have to evaluate $P(B \mid A)$, but we do not have explicit information on $P(A \cap B)$ or $P(A)$. However, given information on $P(B)$, $P(A \mid B)$, and $P(A \mid B^c)$, we can use the total probability rule to find $P(B \mid A)$, as shown in the following definition box.

THE TOTAL PROBABILITY RULE AND BAYES' THEOREM

The posterior probability $P(B \mid A)$ can be found using the information on the prior probability $P(B)$ along with the conditional probabilities $P(A \mid B)$ and $P(A \mid B^c)$ as

$$P(B \mid A) = \frac{P(A \cap B)}{P(A)} = \frac{P(A \cap B)}{P(A \cap B) + P(A \cap B^c)},$$

or equivalently,

$$P(B \mid A) = \frac{P(A \mid B)P(B)}{P(A \mid B)P(B) + P(A \mid B^c)P(B^c)}.$$

In the above formula, we have used Bayes' theorem to update the prior probability $P(B)$ to the posterior probability $P(B \mid A)$. Equivalently, we can use Bayes' theorem to update the prior probability $P(A)$ to derive the posterior probability $P(A \mid B)$ by interchanging the events A and B in the above formula.

EXAMPLE 4.6

In a lie-detector test, an individual is asked to answer a series of questions while connected to a polygraph (lie detector). This instrument measures and records several physiological responses of the individual on the basis that false answers will produce distinctive measurements. Assume that 99% of the individuals who go in for a polygraph test tell the truth. These tests are considered to be 95% reliable. In other words, there is a 95% chance that the test will detect a lie if an individual actually lies. Let there also be a 0.5% chance that the test erroneously detects a lie even when the individual is telling the truth. An individual has just taken a polygraph test and the test has detected a lie. What is the probability that the individual was actually telling the truth?

SOLUTION:

First we define some events and their associated probabilities. Let D and T correspond to the events that the polygraph detects a lie and that an individual is telling the truth, respectively. We are given that $P(T) = 0.99$, implying that $P(T^c) = 1 - 0.99 = 0.01$. In addition, we formulate $P(D \mid T^c) = 0.95$ and $P(D \mid T) = 0.005$. We need to find $P(T \mid D)$ when we are not explicitly given $P(D \cap T)$ and $P(D)$. We can use Bayes' theorem to find

$$P(T \mid D) = \frac{P(D \cap T)}{P(D)} = \frac{P(D \cap T)}{P(D \cap T) + P(D \cap T^c)} = \frac{P(D \mid T)P(T)}{P(D \mid T)P(T) + P(D \mid T^c)P(T^c)}.$$

Although we can use this formula to solve the problem directly, we use Table 4.2 to help solve the problem systematically.

TABLE 4.2 Computing Posterior Probabilities for Example 4.6

Prior Probability	Conditional Probability	Joint Probability	Posterior Probability
$P(T) = 0.99$	$P(D \mid T) = 0.005$	$P(D \cap T) = 0.00495$	$P(T \mid D) = 0.3426$
$P(T^c) = 0.01$	$P(D \mid T^c) = 0.95$	$P(D \cap T^c) = 0.00950$	$P(T^c \mid D) = 0.6574$
$P(T) + P(T^c) = 1$		$P(D) = 0.01445$	$P(T \mid D) + P(T^c \mid D) = 1$

The first column presents prior probabilities and the second column shows related conditional probabilities. We first compute the denominator of Bayes' theorem by using the total probability rule, $P(D) = P(D \cap T) + P(D \cap T^c)$. Joint probabilities are calculated as products of conditional probabilities with their corresponding prior probabilities. For instance, in Table 4.2, in order to obtain $P(D \cap T)$, we multiply $P(D \mid T)$ with $P(T)$, which yields $P(D \cap T) = 0.005 \times 0.99 = 0.00495$. Similarly, we find $P(D \cap T^c) = 0.95 \times 0.01 = 0.00950$. Thus, according to the total probability rule, $P(D) = 0.00495 + 0.00950 = 0.01445$. Finally, $P(T \mid D) = \frac{P(D \cap T)}{P(D \cap T) + P(D \cap T^c)} = \frac{0.00495}{0.01445} = 0.3426$.

The prior probability of an individual telling the truth is 0.99. However, given the new information that the polygraph detected the individual telling a lie, the posterior probability of this individual telling the truth is now revised downward to 0.3426.

Extensions of the Total Probability Rule and Bayes' Theorem

So far we have used the total probability rule as well as Bayes' theorem based on two mutually exclusive and exhaustive events, namely, B and B^c. We can easily extend the analysis to include n mutually exclusive and exhaustive events, $B_1, B_2, \ldots, B_n$.

EXTENSIONS OF THE TOTAL PROBABILITY RULE AND BAYES' THEOREM

If $B_1, B_2, \ldots B_n$ represent n mutually exclusive and exhaustive events, then Bayes' theorem, for any $i = 1, 2, \ldots, n$, extends to

$$P(B_i \mid A) = \frac{P(A \cap B_i)}{P(A \cap B_1) + P(A \cap B_2) + \cdots + P(A \cap B_n)},$$

or equivalently,

$$P(B_i \mid A) = \frac{P(A \mid B_i)P(B_i)}{P(A \mid B_1)P(B_1) + P(A \mid B_2)P(B_2) + \cdots + P(A \mid B_n)P(B_n)}.$$

EXAMPLE 4.7

Scott Myers is a security analyst for a telecommunications firm called Webtalk. Although he is optimistic about the firm's future, he is concerned that its stock price will be considerably affected by the condition of credit flow in the economy. He believes that the probability is 0.20 that credit flow will improve significantly, 0.50 that it will improve only marginally, and 0.30 that it will not improve at all. He also estimates that the probability that the stock price of Webtalk will go up is 0.90 with significant improvement in credit flow in the economy, 0.40 with marginal improvement in credit flow in the economy, and 0.10 with no improvement in credit flow in the economy.

a. Based on Scott's estimates, what is the probability that the stock price of Webtalk goes up?

b. If we know that the stock price of Webtalk has gone up, what is the probability that credit flow in the economy has improved significantly?

SOLUTION:

As always, we first define the relevant events and their associated probabilities. Let S, M, and N denote significant, marginal, and no improvement in credit flow, respectively. Then $P(S) = 0.20$, $P(M) = 0.50$, and $P(N) = 0.30$. In addition, if we allow G to denote an increase in stock price, we formulate $P(G \mid S) = 0.90$, $P(G \mid M) = 0.40$, and $P(G \mid N) = 0.10$. We need to calculate $P(G)$ in part a and $P(S \mid G)$ in part b. Table 4.3 aids in assigning probabilities.

TABLE 4.3 Computing Posterior Probabilities for Example 4.7

Prior Probability	Conditional Probability	Joint Probability	Posterior Probability
$P(S) = 0.20$	$P(G \mid S) = 0.90$	$P(G \cap S) = 0.18$	$P(S \mid G) = 0.4390$
$P(M) = 0.50$	$P(G \mid M) = 0.40$	$P(G \cap M) = 0.20$	$P(M \mid G) = 0.4878$
$P(N) = 0.30$	$P(G \mid N) = 0.10$	$P(G \cap N) = 0.03$	$P(N \mid G) = 0.0732$
$P(S) + P(M) + P(N) = 1$		$P(G) = 0.41$	$P(S \mid G) + P(M \mid G) + P(N \mid G) = 1$

a. In order to calculate $P(G)$, we use the total probability rule, $P(G) = P(G \cap S) + P(G \cap M) + P(G \cap N)$. The joint probabilities are calculated as products of conditional probabilities with their corresponding prior probabilities. For instance, in Table 4.3, $P(G \cap S) = P(G \mid S)P(S) = 0.90 \times 0.20 = 0.18$. Therefore, the probability that the stock price of Webtalk goes up equals $P(G) = 0.18 + 0.20 + 0.03 = 0.41$.

b. According to Bayes' theorem, $P(S \mid G) = \frac{P(G \cap S)}{P(G)} = \frac{P(G \cap S)}{P(G \cap S) + P(G \cap M) + P(G \cap N)}$. We use the total probability rule in the denominator to find $P(G) = 0.18 + 0.20 + 0.03 = 0.41$. Therefore, $P(S \mid G) = \frac{P(G \cap S)}{P(G)} = \frac{0.18}{0.41} = 0.4390$. Note that the prior probability of a significant improvement in credit flow is revised upward from 0.20 to a posterior probability of 0.4390.

EXAMPLE 4.8

We can now answer the questions posed by Alexis Lewis in the introductory case of this chapter. Use the information gathered by Alexis to

a. Formulate relevant conditional, unconditional, and joint probabilities.

b. Calculate the probability of all Americans who support the legalization of marijuana.

SOLUTION:

a. For ease of interpretation, let M, G, B, and S denote "Millennial," "Generation X," "Baby Boomer," and "Silent" generations, respectively. Based on data from the study, the following probability statements can be formulated with respect to the relative size of each generation's voting bloc: $P(M) = 0.31$, $P(G) = 0.25$, $P(B) = 0.31$, $P(S) = 0.13$.

Now let L denote "support for legalizing marijuana." Again, based on data from the study, conditional probabilities can be specified as $P(L \mid M) = 0.71$, $P(L \mid G) = 0.57$, $P(L \mid B) = 0.56$, and $P(L \mid S) = 0.33$.

Therefore, the probability that a randomly selected adult supports legal marijuana and is in the Millennial generation is determined as $P(L \cap M) = 0.71 \times 0.31 = 0.2201$. Similarly, $P(L \cap G) = 0.1425$, $P(L \cap B) = 0.1736$, and $P(L \cap S) = 0.0429$.

b. By combining all generations, we deduce the total probability of support for legalizing marijuana as $P(L) = P(L \cap M) + P(L \cap G) + P(L \cap B) + P(L \cap S) = 0.2201 + 0.1425 + 0.1736 + 0.0429 = 0.5791$.

SYNOPSIS OF INTRODUCTORY CASE

Driven by growing public support, the legalization of marijuana in America has been moving at a breakneck speed in recent years. Changing demographics can help explain how the tide has turned in marijuana's favor, especially with Millennials, who are on the verge of becoming the nation's largest living generation. A recent Pew Research Study provides interesting data regarding support for marijuana legalization. Two factors seem to drive support for the issue: generation (or age group) and the relative size of a generation's voting bloc. Based on data from the study, Millennials and Baby Boomers have the most voting power, each comprising 31% of the voting population; the Generation X and Silent generations represent 25% and 13% of the voting population, respectively. Given other conditional probabilities, we determine that a staggering 57.91% of Americans supported the legalization of marijuana.

To put it in perspective, suppose that there are 1,000 randomly selected adult attendees at a conference. The results imply that there would be about 310 Millennial, 250 Generation X, 310 Baby Boomer, and 130 Silent attendees. Further, the supporters of marijuana legalization would include about 220 Millennial, 143 Generation X, 174 Baby Boomer, and 43 Silent attendees.

Millennials are now as large a political force as Baby Boomers. In general, Millennials tend to be liberal on social issues such as gay rights, immigration, and marijuana. This shift in population has not gone unnoticed by political parties, which all hope to court the more than 75 million of these eligible young voters.

EXERCISES 4.2

Applications

15. Christine has always been weak in mathematics. Based on her performance prior to the final exam in Calculus, there is a 40% chance that she will fail the course if she does not have a tutor. With a tutor, her probability of failing decreases to 10%. There is only a 50% chance that she will find a tutor at such short notice.
    a. What is the probability that Christine fails the course?
    b. Christine ends up failing the course. What is the probability that she had found a tutor?

16. An analyst expects that 20% of all publicly traded companies will experience a decline in earnings next year. The analyst has developed a ratio to help forecast this decline. If the company is headed for a decline, there is a 70% chance that this ratio will be negative. If the company is not headed for a decline, there is a 15% chance that the ratio will be negative. The analyst randomly selects a company and its ratio is negative. What is the posterior probability that the company will experience a decline?

17. The State Police are trying to crack down on speeding on a particular portion of the Massachusetts Turnpike. To aid in this pursuit, they have purchased a new radar gun that promises greater consistency and reliability. Specifically, the gun advertises $\pm$ one-mile-per-hour accuracy 98% of the time; that is, there is a 0.98 probability that the gun will detect a speeder, if the driver is actually speeding. Assume there is a 1% chance that the gun erroneously detects a speeder even when the driver is below the speed limit. Suppose that 95% of the drivers drive below the speed limit on this stretch of the Massachusetts Turnpike.
    a. What is the probability that the gun detects speeding and the driver was speeding?
    b. What is the probability that the gun detects speeding and the driver was not speeding?
    c. Suppose the police stop a driver because the gun detects speeding. What is the probability that the driver was actually driving below the speed limit?

18. According to data from the *National Health and Nutrition Examination Survey*, 33% of white, 49.6% of black, 43% of Hispanic, and 8.9% of Asian women are obese. In a representative town, 48% of women are white, 19% are black, 26% are Hispanic, and the remaining 7% are Asian.
    a. Find the probability that a randomly selected woman in this town is obese.
    b. Given that a woman is obese, what is the probability that she is white?
    c. Given that a woman is obese, what is the probability that she is black?
    d. Given that a woman is obese, what is the probability that she is Asian?

19. An analyst thinks that next year there is a 20% chance that the world economy will be good, a 50% chance that it will be neutral, and a 30% chance that it will be poor. She also predicts probabilities that the performance of a start-up firm, Creative Ideas, will be good, neutral, or poor for each of the economic states of the world economy. The following table presents probabilities for three states of the world economy and the corresponding conditional probabilities for Creative Ideas.

State of the World Economy	Probability of Economic State	Performance of Creative Ideas	Conditional Probability of Creative Ideas
Good	0.20	Good	0.60
		Neutral	0.30
		Poor	0.10
Neutral	0.50	Good	0.40
		Neutral	0.30
		Poor	0.30
Poor	0.30	Good	0.20
		Neutral	0.30
		Poor	0.50

a. What is the probability that the performance of the world economy will be neutral and that of Creative Ideas will be poor?
b. What is the probability that the performance of Creative Ideas will be poor?
c. The performance of Creative Ideas was poor. What is the probability that the performance of the world economy had also been poor?

20. A crucial game of the Los Angeles Lakers basketball team depends on the health of its key player. According to his doctor's report, there is a 40% chance that he will be fully fit to play, a 30% chance that he will be somewhat fit to play, and a 30% chance that he will not be able to play at all. The coach has estimated the chances of winning at 80% if the player is fully fit, 60% if he is somewhat fit, and 40% if he is unable to play.
    a. What is the probability that the Lakers will win the game?
    b. You have just heard that the Lakers won the game. What is the probability that the key player had been fully fit to play in the game?
21. A 2015 national survey by the Washington Post–Kaiser Family Foundation finds that there is a big sex divide between Americans when identifying as feminist or strong feminist. The results of the survey are shown in the following table. In addition, per the 2010 U.S. Census Current Population Survey, 50.8% of the American population is female and 49.2% is male.

Sex	Feminist or Strong Feminist
Female	66%
Male	41%

    a. Calculate the probability that a randomly selected American adult is a female who also identifies as feminist or strong feminist.
    b. Calculate the probability that a randomly selected American adult is a male who also identifies as feminist or strong feminist.
    c. What percentage of American adults identifies as feminist or strong feminist?
    d. If a randomly selected American adult identifies as feminist or strong feminist, what is the probability that this adult is a female?
22. There is a growing public support for marijuana law reform, with polls showing more than half the country is in favor of some form of marijuana legalization. However, opinions on marijuana are divided starkly along political party lines. The results of a recent Pew Research Center survey are shown in the following table. In addition, assume that 27% of Americans identify as Republicans, 30% as Democrats, and 43% as independents.

Political Party	Support
Republican	41%
Democrat	66%
Independent	63%

    a. Calculate the probability that a randomly selected American adult supports marijuana legalization and is a Republican.
    b. Calculate the probability that a randomly selected American adult supports marijuana legalization and is a Democrat.
    c. Calculate the probability that a randomly selected American adult supports marijuana legalization and is an Independent.
    d. What percentage of American adults supports marijuana legalization?
    e. If a randomly selected American adult supports marijuana legalization, what is the probability that this adult is a Republican?

4.3 RANDOM VARIABLES AND DISCRETE PROBABILITY DISTRIBUTIONS

LO 4.3

Describe a discrete random variable and its probability distribution.

We often have to make important decisions in the face of uncertainty. For example, a car dealership has to determine the number of cars to hold on its lot when the actual demand for cars is unknown. Similarly, an investor has to select a portfolio when the actual outcomes of investment returns are not known. This uncertainty is captured by what we call a **random variable**. A random variable summarizes outcomes of an experiment with numerical values.

We generally use the uppercase letter X to denote a random variable and the lowercase letter x to denote the value that X may assume. A **discrete random variable** assumes a countable number of distinct values such as x_1, x_2, x_3, and so on. A **continuous random variable**, on the other hand, is characterized by uncountable values within an interval. Unlike the case of a discrete random variable, we cannot describe the possible values of a continuous random variable X with a list $x_1, x_2, \ldots$ because the value $(x_1 + x_2)/2$, not in the list, might also be possible.

DISCRETE VERSUS CONTINUOUS RANDOM VARIABLES

A random variable is a function that assigns numerical values to the outcomes of an experiment. A discrete random variable assumes a countable number of distinct values. A continuous random variable, on the other hand, is characterized by uncountable values in an interval.

Examples of discrete random variables include the number of sales people who hit their target for the quarter, the number of employees leaving a firm, or the number of firms filing for bankruptcy in a given month. Similarly, the return on a mutual fund, time to completion of a task, or the volume of beer sold as 16 ounces are examples of continuous random variables.

The Discrete Probability Distribution

Every discrete random variable is associated with a **probability distribution** that provides the probability that the random variable X assumes a particular value x, or equivalently, $P(X = x)$. Random variables can also be defined in terms of their **cumulative distribution function**, or, equivalently, $P(X \leq x)$. All discrete probability distributions satisfy the following two properties.

TWO KEY PROPERTIES OF DISCRETE PROBABILITY DISTRIBUTIONS

- The probability of each value x is a value between 0 and 1, or, equivalently, $0 \leq P(X = x) \leq 1$.
- The sum of the probabilities equals 1. In other words, $\Sigma P(X = x_i) = 1$, where the sum extends over all values x of X.

Summary Measures of a Discrete Random Variable

The analysis of probability distributions is useful because it allows us to calculate various probabilities associated with the different values that the random variable assumes. In addition, it allows us to calculate summary measures for a random variable. These summary measures include the mean, the variance, and the standard deviation.

One of the most important probabilistic concepts in statistics is that of the **expected value**, also referred to as the mean. The expected value of the discrete random variable X, denoted by $E(X)$, or simply μ, is a weighted average of all possible values of X. The variance and the standard deviation of a random variable are measures of variability.

SUMMARY MEASURES OF A DISCRETE RANDOM VARIABLE

Consider a discrete random variable X with values $x_1, x_2, x_3, \ldots$, which occur with probabilities $P(X = x_i)$.

The expected value of X, denoted as $E(X)$ or μ, is calculated as

$$E(X) = \mu = \Sigma x_i P(X = x_i).$$

The variance of X, denoted as $Var(X)$ or σ^2, is calculated as

$$Var(X) = \sigma^2 = \Sigma(x_i - \mu)^2 \, P(X = x_i).$$

The standard deviation of X, denoted as $SD(X)$ or σ, is calculated as

$$SD(X) = \sigma = \sqrt{\sigma^2}.$$

EXAMPLE 4.9

Brad Williams is the owner of a large car dealership in Chicago. Brad decides to construct an incentive compensation program that equitably and consistently compensates employees on the basis of their performance. He offers an annual bonus of \$10,000 for superior performance, \$6,000 for good performance, \$3,000 for fair performance, and \$0 for poor performance. Based on prior records, he expects an employee to perform at superior, good, fair, and poor performance levels with probabilities 0.15, 0.25, 0.40, and 0.20, respectively.

a. Calculate the expected value of the annual bonus amount.

b. Calculate the variance and the standard deviation of the annual bonus amount.

c. What is the total annual amount that Brad can expect to pay in bonuses if he has 25 employees?

SOLUTION:

a. Let the random variable X denote the bonus amount (in \$1,000s) for an employee. The first and second columns of Table 4.4 represent the probability distribution of X. The calculations for the mean are provided in the third column. We weigh each outcome by its respective probability, $x_iP(X = x_i)$, and then sum these weighted values. Thus, as shown at the bottom of the third column, $E(X) = \mu = \Sigma x_iP(X = x_i) = 4.2$, or \$4,200.

TABLE 4.4 Calculations for Example 4.9

x_i	$P(X = x_i)$	$x_iP(X = x_i)$	$(x_i - \mu)^2P(X = x_i)$
10	0.15	$10 \times 0.15 = 1.5$	$(10 - 4.2)^2 \times 0.15 = 5.05$
6	0.25	$6 \times 0.25 = 1.5$	$(6 - 4.2)^2 \times 0.25 = 0.81$
3	0.40	$3 \times 0.40 = 1.2$	$(3 - 4.2)^2 \times 0.40 = 0.58$
0	0.20	$0 \times 0.20 = 0$	$(0 - 4.2)^2 \times 0.20 = 3.53$
		Total = 4.2	Total = 9.97

b. The last column of Table 4.4 shows the calculation for the variance. We first calculate each x_i's squared difference from the mean $(x_i - \mu)^2$, weigh each value by the appropriate probability, $(x_i - \mu)^2P(X = x_i)$, and then sum these weighted squared differences. Thus, as shown at the bottom of the last column, $Var(X) = \sigma^2 = \Sigma(x_i - \mu)^2P(X = x_i) = 9.97$, or 9.97 (in (\$1,000s)^2). The standard deviation is the positive square root of the variance, $SD(X) = \sigma = \sqrt{9.97} = 3.158$, or \$3,158.

c. In part a we found that the expected bonus of an employee is \$4,200. Because Brad has 25 employees, he can expect to pay \$4,200 × 25 = \$105,000 in bonuses.

EXERCISES 4.3

Applications

23. Fifty percent of the customers who go to Auto Center for tires buy four tires and 30% buy two tires. Moreover, 18% buy fewer than two tires, with 5% buying none.
    a. What is the probability that a customer buys three tires?
    b. Construct a cumulative probability distribution for the number of tires bought.
24. Jane Wormley is a professor of management at a university. She expects to be able to use her grant money to fund up to two students for research assistance. While she realizes that there is a 5% chance that she may not be able to fund any student, there is an 80% chance that she will be able to fund two students.
    a. What is the probability that Jane will fund one student?
    b. Construct a cumulative probability distribution of the random variable defined as the number of students that Jane will be able to fund.
25. A marketing firm is considering making up to three new hires. Given its specific needs, the management feels that there is a 60% chance of hiring at least two candidates. There is only a 5% chance that it will not make any hires and a 10% chance that it will make all three hires.
    a. What is the probability that the firm will make at least one hire?
    b. Find the expected value and the standard deviation of the number of hires.
26. An appliance store sells additional warranties on its refrigerators. Twenty percent of the buyers buy the limited warranty for $100 and 5% buy the extended warranty for $200. What is the expected revenue for the store from the warranty if it sells 120 refrigerators?
27. Organizers of an outdoor summer concert in Toronto are concerned about the weather conditions on the day of the concert. They will make a profit of $25,000 on a clear day and $10,000 on a cloudy day. They will take a loss of $5,000 if it rains. The weather channel has predicted a 60% chance of rain on the day of the concert. Calculate the expected profit from the concert if the likelihood is 10% that it will be sunny and 30% that it will be cloudy.
28. The manager of a publishing company plans to give a $20,000 bonus to the top 15%, $10,000 to the next 30%, and $5,000 to the next 10% of sales representatives. If the publishing company has a total of 200 sales representatives, what is the expected bonus that the company will pay?
29. You are considering buying insurance for your new laptop computer, which you have recently bought for $1,500. The insurance premium for three years is $80. Over the three-year period there is an 8% chance that your laptop computer will require work worth $400, a 3% chance that it will require work worth $800, and a 2% chance that it will completely break down with a scrap value of $100. Should you buy the insurance?
30. An investor considers investing $10,000 in the stock market. He believes that the probability is 0.30 that the economy will improve, 0.40 that it will stay the same, and 0.30 that it will deteriorate. Further, if the economy improves, he expects his investment to grow to $15,000, but it can also go down to $8,000 if the economy deteriorates. If the economy stays the same, his investment will stay at $10,000. What is the expected value of his investment?

LO 4.4

Calculate probabilities for binomial and Poisson distributions.

4.4 THE BINOMIAL AND THE POISSON DISTRIBUTIONS

Different types of experiments generate different discrete probability distributions. A simple, yet widely used, distribution is called the **discrete uniform distribution**. This distribution has a finite number of values where each value is equally likely. Suppose we know that the weekly production at a facility is between 31 and 40 units and that production follows a discrete uniform distribution. Here, the random variable can only assume one out of ten equally likely values between 31 and 40. For example, the probability that weekly production is 34 is 1/10. Similarly, the probability that weekly production is less than 34 is 3/10.

In this section, we focus on the binomial and the Poisson probability distributions.

The Binomial Distribution

Before we can discuss the binomial distribution, we first must ensure that the experiment satisfies the conditions of a **Bernoulli process**, which is a particular type of experiment described below.

A BERNOULLI PROCESS

A Bernoulli process consists of a series of n independent and identical trials of an experiment such that on each trial:

- There are only two possible outcomes, conventionally labeled success and failure; and
- The probabilities of success and failure remain the same from trial to trial.

We use p to denote the probability of success, and, therefore, $1 - p$ is the probability of failure.

A **binomial random variable** x is defined as the number of successes achieved in the n trials of a Bernoulli process. The possible values of x include $0, 1, \ldots, n$. Many experiments fit the conditions of a Bernoulli process. For instance:

- A customer defaults or does not default on a loan.
- A consumer reacts positively or negatively to a social media campaign.
- A drug is either effective or ineffective.
- A college graduate applies or does not apply to graduate school.

Our goal is to attach probabilities to various outcomes of a Bernoulli process. The result is a **binomial distribution**.

THE BINOMIAL DISTRIBUTION

For a binomial random variable X, the probability of x successes in n Bernoulli trials is

$$P(X = x) = \binom{n}{x} p^x(1 - p)^{n-x} = \frac{n!}{x!(n - x)!}p^x(1 - p)^{n-x}$$

for $x = 0, 1, 2, \ldots, n$. By definition, $0! = 1$.

The formula consists of two parts, which we explain with a scenario where historically 85% of the customers in a store make a purchase. Suppose we want to compute the probability that exactly one of the three customers in the store will make a purchase.

- The first term, $\binom{n}{x} = \frac{n!}{x!(n - x)!}$, tells us how many sequences with x successes and $n - x$ failures are possible in n trials. We refer to the first term as the binomial coefficient, which is really the familiar combination formula used to find the number of ways to choose x objects from a total of n objects, where the order in which the x objects are listed *does not matter*. For instance, in order to calculate the number of sequences that contain exactly one success in three trials of a Bernoulli process, we substitute $x = 1$ and $n = 3$ into the formula and calculate $\binom{n}{x} = \frac{n!}{x!(n - x)!} = \frac{3!}{1!(3 - 1)!} = \frac{3 \times 2 \times 1}{(1) \times (2 \times 1)} = 3$. So there are three sequences having exactly 1 success.
- The second part of the equation, $p^x(1 - p)^{n - x}$, represents the probability of any particular sequence with x successes and $n - x$ failures. For example, we can obtain the probability of one success in three trials as $0.85 \times 0.15 \times 0.15 = (0.85)^1 \times (0.15)^2 = 0.0191$. In other words, each sequence consisting of 1 success in 3 trials has a 1.91% chance of occurring.

We obtain the overall probability of getting 1 success in 3 trials as $P(X = 1) = 3 \times 0.0191 = 0.0573$.

Moreover, we could use the formulas shown in Section 4.3 to calculate the expected value and the variance for any binomial random variable. For the binomial distribution, these formulas simplify to $E(X) = np$ and $Var(X) = np(1 - p)$.

EXAMPLE 4.10

In the United States, about 30% of adults have four-year college degrees (*US Census*, July 31, 2018). Suppose five adults are randomly selected.

a. What is the probability that none of the adults has a college degree?

b. What is the probability that no more than two of the adults have a college degree?

c. What is the probability that at least two of the adults have a college degree?

d. Calculate the expected number of adults with a college degree.

SOLUTION: First, this problem satisfies the conditions for a Bernoulli process with a random selection of five adults, $n = 5$. Here, an adult either has a college degree, with probability $p = 0.30$, or does not have a college degree, with probability $1 - p = 1 - 0.30 = 0.70$.

a. In order to find the probability that none of the adults has a college degree, we let $x = 0$ and find

$$P(X = 0) = \frac{5!}{0!(5 - 0)!} \times (0.30)^0 \times (0.70)^{5-0} = 0.1681$$

In other words, from a random sample of five adults, there is a 16.81% chance that none of the adults has a college degree.

b. We find the probability that no more than two adults have a college degree as

$$P(X \leq 2) = P(X = 0) + P(X = 1) + P(X = 2).$$

We have already found $P(X = 0)$ from part a. So we now compute $P(X = 1)$ and $P(X = 2)$:

$$P(X = 1) = \frac{5!}{1!(5 - 1)!} \times (0.30)^1 \times (0.70)^{5-1} = 0.3602$$

$$P(X = 2) = \frac{5!}{2!(5 - 2)!} \times (0.30)^2 \times (0.70)^{5-2} = 0.3087$$

Next we sum the three relevant probabilities and obtain $P(X \leq 2) = 0.1681 + 0.3602 + 0.3087 = 0.8370$. From a random sample of five adults, there is an 83.7% likelihood that no more than two of them will have a college degree.

c. We find the probability that at least two adults have a college degree as

$$P(X \geq 2) = P(X = 2) + P(X = 3) + P(X = 4) + P(X = 5).$$

A simpler method uses one of the key properties of a probability distribution, which states that the sum of the probabilities over all values of X equals 1. Therefore, $P(X \geq 2)$ can be written as $1 - [P(X = 0) + P(X = 1)]$. We have already calculated $P(X = 0)$ and $P(X = 1)$ from parts a and b, so

$$P(X \geq 2) = 1 - (0.1681 + 0.3602) = 0.4717.$$

From a random sample of five adults, there is a 47.17% likelihood that at least two adults will have a college degree.

d. We calculate the expected number of adults with a college degree as

$$E(X) = np = 5 \times 0.30 = 1.5 \text{ adults}.$$

The Poisson Distribution

Another important discrete probability distribution is the **Poisson distribution**. It is particularly useful in problems that deal with finding the number of occurrences of a certain event over time or space, where space refers to area or region. For simplicity, we call these occurrences "successes." Before we can discuss the Poisson distribution, we first must ensure that our experiment satisfies the conditions of a **Poisson process**.

A POISSON PROCESS

An experiment satisfies a Poisson process if

- The number of successes within a specified time or space interval equals any integer between zero and infinity.
- The number of successes counted in nonoverlapping intervals are independent.
- The probability of success in any interval is the same for all intervals of equal size and is proportional to the size of the interval.

For a Poisson process, we define the number of successes achieved in a specified time or space interval as a **Poisson random variable**. Like the Bernoulli process, many experiments fit the conditions of a Poisson process. For instance:

- The number of customers who use a new banking app in a day.
- The number of spam e-mails received in a month.
- The number of defects in a 50-yard roll of fabric.
- The number of bacteria in a specified culture.

We use the following formula for calculating probabilities associated with a Poisson random variable.

THE POISSON DISTRIBUTION

For a Poisson random variable X, the probability of x successes over a given interval of time or space is

$$P(X = x) = \frac{e^{-\mu}\mu^{x}}{x!},$$

for $x = 0, 1, 2, \ldots,$ where μ is the mean number of successes and $e \approx 2.718$ is the base of the natural logarithm.

If X is a Poisson random variable, then $Var(X) = E(X) = \mu$.

EXAMPLE 4.11

Anne is concerned about staffing needs at the Starbucks that she manages. She believes that the typical Starbucks customer averages 18 visits to the store over a 30-day month.

a. How many visits should Anne expect in a 5-day period from a typical Starbucks customer?

b. What is the probability that a customer visits the chain five times in a 5-day period?

c. What is the probability that a customer visits the chain no more than two times in a 5-day period?

d. What is the probability that a customer visits the chain at least three times in a 5-day period?

SOLUTION: In applications of the Poisson distribution, we first determine the mean number of successes in the relevant time or space interval. We use the Poisson process condition that the probability that success occurs in any interval is the same for all intervals of equal size and is proportional to the size of the interval. Here, the relevant mean will be based on the rate of 18 visits over a 30-day month.

a. Given the rate of 18 visits over a 30-day month, we can write the mean for the 30-day period as $\mu_{30} = 18$. For this problem, we compute the proportional mean for a five-day period as $\mu_5 = 3$ because $\frac{18 \text{ visits}}{30 \text{ days}} = \frac{3 \text{ visits}}{5 \text{ days}}$. In other words, on average, a typical Starbucks customer visits the store three times over a five-day period.

b. In order to find the probability that a customer visits the chain five times in a five-day period, we calculate

$$P(X = 5) = \frac{e^{-3}3^5}{5!} = \frac{(0.0498)(243)}{120} = 0.1008.$$

c. For the probability that a customer visits the chain no more than two times in a five-day period, we find $P(X \leq 2) = P(X = 0) + P(X = 1) + P(X = 2)$. We calculate the individual probabilities, and then find the sum:

$$P(X = 0) = \frac{e^{-3}3^0}{0!} = \frac{(0.0498)(1)}{1} = 0.0498,$$

$$P(X = 1) = \frac{e^{-3}3^1}{1!} = \frac{(0.0498)(3)}{1} = 0.1494, \text{ and}$$

$$P(X = 2) = \frac{e^{-3}3^2}{2!} = \frac{(0.0498)(9)}{2} = 0.2241.$$

Thus, $P(X \leq 2) = 0.0498 + 0.1494 + 0.2241 = 0.4233$. There is approximately a 42% chance that a customer visits the chain no more than two times in a five-day period.

d. We find $P(X \geq 3)$ as $1 - [P(X = 0) + P(X = 1) + P(X = 2)]$. Based on the probabilities in part c, we have $P(X \geq 3) = 1 - [0.0498 + 0.1494 + 0.2241] = 1 - 0.4233 = 0.5767$. Thus, there is about a 58% chance that a customer will frequent the chain at least three times in a five-day period.

Using Excel and R to Obtain Binomial and Poisson Probabilities

As you may have noticed, it is somewhat tedious and cumbersome to solve binomial and Poisson distribution problems using the formulas. This issue becomes even more pronounced when X assumes a wide range of values. In Examples 4.12 and 4.13, we will show how to solve binomial and Poisson distribution problems with Excel and R.

EXAMPLE 4.12

People turn to social media to stay in touch with friends and family members, connect with old friends, catch the news, look for employment, and be entertained. According to a recent survey, 68% of all U.S. adults are Facebook users. Consider a sample of 100 randomly selected American adults.

a. What is the probability that exactly 70 American adults are Facebook users?

b. What is the probability that no more than 70 American adults are Facebook users?

c. What is the probability that at least 70 American adults are Facebook users?

SOLUTION:

We let X denote the number of American adults who are Facebook users. We also know that $p = 0.68$ and $n = 100$.

Using Excel

We use Excel's **BINOM.DIST** function to calculate binomial probabilities. In order to find $P(X = x)$, we enter =BINOM.DIST(x, n, p, 0) where x is the number of successes, n is the number of trials, and p is the probability of success. If we enter a "1" for the last argument in the function, then Excel returns $P(X \leq x)$.

a. In order to find the probability that exactly 70 American adults are Facebook users, $P(X = 70)$, we enter =BINOM.DIST(70, 100, 0.68, 0) and Excel returns 0.0791.

b. In order to find the probability that no more than 70 American adults are Facebook users, $P(X \leq 70)$, we enter =BINOM.DIST(70, 100, 0.68, 1) and Excel returns 0.7007.

c. In order to find the probability that at least 70 American adults are Facebook users, $P(X \geq 70) = 1 - P(X \leq 69)$, we enter =1-BINOM.DIST(69, 100, 0.68, 1) and Excel returns 0.3784.

Using R

We use R's **dbinom** and **pbinom** functions to calculate binomial probabilities. In order to calculate $P(X = x)$, we enter dbinom(x, n, p) where x is the number of successes, n is the number of trials, and p is the probability of success. In order to calculate $P(X \leq x)$, we enter pbinom(x, n, p).

a. In order to find $P(X = 70)$, we enter:

```
> dbinom(70, 100, 0.68)
```

And R returns: 0.07907911.

b. In order to find $P(X \leq 70)$, we enter:

```
> pbinom(70, 100, 0.68)
```

And R returns: 0.7006736.

c. In order to find $P(X \geq 70) = 1 - P(X \leq 69)$, we enter:

```
> 1 - pbinom(69, 100, 0.68)
```

And R returns: 0.3784055.

EXAMPLE 4.13

The sales volume of craft beer continues to grow, amounting to 24% of the total beer market in the U.S. (*USA Today*, April 2, 2019). It has been estimated that 1.5 craft breweries open every day. Assume this number represents an average that remains constant over time.

a. What is the probability that no more than 10 craft breweries open every week?

b. What is the probability that exactly 10 craft breweries open every week?

SOLUTION: We let X denote the number of craft breweries that open every week and compute the weekly mean, $\mu = 1.5 \times 7 = 10.5$.

Using Excel

We use Excel's **POISSON.DIST** function to calculate Poisson probabilities. In order to find $P(X = x)$, we enter =POISSON.DIST(x, μ, 0) where x is the number of successes over some interval and μ is the mean over this interval. If we enter a "1" for the last argument in the function, then Excel returns $P(X \leq x)$.

a. In order to find the probability that no more than 10 craft breweries open every week, $P(X \leq 10)$, we enter =POISSON.DIST(10, 10.5, 1) and Excel returns 0.5207.

b. In order to find the probability that exactly 10 craft breweries open every week, $P(X = 10)$, we enter =POISSON.DIST(10, 10.5, 0) and Excel returns 0.1236.

Using R

We use R's **dpois** and **ppois** functions to calculate Poisson probabilities. In order to calculate $P(X = x)$, we enter dpois(x, μ) where x is the number of successes over some interval and μ is the mean over this interval. In order to calculate $P(X \leq x)$, we enter ppois(x, μ).

a. In order to find $P(X \leq 10)$, we enter:

```
> ppois(10, 10.5)
```

And R returns: 0.5207381.

b. In order to find $P(X = 10)$, we enter:

```
> dpois(10, 10.5)
```

And R returns: 0.1236055.

EXERCISES 4.4

Applications

31. At a local community college, 40% of students who enter the college as freshmen go on to graduate. Ten freshmen are randomly selected.
    a. What is the probability that none of them graduates from the local community college?
    b. What is the probability that at most nine will graduate from the local community college?
    c. What is the expected number that will graduate?

32. As of 2018, 30% of Americans have confidence in U.S. banks, which is still below the pre-recession level of 41% reported in June 2007 (www.gallup.com, June 28, 2018).
    a. What is the probability that fewer than half of four Americans in 2018 have confidence in U.S. banks?
    b. What would have been the corresponding probability in 2007?

33. Approximately 45% of Baby Boomers—those born between 1946 and 1964—are still in the workforce (www.pewresearch.org, May 11, 2015). Six Baby Boomers are selected at random.
    a. What is the probability that exactly one of the Baby Boomers is still in the workforce?

b. What is the probability that at least five of the Baby Boomers are still in the workforce?
c. What is the probability that less than two of the Baby Boomers are still in the workforce?
d. What is the probability that more than the expected number of the Baby Boomers are still in the workforce?

34. According to the Census Bureau projections, Hispanics will comprise 28.6% of the total population in 2060 (*CNN*, March 6, 2019). For comparison, they comprised just 18.1% of the total population in 2018.
    a. What is the expected value and the standard deviation of Hispanics in a random sample of 5,000 people in 2018?
    b. What is the corresponding expected value and the standard deviation projected for 2060?

35. The arduous task of combing and tying up long hair and a desire to assimilate has led to approximately 25% of Sikh youths giving up on wearing turbans.
    a. What is the probability that exactly two in a random sample of five Sikh youths wear a turban?
    b. What is the probability that two or more in a random sample of five Sikh youths wear a turban?
    c. What is the probability that more than the expected number of Sikh youths wear a turban in a random sample of five Sikh youths?
    d. What is the probability that more than the expected number of Sikh youths wear a turban in a random sample of 10 Sikh youths?

36. Researchers from leading universities have shown that divorces are contagious (*Chicago Tribune*, August 16, 2018). A split-up between immediate friends increases a person's own chances of getting divorced from 36% to 63%, an increase of 75%.
    a. Compute the probability that more than half of four randomly selected marriages will end in divorce if the couple's immediate friends have split up.
    b. Redo part a if it is known that none of the couple's immediate friends has split up.

37. Sixty percent of a firm's employees are men. Suppose four of the firm's employees are randomly selected.
    a. What is more likely, finding three men and one woman or two men and two women?
    b. Do you obtain the same answer as in part a if 70% of the firm's employees had been men?

38. The principal of an architecture firm tells her client that there is at least a 50% chance of having an acceptable design by the end of the week. She knows that there is only a 25% chance that any one designer would be able to do so by the end of the week.
    a. Would she be correct in her statement to the client if she asks two of her designers to work on the design, independently?
    b. If not, what if she asks three of her designers to work on the design, independently?

39. Suppose 40% of recent college graduates plan on pursuing a graduate degree. Fifteen recent college graduates are randomly selected.
    a. What is the probability that no more than four of the college graduates plan to pursue a graduate degree?
    b. What is the probability that exactly seven of the college graduates plan to pursue a graduate degree?
    c. What is the probability that at least six but no more than nine of the college graduates plan to pursue a graduate degree?

40. A manager at 24/7 Fitness Center is strategic about contacting open house attendees. With her strategy, she believes that 40% of the attendees she contacts will purchase a club membership. Suppose she contacts 20 open house attendees.
    a. What is the probability that exactly 10 of the attendees will purchase a club membership?
    b. What is the probability that no more than 10 of the attendees will purchase a club membership?
    c. What is the probability that at least 15 of the attendees will purchase a club membership?

41. Fraud detection has become an indispensable tool for banks and credit card companies to combat fraudulent credit card transactions. A fraud detection firm has detected some form of fraudulent activities in 1.31%, and serious fraudulent activities in 0.87%, of transactions. Assume that fraudulent transactions remain stable.
    a. What is the probability that fewer than 2 out of 100 transactions are fraudulent?
    b. What is the probability that fewer than 2 out of 100 transactions are seriously fraudulent?

42. New Age Solar installs solar panels for residential homes. Because of the company's personalized approach, it averages three home installations daily.
    a. What is the probability that New Age Solar installs solar panels in at most four homes in a day?
    b. What is the probability that New Age Solar installs solar panels in at least three homes in a day?

43. On average, there are 12 potholes per mile on a particular stretch of the state highway. Suppose the potholes are distributed evenly on the highway.
    a. Find the probability of finding fewer than two potholes in a quarter-mile stretch of the highway.
    b. Find the probability of finding more than one pothole in a quarter-mile stretch of the highway.

44. A tollbooth operator has observed that cars arrive randomly at an average rate of 360 cars per hour.
    a. Find the probability that two cars arrive during a specified one-minute period.

b. Find the probability that at least two cars arrive during a specified one-minute period.
c. Find the probability that 40 cars arrive between 10:00 am and 10:10 am.

45. A textile manufacturing process finds that on average, two flaws occur per every 50 yards of material produced.
    a. What is the probability of exactly two flaws in a 50-yard piece of material?
    b. What is the probability of no more than two flaws in a 50-yard piece of material?
    c. What is the probability of no flaws in a 25-yard piece of material?

46. Motorists arrive at a Gulf gas station at the rate of two per minute during morning hours.
    a. What is the probability that more than two motorists will arrive at the Gulf gas station during a one-minute interval in the morning?
    b. What is the probability that exactly six motorists will arrive at the Gulf gas station during a five-minute interval in the morning?
    c. How many motorists can an employee expect in her three-hour morning shift?

47. Airline travelers should be ready to be more flexible as airlines once again cancel thousands of flights this summer. The Coalition for Airline Passengers Rights, Health, and Safety averages 400 calls a day to help stranded travelers deal with airlines. Suppose the hotline is staffed for 16 hours a day.
    a. Calculate the average number of calls in a one-hour interval, 30-minute interval, and 15-minute interval.
    b. What is the probability of exactly six calls in a 15-minute interval?
    c. What is the probability of no calls in a 15-minute interval?
    d. What is the probability of at least two calls in a 15-minute interval?

48. According to the Centers for Disease Control and Prevention (CDC), the aging of the U.S. population is translating into many more visits to doctors' offices and hospitals. It is estimated that an average person makes four visits a year to doctors' offices and hospitals.
    a. What are the mean and the standard deviation of an average person's number of monthly visits to doctors' offices and hospitals?
    b. What is the probability that an average person does not make any monthly visits to doctors' offices and hospitals?
    c. What is the probability that an average person makes at least one monthly visit to doctors' offices and hospitals?

49. Last year, there were 24,584 age-discrimination claims filed with the Equal Employment Opportunity Commission. Assume there were 260 working days in the fiscal year for which a worker could file a claim.
    a. Calculate the average number of claims filed on a working day.
    b. What is the probability that exactly 100 claims were filed on a working day?
    c. What is the probability that no more than 100 claims were filed on a working day?

50. American adults are watching significantly less television than they did in previous decades. In 2016, Nielsen reported that American adults are watching an average of five hours and four minutes, or 304 minutes, of television per day.
    a. Find the probability that an average American adult watches more than 320 minutes of television per day.
    b. Find the probability that an average American adult watches more than 2,200 minutes of television per week.

LO 4.5

4.5 THE NORMAL DISTRIBUTION

Describe the normal distribution and calculate its associated probabilities.

Recall that a discrete random variable X assumes a countable number of distinct values such as x_1, x_2, x_3, and so on. A continuous random variable, on the other hand, is characterized by uncountable values because it can take on any value within an interval. Furthermore, we can calculate the probability that a discrete random variable X assumes a particular value x; that is, $P(X = x)$. For instance, for a binomial random variable, we can calculate the probability of exactly one success in n trials; that is, $P(X = 1)$. We cannot make this calculation with a continuous random variable.

The probability that a continuous random variable assumes a particular value x is zero; that is, $P(X = x) = 0$. This occurs because we cannot assign a nonzero probability to each of the uncountable values and still have the probabilities sum to one. Therefore, for a continuous random variable, $P(a \leq X \leq b) = P(a < X < b) = P(a \leq X < b) = P(a < X \leq b)$ because $P(X = a)$ and $P(X = b)$ are both zero.

A continuous random variable is completely described by its probability density function, denoted by $f(x)$. The graph of $f(x)$ approximates the relative frequency polygon for the population. The probability that the variable assumes a value within an interval, say $P(a \leq X \leq b)$, is defined as the area under $f(x)$ between points a and b. Moreover, the entire area under $f(x)$ over all values of x must equal one; this is equivalent to the fact that, for discrete random variables, the probabilities add up to one.

A simple probability distribution for a continuous random variable is called the **continuous uniform distribution**. This distribution is appropriate when the underlying random variable has an equally likely chance of assuming a value within a specified range. Suppose you are informed that your new refrigerator will be delivered between 2:00 pm and 3:00 pm. Let the random variable X denote the delivery time of your refrigerator. This variable is bounded below by 2:00 pm and above by 3:00 pm for a total range of 60 minutes. Here, the probability of delivery between 2:00 pm and 2:30 pm equals 0.50 (=30/60), as does the probability of delivery between 2:30 pm and 3:00 pm. Similarly, the probability of delivery in any 15-minute interval equals 0.25 (=15/60), and so on. Other examples of random variables that follow the continuous uniform distribution include the scheduled flight time between cities and the waiting time for a campus bus. Any specified range for each of these random variables can be assumed to be equally probable.

In this section, we focus on the most widely used continuous probability distribution: the **normal distribution**. It is the familiar bell-shaped distribution, also referred to as the Gaussian distribution. One reason for its extensive use is that it closely approximates the probability distribution for a wide range of random variables of interest. Examples of random variables that closely follow a normal distribution include salaries of employees, cumulative debt of college graduates, and advertising expenditure of firms. Another important function of the normal distribution is that it serves as the cornerstone of statistical inference, a topic discussed in detail in Chapter 5.

A graph depicting the normal probability density function $f(x)$ is often referred to as the normal curve or the bell curve, symmetric around the mean. We generally use the cumulative distribution function $P(X \leq x)$ to compute probabilities for a normally distributed random variable, where $P(X \leq x)$ is simply the area under the normal curve up to the value x. Fortunately, we do not necessarily need the knowledge of integral calculus to compute probabilities for the normal distribution. Instead, we rely on a table to find probabilities. We can also compute probabilities with Excel, R, and other statistical packages. The specifics of how to use the table are explained next.

The Standard Normal Distribution

The **standard normal distribution** is a special case of the normal distribution with a mean equal to zero and a standard deviation (or variance) equal to one. Using the letter Z to denote a random variable with the standard normal distribution, we have $E(Z) = 0$ and $SD(Z) = 1$. As usual, we use the lowercase letter z to denote the value that the standard normal variable Z may assume.

We will first show how to compute probabilities related to the standard normal distribution. Later, we will show that any normal distribution is equivalent to the standard normal distribution when the unit of measurement is changed to measure standard deviations from the mean.

Virtually all introductory statistics texts include the **z table**, that provides areas (probabilities) under the z curve. However, the format of these tables is sometimes different. In this text, the z table provides cumulative probabilities $P(Z \leq z)$; this table appears on two pages in Appendix D and is labeled Table D.1. The left-hand page provides cumulative probabilities for z values less than or equal to zero. The right-hand page shows cumulative probabilities for z values greater than or equal to zero. Given the symmetry of the normal distribution and the fact that the area under the entire curve is one, other probabilities can be easily computed.

THE STANDARD NORMAL DISTRIBUTION

The standard normal random variable Z is a normal random variable with $E(Z) = 0$ and $SD(Z) = 1$. The z table lists cumulative probabilities $P(Z \leq z)$ against positive and negative z values.

Figure 4.4 represents the standard normal probability density function (z distribution). Because the random variable Z is symmetric around its mean of 0, $P(Z < 0) = P(Z > 0) = 0.5$. As is the case with all continuous random variables, we can also write the probabilities as $P(Z \leq 0) = P(Z \geq 0) = 0.5$.

FIGURE 4.4
Standard normal probability density function

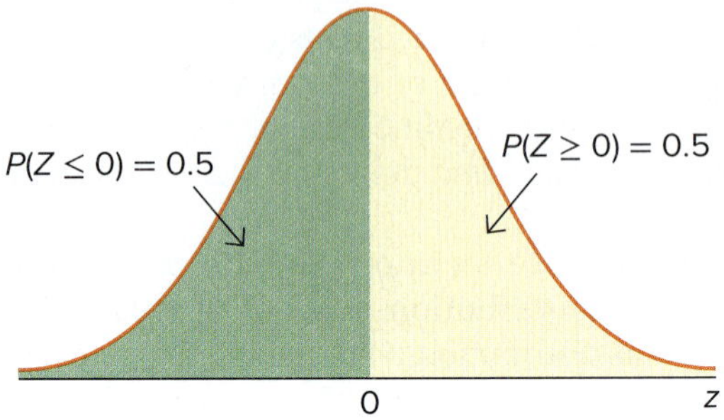

As mentioned earlier, the z table provides cumulative probabilities $P(Z \leq z)$ for a given z. Consider, for example, a cumulative probability $P(Z \leq 1.52)$. Because $z = 1.52$ is positive, we can look up this probability from the right-hand page of the z table in Appendix D; Table 4.5 shows a portion of the table.

TABLE 4.5 Portion of the Right-Hand Page of the *z* Table

z	0.00	0.01	0.02
0.0	0.5000	0.5040	↓
0.1	0.5398	0.5438	↓
⋮	⋮	⋮	⋮
1.5	→	→	0.9357

The first column of the table, denoted as the z column, shows values of z up to the tenth decimal point, while the first row of the table, denoted as the z row, shows hundredths values. Thus, for $z = 1.52$, we match 1.5 on the z column with 0.02 on the z row to find a corresponding probability of 0.9357. The arrows in Table 4.5 indicate that $P(Z \leq 1.52) = 0.9357$. Note that the area to the right of 1.52 can be computed as $P(Z > 1.52) = 1 - P(Z \leq 1.52) = 1 - 0.9357 = 0.0643$.

Suppose we want to find $P(Z \leq -1.96)$. Because z is a negative value, we can look up this probability from the left-hand page of the z table in Appendix D to find $P(Z \leq -1.96) = 0.0250$. As before, the area to the right of -1.96 can be computed as $P(Z > -1.96) = 1 - P(Z \leq -1.96) = 1 - 0.0250 = 0.9750$.

So far we have computed probabilities for given z values. Now we will evaluate z values for given cumulative probabilities; noncumulative probabilities can be evaluated using symmetry. Suppose we need to find z given $P(Z \leq z) = 0.6808$.

Because the probability is already in a cumulative format—that is, $P(Z \leq z) = 0.6808$—we simply look up 0.6808 from the body of the table (right-hand side) to find the corresponding z value from the row/column of z. Table 4.6 shows the relevant portion of the z table. Therefore, $z = 0.47$.

TABLE 4.6 Portion of the z Table

z	0.00	0.01	0.02	0.03	0.04	0.05	0.06	0.07
0.0	0.5000	0.5040	0.5080	0.5120	0.5160	0.5199	0.5239	↑
0.1	0.5398	0.5438	0.5478	0.5517	0.5557	0.5596	0.5636	↑
⋮	⋮	⋮	⋮	⋮	⋮	⋮	⋮	⋮
0.4	←	←	←	←	←	←	←	0.6808

Now suppose we need to find z given $P(Z \leq z) = 0.0643$. Here, z must be negative because the probability to its left is less than 0.50. We look up the cumulative probability 0.0643 from the left-hand page of the z table in Appendix D to find $z = -1.52$. Finally, if the given cumulative probability is not shown in the table, we find the approximate z value. For example, given $P(Z \leq z) = 0.90$, we approximate the value as $z = 1.28$.

The Transformation of Normal Random Variables

Any normal random variable can be transformed into the standard normal random variable to derive the relevant probabilities. In other words, any normally distributed random variable X with mean μ and standard deviation σ can be transformed (standardized) into the standard normal variable Z with mean equal to zero and standard deviation equal to one. We transform X into Z by subtracting from X its mean and dividing by its standard deviation; this is referred to as the **standard transformation**.

THE STANDARD TRANSFORMATION: CONVERTING *X* INTO *Z*

Any normally distributed random variable X with mean μ and standard deviation σ can be transformed into the standard normal random variable Z as

$$Z = \frac{X - \mu}{\sigma}.$$

Therefore, any value x has a corresponding value z given by

$$z = \frac{x - \mu}{\sigma}.$$

We are now in a position to solve any normal distribution problem by first transforming it to the z distribution.

EXAMPLE 4.14

Scores on a management aptitude exam are normally distributed with a mean of 72 and a standard deviation of 8.

a. What is the probability that a randomly selected manager will score above 60?

b. What is the probability that a randomly selected manager will score between 68 and 84?

SOLUTION:

Let X represent scores with $\mu = 72$ and $\sigma = 8$. We will use the standard transformation $z = \frac{x - \mu}{\sigma}$ to solve these problems.

a. The probability that a manager scores above 60 is $P(X > 60)$. Figure 4.5 shows the probability as the shaded area to the right of 60. We derive $P(X > 60) = P\left(Z > \frac{60 - 72}{8}\right) = P(Z > -1.5)$. Because $P(Z > -1.5) = 1 - P(Z \leq -1.5)$, we look up -1.50 in the z table (left-hand side) to get this probability as $1 - 0.0668 = 0.9332$.

FIGURE 4.5 Finding $P(X > 60)$

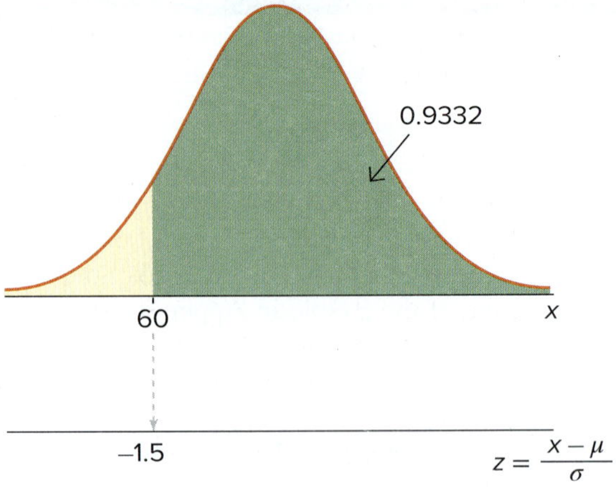

b. When solving for the probability that a manager scores between 68 and 84, we find $P(68 \leq X \leq 84)$. The shaded area in Figure 4.6 shows this probability. We derive $P(68 \leq X \leq 84) = P(\frac{68-72}{8} \leq Z \leq \frac{84-72}{8}) = P(-0.5 \leq Z \leq 1.5)$. We compute this probability using the z table as $P(Z \leq 1.5) - P(Z < -0.5) = 0.9332 - 0.3085 = 0.6247$.

FIGURE 4.6 Finding $P(68 \leq X \leq 84)$

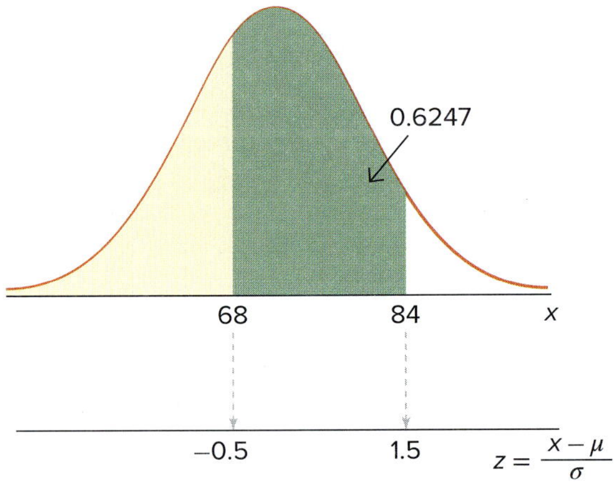

So far we have used the standard transformation to compute probabilities for given x values. We can use the **inverse transformation**, $x = \mu + z\sigma$, to compute x values for given probabilities.

THE INVERSE TRANSFORMATION: CONVERTING Z INTO X

The standard normal variable Z can be transformed to the normally distributed random variable X with mean μ and standard deviation σ as $X = \mu + Z\sigma$.

Therefore, any value z has a corresponding value x given by $x = \mu + z\sigma$.

EXAMPLE 4.15

Scores on a management aptitude examination are normally distributed with a mean of 72 and a standard deviation of 8.

a. What is the lowest score that will place a manager in the top 10% (90th percentile) of the distribution?

b. What is the highest score that will place a manager in the bottom 25% (25th percentile) of the distribution?

SOLUTION: Let X represent scores on a management aptitude examination with $\mu = 72$ and $\sigma = 8$. We will use the inverse transformation $x = \mu + z\sigma$ to solve these problems.

a. The 90th percentile is a numerical value x such that $P(X < x) = 0.90$. We look up 0.90 (or the closest value to 0.90) in the z table (right-hand side) to get $z = 1.28$ and use the inverse transformation to find $x = 72 + 1.28(8) = 82.24$. Therefore, a score of 82.24 or higher will place a manager in the top 10% of the distribution (see Figure 4.7).

FIGURE 4.7 Finding x given $P(X < x) = 0.90$

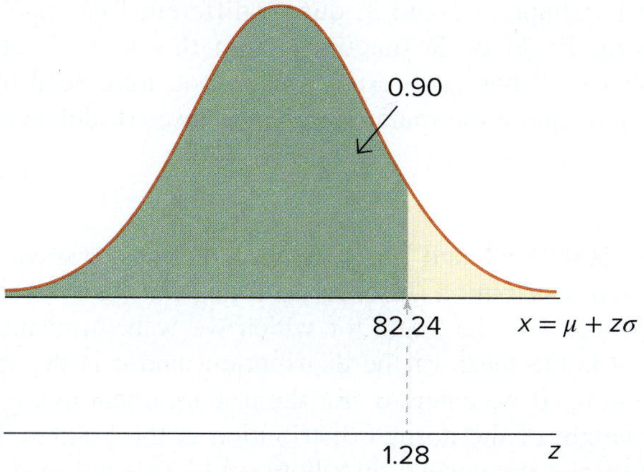

b. The 25th percentile is a numerical value x such that $P(X < x) = 0.25$. Using the z table (left-hand side), we find the corresponding z value that satisfies $P(Z < z) = 0.25$ as -0.67. We then solve $x = 72 - 0.67(8) = 66.64$. Therefore, a score of 66.64 or lower will place a manager in the bottom 25% of the distribution (see Figure 4.8).

FIGURE 4.8 Finding x given $P(X < x) = 0.25$

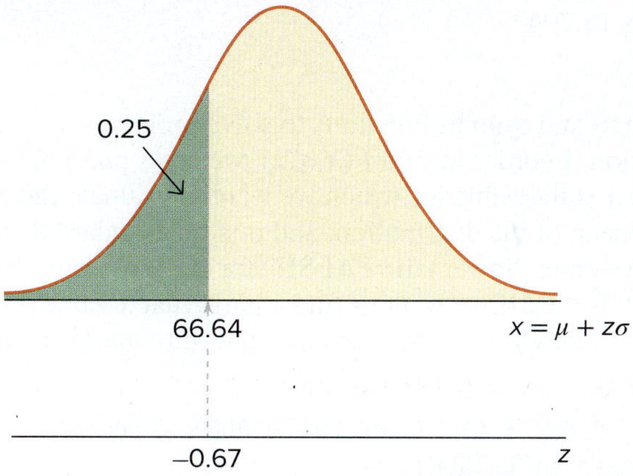

Using Excel and R for the Normal Distribution

Example 4.16 illustrates the use of Excel and R functions with respect to the normal distribution.

EXAMPLE 4.16

The Vanguard Balanced Index Fund seeks to maintain an allocation of 60% to stocks and 40% to bonds. With low fees and a consistent investment approach, this fund ranks fourth out of 792 funds that allocate 50% to 70% to stocks (*US News*, March 2017). Based on historical data, the expected return and standard deviation of this fund are estimated as 7.49% and 6.41%, respectively. Assume that the fund returns are stable and are normally distributed.

a. What is the probability that the fund will generate a return between 5% and 10%?

b. What is the lowest return of the fund that will place it in the top 10% (90th percentile) of the distribution?

SOLUTION: We let X denote the return on the Vanguard Balanced fund. We know that X is normally distributed with $\mu = 7.49$ and $\sigma = 6.41$.

As mentioned in Chapters 2 and 3, due to different fonts and type settings, copying and pasting Excel or R functions from this text directly into Excel or R may cause errors. When such errors occur, you may need to replace special characters such as quotation marks and parentheses or delete extra spaces in the functions.

Using Excel

We use Excel's **NORM.DIST** and **NORM.INV** functions to solve problems pertaining to the normal distribution. In order to find $P(X \leq x)$, we enter =NORM.DIST(x, μ, σ, 1) where x is the value for which we want to evaluate the cumulative probability, μ is the mean of the distribution, and σ is the standard deviation of the distribution. (If we enter "0" for the last argument in the function, then Excel returns the height of the normal distribution at the point x. This feature is useful if we want to plot the normal distribution.) If we want to find a particular x value for a given cumulative probability (*cumulprob*), then we enter =NORM.INV(*cumulprob*, μ, σ).

a. In order to find the probability of a return between 5% and 10%, $P(5 \leq X \leq 10)$, we enter =NORM.DIST(10, 7.49, 6.41, 1) – NORM.DIST(5, 7.49, 6.41, 1). Excel returns 0.3035.

b. In order to find the lowest return that will place it in the top 10% (90th percentile) of the distribution, $P(X > x) = 0.10$, we enter =NORM.INV(0.90, 7.49, 6.41). Excel returns 15.7047.

Using R

We use R's **pnorm** and **qnorm** functions to solve problems associated with the normal distribution. In order to find $P(X \leq x)$, we enter pnorm(x, μ, σ, lower.tail = TRUE) where x is the value for which we want to evaluate the cumulative probability, μ is the mean of the distribution, and σ is the standard deviation of the distribution. If we enter "lower.tail=FALSE" for the last argument in the function, then R returns $P(X > x)$. If we want to find a particular x value for a given cumulative probability (*cumulprob*), then we enter qnorm(*cumulprob*, μ, σ).

a. In order to find $P(5 \leq X \leq 10)$, we enter:

```
> pnorm(10, 7.49, 6.41, lower.tail=TRUE) – pnorm(5, 7.49,
  6.41, lower.tail=TRUE)
```

And R returns: 0.3034746.

b. In order to solve for x to satisfy $P(X > x) = 0.10$, we enter:

```
> qnorm(0.90, 7.49, 6.41)
```

And R returns: 15.70475.

EXERCISES 4.5

Applications

51. The historical returns on a balanced portfolio have had an average return of 8% and a standard deviation of 12%. Assume that returns on this portfolio follow a normal distribution.
    a. What percentage of returns were greater than 20%?
    b. What percentage of returns were below −16%?

52. A professional basketball team averages 105 points per game with a standard deviation of 10 points. Assume points per game follow the normal distribution.
    a. What is the probability that a game's score is between 85 and 125 points?
    b. What is the probability that a game's score is more than 125 points? If there are 82 games in a regular season, in how many games will the team score more than 125 points?

53. The average rent in a city is $1,500 per month with a standard deviation of $250. Assume rent follows the normal distribution.
    a. What percentage of rents are between $1,250 and $1,750?
    b. What percentage of rents are less than $1,250?
    c. What percentage of rents are greater than $2,000?

54. Suppose that the miles-per-gallon (mpg) rating of passenger cars is a normally distributed random variable with a mean and a standard deviation of 33.8 mpg and 3.5 mpg, respectively.
    a. What is the probability that a randomly selected passenger car gets at least 40 mpg?
    b. What is the probability that a randomly selected passenger car gets between 30 and 35 mpg?
    c. An automobile manufacturer wants to build a new passenger car with an mpg rating that improves upon 99% of existing cars. What is the minimum mpg that would achieve this goal?

55. Business interns from a small private college earn an average annual salary of $43,000. Let the salary be normally distributed with a standard deviation of $18,000.
    a. What percentage of business interns make between $40,000 and $50,000?
    b. What percentage of business interns make more than $80,000?

56. A financial advisor informs a client that the expected return on a portfolio is 8% with a standard deviation of 12%. There is a 15% chance that the return would be above 16%. If the advisor is right about her assessment, is it reasonable to assume that the underlying return distribution is normal?

57. According to a company's website, the top 25% of the candidates who take the entrance test will be called for an interview. You have just been called for an interview. The reported mean and standard deviation of the test scores are 68 and 8, respectively. What is the possible range for your test score if you assume that the scores are normally distributed?

58. The time required to assemble an electronic component is normally distributed with a mean and a standard deviation of 16 minutes and 4 minutes, respectively.
    a. Find the probability that a randomly picked assembly takes between 10 and 20 minutes.
    b. It is unusual for the assembly time to be above 24 minutes or below 6 minutes. What proportion of assembly times falls in these unusual categories?

59. According to the Mortgage Banking Association, loans that are 90 days or more past due are considered seriously delinquent (housingwire.com, May 14, 2019). It has been reported that the rate of seriously delinquent loans has an average of 9.1%. Let the rate of seriously delinquent loans follow a normal distribution with a standard deviation of 0.80%.
    a. What is the probability that the rate of seriously delinquent loans is above 8%?
    b. What is the probability that the rate of seriously delinquent loans is between 9.5% and 10.5%?

60. The manager of a night club in Boston stated that 95% of the customers are between the ages of 22 and 28 years. If the age of customers is normally distributed with a mean of 25 years, calculate its standard deviation.

61. An estimated 1.8 million students take on student loans to pay ever-rising tuition and room and board. It is also known that the average cumulative debt of recent college graduates is about $22,500. Let the cumulative debt among recent college graduates be normally distributed with a standard deviation of $7,000. Approximately how many recent college graduates have accumulated student loans of more than $30,000?

62. On average, an American professional football game lasts about three hours, even though the ball is actually in play only 11 minutes (*SB Nation*, April 1, 2019). Assume that game times are normally distributed with a standard deviation of 0.4 hour.
    a. Find the probability that a game lasts less than 2.5 hours.
    b. Find the probability that a game lasts either less than 2.5 hours or more than 3.5 hours.

c. Find the maximum value for the game time that will place it in the bottom 1% of the distribution.

63. A young investment manager tells his client that the probability of making a positive return with his suggested portfolio is 90%. If it is known that returns are normally distributed with a mean of 5.6%, what is the risk, measured by standard deviation, that this investment manager assumes in his calculation?

64. You are considering the risk-return profile of two mutual funds for investment. The relatively risky fund promises an expected return of 8% with a standard deviation of 14%. The relatively less risky fund promises an expected return and standard deviation of 4% and 5%, respectively. Assume that the returns are approximately normally distributed.
    a. Which mutual fund will you pick if your objective is to minimize the probability of earning a negative return?
    b. Which mutual fund will you pick if your objective is to maximize the probability of earning a return above 8%?

65. A new car battery is sold with a two-year warranty whereby the owner gets the battery replaced free of cost if it breaks down during the warranty period. Suppose an auto store makes a net profit of $20 on batteries that stay trouble-free during the warranty period; it makes a net loss of $10 on batteries that break down. The life of batteries is known to be normally distributed with a mean and a standard deviation of 40 and 16 months, respectively.
    a. What is the probability that a battery will break down during the warranty period?
    b. What is the expected profit of the auto store on a battery?
    c. What is the expected monthly profit on batteries if the auto store sells an average of 500 batteries a month?

4.6 WRITING WITH DATA

Case Study

Professor Lang is a professor of economics at Salem State University. She has been teaching a course in Principles of Economics for over 25 years. Professor Lang has never graded on a curve because she believes that relative grading may unduly penalize or benefit a student in an unusually strong or weak class. She always uses an absolute scale for making grades, as shown in the two left columns of Table 4.7.

Jasper White/Image Source

TABLE 4.7 Grading Scales with Absolute Grading versus Relative Grading

Absolute Grading		Relative Grading	
Grade	**Score**	**Grade**	**Probability**
A	92 and above	A	0.10
B	78 up to 92	B	0.35
C	64 up to 78	C	0.40
D	58 up to 64	D	0.10
F	Below 58	F	0.05

A colleague of Professor Lang's has convinced her to move to relative grading because it corrects for unanticipated problems. Professor Lang decides to experiment with grading based on the relative scale as shown in the two right columns of Table 4.7. Using this relative grading scheme, the top 10% of students will get A's, the next 35% B's, and so on. Based on her years of teaching experience, Professor Lang believes that the scores in her course follow a normal distribution with a mean of 78.6 and a standard deviation of 12.4.

Professor Lang wants to use the above information to

1. Calculate probabilities based on the absolute scale. Compare these probabilities to the relative scale.
2. Calculate the range of scores for various grades based on the relative scale. Compare these ranges to the absolute scale.
3. Determine which grading scale makes it harder to get higher grades.

Sample Report—Absolute Grading versus Relative Grading

Many teachers would confess that grading is one of the most difficult tasks of their profession. Two common grading systems used in higher education are relative and absolute. Relative grading systems are norm-referenced or curve-based, in which a grade is based on the student's relative position in class. Absolute grading systems, on the other hand, are criterion-referenced, in which a grade is related to the student's absolute performance in class. In short, with absolute grading, the student's score is compared to a predetermined scale, whereas with relative grading, the score is compared to the scores of other students in the class.

Let X represent a grade in Professor Lang's class, which is normally distributed with a mean of 78.6 and a standard deviation of 12.4. This information is used to derive the grade probabilities based on the absolute scale. For instance, the probability of receiving an A is derived as $P(X \geq 92) = P(Z \geq 1.08) = 0.14$. Other probabilities, derived similarly, are presented in Table 4.8.

TABLE 4.8 Probabilities Based on Absolute Scale and Relative Scale

Grade	Probability Based on Absolute Scale	Probability Based on Relative Scale
A	0.14	0.10
B	0.38	0.35
C	0.36	0.40
D	0.07	0.10
F	0.05	0.05

The second column of Table 4.8 shows that 14% of students are expected to receive A's, 38% B's, and so on. Although these numbers are generally consistent with the relative scale restated in the third column of Table 4.8, it appears that the relative scale makes it harder for students to get higher grades. For instance, 14% get A's with the absolute scale compared to only 10% with the relative scale.

Alternatively, we can compare the two grading methods on the basis of the range of scores for various grades. The second column of Table 4.9 restates the range of scores based on absolute grading. In order to obtain the range of scores based on relative grading, it is once again necessary to apply concepts from the normal distribution. For instance, the minimum score required to earn an A with relative grading is derived by solving for x in $P(X \geq x) = 0.10$. Because $P(X \geq x) = 0.10$ is equivalent to $P(Z \geq z) = 0.10$, it follows that $z = 1.28$. Inserting the proper values of the mean, the standard deviation, and z into $x = \mu + z\sigma$ yields a value of x equal to 94.47. Ranges for other grades, derived similarly, are presented in the third column of Table 4.9.

TABLE 4.9 Range of Scores with Absolute Grading versus Relative Grading

Grade	Range of Scores Based on Absolute Grading	Range of Scores Based on Relative Grading
A	92 and above	94.47 and above
B	78 up to 92	80.21 up to 94.47
C	64 up to 78	65.70 up to 80.21
D	58 up to 64	58.20 up to 65.70
F	Below 58	Below 58.20

Once again comparing the results in Table 4.9, the use of the relative scale makes it harder for students to get higher grades in Professor Lang's courses. For instance, in order to receive an A with relative grading, a student must have a score of at least 94.47 versus a score of at least 92 with absolute grading. Both absolute and relative grading methods have their merits and teachers often make the decision on the basis of their teaching philosophy. However, if Professor Lang wants to keep the grades consistent with her earlier absolute scale, she should base her relative scale on the probabilities computed in the second column of Table 4.8.

Suggested Case Studies

Report 4.1. Enacted in 1998, the Children's Online Privacy Protection Act requires firms to obtain parental consent before tracking the information and the online movement of children; however, the act applies to those children ages 12 and under. Teenagers are often unaware of the consequences of sharing their lives online. Data reapers create huge libraries of digital profiles and sell these profiles to advertisers, who use it to detect trends and micro-target their ads back to teens. For example, a teen searching online for ways to lose weight could become enticed by an ad for dietary supplements, fed into his/her network by tracking cookies. As a preliminary step in gauging the magnitude of teen usage of social networking sites, a researcher surveys 200 teen girls and 200 teen boys. Of teen girls, 166 use social networking sites; of teen boys, 156 use social networking sites.

In a report, use the sample information to

- Determine the probability that a teen uses social networking sites.
- Determine the probability that a teen girl uses a social networking site.
- New legislation would ban Internet companies from sending targeted advertising to children under 16 and give these children and their parents the ability to delete their digital footprint and profile with an "eraser button". Given the probabilities that you calculated with respect to teen usage of social networking sites, do you think that this legislation is necessary? Explain.

Report 4.2. Senior executives at Skyhigh Construction, Inc., participate in a pick-your-salary plan. They choose salaries in a range between $125,000 and $150,000. By choosing a lower salary, an executive has an opportunity to make a larger bonus. If Skyhigh does not generate an operating profit during the year, then no bonuses are paid. Skyhigh has just hired two new senior executives, Allen Grossman and Felicia Arroyo. Each must decide whether to choose Option 1: a base pay of $125,000 with a possibility of a large bonus or Option 2: a base pay of $150,000 with a possibility of a bonus, but the bonus would be one-half of the bonus under Option 1.

Grossman, 44 years old, is married with two young children. He bought his home at the height of the market and has a rather large monthly mortgage payment. Arroyo, 32 years old, just completed her MBA at a prestigious Ivy League university. She is single and has no student loans due to a timely inheritance upon entering graduate school. Arroyo just moved to the area, so she has decided to rent an apartment for at least one year. Given their personal profiles, inherent perceptions of risk, and subjective views of the economy, Grossman and Arroyo construct their individual probability distributions with respect to bonus outcomes shown in Table 4.10.

TABLE 4.10 Grossman's and Arroyo's Probability Distributions

	Probability	
Bonus (in $)	Grossman	Arroyo
0	0.35	0.20
50,000	0.45	0.25
100,000	0.10	0.35
150,000	0.10	0.20

In a report, use the sample information to

- Compute expected values to evaluate payment plans for Grossman and Arroyo.
- Help Grossman and Arroyo decide whether to choose Option 1 or Option 2 for his/her compensation package.

Report 4.3. Akiko Hamaguchi is the manager of a small sushi restaurant called Little Ginza in Phoenix, Arizona. As part of her job, Akiko has to purchase salmon every day for the restaurant. For the sake of freshness, it is important that she buys the right amount of salmon daily. Buying too much may result in wastage and buying too little may disappoint some customers on high-demand days.

Akiko has estimated that the daily consumption of salmon is normally distributed with a mean of 12 pounds and a standard deviation of 3.2 pounds. She has always bought 20 pounds of salmon every day. Lately, she has been criticized by the owners because this amount of salmon was too often resulting in wastage. As part of cost cutting, Akiko is considering a new strategy. She will buy salmon that is sufficient to meet the daily demand of customers on 90% of the days.

In a report, help Akiko use the above information to

- Calculate the probability that the demand for salmon at Little Ginza is above 20 pounds.
- Calculate the probability that the demand for salmon at Little Ginza is below 15 pounds.
- Determine the amount of salmon that should be bought daily so that the restaurant meets demand on 90% of the days.

5 Statistical Inference

LEARNING OBJECTIVES

After reading this chapter, you should be able to:

LO **5.1** **Describe the sampling distribution of the sample mean.**

LO **5.2** **Describe the sampling distribution of the sample proportion.**

LO **5.3** **Construct a confidence interval for the population mean.**

LO **5.4** **Construct a confidence interval for the population proportion.**

LO **5.5** **Conduct a hypothesis test for the population mean.**

LO **5.6** **Conduct a hypothesis test for the population proportion.**

In the last chapter, we had information on population parameters, such as the population proportion or the population mean, for the analysis of discrete and continuous random variables. In many instances, we do not have information on the parameters, so we make statistical inferences on the basis of sample statistics. In this chapter, we first discuss how to evaluate the properties of sample statistics. In particular, we examine the probability distributions of the sample mean and the sample proportion based on simple random sampling.

We then turn our attention to estimation and hypothesis testing, which are the two basic methodologies of statistical inference. In order to estimate an unknown population parameter, we develop and interpret a confidence interval. We use a hypothesis test to challenge the status quo, or some belief about an underlying population parameter. We focus on confidence intervals and hypothesis tests for the population mean and the population proportion.

©Ken Seet/Corbis Images/SuperStock

INTRODUCTORY CASE

Undergraduate Study Habits

Are today's college students studying hard or hardly studying? A study asserts that, over the past six decades, the number of hours that the average college student studies each week has been steadily dropping (*The Wall Street Journal*, April 10, 2019). In 1961, students invested 24 hours per week in their academic pursuits, whereas today's students study an average of 14 hours per week.

Susan Knight is a dean at a large university in California. She wonders if the study trend is reflective of the students at her university. She randomly selects 35 students and asks their average study time per week (in hours). A portion of the responses is shown in Table 5.1.

TABLE 5.1 Number of Hours Spent Studying

25
19
⋮
16

Summary measures: $\bar{x} = 16.3714$ hours and $s = 7.2155$ hours.

FILE
Study_Hours

Susan wants to use the sample information to

1. Determine if the mean study time of students at her university is below the 1961 national average of 24 hours per week.
2. Determine if the mean study time of students at her university differs from today's national average of 14 hours per week.

A synopsis of this case is provided at the end of Section 5.3.

5.1 SAMPLING DISTRIBUTIONS

In many applications, we are interested in the characteristics of a population. For instance, a ride sharing company is interested in the average income (population mean) in a large city. Similarly, a banker is interested in the default probability (population proportion) of mortgage holders. Recall that the population mean and the population proportion are parameters that describe a numerical variable and a categorical variable, respectively. Because it is extremely difficult, if not impossible, to analyze the entire population, we generally make inferences about the characteristics of the population on the basis of a random sample drawn from the population.

It is important to note that there is only one population, but many possible samples of a given size can be drawn from the population. Therefore, a population **parameter** is a constant, even though its value may be unknown. On the other hand, a **statistic**, such as the sample mean or the sample proportion, is a variable whose value depends on the particular sample that is randomly drawn from the population.

> **PARAMETER VERSUS STATISTIC**
>
> A parameter is a constant, although its value may be unknown. A statistic is a variable whose value depends on the chosen random sample.

Consider the income in a large city as the variable of interest. If you decide to make inferences about the population mean income on the basis of a random draw of 38 residents, then the sample mean $\overline{X}$ is the relevant statistic. Note that the value of $\overline{X}$ will change if you choose a different random sample of 38 residents. In other words, $\overline{X}$ is a variable whose value depends on the chosen random sample. The sample mean is commonly referred to as the **estimator**, or the **point estimator**, of the population mean.

In the income example, the sample mean $\overline{X}$ is the estimator of the mean income of residents in the large city. If the average derived from a specific sample is \$54,000, then $\overline{x} = 54{,}000$ is the **estimate** of the population mean. Similarly, if the variable of interest is the default probability of mortgage holders, then the sample proportion of defaults, denoted by $\overline{P}$, from a random sample of 80 mortgage holders is the estimator of the population proportion. If 10 out of 80 mortgage holders in a given sample default, then $\overline{p} = 10/80 = 0.125$ is the estimate of the population proportion.

> **ESTIMATOR AND ESTIMATE**
>
> When a statistic is used to estimate a parameter, it is referred to as an estimator. A particular value of the estimator is called an estimate.

The Sampling Distribution of the Sample Mean

We first focus on the probability distribution of the sample mean $\overline{X}$, which is also referred to as the sampling distribution of $\overline{X}$. Because $\overline{X}$ is a variable, its sampling distribution is simply the probability distribution derived from all possible samples of a given size from the population. Consider, for example, a mean derived from a sample of n observations. Another mean can similarly be derived from a different sample of n observations. If we repeat this process a very large number of times, then the frequency distribution of the sample means can be thought of as its sampling distribution. In particular, we will discuss the expected value and the standard deviation of the sample mean. We will also study the conditions under which the sampling distribution of the sample mean is normally distributed.

LO 5.1

Describe the sampling distribution of the sample mean.

Let the random variable X represent a certain characteristic of a population under study, with an expected value, $E(X) = \mu$, and a variance, $Var(X) = \sigma^2$. For example, X could represent the income of city residents or the return on an investment. We can think of μ and σ^2 as the mean and the variance of an individual observation drawn randomly from the population of interest, or simply as the population mean and the population variance. Let the sample mean $\overline{X}$ be based on a random sample of n observations from this population.

The expected value of $\overline{X}$ is the same as the expected value of the individual observation—that is, $E(\overline{X}) = E(X) = \mu$. In other words, if we were to sample repeatedly from a given population, the average value of the sample means will equal the average value of all individual observations in the population, or, simply, the population mean. This is an important property of an estimator, called unbiasedness, that holds irrespective of whether the sample mean is based on a small or a large sample. An estimator is **unbiased** if its expected value equals the population parameter of interest.

The variance of $\overline{X}$ is equal to $Var(\overline{X}) = \frac{\sigma^2}{n}$. In other words, if we were to sample repeatedly from a given population, the variance of the sample mean will equal the variance of all individual observations in the population, divided by the sample size, n. Note that $Var(\overline{X})$ is smaller than the variance of X, which is equal to $Var(X) = \sigma^2$. This is an intuitive result, suggesting that the variability between sample means is less than the variability between observations. Because each sample is likely to contain both high and low observations, the highs and lows cancel one another, making the variance of $\overline{X}$ smaller than the variance of X. As usual, the standard deviation of $\overline{X}$ is calculated as the positive square root of the variance. However, in order to distinguish the variability between samples from the variability between individual observations, we refer to the standard deviation of $\overline{X}$ as the **standard error** of the sample mean, computed as $se(\overline{X}) = \frac{\sigma}{\sqrt{n}}$.

THE EXPECTED VALUE AND THE STANDARD ERROR OF THE SAMPLE MEAN

The expected value of the sample mean $\overline{X}$ equals the population mean; that is, $E(\overline{X}) = \mu$. The standard error of the sample mean equals the population standard deviation divided by the square root of the sample size; that is, $se(\overline{X}) = \frac{\sigma}{\sqrt{n}}$.

EXAMPLE 5.1

The chefs at a local pizza chain in Cambria, California, strive to maintain the suggested size of their 16-inch pizzas. Despite their best efforts, they are unable to make every pizza exactly 16 inches in diameter. The manager has determined that the size of the pizzas is normally distributed with a mean of 16 inches and a standard deviation of 0.8 inch.

a. What are the expected value and the standard error of the sample mean derived from a random sample of two pizzas?

b. What are the expected value and the standard error of the sample mean derived from a random sample of four pizzas?

c. Compare the expected value and the standard error of the sample mean with those of an individual pizza.

SOLUTION: We know that the population mean $\mu = 16$ and the population standard deviation $\sigma = 0.8$. We use $E(\overline{X}) = \mu$ and $se(\overline{X}) = \frac{\sigma}{\sqrt{n}}$ to calculate the following results.

a. With the sample size $n = 2$, $E(\overline{X}) = 16$ and $se(\overline{X}) = \frac{0.8}{\sqrt{2}} = 0.57$.

b. With the sample size $n = 4$, $E(\overline{X}) = 16$ and $se(\overline{X}) = \frac{0.8}{\sqrt{4}} = 0.40$.

c. The expected value of the sample mean for both sample sizes is identical to the expected value of the individual pizza. However, the standard error of the sample mean with $n = 4$ is lower than the one with $n = 2$. For both sample sizes, the standard error of the sample mean is lower than the standard deviation of the individual pizza. This result confirms that averaging reduces variability.

Sampling from a Normally Distributed Population

An important feature of the sampling distribution of the sample mean $\overline{X}$ is that, irrespective of the sample size n, $\overline{X}$ is normally distributed if the population X from which the sample is drawn is normally distributed. In other words, if X is normally distributed with expected value μ and standard deviation σ, then $\overline{X}$ is also normally distributed with expected value μ and standard error $\sigma/\sqrt{n}$. Moreover, if $\overline{X}$ is normally distributed, then it can be transformed into a standard normal variable Z by subtracting from $\overline{X}$ its mean, and then dividing by its standard error.

SAMPLING FROM NORMALLY DISTRIBUTED POPULATION

For any sample size n, the sampling distribution of $\overline{X}$ is normal if the population X from which the sample is drawn is normally distributed.

EXAMPLE 5.2

Use the information in Example 5.1 to answer the following questions:

a. What is the probability that a randomly selected pizza is less than 15.5 inches?

b. What is the probability that the average of two randomly selected pizzas is less than 15.5 inches?

c. What is the probability that the average of four randomly selected pizzas is less than 15.5 inches?

d. Comment on the computed probabilities.

SOLUTION: Because the population is normally distributed, the sampling distribution of the sample mean is also normal. Figure 5.1 depicts the shapes of the three distributions based on the population mean $\mu = 16$ and the population standard deviation $\sigma = 0.8$.

FIGURE 5.1 Normal distribution of the sample mean

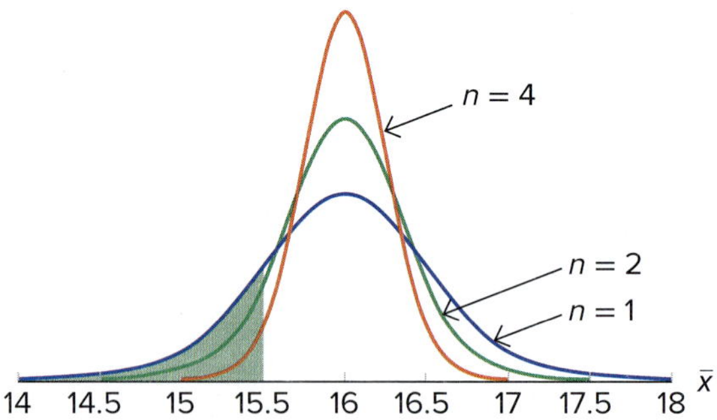

Note that when the sample size $n = 1$, the sample mean $\bar{x}$ is the same as the individual observation x.

a. We use the standard transformation to derive $P(X < 15.5) = P\left(Z < \frac{15.5 - 16}{0.8}\right) = P(Z < -0.63) = 0.2653$. There is a 26.43% chance that an individual pizza is less than 15.5 inches.

b. Here we use the standard transformation to derive $P(\overline{X} < 15.5) = P\left(Z < \frac{15.5 - 16}{0.8/\sqrt{2}}\right) = P(Z < -0.88) = 0.1894$. In a random sample of two pizzas, there is an 18.94% chance that the average size is less than 15.5 inches.

c. Again we find $P(\overline{X} < 15.5)$, but now $n = 4$. Therefore, $P(\overline{X} < 15.5) = P\left(Z < \frac{15.5 - 16}{0.8/\sqrt{4}}\right) = P(Z < -1.25) = 0.1056$. In a random sample of four pizzas, there is a 10.56% chance that the average size is less than 15.5 inches.

d. The probability that the average size is under 15.5 inches, for four randomly selected pizzas, is less than half of that for an individual pizza. This is due to the fact that while X and $\overline{X}$ have the same expected value of 16, the variance of $\overline{X}$ is less than that of X.

The Central Limit Theorem

For making statistical inferences, it is essential that the sampling distribution of $\overline{X}$ is normally distributed. So far we have only considered the case where $\overline{X}$ is normally distributed because the population X from which the sample is drawn is normally distributed. What if the underlying population is not normally distributed?

Here we present the **central limit theorem (CLT)**, which perhaps is the most remarkable result of probability theory. The CLT states that the sum or the average of a large number of independent observations from the same underlying distribution has an approximate normal distribution. The approximation steadily improves as the number of observations increases. In other words, irrespective of whether or not the population X is normally distributed, the sample mean $\overline{X}$ computed from a random sample of size n will be approximately normally distributed as long as n is sufficiently large. How large a sample is necessary? Practitioners often use the normal distribution approximation when $n \geq 30$.

THE CENTRAL LIMIT THEOREM FOR THE SAMPLE MEAN

For any population X with expected value μ and standard deviation σ, the sampling distribution of $\overline{X}$ will be approximately normal if the sample size n is sufficiently large. As a general guideline, the normal distribution approximation is justified when $n \geq 30$.

EXAMPLE 5.3

For the month of May, a coffee chain advertised a Happy Hour between the hours of 3 pm and 5 pm when customers could enjoy a half-price iced coffee. The manager of one of the chains wants to determine if the Happy Hour has had a lingering effect on the amount of money customers now spend on iced coffee.

Before the marketing campaign, customers spent an average of \$4.18 on iced coffee with a standard deviation of \$0.84. Based on 50 customers sampled after the marketing campaign, the average amount spent is \$4.26. If the coffee chain chose not to pursue the marketing campaign, how likely is it that customers will spend an average of \$4.26 or more on iced coffee?

SOLUTION: If the coffee chain did not pursue the marketing campaign, spending on iced coffee would still have mean $\mu = 4.18$ and standard deviation $\sigma = 0.84$. We need to calculate the probability that the sample mean is at least 4.26, or $P(\overline{X} \geq 4.26)$. The population from which the sample is drawn is not known to be normally distributed. However, because $n \geq 30$, from the central limit theorem we know that $\overline{X}$ is approximately normally distributed. Therefore, as shown in Figure 5.2, $P(\overline{X} \geq 4.26) = P\left(Z \geq \frac{4.26 - 4.18}{0.84/\sqrt{50}}\right) = P(Z \geq 0.67) = 1 - 0.7486 = 0.2514$. It is quite plausible (probability = 0.2514) that in a sample of 50 customers, the sample mean is \$4.26 or more even if the coffee chain did not pursue the marketing campaign.

FIGURE 5.2
Finding $P(\overline{X} \geq 4.26)$

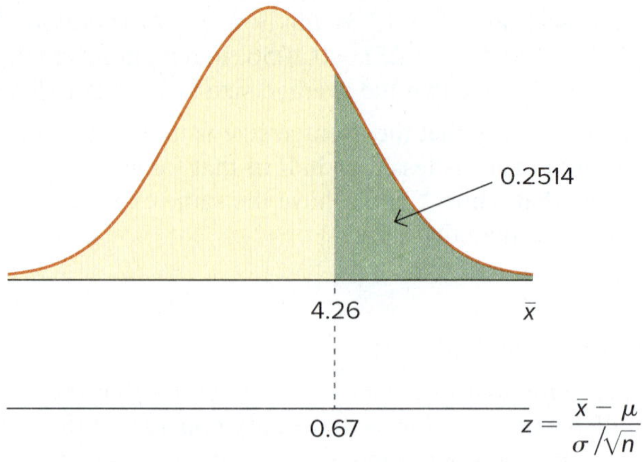

LO 5.2

Describe the sampling distribution of the sample proportion.

The Sampling Distribution of the Sample Proportion

Our discussion thus far has focused on the population mean, but in many business applications, we are concerned with the population proportion. For instance, a banker is interested in the default probability of mortgage holders. Or an online retailer cares about the proportion of customers who make a purchase after receiving a promotional e-mail. In these examples, the parameter of interest is the population proportion p.

As in the case of the population mean, we almost always make inferences about the population proportion on the basis of sample data. Here, the relevant statistic (estimator) is the sample proportion, $\overline{P}$; a particular value (estimate) is denoted by $\overline{p}$. Because $\overline{P}$ is a variable, we need to discuss its sampling distribution.

It turns out that the sampling distribution of $\overline{P}$ is closely related to the binomial distribution. Recall from Chapter 4 that the binomial distribution describes the number of successes X in n trials of a Bernoulli process where p is the probability of success; thus, $\overline{P} = \frac{X}{n}$ is the number of successes X divided by the sample size n. It can be shown that the expected value and the variance of the sampling distribution of $\overline{P}$ are $E(\overline{P}) = p$ and $Var(\overline{P}) = \frac{p(1-p)}{n}$, respectively. Note that because $E(\overline{P}) = p$, it implies that $\overline{P}$ is an unbiased estimator of p. Analogous to our discussion regarding the standard error of the sample mean, we refer to the standard deviation of the sample proportion as the standard error of the sample proportion; that is, $se(\overline{P}) = \sqrt{\frac{p(1-p)}{n}}$.

THE EXPECTED VALUE AND THE STANDARD ERROR OF THE SAMPLE PROPORTION

The expected value of the sample proportion $\overline{P}$ is equal to the population proportion; that is, $E(\overline{P}) = p$. The standard error of the sample proportion $\overline{P}$ equals $se(\overline{P}) = \sqrt{\frac{p(1-p)}{n}}$.

In this text, we make statistical inferences about the population proportion only when the sampling distribution of $\overline{P}$ is approximately normal. From the earlier discussion of the central limit theorem (CLT), we can conclude that $\overline{P}$ is approximately normally distributed when the sample size is sufficiently large. In general, the normal distribution approximation is justified when $np \geq 5$ and $n(1 - p) \geq 5$. Moreover, if $\overline{P}$ is normally distributed, then it can be transformed into a standard normal variable Z by subtracting from $\overline{P}$ its expected value, and then dividing by its standard error.

THE CENTRAL LIMIT THEOREM FOR THE SAMPLE PROPORTION

For any population proportion p, the sampling distribution of $\overline{P}$ is approximately normal if the sample size n is sufficiently large. As a general guideline, the normal distribution approximation is justified when $np \geq 5$ and $n(1 - p) \geq 5$.

EXAMPLE 5.4

A study found that 55% of British firms experienced a cyber-attack in the past year (*BBC*, April 23, 2019).

a. What are the expected value and the standard error of the sample proportion derived from a random sample of 100 firms?

b. In a random sample of 100 firms, what is the probability that the sample proportion is greater than 0.57?

SOLUTION:

a. Given that $p = 0.55$ and $n = 100$, the expected value and the standard error of $\overline{P}$ are $E(\overline{P}) = 0.55$ and $se(\overline{P}) = \sqrt{\frac{0.55(1-0.55)}{100}} = 0.0497$.

b. With $n = 100$, the normal approximation for the sample proportion is justified for $p = 0.55$. As shown in Figure 5.3, we find that $P(\overline{P} \geq 0.57) = P\left(Z \geq \frac{0.57 - 0.55}{\sqrt{\frac{0.55(1-0.55)}{100}}}\right) = P(Z \geq 0.40) = 1 - 0.6554 = 0.3446$.

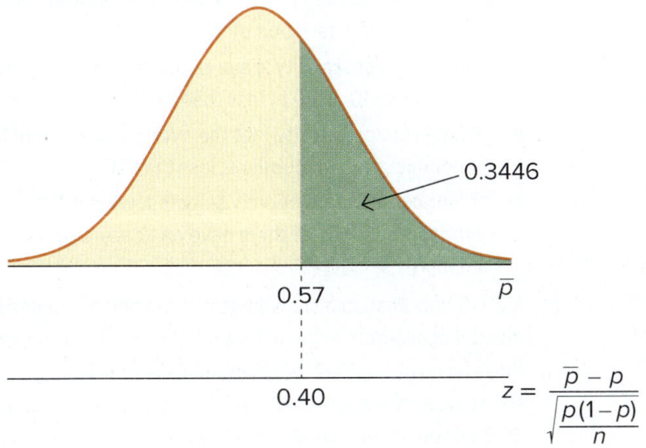

FIGURE 5.3 Finding $P(\overline{P} \geq 0.57)$

With a chance of 34.46%, it is quite plausible that the proportion of British firms who experience a cyber-attack is at least 0.57.

EXERCISES 5.1

Applications

1. According to a survey, high school girls average 100 text messages daily. Assume the population standard deviation is 20 text messages. Suppose a random sample of 50 high school girls is taken.
   a. What is the probability that the sample mean is more than 105?
   b. What is the probability that the sample mean is less than 95?
   c. What is the probability that the sample mean is between 95 and 105?
2. Beer bottles are filled so that they contain an average of 330 ml of beer in each bottle. Suppose that the amount of beer in a bottle is normally distributed with a standard deviation of four ml.
   a. What is the probability that a randomly selected bottle will have less than 325 ml of beer?

b. What is the probability that a randomly selected six-pack of beer will have a mean amount less than 325 ml?
c. What is the probability that a randomly selected 12-pack of beer will have a mean amount less than 325 ml?
d. Comment on the sample size and the corresponding probabilities.

3. The weight of people in a small town in Missouri is known to be normally distributed with a mean of 180 pounds and a standard deviation of 28 pounds. On a raft that takes people across the river, a sign states, "Maximum capacity 3,200 pounds or 16 persons." What is the probability that a random sample of 16 persons will exceed the weight limit of 3,200 pounds?

4. Despite its nutritional value, seafood is only a tiny part of the American diet, with the average American eating just 16 pounds of seafood per year. Janice and Nina both work in the seafood industry and they decide to create their own random samples and document the average seafood diet in their sample. Let the standard deviation of the American seafood diet be seven pounds.
   a. Janice samples 42 Americans and finds an average seafood consumption of 18 pounds. How likely is it to get an average of 18 pounds or more if she had a representative sample?
   b. Nina samples 90 Americans and finds an average seafood consumption of 17.5 pounds. How likely is it to get an average of 17.5 pounds or more if she had a representative sample?
   c. Which of the two women is likely to have used a more representative sample? Explain.

5. A small hair salon in Denver, Colorado, averages about 30 customers on weekdays with a standard deviation of six. It is safe to assume that the underlying distribution is normal. In an attempt to increase the number of weekday customers, the manager offers a $2 discount on five consecutive weekdays. She reports that her strategy has worked because the sample mean of customers during this five-weekday period jumps to 35.
   a. How unusual would it be to get a sample average of 35 or more customers if the manager had not offered the discount?
   b. Do you feel confident that the manager's discount strategy has worked? Explain.

6. Suppose that the typical college student graduates with $28,650 in debt. Let debt among recent college graduates be normally distributed with a standard deviation of $7,000.
   a. What is the probability that the average debt of four recent college graduates is more than $25,000?
   b. What is the probability that the average debt of four recent college graduates is more than $30,000?

7. Forty families gathered for a fund-raising event. Suppose the individual contribution for each family is normally distributed with a mean and a standard deviation of $115 and $35, respectively. The organizers would call this event a success if the total contributions exceed $5,000. What is the probability that this fund-raising event is a success?

8. A doctor is getting sued for malpractice by four of her former patients. It is believed that the amount that each patient will sue her for is normally distributed with a mean of $800,000 and a standard deviation of $250,000.
   a. What is the probability that a given patient sues the doctor for more than $1,000,000?
   b. If the four patients sue the doctor independently, what is the probability that the total amount they sue for is over $4,000,000?

9. Suppose that the miles-per-gallon (mpg) rating of passenger cars is normally distributed with a mean and a standard deviation of 33.8 and 3.5 mpg, respectively.
   a. What is the probability that a randomly selected passenger car gets more than 35 mpg?
   b. What is the probability that the average mpg of four randomly selected passenger cars is more than 35 mpg?
   c. If four passenger cars are randomly selected, what is the probability that all of the passenger cars get more than 35 mpg?

10. Suppose that IQ scores are normally distributed with a mean of 100 and a standard deviation of 16.
   a. What is the probability that a randomly selected person will have an IQ score of less than 90?
   b. What is the probability that the average IQ score of four randomly selected people is less than 90?
   c. If four people are randomly selected, what is the probability that all of them have an IQ score of less than 90?

11. A 2019 Pew Research study finds that the number of undocumented immigrants living in the United States has dropped to the level it was in 2004. While its share has declined, California still accounts for approximately 23% of the nation's estimated 10.5 million undocumented immigrants.
   a. In a sample of 50 undocumented immigrants, what is the probability that more than 20% live in California?
   b. In a sample of 200 undocumented immigrants, what is the probability that more than 20% live in California?
   c. Comment on the reason for the difference between the computed probabilities in parts a and b.

12. Suppose that a study finds that 33% of teenagers text while driving. The study was based on 100 teen drivers.
   a. Discuss the sampling distribution of the sample proportion.
   b. What is the probability that the sample proportion is less than 0.30?
   c. What is the probability that the sample proportion is within ± 0.02 of the population proportion?

13. A car manufacturer is concerned about poor customer satisfaction at one of its dealerships. The management decides to evaluate the satisfaction surveys of its next 40 customers. The dealer will be fined if the number of customers who report favorably is between 22 and 26. The dealership will be dissolved if fewer than 22 customers report favorably. It is known that 70% of the dealer's customers report favorably on satisfaction surveys.
    a. What is the probability that the dealer will be fined?
    b. What is the probability that the dealership will be dissolved?
14. At a new exhibit in the Museum of Science, people are asked to choose between 50 or 100 random draws from a machine. The machine is known to have 60 green balls and 40 red balls. After each draw, the color of the ball is noted and the ball is put back for the next draw. You win a prize if more than 70% of the draws result in a green ball. Would you choose 50 or 100 draws for the game? Explain.
15. Suppose that one in six smartphone users have fallen prey to cyber-attack.
    a. Discuss the sampling distribution of the sample proportion based on a sample of 200 smartphone users. Is it appropriate to use the normal distribution approximation for the sample proportion?
    b. What is the probability that more than 20% of smartphone users in the sample have fallen prey to cyber-attack?

5.2 ESTIMATION

Given sample data, we use the sample statistics to make inferences about the unknown population parameters, such as the population mean and the population proportion. Two basic methodologies emerge from the inferential branch of statistics: estimation and hypothesis testing. Although the sample statistics are based on a portion of the population, they contain useful information to estimate the population parameters and to conduct tests regarding the population parameters. In this section, we focus on estimation.

As mentioned earlier, when a statistic is used to estimate a parameter, it is referred to as a point estimator, or simply an estimator. A particular value of the estimator is called a point estimate or an estimate. Recall that the sample mean $\overline{X}$ is the estimator of the population mean μ, and the sample proportion $\overline{P}$ is the estimator of the population proportion p.

Suppose in a sample of 25 ultra-green cars, we find that the mean miles per gallon (mpg) of the cars is $\bar{x} = 96.52$ mpg; similarly, suppose we calculate the proportion of these cars that get an mpg greater than 100 as $\bar{p} = 0.28$. Thus, the estimate for the mean mpg of all ultra-green cars is 96.52 mpg, and the estimate for the proportion of all ultra-green cars with mpg greater than 100 is 0.28. It is important to note that these estimates are based on a sample of 25 cars and, therefore, are likely to vary between samples. Often it is more informative to provide a range of values—an interval—rather than a single point estimate for the unknown population parameter. This range of values is called a **confidence interval**, also referred to as an interval estimate, for the population parameter.

> **CONFIDENCE INTERVAL**
>
> A confidence interval, or interval estimate, provides a range of values that, with a certain level of confidence, contains the population parameter of interest.

In order to construct a confidence interval for the population mean μ or the population proportion p, it is essential that the sampling distributions of $\overline{X}$ and $\overline{P}$ follow, or approximately follow, a normal distribution. Other methods that do not require the normality condition are not discussed in this text. Recall from Section 5.1 that $\overline{X}$ follows a normal distribution when the underlying population is normally distributed; this result holds irrespective of the sample size n. If the underlying population is not normally distributed, then by the central limit theorem, the sampling distribution of $\overline{X}$ will be approximately normal if the sample size is sufficiently large—that is, when $n \geq 30$. Similarly, the sampling distribution of $\overline{P}$ is approximately normal if the sample size is sufficiently large—that is, when $np \geq 5$ and $n(1 - p) \geq 5$.

The main ingredient for developing a confidence interval is the sampling distribution of the underlying statistic. The sampling distribution of $\overline{X}$, for example, describes how the sample mean varies between samples. Recall that the variability between samples is measured by the standard error of $\overline{X}$. If the standard error is small, it implies that the sample means are not only close to one another, they are also close to the unknown population mean μ.

A confidence interval is generally associated with a **margin of error** that accounts for the standard error of the estimator and the desired confidence level of the interval. The symmetry of the sampling distributions of both the population mean and the population proportion allow us to construct a confidence interval by adding and subtracting the same margin of error to the point estimate.

GENERAL FORMAT OF THE CONFIDENCE INTERVAL FOR μ AND p

The confidence interval for the population mean and the population proportion is constructed as

$$\text{point estimate} \pm \text{margin of error.}$$

An analogy to a simple weather example is instructive. If you feel that the outside temperature is about 50 degrees, then perhaps you can, with a certain level of confidence, suggest that the actual temperature is between 40 and 60 degrees. In this example, 50 degrees is analogous to a point estimate of the actual temperature, and 10 degrees is the margin of error that is added to and subtracted from this point estimate.

Confidence Interval for the Population Mean μ

LO 5.3

Construct a confidence interval for the population mean.

Before constructing a confidence interval for the population mean μ, we first need to introduce a new distribution. Let's see why this is the case.

Recall that if $\overline{X}$ is normally distributed, then any value $\overline{x}$ can be transformed to its corresponding value z as $z = (\overline{x} - \mu)/(\sigma/\sqrt{n})$. In reality, the population standard deviation σ is rarely known. With σ unknown, the standard error of $\overline{X}$, given by $\sigma/\sqrt{n}$, can be conveniently estimated by $s/\sqrt{n}$, where s denotes the sample standard deviation. For convenience, we denote this estimate of the standard error of $\overline{X}$ also by $se(\overline{X}) = s/\sqrt{n}$.

Another standardized statistic, which uses the estimator S in place of σ, is computed as $T = \frac{\overline{X} - \mu}{S/\sqrt{n}}$. The random variable T follows the **Student's *t* distribution**, more commonly known as the ***t* distribution**.

The t distribution is actually a family of distributions, which are similar to the z distribution in that they are all bell-shaped and symmetric around 0. However, all t distributions have slightly broader tails than the z distribution. Each t distribution is identified by the degrees of freedom, or simply, df. The degrees of freedom determine the extent of the broadness of the tails of the distribution; the fewer the degrees of freedom, the broader the tails. Because the t distribution is defined by the degrees of freedom, it is common to refer to it as the t_{df} distribution.

THE t_{df} DISTRIBUTION

If a random sample of size n is taken from a normal population with a finite variance, then the statistic $T = \frac{\overline{X} - \mu}{S/\sqrt{n}}$ follows the t_{df} distribution, where df denotes degrees of freedom.

Locating t_{df} Values and Probabilities

Table 5.2 lists t_{df} values for selected upper-tail probabilities and degrees of freedom df. Table D.2 of Appendix D provides a more complete table. Because the t_{df} distribution is a family of distributions identified by the *df* parameter, the *t* table is not as comprehensive as the *z* table. It only lists probabilities corresponding to a limited number of values. Also, unlike the cumulative probabilities in the *z* table, the *t* table provides the probabilities in the upper tail of the distribution.

TABLE 5.2 Portion of the *t* Table

	Area in Upper Tail, α					
df	0.20	0.10	0.05	0.025	0.01	0.005
1	1.376	3.078	6.314	12.706	31.821	63.657
⋮	⋮	⋮	⋮	⋮	⋮	⋮
10	0.879	1.372	**1.812**	2.228	2.764	3.169
⋮	⋮	⋮	⋮	⋮	⋮	⋮
∞	0.842	1.282	1.645	1.960	2.326	2.576

We use the notation $t_{\alpha,df}$ to denote a value such that the area in the upper tail equals α for a given *df*. In other words, for a random variable T_{df}, the notation $t_{\alpha,df}$ represents a value such that $P(T_{df} \geq t_{\alpha,df}) = \alpha$. Similarly, $t_{\alpha/2,df}$ represents a value such that $P(T_{df} \geq t_{\alpha/2,df}) = \alpha/2$. Figure 5.4 illustrates the notation.

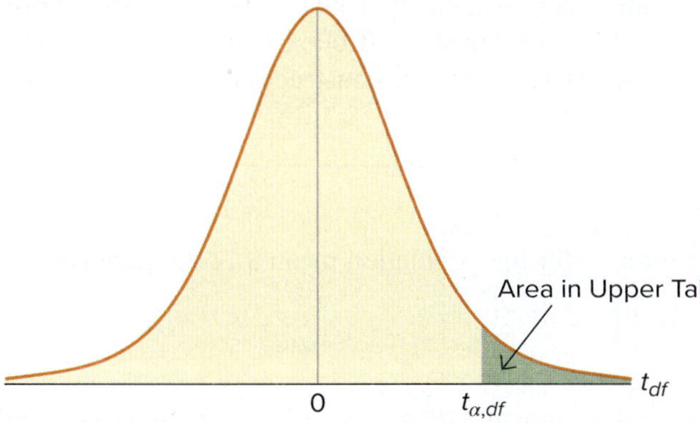

FIGURE 5.4 Graphical depiction of $P(T_{df} \geq t_{\alpha,df}) = \alpha$

When determining the value $t_{\alpha,df}$, we need two pieces of information: (a) the sample size *n* or the degrees of freedom *df*, and (b) α. For instance, suppose we want to find the value $t_{\alpha,df}$ with $\alpha = 0.05$ and $df = 10$; that is, $t_{0.05,10}$. Using Table 5.2, we look at the first column labeled *df* and find the row 10. We then continue along this row until we reach the column $\alpha = 0.05$. The value 1.812 suggests that $P(T_{10} \geq 1.812) = 0.05$. Due to the symmetry of the *t* distribution, we can infer that $P(T_{10} \leq -1.812) = 0.05$. Figure 5.5 shows these results graphically. Also, because the area under the entire t_{df} distribution sums to one, we can infer that $P(T_{10} < 1.812) = 1 - 0.05 = 0.95$, which also equals $P(T_{10} > -1.812)$.

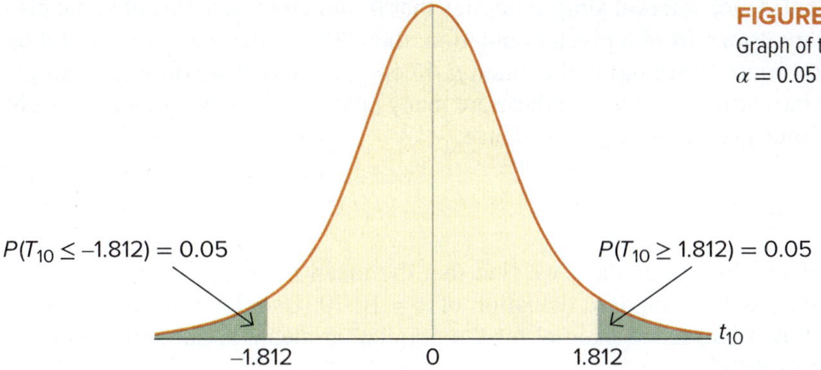

FIGURE 5.5 Graph of the probability $\alpha = 0.05$ on both sides of T_{10}

Sometimes the exact probability cannot be determined from the t table. For example, given $df = 10$, the exact probability $P(T_{10} \geq 1.562)$ is not included in the table. However, this probability is between 0.05 and 0.10 because the value 1.562 falls between 1.372 and 1.812. Similarly, $P(T_{10} < 1.562)$ is between 0.90 and 0.95. We can use Excel, R, and other statistical packages to find exact probabilities.

As mentioned earlier, we construct the confidence interval for μ as point estimate ± margin of error, where the margin of error accounts for the desired confidence level of the interval and the standard error of the sample mean. It can be shown (derivations not provided) that the margin of error is calculated as the product of $t_{\alpha/2,df}$ and $s/\sqrt{n}$, where $t_{\alpha/2,df}$ is often referred to as the reliability factor.

While it is common to report the 95% confidence interval, in theory we can construct an interval of any level of confidence. We now formally let α (alpha) denote the allowed probability of error; in the next section this is referred to as the signficance level. This is the probability that the estimation procedure will generate an interval that does not contain μ. The confidence coefficient $(1 - \alpha)$ is interpreted as the probability that the estimation procedure will generate an interval that contains μ. Thus, the probability of error α is related to the confidence coefficient and the confidence level as follows:

- Confidence coefficient $= 1 - \alpha$, and
- Confidence level $= 100(1 - \alpha)\%$.

For example, the confidence coefficient of 0.95 implies that the probability of error α equals $1 - 0.95 = 0.05$ and the confidence level equals $100(1 - 0.05)\% = 95\%$. Similarly, for the 90% confidence interval, the confidence coefficient equals 0.90 and $\alpha = 1 - 0.90 = 0.10$. The following statement generalizes the construction of a confidence interval for μ.

CONFIDENCE INTERVAL FOR μ

A $100(1 - \alpha)\%$ confidence interval for the population mean μ is computed as

$$\bar{x} \pm t_{\alpha/2,df}\frac{s}{\sqrt{n}} \quad \text{or} \quad \left[\bar{x} - t_{\alpha/2,df}\frac{s}{\sqrt{n}},\ \bar{x} + t_{\alpha/2,df}\frac{s}{\sqrt{n}}\right],$$

where s is the sample standard deviation and $df = n - 1$. This formula is valid only if $\bar{X}$ (approximately) follows a normal distribution.

Confidence intervals are often misinterpreted; we need to exercise care in characterizing them. For instance, suppose we construct a 90% confidence interval for μ. This does *not* imply that the probability that μ falls in the confidence interval is 0.90. Remember that μ is a constant, although its value is not known. It either falls in the interval (probability equals one) or does not fall in the interval (probability equals 0). The randomness comes from $\bar{X}$, not μ, because many possible sample means can be derived from a population. Therefore, it is incorrect to say that the probability that μ falls in some interval is 0.90. The 90% confidence interval simply implies that if numerous samples of some predetermined size are drawn from a given population, then 90% of the intervals formed by the estimating procedure (formula) will contain μ. Keep in mind that we only use a single sample to derive the estimates. Because there are many possible samples, we will be right 90% of the time, thus giving us 90% confidence.

EXAMPLE 5.5

In a sample of 25 ultra-green cars, we find that the mean miles per gallon (mpg) is $\bar{x} = 96.52$ mpg with a standard deviation of $s = 10.70$. Use this information to construct the 90% confidence interval for the population mean. Assume that mpg follows a normal distribution.

SOLUTION: The condition that $\overline{X}$ follows a normal distribution is satisfied since we assumed that mpg is normally distributed. We construct the confidence interval as $\bar{x} \pm t_{\alpha/2,df}\frac{s}{\sqrt{n}}$. For the 90% confidence interval, $\alpha = 0.10$, $\alpha/2 = 0.05$, and, given $n = 25$, $df = 25 - 1 = 24$. Thus, $t_{0.05,24} = 1.711$. The 90% confidence interval for μ is computed as

$$\bar{x} \pm t_{\alpha/2,df}\frac{s}{\sqrt{n}} = 96.52 \pm 1.711\frac{10.70}{\sqrt{25}} = 96.52 \pm 3.66.$$

The 90% confidence interval for the average mpg of all ultra-green cars is between 92.86 mpg and 100.18 mpg.

Using Excel and R to Construct a Confidence Interval for μ

Excel and R are quite useful when constructing confidence intervals. Consider the following example.

EXAMPLE 5.6

Amazon Prime is a $119-per-year service that gives the company's customers free two-day shipping and discounted rates on overnight delivery. Prime customers also get other perks, such as free e-books. Table 5.3 shows a portion of the annual expenditures (in $) for 100 Prime customers. Use Excel and R to construct the 95% confidence interval for the average annual expenditures of all Prime customers. Summarize the results.

TABLE 5.3 Annual Prime Expenditures (in $)

Customer	Expenditures
1	1272
2	1089
⋮	⋮
100	1389

FILE
Prime

SOLUTION: We compute $\bar{x} \pm t_{\alpha/2,df}\frac{s}{\sqrt{n}}$, or, equivalently, we find the lower and upper limits of the confidence interval: $\left[\bar{x} - t_{\alpha/2,df}\frac{s}{\sqrt{n}}, \bar{x} + t_{\alpha/2,df}\frac{s}{\sqrt{n}}\right]$.

Using Excel

a. Open the ***Prime*** data file. Note that the observations for the Expenditures variable are in cells B2 through B101.

b. For a 95% confidence interval, with $n = 100$, we find $t_{0.025,99}$ using = T.INV(0.975,99). Thus, in order to obtain the lower limit, we enter =AVERAGE(B2:B101) – T.INV(0.975,99) *STDEV.S(B2:101)/SQRT(100). For the upper limit, we enter =AVERAGE(B2:B101) + T.INV(0.975,99) *STDEV.S(B2:101)/SQRT(100).

Note: For a one-step approach to constructing a confidence interval in Excel, we can use the *Descriptive Statistics* option in its Analysis Toolpak which we discussed in Chapter 3. In the *Descriptive Statistics* dialog box, we select *Summary statistics* and *Confidence Interval for Mean.* (By default, the confidence level is set at 95%, but you easily enter another level.) In the table that Excel returns, we find the mean and the margin of error which is labeled Confidence Level(95.0%).

Using R

a. Import the ***Prime*** data into a data frame (table) and label it myData.

b. For a 95% confidence interval, with $n = 100$, we find $t_{0.025,99}$ using the **qt** function. Thus, in order to obtain the lower and upper limits, we enter:

```
lower <- mean(myData$Expenditures) – qt(0.975, 99, lower.tail =
TRUE)*sd(myData$Expenditures)/sqrt(100)
upper <- mean(myData$Expenditures) + qt(0.975, 99, lower.tail =
TRUE)*sd(myData$Expenditures)/sqrt(100)
```

Note: For a one-step approach to constructing a confidence interval in R, refer to Example 5.12.

Summary

With 95% confidence, we conclude that the average annual expenditures of all Prime customers fall between \$1,240.24 and \$1,373.64

LO 5.4

Construct a confidence interval for the population proportion.

Confidence Interval for the Population Proportion p

Recall that while the population mean μ describes a numerical variable, the population proportion p is the essential descriptive measure for a categorical variable. The parameter p represents the proportion of successes in the population, where success is defined by a particular outcome.

As in the case of the population mean, we estimate the population proportion on the basis of its sample counterpart. In particular, we use the sample proportion $\overline{P}$ as the point estimator of the population proportion p. Also, although the sampling distribution of $\overline{P}$ is based on the binomial distribution, we can approximate it by the normal distribution for large samples, according to the central limit theorem. This approximation is valid when the sample size n is such that $np \geq 5$ and $n(1 - p) \geq 5$.

Using the normal approximation for $\overline{P}$ with $E(\overline{P}) = p$ and $se(\overline{P}) = \sqrt{p(1-p)/n}$, and analogous to the construction of the confidence interval for the population mean, a $100(1 - \alpha)\%$ confidence interval for the population proportion is $\overline{p} \pm z_{\alpha/2}\sqrt{\frac{p(1-p)}{n}}$, where the notation $z_{\alpha/2}$ (the reliability factor) is the z value associated with the probability of $\alpha/2$ in the upper tail of the standard normal distribution.

This confidence interval is theoretically sound; however, it cannot be implemented because it uses p in the derivation, which is unknown. Because we always use large samples for the normal distribution approximation, we can also conveniently replace p with its estimate $\overline{p}$ in the construction of the interval. Therefore, for $\sqrt{\frac{p(1-p)}{n}}$, we substitute $\sqrt{\frac{\overline{p}(1-\overline{p})}{n}}$. This substitution yields a feasible confidence interval for the population proportion. The following statement generalizes the construction of a confidence interval for p.

CONFIDENCE INTERVAL FOR p

A $100(1 - \alpha)\%$ confidence interval for the population proportion p is computed as

$$\overline{p} \pm z_{\alpha/2}\sqrt{\frac{\overline{p}(1-\overline{p})}{n}} \quad \text{or} \quad \left[\overline{p} - z_{\alpha/2}\sqrt{\frac{\overline{p}(1-\overline{p})}{n}},\ \overline{p} + z_{\alpha/2}\sqrt{\frac{\overline{p}(1-\overline{p})}{n}}\right].$$

This formula is valid only if $\overline{P}$ (approximately) follows a normal distribution.

The normality condition is evaluated at the sample proportion $\bar{p}$. In other words, for constructing a confidence interval for the population proportion p, we require that $n\bar{p} \geq 5$ and $n(1 - \bar{p}) \geq 5$.

EXAMPLE 5.7

In a sample of 25 ultra-green cars, seven of the cars obtained over 100 miles per gallon (mpg). Construct 90% and 99% confidence intervals for the population proportion of all ultra-green cars that obtain over 100 mpg.

SOLUTION: The point estimate for the population proportion is $\bar{p} = 7/25 = 0.28$. Note that the normality condition is satisfied because $np \geq 5$ and $n(1 - p) \geq 5$, where p is evaluated at $\bar{p} = 0.28$. With the 90% confidence level, $\alpha/2 = 0.10/2 = 0.05$; thus, we find $z_{\alpha/2} = z_{0.05} = 1.645$. Substituting the appropriate values into $\bar{p} \pm z_{\alpha/2}\sqrt{\frac{\bar{p}(1-\bar{p})}{n}}$ yields

$$0.28 \pm 1.645\sqrt{\frac{0.28(1 - 0.28)}{25}} = 0.28 \pm 0.148.$$

With 90% confidence, the percentage of cars that obtain over 100 mpg is between 13.2% and 42.8%.

For the 99% confidence interval, we use $\alpha/2 = 0.01/2 = 0.005$ and $z_{\alpha/2} = z_{0.005} = 2.576$ to obtain

$$0.28 \pm 2.576\sqrt{\frac{0.28(1 - 0.28)}{25}} = 0.28 \pm 0.231.$$

At a higher confidence level of 99%, the interval for the percentage of cars that obtain over 100 mpg becomes 4.9% to 51.1%. Given the current sample size of 25 cars, we gain confidence (from 90% to 99%) at the expense of precision, as the corresponding margin of error increases from 0.148 to 0.231.

EXERCISES 5.2

Applications

16. A popular weight loss program claims that with its recommended healthy diet regimen, users lose significant weight within a month. In order to estimate the mean weight loss of all customers, a nutritionist takes a sample of 18 dieters and records their weight loss one month after joining the program. He computes the mean and the standard deviation of weight loss as 12.5 pounds and 9.2 pounds, respectively. He believes that weight loss is likely to be normally distributed.
    a. Calculate the margin of error with 95% confidence.
    b. Calculate the 95% confidence interval for the population mean.
    c. How can the margin of error reported in part a be reduced?
17. FILE ***Customers.*** The manager of The Cheesecake Factory in Memphis reports that on six randomly selected weekdays, the number of customers served was 120, 130, 100, 205, 185, and 220. She believes that the number of customers served on weekdays follows a normal distribution.
    a. Calculate the margin of error with 90% confidence.
    b. Construct the 90% confidence interval for the average number of customers served on weekdays.
    c. How can the margin of error reported in part a be reduced?
18. According to a recent survey, high school girls average 100 text messages daily. Assume that the survey was based on a random sample of 36 high school girls. The sample standard deviation is computed as 10 text messages daily.
    a. Calculate the margin of error with 99% confidence.
    b. What is the 99% confidence interval for the population mean texts that all high school girls send daily?
19. The Chartered Financial Analyst (CFA) designation is fast becoming a requirement for serious investment professionals.

Although it requires a successful completion of three levels of grueling exams, the designation often results in a promising career with a lucrative salary. A student of finance is curious about the average salary of a CFA charterholder. He takes a random sample of 36 recent charterholders and computes a mean salary of $158,000 with a standard deviation of $36,000. Use this sample information to determine the 95% confidence interval for the average salary of a CFA charterholder.

20. The sudoku puzzle has become very popular all over the world. It is based on a 9×9 grid and the challenge is to fill in the grid so that every row, every column, and every 3×3 box contains the digits 1 through 9. A researcher is interested in estimating the average time taken by a college student to solve the puzzle. He takes a random sample of eight college students and records their solving times (in minutes) as 14, 7, 17, 20, 18, 15, 19, 28.
    a. Construct the 99% confidence interval for the average time taken by a college student to solve a sudoku puzzle.
    b. What assumption is necessary to make this inference?

21. FILE ***Stock_Price.*** The monthly closing stock price for a large technology firm for the first six months of the year are reported in the following table.

Month	Price
January	71
February	73
March	76
April	78
May	81
June	75

    a. Calculate the sample mean and the sample standard deviation.
    b. Calculate the 90% confidence interval for the mean stock price of the firm, assuming that the stock price is normally distributed.
    c. What happens to the margin of error if a higher confidence level is used for the interval estimate?

22. Suppose the 90% confidence interval for the mean SAT scores of applicants at a business college is given by [1690, 1810]. This confidence interval uses the sample mean and the sample standard deviation based on 25 observations. What are the sample mean and the sample standard deviation used when computing the interval?

23. A teacher wants to estimate the mean time (in minutes) that students take to go from one classroom to the next. His research assistant uses the sample time of 36 students to report the confidence interval as [8.20, 9.80].
    a. Find the sample mean time used to compute the confidence interval.
    b. Determine the confidence level if the sample standard deviation used for the interval is 2.365.

24. In order to attract more Millennial customers (those born between 1980 and 2000), a new clothing store offers free gourmet coffee and pastry to its customers. The average daily revenue over the past five-week period has been $1,080 with a standard deviation of $260. Use this sample information to construct the 95% confidence interval for the average daily revenue. The store manager believes that the coffee and pastry strategy would lead to an average daily revenue of $1,200. Use the 95% interval to determine if the manager is wrong.

25. FILE ***Debt_Payments.*** The accompanying table shows a portion of average monthly debt payments (Debt in $) for residents of 26 metropolitan areas. Construct 90% and 95% confidence intervals for the population mean. Comment on the width of the intervals.

City	Debt
Washington, D.C.	1285
Seattle	1135
⋮	⋮
Pittsburgh	763

26. FILE ***Economics.*** An associate dean of a university wishes to compare the means on the standardized final exams in microeconomics and macroeconomics. He has access to a random sample of 40 scores from each of these two courses. A portion of the data is shown in the accompanying table.

Micro	Macro
85	48
78	79
⋮	⋮
75	74

    a. Construct 95% confidence intervals for the mean score in microeconomics and the mean score in macroeconomics.
    b. Explain why the widths of the two intervals are different.

27. FILE ***Math_Scores.*** For decades, people have believed that boys are innately more capable than girls in math. In other words, due to the intrinsic differences in brains, boys are believed to be better suited for doing math than girls. Recent research challenges this stereotype, arguing that gender differences in math performance have more to do with culture than innate aptitude. Others argue, however, that while the average may be the same, there is more variability in math ability for boys than girls, resulting in some boys with soaring

math skills. A portion of sample data on math scores of boys and girls is shown in the accompanying table.

Boys	Girls
74	83
89	76
⋮	⋮
66	74

a. Construct 95% confidence intervals for the mean scores of boys and the mean scores of girls. Explain your assumptions.
b. Explain why the widths of the two intervals are different.

28. FILE ***Startups.*** Many of today's leading companies, including Google, Microsoft, and Facebook, are based on technologies developed within universities. Lisa Fisher is a business school professor who believes that a university's research expenditure (Research in $ millions) and the age of its technology transfer office (Duration in years) are major factors that enhance innovation. She wants to know what the average values are for the Research and the Duration variables. She collects data from 143 universities on these variables, a portion of which is shown in the accompanying table.

Research	Duration
145.52	23
237.52	23
⋮	⋮
154.38	9

a. Construct and interpret the 95% confidence interval for the mean research expenditure of all universities.
b. Construct and interpret the 95% confidence interval for the mean duration of all universities.

29. A survey of 1,026 people were asked about what they would do with an unexpected cash gift. Forty-seven percent responded that they would pay off debts.
a. With 95% confidence, what is the margin of error?
b. Construct the 95% confidence interval for the population proportion of people who would pay off debts with an unexpected cash gift.

30. A sample of 5,324 Americans were asked about what matters most to them in a place to live. Thirty-seven percent of the respondents felt job opportunities matter most.
a. Construct the 90% confidence interval for the proportion of Americans who feel that good job opportunities matter most in a place to live.
b. Construct the 99% confidence interval for the proportion of Americans who feel that good job opportunities matter most in a place to live.
c. Which of the above two intervals has a higher margin of error? Explain why.

31. An economist reports that 560 out of a sample of 1,200 middle-income American households actively participate in the stock market.
a. Construct the 90% confidence interval for the proportion of middle-income Americans who actively participate in the stock market.
b. Can we conclude that the percentage of middle-income Americans who actively participate in the stock market is not 50%?

32. In a survey of 1,116 adults, 47% approved of the job that President Trump was doing in handling the economy (*Opinion Today*, July 1, 2019).
a. Compute the 90% confidence interval for the proportion of Americans who approved of President Trump's handling of the economy.
b. What is the resulting margin of error?
c. Compute the margin of error associated with the 99% confidence level.

33. In a recent poll of 760 homeowners in the United States, one in five homeowners reports having a home equity loan that he or she is currently paying off. Using a confidence coefficient of 0.90, construct the confidence interval for the proportion of all homeowners in the United States that hold a home equity loan.

34. Obesity is generally defined as 30 or more pounds over a healthy weight. A recent study of obesity reports 27.5% of a random sample of 400 adults in the United States to be obese.
a. Use this sample information to compute the 90% confidence interval for the adult obesity rate in the United States.
b. Is it reasonable to conclude with 90% confidence that the adult obesity rate in the United States differs from 30%?

35. An accounting professor is notorious for being stingy in giving out good letter grades. In a large section of 140 students in the fall semester, she gave out only 5% A's, 23% B's, 42% C's, and 30% D's and F's. Assuming that this was a representative class, compute the 95% confidence interval of the probability of getting at least a B from this professor.

5.3 HYPOTHESIS TESTING

Each and every, day people make decisions based on their beliefs about the true state of the world. They hold certain things to be true and others to be false, and then act accordingly. For example, an engineer believes that a certain steel cable has a breaking strength of 5,000 pounds or more, and then permits its use at a construction site; a manufacturer believes that a certain process yields capsules that contain precisely 100 milligrams of a drug, and then ships the capsules to a pharmacy; a manager believes that an incoming shipment contains 2%, or fewer, of defects, and then accepts the shipment.

In these cases, and many more, the formation of these beliefs may have started as a mere conjecture, an informed guess, or a proposition tentatively advanced as true. When people formulate a belief in this way, we refer to it as a hypothesis. Sooner or later, however, every hypothesis eventually confronts evidence that either substantiates or refutes it. Determining the validity of an assumption of this nature is called hypothesis testing.

We use hypothesis testing to resolve conflicts between two competing hypotheses on a particular population parameter of interest. We refer to one hypothesis as the **null hypothesis**, denoted H_0, and the other as the **alternative hypothesis**, denoted H_A. We think of the null hypothesis as corresponding to a presumed default state of nature or status quo. The alternative hypothesis, on the other hand, contradicts the default state or status quo.

> **NULL HYPOTHESIS VERSUS ALTERNATIVE HYPOTHESIS**
>
> When constructing a hypothesis test, we define a null hypothesis, denoted H_0, and an alternative hypothesis, denoted H_A. We conduct a hypothesis test to determine whether or not sample evidence contradicts H_0.

The hypothesis testing procedure enables us to make one of two decisions. If sample evidence is inconsistent with the null hypothesis, we reject the null hypothesis. Conversely, if sample evidence is not inconsistent with the null hypothesis, then we do not reject the null hypothesis. It is not correct to conclude that "we accept the null hypothesis" because while the sample information may not be inconsistent with the null hypothesis, it does not necessarily prove that the null hypothesis is true.

Consider an example from the medical field where the null is defined as "an individual is free of a particular disease." Suppose a medical procedure does not detect this disease. On the basis of this limited information, we can only conclude that we are unable to detect the disease (do not reject the null hypothesis). It does not necessarily prove that the person does not have the disease (accept the null hypothesis).

Defining the Null and the Alternative Hypotheses

A very crucial step in a hypothesis test concerns the formulation of the two competing hypotheses because the conclusion of the test depends on how the hypotheses are stated. As a general guideline, whatever we wish to establish is placed in the alternative hypothesis, whereas the null hypothesis includes the status quo. If we are unable to reject the null hypothesis, then we maintain the status quo or "business as usual." However, if we reject the null hypothesis, this establishes that the evidence supports the alternative hypothesis, which may require that we take some kind of action. For instance, if we reject the null hypothesis that an individual is free of a particular disease, then we conclude that the person is sick, for which treatment is prescribed.

In most applications, we require some form of the equality sign in the null hypothesis. (The justification for the equality sign will be provided later.) In general, any statement including one of the three signs "$=$", "$\leq$", or "$\geq$" is valid for the null hypothesis. Given that the alternative hypothesis states the opposite of the null hypothesis, the alternative hypothesis is then specified with a "$\neq$", "$>$", or "$<$" sign.

CONSTRUCTION OF THE COMPETING HYPOTHESES

As a general guideline, we use the alternative hypothesis as a vehicle to establish something new—that is, contest the status quo. In most applications, the null hypothesis regarding a particular population parameter of interest is specified with one of the following signs: $=$, $\leq$, or $\geq$; the alternative hypothesis is then specified with the corresponding opposite sign: $\neq$, $>$, or $<$.

A hypothesis test can be one-tailed or two-tailed. A two-tailed test is defined when the alternative hypothesis includes the sign "$\neq$". For example, H_0: $\mu = \mu_0$ versus H_A: $\mu \neq \mu_0$ and H_0: $p = p_0$ versus H_A: $p \neq p_0$ are examples of two-tailed tests, where μ_0 and p_0 represent hypothesized values of the population mean and the population proportion, respectively. If the null hypothesis is rejected, it suggests that the true parameter does not equal the hypothesized value.

A one-tailed test, on the other hand, involves a null hypothesis that can only be rejected on one side of the hypothesized value. For example, consider H_0: $\mu \leq \mu_0$ versus H_A: $\mu > \mu_0$. Here we can reject the null hypothesis only when there is substantial evidence that the population mean is greater than μ_0. It is also referred to as a right-tailed test because rejection of the null hypothesis occurs on the right side of the hypothesized mean. Another example is a left-tailed test, H_0: $\mu \geq \mu_0$ versus H_A: $\mu < \mu_0$, where the null hypothesis can only be rejected on the left side of the hypothesized mean. One-tailed tests for the population proportion are defined similarly.

In general, we follow three steps when formulating the competing hypotheses:

1. Identify the relevant population parameter of interest.
2. Determine whether it is a one- or two-tailed test.
3. Include some form of the equality sign in the null hypothesis and use the alternative hypothesis to establish a claim.

In the next two examples, our objective is to state the appropriate competing hypotheses.

EXAMPLE 5.8

A trade group predicts that back-to-school spending will average \$606.40 per family this year. A different economic model is needed if the prediction is wrong. Specify the null and the alternative hypotheses to determine if a different economic model is needed.

SOLUTION: Given that we are examining average back-to-school spending, the parameter of interest is the population mean μ. Because we want to be able to determine if the population mean differs from \$606.40 ($\mu \neq 606.40$), we need a two-tailed test and formulate the null and alternative hypotheses as

$$H_0\text{: } \mu = 606.40$$

$$H_A\text{: } \mu \neq 606.40$$

The trade group is advised to use a different economic model if the null hypothesis is rejected.

EXAMPLE 5.9

A television research analyst wishes to test a claim that more than 50% of the households will tune in for a TV episode. Specify the null and the alternative hypotheses to test the claim.

SOLUTION: This is an example of a one-tailed test regarding the population proportion p. Given that the analyst wants to determine whether $p > 0.50$, this claim is placed in the alternative hypothesis, whereas the null hypothesis is just its opposite.

$$H_0: p \leq 0.50$$

$$H_A: p > 0.50$$

The claim that more than 50% of the households will tune in for a TV episode is valid only if the null hypothesis is rejected.

Type I and Type II Errors

Because the decision of a hypothesis test is based on limited sample information, we are bound to make errors. Ideally, we would like to be able to reject the null hypothesis when the null hypothesis is false and not reject the null hypothesis when the null hypothesis is true. However, we may end up rejecting or not rejecting the null hypothesis erroneously. In other words, sometimes we reject the null hypothesis when we should not, or not reject the null hypothesis when we should.

We consider two types of errors in the context of hypothesis testing: a **Type I error** and a **Type II error**. A Type I error is committed when we reject the null hypothesis when the null hypothesis is actually true. On the other hand, a Type II error is made when we do not reject the null hypothesis when the null hypothesis is actually false.

Table 5.4 summarizes the circumstances surrounding Type I and Type II errors. Two correct decisions are possible: not rejecting the null hypothesis when the null hypothesis is true and rejecting the null hypothesis when the null hypothesis is false. Conversely, two incorrect decisions (errors) are also possible: rejecting the null hypothesis when the null hypothesis is true (Type I error) and not rejecting the null hypothesis when the null hypothesis is false (Type II error).

TABLE 5.4 Type I and Type II Errors

Decision	Null hypothesis is true	Null hypothesis is false
Reject the null hypothesis	Type I error	Correct decision
Do not reject the null hypothesis	Correct decision	Type II error

EXAMPLE 5.10

An online retailer is deciding whether or not to build a brick-and-mortar store in a new marketplace. A market analysis determines that the venture will be profitable if average pedestrian traffic exceeds 500 people per day. The competing hypotheses are specified as follows.

$$H_0: \mu \leq 500 \text{ (Do not build brick-and-mortar store.)}$$

$$H_A: \mu > 500 \text{ (Build brick-and-mortar store.)}$$

Discuss the consequences of a Type I error and a Type II error.

SOLUTION: A Type I error occurs when the conclusion to the hypothesis test is to reject H_0 so the retailer builds the brick-and-mortar store, but, in reality, average pedestrian traffic does not exceed 500 people per day and the venture will not be profitable. A Type II error occurs when the conclusion to the hypothesis test is to not reject H_0 so the retailer does not build the brick-and-mortar store, but, in reality, average pedestrian traffic exceeds 500 people per day and the venture would have been profitable. Arguably, the consequences of a Type I error in this example are more serious than those of a Type II error.

It is not always easy to determine which of the two errors has more serious consequences. For given evidence, there is a trade-off between these errors; by reducing the likelihood of a Type I error, we implicitly increase the likelihood of a Type II error, and vice versa. The only way we can reduce both errors is by collecting more evidence. Let us denote the probability of a Type I error by α, the probability of a Type II error by β, and the strength of the evidence by the sample size n. The only way we can lower both α and β is by increasing n. For a given n, however, we can reduce α only at the expense of a higher β and reduce β only at the expense of a higher α. The optimal choice of α and β depends on the relative cost of these two types of errors, and determining these costs is not always easy. Typically, the decision regarding the optimal level of Type I and Type II errors is made by the management of a firm where the job of a data analyst is to conduct the hypothesis test for a chosen value of α.

Hypothesis Test for the Population Mean μ

There are two approaches to implementing a hypothesis test—the p-value approach and the critical value approach. The critical value approach is attractive when a computer is unavailable and all calculations must be done by hand. Most researchers and practitioners, however, favor the p-value approach because virtually every statistical software package reports a p-value. We too will focus on the p-value approach. We implement a four-step procedure that is valid for one- and two-tailed tests regarding the population mean, the population proportion, or any other population parameter of interest.

A hypothesis test regarding the population mean μ is based on the sampling distribution of the sample mean $\overline{X}$. In particular, it uses the fact that $E(\overline{X}) = \mu$ and $se(\overline{X}) = \sigma/\sqrt{n}$. As mentioned in the last section, because σ is rarely known, we estimate $se(\overline{X})$ by $s/\sqrt{n}$. Also, in order to implement the test, it is essential that $\overline{X}$ is normally distributed. Recall that $\overline{X}$ is normally distributed when the underlying population is normally distributed. If the underlying population is not normally distributed, then, by the central limit theorem, $\overline{X}$ is approximately normally distributed if the sample size is sufficiently large—that is, $n \geq 30$.

LO 5.5

Conduct a hypothesis test for the population mean.

The basic principle of hypothesis testing is to first assume that the null hypothesis is true and then determine if sample evidence contradicts this assumption. Suppose a hiring manager wants to establish that the mean retirement age is greater than 67 ($\mu > 67$). It is assumed that retirement age is normally distributed. We can investigate the manager's belief by specifying the competing hypotheses as

$$H_0: \mu \leq 67$$
$$H_A: \mu > 67$$

Let a random sample of 25 retirees produce an average retirement age of 71 with a standard deviation of 9—that is, $\bar{x} = 71$ and $s = 9$. This sample evidence casts doubt on the validity of the null hypothesis because the sample mean is greater than the hypothesized value, $\mu_0 = 67$. However, the discrepancy between $\bar{x}$ and μ_0 does not necessarily imply that the null hypothesis is false. Perhaps the discrepancy can be explained by pure chance. It is common to evaluate this discrepancy in terms of the appropriate test statistic.

TEST STATISTIC FOR μ

The value of the test statistic for the hypothesis test of the population mean μ is computed as

$$t_{df} = \frac{\bar{x} - \mu_0}{s/\sqrt{n}}$$

where μ_0 is the hypothesized value of the population mean and the degrees of freedom $df = n - 1$. This formula is valid only if $\bar{X}$ (approximately) follows a normal distribution.

Note that the value of the test statistic t_{df} is evaluated at $\mu = \mu_0$, which explains why we need some form of the equality sign in the null hypothesis. Given that the population is normally distributed with $n = 25$ (so $df = 24$), $\bar{x} = 71$, and $s = 9$, we compute the value of the test statistic as $t_{24} = \frac{\bar{x} - \mu_0}{s/\sqrt{n}} = \frac{71 - 67}{9/\sqrt{25}} = 2.22$. Therefore, comparing $\bar{x} = 71$ with 67 is identical to comparing $t_{24} = 2.22$ with 0, where 67 and 0 are the means of $\bar{X}$ and T_{24}, respectively.

We now find the ***p*-value**, which is the likelihood of obtaining a sample mean that is at least as extreme as the one derived from the given sample, under the assumption that the null hypothesis is true as an equality—that is, $\mu_0 = 67$. Because in this example $\bar{x} = 71$, we define the extreme value as a sample mean of 71 or higher, so we find the p-value as $P(\bar{X} \geq 71) = P(T_{24} \geq 2.22)$. Table 5.5 shows a portion of the t table. Referencing Table 5.5 for $df = 24$, we find that the exact probability $P(T_{24} \geq 2.22)$ cannot be determined. Because 2.22 lies between 2.064 and 2.492, this implies that the p-value is between 0.01 and 0.025. Using Excel or R (instructions shown shortly), we find that the exact p-value is 0.018. Figure 5.6 shows the computed p-value.

TABLE 5.5 Portion of the *t* Table

	Area in Upper Tail					
df	**0.20**	**0.10**	**0.05**	**0.025**	**0.01**	**0.005**
1	1.376	3.078	6.341	12.706	31.821	63.657
	⋮	⋮	⋮	⋮	⋮	⋮
24	0.857	1.318	1.711	2.064	2.492	2.797

FIGURE 5.6
The p-value for a right-tailed test with $t_{24} = 2.22$

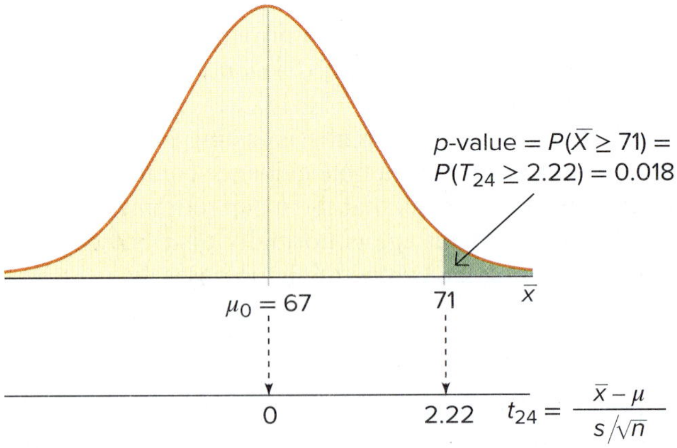

Note that when the null hypothesis is true, there is only a 1.8% chance that the sample mean will be 71 or more. This seems like a very small chance, but is it small enough to allow us to reject the null hypothesis in favor of the alternative hypothesis? Let's see how we define "small enough."

Remember that a Type I error occurs when we reject the null hypothesis when it is actually true. We define the *allowed* probability of making a Type I error as α; we refer to $100\alpha\%$ as the **significance level**. The p-value, on the other hand, is referred to as the *observed* probability of making a Type I error. When using the p-value approach, the decision rule is:

- Reject the null hypothesis if the p-value $< \alpha$, or
- Do not reject the null hypothes if the p-value $\geq \alpha$.

We generally choose a value for α *before* implementing a hypothesis test; that is, we set the rules of the game before playing. Care must be exercised in choosing α because important decisions are often based on the results of a hypothesis test, which in turn depend on α. Most hypothesis tests are conducted using a significance level of 1%, 5%, or 10%, using $\alpha = 0.01$, 0.05, or 0.10, respectively. For example, $\alpha = 0.05$ means that we allow a 5% chance of rejecting a true null hypothesis.

In the retirement age example, suppose we had chosen $\alpha = 0.05$ to conduct the hypothesis test. At this significance level, we reject the null hypothesis because $0.018 < 0.05$. This means that the sample data support the manager's claim that the average retirement age is greater than 67 years old. Individuals may be working past the normal retirement age of 67 because of poor savings and/or because this generation is expected to outlive any previous generation and needs jobs to pay the bills. We should note that if α had been set at 0.01, then the findings would have been different. At this smaller significance level, the evidence does not allow us to reject the null hypothesis ($0.018 > 0.01$). At the 1% significance level, we cannot conclude that the mean retirement age is greater than 67.

In the retirement age example of a right-tailed test, we calculated the p-value as $P(T_{df} \geq t_{df})$. Analogously, for a left-tailed test, the p-value is given by $P(T_{df} \leq t_{df})$. For a two-tailed test, the extreme values exist on both sides of the distribution of the test statistic. Given the symmetry of the t_{df} distribution, the p-value for a two-tailed test is twice that of the p-value for a one-tailed test. It is calculated as $2P(T_{df} \geq t_{df})$ if $t_{df} > 0$ or as $2P(T_{df} \leq t_{df})$ if $t_{df} < 0$.

THE p-VALUE APPROACH

Under the assumption that $\mu = \mu_0$, the p-value is the likelihood of observing a sample mean that is at least as extreme as the one derived from the given sample. Its calculation depends on the specification of the alternative hypothesis.

Alternative Hypothesis	p-value
H_A: $\mu > \mu_0$	Right-tail probability: $P(T_{df} \geq t_{df})$
H_A: $\mu < \mu_0$	Left-tail probability: $P(T_{df} \leq t_{df})$
H_A: $\mu \neq \mu_0$	Two-tail probability: $2P(T_{df} \geq t_{df})$ if $t_{df} > 0$ or $2P(T_{df} \leq t_{df})$ if $t_{df} < 0$

The decision rule is:

- Reject H_0 if the p-value $< \alpha$, or
- Do not reject H_0 if the p-value $\geq \alpha$.

Figure 5.7 shows the three different scenarios of determining the p-value depending on the specification of the competing hypotheses. Figure 5.7a shows the p-value for a left-tailed test. Because the appropriate test statistic follows the t_{df} distribution, we compute the p-value as $P(T_{df} \leq t_{df})$. When calculating the p-value for a right-tailed test (see Figure 5.7b), we find the area to the right of the value of the test statistic t_{df} or, equivalently, $P(T_{df} \geq t_{df})$. Figure 5.7c shows the p-value for a two-tailed test, calculated as $2P(T_{df} \leq t_{df})$ when $t_{df} < 0$ or as $2P(T_{df} \geq t_{df})$ when $t_{df} > 0$.

FIGURE 5.7 The p-values for one- and two-tailed tests

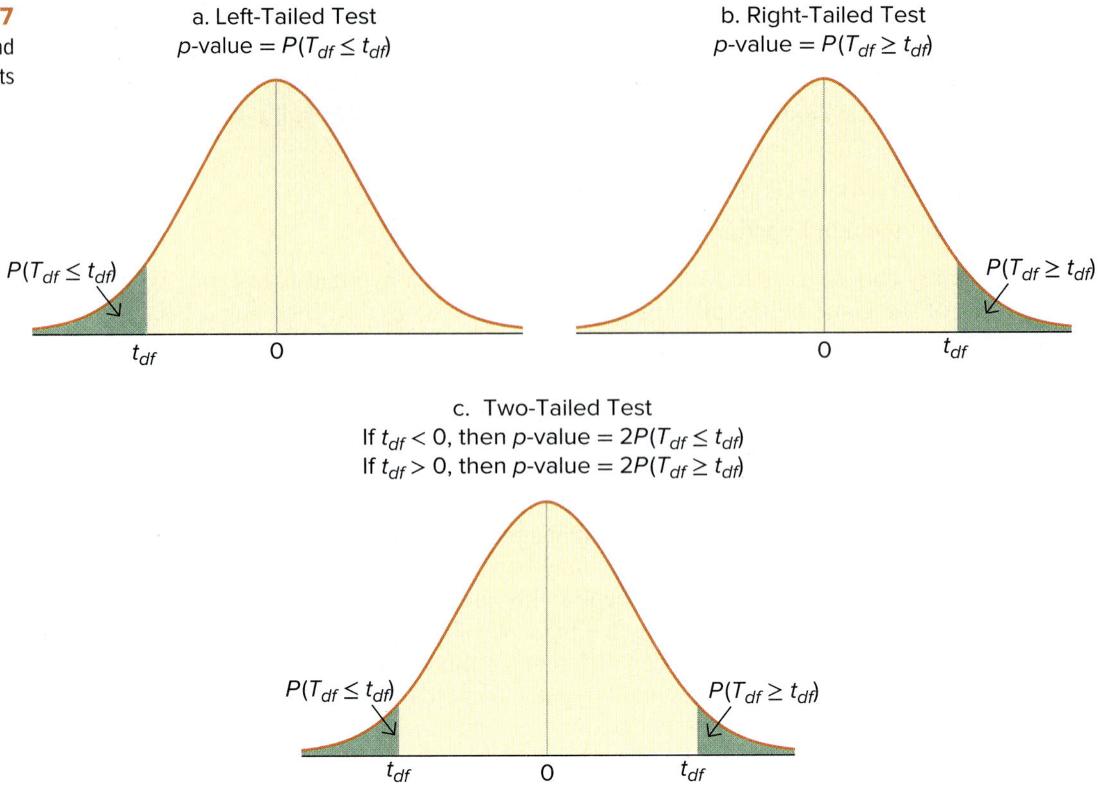

It is important to note that we *cannot* reject H_0 for a right-tailed test if $\bar{x} \leq \mu_0$ or, equivalently, $t_{df} \leq 0$. Consider, for example, a right-tailed test with the hypotheses specified as H_0: $\mu \leq 67$ versus H_A: $\mu > 67$. Here, if $\bar{x} = 65$, there is no need for formal testing because we have no discrepancy between the sample mean and the hypothesized value of the population mean. Similarly, we *cannot* reject H_0 for a left-tailed test if $\bar{x} \geq \mu_0$ or, equivalently, $t_{df} \geq 0$. We will now summarize the four-step procedure using the p-value approach.

THE FOUR-STEP PROCEDURE USING THE p-VALUE APPROACH

Step 1. Specify the null and the alternative hypotheses. We identify the relevant population parameter of interest, determine whether it is a one- or a two-tailed test and, most importantly, include some form of the equality sign in the null hypothesis and place whatever we wish to establish in the alternative hypothesis.

Step 2. Specify the significance level. Before implementing a hypothesis test, we first specify α, which is the *allowed* probability of making a Type I error.

Step 3. Calculate the value of the test statistic and the p-value. When testing the population mean μ, the value of the test statistic is $t_{df} = \frac{\bar{x} - \mu_0}{s/\sqrt{n}}$, where μ_0 is the hypothesized value of the population mean. For a right-tailed test, the p-value is $P(T_{df} \geq t_{df})$, and for a left-tailed test, the p-value is $P(T_{df} \leq t_{df})$. For a two-tailed test, the p-value is $2P(T_{df} \geq t_{df})$ if $t_{df} > 0$, or $2P(T_{df} \leq t_{df})$ if $t_{df} < 0$.

Step 4. State the conclusion and interpret the results. The decision rule is to reject the null hypothesis when the p-value $< \alpha$ and not reject the null hypothesis when the p-value $\geq \alpha$. Clearly interpret the results in the context of the application.

EXAMPLE 5.11

FILE
Study_Hours

In the introductory case to this chapter, the dean at a large university in California wonders if students at her university study less than the 1961 national average of 24 hours per week. She randomly selects 35 students and asks their average study time per week (in hours). From their responses, she calculates a sample mean of 16.3714 hours and a sample standard deviation of 7.2155 hours.

a. Specify the competing hypotheses to test the dean's concern.

b. Calculate the value of the test statistic.

c. Find the p-value.

d. At the 5% significance level, what is the conclusion to the hypothesis test?

SOLUTION:

a. This is an example of a one-tailed test where we would like to determine if the mean hours studied is less than 24; that is, $\mu < 24$. We formulate the competing hypotheses as

$$H_0: \mu \geq 24$$
$$H_A: \mu < 24$$

b. Recall that for any statistical inference regarding the population mean, it is essential that the sample mean $\overline{X}$ is normally distributed. This condition is satisfied because the sample size is greater than 30, specifically $n = 35$. The degrees of freedom, $df = n - 1 = 34$. Given $\overline{x} = 16.3714$ and $s = 7.2155$, we compute the value of the test statistic as

$$t_{34} = \frac{\overline{x} - \mu_0}{s/\sqrt{n}} = \frac{16.3714 - 24}{7.2155/\sqrt{35}} = -6.255.$$

c. Because this is a left-tailed test, we compute the p-value as $P(T_{34} \leq -6.255)$. Referencing the t table for $df = 34$, we can infer that the probability $P(T_{34} \leq -6.255)$, which is equivalent to $P(T_{34} \geq 6.255)$, is less than 0.005. In other words, we approximate the p-value as $P(T_{34} \leq -6.255) < 0.005$. Using Excel or R (instructions shown next), we find that the exact probability is 2.013×10^{-7}.

d. We reject the null hypothesis because the p-value is less than $\alpha = 0.05$. At the 5% significance level, we conclude that the average study time at the university is less than the 1961 national average of 24 hours per week.

Using Excel and R to Test μ

Again we find that functions in Excel and R are quite useful when calculating the value of the test statistic and the exact p-value. Consider the following example.

EXAMPLE 5.12

FILE
Study_Hours

As the introductory case to this chapter mentions, research finds that today's undergraduates study an average of 14 hours per week. Using the sample data from Table 5.1, the dean at a large university in California would like to test if the mean study time of students at her university differs from 14 hours per week. At the 5% significance level, use Excel and R to find the value of the test statistic and the p-value. Summarize the results.

SOLUTION: Because the dean would like to test if the mean study time of students at her university differs from 14 hours per week, we formulate the competing hypotheses as

$$H_0: \mu = 14$$
$$H_A: \mu \neq 14$$

Using Excel

a. Open the ***Study_Hours*** data file. Note that the observations for hours studied are in cells A2 through A36.

b. We find the value of the test statistic, $t_{34} = (\bar{x} - \mu_0)/(s/\sqrt{n})$, using =(AVERAGE(A2:A36)−14)/(STDEV.S(A2:A36)/SQRT(36)). We obtain $t_{34} = 1.9444$.

c. Even though Excel offers a number of functions that generate p-values, we use the **T.DIST.RT** function. Here, for a two-tailed test and a positive value for the test statistic, we enter =2*T.DIST.RT(1.9444, 34) and Excel returns 0.0602.

Using R

a. Import the ***Study_Hours*** data into a data frame (table) and label it myData.

b. We use R's **t.test** function to obtain both the test statistic and the p-value. For options within this function, we use *alternative* to denote the specification of the alternative hypothesis (denoted as "two.sided" for a two-tailed test, "less" for a left-tailed test, and "greater" for a right-tailed test) and *mu* to denote the hypothesized value of the mean. Another feature of this function is that it automatically provides the 95% confidence interval for the mean by default; other levels can be found using the option *conf.level*. We enter

```
> t.test(myData$Hours, alternative="two.sided", mu=14)
```

FIGURE 5.8 R's output using t.test function

```
One Sample t-test
data:  myData$Hours
t = 1.9444, df = 34, p-value = 0.06016
alternative hypothesis: true mean is not equal to 14
95 percent confidence interval:
 13.89281 18.85005
sample estimates:
mean of x
 16.37143
```

Summary

Because the p-value of 0.0602 is not less than $\alpha = 0.05$, we do not reject the null hypothesis. At the 5% significance level, we cannot conclude that the mean study time of students at this large university in California differs from 14 hours per week.

SYNOPSIS OF INTRODUCTORY CASE

A report claims that undergraduates are studying far less today as compared to six decades ago (*The Wall Street Journal*, April 10, 2019). In 1961, students invested 24 hours per week in their academic pursuits, whereas today's students study an average of 14 hours per week. In an attempt to determine whether or not this national trend is present at a large university in California, 35 students are randomly selected and asked their average study time per week (in hours). The sample produces a mean of 16.37 hours with a standard deviation of 7.22 hours.

Asia Images Group/Getty Images

Two hypothesis tests are conducted. The first test examines whether the mean study time of students at this university is below the 1961 national average of 24 hours per week. At the 5% significance level, the sample data suggest that the mean is less than 24 hours per week. The second test investigates whether the mean study time of students at this university differs from today's national average of 14 hours per week. At the 5% significance level, the results do not suggest that the mean study time is different from 14 hours per week.

Thus, the sample results support the overall findings of the report: undergraduates study, on average, 14 hours per week, far below the 1961 average of 24 hours per week. The present analysis, however, does not explain why that might be the case. For instance, it cannot be determined whether students have just become lazier or if, with the advent of the computer, they can access information in less time.

Hypothesis Test for the Population Proportion *p*

LO 5.6

Conduct a hypothesis test for the population proportion.

As discussed earlier, sometimes the variable of interest is categorical rather than numerical. Recall that the population proportion p is the essential descriptive measure for a qualitative variable, and that it is estimated on the basis of its sample counterpart, the sample proportion $\overline{P}$. Although $\overline{P}$ is based on a binomial distribution, it can be approximated by a normal distribution in large samples. This approximation is considered valid when $np \geq 5$ and $n(1 - p) \geq 5$.

Because p is not known, we typically test the sample size requirement under the hypothesized value of the population proportion p_0. In most applications, the sample size is large and the normal distribution approximation is justified. However, when the sample size is not deemed large enough, the statistical methods suggested here for inference regarding the population proportion are no longer valid. The test statistic for p is defined as follows.

TEST STATISTIC FOR *p*

The value of the test statistic for the hypothesis test of the population proportion p is computed as

$$z = \frac{\overline{p} - p_0}{\sqrt{p_0(1 - p_0)/n}}$$

where p_0 is the hypothesized value of the population proportion. This formula is valid only if $\overline{P}$ (approximately) follows a normal distribution.

The following example elaborates on the four-step procedure for a hypothesis test for the population proportion.

EXAMPLE 5.13

Driven by growing public support, the legalization of marijuana in America has been moving at a very rapid rate. Today, 57% of adults say the use of marijuana should be made legal (www.pewresearch.org, October 12, 2016). A health practitioner in Ohio collects data from 200 adults and finds that 102 of them favor marijuana legalization.

a. The health practitioner believes that the proportion of adults who favor marijuana legalization in Ohio is not representative of the national proportion. Specify the competing hypotheses to test her claim.

b. Calculate the value of the test statistic and the p-value.

c. At the 10% significance level, do the sample data support the health practitioner's belief?

SOLUTION:

a. The parameter of interest is the population proportion p. The health practitioner wants to test if the population proportion of those who favor marijuana legalization in Ohio differs from the national proportion of 0.57. We construct the competing hypotheses as

$$H_0: p = 0.57$$
$$H_A: p \neq 0.57$$

b. When evaluated at $p_0 = 0.57$ with $n = 200$, the normality requirement that $np \geq 5$ and $n(1 - p) \geq 5$ is easily satisfied. We use the sample proportion $\bar{p} = 102/200 = 0.51$ to compute the value of the test statistic as

$$z = \frac{\bar{p} - p_0}{\sqrt{p_0(1 - p_0)/n}} = \frac{0.51 - 0.57}{\sqrt{0.57(1 - 0.57)/200}} = -1.71.$$

Given a two-tailed test and $z < 0$, we compute the p-value as $2P(Z \leq z) = 2P(Z \leq -1.71) = 0.0872$.

c. Because the p-value of 0.0872 is less than $\alpha = 0.10$, we reject the null hypothesis. Therefore, at the 10% significance level, the proportion of adults who favor marijuana legalization in Ohio differs from the national proportion of 0.57.

EXERCISES 5.3

Applications

36. Construct the null and the alternative hypotheses for the following tests:
    a. Test if the mean weight of cereal in a cereal box differs from 18 ounces.
    b. Test if the stock price increases on more than 60% of the trading days.
    c. Test if Americans get an average of less than seven hours of sleep.
    d. Define the consequences of Type I and Type II errors for part a.

37. Construct the null and the alternative hypotheses for the following claims:
    a. "I am going to get the majority of the votes to win this election."
    b. "I suspect that your 10-inch pizzas are, on average, less than 10 inches in size."

c. "I will have to fine the company because its tablets do not contain an average of 250 mg of ibuprofen as advertised."

d. Discuss the consequences of Type I and Type II errors for part a.

38. The manager of a large manufacturing firm is considering switching to new and expensive software that promises to reduce its assembly costs. Before purchasing the software, the manager wants to conduct a hypothesis test to determine if the new software does reduce its assembly costs.

a. Would the manager of the manufacturing firm be more concerned about a Type I error or a Type II error? Explain.

b. Would the software company be more concerned about a Type I error or a Type II error? Explain.

39. A polygraph (lie detector) is an instrument used to determine if an individual is telling the truth. These tests are considered to be 95% reliable. In other words, if an individual lies, there is a 0.95 probability that the test will detect a lie. Let there also be a 0.005 probability that the test erroneously detects a lie even when the individual is actually telling the truth. Consider the null hypothesis, "the individual is telling the truth," to answer the following questions.

a. What is the probability of a Type I error?

b. What is the probability of a Type II error?

c. What are the consequences of Type I and Type II errors?

d. What is wrong with the statement, "I can prove that the individual is telling the truth on the basis of the polygraph result"?

40. **FILE** ***Wait_Time.*** The manager of a small convenience store does not want her customers standing in line for too long prior to a purchase. In particular, she is willing to hire an employee for another cash register if the average wait time of the customers is more than five minutes. She randomly observes the wait time (in minutes) of customers during the day as:

3.5	5.8	7.2	1.9	6.8	8.1	5.4

a. Set up the null and the alternative hypotheses to determine if the manager needs to hire another employee.

b. Calculate the value of the test statistic and the p-value. What assumption regarding the population is necessary to implement this step?

c. Decide whether the manager needs to hire another employee at $\alpha = 0.10$.

41. A machine that is programmed to package 1.20 pounds of cereal in each cereal box is being tested for its accuracy. In a sample of 36 cereal boxes, the mean and the standard deviation are calculated as 1.22 pounds and 0.06 pound, respectively.

a. Set up the null and the alternative hypotheses to determine if the machine is working improperly—that is, it is either underfilling or overfilling the cereal boxes.

b. Calculate the value of the test statistic and the p-value.

c. At the 5% level of significance, can you conclude that the machine is working improperly? Explain.

42. This past year, home prices in the Midwest increased by an average of 6.6%. A Realtor collects data on 36 recent home sales in the West. He finds an average increase in home prices of 7.5% with a standard deviation of 2%. Can he conclude that the average increase in home prices in the West is greater than the increase in the Midwest? Use a 5% significance level for the analysis.

43. Based on the average predictions of 45 economists, the U.S. gross domestic product (GDP) will expand by 2.8% this year. Suppose the sample standard deviation of their predictions was 1%. At the 5% significance level, test if the mean forecast GDP of all economists is less than 1%.

44. **FILE** ***MPG.*** The data accompanying this exercise show miles per gallon (MPG) for a sample of 50 hybrid cars.

a. State the null and the alternative hypotheses in order to test whether the average MPG differs from 50.

b. Calculate the value of the test statistic and the p-value.

c. At $\alpha = 0.05$, can you conclude that the average MPG differs from 50?

45. A car manufacturer is trying to develop a new sports car. Engineers are hoping that the average amount of time that the car takes to go from 0 to 60 miles per hour is below six seconds. The manufacturer tested 12 of the cars and clocked their performance times. Three of the cars clocked in at 5.8 seconds, five cars at 5.9 seconds, three cars at 6.0 seconds, and 1 car at 6.1 seconds. At the 5% level of significance, test if the new sports car is meeting its goal to go from 0 to 60 miles per hour in less than six seconds. Assume a normal distribution for the analysis.

46. **FILE** ***Highway_Speeds.*** A police officer is concerned about speeds on a certain section of Interstate 90. The data accompanying this exercise show the speeds of 40 cars on a Saturday afternoon.

a. The speed limit on this portion of Interstate 90 is 65 mph. Specify the competing hypotheses in order to determine if the average speed of cars on Interstate 90 is greater than the speed limit.

b. Calculate the value of the test statistic and the p-value.

c. At $\alpha = 0.01$, are the officer's concerns warranted? Explain.

47. **FILE** ***Debt_Payments.*** The data accompanying this exercise show the average monthly debt payments (Debt, in $) for residents of 26 metropolitan areas.

a. State the null and the alternative hypotheses in order to test whether average monthly debt payments are greater than $900.

b. What assumption regarding the population is necessary to implement this step?

c. Calculate the value of the test statistic and the *p*-value.
d. At $\alpha = 0.05$, are average monthly debt payments greater than $900? Explain.

48. Some first-time home buyers—especially millennials—are raiding their retirement accounts to cover the down payment on a home. An economist is concerned that the percentage of millennials who will dip into their retirement accounts to fund a home now exceeds 20%. He randomly surveys 190 millenials with retirement accounts and finds that 50 are borrowing against them.
   a. Set up the null and the alternative hypotheses to test the economist's concern.
   b. Calculate the value of the test statistic and the *p*-value.
   c. Determine if the economist's concern is justifiable at $\alpha = 0.05$.

49. **FILE** ***Lottery.*** A 2012 survey by Business Week found that Massachusetts residents spent an average of $860.70 on the lottery, more than three times the U.S. average. A researcher at a Boston think tank believes that Massachusetts residents spend less than this amount. He surveys 100 Massachusetts residents and asks them about their annual expenditures on the lottery.
   a. Specify the competing hypotheses to test the researcher's claim.
   b. Calculate the value of the test statistic and the *p*-value.
   c. At the 10% significance level, do the data support the researcher's claim? Explain.

50. The margarita is one of the most common tequila-based cocktails, made with tequila mixed with triple sec and lime or lemon juice, often served with salt on the glass rim. A common ratio for a margarita is 2:1:1, which includes 50% tequila, 25% triple sec, and 25% fresh lime or lemon juice. A manager at a local bar is concerned that the bartender uses incorrect proportions in more than 50% of margaritas. He secretly observes the bartender and finds that he used the correct proportions in only 10 out of 30 margaritas. Test if the manager's suspicion is justified at $\alpha = 0.05$.

51. A politician claims that he is supported by a clear majority of voters. In a recent survey, 24 out of 40 randomly selected voters indicated that they would vote for the politician. Is the politician's claim justified at the 5% level of significance?

52. With increasing out-of-pocket healthcare costs, it is claimed that more than 60% of senior citizens are likely to make serious adjustments to their lifestyle. Test this claim at the 1% level of significance if in a survey of 140 senior citizens, 90 reported that they have made serious adjustments to their lifestyle.

53. A movie production company is releasing a movie with the hopes that many viewers will return to see the movie in the theater for a second time. Their target is to have 30 million viewers, and they want more than 30% of the viewers to want to see the movie again. They show the movie to a test audience of 200 people, and after the movie they asked them if they would see the movie in theaters again. Of the test audience, 68 people said they would see the movie again.
   a. At the 5% level of significance, test if more than 30% of the viewers will return to see the movie again.
   b. Repeat the analysis at the 10% level of significance.

54. **FILE** ***Silicon_Valley.*** According to a 2018 report by CNBC on workforce diversity, about 60% of the employees in high-tech firms in Silicon Valley are white and about 20% are Asian. Women, along with African Americans and Latinxs, are highly underrepresented. Just about 30% of all employees are women, with African Americans and Latinx accounting for only about 15% of the workforce. Tara Jones is a recent college graduate working for a large high-tech firm in Silicon Valley. She wants to determine if her firm faces the same diversity as in the report. She collects sex and ethnicity information on 50 employees in her firm. A portion of the data is shown in the accompanying table.

Sex	Ethnicity
Woman	White
Man	White
⋮	⋮
Man	Nonwhite

   a. At the 5% level of significance, determine if the proportion of women in Tara's firm is different from 0.30.
   b. At the 5% level of significance, determine if the proportion of whites in Tara's firm is more than 0.50.

5.4 WRITING WITH DATA

Ariel Skelley/Blend Images LLC

When using big data, we typically do not construct confidence intervals or perform hypothesis tests. Why is this the case? It turns out that if the sample size is sufficiently large, there is little difference in the estimates of $\overline{X}$ or the estimates of $\overline{P}$ generated by different random samples.

Recall that we use $se(\overline{X}) = \frac{s}{\sqrt{n}}$ to gauge the variability in $\overline{X}$ and $se(\overline{P}) = \sqrt{\frac{\overline{p}(1-\overline{p})}{n}}$ to gauge the variability in $\overline{P}$. In both cases, the variability depends on the size of the sample on which the value of the estimator is based. If the sample size is sufficiently large, then the variability virtually disappears, or, equivalently, $se(\overline{X})$ and $se(\overline{P})$ approach zero. Thus, with big data, it is not very meaningful to construct confidence intervals for the population mean or the population proportion because the margin of error also approaches zero; under these circumstances, when estimating μ or p, it is sufficient to use the estimate of the relevant point estimator.

Recall too that when testing the population mean, the value of the test statistic is calculated as $t_{df} = (\overline{x} - \mu_0)/(s/\sqrt{n})$; and when testing the population proportion, the value of the test statistic is calculated as $z = (\overline{p} - p_0)/(\sqrt{\overline{p}(1-\overline{p})/n})$. With big data, the value of the respective test statistic increases, leading to a small p-value, and thus rejection of the null hypothesis in virtually any scenario.

Thus, if the sample size is sufficiently large, statistical inference is not very useful. In this Writing with Data section, we focus on a case study where the sample size is relatively small.

Case Study

According to a 2018 paper released by the Economic Policy Institute, a nonprofit, nonpartisan think tank in Washington, D.C., income inequality continues to grow in the United States. Over the years, the rich have become richer while working-class wages have stagnated. A local Latino politician has been vocal regarding his concern about the welfare of Latinx. In various speeches, he has stated that the mean salary of Latinx households in his county has fallen below the 2017 mean of approximately $50,000. He has also stated that the proportion of Latinx households making less than $30,000 has risen above the 2017 level of 20%. Both of his statements are based on income data for 36 Latinx households in the county. A portion of the data is shown in Table 5.6.

TABLE 5.6 Latinx Household Income (in $1,000s)

Income
23
63
⋮
47

FILE *Latinx_Income*

Trevor Jones is a newspaper reporter who is interested in verifying the concerns of the local politician. Trevor wants to use the sample information to

1. Determine if the mean income of Latinx households has fallen below the 2017 level of $50,000.
2. Determine if the percentage of Latinx households making less than $30,000 has risen above 20%.

Sample Report—Income Inequality in the United States

One of the hotly debated topics in the United States is that of growing income inequality. This trend, which has picked up post Great Recession, is a reversal of what was seen during and after the Great Depression, where the gap between rich and poor narrowed. Market forces such as increased trade and technological advances have made highly skilled and well-educated workers more productive, thus increasing their pay. Institutional forces, such as deregulation, the decline of unions, and the stagnation of the minimum wage, have contributed to income inequality. Arguably, this income inequality has been felt by minorities, especially African Americans and Latinxs, because a very high proportion of both groups is working class.

A sample of 36 Latinx households resulted in a mean household income of $47,278 with a standard deviation of $19,524. The sample mean is below the 2017 level of $50,000. In addition, eight Latinx households, or approximately 22%, make less than $30,000. Based on these results, a politician concludes that current market conditions continue to negatively impact the welfare of Latinxs. However, it is essential to provide statistically significant evidence to substantiate these claims. Toward this end, formal tests of hypotheses regarding the population mean and the population proportion are conducted. The results of the tests are summarized in Table 5.7.

TABLE 5.7 Test Statistic Values and *p*-Values for Hypothesis Tests

Hypotheses	Test Statistic Value	*p*-value
$H_0: \mu \geq 50$ $H_A: \mu < 50$	$t_{35} = \dfrac{47.278 - 50}{19.524/\sqrt{36}} = -0.837$	0.204
$H_0: p \leq 0.20$ $H_A: p > 0.20$	$z = \dfrac{0.222 - 0.20}{\sqrt{\dfrac{(0.20)(0.80)}{36}}} = 0.333$	0.369

When testing whether the mean income of Latinx households has fallen below the 2017 level of $50,000, a test statistic value of −0.837 is obtained. Given a *p*-value of 0.204, the null hypothesis regarding the population mean, specified in Table 5.7, cannot be rejected at any reasonable level of significance. Similarly, given a *p*-value of 0.369, the null hypothesis regarding the population proportion cannot be rejected. Therefore, sample evidence does not support the claims that the mean income of Latinx households has fallen below $50,000 or that the proportion of Latinx households making less than $30,000 has risen above 20%. Perhaps the politician's remarks were based on a cursory look at the sample statistics and not on a thorough statistical analysis.

Suggested Case Studies

Report 5.1 FILE ***Fidelity_Returns.*** The accompanying data are the annual returns for two mutual funds offered by the investment giant Fidelity for the years 2001–2017. The Fidelity Select Automotive mutual fund invests primarily in companies engaged in the manufacturing, marketing, or sales of automobiles, trucks, specialty vehicles, parts, tires, and related services. The Fidelity Gold mutual fund invests primarily in companies engaged in exploration, mining, processing, or dealing in gold and, to a lesser degree, in other precious metals and minerals. In a report, use the sample information to

- Calculate descriptive statistics to compare the returns of the mutual funds.
- Assess reward by constructing and interpreting 95% confidence intervals for the population mean return. What assumption did you make when constructing the confidence intervals?

Report 5.2 FILE ***Field_Choice.*** A 2018 Pew Research Center survey finds that more than half of Americans (52%) believe that young people do not pursue a degree in science, technology, engineering, or math (STEM) because they feel that these subjects are too hard. Sixty college-bound students are asked about the field they would like to pursue in college. The choices offered in the questionnaire are STEM, Business, and Other; information on a teenager's sex (Male or Female) is also collected. The accompanying data file contains the responses. In a report, use the sample information to

- Compare the 95% confidence interval for the proportion of students who would like to pursue STEM with the proportion who would like to pursue Business. Do the results appear to support the survey's finding? Explain.
- Construct and interpret the 95% confidence interval for the proportion of female students who are college bound.

Report 5.3 FILE ***Wellbeing.*** The Gallup-Healthways Well-Being Index provides an assessment measure of health and well-being of U.S. residents. The overall composite score is calculated on a scale from 0 to 100, where 100 represents fully realized well-being. In 2017, the overall well-being of American residents was reported as 61.5—a decline from 62.1 in 2016. The accompanying data file shows the overall well-being score for a random sample of 35 residents from South Dakota—the state with the highest level of well-being. In a report, use the sample information to

- Determine whether the well-being score of South Dakotans is more than the national average of 61.5 at the 5% significance level.
- Determine if fewer than 40% of South Dakotans report a score below 50 at the 5% significance level.
- Comment on the well-being of South Dakotans given your results.

6 Regression Analysis

LEARNING OBJECTIVES

After reading this chapter, you should be able to:

LO **6.1** **Estimate and interpret a linear regression model.**

LO **6.2** **Interpret goodness-of-fit measures.**

LO **6.3** **Conduct tests of significance.**

LO **6.4** **Address common violations of the OLS assumptions.**

As discussed in Chapter 1, we often group the study of business analytics into three broad categories: descriptive analytics, predictive analytics, and prescriptive analytics. In this chapter, we introduce regression analysis, which is one of the most widely used techniques in predictive analytics. We use regression analysis for two primary purposes: (1) to assess the relationship between variables and (2) to predict the outcome of a target variable on the basis of several input variables. For example, if a firm increases advertising expenditures by $100,000, then we may want to know the likely impact on sales. Or, we may want to predict the price of a house based on its size and location. Regression analysis can be applied in both of these scenarios.

We first explore the ordinary least squares (OLS) method for estimating a linear regression model, where the relationship between the target and the input variables is assumed to be linear. We then examine a number of goodness-of-fit measures and conduct hypothesis tests in order to assess which input variables matter the most. Finally, we examine the importance of the assumptions on the statistical properties of the OLS estimator, as well as the validity of the testing procedures. We address common violations to the model assumptions, the consequences when these assumptions are violated, and offer some remedial measures.

©Rawpixel.com/Shutterstock

INTRODUCTORY CASE

College Scorecard

With college costs and student debt on the rise, the choices that families make when searching for and selecting a college have never been more important. Yet, students and parents struggle to find clear, reliable data on critical questions of college affordability and value. For these reasons, the Department of Education (DOE) published a redesigned College Scorecard that reports the most reliable national data on college costs and students' outcomes at specific colleges.

Fiona Schmidt, a college counselor, believes that the information from the College Scorecard can help her as she advises families. Fiona wonders what college factors influence post-college earnings and wants answers to the following questions: If a college costs more or has a higher graduation rate, should a student expect to earn more after graduation? If a greater percentage of the students are paying down debt after college, does this somehow influence post-college earnings? And finally, does the location of a college affect post-college earnings?

To address these questions, Fiona gathers information from 116 colleges on annual post-college earnings (Earnings in $), the average annual cost (Cost in $), the graduation rate (Grad in %), the percentage of students paying down debt (Debt in %), and whether or not a college is located in a city (City equals 1 if a city location, 0 otherwise). Table 6.1 shows a portion of the data.

FILE *College*

TABLE 6.1 College Scorecard Data, May 2016

School[a]	Earnings	Cost	Grad	Debt	City
St. Ambrose Univ.	44800	22920	62	88	1
Albion College	45100	23429	73	92	0
⋮	⋮	⋮	⋮	⋮	⋮
Wittenburg Univ.	42700	26616	64	90	1

Fiona would like to use the information in Table 6.1 to:

1. Make predictions for post-college earnings using regression analysis.
2. Interpret goodness-of-fit measures for the post-college earnings model.
3. Determine which factors are statistically significant in explaining post-college earnings.

A synopsis of this case is provided at the end of Section 6.3.

LO 6.1

6.1 THE LINEAR REGRESSION MODEL

Estimate and interpret a linear regression model.

Regression analysis is one of the most widely used techniques in predictive analytics. We use it to capture the relationship between two or more variables and to predict the outcome of a target variable based on several input variables. Regression analysis allows us to make assessments and robust predictions by determining which of the relationships matter most and which we can ignore.

We formulate a mathematical model that relates the outcome of a target variable, called the **response variable**, to one or more other input variables, called the **predictor variables**. Consequently, we use information on the predictor variables to describe and/or predict changes in the response variable.

In the introductory case, Fiona wonders what college factors may influence post-college earnings. In another scenario, we may want to predict a firm's sales based on its advertising; estimate an individual's salary based on education and years of experience; predict the selling price of a house on the basis of its size and location; or describe auto sales with respect to consumer income, interest rates, and price discounts. In all of these examples, we can use regression analysis to describe the relationship between the variables of interest.

No matter the response variable that we choose to examine, we cannot expect to predict its exact (unique) value. If the value of the response variable is uniquely determined by the values of the predictor variables, we say that the relationship between the variables is **deterministic**. This is often the case in the physical sciences. For example, momentum p is the product of the mass m and the velocity v of an object; that is, $p = mv$. In most fields of research, however, we tend to find that the relationship between the response variable and the predictor variables is **stochastic**, due to the omission of relevant factors (sometimes not measurable) that influence the response variable. For instance, when trying to predict an individual's salary, the individual's natural ability is often omitted since it is extremely difficult, if not impossible, to quantify.

DETERMINISTIC VERSUS STOCHASTIC RELATIONSHIPS

The relationship between the response variable and the predictor variables is deterministic if the value of the response variable is uniquely determined by the predictor variables; otherwise, the relationship is stochastic.

Our objective is to develop a mathematical model that captures the relationship between the response variable y and the k predictor variables $x_1, x_2, \ldots, x_k$. The model must also account for the randomness that is a part of real life. In order to develop a linear regression model, we start with a deterministic component that approximates the relationship we want to model, and then add a random error term to it, making the relationship stochastic.

The Components of the Linear Regression Model

We use economic theory, intuition, and statistcal measures to determine which predictor variables might best explain the response variable. A regression model treats all predictor variables as numerical, where observations of a categorical variable are first converted into numerical values. Recall from Chapters 1 and 2 that the observations of a numerical variable represent meaningful numbers, whereas the observations of a categorical variable represent different categories. For example, income is a numerical variable, whereas marital status is a categorical variable.

Recall, too, that a dummy variable, also referred to as an indicator or a binary variable, takes on numerical values of 1 or 0 to describe two categories of a categorical variable. For a predictor variable that is a dummy variable, it is common to refer to the category that assumes a value of 0 as the **reference category** or the **benchmark category**. All comparisons are made in relation to the reference category. For example, in the case of a dummy variable categorizing a person's sex, we can define 1 for male and 0 for female. In this case, the reference category would be females. Alternatively, we can define 1 for female and 0 for male, where males would be the reference category.

A DUMMY VARIABLE USED AS A PREDICTOR VARIABLE

A dummy variable takes on numerical values of 1 or 0 to describe two categories of a categorical variable. For a predictor variable that is a dummy variable, we refer to the category that assumes a value of 0 as the reference or benchmark category. All comparisons in the regression analysis are made in relation to the reference category.

If a linear regression model uses only one predictor variable, then the model is referred to as a **simple linear regression model** and is represented as $y = \beta_0 + \beta_1 x_1 + \varepsilon$, where y is the response variable, β_0 and β_1 (the Greek letters read as betas) are the unknown intercept and slope parameters, respectively, x_1 is the predictor variable, and ε is the random error term (the Greek letter read as epsilon). (Technically, we should include the subscript i on all variables, or $y_i = \beta_0 + \beta_1 x_{1i} + \varepsilon_i$. For now, we exclude the subscript i.)

A fundamental assumption underlying the simple linear regression model is that the expected value of y lies on a straight line, denoted by $\beta_0 + \beta_1 x_1$. The expression $\beta_0 + \beta_1 x_1$ is the deterministic component of the simple linear regression model, which can be thought of as the expected value of y for a given value of x. In other words, conditional on x, $E(y) = \beta_0 + \beta_1 x_1$. The slope parameter β_1 determines whether the linear relationship between x and $E(y)$ is positive ($\beta_1 > 0$) or negative ($\beta_1 < 0$); $\beta_1 = 0$ indicates that there is no linear relationship between x and $E(y)$. Figure 6.1 shows the expected value of y for various values of the intercept β_0 and the slope β_1 parameters.

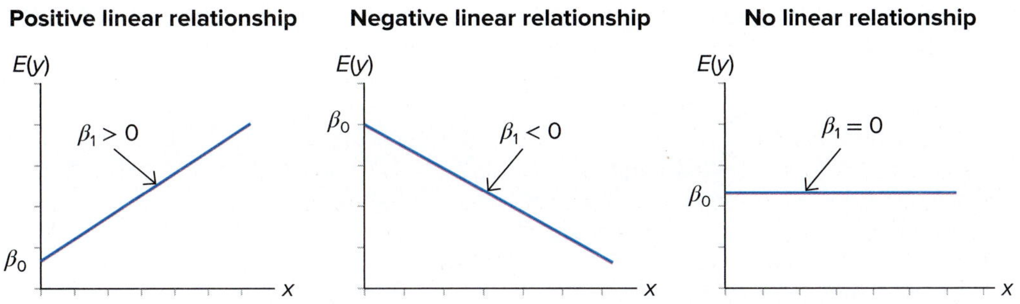

FIGURE 6.1 Examples of a simple linear regression model

We can easily extend the simple linear regression to include more than one predictor variable. The resulting model is referred to as a **multiple linear regression model** and is represented as $y = \beta_0 + \beta_1 x_1 + \beta_2 x_2 + \ldots + \beta_k x_k + \varepsilon$; a common notation is to replace an x with a d if a given predictor variable is a dummy variable. For simplicity, we will refer to the simple linear regression model or the multiple linear regression model as the linear regression model.

The population parameters $\beta_0, \beta_1, \beta_2, \ldots, \beta_k$ used in the linear regression model are unknown and, therefore, must be estimated. As always, we use sample data to estimate the population parameters of interest. Here, sample data consist of n observations on $y, x_1, x_2, \ldots, x_k$.

> **THE LINEAR REGRESSION MODEL**
>
> The linear regression model is defined as
>
> $$y = \beta_0 + \beta_1 x_1 + \beta_2 x_2 + \ldots + \beta_k x_k + \varepsilon,$$
>
> where y is the response variable; $x_1, x_2, \ldots, x_k$ are the k predictor variables; and ε is the random error term. The coefficients $\beta_0, \beta_1, \beta_2, \ldots, \beta_k$ are the unknown parameters to be estimated.

Let $b_0, b_1, b_2, \ldots, b_k$ represent the estimates of $\beta_0, \beta_1, \beta_2, \ldots, \beta_k$, respectively. We form the **sample regression equation** as $\hat{y} = b_0 + b_1x_1 + b_2x_2 + \ldots b_kx_k$, where $\hat{y}$ (read as y-hat) is the predicted value of the response variable given specified values of the predictor variables. For given values of the predictor variables, the observed and the predicted values of the response variable are likely to be different because many factors besides the included predictor variables influence y. We refer to the difference between the observed and the predicted values of y, that is, $y - \hat{y}$, as the **residual** e.

A common approach to obtaining estimates for $\beta_0, \beta_1, \beta_2, \ldots, \beta_k$ is to use the **ordinary least squares (OLS) method**. OLS estimators have many desirable properties if certain assumptions hold. (These assumptions are discussed in Section 6.4.) The OLS method chooses the sample regression equation whereby the error sum of squares, SSE, is minimized, where $SSE = \Sigma(y - \hat{y})^2 = \Sigma e^2$. SSE is the sum of the squared differences between an observed value y and its predicted value $\hat{y}$, or, equivalently, the sum of the squared distances from the regression equation. Thus, using this distance measure, we say that the OLS method produces the equation that is "closest" to the data.

Using calculus, equations have been developed for $b_0, b_1, b_2, \ldots, b_k$ that satisfy the OLS criterion. Virtually every statistical software package computes the necessary output to construct a sample regression equation. In addition, values of all relevant statistics for assessing the model, discussed later in this chapter, are also included with the output.

In order to graphically depict what we have just described with just one predictor variable, consider Figure 6.2 which shows a scatterplot of y against x. Superimposed on the scatterplot is the sample regression line, $\hat{y} = b_0 + b_1x$, that was obtained using OLS. We also show the residual, $e = y - \hat{y}$, for one observation.

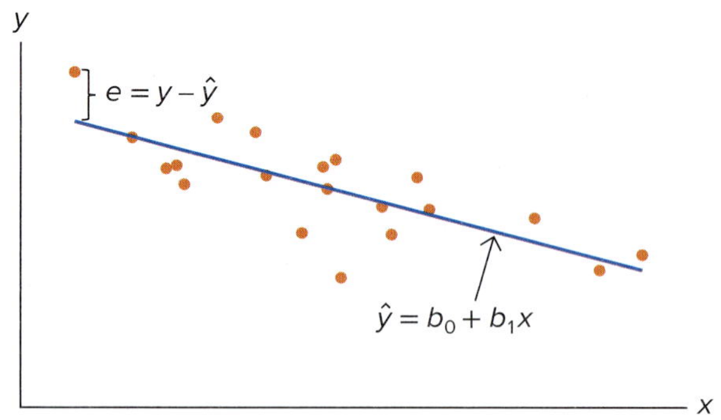

FIGURE 6.2 Scatterplot of y against x with superimposed sample regression line

It is important to be able to interpret the estimated regression coefficients. Mathematically, the intercept estimate b_0 represents the predicted value of $\hat{y}$ when each predictor variable $x_j (j = 1, \ldots, k)$ assumes a value of zero. However, in many applications it is not possible to provide a meaningful interpretation for the intercept. For each predictor variable $x_j (j = 1, \ldots, k)$, the corresponding slope coefficient b_j is the estimate of β_j. The slope coefficient b_j measures the change in the predicted value of the response variable $\hat{y}$ given a unit increase in the associated predictor variable x_j, *holding all other predictor variables constant*. In other words, it represents the partial influence of x_j on $\hat{y}$.

EXAMPLE 6.1

Using the data from Table 6.1, estimate the linear regression model, Earnings = $\beta_0 + \beta_1$Cost + β_2Grad + β_3Debt + β_4City + ε, where Earnings is annual post-college earnings (in \$), Cost is the average annual cost (in \$), Grad is the graduation rate (in %), Debt is the percentage of students paying down debt (in %), and City assumes a value of 1 if the college is located in a city, 0 otherwise.

FILE *College*

a. What is the sample regression equation?

b. Interpret the slope coefficients.

c. Predict annual post-college earnings if a college's average annual cost is \$25,000, its graduation rate is 60%, its percentage of students paying down debt is 80%, and it is located in a city.

SOLUTION: Table 6.2 shows the Excel output from estimating this model. We will provide Excel and R instructions for obtaining regression output at the end of this section.

TABLE 6.2 Regression Results for Example 6.1

Regression Statistics						
Multiple R	0.6552					
R Square	0.4292					
Adjusted R Square	0.4087					
Standard Error	5645.831					
Observations	116					
ANOVA						
	df	SS	MS	F	Significance F	
Regression	4	2660691959	665172990	20.868	7.56E-13	
Residual	111	3538169765	31875403			
Total	115	6198861724				
	Coefficients	Standard Error	t Stat	p-value	Lower 95%	Upper 95%
Intercept	**10004.9665**	7634.3338	1.311	0.1927	−5122.98	25132.91
Cost	**0.4349**	0.1110	3.917	0.0002	0.21	0.65
Grad	**178.0989**	69.1940	2.574	0.0114	40.99	315.21
Debt	**141.4783**	117.2120	1.207	0.2300	−90.79	373.74
City	**2526.7888**	1103.4026	2.290	0.0239	340.32	4713.25

a. As Table 6.2 shows, Excel produces quite a bit of information. In order to answer the questions in Example 6.1, we only need the estimated coefficients, which we have put in boldface in the lower portion of the table. We will address the remaining information in later sections of this chapter. The coefficient estimates, rounded to four decimal places, are $b_0 = 10{,}004.9665$, $b_1 = 0.4349$, $b_2 = 178.0989$, $b_3 = 141.4783$, and $b_4 = 2{,}526.7888$. Thus, the sample regression equation is

$$\widehat{\text{Earnings}} = 10{,}004.9665 + 0.4349\text{Cost} + 178.0989\text{Grad} + 141.4783\text{Debt} + 2{,}526.7888\text{City}.$$

b. All coefficients are positive, suggesting a positive influence of each predictor variable on the response variable. Specifically:

- Holding all other predictor variables constant, if average annual costs increase by $1, then, on average, predicted earnings are expected to increase by b_1; that is, by about $0.4349. This result suggests that spending more on college pays off.
- If the graduation rate increases by 1%, then, on average, predicted earnings are expected to increase by $178.10, holding the other predictor variables constant. Policymakers often debate whether graduation rate can be used as a proxy for a college's academic quality. Perhaps it is not the academic quality but the case that colleges with a higher graduation rate have more motivated students, which translates into higher earnings for these students.
- A one percentage point increase in the percentage of students paying down debt is expected to increase predicted earnings by approximately $141.48, holding the other three predictor variables constant. As it turns out, Debt is not statistically significant at any reasonable level; we will discuss such tests of significance in Section 6.3.
- All else constant, predicted earnings are $2,526.79 higher for graduates of colleges located in a city. This difference is not surprising seeing that students who attend college in a city likely have more internship opportunities, which then often translate into higher-paying jobs after graduation.

c. If a college's average annual cost is $25,000, its graduation rate is 60%, its percentage of students paying down debt is 80%, and it is located in a city, then average post-college earnings for its students are

$$\widehat{\text{Earnings}} = 10{,}004.9665 + 0.4349 \times 25{,}000 + 178.0989 \times 60 + 141.4783 \times 80 + 2{,}526.7888 \times 1 = 45{,}408.7991$$, or approximately $45,409.

Estimating a Linear Regression Model with Excel or R

Using Excel

In order to obtain the regression output in Table 6.2 using Excel, we follow these steps.

FILE
College

A. Open the ***College*** data file.

B. Choose **Data > Data Analysis > Regression** from the menu. (Recall from Chapter 3 that if you do not see the **Data Analysis** option under **Data**, you must add in the **Analysis Toolpak** option.)

C. See Figure 6.3. In the *Regression* dialog box, click on the box next to *Input Y Range*, and then select the data for Earnings. Click on the box next to *Input X Range*, and then *simultaneously* select the data for Cost, Grad, Debt, and City. Select *Labels* because we are using Earnings, Cost, Grad, Debt, and City as headings.

D. Click **OK**.

Using R

In order to obtain the regression output in Table 6.2 using R, we follow these steps.

A. Import the ***College*** data into a data frame (table) and label it myData.

B. By default, R will report the regression output using scientific notation. We opt to turn this option off using the following command:

```
> options(scipen=999)
```

In order to turn scientific notation back on, we would enter options(scipen=0) at the prompt.

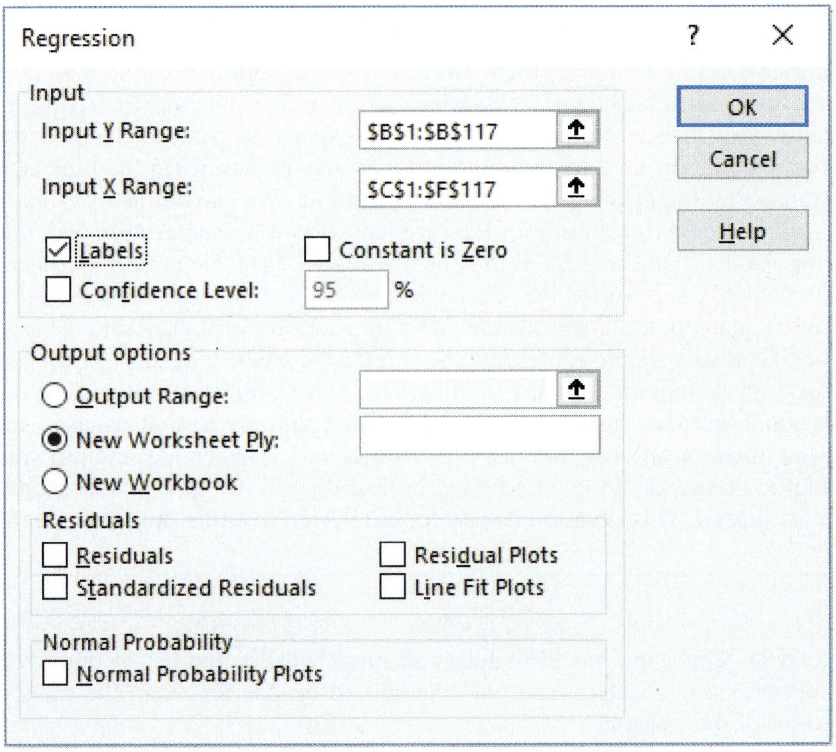

Source: Microsoft Excel

FIGURE 6.3 Excel's Regression dialog box for Example 6.1

C. Use the **lm** function to create a linear model, which we label Multiple. Note that we use the '+' sign to add predictor variables, even if we believe that a negative relationship may exist between the response variable and the predictor variables. You will not see output after you implement this step.

```
> Multiple <- lm(Earnings ~ Cost + Grad + Debt + City, data = myData)
```

D. Use the **summary** function to view the summary regression output. Figure 6.4 shows the R regression output. We have put the intercept and the slope coefficients in boldface. As expected, these values are identical to the ones obtained using Excel.

```
> summary(Multiple)
```

```
Call:
lm(formula = Earnings ~ Cost + Grad + Debt + City, data = myData)

Residuals:
     Min        1Q    Median        3Q       Max
-12375.3   -3065.2    -589.9    2946.5   20189.0

Coefficients:
              Estimate Std. Error t value Pr(>|t|)
(Intercept) 10004.9665  7634.3338   1.311 0.192724
Cost            0.4349     0.1110   3.917 0.000155 ***
Grad          178.0989    69.1940   2.574 0.011373 *
Debt          141.4783   117.2120   1.207 0.229987
City         2526.7888  1103.4026   2.290 0.023912 *
---
Signif. codes:  0 '***' 0.001 '**' 0.01 '*' 0.05 '.' 0.1 ' ' 1

Residual standard error: 5646 on 111 degrees of freedom
Multiple R-squared:  0.4292, Adjusted R-squared:  0.4087
F-statistic: 20.87 on 4 and 111 DF, p-value: 0.0000000000007564
```

FIGURE 6.4 R's regression output for Example 6.1

Categorical Variables with Multiple Categories

So far, we have used a dummy variable to describe a categorical variable with only two categories. Sometimes, a categorical variable may be defined by more than two categories. In such cases, we use multiple dummy variables to capture all categories. For example, the mode of transportation used to commute to work may be described by three categories: Public Transportation, Driving Alone, and Car Pooling. We can define two dummy variables d_1 and d_2, where d_1 equals 1 for Public Transportation, 0 otherwise, and d_2 equals 1 for Driving Alone, 0 otherwise. For this three-category case, we need to define only two dummy variables; Car Pooling, the reference category, is indicated when $d_1 = d_2 = 0$.

Given the intercept term, we exclude one of the dummy variables from the regression, where the excluded variable represents the reference category against which the others are assessed. If we include as many dummy variables as there are categories, then their sum will equal one. For instance, if we add a third dummy d_3 that equals 1 to denote Car Pooling, then for all observations, $d_1 + d_2 + d_3 = 1$. This creates the problem called perfect multicollinearity, a topic discussed in Section 6.4. As we will see, such a model cannot be estimated. This situation is sometimes referred to as the **dummy variable trap**.

AVOIDING THE DUMMY VARIABLE TRAP

If the linear regression model includes an intercept, the number of dummy variables representing a categorical variable should be one less than the number of categories of the variable.

It may be the case that a categorical variable has many categories. Not only is it cumbersome to create many dummy variables, it may not necessarily be informative. In this instance, it typically makes sense to group the categories based on some similarity. For example, when analyzing traffic volume, significant differences may be found between weekdays and weekends instead of between the different days of the week. Therefore, we can simply create one dummy variable to indicate whether it is a weekday or a weekend instead of creating six (7 − 1) dummy variables to indicate the different days of the week.

EXAMPLE 6.2

FILE
Retail

A government researcher is analyzing the relationship between retail sales (Sales in $ millions) and the gross national product (GNP in $ billions). He also wonders whether there are significant differences in retail sales related to the quarters of the year. He collects 10 years of quarterly data and creates dummy variables for the quarters. A portion is shown in Table 6.3.

TABLE 6.3 Data for Example 6.2

Year	Quarter	Sales	GNP
2007	1	921266	14301.854
2007	2	1013371	14512.945
⋮	⋮	⋮	⋮
2016	4	1299699	19134.463

a. Estimate the model $y = \beta_0 + \beta_1 x + \beta_2 d_1 + \beta_3 d_2 + \beta_4 d_3 + \varepsilon$, where y and x represent retail sales and GNP, respectively; d_1 equals 1 if quarter 1, 0 otherwise; d_2 equals 1 if quarter 2, 0 otherwise; and d_3 equals 1 if quarter 3, 0 otherwise. Note that the reference category is quarter 4.

b. Interpret the slope coefficient for quarter 1.

c. What are predicted sales in quarter 2 if GNP is $18,000 (in billions)? For the same value of GNP, what are predicted sales in quarter 4?

SOLUTION:

a. In order to estimate this model, we have to first create three dummy variables d_1, d_2, and d_3 from the Quarter variable. For this example, d_1 will take on the value 1 if Quarter 1, 0 otherwise; d_2 will take on the value 1 if Quarter 2, 0 otherwise; and d_3 will take on the value 1 if Quarter 3, 0 otherwise. We report a portion of the regression results of this model in Table 6.4.

TABLE 6.4 Portion of Regression Results for Example 6.2

	Coefficients	Standard Error	t Stat	p-value
Intercept	47095.6859	53963.3350	0.873	0.3888
GNP	65.0548	3.2151	20.234	6.74E-21
d1	−108765.2580	13638.1967	−7.975	2.21E-09
d2	−30486.2947	13593.5983	−2.243	0.0314
d3	−48805 0461	13570.2660	−3.596	0.0009

b. All else equal, retail sales in quarter 1 are expected to be approximately \$108,765 million less than sales in quarter 4.

c. Given $x = 18{,}000$, we set $d_1 = 0, d_2 = 1, d_3 = 0$ and calculate $\hat{y} = 47{,}095.6859 + 65.0548 \times 18{,}000 - 30{,}486.2947 = 1{,}187{,}594.98$. Or, equivalently, retail sales are predicted to be approximately \$1,187,595 (in millions). For the same GNP value, predicted retail sales in quarter 4 ($d_1 = d_2 = d_3 = 0$) are $\hat{y} = 47{,}095.6859 + 65.0548 \times 18{,}000 = 1{,}218{,}081.28$, or approximately \$1,218,081 (in millions).

EXERCISES 6.1

Applications

1. Using data from 50 workers, a researcher estimates Wage = $\beta_0 + \beta_1$Education + β_2Experience + β_3Age + ε, where Wage is the hourly wage rate and Education, Experience, and Age are the years of higher education, the years of experience, and the age of the worker, respectively. A portion of the regression results is shown in the following table.

	Coefficients	Standard Error	t Stat	p-value
Intercept	7.87	4.09	1.93	0.0603
Education	1.44	0.34	4.24	0.0001
Experience	0.45	0.14	3.16	0.0028
Age	−0.01	0.08	−0.14	0.8920

   a. Interpret the estimates for β_1 and β_2.

   b. Predict the hourly wage rate for a 30-year-old worker with four years of higher education and three years of experience.

2. A sociologist believes that the crime rate in an area is significantly influenced by the area's poverty rate and median income. Specifically, she hypothesizes crime will increase with poverty and decrease with income. She collects data on the crime rate (crimes per 100,000 residents), the poverty rate (in %), and the median income (in \$1,000s) from 41 New England cities. A portion of the regression results is shown in the following table.

	Coefficients	Standard Error	t Stat	p-value
Intercept	−301.62	549.71	−0.55	0.5864
Poverty	53.16	14.22	3.74	0.0006
Income	4.95	8.26	0.60	0.5526

   a. Are the signs as expected on the slope coefficients?

   b. Predict the crime rate in an area with a poverty rate of 20% and a median income of \$50,000.

3. Osteoporosis is a degenerative disease that primarily affects women over the age of 60. A research analyst wants to forecast sales of StrongBones, a prescription drug for treating this debilitating disease. She uses the model Sales = $\beta_0 + \beta_1$Population + β_2Income + ε, where Sales refers to the sales of StrongBones (in \$1,000,000s), Population is the number of women over the age of 60 (in millions), and Income is the average income of women over the age of 60 (in \$1,000s). She collects data on 38 cities across the United States and obtains the following regression results:

	Coefficients	Standard Error	t Stat	p-value
Intercept	10.35	4.02	2.57	0.0199
Population	8.47	2.71	3.12	0.0062
Income	7.62	6.63	1.15	0.2661

a. Interpret the slope coefficients.
b. Predict sales if a city has 1.5 million women over the age of 60 and their average income is $44,000.

4. An executive researcher wants to better understand the factors that explain differences in salaries for marketing majors. He decides to estimate two models: $y = \beta_0 + \beta_1 d_1 + \varepsilon$ (Model 1) and $y = \beta_0 + \beta_1 d_1 + \beta_2 d_2 + \varepsilon$ (Model 2). Here y represents salary, d_1 is a dummy variable that equals 1 for male employees, and d_2 is a dummy variable that equals 1 for employees with an MBA.
   a. What is the reference group in Model 1?
   b. What is the reference group in Model 2?
   c. In these two models, would it matter if d_1 equaled 1 for female employees?

5. House price y is estimated as a function of the square footage of a house x and a dummy variable d that equals 1 if the house has ocean views. The estimated house price, measured in $1,000s, is given by $\hat{y} = 118.90 + 0.12x + 52.60d$.
   a. Compute the predicted price of a house with ocean views and square footage of 2,000 and 3,000, respectively.
   b. Compute the predicted price of a house without ocean views and square footage of 2,000 and 3,000, respectively.
   c. Discuss the impact of ocean views on the house price.

6. **FILE** ***GPA.*** The director of graduate admissions at a large university is analyzing the relationship between scores on the math portion of the Graduate Record Examination (GRE) and subsequent performance in graduate school, as measured by a student's grade point average (GPA). She uses a sample of 24 students who graduated within the past five years. A portion of the data is as follows:

GPA	GRE
3.0	700
3.5	720
⋮	⋮
3.5	780

   a. Find the sample regression equation for the model: $\text{GPA} = \beta_0 + \beta_1 \text{GRE} + \varepsilon$.
   b. What is a student's predicted GPA if he/she scored 710 on the math portion of the GRE?

7. **FILE** ***Education.*** A social scientist would like to analyze the relationship between educational attainment (in years of higher education) and annual salary (in $1,000s). He collects data on 20 individuals. A portion of the data is as follows:

Salary	Education
40	3
53	4
⋮	⋮
38	0

   a. Find the sample regression equation for the model: $\text{Salary} = \beta_0 + \beta_1 \text{Education} + \varepsilon$.
   b. Interpret the coefficient for Education.
   c. What is the predicted salary for an individual who completed seven years of higher education?

8. **FILE** ***Consumption.*** The consumption function, first developed by John Maynard Keynes, captures one of the key relationships in economics. It expresses consumption as a function of disposable income, where disposable income is income after taxes. The accompanying table shows a portion of quarterly data for average U.S. annual consumption (Consumption in $) and disposable income (Income in $) for the years 2000–2016.

Date	Consumption	Income
Q1, 2000	28634	31192
Q2, 2000	28837	31438
⋮	⋮	⋮
Q4, 2016	35987	39254

   a. Find the sample regression equation for the model: $\text{Consumption} = \beta_0 + \beta_1 \text{Income} + \varepsilon$.
   b. In this model, the slope coefficient is called the marginal propensity to consume. Interpret its meaning.
   c. What is predicted consumption if disposable income is $35,000?

9. **FILE** ***Car_Prices.*** The accompanying table shows a portion of data consisting of the price, the age, and the mileage for 20 used sedans.

Price	Age	Mileage
13590	6	61485
13775	6	54344
⋮	⋮	⋮
11988	8	42408

   a. Estimate the sample regression equation that enables us to predict the price of a sedan on the basis of its age and mileage.
   b. Interpret the slope coefficient of Age.
   c. Predict the price of a five-year-old sedan with 65,000 miles.

10. **FILE** ***Engine.*** The maintenance manager at a trucking company wants to build a regression model to forecast the time until the first engine overhaul (Time in years) based on four predictor variables: (1) annual miles driven (Miles in 1,000s), (2) average load weight (Load in tons), (3) average driving speed (Speed in mph), and (4) oil change interval (Oil in 1,000s of miles). Based on driver logs and onboard computers, data have been obtained for a sample of 25 trucks. A portion of the data is shown in the accompanying table.

Time	Miles	Load	Speed	Oil
7.9	42.8	19	46	15
0.9	98.5	25	46	29
⋮	⋮	⋮	⋮	⋮
6.1	61.2	24	58	19

a. For each predictor variable, discuss whether it is likely to have a positive or negative influence on time until the first engine overhaul.
b. Find the sample regression equation for the regression model (use all four predictor variables).
c. Based on part a, are the signs of the regression coefficients logical?
d. Predict the time before the first engine overhaul for a particular truck driven 60,000 miles per year with an average load of 22 tons, an average driving speed of 57 mph, and 18,000 miles between oil changes.

11. **FILE** ***MCAS.*** Education reform is one of the most hotly debated subjects on both state and national policymakers' list of socioeconomic topics. Consider a linear regression model that relates school expenditures and family background to student performance in Massachusetts using 224 school districts. The response variable is the mean score on the MCAS (Massachusetts Comprehensive Assessment System) exam given to 10th graders. Four predictor variables are used: (1) STR is the student-to-teacher ratio in %, (2) TSAL is the average teacher's salary in $1,000s, (3) INC is the median household income in $1,000s, and (4) SGL is the percentage of single-parent households. A portion of the data is shown in the accompanying table.

Score	STR	TSAL	INC	SGL
227.00	19.00	44.01	48.89	4.70
230.67	17.90	40.17	43.91	4.60
⋮	⋮	⋮	⋮	⋮
230.67	19.20	44.79	47.64	5.10

a. For each predictor variable, discuss whether it is likely to have a positive or negative influence on Score.
b. Find the sample regression equation. Are the signs of the slope coefficients as expected?
c. What is the predicted score if STR = 18, TSAL = 50, INC = 60, and SGL = 5?
d. What is the predicted score if everything else is the same as in part c except INC = 80?

12. **FILE** ***Electricity_Cost.*** The facility manager at a pharmaceutical company wants to build a regression model to forecast monthly electricity cost. Three main variables are thought to dictate electricity cost (in $): (1) average outdoor temperature (Avg Temp in °F), (2) working days per month, and (3) tons of product produced. A portion of the past year's monthly data is shown in the accompanying table.

Cost	Avg Temp	Work Days	Tons Produced
24100	26	24	80
23700	32	21	73
⋮	⋮	⋮	⋮
26000	39	22	69

a. For each predictor variable, discuss whether it is likely to have a positive or negative influence on monthly electricity cost.
b. Find the sample regression equation for the regression model (use all three predictor variables).
c. What is the predicted electricity cost in a month during which the average outdoor temperature is 65°, there are 23 working days, and 76 tons are produced?

13. **FILE** ***SAT_1.*** The SAT has gone through many revisions over the years. People argue that female students generally do worse on math tests but better on writing tests. Consider the following portion of data on 20 students who took the SAT test last year. Information includes each student's score on the writing and math sections of the exam, the student's GPA, and a Female dummy variable that equals 1 if the student is female, 0 otherwise.

Writing	Math	GPA	Female
620	600	3.44	0
570	550	3.04	0
⋮	⋮	⋮	⋮
540	520	2.84	0

a. Estimate a linear regression model with Writing as the response variable and GPA and Female as the predictor variables. Compute the predicted writing score for a male student with a GPA of 3.5. Repeat the computation for a female student.
b. Estimate a linear regression model with Math as the response variable and GPA and Female as the predictor variables. Compute the predicted math score for a male student with a GPA of 3.5. Repeat the computation for a female student.

14. **FILE** ***Franchise.*** A president of a large chain of fast-food restaurants collects data on 100 franchises.
a. Estimate the model: $y = \beta_0 + \beta_1 x_1 + \beta_2 x_2 + \varepsilon$ where y is net profit, x_1 is counter sales, and x_2 is drive-through sales. All variables are measured in millions of dollars.
b. Interpret the coefficient attached to drive-through sales.
c. Predict the net profit of a franchise that had counter sales of $6 million and drive-up sales of $4 million.

15. **FILE** ***Arlington.*** A Realtor in Arlington, Massachusetts, is analyzing the relationship between the sale price of a home

(Price in $), its square footage (Sqft), the number of bedrooms (Beds), the number of bathrooms (Baths), and a Colonial dummy variable (Colonial equals 1 if a colonial-style home, 0 otherwise). She collects data on 36 sales in Arlington for the analysis. A portion of the data is shown in the accompanying table.

Price	Sqft	Beds	Baths	Colonial
840000	2768	4	3.5	1
822000	2500	4	2.5	1
⋮	⋮	⋮	⋮	⋮
307500	850	1	1	0

a. Estimate the model: Price $= \beta_0 + \beta_1$Sqft $+ \beta_2$Beds $+ \beta_3$Baths $+ \beta_4$Colonial $+ \varepsilon$.

b. Interpret the coefficients attached to Beds and Colonial.

c. Predict the price of a 2,500-square-foot, colonial-style home with three bedrooms and two bathrooms.

16. **FILE** ***Startups.*** Many of today's leading companies, including Google, Microsoft, and Facebook, are based on technologies developed within universities. Lisa Fisher is a business school professor who would like to analyze university factors that enhance innovation. She collects data on 143 universities for a regression where the response variable is the number of startups (Startups), which is used as a measure for innovation. The predictor variables include the university's research expenditure (Research in $ millions), the number of patents issued (Patents), and the age of its technology transfer office (Duration in years). A portion of the data is shown in the accompanying table.

Startups	Research	Patents	Duration
1	145.52	8	23
1	237.52	16	23
⋮	⋮	⋮	⋮
1	154.38	3	9

a. Estimate: Startups $= \beta_0 + \beta_1$Research $+ \beta_2$Patents $+ \beta_3$Duration $+ \varepsilon$.

b. Predict the number of startups for a university that spent $120 million on research, was issued eight patents, and has had a technology transfer office for 20 years.

c. How much more research expenditure is needed for the university to have an additional predicted startup, with everything else being the same?

17. **FILE** ***Quarterbacks.*** American football is the highest-paying sport on a per-game basis. Given that the quarterback is considered the most important player on the team, he is typically well-compensated. A sports statistician examines the factors that influence a quarterback's salary. He believes that a quarterback's pass completion rate is the most important variable affecting salary. He also wonders how total touchdowns scored and a quarterback's age might impact salary. The statistician collects data on salary (Salary in $ millions), pass completion rate (PC in %), total touchdowns scored (TD), and age for 32 quarterbacks during a recent season. A portion of the data is shown in the accompanying table.

Player	Salary	PC	TD	Age
1	25.5566	65.2	28	27
2	22.0441	60.5	27	26
⋮	⋮	⋮	⋮	⋮
32	0.6260	63.1	26	29

a. Estimate: Salary $= \beta_0 + \beta_1$PC $+ \beta_2$TD $+ \beta_3$Age $+ \varepsilon$.

b. Interpret the slope coefficient attached to TD.

c. Player 8 earned 12.9895 million dollars during the season. According to the model, what is his predicted salary if PCT = 70.6, TD = 34, and Age = 30?

d. Player 16 earned 8.0073 million dollars during the season. According to the model, what is his predicted salary if PCT = 65.5, TD = 28, and Age = 32?

e. Compute and interpret the residual salary for Player 8 and Player 16.

LO 6.2

6.2 MODEL SELECTION

Interpret goodness-of-fit measures.

By simply observing the sample regression equation, we cannot assess how well the predictor variables explain the variation in the response variable. However, several objective "goodness-of-fit" measures do exist that summarize how well the sample regression equation fits the data.

Recall that in the introductory case study, we are interested in analyzing factors that may influence post-college annual earnings (Earnings) for 116 colleges. Here, we will estimate three models, using a combination of four predictor variables, to determine which sample regression equation 'best' explains Earnings. The four predictor variables are the average annual cost (Cost), the graduation rate (Grad), the percentage of students paying down debt (Debt), and whether or not a college is located in a city (City equals 1 if a city location and 0 otherwise). Let the models be specified as follows:

$$\text{Model 1: Earnings} = \beta_0 + \beta_1\text{Cost} + \varepsilon$$
$$\text{Model 2: Earnings} = \beta_0 + \beta_1\text{Cost} + \beta_2\text{Grad} + \beta_3\text{Debt} + \varepsilon$$
$$\text{Model 3: Earnings} = \beta_0 + \beta_1\text{Cost} + \beta_2\text{Grad} + \beta_3\text{Debt} + \beta_4\text{City} + \varepsilon$$

(To simplify, we use the same notation to refer to the coefficients in Models 1, 2, and 3. The coefficients and their estimates may have a different meaning depending on which model we reference. Also, we note that when explaining Earnings, other models do exist; for instance, we could have considered other combinations of predictor variables.)

If you had to choose one of these models to predict annual post-college earnings, which model would you choose? It may be that by using more predictor variables, you can better describe the response variable. However, for a given sample, more is not always better. In order to select the preferred model, we examine several goodness-of-fit measures: the standard error of the estimate (denoted as s_e), the coefficient of determination (denoted as R^2), and the adjusted coefficient of determination (denoted as adjusted R^2). We first discuss these measures in general, and then determine whether Model 1, Model 2, or Model 3 is the preferred model.

The Standard Error of the Estimate, s_e

To simplify, we describe goodness-of-fit measures in the context of a simple linear regression model, and we will refer to Model 1 for this purpose. Figure 6.5 shows a scatterplot of Earnings (y) against Cost (x), as well as the superimposed sample regression line. Recall that the residual e_i represents the difference between the observed value and the predicted value of the response variable for the ith observation—that is, $e_i = y_i - \hat{y}_i$. If all the data points had fallen on the line, then each residual would be zero; in other words, there would be no dispersion between the observed and the predicted values. Because in practice we rarely, if ever, obtain this result, we evaluate models on the basis of the relative magnitude of the residuals. The sample regression equation provides a good fit when the dispersion of the residuals is relatively small.

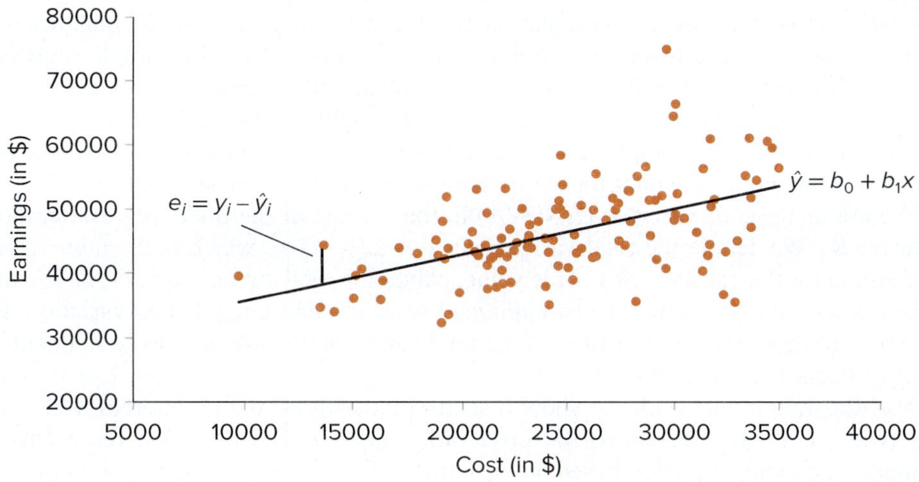

FIGURE 6.5
Scatterplot of Earnings against Cost

A numerical measure that gauges the dispersion from the sample regression equation is the sample variance of the residual, denoted s_e^2. This measure is defined as the average squared difference between y_i and $\hat{y}_i$. The numerator of the formula is the error sum of squares, $SSE = \Sigma(y_i - \hat{y}_i)^2 = \Sigma e_i^2$. Dividing SSE by its respective degrees of freedom $n - k - 1$ yields s_e^2. Recall that k denotes the number of predictor variables in the linear regression model; thus, for a simple linear regression model, k equals one. Instead of s_e^2, we generally report the standard deviation of the residual, denoted s_e, more commonly referred to as the **standard error of the estimate**. As usual, s_e is the positive square root of s_e^2. The standard error of the estimate is measured in the same units of measurement as the response variable. When comparing models with the same response variable, we prefer the model with a smaller s_e. A smaller s_e implies that there is less dispersion of the observed values from the predicted values.

THE STANDARD ERROR OF THE ESTIMATE

The standard error of the estimate s_e is calculated as

$$s_e = \sqrt{\frac{SSE}{n-k-1}},$$

where SSE is the error sum of squares. Theoretically, s_e can assume any value between zero and infinity, $0 \leq s_e < \infty$. When comparing models with the same response variable, the model with the smaller s_e is preferred.

For a given sample size n, increasing the number k of the predictor variables reduces both the numerator (SSE) and the denominator ($n - k - 1$) in the formula for s_e. The net effect, shown by the value of s_e, allows us to determine if the added predictor variables improve the fit of the model. Virtually all statistical software packages report s_e. Excel reports s_e in the *Regression Statistics* portion of the regression output and refers to it as 'Standard Error.' R reports s_e in the bottom portion of the regression output and refers to it as 'Residual standard error.'

The Coefficient of Determination, R^2

Like the standard error of the estimate, the **coefficient of determination** R^2 evaluates how well the sample regression equation fits the data. In particular, R^2 quantifies the sample variation in the response variable y that is explained by the sample regression equation. It is computed as the ratio of the explained variation of the response variable to its total variation. For example, if $R^2 = 0.72$, we say that 72% of the sample variation in y is explained by the sample regression equation. Other factors, which have not been included in the model, account for the remaining 28% of the sample variation.

We use analysis of variance (ANOVA) in the context of the linear regression model to derive R^2. We denote the total variation in y as $\Sigma(y_i - \bar{y})^2$, which is the numerator in the formula for the variance of y. This value, called the total sum of squares, SST, can be broken down into two components: explained variation and unexplained variation. Figure 6.6 illustrates the decomposition of the total variation of y into its two components for a simple linear regression model.

For illustration purposes, we show a scatterplot with all the points removed except one, point A. Point A refers to the observation (x_i, y_i). The blue line represents the estimated regression equation based on the entire sample data; the horizontal and vertical green lines represent the sample means $\bar{y}$ and $\bar{x}$, respectively. The vertical distance between point A and point C is the total difference $y_i - \bar{y}$. For each observation, we square these differences and then find their sum—this amounts to $SST = \Sigma(y_i - \bar{y})^2$, or, equivalently, the total variation in y.

Now, we focus on the distance between point B and point C which is referred to as the explained difference, $\hat{y}_i - \bar{y}$. In other words, this difference can be explained by changes in x. Squaring all such differences and summing them yields the regression sum of squares, SSR, where $SSR = \Sigma(\hat{y}_i - \bar{y})^2$. SSR is a measure of the explained variation in y.

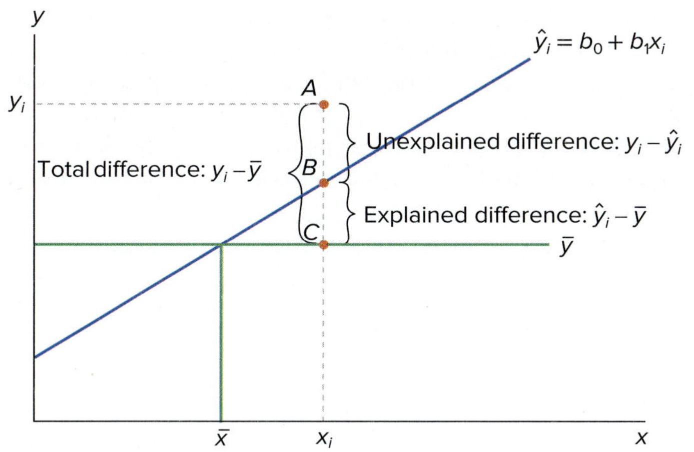

FIGURE 6.6 Total, explained, and unexplained differences

The distance between point A and point B is the unexplained difference. This is the portion that remains unexplained. Squaring all such differences and summing them yields the familiar error sum of squares, $SSE = \Sigma(y_i - \hat{y}_i)^2$.

Thus, the total variation in y can be decomposed into explained and unexplained variation as follows:

$$SST = SSR + SSE.$$

We derive the formula for R^2 by dividing both sides by SST and rearranging:

$$R^2 = SSR/SST = 1 - SSE/SST.$$

> **THE COEFFICIENT OF DETERMINATION, R^2**
>
> The coefficient of determination R^2 is the proportion of the sample variation in the response variable that is explained by the sample regression equation. We compute R^2 as
>
> $$R^2 = SSR/SST, \text{ or equivalently, } R^2 = 1 - SSE/SST,$$
>
> where $SSR = \Sigma(\hat{y}_i - \bar{y})^2$, $SSE = \Sigma(y_i - \hat{y}_i)^2$, and $SST = \Sigma(y_i - \bar{y})^2$.
>
> The value of R^2 falls between zero and one; the closer the value is to one, the better the fit.

Virtually all statistical software packages report R^2. Excel reports R^2 in the *Regression Statistics* section of the regression output and refers to it as R Square; R reports R^2 below the coefficient estimates and refers to it as Multiple R Squared.

Our objective in adding another predictor variable to a linear regression model is to increase the model's usefulness. It turns out that we cannot use R^2 for model comparison when the competing models do not include the same number of predictor variables. This occurs because R^2 never decreases as we add more predictor variables to the model. A popular model selection method in such situations is to choose the model that has the highest adjusted R^2 value, a topic that we discuss next.

The Adjusted R^2

Because R^2 never decreases as we add more predictor variables to the linear regression model, it is possible to increase its value unintentionally by including a group of predictor variables that may have no economic or intuitive foundation in the linear regression model. This is true especially when the number of predictor variables k is large relative to the sample size n. In order to avoid the possibility of R^2 creating a false impression, virtually all software packages include **adjusted R^2**. Unlike R^2, adjusted R^2 explicitly accounts for the sample size n and the number of predictor variables k. It is common to use adjusted R^2 for model selection because it imposes a penalty for any additional predictor variable that is included in the analysis. When comparing models with the same response variable, we prefer the model with the higher adjusted R^2, implying that the model is able to explain more of the sample variation in y.

ADJUSTED R^2

The adjusted coefficient of determination is calculated as

$$\text{Adjusted } R^2 = 1 - (1 - R^2)\left(\frac{n-1}{n-k-1}\right)$$

Adjusted R^2 is used to compare competing linear regression models with different numbers of predictor variables; the higher the adjusted R^2, the better the model.

If SSE is substantially greater than zero and k is large compared to n, then adjusted R^2 will differ substantially from R^2. Adjusted R^2 may be negative, if the correlation between the response variable and the predictor variables is sufficiently low. Both the standard error of the estimate s_e and the adjusted R^2 are useful for comparing linear regression models with different numbers of predictor variables. Adjusted R^2, however, is the more commonly used criterion for model selection.

EXAMPLE 6.3

FILE *College*

Table 6.5 provides goodness-of-fit measures from estimating the following models:

$$\text{Model 1: Earnings} = \beta_0 + \beta_1\text{Cost} + \varepsilon$$
$$\text{Model 2: Earnings} = \beta_0 + \beta_1\text{Cost} + \beta_2\text{Grad} + \beta_3\text{Debt} + \varepsilon$$
$$\text{Model 3: Earnings} = \beta_0 + \beta_1\text{Cost} + \beta_2\text{Grad} + \beta_3\text{Debt} + \beta_4\text{City} + \varepsilon$$

TABLE 6.5 Goodness-of-Fit Measures for Models 1, 2, and 3

	Model 1	Model 2	Model 3
Standard error of the estimate s_e	6,271.4407	5,751.8065	5,645.8306
Coefficient of determination R^2	0.2767	0.4023	0.4292
Adjusted R^2	0.2703	0.3862	0.4087

a. Based on two goodness-of-fit measures, which of the three models is the preferred model.

b. Interpret the coefficient of determination for the preferred model.

c. What percentage of the sample variation in annual post-college earnings is unexplained by the preferred model?

SOLUTION:

a. Model 3 has the lowest standard error of the estimate ($s_e = 5{,}645.8306$) as compared to Model 1 and Model 2. Model 3 also has the highest adjusted R^2 (adjusted $R^2 = 0.4087$). Thus, Model 3 is the preferred model. Note that we cannot use the coefficient of determination R^2 to compare the three models because the models have different numbers of predictor variables.

b. The coefficient of determination R^2 for Model 3 is 0.4292, which means that 42.92% of the sample variation in Earnings is explained by the regression model.

c. If 42.92% of the sample variation in Earnings is explained by changes in the predictor variables in Model 3, then 57.08% (1 – 0.4292) is unexplained by the regression equation. It should not come as a surprise that the regression equation leaves quite a bit of the sample variation in annual post-college earnings unexplained; there are many factors (grade-point average, field of emphasis, natural ability, etc.) that are likely to explain earnings that have not been included in the model.

One Last Note on Goodness-of-Fit Measures

We note that goodness-of-fit measures discussed in this section use the same sample to build the model as well as to assess it. Unfortunately, this procedure does not help us gauge how well the estimated model will predict in an unseen sample. In Chapters 7 through 10, we discuss cross-validation techniques that evaluate predictive models by dividing the original sample into a training set to build (train) the model and a validation set to evaluate (validate) it. The validation set is used to provide an independent performance assessment by exposing the model to unseen data.

EXERCISES 6.2

Applications

18. An analyst estimates the sales of a firm as a function of its advertising expenditures using the model Sales $= \beta_0 + \beta_1$Advertising $+ \varepsilon$. Using 20 observations, he finds that $SSR = 199.93$ and $SST = 240.92$.
    a. What proportion of the sample variation in sales is explained by advertising expenditures?
    b. What proportion of the sample variation in sales is unexplained by advertising expenditures?

19. **FILE** ***Test_Scores.*** The accompanying data file shows the midterm and final scores for 32 students in a statistics course.
    a. Estimate a student's final score as a function of his/her midterm score.
    b. Find the standard error of the estimate.
    c. Find and interpret the coefficient of determination.

20. The director of college admissions at a local university is trying to determine whether a student's high school GPA or SAT score is a better predictor of the student's subsequent college GPA. She formulates two models:

    Model 1. College GPA $= \beta_0 + \beta_1$High School GPA $+ \varepsilon$
    Model 2. College GPA $= \beta_0 + \beta_1$SAT Score $+ \varepsilon$

    She estimates these models and obtains the following goodness-of-fit measures.

	Model 1	Model 2
R^2	0.5595	0.5322
Adjusted R^2	0.5573	0.5298
s_e	40.3684	41.6007

Which model provides a better fit for y? Justify your response with two goodness-of-fit measures.

21. **FILE** ***Property_Taxes.*** The accompanying data file shows the square footage and associated property taxes for 20 homes in an affluent suburb 30 miles outside of New York City.
    a. Estimate a home's property taxes as a linear function of the size of the home (measured by its square footage).
    b. What proportion of the sample variation in property taxes is explained by the home's size?
    c. What proportion of the sample variation in property taxes is unexplained by the home's size?

22. **FILE** ***Car_Prices.*** The accompanying data file shows the selling price of a used sedan, its age, and its mileage. Estimate two models:

    Model 1: Price $= \beta_0 + \beta_1$Age $+ \varepsilon$
    Model 2: Price $= \beta_0 + \beta_1$Age $+ \beta_2$Mileage $+ \varepsilon$

    Which model provides a better fit for y? Justify your response with two goodness-of-fit measures.

23. For a sample of 41 New England cities, a sociologist studies the crime rate in each city (crimes per 100,000 residents) as a function of its poverty rate (in %) and its median income (in \$1,000s). He finds that $SSE = 4{,}182{,}663$ and $SST = 7{,}732{,}451$.
    a. Calculate the standard error of the estimate.
    b. What proportion of the sample variation in crime rate is explained by the variability in the predictor variables? What proportion is unexplained?

24. For a large restaurant chain, a financial analyst uses the following model to estimate a franchise's net profit: $y = \beta_0 + \beta_1 x_1 + \beta_2 x_2 + \varepsilon_i$, where y is net profit, x_1 is counter sales, and x_2 is drive-through sales. For a sample of 100 franchises, she finds that $SSE = 4.4600$ and $SST = 18.3784$.
    a. Calculate the standard error of the estimate.
    b. Calculate and interpret the coefficient of determination.
    c. Calculate the adjusted R^2.
25. **FILE** ***Football.*** Is it defense or offense that wins football games? Consider the following portion of data, which includes a team's winning record (Win in %), the average number of yards gained, and the average number of yards allowed during a recent NFL season.

Team	Win	Yards Gained	Yards Allowed
Arizona Cardinals	46.9	366.8	305.2
Atlanta Falcons	68.8	415.8	371.2
⋮	⋮	⋮	⋮
Washington Redskins	53.1	403.4	377.9

    a. Compare two simple linear regression models where Model 1 predicts Win as a function of Yards Gained and Model 2 predicts Win as a function of Yards Allowed.
    b. Estimate a linear regression model, Model 3, that applies both Yards Gained and Yards Allowed to forecast Win. Is this model an improvement over the other two models? Explain.
26. **FILE** ***Ownership.*** In order to determine if the homeownership rate in the U.S. is linked with income, state-level data on the homeownership rate (Ownership in %) and median household income (Income in $) were collected. A portion of the data is shown in the accompanying table.

State	Ownership	Income
Alabama	73.2	40933
Alaska	65.7	57848
⋮	⋮	⋮
Wyoming	73.0	52201

    a. Estimate and interpret the model Ownership $= \beta_0 + \beta_1$Income $+ \varepsilon$. Is the coefficient attached to Income as expected? Explain.
    b. What is the standard error of the estimate?
    c. Interpret the coefficient of determination. Does this seem like a promising model? Explain.
27. **FILE** ***Return.*** A research analyst is trying to determine whether a firm's price-earnings (P/E) and price-sales (P/S) ratios can explain the firm's stock performance over the past year. A P/E ratio is calculated as a firm's share price compared to the income or profit earned by the firm per share. Generally, a high P/E ratio suggests that investors are expecting higher earnings growth in the future compared to companies with a lower P/E ratio. The P/S ratio is calculated by dividing a firm's share price by the firm's revenue per share for the trailing 12 months. In short, investors can use the P/S ratio to determine how much they are paying for a dollar of the firm's sales rather than a dollar of its earnings (P/E ratio). In general, the lower the P/S ratio, the more attractive the investment. Consider the following portion of data, which includes the year-to-date returns (Return in %) and the P/E and P/S ratios for 30 firms.

Firm	Return	P/E	P/S
1	4.4	14.37	2.41
2	−4.5	11.01	0.78
⋮	⋮	⋮	⋮
30	16.3	13.94	1.94

    a. Estimate Return $= \beta_0 + \beta_1$P/E $+ \beta_2$P/S $+ \varepsilon$. Are the signs on the coefficients as expected? Explain.
    b. Interpret the slope coefficient of the P/S ratio.
    c. What is the predicted return for a firm with a P/E ratio of 10 and a P/S ratio of 2?
    d. What is the standard error of the estimate?
    e. Interpret R^2.
28. **FILE** ***SAT_2.*** It is generally believed that the wealthier a student's family, the higher the student's Scholastic Aptitude Test (SAT) score. Another commonly used predictor for SAT scores is the student's grade point average (GPA). Consider the following portion of data collected on 24 students.

SAT	Income	GPA
1651	47000	2.79
1581	34000	2.97
⋮	⋮	⋮
1940	113000	3.96

    a. Estimate three models:
        (i) SAT $= \beta_0 + \beta_1$Income $+ \varepsilon$,
        (ii) SAT $= \beta_0 + \beta_1$GPA $+ \varepsilon$, and
        (iii) SAT $= \beta_0 + \beta_1$Income $+ \beta_2$GPA $+ \varepsilon$.
    b. Use goodness-of-fit measures to select the best-fitting model.
    c. Use the preferred model to predict SAT given the mean value of the predictor variable(s).

6.3 TESTS OF SIGNIFICANCE

LO 6.3

Conduct tests of significance.

In this section, we continue our assessment of the linear regression model by turning our attention to hypothesis tests about the unknown parameters (coefficients) $\beta_0, \beta_1, \ldots, \beta_k$. In particular, we test for joint and individual significance to determine whether there is evidence of a linear relationship between the response variable and the predictor variables. We note that for the tests to be valid, the OLS estimators $b_0, b_1, \ldots, b_k$ must be normally distributed. This condition is satisfied if the random error term, ε, is normally distributed. If we cannot assume the normality of ε, then the tests are valid only for large sample sizes.

Test of Joint Significance

Consider the following linear regression model, which links the response variable y with k predictor variables $x_1, x_2, \ldots, x_k$:

$$y = \beta_0 + \beta_1 x_1 + \beta_2 x_2 + \ldots + \beta_k x_k + \varepsilon.$$

If all of the slope coefficients equal zero, then all of the predictor variables drop out of the model; this implies that none of the predictor variables has a linear relationship with the response variable. Conversely, if at least one of the slope coefficients does not equal zero, then at least one predictor variable influences the response variable.

When we assess a linear regression model, a test of joint significance is often regarded as a test of the overall usefulness of a regression. This test determines whether the predictor variables $x_1, x_2, \ldots, x_k$ have a joint statistical influence on y. Following the hypothesis testing methodology introduced in Chapter 5, if we reject the null hypothesis that all slope coefficients equal zero, then we are able to conclude that at least one predictor variable influences the response variable. The competing hypotheses for a test of joint significance take the following form:

$$H_0: \beta_1 = \beta_2 = \ldots = \beta_k = 0$$
$$H_A: \text{At least one } \beta_i \neq 0$$

The test statistic for a test of joint significance follows the F distribution. Like the t_{df} distribution, the F distribution is characterized by a family of distributions; however, each distribution depends on two degrees of freedom: the numerator degrees of freedom df_1 and the denominator degrees of freedom df_2. It is common to refer to it as the $F_{(df_1, df_2)}$ distribution.

We calculate the test statistic for a test of joint significance as $F_{(df_1, df_2)} = \frac{MSR}{MSE}$, where $df_1 = k$, $df_2 = n = k - 1$, $MSR = SSR/k$ and $MSE = SSE/(n - k - 1)$. In other words, the $F_{(df_1, df_2)}$ test statistic is a ratio of the mean square regression MSR to the mean square error MSE. The test statistic measures how well the regression equation explains the variability in the response variable. We always employ a right-tailed F test when conducting a test of joint significance since a larger value of $F_{(df_1, df_2)}$ provides us with more evidence to reject the null hypothesis.

A TEST OF JOINT SIGNIFICANCE

For the linear regression model, $y = \beta_0 + \beta_1 x_1 + \beta_2 x_2 + \ldots + \beta_k x_k + \varepsilon$, the following competing hypotheses are used for a test of joint significance:

$$H_0: \beta_1 = \beta_2 = \ldots = \beta_k = 0$$
$$H_A: \text{At least one } \beta_i \neq 0$$

The value of the test statistic is calculated as:

$$F_{(df_1, df_2)} = \frac{SSR/k}{SSE/(n-k-1)} = \frac{MSR}{MSE}$$

where $df_1 = k$, $df_2 = n - k - 1$, SSR is the regression sum of squares, SSE is the error sum of squares, MSR is the mean square regression, and MSE is the mean square error.

- If the null hypothesis is not rejected, then the predictor variables are not jointly significant in explaining the response variable; the model is not useful.
- If the null hypothesis is rejected, then the predictor variables are jointly significant in explaining the response variable; the model is useful.

Most statistical computer packages, including Excel and R, produce an ANOVA table that decomposes the total variability of the response variable y into two components: (1) the variability explained by the regression and (2) the variability that is unexplained. In addition, the value for the $F_{(df_1,df_2)}$ test statistic and its p-value are also provided. Table 6.6 shows the general format of an ANOVA table. Excel explicitly provides an ANOVA table with its regression output, with the p-value reported under the heading Significance F. R provides the value for the $F_{(df_1,df_2)}$ test statistic and its p-value with its regression output, which is sufficient to conduct a test of joint significance. If we use R's **anova** function, R generates an ANOVA table that is even more detailed than the one provided by Excel; R's ANOVA table breaks down the contribution of each predictor variable in explaining the total variability in the response variable.

TABLE 6.6 General Format of an ANOVA Table for Regression

ANOVA	*df*	*SS*	*MS*	*F*	Significance *F*
Regression	k	SSR	$MSR = \frac{SSR}{k}$	$F_{(df_1,df_2)} = \frac{MSR}{MSE}$	$P\left(F_{(df_1,df_2)} \geq \frac{MSR}{MSE}\right)$
Residual	$n-k-1$	SSE	$MSE = \frac{SSE}{n-k-1}$		
Total	$n-1$	SST			

EXAMPLE 6.4

FILE
College

Let's revisit Model 3, from Section 6.2.

$$\text{Model 3: Earnings} = \beta_0 + \beta_1\text{Cost} + \beta_2\text{Grad} + \beta_3\text{Debt} + \beta_4\text{City} + \varepsilon$$

Recall that we chose Model 3 to predict annual post-college earnings because it had the lowest standard error of the estimate and the highest adjusted R^2. We reproduce the ANOVA portion of the regression results in Table 6.7. Conduct a test to determine if the predictor variables are jointly significant in explaining Earnings at $\alpha = 0.05$.

TABLE 6.7 ANOVA portion of Regression Results for Model 3

ANOVA	*df*	*SS*	*MS*	*F*	Significance *F*
Regression	4	2660691959	665172990	20.868	7.56E-13
Residual	111	3538169765	31875403		
Total	115	6198861724			

SOLUTION: When testing whether the predictor variables are jointly significant in explaining Earnings, we set up the following competing hypotheses:

$$H_0: \beta_1 = \beta_2 = \beta_3 = \beta_4 = 0$$
$$H_A: \text{At least one } \beta_j \neq 0.$$

Given $n = 116$ and $k = 4$, we find that $df_1 = k = 4$ and $df_2 = n - k - 1 = 111$. From Table 6.7, we find that

$$F_{(4,111)} = \frac{2{,}660{,}691{,}959/4}{3{,}538{,}169{,}765/111} = \frac{665{,}172{,}990}{31{,}875{,}403} = 20.868.$$

The p-value, $P(F_{(4,111)} \geq 20.868)$, is approximately equal to zero; its exact value is 7.56×10^{-13}. Because the p-value is less than $\alpha = 0.05$, we reject H_0. At the 5% significance level, the predictor variables are jointly significant in explaining Earnings.

Test of Individual Significance

In addition to testing all slope coefficients jointly, we often want to conduct tests on a single coefficient. Again consider the following linear regression model, which links the response variable y with k predictor variables $x_1, x_2, \ldots, x_k$:

$$y = \beta_0 + \beta_1 x_1 + \beta_2 x_2 + \ldots + \beta_k x_k + \varepsilon.$$

If, for example, the slope coefficient β_1 equals zero, then the predictor variable x_1 basically drops out of the equation, implying that x_1 does not influence y. In other words, if β_1 equals zero, then there is no linear relationship between x_1 and y. Conversely, if β_1 does not equal zero, then x_1 influences y.

In general, when we want to test whether the population coefficient β_j is different from, greater than, or less than β_{j0}, where β_{j0} is the hypothesized value of β_j, then the competing hypotheses take one of the following forms:

Two-Tailed Test	Right-Tailed Test	Left-Tailed Test
$H_0: \beta_j = \beta_{j0}$ $H_A: \beta_j \neq \beta_{j0}$	$H_0: \beta_j \leq \beta_{j0}$ $H_A: \beta_j > \beta_{j0}$	$H_0: \beta_j \geq \beta_{j0}$ $H_A: \beta_j < \beta_{j0}$

When testing whether x_j significantly influences y, we set $\beta_{j0} = 0$ and specify a two-tailed test as H_0: $\beta_j = 0$ and H_A: $\beta_j \neq 0$. We could easily specify one-tailed competing hypotheses for a positive linear relationship (H_0: $\beta_j \leq 0$ and H_A: $\beta_j > 0$) or a negative linear relationship (H_0: $\beta_j \geq 0$ and H_A: $\beta_j < 0$).

Although tests of significance are commonly based on $\beta_{j0} = 0$, in some situations we might wish to determine whether the slope coefficient differs from a nonzero value. For instance, if we are analyzing the relationship between students' exam scores on the basis of hours studied, we may want to determine if an extra hour of review before the exam will increase a student's score by more than five points. Here, we formulate the hypotheses as H_0: $\beta_j \leq 5$ and H_A: $\beta_j > 5$. Finally, although in most applications we are interested in conducting hypothesis tests on the slope coefficient(s), there are instances where we may also be interested in testing the intercept, β_0. The testing framework for the intercept remains the same; that is, if we want to test whether the intercept differs from zero, we specify the competing hypotheses as H_0: $\beta_0 = 0$ and H_A: $\beta_0 \neq 0$.

As in all hypothesis tests, the next step is to define the appropriate test statistic.

TEST OF INDIVIDUAL SIGNIFICANCE

For the linear regression model, $y = \beta_0 + \beta_1 x_1 + \beta_2 x_2 + \ldots + \beta_k x_k + \varepsilon$, the following competing hypotheses are used to conduct a test of individual significance:

$$H_0: \beta_j = \beta_{j0}$$
$$H_A: \beta_j \neq \beta_{j0}$$

The value of the test statistic is calculated as

$$t_{df} = \frac{b_j - \beta_{j0}}{se(b_j)},$$

where $df = n - k - 1$, b_j is the estimate for β_j, $se(b_j)$ is the standard error of the estimator b_j, and β_{j0} is the hypothesized value of β_j. If $\beta_{j0} = 0$, the value of the test statistic reduces to $t_{df} = \frac{b_j}{se(b_j)}$.

Suppose the competing hypotheses are H_0: $\beta_j = 0$ versus H_A: $\beta_j \neq 0$.

- If the null hypothesis is not rejected, then x_j is not significant in explaining y.
- If the null hypothesis is rejected, then x_j is significant in explaining y.

We would like to note that while the test of joint significance is important for a multiple linear regression model, it is redundant for a simple linear regression model. In fact, for a simple linear regression model, the p-value of the F-test is identical to that of the t-test on the single slope coefficient. We advise you to verify this fact.

EXAMPLE 6.5

FILE
College

Let's again revisit Model 3.

$$\text{Model 3: Earnings} = \beta_0 + \beta_1\text{Cost} + \beta_2\text{Grad} + \beta_3\text{Debt} + \beta_4\text{City} + \varepsilon$$

We produce a portion of the regression results in Table 6.8. Conduct a hypothesis test to determine whether Cost influences Earnings at the 5% significance level.

TABLE 6.8 Portion of Regression Results for Model 3

	Coefficients	Standard Error	*t* Stat	*p*-value
Intercept	10004.9665	7634.3338	1.311	0.1927
Cost	0.4349	0.1110	3.917	0.0002
Grad	178.0989	69.1940	2.574	0.0114
Debt	141.4783	117.2120	1.207	0.2300
City	2526.7888	1103.4026	2.290	0.0239

SOLUTION: We set up the following competing hypotheses in order to determine whether Cost influences Earnings:

$$H_0: \beta_1 = 0$$
$$H_A: \beta_1 \neq 0$$

From Table 6.8, we find that $b_1 = 0.4349$ and $se(b_1) = 0.1110$. Given earlier information that $n = 116$, we find $df = n - k - 1 = 116 - 4 - 1 = 111$. So, using unrounded calculations, we find the value of the test statistic as $t_{111} = \frac{b_j - \beta_{j0}}{se(b_j)} = \frac{0.4349 - 0}{0.1110} = 3.917$. Note that this calculation is not necessary because virtually all statistical computer packages automatically provide the value of the test statistic and its associated p-value. As usual, the decision rule is to reject H_0 if the p-value $< \alpha$. Because the reported p-value is 0.0002, we reject H_0. At the 5% significance level, Cost is significant in explaining Earnings.

It is important to note that the computer-generated results are valid only in a standard case where a two-tailed test is implemented to determine whether a regression coefficient differs from zero. In Example 6.5 we could use the computer-generated value of the test statistic as well as the corresponding p-value because it represented a standard case. For a one-tailed test with $\beta_{j0} = 0$, the value of the test statistic is valid, but the p-value is not; in most cases, the computer-generated p-value must be divided in half. For a one- or two-tailed test to determine if the regression coefficient differs from a nonzero value, both the computer-generated value of the test statistic and the p-value become invalid. These facts are summarized below.

COMPUTER-GENERATED TEST STATISTIC AND THE p-VALUE

Virtually all statistical packages report a value of the test statistic and its associated p-value for a two-tailed test that assesses whether the regression coefficient differs from zero.

- If we specify a one-tailed test, then we need to divide the computer-generated p-value in half.
- If we test whether the coefficient differs from a nonzero value, then we cannot use the value of the computer-generated test statistic and its p-value.

We would also like to point out that for a one-tailed test with $\beta_{j0} = 0$, there are rare instances when the computer-generated p-value is invalid. This occurs when the sign of b_j (and the value of the accompanying test statistic) is not inconsistent with the null hypothesis. For example, for a right-tailed test, H_0: $\beta_j \leq 0$ and H_A: $\beta_j > 0$, the null hypothesis cannot be rejected if the estimate b_j (and the value of the accompanying test statistic t_{df}) is negative. Similarly, no further testing is necessary if $b_j > 0$ (and thus $t_{df} > 0$) for a left-tailed test. In these rare instances, the reported p-value is invalid.

A Test for a Nonzero Slope Coefficient

In Example 6.5, the null hypothesis included a zero value for the slope coefficient—that is, $\beta_{j0} = 0$. We now motivate a test where the hypothesized value is not zero by using a renowned financial application referred to as the capital asset pricing model (CAPM).

Let R represent the return on a stock or portfolio of interest. Given the market return R_M and the risk-free return R_f, the CAPM expresses the risk-adjusted return of an asset, $R - R_f$, as a function of the risk-adjusted market return, $R_M - R_f$. It is common to use the return of the S&P 500 index for R_M and the return on a Treasury bill for R_f. For empirical estimation, we express the CAPM as

$$R - R_f = \alpha + \beta(R_M - R_f) + \varepsilon.$$

We can rewrite the model as $y = \alpha + \beta x + \varepsilon$, where $y = R - R_f$ and $x = R_M - R_f$. Note that this is essentially a simple linear regression model that uses α and β, in place of the usual β_0 and β_1, to represent the intercept and the slope coefficients, respectively. The slope coefficient β, called the stock's beta, measures how sensitive the stock's return is to changes in the level of the overall market. When β equals 1, any change in the market return leads to an identical change in the given stock return. A stock for which $\beta > 1$ is considered more "aggressive" or riskier than the market, whereas one for which $\beta < 1$ is considered "conservative" or less risky. We also give importance to the intercept coefficient α, called the stock's alpha. The CAPM theory predicts α to be zero, and thus a nonzero estimate indicates abnormal returns. Abnormal returns are positive when $\alpha > 0$ and negative when $\alpha < 0$.

FILE
J&J

EXAMPLE 6.6

Johnson & Johnson (J&J) was founded more than 120 years ago on the premise that doctors and nurses should use sterile products to treat people's wounds. Since that time, J&J products have become staples in most people's homes. Consider the CAPM where the J&J risk-adjusted stock return $R - R_f$ is used as the response variable and the risk-adjusted market return $R_M - R_f$ is used as the predictor variable. A portion of 60 months of data is shown in Table 6.9.

TABLE 6.9 Risk-Adjusted Stock Return of J&J and Market Return

Month	Year	$R - R_f$	$R_M - R_f$
Jan	2012	−0.0129	0.0403
Feb	2012	0.0216	0.0304
⋮	⋮	⋮	⋮
Dec	2016	−0.0221	0.0128

a. Because consumer staples comprise many of the products sold by J&J, its stock is often considered less risky; that is, people need these products whether the economy is good or bad. At the 5% significance level, is the beta coefficient less than one?

b. At the 5% significance level, are there abnormal returns? In other words, is the alpha coefficient significantly different from 0?

SOLUTION: Using the CAPM notation, we estimate the model, $R - R_f = \alpha + \beta(R_M - R_f) + \varepsilon$; the relevant portion of the regression output is presented in Table 6.10.

TABLE 6.10 Portion of CAPM Regression Results for J&J

	Coefficients	Standard Error	*t* Stat	*p*-value
Intercept	0.0048	0.0042	1.127	0.2645
$R_M - R_f$	0.7503	0.1391	5.395	1.32E-06

a. The estimate for the beta coefficient is 0.7503 and its standard error is 0.1391. In order to determine whether the beta coefficient is significantly less than one, we formulate the hypotheses as

$$H_0: \beta \geq 1$$
$$H_A: \beta < 1$$

Given 60 data points, $df = n - k - 1 = 60 - 1 - 1 = 58$. We cannot use the test statistic value or the *p*-value reported in Table 6.10 because the hypothesized value of β is not zero. Using unrounded calculations, we find the value of the test statistic as $t_{58} = \frac{b_j - \beta_{j0}}{se(b_j)} = \frac{0.7503 - 1}{0.1391} = -1.796$. We can use the t table to approximate the *p*-value, $P(t_{58} \leq -1.796)$, as a value that is between 0.025 and 0.05. Using statistical software, we find that the exact *p*-value is 0.039. Because the *p*-value $< \alpha = 0.05$, we reject H_0 and conclude that β is significantly less than one; that is, the return on J&J stock is less risky than the return on the market.

b. Abnormal returns exist when α is significantly different from zero. Thus, the competing hypotheses are H_0: $\alpha = 0$ versus H_A: $\alpha \neq 0$. Because it is a standard case, where the hypothesized value of the coefficient is zero, we can use the reported test statistic value of 1.127 with an associated *p*-value of 0.2645. We cannot reject H_0 at any reasonable level of significance. Therefore, we cannot conclude that there are abnormal returns for J&J stock.

Reporting Regression Results

Regression results are often reported in a "user-friendly" table. Table 6.11 reports the regression results for the three models that attempt to explain annual post-college earnings (Earnings). For Model 1, the predictor variable is the average annual cost (Cost); for Model 2, the predictor variables are Cost, the graduation rate (Grad), and the percentage of students paying down debt (Debt); and for Model 3, the predictor variables are Cost, Grad, Debt, and whether or not a college is located in a city (City equals 1 if a city location, 0 otherwise). If we were supplied with only this table, we would be able to compare these models, construct the sample regression equation of the chosen model, and perform a respectable assessment of the model with the statistics provided. Many tables contain a Notes section at the bottom explaining some of the notation. We choose to put the *p*-values in parentheses under all the estimated coefficients; however, some analysts place the standard errors of the coefficients or the values of the test statistics in parentheses. Whichever format is chosen, it must be made clear to the reader in the Notes section.

TABLE 6.11 Estimates of Alternative Regression Models to Explain Earnings, $n = 116$

	Model 1	Model 2	Model 3
Intercept	28,375.4051* (0.000)	11819.4747 (0.129)	10,004.9665 (0.193)
Cost	0.7169* (0.000)	0.5050* (0.000)	0.4349* (0.000)
Grad	NA	192.6664* (0.007)	178.0989* (0.011)
Debt	NA	104.6573 (0.378)	141.4783 (0.230)
City	NA	NA	2,526.7888* (0.024)
Se	6,271.4407	5,751.8065	5,645.8306
R^2	0.2767	0.4023	0.4292
Adjusted R^2	0.2703	0.3862	0.4087
F-test (p-value)	43.608 (0.000)	25.124 (0.000)	20.868(0.000)

NOTES: Parameter estimates are in the top half of the table with the *p*-values in parentheses; * represents significance at the 5% level. NA denotes not applicable. The lower part of the table contains goodness-of-fit measures.

SYNOPSIS OF INTRODUCTORY CASE

The Department of Education published a redesigned College Scorecard that reports the most reliable national data on college costs and students' outcomes at specific colleges. The availability of clear, reliable data was welcomed by families who are searching for answers to critical questions concerning college affordability and value.

Africa Studio/Shutterstock

In an attempt to determine which college factors 'best' explain annual post-college earnings, three regression models were estimated. A combination of four predictor variables was used in the analysis. The four predictor variables were the average annual cost (Cost), the graduation rate (Grad), the percentage of students paying down debt (Debt), and a City dummy variable that equals 1 if the college is located in a city, 0 otherwise. Goodness-of-fit measures suggested that the model that included all four predictor variables provided the best overall fit, as measured by its lowest standard error of the estimate and its highest adjusted R^2 value. The sample regression equation was $\widehat{\text{Earnings}} = 10{,}004.9665 + 0.4349\text{Cost} + 178.0989\text{Grad} + 141.4783\text{Debt} + 2{,}526.7888\text{City}$. This regression equation implies that if a college's average annual cost is $25,000, its graduation rate is 60%, its percentage of students paying down debt is 80%, and it is located in a city, then average post-college earnings for its students are $45,409.

Further testing of this preferred model revealed that the four predictor variables were jointly significant. Individual tests of significance showed that Cost, Grad, and City were significant at the 5% level; Debt was not significant in explaining Earnings. The coefficient of determination, or R^2, revealed that approximately 43% of the sample variability in annual post-college earnings is explained by the model. Thus, 57% of the sample variability in annual post-college earnings remains unexplained. This is not entirely surprising because factors not included in the model, such as field of emphasis, grade point average, and natural ability, influence annual post-college earnings.

EXERCISES 6.3

Applications

29. In order to examine the relationship between the selling price of a used car and its age, an analyst uses data from 20 recent transactions and estimates Price $= \beta_0 + \beta_1$Age $+ \varepsilon$. A portion of the regression results is shown in the accompanying table.

	Coefficients	Standard Error	*t* Stat	*p*-value
Intercept	21187.94	733.42	28.889	1.56E-16
Age	−1208.25	128.95		2.41E-08

   a. Specify the competing hypotheses in order to determine whether the selling price of a used car and its age are linearly related.
   b. Calculate the value of the test statistic.
   c. At the 5% significance level, is the age of a used car significant in explaining its selling price?
   d. Conduct a hypothesis test at the 5% significance level in order to determine if β_1 differs from −1,000. Show all of the relevant steps.

30. For a sample of 20 New England cities, a sociologist studies the crime rate in each city (crimes per 100,000 residents) as a function of its poverty rate (in %) and its median income (in $1,000s). A portion of the regression results is shown in the accompanying table.

ANOVA	*df*	*SS*	*MS*	*F*	Significance *F*
Regression	2	188246.8	94123.40	35.20	9.04E-07
Residual	17	45457.32	2673.96		
Total	19	233704.1			

	Coefficients	Standard Error	*t* Stat	*p*-value
Intercept	−301.7927	549.7135	−0.549	0.590
Poverty	53.1597	14.2198	3.738	0.002
Income	4.9472	8.2566	0.599	0.557

   a. Specify the sample regression equation.
   b. At the 5% significance level, are the poverty rate and income jointly significant in explaining the crime rate?
   c. At the 5% significance level, show whether the poverty rate and the crime rate are linearly related.
   d. Determine whether income influences the crime rate at the 5% significance level.

31. Akiko Hamaguchi is a manager at a small sushi restaurant in Phoenix, Arizona. Akiko is concerned that the weak economic environment has hampered foot traffic in her area, thus causing a dramatic decline in sales. In order to offset the decline in sales, she has pursued a strong advertising campaign. She believes advertising expenditures have a positive influence on sales. To support her claim, Akiko estimates the following linear regression model: Sales $= \beta_0 + \beta_1$Unemployment $+ \beta_2$Advertising $+ \varepsilon$. A portion of the regression results is shown in the accompanying table.

ANOVA	*df*	*SS*	*MS*	*F*	Significance *F*
Regression	2	72.6374	36.3187	8.760	0.003
Residual	14	58.0438	4.1460		
Total	16	130.681			

	Coefficients	Standard Error	*t* Stat	*p*-value
Intercept	17.5060	3.9817	4.397	0.007
Unemployment	−0.6879	0.2997	−2.296	0.038
Advertising	0.0266	0.0068	3.932	0.002

   a. At the 5% significance level, test whether the predictor variables jointly influence sales.
   b. At the 1% significance level, test whether the unemployment rate is negatively related with sales.
   c. At the 1% significance level, test whether advertising expenditures are positively related with sales.

32. A researcher estimates the following model relating the return on a firm's stock as a function of its price-to-earnings ratio and its price-to-sales ratio: Return $= \beta_0 + \beta_1$P/E $+ \beta_2$P/S $+ \varepsilon$. A portion of the regression results is shown in the accompanying table.

ANOVA	*df*	*SS*	*MS*	*F*	Significance *F*
Regression	2	918.746	459.3728	2.817	0.077
Residual	27	4402.786	163.0661		
Total	29	5321.532			

	Coefficients	Standard Error	*t* Stat	*p*-value
Intercept	−12.0243	7.886858	−1.525	0.139
P/E	0.1459	0.4322	0.338	0.738
P/S	5.4417	2.2926	2.374	0.025

a. Specify the sample regression equation.
b. At the 10% significant level, are P/E and P/S jointly significant? Show the relevant steps of the test.
c. Are both predictor variables individually significant at the 10% significance level? Show the relevant steps of the test.

33. **FILE** ***Fertilizer.*** A horticulturist is studying the relationship between tomato plant height and fertilizer amount. Thirty tomato plants grown in similar conditions were subjected to various amounts of fertilizer (in ounces) over a four-month period, and then their heights (in inches) were measured.
a. Estimate the regression model: Height $= \beta_0 + \beta_1$Fertilizer $+ \varepsilon$.
b. At the 5% significance level, determine if an ounce of fertilizer increases height by more than three inches. Show the relevant steps of the test.

34. **FILE** ***Dexterity.*** Finger dexterity, the ability to make precisely coordinated finger movements to grasp or assemble very small objects, is important in jewelry making. Thus, the manufacturing manager at Gemco, a manufacturer of high-quality watches, wants to develop a regression model to predict the productivity, measured by watches per shift, of new employees based on the time required (in seconds) to place three pins in each of 100 small holes using tweezers. He has subjected a sample of 20 current employees to the O'Connor dexterity test in which the time required to place the pins and the number of watches produced per shift are measured.
a. Estimate the regression model: Watches $= \beta_0 + \beta_1$Time $+ \varepsilon$.
b. The manager claims that for every extra second taken on placing the pins, the number of watches produced decreases by more than 0.02. Test this claim at the 5% significance level. Show the relevant steps of the test.

35. **FILE** ***Engine.*** The maintenance manager at a trucking company wants to build a regression model to forecast the time until the first engine overhaul (Time in years) based on four predictor variables: (1) annual miles driven (Miles in 1,000s), (2) average load weight (Load in tons), (3) average driving speed (Speed in mph), and (4) oil change interval (Oil in 1,000s miles). Based on driver logs and onboard computers, data have been obtained for a sample of 25 trucks.
a. Estimate the time until the first engine overhaul as a function of all four predictor variables.
b. At the 10% significance level, are the predictor variables jointly significant? Show the relevant steps of the test.
c. Are the predictor variables individually significant at the 10% significance level? Show the relevant steps of the test.

36. **FILE** ***Electricity_Cost.*** The facility manager at a pharmaceutical company wants to build a regression model to forecast monthly electricity cost. Three main variables are thought to dictate electricity cost: (1) average outdoor temperature (Temp in °F), (2) working days per month (Days), and (3) tons of product produced (Tons).
a. Estimate the regression model.
b. At the 10% significance level, are the predictor variables jointly significant? Show the relevant steps of the test.
c. Are the predictor variables individually significant at the 10% significance level? Show the relevant steps of the test.

37. **FILE** ***Caterpillar.*** Caterpillar, Inc., manufactures and sells heavy construction equipment worldwide. The performance of Caterpillar's stock is likely to be strongly influenced by the economy. For example, during the Great Recession, the value of Caterpillar's stock plunged dramatically. Monthly data for Caterpillar's risk-adjusted return ($R - R_f$) and the risk-adjusted market return ($R_M - R_f$) are collected for a five-year period ($n = 60$). A portion of the data is shown in the accompanying table.

Month	Year	$R - R_f$	$R_M - R_f$
Jan	2012	0.051024	0.040289
Feb	2012	−0.068230	0.030432
⋮	⋮	⋮	⋮
Dec	2016	0.026386	0.012784

a. Estimate the CAPM model for Caterpillar, Inc. Show the regression results in a well-formatted table.
b. At the 5% significance level, determine if investment in Caterpillar is riskier than the market (beta significantly greater than 1).
c. At the 5% significance level, is there evidence of abnormal returns?

38. **FILE** ***Arlington.*** A Realtor examines the factors that influence the price of a house in Arlington, Massachusetts. He collects data on 36 house sales (Price in $) and notes each

house's square footage (Sqft), the number of bedrooms (Beds), the number of bathrooms (Baths), and a Colonial dummy variable (Colonial equals 1 if house is colonial, 0 otherwise). A portion of the data is shown in the accompanying table.

Price	Sqft	Beds	Baths	Colonial
840000	2768	4	3.5	1
822000	2500	4	2.5	1
⋮	⋮	⋮	⋮	⋮
307500	850	1	1	0

a. Estimate Price $= \beta_0 + \beta_1$Sqft $+ \beta_2$Beds $+ \beta_3$Baths $+ \beta_4$Colonial $+ \varepsilon$. Show the regression results in a well-formatted table.
b. At the 5% significance level, are the predictor variables jointly significant in explaining Price?
c. At the 5% significance level, are all predictor variables individually significant in explaining Price?

39. FILE ***Final_Test.*** On the first day of class, an economics professor administers a test to gauge the math preparedness of her students. She believes that the performance on this math test and the number of hours studied per week on the course are the primary factors that predict a student's score on the final exam. She collects data from 60 students, a portion of which is shown in the accompanying table.

Final	Math	Hours
94	92	5
74	90	3
⋮	⋮	⋮
63	64	2

a. Estimate the sample regression equation that enables us to predict a student's final exam score on the basis of his/her math score and the number of hours studied per week.
b. At the 5% significance level, are a student's math score and the number of hours studied per week jointly significant in explaining a student's final exam score?
c. At the 5% significance level, is each predictor variable individually significant in explaining a student's final exam score?

40. FILE ***Union_Pay.*** An automotive workers union, in conjunction with top management, is negotiating a new hourly pay policy for union workers based on three variables: (1) job class, (2) years with the company, and (3) years as a union member at any company. The goal is to develop an equitable model that can objectively specify hourly pay, thereby reducing pay disparity grievances. Fifty union workers have been sampled and will be used as the basis for the pay model. A portion of the data is shown in the accompanying table.

Hourly Pay	Job Class	Years with Company	Years in Union
15.90	24	12	7
23.70	52	17	14
⋮	⋮	⋮	⋮
26.70	43	2	2

a. Report the sample regression equation of the appropriate model.
b. At the 5% significance level, are the predictor variables jointly significant? Are they individually significant?
c. Predict hourly pay for a worker in Job Class 48 with 18 years of experience at the company and 14 years with the union.

41. FILE ***Yields.*** While the Federal Reserve controls short-term interest rates, long-term interest rates essentially depend on supply/demand dynamics, as well as longer-term interest rate expectations. In order to examine the relationship between short-term and long-term interest rates, monthly data were collected on the three-month Treasury yield (in %) and the 10-year Treasury yield (in %). A portion of the data is shown in the accompanying table.

Month	Year	3-month	10-year
Jan	2016	0.26	2.09
Feb	2016	0.31	1.78
⋮	⋮	⋮	⋮
Dec	2017	1.32	2.40

a. Estimate and interpret a sample regression equation using the 10-year yield as the response variable and the three-month yield as the predictor variable.
b. Interpret the coefficient of determination.
c. At the 5% significance level, is the three-month-yield significant in explaining the 10-year yield?
d. Many wonder whether a change in the three-month yield implies the same change in the 10-year yield. At the 5% significance level, is this belief supported by the data?

42. FILE ***BMI.*** According to the World Health Organization, obesity has reached epidemic proportions globally. While obesity has generally been linked with chronic disease and disability, researchers argue that it may also affect salaries. In other words, the body mass index (BMI) of an employee is a predictor for salary. (A person is considered overweight if his/ her BMI is at least 25 and obese if BMI exceeds 30.)

The accompanying table shows a portion of salary data (in $1,000s) for 30 college-educated men with their respective BMI and a dummy variable that equals 1 for a white man and 0 otherwise.

Salary	BMI	White
34	33	1
43	26	1
⋮	⋮	⋮
45	21	1

a. Estimate a model for Salary using BMI and White as the predictor variables. Determine if BMI influences salary at the 5% level of significance.

b. What is the estimated salary of a white college-educated man with a BMI of 30? Compute the corresponding salary of a nonwhite man.

43. **FILE** ***Wage.*** A researcher wonders whether males get paid more, on average, than females at a large firm. She interviews 50 employees and collects data on each employee's hourly wage (Wage in $), years of higher education (Educ), years of experience (Exper), age (Age), and a Male dummy variable that equals 1 if male, 0 otherwise. A portion of the data is shown in the accompanying table.

Wage	Educ	Exper	Age	Male
37.85	11	2	40	1
21.72	4	1	39	0
⋮	⋮	⋮	⋮	⋮
24.18	8	11	64	0

a. Estimate $\text{Wage} = \beta_0 + \beta_1\text{Educ} + \beta_2\text{Exper} + \beta_3\text{Age} + \beta_4\text{Male} + \varepsilon$.

b. Predict the hourly wage of a 40-year-old male employee with 10 years of higher education and five years of experience. Predict the hourly wage of a 40-year-old female employee with the same qualifications.

c. Interpret the estimated coefficient for Male. Is the variable Male significant at the 5% level? Do the data suggest that sex discrimination exists at this firm?

44. **FILE** ***Quotations.*** The labor estimation group at Sturdy Electronics, a contract electronics manufacturer of printed circuit boards, wants to simplify the process it uses to quote production costs to potential customers. It has identified the primary drivers for production time (and thus production cost) as being the number of electronic parts that can be machine-installed and the number of parts that must be manually installed. Accordingly, it wishes to develop a multiple regression model to predict production time, measured as minutes per board, using a random sample of 25 recent product quotations. A portion of the data is shown in the accompanying table.

Production Time	Machine Parts	Manual Parts
9.1	275	14
10.8	446	12
⋮	⋮	⋮
15.5	618	16

a. What is the sample regression equation?

b. Predict production time for a circuit board with 475 machine-installed components and 16 manually installed components.

c. What proportion of the sample variability in production time is explained by the two predictor variables?

d. At the 5% significance level, are the predictor variables jointly significant? Are they individually significant?

45. **FILE** ***Ice_Cream.*** A manager at an ice cream store is trying to determine how many customers to expect on any given day. Overall business has been relatively steady over the past several years, but the customer count seems to have ups and downs. He collects data over 30 days and records the number of customers, the high temperature (in degrees Fahrenheit), and whether the day fell on a weekend (Weekend equals 1 if weekend, 0 otherwise). A portion of the data is shown in the accompanying table.

Customers	Temperature	Weekend
376	75	0
433	78	0
⋮	⋮	⋮
401	68	0

a. Estimate $\text{Customers} = \beta_0 + \beta_1\text{Temperature} + \beta_2\text{Weekend} + \varepsilon$.

b. How many customers should the manager expect on a Sunday with a forecasted high temperature of 80°?

c. Interpret the estimated coefficient for Weekend. Is it significant at the 5% level? How might this affect the store's staffing needs?

46. **FILE** ***QuickFix.*** The general manager of QuickFix, a chain of quick-service, no-appointment auto repair shops, wants to develop a model to forecast monthly vehicles served at any particular shop based on four factors: garage bays, population within five-mile radius (Population in 1,000s), interstate

highway access (Access equals 1 if convenient, 0 otherwise), and time of year (Winter equals 1 if winter, 0 otherwise). He believes that, all else equal, shops near an interstate will service more vehicles and that more vehicles will be serviced in the winter due to battery and tire issues. A sample of 19 locations has been obtained. A portion of the data is shown in the accompanying table.

Vehicles Served	Garage Bays	Population	Access	Winter
200	3	15	0	0
351	3	22	0	1
⋮	⋮	⋮	⋮	⋮
464	6	74	1	1

a. Estimate the regression equation relating vehicles serviced to the four predictor variables.
b. Interpret each of the slope coefficients.
c. At the 5% significance level, are the predictor variables jointly significant? Are they individually significant? What about at the 10% significance level?
d. What proportion of the variability in vehicles served is explained by the four predictor variables?
e. Predict vehicles serviced in a nonwinter month for a particular location with five garage bays, a population of 40,000, and convenient interstate access.

47. **FILE** ***Industry.*** Consider a regression model that links a CEO's compensation (in $ millions) with the total assets of the firm (in $ millions) and the firm's industry. Dummy variables are used to represent four industries: Manufacturing Technology d_1, Manufacturing Other d_2, Financial Services d_3, and Nonfinancial Services d_4. A portion of the data for the 455 CEOs is shown in the accompanying table.

CEO	y	x	d_1	d_2	d_3	d_4
1	16.58	20917.5	1	0	0	0
2	26.92	32659.5	1	0	0	0
⋮	⋮	⋮	⋮	⋮	⋮	⋮
450	2.30	44875.0	0	0	1	0

a. Estimate the model: $y = \beta_0 + \beta_1 x + \beta_2 d_1 + \beta_3 d_2 + \beta_4 d_3 + \varepsilon$, where y and x denote compensation and assets, respectively. Here the reference category is the nonfinancial services industry.
b. Interpret the estimated coefficients.
c. Use a 5% level of significance to determine which industries, relative to the nonfinancial services industry, have different executive compensation.
d. Reformulate the model to determine, at the 5% significance level, if compensation is higher in Manufacturing Other than in Manufacturing Technology. Your model must account for total assets and all industry types.

48. **FILE** ***Retail.*** A government researcher is analyzing the relationship between retail sales (in $ millions) and the gross national product (GNP in $ billions). He also wonders whether there are significant differences in retail sales related to the quarters of the year. He collects 10 years of quarterly data. A portion is shown in the accompanying table.

Year	Quarter	Sales	GNP
2007	1	921266	14301.854
2007	2	1013371	14512.945
⋮	⋮	⋮	⋮
2016	4	1299699	19134.463

a. Estimate $y = \beta_0 + \beta_1 x + \beta_2 d_1 + \beta_3 d_2 + \beta_4 d_3 + \varepsilon$, where y and x represent retail sales and GNP, respectively; d_1 equals 1 if quarter 1, 0 otherwise; d_2 equals 1 if quarter 2, 0 otherwise; and d_3 equals 1 if quarter 3, 0 otherwise. Note that the reference category is quarter 4.
b. Predict retail sales in quarters 2 and 4 if GNP equals $16,000 billion.
c. Which of the quarterly sales are significantly different from those of the 4th quarter at the 5% level?
d. Reformulate the model to determine, at the 5% significance level, if sales differ between quarter 2 and quarter 3. Your model must account for all quarters.

49. **FILE** ***Longevity.*** According to the Centers for Disease Control and Prevention, life expectancy at age 65 in the United States is about 18.7 years. Medical researchers have argued that while excessive drinking is detrimental to health, drinking a little alcohol every day, especially wine, may be associated with an increase in life expectancy. Others have also linked longevity with income and a person's sex. The accompanying table shows a portion of data relating to the length of life after 65; average income (in $1,000s) at a retirement age of 65; a Female dummy variable that equals 1 if the individual is female, 0 otherwise; and the average number of alcoholic drinks consumed per day.

Life	Income	Female	Drinks
19.00	64	0	1
19.30	43	1	3
⋮	⋮	⋮	⋮
20.24	36	1	0

a. Use the data to model life expectancy at 65 on the basis of Income, Female, and Drinks.
b. Conduct a one-tailed test at $\alpha = 0.01$ to determine if females live longer than males.
c. Predict the life expectancy at 65 of a male with an income of $40,000 and an alcohol consumption of two drinks per day; repeat the prediction for a female.

50. **FILE** ***SAT_3.*** A researcher from the Center for Equal Opportunity wants to determine if SAT scores of admitted students at a large state university differed by ethnicity. She collects data on SAT scores and ethnic background for 200 admitted students. A portion of the data is shown in the accompanying table.

SAT	Ethnicity
1515	White
1530	Latinx
⋮	⋮
1614	White

a. Estimate the model $y = \beta_0 + \beta_1 d_1 + \beta_2 d_2 + \beta_3 d_3 + \varepsilon$, where y represents a student's SAT score; d_1 equals 1 if the student is white, 0 otherwise; d_2 equals 1 if the student is black, 0 otherwise; and d_3 equals 1 if the student is Asian, 0 otherwise. Note that the reference category is Latinx. What is the predicted SAT score for an Asian student? For a Latinx student?

b. At the 5% significance level, determine if the SAT scores of Asian students differ from those of Latinx students.

c. Reformulate the model to determine if the SAT scores of white students are lower than the SAT scores of Asian students at the 5% significance level. Your model must account for all ethnic categories.

6.4 MODEL ASSUMPTIONS AND COMMON VIOLATIONS

So far we have focused on the estimation and the assessment of linear regression models. It is important to understand that the statistical properties of the ordinary least squares (OLS) estimator, as well as the validity of the testing procedures, depend on the assumptions of the classical linear regression model. In this section, we discuss these assumptions. We also address common violations to the assumptions, discuss the consequences when the assumptions are violated, and, where possible, offer some remedies.

Required Assumptions of Regression Analysis

In this chapter, we have estimated the classical linear regression model using the ordinary least squares (OLS) methodology. We have also examined various goodness-of-fit measures and conducted hypothesis tests in order to assess which predictor variables matter the most. However, when we apply any of these techniques, we require that certain assumptions hold. The following are the assumptions that underlie the classical linear regression model:

1. The regression model given by $y = \beta_0 + \beta_1 x_1 + \beta_2 x_2 + \ldots + \beta_k x_k + \varepsilon$ is *linear in the parameters* $\beta_0, \beta_1, \ldots, \beta_k$.
2. Conditional on $x_1, x_2, \ldots, x_k$, the error term has an *expected value of zero,* or $E(\varepsilon) = 0$. This implies that $E(y) = \beta_0 + \beta_1 x_1 + \beta_2 x_2 + \ldots + \beta_k x_k$.
3. There is no exact linear relationship among the predictor variables; or, in statistical terminology, there is *no perfect multicollinearity.*
4. Conditional on $x_1, x_2, \ldots, x_k$, the variance of the error term ε is the same for all observations; or, in statistical terminology, there is *no heteroskedasticity.* The assumption is violated if observations have a *changing variability.*
5. Conditional on $x_1, x_2, \ldots, x_k$, the error term ε is uncorrelated across observations; or, in statistical terminology, there is *no serial correlation.* The assumption is violated if *observations are correlated.*
6. The error term ε is not correlated with any of the predictor variables $x_1, x_2, \ldots, x_k$; or, in statistical terminology, there is *no endogeneity.* In general, this assumption is violated if important *predictor variables are excluded.*
7. Conditional on $x_1, x_2, \ldots, x_k$, the error term ε is *normally distributed.* This assumption allows us to construct interval estimates and conduct tests of significance. If ε is not normally distributed, the interval estimates and the hypothesis tests are valid only for large sample sizes.

Under the assumptions of the classical linear regression model, the OLS estimators have desirable properties. In particular, the OLS estimators of the regression coefficients β_j are unbiased; that is, $E(b_j) = \beta_j$. Moreover, among all linear unbiased estimators, they have minimum variations between samples. These desirable properties of the OLS estimators become compromised as one or more model assumptions are violated. Aside from coefficient estimates, the validity of the significance tests is also impacted by the assumptions. For certain violations, the estimated standard errors of the OLS estimators are inappropriate; in these cases, it is not possible to make meaningful inferences from the t and the F test results.

The assumptions of the classical linear regression model are, for the most part, based on the error term ε. Because the residuals, or the observed error term, $e = y - \hat{y}$, contain useful information regarding ε, it is common to use the residuals to investigate the assumptions. In this section, we will rely on **residual plots** to detect some of the common violations to the assumptions. These graphical plots are easy to use and provide informal analysis of the estimated regression models. Formal tests are beyond the scope of this text.

RESIDUAL PLOTS

For the regression model, $y = \beta_0 + \beta_1 x_1 + \beta_2 x_2 + \ldots + \beta_k x_k + \varepsilon$, the residuals are computed as $e = y - \hat{y}$, where $\hat{y} = b_0 + b_1 x_1 + b_2 x_2 + \ldots + b_k x_k$. These residuals can be plotted sequentially or against a predictor variable x_j to look for model inadequacies.

It is common to plot the residuals e on the vertical axis and the predictor variable x_j or the predicted values $\hat{y}$ on the horizontal axis. Such plots are useful for detecting departures from linearity as well as constant variability. If the regression is based on time series data, we can plot the residuals sequentially to detect if the observations are correlated.

Residual plots can also be used to detect outliers. Recall from Chapter 3 that outliers are observations that stand out from the rest of the data. For an outlier observation, the resulting residual will appear distinct in a plot; it will stand out from the rest. While outliers can greatly impact the estimates, it is not always clear what to do with them. Outliers may indicate bad data due to incorrectly recorded (or included) observations in the data set. In such cases, the relevant observation should be corrected or simply deleted. Alternatively, outliers may just be due to random variations, in which case the relevant observations should remain. In any event, residual plots help us identify potential outliers so that we can take corrective actions, if needed.

In Figure 6.7, we present a hypothetical residual plot when none of the assumptions has been violated. Note that all the points are randomly dispersed around the 0 value of the residuals. Also, there is no evidence of outliers because no residual stands out from the rest. Any discernible pattern of the residuals indicates that one or more assumptions have been violated.

FIGURE 6.7 Residual plot of a correctly specified model

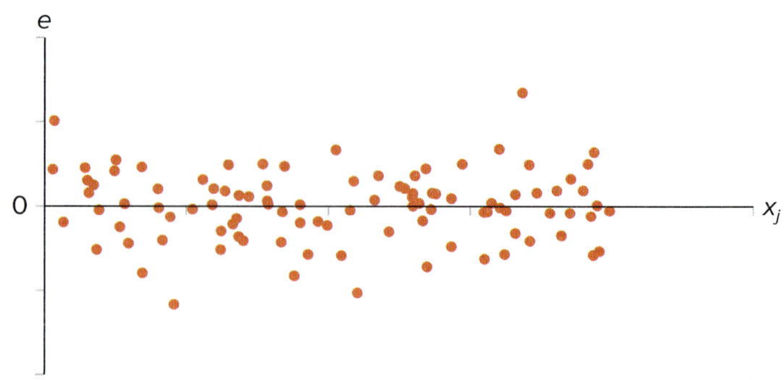

We discuss how to obtain residual plots in Excel and R at the end of this section, but first we describe common violations of the assumptions and offer remedies.

Common Violation 1: Nonlinear Patterns

LO 6.4

Address common violations of the OLS assumptions.

Linear regression models are often justified on the basis of their computational simplicity. The simple linear regression model $y = \beta_0 + \beta_1 x + \varepsilon$ implies that if x goes up by one unit, we expect y to change by β_1, irrespective of the value of x. However, in many applications, the relationship cannot be represented by a straight line and, therefore, must be captured by an appropriate curve. It is always good to rely on economic theory and intuition to determine if the linearity assumption is appropriate. We confirm our intuition by analyzing scatterplots or residual plots. The OLS estimates can be quite misleading if there are obvious nonlinear patterns in the data.

Detection

We can use residual plots to identify nonlinear patterns. Linearity is justified if the residuals are randomly dispersed across the values of a predictor variable. A discernible trend in the residuals is indicative of nonlinear patterns.

EXAMPLE 6.7

A sociologist wishes to study the relationship between age and happiness. He interviews 24 individuals and collects data on age and happiness, measured on a scale from 0 to 100. A portion of the data is shown in Table 6.12. Examine the linearity assumption in the regression model, Happiness $= \beta_0 + \beta_1$Age $+ \varepsilon$.

FILE
Happiness_Age

TABLE 6.12 Happiness and Age

Happiness	Age
62	49
66	51
⋮	⋮
72	69

SOLUTION: We start the analysis with a scatterplot of Happiness against Age. Figure 6.8 shows the scatterplot and the superimposed trend line, which is based on the sample regression equation $\widehat{\text{Happiness}} = 56.18 + 0.28\text{Age}$. It is fairly clear from Figure 6.8 that the linear regression model does not appropriately capture the relationship between Happiness and Age. In other words, it is misleading to conclude that a person's happiness increases by 0.28 unit every year.

FIGURE 6.8 Scatterplot and the superimposed trendline (Example 6.7)

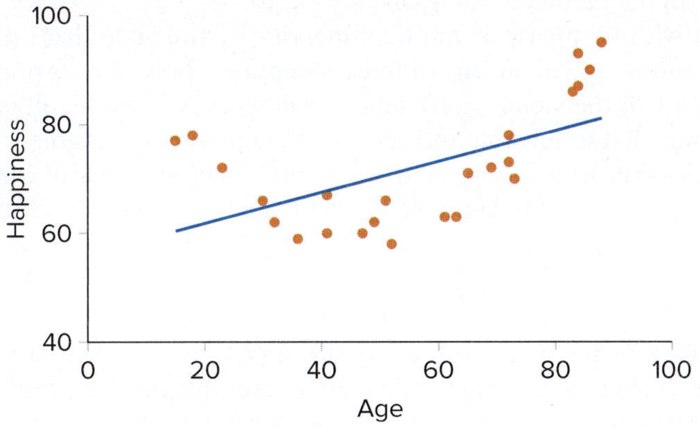

Figure 6.9 is a residual plot that further explores the linearity assumption of the regression model.

FIGURE 6.9 Residual plot against Age (Example 6.7)

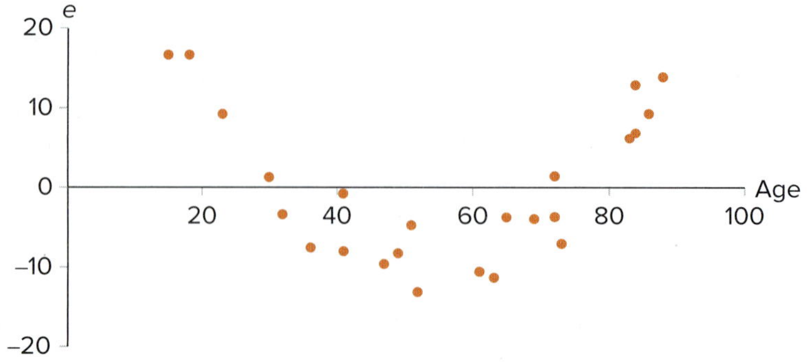

It shows that there is an obvious trend with the residuals decreasing until the age of 50 and steadily increasing thereafter. The linear regression model is inappropriate as it underestimates at lower and higher age levels and overestimates in the middle. This result is consistent with a 2018 study in *The Journal of Happiness* that shows that happiness initially decreases with age and then increases with age.

Remedy

Linear regression models are often used as a first pass for most empirical work. In many instances, they provide a very good approximation for the actual relationship. However, if residual plots exhibit strong nonlinear patterns, the inferences made by a linear regression model can be quite misleading. In such instances, we should employ nonlinear regression methods based on simple transformations of the response and the predictor variables; these methods are discussed in the next chapter.

Common Violation 2: Multicollinearity

Perfect multicollinearity exists when two or more predictor variables have an exact linear relationship. Consider the model $y = \beta_0 + \beta_1 x_1 + \beta_2 x_2 + \varepsilon$, where y is bonus, x_1 is the number of cars sold, and x_2 is the number of cars remaining in the lot. If all car salesmen started with the same inventory, we have a case of *perfect* multicollinearity ($x_2 =$ Constant $- x_1$). Perfect multicollinearity is easy to detect because the model cannot be estimated. However, if x_2 represents the proportion of positive reviews from customers, we have *some* multicollinearity because the number of cars sold and the proportion of positive reviews are likely to be correlated. In most applications, some degree of correlation exists between the predictor variables.

The problem with (nonperfect) multicollinearity is similar to that of small samples. Multicollinearity does not violate any of the assumptions; however, its presence results in imprecise estimates of the slope coefficients. In other words, multicollinearity makes it difficult to disentangle the separate influences of the predictor variables on the response variable. If multicollinearity is severe, we may find insignificance of important predictor variables. Seemingly wrong signs of the estimated regression coefficients may also indicate multicollinearity.

Detection

The detection methods for multicollinearity are mostly informal. If we find a high R^2 and a significant F statistic coupled with individually insignificant predictor variables, then multicollinearity may be an issue. We can also examine the correlations between the predictor variables to detect severe multicollinearity. One guideline suggests that multicollinearity is severe if the sample correlation coefficient between any two predictor variables is more than 0.80 or less than −0.80. The variance inflation factor (VIF) is another measure that can detect a high correlation between three or more predictor variables even if no pair of predictor variables has a particularly high correlation. The smallest possible value of VIF is one (absence of multicollinearity). Multicollinearity may be a problem if the VIF exceeds five or 10. A more detailed discussion of the VIF is beyond the scope of this text.

EXAMPLE 6.8

Examine the multicollinearity issue in a linear regression model that uses median home values (in $) as the response variable and median household incomes (in $), per capita incomes (in $), and the percentage of owner-occupied homes as the predictor variables. A portion of 2010 data for all states in the United States is shown in Table 6.13.

TABLE 6.13 Home Values and Other Factors

FILE *Home_Values*

State	Home Value	HH Income	Per Cap Inc	Pct Owner Occ
Alabama	117600	42081	22984	71.1
Alaska	229100	66521	30726	64.7
⋮	⋮	⋮	⋮	⋮
Wyoming	174000	53802	27860	70.2

SOLUTION: We estimate three models to examine the multicollinearity issue; Table 6.14 presents the regression results.

TABLE 6.14 Summary of Model Estimates (Example 6.8)

Variable	Model 1	Model 2	Model 3
Intercept	417,892.04* (0.001)	348,187.14* (0.002)	285,604.08 (0.083)
HH Income	9.04* (0.000)	7.74* (0.000)	NA
Per Cap Inc	−3.27 (0.309)	NA	13.21* (0.000)
Pct Owner Occ	−8,744.30* (0.000)	−8,027.90* (0.000)	−6,454.08* (0.001)
Adjusted R^2	0.8071	0.8069	0.6621

Notes: The table contains parameter estimates with *p*-values in parentheses; * represents significance at the 5% level. NA denotes not applicable. Adjusted R^2, reported in the last row, is used for model selection.

Model 1 uses all three predictor variables to explain home values. Surprisingly, the per capita income variable has a negative estimated coefficient of −3.27 and, with a *p*-value of 0.31, is not even statistically significant at the 5% level. Multicollinearity might be the reason for this surprising result because household income and per capita income are likely to be correlated. We compute the sample correlation coefficient between these two variables as 0.8582, which suggests that multicollinearity is severe. We estimate two more models where one of these collinear variables is removed; Model 2 removes per capita income and Model 3 removes household income. Note that per capita income in Model 3 now exerts a positive and significant influence on home values. Between these two models, Model 2 is preferred to Model 3 because of its higher adjusted R^2 (0.8069 > 0.6621). The choice between Model 1 and Model 2 is unclear. In general, Model 1, with the highest adjusted R^2 value of 0.8071, is preferred if the sole purpose of the analysis is to make predictions. However, if the coefficient estimates need to be evaluated, then Model 2 may be the preferred choice.

Remedy

Inexperienced researchers tend to include too many predictor variables in their quest not to omit anything important and, in doing so, may include redundant variables that essentially measure the same thing. When confronted with multicollinearity, a good remedy is to drop one of the collinear variables. The difficult part is to decide which of the collinear variables is redundant and, therefore, can safely be removed. Another option is to obtain more data because the sample correlation may get weaker as we include more observations. Sometimes it helps to express the predictor variables differently so that they are not collinear. At times, the best approach may be to *do nothing* when there is a justification to include all predictor variables. This is especially so if the estimated model yields a high R^2, which implies that the estimated model is good for making predictions.

Common Violation 3: Changing Variability

The assumption of constant variability of observations often breaks down in studies with cross-sectional data. Consider the model $y = \beta_0 + \beta_1 x + \varepsilon$, where y is a household's consumption expenditure and x is its disposable income. It may be unreasonable to assume that the variability of consumption is the same across a cross-section of household incomes. For example, we would expect higher-income households to have a higher variability in consumption as compared to lower-income households. Similarly, home prices tend to vary more as homes get larger, and sales tend to vary more as firm size increases.

In the presence of changing variability, the OLS estimators are still unbiased. However, the estimated standard errors of the OLS estimators are inappropriate. Consequently, we cannot put much faith in the standard t or F tests because they are based on these estimated standard errors.

Detection

We can use residual plots to gauge changing variability. The residuals are generally plotted against each predictor variable x_j; for a multiple regression model, we can also plot them against the predicted value $\hat{y}$. There is no violation if the residuals are randomly dispersed across the values of x_j. On the other hand, there is a violation if the variability increases or decreases over the values of x_j.

EXAMPLE 6.9

Consider a simple regression model that relates monthly sales (Sales in \$1,000s) from a chain of convenience stores with the square footage (Sqft) of the store. A portion of the data used for the analysis is shown in Table 6.15. Estimate the model and use a residual plot to determine if the observations have a changing variability.

FILE
Convenience_Stores

TABLE 6.15 Sales and Square Footage of Convenience Stores

Sales	Sqft
140	1810
160	2500
⋮	⋮
110	1470

SOLUTION: The sample regression is given by

$$\widehat{Sales} = 22.0795 + 0.0591Sqft,$$
$$(se) \quad (10.4764) \quad (0.0057)$$

where we have put the standard errors of the coefficients in parentheses. We will reference these values when we incorporate R instructions at the end of this section.

A residual plot of the estimated model is shown in Figure 6.10. Note that the residuals seem to fan out across the horizontal axis. Therefore, we conclude that changing variability is a likely problem in this application relating sales to square footage. This result is not surprising because you would expect sales to vary more as square footage increases. For instance, a small convenience store is likely to include only bare essentials for which there is a fairly stable demand. A larger store, on the other hand, may include specialty items, resulting in more fluctuation in sales.

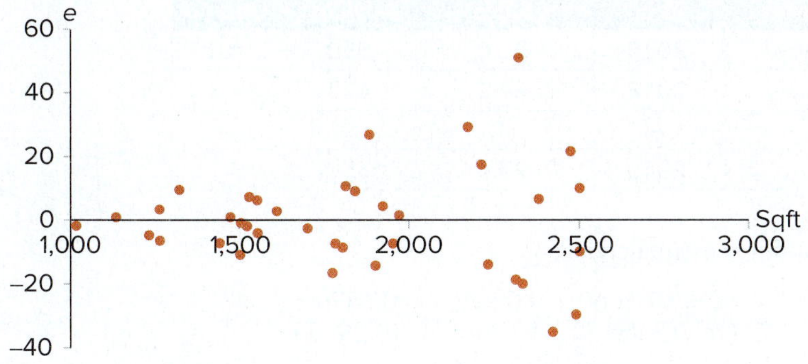

FIGURE 6.10 Residual plot against square footage (Example 6.9)

Remedy

As mentioned earlier, in the presence of changing variability, the OLS estimators are unbiased, but their estimated standard errors are inappropriate. Therefore, OLS still provides reasonable coefficient estimates, but the t and the F tests are no longer valid. This has prompted some researchers to use the OLS estimates along with a correction for the standard errors, often referred to as robust standard errors. Unfortunately, the current version of Excel does not include a correction for the standard errors. However, it is available on many statistical computer packages, including R. At the end of this section, we use R to make the necessary correction in Example 6.9. With robust standard errors, we can then perform legitimate t-tests.

Common Violation 4: Correlated Observations

When obtaining the OLS estimators, we assume that the observations are uncorrelated. This assumption often breaks down in studies with time series data. Variables such as sales, employment, and asset returns exhibit business cycles. As a consequence, successive observations are likely to be correlated.

In the presence of correlated observations, the OLS estimators are unbiased, but their estimated standard errors are inappropriate. Generally, these standard errors are distorted downward, making the model look better than it really is with a spuriously high R^2. Furthermore, the t and F tests may suggest that the predictor variables are individually and jointly significant when this is not true.

Detection

We can plot the residuals sequentially over time to look for correlated observations. If there is no violation, then the residuals should show no pattern around the horizontal axis. A violation is indicated when a positive residual in one period is followed by positive residuals in the next few periods, followed by negative residuals for a few periods, then positive residuals, and so on. Although not as common, a violation is also indicated when a positive residual is followed by a negative residual, then a positive residual, and so on.

EXAMPLE 6.10

Consider $y = \beta_0 + \beta_1 x_1 + \beta_2 x_2 + \varepsilon$, where y represents sales (in \$1,000s) at a sushi restaurant and x_1 and x_2 represent advertising costs (in \$) and the unemployment rate (in %), respectively. A portion of monthly data from January 2018 to May 2019 is given in Table 6.16. Inspect the behavior of the residuals to comment on serial correlation.

FILE
Sushi_Restaurant

TABLE 6.16 Sales, Advertising Costs, and Unemployment Data

Month	Year	Sales	AdsCost	Unemp
January	2018	27.0	550	4.6
February	2018	24.2	425	4.3
⋮	⋮	⋮	⋮	⋮
May	2019	27.4	550	9.1

SOLUTION: The model is estimated as

$$\begin{array}{l} \hat{y} = 17.5060 + 0.0266x_1 - 0.6879x_2, \\ (se)\ (3.9817)\quad (0.0068)\quad (0.2997) \end{array}$$

where we have put the standard errors of the coefficients in parentheses. We will reference these values when we incorporate R instructions at the end of this section.

In order to detect serial correlation, we plot the residuals sequentially against time t, where t is given by 1, 2, . . . , 17 for the 17 months of time series data. Figure 6.11 shows a wavelike movement in the residuals over time, first clustering below the horizontal axis, then above the horizontal axis, and so on. Given this pattern around the horizontal axis, we conclude that the observations are correlated.

FIGURE 6.11 Scatterplot of residuals against time t

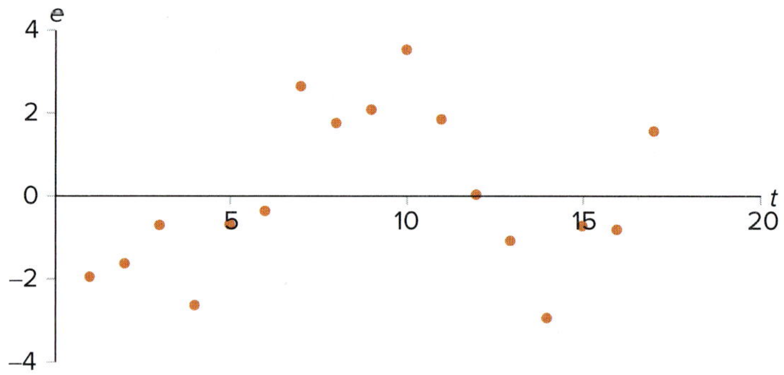

Remedy

As mentioned earlier, in the presence of correlated observations, the OLS estimators are unbiased, but their standard errors are inappropriate and generally distorted downward, making the model look better than it really is. Therefore, OLS still provides reasonable coefficient estimates, but the t and the F tests are no longer valid. This has prompted some researchers to use the OLS estimates but correct the standard errors, often referred to as robust standard errors. As in the case of changing variability, the current version of Excel does not include this correction. However, it is available on many statistical computer packages, including R. At the end of this section, we use R to make the necessary correction in Example 6.10. We can perform legitimate t-tests once the standard errors have been corrected.

Common Violation 5: Excluded Variables

Another crucial assumption in a linear regression model is that the error term is not correlated with the predictor variables. In general, this assumption breaks down when important predictor variables are excluded. If one or more of the relevant predictor variables are excluded, then the resulting OLS estimators are biased. The extent of the bias depends on the degree of the correlation between the included and the excluded predictor variables—the higher the correlation, the greater the bias.

Suppose we want to estimate $y = \beta_0 + \beta_1 x + \varepsilon$, where y is salary and x is years of education. This model excludes innate ability, which is an important ingredient for salary. Note that the omitted innate ability is correlated with years of education. Now consider someone who is highly educated and also commands a high salary. The model will associate high salary with education, when, in fact, it may be the person's unobserved high level of innate ability that has raised both education and salary. In sum, this violation leads to unreliable coefficient estimates; some estimates may even have the wrong signs.

Remedy

It is important that we include all relevant predictor variables in the regression model. An important first step before running a regression model is to compile a comprehensive list of potential predictor variables. We can then build down to perhaps a smaller list of predictor variables using the adjusted R^2 criterion. Sometimes, due to data limitations, we are unable to include all relevant variables. For example, innate ability may be an important predictor variable for a model that explains salary, but we are unable to include it because innate ability is not observable. In such instances, we use a technique called the instrumental variable technique, which is outside the scope of this text.

Summary

It takes practice to become an effective user of the regression methodology. We should think of regression modeling as an iterative process. We start with a clear understanding of what the regression model is supposed to do. We define the relevant response variable and compile a comprehensive list of potential predictor variables. The emphasis should be to pick a model that makes economic and intuitive sense and avoid predictor variables that more or less measure the same thing, thus causing multicollinearity. We then apply this model to data and refine and improve its fit. Specifically, from the comprehensive list, we build down to perhaps a smaller list of predictor variables using significance tests and goodness-of-fit measures such as the standard error of the estimate and the adjusted R^2. It is important that we explore residual plots to look for signs of changing variability and correlated observations in cross-sectional and time series studies, respectively. If we identify any of these two violations, we can still trust the point estimates of the regression coefficients. However, we cannot place much faith in the standard t or F tests of significance unless we employ the necessary correction.

Using Excel and R to Construct Residual Plots

We first replicate Figure 6.10 from Example 6.9 in Excel and R. Because we found that changing variability was an issue in Example 6.9, we show how to calculate robust standard errors in R.

We then replicate Figure 6.11 from Example 6.10. Because we found that correlated observations were an issue in Example 6.10, we show how to calculate robust standard errors in R.

FILE
Convenience_Stores

Using Excel to Replicate Figure 6.10

A. Open the ***Convenience_Stores*** data file.

B. Choose **Data > Data Analysis > Regression** from the menu.

C. For *Input Y Range*, select the Sales data, and for *Input X Range*, select the Sqft data.

D. Select *Residual Plots*.

E. Click **OK.** You should see a graph that resembles Figure 6.10. Formatting (regarding colors, axes, etc.) can be done by selecting **Format** from the menu.

Using R to Replicate Figure 6.10 and Obtain Robust Standard Errors

A. Import the ***Convenience_Stores*** data into a data frame (table) and label it myData.

B. Install and load the *sandwich* package. We use this package to calculate robust standard errors. Enter:

```
> install.packages("sandwich")
> library(sandwich)
```

C. Use the **lm** function to create a linear regression model (object), labeled Simple. Enter:

```
> Simple <- lm(Sales~Sqft, data=myData)
```

D. Use the **resid** function to obtain the residuals from the simple linear regression model, labeled Simple_Residuals. Enter:

```
> Simple_Residuals <- resid(Simple)
```

E. Use the **plot** function to create a scatterplot of the residuals against the predictor variable, Sqft. We also use the *xlab* and *ylab* options to add labels to the *x*- and *y*-axes. Enter:

```
> plot(Simple_Residuals ~ myData$Sqft, xlab = "Sqft", ylab = "e")
```

The scatterplot that R returns should resemble Figure 6.10.

F. Use the **vcovHC** function in the *sandwich* package to calculate robust standard errors for the OLS estimators. By using the option *type* = "HC1", we are asking R to apply a widely used formula for calculating robust standard errors (other designations within *type* are available in R). Enter:

```
> vcovHC(Simple, type="HC1")
```

R returns:

```
             (Intercept)          Sqft
(Intercept)  91.45127988  -6.095285e-02
Sqft         -0.06095285   4.149344e-05
```

The above output represents the variance-covariance matrix, where the diagonal elements contain the variances and the off-diagonal elements contain the covariances of the OLS estimators. Because we are interested in the standard errors, we simply take the square roots of the diagonal values of the matrix (see values in boldface). In order to find the standard errors, labeled as Simple_SE, enter:

```
> Simple_SE <- diag(vcovHC(Simple,type="HC1"))^0.5
> Simple_SE
```

```
(Intercept)        Sqft
9.56301625  0.00644154
```

The corrected standard errors for the intercept and Sqft are 9.5630 and 0.0064, respectively. Recall from Example 6.9 that the OLS-generated standard errors for the intercept and Sqft were 10.4764 and 0.0057, respectively. So now we can easily compute the *t*-test of significance using the OLS estimates with the corrected standard errors.

Using Excel to Replicate Figure 6.11

FILE
Sushi_Restaurant

A. Open the ***Sushi_Restaurant*** data file.

B. Choose **Data > Data Analysis > Regression** from the menu.

C. For *Input Y Range*, select the Sales data, and for *Input X Range*, simultaneously select the AdsCost and Unemp data.

D. Select *Residuals*. Click **OK.**

E. Given the regression output, select the residual data and choose **Insert > Scatter**; choose the option on the top left. (If you are having trouble finding this option after selecting **Insert**, look for the graph with data points above **Charts**.) You should see a graph that resembles Figure 6.11. Formatting (regarding colors, axes, etc.) can be done by selecting **Format** from the menu.

Using R to Replicate Figure 6.11 and Obtain Robust Standard Errors

A. Follow steps A through D from the instructions for Using R to Replicate Figure 6.10, except import the ***Sushi_Restaurant*** data file and create a linear regression model (object), labeled Multiple, which expresses Sales as a function of AdsCost and Unemp. Retrieve the residuals and label them as Multiple_Residuals.

B. First use the **seq** function to create a time variable, labeled as T, that has the same number of observations as Multiple_Residuals; then use the **plot** function. We also use the **abline** function to insert a line at the *x*-axis. Enter:

```
> T <- seq(from = 1, to = length(Multiple_Residuals))
> plot(Multiple_Residuals ~ T, xlab = "time", ylab = "e")
> abline(h = 0)
```

The scatterplot that R returns should resemble Figure 6.11.

C. Use the **NeweyWest** function in the *sandwich* package to calculate robust standard errors for the OLS estimators. By using the option *prewhite*=FALSE, we are asking for the most basic correction (many other options are available in R). Enter:

```
> NeweyWest(Multiple, prewhite=FALSE)
```

R returns:

```
            (Intercept)       AdsCost         Unemp
(Intercept) 18.10230474 -2.342228e-02 -5.592667e-01
AdsCost     -0.02342228  4.056877e-05 -9.819913e-05
Unemp       -0.55926668 -9.819913e-05  9.036499e-02
```

The output represents the variance-covariance matrix, where the diagonal elements contain the variances and the off-diagonal elements contain the covariances of the OLS estimators. Because we are interested in the standard errors, we simply take the square roots of the diagonal values of the matrix (see values in boldface). In order to find the standard errors, labeled as Multiple_SE, enter:

```
> Multiple_SE<-diag(NeweyWest(Multiple))^0.5
> Multiple_SE

(Intercept) AdsCost Unemp
4.773375748 0.006961572 0.354646071
```

The corrected standard errors for the intercept, AdsCost, and Unemp are 4.7734, 0.0070, and 0.3546, respectively. Recall from Example 6.10 that the OLS-generated standard errors for the intercept, AdsCost, and Unemp were 3.9817, 0.0068, and 0.2997, respectively. The corrected standard errors are all higher than the OLS estimates, which is typically what we expect when correlated observations are an issue in a regression model. We can now easily compute the *t*-test of significance using the OLS estimates with the corrected standard errors.

EXERCISES 6.4

Mechanics

51. Using 20 observations, the multiple regression model $y = \beta_0 + \beta_1 x_1 + \beta_2 x_2 + \varepsilon$ was estimated. A portion of the regression results is as follows:

	df	*SS*	*MS*	*F*	Significance *F*	
Regression	2	2.12E+12	1.06E+12	56.556	3.07E-08	
Residual	17	3.19E+11	1.88E+10			
Total	19	2.44E+12				
	Coefficients	Standard Error	*t* Stat	*p*-value	Lower 95%	Upper 95%
Intercept	−987557	131583	−7.505	0.000	−1265173	−709941
x_1	29233	32653	0.895	0.383	−39660	98125
x_2	30283	32645	0.928	0.367	−38592	99158

a. At the 5% significance level, are the predictor variables jointly significant?
b. At the 5% significance level, is each predictor variable individually significant?
c. What is the likely problem with this model?

52. A simple linear regression, $y = \beta_0 + \beta_1 x + \varepsilon$, is estimated with cross-sectional data. The resulting residuals *e* along with the values of the predictor variable *x* are shown in the accompanying table.

x	1	2	5	7	10	14	15	20	24	30
e	−2	1	−3	2	4	−5	−6	8	11	−10

a. Graph the residuals *e* against the values of the predictor variable *x* and look for any discernible pattern.
b. Which assumption is being violated? Discuss its consequences and suggest a possible remedy.

53. A simple linear regression, $y = \beta_0 + \beta_1 x + \varepsilon$, is estimated with time series data. The resulting residuals *e* and the time variable *t* are shown in the accompanying table.

t	1	2	3	4	5	6	7	8	9	10
e	−5	−4	−2	3	6	8	4	−5	−3	−2

a. Graph the residuals against time and look for any discernible pattern.
b. Which assumption is being violated? Discuss its consequences and suggest a possible remedy.

Applications

54. **FILE** ***Television.*** Like books and stories, television not only entertains, it also exposes a child to new information about the world. While watching too much television is harmful, a little bit may actually help. Researcher Matt Castle gathers information on the grade point average (GPA) of 28 middle-school children and the number of hours of television they watched per week. Examine the linearity assumption in the regression model $\text{GPA} = \beta_0 + \beta_1\text{Hours} + \varepsilon$.

55. **FILE** ***Delivery.*** Quick2U, a delivery company, would like to standardize its delivery charge model for shipments (Charge in $) such that customers will better understand their delivery costs. Three predictor variables are used: (1) distance (in miles), (2) shipment weight (in lbs), and (3) number of boxes. A sample of 30 recent deliveries is collected; a portion of the data is shown in the accompanying table.

Charge	Distance	Weight	Boxes
92.50	29	183	1
157.60	96	135	3
⋮	⋮	⋮	⋮
143.00	47	117	7

a. Estimate the model $\text{Charge} = \beta_0 + \beta_1\text{Distance} + \beta_2\text{Weight} + \beta_3\text{Boxes} + \varepsilon$ and examine the joint and individual significance of the predictor variables at the 1% level.
b. Is there any evidence of multicollinearity?
c. Graph the residuals against the predicted values and determine if there is any evidence of changing variability.

56. Consider the results of a survey where students were asked about their GPA and also to break down their typical 24-hour day into study, leisure (including work), and sleep. Consider the model $\text{GPA} = \beta_0 + \beta_1\text{Study} + \beta_2\text{Leisure} + \beta_3\text{Sleep} + \varepsilon$.
a. What is wrong with this model?
b. Suggest a simple way to reformulate the model.

57. **FILE** ***AnnArbor_Rental.*** Consider the monthly rent (Rent in $) of a home in Ann Arbor, Michigan, as a function of the number of bedrooms (Beds), the number of bathrooms (Baths), and square footage (Sqft).
a. Estimate $\text{Rent} = \beta_0 + \beta_1\text{Beds} + \beta_2\text{Baths} + \beta_3\text{Sqft} + \varepsilon$.
b. Which of the predictor variables might cause changing variability? Explain.
c. Use residual plots to verify your economic intuition.

58. **FILE** ***Work_Experience.*** Consider the data on salary (in $) and work experience (in years) of 100 employees in a marketing firm. Estimate the model $\text{Salary} = \beta_0 + \beta_1\text{Experience} + \varepsilon$.
a. Explain why you would be concerned about changing variability in this application.
b. Use a residual plot to confirm your economic intuition.

59. **FILE** ***Healthy_Living.*** Healthy living has always been an important goal for any society. Consider a regression model that conjectures that fruits and vegetables (FV) and regular exercising have a positive effect on health and smoking has a negative effect on health. The sample consists of the

percentage of these variables observed in various states in the United States. A portion of the data is shown in the accompanying table.

State	Healthy	FV	Exercise	Smoke
AK	88.7	23.3	60.6	14.6
AL	78.3	20.3	41.0	16.4
⋮	⋮	⋮	⋮	⋮
WY	87.5	23.3	57.2	15.2

a. Estimate the model Healthy $= \beta_0 + \beta_1$FV $+ \beta_2$Exercise $+ \beta_3$Smoke $+ \varepsilon$.

b. Analyze the data to determine if multicollinearity and changing variability are present.

60. **FILE** ***J&J.*** A capital asset pricing model (CAPM) for Johnson & Johnson (J&J) was discussed in Example 6.6. The model uses the risk-adjusted stock return $R - R_f$ for J&J as the response variable and the risk-adjusted market return $R_M - R_f$ as the predictor variable. Because serial correlation may occur with time series data, it is prudent to inspect the behavior of the residuals. Construct a scatterplot of the residuals against time to comment on correlated observations.

61. **FILE** ***Consumption.*** The consumption function is one of the key relationships in economics, where consumption is a function of disposable income. The accompanying table shows a portion of quarterly data for average U.S. annual consumption (Consumption in \$) and disposable income (Income in \$) for the years 2000–2016.

Date	Consumption	Income
Q1, 2000	28634	31192
Q2, 2000	28837	31438
⋮	⋮	⋮
Q4, 2016	35987	39254

a. Estimate Consumption $= \beta_0 + \beta_1$Income $+ \varepsilon$. Plot the residuals against time to determine if there is a possibility of correlated observations.

b. Discuss the consequences of correlated observations and suggest a possible remedy.

62. **FILE** ***Mowers.*** The marketing manager at Turfco, a lawn mower company, believes that monthly sales across all outlets (stores, online, etc.) are influenced by three key variables: (1) outdoor temperature (in °F), (2) advertising expenditures (in \$1,000s), and (3) promotional discounts (in %). A portion of the monthly sales data for the past two years is shown in the accompanying table.

Sales	Temperature	Advertising	Discount
17235	33	15	5.0
19854	42	25	5.0
⋮	⋮	⋮	⋮
22571	44	21	5.0

a. Estimate Sales $= \beta_0 + \beta_1$Temperature $+ \beta_2$Advertising $+ \beta_3$Discount $+ \varepsilon$, and test for the joint and individual significance of the predictor variables at the 5% level.

b. Examine the data for evidence of multicollinearity. Provide two reasons why it might be best to do nothing about multicollinearity in this application.

c. Examine the residual plots for evidence of changing variability.

6.5 WRITING WITH BIG DATA

When using regression analysis with big data, we often do not place much value in tests of significance. Why is this the case? It turns out that if the sample size is sufficiently large, then the relationship between each predictor variable and the response variable will be statistically significant even when the relationship is not economically meaningful.

What occurs in these instances is that there is little difference in the estimates of β_j generated by different large random samples. Recall that we use $se(b_j)$ to gauge the variability in b_j, and this variability depends on two factors: (1) how closely the members of the population mirror the relationship between x_j and y that is implied by β_j, and (2) the size of the sample on which the value of the estimator b_j is based. If the sample size is sufficiently large, then the variability virtually disappears, or, equivalently, $se(b_j)$ approaches zero. As $se(b_j)$ approaches zero, the value of the t_{df} test statistic (calculated as $t_{df} = b_j/se(b_j)$) increases, leading to a small p-value, and thus rejection of the null hypothesis of insignificance.

Therefore, if the sample size is sufficiently large, statistical significance does not necessarily imply that a relationship is economically meaningful. It is for this reason that when confronted with big data and assessing various models, we tend to rely on economic intuition and model validation rather than tests of significance. In Chapters 7 through 10, we will rely on cross-validation techniques in order to assess various models.

Case Study

FILE
House_Price

Develop a predictive model for the price of a house in the college town of Ames, Iowa. Before evaluating various models, you first have to filter out the ***House_Price*** data to get the appropriate subset of observations for selected variables. After you have obtained the preferred model, summarize your findings as well as predict the price of a house in Ames, Iowa, given typical values of the predictor variables.

Sample Report—Investing In College Town Real Estate

Investing in college town real estate can be a smart move. First, students offer a steady stream of rental demand as many cash-strapped public universities are unable to house their students beyond freshman year. Second, this demand is projected to grow. The National Center for Education Statistics predicts that college enrollment in the U.S. will reach 19.8 million students by 2025, an increase of 14% from its 2014 enrollment of 17.3 million.

Shutterstock/Dmytro Zinkevych

A regression analysis is conducted to determine the factors that influence the sale price of a single-family house in Ames, Iowa—home to Iowa State University. For a sample of 209 single-family houses in 2016, the following data are collected: the house's sale price (Price in $), the number of bedrooms (Beds), the number of bathrooms (Baths), the square footage (Sqft), and the lot size (LSize in square feet). Table 6.17 shows the mean values of the relevant variables for newer houses (those built in 2000 or after), old houses (those built prior to 2000), and for all houses in the sample. Median values are shown in parentheses.

TABLE 6.17 The Mean (Median) of Variables for New, Old, and All Houses

Variables	New Houses	Old Houses	All Houses
Price	326,134 (292,000)	209,552 (190,500)	230,191 (215,000)
Beds	3.68 (4.00)	3.22 (3.00)	3.30 (3.00)
Baths	3.06 (3.00)	2.20 (2.00)	2.36 (2.00)
Sqft	1,867 (1,691)	1,596 (1,444)	1,644 (1,515)
LSize	18,137 (10,361)	19,464 (10,123)	19,229 (10,171)
Number of Observations	37	172	209

The average sale price for the newer houses is substantially more than that for the older houses. For all houses, given that the mean is higher than the median, the house price distribution is positively skewed, indicating that a few expensive houses have pulled up the mean above the median. The square footage and the lot size are also positively skewed. Finally, relatively newer houses have more bedrooms, bathrooms, and square footage but a smaller lot size. This is consistent with a 2017 article in *Building* magazine that found that newer houses have become 24% bigger over the past 15 years, while lot sizes have shrunk 16%.

In order to analyze the factors that may influence the price of a house, the following linear regression model with all the referenced predictor variables is considered:

$$\text{Price} = \beta_0 + \beta_1 \text{Beds} + \beta_2 \text{Baths} + \beta_3 \text{Sqft} + \beta_4 \text{Lsize} + \beta_5 \text{New} + \varepsilon$$

where New is a dummy variable that equals 1 if the house was built in 2000 or after, 0 otherwise. It is expected that Beds, Bath, Sqft, and Lsize will have a positive relationship with Price; that is, a house with more bedrooms and bathrooms is expected to obtain a higher price than one with fewer bedrooms and bathrooms. Similarly, a bigger house, or one on a bigger lot, is expected to obtain a higher price. A newer house, one with all the latest updates, is expected to obtain a higher price as compared to an older house in need of work. Column 2 of Table 6.18 shows the regression results from estimating this complete model.

TABLE 6.18 Estimates of Alternative Regression Models to Predict House Price, $n = 209$

Variables	Complete Model	Restricted Model
Intercept	95.82 (0.996)	5,815.38 (0.672)
Beds	3,124.63 (0.623)	NA
Baths	30,971.41* (0.000)	31,985.61* (0.000)
Sqft	76.98* (0.000)	78.36* (0.000)
Lsize	0.43* (0.000)	0.43* (0.000)
New	68,248.89* (0.000)	68,415.54* (0.000)
s_e	64,612.08	64,492.0062
R^2	0.6689	0.6685
Adjusted R^2	0.6608	0.6620
F-stat (*p*-value)	82.03* (0.000)	102.86* (0.000)

Notes: Parameter estimates are in the top half of the table with the *p*-values in parentheses; * represents significance at the 5% level. NA denotes not applicable. The lower part of the table contains goodness-of-fit measures.

All predictor variables with the exception of Beds are correctly signed and statistically significant. Perhaps the lack of significance of Beds is due to multicollinearity because the number of bedrooms is likely to be correlated with the number of bathrooms as well as square footage. An alternative explanation might be that additional bedrooms add value only in houses with large square footage. For comparison, a restricted model is estimated that omits Beds from the list of predictor variables; see Column 3 of Table 6.18 for the results.

The following observations are made:

- The restricted model is preferred because it has the lower standard error of the estimate s_e and the higher adjusted R^2.
- Holding other factors constant, an additional bathroom adds about $31,986 in value. Similarly, a 100-square-foot increase in a house adds $7,836 in value and a 1,000-square-foot increase in the lot size adds $430 in value. Finally, there is a premium of $68,416 for relatively newer houses.
- The coefficient of determination reveals that 66.85% of the variability in sale price is explained by the predictor variables, implying that approximately 33.15% is unexplained. This is not surprising because other factors, such as the condition of the house or its proximity to nearby amenities, are likely to influence the sales price.
- Suppose a 1,600-square-foot house with two bathrooms sits on a 15,000-square-foot lot. Given the preferred model, its predicted sale price is $269,969 for a relatively newer house and $201,553 for an older house.

Suggested Case Studies

Many different regression models can be estimated and assessed with the big data that accompany this text. Here are some suggestions.

Report 6.1 **FILE** ***House_Price.*** Choose two comparable college towns. Find the model that best predicts the sale price of a house. Make sure to include a dummy variable that accounts for the possibility of differences in the sale price due to the location.

Report 6.2 **FILE** ***College_Admissions.*** Choose a college of interest and use the sample of enrolled students to best predict a student's college grade point average. Use goodness-of-fit measures to find the best predictive model. In order to estimate these models, you have to first filter the data to include only the enrolled students.

Report 6.3 **FILE** ***NBA.*** Develop and compare two models for predicting a player's salary based on offensive performance measures and defensive performance measures, respectively. In order to estimate these models, you have to first filter the data to include only career statistics based on regular seasons. Exclude players with no information on salary.

Report 6.4 **FILE** ***Longitudinal_Surveys.*** Develop a linear regression model for predicting the weight of a respondent in 1981. Use goodness-of-fit measures to find the appropriate predictor variables. In order to estimate these models, you have to first filter the data to exclude missing observations.

Report 6.5 **FILE** ***TechSales_Reps.*** Develop a linear regression model for predicting the salary of a sales representative for both software and hardware industries. Create dummy variables to capture personality type and discuss their role, along with the other relevant predictor variables, in predicting salary.

7 Advanced Regression Analysis

LEARNING OBJECTIVES

After reading this chapter, you should be able to:

- LO **7.1** **Estimate and interpret regression models with interaction variables.**
- LO **7.2** **Estimate and interpret nonlinear regression models.**
- LO **7.3** **Estimate and interpret linear probability and logistic regression models.**
- LO **7.4** **Use cross-validation techniques to evaluate regression models.**

In Chapter 6, we discussed linear regression models where the partial effect of a predictor variable on the response variable was constant and did not depend on other predictor variables in the model. For example, when evaluating the price of a house, we assumed that an additional bedroom resulted in the same increase in the price of a house regardless of its square footage.

In this chapter, we estimate and interpret regression models with interaction variables. These variables allow the partial effect of a predictor variable to depend on the value of the other predictor variables. Continuing with the house price example, an additional bedroom may have a higher impact on a house price with a larger square footage. We then turn our attention to regression models for nonlinear relationships. These models are useful when the relationship between the predictor variable and the response variable cannot be represented by a straight line. In the house price example, an additional bedroom may have a higher impact on the price of a house when going from one to two bedrooms than from four to five bedrooms.

So far, we have used regression models to predict the value of a numerical response variable. We extend the analysis to estimate and interpret the linear and the logistic regression models for predicting the value of a binary or dummy response variable. For example, we may want to predict the probability that mortgage applicants will default on their payments, based on predictor variables such as the loan-to-value ratio, income level of the borrower, etc. Finally, we employ cross-validation techniques for regression models where we partition the original sample into a training set to train the model and a validation set to evaluate the model.

©JrCasas/Shutterstock

INTRODUCTORY CASE

Gender Gap in Manager Salaries

The salary difference between men and women has shrunk over the years, particularly among younger workers, but it still persists. According to a Pew Research Center analysis, women earned 82% of what men earned in 2017 (http://www.pewresearch.org, April 9, 2018). Ara Lily is completing her MBA degree from Bentley University, located just outside Boston. She is upset that the gender gap in salaries continues to exist in the American workplace. For a class project, she decides to analyze the gender gap in salaries of project managers. Ara gains access to the salary (in $1,000s) for 200 project managers in small- to middle-sized firms in the Boston area. In addition, she has data on the firm size, the manager's experience (in years), whether the manager is a female (Female equals 1 if female, 0 otherwise), and whether the manager has a graduate degree (Grad equals 1 if graduate degree, 0 otherwise). Table 7.1 shows a portion of the data.

TABLE 7.1 Salary and Other Information on Project Managers ($n = 200$)

Salary	Size	Experience	Female	Grad
111	233	11	0	1
137	327	18	0	0
⋮	⋮	⋮	⋮	⋮
117	202	19	0	0

FILE *Gender_Gap*

Ara would like to use the information in Table 7.1 to:

1. Analyze the determinants of a project manager's salary.
2. Estimate and interpret a regression model with relevant interaction variables.
3. Determine whether there is evidence of a gender gap in salaries.

A synopsis of this case is provided at the end of Section 7.1.

7.1 REGRESSION MODELS WITH INTERACTION VARIABLES

LO 7.1

Estimate and interpret regression models with interaction variables.

As discussed in Chapter 6, regression analysis is one of the most widely used techniques in predictive analytics for predicting the value of the response (target) variable on the basis of several predictor variables; other techniques are discussed in Chapters 8, 9, and 10. Recall that the linear regression model is specified as $y = \beta_0 + \beta_1 x_1 + \beta_2 x_2 + \ldots + \beta_k x_k + \varepsilon$, where y is the response variable, $x_1, x_2, \ldots, x_k$ are the k predictor variables, and ε is the random error term. The coefficients $\beta_0, \beta_1, \beta_2, \ldots, \beta_k$ are the unknown parameters to be estimated. We use the method of ordinary least squares to derive the sample regression equation as $\hat{y} = b_0 + b_1 x_1 + b_2 x_2 + \ldots + b_k x_k$, where $\hat{y}$ is the predicted value of the response variable given specified values of the predictor variables. For each predictor variable x_j ($j = 1, \ldots, k$), the corresponding slope coefficient b_j measures the change in the predicted value of the response variable $\hat{y}$ given a unit increase in the associated predictor variable x_j, *holding all other predictor variables constant.* In other words, b_j represents the partial (or marginal) effect of x_j on $\hat{y}$. (Note that the partial effect is simply the partial derivative of $\hat{y}$ with respect to x_j.)

It is important to note that the partial effect of a predictor variable in the above regression model does not depend on the values of any other predictor variable. Sometimes, it is natural for the partial effect to depend on another predictor variable. For example, when evaluating the price of a house, it is commonly assumed that an additional bedroom results in the same increase in the house price regardless of the square footage of the house. However, this assumption may be unrealistic because, for larger houses, an additional bedroom often results in a higher increase in house prices. In other words, there is an **interaction effect** between the number of bedrooms and the square footage of the house. We capture this effect by incorporating interaction variables in the regression model.

> **INTERACTION EFFECT IN A REGRESSION MODEL**
>
> The interaction effect in a regression model occurs when the partial effect of a predictor variable on the response variable depends on the value of another predictor variable.

Consider a regression model with two predictor variables: $y = \beta_0 + \beta_1 x_1 + \beta_2 x_2 + \varepsilon$. (The analysis can easily be extended to include more predictor variables.) The interaction variable $x_1 x_2$ is defined as a product of the two predictor variables and is included in the regression as: $y = \beta_0 + \beta_1 x_1 + \beta_2 x_2 + \beta_3 x_1 x_2 + \varepsilon$. This regression model is estimated as $\hat{y} = b_0 + b_1 x_1 + b_2 x_2 + b_3 x_1 x_2$. Note that the partial effect of x_1 on $\hat{y}$ is now given by $b_1 + b_3 x_2$, which depends on the value of x_2. Similarly, the partial effect of x_2 on $\hat{y}$, given by $b_2 + b_3 x_1$, depends on the value of x_1.

As discussed in Chapter 6, the predictor variables can be both numerical and dummy variables, denoted by x and d, respectively. Recall that we use a dummy variable to describe a categorical variable with two categories. We will consider three types of interaction variables: (a) the interaction of two dummy variables, (b) the interaction of a dummy variable with a numerical variable, and (c) the interaction of two numerical variables.

The Interaction of Two Dummy Variables

Consider a regression model with two dummy variables, d_1 and d_2, along with an interaction variable $d_1 d_2$: $y = \beta_0 + \beta_1 d_1 + \beta_2 d_2 + \beta_3 d_1 d_2 + \varepsilon$. This model is estimated as $\hat{y} = b_0 + b_1 d_1 + b_2 d_2 + b_3 d_1 d_2$. The partial effect of d_1 on $\hat{y}$, given by $b_1 + b_3 d_2$, equals b_1 if $d_2 = 0$

and $b_1 + b_3$ if $d_2 = 1$. Similarly the partial effect of d_2 on $\hat{y}$ is $b_2 + b_3d_1$, which depends on the value of d_1. Models with the interaction variables are easy to estimate. In addition, tests of significance can be conducted on all variables, including the interaction variable. Example 7.1 illustrates the interaction between two dummy variables.

EXAMPLE 7.1

According to the National Association of Colleges and Employers, in 2016 the top-paid business graduates at the bachelor's degree level were expected to be those with a concentration in management information systems (MIS). This was due, in large part, to the concentration's linkage with the exploding field of data analytics. At a University of California campus, data were collected on the starting salary of business graduates (Salary in \$1,000s) along with their cumulative GPA, whether they have an MIS concentration (MIS = 1 if yes, 0 otherwise), and whether they have a statistics minor (Statistics = 1 if yes, 0 otherwise). A portion of the data is shown in Table 7.2.

TABLE 7.2 Starting Salary of Business Majors (n =120)

FILE *Salary_MIS*

Salary	GPA	MIS	Statistics
72	3.53	1	0
66	2.86	1	0
⋮	⋮	⋮	⋮
66	3.65	0	0

a. Estimate and interpret the effect of GPA, MIS, and Statistics on Salary. Predict the salary of a business graduate with and without the MIS concentration and the statistics minor. Use a GPA of 3.5 for making predictions.

b. Extend the model from part a to include the interaction between MIS and Statistics. Predict the salary of a business graduate with and without the MIS concentration and the statistics minor. Use a GPA of 3.5 for making predictions.

SOLUTION:

Table 7.3 shows the regression results for part a (see Model 1) and for part b (see Model 2).

TABLE 7.3 Regression Results of the Starting Salary of Business Graduates

Variable	Model 1	Model 2
Constant	44.0073* (0.000)	44.0993* (0.000)
GPA	6.6227* (0.000)	6.7109* (0.000)
MIS	6.6071* (0.000)	5.3250* (0.000)
Statistics	6.7309* (0.000)	5.5350* (0.000)
MIS × Statistics	NA	3.4915* (0.004)
Adjusted R^2	0.7901	0.8029

Notes: Parameter estimates are followed with the p-values in parentheses; NA denotes not applicable; * represents significance at the 5% level.

a. We refer to the second column of Table 7.3 to derive the estimated equation as $\widehat{\text{Salary}} = 44.0073 + 6.6227\text{GPA} + 6.6071\text{MIS} + 6.7309\text{Statistics}$. Note that with the positive coefficients and the p-values of approximately 0, all predictor variables exert a positive and significant influence on the starting salary of business graduates. The MIS concentration and a statistics minor are predicted to fetch an additional starting salary of \$6,607 and \$6,731, respectively. For a GPA of 3.5, we compute the predicted salary for a business graduate with neither an MIS concentration nor a Statistics minor as $44.0073 + 6.6227 \times 3.5 + 6.6071 \times 0 + 6.7309 \times 0 = \$67,187$. For a GPA of 3.5, the predicted salaries for business graduates are \$73,794 with an MIS concentration only, \$73,918 with a Statistics minor only, and \$80,525 with both an MIS concentration and a Statistics minor.

b. To estimate Model 2, we need to create a data column for the interaction variable MIS × Statistics. The entries for the new column are computed by multiplying the column entries of MIS and Statistics. For example, the first entry is computed as $1 \times 0 = 0$; other entries are computed similarly. We refer to the third column of Table 7.3 to derive the estimated equation as $\widehat{\text{Salary}} = 44.0993 + 6.7109\text{GPA} + 5.3250\text{MIS} + 5.5350\text{Statistics} + 3.4915(\text{MIS} \times \text{Statistics})$. Like the earlier predictor variables, the interaction variable is also positive and statistically significant at the 5% level. All else constant, the slope coefficient attached to the interaction variable implies that the value of an MIS concentration is enhanced by about \$3,492 when it is accompanied with a Statistics minor. Likewise, the value of a Statistics minor is enhanced by \$3,492 when accompanied with an MIS concentration. Model 2 provides a better fit because it has a higher value of the adjusted R^2 than Model 1 $(0.8029 > 0.7901)$. For a GPA of 3.5, we compute the predicted salary for a business graduate who has neither an MIS concentration nor a Statistics minor as $44.0993 + 6.7109 \times 3.5 + 5.3250 \times 0 + 5.5350 \times 0 + 3.4915(0 \times 0) = \$67,588$. For a GPA of 3.5, the predicted salaries for business graduates are \$72,913 with an MIS concentration only, \$73,123 with a Statistics minor only, and \$81,939 with both an MIS concentration and a Statistics minor.

The Interaction of a Dummy Variable and a Numerical Variable

Consider a regression model with a numerical variable x and a dummy variable d along with an interaction variable xd: $y = \beta_0 + \beta_1 x + \beta_2 d + \beta_3 xd + \varepsilon$. This model is estimated as $\hat{y} = b_0 + b_1 x + b_2 d + b_3 xd$. The partial effect of x on $\hat{y}$, given by $b_1 + b_3 d$, equals b_1 if $d = 0$ and $b_1 + b_3$ if $d = 1$. The partial effect of d on $\hat{y}$, given by $b_2 + b_3 x$, is difficult to interpret because it depends on the value of the numerical variable x. It is common to interpret this partial effect at the variable's sample mean $\bar{x}$ (or some other value of interest). Therefore, at the average value of x, the partial effect of d on $\hat{y}$ is equal to $b_2 + b_3\bar{x}$. The next example illustrates the interaction between a dummy variable and a numerical variable.

EXAMPLE 7.2

Important risk factors for high blood pressure reported by the *National Institute of Health* include weight and ethnicity. High blood pressure is common in adults who are overweight and are African American. According to the American Heart Association, the systolic pressure (top number) should be below 120. In a recent study, a public policy researcher in Atlanta surveyed 110 adult men about 5′10″ in height and in the 55–60 age group. Data were collected on their systolic pressure, weight (in pounds), and race (Black = 1 for African American, 0 otherwise); a portion of the data is shown in Table 7.4.

TABLE 7.4 Systolic Pressure of Adult Men ($n = 110$)

Systolic	Weight	Black
196	254	1
151	148	0
⋮	⋮	⋮
170	228	0

FILE
BP_Race

a. Estimate and interpret the effect of Weight and Black on systolic pressure. Predict the systolic pressure of black and non-black adult men with a weight of 180 pounds.

b. Extend the model in part a to include the interaction between Weight and Black. Predict the systolic pressure of black and nonblack adult men with a weight of 180 pounds.

SOLUTION:

Table 7.5 shows the regression results for part a (see Model 1) and for part b (see Model 2).

TABLE 7.5 Regression Results of the Systolic Pressure of Adult Men

Variable	Model 1	Model 2
Constant	80.2085* (0.000)	70.8312* (0.000)
Weight	0.3901* (0.000)	0.4362* (0.000)
Black	6.9082* (0.001)	30.2482* (0.006)
Weight × Black	NA	−0.1118* (0.029)
Adjusted R^2	0.7072	0.7175

Notes: Parameter estimates are followed with the *p*-values in parentheses; NA denotes not applicable; * represents significance at the 5% level.

a. We refer to the second column of Table 7.5 to derive the estimated equation as $\widehat{\text{Systolic}} = 80.2085 + 0.3901\text{Weight} + 6.9082\text{Black}$. Both predictor variables are statistically significant at the 5% level (p-values < 0.05). For any given weight, black men are predicted to have about seven units of higher systolic pressure than their nonblack counterparts. This result is consistent with the National Institute of Health report. For a weight of 180 pounds, the predicted systolic pressure of a black man is $80.2085 + 0.3901 \times 180 + 6.9082 \times 1 = 157$. The corresponding systolic pressure for a nonblack man is 150.

b. To estimate Model 2, we need to create a data column for the interaction variable Weight × Black. The data entries for the new column are computed by multiplying the column entries of Weight and Black. For example, the first entry is computed as $254 \times 1 = 254$; other entries are computed similarly. We refer to the third column of Table 7.5 to derive the estimated equation as $\widehat{\text{Systolic}} = 70.8312 + 0.4362\text{Weight} + 30.2482\text{Black} - 0.1118(\text{Weight} \times \text{Black})$.

The interaction variable is negative and statistically significant at the 5% level. The negative coefficient is interesting as it implies that black men carry their weight better in terms of the systolic pressure than their nonblack counterparts. Model 2 is more suitable for prediction because it has a higher value of the adjusted R^2 than Model 1 (0.7175 > 0.7072). For a weight of 180 pounds, the predicted systolic pressure of a black man is $70.8312 + 0.4362 \times 180 + 30.2482 \times 1 - 0.1118(180 \times 1) = 159$. The corresponding systolic pressure for a nonblack man is 149.

The Interaction of Two Numerical Variables

Consider a regression model with two numerical variables, x_1 and x_2, along with an interaction variable x_1x_2: $y = \beta_0 + \beta_1x_1 + \beta_2x_2 + \beta_3x_1x_2 + \varepsilon$. This model is estimated as $\hat{y} = b_0 + b_1x_1 + b_2x_2 + b_3x_1x_2$. Here the partial effects of both predictor variables are difficult to interpret. For example, the partial effect of x_1 on $\hat{y}$, given by $b_1 + b_3x_2$, depends on the given value of x_2. Similarly, the partial effect of x_2 on $\hat{y}$, given by $b_2 + b_3x_1$, depends on the given value of x_1. As in the case of the interaction of a dummy variable and a numerical variable, it is common to evaluate the partial effects at the sample means $\bar{x}_1$ and $\bar{x}_2$ (or some other values of interest). Therefore, we can use the sample means to evaluate the partial effect of x_1 on $\hat{y}$ as $b_1 + b_3\bar{x}_2$ and the partial effect of x_2 on $\hat{y}$ as $b_2 + b_3\bar{x}_1$. The next example illustrates the interaction between two numerical variables.

EXAMPLE 7.3

The Master's in Business Administration (MBA), once a flagship program in business schools, has lost its appeal in recent years (*The Wall Street Journal*, June 5, 2019). While elite schools like Harvard, Wharton, and Chicago are still attracting applicants, other schools are finding it much harder to entice students. As a result, business schools are focusing on specialized master's programs to give graduates the extra skills necessary to be career ready and successful in more technically challenging fields.

An educational researcher is trying to analyze the determinants of the applicant pool for the specialized Master of Science in Accounting (MSA) program at medium-sized universities in the United States. Two important determinants are the marketing expense of the business school and the percentage of the MSA alumni who were employed within three months after graduation. Consider the data collected on the number of applications received (Applicants), marketing expense (Marketing, in $1,000s), and the percentage employed within three months (Employed); a portion of the data is shown in Table 7.6.

FILE
Marketing_MSA

TABLE 7.6 Applications Received for MSA ($n = 80$)

Applicants	Marketing	Employed
60	173	61
71	116	83
⋮	⋮	⋮
69	70	92

a. Estimate and interpret the effect of Marketing and Employed on the number of applications received. For a given marketing expense of $80,000, predict the number of applications received if 50% of the graduates were employed within three months. Repeat the analysis with 80% employed within three months.

b. Extend the model in part a to include the interaction between Marketing and Employed. For a given marketing expense of \$80,000, predict the number of applications received if 50% of the graduates were employed within three months. Repeat the analysis with 80% employed within three months.

SOLUTION:

Table 7.7 shows the regression results for part a (see Model 1) and for part b (see Model 2).

TABLE 7.7 Regression Results of the Applications Received for MSA

Variable	Model 1	Model 2
Constant	−49.5490* (0.000)	−16.6356 (0.316)
Marketing	0.3550* (0.000)	0.0865 (0.460)
Employed	1.0149* (0.000)	0.5405* (0.019)
Marketing × Employed	NA	0.0039* (0.020)
Adjusted R^2	0.7254	0.7410

Notes: Parameter estimates are followed with the *p*-values in parentheses; NA denotes not applicable; * represents significance at the 5% level.

a. We refer to the second column of Table 7.7 to derive the estimated equation as $\widehat{\text{Applicants}} = -49.5490 + 0.3550\text{Marketing} + 1.0149\text{Employed}$. Both predictor variables are statistically significant at the 5% level (*p*-values < 0.05). For any given value of Employment, a \$10,000 increase in the marketing expense is predicted to bring in 3.55 more applicants. Similarly, for any value of Marketing, a 10% increase in Employed brings in 10.149 more applicants. If Marketing equals 80 and Employed equals 50, then the predicted number of applicants is $-49.5490 + 0.3550 \times 80 + 1.0149 \times 50 = 30$. For the same marketing expenditure, if there is a 30 percentage point increase in Employed $(= 80 - 50)$, then the predicted number of applicants increases by 30 $(= 1.0149 \times 30)$ to 60 applicants.

b. To estimate Model 2, we need to create a data column for the interaction variable Marketing × Employed. The data entries for the new column are computed by multiplying the column entries of Marketing and Employed. For example, the first entry is computed as $173 \times 61 = 10{,}533$; other entries are computed similarly. We refer to the third column of Table 7.7 to derive the estimated equation as $\widehat{\text{Applicants}} = -16.6356 + 0.0865\text{Marketing} + 0.5405\text{Employed} + 0.0039(\text{Marketing} \times \text{Employed})$. Interestingly, the Marketing variable is no longer significant at the 5% level; however, its interaction with Employed is significant. In other words, the marketing effort by the business schools is effective only if the school has a good record in placing students after graduation. Model 2 is the preferred model for predictions because it has a higher value of the adjusted R^2 than Model 1 (0.7410 > 0.7254). If Marketing equals 80 and Employed equals 50, then the predicted number of applicants is $-16.6356 + 0.0865 \times 80 + 0.5405 \times 50 + 0.0039(80 \times 50) = 33$. For the same marketing expenditure, if the percentage of MSA alumni finding employment within three months jumps to 80%, then the predicted number of applicants is 59.

EXAMPLE 7.4

The objective outlined in the introductory case is to analyze a possible gender gap in the salaries of project managers. Use the data in Table 7.1 for the following analysis.

FILE
Gender_Gap

a. Evaluate the determinants of a project manager's salary.

b. Estimate and interpret a regression model with relevant interaction variables.

c. Determine whether there is evidence of a gender gap in salaries.

SOLUTION:

a. In addition to the predictor variables Size, Experience, Female, and Grad denoting, respectively, the firm size, the manager's experience, whether the manager is a female, and whether the manager has a graduate degree, we also consider important interactions. By interacting Female with Experience and Female with Grad, the influence of experience on salary or a graduate degree on salary now depends on whether the manager is female or male. Similarly, by interacting Experience with Size, we consider the partial effect of Experience to depend on Size and the partial effect of Size to depend on Experience.

b. In order to estimate the regression, we first create three new interaction variables. Table 7.8 shows the regression results.

TABLE 7.8 Regression Results for the Project Manager's Salary; $n = 200$

Variable	Coefficient	p-value
Constant	41.9298*	0.002
Size	−0.0432	0.388
Experience	1.9286*	0.035
Female	−4.3688	0.654
Grad	15.4357*	0.000
Female × Experience	−1.3915*	0.026
Female × Grad	4.2128	0.269
Size × Experience	0.0105*	0.002
R^2	0.7437	
F-test (p-value)	79.5934* (0.000)	

Notes: * represents significance at the 5% level.

Overall, 74.37% of the sample variations in salaries is explained by the sample regression equation. The predictor variables are jointly significant at any significance level, given the F-statistic value of 79.5934 with an approximate p-value of 0. Because Size and Female are not individually significant at the 5% level, one may be tempted to infer that there are no salary differences between males and females and between firms of different sizes. This inference, however, is erroneous as it ignores the significance of the interaction variables Female × Experience and Size × Experience. The negative coefficient of Female × Experience implies that for every year of experience, the gender gap increases by about $1,392. Similarly, the positive coefficient of Size × Experience implies that managers get a higher salary increase for every year of experience in relatively larger firms. Project managers with a graduate degree make about $15,436 more in salaries; this additional salary is not statistically different between male and female managers.

To better understand the gender gap, Figure 7.1 shows the predicted salary for male and female managers with respect to experience using the sample average firm size of 244.72 employees and a manager with a graduate degree. Qualitatively, the results will not change if we reference a different sized firm and/or an employee without a graduate degree. We find that initially the salary gap between male and female managers is minimal; however, the gap increases with experience. For example, with 20 years of experience, the predicted salaries of male and female managers are about \$137,000 and \$109,000, respectively.

FIGURE 7.1 Salary of male and female managers

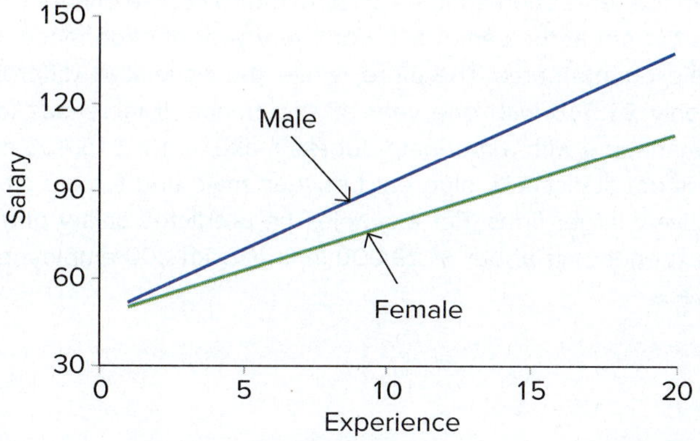

Similarly, to better understand the effect of firm size on salary, Figure 7.2 shows the predicted salary of a male employee with a graduate degree in firms with 200 and 400 employees. We find that, initially, the predicted salary is relatively higher in smaller firms with 200 employees as compared to firms with 400 employees. This, however, changes with experience. For example, with 20 years of experience, the predicted salaries of male managers in firms with 200 and 400 employees are about \$129,000 and \$163,000, respectively.

FIGURE 7.2 Salary of male managers in firms with 200 and 400 employees

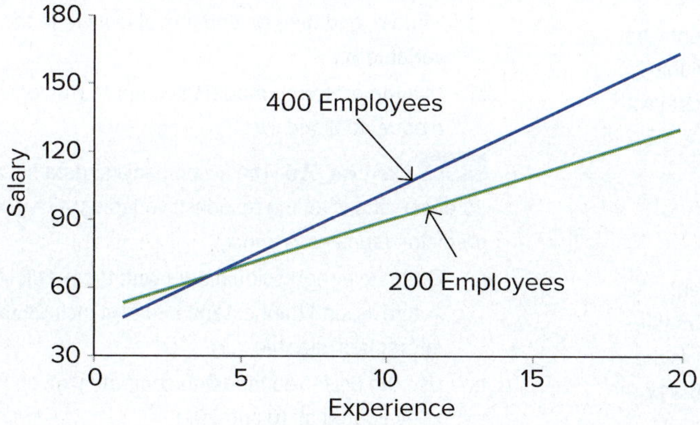

c. We find evidence of a gender gap in the salaries of project managers despite the fact that the Female variable is insignificant at the 5% level. The significance of the interaction of Female and Experience implies that for every year of experience, the gender gap increases by about \$1,392, becoming \$28,000 after 20 years of experience.

SYNOPSIS OF INTRODUCTORY CASE

Millennial women are closing the salary gap with men; however, the gender gap in the United States still persists (Washington Post, May 14, 2019). It is well documented that women are less likely than men to hold management roles and those who do make about 20% less than men. In this report, the gender gap in salaries of project managers is analyzed for small- to middle-sized firms in the Boston area. The predictor variables used for the analysis include firm size, work experience, female and graduate degree dummy variables, and interactions between female with experience, female with graduate degree, and experience with firm size. Overall, 74.37% of the sample variations in salaries is explained by the sample regression equation, and the predictor variables are jointly significant at any level.

Several interesting results emerge from the regression analysis. First, over the course of their career, salaries of both male and female managers increase but not at the same rate. For every year of experience, male managers get about $1,392 more than their female counterparts. Therefore, while the estimated difference in salaries between male and female managers is only $1,548 with one year of experience, it increases to $27,987 with 20 years of experience. Second, project managers with a graduate degree make about $15,436 more in salaries, and this premium for a graduate degree is not statistically different between male and female managers. Finally, experience pays off, especially so in relatively larger firms. For example, the predicted salary of a male manager with a graduate degree and 20 years of experience is about $129,000 in firms with 200 employees, whereas it is about $163,000 in firms with 400 employees.

EXERCISES 7.1

Mechanics

1. Consider a linear regression model where y represents the response variable and x, d_1, and d_2 are the predictor variables. Both d_1 and d_2 are dummy variables, each assuming values 1 or 0. A regression model with x, d_1, d_2, and d_1d_2, where d_1d_2 is the interaction variable, is estimated as $\hat{y} = -1.34 + 1.02x + 3.08d_1 - 1.29d_2 + 0.58d_1d_2$.
   a. Compute $\hat{y}$ for $x = 5$, $d_1 = 1$, and d_2 equal to 0 and 1.
   b. Compute $\hat{y}$ for $x = 5$, $d_1 = 0$, and d_2 equal to 0 and 1.
2. Consider a linear regression model where y represents the response variable and x and d are the predictor variables; d is a dummy variable assuming values 1 or 0. A model with x, d, and the interaction variable xd is estimated as $\hat{y} = 5.2 + 0.9x + 1.4d + 0.2xd$.
   a. Compute $\hat{y}$ for $x = 10$ and $d = 1$.
   b. Compute $\hat{y}$ for $x = 10$ and $d = 0$.
3. Consider a linear regression model where y represents the response variable and x_1 and x_2 are the predictor variables. A regression model with x_1, x_2, and x_1x_2, where x_1x_2 is the interaction variable, is estimated as $\hat{y} = 123.12 + 6.91x_1 - 1.53x_2 - 0.12x_1x_2$.
   a. Compute $\hat{y}$ for $x_1 = 12$ and x_2 equal to 20 and 30.
   b. Compute $\hat{y}$ for $x_1 = 24$ and x_2 equal to 20 and 30.
4. FILE ***Exercise_7.4.*** The accompanying data file contains 20 observations on the response variable y along with the predictor variables x, d_1, and d_2.
   a. Estimate a regression model with the predictor variables x, d_1, and d_2, and then extend it to also include the interaction variable d_1d_2.
   b. Use the preferred model to compute $\hat{y}$ given $x = 20$, $d_1 = 1$, and d_2 equal to 0 and 1.
5. FILE ***Exercise_7.5.*** The accompanying data file contains 20 observations on the response variable y along with the predictor variables x and d.
   a. Estimate a regression model with the predictor variables x and d, and then extend it to also include the interaction variable xd.
   b. Use the preferred model to compute $\hat{y}$ given $x = 15$ and d equal to 0 and 1.
6. FILE ***Exercise_7.6.*** The accompanying data file contains 20 observations on the response variable y along with the predictor variables x_1 and x_2.
   a. Estimate a regression model with the predictor variables x_1 and x_2, and then extend it to also include the interaction variable x_1x_2.
   b. Use the preferred model to compute $\hat{y}$ given $x_1 = 30$ with x_2 evaluated at 10 and 20.

Applications

7. FILE ***Overweight.*** According to the U.S. Department of Health and Human Services, African American women have the highest rates of being overweight compared to other groups in the

United States. Individuals are considered overweight if their body mass index (BMI) is 25 or greater. Data are collected from 120 individuals. The following table shows a portion of data on each individual's BMI; a Female dummy variable that equals 1 if the individual is female, 0 otherwise; and a Black dummy variable that equals 1 if the individual is African American, 0 otherwise.

BMI	Female	Black
28.70	0	1
28.31	0	0
⋮	⋮	⋮
24.90	0	1

a. Estimate the model, BMI $= \beta_0 + \beta_1$Female $+ \beta_2$Black $+ \beta_3$(Female $\times$ Black) $+ \varepsilon$, to predict the BMI for white males, white females, black males, and black females.

b. Is the difference between white females and white males statistically significant at the 5% level?

c. Is the difference between white males and black males statistically significant at the 5% level?

8. **FILE** ***Diversity_Silicon.*** Silicon Valley tech companies are under pressure to increase diversity as most of their employees are white and Asian men (*Bloomberg*, August 16, 2017). Black and Hispanic people, especially women, are grossly underrepresented. In order to analyze if the lack of diversity is influenced by a lack of diversity in the founding leadership team, data are collected on the percentage of white and Asian men (Majority Male) in Silicon Valley tech companies and whether the founding members included a woman (Female) and/or a Black or Hispanic man (Minority Male). A portion of the data is shown in the accompanying table.

Majority Male	Female	Minority Male
100	0	1
80	1	0
⋮	⋮	⋮
80	0	0

a. Estimate and interpret the effect of Female, Minority Male, and the interaction between Female and Minority Male.

b. Predict the percentage of White and Asian men if the founding members included a woman but no Black or Hispanic men. Repeat the analysis if the founding members included a woman and a Hispanic man.

9. **FILE** ***IceCream.*** In a recent survey, ice cream truck drivers in Cincinnati, Ohio, reported that they make about $280 in income on a typical summer day. The income was generally higher on days with longer work hours, particularly hot days, and on holidays. Irma follows an ice cream truck driver for five weeks. She collects the information on the driver's daily income (Income), number of hours on the road (Hours), whether it was a particularly hot day (Hot = 1 if the high temperature was above 85°F, 0 otherwise), and whether it was a Holiday (Holiday = 1, 0 otherwise). A portion of the data is shown in the accompanying table.

Income	Hours	Hot	Holiday
196	5	1	0
282	8	0	0
⋮	⋮	⋮	⋮
374	6	1	1

a. Estimate and interpret the effect of Hours, Hot, and Holidays on Income. Predict the income of a driver working 6 hours on a hot holiday. What if it was not a holiday?

b. Extend the above model to include the interaction between Hot and Holiday. Predict the income of a driver working 6 hours on a hot holiday. What if it was not a holiday?

10. **FILE** ***Mobile_Devices.*** Americans are spending an average of two hours and 37 minutes daily on smartphones and other mobile devices to connect to the world of digital information (*Business Insider*, May 25, 2017). The usage of mobile devices is especially high for affluent, college-educated urban/suburban dwellers. A survey was conducted on customers in the 50-mile radius of Chicago. Participants were asked the average daily time they spent on mobile devices (Usage, in minutes), their household income (Income, in $1,000s), if they lived in a rural area (Rural =1 if rural, 0 otherwise), and if they had a college degree (College = 1 if college graduate, 0 otherwise). A portion of the data is shown in the accompanying table.

Usage	Income	Rural	College
172	146	0	0
165	198	0	1
⋮	⋮	⋮	⋮
110	31	0	1

a. Estimate and interpret a regression model for the mobile device usage based on Income, Rural, College, and the interaction between Rural and College. Explain the rationale for using the interaction variable.

b. Predict the mobile device usage for a college-educated person with a household income of $120,000 and living in a rural area. What would be the corresponding usage for someone living in a urban/suburban area?

c. Discuss the impact of a college degree on salary.

11. **FILE** ***Urban.*** A sociologist is looking at the relationship between consumption expenditures of families in the United States (Consumption in $), family income (Income in $), and whether or not the family lives in an urban or rural community (Urban = 1 if urban, 0 otherwise). She collects data on

50 families across the United States, a portion of which is shown in the accompanying table.

Consumption	Income	Urban
62336	87534	0
60076	94796	1
⋮	⋮	⋮
59055	100908	1

a. Estimate Consumption $= \beta_0 + \beta_1$Income $+ \varepsilon$. Compute the predicted consumption expenditures of a family with income of $75,000.

b. Include a dummy variable Urban to predict consumption for a family with income of $75,000 in urban and rural communities.

c. Include a dummy variable Urban and an interaction variable (Income × Urban) to predict consumption for a family with income of $75,000 in urban and rural communities.

d. Which of the preceding models is most suitable for the data? Explain.

12. **FILE** ***Pick_Errors.*** The distribution center for an online retailer has been experiencing quite a few "pick errors" (i.e., retrieving the wrong item). Although the warehouse manager thinks most errors are due to inexperienced workers, she believes that a training program also may help to reduce them. Before sending all employees to training, she examines data from a pilot study of 30 employees. Information is collected on the employee's annual pick errors (Errors), experience (Exper in years), and whether or not the employee attended training (Train equals 1 if the employee attended training, 0 otherwise). A portion of the data is shown in the accompanying table.

Errors	Exper	Train
13	9	0
3	27	0
⋮	⋮	⋮
4	24	1

a. Estimate two models:
Errors $= \beta_0 + \beta_1$Exper $+ \beta_2$Train $+ \varepsilon$, and
Errors $= \beta_0 + \beta_1$Exper $+ \beta_2$Train $+ \beta_3$ (Exper × Train) $+ \varepsilon$.

b. Which model provides a better fit in terms of adjusted R^2 and the significance of the predictor variables at the 5% level?

c. Use the chosen model to predict the number of pick errors for an employee with 10 years of experience who attended the training program, and for an employee with 20 years of experience who did not attend the training program.

d. Give a practical interpretation for the positive interaction coefficient.

13. **FILE** ***BMI.*** According to the World Health Organization, obesity has reached epidemic proportions globally. While obesity has generally been linked with chronic disease and disability, researchers argue that it may also affect wages. In other words, the body mass index (BMI) of an employee is a predictor for salary. (A person is considered overweight if his/her BMI is at least 25 and obese if BMI exceeds 30.) The accompanying table shows a portion of salary data (in $1,000s) for 30 college-educated men with their respective BMI and a dummy variable that represents 1 for a white man and 0 otherwise.

Salary	BMI	White
34	33	1
43	26	1
⋮	⋮	⋮
45	21	1

a. Estimate a model for Salary with BMI and White as the predictor variables.

b. Reestimate the model with BMI, White, and a product of BMI and White as the predictor variables.

c. Which of the models is more suitable? Explain. Use this model to estimate the salary for a white college-educated man with a BMI of 30. Compute the corresponding salary for a nonwhite man.

14. **FILE** ***Compensation.*** To encourage performance, loyalty, and continuing education, the human resources department at a large company wants to develop a regression-based compensation model (Comp in $ per year) for midlevel managers based on three variables: (1) business-unit profitability (Profit in $1000s per year), (2) years with the company (Years), and (3) whether or not the manager has a graduate degree (Grad equals 1 if graduate degree, 0 otherwise). The accompanying table shows a portion of data collected for 36 managers.

Comp	Profit	Years	Grad
118100	4500	37	1
90800	5400	5	1
⋮	⋮	⋮	⋮
85000	4200	29	0

a. Estimate the following model for compensation:
Comp $= \beta_0 + \beta_1$Profit $+ \beta_2$Years $+ \beta_3$Grad $+ \beta_4$(Profit × Grad) $+ \beta_5$(Years × Grad) $+ \varepsilon$.

b. At the 5% significance level, is the overall regression model significant?

c. Which predictor variables and interaction terms are significant at $\alpha = 0.05$?

d. Use the (full) model to determine compensation for a manager having 15 years with the company, a graduate degree, and a business-unit profit of $4,800(000) last year.

15. **FILE** ***IPO.*** One of the theories regarding initial public offering (IPO) pricing is that the initial return (the percentage

change from offer to open price) on an IPO depends on the price revision (the percentage change from pre-offer to offer price). Another factor that may influence the initial return is a dummy variable that equals 1 for high-tech firms and 0 otherwise. The following table shows a portion of data on 264 IPO firms.

Initial Return	Price Revision	High Tech
33.93	7.14	0
18.68	−26.39	0
⋮	⋮	⋮
0.08	−29.41	1

a. Estimate a model with the initial return as the response variable and the price revision and the high-tech dummy variable as the predictor variables.

b. Reestimate the model with price revision along with the dummy variable and the product of the dummy variable and the price revision.

c. Which of these models is the preferred model? Explain. Use this model to estimate the initial return for a high-tech firm with a 15% price revision. Compute the corresponding initial return for a firm that is not high tech.

16. **FILE** ***GPA_College.*** It is often claimed that the SAT is an important indicator of the grades students will earn in the first year of college. The admission officer at a state university wants to analyze the relationship between the first-year GPA in college (College GPA) and the SAT score of the student (SAT), the unweighted high school GPA (HS GPA), and the student's race (White equals 1 if the student is white, 0 otherwise). A portion of the data is shown in the accompanying table.

College GPA	SAT	HS GPA	White
4.00	1560	4.00	1
1.78	1060	2.18	0
⋮	⋮	⋮	⋮
3.38	1460	4.00	0

a. Estimate and interpret a regression model for college GPA using SAT, HS GPA, White, and the interactions of SAT with HS GPA and SAT with White as predictor variables.

b. Predict the first-year college GPA of a white student with a high school GPA of 3.2 and SAT scores of 1200, 1300, and 1400. Make a corresponding prediction for a non-white student.

17. **FILE** ***Health_Factors.*** According to the World Health Organization, the health of an individual, to a large extent, is determined by factors such as income, education, genetics, and social connections. In a survey, 120 American adults are asked how they rated their health (Health) and social connections (Social) on a scale of 1 to 100. Information is also gathered on their household income (Income, in $1,000s), and college education (College equals 1 if they have completed bachelor's degree, 0 otherwise). A portion of the data is shown in the accompanying table.

Health	Social	Income	College
52	58	80	0
55	68	43	0
⋮	⋮	⋮	⋮
58	90	35	0

a. Estimate and interpret a regression model for Health using Social, Income, and College as the predictor variables. Predict the health rating of a college-educated person given Social = 80 and Income = 100. What if the person is not college-educated?

b. Estimate and interpret an extended model that includes the interactions of Social with Income and Social with College. Predict the health rating of a college-educated person given Social = 80 and Income = 100. What if the person is not college-educated?

c. Explain which of the above two models is preferred for making predictions.

18. **FILE** ***College.*** With college costs and student debt on the rise, the choices that families make when searching for and selecting a college have never been more important. Consider the information from 116 colleges on annual post-college earnings of graduates (Earnings in $), the average annual cost (Cost in $), the graduation rate (Grad in %), the percentage of students paying down debt (Debt in %), and whether or not a college is located in a city (City equals 1 if a city location, 0 otherwise). A portion of the data is shown in the accompanying table.

Earnings	Cost	Grad	Debt	City
44800	22920	62	88	1
45100	23429	73	92	0
⋮	⋮	⋮	⋮	⋮
42700	6616	64	90	1

a. Estimate a regression model for the annual post-college earnings on the basis of Cost, Grad, Debt, City, and the interaction between Cost and Grad. Interpret the estimated coefficient of the interaction variable.

b. Predict the annual post-college earnings of graduates of a college in a city with a graduation rate of 60%, Debt of 80% and the average annual cost of $20,000, $30,000, and $40,000.

c. Repeat the above analysis with a graduation rate of 80%.

19. **FILE** ***Rental.*** Jonah has worked as an agent for rental properties in Cincinnati, Ohio, for almost 10 years. He understands that the premium for additional bedrooms is more in larger as compared to smaller homes. Consider the monthly data on rent (Rent, in $) along with square footage (Sqft), number of bedrooms (Bed), and number of bathrooms (Bath). A portion of the data is shown in the accompanying table.

Rent	Sqft	Bed	Bath
2300	2050	3	3
1240	680	2	1
⋮	⋮	⋮	⋮
2800	2370	4	3

a. Estimate a regression model for monthly rent on the basis of Bed, Bath, Sqft, and the interaction between Bed and Sqft. Interpret the estimated coefficient of the interaction variable.

b. Predict the monthly rent of homes with a square footage of 1,600, 2 baths, and the number of bedrooms equal to 2, 3, and 4. Compute the incremental predicted rent as the number of bedrooms increases from 2 to 3 and 3 to 4.

c. Repeat the above analysis with a square footage of 2,400.

LO 7.2

7.2 REGRESSION MODELS FOR NONLINEAR RELATIONSHIPS

Estimate and interpret nonlinear regression models.

Regression analysis not only empirically validates whether a relationship exists between variables, but also quantifies the strength of the relationship. So far, we have considered only linear regression models. There are numerous applications where the relationship between the predictor variable and the response variable cannot be represented by a straight line and, therefore, must be captured by an appropriate curve. In fact, the choice of a functional form is a crucial part of specifying a regression model.

In this section, we discuss some common nonlinear regression models by making simple transformations of the variables. These transformations include squares and natural logarithms, which capture interesting nonlinear relationships while still allowing easy estimation within the framework of the linear regression model. We use goodness-of-fit measures to choose between alternative model specifications.

The Quadratic Regression Model

Linear regression models are often justified on the basis of their computational simplicity. An implication of a simple linear regression model, $y = \beta_0 + \beta_1 x + \varepsilon$, is that if x goes up by one unit, the expected value of y changes by β_1, irrespective of the value of x. However, in many applications, the relationship between the variables cannot be represented by a straight line. We note that the linearity assumption discussed in Chapter 6 places the restriction of linearity on the parameters and not on the variables. Consequently, we can capture many interesting nonlinear relationships, within the framework of the linear regression model, by simple transformations of the response and/or the predictor variables.

If you ever studied microeconomics, you may have learned that a firm's (or industry's) average cost curve tends to be "U-shaped." Due to economies of scale, the average cost y of a firm initially decreases as output x increases. However, as x increases beyond a certain point, its impact on y turns positive. Other applications show the influence of the predictor variable initially positive but then turning negative, leading to an "inverted U-shape." The **quadratic regression model** is appropriate when the slope, capturing the influence of x on y, changes in magnitude as well as sign.

A quadratic regression model with one predictor variable is specified as $y = \beta_0 + \beta_1 x + \beta_2 x^2 + \varepsilon$; we can easily extend it to include multiple predictor variables. The expression $\beta_0 + \beta_1 x + \beta_2 x^2$ is the deterministic component of a quadratic regression model. In other words, conditional on x, $E(y) = \beta_0 + \beta_1 x + \beta_2 x^2$.

Figure 7.3 shows two scatterplots of sample data with superimposed trendlines that were generated by estimating the quadratic regression model. Although the estimated simple linear regression model is not included in either panel, it is clear that the quadratic regression model provides a better fit for both scatterplots.

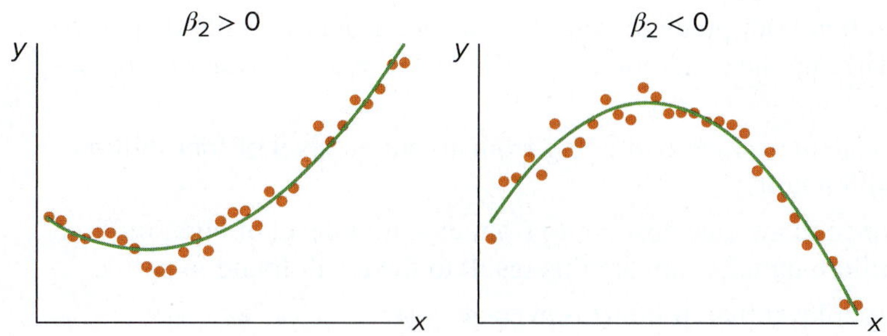

FIGURE 7.3 Scatterplot of *y* against *x* with trendline generated from estimating the quadratic regression model

It is important to be able to determine whether a quadratic regression model provides a better fit than the linear regression model. Recall from Chapter 6 that we cannot compare these models on the basis of their respective R^2 values because the quadratic regression model uses one more parameter than the linear regression model. For comparison purposes, we use adjusted R^2, which imposes a penalty for the additional parameter.

In order to estimate the quadratic regression model $y = \beta_0 + \beta_1 x + \beta_2 x^2 + \varepsilon$, we have to first create a variable x^2 that contains the squared values of x. The quadratic model is estimated in the usual way as $\hat{y} = b_0 + b_1 x + b_2 x^2$, where b_1 and b_2 are the estimates of β_1 and β_2, respectively.

Interpretation of coefficients in the quadratic regression model: It does not make sense to think of b_1 in the estimated quadratic regression equation as being the effect of changing x by one unit, holding the square of x constant. In nonlinear models, the sample regression equation is best interpreted by calculating, and even graphing, the predicted effect on the response variable over a range of values for the predictor variable. We will elaborate on this point in Examples 7.5 and 7.6.

Evaluating the marginal effect of *x* on *y* in the quadratic regression model: It is important to evaluate the estimated marginal (partial) effect of the predictor variable x on the predicted value of the response variable; that is, we want to evaluate the change in $\hat{y}$ due to a one-unit increase in x. In the estimated linear regression equation $\hat{y} = b_0 + b_1 x$, the partial (marginal) effect is constant, estimated by the slope coefficient b_1. In a quadratic regression model, it can be shown that the partial effect of x on $\hat{y}$ can be approximated by $b_1 + 2b_2 x$. This partial effect, unlike in the case of a linear regression model, depends on the value at which x is evaluated. In addition, $\hat{y}$ reaches a maximum ($b_2 < 0$) or minimum ($b_2 > 0$) when the partial effect equals zero. The value of x when this happens is obtained from solving the equation $b_1 + 2b_2 x = 0$, as $x = \frac{-b_1}{2b_2}$. (Note that the optimum is obtained where the first derivative, $b_1 + 2b_2 x$, equals zero and the second derivative, $2b_2$, is negative for a maximum and positive for a minimum.)

THE QUADRATIC REGRESSION MODEL

In a quadratic regression model $y = \beta_0 + \beta_1 x + \beta_2 x^2 + \varepsilon$, the coefficient β_2 determines whether the relationship between x and y is U-shaped ($\beta_2 > 0$) or inverted U-shaped ($\beta_2 < 0$).

Predictions with a quadratic model are made by $\hat{y} = b_0 + b_1 x + b_2 x^2$. It is advisable to use unrounded coefficients for making predictions.

EXAMPLE 7.5

Consider the quadratic regression of the average cost (AC, in \$) on annual output (Output, in millions of units). The estimated regression equation using the predictor variables Output and Output^2 is given by $\widehat{AC} = 10.5225 - 0.3073$ Output + 0.0210

Output^2. It is found that both predictor variables are statistically significant at the 5% level, thus confirming the quadratic effect. Use the estimates to answer the following questions.

a. What is the change in average cost going from an output level of four million units to five million units?

b. What is the change in average cost going from an output level of eight million units to nine million units? Compare this result to the result found in part a.

c. What is the output level that minimizes average cost?

SOLUTION:

a. The predicted average cost for a firm that produces four million units is:

$$\widehat{AC} = 10.5225 - 0.3073(4) + 0.0210(4^2) = \$9.63.$$

The predicted average cost for a firm that produces five million units is:

$$\widehat{AC} = 10.5225 - 0.3073(5) + 0.0210(5^2) = \$9.51.$$

An increase in output from four to five million units results in a \$0.12 decrease in predicted average cost.

b. The predicted average cost for a firm that produces eight million units is:

$$\widehat{AC} = 10.5225 - 0.3073(8) + 0.0210(8^2) = \$9.41.$$

The predicted average cost for a firm that produces nine million units is:

$$\widehat{AC} = 10.5225 - 0.3073(9) + 0.0210(9^2) = \$9.46.$$

An increase in output from eight to nine million units results in a \$0.05 increase in predicted average cost. Comparing this result to the one found in part a, we note that a one-unit change in x depends on the value at which x is evaluated.

c. Given $b_1 = -0.3073$ and $b_2 = 0.0210$, the output level that minimizes average cost is $x = \frac{-b_1}{2b_2} = \frac{-(-0.3073)}{2 \times 0.0210} = 7.32$ million units.

Let's now turn to an example with an inverted U-shaped relationship.

EXAMPLE 7.6

In the United States, age discrimination is illegal, but its occurrence is hard to prove (*The New York Times*, August 7, 2017). Even without discrimination, it is widely believed that wages of workers decline as they get older. A young worker can expect wages to rise with age only up to a certain point, beyond which wages begin to fall. Ioannes Papadopoulos works in the human resources department of a large manufacturing firm and is examining the relationship between wages (in \$), years of education, and age. Specifically, he wants to verify the quadratic effect of age on wages. He gathers data on 80 workers in his firm with information on their hourly wage, education, and age. A portion of the data is shown in Table 7.9.

FILE
Wages

TABLE 7.9 Hourly Wage of Americans ($n = 80$)

Wage	Education	Age
17.54	12	76
20.93	10	61
⋮	⋮	⋮
23.66	12	49

a. Plot Wage against Age and evaluate whether the linear or the quadratic regression model better captures the relationship. Verify your choice by using the appropriate goodness-of-fit measure.

b. Use the appropriate model to predict hourly wages for someone with 16 years of education and age equal to 30, 50, or 70.

c. According to the model, at what age will someone with 16 years of education attain the highest wages?

SOLUTION:

a. Figure 7.4 shows a scatterplot of Wage against Age. We superimpose linear and quadratic trendlines on the scatterplot. It seems that the quadratic regression model provides a better fit for the data as compared to the linear regression model.

FIGURE 7.4 Scatterplot of Wage versus Age

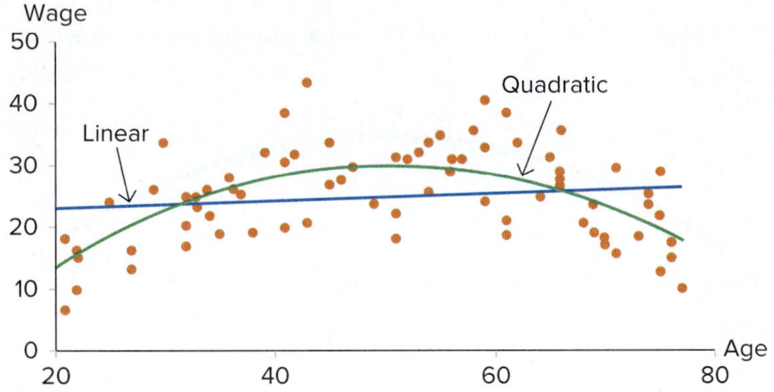

We estimate two models.

Linear Regression Model: Wage $= \beta_0 + \beta_1$Education $+ \beta_2$Age $+ \varepsilon$

Quadratic Regression Model: Wage $= \beta_0 + \beta_1$Education $+ \beta_2$Age $+ \beta_3$Age$^2 + \varepsilon$

For ease of exposition, we use the same notation for the coefficients in the linear and the quadratic models even though they have a different meaning depending on the model we reference. Table 7.10 shows the relevant regression results for the linear and the quadratic regression models.

TABLE 7.10 Estimates of the Linear and the Quadratic Regression Models for Example 7.6

Variable	Linear Regression Model	Quadratic Regression Model
Intercept	2.6381 (0.268)	−22.7219* (0.000)
Education	1.4410* (0.000)	1.2540* (0.000)
Age	0.0472 (0.127)	1.3500* (0.000)
Age^2	NA	−0.0133* (0.000)
Adjusted R^2	0.6088	0.8257

Notes: Parameter estimates are in the main body of the table with the p-values in parentheses; NA denotes not applicable; * represents significance at the 5% level. The last row presents adjusted R^2 for model comparison.

Note that in the linear regression model, Age has an estimated coefficient of only 0.0472, which is not statistically significant (p-value = 0.127) even at the 10% significance level. However, results change dramatically when Age^2 is included along with Age. In the quadratic regression model, both of these variables, with p-values of approximately 0, are statistically significant at any reasonable level. Also, the adjusted R^2 is higher for the quadratic regression model (0.8257 > 0.6088), making it a better choice for prediction. This conclusion is consistent with our visual impression from the scatterplot in Figure 7.4, which suggested a weak linear but strong quadratic relationship between age and hourly wage.

b. The predicted hourly wage for a 30-year-old person with 16 years of education is

$$\widehat{Wage} = -22.7219 + 1.2540 \times 16 + 1.3500 \times 30 - 0.0133 \times 30^2 = \$25.87.$$

Similarly, the predicted hourly wage for a 50- and a 70-year-old person is \$31.59 and \$26.67, respectively.

c. In part b, we predicted the hourly wage for 30-, 50-, and 70-year-old persons with 16 years of education. Therefore, of the three ages considered, a 50-year-old person earns the highest wage. In Figure 7.5, we plot the predicted wage with 16 years of education and vary age from 20 to 80 with increments of 1.

FIGURE 7.5 Predicted wages with 16 years of education and varying age

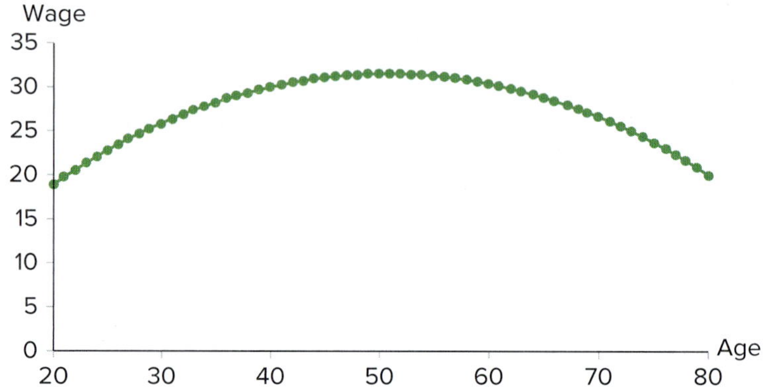

In order to determine the optimal age at which the wage is maximized, we also solve $x = \frac{-b_2}{2b_3} = \frac{-(1.3500)}{2(-0.0133)} = 50.75$. The optimal age at which the wage is maximized is about 51 years, with a wage of about \$31.60. It is worth noting that at a different education level, predicted wages will not be the same, yet the highest wage will still be achieved at the same 51 years of age. We advise you to plot a similar graph with 12 years of education and varying age levels.

Regression Models with Logarithms

Consider an estimated linear regression of annual food expenditure y on annual income x: $\hat{y} = 9{,}000 + 0.20x$. An estimated slope coefficient value of $b_1 = 0.20$ implies that a \$1,000 increase in annual income would lead to a \$200 increase in annual food expenditure, irrespective of whether the income increase is from \$20,000 to \$21,000 or from \$520,000 to \$521,000. This is yet another example where the linearity assumption is not justified. Because we would expect the impact to be smaller at high income levels, it may be more meaningful to analyze what happens to food expenditure as income increases by a certain percentage rather than by a certain dollar amount.

Another commonly used transformation is based on the natural logarithm that converts changes in a variable into percentage changes.

THE LOGARITHMIC TRANSFORMATION

The natural logarithm converts changes in a variable into percentage changes.

The logarithmic transformation is useful because many relationships are naturally expressed in terms of percentages. For instance, it is common to log-transform variables such as incomes, house prices, and sales. On the other hand, variables such as age, experience, and scores are generally expressed in their original form. We rely on both economic intuition as well as statistical measures to find the appropriate form for the variables.

We first illustrate log models with only one predictor variable, which we later extend to a multiple regression model.

The Log-Log Regression Model

In the **log-log regression model**, both the response variable and the predictor variable are transformed into natural logs. We can write this model as

$$\ln(y) = \beta_0 + \beta_1 \ln(x) + \varepsilon,$$

where $\ln(y)$ is the log-transformed response variable and $\ln(x)$ is the log-transformed predictor variable. With these transformations, the relationship between y and x is captured by a curve whose shape depends on the sign and magnitude of the slope coefficient β_1. Figure 7.6 shows two scatterplots of sample data with superimposed trendlines. Each trendline was generated by estimating the log-log regression model. Although the estimated simple linear regression model is not included in either panel, it is clear that the log-log regression model provides a better fit for both scatterplots.

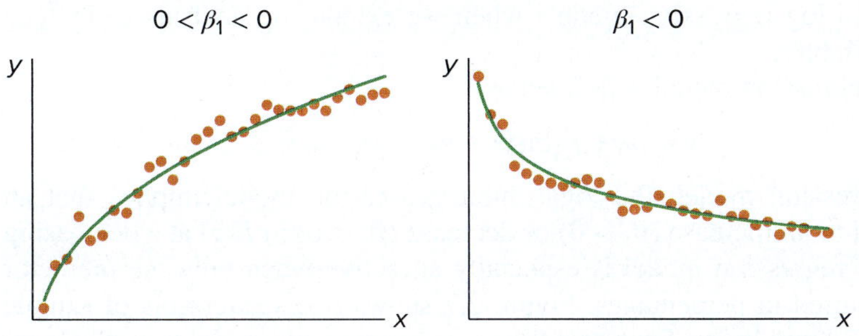

FIGURE 7.6 Scatterplot of y against x with trendline generated from estimating the log-log regression model

For $0 < \beta_1 < 1$, the log-log regression model implies a positive relationship between x and $E(y)$; as x increases, $E(y)$ increases at a slower rate. This may be appropriate in the food expenditure example where we expect food expenditure to react positively to changes in income, with the impact diminishing at higher income levels. If $\beta_1 < 0$, it suggests a negative relationship between x and $E(y)$; as x increases, $E(y)$ decreases at a slower rate. Finally, $\beta_1 > 1$ implies a positive and increasing relationship between x and y; this case is not shown in Figure 7.6. For any application, the estimated value of β_1 is determined by the data.

Note that while the log-log regression model is nonlinear in the variables, it is still linear in the coefficients, thus satisfying the requirement of the linear regression model. The only requirement is that we have to first transform both variables into logs before running the regression. We should also point out that in the log-log regression model, the slope coefficient β_1 measures the approximate percentage change in y for a small percentage change in x. In other words, β_1 is a measure of elasticity. In the log-log regression model, if y represents the quantity demanded of a particular good and x is its unit price, then β_1 measures the price elasticity of demand, a parameter of considerable economic interest. Suppose $\beta_1 = -1.2$; then a 1% increase in the price of this good is expected to lead to about a 1.2% decrease in its quantity demanded.

Finally, even though the response variable is transformed into logs, we still make predictions in regular units. Given $\widehat{\ln(y)} = b_0 + b_1 \ln(x)$, you may be tempted to use the anti-log function to make predictions in regular units as $\hat{y} = \exp(\widehat{\ln(y)}) = \exp(b_0 + b_1 \ln(x))$, where b_0 and b_1 are the coefficient estimates. However, this transformation is known to systematically underestimate the expected value of y. One relatively simple correction is to make predictions as $\hat{y} = \exp(b_0 + b_1\ln(x) + s_e^2/2)$, where s_e is the standard error of the estimate from the log-log regression model. This correction is easy to implement because virtually all statistical packages report s_e.

THE LOG-LOG REGRESSION MODEL

The log-log regression model is specified as $\ln(y) = \beta_0 + \beta_1\ln(x) + \varepsilon$, and β_1 measures the approximate percentage change in $E(y)$ when x increases by 1%.

Predictions with the log-log regression model are made by $\hat{y} = \exp(b_0 + b_1\ln(x) + s_e^2/2)$, where b_0 and b_1 are the coefficient estimates and s_e is the standard error of the estimate. It is advisable to use unrounded coefficients for making predictions.

The Logarithmic Regression Model

The log-log specification transforms all variables into logs. It is also common to employ the **semi-log regression model**, in which not all variables are transformed into logs. We will discuss two types of semi-log regression models in the context of the simple linear regression model. A semi-log model that transforms only the predictor variable is often called the **logarithmic regression model**, and the semi-log model that transforms only the response variable is often called an **exponential regression model**. We can have many variants of semi-log regression models when we extend the analysis to include multiple predictor variables.

The logarithmic regression model is defined as

$$y = \beta_0 + \beta_1\ln(x) + \varepsilon.$$

Like the log-log regression model, the logarithmic regression model implies that an increase in x will lead to an increase ($\beta_1 > 0$) or decrease ($\beta_1 < 0$) in $E(y)$ at a decreasing rate. The logarithmic regression model is especially attractive when only the predictor variable is better captured in percentages. Figure 7.7 shows two scatterplots of sample data with superimposed trendlines. Each trendline was generated by estimating the logarithmic regression model. Although the estimated simple linear regression model is not included in either panel, it is clear that the logarithmic regression model provides a better fit for both scatterplots. Because the log-log and the logarithmic regression models can allow similar shapes, the choice between the two models can be tricky. We will compare models later in this section.

FIGURE 7.7 Scatterplot of y against x with trendline generated from estimating the logarithmic regression model

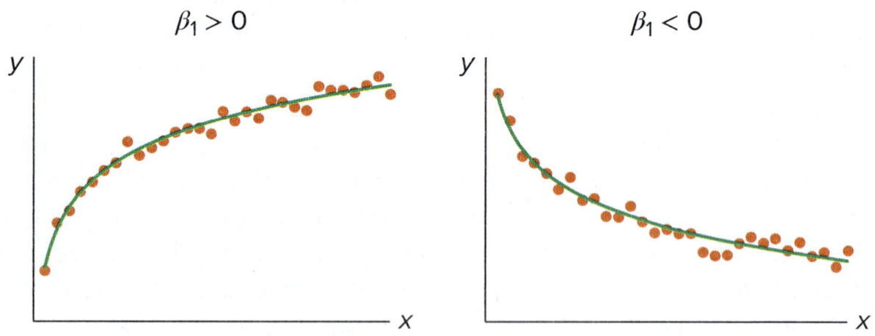

In the logarithmic regression model, the response variable is specified in regular units, but the predictor variable is transformed into logs. Therefore, $\beta_1 \times 0.01$ measures the approximate unit change in $E(y)$ when x increases by 1%. For example, if $\beta_1 = 5{,}000$, then a 1% increase in x leads to a 50 unit ($= 5{,}000 \times 0.01$) increase in $E(y)$. Because the response variable is already specified in regular units, no further transformation is necessary when making predictions.

> **THE LOGARITHMIC REGRESSION MODEL**
>
> The logarithmic regression model is specified as $y = \beta_0 + \beta_1 \ln(x) + \varepsilon$, and $\beta_1 \times 0.01$ measures the approximate change in $E(y)$ when x increases by 1%.
>
> Predictions with the logarithmic model are made by $\hat{y} = b_0 + b_1 \ln(x)$, where b_0 and b_1 are the coefficient estimates. It is advisable to use unrounded coefficients for making predictions.

The Exponential Regression Model

Unlike the logarithmic regression model, in which we were interested in finding the unit change in $E(y)$ for a 1% increase in x, the exponential regression model allows us to estimate the percent change in $E(y)$ when x increases by one unit. The exponential regression model is defined as

$$\ln(y) = \beta_0 + \beta_1 x + \varepsilon.$$

Figure 7.8 shows shows two scatterplots of sample data with superimposed trendlines. Each trendline was generated by estimating the exponential regression model. Although the estimated simple linear regression model is not included in either panel, it is clear that the exponential regression model provides a better fit for both scatterplots.

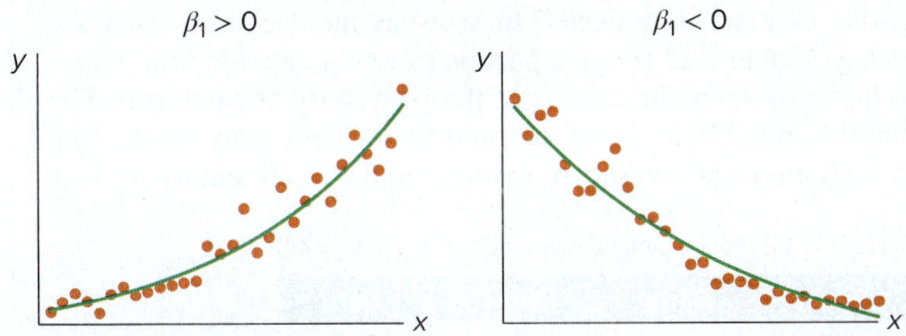

FIGURE 7.8 Scatterplot of y against x with trendline generated from estimating the exponential regression model

For the exponential model, $\beta_1 \times 100$ measures the approximate percentage change in $E(y)$ when x increases by one unit; the exact percentage change can be calculated as $(\exp(\beta_1) - 1) \times 100$. For example, a value of $\beta_1 = 0.05$ implies that a one-unit increase in x leads to an approximate 5% (= 0.05×100) increase in $E(y)$, or more precisely, a 5.1271% (= $(\exp(0.05) - 1) \times 100$) increase in $E(y)$. In applied work, we often see this model used to describe the rate of growth of certain economic variables, such as population, employment, salaries, and sales. As in the case of the log-log regression model, we make a correction for making predictions because the response variable is measured in logs.

> **THE EXPONENTIAL REGRESSION MODEL**
>
> The exponential regression model is specified as $\ln(y) = \beta_0 + \beta_1 x + \varepsilon$, and $\beta_1 \times 100$ measures the approximate percentage change in $E(y)$ when x increases by one unit.
>
> Predictions with the exponential regression model are made by $\hat{y} = \exp(b_0 + b_1 x + s_e^2/2)$, where b_0 and b_1 are the coefficient estimates and s_e is the standard error of the estimate. It is advisable to use unrounded coefficients for making predictions.

While these log models are easily estimated within the framework of a linear regression model, care must be exercised in making predictions and interpreting the estimated slope coefficient. When interpreting the slope coefficient, keep in mind that logs essentially convert changes in variables into percentage changes. Table 7.11 summarizes the results.

TABLE 7.11 Summary of the Linear, Log-Log, Logarithmic, and Exponential Regression Models

Model	Predicted Value	Estimated Slope Coefficient
$y = \beta_0 + \beta_1 x + \varepsilon$	$\hat{y} = b_0 + b_1 x$	b_1 measures the change in $\hat{y}$ when x increases by one unit.
$\ln(y) = \beta_0 + \beta_1 \ln(x) + \varepsilon$	$\hat{y} = \exp(b_0 + b_1 \ln(x) + s_e^2/2)$	b_1 measures the approximate percentage change in $\hat{y}$ when x increases by 1%.
$y = \beta_0 + \beta_1 \ln(x) + \varepsilon$	$\hat{y} = b_0 + b_1 \ln(x)$	$b_1 \times 0.01$ measures the approximate change in $\hat{y}$ when x increases by 1%.
$\ln(y) = \beta_0 + \beta_1 x + \varepsilon$	$\hat{y} = \exp(b_0 + b_1 x + s_e^2/2)$	$b_1 \times 100$ measures the approximate percentage change in $\hat{y}$ when x increases by one unit.

It is advisable to use unrounded coefficients for making predictions.

FILE
AnnArbor

EXAMPLE 7.7

Real estate investment in college towns promises good returns (*The College Investor*, August 22, 2017). First, students offer a steady stream of rental demand as cash-strapped public universities are unable to house their students beyond freshman year. Second, this demand is projected to grow as more children of baby boomers head to college. Table 7.12 shows a portion of rental data for Ann Arbor, Michigan, which is home to the main campus of the University of Michigan. The data include the monthly rent (Rent, in \$), the number of bedrooms (Beds), the number of bathrooms (Baths), and the square footage (Sqft) for 40 rentals.

TABLE 7.12 Rental Data for Ann Arbor, Michigan ($n = 40$)

Rent	Beds	Baths	Sqft
645	1	1	500
675	1	1	648
⋮	⋮	⋮	⋮
2400	3	2.5	2700

a. Plot rent against each of the three predictor variables and evaluate whether the relationship is best captured by a line or a curve. Identify variables that may require a log-transformation.

b. Estimate the linear and the relevant log regression models to predict rent for a 1,600-square-foot rental with 3 bedrooms and 2 bathrooms.

SOLUTION:

Given the nature of Beds and Baths, we will specify these variables only in regular units. We will, however, consider log-transformations for Rent and Sqft because their changes are often expressed in percentages.

a. In Figure 7.9, we plot Rent against (a) Beds and (b) Baths and superimpose linear and exponential trendlines (recall that the exponential regression model log-transforms only the response variable).

It is hard to tell from Figure 7.9 whether the relationship between Rent and Beds or Rent and Baths is better captured by a line or a curve. We will use goodness-of-fit measures for the selection.

We now plot Rent against Sqft in Figure 7.10. Here, it appears that the relationship between Rent and Sqft is better captured by a curve than a line.

FIGURE 7.9 Comparing Rent against (a) Beds and (b) Baths

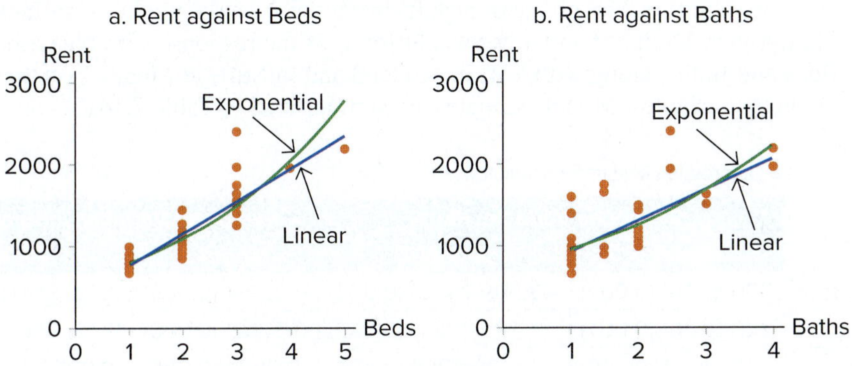

FIGURE 7.10 Comparing Rent against Sqft

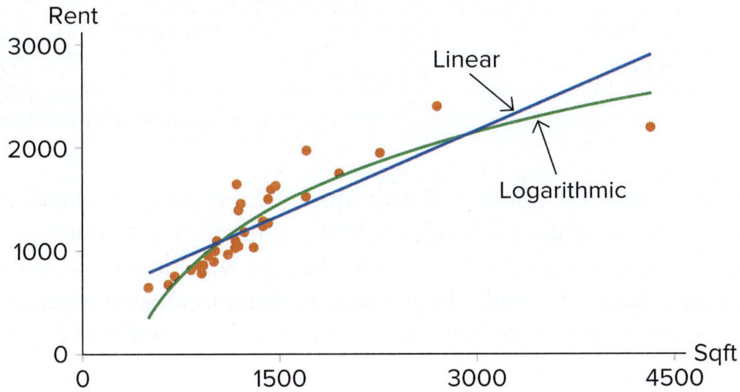

The logarithmic regression model that log-transforms Sqft fits the data better than the linear model, suggesting that as square footage increases, rent increases at a decreasing rate. In other words, the increase in Rent is higher when Sqft increases from 1,000 to 2,000 than from 2,000 to 3,000. Two other models worth considering are the exponential regression model, where only Rent is log-transformed, and the log-log regression model, where both Rent and Sqft are log-transformed. In order to avoid a "cluttered" figure, these trendlines are not superimposed on the scatterplot; however, we will formally evaluate all models.

b. While the preceding visual tools are instructive, we evaluate four models and use goodness-of-fit measures to select the most appropriate model for prediction.

Model 1: $\text{Rent} = \beta_0 + \beta_1 \text{Beds} + \beta_2 \text{Baths} + \beta_3 \text{Sqft} + \varepsilon$
Model 2: $\text{Rent} = \beta_0 + \beta_1 \text{Beds} + \beta_2 \text{Baths} + \beta_3 \ln(\text{Sqft}) + \varepsilon$
Model 3: $\ln(\text{Rent}) = \beta_0 + \beta_1 \text{Beds} + \beta_2 \text{Baths} + \beta_3 \text{Sqft} + \varepsilon$
Model 4: $\ln(\text{Rent}) = \beta_0 + \beta_1 \text{Beds} + \beta_2 \text{Baths} + \beta_3 \ln(\text{Sqft}) + \varepsilon$

In order to estimate these models, we first log-transform Rent and Sqft; see the last two columns of Table 7.13.

TABLE 7.13 Transforming Rent and Sqft into Logs

Rent	Beds	Baths	Sqft	ln(Rent)	ln(Sqft)
645	1	1	500	6.4693	6.2146
675	1	1	648	6.5147	6.4739
⋮	⋮	⋮	⋮	⋮	⋮
2400	3	2.5	2700	7.7832	7.9010

In Models 1 and 2, we use Rent as the response variable with Beds and Baths, along with Sqft in Model 1 and ln(Sqft) in Model 2, as the predictor variables. Similarly, in Models 3 and 4, we use ln(Rent) as the response variable with Beds and Baths, along with Sqft in Model 3 and ln(Sqft) in Model 4, as the predictor variables. Model estimates are summarized in Table 7.14.

TABLE 7.14 Regression Results for Example 7.7

	Response Variable: Rent		Response Variable: ln(Rent)	
	Model 1	**Model 2**	**Model 3**	**Model 4**
Intercept	300.4116* (0.001)	−3,909.7415* (0.001)	6.3294* (0.000)	3.3808* (0.000)
Beds	225.8100* (0.001)	131.7781* (0.040)	0.2262* (0.000)	0.1246* (0.009)
Baths	89.2661 (0.119)	36.4255 (0.494)	0.0831 (0.060)	0.0254 (0.514)
Sqft	0.2096* (0.028)	NA	0.0001 (0.362)	NA
ln(Sqft)	NA	675.2648* (0.000)	NA	0.4742* (0.001)
s_e	193.1591	172.2711	0.1479	0.1262
R^2	0.8092	0.8482	0.8095	0.8613

Notes: Parameter estimates are followed with the *p*-values in parentheses; NA denotes not applicable; * represents significance at the 5% level.

For the most part, the number of bedrooms and the square footage are statistically significant at the 5% level, while the number of bathrooms is insignificant. We use the model results to predict the rent for a 1,600-square-foot rental with 3 bedrooms and 2 bathrooms. In order to make a prediction with Models 3 and 4, which are both based on ln(Rent), we will add the correction term $s_e^2/2$.

$$\text{Model 1: } \widehat{\text{Rent}} = 300.4116 + 225.8100(3) + 89.2661(2) + 0.2096(1{,}600) = \$1{,}492$$

$$\text{Model 2: } \widehat{\text{Rent}} = -3{,}909.7415 + 131.7781(3) + 36.4255(2) + 675.2648 \times \ln(1{,}600) = \$1{,}540$$

$$\text{Model 3: } \widehat{\text{Rent}} = \exp(6.3294 + 0.2262(3) + 0.0831(2) + 0.0001(1{,}600) + 0.1479^2/2) = \$1{,}549$$

$$\text{Model 4: } \widehat{\text{Rent}} = \exp(3.3808 + 0.1246(3) + 0.0254(2) + 0.4742 \times \ln(1{,}600) + 0.1262^2/2) = \$1{,}498$$

The predicted rent ranges from \$1,492 in Model 1 to \$1,549 in Model 3. We would like to know which model provides the best prediction, as we discuss next.

Comparing Linear and Log-Transformed Regression Models

As seen in Example 7.7, it is often not clear which regression model is best suited for an application. While we can use economic intuition and scatterplots for direction, we also justify our selection on the basis of goodness-of-fit measures. In Chapter 6, we introduced R^2 to compare models based on the same number of predictor variables; we compared adjusted R^2 if the number of predictor variables was different. Such comparisons are valid only when the response variable of the competing models is the same. Because R^2 measures the percentage of sample variations of the response variable explained by the model, we cannot compare the percentage of explained variations of y with that of $\ln(y)$. Comparing models based on the computer-generated R^2, which does not differentiate between y and $\ln(y)$, is like comparing apples with oranges. For a valid comparison, we need to compute the percentage of explained variations of y, the appropriate R^2, even though the estimated model uses $\ln(y)$ as the response variable. In Chapter 6, we calculated $R^2 = SSR/SST = 1 - SSE/SST$. Here, we will use an alternative way by squaring the sample correlation coefficient of y and $\hat{y}$.

AN ALTERNATIVE WAY TO CALCULATE THE COEFFICIENT OF DETERMINATION, R^2

The coefficient of determination, R^2, can be computed as $R^2 = (r_{y\hat{y}})^2$, where $r_{y\hat{y}}$ is the sample correlation coefficient between y and $\hat{y}$.

Example 7.8 elaborates on the method with the use of Excel and R.

Using Excel and R to Compare Linear and Log-Transformed Regression Models

EXAMPLE 7.8

FILE *AnnArbor*

Revisit the four regression models in Example 7.7 and determine which model is best suited for making predictions.

SOLUTION:

From Table 7.14, Model 4 has the highest computer-generated R^2 value of 0.8613. However, this does not mean that Model 4 is necessarily the best, since R^2 is based on Rent for Models 1 and 2 and on ln(Rent) for Models 3 and 4. Therefore, while we can infer that Model 2 is superior to Model 1 (0.8482 > 0.8092) and Model 4 is superior to Model 3 (0.8613 > 0.8095), we cannot directly compare Models 2 and 4 based on the computer-generated R^2. For a valid comparison, we compute R^2 for Model 4 from scratch; that is, R^2 is based on Rent, even though it uses ln(Rent) for estimation.

For Model 4, we first compute $\widehat{\text{Rent}} = \exp(b_0 + b_1\text{Beds} + b_2\text{Baths} + b_3\ln(\text{Sqft}) + s_e^2/2)$ for the given sample values of the predictor variables. For example, for the first sample observation, with Beds = 1, Baths = 1, and Sqft = 500, the predicted rent is computed as

$$\widehat{\text{Rent}} = \exp(3.3808 + 0.1246(1) + 0.0254(1) + 0.4742 \times \ln(500) + 0.1262^2/2) = \$656.$$

The predicted rent for other sample observations is calculated similarly. Excel and R are quite useful in performing the calculations for the predicted values for Rent, as well as generating a value of R^2 for Model 4 based on Rent rather than ln(Rent).

USING EXCEL

a. Open the ***AnnArbor*** data file. Convert the Rent and Sqft variables into their respective logarithms by using Excel's **ln** function.

b. Estimate Model 4 by choosing **Data > Data Analysis > Regression** from the menu. For *Input Y Range*, select the ln(Rent) data, and for *Input X Range*, simultaneously select the Beds, Baths, and ln(Sqft) data. If you check the *Residuals* box, then Excel provides the predicted values for the ln(Rent), or $\widehat{\ln(\text{Rent})}$. Select this box, and then click **OK.**

c. For convenience, paste the values for $\widehat{\ln(\text{Rent})}$ next to the observed values for Rent on the spreadsheet; the first two columns of Table 7.15 show a portion of the results. Next, we want to calculate $\widehat{\text{Rent}} = \exp(b_0 + b_1\text{Beds} + b_2\text{Baths} + b_3\ln(\text{Sqft}) + s_e^2/2)$. Given the Excel-produced predicted values for ln(Rent), this equation simplifies to $\widehat{\text{Rent}} = \exp(\widehat{\ln(\text{Rent})} + s_e^2/2)$. Substituting the standard error of the estimate s_e from Model 4 into this equation yields $\widehat{\text{Rent}} = \exp(\widehat{\ln(\text{Rent})} + 0.1262^2/2)$. (For a more precise estimate, you can use the unrounded value for s_e from the regression output.) The third column of Table 7.15 shows a portion of the results.

TABLE 7.15 Excel-Produced Predicted Values for Model 4

Rent	$\widehat{\ln(\text{Rent})}$	$\widehat{\text{Rent}} = \exp(\widehat{\ln(\text{Rent})} + 0.1262^2/2)$
645	6.4778	655.7334
675	6.6007	742.5210
⋮	⋮	⋮
2400	7.5648	1944.5760

d. Finally, use Excel's **CORREL** function to calculate the correlation between Rent and $\widehat{\text{Rent}}$ (columns 1 and 3 in Table 7.15) as $r_{y\hat{y}} = 0.8691$. Square the sample correlation coefficient to find the coefficient of determination, $R^2 = (0.8691)^2 = 0.7554$. We can now compare this value with the computer-generated value for Model 2 that is correctly based on Rent and conclude that Model 2 is better suited for making predictions because $0.8482 > 0.7554$.

USING R

a. Import the ***AnnArbor*** data into a data frame (table) and label it myData.

b. As shown in Chapter 6, we use the **lm** function to create a regression model or, in R terminology, an object. We label this object as Model4. We also use the **log** function for the natural log transformation of the variables Rent and Sqft. Enter:

```
> Model4 <- lm(log(Rent) ~ Bed+Bath+log(Sqft), data=myData)
> summary(Model4)
```

c. We then generate predicted values for Model4, or $\widehat{\ln(\text{Rent})}$, using the **predict** function. Within the function, we indicate the name of the model or object. We label $\widehat{\ln(\text{Rent})}$ as Pred_lnRent. Enter:

```
> Pred_lnRent<-predict(Model4)
```

d. Next, we want to calculate the predicted values for Rent: $\widehat{\text{Rent}} = \exp(\widehat{\ln(\text{Rent})} + s_e^2/2)$. We label $\widehat{\text{Rent}}$ as Pred_Rent. We could use the standard error of the estimate of 0.1262 that is provided in the model summary output. However, we first obtain the unrounded value, which provides a more precise estimate; we label this value as SE. Enter:

```
> SE<-summary(Model4)$sigma
> Pred_Rent<-exp(Pred_lnRent+SE^2/2)
```

e. Finally, we use R's **cor** function to calculate the correlation between Rent and $\widehat{\text{Rent}}$. We square this value to find the coefficient of determination, R^2. Enter:

```
> cor(myData$Rent, Pred_Rent)^2
```

And R returns 0.7554188. This result is the same as the one that we obtained with Excel; it would be identical to the last digit if we had used the unrounded value for s_e from the Excel output. We again conclude that Model 2, with an R^2 equal to 0.8482, is better suited than Model 4 for making predictions.

EXERCISES 7.2

Mechanics

20. Consider the estimated quadratic model $\hat{y} = 20 + 1.9x - 0.05x^2$.
    a. Predict y when x equals 10, 20, and 30.
    b. Find the value of x at which the predicted y is optimized. At this x value, is the predicted y maximized or minimized.

21. Consider the following sample regressions for the linear and quadratic models along with their respective R^2 and adjusted R^2.

	Linear	Quadratic
Intercept	13.3087	1.7656
x	0.3392	4.0966
x^2	NA	−0.2528
R^2	0.1317	0.5844
Adjusted R^2	0.0232	0.4657

    a. Use the appropriate goodness-of-fit measure to justify which model fits the data better.
    b. Given the best-fitting model, predict y for $x = 4$, 8, and 12.

22. Consider the sample regressions for the linear, the logarithmic, the exponential, and the log-log models. For each of the estimated models, predict y when x equals 50.

	Response Variable: y		Response Variable: ln(y)	
	Model 1	Model 2	Model 3	Model 4
Intercept	18.52	−6.74	1.48	1.02
x	1.68	NA	0.06	NA
ln(x)	NA	29.96	NA	0.96
s_e	23.92	19.71	0.12	0.10

23. Consider the following sample regressions for the linear and the logarithmic models.

	Linear	Logarithmic
Intercept	6.7904	−5.6712
x	1.0607	NA
ln(x)	NA	10.5447*
s_e	2.4935	1.5231
R^2	0.8233	0.9341
Adjusted R^2	0.8013	0.9259

    a. Justify which model fits the data better.
    b. Use the selected model to predict y for $x = 10$.

24. Consider the following sample regressions for the log-log and the exponential models.

	Log-Log	Exponential
Intercept	1.8826	2.0219
x	NA	0.0513
ln(x)	0.3663	NA
s_e	0.3508	0.2922
R^2	0.5187	0.6660
Adjusted R^2	0.4585	0.6242

    a. Justify which model fits the data better.
    b. Use the selected model to predict y for $x = 20$.

Applications

25. FILE ***Television.*** Numerous studies have shown that watching too much television hurts school grades. Others have argued that television is not necessarily a bad thing for children (*Psychology Today*, October 22, 2012). Like books and stories, television not only entertains, it also exposes a child to new information about the world. While watching too much television is harmful, a little bit may actually help. Researcher Matt Castle gathers information on the grade point average (GPA) of 28 middle school children and the number of hours of television they watched per week. A portion of the data is shown in the accompanying table.

GPA	Hours
3.24	19
3.10	21
⋮	⋮
3.31	4

    a. Estimate a quadratic regression model where the GPA of middle school children is regressed on hours and hours-squared.
    b. Is the quadratic term in this model justified? Explain.
    c. Find the optimal number of weekly hours of TV for middle school children.

26. FILE ***Sales_Reps.*** Brendan Connolly manages the human resource division of a high-tech company. He has access to the salary information of 300 sales reps along with their age, sex (Female), and the net promoter score (NPS) that indicates customer satisfaction. A portion of the data is shown in the accompanying table.

Salary	Age	Female	NPS
97000	44	0	9
50000	34	0	4
⋮	⋮	⋮	⋮
88000	36	0	10

a. Estimate and interpret a quadratic model using the natural log of salary as the response variable and Age, Age^2, Female, and NPS as the predictor variables.

b. Determine the optimal level of age at which the natural log of salary is maximized.

c. At the optimal age, predict the salary of male and female sales reps with NPS = 8.

27. **FILE** ***Fertilizer2.*** A horticulturist is studying the relationship between tomato plant height and fertilizer amount. Thirty tomato plants grown in similar conditions were subjected to various amounts of fertilizer (in ounces) over a four-month period, and then their heights (in inches) were measured. A portion of the data is shown in the accompanying table.

Height	Fertilizer
20.4	1.9
29.1	5.0
⋮	⋮
36.4	3.1

a. Estimate the linear regression model $\text{Height} = \beta_0 + \beta_1\text{Fertilizer} + \varepsilon$.

b. Estimate the quadratic regression model $\text{Height} = \beta_0 + \beta_1\text{Fertilizer} + \beta_2\text{Fertilizer}^2 + \varepsilon$. Find the fertilizer amount at which the height reaches a minimum or maximum.

c. Use the best-fitting model to predict, after a four-month period, the height of a tomato plant that received 3.0 ounces of fertilizer.

28. **FILE** ***Circuit_Boards.*** The operators manager at an electronics company believes that the time required for workers to build a circuit board is not necessarily proportional to the number of parts on the board. He wants to develop a regression model to predict time (in minutes) based on part quantity. He has collected data for the last 25 boards. A portion of this data is shown in the accompanying table.

Time	Parts
30.8	62
9.8	32
⋮	⋮
29.8	60

a. Estimate the linear regression model to predict time as a function of the number of parts (Parts). Then estimate the quadratic regression model to predict time as a function of Parts and Parts squared.

b. Evaluate the two models in terms of variable significance ($\alpha = 0.05$) and adjusted R^2.

c. Use the best-fitting model to predict how long it would take to build a circuit board consisting of 48 parts.

29. **FILE** ***Inventory_Cost.*** The inventory manager at a warehouse distributor wants to predict inventory cost (Cost in \$) based on order quantity (Quantity in units). She thinks it may be a nonlinear relationship because its two primary components move in opposite directions: (1) order processing cost (costs of procurement personnel, shipping, transportation), which *decreases* as order quantity increases (due to fewer orders needed), and (2) holding cost (costs of capital, facility, warehouse personnel, equipment), which *increases* as order quantity increases (due to more inventory held). She has collected monthly inventory costs and order quantities for the past 36 months. A portion of the data is shown in the accompanying table.

Cost	Quantity
844	54.4
503	52.1
⋮	⋮
870	55.5

a. Create a scatterplot of inventory cost as a function of quantity. Superimpose the linear trendline and the quadratic trendline.

b. Estimate the linear regression model to predict inventory cost as a function of order quantity. Then estimate the quadratic regression model to predict inventory cost as a function of order quantity and order quantity squared.

c. Evaluate the two models in terms of significance tests ($\alpha = 0.05$) and adjusted R^2.

d. Use the best-fitting model to predict monthly inventory cost for an order quantity of 800 units.

30. **FILE** ***Dexterity.*** A manufacturing manager uses a dexterity test on 120 current employees in order to predict watch production based on time to completion (in seconds) and a Male dummy variable. A portion of the data is shown in the accompanying table.

Watches	Time	Male
28	503	1
33	534	1
⋮	⋮	⋮
24	518	1

a. Estimate the linear model $\text{Watches} = \beta_0 + \beta_1\text{Time} + \beta_2\text{Male} + \varepsilon$. Interpret the slope coefficient for Time. If the time required to complete the dexterity test is 550 seconds, what is the predicted watch production for male and female employees?

b. Estimate the logarithmic model $\text{Watches} = \beta_0 + \beta_1\ln(\text{Time}) + \beta_2\text{Male} + \varepsilon$. Interpret the slope coefficient for ln(Time).

If the time required to complete the dexterity test is 550 seconds, what is the predicted watch production for male and female employees?

c. Which model provides a better fit? Explain.

31. **FILE** ***Wine_Pricing.*** Professor Orley Ashenfelter of Princeton University is a pioneer in the field of wine economics. He claims that, contrary to old orthodoxy, the quality of wine can be explained mostly in terms of weather conditions. Wine romantics accuse him of undermining the whole wine-tasting culture. In an interesting co-authored paper that appeared in *Chance* magazine in 1995, he ran a multiple regression model where quality, measured by the average vintage price relative to 1961, is used as the response variable y. The predictor variables were the average temperature x_1 (in degrees Celsius), the amount of winter rain x_2 (in millimeters), the amount of harvest rain x_3 (in millimeters), and the years since vintage x_4. A portion of the data is shown in the accompanying table.

y	x_1	x_2	x_3	x_4
0.3684	17.1167	600	160	31
0.6348	16.7333	690	80	30
⋮	⋮	⋮	⋮	⋮
0.1359	16.0000	578	74	3

a. Estimate the linear model $y = \beta_0 + \beta_1 x_1 + \beta_2 x_2 + \beta_3 x_3 + \beta_4 x_4 + \varepsilon$. What is the predicted price if $x_1 = 16$, $x_2 = 600$, $x_3 = 120$, and $x_4 = 20$?

b. Estimate the exponential model $\ln(y) = \beta_0 + \beta_1 x_1 + \beta_2 x_2 + \beta_3 x_3 + \beta_4 x_4 + \varepsilon$. What is the predicted price if $x_1 = 16$, $x_2 = 600$, $x_3 = 120$, and $x_4 = 20$?

c. Use R^2 to select the appropriate model for prediction.

32. **FILE** ***Electricity.*** The facility manager at a pharmaceutical company wants to build a regression model to forecast monthly electricity cost (Cost in \$). Three main variables are thought to influence electricity cost: (1) average outdoor temperature (Temp in °F), (2) working days per month (Days), and (3) tons of product produced (Tons). A portion of the past monthly data on 80 observations is shown in the accompanying table.

Cost	Temp	Days	Tons
16747	46	22	75
7901	31	24	98
⋮	⋮	⋮	⋮
11380	56	28	84

a. Estimate the linear model $\text{Cost} = \beta_0 + \beta_1\text{Temp} + \beta_2\text{Days} + \beta_3\text{Tons} + \varepsilon$. What is the predicted electricity cost in a month during which the average outdoor temperature is 65°, there are 23 working days, and 76 tons are produced?

b. Estimate the exponential model $\ln(\text{Cost}) = \beta_0 + \beta_1\text{Temp} + \beta_2\text{Days} + \beta_3\text{Tons} + \varepsilon$. What is the predicted electricity cost in a month during which the average outdoor temperature is 65°, there are 23 working days, and 76 tons are produced?

c. Based on R^2, which model provides the better fit?

33. **FILE** ***Davis_Rental.*** Chad Dobson has heard about the positive outlook for real estate investment in college towns. He is interested in investing in Davis, California, which houses one of the University of California campuses. He has access to monthly rents (in \$) for 27 houses, along with three characteristics of the home: number of bedrooms (Beds), number of bathrooms (Baths), and square footage (Sqft). A portion of the data is shown in the accompanying table.

Rent	Beds	Baths	Sqft
2950	4	4	1453
2400	4	2	1476
⋮	⋮	⋮	⋮
744	2	1	930

a. Estimate the linear model that uses Rent as the response variable. Estimate the exponential model that uses log of Rent as the response variable.

b. Compute the predicted rent for a 1,500-square-foot house with 3 bedrooms and 2 bathrooms for the linear and the exponential models (ignore the significance tests).

c. Use R^2 to select the appropriate model for prediction.

34. **FILE** ***Savings_Rate.*** The accompanying table shows a portion of the monthly data on the personal savings rate (Savings in %) and personal disposable income (Income in \$ billions) in the U.S. from January 2007 to November 2010.

Date	Savings	Income
Jan 2007	2.2	10198.2
Feb 2007	2.3	10252.9
⋮	⋮	⋮
Nov 2010	5.5	11511.9

a. Estimate the linear model $\text{Savings} = \beta_0 + \beta_1\text{Income} + \varepsilon$ and the log-log model, $\ln(\text{Savings}) = \beta_0 + \beta_1\ln(\text{Income}) + \varepsilon$. For each model, predict Savings if Income = \$10,500.

b. Which is the preferred model? Explain.

35. **FILE** ***Learning_Curve.*** Learning curves are used in production operations to estimate the time required to complete a repetitive task as an operator gains experience. Suppose a production manager has compiled 30 time values (in minutes) for a particular operator as she progressed down the learning curve during the first 100 units. A portion of this data is shown in the accompanying table.

Time per Unit	Unit Number
18.30	3
17.50	5
⋮	⋮
5.60	100

a. Create a scatterplot of time per unit against units built. Superimpose the linear trendline and the logarithmic trendline to determine visually the best-fitting model.
b. Estimate the simple linear regression model and the logarithmic regression model for predicting time per unit using unit number as the predictor variable.
c. Based on R^2, use the best-fitting model to predict the time that was required for the operator to build Unit 50.

36. **FILE** ***Happiness.*** Numerous attempts have been made to understand happiness. Because there is no unique way to quantify it, researchers often rely on surveys to capture a subjective assessment of well-being. One study finds that holding everything else constant, people seem to be least happy when they are in their 40s (*Psychology Today*, April 27, 2018). Another study suggests that money does buy happiness, but its effect diminishes as incomes rise above $75,000 a year (*Money Magazine*, February 14, 2018). Consider survey data of 100 working adults' self-assessed happiness on a scale of 0 to 100, along with their age and annual income. A portion of the data is shown in the accompanying table.

Happiness	Age	Income
69	49	52000
83	47	123000
⋮	⋮	⋮
79	31	105000

a. Estimate and interpret a regression model for Happiness based on Age, Age^2, and ln(Income).
b. Predict happiness with Income equal to $80,000 and Age equal to 30, 45, and 60 years.
c. Predict happiness with Age equal to 60 and Income equal to $25,000, $75,000, $125,000.

37. **FILE** ***Production_Function.*** Economists often examine the relationship between the inputs of a production function and the resulting output. A common way of modeling this relationship is referred to as the Cobb-Douglas production function. This function can be expressed as $\ln(Q) = \beta_0 + \beta_1\ln(L) + \beta_2\ln(K) + \varepsilon$, where Q stands for output, L for labor, and K for capital. The accompanying table lists a portion of data relating to the U.S. agricultural industry in the year 2004.

State	Output	Labor	Capital
AL	3.1973	2.7682	3.1315
AR	7.7006	4.9278	4.7961
⋮	⋮	⋮	⋮
WY	1.2993	1.6525	1.5206

a. Estimate $\ln(Q) = \beta_0 + \beta_1\ln(L) + \beta_2\ln(K) + \varepsilon$. What is the predicted change in output if labor increases by 1%, holding capital constant?
b. Holding capital constant, can we conclude at the 5% level that a 1% increase in labor will increase the output by more than 0.5%?

38. **FILE** ***Smoking.*** A nutritionist wants to understand the influence of income and healthy food on the incidence of smoking. He collects data on the percentage of smokers in each state in the U.S., the percentage of the state's population that regularly eats fruits and vegetables, and the state's median income (in $). A portion of the data is shown in the accompanying table.

State	Smoke	Fruits/Vegetables	Income
AK	14.6	23.3	61604
AL	16.4	20.3	39980
⋮	⋮	⋮	⋮
WY	15.2	23.3	52470

a. Estimate $\text{Smoke} = \beta_0 + \beta_1\text{Fruits/Vegetables} + \beta_2\text{Income} + \varepsilon$.
b. Compare this model with a model that log-transforms the income variable.

LO 7.3

7.3 LINEAR PROBABILITY AND LOGISTIC REGRESSION MODELS

Estimate and interpret linear probability and logistic regression models.

So far we have considered regression models where dummy (binary) variables are used as predictor variables. In this section, we analyze **binary choice (classification) models** where the response variable is a binary variable.. The consumer choice literature is replete with applications such as whether or not to buy a house, join a health club, or go to graduate school. At the firm level, managers make decisions such as whether or not to run a marketing campaign, restructure debt, or approve a loan. In all such applications, the response variable is binary, where one of the choices can be designated as 1 and the other as 0. Usually, this choice can be related to a host of factors—the predictor variables. For instance, whether or not a family buys a house depends on predictor variables such as household income, mortgage rates, and so on.

The Linear Probability Model

Consider a simple linear regression model $y = \beta_0 + \beta_1 x + \varepsilon$, where y is a binary variable; we can easily extend the model to include multiple predictor variables. The linear regression model applied to a binary response variable is called the **linear probability model (LPM)**.

> **THE LINEAR PROBABILITY MODEL**
>
> The linear probability model is specified as $y = \beta_0 + \beta_1 x + \varepsilon$, where y assumes a 1 or 0 value. Predictions with this model are made by $\hat{y} = b_0 + b_1 x$, where b_0 and b_1 are the estimates of the population parameters β_0 and β_1, and $\hat{y} = \hat{p}$ is the predicted probability of success.

EXAMPLE 7.9

FILE *Mortgage*

The subprime mortgage crisis of 2006 that eventually lead to the Great Recession forced financial institutions to be extra stringent in granting mortgage loans. Thirty recent mortgage applications are obtained to analyze the mortgage approval rate. The response variable y equals 1 if the mortgage loan is approved, 0 otherwise. It is believed that approval depends on the percentage of the down payment x_1 and the percentage of the income-to-loan ratio x_2. Table 7.16 shows a portion of the data.

TABLE 7.16 Mortgage Application Data

y	x_1	x_2
1	16.35	49.94
1	34.43	56.16
⋮	⋮	⋮
0	17.85	26.86

a. Estimate and interpret the linear probability model $y = \beta_0 + \beta_1 x_1 + \beta_2 x_2 + \varepsilon$.

b. Predict the loan approval probability for an applicant with a 20% down payment and a 30% income-to-loan ratio. What if the down payment was 30%?

SOLUTION:

a. Table 7.17 shows a portion of the regression results. The estimated regression equation is $\hat{p} = \hat{y} = -0.8682 + 0.0188x_1 + 0.0258x_2$. With p-values of 0.012 and 0.000, respectively, both predictor variables exert a positive and statistically significant influence on loan approval, at a 5% level. Also, holding the income-to-loan ratio constant, $b_1 = 0.0188$ implies that a 1-percentage-point increase in down payment increases the approval probability by 0.0188, or by 1.88%. Similarly, holding down payment constant, a 1-percentage-point increase in the income-to-loan ratio increases the approval probability by 0.0258, or by 2.58%.

TABLE 7.17 The Linear Probability Model Results for Example 8.9

	Coefficients	Standard Error	*t* Stat	*p*-Value
Intercept	−0.8682	0.2811	−3.089	0.005
x_1	0.0188	0.0070	2.695	0.012
x_2	0.0258	0.0063	4.107	0.000

b. The predicted loan approval probability for an applicant with a 20% down payment and a 30% income-to-loan ratio is $\hat{p} = -0.8682 + 0.0188 \times 20 + 0.0258 \times 30 = 0.2818$. Similarly, the predicted loan approval probability with a down payment of 30% is $\hat{p} = -0.8682 + 0.0188 \times 30 + 0.0258 \times 30 = 0.4698$. In other words, as down payment increases by 10 percentage points, the predicted probability of loan approval increases by 0.1880 (= 0.4698 – 0.2818), which is essentially the estimated slope, 0.0188, multiplied by 10. The estimated slope coefficient for the percentage of income-to-loan variable can be interpreted similarly.

Although it is easy to estimate and interpret the linear probability model, it has some shortcomings. The major shortcoming is that it can produce predicted probabilities that are greater than 1 or less than 0. For instance, for a down payment of 60%, with the same income-to-loan ratio of 30%, we get a predicted loan approval probability of $\hat{p} = -0.8682 + 0.0188 \times 60 + 0.0258 \times 30 = 1.0338$, a probability greater than 1! Similarly, for a down payment of 5%, the model predicts a negative probability, $\hat{p} = -0.8682 + 0.0188 \times 5 + 0.0258 \times 30 = -0.0002$. Furthermore, the linearity of the relationship may also be questionable. For instance, we would expect a big increase in the probability of loan approval if the applicant makes a down payment of 30% instead of 20%. This increase in probability is likely to be much smaller if the same 10-percentage-point increase in down payment is from 60% to 70%. The linear probability model cannot differentiate between these two scenarios. For these reasons, we introduce the logistic regression model, which is a more appropriate probability model for binary response variables.

The Logistic Regression Model

Recall that in an estimated linear probability model, $\hat{p} = \hat{y} = b_0 + b_1x$, the influence of x on $\hat{p}$, captured by the estimated slope b_1, is constant. Furthermore, for any given slope, we can find some value of x for which the predicted probability is outside the [0,1] interval. For meaningful analysis, we would like a nonlinear specification that constrains the predicted probability between 0 and 1.

Consider the following logistic specification

$$\hat{p} = \frac{\exp(b_0 + b_1x)}{1 + \exp(b_0 + b_1x)}$$

where $\exp(b_0 + b_1x) = e^{b_0+b_1x}$ and $e \approx 2.718$. The logistic specification ensures that the estimated probability is between 0 and 1 for all values of x.

The logistic regression model cannot be estimated with standard ordinary least squares (OLS) procedures. Instead, we rely on the method of **maximum likelihood estimation (MLE)**. While the MLE of the logistic regression model is not supported by Excel, it can easily be estimated with most statistical packages, including Analytic Solver and R. Given the relevance of the logistic regression model in business applications, it is important to be able to interpret and make predictions with the estimated model.

THE LOGISTIC REGRESSION MODEL

The logistic regression model is a nonlinear model that can be estimated with most statistical packages. Predictions with this model are made by

$$\hat{p} = \frac{\exp(b_0 + b_1x)}{1 + \exp(b_0 + b_1x)}$$

where b_0 and b_1 are the estimates of the population parameters β_0 and β_1 and $\hat{p}$ is the predicted probability of success.

Figure 7.11 highlights the relationship between the predicted probability $\hat{p}$ and the predictor variable x for the linear probability model and the logistic regression model, given $b_1 > 0$. Note that in the linear probability model, the probability falls below 0 for small values of x and exceeds 1 for large values of x. The probabilities implied by the logistic regression model, however, are always constrained in the [0,1] interval. (For ease of exposition, we use the same notation to refer to the coefficients in the linear probability model and the logistic regression model. We note, however, that these coefficients and their estimates have a different meaning depending on which model we are referencing.)

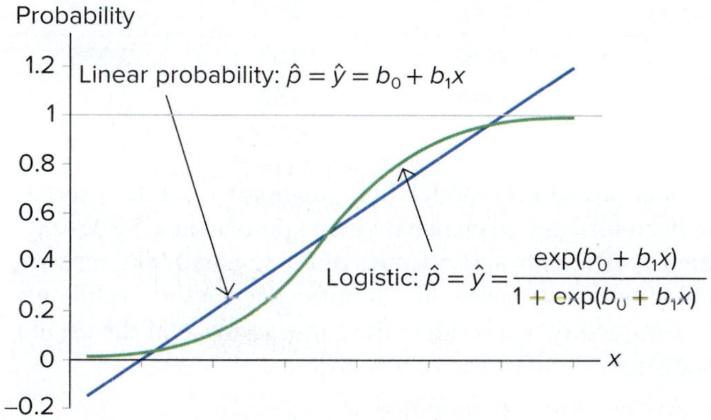

FIGURE 7.11 Predicted probabilities for linear probability and logistic regression models, with $b_1 > 0$

It is important to be able to interpret the regression coefficients of the logistic regression model. In a linear probability model, the interpretation of a regression coefficient is straightforward. For instance, if the estimated linear probability model is $\hat{p} = -0.20 + 0.03x$, it implies that for every 1-unit increase in x, the predicted probability $\hat{p}$ increases by 0.03. We note that $\hat{p}$ increases by 0.03, whether x increases from 10 to 11 or from 20 to 21.

Now consider the estimated logistic regression model, $\hat{p} = \frac{\exp(-2.10 + 0.18x)}{1 + \exp(-2.10 + 0.18x)}$. Because the regression coefficient $b_1 = 0.18$ is positive, we can infer that x exerts a positive influence on $\hat{p}$. However, the exact impact based on the estimated regression coefficient is not obvious. A useful method to interpret the estimated coefficient is to highlight the changing impact of x on $\hat{p}$. For instance, given $x = 10$, we compute the predicted probability as $\hat{p} = \frac{\exp(-2.10 + 0.18 \times 10)}{1 + \exp(-2.10 + 0.18 \times 10)} = 0.4256$. Similarly, for $x = 11$, the predicted probability is $\hat{p} = 0.4700$. Therefore, as x increases by one unit from 10 to 11, the predicted probability increases by 0.0444. However, the increase in $\hat{p}$ will not be the same if x increases from 20 to 21. We can show that $\hat{p}$ increases from 0.8176 when $x = 20$ to 0.8429 when $x = 21$, for a smaller increase of 0.0253. Note that when x is relatively large, its reduced influence on the predicted probability is consistent with the depiction of logistic probabilities in Figure 7.11.

EXAMPLE 7.10

Let's revisit Example 7.9.

a. Estimate and interpret the logistic regression model for the loan approval outcome y based on the applicant's percentage of down payment x_1 and the income-to-loan ratio x_2.

b. For an applicant with a 30% income-to-loan ratio, predict loan approval probabilities with down payments of 20% and 30%.

c. Compare the predicted probabilities based on the estimated logistic regression model with those from the estimated linear probability model in Example 7.9.

SOLUTION:

a. We use R to produce the logistic regression results shown in Table 7.18. (Instructions for estimating the logistic regression model with Analytic Solver and R are provided at the end of this section.)

TABLE 7.18 Logistic Regression Results for Example 7.10

	Estimate	Std. Error	z value	P (>|z|)
(Intercept)	−9.3671	3.1958	−2.931	0.003
x_1	0.1349	0.0640	2.107	0.035
x_2	0.1782	0.0646	2.758	0.006

As in the case of the linear probability model, both predictor variables exert a positive and statistically significant influence on loan approval at a 5% level, given positive estimated coefficients and p-values of 0.035 and 0.006, respectively. (In maximum likelihood estimation, the significance tests are valid only with large samples. Consequently, we conduct the z test, in place of the usual t test, to evaluate the statistical significance of a coefficient.)

b. The estimated probability equation is computed as

$$\hat{p} = \frac{\exp(-9.3671 + 0.1349x_1 + 0.1782x_2)}{1 + \exp(-9.3671 + 0.1349x_1 + 0.1782x_2)}.$$

The predicted loan approval probability with $x_1 = 20$ and $x_2 = 30$ is

$$\hat{p} = \frac{\exp(-9.3671 + 0.1349 \times 20 + 0.1782 \times 30)}{1 + \exp(-9.3671 + 0.1349 \times 20 + 0.1782 \times 30)} = 0.2103.$$

Similarly, the predicted loan approval probability with $x_1 = 30$ and $x_2 = 30$ is 0.5065. Note that, given an income-to-loan ratio of 30%, the predicted probability increases by 0.2962 (= 0.5065 – 0.2103) when the down payment increases from 20% to 30%. For the same income-to-loan ratio of 30%, it can be shown that the increase in the predicted probability is only 0.0449 (= 0.9833 – 0.9384) when the down payment increases from 50% to 60%.

c. Table 7.19 provides predicted probabilities for the linear probability and the logistic regression models for selected values of x_1 given $x_2 = 30$.

TABLE 7.19 Predicted Probabilities for the Linear Probability and the Logistic Regression Models

x_1	x_2	Linear Probability	Logistic
5	30	−0.0002	0.0340
20	30	0.2818	0.2103
30	30	0.4698	0.5065
50	30	0.8458	0.9384
60	30	1.0338	0.9833

As discussed earlier, with the linear probability model, the predicted probabilities can be negative or greater than one. The probabilities based on the logistic regression model stay between zero and one for all possible values of the predictor variables. Therefore, whenever possible, it is preferable to use the logistic regression model over the linear probability model in binary choice models.

Sometimes, analysts prefer to interpret the estimated logistic model in terms of the odds ratio. The odds ratio is defined as the ratio of the probability of success $P(y = 1)$ to the probability of failure $P(y = 0)$, or simply $\hat{p}/1 - \hat{p}$. The odds ratio metric is especially popular in sports and gambling.

Accuracy of Binary Choice Models

There is no universal goodness-of-fit measure for binary choice models that can be used to assess how well the model fits the data. Unlike in the case of the linear regression models, we cannot assess the performance of binary choice models based on the standard error of the estimate s_e, the coefficient of determination R^2, or adjusted R^2. The residual analysis is meaningless because the response variable can only take values 0 and 1, which then corresponds to two values for the residuals: $-\hat{y}$ for $y = 0$ and $1 - \hat{y}$ for $y = 1$.

It is common to assess the performance of linear probability and logistic regression models on the basis of the accuracy rates defined as the percentage of correctly classified observations. Using a default cutoff of 0.5, we compare the binary values of the response variable y with the binary predicted values that equal one if $\hat{y} \geq 0.5$ and zero if $\hat{y} < 0.5$, where $\hat{y}$ is the estimated probability. The accuracy rate is calculated as the number of correct predictions divided by the total number of observations.

THE ACCURACY RATE OF A BINARY CHOICE MODEL

Using the default cutoff of 0.5, the binary predicted values are calculated as 1 for $\hat{y} \geq 0.5$ and 0 for $\hat{y} < 0.5$. These values are then compared with the y values to compute the accuracy rate of the model as:

$$\frac{\text{number of correct predictions}}{\text{total number of observations}} \times 100$$

Although the accuracy measure is useful, it can sometimes be misleading. In applications with many ones and a few zeros, or many zeros and a few ones, the percentage of correctly classified observations can be high even when the model predicts the less likely outcome poorly. For example, in the case of fraud detection, we are interested primarily in identifying the fraudulent cases where the number of fraudulent cases often account for a very small percentage (less than 1%) of the total number of cases. A fraud detection model that classifies all the nonfraudulent cases correctly but misses most of the fraudulent cases is not very useful despite having an extremely high accuracy rate (> 99%). For this reason, it is better to report the percentage of correctly classified observations for both outcomes of the binary response variable, referred to as the sensitivity and the specificity measures.

Note that the relevance of performance measures, including accuracy, sensitivity, and specificity, depends on their related misspecification costs. Although the default for the cutoff value is 0.50, the analyst may choose a higher or lower cutoff value to improve a particular performance measure. Further details on performance measures and cutoff values are provided in Chapter 8.

EXAMPLE 7.11

For the mortgage approval example, compare the accuracy rates of the estimated linear probability model (LPM) with the estimated logistic regression model.

SOLUTION:

In order to compute the accuracy rates, we first find the predicted approval probabilities given the sample values of the predictor variables. For the first sample observation, we find the predicted approval as:

$$\hat{y} = -0.8682 + 0.0188 \times 16.35 + 0.0258 \times 49.94 = 0.7276 \text{ (LPM), and}$$

$$\hat{y} = \frac{\exp(-9.3671 + 0.1349 \times 16.35 + 0.1782 \times 49.94)}{1 + \exp(-9.3671 + 0.1349 \times 16.35 + 0.1782 \times 49.94)} = 0.8504 \text{ (Logistic).}$$

Because the predicted values for both models are greater than 0.5, their corresponding binary predicted values are one. Predictions for other sample observations are computed similarly; see Table 7.20 for a portion of these predictions.

TABLE 7.20 Computing the Accuracy Rates of Binary Choice Models

			Prediction		Binary Prediction	
y	x_1	x_2	LPM	Logistic	LPM	Logistic
1	16.35	49.94	0.7276	0.8504	1	1
1	34.43	56.16	1.2280	0.9950	1	1
⋮	⋮	⋮	⋮	⋮	⋮	⋮
0	17.85	26.86	0.1604	0.1022	0	0

We find that out of 30 observations, the binary predicted values match the values of y in 25 and 26 of the cases for the linear probability model and the logistic regression model, respectively. Therefore, the accuracy rate is 83.33% for the linear probability model and 86.67% for the logistic regression model. We infer that the logistic model provides better predictions than the linear probability model.

FILE
Mortgage

Using Analytic Solver and R to Estimate the Logistic Regression Model

Analytic Solver and R are useful when estimating the logistic regression model and finding the corresponding accuracy rates; we use the Mortgage data to replicate the results for Examples 7.10 and 7.11.

Using Analytic Solver

Before following the Analytic Solver instructions, make sure that you have read Appendix B ("Getting Started with Excel and Excel Add-Ins").

A. Open the ***Mortgage*** data file.

B. Choose **Data Mining > Classify > Logistic Regression** from the menu.

C. See Figure 7.12. Click on the ellipsis ... next to the *Data range* and highlight cells A1:C31. Make sure that the box preceding *First Row Contains Headers* is checked. The *Variables in Input Data* box will populate. Select and move variables x_1 and x_2 to *Selected Variables* box and y to *Output Variable* box. Accept other defaults and click *Next*.

FIGURE 7.12 Logistic regression dialog box

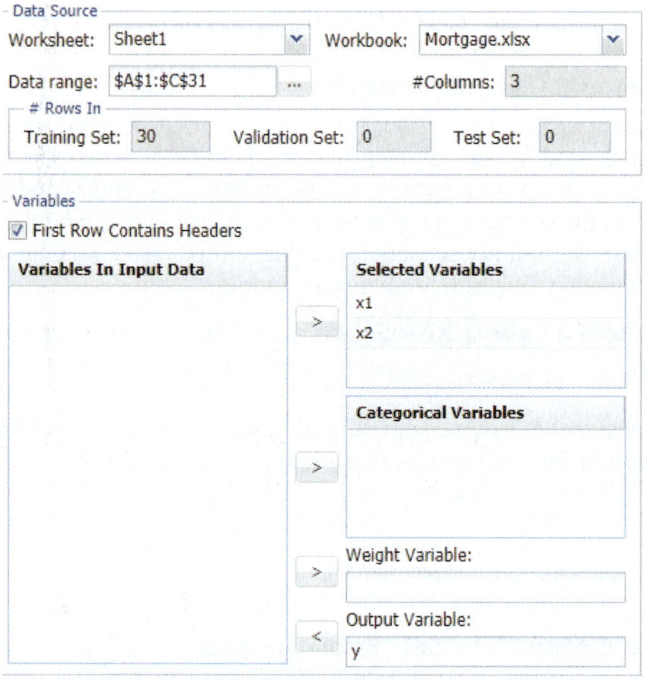

Source: Microsoft Excel

D. Check *Variance-Covariance Matrix* under *Regression: Display*; this is used to compute the standard errors for the significance tests. Click *Next* and accept the defaults. Click *Finish*.

E. Analytic Solver will produce a lot of output in separate worksheets. The top part of Figure 7.13 shows the relevant portion from the LogReg_Output worksheet.

FIGURE 7.13 Analytic Solver's relevant output for Examples 7.10 and 7.11

Coefficients

Predictor	Estimate
Intercept	-9.36708522
x1	0.13489783
x2	0.17822455

Variance-Covariance Matrix of Coefficients

Predictor	Intercept	x1	x2
Intercept	10.2143689	-0.1516609	-0.18255
x1	-0.15166087	0.0040976	0.001585
x2	-0.18255415	0.00158538	0.004177

Metrics

Metric	Value
Accuracy (#correct)	26
Accuracy (%correct)	86.66667

Source: Microsoft Excel

Note that the coefficient estimates are the same as those reported in Table 7.18. In order to find the standard errors, we take the positive square root of the diagonal elements of the variance-covariance matrix. For example, the standard error of $b_1 = \sqrt{0.0040976} = 0.0640$, which is the same as in Table 7.18. The z-value is calculated as $z = \frac{b_1}{se(b_1)} = \frac{0.1349}{0.0640} = 2.107$.

F. The bottom part of Figure 7.13 shows output from the LogReg_TrainingScore worksheet. We find that 26 observations, or 86.66667%, are correctly classified. Again, these results are the same as we derived in Example 7.11.

Using R

A. Import the ***Mortgage*** data into a data frame (table) and label it myData.

B. We use the **glm** function to construct a logistic regression model object, which is a generalized version of the **lm** function; we label this object as Logistic_Model. Within the function, we first specify y as a function of x_1 and x_2 and then use the *family* option to denote the type of model. Finally, we specify the data frame. Like the **lm** function, we will not see any immediate output after we enter the command. We use the *summary* function to obtain the output. Enter:

```
> Logistic_Model <- glm(y ~ x1 + x2, family = binomial(link = logit), data = myData)
> summary(Logistic_Model)
```

Figure 7.14 shows the R regression output. Note that the estimated logistic regression model results are the same as those reported in Table 7.18.

FIGURE 7.14 R's relevant output for Example 7.11

```
Coefficients:
              Estimate    Std. Error  z value   Pr(>|z|)
(Intercept)   -9.36709     3.19580    -2.931    0.00338  **
x1             0.13490     0.06401     2.107    0.03508  *
x2             0.17822     0.06463     2.758    0.00582  **
---
Signif. codes:   0 '***' 0.001 '**' 0.01 '*' 0.05 '.' 0.1 ' ' 1
```

C. We use the **predict** function to compute the predicted probabilities for the given sample values, labeled as Pred. Enter:

```
> Pred <- predict(Logistic_Model, type = "response")
```

D. We use the **round** function to construct the binary predicted values, labeled as Binary. If a predicted probability is 0.50 or more, then its corresponding binary value is 1; if a predicted probability is less than 0.5, then its corresponding binary value is 0. Enter:

```
> Binary <- round(Pred)
```

E. Both y and Binary now contain 0 and 1 values. We want to find the proportion of the values in the sample for which y equals Binary. Recall from Chapter 2 that the double equal sign (==) is used to compare the values of y and Binary. If the two values are the same, the operator returns 1, and 0 otherwise. We use the **mean** function to compute the proportion of correctly classified observations; we multiply by 100 to get a percentage. Enter:

```
> 100 * mean(myData$y == Binary)
```

R returns: [1] 86.66667.

EXERCISES 7.3

Mechanics

39. Consider a binary response variable y and a predictor variable x that varies between 0 and 4. The linear probability model is estimated as $\hat{y} = -1.11 + 0.54x$.
    a. Compute the estimated probability for $x = 2$ and $x = 3$.
    b. For what values of x is the estimated probability negative or greater than 1?

40. Consider a binary response variable y and a predictor variable x. The following table contains the parameter estimates of the linear probability model (LPM) and the logistic regression model, with the associated p-values shown in parentheses.

Variable	LPM	Logistic
Intercept	−0.72 (0.04)	−6.20 (0.04)
x	0.05 (0.06)	0.26 (0.02)

    a. Test for the significance of the intercept and the slope coefficients at the 5% level in both models.
    b. What is the predicted probability implied by the linear probability model for $x = 20$ and $x = 30$?
    c. What is the predicted probability implied by the logistic regression model for $x = 20$ and $x = 30$?

41. Consider a binary response variable y and two predictor variables x_1 and x_2. The following table contains the parameter estimates of the linear probability model (LPM) and the logistic regression model, with the associated p-values shown in parentheses.

Variable	LPM	Logistic
Intercept	−0.40 (0.03)	−2.20 (0.01)
x_1	0.32 (0.04)	0.98 (0.06)
x_2	−0.04 (0.01)	−0.20 (0.01)

    a. Comment on the significance of the variables.
    b. What is the predicted probability implied by the linear probability model for $x_1 = 4$ with x_2 equal to 10 and 20?
    c. What is the predicted probability implied by the logistic regression model for $x_1 = 4$ with x_2 equal to 10 and 20?

42. Using 30 observations, the following output was obtained when estimating the logistic regression model.

	Estimate	Std. Error	z value	$P(>\|z\|)$
Intercept	−0.188	0.083	2.27	0.024
x	3.852	1.771	2.18	0.030

    a. What is the predicted probability when $x = 0.40$?
    b. Is x significant at the 5% level?

43. **FILE** ***Exercise_7.43.*** The accompanying data file contains 20 observations on the binary response variable y along with the predictor variables x_1 and x_2.
    a. Estimate the linear probability model to compute $\hat{y}$ for $x_1 = 12$ and $x_2 = 8$.
    b. Estimate the logistic regression model to compute $\hat{y}$ for $x_1 = 12$ and $x_2 = 8$.

44. **FILE** ***Exercise_7.44.*** The accompanying data file contains 20 observations on the binary response variable y along with the predictor variables x_1 and x_2.
    a. Estimate and interpret the linear probability model and the logistic regression model.
    b. Compute the accuracy rates of both models.
    c. Use the preferred model to compute $\hat{y}$ for $x_1 = 60$ and $x_2 = 18$.

Applications

45. **FILE** ***Purchase.*** Annabel, a retail analyst, has been following Under Armour, Inc., the pioneer in the compression-gear market. Compression garments are meant to keep moisture away from a wearer's body during athletic activities in warm and cool weather. Annabel believes that the Under Armour brand attracts a younger customer, whereas the more established companies, Nike and Adidas, draw an older clientele. In order to test her belief, she collects data on the age of the customers and whether or not they purchased Under Armour (Purchase; 1 for purchase, 0 otherwise). A portion of the data is shown in the accompanying table.

Purchase	Age
1	30
0	19
⋮	⋮
1	24

    a. Estimate the linear probability model using Under Armour as the response variable and Age as the predictor variable.
    b. Compute the predicted probability of an Under Armour purchase for a 20-year-old customer and a 30-year-old customer.
    c. Test Annabel's belief that the Under Armour brand attracts a younger customer, at the 5% level.

46. **FILE** ***Purchase.*** Refer to the previous exercise for a description of the data set. Estimate the logistic regression model where the Under Armour purchase depends on age.
    a. Compute the predicted probability of an Under Armour purchase for a 20-year-old customer and a 30-year-old customer.

b. Test Annabel's belief that the Under Armour brand attracts a younger customer, at the 5% level.

47. FILE ***Parole.*** More and more parole boards are using risk assessment tools when trying to determine an individual's likelihood of returning to crime (*Prison Legal News*, February 2, 2016). Most of these models are based on a range of character traits and biographical facts about an individual. Many studies have found that older people are less likely to re-offend than younger ones. In addition, once released on parole, women are not likely to re-offend. A sociologist collects data on 20 individuals who were released on parole two years ago. She notes if the parolee committed another crime over the last two years (Crime equals 1 if crime committed, 0 otherwise), the parolee's age at the time of release, and the parolee's sex (Male equals 1 if male, 0 otherwise). The accompanying table shows a portion of the data.

Crime	Age	Male
1	25	1
0	42	1
⋮	⋮	⋮
0	30	1

a. Estimate the linear probability model where crime depends on age and the parolee's sex.

b. Are the results consistent with the claims of other studies with respect to age and the parolee's sex?

c. Predict the probability of a 25-year-old male parolee committing another crime; repeat the prediction for a 25-year-old female parolee.

48. FILE ***Parole.*** Refer to the previous exercise for a description of the data set.

a. Estimate the logistic regression model where crime depends on age and the parolee's sex.

b. Are the results consistent with the claims of other studies with respect to age and the parolee's sex?

c. Predict the probability of a 25-year-old male parolee committing another crime; repeat the prediction for a 25-year-old female parolee.

49. FILE ***Health_Insurance.*** According to the 2017 census, just over 90% of Americans have health insurance (*CNBC*, May 22, 2018). However, a higher percentage of Americans on the lower end of the economic spectrum are still without coverage. Consider a portion of data in the following table relating to insurance coverage (1 for coverage, 0 for no coverage) for 30 working individuals in Atlanta, Georgia. Also included in the table is the percentage of the premium paid by the employer and the individual's income (in $1,000s).

Insurance	Premium Percentage	Income
1	0	88
0	0	60
⋮	⋮	⋮
0	60	60

a. Analyze the linear probability model for insurance coverage with premium percentage and income used as the predictor variables.

b. Consider an individual with an income of $60,000. What is the probability that she has insurance coverage if her employer contributes 50% of the premium? What if her employer contributes 75% of the premium?

50. FILE ***Health_Insurance.*** Refer to the previous exercise for a description of the data set. Estimate the logistic regression model where insurance coverage depends on premium percentage and income. Consider an individual with an income of $60,000. What is the probability that she has insurance coverage if her employer contributes 50% of the premium? What if her employer contributes 75% of the premium?

51. FILE ***Assembly.*** Because assembly line work can be tedious and repetitive, it is not suited for everybody. Consequently, a production manager is developing a binary choice regression model to predict whether a newly hired worker will stay in the job for at least one year (Stay equals 1 if a new hire stays for at least one year, 0 otherwise). Three predictor variables will be used: (1) Age; (2) a Female dummy variable that equals 1 if the new hire is female, 0 otherwise; and (3) an Assembly dummy variable that equals 1 if the new hire has worked on an assembly line before, 0 otherwise. The accompanying table shows a portion of data for 32 assembly line workers.

Stay	Age	Female	Assembly
0	35	1	0
0	26	1	0
⋮	⋮	⋮	⋮
1	38	0	1

a. Estimate and interpret the linear probability model and the logistic regression model where being on the job one year later depends on Age, Female, and Assembly.

b. Compute the accuracy rates of both models.

c. Use the preferred model to predict the probability that a 45-year-old female who has not worked on an assembly line before will still be on the job one year later. What if she has worked on an assembly line before?

52. FILE ***CFA.*** The Chartered Financial Analyst (CFA) designation is the de facto professional certification for the financial

industry. Employers encourage their prospective employees to complete the CFA exam. Daniella Campos, an HR manager at SolidRock Investment, is reviewing 10 job applications. Given the low pass rate for the CFA Level 1 exam, Daniella wants to know whether or not the 10 prospective employees will be able to pass it. Historically, the pass rate is higher for those with work experience and a good college GPA. With this insight, she compiles the information on 263 current employees who took the CFA Level I exam last year, including the employee's success on the exam (1 for pass, 0 for fail), the employee's college GPA, and years of work experience. A portion of the data is shown in the accompanying table.

Pass	GPA	Experience
1	3.75	18
0	2.62	17
⋮	⋮	⋮
0	2.54	4

a. Estimate the linear probability model to predict the probability of passing the CFA Level I exam for a candidate with a college GPA of 3.80 and five years of experience.

b. Estimate the logistic regression model to predict the probability of passing the CFA Level I exam for a candidate with a college GPA of 3.80 and five years of experience.

53. **FILE** ***Admit.*** Unlike small selective colleges that pay close attention to personal statements, teacher recommendations, etc., large, public state university systems primarily rely on a student's grade point average (GPA) and scores on the SAT or ACT for the college admission decisions. Data were collected for 120 applicants on college admission (Admit equals 1 if admitted, 0 otherwise) along with the student's GPA and SAT scores. A portion of the data is shown in the accompanying table.

Admit	GPA	SAT
1	3.10	1550
0	2.70	1360
⋮	⋮	⋮
1	4.40	1320

a. Estimate and interpret the appropriate linear probability and the logistic regression models.

b. Compute the accuracy rates of both models.

c. Use the preferred model to predict the probability of admission for a college student with GPA = 3.0 and SAT = 1400. What if GPA = 4.0?

54. **FILE** ***Divorce.*** Divorce has become an increasingly prevalent part of American society. According to a 2019 Gallup poll, 77% of U.S. adults say divorce is morally acceptable, which is a 17-point increase since 2001 (*Gallup*, May 29, 2019). In general, the acceptability is higher for younger adults who are not very religious. A sociologist conducts a survey in a small Midwestern town where 200 American adults are asked about their opinion on divorce (Acceptable equals 1 if morally acceptable, 0 otherwise), religiosity (Religious equals 1 if very religious, 0 otherwise), and their age. A portion of the data is shown in the accompanying table.

Acceptable	Age	Religious
1	78	0
1	20	0
⋮	⋮	⋮
1	22	0

a. Estimate and interpret the appropriate linear probability and the logistic regression models.

b. Compute the accuracy rates of both models.

c. Use the preferred model to predict the probability that a 40-year old, very religious adult will find divorce morally acceptable. What if the adult is not very religious?

55. **FILE** ***STEM.*** Several studies have reported lower participation in the science, technology, engineering, and mathematics (STEM) careers by female and minority students. A high school counselor surveys 240 college-bound students, collecting information on whether the student has applied to a STEM field (1 if STEM, 0 otherwise), whether or not the student is female (1 if female, 0 otherwise), white (1 if white, 0 otherwise), and Asian (1 if Asian, 0 otherwise). Also included in the survey is the information on the student's high school GPA and the SAT scores. A portion of the data is shown in the accompanying table.

STEM	GPA	SAT	White	Female	Asian
0	3.70	1420	0	0	1
0	4.40	1240	0	1	1
⋮	⋮	⋮	⋮	⋮	⋮
0	3.80	1390	0	1	0

a. Estimate and interpret the logistic regression model using STEM as the response variable, and GPA, SAT, White, Female, and Asian as the predictor variables.

b. Find the predicted probability that a white male student will apply to a STEM field with GPA = 3.4 and SAT = 1400. Find the corresponding probabilities for an Asian male and a male who is neither white nor Asian.

c. Find the predicted probability that a white female student will apply to a STEM field with GPA = 3.4 and SAT = 1400. Find the corresponding probabilities for an Asian female and a female who is neither white nor Asian.

LO 7.4

7.4 CROSS-VALIDATION METHODS

Use cross-validation techniques to evaluate regression models.

In Section 6.2, we discussed goodness-of-fit measures—the standard error of the estimate s_e, the coefficient of determination R^2, and the adjusted R^2—that summarize how well the sample regression equation fits the data in linear regression models. Similarly, in Section 7.3, we assessed the performance of binary choice models on the basis of their accuracy rates. All these measures help us assess predictability in the sample data that was also used to build the model. Unfortunately, these measures do not help us gauge how well an estimated model will predict in an unseen sample.

It is possible for a model to perform really well with the data set used for estimation, but then perform miserably once a new data set is used. Recall that in linear regression models, we can easily improve the fit, as measured by R^2, by including a whole bunch of predictor variables, some of which may have no economic justification. We often call modelling of this sort **overfitting**. Overfitting occurs when an estimated model begins to describe the quirks of the data rather than the real relationships between variables. By making the model conform too closely to the given data, the model's predictive power is compromised. The overfit model will fail to describe the behavior in a new sample that has its own quirks. Although the adjusted R^2 imposes a penalty for additional predictor variables, the measure still suffers from the fact that the same data are used for both estimation and assessment.

OVERFITTING

Overfitting occurs when a regression model is made overly complex to fit the quirks of given sample data. By making the model conform too closely to the sample data, its predictive power is compromised.

A useful method to assess the predictive power of a model is to test it on a data set not used in estimation. **Cross-validation** is a technique that evaluates predictive models by partitioning the original sample into a **training set** to build (train) the model and a **validation set** to evaluate (validate) it. Although training set performance can be assessed, it may result in overly optimistic estimates because it is based on the same data as were used to build the model. Therefore, a validation set is used to provide an independent performance assessment by exposing the model to unseen data. Sometimes, the data are partitioned into an optional third set called a test data set; further detail is provided in Chapters 8, 9, and 10.

CROSS-VALIDATION

Cross-validation is a technique in which the sample is partitioned into a training set to estimate the model and a validation set to assess how well the estimated model predicts with unseen data.

In this section, we will examine two cross-validation methods: the **holdout method** and the ***k*-fold cross-validation method**. For both methods, it is common to use the root mean squared error (RMSE) on the validation set to assess the linear regression models, where $\text{RMSE} = \sqrt{\frac{\Sigma(y-\hat{y})^2}{n^*}}$ and n^* is the number of observations in the validation set. Recall that RMSE is the square root of mean squared error (MSE). In addition to RMSE, other important performance measures include the mean absolute deviation (MAD) and the mean absolute percentage error (MAPE); these measures are discussed in Chapter 8. To assess binary choice models, we use the accuracy rate computed as the percentage of correctly classified observations in the validation set; other performance measures are discussed in Chapter 8.

Note that the predictability is likely to be higher in the training set as compared to the validation set because the model is built from the training set. In other words, the RMSE will be lower, and the accuracy rate will be higher, in the training set as compared to the validation set. In general, a large discrepancy between the RMSE (or the accuracy rates) of the training and validation sets is indicative of the overfitting problem discussed earlier; the model fits the training data set very well but fails to generalize to an unseen data set.

The Holdout Method

The simplest of the cross-validation methods is the holdout method. The sample data set is partitioned into two independent and mutually exclusive data sets—the training set and the validation set. Figure 7.15 shows the partitioning of the sample data into two distinct sets. There is no rule as to how the sample data should be partitioned. Ideally, we should make random draws when partitioning the data. For illustration purposes, we will use the first 75% of the observations for the training set and the remaining 25% of the observations for the validation set. It is easy to make random draws in Analytic Solver and R for the partitioning of the data.

FIGURE 7.15 Partitioning the sample for the holdout method

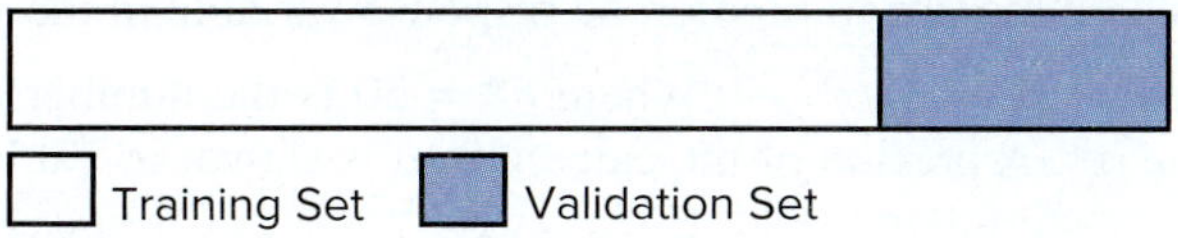

The holdout method is implemented as follows:

A. We partition the sample data into two parts, labeled training set and validation set.

B. We use the training set to estimate competing models.

C. We use the estimates from the training set to predict the response variable in the validation set.

D. We calculate the RMSE (or the accuracy rate) for each competing model. The preferred model will have the smallest RMSE (or the largest accuracy rate).

Ideally, we would like the model with the best performance in the training set to also have the best performance in the validation set. For example, we would like that the linear regression model with the highest adjusted R^2 also have the lowest RMSE in the validation set. As discussed earlier, conflicting results between the two is a sign of overfitting. Data analytics professionals generally rely on cross-validation for model selection if they have a sufficient number of observations in the training and the validation sets for effective estimation and assessment, respectively. After selecting the best model, we generally reestimate this model with the entire data set for making predictions.

EXAMPLE 7.12

FILE *Gender_Gap*

The objective outlined in the introductory case is to analyze the gender gap in salaries of project managers. Consider two models to analyze a project manager's salary. For predictor variables, Model 1 uses Size, Experience, Female, and Grad, whereas Model 2 also includes the interactions between Female with Experience, Female with Grad, and Size with Experience. Use the holdout method to compare the predictability of both models using the first 150 observations for training and the remaining 50 observations for validation.

SOLUTION:

We use the training set with 150 observations to estimate Model 1 and Model 2. The estimates are presented in Table 7.21.

TABLE 7.21 Estimates of the Competing Models, Example 7.12

Variable	Model 1	Model 2
Constant	7.4453	56.1077
Size	0.1136	−0.1185
Experience	4.2250	1.0891
Female	−23.2909	7.3771
Grad	15.6116	15.2640
Female × Experience	NA	−2.0428
Female × Grad	NA	2.2042
Size × Experience	NA	0.0150
Adjusted R^2	0.6896	0.7284

Notes: Parameter estimates; NA denotes not applicable.

Based on the training set, Model 2 is more suitable for prediction because it has a higher adjusted R^2 than Model 1 (0.7284 > 0.6896). There is no guarantee, however, that Model 2 will also have a better predictability in the validation set. We use the estimated models to predict the response variable in the validation set and compute the RMSE $= \sqrt{\frac{\Sigma(y - \hat{y})^2}{n^*}}$, where $n^* = 50$ is the number of observations in the validation set. A portion of the calculations is shown in Table 7.22.

TABLE 7.22 Analysis of the Holdout Method, Example 7.12

Observation	y	$\hat{y}$ (Model 1)	$\hat{y}$ (Model 2)
151	117	113.2913	105.8106
152	125	121.3257	126.1153
⋮	⋮	⋮	⋮
200	117	110.6685	110.4045
RMSE		11.31	12.54

Interestingly, Model 2, with a better performance in the training set, does poorer in the validation set (12.54 > 11.31). Based on the results, Model 1 would be preferred for prediction.

FILE
AnnArbor

EXAMPLE 7.13

In Example 7.8, we used in-sample measures to compare two models, where Model 1 used Rent and Model 2 used ln(Rent) as the response variable. Recall that these models were referred to as Models 2 and 4, respectively, and the predictor variables for both models included Beds, Baths, and ln(Sqft). Use the holdout method to compare the predictability of the two competing models, using the first 30 observations for training and the remaining 10 observations for validation.

SOLUTION:

We use the training set with 30 observations to estimate Model 1 and Model 2. The estimates are presented in Table 7.23.

TABLE 7.23 Estimates of the Competing Models, Example 7.13

Variable	Model 1	Model 2
Constant	−2674.2552	2.5742
Beds	123.6672	0.0975
Baths	18.0267	−0.0025
Ln(Sqft)	496.9671	0.6004
s_e	104.2082	0.0854

Notes: Standard error of the estimate s_e is used for making predictions with Model 2.

We use the estimated models to predict the response variable in the validation set and compute the resulting RMSE $= \sqrt{\frac{\Sigma(y - \hat{y})^2}{n^*}}$, where $n^* = 10$ is the number of observations in the validation set. A portion of the calculations is shown in Table 7.24.

TABLE 7.24 Analysis of the Holdout Method, Example 7.13

Observation	y	$\hat{y}$ (Model 1)	$\hat{y}$ (Model 2)
31	1518	1447.4587	1523.5103
32	1600	1328.9161	1385.7901
⋮	⋮	⋮	⋮
40	2400	1668.3540	2013.7291
RMSE		362.52	422.25

Thus, Model 1 is considered a better predictor than Model 2 (362.52 < 422.25) based on this cross-validation method. These results are consistent with the analysis with in-sample measures in Example 7.8.

In Example 7.14, we use the holdout method to assess binary choice models.

EXAMPLE 7.14

FILE *Spam*

Peter Derby works as a cyber security analyst at a private equity firm. His colleagues at the firm have been inundated by a large number of spam e-mails. Peter has been asked to implement a spam detection system on the company's e-mail server. He analyzes a sample of 500 spam and legitimate e-mails with the following relevant variables: spam (1 if spam, 0 otherwise), the number of recipients, the number of hyperlinks, and the number of characters in the message. A portion of the data is shown in the accompanying table.

TABLE 7.25 Spam Data ($n = 500$)

Record	Spam	Recipients	Hyperlinks	Characters
1	0	19	1	47
2	0	15	1	58
⋮	⋮	⋮	⋮	⋮
500	1	13	2	32

a. Use the holdout method to compare the accuracy rates of two competing logistic models for spam, using the first 375 observations for training and the remaining 125 observations for validation. Model 1 uses Recipients, Hyperlinks, and Characters as predictor variables, whereas Model 2 drops the predictor variable(s) found to be statistically insignificant in Model 1.

b. Re-estimate the preferred model to predict the probability of spam if the number of recipients, hyperlinks, and characters are 20, 5, and 60, respectively.

SOLUTION:

a. We use the training set with 375 observations to estimate two logistic models; see Table 7.26 for the estimates. Note that in Model 1, the variable, Characters, is not statistically significant at the 5% level and is, therefore, dropped in Model 2.

TABLE 7.26 Estimates of the pam Data ($n = 500$)

Variable	Model 1	Model 2
Constant	−5.1778* (0.000)	−5.8045* (0.000)
Recipients	0.1765* (0.000)	0.1806* (0.000)
Hyperlinks	0.5473* (0.000)	0.5402* (0.000)
Characters	−0.0104 (0.074)	NA

Notes: Parameter estimates are followed with the *p*-values in parentheses; NA denotes not applicable; * represents significance at the 5% level.

To compute the accuracy rates of the estimated logistic binary choice models, we first compute the predicted probabilities of the models in the validation set; a portion of the calculations is shown in Table 7.27.

TABLE 7.27 Analysis of the Holdout Method, Example 7.14

Record	Spam	Prediction		Binary Prediction	
		Model 1	Model 2	Model 1	Model 2
376	0	0.4734	0.5367	0	1
377	0	0.6963	0.7037	1	1
⋮	⋮	⋮	⋮	⋮	⋮
500	1	0.1070	0.0850	0	0

By converting the predicted probabilities into binary predictions and comparing them with the actual spam data, we find that the accuracy rates for Model 1 and Model 2 are 68.00% and 65.60%, respectively. Based on these rates, we infer that Model 1 is superior to Model 2 (68.00% > 65.60%).

b. We re-estimate Model 1 with all 500 observations to predict the spam probability with the number of recipients, hyperlinks, and characters as 20, 5, and 60, respectively, as:

$$\widehat{Spam} = \frac{\exp(-3.8243 + 0.1075 \times 20 + 0.5133 \times 5 - 0.0141 \times 60)}{1 + \exp(-3.8243 + 0.1075 \times 20 + 0.5133 \times 5 - 0.0141 \times 60)} = 0.51.$$

Using Analytic Solver and R for the Holdout Method for the Logistic Regression Model

Analytic Solver and R are easy to use for partitioning the data, estimating models with the training set, and deriving the necessary cross-validation measures. As mentioned earlier, we generally use random draws for partitioning the sample data into the training and validation sets. Here, for replicating purposes, we will continue to use the latter part of the sample data for the validation set. We use the ***Spam*** data to replicate the results in Example 7.14 for Model 1; results for Model 2 can be derived similarly.

FILE *Spam*

Using Analytic Solver

A. Open the ***Spam*** data file. In column F of the data file, create a variable called Flag with the letter T for the first 375 observations and the letter V for the remaining 125 observations; here T and V denote training and validation, respectively.

B. From the menu, choose **Data Mining > Partition > Standard Partition.**

Specify the *Data range* by highlighting cells A1:F501. Select and move variables Spam, Recipients, Hyperlinks, and Characters to the *Selected Variables* box. Although there is an option to pick up rows randomly, for *Partitioning Options*, we select *Use partition variable.* Select and move Flag to the *Use partition variable* box; see the relevant portion of the screen shot in Figure 7.16. Click *OK.* The STDPartition worksheet now contains partitioned data with 375 observations in the training set and 125 observations in the validation set.

FIGURE 7.16 Partitioning the sample with Analytic Solver

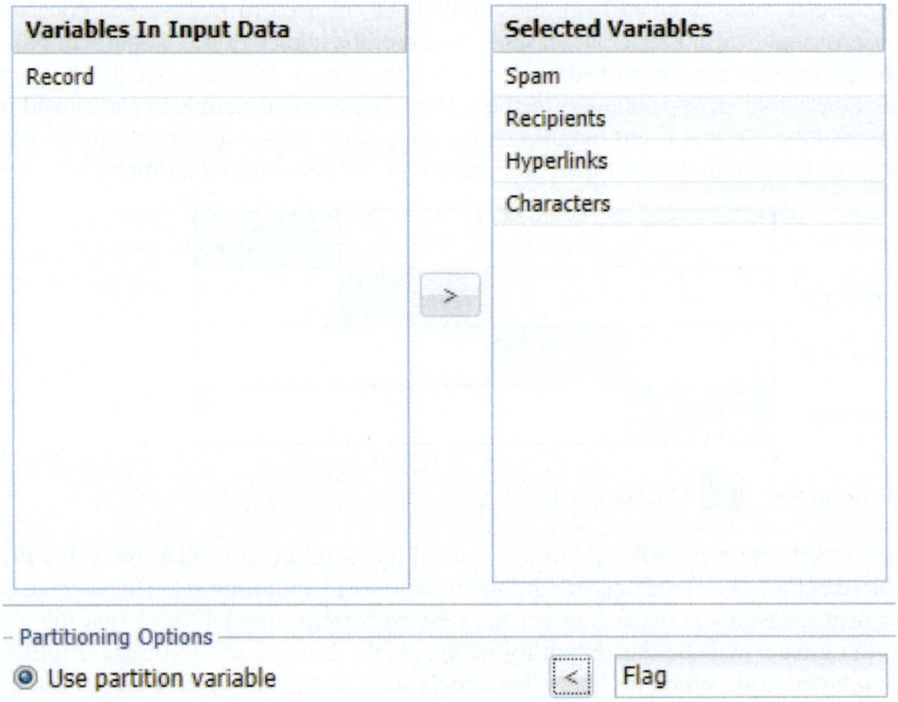

Source: Microsoft Excel

C. Make sure the STDPartition worksheet is active, then choose **Data Mining > Classify > Logistic Regression**. Select and move variables Recipients, Hyperlinks, and Characters to the *Selected Variables* box and Spam to the *Output Variable* box. Click *Finish.* In the LogReg_ValidationScore worksheet, you will find Accuracy (%correct) equal to 68. This is the same as derived for Model 1 in Example 7.14.

Using R

A. Import the ***Spam*** data into a data frame (table) and label it myData.

B. We partition the sample into training and validation sets, labeled TData and VData, respectively. Enter:

```
> TData <- myData[1:375,]
> VData <- myData[376:500,]
```

C. We use the training set, TData, to estimate Model 1. Enter:

```
>Model1 <- glm(Spam ~ Recipients+Hyperlinks+Characters,
  family=binomial(link = logit), data = TData)
```

D. We use the estimates to make predictions for VData and then convert them into a binary prediction. Finally, we compute the accuracy rate in the validation set. Enter:

```
> Pred1 <- predict(Model1, VData, type="response")
> Binary1 <- round(Pred1)
> 100*mean(VData$Spam == Binary1)
R returns: [1] 68
```

This is the same as derived for Model 1 in Example 7.14.

The *k*-Fold Cross-Validation Method

The main limitation of the holdout method is that the experiment is performed only once where the estimates obtained from the training set are used to make predictions for the response variable with the validation set. Therefore, the choice of the model will be sensitive to how the data are partitioned. A popular method that is less sensitive to data partition is called the *k*-fold cross-validation method. Here, the original sample is partitioned into k subsets, and the one that is left out in each iteration is the validation set. In other words, we perform the holdout method k times. In Figure 7.17, we show the experiments with $k = 4$.

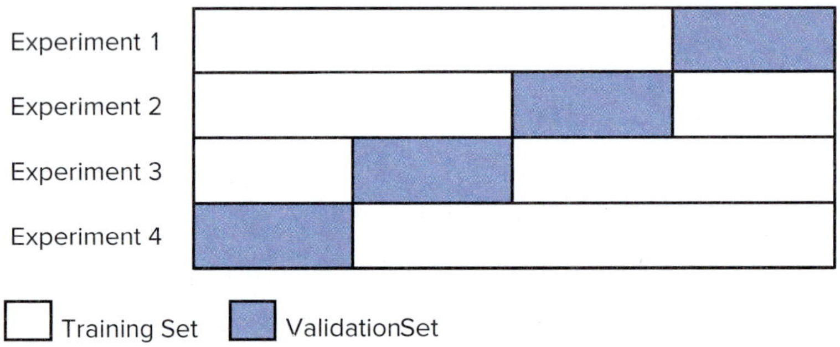

FIGURE 7.17 Partitioning the sample for the *k*-fold method

As mentioned above, in each experiment, one of the k subsets is used as the validation set and the remaining $k - 1$ subsets are put together to form a training set. The average of the assessment measures is used to select the best-performing model. Note that the greater the k, the greater will be the reliability of the k-fold method and the greater will be its computational cost. When k equals the sample size, the resulting method is also called the **leave-one-out cross-validation method**, where you leave out just one observation for the validation set.

> **THE HOLDOUT AND THE *k*-FOLD CROSS-VALIDATION METHODS**
>
> In the holdout method, the sample data set is partitioned into two independent and mutually exclusive data sets—the training set and the validation set. In the *k*-fold cross-validation method, the sample data are partitioned into k subsets, where one

of the k subsets is used as the validation set and the remaining $k - 1$ subsets are put together to form a training set. By averaging the assessment measures, the k-fold cross-validation method is less sensitive to data partitioning than the holdout method.

EXAMPLE 7.15

FILE
Gender_Gap

In Example 7.12, we used the holdout method to assess two models for analyzing a project manager's salary. For predictors, Model 1 used Size, Experience, Female, and Grad. Model 2 extends the model by also including the interactions between Female with Experience, Female with Grad, and Size with Experience. Use the k-fold cross-validation method to compare the predictability of the models using $k = 4$.

SOLUTION:

We assess both models four times with the validation set formed by the observations 151–200, 101–150, 51–100, and 1–50, respectively. Each time the training set includes the remaining observations for estimating the regression models. In Table 7.28, we also present RMSE $= \sqrt{\frac{\Sigma(y - \hat{y})^2}{n^*}}$ for both models, where $n^* = 50$ is the number of observations in the validation set.

TABLE 7.28 RMSE for the k-Fold Cross-Validation Method with $k = 4$, Example 7.15

Observations in Validation Set	Model 1	Model 2
151–200	11.31	12.54
101–150	12.26	11.88
51–100	13.30	12.09
1–50	13.76	13.46
Average	12.66	12.49

In Example 7.12 we had noted that Model 1 performed better in the validation set even though it did poorer in the testing set. With the k-fold cross-validation method, we observe that the performance of Model 1 is better only when observations 151–200 are used in the validation set. For every other partitioning, Model 2 is better, giving it a lower average RMSE ($12.49 < 12.66$). We conclude that Model 2 is a superior model for prediction. Whenever possible, it is better to use the more reliable k-fold cross-validation method.

We can similarly assess the predictability of binary choice models with the k-fold cross-validation method, using the average accuracy rate for model comparison.

As you may have noticed, the k-fold cross-validation method is quite involved. Software packages such as R provide several ways to automatize the process. In this chapter, we focus primarily on the partitioning based on fixed draws of the observations. For instance, in Example 7.15, we partitioned the data into four equal parts, based on how the data appeared in the sample. Software packages often use random draws of the observations for the partitioning. Consequently, the results from these packages are not identical to the ones we obtain with fixed partitioning; for the most part, however, the decision is not impacted by the method used. In Appendix 7.1, we introduce the popular *caret* package in R for implementing the k-fold cross-validation method, which we will revisit in Chapters 9 and 10.

EXERCISES 7.4

Mechanics

56. **FILE** ***Exercise_7.56.*** The accompanying data file contains 40 observations on the response variable *y* along with the predictor variables *x* and *d*. Consider two linear regression models where Model 1 uses the variables *x* and *d* and Model 2 extends the model by including the interaction variable *xd*. Use the holdout method to compare the predictability of the models using the first 30 observations for training and the remaining 10 observations for validation.

57. **FILE** ***Exercise_7.57.*** The accompanying data file contains 40 observations on the response variable *y* along with the predictor variables x_1 and x_2. Use the holdout method to compare the predictability of the linear model with the exponential model using the first 30 observations for training and the remaining 10 observations for validation.

58. **FILE** ***Exercise_7.58.*** The accompanying data file contains 40 observations on the binary response variable *y* along with the predictor variables x_1 and x_2. Use the holdout method to compare the accuracy rates of the linear probability model with the logistic regression model using the first 30 observations for training and the remaining 10 observations for validation.

Applications

59. **FILE** ***IceCream.*** The accompanying data file contains 35 observations for an ice cream truck driver's daily income (Income in $), number of hours on the road (Hours), whether it was a particularly hot day (Hot = 1 if the high temperature was above 85°F, 0 otherwise), and whether it was a Holiday (Holiday = 1, 0 otherwise). Consider two models where Model 1 predicts Income on the basis of Hours, Hot, and Holiday and Model 2 also includes the interaction between Hot and Holiday. Use the holdout method to compare the predictability of the models using the first 24 observations for training and the remaining 11 observations for validation.

60. **FILE** ***Mobile_Devices.*** The accompanying data file contains survey data for 80 participants with information on average daily time spent on mobile devices (Usage, in minutes), household income (Income, in $1,000s), lived in a rural area (Rural = 1 if rural, 0 otherwise), and had a college degree (College = 1 if college graduate, 0 otherwise). Consider two predictive models for mobile device usage where Model 1 is based on Income, Rural, and College and Model 2 also includes the interaction between Rural and College.
    a. Use the holdout method to compare the predictability of the models using the first 60 observations for training and the remaining 20 observations for validation.
    b. Use the *k*-fold cross-validation method to compare the predictability of the models using $k = 4$.

61. **FILE** ***BMI.*** The accompanying data file contains salary data (in $1,000s) for 30 college-educated men with their respective BMI and a dummy variable that represents 1 for a white man and 0 otherwise. Model 1 predicts Salary using BMI and White as predictor variables. Model 2 includes BMI and White along with an interaction between the two.
    a. Use the holdout method to compare the predictability of the models using the first 20 observations for training and the remaining 10 observations for validation.
    b. Use the *k*-fold cross-validation method to compare the predictability of the models using $k = 3$.

62. **FILE** ***Pick_Errors.*** The accompanying data file contains information on 30 employee's annual pick errors (Errors), experience (Exper in years), and whether or not the employee attended training (Train equals 1 if the employee attended training, 0 otherwise). Model 1 predicts Errors using Exper and Train as predictor variables. Model 2 includes Exper and Train along with an interaction between the two.
    a. Use the holdout method to compare the predictability of the models using the first 20 observations for training and the remaining 10 observations for validation.
    b. Use the *k*-fold cross-validation method to compare the predictability of the models using $k = 3$.

63. **FILE** ***Health_Factors.*** The accompanying data file contains survey information on 120 American adults who rated their health (Health) and social connections (Social) on a scale of 1 to 100. The file also contains information on their household income (Income, in $1,000s) and college education (College equals 1 if they have completed a bachelor's degree, 0 otherwise). Consider two linear regression models for Health. Model 1 uses Social, Income, and College as the predictor variables, whereas Model 2 also includes the interactions of Social with Income and Social with College.
    a. Use the holdout method to compare the predictability of the models using the first 90 observations for training and the remaining 30 observations for validation.
    b. Use the *k*-fold cross-validation method to compare the predictability of the models using $k = 4$.

64. **FILE** ***Rental.*** The accompanying data file contains monthly data on rent (Rent, in $) along with square footage (Sqft), number of bedrooms (Bed), and number of bathrooms (Bath) of 80 rental units. Consider two linear regression models for Rent. Model 1 uses Bed, Bath, and Sqft, whereas Model 2 also allows the interaction between Bed and Sqft.
    a. Use the holdout method to compare the predictability of the models using the first 60 observations for training and the remaining 20 observations for validation.
    b. Use the *k*-fold cross-validation method to compare the predictability of the models using $k = 4$.

65. FILE ***Crew_Size.*** The accompanying data file contains weekly data on crew size (the number of workers) and productivity (jobs/week) over the past 27 weeks. A linear regression model and a quadratic regression model are considered for predicting productivity on the basis of crew size.
   a. Use the holdout method to compare the predictability of the models using the first 18 observations for training and the remaining 9 observations for validation.
   b. Use the k-fold cross-validation method to compare the predictability of the models using $k = 3$.

66. FILE ***Happiness.*** The accompanying data file contains information on 100 working adults' self-assessed happiness on a scale of 0 to 100, along with their age and annual income. Consider two quadratic models for happiness. Model 1 is based on age, age^2, and income. Model 2 is based on age, age^2, and ln(income).
   a. Use the holdout method to compare the predictability of the models using the first 75 observations for training and the remaining 25 observations for validation.
   b. Use the k-fold cross-validation method to compare the predictability of the models using $k = 4$.

67. FILE ***Electricity.*** Consider a regression model for predicting monthly electricity cost (Cost in $) on the basis of average outdoor temperature (Temp in °F), working days per month (Days), and tons of product produced (Tons). The accompanying data file contains data on 80 observations. Use the holdout method to compare the predictability of the linear and the exponential regression models using the first 60 observations for training and the remaining 20 observations for validation.

68. FILE ***Arlington_Homes.*** The accompanying data file contains information on the sale price (in $) for 36 single-family homes in Arlington, Massachusetts. In order to analyze house price, the predictor variables include the house's square footage (Sqft), the number of bedrooms (Beds), the number of bathrooms (Baths), and whether or not it is a colonial (Col = 1 if colonial, 0 otherwise).
   a. Use the holdout method to compare the predictability of the linear and the exponential models using the first 24 observations for training and the remaining 12 observations for validation.
   b. Use the k-fold cross-validation method to compare the predictability of the models using $k = 3$.

69. FILE ***Purchase.*** Consider the accompanying data to predict an Under Armour purchase (Purchase; 1 for purchase, 0 otherwise) on the basis of customer age.
   a. Use the holdout method to compare the accuracy rates of the linear probability model (Model 1) and the logistic regression model (Model 2) using the first 20 observations for training and the remaining 10 observations for validation.
   b. Use the k-fold cross-validation method to compare the accuracy of the models using $k = 3$.

70. FILE ***Divorce.*** Consider the accompanying data to analyze how people view divorce (Acceptable equals 1 if morally acceptable, 0 otherwise) on the basis of age and religiosity (Religious equals 1 if very religious, 0 otherwise).
   a. Use the holdout method to compare the accuracy rates of two competing logistic models for divorce, using the first 150 observations for training and the remaining 50 observations for validation. Model 1 uses Age and Religious as predictor variables, whereas Model 2 also incudes the interaction between Age and Religious.
   b. Use the k-fold cross-validation method to compare the accuracy of the models using $k = 4$.

7.5 WRITING WITH BIG DATA

FILE
College_Admission

As mentioned in Chapter 6, when using regression analysis with big data, the emphasis is placed on the model's predictability and not necessarily on tests of significance. In this section, we will use logistic regression models for predicting college admission and enrollment decisions. Before running the models, we have to first filter out the ***College_Admission*** data to get the appropriate subset of observations for selected variables. We encourage you to replicate the results in the report.

Case Study

Create a sample report to analyze admission and enrollment decisions at the school of arts & letters in a selective four-year college in North America. For predictor variables, include the applicant's sex, ethnicity, grade point average, and SAT scores. Make predictions for the admission probability and the enrollment probability using typical values of the predictor variables.

Sample Report—College Admission and Enrollment

Rawpixel.com/Shutterstock

College admission can be stressful for both students and parents as there is no magic formula when it comes to admission decisions. Two important factors considered for admission are the student's high school record and performance on standardized tests. According to the National Association for College Admission Counseling (NACAC), a student's high school record carries more weight than standardized test scores.

Just as prospective students are anxious about receiving an acceptance letter, most colleges are concerned about meeting their enrollment targets. The number of acceptances a college sends out depends on its enrollment target and admissions yield, defined as the percentage of students who enroll at the school after being admitted. It is difficult to predict admissions yield as it depends on the college's acceptance rate as well as the number of colleges to which students apply. As the number of applications for admission and the number of acceptances increase, the yield decreases.

In this report, we analyze factors that affect the probability of college admission and enrollment at a school of arts & letters in a selective four-year college in North America. Predictors include the applicant's high school GPA, SAT score,[1] and the Male, White, and Asian dummy variables capturing the applicant's sex and ethnicity. In Table 7.29, we present the representative applicant profile.

TABLE 7.29 Applicant Profile for the School of Arts & Letters

Variable	Applied	Admitted	Enrolled
Male Applicant (%)	30.76	27.37	26.68
White Applicant (%)	55.59	61.13	69.83
Asian Applicant (%)	12.42	11.73	8.73
Other Applicant (%)	31.99	27.14	21.45
High School GPA (Average)	3.50	3.86	3.74
SAT Score (Average)	1,146	1,269	1,229
Number of Applicants	6,964	1,739	401

Of the 6,964 students who applied to the school of arts & letters, 30.76% were males; in addition, the percentages of white and Asian applicants were 55.59% and 12.42%, respectively, with about 32.00% from other ethnicities. The average applicant had a GPA of 3.50 and an SAT score of 1146. Table 7.29 also shows that 1,739 (or 24.97%) applicants were granted admission, of which 401 (23.06%) decided to enroll. As expected, the average GPA and SAT scores of admitted applicants are higher than those who applied and those who enrolled, but to a lesser extent.

Two logistic regression models are estimated using the same predictor variables, one for predicting the admission probability and the other for predicting the enrollment probability. The entire pool of 6,964 applicants is used for the first regression, whereas 1,739 admitted applicants are used for the second regression. The results are presented in Table 7.30.

With accuracy rates of 81% and 77%, respectively, both models do a good job with predicting probabilities. It seems that the sex of the applicant plays no role in the admission or enrollment

[1]The higher of SAT and ACT scores is included in the data where for comparison, ACT scores on reading and math are first converted into SAT scores.

TABLE 7.30 Logistic Regressions for College Admission and Enrollment

Variable	Admission	Enrollment
Constant	−17.5732* (−37.41)	7.2965* (8.48)
Male Dummy Variable	0.0459 (0.61)	−0.1433 (−1.05)
White Dummy Variable	−0.3498* (−4.43)	0.7653* (5.15)
Asian Dummy Variable	−0.4140* (−3.57)	−0.0074 (−0.03)
High School GPA	2.7629* (25.74)	−1.4265* (−7.17)
SAT Score	0.0056* (20.93)	−0.0028* (−5.99)
Accuracy (%)	81	77
Number of Observations	6,964	1,739

Notes: Parameter estimates are in the top half of the table with the z-statistics given in parentheses; * represents significance at the 5% level. Accuracy (%) measures the percentage of correctly classified observations.

decisions. Interestingly, both white and Asian applicants have a lower probability of admission than those from other ethnicities. Perhaps this is due to affirmative action, whereby colleges admit a proportionally higher percentage of underrepresented applicants. As expected, quality applicants, in terms of both GPA and SAT, are pursued for admission.

On the enrollment side, admitted applicants who are white are more likely to enroll than all other admitted applicants. Finally, admitted applicants with high GPA and high SAT scores are less likely to enroll at this college. This is not surprising because academically strong applicants will have many offers, which lowers the probability that an applicant will accept the admission offer of a particular college.

In order to further interpret the influence of SAT scores on college admission and enrollment, we compute predicted admission and enrollment probabilities for representative males from all ethnicities with a GPA of 3.8 and SAT scores varying between 1000 and 1600. The results are shown in Figures 7.18 and 7.19.

FIGURE 7.18 Predicted Admission Probability

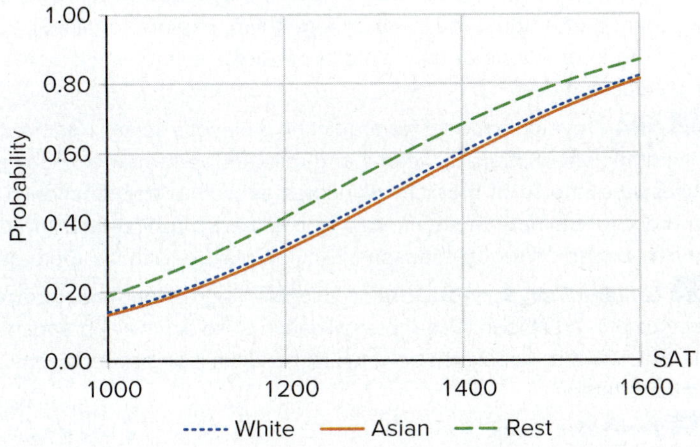

Consider the case of a representative male applicant with an SAT score of 1300. For a white male, the predicted probabilities of admission and enrollment are 47% and 24%, respectively. The corresponding probabilities are 45% and 13%, respectively, for Asians and 55% and 13%, respectively, for all other ethnicities. The probabilities get closer as SAT scores increase. Higher

FIGURE 7.19 Predicted Enrollment Probability

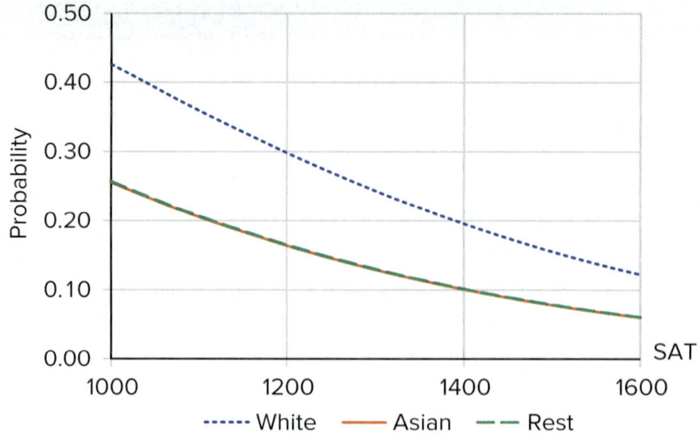

admission rate for underrepresented applicants is consistent with the admission practices at other colleges that believe that diversity enriches the educational experience for all.

Unfortunately, despite a higher admission rate, the lower admission yield at this college for underrepresented applicants makes the percentage of those who actually enroll even lower than the percentage of those who apply. As we can observe in Table 7.18, about 23% of underrepresented applicants applied for admission, but the percentage of those who enrolled dropped to 21.45%. This is consistent with an article in *The New York Times* (August 24, 2017) that found that black and Hispanic students are more underrepresented at the nation's top colleges and universities than they were 35 years ago. The yield for Asian applicants is the lowest at 8.73%. It is advised that the college explore the reasons for the especially low admission yield of nonwhite applicants and finds ways to raise it.

Suggested Case Studies

Many predictive models can be estimated and assessed with the big data that accompany this text. Here are some suggestions.

Report 7.1 FILE ***College_Admissions***. Choose a college of interest and use the sample of enrolled students to best predict a student's college grade point average. Explore interactions of the relevant predictor variables and use cross validation to select the best predictive model. In order to estimate these models, you have to first filter the data to include only the enrolled students.

Report 7.2 FILE ***House_Price***. Choose two comparable college towns. Develop a predictive model for the sale price of a house for each college town. Explore log-linear transformations, dummy variables, and interactions of the relevant predictor variables. Use cross validation to select the best predictive model.

Report 7.3 FILE ***NBA***. Develop a model for predicting a player's salary. For predictor variables, consider age (quadratic effect), height, weight, and relevant performance measures. Use cross validation to assess the choice of predictor variables as well as the functional form (linear or exponential). In order to estimate these models, you will have to first filter the data to include only career statistics based on regular seasons. Exclude players with no information on salary.

Report 7.4 FILE ***Longitudinal_Survey***. Develop a logistic regression model for predicting if the respondent is outgoing in adulthood. Use cross validation to select the appropriate predictor variables. In order to estimate this model, you have to first handle missing observations using the missing or the imputation strategy.

Report 7.5 FILE ***TechSales_Reps***. The net promoter score (NPS) is a key indicator of customer satisfaction and loyalty. Use data on employees in the software product group with a college degree to develop the logistic regression model for predicting if a sales rep will score an NPS of 9 or more. Use cross validation to select the appropriate predictor variables. In order to estimate this model, you have to first construct the (dummy) target variable, representing NPS ≥ 9 and subset the data to include only the employees who work in the software product group with a college degree.

APPENDIX 7.1 The Caret Package in R for the *k*-fold Cross-Validation Method

The *caret* package (short for Classification And Regression Training) in R is a set of functions that attempt to streamline the process for creating predictive models. It is extremely useful for implementing the *k*-fold cross-validation method. We introduce it here, and will revisit it in Chapters 9 and 10. (As discussed in Appendix C, we note that the following instructions are based on **R version 3.5.3**. They may not work for different versions of R.)

Using the Caret Package to Assess the Linear Regression Model

FILE *Gender_Gap*

For illustration, we will use the ***Gender_Gap*** data to replicate the results of Example 7.15.

A. Import the ***Gender_Gap*** data into a data frame (table) and label it myData.

B. Install and load the *caret* package. Enter:

```
> install.packages("caret")
> library(caret)
```

On some computers, you might also need to install other packages that support the *caret* package using the command

```
> install.packages("caret", dependencies = c("Depends", "Suggests")).
```

C. We use the **trainControl** and the **train** functions. For options within the **trainControl** function, we use *method* to specify the sampling method (here denoted as "cv" for cross-validation) and *number* to indicate the number of folds. Enter:

```
> myControl <- trainControl(method = "cv", number = 4)
```

D. Within the **train** function, we specify the model, and then set the following options: *data* (to indicate the data frame), *method* (here denoted as "lm" for linear model) and *trControl* (to indicate the variable defined when using the **trainControl** function). We show the steps for Model 1 and Model 2. Enter:

```
> Model1 <- train(Salary~ Size + Experience + Female + Grad,
  data = myData, method = "lm", trControl = myControl)
> Model1
> Model2 <- train(Salary~ Size + Experience + Female + Grad
  + Female*Experience + Female*Grad + Size*Experience, data = myData,
  method = "lm", trControl = myControl)
> Model2
```

R reports the average RMSE as well as other measures. The average RMSE is 12.60 for Model 1 and 12.38 for Model 2 (results will vary). These values are fairly close but not identical to those reported in Table 7.28. The reason for the difference is that R uses random draws for determining the training and validation sets, whereas we used fixed draws in Example 7.15; re-running the R command will give you a slightly different result. With both methods, however, we find that Model 2 is better for prediction purposes.

We can easily modify the **trainControl** function to implement a repeated *k*-fold cross-validation method. For instance, suppose we wanted to implement a four-fold cross-validation that is repeated five times. We would modify the earlier function as:

```
> myControl <- trainControl(method = "repeatedcv", number = 4, repeats = 5).
```

Using the Caret Package to Assess the Logistic Regression Model

FILE *Spam*

For illustration, we use the ***Spam*** data that was used to assess Model 1 and Model 2 in Example 7.14. The first three steps are similar to those used when assessing the linear regression model.

A. Import the ***Spam*** data into a data frame (table) and label it myData.

B. Install and load the *caret* package. Enter:

```
> install.packages("caret")
> library(caret)
```

C.
```
> myControl <- trainControl(method = "cv", number = 4)
```

D. Before estimating the logistic regression model, we must convert *y* from numeric type into factor type so that R treats it as a categorical variable with two classes; in other words, a dummy variable. We use the **as.factor** function to accomplish this task. Enter:

```
> myData$Spam <- as.factor(myData$Spam)

> Model1 <- train(Spam ~ Recipients + Hyperlinks + Characters,
  data = myData, trControl = myControl, method = "glm", family =
  binomial(link=logit), metric = "Accuracy")

> Model1

> Model2 <- train(Spam ~ Recipients + Hyperlinks, data = myData,
  trControl = myControl, method = "glm", family = binomial(link=logit),
  metric = "Accuracy")

> Model2
```

R reports the accuracy of 78.59% for Model 1 and 76.60% for Model 2 (results will vary). As in Example 7.14, we find that Model 1 is better for making predictions.

Again, we can implement a four-fold cross-validation that is repeated five times by modifying the earlier function as:

```
> myControl <- trainControl(method = "repeatedcv", number = 4, repeats = 5).
```

8 Introduction to Data Mining

LEARNING OBJECTIVES

After reading this chapter, you should be able to:

LO **8.1** **Describe the data mining process.**

LO **8.2** **Implement similarity measures.**

LO **8.3** **Assess the predictive performance of data mining models.**

LO **8.4** **Conduct principal component analysis.**

Data mining is the process of applying analytical techniques to a data set to find hidden structures, patterns, and relationships among variables. These techniques go beyond data visualization and summary measures discussed in Chapter 3 and linear and logistic regression models discussed in Chapters 6 and 7. In this chapter, we first provide an overview of data mining, the data mining process, and the two primary data mining techniques: supervised (or predictive or directed) and unsupervised (or descriptive or undirected) data mining.

We then explore three key issues that are relevant to data mining: similarity measures, predictive performance assessment, and dimension reduction. Similarity measures gauge whether a group of observations are similar or dissimilar to one another and are essential ingredients for data mining techniques. Assessment of predictive performance is a critical step for model selection in supervised data mining where we partition the original sample into a training set to build (train) the model, a validation set to assess (evaluate) the model, and an optional test data set. Several performance measures are developed to assess how well an estimated model performs in an unseen sample.

Finally, principal component analysis, a dimension reduction technique, is discussed. This technique reduces the number of variables in the data set to a smaller set of principal components that retain most of the crucial information in the original data. These concepts are the prerequisite knowledge for understanding the supervised and unsupervised data mining techniques discussed later in Chapters 9, 10, and 11.

©easy camera/Shutterstock

INTRODUCTORY CASE

Social Media Marketing

Alissa Bridges is the marketing director of FashionTech, an online apparel retailer that specializes in activewear for both men and women. The target market for FashionTech includes individuals between the ages of 18 and 35 with an active and/or outdoors lifestyle who look for both fashion and value in their apparel purchase. The company markets its products via a variety of media channels including TV ads, quarterly catalogs, product placements, search engines, and social media. Alissa has hired a social media marketing firm, MarketWiz, to develop predictive models that would help FashionTech acquire new customers as well as increase sales from existing customers. Using FashionTech's historical social media marketing and sales data, MarketWiz develops two types of predictive models.

- A classification model that predicts potential customers' purchase probability from FashionTech within 30 days of receiving a promotional message in their social media account.
- Two prediction models that predict the one-year purchase amounts of customers acquired through social media channels.

In order to assess the performance of the predictive models, Alissa's team would like to use the validation data set to:

1. Evaluate how accurately the classification model classifies potential customers into the purchase and no-purchase classes.
2. Compare the performance of prediction models that estimate the one-year purchase amounts of customers acquired through social media channels.

A synopsis of this introductory case is presented at the end of section 8.3.

8.1 DATA MINING OVERVIEW

The terms artificial intelligence, machine learning, and data mining describe applications of computer software used to obtain insightful solutions that traditional data analysis techniques may not be able to achieve. In a very broad sense, **artificial intelligence** is used to describe computer systems that demonstrate human-like intelligence and cognitive functions, such as deduction, pattern recognition, and the interpretation of complex data.

In 1959, IBM computer scientist Arthur Samuel coined the term **machine learning**. It describes an application of artificial intelligence that allows the computer to learn automatically without human intervention or assistance. Machine learning techniques can uncover hidden patterns and relationships in data and use self-learning algorithms to evaluate results and improve performance over time. Uber, a popular ride-hailing service, uses machine learning algorithms to predict rider demand to strategically dispatch drivers to various locations.

Data mining describes the process of applying a set of analytical techniques necessary for the development of machine learning and artificial intelligence. The goal of data mining is to uncover hidden patterns and relationships in data, which allows us to gain insights and derive relevant information to help make decisions. As we will discuss in the next three chapters, data mining techniques are used for data segmentation, pattern recognition, classification, and prediction. For example, a retail company might be interested in studying consumer behavior and group customers into different market segments so that it can design and customize a promotion campaign unique to each segment. The company can also use information from previous promotion campaigns to help predict future behaviors of existing and prospective customers.

In many ways, the definitions of these terms overlap, and there are no definitive boundaries among them. For example, a public transportation department might use data mining tools to analyze traffic data from the previous months to set general guidelines for the timing of traffic lights throughout a city, while employing machine learning algorithms to make small adjustments on individual traffic lights based on real-time traffic information during rush hours, and use artificial intelligence techniques to make decisions when dealing with occasional problems with traffic congestion and accidents that involve complex circumstances. As such, data mining is often recognized as a building block of machine learning and artificial intelligence.

ARTIFICIAL INTELLIGENCE, MACHINE LEARNING, AND DATA MINING

The terms artificial intelligence, machine learning, and data mining are often grouped together or used interchangeably because their definitions tend to overlap with no clear boundaries. The following general definitions for these terms simply reinforce this fact:

- Artificial intelligence is a computer system that can demonstrate human-like intelligence and cognitive functions, such as deduction, pattern recognition, and the interpretation of complex data.
- Machine learning describes techniques that integrate self-learning algorithms designed to evaluate results and to improve performance over time.
- Data mining is a process of applying a set of analytical techniques designed to uncover hidden patterns and relationships in data.

LO 8.1

Describe the data mining process.

The Data Mining Process

Data mining is a complex process of examining large sets of data for identifying patterns and then using them for valuable business insights. Due to the recent explosion in the field of data mining, there is a growing need for the establishment of standards in the area. When conducting data mining analysis, practitioners generally adopt either the Cross-Industry Standard Process for Data Mining (**CRISP-DM**) methodology or the Sample, Explore, Modify, Model, and Assess (**SEMMA**) methodology. With either methodology, it is important to fully understand the surrounding socioeconomic climate, business goals, and underlying issues at hand prior to preparing the data and choosing analysis techniques. We now elaborate on each methodology.

CRISP-DM

CRISP-DM was developed in the 1990s by a group of five companies: SPSS, TeraData, Daimler AG, NCR, and OHRA. CRISP-DM consists of six major phases: business understanding, data understanding, data preparation, modeling, evaluation, and deployment. The six phases can be summarized as follows:

1. Business understanding: The first phase focuses on understanding the data mining project and its objectives. Information about the situational context around the data mining project (e.g., resources and data availability) is gathered during this phase in order to define specific objectives (e.g., predict the number of units sold to a customer segment or increase the sales in a particular region) as well as the project schedule and deliverables.
2. Data understanding: This phase involves collecting relevant data and conducting a preliminary analysis to understand the data. Results from these initial analyses may lead to ideas and potential hypotheses for subsequent data mining phases.
3. Data preparation: Specific tasks in this phase include record and variable selection, data wrangling, and cleansing for subsequent analyses. For example, certain data mining techniques may require subsetting and/or transformation of numerical and categorical data. These, along with other topics, related to data wrangling were discussed in Chapter 2.
4. Modeling: This phase involves the selection and execution of data mining techniques, including linear and logistic regression models discussed earlier. Certain analysis techniques require specific formats and types of variables in the data set. For example, a traditional naïve Bayes technique (discussed in Chapter 9) can only work with categorical variables. As such, we may need to step back to the data preparation phase to convert or transform data. We also need to document the assumptions that we make (e.g., normal distribution, treatment of missing values, etc.) and set parameter values for the model. For data mining, we often need to set aside portions of a data set for training and validating the model(s).
5. Evaluation: After developing data mining models, we evaluate the performance of competing models based on specific criteria (discussed later in this chapter) in order to select the best model that meets the business objectives of the project. We then review and interpret the results in the context of the business objectives described in the first phase. At the end of each regression and data mining chapter in this text, we include a section called "Writing with Big Data" where a written report presents the results, interpretation, and recommendations based on the knowledge gained from the analysis.
6. Deployment: During this final phase, we develop a set of actionable recommendations based on the analysis results. Similar to other business projects, we need a strategy for deployment, monitoring, and feedback. The CRISP-DM model was conceived as a life cycle, implying the cyclical nature of data mining projects. Once recommendations are implemented, we may gain additional insights that trigger subsequent data mining projects.

Figure 8.1 shows the steps of the CRISP-DM methodology.

FIGURE 8.1 CRISP-DM data mining methodology

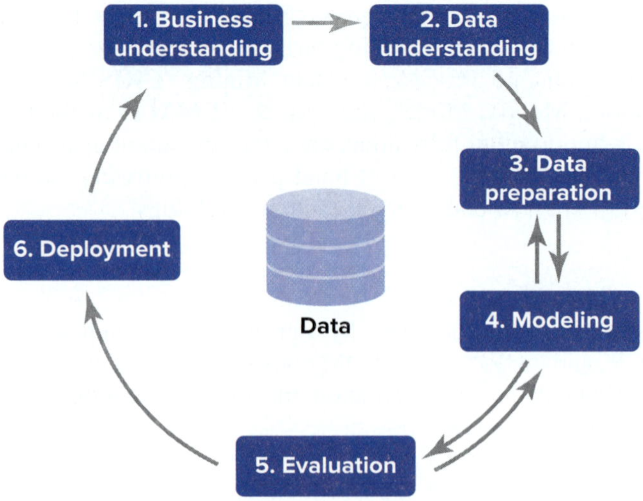

SEMMA

Some practitioners of data mining prefer the SEMMA methodology. Developed by the SAS Institute, this methodology focuses on a core set of tasks and provides a step-by-step process for analyzing data. The five steps of the SEMMA methodology can be summarized as follows:

1. Sample: The first step focuses on identifying appropriate variables, merging or dividing data sets, and drawing a sample of data for subsequent analyses.
2. Explore: Various exploratory data analysis techniques are implemented, including data visualization and summary measures, to gain a thorough understanding of the data.
3. Modify: Similar to the data preparation phase in the CRISP-DM methodology, relevant variables are selected, created, and/or transformed in order to prepare the data set for subsequent analyses.
4. Model: Similar to the modeling phase in the CRISP-DM methodology, analysis techniques and models are chosen and applied to the data, and results are produced.
5. Assess: Results from different models are presented to the end users. The users then compare the outcomes and performance of the competing models. In some cases, new observations are scored using the insights gained from the model(s).

Figure 8.2 shows the steps of the SEMMA methodology.

FIGURE 8.2 SEMMA data mining methodology

THE DATA MINING PROCESS

Two important methodologies when conducting data mining analysis are Cross-Industry Standard Process for Data Mining (CRISP-DM) and Sample, Explore, Modify, Model, and Assess (SEMMA).

- CRISP-DM includes six major phases in the data mining process: business understanding, data understanding, data preparation, modeling, evaluation, and deployment.
- SEMMA includes five major steps in the data mining process: sample, explore, modify, model, and assess.

Both CRISP-DM and SEMMA provide good coverage of the sequential steps, starting with problem identification, data exploration, data collection, data processing, analysis, performance evaluation, and implementation. It is important to note that not every step of these processes is needed for all data mining applications. Also, in practice, the data preparation phase in CRISP-DM and the modify step in SEMMA play a significant role in the data mining process. An analyst or analytics team tends to spend a sizable portion of the project time (often 80%) on understanding, cleansing, transforming and preparing data leading up to the modeling activities. Several surveys conducted by KD Nuggets, a leading website on data analytics, suggest that the CRISP-DM methodology is more popular than the SEMMA methodology. Many find CRISP-DM a true methodology as it offers a holistic approach to data mining with detailed phases, tasks, and activities.

Supervised and Unsupervised Data Mining

Data mining uses many kinds of computational algorithms to identify hidden patterns and relationships in data. These algorithms are classified into supervised and unsupervised techniques, depending on the way they "learn" about data to make predictions or identify patterns. For developing predictive models, one tends to employ **supervised data mining** techniques. **Unsupervised data mining** techniques are especially effective for data exploration, dimension reduction, and pattern recognition. The key distinction between supervised and unsupervised techniques is that, in supervised data mining, the target variable is identified. In Chapters 6 and 7, we refer to the target variable as a response variable, which is the name often used in statistics. The historical values of the target variable exist in the data set so that data mining algorithms can examine the impact of the predictor variables on the target variable. On the contrary, in unsupervised data mining, no target variable is identified.

Supervised Data Mining

Some of the most commonly used supervised data mining algorithms are based on classic statistical techniques. The linear regression model and the logistic regression model, discussed in Chapters 6 and 7, are examples of supervised techniques. These models are used to predict the outcomes of a target variable based on several predictor variables. The mathematical model relates the outcome of the target variable (commonly referred to as y) to one or more predictor variables (commonly referred to as $x_1, x_2, \ldots, x_k$). Consequently, we use information on the predictor variables to predict and/or describe changes in the target variable. A regression model is therefore "trained" or "supervised" because the known values of the target variable are used to build the model. In addition, performance of the model can be evaluated based on the extent to which the predicted values deviate from the actual values of the target variable. There are several other machine learning algorithms that are widely used in supervised data mining. We will discuss three of these techniques including k-Nearest Neighbors, naïve Bayes, and Decision Trees in Chapters 9 and 10.

Common applications of supervised data mining include **classification** and **prediction models**. In a classification model, the target variable is categorical. The objective of a classification model is to predict the class memberships of new cases. For example, a marketing manager may classify a list of prospective customers as buyers and nonbuyers. A financial analyst may classify a stock into one of the following three classes: buy, hold, and sell. In a prediction model, the target variable is numerical. Examples of prediction models include predicting the spending of a customer, the selling price of a house, or the length of hospital stay after a medical procedure.

> **SUPERVISED DATA MINING**
>
> In supervised data mining, the target (response) variable is known. Common applications of supervised learning include classification and prediction models.
>
> - In a classification model, the target variable is categorical. The objective of the classification model is to predict the class membership of a new case.
> - In a prediction model, the target variable is numerical. The objective of the prediction model is to predict the numeric value of a new case.

Unsupervised Data Mining

Unsupervised data mining requires no knowledge of the target variable. It is called unsupervised because, unlike supervised learning, the algorithms allow the computer to identify complex processes and patterns without any specific guidance from the analyst. In the field of business analytics, unsupervised learning is considered to be an important part of exploratory data analysis and descriptive analytics. It is also used prior to conducting supervised learning in order to understand the data set, formulate questions, or summarize data.

Common applications of unsupervised learning include **dimension reduction** and **pattern recognition**. Dimension reduction (discussed later in this chapter) refers to the process of converting a set of high-dimensional data (data with a large number of variables) into data with a smaller number of variables without losing much of the information in the original data. It is an important step before deploying other data mining methods to reduce information redundancy and improve model stability. Dimension reduction is especially relevant to today's big data environment. For example, data collected by sensors or other Internet of things (IoT) devices tend to have a large number of variables (high-dimensional) and a lot of redundancy in the information they carry. Reducing the dimensionality of these data sets will help bring out the important patterns in data and build more stable predictive models.

Pattern recognition is the process of recognizing patterns using machine learning techniques (discussed in Chapter 11). A pattern may be recurring sequences of behaviors of customers, frequent combinations of words in documents, recognizable features of objects, or common characteristics of things that belong to the same group. For example, retail companies use pattern recognition techniques to group customers into different market segments in order to customize product and service offerings that are of interest to each segment.

UNSUPERVISED DATA MINING

In unsupervised data mining, there is no target variable. Common applications of unsupervised learning include dimension reduction and pattern recognition.

- Dimension reduction is the process of converting a set of high-dimensional data into data with lesser dimensions.
- Pattern recognition is the process of recognizing patterns in the data using machine learning techniques.

The next few sections of this chapter explore three key concepts relevant to data mining: similarity measures, performance evaluation, and dimension reduction techniques. They are the prerequisite knowledge for understanding the data mining techniques discussed in Chapters 9, 10, and 11.

8.2 SIMILARITY MEASURES

We first explore **similarity measures**, which gauge whether a group of observations are similar or dissimilar to one another. These measures are important for understanding both supervised and unsupervised data mining techniques discussed later in the text. In Chapter 9, for example, similarity measures are used to identify observations that are similar to each other or close neighbors in the *k*-Nearest Neighbors (KNN) technique. In Chapter 11, cluster analysis finds similarities among observations in the data and groups them into meaningful clusters based on similar characteristics. Clusters are formed in such a way that observations are similar within a group but dissimilar across groups.

LO 8.2

Implement similarity measures.

Similarity measures are based on the distance between pairwise observations (records) of the variables. A small distance between the observations implies a high degree of similarity, whereas a large distance between the observations implies a low degree of similarity. In this chapter, we represent all k variables as $x_1, x_2, \ldots, x_k$.

Consider three observations for the variables, x_1 and x_2, shown in Table 8.1.

TABLE 8.1 Three Pairwise Observations for x_1 and x_2

Observation	x_1	x_2
1	3	4
2	4	5
3	10	1

Figure 8.3 plots the observations. We can clearly see that observations 1 and 2 are closer to each other, implying that they are "similar" to each other. Also, we can see that observation 3 is dissimilar from observations 1 and 2. In this section, we present a more formal way to measure similarity among observations for numerical and categorical variables.

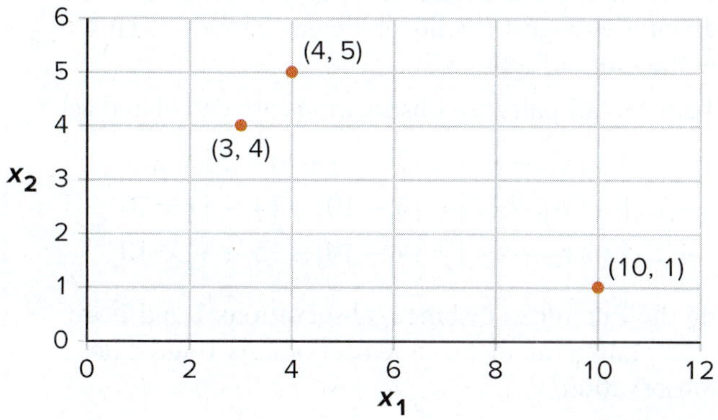

FIGURE 8.3 Plot of three pairwise observations

Similarity Measures for Numerical Data

The **Euclidean distance** is one of the most widely used measures for evaluating similarity with numerical variables. It is defined as the length of a straight line between two observations. For a data set with k variables, the Euclidean distance between the ith and jth observations is calculated as:

$$\text{Euclidian distance} = \sqrt{(x_{1i} - x_{1j})^2 + (x_{2i} - x_{2j})^2 + (x_{3i} - x_{3j})^2 + \cdots + (x_{ki} - x_{kj})^2},$$

where x_{ki} and x_{kj} represent the ith and jth observations for the kth variable.

The **Manhattan distance** is the shortest distance between two observations if you are only allowed to move horizontally or vertically. Referring to the city of Manhattan, which is laid out in square blocks, the Manhattan distance between two points is the shortest path for a vehicle to travel from one point to another in the city. For a data set with k variables, the Manhattan distance between the ith and jth observations is calculated as:

$$\text{Manhattan distance} = |x_{1i} - x_{1j}| + |x_{2i} - x_{2j}| + |x_{3i} - x_{3j}| + \cdots + |x_{ki} - x_{kj}|,$$

where x_{ki} and x_{kj} represent the ith and jth observations for the kth variable.

EXAMPLE 8.1

Refer back to Table 8.1, where three observations are reported for variables x_1 and x_2.

a. Calculate and interpret the Euclidean distance between all pairwise observations.

b. Calculate and interpret the Manhattan distance between all pairwise observations.

SOLUTION:

a. The Euclidean distances between all pairwise observations are calculated as:

Observations 1 and 2:
$$\sqrt{(x_{11} - x_{12})^2 + (x_{21} - x_{22})^2} = \sqrt{(3 - 4)^2 + (4 - 5)^2} = 1.41$$

Observations 1 and 3:
$$\sqrt{(x_{11} - x_{13})^2 + (x_{21} - x_{23})^2} = \sqrt{(3 - 10)^2 + (4 - 1)^2} = 7.62$$

Observations 2 and 3:
$$\sqrt{(x_{12} - x_{13})^2 + (x_{22} - x_{23})^2} = \sqrt{(4 - 10)^2 + (5 - 1)^2} = 7.21$$

Using the Euclidean measure to gauge similarity, observations 1 and 2 are the most similar with the shortest Euclidean distance of 1.41. Observations 1 and 3 are the most dissimilar given the longest Euclidean distance of 7.62. This conclusion is reinforced by the plot in Figure 8.3.

b. The Manhattan distances between all pairwise observations are calculated as:

Observations 1 and 2: $|x_{11} - x_{12}| + |x_{21} - x_{22}| = |3 - 4| + |4 - 5| = 2$

Observations 1 and 3: $|x_{11} - x_{13}| + |x_{21} - x_{23}| = |3 - 10| + |4 - 1| = 10$

Observations 2 and 3: $|x_{12} - x_{13}| + |x_{22} - x_{23}| = |4 - 10| + |5 - 1| = 10$

Like the results found using the Euclidean distance, observations 1 and 2 are the most similar based on the Manhattan distance. Observations 1 and 2 are now equally dissimilar to observation 3.

EUCLIDIAN AND MANHATTAN DISTANCES

For numerical data, similarity measures are based on the distance between pairwise observations (records) of the variables. For a data set with k variables, the Euclidean and the Manhattan distances between the ith and jth observations are calculated as:

$$\text{Euclidian distance} = \sqrt{(x_{1i} - x_{1j})^2 + (x_{2i} - x_{2j})^2 + (x_{3i} - x_{3j})^2 + \cdots + (x_{ki} - x_{kj})^2}$$

and

$$\text{Manhattan distance} = |x_{1i} - x_{1j}| + |x_{2i} - x_{2j}| + |x_{3i} - x_{3j}| + \cdots + |x_{ki} - x_{kj}|,$$

where x_{ki} and x_{kj} represent the ith and jth observations for the kth variable.

As shown in Example 8.1, different distance measures do not always lead to the same inference. The Euclidian distance is known to be more influenced by outliers than the Manhattan distance. In Example 8.1, the third observation is clearly an outlier, and, therefore, the Manhattan distance may be more appropriate. Most data mining algorithms, however, employ the Euclidian distance.

Standardization and Normalization

When a data set contains multiple variables, the scale of each variable can influence the distance measure and how we determine the similarity between two observations. For example, when comparing consumer information, data such as annual incomes tend to have a greater scale than, say, the number of hours spent online per week simply by the fact that annual incomes are larger numbers. As a result, annual income will have greater influence on the similarity measure than the number of hours spent online per week.

This difference in scale distorts the true distance between observations and can lead to inaccurate results. It is common, therefore, to make the observations unit-free by **standardizing** or **normalizing** numerical data before calculating the similarity measure for the data mining techniques. These transformations of numerical data ensure that each variable receives an equal weight when the similarity measure is calculated.

One common way to standardize the data is to compute z-scores, which were discussed in Chapter 3. Recall that the z-score measures the distance of a given observation from the sample mean in terms of standard deviations. In order to find the z-score for the ith observation of the kth variable, denoted z_{ki}, we calculate:

$$z_{ki} = \frac{x_{ki} - \bar{x}_k}{s_k},$$

where x_{ki} is the ith observation of the kth variable, and $\bar{x}_k$ and s_k are the mean and the standard deviation of the kth variable, respectively.

Another widely used transformation method is min-max normalization, which subtracts the minimum value from the observation and then divides the difference by the range (maximum value − minimum value). This approach rescales each value to be between 0 and 1. In order to find the min-max normalized value for the ith observation of the kth variable, denoted q_{ki}, we calculate:

$$q_{ki} = \frac{x_{ki} - min_k}{range_k},$$

where x_{ki} is the ith observation of the kth variable, and min_k and $range_k$ are the minimum value and the range of the kth variable, respectively.

STANDARDIZING AND NORMALIZING NUMERICAL DATA

The z-score standardization and min-max normalization are two conversion techniques that make the numerical data independent of scale. The z-score standardization for the ith observation of the kth variable, z_{ki}, is calculated as:

$$z_{ki} = \frac{x_{ki} - \bar{x}_k}{s_k},$$

where x_{ki} is the ith observation of the kth variable, and $\bar{x}_k$ and s_k are the mean and the standard deviation of the kth variable, respectively. The min-max normalized value for the ith observation of the kth variable, q_{ki}, is calculated as:

$$q_{ki} = \frac{x_{ki} - min_k}{range_k},$$

where x_{ki} is the ith observation of the kth variable, and min_k and $range_k$ are the minimum value and the range of the kth variable, respectively.

A Note on the Term Normalization

It is important to note that the term 'normalization' has several meanings in statistics. Generally, it refers to a process that makes the numerical data independent of scale. Sometimes, the term is even used for the z-score standardization; Analytic Solver uses the term 'normalization' to convert the numerical data into z-scores. In this text, we prefer to use the term min-max normalization to avoid confusion.

Example 8.2 demonstrates how to standardize and normalize data.

EXAMPLE 8.2

Consider a sample of five consumers with their annual income (Income, in \$) and hours spent online per week (Hours Spent) shown in columns 1–3 of Table 8.2. The distance measures calculated from raw data can be distorted because the annual income values are much larger than the values of hours spent online per week.

TABLE 8.2 Annual Income and Hours Spent

Name	Income	Hours Spent	Standardized Income	Standardized Hours Spent	Normalized Income	Normalized Hours Spent
Jane	125,678	2.5	1.2473	−1.5071	1.0000	0.0000
Kevin	65,901	10.1	−1.1892	1.0382	0.0000	1.0000
Dolores	75,550	5.8	−0.7959	−0.4019	0.1614	0.4342
Deshaun	110,250	9.0	0.6184	0.6698	0.7419	0.8553
Mei	98,005	7.6	0.1194	0.2010	0.5371	0.6711

a. Use z-scores to standardize the observations for Income and Hours Spent.

b. Use the min-max transformation to normalize the observations for Income and Hours Spent.

SOLUTION:

a. In order to standardize the observations for Income, we first calculate its average and the standard deviation as \$95,077 and \$24,534.45, respectively. We then divide the difference between each observation and the mean by the standard deviation. For Jane, we find the standardized Income value as:

$$z_{\text{Income Jane}} = \frac{x_{\text{Income Jane}} - \bar{x}_{\text{Income}}}{s_{\text{Income}}} = \frac{125{,}678 - 95{,}077}{24{,}534.45} = 1.2473.$$

Therefore, Jane's income is 1.2473 standard deviations above the average income of all consumers in the sample. Standardized values for all Income observations are shown in column 4 of Table 8.2. Kevin's annual income, for example, is 1.1892 standard deviations below the average income.

Standardized values for Hours Spent are found similarly using an average and standard deviation of 7.0 hours and 2.99 hours, respectively. Column 5 of Table 8.2 shows these standardized values. The standardized values have a similar scale, and, therefore, they will receive an equal weight when calculating the distance measure.

b. In order to normalize the observations for Income, we first find the minimum and maximum values for Income as \$65,901 and \$125,678, respectively, and then calculate the range as \$59,777. We then divide the difference between each observation and the minimum value by the range. For Jane, we find the min-max normalized value for Income as:

$$q_{\text{Income Jane}} = \frac{x_{\text{Income Jane}} - min_{\text{Income}}}{range_{\text{Income}}} = \frac{125{,}678 - 65{,}901}{59{,}777} = 1.$$

Because the min-max normalization rescales each observation between 0 and 1, Jane, with the highest annual income, has a min-max normalized income of 1, and Kevin, with the lowest annual income, has a min-max normalized income of 0. The min-max normalized values for Income are shown in column 6 of Table 8.2.

The min-max normalization values for Hours Spent are found similarly using minimum and maximum values of 2.5 hours and 10.1 hours, respectively. Column 7 of Table 8.2 shows the min-max normalization values for Hours Spent. As in the case of standardized values, the min-max normalized values have a similar scale, and, therefore, they will receive an equal weight when calculating the distance measure.

Similarity Measures for Categorical Data

Euclidean and Manhattan distance measures are suitable for numerical variables. When dealing with categorical variables, we rely on other measures of similarity. For example, you may be interested in analyzing types of cars, where the values of the categorical variable include sedan, sport utility, truck, minivan, etc. Recall that a categorical variable with only two categories is called a binary variable. For example, when analyzing loans, the values of the binary variable include approved or not approved. Two commonly used measures for categorical and binary data are the matching coefficient and Jaccard's coefficient.

Matching Coefficient

The **matching coefficient** for a categorical variable is based on matching values to determine similarity among observations (records). The matching coefficient between two observations is:

$$\text{Matching coefficient} = \frac{\text{Number of variables with matching outcomes}}{\text{Total number of variables}}$$

The higher the value of the matching coefficient, the more similar the two observations are. A matching coefficient value of one implies a perfect match.

EXAMPLE 8.3

Consider the list of college students in Table 8.3. Each record shows the student's major, field, sex, and whether or not the student is on the Dean's List. Compute the matching coefficient between all pairs of students and determine how similar or dissimilar they are from each other.

TABLE 8.3 Characteristics of College Students

Student	Major	Field	Sex	Dean's list
1	Business	MIS	Female	Yes
2	Engineering	Electrical	Male	Yes
3	Business	Accounting	Female	No

SOLUTION:

Comparing students 1 and 2, only one of the four variables (i.e., Dean's List) has a matching value. Therefore, the matching coefficient equals 1/4 = 0.25. Comparing students 1 and 3, two of the four variables (i.e., Major and Sex) have a matching value. Therefore, the matching coefficient equals 2/4 = 0.50. Comparing students 2 and 3, none of the four variables has a matching value. Therefore, the matching coefficient equals 0/4 = 0.

Based on the matching coefficients for these three students, students 1 and 3 are the most similar to each other, whereas students 2 and 3 are the most dissimilar.

Jaccard's Coefficient

The matching coefficient makes no distinction between positive outcomes (e.g., made a purchase) and negative outcomes (e.g., did not make a purchase) and, therefore may provide a misleading measure of similarity. Consider, for example, consumer purchasing behavior at a grocery store where thousands of products are available. Intuitively, two consumers purchasing the same products exhibit similar behavior. However, if one consumer purchases only a Hostess cupcake, and the other purchases only organic apples, most people would conclude that these two consumers are not similar. However, a simple matching coefficient will account for the fact that neither of the customers purchased thousands of other products that are available and, therefore, erroneously produce a very high value of the matching coefficient.

Jaccard's coefficient, named after French scientist Paul Jaccard, is a more appropriate measure of similarity in situations where negative outcomes are not as important as positive outcomes. It is computed as:

$$\text{Jaccard's coefficient} = \frac{\text{Number of variables with matching positive outcomes}}{(\text{Total number of variables}) - \begin{pmatrix}\text{Number of variables with}\\ \text{matching negative outcomes}\end{pmatrix}}$$

EXAMPLE 8.4

A retail store collects point of sales information that shows whether or not five products were included in each sales transaction. This information is captured in Table 8.4. A 'yes' indicates a positive outcome, while a 'no' indicates a negative outcome. For example, Transaction 1 indicates that a consumer purchases a computer keyboard, a mouse, and a headphone. Compute and compare matching coefficients and Jaccard's coefficients for all sets of pairwise transactions.

TABLE 8.4 Retail Transactions

Transaction	Keyboard	Memory card	Mouse	USB drive	Headphone
1	Yes	No	Yes	No	Yes
2	Yes	Yes	Yes	No	No
3	No	No	No	No	Yes
4	Yes	No	No	No	No

SOLUTION:

We demonstrate how to calculate the matching coefficient and the Jaccard coefficient between transactions 1 and 2. For the matching coefficient, transactions 1 and 2 have three matching values: keyboard, mouse, and USB drive. Given that there are five products (so five variables), the matching coefficient is calculated as 3/5 = 0.6. For the Jaccard's coefficient, the two transactions have two matching positive outcomes (keyboard and mouse) and one matching negative outcome (USB drive). Therefore, the Jaccard's coefficient for the pair is calculated as 2/(5 − 1) = 0.50. The coefficients for the remaining pairs are calculated similarly and are shown in Table 8.5.

TABLE 8.5 Comparing Matching Coefficients with Jaccard's Coefficients

Transactions	Matching coefficients	Jaccard's coefficients
1 and 2	3/5 = 0.6	2/4 = 0.50
1 and 3	3/5 = 0.6	1/3 = 0.33
1 and 4	3/5 = 0.6	1/3 = 0.33
2 and 3	1/5 = 0.2	0/4 = 0.00
2 and 4	3/5 = 0.6	1/3 = 0.33
3 and 4	3/5 = 0.6	0/2 = 0.00

Table 8.5 shows that both measures produce the highest coefficient for transactions 1 and 2, implying that these transactions are most similar. However, some

notable differences arise. For example, the matching coefficients yield a higher value when comparing transactions with matching negative outcomes (for example, transactions 1 and 3; transactions 1 and 4; etc.). The absence of particular products in a sales transaction (i.e., negative outcomes) is usually not as important as the positive outcomes, and including the negative outcomes in the similarity measure is misleading. Consider transactions 3 and 4. The fact that the two customers did not purchase the same three products (memory card, mouse, and USB drive) may not imply any similarity between the two transactions or customers at all. Jaccard's coefficient makes the appropriate adjustment and with a Jaccard's coefficient of 0 suggests that the two transactions are dissimilar. The matching coefficient of 0.6, on the other hand, erroneously suggests a relatively high similarity because of the number of matching negative outcomes.

MATCHING AND JACCARD'S COEFFICIENTS

Matching and Jaccard's coefficients are similarity measures for categorical data. For a data set with k variables, the matching coefficient between the ith and the jth observations (records) is calculated as:

$$\text{Matching coefficient} = \frac{\text{Number of variables with matching outcomes}}{\text{Total number of variables}}.$$

For a data set with k variables, the Jaccard's coefficient between the ith and the jth observations is calculated as:

$$\text{Jaccard's coefficient} = \frac{\text{Number of variables with matching positive outcomes}}{\begin{pmatrix}\text{Total number of}\\ \text{variables}\end{pmatrix} - \begin{pmatrix}\text{Number of variables with}\\ \text{matching negative outcomes}\end{pmatrix}}.$$

The Jaccard's coefficient is appropriate when it is more informative to match only positive outcomes between two observations.

EXERCISES 8.2

Note: For exercises in this section, it is advisable to use unrounded numbers in the calculations.

Mechanics

1. **FILE** ***Exercise_8.1.*** The accompanying data file contains 10 observations with two variables, x_1 and x_2.
   a. Using the original values, compute the Euclidean distance between the *first two observations*.
   b. Using the original values, compute the Manhattan distance between the first two observations.
   c. Based on the entire data set, calculate the sample mean and standard deviation for x_1 and x_2. Use z-scores to standardize the values, and then compute the Euclidean distance between the first two observations.
   d. Based on the entire data set, find the minimum and maximum values for x_1 and x_2. Use the min-max transformation to normalize the values, and then compute the Euclidean distance between the first two observations.
2. **FILE** ***Exercise_8.2.*** The accompanying data file contains 10 observations with three variables, x_1, x_2, and x_3.
   a. Using the original values, compute the Euclidean distance between the *first two observations*.
   b. Using the original values, compute the Manhattan distance between the first two observations.
   c. Based on the entire data set, calculate the sample mean and standard deviation for the three variables. Use z-scores to standardize the values, and then compute the Euclidean distance between the first two observations.
   d. Based on the entire data set, find the minimum and maximum values for the three variables. Use the min-max transformation to normalize the values, and then

compute the Euclidean distance between the first two observations.

3. **FILE** ***Exercise_8.3.*** The accompanying data file contains 28 observations with three variables, x_1, x_2, and x_3.
   a. Using the original values, compute the Euclidean distance for all possible pairs of the *first three observations*.
   b. Based on the entire data set, calculate the sample mean and standard deviation for the three variables. Use z-scores to standardize the values, and then compute the Euclidean distance for all possible pairs of the first three observations. Compare the results with part a.
   c. Using the original values, and then the z-score standardized values, compute the Manhattan distance for all possible pairs of the first three observations.
4. **FILE** ***Exercise_8.4.*** The accompanying data file contains 19 observations with two variables, x_1 and x_2.
   a. Using the original values, compute the Euclidean distance for all possible pairs of the *first three observations*.
   b. Based on the entire data set, find the minimum and maximum values for the three variables. Use the min-max transformation to normalize the values, and then compute the Euclidean distance for all possible pairs of the first three observations.
   c. Using the original values, and then the min-max normalized values, compute the Manhattan distance for all possible pairs of the first three observations.
5. **FILE** ***Exercise_8.5.*** The accompanying data file contains 10 observations with two variables, x_1 and x_2.
   a. Based on the entire data set, calculate the sample mean and standard deviation of the two variables. Using the original values, and then the z-score standardized values, compute the Euclidean distance for all possible pairs of the *first three observations*.
   b. Using the original values, and then the z-score standardized values, compute the Manhattan distance for all possible pairs of the *first three observations*.
6. **FILE** ***Exercise_8.6.*** The accompanying data file contains 12 observations with three variables, x_1, x_2, and x_3.
   a. Based on the entire data set, calculate the sample mean and standard deviation for the three variables. Using the original values, and then the z-score standardized values, compute the Euclidean distance for all possible pairs of the *first three observations*.
   b. Based on the entire data set, find the minimum and maximum values of the three variables. Using the original values, and then the min-max normalized values, compute the Manhattan distance for all possible pairs of the *first three observations*.
7. **FILE** ***Exercise_8.7.*** The accompanying data file contains five observations with three categorical variables, x_1, x_2, and x_3.
   a. Compute the matching coefficient for all pairwise observations.
   b. Identify the observations that are most and least similar to each other.
8. **FILE** ***Exercise_8.8.*** The accompanying file contains four observations with four categorical variables, x_1, x_2, x_3, and x_4.
   a. Compute the matching coefficient for all pairwise observations.
   b. Identify the pair of observations that are most and least similar to each other.
9. **FILE** ***Exercise_8.9.*** The accompanying file contains six observations with four binary variables, x_1, x_2, x_3, and x_4.
   a. Compute the matching coefficient for all pairwise observations. Identify the pair of observations that are most and least similar to each other.
   b. Compute the Jaccard's coefficient for all pairwise observations. Identify the pair of observations that are most and least similar to each other.

Applications

10. **FILE** ***Employees.*** Consider the following portion of data that lists the starting salaries (in $1,000) of newly hired employees and their college GPAs:

Employee	Salary	GPA
1	72	3.53
2	66	2.86
3	72	3.69
⋮	⋮	⋮
11	59	3.49

   a. Without transforming the values, compute the Euclidean distance for all possible pairs of the first three employees. Make sure to exclude the employee numbers in the calculations.
   b. Compute the z-score standardized values for salary and GPA, and then compute the Euclidean distance for all possible pairs of the first three employees. Discuss the impact that standardization has on the similarity distance.
   c. Using the z-score standardized values, compute the Manhattan distance for all possible pairs of the first three employees. Discuss the differences between the Euclidean and Manhattan distances.
11. **FILE** ***Online_Retailers.*** Consider the following portion of data that lists information about an online retailer's annual revenues (Revenue in $), the number of products available on the retailer's website (SKUs), and the number of visits to the website per day (Visits):

Website ID	Revenue	SKUs	Visits
001	2,984,567	34,567	546,799
002	1,230,956	22,398	342,455
⋮	⋮	⋮	⋮
010	2,278,890	28,773	333,219

a. Without transforming the values, compute the Euclidean distance for all pairwise observations of websites 001, 003, and 005 based on annual revenues, SKUs, and visits per day. Make sure to exclude the Website IDs from your calculation.
b. Compute the min-max normalized values for annual revenues, SKUs, and visits per day, and then compute the Euclidean distance for all pairwise observations of websites 001, 003, and 005. Discuss the differences in parts a and b. Make sure to exclude the Website IDs from your calculation.
c. Using the min-max normalized values, compute the Manhattan distance for all pairwise observations of websites 001, 003, and 005. Discuss the difference between the Euclidean and Manhattan distances. Make sure to exclude the Website IDs from your calculation.

12. **FILE** ***Vehicles.*** Consider the following portion of data that shows vehicle information based on three variables: Type of vehicle, whether or not the vehicle has all-wheel drive (AWD), and whether the vehicle's transmission is automatic or manual.

Vehicle	Type	AWD	Transmission
1	SUV	Yes	Automatic
2	Sedan	No	Manual
⋮	⋮	⋮	⋮
56	SUV	No	Automatic

a. Using the first five vehicles, compute the matching coefficient for all pairwise observations based on Type, AWD, and Transmission.
b. Identify and describe the vehicles that are most and least similar to each other. Explain the characteristics of these vehicles.

13. **FILE** ***Home_Loan.*** Consider the following portion of data that includes information about home loan applications. Variables on each application include (1) whether the application is conventional or subsidized by the federal housing administration (LoanType), (2) whether the property is a single-family or multi-family home (PropertyType), and (3) whether the application is for a first-time purchase or refinancing (Purpose).

Application	LoanType	PropertyType	Purpose
1	Conventional	Single-family	Purchase
2	Conventional	Multi-family	Refinancing
⋮	⋮	⋮	⋮
103	Federal Housing	Single-family	Purchase

a. Using the first five applications, compute the matching coefficients for all pairwise observations based on LoanType, PropertyType, and Purpose.
b. Identify and describe the loan applications that are most and least similar to each other. Explain the characteristics of these loan applications.

14. **FILE** ***University_Students.*** Information is collected on university students. The variables of interest include (1) whether a student is an undergraduate or graduate student (Level of education), (2) whether or not the student is a math major, (3) whether or not the student is a statistics minor, and (4) whether a student is male or female. A portion of the data is shown in the accompanying table.

Student	Level of education	Math major?	Statistics minor?	Sex
1	Graduate	Yes	Yes	F
2	Undergraduate	Yes	No	M
⋮	⋮	⋮	⋮	⋮
8	Graduate	Yes	Yes	M

a. Using the first five students, compute the matching coefficients for all pairwise observations based on the four variables.
b. Identify and describe students who are most and least similar to each other.

15. **FILE** ***Bookstore.*** Consider the following data that shows a portion of point of sales transactions from a local bookstore. Each binary variable indicates whether or not a particular book genre is purchased within a transaction.

Transaction	Sci-fi	Travel guide	Self help	Biography	Children's book
1	0	0	1	1	1
2	1	0	1	0	1
⋮	⋮	⋮	⋮	⋮	⋮
101	0	0	0	0	1

a. Using the first five sales transactions, compute the matching coefficients for all pairwise observations for the five binary variables.
b. Using the first five sales transactions, compute Jaccard's coefficients for all pairwise observations for the five binary variables.
c. Based on the results from parts a and b, identify and describe the transactions that are most and least similar to each other. Discuss the difference between the results from parts a and b.

16. **FILE** ***Grocery_Store.*** Consider the following data that show a portion of the point of sales transactions from a grocery store. Each binary variable indicates whether or not a product is purchased as part of the transaction.

Transaction	Meat	Produce	Baked goods	Candy
1	1	0	1	1
2	1	1	0	1
⋮	⋮	⋮	⋮	⋮
258	1	1	1	0

a. Using the first five sales transactions, compute the matching coefficients for all pairwise observations for the four binary variables.

b. Using the first five sales transactions, compute Jaccard's coefficients for all pairwise observations for the four binary variables.

c. Based on the results from parts a and b, identify and describe the transactions that are most and least similar to each other. Discuss the difference between the results from parts a and b.

17. **FILE** ***Fast_Food.*** Consider the following data that show a portion of the sales transactions from a local fast-food restaurant. Each binary variable indicates whether or not a product is purchased as part of the sales transaction.

Transaction	Hamburgers	Fries	Soda
1	0	1	0
2	1	1	0
⋮	⋮	⋮	⋮
238	0	1	1

a. Using the first five sales transactions, compute the matching coefficients for all pairwise observations for the three binary variables.

b. Using the first five sales transactions, compute Jaccard's coefficients for all pairwise observations for the three binary variables.

c. Based on the results from parts a and b, identify and describe the transactions that are most and least similar to each other. Discuss the difference between the results from parts a and b.

LO 8.3

8.3 PERFORMANCE EVALUATION

Assess the predictive performance of data mining models.

In this section we assess the predictive performance of data mining models, including linear and the logistic regression models discussed in Chapters 6 and 7. Recall that it is important to develop performance measures that evaluate how well an estimated model will perform in an unseen sample, rather than making the evaluation solely on the basis of the sample data used to build the model.

In Chapter 7, we discussed cross-validation techniques where we partition the original sample into a training set to build (train) the model and a validation set to assess (evaluate) the model. We used the root mean squared error (RMSE) to evaluate linear regression models and the accuracy rate to evaluate logistic regression models. In this chapter, we extend the analysis to include several other performance measures that can be applied to all supervised data mining models.

Data Partitioning

Data partitioning is the process of dividing a data set into a training, a validation, and, in some situations, an optional test data set. A common data partitioning practice is a two-way random partitioning of the data to generate a training data set and a validation data set. We use random partitioning, as opposed to fixed draws discussed in Chapter 7, to avoid any bias in the selection of the training and validation data sets. The training data set, which often contains the larger portion of the data, "trains" data mining algorithms to identify the relationship between the predictor variables and the target (response) variable. The validation data set, which is not involved in model building, is used to provide an unbiased assessment of the predictive performance of data mining models.

The model built from the training data set is used to predict the values of the target variable in the validation data set. These predicted values are then compared to the actual values of the target variable of the validation data set to evaluate the performance of the model. The performance measures obtained from this process can be used to help assess model performance, fine-tune the model, or compare the performance of competing models.

A common practice is to partition 60% of the data into the training data set and 40% of the data into the validation data set. However, sometimes, the 70%/30% training/validation partitioning is used if the model building process can benefit from a larger training data set. As explained in Chapter 7, we can implement cross-validation with the holdout as well as *k*-fold methods.

In supervised data mining, we sometimes use three-way random partitioning of the data to generate training, validation, and test data sets. The third data partition, called a test data set, which is not involved in either model building or model selection, is created to evaluate how well the final model would perform on a new data set that it has never seen before. As in the case of two-way partitioning, data are usually partitioned randomly to create unbiased training, validation, and test data sets. In the three-way random partitioning method, 50% training/30% validation/20% test partitioning is often recommended. The three-way random partitioning is usually implemented with the holdout method, as opposed to *k*-fold cross-validation.

> **DATA PARTITIONING**
>
> Data partitioning is the process of dividing a data set into a training, a validation, and an optional test data set. The training data set is used to generate one or more models. The validation data set is used to fine-tune or compare the performance of competing models, The optional test data set is used to assess the performance of the final model on a new data set.

Oversampling

Sometimes the target class that we wish to classify is very rare, which reduces the usefulness of classification models. For example, in order to build a classification model that informs an online retailer about which prospective customers are likely to respond to a promotional e-mail, the retailer conducts an experiment by sending promotional e-mail messages to 10,000 potential customers of which only 200 customers respond, resulting in a response rate of tow %. The resulting data from this experiment would consist mostly of non-responders with little information to distinguish them from the target class of responders. If this retailer attempts to build classification models, the best-performing model might be the one that suggests no prospective customers will respond to the promotional e-mail message as the model would have an extremely high accuracy rate of 98%. Nevertheless, the best-performing model in this application might be useless to the retailer.

A common solution to this problem is called **oversampling**. The oversampling technique involves intentionally selecting more samples from one class than from the other class or classes in order to adjust the class distribution of a data set. Rare target class cases will be more represented in the data set if they are oversampled. This would lead to predictive models that are more useful in predicting the target class cases.

In the promotional e-mail example, the retailer may choose to oversample the rare target class cases by including most, if not all, responders and reduce the number of non-responders so that the resulting data set constitutes a healthy combination of responders and non-responders.

> **OVERSAMPLING**
>
> The oversampling procedure overweights the rare class relative to the other class or classes in order to adjust the class distribution of a data set.

As a common practice, only the training data set is oversampled. Observations in the validation and test data sets maintain the original class proportions so that the resulting performance estimates will be more representative of the reality.

Performance Evaluation in Supervised Data Mining

In Section 6.2, we used goodness-of-fit measures such as R^2 and adjusted R^2 to assess how well the regression model fits or explains the data. Nevertheless, a model that fits a set of in-sample data well may not predict new observations accurately due to the possibility of **overfitting**. Recall from Section 7.4 that overfitting occurs when a model corresponds too closely to a set of data but fails to predict future observations reliably. In other words, an overfit model accounts for the noise in a particular set of data rather than the underlying patterns that can be generalized to future observations. Overfitting may become more severe as the model complexity increases (for example, as more predictor variables are included in the model).

> **OVERFITTING**
>
> Overfitting occurs when a predictive model is made overly complex to fit the quirks of given sample data. By making the model conform too closely to the sample data, its predictive power is compromised.

Data partitioning and cross-validation can be used to detect overfitting and provide objective assessment of the predictive performance of models. Suppose a model is developed using a training data set and is then assessed by inspecting the performance measures obtained from the validation data set. As shown in Figure 8.4, while the performance of the model on the training data set tends to improve (i.e., predictive error rate decreases) as the model gets more and more complex, the model performance on the validation data set will improve initially but deteriorate after a certain point. In addition to providing an unbiased performance evaluation of the model, the validation data set is often used to identify the optimal model complexity in some supervised data mining techniques (e.g., KNN and decision trees discussed in Chapters 9 and 10).

FIGURE 8.4 The relationship between error rate and model complexity

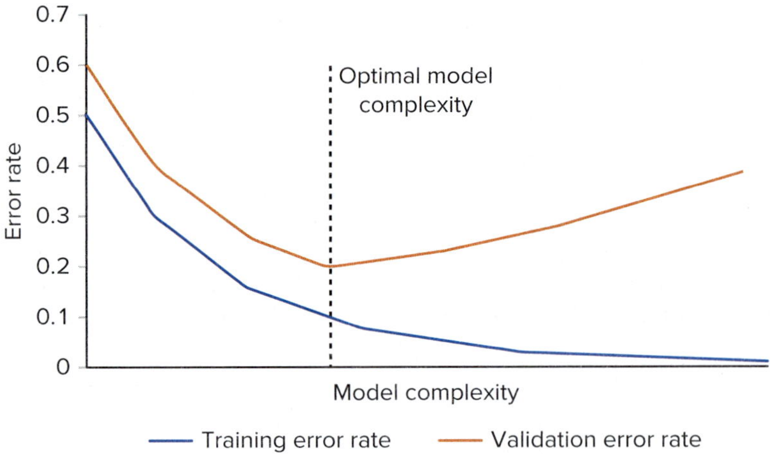

We will now discuss the assessment of classification models where the target variable is categorical, and prediction models where the target variable is numerical. Performance measures used in classification and prediction models are different; therefore, they are discussed separately in the following subsections.

Performance Evaluation for Classification Models

Performance measures for classification models can be computed from a confusion matrix, a table that summarizes classification outcomes obtained from the validation data set. Table 8.6 shows a confusion matrix for a binary classification problem. Assume that the target class, also called the success class, is Class 1 and that the nontarget class is Class 0. From the confusion matrix we see that two correct classifications are possible:

- True positive (TP) is a Class 1 observation that is correctly classified by the model, and
- True negative (TN) is a Class 0 observation that is correctly classified by the model.

Conversely, two incorrect classifications are possible:

- False positive (FP) is a Class 0 observation that is incorrectly classified as a Class 1 observation by the model, and
- False negative (FN) is a Class 1 observation that is incorrectly classified as a Class 0 observation by the model.

TABLE 8.6 Confusion Matrix

Actual Class	Predicted Class 1	Predicted Class 0
Class 1	No. of true positives (TP)	No. of false negatives (FN)
Class 0	No. of false positives (FP)	No. of true negatives (TN)

The followings are common performance measures for classification models:

The **misclassification rate**, also called **error rate**, is the overall proportion of observations that are misclassified. In other words, the misclassification rate measures how often the predictive model makes an incorrect prediction. It is computed using the following equation:

$$\text{Misclassification rate} = \frac{\text{FP} + \text{FN}}{\text{TP} + \text{TN} + \text{FP} + \text{FN}}$$

The **accuracy rate** is the overall proportion of observations that are classified correctly. As it measures how often the predictive model makes a correct prediction, we can think of the accuracy rate as the opposite measure of the misclassification rate. It is computed using the following equation:

$$\text{Accuracy rate} = 1 - \text{Misclassification rate} = \frac{\text{TP} + \text{TN}}{\text{TP} + \text{TN} + \text{FP} + \text{FN}}$$

Sensitivity, also called **recall**, is the proportion of target class cases that are classified correctly. It is computed using the following equation:

$$\text{Sensitivity} = \frac{\text{TP}}{\text{TP} + \text{FN}}$$

To better understand the importance of the sensitivity rate, consider an example of a model, say, for predicting breast cancer among a group of patients. A predictive model with 100% sensitivity would correctly identify all patients who have cancer. A model with 60% sensitivity would correctly identify only 60% of the patients with cancer (true positives) but leave the remaining 40% with the cancer undetected and untreated (false negatives). Developing a predictive model with a high sensitivity is clearly important to help identify patients with a life-threatening but treatable disease.

Precision, also called **positive predictive value**, is the proportion of the predicted target class cases that actually belong to the target class. It differs from sensitivity in that the denominator is based on *predicted* Class 1 cases instead of *actual* Class 1 cases. Precision is computed using the following equation:

$$\text{Precision} = \frac{\text{TP}}{\text{TP} + \text{FP}}$$

Consider again the predictive model for breast cancer. While the sensitivity rate measures the proportion of the patients with the cancer who test positive (true positives as a proportion of those who have the cancer), the precision rate measures the proportion of the patients with a positive test who in fact have the cancer (true positives as a proportion of those with a positive test). A predictive model with a low precision rate would unnecessarily subject many patients who are cancer-free to undergo further medical tests and treatments (false positives).

Specificity is the proportion of nontarget class cases that are classified correctly. It is computed using the following equation:

$$\text{Specificity} = \frac{\text{TN}}{\text{TN} + \text{FP}}$$

Again, consider the predictive model for breast cancer. A predictive model with 100% specificity would correctly identify all patients without the cancer. A model with 75% specificity would correctly identify 75% of the patients as cancer-free (true negatives), but the remaining 25% of patients who are cancer-free are classified by the model as having the cancer (false positives). These 25% of patients may be unnecessarily subjected to further medical tests or treatments.

CLASSIFICATION PERFORMANCE MEASURES

Common performance measures for classification models include the following:

- The misclassification rate, also called error rate, is the overall proportion of observations that are misclassified.
- The accuracy rate is the overall proportion of observations that are classified correctly.
- The sensitivity, also called recall, is the proportion of target class cases that are classified correctly.
- The precision, also called positive predictive value, is the proportion of the predicted target class cases that belong to the target class.
- The specificity is the proportion of nontarget class cases that are classified correctly.

These performance measures collectively represent the performance of a classification model. When the misclassification costs are symmetric for both target and nontarget class cases, the overall misclassification rate and accuracy rate are good indicators of model performance. However, emphasis may be placed on sensitivity or specificity measures when the misclassification costs are asymmetric, and/or the proportion of the target class observations is very small.

Consider the social media marketing example from the introductory case. The cost of misclassifying a buying customer as a nonbuying customer (e.g., loss in profit) is often much higher than the cost of misclassifying a non-buying customer as a buying customer (e.g., cost of sending marketing materials). In such cases, marketers tend to pay more attention to the sensitivity measure than to the overall accuracy as the sensitivity measure indicates the proportion of buyers the classification model is able to identify correctly. In addition, actual buyers tend to represent only a small portion of all the prospective buyers. Here, the accuracy rate may be misleading as a high overall accuracy rate may be a result of classifying the large number of non-buyers correctly, which is not indicative of a successful marketing campaign.

In practice, in order to assess the performance of a classification model, we often compare the model with a baseline or benchmark. A common baseline approach is to compare the accuracy rate of the model with that of a naïve rule where all cases are classified into the most predominant class. Additional information and examples for the naïve rule baseline are available in Chapters 9 and 10.

EXAMPLE 8.5

Recall the FashionTech example from the introductory case where Class 1 (target) is the group of social media users who purchase at least one product within 30 days of receiving a promotional message and Class 0 (nontarget) is the group of social media users who do not make a purchase after receiving a promotional message. Table 8.7 shows the confusion matrix that is obtained after applying the classification model to the validation data set of 200 observations. [Shortly, we show how we create the confusion matrix in Excel.]

TABLE 8.7 Confusion Matrix for the FashionTech Example

Actual Class	Predicted Class 1	Predicted Class 0
Class 1	29	19
Class 0	19	133

a. Interpret the four classifications in the confusion matrix.

b. Calculate and interpret the accuracy rate.

c. Calculate and interpret sensitivity and specificity.

SOLUTION:

a. The values in the confusion matrix are interpreted as follows:

- True positives (TP): There are 29 FashionTech customers who made a purchase and were correctly classified as buyers by the classification model, so TP = 29.
- True negatives (TN): There are 133 FashionTech customers who did not make a purchase and were correctly classified as nonbuyers by the classification model, so TN = 133.
- False positives (FP): There are 19 nonpurchasing FashionTech customers who were incorrectly classified as buyers by the classification model (the lower left cell of Table 8.7), so FP = 19, and
- False negatives (FN): There are 19 FashionTech customers who made a purchase but were classified by the classification model as nonbuyers (the upper right cell of Table 8.7), so FN = 19.

b. The accuracy rate is calculated as $\frac{TP + TN}{TP + TN + FP + FN} = \frac{29 + 133}{29 + 133 + 19 + 19} = 0.81$; this measure implies that 81% of the observations are correctly classified.

c. The sensitivity is calculated as $\frac{TP}{TP + FN} = \frac{29}{29 + 19} = 0.64$; this is the proportion of buyers that the classification model is able to identify correctly. The specificity is calculated as $\frac{TN}{TN + FP} = \frac{133}{133 + 19} = 0.875$; this is the proportion of non-buyers that the classification model is able to identify correctly. As mentioned earlier, in this application the sensitivity measure is the more useful performance measure.

Using Excel to Obtain the Confusion Matrix and Performance Measures

The confusion matrix in Table 8.7 is based on the ***Class_Prob*** data set that was generated by the FashionTech firm from the introductory case. Each row in the data set includes the actual class to which the observation belongs (ActualClass) and the probability of the target class (TargetProb) predicted by an estimated classification model; FashionTech did not provide the model details. A portion of the data is shown in Table 8.8.

FILE
Class_Prob

TABLE 8.8 A Portion of the FashionTech Firm Data Set

ActualClass	TargetProb
1	0.77585787
0	0.04709009
⋮	⋮
0	0.38111670

Here, we show step-by-step Excel instructions to build a confusion matrix for an estimated classification model given the target probabilities; specifically, we replicate Table 8.7. (In Chapters 9 and 10, we discuss how Analytic Solver and R estimate classification models, generate a confusion matrix as well as performance measures)

A. Open the ***Class_Prob*** data file.

B. Derive the predicted class based on a default cutoff of 0.5; in other words, the predicted class equals one if the target probability is greater than or equal to 0.5, zero otherwise. Enter the column heading "PredClass" in cell C1. Enter the formula = IF(B2 >=0.5, 1, 0) in cell C2. Fill the range C3:C201 using the formula in C2.

C. Compute the values for the four classifications of the confusion matrix as follows:
   - Enter the column heading "True Positive" in cell D1. Enter the formula = IF (AND(A2 = 1, C2 = 1), 1, 0) in cell D2. Fill the range D3:D201 using the formula in D2.
   - Enter the column heading "True Negative" in cell E1. Enter the formula = IF(AND (A2 = 0, C2 = 0), 1, 0) in cell E2. Fill the range E3:E201 using the formula in E2.
   - Enter the column heading "False Positive" in cell F1. Enter the formula = IF(AND (A2 = 0, C2 = 1), 1, 0) in cell F2. Fill the range F3:F201 using the formula in F2.
   - Enter the column heading "False Negative" in cell G1. Enter the formula = IF (AND(A2 = 1, C2 = 0), 1, 0) in cell G2. Fill the range G3:G201 using the formula in G2.

D. Build the confusion matrix by entering the formulas as shown in Table 8.9. The resulting table should be identical to Table 8.7.

TABLE 8.9 Excel Formulas for the Confusion Matrix

Actual Class	Predicted Class 1	Predicted Class 0
Class 1	=COUNTIF(D2:D201, 1)	=COUNTIF(G2:G201, 1)
Class 0	=COUNTIF(F2:F201, 1)	=COUNTIF(E2:E201, 1)

Selecting Cut-off Values

In the context of the binary choice models presented in section 7.3, we computed the probability that a new mortgage loan application will be approved (Class 1) or denied (Class 0). If the predicted probability value was greater than or equal to 0.5, we classified the new loan application as belonging to Class 1 (approved), and Class 0 (denied) otherwise. In other words, we used a default cutoff value of 0.5. Classification techniques in all supervised data mining follow a similar process where the class membership is determined by comparing the predicted probability of the target class to a predetermined cutoff value, the minimum required probability of belonging to the target class. In some applications, however, the analyst may choose to increase or decrease the cutoff value to classify fewer or more observations into the target class due to asymmetric misclassification costs or uneven class distributions. As a result, the choice of the cutoff value can influence the confusion matrix and the resulting performance measures. Example 8.6 highlights the impact of the cutoff value on the performance measures of a classification model.

EXAMPLE 8.6

Table 8.10 shows the actual class and the predicted target class probability for 10 observations of a categorical variable. The table also includes the predicted target class memberships based on five different cutoff values.

TABLE 8.10 Actual and Predicted Class Memberships Given Various Cutoffs

		Target Class	Predicted Target Class by Cutoffs				
Obs.	**Actual Class**	**Probability**	**0.15**	**0.25**	**0.50**	**0.75**	**0.85**
1	1	0.73	1	1	1	0	0
2	1	0.48	1	1	0	0	0
3	0	0.22	1	0	0	0	0
4	1	0.33	1	1	0	0	0
5	0	0.52	1	1	1	0	0
6	0	0.10	0	0	0	0	0
7	1	0.98	1	1	1	1	1
8	0	0.05	0	0	0	0	0
9	0	0.12	0	0	0	0	0
10	1	0.78	1	1	1	1	0

a. Calculate the misclassification rate with a cutoff value of 0.25 and a cutoff value of 0.75.

b. Compute the sensitivity and precision with a cutoff value of 0.25 and a cutoff value of 0.75.

c. Report and interpret performance measures with all five cutoff values.

SOLUTION:

a. Recall that the misclassification rate is the overall proportion of observations that are misclassified. With a cutoff value of 0.25, we note that there is only one observation, the 5th, that is not correctly classified; therefore, the misclassification rate is computed as 1/10 = 0.10. With a cutoff value of 0.75, observations 1st, 2nd, and 4th are not correctly classified, resulting in the misclassification rate of 3/10 = 0.30.

b. Recall that the sensitivity is the proportion of the target class cases that are classified correctly. With a cutoff value of 0.25, we find that all five actual Class 1 observations are correctly classified as the target classes, so the sensitivity is 5/5 = 1. With a cutoff value of 0.75, the sensitivity decreases to 2/5 = 0.40. Recall that the precision is the proportion of the predicted target class cases that actually belong to the target class. With a cutoff value of 0.25, we note that of the six predicted target class cases, five of the cases belong to the target class, so the precision is 5/6 = 0.833. With a cutoff value of 0.75, the precision increases to 2/2 = 1.

c. Table 8.11 shows performance measures for the different cutoff values in Table 8.10.

TABLE 8.11 Classification Performance Measures

Cutoff	Misclassification Rate	Accuracy Rate	Sensitivity	Precision	Specificity
0.15	0.20	0.80	1.00	0.714	0.60
0.25	0.10	0.90	1.00	0.833	0.80
0.50	0.30	0.70	0.60	0.750	0.80
0.75	0.30	0.70	0.40	1.000	1.00
0.85	0.40	0.60	0.20	1.000	1.00

As mentioned earlier, and as shown in Table 8.11, the choice of the cutoff value can greatly influence the confusion matrix and performance measures. Although the default for the cutoff value for binary choice models is 0.50, the analyst may choose a higher or lower cutoff value to classify fewer or more observations into the target class to adjust for asymmetric misclassification costs or uneven class distribution.

Performance Charts for Classification

It is sometimes more informative to have graphic representations to assess the predictive performance of data mining models. The most popular performance charts are the cumulative lift chart, the decile-wise lift chart, and the receiver operating characteristic (ROC) curve.

Cumulative Lift Chart

A **cumulative lift chart** (also called a cumulative gains chart or a lift chart) shows the improvement that a predictive model provides over a random selection in capturing the target class cases. It also allows us to determine the point at which the model's predictions become less useful. Figure 8.5 displays a cumulative lift chart for a classification model. The chart shows the number (percentage) of the target class cases gained by targeting a number (percentage) of all the cases. The *x* axis indicates the number of cases selected. The *y* axis indicates the cumulative number of target class (Class 1) cases identified by the model. The orange diagonal line represents the baseline model where observations are randomly selected, without using predictive models. The slope of the diagonal line is the number of Class 1 cases divided by the total number of cases, or the probability of a randomly selected case belonging to Class 1. Suppose 475 of the 5,000 total cases belong to Class 1. The probability of a randomly selected case belonging to Class 1, or the slope of the diagonal line, is 475/5,000 = 0.095; note that in Figure 8.5, the slope of the diagonal line is 190/2000 = 0.095.

FIGURE 8.5 The cumulative lift chart

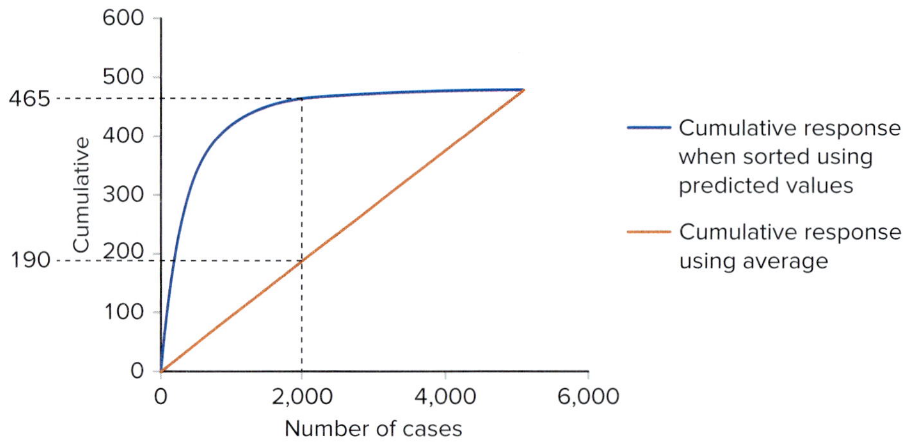

The blue upper curve in Figure 8.5 is called the lift curve, which represents the ability of the classification model to identify Class 1 cases (for example, buyers). To construct a lift curve, the observations in the validation data set are sorted in descending order based on their predicted probability of belonging to the target class (i.e., Class 1). The lift curve in Figure 8.5 shows that if we select the top 2,000 observations with the highest predicted probability of belonging to Class 1, we will capture 465 Class 1 observations. If we randomly select 2,000 observations, we will likely capture only 190 Class 1 observations. The ratio of the number of Class 1 observations captured by the model to the number captured by random selection is called the lift.

The cumulative lift chart in Figure 8.5 shows that when we select 2,000 observations, the model provides a lift of 465/190 or 2.447. This means that among the top 2,000 observations selected by the model, we are able to capture 2.447 times as many Class 1 observations as compared to the 2,000 observations selected randomly. Therefore, the cumulative lift chart shows how well a predictive model can capture the target class cases, compared to random selection. A high lift number is desirable in most applications ranging from marketing to fraud detection as it means that we are able to capture a large proportion of the target class cases by only focusing on a small portion of cases with a high predicted probability. A lift curve that is above the baseline is indicative of good predictive performance of the model. The further above the baseline the lift curve lies, the better the model's ability to identify target class cases.

Decile-wise Lift Chart

The **decile-wise lift chart** conveys similar information as the cumulative lift chart but presents the information in 10 equal-sized intervals (e.g., every 10% of the observations). It is usually presented as a bar chart where the *y* axis represents the ratio of the target class cases identified by the model to that identified through random selection. A decile-wise lift chart is shown in Figure 8.6.

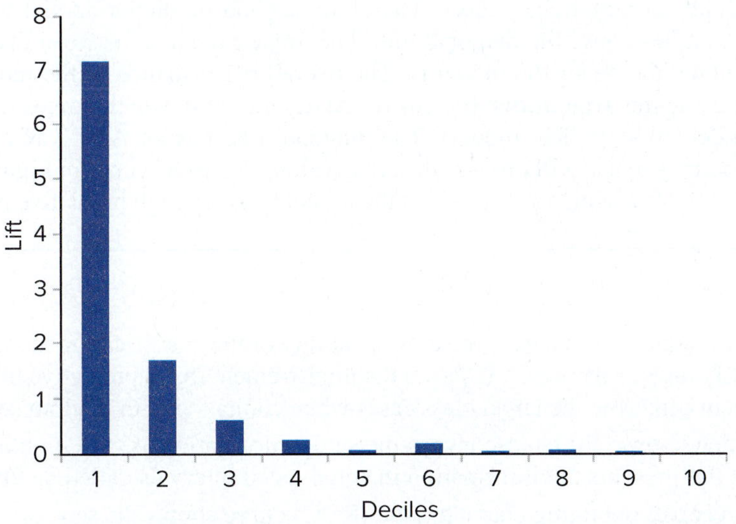

FIGURE 8.6 The decile-wise lift chart

Figure 8.6 shows that the lift for the first 10% of the observations (first bar) is about 7.1, which means that the top 10% of the observations selected by the model contain 7.1 times as many Class 1 cases as the 10% of the observations that are randomly selected. It also allows us to determine the point at which the model's predictions become less useful. For example, after the second decile, the lift values dip below one, suggesting that the model will capture fewer target class cases than random selection in the subsequent deciles. Therefore, in this case, we want to focus on the first 20% of the observations that have the highest predicted probabilities of belonging to the target class if our goal is to capture the target class cases (e.g., in a marketing campaign or when detecting fraudulent credit card transactions).

Receiver Operating Characteristic (ROC) Curve

The **receiver operating characteristic (ROC) curve** shows the sensitivity and specificity measures across all cutoff values and how accurately the model is able to classify both target and nontarget class cases overall. An ROC curve is shown in Figure 8.7. The x-axis of the ROC curve is equal to 1 – Specificity, which ranges from 0 (classifying 100% of the nontarget class cases correctly) to 1 (classifying 0% of the nontarget class cases correctly), and the y-axis is equal to sensitivity, which also ranges from 0 (classifying 0% of the target class cases correctly) to 1 (classifying 100% of the target class cases correctly); therefore, the perfect point on the diagram is point (0,1) as it indicates that the model is able to correctly classify 100% of both the target and nontarget class cases simultaneously.

FIGURE 8.7 The ROC curve

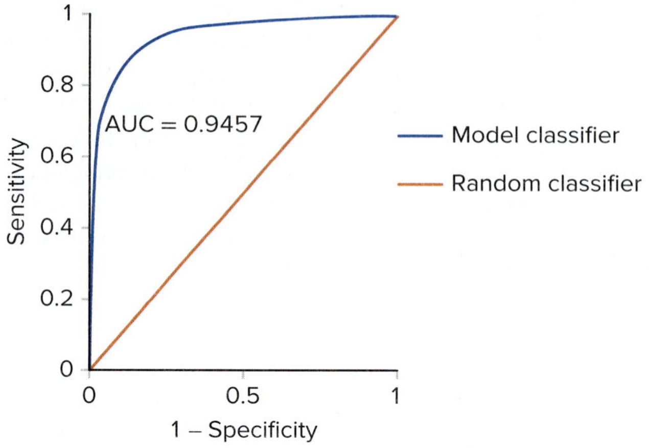

Figure 8.7 shows the ROC curve along with the orange diagonal line that represents a baseline model that randomly assigns the observations to the two classes based on the prior probability of target class cases. Therefore, a good predictive model would have a ROC curve that lies above the diagonal line. The greater the area between the ROC curve and the baseline, the better the model is. The overall performance of the model can also be assessed using the **area under the curve (AUC)** measure, which ranges from 0 (worst possible model) to 1 (perfect model). The diagonal line has an AUC value of 0.5. The software product you use will provide the AUC value. The ROC curve in Figure 8.7 has an AUC value of 0.9457, which suggests that the model has very high predictive performance.

SUMMARY OF CLASSIFICATION PERFORMANCE DIAGRAMS

- The cumulative lift chart represents the ability of the classification model to identify target class cases. It shows the improvement that a predictive model provides in capturing the target class cases when compared with random selection.
- The decile-wise lift chart conveys the same information as the cumulative lift chart but presents the information in equal-sized intervals called deciles.
- The receiver operating characteristic (ROC) curve shows the sensitivity and the specificity measures across all cutoff values and how accurately the model is able to classify both target and nontarget class cases.

EXAMPLE 8.7

Let's go back to the introductory case where Alissa and her team at FashionTech want to assess the performance of predictive models developed by MarketWiz. Alissa and her team constructed a cumulative lift chart, a decile-wise lift chart, and a ROC curve; see Figure 8.8. Interpret these performance charts. [Shortly, we show how to create these graphs in Excel.]

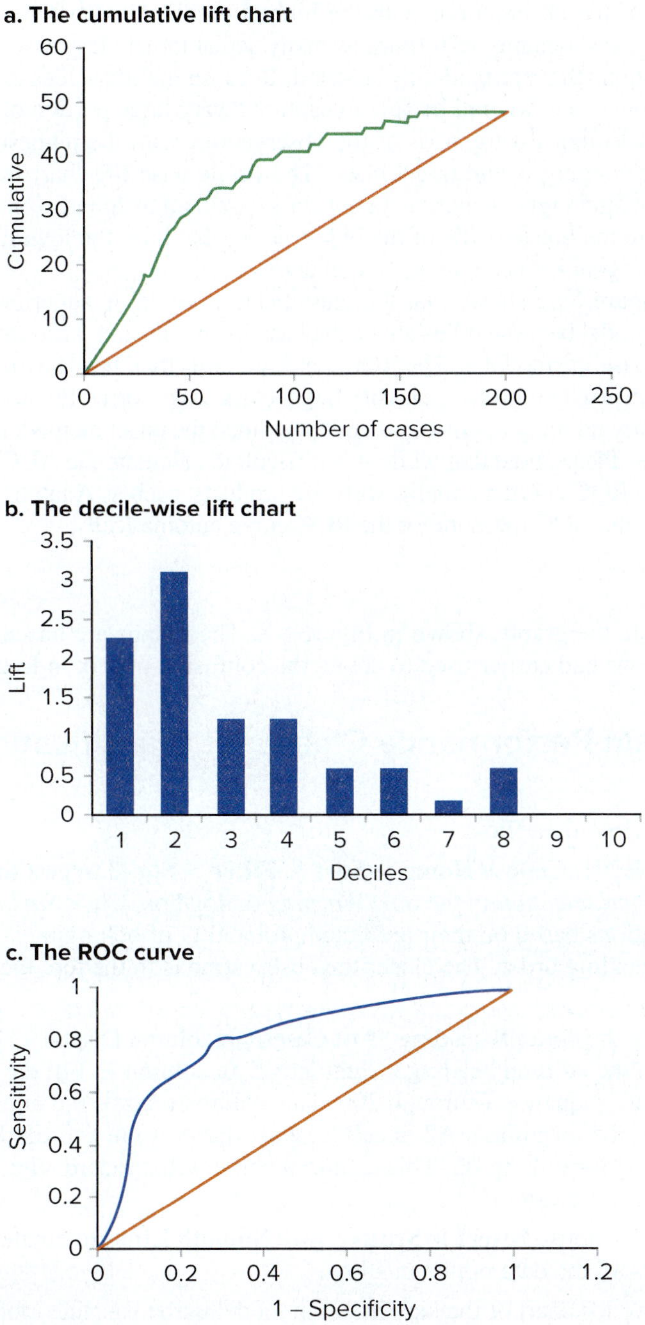

FIGURE 8.8 Performance charts for Example 8.7

SOLUTION:

The cumulative lift curve in Figure 8.8a shows that the classification model is superior compared to the baseline model because it lies above the baseline model. The chart shows that if 50 observations (25% of the total observations) with the highest predicted probability of belonging to Class 1 are selected, we would be able to capture 30 of the 48 actual Class 1 cases, or 30/48 = 0.625, or 62.5%. In the baseline model where the cases are randomly selected, we would only be able to capture 12/48 = 0.25, or 25% of the Class 1 cases. Therefore, at 50 cases, the lift of the classification model is 0.625/0.25 = 2.5.

The decile-wise lift chart in Figure 8.8b shows the improvement (lift) that the classification model provides in capturing the target class cases for each decile compared to the baseline model. For example, the lift for the first decile is 2.29, which implies that the top 10% of the observations with the highest predicted probability of belonging to the target class contains 2.29 times as many actual target class cases as the 10% of the observations that are randomly selected. Because the lift values of the first four deciles are above one, we will be able to capture a very large portion of the target class cases by selecting the top 40% of the observations with the highest predicted probability of belonging to the target class. The decile-wise lift chart in Figure 8.8b also shows that after eight deciles, no target class cases can be found. This suggests that we can ignore the bottom 20% of the observations that have the lowest predictive probability if our goal is to capture the target class cases.

The ROC curve in Figure 8.8c shows that the classification model is superior compared to the baseline model because it lies above the baseline model and is closer to the point (0,1) than the baseline model is. The ROC curve suggests that the classification model has higher sensitivity (ability to classify target class cases correctly) and specificity (ability to classify nontarget class cases correctly) than the baseline model has across all cutoff values. Please note that while it is difficult to calculate the AUC measure when you plot the ROC curve manually, software products, such as Analytic Solver and R, will provide the AUC measure for the ROC curve automatically.

We now use Excel to replicate the graphs shown in Figure 8.8. The graphs are based on the ***Class-Prob*** data file that we had earlier used to create the confusion matrix in Excel.

Using Excel to Obtain Performance Charts for Classification

The Cumulative Lift Chart

FILE
Class_Prob

A. Open the original ***Class_Prob*** data file.

B. Select the data range B1:B201. Choose **Home > Sort & Filter > Sort Largest to Smallest**. Select *Expand the selection* in the *Sort Warning* dialog box. Click *Sort.* This sorts all the observations based on their predicted probability of belonging to the target class in descending order. The closer the observation is to the top, the higher the probability.

C. Create a new column with the column heading "# of Cases" in column D and another new column with the column heading "Cumulative" in column E. Fill the cells D2:D201with the data sequence 1 through 200. This column records the number of observations. Enter the formulas =A2 in cell E2 and =E2 + A3 in cell E3. Fill the range E4:E201 with the formula in E3. This creates a column that records the cumulative number of Class 1 cases.

D. Select the range D1:E201. Choose **Insert > Scatter with Smooth Lines** to create a scatter chart that connects all the data points in a line.

E. To compare the cumulative lift chart of the classification model to the baseline model, add a diagonal line that connects points (0,0) and (200,48). As there are 48 actual Class 1 cases among the 200 cases, each case has the probability of 48/200 = 0.24 of belonging to Class 1. Right-click the chart area and choose *Select Data.* Click the *Add* button in the *Select Data Source* dialog box. Enter "Baseline Model" in the *Series name:* box. Enter "0, 200" in the *Series X values:* box. Enter "0, 48" in the *Series Y values:* box. Click **OK** twice. [Formatting regarding the chart title, axis titles, etc. can be done by selecting **Format > Add Chart Element** from the menu.]

The Decile-Wise Lift Chart

FILE
Class_Prob

A. Open the original ***Class_Prob*** data file and sort the data as described in part B for the cumulative lift chart.

B. We need to compute the ratio of the number of Class 1 cases identified in each decile (200 × 0.10 = 20 cases in each decile) to the number of Class 1 cases that we would have identified if 10% of the cases were selected randomly.

First type the column heading "# of Class 1 Cases in Each Decile" in D1 and "Decile-Wise Lift" in E1. In order to find the number of Class 1 cases identified in the first decile—the numerator of the ratio for the first decile—type =SUM(A2:A21) in D2. Similarly, to find the number of Class 1 cases identified in the second decile, type =SUM(A22:A41) in D3. The other eight deciles are found in a like manner. Because there are a total of 48 Class 1 cases, the number of Class 1 cases among the randomly selected 10% of the cases would be $48 \times 0.10 = 4.8$ cases; this is the denominator of the ratio for all deciles. Enter the formula =D2/4.8 in cell E2 to compute the lift for the first decile. Fill the range E3:E11 with the formula in E2. This computes the lift values for the rest of the 9 deciles.

C. Select the range E2:E11. Choose **Insert > Insert Column or Bar Chart > Clustered Columns** to create a column chart. [Formatting (regarding the chart title, axis titles, etc.) can be done by selecting **Format > Add Chart Element** from the menu.]

The ROC Curve

Earlier, we used the ***Class_Prob*** data to derive the confusion matrix and the resulting performance measures with a default cutoff value of 0.5. In order to construct the ROC curve, we follow the same procedure to find performance measures for the various cutoff values. We created the ***Spec_Sens*** data set, which contains the specificity and sensitivity measures for cutoff values ranging from 0 to 1 in 0.05 increments. The data set has the following columns: the cutoff value (Cutoff), the specificity value (Specificity), and the sensitivity value (Sensitivity). A portion of the data is shown in Table 8.12.

TABLE 8.12 A portion of the Spec_Sens data set

Cutoff	Specificity	Sensitivity
0	0	1
0.05	0.296053	0.958333
⋮	⋮	⋮
1	1	0

FILE *Spec_Sens*

A. Open the ***Spec_Sens*** data file.

B. Select column C. Right-click and choose Insert to insert a column. Type the column heading "1 – Specificity" in the new column. Insert the formula = 1–B2 in cell C2. Fill the range C3:C22 with the formula in C2. The new column computes the 1 – Specificity values for all the cutoff values in column A.

C. Select the range C1:D22. Choose **Insert > Scatter with Smooth Lines** to create a scatter chart that connects all the data points in a line. Change the chart title to "ROC Curve". Change the x-axis title to "1 – Specificity". Change the y-axis title to "Sensitivity".

D. To compare the ROC curve of the classification model to that of the baseline model, you will add a diagonal line that connects points (0,0) and (1,1). Right-click the chart area and choose *Select Data.* Click the *Add* button in the *Select Data Source* dialog box. Enter "Baseline Model" in the *Series name:* box. Enter "0, 1" in the *Series X values:* box. Enter "0, 1" in the *Series Y values:* box. Click **OK** twice.

Performance Evaluation for Prediction

We now consider the performance measures for prediction models where the target variables have numerical values. Similar to the performance measures for regression models that were discussed in Chapters 6 and 7, prediction performance of supervised data mining models is assessed by computing the **prediction error** e, which is the difference between the actual value y and predicted value $\hat{y}$ of the target variable. It is calculated as

$$e = y - \hat{y}.$$

Note that prediction errors are calculated in the same way as the residuals, but they are calculated using the validation data set rather than the training data set. As with regression models, low values for the prediction error e are preferred. The following definition box highlights five performance measures: (1) the root mean square error (RMSE), (2) the mean error (ME) or the average error (AE), (3) the mean absolute deviation (MAD) or mean absolute error (MAE), (4) the mean percentage error (MPE), and (5) the mean absolute percentage error (MAPE).

PREDICTION PERFORMANCE MEASURES

All performance measures are based on the prediction error, $e = y - \hat{y}$, given n observations in the validation data set.

- The **root mean square error (RMSE)** is similar to the standard error of the estimate in the linear regression model except that it is calculated for the validation data set, rather than the training data set. It is calculated as $\text{RMSE} = \sqrt{\frac{\Sigma e_i^2}{n}}$. Because RMSE uses squared prediction errors, it penalizes models with large prediction errors when used for comparing models.
- The **mean error (ME)** or the **average error (AE)** is the average of the prediction errors and is calculated as $\text{ME} = \frac{\Sigma e_i}{n}$. Because positive and negative errors offset each other, average error is used as a measure of prediction *bias*. On average, a positive ME implies the model underpredicts, a negative ME implies it overpredicts, and an ME close to zero implies that the predictions are unbiased.
- The **mean absolute deviation (MAD)** or **mean absolute error (MAE)** is the average absolute error and is calculated as $\text{MAD} = \frac{\Sigma |e_i|}{n}$. MAD measures the average *magnitude* of the errors, without considering their direction. Because errors are not squared, models with large errors are not penalized as heavily as in RMSE.
- The **mean percentage error (MPE)** is the average percentage error and is calculated as $\text{MPE} = \left(\frac{1}{n}\Sigma\frac{e_i}{y_i}\right) \times 100$. Because the positive and negative percentage errors can offset each other, MPE is often used as a measure of prediction bias; however, it does not reflect the magnitude of the errors.
- The **mean absolute percentage error (MAPE)** is the average absolute percentage error and is calculated as $\text{MAPE} = \left(\frac{1}{n}\Sigma\left|\frac{e_i}{y_i}\right|\right) \times 100$. It shows the error as a percentage of the actual value, giving a sense of the magnitude of the errors.

The two most commonly used performance measures that capture the magnitude of the errors are RMSE and MAD. They both range from 0 to ∞, with lower values indicating a better prediction model. Because RMSE gives a relatively high weight to large errors, it is more useful when large errors are particularly undesirable. Note that RMSE will always be larger or equal to MAD; RMSE = MAD only if all of the errors have the same magnitude.

There is no way to define a "good" value for RMSE and MAD because they both assume the same units as the original target variable. For example, the RMSE and MAD values will change depending on whether the purchase amounts are expressed in U.S. dollars or in euros. This makes these measures difficult to interpret in isolation, although they are useful for model selection. The model with the lowest RMSE or MAD will always be preferred over competing models, irrespective of the currency used in the calculations. The main attraction of MAPE is that it is in percentage terms and, therefore, it is somewhat easy to interpret.

EXAMPLE 8.8

Recall from the introductory case that Alissa and her team at FashionTech want to assess the performance of predictive models developed by MarketWiz. Two prediction models were designed to predict the one-year purchase amounts for customers acquired through social media channels. After applying the prediction models to the validation data set of 200 observations, Alissa and her team generated the ***Prediction*** data set, which contains the predicted one-year purchase amounts for the 200 observations. Each row of the data set includes the actual target value (ActVal) and the corresponding predicted value for two models (PredVal1 and PredVal2). A portion of the data is shown in Table 8.13.

FILE *Prediction*

TABLE 8.13 Actual and Predicted Values

ActVal	PredVal1	PredVal2
1326.50	1189.60	1169.60
546.00	493.30	506.30
⋮	⋮	⋮
689.50	481.50	493.50

Using the data from Table 8.13, the five performance measures, RMSE, ME, MAD, MPE, and MAPE, for both prediction models were calculated. These measures are shown in Table 8.14. Use these measures to compare the performance of the models. [Shortly, we show how we compute these measures in Excel.]

TABLE 8.14 Prediction Performance Measures

Performance Measure	Model 1	Model 2
RMSE	171.3489	174.1758
ME	11.2530	12.0480
MAD	115.1650	117.9920
MPE	−2.05%	−2.08%
MAPE	15.51%	15.95%

SOLUTION:

For both models, ME and MPE, as measures of prediction bias, offer conflicting results. The positive values of ME suggest that predictions for both models tend to underestimate the purchase amounts, while negative values of MPE suggest that predictions tend to slightly overestimate the purchase amounts percentwise. Because Model 1 exhibits lower values of all performance measures, we conclude that Model 1 has the lower prediction bias as well as lower magnitude of the errors. Therefore, Model 1 is the preferred model to predict the one-year purchase amounts for customers acquired through social media channels.

Using Excel to Obtain Performance Measures for Prediction

We replicate the performance measures for Model 1 shown in Table 8.14; performance measures for Model 2 can be computed similarly.

FILE *Prediction*

A. Open the ***Prediction*** data file.

B. Create a new column in column D to compute the prediction error for each observation. Type the column heading "Error" in cell D1. Enter the formula = A2−B2 in cell D2. Fill the range D3:D201 with the formula.

C. Create a new column in column E to compute the squared prediction error for each observation. Type the column heading "Squared Error" in cell E1. Enter the formula =D2^2 in cell E2. Fill the range E3:E201 with the formula.

D. Create a new column in column F to compute the absolute prediction error for each observation. Type the column heading "Absolute Error" in cell F1. Enter the formula =ABS(D2) in cell F2. Fill the range F3:F201 with the formula.

E. Create a new column in column G to compute the prediction error as a percentage of the actual value for each observation. Type the column heading "Percent Error" in cell G1. Enter the formula =D2/A2 in cell G2. Fill the range G3:G201 with the formula.

F. Create a new column in column H to compute the absolute percent error for each observation. Type the column heading "Absolute Percent Error" in cell H1. Enter the formula =ABS(G2) in cell H2. Fill the range H3:H201 with the formula.

G. Compute the performance measures anywhere in the worksheet by entering the formulas as shown in Table 8.15. The resulting table should be identical to the second column of Table 8.14.

TABLE 8.15 Excel Formulas for Prediction Performance Measures

Performance Measures	Formula
RMSE	=SQRT(SUM(E2:E201)/200)
ME	=SUM(D2:D201)/200
MAD	=SUM(F2:F201)/200
MPE	=SUM(G2:G201)/200
MAPE	=SUM(H2:H201)/200

SYNOPSIS OF INTRODUCTORY CASE

Wayhome studio/Shutterstock

With an objective to help FashionTech acquire new customers as well as increase sales from existing customers, MarketWiz develops predictive models for the online apparel retailer. A classification model is estimated that predicts purchase probability from FashionTech within 30 days of receiving a promotional message in their social media account. A confusion matrix using 0.5 as the cutoff value is constructed to assess the performance of the model, using 200 observations in the validation data set. The confusion matrix shows that 29 buyers and 133 nonbuyers are correctly classified by the model, suggesting an accuracy rate of 0.81.

A sensitivity measure of 0.6042 and a specificity measure of 0.8750 suggest that the model is better at classifying nonbuyers correctly than classifying buyers correctly. Because the confusion matrix and the performance measures are sensitive to the chosen cutoff value to classify the observations, MarketWiz explains that if the cutoff value is lowered, then the model will classify more buyers correctly but at the same time classify more nonbuyers incorrectly. Because the cost of sending social media messages is low, FashionTech agrees to lower the cutoff to 0.25 to increase sensitivity to 0.8125.

The performance of the model is also assessed graphically using the cumulative lift chart, decile-wise lift chart, and ROC curve. The cumulative lift and decile-wise lift charts show that the model can capture almost all the actual buyers by targeting only a portion of social media users with the highest predicted probability of purchasing. The ROC curve shows that the model performs better than the baseline model (random guess) across all cutoff values in terms of sensitivity and specificity. Overall, the estimated classification model does a good job classifying potential customers into the purchase and no-purchase classes.

Two models are estimated to predict the one-year purchase amounts for customers acquired through social media channels. In order to compare the performance of the models, several performance measures are calculated using 200 observations in the validation data set. Because the first estimated model exhibits lower values for all performance measures, we conclude that the first model has lower prediction bias as well as lower magnitude of the errors when compared with the second model. Therefore, the first model is the preferred model to predict the one-year purchase amounts for customers acquired through social media channels.

EXERCISES 8.3

Mechanics

18. **FILE** ***Exercise_8.18.*** Construct a confusion matrix using the accompanying data set that lists actual and predicted class memberships for 10 observations.

19. Compute the misclassification rate, accuracy rate, sensitivity, precision, and specificity for the following confusion matrix.

Actual Class	Predicted Class 1	Predicted Class 0
Class 1	120	67
Class 0	35	278

20. Compute the misclassification rate, accuracy rate, sensitivity, precision, and specificity for the following confusion matrix.

Actual Class	Predicted Class 1	Predicted Class 0
Class 1	254	10
Class 0	87	649

21. Compute the misclassification rate, accuracy rate, sensitivity, precision, and specificity for the following confusion matrix.

Actual Class	Predicted Class 1	Predicted Class 0
Class 1	295	378
Class 0	379	3948

22. Compute the misclassification rate, accuracy rate, sensitivity, precision, and specificity for the following confusion matrix.

Actual Class	Predicted Class 1	Predicted Class 0
Class 1	1,367	25
Class 0	35	1,573

23. **FILE** ***Exercise_8.23.*** Answer the following questions using the accompanying data set that lists the actual class memberships and predicted Class 1 (target class) probabilities for 10 observations.
    a. Compute the misclassification rate, accuracy rate, sensitivity, precision, and specificity using the cutoff value of 0.5.
    b. Compute the misclassification rate, accuracy rate, sensitivity, precision, and specificity using the cutoff value of 0.25.
    c. Compute the misclassification rate, accuracy rate, sensitivity, precision, and specificity using the cutoff value of 0.75.

24. Use the data in the preceding exercise.
    a. What is the lift that the classification model provides if 5 observations are selected by the model compared to randomly selecting 5 observations?
    b. What is the lift that the classification model provides if 8 observations are selected by the model compared to randomly selecting 8 observations?

25. **FILE** ***Exercise_8.25.*** Answer the following questions using the accompanying data set that lists the actual class memberships and predicted Class 0 (nontarget class) probabilities for 10 observations.
    a. Compute the misclassification rate, accuracy rate, sensitivity, precision, and specificity using the cutoff value of 0.5.
    b. Compute the misclassification rate, accuracy rate, sensitivity, precision, and specificity using the cutoff value of 0.25.
    c. Compute the misclassification rate, accuracy rate, sensitivity, precision, and specificity using the cutoff value of 0.75.

26. Use the data in the preceding exercise.
    a. What is the lift that the classification model provides if 5 observations are selected by the model compared to randomly selecting 5 observations?
    b. What is the lift that the classification model provides if 8 observations are selected by the model compared to randomly selecting 8 observations?

27. **FILE** ***Exercise_8.27.*** Compute the RMSE, ME, MAD, MPE, and MAPE using the accompanying data set that lists the actual and predicted values for 10 observations.

28. **FILE** ***Exercise_8.28.*** Compute the RMSE, ME, MAD, MPE, and MAPE using the accompanying data set that lists the actual and predicted values for 10 observations.

Applications

29. A mail-order catalog company has developed a classification model to predict whether a prospective customer will place an order if he or she receives a catalog in the mail. If the prospective customer is predicted to place an order, then he or she is classified in Class 1; otherwise, he or she is classified in Class 0. The validation data set results in the following confusion matrix.

Actual Class	Predicted Class 1	Predicted Class 0
Class 1	75	25
Class 0	84	816

a. Compute the misclassification rate, accuracy rate, sensitivity, precision, and specificity of the classification model.

b. The confusion matrix was generated based on a cutoff rate of 0.5. If the cutoff rate is decreased to 0.25, will the sensitivity value increase or decrease? What about the specificity value?

c. If the profit from an order is much higher than the cost of sending a catalog, would the company benefit from a higher or lower cutoff rate for classifying prospective customers in Class 1 and Class 0?

30. Randy Johnson is an insurance adjustor for a national auto insurance company. Using historical insurance claim data, Randy has built an insurance fraud detection model with the help of a data analyst. Applying the model on the validation data set generated the following confusion matrix. A fraudulent insurance claim is a Class 1 case while a nonfraudulent claim is a Class 0 case.

Actual Class	Predicted Class 1	Predicted Class 0
Class 1	130	170
Class 0	2,402	27,298

a. Compute the misclassification rate, accuracy rate, sensitivity, precision, and specificity of the classification model.

b. Should the data be oversampled to produce a more reliable classification model?

c. The confusion matrix was generated based on a cutoff rate of 0.5. If the cost of missing a fraudulent insurance claim is much higher than the cost of investigating a potentially fraudulent insurance claim, should the cutoff rate be increased or decreased when classifying claims?

31. **FILE** ***Credit_Cards.*** A national bank has developed a predictive model for identifying customers who are more likely to accept a credit card offer. If a customer is predicted to accept the credit card offer, he or she is classified into Class 1; otherwise, he or she is classified into Class 0. Applying the model to the validation data set generated a table that lists the actual class membership and predicted Class 1 probability of the 100 observations in the validation data set. A portion of the table is shown below.

Customer	Actual Class	Predicted Class 1 Probability
1	1	0.22
2	0	0.54
⋮	⋮	⋮
100	1	0.5

a. Specify the predicted class membership for the validation data set using the cutoff values of 0.25, 0.5, and 0.75. Produce a confusion matrix in Excel based on the classification results from each cutoff value.

b. Compute the misclassification rate, accuracy rate, sensitivity, precision, and specificity of the classification model for each of the three cutoff values specified in part a.

c. Create a cumulative lift chart and a decile-wise lift chart for the classification model.

d. What is the lift that the classification model provides if 20% of the observations are selected by the model compared to randomly selecting 20% of the observations?

e. What is the lift that the classification model provides if 50% of the observations are selected by the model compared to randomly selecting 50% of the observations?

32. **FILE** ***IT_Professionals.*** Kenzi Williams is the Director of Human Resources of a high-tech company. In order to manage the high turnover rate of the IT professionals in her company, she has developed a predictive model for identifying software engineers who are more likely to leave the company within the first year. If the software engineer is predicted to leave the company within a year, he or she is classified into Class 1; otherwise, he or she is classified into Class 0. Applying the model to the validation data set generated a table that lists the actual class membership and predicted Class 1 probability of the 100 observations in the validation data set. A portion of the table is shown below.

Employee	Actual Class	Predicted Class 1 Probability
1	0	0.09
2	0	0.22
⋮	⋮	⋮
100	1	0.41

a. Specify the predicted class membership for the validation data set using the cutoff values of 0.25, 0.5, and 0.75. Produce a confusion matrix based on the classification results from each cutoff value.

b. Compute the misclassification rate, accuracy rate, sensitivity, precision, and specificity of the classification model from each of the three cutoff values specified in part a.
c. Create a cumulative lift chart and a decile-wise lift chart for the classification model.
d. What is the lift that the classification model provides if 20% of the observations are selected by the model compared to randomly selecting 20% of the observations?
e. What is the lift that the classification model provides if 50% of the observations are selected by the model compared to randomly selecting 50% of the observations?

33. FILE ***Gamers.*** Monstermash, an online game app development company, has built a predictive model to identify gamers who are likely to make in-app purchases. The model classifies gamers who are likely to make in-app purchases in Class 1 and gamers who are unlikely to make in-app purchases in Class 0. Applying the model on the validation data set generated a table that lists the actual class and Class 1 probability of the gamers in the validation data set. A portion of the table is shown below.

Gamer	Actual Class	Predicted Class 1 Probability
1	0	0.022666
2	0	0.032561
⋮	⋮	⋮
920	0	0.040652

a. Specify the predicted class membership for the validation data set using the cutoff values of 0.25, 0.5, and 0.75. Produce a confusion matrix based on the classification results from each cutoff value.
b. Compute the misclassification rate, accuracy rate, sensitivity, precision, and specificity of the classification model from each of the three cutoff values specified in part a.
c. Create the cumulative lift chart, decile-wise lift chart and ROC curve for the classification model.
d. What is the lift that the classification model provides if 20% of the observations are selected by the model compared to randomly selecting 20% of the observations?
e. What is the lift that the classification model provides if 50% of the observations are selected by the model compared to randomly selecting 50% of the observations?

34. FILE ***House_Prices.*** A real estate company has built two predictive models for estimating the selling price of a house. Using a small test data set of 10 observations, it tries to assess how the prediction models would perform on a new data set. The following table lists a portion of the actual prices and predicted prices generated by the two predictive models.

House	Actual Price	Predicted Price1	Predicted Price 2
1	$230,500	$254,000	$256,000
2	$209,900	$215,500	$223,400
⋮	⋮	⋮	⋮
10	$328,900	$340,000	$324,500

a. Compute the ME, RMSE, MAD, MPE, and MAPE for the two predictive models.
b. Are the predictive models over- or underestimating the actual selling price on average?
c. Compare the predictive models to a base model where every house is predicted to be sold at the average price of all the houses in the training data set, which is $260,500. Do the predictive models built by the real estate company outperform the base model in terms of RMSE?
d. Which predictive model is the better-performing model?

35. FILE ***Customer_Spending.*** Mary Grant, a marketing manager of an online retailer, has built two predictive models for estimating the annual spending of new customers. Applying the models to the 100 observations in the validation data set generates a table that lists the customers' actual spending and predicted spending. A portion of the data set is shown below.

Customer	Actual Spending	Predicted Spending 1	Predicted Spending 2
1	555	587	487
2	190	198	182
⋮	⋮	⋮	⋮
100	464	380	312

a. Compute the ME, RMSE, MAD, MPE, and MAPE for the two predictive models.
b. Are the predictive models over- or underestimating the actual selling price on average?
c. Compare the RMSE and MAD of the two predictive models. Which predictive model performs better?
d. Compare the better-predictive model to a base model where every customer is predicted to have the average spending of the cases in the training data set, which is $290. Does the better-predictive model built by Mary outperform the base model in terms of RMSE?

LO 8.4

8.4 PRINCIPAL COMPONENT ANALYSIS

Conduct principal component analysis.

In many real-world situations, we may find a data set with a large number of variables. This is especially true in scientific, medical, and consumer research. Data sets that contain many variables (dimensions) are referred to as high-dimensional data. Sometimes the number of variables even exceeds the number of observations in the data set. In some cases, we may be able to eliminate some of the redundant variables, but in many other cases simply dropping the variables might result in losing valuable information.

Principal component analysis (PCA) is a useful dimension reduction technique that is especially effective when we want to reduce the number of variables but cannot completely eliminate any variables from the predictive model without losing important information. PCA transforms a large number of possibly correlated variables into a smaller number of uncorrelated variables called principal components. These principal components allow us to summarize the data with a smaller number of representative variables that collectively explain most of the variability in the data.

PCA is considered an unsupervised data mining technique that allows us to select a relatively small number of principal components that drive most of the patterns found in the data. It can, for example, be used to visualize and pre-process data before applying other unsupervised learning methods such as clustering. We can also use PCA with supervised learning methods, such as linear regression and logistic regression, where a large number of predictor variables can be substituted with a smaller number of principal components.

Given n observations, the main task is to find a sequence of principal components $PC_1, PC_2, \ldots, PC_m$, which are the weighted linear combination of the k original variables $x_1, x_2, \ldots, x_k$, where $m \leq k$. The derivation of the weights involves a mathematical technique in linear algebra called eigen decomposition, which is outside of the scope of this text. Here, we simply use Analytic Solver and R to derive the weights, the corresponding principal components, and the variability that they account for in the data. These mutually uncorrelated principal components are fewer in number than the original variables, yet they retain most of the information in the data.

PRINCIPAL COMPONENT ANALYSIS

When faced with a large set of correlated variables, principal component analysis summarizes this set with a smaller number of representative variables, called principal components. Principal components are uncorrelated variables whose values are the weighted linear combinations of the original variables. The first principal component accounts for most of the variability in the data, followed by the second principal component, and so on.

FILE
CandyBars

To illustrate how PCA works, we use a simple example. Table 8.16 shows a portion of data that lists the following nutritional content for 37 candy bars: the calories per serving

TABLE 8.16 Nutritional Content for Candy Bars ($n = 37$)

Brands	Calories	Fat	Protein	Carb
Peanut Butter Twix	311.0	18.5	5.3	31.4
Baby Ruth	275.0	13.0	3.2	39.0
⋮	⋮	⋮	⋮	⋮
Twizzlers Cherry Nibs	139.0	1.1	1.0	31.7

(Calories), total fat (Fat in grams), protein (Protein in grams), and carbohydrates (Carb in grams). For ease of exposition, we will show how a single principal component can capture most of the variability between two of the variables: Fat (denoted as x_1) and Protein (denoted as x_2).

Figure 8.9 shows a scatterplot of x_1 (Fat) and x_2 (Protein).

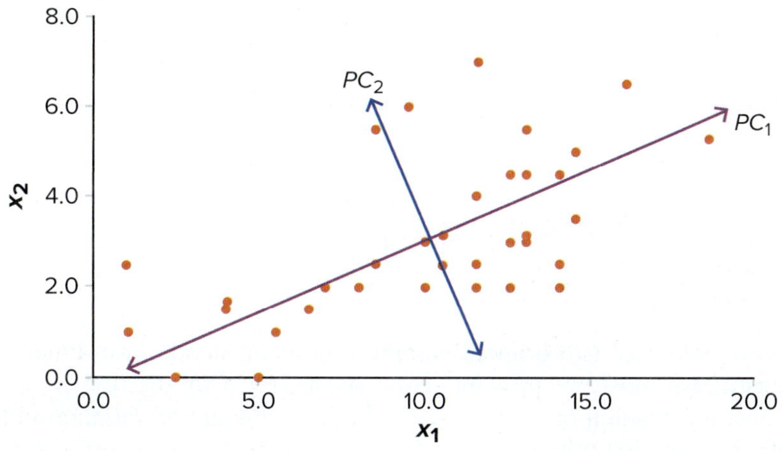

FIGURE 8.9 Scatterplot of variables x_1 and x_2

When we analyze data, we are usually interested in the information associated with the variation in the data. If there is no variation in the data (all data points have the same values), there would be nothing for us to study! Therefore, the direction where there is the most variation contains the most information. The first principal component, represented by the purple line in Figure 8.9, is designated along the direction where the data vary the most. Visually, this line captures the largest amount of variability in the data. Alternatively, we can interpret the first principal component as the line that is closest to the data.

We can also think of the values of the first principal component as a weighted linear combination of the x_1 and x_2 values. In Figure 8.9, there appears to be a linear relationship between x_1 and x_2, and so it is reasonable to expect that a linear combination of the x_1 and x_2 values will adequately capture that relationship. In other words, the first principal component appears to capture most of the information contained in the two variables. As mentioned earlier, PCA is effective especially when the variables are highly correlated.

The second principal component PC_2 is a linear combination of the variables that is uncorrelated with PC_1 and captures the second largest variability in the data. In Figure 8.9, the blue line represents the second principal component of the data, where PC_2 is perpendicular to (or, in a more formal term, orthogonal to) or uncorrelated with PC_1.

By applying PCA to a data set, we ensure that all of the resulting principal components are uncorrelated with each other, while collectively capturing almost all of the information (variation) contained in the data. In our example, the first principal component (purple line) represents a very large portion of the total variation in the data, and the second principal component (blue line) represents much of the remaining variation.

In Figure 8.10, the data points have been rotated so that the first and second principal component directions coincide with the axes. Note that the data have not changed; we are simply looking at the data from a different angle. The positions of the data points relative to each other remain the same. The only things that have changed are the axes used to derive the coordinates of the data points. Another difference here is that the old axes were well defined and easily understood; they represented the fat and protein content of candy bars. The new axes, however, are more abstract and simply represent weighted linear combinations of the original variables. The values of the first and second principal components for each data point are the projected values of x_1 and x_2 on the new axes.

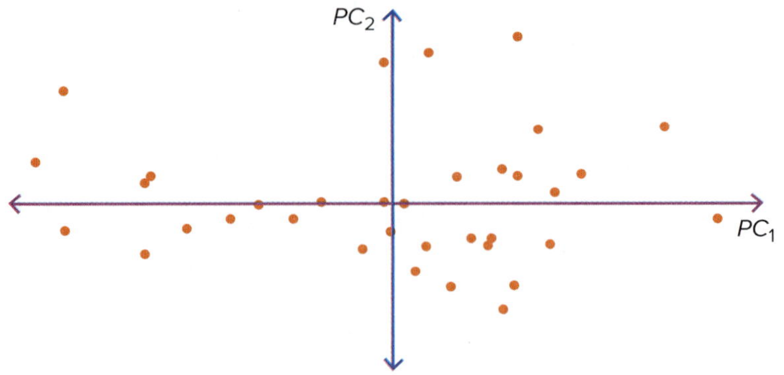

FIGURE 8.10 Scatterplot of the rotated data

In this example with two original variables, or, equivalently, two-dimensional data, we can construct at most two principal components. Even so, the first component contains the most information on x_1 and x_2. As the large amount of variation in the data is now captured by the first principal component PC_1, substituting the original variables x_1 and x_2 with PC_1 will result in little loss of information. In other words, we can replace two original variables x_1 and x_2 with one principal component PC_1 without losing a lot of information. PCA is sensitive to the scale of the data. In the candy bar example, because fat has more variability than protein, it will dominate the PCA results, if not standardized. Therefore, it is recommended that data be standardized (e.g., converted to z-scores) prior to performing PCA.

When using Analytic Solver or R to perform PCA, quite a bit of output is generated. We focus on the weights for computing the PC scores and the variance distribution. Figure 8.11 summarizes this portion of output for the candy bar example. (Instructions for conducting PCA in Analytic Solver and R will be provided shortly.)

FIGURE 8.11 PCA results for the candy bar example

a. Weights for Fat and Protein

Feature\Component	PC_1	PC_2
Fat (g)	0.707107	−0.70711
Protein (g)	0.707107	0.707107

b. Variance Distribution

	PC_1	PC_2
Variance	1.784387	0.215613
Variance Percentage	89.21933	10.78067
Cumulative Variance %	89.21933	100

c. Original Values, *z*-Scores, and PC Scores

Item	Fat	Protein	Fat (z-score)	Protein (z-score)	PC_1 score	PC_2 score
3 Musketeers	6.5	1.5	−0.7860	−0.8982	−1.1910	−0.0793
5th Avenue	12.5	4.5	0.0929	0.4409	0.3775	0.2461
⋮	⋮	⋮	⋮	⋮	⋮	⋮
York Peppermint Pattie	4	1.5	−1.1523	−0.8982	−1.4499	0.1796

The PC scores shown in the last two columns of Figure 8.11c are based on the weights shown in Figure 8.11a. The following equation is used to compute the mth principal component score for the ith observation, denoted as $PC_{m,i}$:

$$PC_{m,i} = w_{m1} z_{1i} + w_{m2} z_{2i} + \cdots + w_{mk} z_{ki},$$

where w_{mk} is the weight for the kth variable of the mth principal component and z_{ki} is the standardized value for the ith observation of the kth variable.

For example, let's calculate the PC_1 score for the first candy bar, three Musketeers, denoted $PC_{1,3M}$. Figure 8.11a shows that the weights for fat and protein are both 0.707107, so $w_{11} = 0.707107$ and $w_{12} = 0.707107$. Figure 8.11c shows that the standardized values for three Musketeer's fat and protein content are −0.7860 and −0.8982, respectively, so $z_{11} = -0.7860$ and $z_{21} = -0.8982$. We calculate $PC_{1,3M}$ as:

$$PC_{1,3M} = w_{11}z_{11} + w_{12}z_{21} = 0.707107 \times -0.7860 + 0.707107 \times -0.8982 = -1.1910.$$

The PC_1 scores for each candy bar appear in the second-to-last column in Figure 8.11c. Similarly, the PC_2 score for three Musketeers, denoted $PC_{2,3M}$, is calculated as:

$$PC_{2,3M} = w_{21}z_{11} + w_{22}z_{21} = -0.70711 \times -0.7860 + 0.707107 \times -0.8982 = -0.0793.$$

The PC_2 scores for each candy bar appear in the last column in Figure 8.11c.

Figure 8.11b shows the distribution of variance across all the principal components. PC_1 accounts for 89.22% of the total variance while PC_2 only accounts for 10.78% of the variance. PCA has redistributed the variance in the data so that using PC_1 alone will result in very little loss of information.

So far, we have worked with two-dimensional data with which we can construct at most two principal components. If we had k original variables, $x_1, x_2, \ldots, x_k$, then up to k principal components could be constructed. For example, with the ***CandyBars*** data on calories, fat, protein and carb, we could have constructed up to four principal components for the analysis. The amount of variance explained decreases from the first principal component to the last principal component. Therefore, the first few principal components often represent a very large portion of the total variance (or information) in the data. This allows us to significantly reduce the number of dimensions by only including the first few principal components instead of the entire list of original variables without losing a lot of information. In practice, a predetermined percentage of variance explained (e.g., 80%) is used as a threshold to determine the number of principal components to retain. In addition, the principal components are uncorrelated; therefore, multicollinearity would not be an issue in subsequent data mining analysis.

Using Analytic Solver and R to Perform Principal Component Analysis

In Example 8.9, we will demonstrate how to use Analytic Solver and R to perform PCA with 12 variables.

EXAMPLE 8.9

Consider country-level health and population measures for 38 countries from World Bank's 2000 Health Nutrition and Population Statistics database. For each country, the measures include death rate per 1,000 people (Death Rate, in %), health expenditure per capita (Health Expend, in US$), life expectancy at birth (Life Exp, in years), male adult mortality rate per 1,000 male adults (Male Mortality), female adult mortality rate per 1,000 female adults (Female Mortality), annual population growth (Population Growth, in %), female population (Female Pop, in %), male population (Male Pop, in %), total population (Total Pop), size of labor force (Labor Force), births per woman (Fertility Rate), and birth rate per 1,000 people (Birth Rate). A portion of the data is shown in Table 8.17.

FILE
Health

TABLE 8.17 Country-Level Health and Population Measures

Country Name	Death Rate	Health Expend	. . .	Birth Rate
Argentina	7.80	706.90	. . .	19.41
Austria	9.60	2415.78	. . .	9.80
⋮	⋮	⋮	⋮	⋮
Switzerland	8.70	3540.86	. . .	10.90

SOLUTION:

As mentioned earlier, PCA is especially effective when the variables are highly correlated. The correlation analysis on the ***Health*** data reveals strong correlation between many of the variables. For example, the correlation coefficient between male and female mortality rates is 0.95, indicating a strong positive correlation between the two variables. The correlation measure tells us that some of the information in male mortality of a country in the form of variance is duplicated in female mortality. However, if we remove one of the variables from the data set, we may lose a sizable portion of the variance (information) in the data. Applied to a data set with a large number of correlated variables, PCA can significantly reduce data dimensions while retaining almost all of the information in the data.

Next, we demonstrate how to use Analytic Solver and R to perform PCA on the Health and Population data set. We also summarize the findings.

Using Analytic Solver

a. Open the ***Health*** data file.

b. From the menu, choose **Data Mining > Transform > Principal Components**.

c. See Figure 8.12. Click on the ellipsis button next to the *Data range* and highlight cells \$A\$1:\$M\$39. Make sure that the box *First Row Contains Headers* is checked. The *Variables In Input Data* box will populate. Select and move all the variables except *Country Name* to *Selected Variables* box. Accept other defaults and click *Next.*

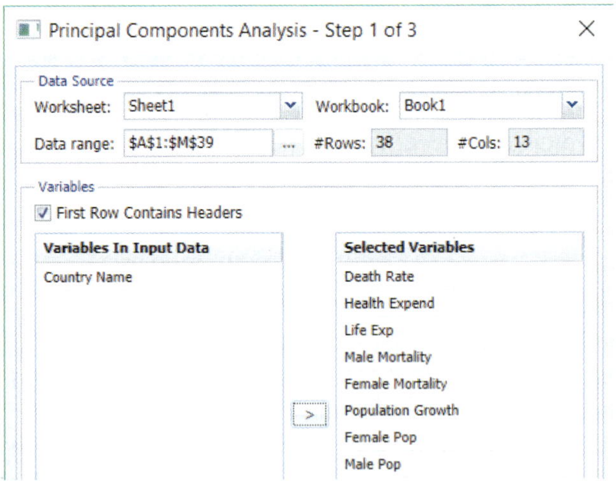

FIGURE 8.12 Principal component analysis dialogue box—step 1 of 3

Source: Microsoft Excel

d. See Figure 8.13. Analytic Solver offers you two options for the number of principal components to display in the results. The first option is to display a fixed number of principal components. The total number of principal components that can be calculated is the same number as the number of variables. Therefore, the maximum number of principal components to display in this example is 12. The other option allows you to display the smallest number of components that collectively explain at least a certain percentage of the total variance in the data, where the default threshold is 95%. Choose the option to display all 12 components.

Analytic Solver also offers you the option of choosing one of the two methods for performing PCA: using the covariance matrix or the correlation matrix. Recall that the correlation coefficients are unit-free and, therefore, choosing the *Use Correlation Matrix* option is equivalent to using standardized data for PCA. As mentioned earlier, it is recommended that data be standardized (converted to z-scores) prior to performing PCA when the scales are different. The scales of the data in the ***Health*** data set vary significantly; therefore, we will choose the *Use Correlation Matrix* option to remove the impact of data scale on the results. Click *Next.*

FIGURE 8.13 Principal component analysis dialogue box—step 2 of 3

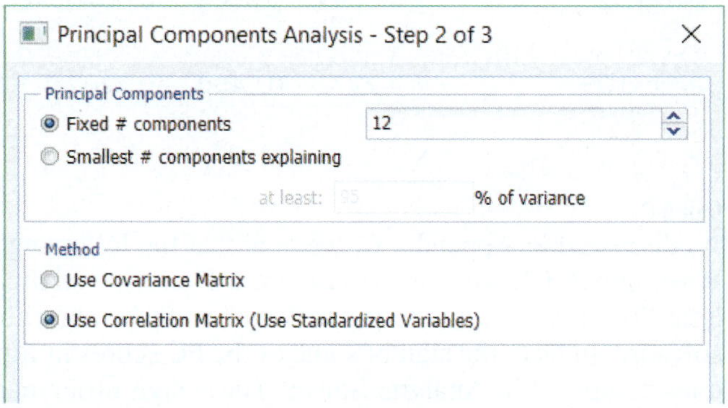

Source: Microsoft Excel

e. In the final dialog box, make sure the box next to *Show principal components score* is checked. Click *Finish.*

Analytic Solver inserts two new worksheets (PCA_Output and PCA_Scores). Figure 8.14c shows a portion of the principal component scores for the 38 countries from the PCA_Scores worksheet. Here, Record 1 refers to Argentina, Record 2 refers to Austria, and so on. Recall that the principal component scores are the weighted linear combinations of the original variables. Figures 8.14a and 8.14b summarize the results from the PCA_Output worksheet, showing the weights used to calculate the principal component scores and the amount of variance accounted for by each principal component. We see that the first principal component accounts for a very large portion, 46.6189%, of the total variance in the data. Among the original variables, Life Exp has the most weight, in absolute terms, for the first principal component, followed by Birth Rate. Cumulatively, the first four principal components account for 93.3486% of the total variance in the data, suggesting that if we reduce the dimension of the data from the original 12 variables to the four newly calculated principal components, we would still be able to retain almost all the information in the data.

It is important to note that different versions of Analytic Solver and Excel may yield slightly different results, especially for a very small value such as the principal component scores, weights, and variances for PC_{12}. The results for the other principal components (i.e., the first four components in the current example) should remain consistent across versions.

FIGURE 8.14 PCA results using Analytic Solver

a. Variance Distribution

Feature\Component	PC_1	PC_2	PC_3	PC_4	. . .	PC_{12}
Variance %	46.6189	24.6953	15.3240	6.7104	. . .	−5.7829E-13
Cumulative Variance %	46.6189	71.3142	86.6382	93.3486	. . .	100

b. Principal Component Weights

Feature\Component	PC_1	PC_2	PC_3	PC_4	. . .	PC_{12}
Death Rate	−0.1261	0.4250	0.1651	−0.5040	. . .	−1.1245E-12
Health Expend	0.2780	0.0809	−0.0621	−0.7674	. . .	1.0678E-12
⋮	⋮	⋮	⋮	⋮	⋮	⋮
Birth Rate	−0.4071	0.0213	−0.0731	−0.0211	. . .	1.9357E-12

c. Principal Component Scores

Record ID	PC_1	PC_2	PC_3	PC_4	. . .	PC_{12}
Record 1	0.0966	0.4045	−0.2255	0.6312	. . .	−1.07E-12
Record 2	2.0092	0.9664	−0.0020	−0.4192	. . .	4.585E-13
⋮	⋮	⋮	⋮	⋮	⋮	⋮
Record 38	2.2972	0.5450	−0.3202	−1.1028	. . .	7.811E-13

Using R

As discussed in Appendix C, we note that the following instructions are based on **R version 3.5.3.** Also, the results from R may be slightly different from the Analytic Solver results due to the differences in the algorithms employed by the two software. In fact, the sign of some of the PC scores in R may be the opposite of the ones computed in Analytic Solver. These sign differences, however, will have no impact on the resulting data mining techniques.

a. Import the ***Health*** data into a data frame (table) and label it myData.

b. Display a few observations in the myData data frame to inspect the data using the **head** function. Enter:

```
> head(myData)
```

c. We exclude the Country Name variable (1st variable) from the analysis, standardize the rest of the variables, and store their standardized values in a data frame called myData.st. Use the **scale** function to standardize the data. Enter:

```
> myData.st <- scale(myData[ , -1])
```

d. We use the **prcomp** function to perform PCA and use the **summary** function to display the PCA results. Enter:

```
> pca <- prcomp(myData.st)
> summary(pca)
```

Figure 8.15a shows a portion of the PCA results. As you can see from the cumulative proportion row in the table, the first four principal components account for 93.35% of the total variance in the data. This is consistent with the result from Analytic Solver even though the exact cumulative proportion of variance is slightly different.

e. To review the weights for computing the principal components, we display the **rotation** property of the PCA results. Enter:

```
> pca$rotation
```

Figure 8.15b shows a portion of the weights. Again, the weights are very similar to the ones produced by Analytic Solver.

FIGURE 8.15 PCA results using R

a. R's summary results

```
Importance of components%s:
                          PC1     PC2     PC3     PC4    ...      PC12
Standard deviation     2.3652  1.7215  1.3561  0.8974    ...  3.345e-17
Proportion of variance 0.4662  0.2470  0.1532  0.0671    ...  0.000e+00
Cumulative Proportion  0.4662  0.7131  0.8664  0.9335    ...  1.000e+00
```

b. R's PCA weights

```
                    PC1         PC2          PC3          PC4    ...          PC12
Death.Rate   0.12614475  0.42498298  -0.16514637  -0.50397341    ...  -7.138364e-17
Health.Expend -0.27803071 0.08089049  0.06210637  -0.76743206    ...   1.446584e-16
     ⋮            ⋮           ⋮            ⋮            ⋮          ⋮         ⋮
Birth.Rate   0.40706962  0.02131421   0.07310887  -0.02106416    ...   1.614795e-17
```

c. R's Principal components

```
            PC1          PC2          PC3           PC4      ...          PC12
[1,]  -0.09655764   0.40453066  0.225491452   0.631209232    ...  -4.286392e-17
[2,]  -2.00916845   0.96638977  0.002007443  -0.419234070    ...  -1.816474e-18
  ⋮         ⋮            ⋮            ⋮             ⋮          ⋮         ⋮
[38,] -2.29716742   0.54503126  0.320183989  -1.102757401    ...   1.099835e-16
```

f. To review the principal component scores, we display the **x** property of the PCA results. Enter:

```
> pca$x
```

Figure 8.15c displays a portion of the principal component scores of the observations. In general, the results are consistent with those produced by Analytic Solver.

g. In order to list countries (1st variable) along with the principle component scores, we first use the **data.frame** statement to combine the myData data frame with the principal component scores. We then remove columns 2 to 13, which contain the original variables in the myData data frame. We display a few observations in the new data frame using the **head** function. Enter:

```
> newData <- data.frame(myData, pca$x)
> newData <- newData[ , -(2:13)]
> head(newData)
```

As mentioned earlier, PCA allows us to significantly reduce the dimension of the data by replacing a large number of original variables with a few uncorrelated principal components that retain a very large portion of the information in the data. However, these advantages come at a price. As principal components are simply the weighted linear combinations of the original variables, they are abstract and cannot be easily interpreted. In addition, PCA only works with numerical data.

EXERCISES 8.4

Note: AS and R indicate that the exercises must be solved using Analytic Solver and R, respectively.

Mechanics

36. FILE *Exercise_8.36.* AS Perform principal component analysis on the accompanying data set.
   a. Use the data with the covariance matrix to compute the first two principal components. What are the weights for computing the first principal component scores? What percent of the total variability is accounted for by the first principal component?
   b. Use the data with the correlation matrix to compute the first two components. What are the weights for computing the first principal component scores? What percent of the total variability is accounted for by the first principal component?
   c. Comment on the differences in the results of parts a and b.

37. FILE *Exercise_8.37.* AS Perform principal component analysis on the accompanying data set.
   a. Use the data with the covariance matrix and choose *Smallest # components explaining at least:* 85% of variance. How many principal components were

created? What percent of total variance is accounted for by the calculated principal components? What are the weights for computing the first principal component scores?

b. Use the data with the correlation matrix to perform PCA. Keep all the other options the same as in part a. How many principal components were created? What percent of total variance is accounted for by the calculated principal components? What are the weights for computing the first principal component scores?

38. **FILE** ***Exercise_8.38.*** **AS** Perform principal component analysis on the accompanying data set.

a. Use the data with the covariance matrix to compute the seven principal components. How many principal components do you need to retain in order to account for 80% of the total variance? What are the weights for computing the first principal component scores?

b. Use the data with the correlation matrix to compute the seven principal components. How many principal components do you need to retain in order to account for 80% of the total variance? What are the weights for computing the first principal component scores?

c. Comment on the differences in the results of part a and b.

39. **FILE** ***Exercise_8.39.*** **R** Standardize the accompanying data set, and then perform principal component analysis.

a. What percent of total variance is accounted for by the first three principal components?

b. What are the weights for computing the first principal component scores?

c. What is the first principal component score for the first observation?

40. **FILE** ***Exercise_8.40.*** **R** Standardize the accompanying data set, and then perform principal component analysis.

a. How many principal components do you need to account for at least 80% of the total variance?

b. What are the weights for computing the first principal component scores?

c. What is the second principal component score for the first observation?

41. **FILE** ***Exercise_8.41.*** **AS** Perform principal component analysis on the accompanying data set.

a. Use standardized data to compute the principal components. Select the number of principal components that account for at least 80% of the total variance. How many principal components are displayed by Analytic Solver?

b. What are the weights for computing the first principal component scores? What is the second principal component score for the first observation?

42. The following table displays the weights for computing the principal components and the data for two observations.

Weight	PC_1	PC_2
x_1	−0.892	0.452
x_2	−0.452	−0.892
	x_1	x_2
Observation 1	4.04	12.77
Observation 2	4.10	12.18

a. The mean and standard deviation for x_1 are 3.5 and 1.2, respectively. The mean and standard deviation for x_2 are 11.75 and 3.8, respectively. Compute the z-scores for the x_1 and x_2 values for the two observations.

b. Compute the first principal component score for observation 1.

c. Compute the second principal component score for observation 2.

43. The following table displays the weights for computing the principal components and the data for two observations.

Weight	PC_1	PC_2
x_1	−0.81	0.59
x_2	−0.59	−0.81
	x_1	x_2
Observation 1	7.30	342.90
Observation 2	3.20	258.60

a. The mean and standard deviation for x_1 are 5.8 and 2.4, respectively. The mean and standard deviation for x_2 are 380.5 and 123.4, respectively. Compute the z-scores for the x_1 and x_2 values for the two observations.

b. Compute the first principal component score for observation 1.

c. Compute the second principal component score for observation 2.

44. The following table displays the weights for computing the principal components and the standardized data (z-scores) for three observations.

Weight	PC_1	PC_2	PC_3
x_1	−0.57	0.62	0.55
x_2	−0.64	0.09	−0.76
x_3	0.52	0.78	−0.34
	z_1	z_2	z_3
Observation 1	0.71	0.33	−0.36
Observation 2	2.81	2.44	−1.41
Observation 3	−0.76	−1.18	1.37

a. Compute the first principal component score for observation 1.

b. Compute the second principal component score for observation 2.

c. Compute the third principal component score for observation 3.

45. The following Analytic Solver results were generated by a principal component analysis.

	PC_1	PC_2	PC_3	PC_4	PC_5
Variance %	76.2656	13.6728	8.9626	0.8751	0.2239
Cumulative Variance %	76.2656	89.9384	98.9010	99.7761	100

a. How many original variables are in the data set?

b. What percent of variance does the third principal component account for?

c. How many principal components need to be retained in order to account for at least 95% of the total variance in the data?

46. The following R results were generated by a principal component analysis.

```
Importance of components%s:
                        PC1     PC2     PC3     PC4      ...   PC9
Standard deviation      2.0294  1.7895  1.1338  0.83607  ...   1.538e-16
Proportion of variance  0.4217  0.3279  0.1316  0.07158  ...   0.000e+00
Cumulative proportion   0.4217  0.7497  0.8813  0.95288  ...   1.000e+00
```

a. How many original variables are in the data set?

b. What percent of variance does the third principal component account for?

c. How many principal components need to be retained in order to account for at least 85% of the total variance in the data?

Applications

47. FILE ***Development.*** The accompanying data set contains some economic indicators for 11 African countries collected by the World Bank in 2015. The economic indicators include annual % growth in agriculture (Agriculture), annual % growth in exports (Exports), annual % growth in final consumption (Final consumption), annual % growth in GDP (GDP growth), and annual % growth in GDP per capita (GDP per capita growth). A portion of the data set is shown in the accompanying table.

Country	Agriculture	Exports	...	GDP per capita growth
Burkina Faso	−3.4761	1.3822	...	0.8848
Burundi	−2.9826	−9.9000	...	−6.8177
⋮	⋮	⋮	⋮	⋮
Mali	6.9242	4.6719	...	2.8988

a. Perform correlation analysis on the data. Discuss the correlation between the variables in the data set. Which variable pair has the highest correlation?

b. Conduct principal component analysis on all the variables in the data set. Standardize the data prior to the analysis or use the correlation matrix if you are using Analytic Solver.

c. Allow the maximum number of principal components to be calculated by the software. How many principal components are computed? What percent of the total variability is accounted for by the first three principal components? How many principal components must be retained in order to account for at least 80% of the total variance in the data?

d. Which original variable is given the highest weight to compute the first principal component? Which original variable is given the highest weight to compute the second principal component?

e. Create a new data set that contains the country names and the principal components that account for at least 80% of the total variance in the data.

48. FILE ***Football_Players.*** AS Beza Gordon-Smith is a high school senior in northern California who loves watching football. She keeps track of football results and statistics of the quarterbacks of each high school team. The accompanying table shows a portion of the data that Beza has recorded, with the following variables: the player's number that Beza assigns to each quarterback (Player), team's mascot (Team), completed passes (Comp), attempted pass (Att), completion percentage (Pct), total yards thrown (Yds), average yards per attempt (Avg), yards thrown per game (Yds/G), number of touchdowns (TD), and number of interceptions (Int).

Player	Team	Comp	...	Int
1	Albatrosses	154	...	6
2	Bobcats	341	...	5
⋮	...	⋮	⋮	⋮
43	Salamanders	263	...	4

a. Conduct principal component analysis on all variables, except the players' number, in the data set. Should you use the covariance matrix or the correlation matrix for the analysis in this case? Explain.

b. Allow the maximum number of principal components to be calculated by the software. How many principal components are computed? What percent of the total variability is accounted for by the first three principal components? How many principal components must be retained in order to account for at least 80% of the total variance in the data?

c. Which original variable is given the highest weight to compute the first principal component? Which original variable is given the highest weight to compute the second principal component?

d. What is the principal component 1 score for the first record (Player 1)?

49. **FILE** ***Baseball_Players.*** **R** Ben Derby is a scout for a college baseball team. He attends many high school games and practices each week in order to evaluate potential players to recruit during each college recruitment season. He also keeps detailed records about each prospective player. His college team is in particular need to add another hitter to its roster next season. Luckily, Ben has information on 144 high school players who have played at least 100 games during the previous season. portion of the data is shown in the accompanying table that includes the following variables: Player's ID (Player), the number of games played (G), at bats (AB), runs (R), hits (H), homeruns (HR), runs batted in (RBI), batting average (AVG), on base percentage (OBP), and slugging percentage (SLG).

Player	G	AB	...	SLG
1	156	621	...	0.552
2	142	451	...	0.501
⋮	⋮	⋮	⋮	⋮
144	144	524	...	0.573

a. Conduct principal component analysis on all the variables, except the player's ID, in the data set. Standardize the data prior to the analysis.

b. How many principal components are computed? How many principal components must be retained to account for at least 80% of the total variance in the data?

c. Display the weights used to compute the first principal component scores.

d. Create a new data set that contains the players' names and the principal components that account for at least 80% of the total variance in the data.

50. **FILE** ***Internet_Addiction.*** Internet addiction has been found to be a widespread problem among university students. A small liberal arts college in Colorado conducted a survey of Internet addiction among its students using the Internet Addiction Test (IAT) developed by Dr. Kimberly Young. The IAT contains 20 questions that measure various aspects of Internet addiction. Individuals who score high on the IAT are more likely to have problematic Internet use. Also included in the data are the sex of the students (Sex, 1 for female and 0 for male) and whether or not they study at the graduate level (1 for Graduate and 0 for Undergraduate). A portion of the data set is shown in the accompanying table.

Record	IAT1	IAT2	...	Graduate
1	2	2	...	1
2	2	3	...	0
⋮	⋮	⋮	⋮	⋮
350	1	2	...	0

a. Conduct principal component analysis on all the variables except the Record Number. Should you standardize the data? Explain.

b. How many principal components are computed? What percent of the total variability is accounted for by the first principal component? How many principal components must be retained in order to account for at least 80% of the total variance in the data?

c. Which original variable is given the highest weight to compute the first principal component? Which original variable is given the highest weight to compute the second principal component?

d. What is the principal component 1 score for the first record?

51. **FILE** ***Nutritional_Facts.*** **R** Jenny, a first-year Nutrition Studies student at Hillside College, is conducting research on various common food items and their nutritional facts. She compiled a data set that contains the nutrition facts on 30 common food items. Jenny feels that many of the nutritional facts of these food items are highly correlated and wonders if there is a way to reduce the dimensionality of the data set by creating principal components. A portion of the data set is shown in the accompanying table. (Values are based on 100 grams of the food items.)

Name	Calories	Total fat	...	Protein
Banana	89	0.3	...	1.1
Egg	155	11	...	13
⋮	⋮	⋮	⋮	⋮
Tuna	184	6	...	30

a. Conduct principal component analysis on all the variables except the Name variable. Should you standardize the data? Explain.

b. How many principal components are computed? What percent of the total variability is accounted for by the first principal component? How many principal components must be retained in order to account for at least 80% of the total variance in the data?

c. Display the weights used to compute the first principal component scores.

d. Create a new data set that contains the names of the food items and the principal components that account for at least 80% of the total variance in the data.

52. FILE ***Happiness.*** Since 2014, the United Nations has conducted annual studies that measure the level of happiness among its member countries. Experts in social science and psychology are commissioned to collect relevant data and define measurements related to happiness. Happiness measurements are based on survey questions such as how people feel about their life (i.e., life ladder), levels of positive and negative emotion, freedom to make choices (Life choices), and aggregate indicators such as social support, life expectancy, and relative household income. These data are converted into numerical scores for each member country. The accompanying table shows a portion of the United Nation's happiness data.

Country	Life Ladder	Social support	...	Household income
Albania	4.5111	0.6384	...	0.4165
Argentina	6.4272	0.8828	...	0.3321
⋮	⋮	⋮	⋮	⋮
Zimbabwe	3.7354	0.7684	...	0.5967

a. Conduct principal component analysis on all the variables except the Country variable. Should you standardize the data? Explain.
b. What percent of the total variability is accounted for by the first principal component? How many principal components must be retained in order to account for at least 80% of the total variance in the data?
c. Display the weights used to compute the first principal component scores. Which original variable is given the highest weight to compute the second principal component?
d. What is the principal component 1 score for the first record (Albania)?

53. FILE ***Tennis.*** R In tennis, how well a player serves and returns serves often determine the outcome of the game. Coaches and players track these numbers and work tirelessly to make improvement. The accompanying table shows a sample of data that includes local youth tennis players. The relevant variables include the number of aces (Aces), number of double faults (DF), first serve percentage (1ST SRV), first serve win percentage (1ST SRV WIN), break point saved percentage (BP SVD), percentage of service games won (SRV WIN), first serve return win percentage (1ST RTN WIN), percentage of return games won (RTN WON), and break point conversion percentage (BP CONV).

Player	Aces	DF	...	BP CONV
1	96	144	...	48.2
2	180	164	...	50.3
⋮	⋮	⋮	⋮	⋮
40	49	62	...	48.5

a. Conduct principal component analysis on all variables except the Player variable and display the weights used to compute the first principal component scores.
b. Which original variable is given the highest weight to compute the first principal component? Which original variable is given the highest weight to compute the second principal component?
c. Create a new data set that contains the Player column and the principal components that account for at least 90% of the total variance in the data.

54. FILE ***Stocks.*** Investors usually consider a variety of information to make investment decisions. The accompanying table displays a sample of large publicly traded corporations and their financial information. Relevant information includes stock price (Price), dividend as a percentage of share price (Dividend), price to earnings ratio (PE), earnings per share (EPS), book value, lowest and highest share prices within the past 52 weeks (52 wk low and 52 wk high), market value of the company's shares (Market cap), and earnings before interest, taxes, depreciation, and amortization (EBITDA in $billions).

Name	Price	Dividend	...	EBITDA
3M	189.09	2.48	...	8.70
Abbott Lab	45.00	2.34	...	4.59
⋮	⋮	⋮	⋮	⋮
Zoetis	53.07	0.79	...	1.70

a. Conduct principal component analysis on all the variables except the Name variable. Should you standardize the data? Explain.
b. What percent of the total variability is accounted for by the first principal component? How many principal components must be retained in order to account for at least 80% of the total variance in the data?
c. Which original variable is given the highest weight to compute the first principal component? Which original variable is given the highest weight to compute the second principal component?
d. What is the principal component 1 score for the first record (3M)?

8.5 WRITING WITH BIG DATA

An inherent problem that comes with big data is that data sets may be complex and contain many variables (dimensions). To reduce information redundancy and improve the stability of the resulting models, it is recommended that dimension reduction techniques be implemented to result in a more manageable number of variables that capture most, if not all, of the information in the original data. Dimension reduction techniques, such as principal component analysis, are effective in achieving this goal and are often performed prior to model building activities.

FILE
NBA

Case Study

Merrick Stevens is a sports analyst working for ACE Sports Management, a sports agency that represents over 200 athletes. Merrick is tasked with analyzing sports-related data and developing a predictive model for the National Basketball Association (NBA). He uses the ***NBA*** data set that contains information on 30 competing NBA teams and 455 players. The player statistics are for several seasons as well as for their career. Because a player's salary is based on his performance over multiple seasons, Merrick decides to only look at the career regular season data rather than data of a particular season.

Given the large number of predictor variables that may explain a player's salary, Merrick decides to investigate whether principal component analysis may be advantageous as a first step in model building.

Sample Report – Dimension Reduction of the NBA Player Data

An NBA player's salary is determined by a wide range of variables. Prior to constructing a model that can be used to predict an NBA player's salary, data are collected for 23 possible predictor variables for 455 NBA players. These variables include physicality variables, such as a player's age, height, and weight, as well as performance variables, such as the number of games played, the number of baskets made, the number of three-pointers made, and so forth.

Marcio Sanchez/Ap/Pool/EPA/Shutterstock

High correlations between many of the predictor variables suggest that information redundancy exists in the data. In order to eliminate potential multicollinearity problems and improve model stability in the resulting salary model, dimension reduction using principal component analysis (PCA) is performed on the 23 predictor variables.

Prior to performing the PCA analysis, the data are standardized in order to remove the impact of data scales. The PCA analysis is not restricted with respect to the number of principle components to produce; thus, given that the analysis used 23 predictor variables, 23 principal components are estimated. Table 8.18 shows a portion of the PCA output with respect to weights and variances. The first principal component accounts for 44.1218% of the total variance, and Points (Average points per game) has the largest weight for the first principal component. Referencing the Cumulative Variance % row in Table 8.18, it is found that the first seven principal components account for almost 90% of the total variance in the original data.

TABLE 8.18 Principal Component Weights and Variances

Feature\ Component	PC_1	PC_2	PC_3	PC_4	PC_5	PC_6	PC_7	...	PC_{23}
Age	−0.1455	0.0233	−0.6712	−0.0200	−0.0559	0.0590	−0.0325	...	0.0017
Height	0.0172	0.0233	−0.6712	−0.0200	−0.0288	−0.0919	0.1066	...	0.0005
⋮	⋮	⋮	⋮	⋮	⋮	⋮	⋮	⋮	⋮
Points	−0.3024	−0.0244	0.0910	0.0631	0.0463	−0.2248	−0.0008	...	−0.7888
Variance %	44.1218	24.3615	6.8076	5.2865	3.2806	2.9727	2.7560	...	0.0175
Cumulative Variance %	44.1218	68.4832	75.2909	80.5774	83.8580	86.8307	89.5867	...	100

In future analyses, it is advisable to use the first seven principal components as the predictor variables for building models that predict an NBA player's salary. A portion of the principal component scores for the first seven principal components are displayed in Table 8.19. By using the seven principle components instead of the original 23 predictor variables, information redundancy has been removed. In addition, a large number of highly correlated predictor variables have been replaced with a smaller set of uncorrelated principal components that retain at least 90% of the information in the original data.

TABLE 8.19 Principal Component Scores

Player	PC_1	PC_2	PC_3	PC_4	PC_5	PC_6	PC_7
Metta World Peace	−4.6778	−0.3177	−1.9019	0.4324	−1.4056	0.6642	0.9347
Elton Brand	−5.4075	4.3766	−1.9281	−0.7296	0.2911	0.4351	0.7778
Kobe Bryant	−9.5196	−1.3329	−1.9168	−0.5547	0.2608	−2.1314	1.2170
⋮	⋮	⋮	⋮	⋮	⋮	⋮	⋮
Luis Montero	5.9482	−1.5002	−0.3373	−0.7296	1.5916	−0.5624	2.1202

Suggested Case Studies

Principal component analysis can be applied to many situations and different data sets, especially the big data that accompany this text. Here are some suggestions.

Report 8.1 **FILE** ***Longitudinal_Information.*** Subset the data to select only those individuals who lived in an urban area. Reduce the dimensionality of the data by converting numerical variables such as age, height, weight, number of years of education, number of siblings, family size, number of weeks employed, self-esteem scale, and income into a smaller set of principal components that retain at least 90% of the information in the original data. Note: You will need to standardize the data prior to PCA as the scales of the variables are different.

Report 8.2 **FILE** ***College_Admissions.*** Select the data for one of the three colleges. Reduce the dimensionality of the data by converting numerical variables such as high school GPAs, MCA GPAs, SAT scores, and ACT scores into a smaller set of principal components that retain at least 90% of the information in the original data. Then use the principal components as predictor variables for building models for predicting admission.

Report 8.3 **FILE** ***House_Price.*** Choose one of the college towns in the data set. Reduce the dimensionality of the data by converting numerical variables such as number of bedrooms, number of bathrooms, home square footage, lot square footage, and age of the house into a smaller set of principal components that retain at least 90% of the information in the original data. Then use the principal components as predictor variables for building models for predicting sale prices of houses.

Report 8.4 **FILE** ***TechSales_Reps.*** Subset the data to include only the employees who work in the hardware division and have a college degree. Reduce the dimensionality of the data by converting numerical variables such as age, years with the company, number of certifications, feedback scores, and salary into a smaller set of principal components that retain at least 85% of the information in the original data. Then use the principal components as predictor variables for building models for predicting the net promoter score (NPS).

9 Supervised Data Mining: *k*-Nearest Neighbors and Naïve Bayes

LEARNING OBJECTIVES

After reading this chapter, you should be able to:

LO **9.1** **Explain key differences among supervised data mining techniques.**

LO **9.2** **Apply the *k*-nearest neighbors method to classify new records.**

LO **9.3** **Apply the naïve Bayes method to classify new records.**

In Chapters 9 and 10, we discuss supervised data mining, also referred to as predictive or directed data mining. These models are used to predict the outcome of a target variable based on several predictor variables. As mentioned in Chapter 8, supervised data mining includes classification and prediction models. In a classification model, the target variable is categorical, and the objective is to classify class memberships of new cases. Examples include classifying a list of prospective customers as buyers and nonbuyers or classifying a financial asset as buy, hold, and sell. In a prediction model, the target variable is numerical, and the objective is to predict its numerical value. Examples include predicting consumer spending, the selling price of a house, or the time it takes to recover from a medical procedure.

Linear and logistic regression models, discussed in Chapter 6 and 7, are important prediction and classification models, respectively. In this chapter, we explore two widely used supervised data mining techniques: *k*-nearest neighbors and naïve Bayes. Another popular technique called decision trees will be discussed in Chapter 10. The *k*-nearest neighbors method is a data-driven technique that classifies or predicts the new case by identifying the *k* nearest neighbors of the new case based on the predictor variables. The naïve Bayes method, a classification technique, computes the posterior probability that a new case will belong to a target class based on its prior probability and the conditional probabilities of the predictor variables. These data mining techniques are frequently used to build predictive models in a wide range of business scenarios.

©Halfpoint/Shutterstock

INTRODUCTORY CASE

24/7 Fitness Center Annual Membership

24/7 Fitness Center is a high-end full-service gym and recruits its members through advertisements and monthly open house events. Each open house attendee is given a tour and a one-day pass. Potential members register for the open house event by answering a few questions about themselves and their exercise routine. The fitness center staff places a follow-up phone call with the potential member and sends information to open house attendees by mail in the hopes of signing the potential member up for an annual membership.

Janet Williams, a manager at 24/7 Fitness Center, wants to develop a data-driven strategy for selecting which new open house attendees to contact. She has compiled information from 1,000 past open house attendees in the Gym_Data worksheet of the ***Gym*** data file. The data include whether or not the attendee purchases a club membership (Enroll equals 1 if purchase, 0 otherwise), the age and the annual income of the attendee, and the average number of hours that the attendee exercises per week. Janet also collects the age, income, and number of hours spent on weekly exercise from 23 new open house attendees and maintains a separate worksheet called Gym_Score in the ***Gym*** data file. Because these are new open house attendees, there is no enrollment information on this worksheet. A portion of the two worksheets is shown in Table 9.1.

FILE *Gym*

TABLE 9.1 24/7 Fitness Data

a. The *Gym_Data* Worksheet

Enroll	Age	Income	Hours
1	26	18000	14
0	43	13000	9
⋮	⋮	⋮	⋮
0	48	67000	18

b. The *Gym_Score* Worksheet

Age	Income	Hours
22	33000	5
23	65000	9
⋮	⋮	⋮
51	88000	6

Janet would like to use the data to accomplish the following tasks.

1. Develop a data-driven classification model for predicting whether or not a potential gym member will purchase a gym membership.
2. Identify which of the 23 new open house attendees are likely to purchase a gym membership.

A synopsis of this case is provided in Section 9.2.

9.1 INTRODUCTION TO SUPERVISED DATA MINING

Supervised data mining techniques include classification models where the target variable is categorical and prediction models where the target variable is numerical. Examples of classification models include predicting whether or not a consumer will make a purchase, a mortgage will be approved, a patient will have a certain illness, and an e-mail will be a spam. Similarly, examples of prediction models include predicting the sale price of a house, the salary of a business school graduate, the total sales of a firm, and the debt payment of a consumer.

Linear and logistic regression models, discussed in Chapter 6 and 7, are important prediction and classification models, respectively. In this chapter, we extend the analysis by including two widely used data mining techniques: *k*-nearest neighbors and naïve Bayes. Chapter 10 provides extensive coverage of classification and regression trees and ensemble trees.

In supervised data mining, it is important to be able to classify or predict the outcome of a new case; as mentioned in earlier chapters, we use the terms case, record, and observation interchangeably in this text. For example, in the introductory case, the manager of 24/7 Fitness Center is interested in whether or not an open house attendee is likely to purchase a gym membership. The classification is based on given values of predictor variables and is called **scoring a record**. Scoring is straightforward in linear and logistic regression models where the estimated equation allows us to obtain the predicted values of a target variable for given predictor values. Because such an estimated equation does not exist in supervised data mining techniques, we rely on built-in algorithms in Analytic Solver and R to score new records. Throughout Chapters 9 and 10, we will provide two worksheets for each solved example where the "data" worksheet allows us to find the preferred data mining technique that we use to predict new records in the "score" worksheet.

> **SCORING A RECORD**
>
> A process for classifying or predicting the value of the target variable of a new record for given values of predictor variables.

As discussed in Sections 7.4 and 8.3, the problem of overfitting occurs when a predictive model is made overly complex to fit the quirks of given sample data. It is possible for a model to perform really well with the data set used for estimation, but then perform miserably once a new data set is used. To address this issue, we partition the data into training, validation, and optional test data sets. The training data set is used to generate one or more models. The validation data set is used to evaluate the performance of the models and select the best model. The optional test data set is used to assess the performance of the final model on a new data set. Hands-on examples for data partitioning and cross-validation in Analytic Solver and R will be provided later in this chapter.

We also discussed several performance measures to assess predictive models in Section 8.3. For classification, a confusion matrix is used to summarize all outcomes obtained from the validation or test data set. These outcomes include true positive (TP) and true negative (TN), where the observations are classified correctly by the model. Similarly, false positive (FP) and false negative (FN) outcomes imply that the observation is incorrectly classified by the model. Based on these outcomes, performance measures such as the accuracy rate, the sensitivity, and the specificity are computed. We also use graphical representations such as the cumulative lift chart, the decile-wise lift chart, and the receiver operating characteristic (ROC) curve to assess model performance. For prediction models, we considered the prediction error, defined as the difference between the actual and the predicted value of the numerical target variable. We discussed several performance measures that capture the magnitude of the prediction errors, including the root mean square error (RMSE), the mean error (ME), the mean absolute deviation (MAD) or mean absolute error (MAE), the mean percentage error (MPE), and the mean absolute percentage error (MAPE). In this chapter, we will simply interpret predictive models and assess their performance using Analytic Solver and R.

Comparison of Supervised Data Mining Techniques

LO 9.1

Explain key differences among supervised data mining techniques.

Each data mining technique has its advantages and limitations. As discussed in Chapter 8, in practice, people tend to develop several predictive models based on different techniques and choose the best model based on performance and other practical considerations. Here, we summarize key differences among supervised data mining techniques.

Linear and logistic regression models, discussed in Chapters 6 and 7, are the most ubiquitous data mining techniques with a wide range of practical applications. Regression results describe the relationship between predictor and target variables in a manner that is easily interpretable. Regression techniques have been extensively studied and were used as early as in the 1800s in a study to predict locations of asteroids. Since then scientists and practitioners have applied this concept in a countless number of studies, applications, and research.

The *k*-nearest neighbors (KNN) method is a relatively simple data mining tool whose underlying concepts are easy to understand. It has been widely used for developing recommendation systems among online companies. Consumer information such as book purchases and movie or TV viewing habits is used for training KNN algorithms to offer personalized recommendations for new books, movies, or TV shows. Online companies that sell or offer these products can develop a data collection system that efficiently captures such information. The KNN method has been found to be very effective as a classifier, such as producing accurate product recommendations; however, it is not as popular for prediction problems. In this chapter, we use KNN only for classification.

Naïve Bayes classifiers are relatively fast, even when applied to big data. The underlying concept is also simple and relatively easy to understand. It is often used in commercial spam e-mail filters; in fact, it is one of the oldest and most effective spam filtering techniques. Unlike other techniques such as keyword filtering, blacklists, and whitelists, naïve Bayes classifiers can "learn" and recognize new spam e-mails as well as allow individual users to train the naïve Bayes algorithm by personally classifying e-mails as spam or nonspam. In addition, the e-mail information can usually be captured and reduced into a data set that consists solely of categorical variables, which is a requirement for traditional naïve Bayes methods.

Classification and regression trees (CART), discussed later in Chapter 10, have many advantages. The tree representations are very simple to understand, and the rule-based results are easy to interpret. CART algorithms also require a relatively small amount of data and can handle both numerical and categorical variables at the same time. Because it is a nonparametric method, it doesn't rely on the data belonging to any underlying distributions, which is pertinent to many real-world situations. As a result, it has been used in a wide variety of applications such as fraud detection, diagnosis of medical conditions, stock trading decisions, and prediction of student success in college.

While decision trees are highly popular, they are sensitive to changes in the data. Even small changes in the data may render drastically different trees and results. Ensemble tree models, which combine multiple single-tree models into an ensemble model, are often credited to produce better and more stable predictive performance than a single-tree model.

Two other techniques that are beyond the scope of this text—discriminant analysis and neural networks—are also included in the discussion here as reference. Discriminant analysis is a robust classification technique that, like decision trees, provides information about predictor importance. However, it assumes that predictor variables are normally distributed with equal variance and, thus, is only suitable for numerical predictor variables.

Neural networks can be used for both classification and prediction. They mimic the neural structure of the brain using learning, memory, and generalization. As a result, neural networks can capture highly complex relationships in the data and are used as a building block of sophisticated machine learning systems (often called deep learning). A much-publicized neural network application, Google's self-driving car project called Waymo, claims to have used millions of data points to train the car to recognize, adapt, and safely respond to pedestrians and objects on public roads. Despite their sophistication, neural networks do not provide insight into the rationale used for classifications or predictions and lack interpretability. Many practitioners liken neural networks to a "black box" and find it difficult to justify the results to a nontechnical audience.

A summary of advantages and limitations of popular supervised data mining techniques is presented in Table 9.2. The nature and some of the prerequisites of these techniques lend themselves to certain types of analysis and applications.

TABLE 9.2 Comparison of Supervised Techniques

Technique	Advantages	Limitations
Linear regression (Chapter 6 and Sections 7.1 and 7.2)	Widely used; computationally efficient; yields "best" mathematical function with interpretable parameters and predictor importance information	Only for prediction; can be affected by nonlinearity, collinearity between predictor variables, and other violations of the assumptions
Logistic regression (Section 7.3)	Computationally efficient; provides predictor importance information and probabilistic interpretation	Only for classification; can be affected by collinearity between predictor variables
k-nearest neighbors (Section 9.2)	Used both for classification and prediction but is particularly effective as a classifier; easy to understand; does not assume any underlying distribution in the data	Provides no information on predictor importance; searches the entire training data set, and therefore, is computationally expensive
Naïve Bayes (Section 9.3)	Simple, efficient, and effective	Only for classification; assumes independence among predictors; predictors must be categorical or transformed into categories (binning)
Classification and regression trees (CART) (Sections 10.2 and 10.3)	Used both for classification and prediction; easy to understand and interpret; easily explained and justified to non-technical decision makers; provides predictor importance information; does not assume any underlying distribution in the data; robust when dealing with outliers and missing values	Cannot capture interactions among variables; sensitive to changes in data; single trees are prone to overfitting
Ensemble tree models (Section 10.4)	Used both for classification and prediction; addresses the overfitting issue of single tree models	Do not provide the tree diagram, thus lack interpretability
Discriminant analysis (Not covered in text)	Provides predictor importance information; accounts for interactions between predictor variables	Only for classification; assumes predictor variables are normally distributed with equal variance; uses only numerical predictor variables
Neural networks (Not covered in text)	Used both for classification and prediction; flexible; captures complex relationships	Provides little insight into relationships or results; hard to explain or interpret; lacks interpretability; computationally burdensome

LO 9.2

9.2 THE *k*-NEAREST NEIGHBORS METHOD

Apply the *k*-nearest neighbors method to classify new records.

In this section, we explore a supervised data mining technique called the *k*-nearest neighbors method, often abbreviated KNN. The KNN method has been used in numerous applications including consumer credit rating assessment, loan application evaluation, fraud detection, and medical diagnosis. It is one of the simplest, yet most frequently used data mining techniques for classification when the response variable is categorical and for prediction when the response variable is numerical. Also, traditional KNN algorithms require predictor variables to be numerical; therefore, data transformation may need to be performed to convert categorical predictor variables into numerical values. For a discussion on transforming categorical data, refer to Section 2.5 of this text.

The KNN method is known to be a very effective classifier; however, it is much less popular as a predictor. In this section, we focus primarily on classification problems where the target variable is binary.

KNN belongs to a category of data mining techniques called memory-based reasoning. The premise of memory-based reasoning is that we tend to guide our decisions using the memories of similar situations we experienced in the past. A credit card company can use KNN to evaluate a new credit card application based on information from similar customers. The KNN algorithm considers the existing credit card holders that are most similar to the new credit card applicant as its "nearest neighbors" and uses the existing information to decide on whether or not to approve the new application. In the medical field, doctors and nurses can use the KNN algorithm to compare past patients to help determine whether or not a new patient has a similar disease. Past patients with similar symptoms are considered "nearest neighbors" of the new patient, and their information can be used to help diagnose new patients.

THE *k*-NEAREST NEIGHBORS (KNN) METHOD

A memory-based reasoning technique that uses observations from the past that are most similar to the new observation to classify or predict the value of the target variable.

To better understand how the KNN algorithm works, consider a mortgage company trying to determine whether or not a new applicant is likely to default on his or her home loan. The new applicant is 36 years old and has an annual income of $64,000. The mortgage company extracts information from 10 previous customers with similar income (in $1,000s) and age characteristics, as well as whether or not the customer defaulted on the loan. Table 9.3 shows the data.

TABLE 9.3 Characteristics of Home Loan Customers

Customer ID	Income	Age	Default
001	65	35	Yes
002	59	34	No
003	71	40	No
004	67	32	No
005	60	31	Yes
006	59	37	No
007	72	42	No
008	63	34	No
009	64	38	No
010	71	34	Yes

The KNN algorithm works by identifying a number of existing observations (i.e., past loan applicants) that are most similar to the new observation (i.e., the new applicant) in order to classify the new observation. Thus, central components of the KNN algorithm are (1) the chosen similarity measure and (2) the number of nearest neighbors (k) to consider. In practice, the KNN algorithm often uses the Euclidean distance to measure the similarity between observations. In the mortgage approval example, given the differences in scale of the Age and Income variables, we would standardize these variables before calculating the Euclidean distance between observations. Similarity measures, the Euclidean distance, and the standardization of variables are discussed in Section 8.2.

To demonstrate this process, Figure 9.1 shows a scatterplot of Age against Income for the 10 past customers, where customers who defaulted on the loan are labeled with a red marker and customers who did not default are labeled with a blue marker. We add the new applicant to the scatterplot as a green triangle and identify the three "nearest neighbors" in the green circle. In other words, we choose the value of $k = 3$ in the KNN algorithm.

The nearest neighbors can also be determined mathematically using the Euclidean distance between the new applicant and other applicants in the data set. In this scenario, only one of the three nearest neighbors defaulted on his or her home loan (one red marker among the three nearest neighbors in the green circle). As a result, we estimate that the probability that the new applicant will default is 1/3 = 0.33. The mortgage company can then compare the probability to a predetermined cutoff point in order to decide whether to approve or reject the new applicant. If the company uses 0.5 as the default probability cutoff point, the new loan applicant will be classified as being unlikely to default and will receive an approval on the loan application. However, if the cutoff is 0.25, the new loan applicant will be classified as being likely to default; we discussed cutoff values and their influence on the classification in Section 8.3.

As you can see from this example, the choice of k will result in different classification results. For example, if $k = 1$, then we use the nearest neighbor (the red marker) to determine the class membership of the new applicant. Now, the probability that the new applicant will default becomes 1/1 = 1.

FIGURE 9.1
Age and Income of home loan applicants

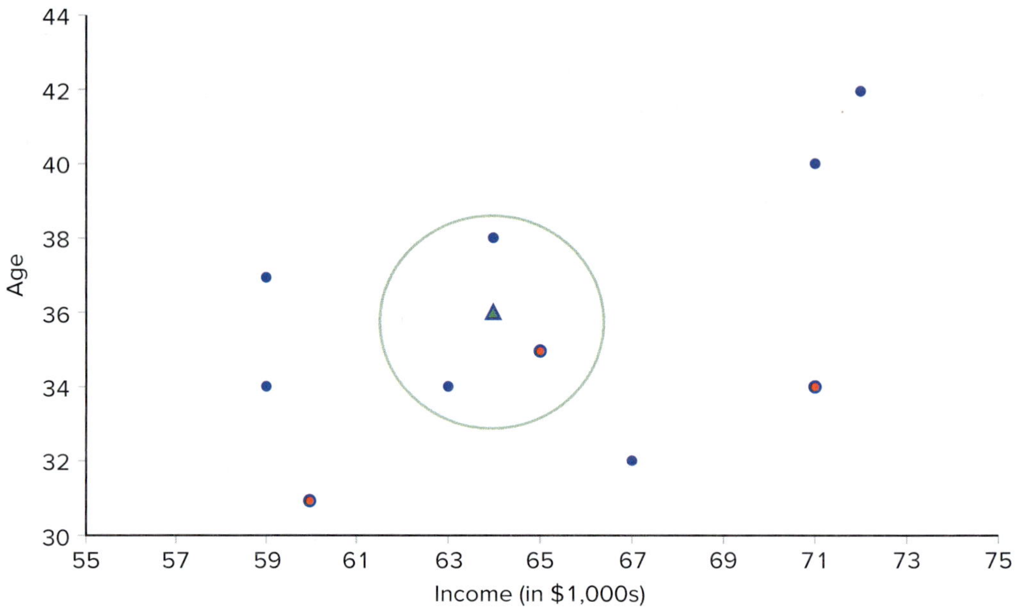

Because the KNN method is a supervised data mining technique, data partitioning is used to determine its performance and to optimize model complexity. The nearest neighbor observations are identified in the training data set. Most practitioners try to minimize the error rate in the KNN method by experimenting with a range of k values and their corresponding performance measures from the validation data set in order to determine the optimal k value. In some software applications such as Analytic Solver, the test data set is used to assess the performance of the final predictive model and the optimal k value. The KNN algorithm can also classify new observations based on the existing observations that are most similar to the new observation. As mentioned earlier, this process is called scoring a new record based on the values of the predictor variables. As presented in Figure 9.1, the KNN algorithm first searches the entire training data set for the most similar observations, and then provides a score for a new observation.

Unlike a traditional analysis with linear and logistic regression models, the KNN algorithm does not assume any underlying distribution in the data for making predictions. This nonparametric approach makes the KNN method very useful in a practical situation because real-world data do not always follow theoretical assumptions. Despite its simplicity, the KNN method often produces highly accurate results. Because the KNN algorithm searches the entire training data set for close neighbors, the process can be quite time-consuming and computationally intensive, especially with a large amount of data. Fortunately, several computer software programs include the KNN algorithm. Example 9.1 illustrates how to perform KNN classification using Analytic Solver and R.

EXAMPLE 9.1

FILE *Gym*

Recall from the introductory case that Janet Williams, the membership manager at 24/7 Fitness Center, has collected data from 1,000 past open house attendees (Gym_Data worksheet) and 23 new open house attendees (Gym_Score worksheet). The data include the age and the annual income of the attendee, the average number of hours that the attendee exercises per week, and for the Gym_Data worksheet, whether or not the attendee purchases a membership. Janet is interested in a model that will help her identify attendees who are likely to purchase a membership. Perform KNN analysis to estimate a classification model and evaluate its performance. Report the relevant performance measures and score new records.

SOLUTION:

Using Analytic Solver

As discussed in Chapters 7 and 8, to develop and evaluate a classification model, we generally perform cross-validation using either the holdout method or the *k*-fold method. Analytic Solver provides a procedure for the holdout method and allows for partitioning a data set into training, validation, and test data sets. In this chapter, we partition our data set in Analytic Solver as follows: 50% for training, 30% for validation, and 20% for test. Here, an independent assessment of the predictive performance of the KNN model is conducted with the test data set that is not used in the model development.

a. Open the ***Gym*** data file and go to the Gym_Data worksheet.
b. Choose **Data Mining** > **Partition** > **Standard Partition**.
c. See Figure 9.2. Click on the ellipsis button next to *Data Range* and highlight cells \$A\$1:\$D\$1001. Make sure that the box *First Row Contains Headers* is

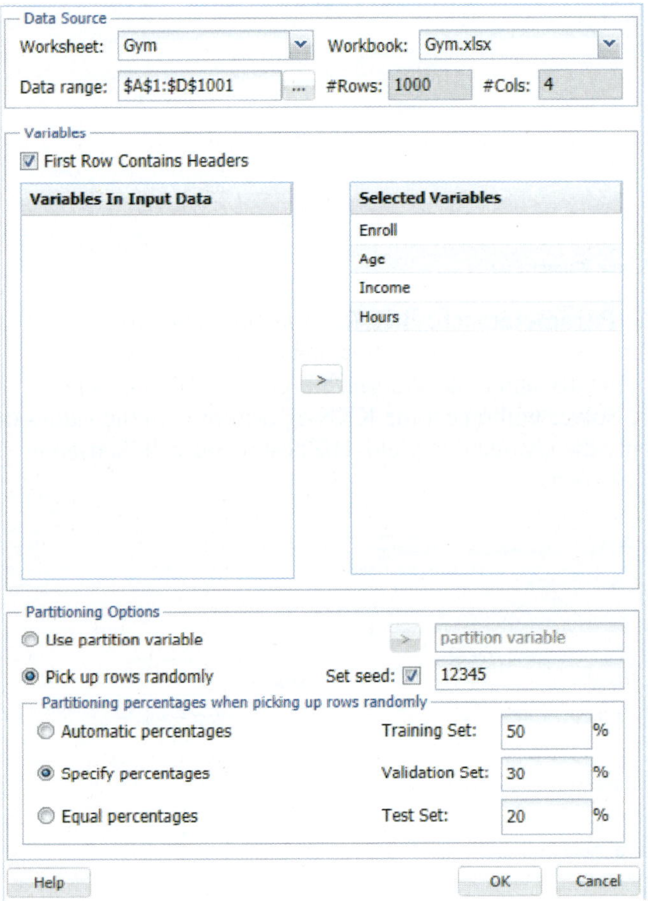

Source: Microsoft Excel

FIGURE 9.2 Analytic Solver's standard data partition

checked. The *Variables in Input Data* box will populate. Select and move all the variables to the *Selected Variables* box. Choose *Specify percentages* with 50% for Training Set, 30% for Validation Set, and 20% for Test Set. Accept other defaults. Click **OK**.

d. Analytic Solver will create a new worksheet called STDPartition with the partitioned data. In the *Partition Summary* table of this worksheet, you should see the following number of observations in each partition: 500 for Training, 300 for Validation, and 200 for Testing.

e. Choose **Data Mining** > **Classify** > **k-Nearest Neighbors**. See Figure 9.3. Make sure that the STDPartition worksheet is active. In the **Data** tab, select and move Age, Income, and Hours to the *Selected Variables* box. Select Enroll as the *Output Variable*. Accept the other defaults and click *Next*.

FIGURE 9.3
The KNN classification

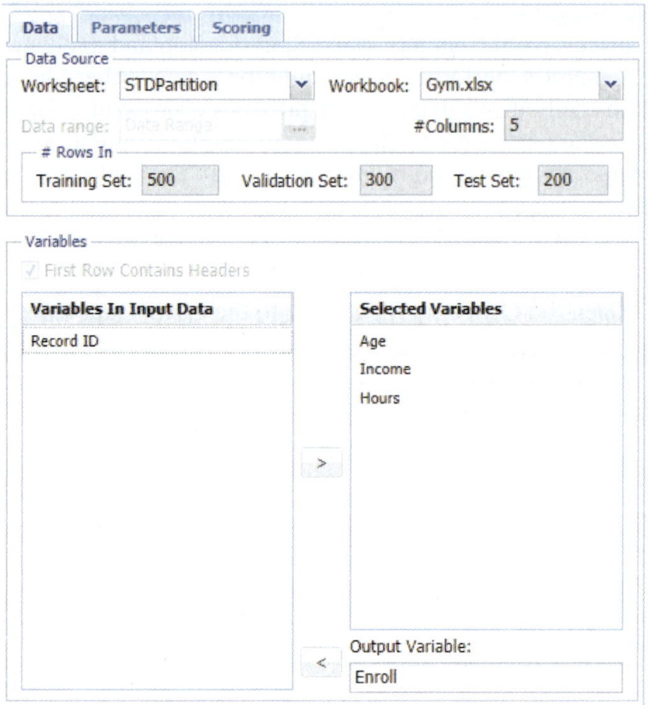

Source: Microsoft Excel

f. See Figure 9.4. In the **Parameters** tab, click *Rescale Data* and check the *Rescale Data* checkbox. Select *Standardization* and click **Done**. In the # Neighbors (*K*) box, input 10, and under *Nearest Neighbors: Search*, select *Search 1..K*. Analytic Solver will repeat the KNN algorithm with the values of *k* from 1 to 10, but only the *k* value that yields the best result will be used in subsequent steps. Click *Next*.

FIGURE 9.4
The KNN parameters options

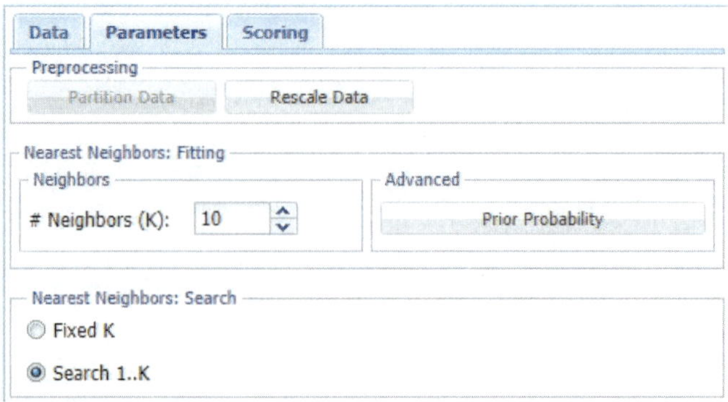

Source: Microsoft Excel

g. See Figure 9.5. In the **Scoring** tab, check the *Summary Report* boxes for *Score Training Data*, *Score Validation Data*, and *Score Test Data*. Also check the *Lift Charts* box for *Score Test Data*. Check the *In Worksheet* checkbox under the *Score New Data* section. Under the **New Data (WS)** tab, select Gym_Score in the *Worksheet* box and enter \$A\$1:\$C\$24 in the *Data Range*. These 23 records of potential members will be scored by the KNN classification algorithm. Make sure the *First Row Contains Headers* box is checked and click the *Match By Name* button. Click *Finish*.

Source: Microsoft Excel

FIGURE 9.5
Analytic Solver's scoring options

Analytic Solver will create seven new worksheets. The KNNC_Output worksheet displays the misclassification percentage for each value of k using the validation data set. Recall from Chapter 8 that the misclassification rate is the overall proportion of cases that are classified incorrectly (false positives and false negatives combined). Figure 9.6 shows that the lowest misclassification rate is reached at the k value of 3, which is 8%. Therefore, $k = 3$ is used in the subsequent calculations.

K	% Misclassification
1	11.66666667
2	11.33333333
3	8
4	9.333333333
5	9.333333333
6	10.33333333
7	10.66666667
8	10
9	10
10	8.666666667

Source: Microsoft Excel

FIGURE 9.6
Misclassification rates

The KNNC_TrainingScore, KNNC_ValidationScore, and KNNC_TestScore worksheets display the classification results for the training, validation, and test data sets, with $k = 3$. Figure 9.7 summarizes the main results from the test data set. Here, we focus on the most notable performance measures for this application. The accuracy rate indicates that 89.5% of the observations are correctly classified; thus, 10.5% are incorrectly classified (see the error rate). Normally, the performance measures from the training data will be better than the results obtained from the validation or test data. However, if the performance values from the training data are considerably better than the values from the validation and the test data, overfitting might be an issue. In the 24/7 Fitness Center case, the KNN algorithm can accurately predict the outcome for 94.6% of the observations in the training data and 92% of the observations in the validation data (performance measures not shown here), while the accuracy rate is slightly lower for the test data, (89.5%), which indicates that some overfitting may exist. However, the differences may not be large enough to suggest any severe overfitting problems. The sensitivity of 0.90 is the proportion of buyers that the model is able to identify correctly, while the specificity of 0.89 is the proportion of the nonbuyers that the model is able to identify correctly.

FIGURE 9.7 Classification summary tables

Confusion Matrix

Actual\Predicted	0	1
0	107	13
1	8	72

Error Report

Class	# Cases	# Errors	% Error
0	120	13	10.83333
1	80	8	10
Overall	200	21	10.5

Metrics

Metric	Value
Accuracy (#correct)	179
Accuracy (%correct)	89.5
Specificity	0.891667
Sensitivity (Recall)	0.9
Precision	0.847059
F1 score	0.872727
Success Class	1
Success Probability	0.5

Source: Microsoft Excel

To answer the question of whether the resulting KNN model has good predictive performance or not, we can compare the accuracy rate of the model to that of the naïve rule, where all cases are classified into the predominant class. For example, because there are 80 target class (Enrolled in the gym) cases among the 200 test data cases, the naïve rule would assume that each case has the probability of 80/200 or 0.4 of belonging to the target class. Using the cutoff rate of 0.5, the naïve rule will classify all cases into the non-target class (Do not enroll in the gym) and produce an accuracy rate of $(200 - 80) \div 200 = 0.60$, sensitivity of 0, and specificity of 1. Therefore, we conclude that the KNN model has better predictive performance than the naïve rule does, especially if the goal is to identify target class cases.

As illustrated in Example 8.6 in Chapter 8, the choice of the cutoff value can influence the confusion matrix and the resulting performance measures. By default, Analytic Solver uses 0.5 as the cutoff value for binary choice models. The analyst may choose to increase or decrease the cutoff value to classify fewer or more observations into the target class due to asymmetric misclassification costs or uneven class distributions.

In this example, the opportunity cost of missing a potential gym member who would have purchased a gym membership is likely to be higher than the cost of reaching out to a potential gym member who ends up not purchasing a gym membership. Furthermore, among the 1,000 past open house attendees in the data set,

403 purchased gym memberships suggesting that the probability of an open house attendee purchasing the gym membership is 403 ÷ 1,000 = 0.403 instead of the default probability of 0.5 for a binary choice situation with equal class distribution.

In this case, the manager of the fitness center may reduce the cutoff value to a lower value than 0.5 in order to classify more cases into the target class in order to achieve a higher sensitivity value. To assess predictive performance using a different cutoff value in Analytic Solver, input the desired cutoff value, for example, 0.25, in the *Success Probability Cutoff:* box in the **Data** tab in step e. You may want to experiment with a number of different cutoff values to examine their impact on the performance measures.

Figure 9.8 summarizes the output found on the KNNC_TestLiftChart worksheet. Because Analytic Solver uses the training and validation data to determine the best *k* value, it uses the test data and the charts displayed on the KNNC_TestLiftChart worksheet to provide an independent assessment of the KNN classification.

In the cumulative lift chart, the blue line represents the results from the KNN model, and the diagonal red line represents a model that randomly classifies potential gym members (baseline model). In this case, the blue line from the KNN model lies well above the red diagonal line, indicating that the KNN model performs

FIGURE 9.8 Performance charts for KNN

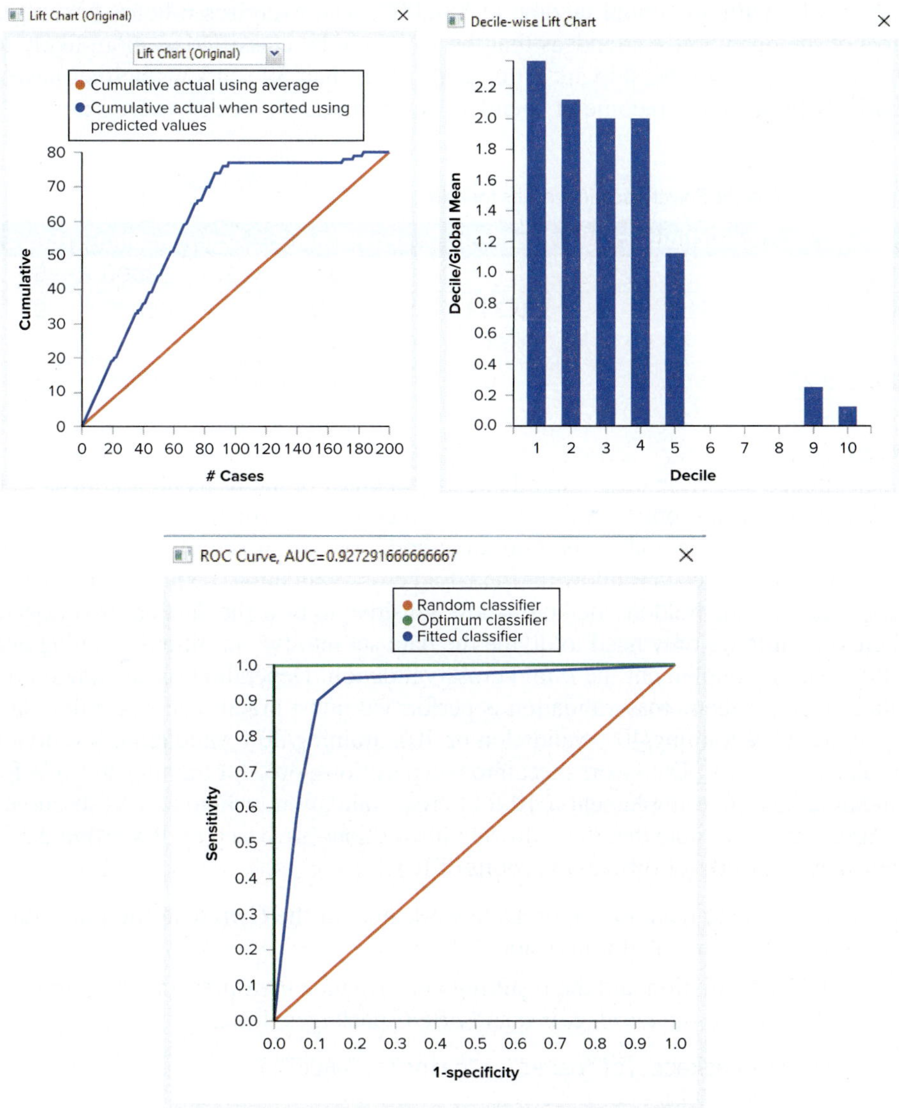

considerably better in terms of predicting whether or not potential gym members will purchase a gym membership as compared to the baseline model.

The decile-wise lift chart shows that the first 10% of potential members selected by the KNN model include about 2.375 times as many individuals who would actually purchase a gym membership than a randomly selected 10% of potential members. (The value 2.375 is obtained from the decile table, which is not shown.) Moreover, the decile-wise lift chart shows that almost all of the Class 1 cases (that is, purchased a gym membership) have been identified within the first five deciles of cases with the highest predicted probability of belonging to Class 1. Similarly, the blue line from the KNN model in the ROC curve lies well above the red diagonal line. The area under the ROC curve, or AUC, is very high (0.9273), indicating that the KNN model performs extremely well in terms of sensitivity and specificity across all possible cutoff values.

On the KNNC_NewScore worksheet, the 23 records of potential members are scored. The Prediction: Enroll column displays the classification result for each record. The KNN model predicts that six of the 23 attendees will purchase a gym membership. We combine the information from the KNNC_NewScore worksheet with the information that Janet collected for the 23 attendees at the most recent open house.

Table 9.4 shows a portion of the scoring results. From this grouping, Janet and her staff should target the second attendee—a 23-year-old, with an annual income of $65,000, who exercises 9 hours per week—as well as the last attendee—a 51-year-old, with an annual income of $88,000, who exercises 6 hours per week. Most of the open house attendees that the KNN model classified as more likely to purchase a gym membership are individuals older than 50 years who either have a relatively high annual income or spend at least 9 hours on weekly exercise.

TABLE 9.4 Analytic Solver's scoring results for KNN

Record ID	Prediction: Enroll	PostProb: 0	PostProb: 1	Age	Income	Hours
Record 1	0	1	0	22	33000	5
Record 2	1	0.3333	0.6667	23	65000	9
⋮	⋮	⋮	⋮	⋮	⋮	⋮
Record 23	1	0	1	51	88000	6

Using R

As mentioned earlier, in order to evaluate the accuracy of the KNN algorithm as well as determine the appropriate value of *k*, we generally perform cross-validation using either the holdout method or the *k*-fold method, both discussed in Chapter 7. Most data mining packages in R allow for the *k*-fold cross-validation method, which, when compared with the holdout method, is less sensitive to how the data are partitioned. Therefore, in R we only need to divide the data set into two partitions, training and validation, and implement the *k*-fold cross-validation. Depending on the amount of data available, when cross-validation is performed, most practitioners partition data into either 60% training/40% validation or 70% training/30% validation. We divide the data in the Gym_Data worksheet into two partitions, 60% for training and 40% for validation, and then implement a 10-fold cross-validation technique. (As discussed in Appendix C, we note that the following instructions are based on **R version 3.5.3**. They may not work for different versions of R.)

a. Import the data from the Gym_Data worksheet of the ***Gym*** data file into a data frame (table) and label it myData.

b. For KNN estimation and the resulting performance measures and diagrams, install and load the *caret*, *gains*, and *pROC* packages. Enter:

```
> install.packages(c("caret", "gains", "pROC"))
> library(caret)
```

```
> library(gains)
> library(pROC)
```

On some computers, you might also need to install other packages that support the *caret* package using the command `> install.packages("caret", dependencies = c("Depends", "Suggests"))`. Also, if prompted by R Studio, install and load the *car* package.

c. We use the **scale** function to standardize the Age, Income, and Hours variables; store the standardized values in a new data frame called myData1; and append the original Enroll variable back to myData1. We use the **as.factor** function to convert the target variable (Enroll) into a categorical data type. To simplify the R code, we use the **colnames** function to rename myData1$myData.Enroll (in column 4) to myData1$Enroll. Enter:

```
> myData1 <- scale(myData[2:4])
> myData1 <- data.frame(myData1, myData$Enroll)
> colnames(myData1)[4] <- 'Enroll'
> myData1$Enroll <- as.factor(myData1$Enroll)
```

d. To partition the data into 60% training and 40% validation sets, we use the **createDataPartition** function and specify Enroll as the target variable. To ensure consistency, we use the **set.seed** function to set the random seed to 1. Enter:

```
> set.seed(1)
> myIndex <- createDataPartition(myData1$Enroll, p=0.6,
list = FALSE)
> trainSet <- myData1[myIndex,]
> validationSet <- myData1[-myIndex,]
```

The data set is partitioned into 60% for training and 40% for validation with the option $p = 0.6$. The 60% training set is assigned to an object called **trainSet** and the other 40% is assigned to the **validationSet** object. In order to maintain the same ratio of target and nontarget class cases for both the training and validation data sets, R partitions 601 cases into the training data set and 399 cases into the validation set.

e. We use the **trainControl** function to implement a 10-fold cross-validation by setting the option *method* equal to "cv" and the option *number* equal to 10. Enter:

```
> myCtrl <- trainControl(method = "cv", number = 10)
```

f. We use the **expand.grid** function to specify possible *k* values from 1 to 10 and store the results in an object called myGrid. The optimal *k* value is determined based on accuracy. The possible range of *k* values may vary; you may experiment with a different range by changing the numbers in the statement. Enter:

```
> myGrid <- expand.grid(.k=c(1:10))
```

g. To implement the KNN method with the training data set with option values specified in steps e and f, we use the **train** function and store the results in an object called KNN_fit. To ensure consistency of the cross-validation results, we again use the **set.seed** function to fix a random seed. Enter:

```
> set.seed(1)
> KNN_fit <- train(Enroll ~., data = trainSet, method = "knn",
trControl=myCtrl, tuneGrid = myGrid)
> KNN_fit
```

Note that the Enroll variable is specified as a target variable and "knn" is specified as the classification method. The KNN results are shown in Figure 9.9.

The value $k = 6$ yields the highest accuracy rate (0.9102695) and will be used in subsequent steps.

FIGURE 9.9
KNN training results

k	Accuracy	Kappa
1	0. 8586839	0. 7068705
2	0. 8636556	0. 7161206
3	0. 8986302	0. 7913498
4	0. 8737941	0. 7394298
5	0. 9052978	0. 8049542
6	0. 9102695	0. 8148253
7	0. 9036584	0. 8015972
8	0. 9052422	0. 8040322
9	0. 9068806	0. 8071254
10	0. 9051584	0. 8044090

h. We apply the KNN model, which uses $k = 6$, on the validation data set using the **predict** function, and then we use the **confusionMatrix** function to create a confusion matrix. Enter:

```
> KNN_Class <- predict(KNN_fit, newdata = validationSet)
> confusionMatrix(KNN_Class,validationSet$Enroll, positive = '1')
```

Note that we identify Class 1 (Enrolled in the gym) as the positive or success class. In other situations, the positive class may be different. Also, the Enroll variable in the validation set is identified as the target variable. Relevant output is shown in Figure 9.10. The confusion matrix results from the validation set indicate a high classification accuracy (0.9148), sensitivity (0.8944), and specificity (0.9286). Refer to Section 8.3 for additional details of these performance measures.

FIGURE 9.10
Confusion matrix for KNN

```
Confusion Matrix and Statistics

          Reference
prediction   0   1
         0 221  17
         1  17 144

               Accuracy : 0.9148
                 95% CI : (0.883, 0.9403)
    No Information Rate : 0.5965
    P-Value [Acc > NIR] : <2e-16

                  Kappa : 0.823

 Mcnemar's Test P-Value : 1

            Sensitivity : 0.8944
            Specificity : 0.9286
         Pos Pred Value : 0.8944
         Neg Pred Value : 0.9286
             Prevalence : 0.4035
         Detection Rate : 0.3609
   Detection Prevalence : 0.4035
      Balanced Accuracy : 0.9115

       'Positive' Class : 1
```

To evaluate the predictive performance of the KNN model, we can compare its performance measures to those of the naïve rule, where all cases are classified into the predominant class. Because there are 161 target class (Enrolled in the gym) cases among the 399 validation data cases, the naïve rule would classify all cases into the non-target class (Do not enroll in the gym) and produce an accuracy rate of $(399 - 161) \div 399 = 0.5965$, sensitivity of 0, and specificity of 1. Therefore, the KNN model shows better predictive performance than the naïve rule does, especially if the goal is to identify target class cases.

As illustrated in Example 8.6 in Chapter 8, the choice of the cutoff value can influence the confusion matrix and the resulting performance measures. By default, R uses 0.5 as the cutoff value for binary choice models. The analyst may choose to increase or decrease the cutoff value to classify fewer or more observations into the target class due to asymmetric misclassification costs or uneven class distributions. In this example, the opportunity cost of missing a potential gym member who would have purchased a gym membership is likely to be higher than the cost of reaching out to a potential gym member who ends up not purchasing a gym membership. Furthermore, among the 1,000 past open house attendees in the data set, 403 purchased gym memberships suggesting that the probability of an open house attendee purchasing the gym membership is $403 \div 1{,}000 = 0.403$ instead of the default probability of 0.5 for a binary choice situation with equal class distribution. In this case, the manager of the fitness center may reduce the cutoff value to a lower value than 0.5 in order to classify more cases into the target class in order to achieve a higher sensitivity value. This is illustrated in step i.

i. To evaluate the predictive performance of the KNN model using a different cutoff value in R, we first compute the probability of each case belonging to the target class instead of its class membership. In the **predict** function, we set the *type* option equal to 'prob' to predict the probability values. Enter:

```
> KNN_Class_prob <- predict(KNN_fit, newdata = validationSet,
type ='prob')
> KNN_Class_prob
```

Figure 9.11 shows the probabilities associated with the first few cases. As you can see, the first column lists the probabilities of the cases belonging to Class 0 (Not enrolled in the gym), while the second column lists the probabilities of the cases belonging to Class 1 (Enrolled in the gym). To determine the class memberships of cases using a cutoff value other than the default probability of 0.5 (for example, 0.25, in order to accurately classify more Class 1 cases), we compare the values in the second column to the new cutoff value.

	0	1
1	1.0000000	0.0000000
2	0.3333333	0.6666667
3	1.0000000	0.0000000
4	1.0000000	0.0000000
5	1.0000000	0.0000000
6	1.0000000	0.0000000
7	0.1666667	0.8333333

FIGURE 9.11
Predicted probabilities

j. To construct a confusion matrix using the new cutoff value of 0.25, we use the **ifelse** function to determine the class memberships. We use the **as.factor** function to convert the class membership to factor, which is the same data type as the target variable, Enroll. Enter:

```
> confusionMatrix(as.factor(ifelse(KNN_Class_prob[,2]>0.25,
'1', '0')), validationSet$Enroll, positive = '1')
```

The resulting confusion matrix (not shown here) provides the performance measures of the KNN model using the cutoff value of 0.25. Please verify that in the new confusion matrix, accuracy, sensitivity, and specificity are 0.8797, 0.9627, and 0.8235, respectively. Although the overall accuracy is lower than before, the new cutoff value allows the manager of the fitness club to identify more target class cases correctly as signified by the higher sensitivity value.

k. To create a cumulative gain table and a cumulative lift chart, we need to convert the Enroll variable back as a numerical data type as required by the *gains* package. Enter:

```
> validationSet$Enroll <- as.numeric(as.character(validationSet$En
roll))
```

l. We generate the cumulative gains lift table using the **gains** function. The **gains** function requires two arguments: actual class memberships and predicted target class probabilities. Enter:

```
> gains_table <- gains(validationSet$Enroll, KNN_Class_prob[,2])
> gains_table
```

Figure 9.12 shows the relevant results. By default, the cumulative gains table divides the cases into 10 groups based on their probabilities of belonging to the target class. The last column of Figure 9.12 shows the average probability for each group. (Note: These values are rounded to two digits after the decimal point.) In R, in situations where there are less than ten possible probability values, the cumulative gains table and decile-wise lift chart will show less than 10 groups.

FIGURE 9.12 Cumulative gains table

Depth of File	N	Cume N	Mean Resp	Cume Mean Resp	Cume Pct of Total Resp	Lift Index	Cume Lift	Mean Model Score
15	59	59	0.93	0.93	34.2%	231	231	1.00
30	62	121	0.90	0.92	68.9%	224	227	0.83
31	1	122	1.00	0.92	69.6%	248	228	0.71
38	28	150	0.93	0.92	85.7%	230	228	0.67
43	21	171	0.57	0.88	93.2%	142	217	0.50
43	1	172	0.00	0.87	93.2%	0	216	0.43
49	24	196	0.21	0.79	96.3%	52	196	0.33
49	1	197	0.00	0.79	96.3%	0	195	0.29
58	34	231	0.09	0.68	98.1%	22	170	0.17
100	168	399	0.02	0.40	100.0%	4	100	0.00

m. We use the **plot** function to create the cumulative lift chart as shown in Figure 9.13. The first command plots the lift curve for the KNN model, and the second command draws a dashed diagonal line to indicate the baseline model. Enter:

```
> plot(c(0, gains_table$cume.pct.of.total*sum(validationSet
$Enroll)) ~ c(0, gains_table$cume.obs),xlab = "# of cases",
ylab="Cumulative", main="Cumulative Lift Chart", type = "l")
> lines(c(0, sum(validationSet$Enroll)) ~ c(0,
dim(validationSet)[1]), col="red", lty=2)
```

FIGURE 9.13 R's cumulative lift chart

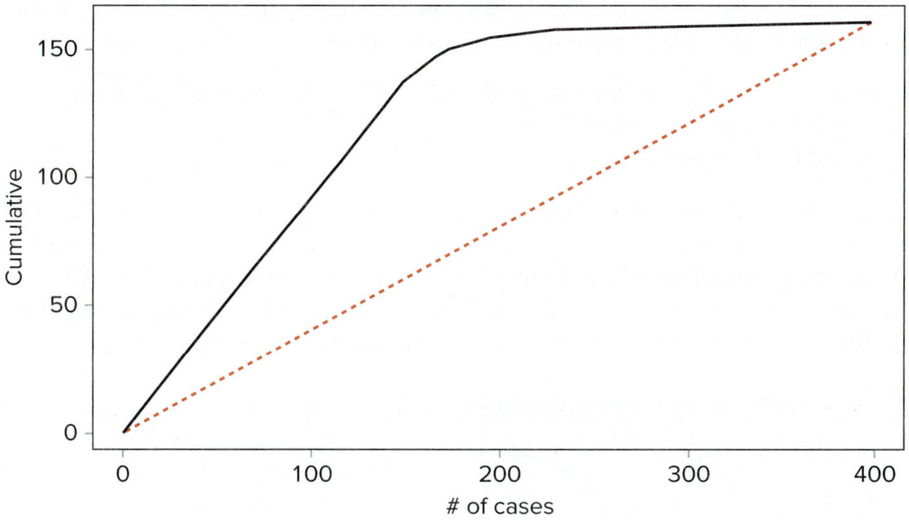

n. To plot the decile-wise lift chart, we use the **barplot** function to plot a bar chart. Enter:

```
> barplot(gains_table$mean.resp/mean(validationSet$Enroll),
names.arg=gains_table$depth, xlab="Percentile", ylab="Lift", ylim
= c(0,3), main = "Decile-Wise Lift Chart")
```

The decile-wise lift chart is displayed in Figure 9.14. The decile-wise lift chart shows that if the 24/7 Fitness Center contacts the top 15% of the potential gym members with the highest predicted probability of enrolling, the gym would be able to capture 2.31 times as many potential members who actually

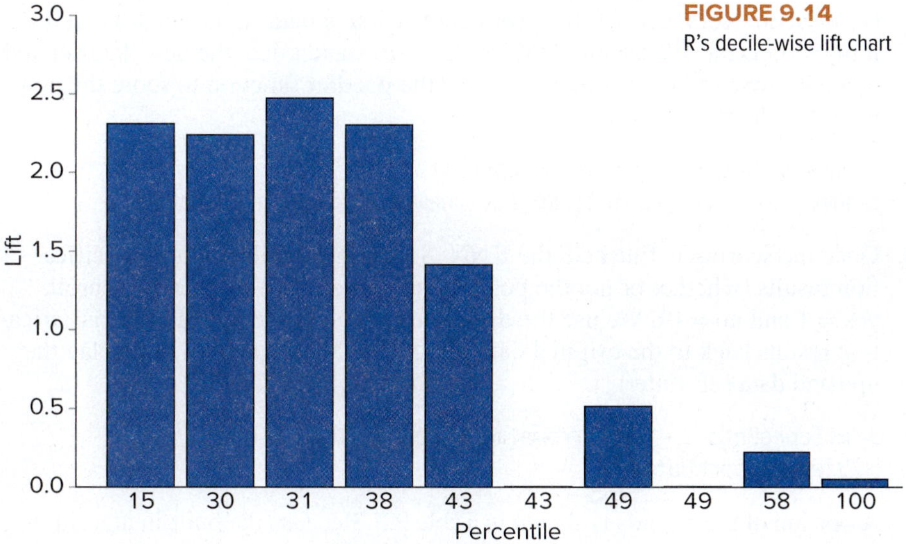

FIGURE 9.14
R's decile-wise lift chart

purchase the gym membership, compared to a scenario where the 24/7 Fitness Center randomly selects 15% of the potential members to contact. The KNN model shows superior predictive power compared to the baseline model.

o. We use the **roc** function, which produces a **roc** object that can be used to plot the ROC curve. We then use the **plot.roc** function to plot the ROC curve and the **auc** function to retrieve the AUC value. Enter:

```
> roc_object<- roc(validationSet$Enroll, KNN_Class_prob[,2])
> plot.roc(roc_object)
> auc(roc_object)
```

The area under the ROC curve, or AUC, is very high (0.9532), indicating that the KNN model performs extremely well in predicting the gym enrollment among potential members. Figure 9.15 displays the ROC curve. The KNN model performs better than the baseline model (shown as the green diagonal line) in terms of sensitivity and specificity across all cutoff values.

FIGURE 9.15 R's ROC curve, with AUC = 0.9532

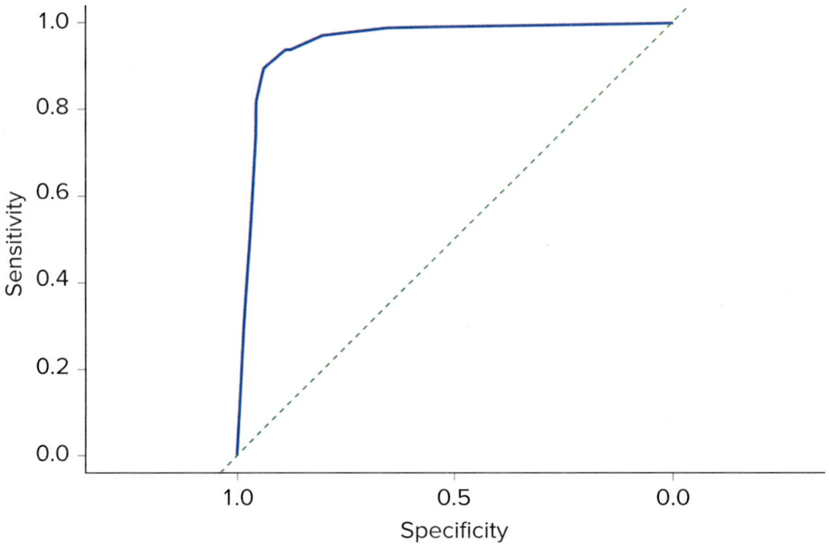

p. To score the records of the potential gym members, we import data from the Gym_Score worksheet of the ***Gym*** data file into a data frame (table) and name it myScoreData. We use the **scale** function to standardize the new data set and name it myScoreData1. Finally, we use the **predict** function to score the new records. Enter:

```
> myScoreData1 <- scale(myScoreData)
> KNN_Score <- predict(KNN_fit, newdata = myScoreData1)
```

q. Once the scoring is finished, the KNN_Score object will contain classification results (whether or not the potential gym members are likely to enroll: yes = 1 and no = 0). We use the **data.frame** function to append the classification results back to the original data set and the **View** function to display the updated data set. Enter:

```
> myScoreData <- data.frame(myScoreData, KNN_Score)
> View(myScoreData)
```

A portion of the records is shown in Table 9.5. Because the built-in algorithms are not the same, Analytic Solver and R yield different classification outcomes. The R results suggest that the 24/7 Fitness Center should focus on contacting potential gym members who are older than 40 years with a high annual income.

TABLE 9.5 R's Scoring Results for KNN

Record	Age	Income	Hours	KNN_Score
1	22	33000	5	0
2	23	65000	9	0
⋮	⋮	⋮	⋮	⋮
23	51	88000	6	1

As mentioned earlier, the KNN method is most often used for classification where the target variable is categorical. However, it can also be used for predicting a target variable with a numerical value. To predict the value of a new record, the KNN method uses a similar approach with the Euclidean distance to identify the nearest neighbors, but instead uses the *average* of its *k* nearest neighbors to estimate the value of the new record's target variable. As discussed in Chapter 8, instead of misclassification or accuracy rates, to evaluate the performance of the KNN prediction, we use prediction metrics such as the root mean square error (RMSE) and the mean absolute deviation (MAD). Functions for KNN prediction can be found in both Analytic Solver and R. However, because practitioners use the KNN method mostly for classification purposes, we focus solely on using the KNN method for classification in this text.

SYNOPSIS OF INTRODUCTORY CASE

Gyms and exercise facilities usually have a high turnover rate among their members. Like other gyms, 24/7 Fitness Center relies on recruiting new members on a regular basis in order to sustain its business and financial well-being. Completely familiar with data analytics techniques, Janet Williams, a manager at 24/7 Fitness Center, uses the KNN method to analyze data from the gym's past open house. She wants to gain a better insight into which attendees are likely to purchase a gym membership after attending this event.

Overall, Janet finds that the KNN analysis provides reasonably high accuracy in predicting whether or not potential gym members will purchase a membership. The accuracy, sensitivity, and specificity rates from the test data set are well above 80%. More importantly, the KNN analysis identifies individual open house attendees who are likely to purchase a gym membership. For example, the analysis results indicate that open house attendees who are 50 years or older with a relatively high annual income and those in the same age group who spend at least nine hours on weekly exercise are more likely to enroll after attending the open house. With these types of actionable insights, Janet decides to train her staff to regularly analyze the monthly open house data in order to help 24/7 Fitness Center grow its membership base.

EXERCISES 9.2

Note: These exercises can be solved using Analytic Solver and/or R. The answers, however, will depend on the software package used. All answers in R are based on version 3.5.3. For Analytic Solver, partition data sets into 50% training, 30% validation, and 20% test and use 12345 as the default random seed. For R, partition data sets into 60% training and 40% validation and implement the 10-fold cross-validation. Use the statement set.seed(1) to specify the random seed for data partitioning and cross-validation. When searching for the optimal value of *k*, search within possible *k* values from 1 to 10 for both Analytic Solver and R. Some data files have two worksheets (for example, Exercise_9.3_Data and Exercise_9.3_Score worksheets) for model development and scoring new records.

Mechanics

1. **FILE** ***Exercise_9.1***. The accompanying file contains 60 observations with the binary target variable *y* along with the predictor variables x_1 and x_2.
   a. Perform KNN analysis. What is the optimal value of *k?*
   b. Report the accuracy, specificity, sensitivity, and precision rates for the test data set (for Analytic Solver) or validation data set (for R).

2. **FILE** ***Exercise_9.2.*** The accompanying file contains 111 observations with the binary target variable *y* along with the predictor variables x_1, x_2, x_3, and x_4.
   a. Perform KNN analysis on the data set. What is the optimal value of *k*?
   b. Report the accuracy, specificity, sensitivity, and precision rates for the test data set (for Analytic Solver) or validation data set (for R).
   c. Comment on the performance of the KNN classification model.
3. **FILE** ***Exercise_9.3.*** The accompanying file contains 80 observations with the binary target variable *y* along with the predictor variables x_1, x_2, x_3, and x_4.
   a. Perform KNN analysis on the data set. What is the optimal value of *k*?
   b. What is the misclassification rate for the optimal *k*?
   c. Report the accuracy, specificity, sensitivity, and precision rates for the test data set (for Analytic Solver) or validation data set (for R).
   d. What is the area under the ROC curve (or the AUC value)?
   e. Score the new observations in the Exercise_9.3_Score worksheet. What is the predicted response value of the first observation?
4. **FILE** ***Exercise_9.4.*** The accompanying file contains 200 observations with the binary target variable *y* along with the predictor variables x_1, x_2, x_3, x_4, and x_5.
   a. Perform KNN analysis on the data set. What is the optimal value of *k*?
   b. What is the misclassification rate for the optimal *k*?
   c. Report the accuracy, specificity, sensitivity, and precision rates for the test data set (for Analytic Solver) or validation data set (for R).
   d. Change the cutoff value to 0.2. Report the accuracy, specificity, sensitivity, and precision rates for the test data set (for Analytic Solver) or the validation data set (for R).
   e. Comment on the performance of the KNN classification model.
5. **FILE** ***Exercise_9.5.*** The accompanying file contains 1,000 observations with the binary target variable *y* along with the predictor variables x_1, x_2, and x_3.
   a. Perform KNN analysis on the data set. What is the optimal value of *k*?
   b. What is the misclassification rate for the optimal *k*?
   c. Report the accuracy, specificity, sensitivity, and precision rates and the AUC value for the test data set (for Analytic Solver) or validation data set (for R).
   d. Comment on the performance of the KNN classification model.
6. **FILE** ***Exercise_9.6.*** The accompanying file contains 2,000 observations with the binary target variable *y* along with the predictor variables x_1, x_2, and x_3.
   a. Perform KNN analysis on the data set. What is the optimal value of *k*?
   b. Report the accuracy, specificity, sensitivity, and precision rates and the AUC value for the test data set (for Analytic Solver) or validation data set (for R).
   c. Compare the specificity and sensitivity rates and comment on the performance of the KNN classification model.
   d. Display the cumulative lift chart, decile-wise lift chart, and ROC curve.
7. **FILE** ***Exercise_9.7.*** The accompanying file contains 400 observations with the binary response variable *y* along with the predictor variables x_1, x_2, x_3, and x_4.
   a. Perform KNN analysis on the data set. What is the optimal value of *k*?
   b. Report the accuracy, specificity, sensitivity, and precision rates and the AUC value for the test data set (for Analytic Solver) or validation data set (for R).
   c. What is the lift value of the leftmost bar shown in the decile-wise lift chart?
   d. Score the new observations in the Exercise_9.7_Score worksheet. What are the predicted response values of the first two new observations?

Applications

8. **FILE** ***Admit.*** Universities often rely on a high school student's grade point average (GPA) and scores on the SAT or ACT for the college admission decisions. Consider the data for 120 applicants on college admission (Admit equals 1 if admitted, 0 otherwise) along with the student's GPA and SAT scores. A portion of the Admit_Data worksheet is shown in the accompanying table.

Admit	GPA	SAT
1	3.10	1550
0	2.70	1360
⋮	⋮	⋮
1	4.40	1320

   a. Perform KNN analysis to estimate a classification model for college admission decisions in the Admit_Data worksheet and score new applications in the Admit_Score worksheet. What is the optimal value of *k*?
   b. Report and interpret the overall accuracy, specificity, sensitivity, and precision rates for the test data set (for Analytic Solver) or validation data set (for R).
   c. What is the area under the ROC curve (or the AUC value)? Comment on the performance of the KNN classification model.
   d. What is the predicted admission outcome for the first new application?
9. **FILE** ***CFA.*** The Chartered Financial Analyst (CFA) designation is the de facto professional certification for the financial

industry. Employers encourage their prospective employees to complete the CFA exam. Daniella Campos, an HR manager at SolidRock Investment, is reviewing 10 job applications. Given the low pass rate for CFA Level 1, Daniella wants to know whether or not the 10 prospective employees will be able to pass the CFA Level 1 exam. Historically, the pass rate is higher for those with work experience and a good GPA in college. With this insight, she compiles the information on 63 current employees who took the CFA Level I exam last year, including the employee's success on the exam (1 for pass, 0 for fail), the employee's college GPA, and years of work experience. A portion of the CFA_Data worksheet is shown in the accompanying table.

Pass	GPA	Experience
1	3.20	11
1	3.75	15
⋮	⋮	⋮
1	3.21	6

a. Perform KNN analysis to estimate a classification model for the CFA Level 1 exam using the CFA_Data worksheet and score the 10 job applicants in the CFA_Score worksheet. What are the misclassification rates for $k = 3$, 4, and 5?

b. What is the optimal value of k? Report the overall accuracy, specificity, sensitivity, and precision rates for the test data set (for Analytic Solver) or validation data set (for R).

c. What is the predicted CFA Level 1 outcome for the first job applicant?

10. **FILE** ***SocialMedia.*** A social media marketing company is conducting consumer research to see how the income level and age might correspond to whether or not consumers respond positively to a social media campaign. Aliyah Turner, a new college intern, is assigned to collect data from the past marketing campaigns. She compiled data on 284 consumers who participated in the marketing campaigns in the past, including income (in $1,000s), age, and whether or not each individual responded to the campaign (1 if yes, 0 otherwise). A portion of the SocialMedia_Data worksheet is shown in the accompanying table.

Social Media	Income	Age
0	103.3	67
0	61.4	34
⋮	⋮	⋮
1	91.3	40

a. Perform KNN analysis to estimate a classification model for the social media campaign using the SocialMedia_Data worksheet and score new consumer records in the SocialMedia_Score worksheet. What is the optimal value of k?

b. Report and interpret the overall accuracy, specificity, sensitivity, and precision rates for the test data set (for Analytic Solver) or validation data set (for R).

c. What is the area under the ROC curve (or the AUC value)? Comment on the performance of the KNN classification model.

d. What is the predicted outcome for the first new consumer record?

e. Change the cutoff value to 0.3. Report the accuracy, specificity, sensitivity, and precision rates for the test data set (for Analytic Solver) or validation data set (for R).

11. **FILE** ***Spam.*** Peter Derby works as a cyber security analyst at a private equity firm. His colleagues at the firm have been inundated by a large number of spam e-mails. Peter has been asked to implement a spam detection system on the company's e-mail server. He reviewed a sample of 500 spam and legitimate e-mails with relevant variables: spam (1 if spam, 0 otherwise), the number of recipients, the number of hyperlinks, and the number of characters in the message. A portion of the Spam_Data worksheet is shown in the accompanying table.

Spam	Recipients	Hyperlinks	Characters
0	19	1	47
0	15	1	58
⋮	⋮	⋮	⋮
1	13	2	32

a. Perform KNN analysis to estimate a classification model for spam detection using the Spam_Data worksheet and score new e-mails in the Spam_Score worksheet. What is the optimal value of k?

b. Report the overall accuracy, specificity, sensitivity, and precision rates for the test data set (for Analytic Solver) or validation data set (for R).

c. What is the area under the ROC curve (or AUC value)?

d. What is the predicted outcome for the first new e-mail?

12. **FILE** ***Security.*** Law enforcement agencies monitor social media sites on a regular basis, as a way to identify and assess potential crimes and terrorism activities. For example, certain keywords on Facebook pages are tracked, and the data are compiled into a data mining model to determine whether or not the Facebook page is a potential threat. Officer Matthew Osorio is assigned to explore data mining techniques that can be used for this purpose. He starts by experimenting with KNN algorithms to monitor and assess social media sites with war-related terms such as "warfare," "bomb," and "attack" as well as suspicious keywords such as "extremist," "radical," and "conspiracy." He collects a data set with 300 observations, a portion of which is shown in the accompanying table. Each record in the data set includes the following variables: Threat (1 if yes, 0 otherwise), the number of suspicious words (WarTerms and Keywords), and the number of hyperlinks to or mentioning of suspicious sites.

Threat	WarTerms	Keywords	Links
0	6	5	5
0	3	5	8
⋮	⋮	⋮	⋮
1	4	4	2

a. Perform KNN analysis on the data set. What is the optimal value of *k*?
b. What is the misclassification rate for the optimal *k*?
c. Report and interpret the accuracy, specificity, sensitivity, and precision rates for the test data set (for Analytic Solver) or validation data set (for R).
d. Generate the cumulative lift chart. Does the entire lift curve lie above the baseline?
e. Generate the decile-wise lift chart. What is the lift value of the leftmost bar?
f. Generate the ROC curve. What is the area under the ROC curve (or the AUC value)?
g. Comment on the performance of the KNN classification model.

13. **FILE** ***HR.*** Daniel Lara, a human resources manager at a large tech consulting firm, has been reading about using analytics to predict the success of new employees. With the fast-changing nature of the tech industry, some employees have had difficulties staying current in their field and have missed the opportunity to be promoted into a management position. Daniel is particularly interested in whether or not a new employee is likely to be promoted into a management role after 10 years with the company. He gathers information on 300 current employees who have worked for the firm for at least 10 years. The information was based on the job application that the employees provided when they originally applied for a job at the firm. For each employee, the following variables are listed: Promoted (1 if promoted within 10 years, 0 otherwise), GPA (college GPA at graduation), Sports (number of athletic activities during college), and Leadership (number of leadership roles in student organizations). A portion of the HR_Data worksheet is shown in the accompanying table.

Promoted	GPA	Sports	Leadership
0	3.28	0	2
1	3.93	6	3
⋮	⋮	⋮	⋮
0	3.54	5	0

a. Use the HR_Data worksheet to help Daniel perform KNN analysis to determine whether or not an employee is likely to be promoted into a management role after 10 years with the company. Score the records of the 10 new employees in the HR_Score worksheet. What is the optimal *k*? What is the predicted outcome for the first new employee?
b. What is the misclassification rate for the optimal *k*?
c. Report the accuracy, specificity, sensitivity, and precision rates for the test data set (for Analytic Solver) or validation data set (for R).
d. Display the cumulative lift chart, decile-wise chart, and ROC curve.
e. Comment on the performance of the KNN classification model. Is the KNN classification an effective way to predict an employee's success?

14. **FILE** ***Heart.*** In recent years, medical research has incorporated the use of data analytics to find new ways to detect heart disease in its early stage. Medical doctors are particularly interested in accurately identifying high-risk patients so that preventive care and intervention can be administered in a timely manner. A readily available set of information such as the patient's age (Age), blood pressure (BP Systolic and BP Diastolic), and BMI, along with an indicator whether or not the patient has heart disease (Disease = 1 if heart disease, 0 otherwise). A portion of the data set is provided in the accompanying table.

Disease	Age	Systolic	Diastolic	BMI
0	44	112	111	17
1	55	128	90	27
⋮	⋮	⋮	⋮	⋮
0	29	144	85	32

a. Perform KNN analysis on the data set. What is the optimal value of *k*?
b. What is the misclassification rate for the optimal *k*?
c. Report the accuracy, specificity, sensitivity, and precision rates for the test data set (for Analytic Solver) or validation data set (for R).
d. Display the cumulative lift chart, decile-wise chart, and ROC curve.
e. Comment on the performance of the KNN classification model. Is the KNN classification an effective way to predict heart disease?

15. **FILE** ***Retail.*** Online retailers often use a recommendation system to suggest new products to consumers. Consumers are compared to others with similar characteristics such as past purchases, age, income, and education level. A data set, such as the one shown in the accompanying table, is often used as part of a product recommendation system in the retail industry. The variables used in the system include whether or not the consumer eventually purchases the suggested item (Purchase = 1 if purchased, 0 otherwise), the consumer's age (Age in years), income (Income, in $1,000s), and number of similar items previously purchased (PastPurchase).

Purchase	Age	Income	PastPurchase
1	48	99	21
1	47	32	0
⋮	⋮	⋮	⋮
0	34	110	2

a. Perform KNN analysis on the Retail_Data worksheet to determine whether or not a consumer is likely to make a purchase. Score the records of the 10 new consumers in the Retail_Score worksheet. What is the optimal k? What is the predicted outcome for the first new consumer?
b. What is the misclassification rate for the optimal k?
c. Report the accuracy, specificity, sensitivity, and precision rates for the test data set (for Analytic Solver) or validation data set (for R).
d. Generate the decile-wise lift chart. What is the lift value of the leftmost bar?
e. Generate the ROC curve. What is the area under the ROC curve (or the AUC value)?
f. Comment on the performance of the KNN classification model. Is the KNN classification an effective way to develop a recommendation system?

16. **FILE** ***Solar.*** New Age Solar sells and installs solar panels for residential homes. The company's sales representatives contact and pay a personal visit to potential customers to present the benefits of installing solar panels. This high-touch approach works well as the customers feel that they receive personal services that meet their individual needs, but it is more expensive than other, mass-marketing approaches. The company wants to be very strategic about visiting potential customers who are more likely to install solar panels. The company has compiled a data set of past home visits by sales reps. The data include the age and annual income (in $1,000s) of the potential customer and whether or not the customer purchases the solar panels (Install: Y/N). A portion of the Solar_Data worksheet is shown in the accompanying table.

Income	Age	Install
115	45	N
68	31	Y
⋮	⋮	⋮
73	34	N

a. Perform KNN analysis on the Solar_Data worksheet to determine whether or not a potential customer is likely to purchase solar panels. Score the records of the 11 new potential customers in the Solar_Score worksheet. What is the optimal k? What is the predicted outcome for the first new potential customer?
b. What is the misclassification rate for the optimal k?
c. Report the accuracy, specificity, sensitivity, and precision rates for the test data set (for Analytic Solver) or validation data set (for R).
d. Display the cumulative lift chart, decile-wise chart, and ROC curve.
e. Based on your answers in part c and d, is KNN an effective way to classify potential customers?

17. **FILE** ***Machine.*** Being able to predict machine failures before they happen can save millions of dollars for manufacturing companies. Manufacturers want to be able to perform preventive maintenance or repairs in advance to minimize machine downtime and often install electronic sensors to monitor the machines and their surrounding environment. However, the more sophisticated the machine, the more difficult it is to diagnose and predict the failure rate. Data mining has been used to analyze environmental factors to predict whether or not complex machines such as nanotechnology equipment will fail from one production period to another. The accompanying data set contains 480 observations and three environmental variables: level of humidity in the room where the equipment is located (Humid, in percentage); overall temperature in the room (Temp, in Fahrenheit); and a target variable that indicates whether or not the equipment broke down during the next production period (Breakdown = 1 if breakdown, 0 otherwise).

Humid	Temp	Breakdown
9.36	79.99	0
10.37	61.89	0
⋮	⋮	⋮
15.02	38.02	1

a. Perform KNN analysis on the data set. What is the optimal value of k?
b. What is the misclassification rate for the optimal k?
c. Report the accuracy, specificity, sensitivity, and precision rates for the test data set (for Analytic Solver) or validation data set (for R).
d. What is the area under the ROC curve (or the AUC value)?
e. Based on your answers in part c and d, is KNN an effective way to classify potential customers?
f. Change the cutoff value to 0.3. Report the accuracy, specificity, sensitivity, and precision rates for the test data set (for Analytic Solver) or validation data set (for R).

LO 9.3

9.3 THE NAÏVE BAYES METHOD

Apply the naïve Bayes method for classification.

The naïve Bayes method represents a family of classification models that allows us to predict the probability that a record belongs to a particular class. It is based on Bayes' theorem discussed in Chapter 4. Recall that Bayes' theorem uses new information to update a *prior* probability to form a *posterior* probability.

Suppose the target variable is defined by two classes: a potential customer will make a purchase and a potential customer will not make a purchase. Here, we can estimate the prior probability using the proportion of customers who made a purchase. If we use a customer's sex as a predictor variable, the posterior probability is estimated conditional on the sex of the potential customer, male or female. Similarly, other predictor variables, which must be categorical or transformed into categories, are used to estimate posterior probabilities. It is important to note that estimating posterior probabilities can be cumbersome when the number of predictor variables is large.

For computational simplicity, the naïve Bayes classifier assumes that the predictor variables are independent. This independence assumption is often not realistic, hence the label "naïve." While the assumption of variable independence does not capture the possible interaction between predictor variables, this simple method can perform well in many real-world situations, compared to a more sophisticated classification method, especially in situations where ranking cases in terms of their probabilities of belonging to the target class is the primary objective. The underlying concept of naïve Bayes is quite simple to understand, easy to implement, and especially attractive when applied to applications with large data sets such as target marketing, medical diagnosis, spam detection, textual document classification, and face recognition.

THE NAÏVE BAYES METHOD

The naïve Bayes method represents a family of classification models based on Bayes' theorem. Even though it makes a strong independence assumption between categorical predictor variables, it tends to perform well in many real-world applications.

In Chapter 4, we used Bayes' theorem, defined as $P(B|A) = \frac{P(B)P(A|B)}{P(A)}$, to update the prior probability $P(B)$ to the posterior probability $P(B|A)$. Consider a simple classification model where the target variable y and the predictor variable x are both binary. Here, we use Bayes' theorem to get $P(y|x) = \frac{P(y)P(x|y)}{P(x)}$. Continuing with the customer purchase example, let y equal 1 if a potential customer makes a purchase, 0 otherwise, and let x equal 1 if male, 0 otherwise. Table 9.6 shows the number of observations in each class of the training data set.

TABLE 9.6 Counts in the Training Data Set

	Male ($x = 1$)	Female ($x = 0$)
Purchase ($y = 1$)	30	50
No Purchase ($y = 0$)	20	100

We use the relevant proportions to compute the conditional probability of making (not making) a purchase given that the potential customer is a male (female), as:

$$P(y = 1|x = 1) = 30/50 = 0.60; P(y = 0|x = 1) = 20/50 = 0.40$$

If the potential customer is female, we derive the conditional probability as:

$$P(y = 1|x = 0) = 50/150 = 0.333; P(y = 0|x = 0) = 100/150 = 0.667$$

In this simple example, we assign a male customer to the "purchase" class because $0.60 > 0.40$ and a female customer to the "no purchase" class because $0.333 < 0.667$. Two things are noteworthy in this example. First, it uses a categorical predictor variable, a customer's sex, with multiple records for both male and female customers. If we had used a numerical variable like income as a predictor variable, it would have been highly unlikely to find multiple records at all levels of income. In practice, it is common to use numerical predictor variables but first transform them into categories. Second, it is highly unlikely to find a classification model that employs only one predictor variable. Often, several predictor variables are used for classification. We will now address both of these issues.

Continuing with the customer purchase example, let y represent whether or not a potential customer makes a purchase. Let $x_1, x_2, \ldots, x_k$ represent the k predictor variables, which now may include a customer's sex, income, age, and college education. The extended Bayes' theorem describes the probability of y given values of x_1 through x_k as:

$$P(y|x_1, x_2, \ldots, x_k) = \frac{P(y)P(x_1, x_2, \ldots, x_k|y)}{P(x_1, x_2, \ldots, x_k)}$$

Assuming that x_1 through x_k are independent of each other, the probability of y given values of x_1 through x_k can be simplified as:

$$P(y|x_1, x_2, \ldots, x_k) = \frac{P(y)(P(x_1|y)P(x_2|y)\ldots P(x_k|y))}{P(x_1, x_2, \ldots, x_k)}$$

This simplification significantly improves the efficiency of the naïve Bayes classifiers over other classification methods, especially when performed on a large data set and/or with a large number of predictor variables. If a retailer wants to classify potential customers as $y = 1$ for purchase, 0 otherwise, we would compute and compare the following two probability values:

$$P(y = 1|x_1, x_2, \ldots, x_k) = \frac{P(y = 1)(P(x_1|y = 1)P(x_2|y = 1)\ldots P(x_k|y = 1))}{P(x_1, x_2, \ldots, x_k)}$$

$$P(y = 0|x_1, x_2, \ldots, x_k) = \frac{P(y = 0)(P(x_1|y = 0)P(x_2|y = 0)\ldots P(x_k|y = 0))}{P(x_1, x_2, \ldots, x_k)}$$

If $P(y = 1|x_1, x_2, \ldots, x_k)$ is higher, then we conclude that the potential customer will make a purchase; i.e., $\hat{y} = 1$. Similarly, if $P(y = 0|x_1, x_2, \ldots, x_k)$ is higher, then we conclude that the potential customer will not make a purchase; i.e., $\hat{y} = 0$. In case of ties, various methods such as a random tiebreaker or a selection that favors the most frequent outcome, or an alphabetical order might be used.

As mentioned earlier, a naïve Bayes classifier is performed on a data set where all predictor variables are categorical. To capture the influence of continuous variables, they must first be converted into discrete categories, a process called "binning," which was detailed in Chapter 2. For example, incomes could easily be converted into discrete values or bins as 1 = [0, $50,000), 2 = [$50,000, $100,000), and 3 = [$100,000, $500,000), and so on. There is also a special family of naïve Bayes classifiers called the Gaussian naïve Bayes where continuous variables are assumed to follow a normal distribution, and the density functions are used to estimate conditional probabilities for the naïve Bayes classifier; this technique, however, is beyond the scope of this text.

Another potential issue with the naïve Bayes classifier is a situation that includes a rare outcome such as classifying patients with a rare disease. The problem occurs when this rare outcome is not present in the training data set. According to the formulas shown earlier, the probability of this rare outcome would be estimated as 0, and none of the new records would be classified or assigned to this category. To overcome this problem, most naïve Bayes algorithms allow a replacement of zero probability values with a nonzero value (usually with a value of 1). This technique is called smoothing or Laplace smoothing.

Because the naïve Bayes method is a supervised data mining technique, data partitioning is used to assess model performance. Unlike the KNN method, the naïve Bayes method does not use the validation data set to optimize model complexity (e.g., finding the optimal value for k); therefore, it is customary to partition the data into training and validation sets only. The training data are used to compute the conditional probabilities, whereas the validation data are used to assess the performance of the naïve Bayes model on a previously unseen data set.

The naïve Bayes classifier essentially uses relevant proportions to estimate conditional probabilities for each class of the target variable and for all combinations of the predictor variable values in the training data set. Although simple in principle, this approach can get quite cumbersome when performed with a large number of predictor variables. Fortunately, several software packages routinely implement the naïve Bayes procedure. In Example 9.2, we will illustrate this procedure with Analytics Solver and R.

EXAMPLE 9.2

FILE *Census*

An institute for public policy in Washington, D.C., hires a number of college interns every summer. This year, Sara Anderson, a third-year Economics major from Massachusetts, is selected as one of the research interns. Her first assignment is to conduct data analysis to help congressional offices gain a better understanding of U.S. residents whose incomes are below the poverty level. To complete her assignment, Sara extracts a relevant data set maintained by the U.S. Census Bureau. The data set has 9,980 observations and is stored in the Census_Data worksheet of the ***Census*** data file. Each observation contains an individual's marital status (Married; yes/no), sex (Female; yes/no), ethnicity (White; yes/no), age groups (Age: 1 for [18, 25), 2 for [25, 35), 3 for [35, 45), 4 for [45, 55), and 5 for 55 years and older), whether or not the individual receives college-level education (Edu; yes/no), and whether or not the individual's income is below the poverty level (Poverty = 1 if living in poverty, 0 otherwise). In addition, she keeps records of 66 new individuals with the predictor variables in the Census_Score worksheet of the ***Census*** data file for scoring based on the naïve Bayes classifier. A portion of the two worksheets is shown in Table 9.7.

TABLE 9.7 A Portion of Census Data

a. *Census_Data* Worksheet

Married	Female	White	Age	Edu	Poverty
Y	N	Y	1	N	0
Y	N	Y	1	N	0
⋮	⋮	⋮	⋮	⋮	⋮
N	Y	N	5	N	1

b. *Census_Score* Worksheet

Married	Female	White	Age	Edu
N	Y	Y	5	N
N	Y	Y	5	N
⋮	⋮	⋮	⋮	⋮
Y	N	Y	5	Y

Help Sara develop a naïve Bayes classification model to classify whether or not an individual is likely to live in poverty using all five predictor variables. Report the relevant performance measures and score new observations.

SOLUTION:

Using Analytic Solver

a. Open the ***Census*** data file and go to the Census_Data worksheet.

b. Choose **Data Mining** > **Partition** > **Standard Partition**.

c. For *Data Range*, highlight cells $A$1:$F$9981 and check the box *First Row Contains Headers*. The *Variables in Input Data* box will populate. Choose *Automatic percentages* with 60% for Training Set and 40% for Validation Set. Accept other defaults and click **OK**.

d. Analytic Solver will create a new worksheet called STDPartition with the partitioned data. Make sure that the STDPartition worksheet is active. Choose **Data Mining > Classify > Naive Bayes**.

e. In the **Data** tab, select and move Married, Female, White, Age, and Edu to *Selected Variables* box. Select Poverty as the *Output Variable*. Accept the other defaults and click *Next*. Note: If a cutoff value other than the default 0.5 is used, input the desired cutoff value (e.g. 0.75) in the *Success Probability Cutoff*: box in this step.

f. In the **Parameters** tab, note that Analytic Solver provides an option for Laplace smoothing. In this case, there are no missing values for any outcome categories in the training data set, and therefore, there is no need for smoothing. Uncheck the box next to *Laplace Smoothing*. Click on the **Scoring** tab.

g. Check the *Summary Report* boxes for *Score Training Data* and *Score Validation Data*. Also check the *Lift Charts* box for *Score Validation Data*. Check the *In Worksheet* box under the *Score New Data* section. A new tab called **New Data (WS)** will open. In the *Worksheet* dropdown box, select Census_Score, select the data range $A$1:SES67, click *Match By Name*, and *Finish*.

Analytic Solver will create six new worksheets. The NB_Output worksheet summarizes the naïve Bayes input parameters that we specified earlier. The NB_TrainingScore and NB_ValidationScore worksheets display the confusion matrix and model performance metrics for the training and validation data sets, respectively. The confusion matrix and accuracy statistics for the validation data set are shown in Figure 9.16.

FIGURE 9.16 Analytic Solver's classification summary tables for naïve Bayes

Confusion Matrix

Actual\Predicted	0	1
0	452	428
1	377	2735

Error Report

Class	# Cases	# Errors	% Error
0	880	428	48.63636
1	3112	377	12.1144
Overall	3992	805	20.16533

Metrics

Metric	Value
Accuracy (#correct)	3187
Accuracy (%correct)	79.83467
Specificity	0.513636
Sensitivity (Recall)	0.878856
Precision	0.864685
F1 score	0.871713
Success Class	1
Success Probability	0.5

Source: Microsoft Excel

While the overall accuracy is 79.83%, there is a considerable difference between specificity (51.36%) and sensitivity (87.89%). This indicates that, by using a default cutoff value of 0.5, the model is more accurate in classifying people in poverty (Class 1) than classifying people who are not in poverty (Class 0).

The performance of the naïve Bayes classifier can also be evaluated graphically using the cumulative lift chart, the decile-wise chart, and the ROC curve for the test data, as shown in Figure 9.17. The lift chart and the decile-wise lift chart show that the naïve Bayes classifier performs better than the baseline model. The ROC curve also shows that the naïve Bayes classifier performs better than the baseline model in terms of sensitivity and specificity across all cutoff values. The area under curve (AUC) is 0.8465, which is closer to the optimum classifier (AUC = 1) than to the random classifier (AUC = 0.5).

FIGURE 9.17 Analytic Solver's performance charts for naïve Bayes

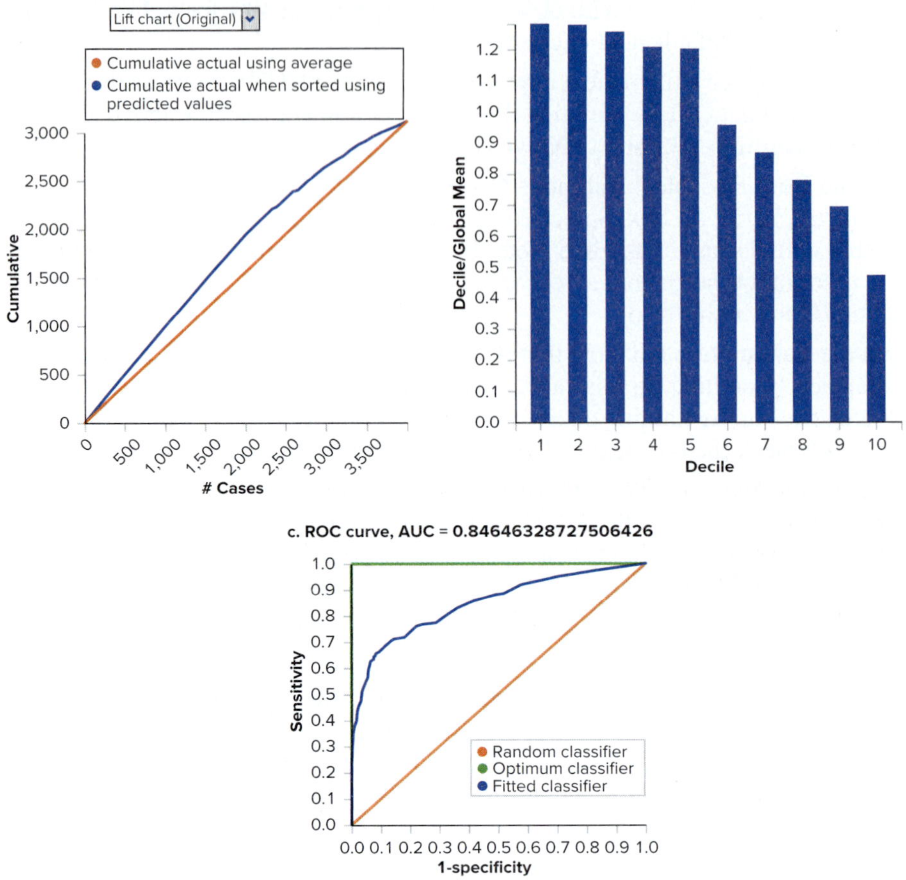

The NB_NewScore worksheet shows the classification predictions for the new records from the Census_Score worksheet. For each observation, the naïve Bayes classifier displays the predicted value (poverty = 1 or 0, and the probabilities for both outcomes). Table 9.8 shows a portion of the classification outcomes and the original predictor variables. The naïve Bayes model classified individuals who are married male with a college education as unlikely to live in poverty.

TABLE 9.8 Naïve Bayes Scoring Results

Record ID	Prediction: Poverty	PostProb: 0	PostProb: 1	Married	Female	White	Age	Edu
Record 1	1	0.0169	0.9831	N	Y	Y	5	N
Record 2	1	0.0169	0.9831	N	Y	Y	5	N
⋮	⋮	⋮	⋮	⋮	⋮	⋮	⋮	⋮
Record 66	0	0.6902	0.3098	Y	N	Y	5	Y

Using R

As before, we will use the *caret* package for classification with k-fold cross-validation. So, we will divide the data into two partitions for training and validation. (Again, we note that the following instructions are based on **R version 3.5.3**. They may not work for different versions of R.)

a. Import the data from the Census_Data worksheet of the ***Census*** data file into a data frame (table) and label it myData.

b. The *caret* and *klaR* packages contain necessary functions for partitioning the data, k-fold cross-validation, and naïve Bayes classification. Also, similar to the KNN example, a cumulative lift chart, decile-wise chart, and ROC curve can be generated for visual inspection of the model performance using the *gains* and *pROC* packages. Install and load all packages, if you have not already done so. Enter:

```
> install.packages("caret")
> install.packages("klaR")
> install.packages("gains")
> install.packages("pROC")
> library(caret)
> library(klaR)
> library(gains)
> library(pROC)
```

c. We use the **as.factor** command to convert the poverty variable into a categorical type. Enter:

```
> myData$Poverty <- as.factor(myData$Poverty)
```

d. As in the KNN example, we use the **set.seed** command to set the random seed to one for consistency. We use the **createDataPartition** function to partition the data into training (60%) and validation (40%). Enter:

```
> set.seed(1)
> myIndex <- createDataPartition(myData$Poverty, p=0.6, list = FALSE)
> trainSet <- myData[myIndex,]
> validationSet <- myData[-myIndex,]
```

e. We use the **trainControl** function to specify a 10-fold cross-validation process. On the training data set, we use the **train** function and set the *method* option equal to "nb", which stands for naïve Bayes. The Poverty variable is identified as the target variable. To ensure consistency of the cross-validation results, we again use the **set.seed** function to fix a random seed. Enter:

```
> myCtrl <- trainControl(method='cv', number=10)
> set.seed(1)
> nb_fit <- train(Poverty ~., data = trainSet, method = "nb",
trControl=myCtrl)
> nb_fit
```

Figure 9.18 displays the naïve Bayes results. The naïve Bayes classifier generates two accuracy rates based on the underlying distribution of the target variables and uses the option that yields a higher accuracy (77.29% in this case) in the final model.

FIGURE 9.18 Naïve Bayes results

```
Naive Bayes

5989 samples
   5 predictor
   2 classes: '0', '1'

No pre-processing
Resampling: Cross-Validated (10 fold)
Summary of sample sizes: 5390, 5390, 5390, 5390, 5390, 5391, ...
Resampling results across tuning parameters:

   usekernel  Accuracy   Kappa
   FALSE      0.7580586  0.3954072
    TRUE      0.7729170  0.4171048
```

f. We use the **predict** and **confusionMatrix** functions to validate the model on the validation data set and produce a confusion matrix. Enter:

```
> nb_class <- predict(nb_fit, newdata = validationSet)
> confusionMatrix(nb_class, validationSet$Poverty, positive = '1')
```

Note that in the **confusionMatrix** statement, we specify the value '1' in the poverty variable as a positive or success class. The accuracy value (75.65%) remains consistent with results from the training data set. Unlike in Analytic Solver, the naïve Bayes model in R yields sensitivity and specificity values that are close to each other (76.73% and 71.80%, respectively). Again, the algorithms in the two software are not the same and yield different results. A portion of the R results is shown in Figure 9.19.

FIGURE 9.19 Confusion matrix

```
Confusion Matrix and Statistics

          Reference
Prediction    0    1
         0  629  725
         1  247 2390

               Accuracy : 0.7565
                        :
            Sensitivity : 0.7673
            Specificity : 0.7180
         Pos Pred Value : 0.9063
```

We can also use other cutoff values, instead of the default value of 0.5, to create the confusion matrix. For example, use the following commands to specify a cutoff value of 0.75:

```
>nb_class_prob <- predict(nb_fit, newdata=validationSet, type=
'prob')
>confusionMatrix(as.factor(ifelse(nb_class_prob[,2]>0.75, '1',
'0')), validationSet$Poverty, positive = '1')
```

g. To create the two lift charts and ROC curve, we first need to compute a cumulative gains table by using the **predict** and **gains** functions. Note that the poverty variable was converted into a categorical type in a previous step. The **gains** function requires the variable to be converted back to a numerical type. Enter:

```
> nb_class_prob <- predict(nb_fit, newdata=validationSet,
type='prob')
> validationSet$Poverty <- as.numeric(validationSet$Poverty)
> gains_table <- gains(validationSet$Poverty, nb_class_prob[,2])
> gains_table
```

Figure 9.20 shows the gains table.

FIGURE 9.20 Gains table

Depth of File	N	Cume N	Mean Resp	Cume Mean Resp	Cume Pct of Total Resp	Lift Index	Cume Lift	Mean Model Score
12	490	490	2.00	2.00	13.8%	112	112	1.00
20	311	801	2.00	2.00	22.5%	112	112	0.99
:	:	:	:	:	:	:	:	:
100	216	3991	1.35	1.78	100.0%	76	100	0.24

h. We use the **plot** and **line** functions to create the cumulative lift chart as shown in Figure 9.21. Enter:

```
> plot(c(0, gains_table$cume.pct.of.total*sum(validationSet$
Poverty)) ~ c(0, gains_table$cume.obs),xlab = "# of cases",
ylab="Cumulative", type ="l")
> lines(c(0, sum(validationSet$Poverty)) ~ c(0, dim(validationSet)
[1]), col="red", lty=2)
```

FIGURE 9.21 The cumulative lift chart

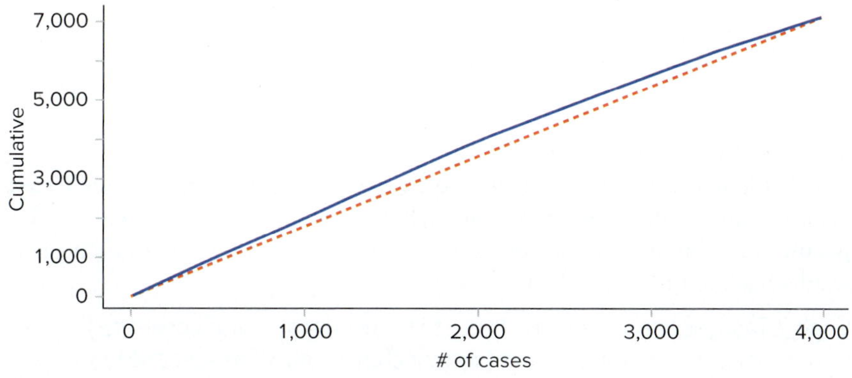

i. We use the **barplot** function to create a decile-wise chart as shown in Figure 9.22. Enter:

```
> barplot(gains_table$mean.resp/mean(validationSet$Poverty), names.
arg=gains_table$depth, xlab="Percentile", ylab="Lift", ylim =
c(0,1.5), main = "Decile-Wise Lift Chart")
```

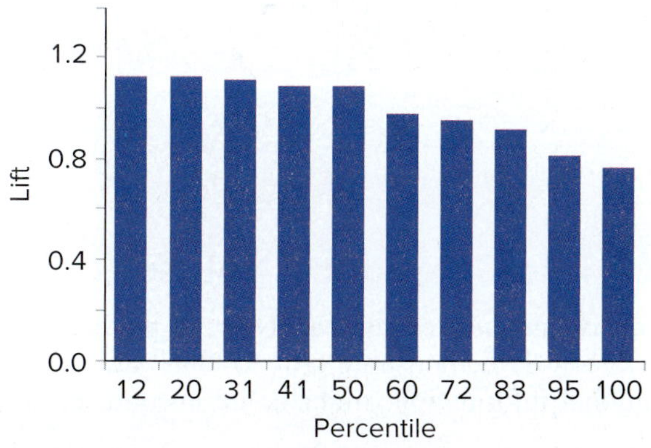

FIGURE 9.22
The decile-wise lift chart

j. We use the **roc**, **plot.roc**, and **auc** functions to create the ROC curve and compute the area under the curve. Enter:

```
> roc_object<- roc(validationSet$Poverty, nb_class_prob[,2])
> plot.roc(roc_object)
> auc(roc_object)
```

The area under the ROC curve, or AUC, is 0.8437, indicating that the naïve Bayes model performs well in predicting whether an individual is in poverty or not. Figure 9.23 displays the ROC curve, which shows that model performs better than the baseline model (shown as the green diagonal line) in terms of sensitivity and specificity across all cutoff values.

FIGURE 9.23 The ROC curve

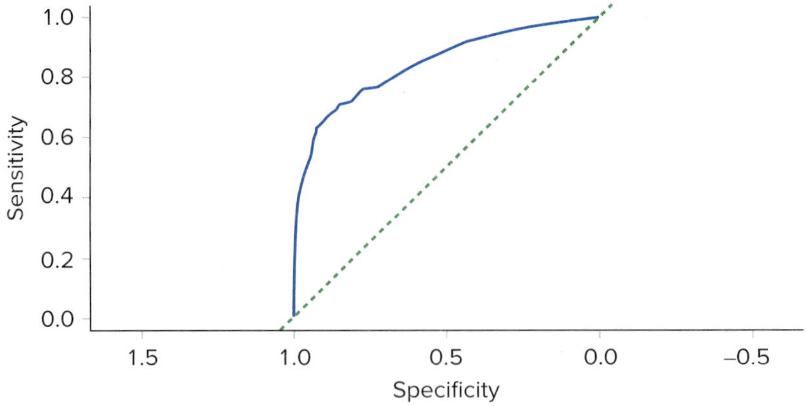

k. Import the new observations from the Census_Score worksheet of the ***Census*** data file into a data frame (table) and label it myScoreData. We then use the **predict** function to score the 66 new records and append the classification results back to the original data. Enter:

```
> nb_class_score <- predict(nb_fit, newdata = myScoreData)
> myScoreData <- data.frame(myScoreData, nb_class_score)
```

Table 9.9 shows R's scoring results. Similar to the Analytic Solver model, the KNN model in R tends to classify new records who are married male with a college education as unlikely to live in poverty.

TABLE 9.9 R's Scoring Results for Naïve Baye

Record	Married	Female	White	Age	Edu	nb_ class_ score
1	N	Y	Y	5	N	1
2	N	Y	Y	5	N	1
⋮	⋮	⋮	⋮	⋮	⋮	⋮
66	Y	N	Y	5	Y	0

Transforming Numerical into Categorical Values

As mentioned earlier, in order to perform a naïve Bayes analysis, all predictor variables must be categorical. Here, we will briefly demonstrate how to "bin" numerical values into discrete categories; for additional information, students are encouraged to review related sections in Chapter 2.

In the introductory case, Janet Williams, the membership manager at a 24/7 Fitness Center, is holding an open house event and collecting information from potential members. She wants to explore naïve Bayes for determining whether or not potential members are likely to purchase a gym membership. However, because the predictor variables, Age, Income, and Hours, are numerical, she has to first convert them into discrete categories.

FILE
Gym

Using the data from the Gym_Data worksheet, we will outline the procedure for binning the Age variable; other variables can be binned similarly. Note that the values of the Age variable range from 21 to 68. Suppose we want to bin Age into five categories.

In Analytic Solver, go to **Data Mining > Data Analysis > Transform > Transform Continuous Data > Bin**. Click on the ellipsis next to *Data range* and highlight cells $A$1:$D$1001. Select Age to convert it into a binned variable called Binned_Age and select 5 for *#bins for variable*. Select *Equal interval*. Click on *Apply to Selected Variable* and click *Finish*. The Bin_Transform worksheet will show the binned Age variable ranging from one to five. The new variable can be copied and pasted back to the original

Gym_Data worksheet and used in the naïve Bayes method and other analysis techniques that require categorical variables.

In R, we first import the data from the Gym_Data worksheet into R and call the resulting data frame Binning. The following statement forces the first bin to start at 20 years and cap the last bin at 70 years with each interval value set at 10 years.

```
> age_bins <- cut(Binning$Age, breaks = seq(20, 70, by = 10))
```

The age_bins variable can now be appended back to the original data frame and used in the analysis that requires categorical variables.

Generally, we adjust the binning options according to the data or conceptual design. For example, if we want to compare low- versus high-income individuals, then we might want to bin the Income variable into two categories. Additional discussions on this topic can be found in Chapter 2.

EXERCISES 9.3

Note: These exercises can be solved using Analytic Solver and/or R. The answers, however, will depend on the software package used. All answers in R are based on version 3.5.3. For Analytic Solver, partition the data into 60% training and 40% validation and use 12345 as the default random seed. For R, partition the data into 60% training and 40% validation and implement the 10-fold cross-validation. Use the statement set.seed(1) to specify the random seed one for data partitioning and cross-validation. Some data files have two worksheets (e.g., Exercise_9.18_Data and Exercise_9.18_Score worksheets) for model development and scoring new records.

Mechanics

18. **FILE** ***Exercise_9.18.*** The accompanying data set contains three predictor variables (x_1, x_2, and x_3) and the target variable (y). Partition the data in the Exercise_9.18_Data worksheet to develop a naïve Bayes classification model where "Yes" denotes the positive or success class for y. Score the 10 new observations on the Exercise_9.18_Score worksheet.
    a. Report the accuracy, sensitivity, and specificity rates for the validation data set.
    b. Generate the decile-wise lift chart. What is the lift value of the leftmost bar? What does this value imply?
    c. Generate the ROC curve. What is the area under the ROC curve (or the AUC value)?
    d. Report the scoring results for the first three new observations.

19. **FILE** ***Exercise_9.19.*** The accompanying data set contains three predictor variables (x_1, x_2, and x_3) and the target variable (y). Partition the data in the Exercise_9.19_Data worksheet to develop a naïve Bayes classification model where "Y" denotes the positive or success class for y. Score the five new observations on the Exercise_9.19_Score worksheet.
    a. Report the accuracy, sensitivity, and specificity rates for the validation data set.
    b. What is the area under the ROC curve (or AUC value)?
    c. Report the scoring results for the five new observations.

20. **FILE** ***Exercise_9.20.*** The accompanying data set contains four predictor variables (x_1, x_2, x_3, and x_4) and the target variable (y). Partition the data in the Exercise_9.20_Data worksheet to develop a naïve Bayes classification model where "1" denotes the positive or success class for y. Score the five new observations on the Exercise_9.20_Score worksheet.
    a. Report the accuracy, sensitivity, and specificity rates for the validation data set.
    b. Generate the cumulative lift chart. Does the entire lift curve lie above the baseline?
    c. Generate the ROC curve. What is the area under the ROC curve (or the AUC value)?
    d. Report the scoring results for the five new observations.
    e. Develop the naïve Bayes model with only x_1, x_2, and y in the naïve Bayes model. Repeat parts a through c and compare the results.

21. **FILE** ***Exercise_9.21.*** The accompanying data set contains three predictor variables (x_1, x_2, and x_3) and the target variable (y). Partition the data to develop a naïve Bayes classification model where "1" denotes the positive or success class for y.
    a. Report the accuracy, sensitivity, and specificity rates for the validation data set.
    b. Generate the decile-wise lift chart. What is the lift value of the leftmost bar? What does this value imply?
    c. Generate the ROC curve. What is the area under the ROC curve (or the AUC value)?
    d. Can the naïve Bayes model be used to effectively classify the data? Explain your answer.

22. **FILE** ***Exercise_9.22.*** The accompanying data set contains three predictor variables (x_1, x_2, and x_3) and the target variable (y). Partition the data to develop a naïve Bayes classification model where "1" denotes the positive or success class for y.
    a. Report the accuracy, sensitivity, specificity, and precision rates for the validation data set.
    b. Generate the cumulative lift chart. Does the entire lift curve lie above the baseline?

c. Generate the ROC curve. What is the area under the ROC curve (or the AUC value)?

d. Can the naïve Bayes model be used to effectively classify the data? Explain your answer.

23. **FILE** ***Exercise_9.23.*** The accompanying data set contains two predictor variables (x_1 and x_2) and the target variable (y). Partition the data to develop a naïve Bayes classification model where "1" denotes the positive or success class for y.

a. Report the accuracy, sensitivity, specificity, and precision rates for the validation data set.

b. Generate the decile-wise lift chart. What is the lift value of the leftmost bar?

c. Generate the ROC curve. What is the area under the ROC curve (or the AUC value)?

d. Can the naïve Bayes model be used to effectively classify the data? Explain.

24. **FILE** ***Exercise_9.24.*** The accompanying data set contains three predictor variables (x_1, x_2, and x_3) and the target variable (y).

a. Bin predictor variables x_1, x_2, and x_3. For Analytic Solver, choose the *Equal count* option and three bins for each of the three variables. For R, bin x_1 into [0, 6), [6, 14), and [14, 30); x_2 into [0, 10), [10, 20), and [20, 61); and x_3 into [0, 3), [3, 5), and [5, 10). What are the bin numbers for the variables of the first two observations?

b. Partition the transformed data to develop a naïve Bayes classification model where "1" denotes the positive or success class for y. Report the accuracy, sensitivity, specificity, and precision rates for the validation data set.

c. Generate the ROC curve. What is the area under the ROC curve (or the AUC value)?

d. Change the cutoff value to 0.2. Report the accuracy, sensitivity, specificity, and precision rates for the validation data set.

25. **FILE** ***Exercise_9.25.*** The accompanying data set contains three predictor variables (x_1, x_2, and x_3) and the target variable (y).

a. Bin predictor variables x_1 and x_2. For Analytic Solver, choose the *Equal count* option and three bins for each of the three variables. For R, bin x_1 into [0, 60), [60, 400), and [400, 30000); and x_2 into [0, 160), [160, 400), and [400, 800). What are the bin numbers for the variables of the first two observations?

b. Partition the transformed data to develop a naïve Bayes classification model where "1" denotes the positive or success class for y. Report the accuracy, sensitivity, specificity, and precision rates for the validation data set.

c. Generate the ROC curve. What is the area under the ROC curve (or the AUC value)?

26. **FILE** ***Exercise_9.26.*** The accompanying data set contains three predictor variables (x_1, x_2, and x_3) and the target variable (y).

a. Bin predictor variables x_1, x_2, and x_3. For Analytic Solver, choose the *Equal interval* option and 2 bins for each of the three variables. For R, bin x_1 into [0, 125) and [125, 250); x_2 into [0, 30) and [30, 60); and x_3 into [0, 30) and [30, 60). What are the bin numbers for the variables of the first two observations?

b. Partition the transformed data to develop a naïve Bayes classification model where "1" denotes the positive or success class for y. Report the accuracy, sensitivity, specificity, and precision rates for the validation data set.

c. Generate the ROC curve. What is the area under the ROC curve (or the AUC value)?

d. Change the cutoff value to 0.4. Report the accuracy, sensitivity, specificity, and precision rates for the validation data set.

27. **FILE** ***Exercise_9.27.*** The accompanying data set contains four predictor variables (x_1, x_2, x_3, and x_4) and the target variable (y).

a. Bin predictor variables x_1, x_2, x_3, and x_4. For Analytic Solver, choose the *Equal interval* option and 2 bins for each of the four variables. For R, bin x_1 into [0, 40000) and [40000, 80000); x_2 into [0, 50) and [50, 100); x_3 into [50, 75) and [75, 100); and x_4 into [0, 20000) and [20000, 40000). What are the bin numbers for the variables of the first two observations?

b. Partition the transformed data to develop a naïve Bayes classification model where "1" denotes the positive or success class for y. Report the accuracy, sensitivity, specificity, and precision rates for the validation data set.

c. Generate the ROC curve. What is the area under the ROC curve (or the AUC value)?

d. Can the naïve Bayes model be used to effectively classify the data? Explain your answer.

Applications

28. **FILE** ***International.*** Every year, hundreds of thousands of international students apply to graduate programs in the United States. Two of the most important admissions criteria are undergraduate GPAs and TOEFL scores. An English language preparation school in Santiago, Chile, wants to examine the acceptance records of its former students who had applied to graduate school in the United States during the past two years. The results will be used to help advise new students about their chance of acceptance to their first choice of graduate programs. A portion of the data set is shown in the accompanying table with the following variables: Accept (1 if accepted, 0 otherwise); GPA (1 for below 3.00, 2 for 3.00–3.49, 3 for 3.50 and above); and TOEFL (H for 80 or above, L for below 80).

Accept	GPA	TOEFL
1	1	H
0	1	H
⋮	⋮	⋮
0	1	L

a. Partition the data to develop a naïve Bayes classification model. Report the accuracy, sensitivity, specificity, and precision rates for the validation data set.
b. Generate the ROC curve. What is the area under the ROC curve (or AUC value)?
c. Can the naïve Bayes model be used to effectively classify the data? Explain your answer.

29. **FILE** ***OnlineRetail.*** An online retailer is offering a new line of running shoes. The retailer plans to send out an e-mail with a discount offer to some of its existing customers and wants to know if it can use data mining analysis to predict whether or not a customer might respond to its e-mail offer. The retailer prepares a data set of 170 existing customers who had received online promotions in the past, which include the following variables: Purchase (1 if purchase, 0 otherwise); Age (1 for 20 years and younger, 2 for 21 to 30 years, 3 for 31 to 40 years, 4 for 41 to 50 years, and 5 for 51 and older); Income (1 for $0 to $50K, 2 for $51K to $80K, 3 for $81K to $100K, 4 for $100K+); and PastPurchase (1 for no past purchase, 2 for 1 or 2 past purchases, 3 for 3 to 6 past purchases, 4 for 7 or more past purchases). A portion of the data set is shown in the accompanying table.

Purchase	Age	Income	PastPurchase
1	4	3	4
1	4	1	1
⋮	⋮	⋮	⋮
1	3	4	3

a. Partition the data to develop a naïve Bayes classification model. Report the accuracy, sensitivity, specificity, and precision rates for the validation data set.
b. Generate the decile-wise lift chart. What is the lift value of the leftmost bar? What does this value imply?
c. Generate the ROC curve. What is the area under the ROC curve (or AUC value)?
d. Can the naïve Bayes model be used to effectively classify the data? Explain your answer.

30. **FILE** ***MedSchool.*** Admission to medical schools in the United States is highly competitive. The acceptance rate to the top medical schools could be as low as 2% or 3%. With such a low acceptance rate, medical school admissions consulting has become a growing business in many cities. In order to better serve his clients, Paul Foster, a medical school admissions consultant, wants to build a data-driven model to predict whether or not a new applicant is likely to get accepted into one of the top 10 medical schools. He collected a database of 1,992 past applicants to the top 10 medical schools with the following information: Sex (F = female, M = male), CollegeParent (1 if parents with college degrees, 0 otherwise), GPA (1 if undergraduate GPA of 3.50 or higher, 0 otherwise), Med (1 if accepted to the top 10 medical school, 0 otherwise). A portion of the data set is shown in the accompanying table.

Sex	CollegeParent	GPA	Med
F	1	1	1
M	1	0	1
⋮	⋮	⋮	⋮
M	0	0	0

a. Partition the data to develop a naïve Bayes classification model. Report the accuracy, sensitivity, specificity, and precision rates for the validation data set.
b. Generate the decile-wise lift chart. What is the lift value of the leftmost bar? What does this value imply?
c. Generate the ROC curve. What is the area under the ROC curve (or AUC value)?
d. Can the naïve Bayes model be used to effectively classify the medical school applicant data? Explain your answer.

31. **FILE** ***CreditCard.*** A home improvement retail store is offering its customers store-branded credit cards that come with a deep discount when used to purchase in-store home improvement products. To maintain the profitability of this marketing campaign, the store manager would like to make these offers only to the customers who are likely to carry a high monthly balance on the credit card. A data set obtained from a nationwide association of home improvement stores contains records of 500 consumers who carry similar credit cards offered by other home improvement stores. Relevant variables include Sex (Female or Male), Education (1 if did not finish college, 2 if undergraduate degree, 3 if graduate degree), Children (1 if have children, 0 otherwise), Age (1 if below 20 years old, 2 if 20–29 years, 3 if 30–39 years, 4 if 40–49 years, 5 if 50–59 years, 6 if 60 years and older). Balance is the target variable where one indicates the customer maintains a high monthly balance, and 0 otherwise. A portion of the CreditCard_Data worksheet is shown in the accompanying table.

Sex	Education	Children	Age	Balance
Female	2	Yes	3	1
Male	1	No	4	0
⋮	⋮	⋮	⋮	⋮
Female	2	Yes	3	0

a. Partition the data to develop a naïve Bayes classification model. Report the accuracy, sensitivity, specificity, and precision rates for the validation data set.
b. Generate the ROC curve. What is the area under the ROC curve (or AUC value)?
c. Interpret the performance measures and evaluate the effectiveness of the naïve Bayes model.
d. Score the new customer records in the CreditCard_Score worksheet. What is the scoring result of the first customer record?
e. Change the cutoff value to 0.3. Report the accuracy, sensitivity, specificity, and precision rates for the validation data set.

32. **FILE** ***Volunteer.*** A community center is launching a campaign to recruit local residents to help maintain a protected nature preserve area that encompasses extensive walking trails, bird watching blinds, wild flowers, and animals. The community center wants to send out a mail invitation to selected residents and invite them to volunteer their time to help but does not have the financial resources to launch a large mailing campaign. As a result, they solicit help from the town mayor to analyze a data set of 5,000 local residents and their past volunteer activity, stored in the Volunteer_Data worksheet. The data include Sex (F/M), Married (Y = married, N = not married), College (1 if college degree, 0 otherwise), Income (1 if annual income of $50K and above, 0 otherwise), and Volunteer (1 if participated in volunteer activities, 0 otherwise). They want to use the analysis results to help select potential residents who are likely to accept the invitation to volunteer. A portion of the data set from the mayor is shown in the accompanying table.

Sex	Married	College	Income	Volunteer
F	N	0	0	1
F	Y	1	0	1
⋮	⋮	⋮	⋮	⋮
F	Y	1	1	1

a. Partition the data to develop a naïve Bayes classification model. Report the accuracy, sensitivity, specificity, and precision rates for the validation data set.
b. Generate the ROC curve and decile-wise lift chart. What is the area under the ROC curve (or AUC value)? What is the lift of the leftmost bar of the decile-wise lift chart?
c. Score the new volunteer records in the Volunteer_Score worksheet. What is the scoring result of the first customer record?

33. **FILE** ***Vacation.*** Nora Jackson owns a number of vacation homes on a beach. She works with a consortium of rental home owners to gather a data set to build a classification model to predict the likelihood of potential customers renting a beachfront home during holidays. A portion of the data set is shown in the accompanying table with the following variables: whether the potential customer owns a home (Own = 1 if yes, 0 otherwise), whether the customer has children (Children = 1 if yes, 0 otherwise), the customer's age in years (Age), annual income (Income), and whether or not the customer has previously rented a beachfront house (Rental = 1 if yes , 0 otherwise).

Own	Children	Age	Income	Rental
0	1	41	64000	0
1	0	64	22000	0
⋮	⋮	⋮	⋮	⋮
0	0	67	146000	1

a. Bin the Age and Income variables as follows. For Analytic Solver, choose the *Equal count* option and two bins for each of the two variables. For R, bin Age into [22, 45) and [45, 85) and Income into [0, 85000) and [85000, 300000). What are the bin numbers for Age and Income of the first two observations?
b. Partition the transformed data to develop a naïve Bayes classification model. Report the accuracy, sensitivity, specificity, and precision rates for the validation data set.
c. Generate the decile-wise lift chart. What is the lift value of the leftmost bar?
d. Generate the ROC curve. What is the area under the ROC curve (or AUC value)?
e. Interpret the performance measures and evaluate the effectiveness of the naïve Bayes model.

34. **FILE** ***InGame.*** A mobile gaming company wants to study a group of its existing customers about their in-game purchases. A data set, a portion of which is shown in the accompanying table, is extracted and includes how old the customer is (Age), Sex (1 if female, 0 otherwise), the amount of weekly play time in hours (Hours), whether or not the customer's mobile phone is linked to a Facebook account (Facebook = 1 if yes, 0 otherwise), and whether or not the customer has made an in-game purchase (Buy = 1 if yes, 0 otherwise).

Age	Sex	Hours	Facebook	Buy
35	1	21	0	1
34	0	2	1	1
⋮	⋮	⋮	⋮	⋮
49	1	26	1	1

a. Bin the Age and Hours variables as follows. For Analytic Solver, choose the *Equal interval* option and two bins for each of the two variables. For R, bin Age into [15, 40) and [40, 65) and Hours into [0, 20) and [20, 40). What are the bin numbers for Age and Hours for the first two observations?

b. Partition the transformed data to develop a naïve Bayes classification model. Report the accuracy, sensitivity, specificity, and precision rates for the validation data set.

c. Generate the ROC curve. What is the area under the ROC curve (or AUC value)?

d. Interpret the performance measures and evaluate the effectiveness of the naïve Bayes model.

35. **FILE** ***Grit.*** *Forbes* magazine published an article that studied career accomplishments and factors that might contribute to career success (August 30, 2018). It turns out that career success has less to do with talents and is not necessarily influenced by test scores or IQ scores. Rather, "grit," or a combination of persistence and passion, was found to be a good indicator of a person's career success. Tom Weyerhaeuser, an HR manager at an investment bank, is conducting a campus recruitment and wants to know how he might be able to measure "grit." He thought that he could ask each job candidate about his or her GPA, athletic activities, leadership roles in college, study abroad experience, and employment during college as a way to gauge whether or not each candidate has the persistence and passion to succeed in the investment banking industry. He extracts data from the corporate HR database on 157 current employees with variables indicating whether or not they currently hold an upper-management position (Success = 1 if yes, 0 otherwise), had a part-time job in college (Job = 1 if yes, 0 othwerwise), graduated with a GPA higher than 3.5 (GPA = 1 if yes, 0 otherwise), represented their university in athletic activities (Sports = 1 if yes, 0 otherwise), and had a leadership role in college organizations (Leadership = 1 if yes, 0 otherwise). A portion of the Grit_Data worksheet is shown in the accompanying table.

Success	Job	GPA	Sports	Leadership
0	0	0	1	1
0	1	0	0	0
⋮	⋮	⋮	⋮	⋮
0	1	0	0	1

a. Partition the data to develop a naïve Bayes classification model. Report the accuracy, sensitivity, specificity, and precision rates for the validation data set.

b. Generate and display the cumulative lift chart, the decile-wise lift chart, and the ROC curve.

c. Generate the ROC curve. What is the area under the ROC curve (or AUC value)?

d. Interpret the performance measures and evaluate the effectiveness of the naïve Bayes model.

e. Score the new job applicants in the Grit_Score worksheet. What is the predicted outcome of the first applicant?

36. **FILE** ***Graduation.*** Predicting whether or not an entering freshman student will drop out of college has been a challenge for many higher education institutions. Nelson Touré, a senior student success adviser at an ivy-league university, has been asked to investigate possible indicators that might allow the university to be more proactive to provide support for at-risk students. Nelson reviews a data set of 200 former students and selects the following variables to include in his study: Graduate (Graduate = 1 if graduated, 0 otherwise); whether or not the student received a passing grade in his or her first calculus, statistics, or math course (Math = 1 if yes, 0 otherwise); whether or not the student received a passing grade in his or her first English or communications course (Language = 1 if yes, 0 otherwise); whether or not the student had any contact with the advising center during his or her first semester (Advise = 1 if yes, 0 otherwise); and whether or not the student lived on campus during his or her first year at college (Dorm = 1 if yes, 0 otherwise). A portion of the data is shown in the accompanying table.

Graduate	Math	Language	Advise	Dorm
1	1	0	0	1
0	0	1	0	1
⋮	⋮	⋮	⋮	⋮
1	1	1	1	1

a. Partition the data to develop a naïve Bayes classification model. Report the accuracy, sensitivity, specificity, and precision rates for the validation data set.

b. Generate the cumulative lift chart. Does the entire lift curve lie above the baseline?

c. Generate the ROC curve. What is the area under the ROC curve (or the AUC value)?

d. Interpret the results and evaluate the effectiveness of the naïve Bayes model.

37. **FILE** ***Fraud.*** Credit card fraud is becoming a serious problem for the financial industry and can pose a considerable cost to banks, credit card issuers, and consumers. Fraud detection using data mining techniques has become an indispensable tool for banks and credit card companies to combat fraudulent transactions. A sample credit card data set contains the following variables: Fraud (1 if fraudulent activities, 0 otherwise), Amount (1 if low, 2 if medium, 3 if high), Online (1 if online transactions, 0 otherwise), and Prior (1 if products that the card holder previously purchased, 0 otherwise). A portion of the data set is shown in the accompanying table.

Fraud	Amount	Online	Prior
0	2	0	1
0	3	0	0
⋮	⋮	⋮	⋮
0	2	0	1

a. Partition the data to develop a naïve Bayes classification model. Report the accuracy, sensitivity, specificity, and precision rates for the validation data set.

b. Generate the decile-wise lift chart. What is the lift value of the leftmost bar? What does this value imply?
c. Generate the ROC curve. What is the area under the ROC curve (or AUC value)?
d. Interpret the performance measures and evaluate the effectiveness of the naïve Bayes model.
e. Change the cutoff value to 0.1. Report the accuracy, sensitivity, specificity, and precision rates for the validation data set.

38. **FILE** ***Insurance.*** Insurance companies use a number of factors to help determine the premium amount for car insurance coverage. Discounts or a lower premium may be given based on factors including credit scores, history of at-fault accidents, age, and sex. Consider the insurance discount data set from 200 existing drivers. The following variables are included in the data set: Discount (1 if yes, 0 otherwise), Female (1 if female, 0 otherwise), Credit (1 if low, 2 if medium, 3 if high scores), AtFault (1 if history of at-fault accidents, 0 otherwise), and Age (1 if 25 years and older, 0 otherwise). A portion of the data is shown in the accompanying table.

Discount	Female	Credit	AtFault	Age
1	0	2	0	0
0	0	3	0	1
⋮	⋮	⋮	⋮	⋮
1	1	1	1	1

a. Partition the data to develop a naïve Bayes classification model. Report the accuracy, sensitivity, specificity, and precision rates for the validation data set.
b. Display the cumulative lift chart, the decile-wise lift chart, and the ROC curve.
c. Generate the ROC curve. What is the area under the ROC curve (or AUC value)?
d. Interpret the performance measures and evaluate the effectiveness of the naïve Bayes model.

39. **FILE** ***Solar.*** Refer to Exercise 9.16 for the description of a solar panel company called New Age Solar and the Solar_Data worksheet.

a. Bin the Age and Income variables in the Solar_Data worksheet as follows. For Analytic Solver, choose the *Equal count* option and two bins for each of the two variables. For R, bin Age into [30, 50) and [50, 90) and Income into [30, 85) and [85, 140). What are the bin numbers for Age and Income of the first two observations?
b. Partition the transformed data and develop a naïve Bayes classification model. Report the accuracy, sensitivity, specificity, and precision rates for the validation data set.
c. Generate the ROC curve. What is the area under the ROC curve (or AUC value)?
d. Interpret the results and evaluate the effectiveness of the naïve Bayes model.

40. **FILE** ***Depression.*** Michelle McGrath is a college student working to complete an undergraduate research project to fulfill her psychology degree requirements. She is interested in how physical and behavioral factors might be used to predict an individual's risk of having depression. After receiving an approval from her adviser, she sends out a survey to local residents asking for their age (Age, in years), years of education (Education), the number of hours per month they engaged in moderate or vigorous physical activities (Hours), and whether or not they have experienced depression (Depression: Y/N). A portion of the data from 261 respondents is shown in the accompanying table.

Age	Education	Hours	Depression
44	12	20	Y
49	9	30	Y
⋮	⋮	⋮	⋮
69	15	34	Y

a. Bin the Age, Education, and Hours variables as follows. For Analytic Solver, choose the *Equal interval* option and three bins for each of the variables. For R, bin Age into [20, 40), [40,60), and [60, 81), Education into [9, 12), [12, 16), and [16, 20), and Hours into [0, 55), [55, 105), and [105, 150). What are the bin numbers for the variables of the first two observations?
b. Partition the transformed data and develop a naïve Bayes classification model. Report the accuracy, sensitivity, specificity, and precision rates for the validation data set.
c. Generate the ROC curve. What is the area under the ROC curve (or AUC value)?
d. Interpret the results and evaluate the effectiveness of the naïve Bayes model.

9.4 WRITING WITH BIG DATA

FILE
College_Admission

In this chapter, we discussed two well-known supervised data mining techniques for classification problems: the KNN method and the naïve Bayes method. In the introductory case, we used the KNN method to analyze gym membership data that have numerical predictor variables to predict whether or not a potential member will purchase a gym membership. The naïve Bayes method, however, requires categorical predictor variables. In the Big Data case presented next, we will transform numerical predictor variables into categorical variables and use the naïve Bayes method to predict the college admissions of high school students. Details on data wrangling and transformation are discussed in Chapter 2.

Case Study

Every year, millions of high school students apply and vie for acceptance to a college of their choice. For many students and their parents, this requires years of preparation, especially for those wishing to attend a top-ranked college. In high schools, students usually work with college advisors to research different colleges and navigate the admissions process.

Elena Sheridan, a college counselor at Beachside High School, is working with 14 students who are interested in applying to the same selective four-year college. She is asked by her school principal to prepare a report that analyzes the chances of the 14 students getting accepted into one of the three academic programs. In a database of past college applicants available to counselors at Beachside High, predictor variables include the student's high school GPA, SAT score, and the Male, White, and Asian dummy variables that capture the student's sex and ethnicity. Elena also wants to know whether or not the parents' education can be a predictor of a student's college acceptance and plans to include the education level of both parents in her analysis.

Based on her conversation with college counselors at other high schools, she believes that high school students with a GPA of 3.5 or above have a much higher chance of getting accepted into a selective college. She also thinks that SAT scores of at least 1,200 substantially increase the chance of acceptance. To test these anecdotal assumptions, Elena wants to convert the GPAs and SAT scores into the categories corresponding to these thresholds. In addition, the database has a target variable indicating whether or not the past applicant was accepted to the college.

Develop the naïve Bayes classification model and create a report that presents an analysis of the factors that may influence whether or not a high school student is admitted to a selective four-year college. Predictor variables should include the applicant's sex, ethnicity, parents' education levels, GPA, and SAT scores. Transform the GPAs and SAT scores into appropriate categorical variables. Make predictions whether or not each of the 14 high school students at Beachside High in the College_Admission_Score worksheet will be admitted.

Sample Report – College Admissions

High school students work hard to excel academically and set themselves apart with extracurricular achievements. Getting into the right college and choosing the right major can help start them out on a successful professional career.

My Life Graphic/Shutterstock

The college admissions data set that is available to Beachside High School counselors includes records of past students who had applied to a selective four-year college that has three academic units: School of Arts and Letters, School of Business and Economics, and School of Mathematics and Sciences. The data set is used to develop classification models based on a naïve Bayes algorithm to predict whether or not the 14 high-achieving students at Beachside High will be admitted to any of the three academic units at the college.

The 14 current students are the top students in their graduating class. However, because the admission process can be highly competitive, some of these students might not get admitted to the college they wish to attend. Moreover, different academic programs may have different admission criteria. As a result, a naïve Bayes classification model is developed for each of the three academic schools based on the following variables: parents' education, high school

GPAs, SAT scores, and the male, white, and Asian indicators. Because the naïve Bayes algorithm requires that all predictor variables are categorical, GPAs and SAT scores are converted into binary values where GPAs that are at least 3.50 are denoted as 1, 0 otherwise, and SAT scores that are at least 1,200 are denoted as 1, 0 otherwise. A summary of the students' demographic and academic information is as follows.

- Of the 14 students, eight of them are female. Four students are of Asian descent, and six are nonwhite.
- The average high school GPA and SAT score of the 14 students are 3.64 and 1,261, respectively.
- Nine students have a current GPA of 3.50 or higher, and 10 students scored at least 1,200 on the SAT exam.
- All but three students have at least one parent who completed a four-year college degree.

Even though the current students have not decided which academic program they want to pursue, most of them express an interest in the School of Arts and Letters. The data set has 6,964 records of past applicants to this program, which are partitioned into training, validation, and test data sets. Based on the test data set, the naïve Bayes model for the School of Arts and Letters has an overall accuracy rate of 75.81%. The specificity and sensitivity rates are 84.65% and 48.83%, respectively.

A summary of performance measures of the classification models for the three academic schools is shown in Table 9.10. The naïve Bayes model predicts that only four of our 14 top students will be admitted to the School of Arts and Letters. This program appears to be the most selective of the three academic units. The scoring results of the 14 students for each of the three academic schools are presented in Table 9.11.

TABLE 9.10 Performance Measures of Naïve Bayes Classifiers

Schools	Accuracy (%)	Specificity (%)	Sensitivity (%)	AUC (%)	Lift Ratio: 1st Decile
Arts & Letters	75.81	84.65	48.83	78.35	2.21
Business & Economics	77.44	83.20	67.86	83.49	2.14
Math. & Sciences	76.24	79.81	69.19	81.66	2.07

The School of Business and Economics is also a popular choice among the current students. The data set has 4,103 records of past applicants to this program, which are partitioned into training, validation, and test data sets. The accuracy, specificity, and sensitivity rates based on the test data are 77.44%, 83.20%, and 67.86%, respectively. The model predicts that six out of the 14 students will be admitted into this program.

A similar naïve Bayes classifier is developed based on the 6,272 records of past applicants to the School of Mathematics and Sciences. As presented in Table 9.10, the accuracy, specificity, and sensitivity rates based on the test data are 76.24%, 79.81%, and 69.19%, respectively. Based on the scoring results, six out of the 14 students are likely to be admitted into this program. These are the same six students that the previous model classifies as likely to be admitted into the School of Business and Economics.

Based on the overall accuracy rate, the naïve Bayes classifiers perform reasonably well. The lift ratios and the decile-wise lift chart also indicate that the naïve Bayes classifiers are more effective than a baseline random model. As shown in Table 9.10, the lift values of the first decile of the three models are above 2.0, and the AUC values are around 80%. However, compared to other performance measures, the sensitivity rate of the models is relatively low, especially for the School of Arts and Letters. This may be because the schools also use qualitative information that is not captured in the database, making it difficult to correctly classify all of the past applicants who were admitted to the college (i.e., identifying true positive cases). The qualitative factors that are relevant to the admission process include letters of recommendations, written essays, and, for the School of Arts and Letters, a student's artwork.

Table 9.11 presents the scoring results of the 14 current students. In general, the only students who are likely to be admitted into any of the three academic programs are those who maintain a GPA of at least 3.50 and score 1,200 or above on the SAT exam. Out of the 14 students, only six of them meet both criteria. A high GPA or a high SAT score alone is not likely to result in an acceptance to the college.

These data-driven results confirm the anecdotal intuition that a GPA of 3.50 and an SAT score of 1,200 are the minimum thresholds that students at Beachside High need to achieve in order to be admitted into a more selective college or university. Moreover, the School of Arts and Letters appears to be more selective than the other two schools. Only four of the six students with a GPA above 3.50 and an SAT score above 1,200 are likely to get accepted into this program. With this information, it is advised that some of the 14 students wishing to attend the School of Arts and Letters apply to additional colleges and universities with a similar degree program as a back-up plan.

TABLE 9.11 Prediction Results for the 14 Students

			Admission Prediction:		
ID	GPA at Least 3.50	SAT at Least 1,200	Arts & Letters	Business & Economics	Math. & Sciences
1	Y	Y	Y	Y	Y
2	Y	N	N	N	N
3	N	Y	N	N	N
4	N	Y	N	N	N
5	N	Y	N	N	N
6	Y	Y	N	Y	Y
7	Y	N	N	N	N
8	N	Y	N	N	N
9	Y	Y	Y	Y	Y
10	Y	Y	Y	Y	Y
11	N	N	N	N	N
12	Y	Y	Y	Y	Y
13	Y	Y	N	Y	Y
14	Y	N	N	N	N

Suggested Case Studies

Supervised data mining techniques can be applied to many situations and different data sets. The following are some suggestions based on the Big Data sets that are provided with this text.

Report 9.1 **FILE** ***Longitudinal_Survey***. Subset the data to include only those individuals who lived in an urban area. Predict whether or not an individual's marriage will end up in a divorce, a separation, or a remarriage using predictor variables such as sex, parents' education, height, weight, number of years of education, self-esteem scale, and whether the person is outgoing as a kid and/or adult. Note: You may need to remove observations with missing values prior to the analysis.

Report 9.2 **FILE** ***Longitudinal_Survey.*** Subset the data to include only those individuals who lived in a non-urban area. Predict whether or not an individual will have full-time employment (i.e., work for 52 weeks) using predictor variables such as parents' education, race, self-esteem score, and whether the person is outgoing as a kid. Note: You may need to remove observations with missing values prior to the analysis.

Report 9.3 **FILE** ***TechSales_Reps.*** Subset the data set to include only college-educated sales professionals in the software product group. Predict whether the sales professional will receive a high (9 or 10) net promoter score (NPS) or not using predictor variables such as age, sex, tenure with the company, number of professional certificates acquired, annual evaluation score, and personality type. Note: You may need to perform data transformation in order to meet the requirements of the analytics technique.

Report 9.4 FILE ***College_Admissions.*** Subset the data to include only one of the colleges. Predict whether an admitted applicant will eventually decide to enroll at the college using predictor variables such as gender, race, high school GPA, SAT/ACT score, and parents' education level.

Report 9.5 FILE ***Car_Crash.*** Subset the data to include only the accidents that occured in one city or during one month. Predict whether or not a car crash will result in fatality or severe injuries by using predictor variables such as the weather condition, amount of daylight, and whether or not the accident takes place on a highway.

10 Supervised Data Mining: Decision Trees

LEARNING OBJECTIVES

After reading this chapter, you should be able to:

LO **10.1** **Apply classification trees to classify new records.**

LO **10.2** **Apply regression trees to predict new records.**

LO **10.3** **Apply ensemble tree models to classify new records.**

In the last chapter, we examined two widely used supervised data mining techniques: the *k*-nearest neighbors (KNN) method and the naïve Bayes method. Recall that the KNN method is a data-driven technique that classifies a new case by identifying the *k*-nearest neighbors of the new case based on numerical predictor variables. The naïve Bayes method, another classification technique, computes the posterior probability that a new case will belong to a target class based on its prior probability and the conditional probabilities of categorical predictor variables.

In this chapter, we focus on another popular supervised data mining technique called decision trees. Decision trees can be constructed using both numerical and categorical predictor variables and are used for both classification and prediction problems. We start with a detailed discussion of the classification and regression trees (CART) method, which is considered one of the most transparent and easily interpretable data mining techniques. At the end of the chapter, we also discuss a methodology called ensemble trees, where multiple decision trees are combined to improve the predictive performance of the model and reduce overfitting.

©Andy Dean Photography/Shutterstock

INTRODUCTORY CASE

Home Equity Line of Credit from Sunnyville Bank

Established in 1990, Sunnyville Bank is a local community bank serving businesses, individuals, and nonprofit organizations throughout southern California. The bank is committed to offering personalized services and a wide range of banking products and services that match those of larger financial institutions. For the last five years, Sunnyville Bank has been named "Best Local Bank" by residents of southern California.

Hayden Sellar, the retail banking manager of Sunnyville Bank, was taken by surprise when he heard of a recent decline in the bank's home equity line of credit (HELOC) business. Hayden does not believe that the decline is due to the competitiveness of the bank's interest rates. After all, customers choose to bank with Sunnyville for the superior service, not just for low prices. Hayden's intuition suggest that Sunnyville Bank has not been targeting the right customers to market its HELOC products.

As an experiment, Hayden compiles data on 500 past customers to whom Sunnyville Bank marketed its HELOC products. The data include the age, sex, income, and whether or not the customer responded to the HELOC offer (HELOC equals 1 if responded, 0 otherwise). Table 10.1a shows a portion of this data, labeled the HELOC_Data worksheet. Hayden also collects the age, sex and income from 20 new bank customers. Table 10.1b shows a portion of these data, labeled the HELOC_Score worksheet. Hayden plans to use the predictive model generated from historical data to predict whether these new customers will respond to a HELOC offer. Both worksheets are located in the ***HELOC*** data file.

FILE *HELOC*

TABLE 10.1 Bank Customers and Their Response to a HELOC Offer

a. The HELOC_Data worksheet

Age	Sex	Income	HELOC
30	Female	101000	0
25	Male	86000	0
⋮	⋮	⋮	⋮
47	Male	33000	1

b. The HELOC_Score worksheet

Age	Sex	Income
25	Female	45000
23	Male	22000
⋮	⋮	⋮
51	Male	43000

Hayden would like to use the data to accomplish the following tasks.

1. Develop a classification tree for predicting whether or not a bank customer will respond to a HELOC offer.
2. Identify which of the 20 new customers are likely to respond to a HELOC offer.

A synopsis of this case is provided in Section 10.2.

10.1 INTRODUCTION TO CLASSIFICATION AND REGRESSION TREES (CART)

Decision trees are a popular supervised data mining technique with a wide range of applications. Their appeal lies in the fact that the output is displayed as one or more upside-down trees that are easy to interpret. In general, a decision tree represents a set of If-Then rules, whereby answers to these statements will eventually lead to a solution to the application at hand.

Imagine a business decision such as the one in the introductory case where a bank manager tries to decide which customers are likely to respond to the bank's home equity line of credit (HELOC) offer. Figure 10.1 shows a hypothetical decision tree applied to the HELOC example. The top node of the decision tree is called the root node. The root node is the first variable to which a split value is applied. The left branch from the root node represents the cases whose variable values are less than (<) the split value, and the right branch represents the cases whose variable values are greater than or equal to (≥) the split value. Figure 10.1 shows that the root node is the Age variable. Customers who are younger than 50 years old are placed in the left branch, and customers who are at least 50 years old are placed in the right branch. These branches often lead to interior nodes where more decision rules are applied.

In this simplified example, the Income variable is an interior node. The split value for a variable can be different if it originates from a different branch. Here, the split value for Income is \$100,000 for those customers younger than 50 years old, whereas it is \$50,000 for those customers at least 50 years old. The bottom nodes of the decision tree are called leaf nodes or terminal nodes, and this is where the classification or prediction outcomes are given. In the HELOC example, the leaf node indicates whether or not the customer will respond to the HELOC offer.

FIGURE 10.1
A simplified decision tree

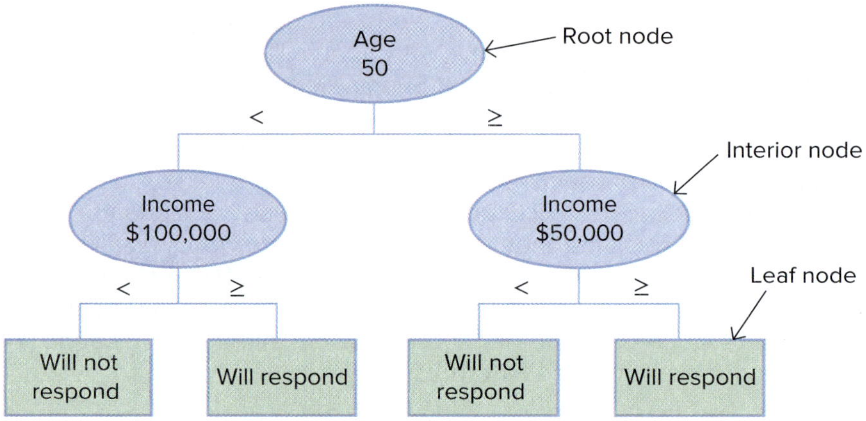

The following four rules can be derived from Figure 10.1:

- If Age < 50 and Income < \$100,000, then the customer will not respond.
- If Age < 50 and Income ≥ \$100,000, then the customer will respond.
- If Age ≥ 50 and Income < \$50,000, then the customer will not respond.
- If Age ≥ 50 and Income ≥ \$50,000, then the customer will respond.

The bank manager can then apply these rules to future customers when marketing the bank's HELOC products.

Classification and Regression Trees (CART)

As the HELOC example shows, a decision tree sorts or splits the cases based on the values of predictor variables (such as Age < 50 versus Age ≥ 50) into subsets of cases. At each node, potential customers are sorted or split into groups depending on their age or income. This process is repeated at each level of the decision tree until each subset contains only the cases with similar values for the target variable. The process is recursive because every split is dependent on the previous splits. In Figure 10.1, for example, the split on the Income variable is dependent on the previous split on the Age variable. Each of the final four subsets (the green rectangular boxes) contains cases with the same value of the target variable, that is, whether or not the customer will respond. A leaf node such as these four subsets is called a **pure subset** where each leaf node contains cases with the same value of the target variable and, therefore, there is no need to further split it.

The decision tree in Figure 10.1 is kept simple intentionally to help illustrate the relevant concepts. It is important to understand that for real-world, large, and complex data sets, it will require many interior nodes to reach pure subsets. Sometimes, it may not even be possible to reach purity in the case of identical observations with different values of the target variable.

> **PURE SUBSETS**
>
> Pure subsets consist of leaf nodes that contain cases with the same value of the target variable. There is no need to further split pure subsets.

This successive split or partitioning of the cases into pure subsets is the primary building block of the **classification and regression trees** (CART) algorithm. Decision trees produced by the CART algorithm are binary, meaning that there are two branches for each decision node. When the target variable is categorical, the CART algorithm produces a **classification tree** to predict the class memberships of new cases. When the target variable is numerical, the CART algorithm produces a **regression tree** to estimate the numeric values of the target variable of new cases.

> **CLASSIFICATION AND REGRESSION TREES (CART)**
>
> The CART algorithm successively splits the cases into increasingly homogeneous subsets based on the values of the predictor variables.
>
> - When the target variable is categorical, the CART algorithm produces a classification tree to predict the class memberships of future cases.
> - When the target variable is numerical, the CART algorithm produces a regression tree to predict the value of the outcome variable of future cases.

Like other supervised data mining methods discussed in Chapter 9, a decision tree is usually built using partitioned data sets. It is common practice to partition data into three sets: training, validation, and test data sets. The CART algorithm will first grow the tree using the training data set by selecting the optimal splits of all predictor variables and all possible split values until no further splits can be made. This is usually achieved when all the leaf nodes only contain cases that belong to the same class for classification trees or have the same outcome value for regression trees. In other words, the leaf nodes are all pure subsets. The decision tree produced in this step is called a **full tree**, also called a full-grown tree or maximal tree, as it represents the maximum number of splits the CART algorithm can make to identify pure subsets.

A full tree, however, tends to overfit the data, resulting in low predictive performance when applied to new cases. This is especially true for the decision nodes and branches close to the end of the tree as these splits are based on a very small number of cases and tend to fit the noise rather than the underlying patterns of the data. A validation, and sometimes even a test, data set is used to assess the performance of a decision tree and the possible issue of overfitting.

In CART, the validation data set is used to optimize the complexity of the tree by "pruning" the full tree to a simpler tree that generalizes better to new data. Pruning is the process of removing branches of the decision tree to improve its ability to predict new cases more accurately. The pruning process results in a set of candidate decision trees with different levels of complexity. Performance measures such as the misclassification rate for the classification tree or the root mean square error (RMSE) for the regression tree from the validation data set are then compared to identify the tree that produces the lowest error rate, called the **minimum error tree**. The minimum error tree is the smallest (least complex) tree that produces the smallest classification or prediction error on the validation data set among all the candidate trees. Alternatively, the **best-pruned tree**, which is the smallest (least complex) tree with a validation error within one standard error of the minimum error tree, can be used as the final decision tree. Because the validation data set is a sample from the original data, relaxing the tree selection criterion by one standard error accounts for the sampling error. Finally, an independent assessment of the predictive performance of the tree is sometimes conducted by applying the final tree to the test data set.

While the underlying concept remains the same, different software packages tend to perform data mining techniques differently. As illustrated in the KNN example in Chapter 9, Analytic Solver uses the validation data set to determine the optimal model complexity, whereas R uses the cross-validation technique. Similarly for the decision tree method, while Analytic Solver uses three-way partitioning (i.e., train, validation, and test data) for building and pruning decision trees, R implements a k-fold cross-validation process for pruning decision trees and therefore uses two-way partitioning (i.e., only train and validation data). For a detailed disucssion on the cross-validation method, refer to section 7.4 of this text.

VARIOUS DECISION TREES

The full tree is a fully grown decision tree that represents the maximum number of splits the CART algorithm is willing to make in order to identify pure subsets. As the full tree tends to overfit and does not generalize well to new data, the full tree is often pruned by removing the weaker branches to create the minimum error tree or the best-pruned tree.

- The minimum error tree is the least complex tree with the smallest validation error.
- The best-pruned tree is the least complex tree with a validation error within one standard error of the minimum error tree.

The decision tree methodology has a number of characteristics that make it highly popular. First, the technique is versatile and can deal with both categorical and numerical target variables. Second, the tree diagram and the If-Then rules are easy to understand, interpret, and implement in real-world situations even for a non-technical audience. Third, the selection of the most discriminatory predictor variables is automatic through the recursive partitioning and pruning processes. The most important predictors appear at the top of the tree diagram. The variable importance information can help refine future data collection efforts. Fourth, because the methodology is data-driven, it does not assume a particular type of relationship between the predictor and the target variables as assumed in linear and logistic regression models. Moreover, the methodology can handle incomplete data and is not affected by outliers, and, therefore, requires relatively less effort for data preparation.

At the same time, however, it does require a relatively large training data set to build a reasonably accurate model, and the computational cost increases exponentially as the number of predictor variables and observations increase. Furthermore, due to the recursive partitioning process used in the CART algorithm, small changes to the training data set will result in drastically different trees. Later in this chapter, we will discuss ensemble trees, which are designed to improve model stability.

10.2 CLASSIFICATION TREES

LO 10.1

Apply classification trees to classify new records.

In this section, we focus on applications of decision trees where the outcome variable is binary. The decision trees generated in these applications are called classification trees. As mentioned earlier, the CART algorithm uses a recursive partitioning process to split the cases into increasingly pure subsets to build the tree. In a classification problem with a binary target variable, a subset is considered "pure" when it contains cases that all belong to the same class (100% and 0% split between classes). A subset with the highest degree of impurity is when half of the cases belong to one class and the other half belong to the other (50% and 50% split between classes). Impurity is therefore measured by how well the two classes are separated. In order to build a decision tree, we need to understand the possible split points on each predictor variable and how the CART algorithm determines the optimal splits.

Identifying Possible Split Points

Consider the HELOC example from the introductory case. Recall that the bank manager has collected data from 500 past customers that include the customer's age, sex, income, and whether or not the customer responded to the HELOC offer (HELOC equals 1 if responded, 0 otherwise). Table 10.2 shows a portion of 20 randomly selected cases from this data set that are labeled ***HELOC_Data_20***. These 20 cases as a training data set are used only for illustration to develop a classification tree with two predictor variables: Age and Income.

FILE
HELOC_Data_20

TABLE 10.2 The ***HELOC_Data_20*** worksheet

Age	Income	HELOC
44	99000	0
63	158000	1
⋮	⋮	⋮
40	97000	0

The CART algorithm uses the midpoints between consecutive cases of the predictor variable as possible split points. For example, the ages of the 20 cases can be sorted in ascending order into the following data array:

{23, 24, 25, 35, 36, 37, 39, 40, 43, 44, 45, 47, 51, 59, 62, 63}

(Note that some values have multiple occurrences, but for determining splitting points, each value only needs to appear once in the array.)

Therefore, the first possible split point is calculated as (23 + 24)/ 2 = 23.5, the next possible split point is calculated as (24 + 25)/ 2 = 24.5, and the remaining possible split points are found in the same way. The following data array shows all possible split points for Age:

{23.5, 24.5, 30, 35.5, 36.5, 38, 39.5, 41.5, 43.5, 44.5, 46, 49, 55, 60.5, 62.5}

EXAMPLE 10.1

What are the possible split points on the Income variable for the 20 cases in Table 10.2?

SOLUTION: First, we sort the values for Income in ascending order to produce the following data array:

{4000, 11000, 14000, 17000, 32000, 47000, 50000, 53000, 64000, 65000, 68000, 77000, 93000, 95000, 97000, 98000, 99000, 105000, 109000, 158000}

Next, we find the midpoints between consecutive cases. The first split value is found as (4000 + 11000)/ 2 = 7500, the next possible split point is calculated as (11000 + 14000)/ 2 = 12500. The following data array shows all possible split points for Income:

{7500, 12500, 15500, 24500, 39500, 48500, 51500, 58500, 64500, 66500, 72500, 85000, 94000, 96000, 97500, 98500, 102000, 107000, 133500}

After identifying all the possible split points on the two variables, the next step is to find the optimal partition that minimizes impurity in the two resulting subsets. Recall that the impurity of a node in a decision tree is measured by how well the classes are separated from one another. There are several different ways to measure impurity, including the Gini impurity index, entropy index, and Chi-Square test; in this chapter, we use the Gini impurity index to illustrate how to identify the optimal splits for producing a classification tree.

The Gini Impurity Index

The Gini impurity index, or simply the Gini index, measures the degree of impurity of a set of cases in a multiclass classification context. Using m as the number of classes of the target variable, the Gini index is computed as

$$\text{Gini index} = 1 - \Sigma_{k=1}^{m} P_k^2,$$

where $P_k = \dfrac{\text{Total number of cases that belong to class } k}{\text{Total number of cases}}$.

For a binary classification problem ($m = 2$), the Gini index of a set of cases ranges from 0 (highest purity) to 0.5 (highest impurity). For example, if all the cases in the set belong to Class 0 and none belongs to Class 1, then the Gini index is $1 - (1^2 + 0^2) = 0$. On the other hand, if half of the cases belong to Class 0 and the other half of the cases belong to Class 1, then the Gini index is $1 - (0.5^2 + 0.5^2) = 0.5$. As mentioned earlier, we have the highest degree of impurity when half of the cases belong to one class and the other half belong to the other. With any other split, the Gini index will be less than 0.5. For example, if 90% of the cases belong to Class 0 and 10% of the cases belong to Class 1, then the Gini index is $1 - (0.90^2 + 0.10^2) = 0.18$, implying that it is relatively pure as its value is closer to 0 than to 0.5. During the recursive partitioning process, the CART algorithm determines the optimal split at each step by comparing the Gini indexes for all possible splits across all variables. The optimal split is the one that produces the smallest Gini index. In Examples 10.2, 10.3, and 10.4, we illustrate the steps in the recursive partitioning process to determine the optimal splits using the Gini index.

EXAMPLE 10.2

Let's return to the HELOC example with the 20 randomly selected customers. Figure 10.2 shows a plot of Income against Age for these 20 cases. The 15 blue dots represent customers who did not respond to the HELOC offer (Class 0), whereas the five red dots represent customers who responded to the HELOC offer (Class 1). Using the information in Figure 10.2, find the overall Gini index.

FIGURE 10.2 Plot of Income against Age for $n = 20$

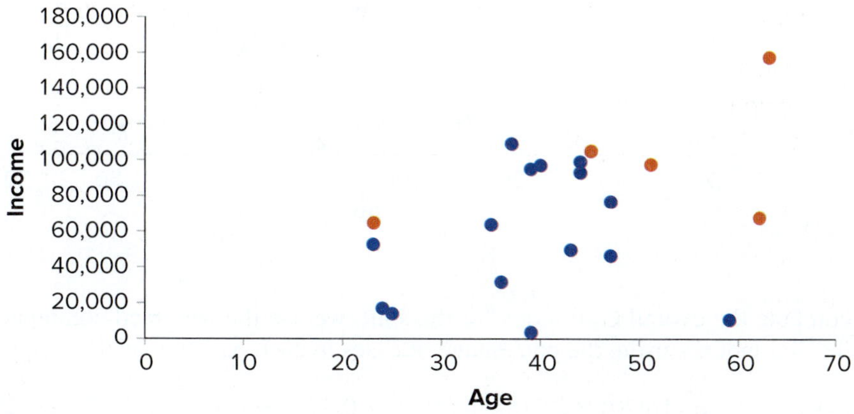

SOLUTION: Among the 20 cases, five cases belong to Class 1 while the rest of the cases belong to Class 0. The Gini index for the 20 cases can be computed as follows:

$$\text{Gini}_{20\text{ cases}} = 1 - [(15/20)^2 + (5/20)^2] = 1 - [0.5625 + 0.0625] = 0.3750$$

This group of 20 cases is an impure subset as 15 cases belong to Class 0 and five cases belong to Class 1 (75% and 25% split).

Example 10.3 demonstrates the next step in the recursive partitioning process that reduces impurity to construct a classification tree.

EXAMPLE 10.3

We continue with the HELOC example as applied to the 20 randomly selected cases from Table 10.2. Earlier, we calculated the possible split points for the Age variable. One of the possible split points is when Age = 49. Figure 10.3 shows a black vertical line at Age = 49. The subset on the left includes all the cases whose ages are less than 49, and the subset on the right contains all the cases whose ages are greater than or equal to 49. Use Figure 10.3 to compute the Gini index given an Age split of 49.

SOLUTION: For the 16 cases in the left subset (Age < 49), two belong to Class 1 and 14 belong to Class 0. For the four cases in the right subset (Age ≥ 49), one belongs to Class 1 and three belong to Class 0. Therefore, the Gini indexes for the two subsets are:

$$\text{Gini}_{\text{Age}<49} = 1 - [(14/16)^2 + (2/16)^2] = 1 - [0.7656 + 0.0156] = 0.2188$$

$$\text{Gini}_{\text{Age}\geq 49} = 1 - [(1/4)^2 + (3/4)^2] = 1 - [0.0625 + 0.5625] = 0.3750$$

FIGURE 10.3 Split at Age = 49

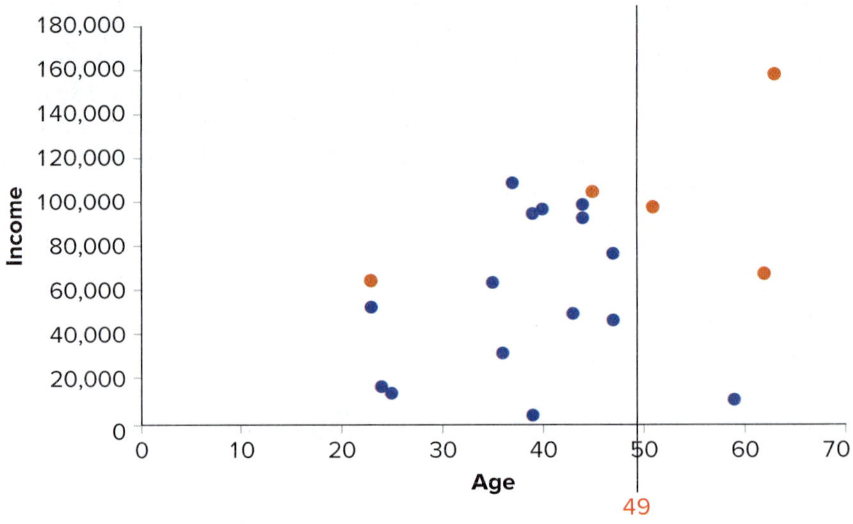

To compute the overall Gini index for the split, we use the weighted combination of the Gini indexes using the percentage of cases in each partition as the weight:

$$\text{Gini}_{\text{split:Age=49}} = (16/20) \times 0.2188 + (4/20) \times 0.3750 = 0.1750 + 0.075 = 0.25$$

Partitioning the cases using an Age split value of 49 has reduced the Gini index from 0.375 to 0.25. The best split on a predictor is chosen by comparing the Gini indexes across all possible splits for the predictor. In our example, if you compute the Gini indexes for all possible splits for Age, you will find that the split value of 49 produces the smallest Gini index; therefore, this split is chosen as the best split for Age.

Because we have not produced a pure subset from the 20 cases in the HELOC example, we will continue the recursive partitioning process using the Income variable. Consider Example 10.4.

EXAMPLE 10.4

Recall from Example 10.1 that one of the possible split points on the Income variable is when Income = 64,500. Figure 10.4 shows a horizontal black line at Income = 64,500. This split creates top and bottom partitions. Compute the overall Gini index given an Income split of 64,500.

SOLUTION: For the 11 cases in the top subset (Income ≥ 64,500), five belong to Class 1 and six belong to Class 0. For the nine cases in the bottom subset (Income < 64,500), none belongs to Class 1 and nine belong to Class 0. Therefore, the Gini indexes for the two subsets are

$$\text{Gini}_{\text{Income}\geq 64500} = 1 - [(6/11)^2 + (5/11)^2] = 1 - [0.2975 + 0.2066] = 0.4959$$

$$\text{Gini}_{\text{Income}<64500} = 1 - [(9/9)^2 + (0/9)^2] = 1 - (1 + 0) = 0$$

The Gini index for this split is computed as

$$\text{Gini}_{\text{spilt:Income=64500}} = (11/20) \times 0.4959 + (9/20) \times 0 = 0.2727 + 0 = 0.2727$$

FIGURE 10.4 Split at Income = $64,500

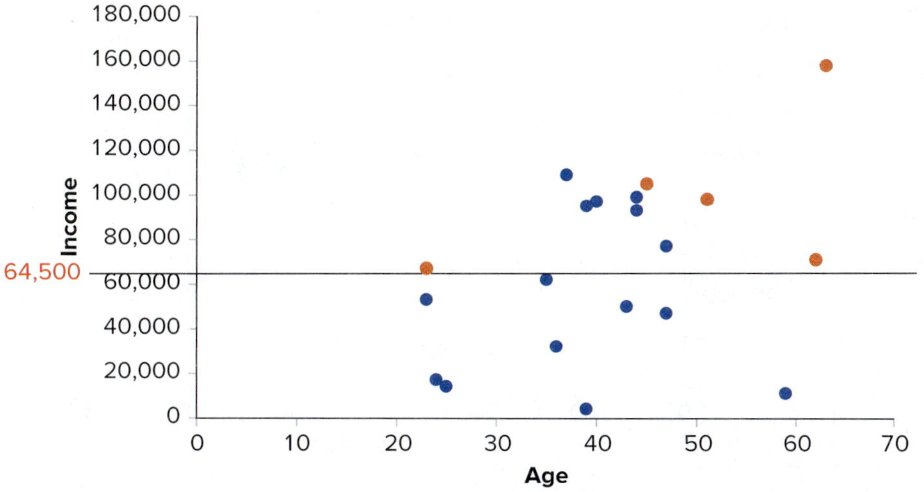

It can be shown that the split with Income = 64,500 produces the smallest Gini index across all possible Income splits. Note that the splits at Age = 49 and Income = 64,500 (Examples 10.3 and 10.4) produce a Gini index that is better than the original Gini index computed in Example 10.2. Next, we will start constructing a decision tree by considering the Gini index values from the two Age and Income splits.

Building the Decision Tree

In the HELOC example with the Age and Income predictor variables, we compare the Gini indexes of the best splits for the two predictors. The split using Age = 49 produces the most reduction in impurity across all possible splits for the two predictors because its Gini index is the smallest (0.25 < 0.2727). Therefore, Age is used as the root node on the decision tree with a split of 49. Figure 10.5 shows this result.

Next, we find the probability that a customer responds to the HELOC offer given the customer's age. In general, this probability is found by finding the proportion of cases in a partition that belongs to the target class. In the HELOC example, the probability that a customer is younger than 49 years old and responds to the HELOC offer (the target class or Class 1) is 2/16 = 0.125 (see Figure 10.3). Similarly, the probability that a customer is 49 years old or older and responds to the HELOC offer is 3/4 = 0.75.

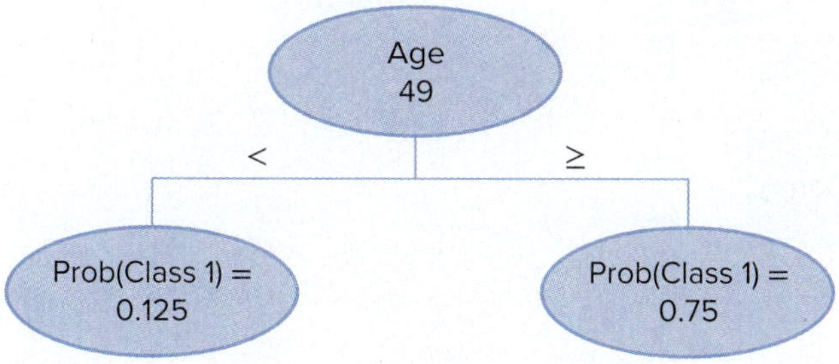

FIGURE 10.5 Root node partition

To grow the decision tree, the process is repeated for all the partitions until no splits can further reduce impurity. In other words, the recursive process terminates when it can no longer produce a lower Gini index or when all the partitions become pure subsets (i.e., the Gini index = 0). Figure 10.6 shows the result of the entire recursive partitioning process. Note that Age is split at 23.6 and 49 and Income is split at 39,500; 59,000; 102,000; and 107,000. In this case, all partitions are pure subsets.

FIGURE 10.6
Recursive partitioning results

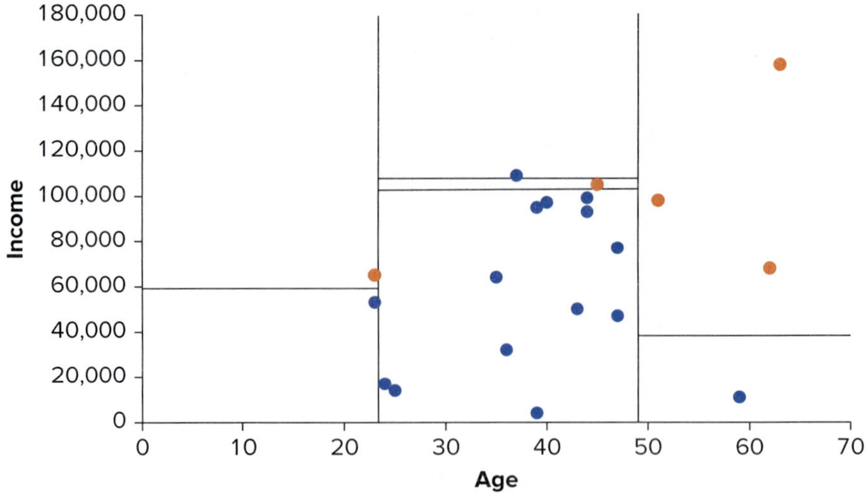

The recursive partitioning process produces the full-grown tree in Figure 10.7. Within the older age group (49 years and older), those who earn at least \$39,500 in annual income are likely to respond to the HELOC offer. Among the younger age groups, individuals who are younger than 23.5 years with an annual income of at least \$59,000 are likely to respond to the offer. Individuals who are between 24 and 49 years old and earn an annual income between \$102,000 and \$107,000 are also likely to respond to the offer.

FIGURE 10.7 Full-grown classification tree

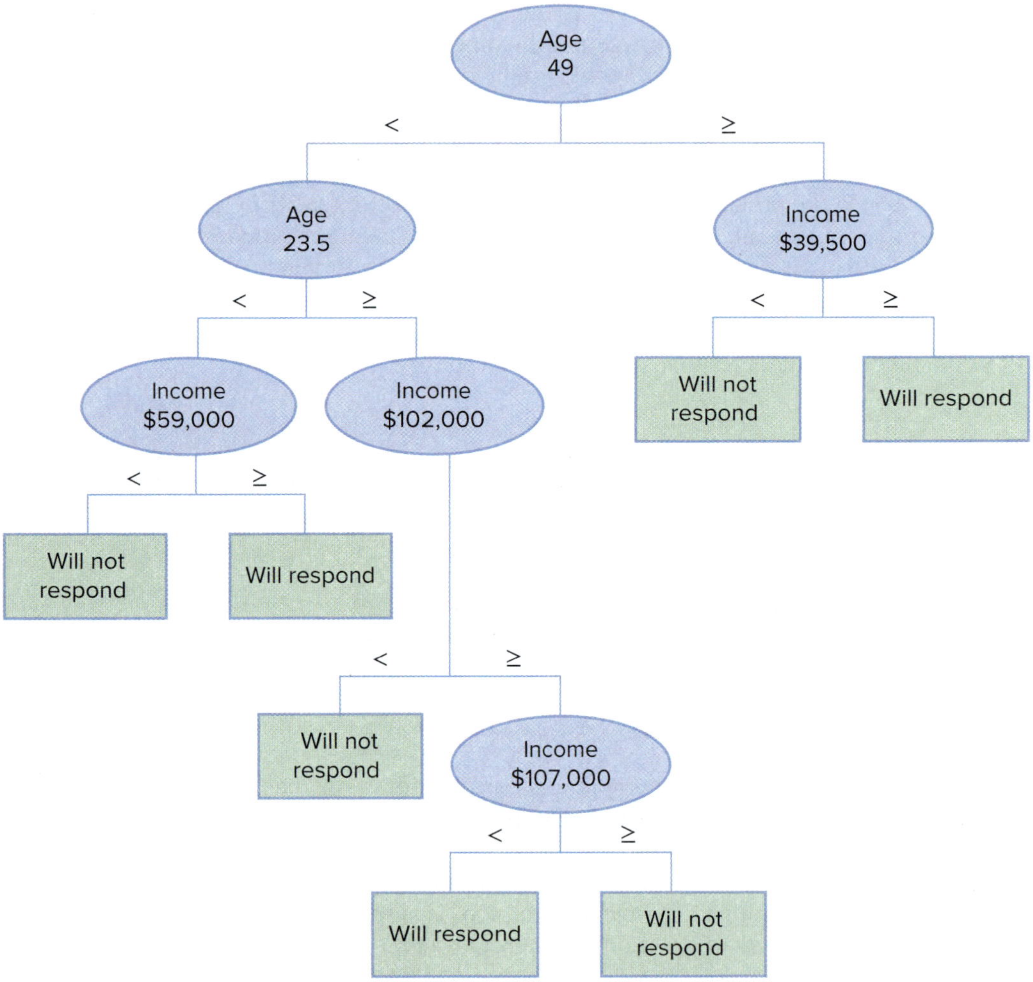

While the classification tree produced in this example is relatively simple due to the fact that we use a small data set with only 20 observations and two predictor variables, a large data set with many predictor variables will likely generate a very complex tree with many levels of decision nodes. As the number of partitions increases, the misclassification rate from the training data set will decrease and eventually reach 0 when all partitions include only cases that belong to the same class. However, for a new data set (e.g., validation data), the misclassification rate will likely decrease initially but increase after a certain point due to overfitting. Therefore, pruning is an important step to optimize the complexity of the final decision tree.

Pruning the Decision Tree

Table 10.3 shows five additional randomly selected observations from the HELOC_Data worksheet that we use as validation data to prune the fully grown classification tree in Figure 10.7.

TABLE 10.3 Validation Data

Age	Sex	Income	HELOC
50	Female	35000	0
23	Male	60000	0
56	Male	87000	1
42	Female	90000	0
62	Male	71000	1

A simple approach to prune a classification tree is to reduce the misclassification rate in the validation data set by replacing a branch of the tree with a leaf node; soon we will show how we build and prune a classification tree with Analytic Solver and R. For example, Figure 10.8 shows a pruned tree where what used to be an interior node with a split point where Age = 23.5 is now replaced with a leaf node. Because the majority of the cases that reach this node belong to Class 0, the leaf node predicts that customers in this subset will not respond to the HELOC offer. This simpler tree yields the best classification performance on the validation data set. All five observations in the validation data are correctly classified. If we score the validation data using the full-grown tree in Figure 10.7, we would get an accuracy rate of 80% as the second observation is misclassified.

Unlike the full-grown tree, the tree obtained from the pruning process is much simpler. The following three rules can be derived from the optimized tree:

- If Age < 49, then the customer will not respond.
- If Age ≥ 49 and Income < $39,500, then the customer will not respond.
- If Age ≥ 49 and Income ≥ $39,500, then the customer will respond.

The optimized tree shows that individuals whose age is 49 or older and income is $39,500 or higher are likely to respond to a HELOC offer from the bank. As this example demonstrates, pruning is effective in determining the optimal complexity of a decision tree and reducing the chance of overfitting.

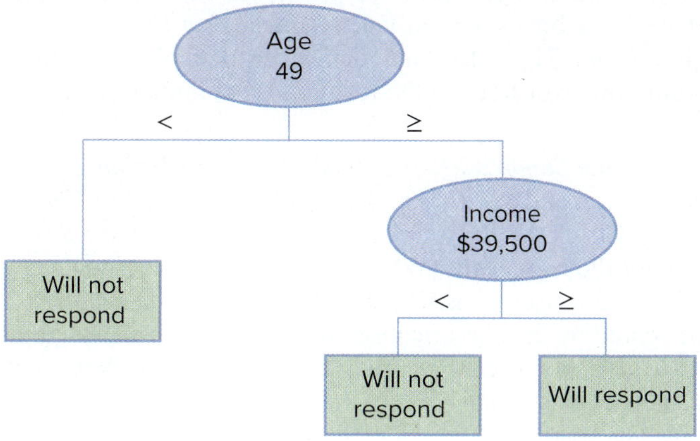

FIGURE 10.8 Resulting decision tree

Using Analytic Solver and R to Develop a Classification Tree

We now demonstrate how to use Analytic Solver and R to build classification trees, using the complete data set. Consider Example 10.5.

FILE
HELOC

EXAMPLE 10.5

Recall from the introductory case that Hayden Sellar, the bank manager of Sunnyville Bank, wants to use historical data from 500 bank customers to develop a classification model for determining whether or not new bank customers will respond to a HELOC offer. He also thinks that Sunnyville Bank is not targeting the right customers when marketing its HELOC products and hopes that the classification model will offer actionable insights for his company. Hayden plans to assess the performance of the model and then classify 20 new bank customers as likely or unlikely to respond to a HELOC offer. Use Analytic Solver and R to build the preferred classification tree, and then use this tree to score the new cases.

SOLUTION:

Using Analytic Solver

a. Open the HELOC_Data worksheet of the ***HELOC*** data file.

b. Choose **Data Mining > Partition** (under the *Data Mining* group) > **Standard Partition**.

c. In the *Standard Data Partition* dialog box, we select the data range $A$1:$D$501 and move Age, Sex, Income, and HELOC to the *Selected Variables* box. Select *Pick up rows randomly* and check the *Set seed* checkbox to use the default random seed of 12345. Choose *Specify percentages* to allocate 50%, 30%, and 20% of the data to training, validation, and test sets, respectively. Click **OK**.

d. Analytic Solver will create a new worksheet called STDPartition with the partitioned data. With the STDPartition worksheet active, choose **Data Mining > Classify > Classification Tree** to open the *Classification Tree* dialog box. In the **Data** tab, select and move the predictor variables Age and Income to the *Selected Variables* box and Sex to the *Categorical Variables* box. Select HELOC as the *Output Variable*. Accept other defaults. Click *Next*.

e. In the **Parameters** tab, check the *Prune (Using Validation Set)* checkbox and click on the *Tree for Scoring* button. Select *Best Pruned*. Click *Done*. This selection tells Analytic Solver to score cases using the best-pruned tree to evaluate the performance of the classification tree and score new cases. Check the *Show Feature Importance* checkbox and click on the *Trees to Display* button. Check the boxes next to *Fully Grown*, *Best Pruned*, and *Minimum Error*. Click *Done*. This tells Analytic Solver to display the full, best-pruned, and minimum error trees in the results. Accept other defaults. Click *Next*.

f. In the **Scoring** tab, check the *Summary Report* boxes for *Score Training Data, Score Validation Data,* and *Score Test Data.* Also check the *Lift Charts* box for *Score Test Data.* Check the *In Worksheet* check box under the *Score New Data* section. Under the **New Data (WS)** tab, select HELOC_Score in the *Worksheet* box. These 20 cases of new bank customers in *Data Range* $A$1:$C$21 will be scored by the classification tree algorithm. Make sure the *First Row Contains Headers* box is checked and click the *Match By Name* button. Accept other defaults. Click *Finish*.

The CT_Output worksheet shows a prune log that reports the error rate depending on the number of decision nodes. Table 10.4 shows a portion of the prune log listing error rates against decision nodes. The simplest tree with the minimum validation error rate of 0.16 occurs at three decision nodes.

TABLE 10.4 Analytic Solver's Prune Log

# Decision Nodes	Error Rate
0	0.2267
1	0.2267
2	0.2267
3	0.1600
4	0.2000
5	0.2000
6	0.2000

Is there a simpler tree with a validation error rate that is within one standard error of the minimum validation error rate? To answer this question, we have to inspect the tree diagrams. The CT_FullTree worksheet shows the full tree. The full tree is quite complex with many decision nodes. Due to its size, the full tree is not displayed here. The CT_BestTree and CT_MinErrorTree worksheets show the best-pruned and minimum error trees. When comparing these two tree diagrams, we find the best-pruned and minimum error trees are the same. In this example, therefore, no simpler tree with a validation error rate that is within one standard error of the minimum validation error rate can be found.

The best-pruned and minimum error tree is displayed in Figure 10.9. The tree is relatively simple with three decision nodes and seven total nodes if the terminal nodes are included. The predictor variable in the root node is Sex. Because Sex is a categorical variable, Analytic Solver uses the generic value "Set" as the split value.

FIGURE 10.9 Analytic Solver's best-pruned classification tree

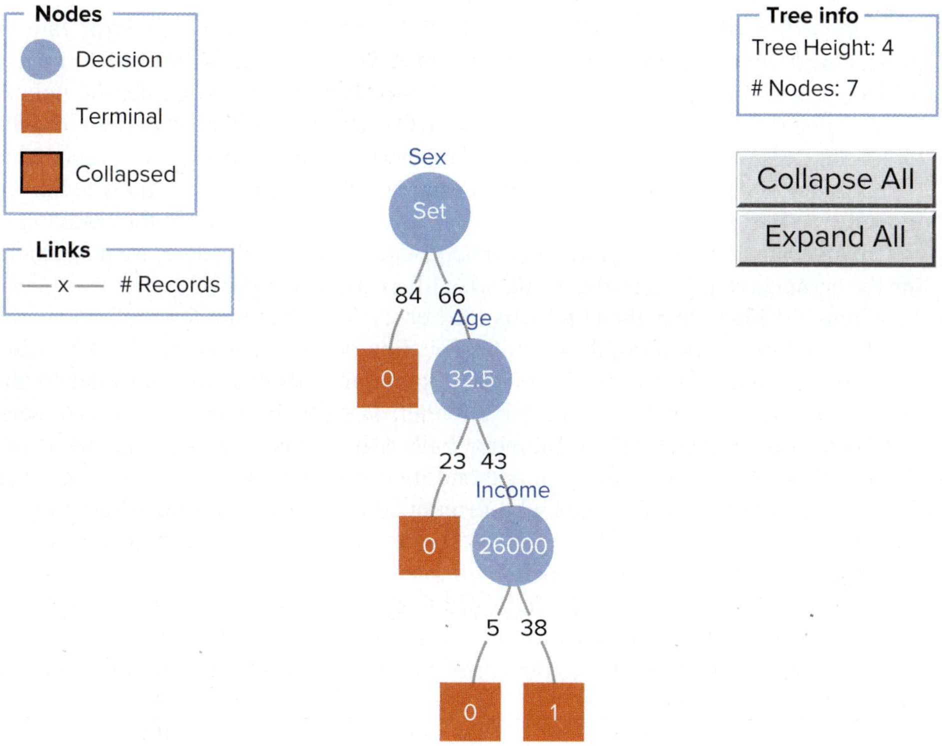

To find out what it means, we place our mouse pointer over the root node, and the following text would appear above the tree:

Decision Node:

Go left if Sex is from set {Female}

Go right if Sex is not from set {Female}

A number of If-Then rules can be derived from the classification tree. For example, one rule is that if the customer is a male who is younger than 32.5 years old, then he will not respond to a HELOC offer. Another rule suggests that if a customer is a male who is 32.5 years or older with an income greater than $26,000, then he will respond to a HELOC offer. Finally, and perhaps more importantly, the classification tree indicates that female customers are not likely to respond to the HELOC offer, confirming the bank manager's intuition that the current marketing campaign is not targeting all the right customers.

Because the validation data were used for pruning, the performance of the classification tree on new data should be assessed using the test data set. To assess the performance of the resulting classification tree, we turn to Testing: Classification Summary in the CT_TestScore worksheet, a portion of which is shown in Figure 10.10.

FIGURE 10.10 Analytic Solver's summary measures

Confusion Matrix

Actual\Predicted	0	1
0	63	11
1	12	14

Error Report

Class	# Cases	# Errors	% Error
0	74	11	14.86486486
1	26	12	46.15384615
Overall	100	23	23

Metrics

Metric	Value
Accuracy (#correct)	77
Accuracy (%correct)	77
Specificity	0.851351351
Sensitivity (Recall)	0.538461538
Precision	0.56
F1 score	0.549019608
Success Class	1
Success Probability	0.5

Source: Microsoft Excel

The performance measures show that the model has an overall error rate of 23%, sensitivity of 0.5385, and specificity of 0.8514. Note that these performance measures are highly sensitive to the cutoff value used. In this example, the default cutoff value is 0.5. If we lower the cutoff value, more cases will be classified into the target class, resulting in different values for the performance measures. To evaluate the performance of the classification tree using a different cutoff value, in Analytic Solver, input the desired cutoff value in the *Success Probability Cutoff:* box in the **Data** tab in step d. To evaluate model performance independent of the cutoff value, we now examine the cumulative lift chart, the decile-wise lift chart, and the ROC curve.

Figure 10.11a shows the cumulative lift chart. The blue line lies well above the red diagonal line, indicating that the classification tree performs considerably better in terms of predicting whether or not a potential customer will respond to the HELOC offer, compared to the baseline model. The lift chart shows that if we send a HELOC offer to the 50 bank customers (half of the test data sample size) who have the highest predicted probability of responding to the offer, we will be able to reach 22 out of 26 (84.6%) individuals who responded to a HELOC offer. Alternately, if we send the offer to 50 randomly chosen customers, we would reach only 13 of the customers who responded to the offer.

Figure 10.11b shows the decile-wise lift chart. The first 10% of potential customers selected by the classification tree, for example, include 1.92 times as many customers who would respond to the HELOC offer, compared to a random selection of 10% of potential customers.

Finally, the ROC curve (see Figure 10.11c) shows that the classification tree performs much better than the baseline model in terms of sensitivity and specificity across all cutoff values. The area under the curve (AUC) is 0.7710, which is closer to the optimum classifier (AUC = 1) as compared to the random classifier (AUC = 0.5).

FIGURE 10.11 Analytic Solver's performance charts

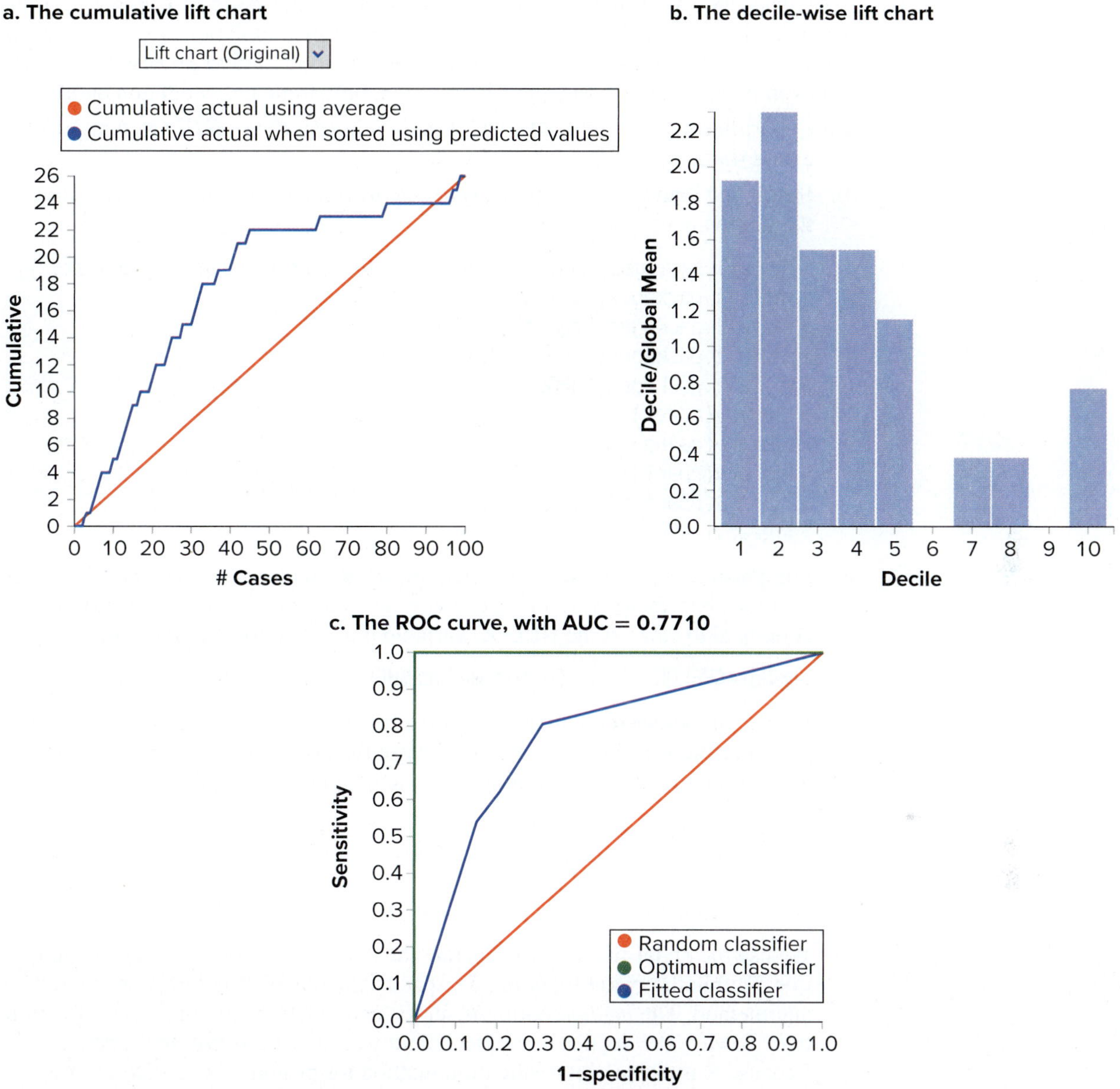

The CT_NewScore worksheet shows the classification predictions for the 20 records of new customers. The results are summarized in Table 10.5. As shown

TABLE 10.5 Analytic Solver's Scoring Results

Record ID	Prediction: HELOC	PostProb: 0	PostProb: 1	Age	Sex	Income
Record 1	0	0.9191	0.0809	25	Female	45000
Record 2	0	0.7368	0.2632	23	Male	22000
⋮	⋮	⋮	⋮	⋮	⋮	⋮
Record 20	1	0.2969	0.7031	51	Male	43000

in the Prediction: HELOC column, the first two potential customers are classified as not likely to respond to a HELOC offer, while the last customer is likely to respond. The PostProb:0 and PostProb:1 columns provide the predicted probabilities of the customer belonging to Class 0 and Class 1, respectively.

Using R

The most popular algorithms for building decision trees in R can be found in the *rpart* package. As in the case of the KNN method discussed in Chapter 9, while Analytic Solver uses three-way partitioning (i.e., train, validation, and test data) for building decision trees, R implements a *k*-fold cross-validation process for pruning decision trees using two-way partitioning (i.e., only train and validation data).

a. Import the data from the HELOC_Data worksheet of the ***HELOC*** data file into a data frame (table) and label it myData.

b. Install and load the *caret*, *gains*, *rpart*, *rpart.plot*, and *pROC* packages using the following commands. Enter:

```
>install.packages("caret", dependencies = c("Depends", "Suggests"))
>install.packages("gains")
>install.packages("rpart")
>install.packages("rpart.plot")
>install.packages("pROC")
>library(caret)
>library(gains)
>library(rpart)
>library(rpart.plot)
>library(pROC)
```

c. For constructing a classification tree model, R requires that the target variable, HELOC, be a factor variable, a categorical data type. We use the **as.factor** command to convert the HELOC variable into a categorical type. Enter:

```
>myData$HELOC <- as.factor(myData$HELOC)
```

d. We use the **set.seed** command to set the random seed to 1, thus generating the same partitions as in this example. We use the **createDataPartition** function to partition the data into training (70%) and validation (30%). Enter:

```
>set.seed(1)
>myIndex <- createDataPartition(myData$HELOC, p=0.7, list = FALSE)
>trainSet <- myData[myIndex,]
>validationSet <- myData[-myIndex,]
```

e. We use the **rpart** function to generate the default classification tree, default_tree. Within the **rpart** function, we specify the model structure, data source, and method. The *method* option is set to "class" for developing a classification tree. To view the details about the default tree, use the **summary** function. Because R uses the cross-validation method for pruning the tree, to ensure consistency of the cross-validation results, we use the **set.seed** function to set a random seed of 1. Enter:

```
>set.seed(1)
>default_tree <- rpart(HELOC ~ ., data=trainSet, method="class")
>summary(default_tree)
```

f. To view the classification tree visually, use the **prp** function. The *type* option is set equal to 1 so that all nodes except the leaf nodes are labeled in the tree diagram. The *extra* option is set equal to 1 so that the number of observations that fall into each node are displayed. The *under* option is set equal to TRUE to put the number of cases under each decision node in the diagram. Enter:

```
>prp(default_tree, type=1, extra=1, under = TRUE)
```

Figure 10.12 shows the default classification tree. The first decision node is on the Sex variable, followed by Age and Income splits. Note that R presents decision trees in a slightly different format as Analytic Solver does. The root node provides information about how to interpret the tree. For example, in Figure 10.12, the root node shows that if Sex is "Female" then go to the left branch, otherwise go to the right branch. The subsequent decision nodes follow the same format. For example, the second decision node suggests that if Age is less than 25 then go to the left branch, otherwise go to the right branch.

FIGURE 10.12 R's default classification tree

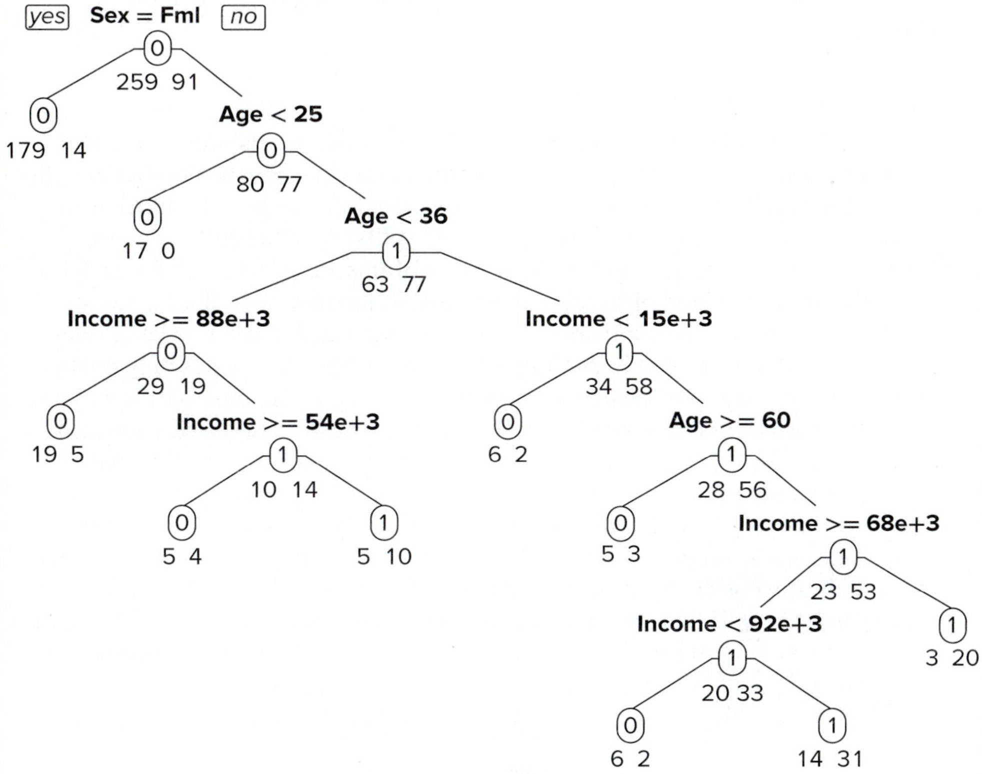

How are the number of splits determined in the default classification tree? The **rpart** function uses the complexity parameter (cp) to determine when to stop growing the tree. If the cost of adding another split to the tree exceeds the value of cp, then the tree growth will not continue. The default cp value for the **rpart** function is 0.01. However, in most cases, it is very difficult to know which cp value will produce the best-performing tree beforehand. Therefore, a common practice is to grow the full tree and then prune it to a less-complex tree based on the classification errors produced by a built-in cross-validation process of the **rpart** function. By identifying the value of cp associated with the smallest cross-validated classification error, we can create the minimum error tree. Alternatively, we can produce the best-pruned tree, which is the smallest tree with an error rate that is within one standard error of the minimum error rate. Next, we will demonstrate the pruning process to optimize the complexity of the tree.

g. We first grow the full tree by using the **rpart** function. We set the options *cp* equal to 0, *minsplit* equal to 2, and *minbucket* equal to 1. The *minsplit* option specifies the minimum number of observations in the parent node that can be split further, and the *minbucket* option specifies the minimum number of observations that are allowed in the leaf node. These settings ensure that the largest possible tree will be produced. We plot the full tree using the **prp**

function. Again, to ensure consistency of the cross-validation results, we specify a random seed of 1 using the **set.seed** function. Enter:

```
>set.seed(1)
>full_tree <- rpart(HELOC ~ ., data= trainSet, method="class",
cp=0, minsplit=2, minbucket=1)
>prp(full_tree, type=1, extra=1, under = TRUE)
```

The full tree in this case is very complex, so it is not displayed here.

h. To identify the value of cp that is associated with the smallest cross-validated classification error, we use the **printcp** function to display the complexity parameter table. Enter:

```
>printcp(full_tree)
```

Figure 10.13 displays the complexity parameter table for the nine candidate trees with increasing complexity. The nsplit column shows the number of splits for each tree. The number of leaf nodes for each tree can be calculated using nsplit + 1. For example, the last tree has 82 splits, so it has 83 leaf nodes.

The rel error column shows the fraction of misclassified cases for each tree relative to the fraction of misclassified cases in the root node if all cases are classified into the predominant class. As you can see, the last tree has a relative error of 0 because it is the fully grown tree whose leaf nodes only contain cases that belong to the same class; therefore, there are no misclassified cases.

The xerror column shows the cross-validation errors associated with each candidate tree. It is the recommended measure for identifying the tree that can potentially perform well on new data sets. As you can see from the xerror column, the cross-validation errors decrease initially as the classification tree becomes more complex and then increase after a certain point. This is common and indicative of the overfitting problems with complex tree models. The fourth tree, with six splits, has the lowest cross-validation error (0.83516 relative to the cross-validation error of the root node); therefore, it is the minimum error tree.

The xstd column can be used to identify the best-pruned tree, which is the smallest tree with an error that is within one standard error of the minimum

FIGURE 10.13 R's complexity parameter table

```
Classification tree:
rpart(formula = HELOC ~ ., data = trainSet, method = "class",
    cp = 0, minsplit = 2, minbucket = 1)

Variables actually used in tree construction:
[1] Age    Sex Income

Root node error: 91/350 = 0.26

n= 350

         CP nsplit rel error  xerror     xstd
1 0.0769231      0   1.00000 1.00000 0.090177
2 0.0732601      2   0.84615 1.02198 0.090810
3 0.0439560      5   0.62637 0.97802 0.089524
4 0.0164835      6   0.58242 0.83516 0.084763
5 0.0109890      8   0.54945 0.86813 0.085945
6 0.0073260     17   0.45055 0.84615 0.085163
7 0.0054945     28   0.36264 0.91209 0.087442
8 0.0043956     58   0.13187 0.94505 0.088507
9 0.0000000     82   0.00000 0.95604 0.088851
```

error tree. In this case, no simpler tree has a cross-validation error that meets this criterion. In other words, no simpler tree has a relative cross-validation error that is less than 0.83516+0.084763 or 0.919923. Therefore, the best-pruned tree and minimum error tree are the same tree. However, in many cases, you may find that the best-pruned and minimum error trees are two different trees.

Figure 10.14 displays a hypothetical complexity parameter table from another classification tree. In this case, the third tree, with five splits, has a relative cross-validation error (0.87912) that is within one standard error of the minimum error (0.81319 + 0.083945 = 0.897135); hence, the third tree, with five splits, is the best-pruned tree. Next, we use the value of cp associated with the third tree to produce our pruned tree.

FIGURE 10.14 A hypothetical complexity parameter table in R

	CP	nsplit	rel error	xerror	xstd	
1	0.0769231	0	1.00000	1.00000	0.090177	
2	0.0732601	2	0.84615	0.97802	0.089524	
3	0.0439560	5	0.62637	0.87912	0.086328	← Best-pruned tree
4	0.0164835	6	0.58242	0.87912	0.086328	
5	0.0109890	8	0.54945	0.81319	0.083945	← Minimum error tree
6	0.0073260	17	0.45055	0.92308	0.087802	
7	0.0054945	28	0.36264	0.93407	0.088157	
8	0.0043956	58	0.13187	0.97802	0.089524	
9	0.0000000	82	0.00000	1.03297	0.091119	

i. We use the **prune** function to create the pruned tree by using the cp value associated with the fourth tree. Please note that the cp values provided in R results are rounded to seven digits after the decimal points. To ensure that we do not use a cp value that is less than the actual cp value, we use a cp value that is slightly larger than the cp value displayed in the table but lower than the cp value for the next smaller tree. In this case, we will use 0.0164836, a number that is slightly larger than the cp number associated with the fourth tree (0.0164835). We display the pruned tree using the **prp** function. Enter:

```
>pruned_tree <- prune(full_tree, cp=0.0164836)
>prp(pruned_tree, type=1, extra=1, under = TRUE)
```

Figure 10.15 displays the pruned tree, which has six splits and seven leaf nodes. Note that this is a much simpler tree with fewer branches, compared to the default tree in Figure 10.12. Next, we will evaluate the performance of the pruned tree using the validation data set.

j. We predict the class memberships of the observations in the validation data set using the **predict** function. We set the *type* option equal to "class" so that the class membership is produced instead of its probability. Enter:

```
>predicted_class <- predict(pruned_tree, validationSet,
type="class")
```

k. The confusion matrix can be created by comparing the predicted class memberships and actual class memberships of the validation data set. We use the **confusionMatrix** function to produce the confusion matrix and various performance measures. The *positive = "1"* option specifies 1 as the target class (respond to a HELOC offer). Enter:

```
>confusionMatrix(predicted_class, valid.data$HELOC, positive="1")
```

FIGURE 10.15 R's pruned tree

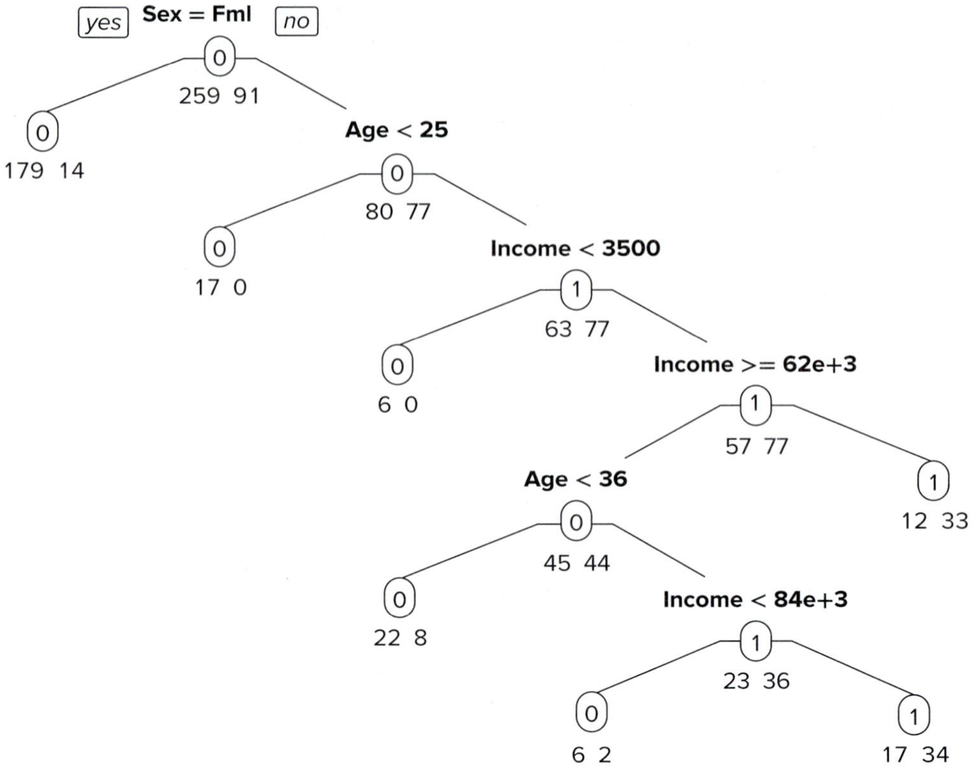

Figure 10.16 reports the confusion matrix and relevant performance measures. The model has an overall accuracy rate of 76.67%, sensitivity of 0.4872, and specificity of 0.8649. These measures suggest that, while the overall accuracy rate is relatively high, the model classifies a much larger portion of the non-target class (customers who do not respond to HELOC offers) cases than

FIGURE 10.16 R's summary measures

```
Confusion Matrix and Statistics

          Reference
Prediction  0  1
         0 96 20
         1 15 19

               Accuracy : 0.7667
                 95% CI : (0.6907, 0.8318)
    No Information Rate : 0.74
    P-Value [Acc > NIR] : 0.2602

                  Kappa : 0.3673

 Mcnemar's Test P-Value : 0.4990

            Sensitivity : 0.4872
            Specificity : 0.8649
         Pos Pred Value : 0.5588
         Neg Pred Value : 0.8276
             Prevalence : 0.2600
         Detection Rate : 0.1267
   Detection Prevalence : 0.2267
      Balanced Accuracy : 0.6760

       'Positive' class : 1
```

target class (customers who respond to HELOC offers) cases correctly using the default cutoff rate of 0.5. As noted earlier, these performance measures are highly sensitive to the cutoff value. In this example, the default cutoff value of 0.5 is much higher than the proportion of target class cases in the data set, which is 0.26. By lowering the cutoff value to be close to the actual class distribution, we will be able to classify more cases into the target class and improve the sensitivity measure. This is illustrated in the following steps.

l. To evaluate the predictive performance of the classification tree model using a different cutoff value in R, we first compute the probability of each validation case belonging to the target class instead of its class membership. In the **predict** function, we set the *type* option equal to 'prob' to predict the probability values. Enter:

```
>predicted_prob <- predict(pruned_tree, validationSet, type="prob")
>head(predicted_prob)
```

Figure 10.17 shows the probabilities associated with the first few cases. The first column lists the probabilities of the cases belonging to Class 0, while the second column lists the probabilities of the cases belonging to Class 1. To determine the class memberships of cases using a cutoff value other than the default value of 0.5 (for example, 0.26, in order to accurately classify more Class 1 cases), we compare the values in the second column to the new cutoff value.

```
          0          1
1 0.9274611 0.07253886
2 0.7333333 0.26666667
3 1.0000000 0.00000000
4 0.3333333 0.66666667
5 0.7500000 0.25000000
6 0.2666667 0.73333333
```

FIGURE 10.17
R's predicted probabilities

m. To construct a confusion matrix using the new cutoff value of 0.26, we use the **ifelse** function to determine the class memberships. We use the **as.factor** function to convert the class membership to factor, which is the same data type as the target variable, HELOC. Enter:

```
>confusionMatrix(as.factor(ifelse(predicted_prob[,2]>0.26, '1',
'0')), validationSet$HELOC, positive = '1')
```

The resulting confusion matrix (not shown here) provides the performance measures of the pruned decision tree using the cutoff value of 0.26. Please verify that in the new confusion matrix, accuracy, sensitivity, and specificity are 0.7667, 0.6410, and 0.8108, respectively. The new cutoff value allows the manager of the bank to identify more target class cases correctly as signified by the higher sensitivity value.

To evaluate model performance independent of the cutoff value, we now examine the cumulative lift chart, the decile-wise lift chart, and the ROC curve.

n. We first convert the target variable (HELOC) to a numerical data type as required by the *gains* package using the **as.numeric** function. We generate the cumulative lift table using the **gains** function. The **gains** function requires two inputs: actual class memberships and predicted target class probabilities. Because in Figure 10.17, '1' is the target class, we refer to column two for the predicted target class probabilities. Enter:

```
>validationSet$HELOC <- as.numeric(as.character(validationSet$HELOC))
>gains_table <- gains(validationSet$HELOC, predicted_prob[,2])
>gains_table
```

Figure 10.18 shows the cumulative gains table. Because there are only six possible target class probabilities in the pruned tree—0.73, 0.67, 0.27, 0.25, 0.07, and 0.00—that can be assigned to each case, the gains function generates only six groups instead of the default 10 groups, one for each unique probability value. (Note: These values are rounded to two digits after the decimal point. That is why you will get the warning: Fewer distinct predicted values than groups requested.)

FIGURE 10.18 R's cumulative gains table

Depth of File	N	Cume N	Mean Resp	Cume Mean Resp	Cume Pct of Total Resp	Lift Index	Cume Lift	Mean Model Score
14	21	21	0.52	0.52	28.2%	201	201	0.73
23	13	34	0.62	0.56	48.7%	237	215	0.67
31	12	46	0.50	0.54	64.1%	192	209	0.27
37	9	55	0.78	0.58	82.1%	299	224	0.25
92	83	138	0.08	0.28	100.0%	32	109	0.07
100	12	150	0.00	0.26	100.0%	0	100	0.00

o. Because the R instructions for the cumulative lift chart, the decile-wise lift chart, and the ROC curve have been discussed in detail in Chapter 9, we group the commands here. Enter:

```
>plot(c(0, gains_table$cume.pct.of.total*sum(validationSet$
HELOC)) ~ c(0, gains_table$cume.obs), xlab = "# of cases",
ylab="Cumulative", main="Cumulative Lift Chart", type ="l")
>lines(c(0, sum(validationSet$HELOC)) ~ c(0, dim(validationSet)
[1]), col="red", lty=2)
>barplot(gains_table$mean.resp/mean(validationSet$HELOC),
names.arg=gains_table$depth, xlab="Percentile", ylab="Lift",
ylim=c(0,3), main = "Decile- Wise Lift Chart")
>roc_object<- roc(validataionSet$HELOC, predicted_prob[,2])
>plot.roc(roc_object)
>auc(roc_object)
```

Figure 10.19a displays the cumulative lift chart. The chart shows that the classification model shows superior predictive power compared to the default model. Sunnyville Bank can reach a larger portion of potential customers who will actually respond to the HELOC offer by targeting a smaller percentage of the potential customers with the highest predicted probability of responding to the offer. Figure 10.19b displays the decile-wise lift chart. If Sunnyville Bank sends offers to the top 14% of the potential customers with the highest predicted probability of responding to a HELOC offer, it would be able to capture twice as many individuals who actually respond to the HELOC offer as compared to if 14% of the customers are randomly selected. Figure 10.19c displays the ROC curve. Again, this curve shows that the classification tree model outperforms the baseline model in terms of sensitivity and specificity across all cutoff values. The AUC value of 0.805 also reinforces this finding.

p. Finally, to score the 20 new cases, we import the data from the HELOC_Score worksheet of the ***HELOC*** data file into a data frame (table) called myScoreData and use the **predict** function to produce the predicted class memberships and probabilities for the new cases using our classification tree. Enter:

```
>predicted_class_score <- predict(pruned_tree, myScoreData,
type="class")
>predicted_class_score
>predicted_class_prob <- predict(pruned_tree, myScoreData,
type="prob")
>predicted_class_prob
```

FIGURE 10.19 R's performance charts

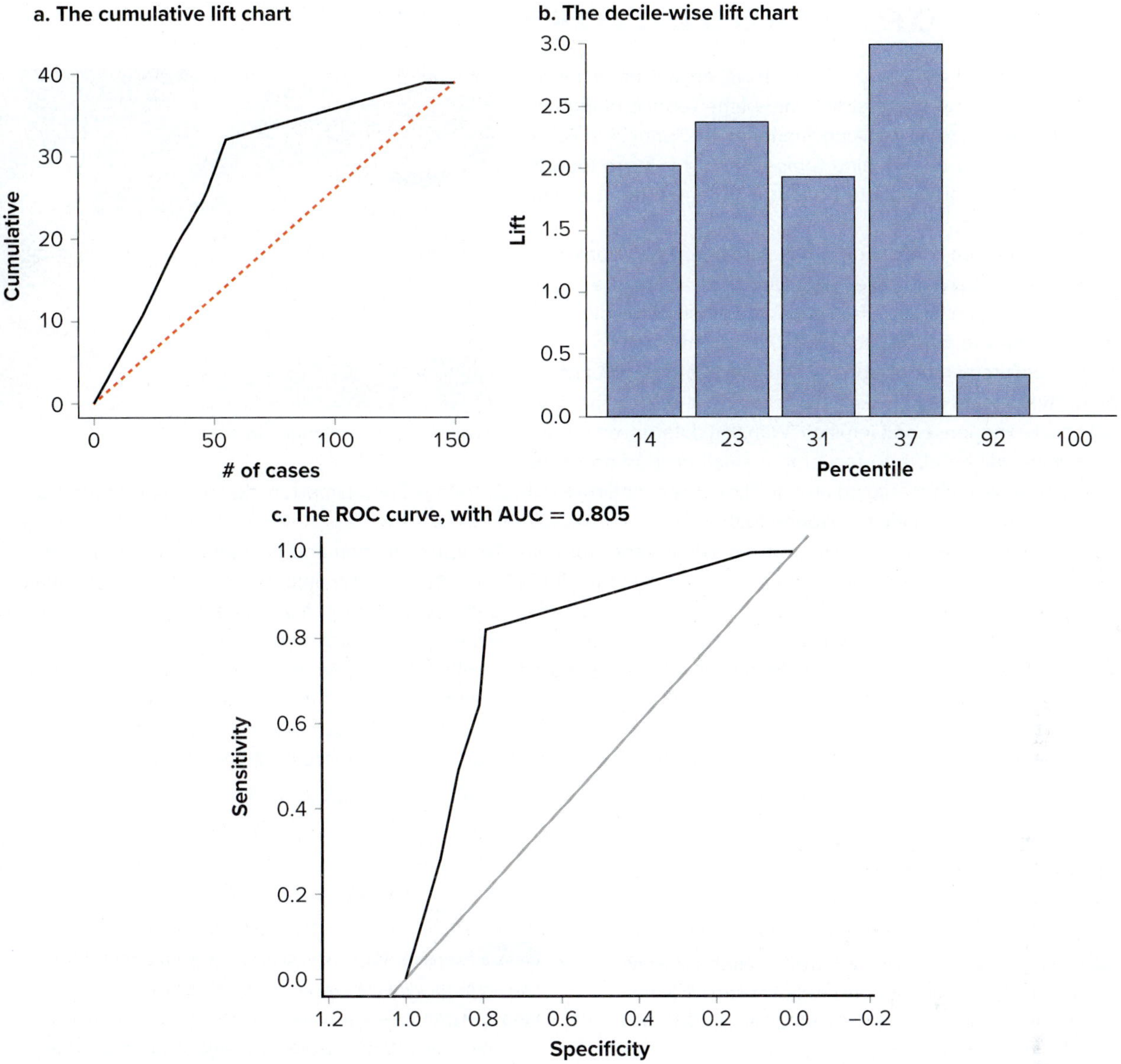

The scoring results are summarized in Table 10.6. The predicted classes for the cases are similar to those predicted by the classification tree constructed in Analytic Solver although the probabilities are slightly different due to the differences in constructing the trees.

TABLE 10.6 R's Scoring Results

Record ID	Prediction: HELOC	PostProb: 0	PostProb: 1	Age	Sex	Income
Record 1	0	0.9275	0.0725	25	Female	45000
Record 2	0	1	0	23	Male	22000
⋮	⋮	⋮	⋮	⋮	⋮	⋮
Record 20	1	0.2667	0.7333	51	Male	43000

SYNOPSIS OF INTRODUCTORY CASE

Syda Productions/Shutterstock

Data-driven marketing decisions can help an organization better target potential customers and at the same time reduce marketing costs. Hayden Sellar, retail banking manager of Sunnyville Bank, is excited about using data mining tools to help his team identify customers who are more likely to be interested in certain banking products and services.

Experimenting with a relatively small sample of 500 bank customers who previously received HELOC offers from the bank, Hayden and his team built a classification tree to predict which new customers are likely to respond to HELOC offers. The model offers a classification accuracy rate of about 77%, which is a significant improvement over what Hayden and his team were able to achieve using only past experience and intuition. With this data-driven model, Sunnyville Bank will be able to focus on a small proportion of the customers who have high predicted probabilities of responding to HELOC offers. For example, male customers in their late 30s with high income are likely to respond to the offer.

A closer study of the tree diagram also reveals a rather troubling issue for Hayden and his team. The decision tree predicts that female customers are not likely to respond to the HELOC offer. At the same time, Hayden knows that female customers account for a substantial portion of Sunnyville customers. Could the alarmingly low percentage of female customers who are interested in HELOC products be due to the unconscious bias in the bank's marketing materials? To answer this question, Hayden and his team decide to review the previous ads of HELOC products. As they expected, all previous HELOC ads indeed seem to have a bias toward male customers. This confirms Hayden's intuition that Sunnyville's current marketing strategy is not targeting the right customers. As a result, he has scheduled to meet and work with the bank's marketing team to eliminate any unconscious bias in its marketing materials and focus more on the female customers.

EXERCISES 10.2

Note: **AS** and **R** indicate that the exercise problems must be solved using Analytic Solver and R, respectively. For Analytic Solver, partition data sets into 50% training, 30% validation, and 20% test and use 12345 as the default random seed. For R, partition data sets into 70% training and 30% validation. Use the statement set.seed(1) to specify the random seed of 1 for both data partitioning and cross-validation. Some data files have two worksheets (for example, Exercise_10.7_Data and Exercise_10.7_Score worksheets) for model development and scoring new records. If the predictor variable values are in the character format, then treat the predictor variable as a categorical variable. Otherwise, treat the predictor variable as a numerical variable.

Mechanics

1. **FILE** ***Exercise_10.1.*** The accompanying data set contains two predictor variables, age and income, and one binary target variable, newspaper subscription (subscribe), indicating whether or not the person subscribes to a newspaper. A media company wants to create a decision tree for predicting whether or not a person will subscribe to the newspaper.
   a. List the possible split values for age in ascending order.
   b. List the possible split values for income in ascending order.
2. **FILE** ***Exercise_10.2.*** The accompanying data set contains two predictor variables, average annual number of sunny days (days) and average annual precipitation (precipitation), and one numeric target variable, average annual crop yield in bushels per acre (yield). An agricultural researcher wants to create a decision tree for predicting the annual crop yield in bushels per acre for various areas.
   a. List the possible split values for days in ascending order.
   b. List the possible split values for precipitation in ascending order.
3. After a data set was partitioned, the first partition contains 43 cases that belong to Class 1 and 12 cases that belong to Class 0, and the second partition contains 24 cases that belong to Class 1 and 121 cases that belong to Class 0.
   a. Compute the Gini impurity index for the root node.
   b. Compute the Gini impurity index for partition 1.
   c. Compute the Gini impurity index for partition 2.
   d. Compute the Gini impurity index for the split.
4. After a data set was partitioned using the split value of 45.5 for age. The age < 45.5 partition contains 22 patients with a diabetes diagnosis and 178 patients without a diabetes diagnosis, and the age ≥ 45.5 partition contains 48 patients

with a diabetes diagnosis and 152 patients without a diabetes diagnosis.

a. Compute the Gini impurity index for the root node.
b. Compute the Gini impurity index for the age < 45.5 partition.
c. Compute the Gini impurity index for the age ≥ 45.4 partition.
d. Compute the Gini impurity index for the split.
e. State the rules generated from this split.

5. **FILE** ***Exercise_10.5.*** Use the accompanying data set to answer the following questions.
   a. Which split value for age would best separate the newspaper subscribers from nonsubscribers based on the Gini impurity index?
   b. Which split value for income would best separate the newspaper subscribers from nonsubscribers based on the Gini impurity index?
   c. Between the best split values for age and income, which one should be chosen as the first split for a decision tree that predicts whether someone is a newspaper subscriber or not?
   d. State the rules generated from this split.
6. The classification tree below relates type of wine (A, B, or C) to alcohol content, flavonoids, malic acid, and magnesium. Classify each of the following wines of unknown class.
   a. Wine with alcohol = 13.3, flavanoids = 1.95, malic acid = 1.03, and magnesium = 114
   b. Wine with alcohol = 11.8, flavanoids = 2.44, malic acid = 0.97, and magnesium = 103
   c. Wine with alcohol = 12.9, flavanoids = 2.21, malic acid = 1.22, and magnesium = 99

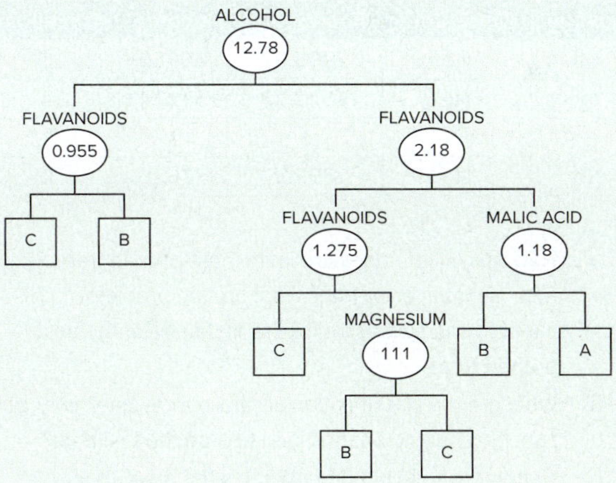

7. **FILE** ***Exercise_10.7.*** **AS** The accompanying data set in the Exercise_10.7_Data worksheet contains four predictor variables (x_1 to x_4) and one binary target variable (y). Select the best-pruned tree for scoring and display the full-grown, best-pruned, and minimum error trees.
   a. What is the minimum error in the prune log for the validation data? How many decision nodes are associated with the minimum error?
   b. Display the best-pruned tree. How many leaf nodes are in the best-pruned tree? How many leaf nodes are in the minimum error tree?
   c. What are the predictor variable and split value for the first split of the best-pruned tree?
   d. What are the classification accuracy rate, sensitivity, specificity, and precision of the best-pruned tree on the test data?
   e. Generate the decile-wise lift chart of the best-pruned tree on the test data. What is the lift value of the leftmost bar of the decile-wise lift chart? What does this value imply?
   f. Generate the ROC curve of the best-pruned tree on the test data. What is the area under the ROC curve (or AUC value)?
   g. Score the new observations in the Exercise_10.7_Score worksheet using the best-pruned tree. What is the predicted response value of the new observations? What is the Class 1 probability of the first observation? Round your answers to four decimal places.
8. **FILE** ***Exercise_10.8.*** **AS** The accompanying data set in the Exercise_10.8_Data worksheet contains four predictor variables (x_1 to x_4) and one binary target variable (y). Select the best-pruned tree for scoring and display the full-grown, best-pruned, and minimum error trees.
   a. What is the minimum error in the prune log for the validation data? How many decision nodes are associated with the minimum error?
   b. Display the best-pruned tree. How many leaf nodes are in the best-pruned tree? How many leaf nodes are in the minimum error tree?
   c. What are the predictor variable and split value for the first split of the best-pruned tree?
   d. What are the classification accuracy rate, sensitivity, specificity, and precision of the best-pruned tree on the test data?
   e. Generate the lift chart of the best-pruned tree on the test data. Does the entire lift curve lie above the baseline?
   f. Generate the ROC curve of the best-pruned tree on the test data. What is the area under the ROC curve (or AUC value)?
   g. Score the new observations in the Exercise_10.8_Score worksheet using the best-pruned tree. What is the predicted response value of the new observations? What is the Class 1 probability of the first observation? Round your answers to four decimal places.
9. **FILE** ***Exercise_10.9.*** **R** The accompanying data set contains five predictor variables (x_1 to x_5) and one binary target variable (y). Follow the instructions below to create classification trees using the Exercise_10.9_Data worksheet.

a. Use the **rpart** function to build a default classification tree. Display the default classification tree. How many leaf nodes are in the default classification tree? What are the predictor variable and split value for the first split of the default classification tree (root node)?
b. Use the **rpart** function to build a fully-grown classification tree. Display the cp table. What is the cp value associated with the lowest cross-validation error? How many splits are in the minimum error tree?
c. Is there a simpler tree within one standard error of the cross-validation error of the minimum error tree? If there is, then what is the cp value associated with the best-pruned tree?
d. Use the prune function to prune the full tree to the minimum error tree. Display the minimum error tree. How many leaf nodes are in the minimum error tree?
e. Assign Class 1 to be the positive class. What are the accuracy, sensitivity, specificity, and precision of the minimum error tree on the validation data?
f. Generate the cumulative lift chart and decile-wise lift chart of the minimum error tree on the validation data. Does the entire lift curve lie above the baseline? What is the lift value of the leftmost bar of the decile-wise lift chart? What does this value imply?
g. Generate the ROC curve of the minimum error tree on the validation data. What is the area under the ROC curve (or AUC value)?
h. Score the new observations in the Exercise_10.9_Score worksheet. What is the predicted response value of the new observations? What is the Class 1 probability of the first observation? Round your answers to four decimal places.

10. FILE ***Exercise_10.10.*** R The accompanying data set contains four predictor variables (x_1 to x_4) and one binary target variable (y). Follow the instructions below to create classification trees using the Exercise_10.10_Data worksheet.

a. Use the **rpart** function to build a default classification tree. Display the default classification tree. How many leaf nodes are in the default classification tree? What are the predictor variable and split value for the first split of the default classification tree (root node)?
b. Use the **rpart** function to build a fully-grown classification tree. Display the cp table. What is the cp value associated with the lowest cross-validation error? How many splits are in the minimum error tree?
c. Is there a simpler tree within one standard error of the cross-validation error of the minimum error tree? If there is, then what is the cp value associated with the best-pruned tree?
d. Use the prune function to prune the full tree to the best-pruned tree or minimum error tree if the answer to part c is "No." Display the pruned tree. How many leaf nodes are in the pruned tree?
e. Assign Class 1 to be the positive class. What are the accuracy, sensitivity, specificity, and precision of the pruned tree on the validation data?
f. Generate the decile-wise lift chart of the pruned tree on the validation data. What is the lift value of the leftmost bar of the decile-wise lift chart? What does this value imply?
g. Generate the ROC curve of the pruned tree on the validation data. What is the area under the ROC curve (or AUC value)?
h. Score the new observations in the Exercise_10.10_Score worksheet using the pruned tree. What is the predicted response value of the new observations? What is the Class 1 probability of the first observation? Round your answers to four decimal places.

Applications

11. FILE ***Travel_Plan.*** AS Jerry Stevenson is the manager of a travel agency. He wants to build a model that can predict whether or not a customer will travel within the next year. He has compiled a data set that contains the following variables: whether the individual has a college degree (College), whether the individual has credit card debt (CreditCard), annual household spending on food (FoodSpend), annual income (Income), and whether the customer has plans to travel within the next year (TravelPlan, 1 = has travel plans, 0 = does not have travel plans). A portion of the Travel_Plan_Data worksheet is shown in the accompanying table. Create a classification tree model for predicting whether or not the customer will travel within the next year (TravelPlan). Select the best-pruned tree for scoring and display the full-grown, best-pruned, and minimum error trees.

College	CreditCard	FoodSpend	Income	TravelPlan
No	No	2905.97	65982	1
Yes	No	4677.03	57274	1
⋮	⋮	⋮	⋮	⋮
No	No	1892.37	77626	0

a. How many leaf nodes are in the best-pruned tree and minimum error tree? What are the predictor variable and split value for the root node of the best-pruned tree?
b. What are the classification accuracy rate, sensitivity, and specificity of the best-pruned tree on the test data?
c. Generate the ROC curve. What is the area under the ROC curve (or AUC value)?
d. Score the two new customers in the Travel_Plan_Score worksheet using the best-pruned tree. What is the probability of the first customer having plans to travel within the next year? What is the probability for the second customer?

12. **FILE** ***Travel_Plan.*** **R** Refer to the previous exercise for a description of the problem and data set. Build a default classification tree to predict whether a customer has plans to travel within the next year. Display the default classification tree.

   a. How many leaf nodes are in the tree? What are the predictor variable and the split value for the first split of the default classification tree?
   b. Build a full-grown tree. Which cp value is associated with the lowest cross-validation error? How many splits are in the minimum error tree?
   c. Is there a simpler tree with a cross-validation error that is within one standard error of the minimum cross-validation error? If there is, then which cp value is associated with the best-pruned tree?
   d. Prune the full tree to the best-pruned tree or the minimum error tree if the answer to part c is "No." Display the tree. How many leaf nodes are in the pruned tree?
   e. Create a confusion matrix and display the various performance measures. Assign Class 1 to be the positive class. What are the accuracy, sensitivity, specificity, and precision of the pruned tree on the validation data?
   f. Display the cumulative lift chart, the decile-wise lift chart, and the ROC curve of the minimum error tree on the validation data. Comment on the performance of the classification tree.
   g. Score the two new customers in the Travel_Plan_Score worksheet using the pruned tree. What is the probability of the first customer having plans to travel within the next 12 months? What is the probability for the second customer? Round your answers to four decimal places.

13. **FILE** ***Continue_Edu.*** **R** Samantha Brown is Director of Continuing Education of a major university. The Continuing Education department offers a wide range of five-week courses to the community during the summer. Samantha would like to find out which community members are more likely to enroll in these summer courses. She has compiled a data set of 2,000 community members that includes the following variables: age (Age), years of marriage (Marriage), annual income (Income), education level (Edu), whether the person owns his or her residence (Own), whether the person owns a pet (Pet), whether the person lives in the city or suburb (City), and whether the person has enrolled in at least one continuing education course from the university before (ContinueEdu, 1 = enrolled, 0 otherwise). A portion of the Continue_Edu_Data worksheet is shown in the accompanying table. Build a default classification tree to predict whether a community member is likely to enroll in summer courses. Display the default classification tree.

Age	Marriage	Income	Edu	Own	Pet	City	ContinueEdu
78	50	64000	1	0	1	1	0
64	35	22000	3	1	0	1	0
⋮	⋮	⋮	⋮	⋮	⋮	⋮	⋮
67	38	146000	1	0	1	1	0

   a. How many leaf nodes are in the tree? What are the predictor variable and the split value for the first split of the default classification tree?
   b. Build a full-grown tree. Which cp value is associated with the lowest cross-validation error? How many splits are in the minimum error tree?
   c. Is there a simpler tree with a cross-validation error that is within one standard error of the minimum cross-validation error? If there is, then which cp value is associated with the best-pruned tree?
   d. Prune the full tree to the best-pruned tree or the minimum error tree if the answer to part c is "No." Display the tree. How many leaf nodes are in the pruned tree?
   e. Create a confusion matrix and display the various performance measures. Assign Class 1 to be the positive class. What are the accuracy, sensitivity, specificity, and precision of the pruned tree on the validation data?
   f. Change the cutoff value to 0.1. Report the accuracy, sensitivity, specificity, and precision rates of the pruned tree on the validation data.
   g. Generate the decile-wise lift chart. What is the lift value of the leftmost bar of the decile-wise lift chart?
   h. Generate the ROC curve. What is the area under the ROC curve (or AUC value)?
   i. Score the two new individuals in the Continue_Edu_Score worksheet using the pruned tree. What is the probability of the first community member enrolling in summer courses? What is the probability for the second community member? Round your answers to four decimal places.

14. **FILE** ***Continue_Edu.*** **AS** Refer to the previous exercise for a description of the problem and data set. Create a classification tree model for predicting whether the community member is likely to enroll in summer courses (ContinueEdu). Select the best-pruned tree for scoring and display the full-grown, best-pruned, and minimum error trees.

   a. How many leaf nodes are in the best-pruned tree and minimum error tree? What are the predictor variable and split value for the root node of the best-pruned tree?
   b. What are the accuracy rate, sensitivity, and specificity of the best-pruned tree on the test data?
   c. Display the cumulative lift chart, the decile-wise lift chart, and the ROC curve. Comment on the performance of the classification model?
   d. Score the two new cases in the Continue_Edu_Score worksheet using the best-pruned tree. What is the probability of the first community member enrolling in summer classes? What is the probability for the second community member?

15. **FILE** ***Church.*** **AS** The following data set in the Church_Data worksheet is used to classify individuals as likely or unlikely to attend church using five predictor variables: years of education (Educ), annual income (Income in $), age, sex

(F = female, M = male), and marital status (Married, Y = yes, N = no). The outcome variable is Church (1 = attends, 0 otherwise). Create a classification tree model for predicting whether the individual is likely to attend church. Select the best-pruned tree for scoring and display the full-grown, best-pruned, and minimum error trees.

Education	Income	Age	Sex	Married	Church
8	97700	71	F	N	1
18	3900	35	F	Y	1
⋮	⋮	⋮	⋮	⋮	⋮
18	151400	49	F	Y	1

a. How many leaf nodes are in the best-pruned tree and minimum error tree? What are the rules that can be derived from the best-pruned tree?

b. What are the accuracy rate, sensitivity, specificity, and precision of the best-pruned tree on the test data?

c. Generate the ROC curve. What is the area under the ROC curve (or AUC value)?

d. Score the cases in the Church_Score worksheet using the best-pruned tree. What percentage of the individuals in the score data set are likely to go to church based on a cutoff probability value of 0.5?

16. FILE ***Church.*** R Refer to the previous exercise for a description of the problem and data set. Build a default classification tree to predict whether an individual is likely to attend church. Display the default classification tree.

a. How many leaf nodes are in the tree? What are the predictor variable and the split value for the first split of the default classification tree? What are the rules that can be derived from the root node?

b. Build a full-grown tree. Which cp value is associated with the lowest cross-validation error?

c. Is there a simpler tree with a cross-validation error that is within one standard error of the minimum cross-validation error? If there is, then which cp value is associated with the best-pruned tree? How many splits are in the best-pruned tree?

d. Prune the full tree to the best-pruned tree or the minimum error tree if the answer to part c is "No." Create a confusion matrix and display the various performance measures. Assign Class 1 to be the positive class. What are the accuracy, sensitivity, specificity, and precision of the pruned tree on the validation data?

e. Display the cumulative lift chart, the decile-wise lift chart, and the ROC curve of the minimum error tree on the validation data. Comment on the performance of the classification tree.

f. Score the cases in the Church_Score worksheet using the best-pruned tree. What percentage of the individuals in the score data set are likely to go to church based on a cutoff probability value of 0.5?

17. FILE ***Mobile_Banking.*** AS Sunnyville Bank wants to identify customers who may be interested in its new mobile banking app. The worksheet called Mobile_Banking_Data contains 500 customer records collected from a previous marketing campaign for the bank's mobile banking app. Each observation in the data set contains the customer's age (Age), sex (Male/Female), education level (Edu, ranging from one to three), income (Income in $1,000s), whether the customer has a certificate of deposit account (CD), and whether the customer downloaded the mobile banking app (App equals 1 if downloaded, 0 otherwise). A portion of the data set is shown in the accompanying table. Create a classification tree model for predicting whether a customer will download the mobile banking app. Assign one as the success class as we are more interested in identifying customers who download the app. Select the best-pruned tree for scoring and display the full-grown, best-pruned, and minimum error trees.

Age	Sex	Edu	Income	CD	App
32	Male	1	0	Yes	0
40	Female	1	1	No	0
⋮	⋮	⋮	⋮	⋮	⋮
26	Female	3	215	Yes	1

a. How many leaf nodes are in the best-pruned tree and minimum error tree? What are the predictor variable and split value for the root node of the best-pruned tree?

b. What are the accuracy rate, sensitivity, specificity, and precision of the best-pruned tree on the test data?

c. Generate the decile-wise lift chart. What is the lift value of the leftmost bar of the decile-wise lift chart? What does it imply?

d. Generate the ROC curve. What is the area under the ROC curve (or AUC value)?

e. Score the 20 customers in the Mobile_Banking_Score worksheet using the best-pruned tree. How many of the 20 new customers will likely download the mobile banking app based on your classification model? What is the probability of the first new customer downloading the app?

18. FILE ***Mobile_Banking.*** R Refer to the previous exercise for a description of the problem and data set. Build a default classification tree to predict whether a customer will download the mobile banking app. Display the default classification tree.

a. How many leaf nodes are in the tree? What are the predictor variable and split value for the first split of the default classification tree? State the rule that can be derived from the first leaf node from the top of the tree diagram.

b. Build a full-grown tree. Which cp value is associated with the lowest cross-validation error?

c. Is there a simpler tree with a cross-validation error that is within one standard error of the minimum cross-validation error? If there is, then which cp value is associated with the best-pruned tree? How many splits are in the best-pruned tree?

d. Prune the full tree to the best-pruned tree or the minimum error tree if the answer to part c is "No." Display the tree. Create a confusion matrix and display the various performance measures. Assign Class 1 to be the positive class. What are the accuracy, sensitivity, specificity, and precision of the pruned tree on the validation data?

e. Generate the decile-wise lift chart. What is the lift value of the leftmost bar of the decile-wise lift chart?

f. Generate the ROC curve. What is the area under the ROC curve (or AUC value)?

g. Score the 20 new customers in the Mobile_Banking_Score worksheet using the pruned tree. How many customers will likely download the mobile banking app based on your classification model? What is the probability of the first customer to download the mobile banking app? Round your answer to 4 decimal places.

19. **FILE** ***Graduate.*** **R** Dereck Anderson is an institutional researcher at a major university. The university has set a goal to increase the number of students who graduate within four years by 20% in five years. Dereck is asked by his boss to create a model that would flag any student who has a high likelihood of not being able to graduate within four years. He has compiled a data set of 2,000 previous students of the university that contains the following variables: sex (M/F), whether the student is Caucasian (White), high school GPA (HS GPA), SAT score (SAT), College GPA (GPA), whether the student's parents are college educated (College Parent), and whether the student graduated within four years (Grad). A portion of the *Graduate_Data* worksheet is shown in the accompanying table. Build a default classification tree to predict whether the student will be able to graduate within four years (Grad). Display the classification tree.

Sex	White	HS GPA	SAT	GPA	College Parent	Grad
F	1	4.14	1410	2.949	1	1
M	1	3.3	1260	2.789	1	1
⋮	⋮	⋮	⋮	⋮	⋮	⋮
M	0	3.08	950	2.09	0	0

a. What are the predictor variable and the split value for the first split of the default classification tree? State the rules that can be derived from the root node.

b. Build a full-grown tree. Which cp value is associated with the lowest cross-validation error?

c. Is there a simpler tree with a cross-validation error that is within one standard error of the minimum cross-validation error? If there is, then which cp value is associated with the best-pruned tree?

d. Prune the full tree to the best-pruned tree or the minimum error tree if the answer to part c is "No." Display the tree. Is the pruned tree the same tree as the default tree created in a?

e. Create a confusion matrix and display the various performance measures. Assign Class 1 to be the positive class. What are the accuracy, sensitivity, specificity, and precision of the pruned tree on the validation data?

f. Generate the cumulative lift chart. Does the lift curve lie above the baseline? What does this mean?

g. Generate the ROC curve. What is the area under the ROC curve (or AUC value)? What does the AUC value imply?

h. Score the three university students in the Graduate_Score worksheet using the pruned tree. How many of these three students will be able to graduate within four years according to your model?

20. **FILE** ***Graduate.*** **AS** Refer to the previous exercise for a description of the problem and data set. Create a classification tree model for predicting whether the student will be able to graduate within four years (Grad). Assign 0 as the success class as we are more interested in identifying students who are at the risk of not being able to graduate within four years. Select the best-pruned tree for scoring and display the full-grown, best-pruned, and minimum error trees.

a. How many leaf nodes are in the best-pruned tree and minimum error tree? What are the rules that can be derived from the best-pruned tree?

b. What are the accuracy rate, sensitivity, specificity, and precision of the best-pruned tree on the test data?

c. Generate the cumulative lift chart. Does the lift curve lie above the baseline? What does this mean?

d. Generate the ROC curve. What is the area under the ROC curve (or AUC value)?

e. Score the three university students in the Graduate_Score worksheet using the best-pruned tree. Will these three students be able to graduate within four years according to your model?

21. **FILE** ***In_App_Pur.*** **AS** Monstermash, an online game app development company, wants to be able to predict which gamers are likely to make in-app purchases. Ranon Weatherby, the company's data analyst, has compiled a data set about customers that contains the following variables: customer age (Age), sex (1 if male, 0 otherwise), household income (Income in $1,000s), the number of years playing online games (Years), the number of hours playing online games per week (Hours), whether the customer has a credit card (CreditCard), whether the customer has a Facebook profile (Facebook), and whether the customer has made in-app purchases before (Buy). A portion of the In_App_Pur_Data worksheet is shown in the accompanying table. Create a classification tree model for predicting whether the customer will make in-app purchases (Buy). Select the best-pruned tree for scoring and display the full-grown, best-pruned, and minimum error trees.

Age	Sex	Income	Years	Hours	CreditCard	Facebook	Buy
40	0	139	3	25	1	1	0
26	0	138	7	4	1	1	0
⋮	⋮	⋮	⋮	⋮	⋮	⋮	⋮
44	1	64	9	26	1	0	1

a. How many leaf nodes are in the best-pruned tree and minimum error tree? What are the predictor variable and split value for the root node of the best-pruned tree?
b. Describe the rules produced by the best-pruned tree.
c. What are the accuracy rate, sensitivity, specificity, and precision of the best-pruned tree on the test data?
d. Display the cumulative lift chart, the decile-wise lift chart, and the ROC curve, does the classification model outperform the baseline model? What is the area under the ROC curve (or AUC value)?
e. Score the two new customers in the In_App_Pur_Score worksheet using the best-pruned tree. Will the first new customer make in-app purchases according to your model? What about the second new customer? What are the probabilities of the two new customers to make in-app purchases?

22. FILE *In_App_Pur.* R Refer to the previous exercise for a description of the problem and data set. Build a default classification tree to predict whether the gamer will make in-app purchases. Display the classification tree.

a. What are the predictor variable and the split value for the first split of the default classification tree?
b. Build a full-grown tree. Which cp value is associated with the lowest cross-validation error?
c. Is there a simpler tree with a cross-validation error that is within one standard error of the minimum cross-validation error? If there is, then which cp value is associated with the best-pruned tree?
d. Prune the full tree to the best-pruned tree or the minimum error tree if the answer to part c is "No." Create a confusion matrix and display the various performance measures. Assign Class 1 to be the positive class. What are the accuracy, sensitivity, and specificity of the minimum error tree on the validation data?
e. Display the cumulative lift chart, the decile-wise lift chart, and the ROC curve of the minimum error tree on the validation data. Comment on the performance of the classification tree.
f. Score the two gamers in the In_App_Pur_Score worksheet using the pruned tree. What is the probability of the first gamer making in-app purchases according to your classification model? What is the probability for the second gamer?

LO 10.2

Apply regression trees to predict new records.

10.3 REGRESSION TREES

In Section 10.2, we presented classification trees, where the target variable assumed a categorical value. We now discuss regression trees, where the target variable assumes a numerical value. Like classification trees, regression trees can be constructed using the CART algorithm. The CART algorithm operates similarly for classification and regression trees, with the following three important differences.

First, as the target variable of the regression tree is numerical, the predicted value is the average value of the previous cases that belong to the same leaf node. Consider, for example, a regression tree for predicting customer spending over a 12-month period. Let one of the leaf nodes consist of four cases in the training data set with the following customer spending values: 259.00, 412.50, 139.75, and 188.45. When scoring any new customer that falls into this leaf node, the predicted spending amount for the new customer is the average of the four values, or $\frac{259.00 + 412.50 + 139.75 + 188.45}{4} = 249.925$.

Second, while the CART algorithm uses the Gini index to measure impurity in the classification tree, it uses the mean squared error (MSE) to measure impurity in a regression tree. Recall that the MSE is calculated as the average sum of the squared differences between the actual and the predicted values of the target variable in each leaf node or subset. If the exact values of all cases in a subset are predicted accurately, then the MSE equals 0, indicating that the subset is pure. There is no upper limit for the MSE for an impure subset. The higher the MSE, the more impure the subset is. In principle, a recursive partitioning process for a regression tree is similar to the classification tree process presented in Examples 10.1 through 10.5. As such, in Example 10.6, we will only demonstrate how the CART algorithm computes the MSE to determine the splits of a regression tree.

Finally, as a regression tree is a prediction technique, the performance of the tree is evaluated using the performance measures for prediction that were discussed in Section 8.3; that is, we use the root mean square error (RMSE), the mean error (ME), the mean absolute deviation (MAD) or mean absolute error (MAE), the mean percentage error (MPE), and the mean absolute percentage error (MAPE).

In Section 10.2, we showed business insights gained from the classification tree that Hayden and his team built for predicting which new customers are likely to respond to HELOC offers from Sunnyville Bank. Encouraged by these insights, Hayden has an idea for another data mining project. His retail banking team is interested in attracting high-value customers, defined as those who routinely maintain high balances in their accounts with Sunnyville Bank. Hayden hopes that a predictive model can help his team identify and focus on this group of high-value customers. He compiles a data file, ***Balance,*** that has two worksheets, Balance_Data and Balance_Score. Table 10.7a shows a portion of the Balance_Data worksheet, which contains the information from 500 current customers including the customer's age (Age, in years), sex (Sex), annual income (Income), and the average monthly account balance (Balance). Table 10.7b shows a portion of the Balance_Score worksheet, which includes the age, sex, and income of 20 potential customers. Ultimately, Hayden wants to build a predictive model using the data of current customers to predict the average account balance for the 20 potential customers.

TABLE 10.7 The ***Balance*** Data

FILE
Balance

a. The *Balance_Data* Worksheet

Age	Sex	Income	Balancec
38	Female	60000	3250
20	Male	41000	3546
⋮	⋮	⋮	⋮
50	Female	17000	2529

b. The *Balance_Score* Worksheet

Age	Sex	Income
35	Female	65000
56	Male	160000
⋮	⋮	⋮
52	Female	155000

Before building a prediction tree, we first show how to identify possible split points using a smaller data set.

Identifying Possible Split Points

Similar to the classification tree, one of the first steps in constructing a regression tree is to identify possible splits of the predictor variables. In principle, a recursive partitioning process for a regression tree is similar to the classification tree process presented in Section 10.2. In Example 10.6, we demonstrate how the CART algorithm computes the MSE to determine the splits of a regression tree.

EXAMPLE 10.6

For illustration, we use only a small data set of 20 randomly selected bank customers from the Balance_Data worksheet. Table 10.8 shows a portion of the data, which is stored in the Balance_Data_20 worksheet. Select the optimal split for the Age variable based on the MSE impurity measure.

TABLE 10.8 The ***Balance_Data_20*** worksheet

FILE
Balance_Data_20

Age	Balance
43	1775
34	3675
⋮	⋮
26	10761

SOLUTION: Similar to Example 10.1, we identify the possible split points by finding the midpoints between the consecutive values of Age. The ages of the 20 potential customers are first sorted in ascending order in the following data array:

$$\{18, 20, 24, 26, 28, 29, 31, 33, 34, 43, 45, 46, 48, 52, 58\}$$

(Note that some values have multiple occurrences, but for determining splitting points, each value only appears once in the array.)

Therefore, the first possible split point is calculated as (18 + 20)/ 2 = 19, the next possible split point is calculated as (20 + 24)/ 2 = 22, and the remaining possible split points are found in a like manner, as shown in the following data array:

$$\{19, 22, 25, 27, 28.5, 30, 32, 33.5, 38.5, 44, 45.5, 47, 50, 55\}$$

Consider two of the possible splits, 30 and 32. We will compute and compare the MSE for the two split values to find the preferred split. Recall that the MSE is the average sum of the squared differences between the actual account balances and predicted account balances in each partition. A split at Age = 30 creates two partitions: customers whose ages are less than 30 (8 cases) and customers whose ages are equal to or greater than 30 (12 cases). The average bank account balances of the two partitions are \$7,811.25 and \$4,445, respectively. This suggests that if we create a regression tree with one decision node that splits Age at the value of 30, all potential customers younger than 30 years will have a predicted balance of \$7,811.25, whereas all customers 30 years or older will have a predicted balance of \$4,445. For the Age = 30 split, the MSE for each partition is calculated as

$$\begin{aligned} MSE_{Age<30} &= (1/8) \times [(11{,}062 - 7{,}811.25)^2 + (758 - 7{,}811.25)^2 \\ &+ (3{,}675 - 7{,}811.25)^2 + (24{,}011 - 7{,}811.25)^2 + (4{,}825 - 7{,}811.25)^2 \\ &+ (2{,}861 - 7{,}811.25)^2 + (4{,}537 - 7{,}811.25)^2 + (10{,}761 - 7{,}811.25)^2] \\ &= 49{,}087{,}572.2 \end{aligned}$$

$$\begin{aligned} MSE_{Age\geq 30} &= (1/12) \times [(1{,}775 - 4{,}445)^2 + (3{,}675 - 4{,}445)^2 + (4{,}244 - 4{,}445)^2 \\ &+ (4{,}962 - 4{,}445)^2 + (3{,}743 - 4{,}445)^2 + (8{,}290 - 4{,}445)^2 + (6{,}188 - 4{,}445)^2 \\ &+ (14{,}390 - 4{,}445)^2 + (4{,}282 - 4{,}445)^2 + (57 - 4{,}445)^2 + (428 - 4{,}445)^2 \\ &+ (1{,}306 - 4{,}445)^2] = 14{,}209{,}843.0 \end{aligned}$$

To compute the overall MSE for the split, we calculate the weighted combination of the MSEs using the percentage of cases in each partition as the weight:

$$MSE_{split(Age=30)} = (8/20) \times 49{,}087{,}572.2 + (12/20) \times 14{,}209{,}843 = 28{,}160{,}934.7$$

Similarly, a split at Age = 32 creates two partitions as well: customers whose ages are less than 32 (9 cases) and customers whose ages are equal to or greater than 32 (11 cases). The average bank account balances for the two partitions are \$7,494.667 and \$4,398, respectively. For the Age = 32 split, the MSE for each partition is calculated as

$$\begin{aligned} MSE_{Age<32} &= (1/9) \times [(4{,}962 - 7{,}494.667)^2 + (11{,}062 - 7{,}494.667)^2 \\ &+ (758 - 7{,}494.667)^2 + (3{,}675 - 7{,}494.667)^2 + (24{,}011 - 7{,}494.667)^2 \\ &+ (4{,}825 - 7{,}494.667)^2 + (2{,}861 - 7{,}494.667)^2 + (4{,}537 - 7{,}494.667)^2 \\ &+ (10{,}761 - 7{,}494.667)^2] = 44{,}435{,}197.6 \end{aligned}$$

$$\begin{aligned} MSE_{Age\geq 32} &= (1/11) \times [(1{,}775 - 4{,}398)^2 + (3{,}675 - 4{,}398)^2 + (4{,}244 - 4{,}398)^2 \\ &+ (3{,}743 - 4{,}398)^2 + (8{,}290 - 4{,}398)^2 + (6{,}188 - 4{,}398)^2 + (14{,}390 - 4{,}398)^2 \\ &+ (4{,}282 - 4{,}398)^2 + (57 - 4{,}398)^2 + (428 - 4{,}398)^2 + (1{,}306 - 4{,}398)^2] \\ &= 15{,}475{,}138.9 \end{aligned}$$

The overall MSE for the split is calculated as

$$MSE_{split(Age=32)} = (9/20) \times 44{,}435{,}197.6 + (11/20) \times 15{,}475{,}138.9 = 28{,}507{,}165.3$$

The MSE value of the Age = 30 split is slightly smaller than that of the Age = 32 split, suggesting that the Age = 30 split generates a lower level of impurity; therefore, Age = 30 is a better split for constructing the regression tree. In fact, if we compute the MSE values for all the possible splits for Age in our example, we would find that the split at Age = 30 produces the smallest MSE. Therefore, the Age = 30 split is chosen as the best split for Age. Figure 10.20 shows the regression tree when Age is the only predictor variable used in the analysis.

FIGURE 10.20 Regression tree if Age only predictor

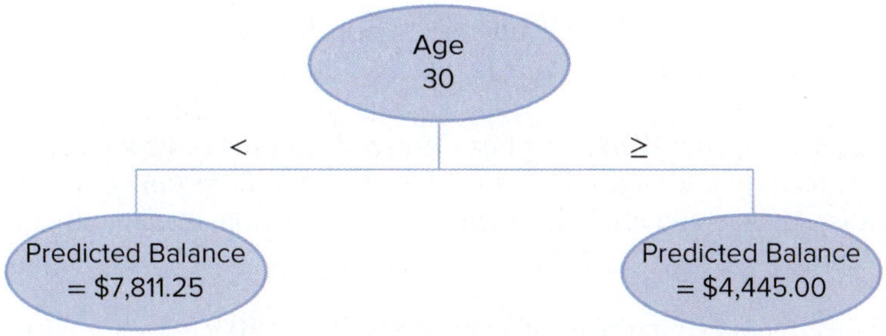

As mentioned earlier, the recursive partitioning process used for classification trees also applies to regression trees. Using the MSE as the criterion, a regression tree can be constructed by selecting the best split at each recursive partitioning step across all predictor variables. We will now develop a prediction tree with Analytic Solver and R.

Using Analytic Solver and R to Develop a Prediction Tree

FILE
Balance

EXAMPLE 10.7

Hayden wants to use historical data from 500 bank customers to develop a prediction model for predicting a customer's account balance. He also plans to assess the performance of the regression tree and then score 20 new customers. Use Analytic Solver and R to build the preferred prediction tree, and then use this tree to score the new cases.

SOLUTION:

Using Analytic Solver

a. Open the Balance_Data worksheet of the ***Balance*** data file.

b. Choose **Data Mining > Partition** (under the *Data Mining* group) > **Standard Partition.**

c. In the *Standard Data Partition* dialog box, we select the data range $A$1:$D$501 and move Age, Sex, Income, and Balance to the *Selected Variables* box. Select *Pick up rows randomly* and check the *Set seed* checkbox to use the default random seed of 12345. Select *Specify percentages* to allocate 50%, 30%, and 20% of the data to training, validation, and test sets, respectively. Click **OK.**

d. Analytic Solver will create a new worksheet called STDPartition with the partitioned data. With the STDPartition worksheet active, choose **Data Mining > Predict > Regression Tree** to open the *Regression Tree* dialog box.

In the **Data** tab, move the predictor variables Age and Income to the *Selected Variables* box and Sex to the *Categorical Variables* box. Select and move the target variable, Balance, to the *Output Variable* box. Accept other defaults. Click *Next*.

e. In the **Parameters** tab, check the *Prune (Using Validation Set)* checkbox and click on the *Tree for Scoring* button. Select *Best Pruned*, then click *Done*. This selection tells Analytic Solver to score cases using the best-pruned tree. Click on the *Trees to Display* button. Check the checkboxes next to *Fully Grown*, *Best Pruned*, and *Minimum Error*, then click *Done*. Accept other defaults. Click *Next*.

f. In the **Scoring** tab, Check the *Summary Report* boxes for *Score Training Data, Score Validation Data,* and *Score Test Data.* Check the *In Worksheet* check box under the *Score New Data* section. Under the **New Data (WS)** tab, select Balance_Score in the *Worksheet* box. These 20 records of new bank customers will be scored by the regression tree. Make sure the *First Row Contains Headers* box is checked and click the *Match by Name* button. Accept other defaults. Click *Finish*.

Analytic Solver creates a number of worksheets. Table 10.9 shows a portion of the prune log, which is found in the RT_Output worksheet. The prune log shows that the simplest tree with the minimum validation MSE of 34,625,847.56 occurs at two decision nodes. Because no smaller tree has a validation MSE within one standard error of this value, the minimum error tree and best-pruned tree coincide in this example.

TABLE 10.9 Analytic Solver's Prune Log

# Decision Nodes	Cost Complexity	Validation MSE
0	10010714.87	47757025.42
1	8713455.60	39391178.20
2	7016220.13	34625847.56
3	7091273.75	35733534.52
4	6440499.50	35411119.80
5	5154901.31	35536360.84
6	5764821.26	36632166.92

The RT_FullTree worksheet shows the full tree. The full tree is quite complex with many decision nodes. Due to its size, the full tree is not displayed here. The RT_BestTree and RT_MinErrorTree worksheets show the best-pruned and minimum error trees, respectively. As mentioned earlier, the two trees are identical in this example. Figure 10.21 displays the tree. It is relatively simple with two decision nodes and five total nodes if the terminal nodes are included. The following If-Then rules can be derived:

- If the customer's annual income is at least $157,500, then the predicted account balance is $15,448.3.
- If the customer's annual income is at least $72,500 but less than $157,500, then the predicted account balance is $7,630.6.
- If the customer's annual income is less than $72,500, then the predicted balance is $3,200.6.

The regression tree suggests that bank customers who have high income tend to maintain high balances in their checking accounts. Age and Sex have no impact on predicting Balance.

FIGURE 10.21 Analytic Solver's minimum error and best-pruned regression tree

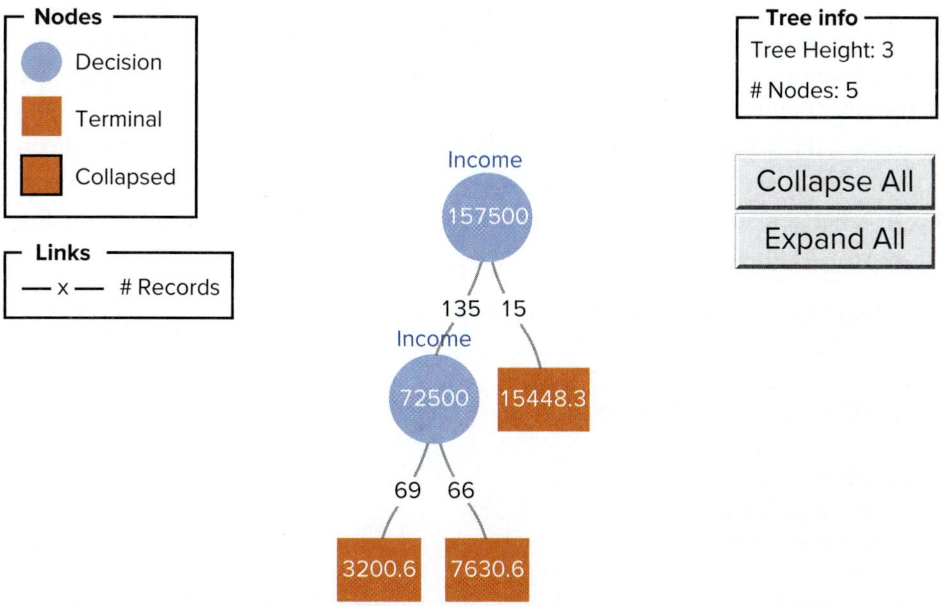

Because the validation data were used for pruning, the performance of the regression tree on a new data set should be assessed using the test data set. A portion of the performance measures in Testing: Prediction Summary in the RT_TestScore worksheet is shown in Table 10.10. The RMSE implies that the standard error of the average checking account balance prediction is $6,151.07, and the MAD implies that the predicted balances on average differ from the actual balance by $4,326.83.

TABLE 10.10 Analytic Solver's Performance Measures

Performance Measure	Value
RMSE	6151.07
MAD	4326.83

Sometimes the prediction errors implied by the performance measures appear large. This is quite common for regression trees when the data do not have a very clear and simple pattern. However, if you rank order the customers based on their predicted balances from the highest to lowest, you will find that the regression tree model does a relatively good job in predicting whether the customer tends to have a high or a low account balance. Therefore, in many cases, predicting the values of the target variable may not be the ultimate goal of a regression tree model. In our example, Hayden will likely use the regression tree model to identify customers who tend to have higher account balances instead of trying to predict the actual balances. The RT_NewScore worksheet shows the predicted balances of the 20 new customers using our regression tree. A portion of the predicted balances are shown in Table 10.11.

TABLE 10.11 Analytic Solver's Scoring Results

Record ID	Prediction: Balance	Age	Sex	Income
Record 1	3200.60	35	Female	65000
Record 2	15448.29	56	Male	160000
⋮	⋮	⋮	⋮	⋮
Record 20	7630.60	52	Female	155000

Using R

As mentioned earlier in the construction of classification trees, R's built-in cross-validation process means that there is no need to separate the data into three partitions as we did when using Analytics Solver. Here, we separate the data into two partitions: training and validation data sets.

a. Import the data from the Balance_Data worksheet of the ***Balance*** data file into a data frame (table) and label it myData.

b. Install and load the *caret*, *rpart*, *rpart.plot*, and *forecast* packages using the following command if you have not already done so. Enter:

```
>install.packages("caret", dependencies = c("Depends", "Suggests"))
>install.packages("rpart")
>install.packages("rpart.plot")
>install.packages("forecast")
>library(caret)
>library(rpart)
>library(rpart.plot)
>library(forecast)
```

c. By setting the random seed to 1, we will generate the same partitions as shown in this example. As the construction of a decision tree is a data-driven process and can benefit from a large training set, we use the **createDataPartition** function to randomly allocate 70% of the data into the training data set and 30% into the validation data set. Enter:

```
>set.seed(1)
>myIndex <- createDataPartition(myData$Balance, p=0.7, list =
FALSE)
>trainSet <- myData[myIndex,]
>validationSet <- myData[-myIndex,]
```

d. We use the **rpart** function to generate the default classification tree labeled default_tree. Within the **rpart** function, we specify the model structure, data source, and method. The *method = "anova"* option tells the function to build a regression tree to estimate a numerical target value. To view the details of the default tree, use the **summary** function. To ensure consistency of the cross-validation results, we use the **set.seed** function to fix the random seed to 1. Enter:

```
>set.seed(1)
>default_tree <- rpart(Balance ~ ., data=trainSet, method="anova")
>summary(default_tree)
```

e. To view the regression tree visually, we use the **prp** function. The *type* option is set equal to 1 so that all nodes except the leaf nodes are labeled in the tree diagram. The *extra* option is set equal to 1 so that the number of observations that fall into each node are displayed. The *under* option is set equal to TRUE in order to put the number of cases under each decision node in the diagram. Enter:

```
>prp(default_tree, type=1, extra=1, under = TRUE)
```

Figure 10.22 shows the default regression tree for predicting average balance.

FIGURE 10.22 R's default regression tree

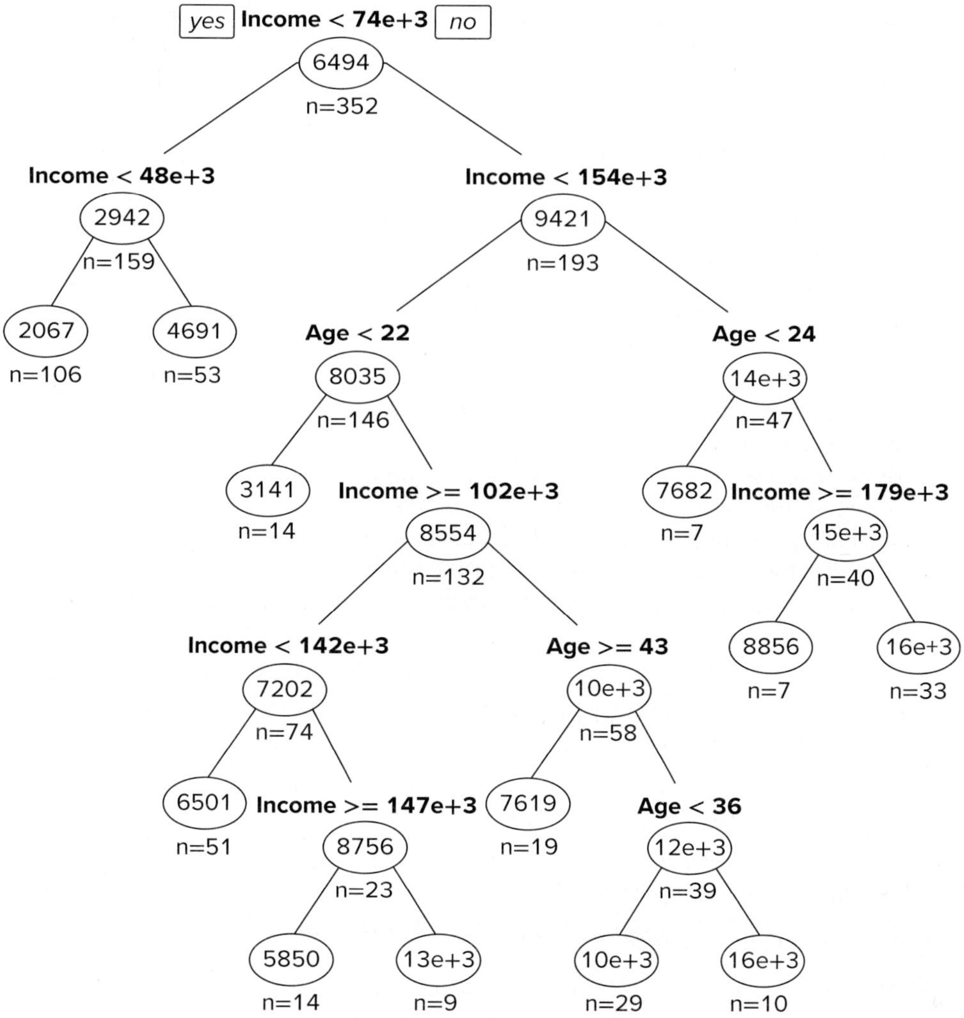

As discussed earlier, to find the optimal decision tree, a common practice is to grow the full tree and then prune it to a less-complex tree based on the prediction errors produced by the cross-validation process of the **rpart** function. By identifying the value of the complexity parameter (cp) associated with the smallest cross-validated prediction error, we can create the minimum error tree. Next, we demonstrate the pruning process to optimize the complexity of the tree.

f. We first grow the full tree by using the **rpart** function. We set the options *cp* equal to 0, *minsplit* equal to 2, and *minbucket* equal to 1. As discussed in the classification tree section, these settings ensure that the largest possible tree will be produced. We plot the full tree using the **prp** function. Again, to ensure consistency of the cross-validation results, we set the random seed to 1. Enter:

```
>set.seed(1)
>full_tree <- rpart(Balance ~ ., data= trainSet, method="anova",
cp=0, minsplit=2, minbucket=1)
>prp(full_tree, type=1, extra=1, under = TRUE)
```

The full tree in this case is very complex so it is not displayed here.

g. To identify the value of cp that is associated with the smallest cross-validated prediction error, we use the **printcp** function. Enter:

```
>printcp(full_tree)
```

Due to the complexity of the full tree, 273 subtree options are displayed in the cp table. Figure 10.23 displays a portion of the complexity parameter table showing the first eight candidate trees with increasing complexity. The nsplit column shows the number of splits for each tree. The rel error column shows the prediction error for each tree, relative to the prediction error of the root node if all cases are given the predicted balance that equals the average of all balances. The prediction performance of the trees needs to be evaluated by inspecting the cross-validation errors associated with each tree; see the xerror column. The third tree, with two splits, has the lowest cross-validation error (xerror = 0.72172); therefore, it is the minimum error tree. The xstd column (standard error) can be used to identify the best-pruned tree, which is the smallest tree whose cross-validation error falls within one standard error of the minimum error tree (0.72172 + 0.10521 = 0.82693). In this case, the second tree, with just one split, has a cross-validation error of 0.78354, which is within the range; hence, the best-pruned tree is the second tree. Next, we use the value of cp associated with the second tree to produce our best-pruned tree.

FIGURE 10.23 R's complexity parameters

```
Regression tree:
rpart(formula = Balance ~ ., data = trainSet, method = "anova",
     cp = 0, minsplit = 2, minbucket = 1)

Variables actually used in tree construction:
[1] Age    Sex  Income

Root node error: 1.5323e+10/352 = 43532223

n= 352

         CP nsplit relerror   xerror    xstd
1 2.3884e-01   0   1.0000000 1.00736 0.12558
2 7.5218e-02   1   0.7611608 0.78354 0.10941  ← Best-pruned tree
3 2.4196e-02   2   0.6859424 0.72172 0.10521  ← Minimum error tree
4 2.0775e-02   3   0.6617459 0.81956 0.12570
5 2.0084e-02   4   0.6409709 0.86702 0.12851
6 1.8255e-02   5   0.6208865 0.87927 0.12873
7 1.6691e-02   6   0.6026315 0.87122 0.12825
8 1.5877e-02  10   0.5358656 1.02948 0.16621
```

h. We use the **prune** function to create the best-pruned tree by using the cp value associated with the second tree. Again, to avoid issues caused by rounding, we use a cp value that is slightly larger than the cp value associated with the second tree but lower than that of the next smaller tree. In this case, we will use 7.5219e-02. We display the pruned tree using the **prp** function. Enter:

```
>pruned_tree <- prune(full_tree, cp=7.5219e-02)
>prp(pruned_tree, type=1, extra=1, under = TRUE)
```

Figure 10.24 displays the tree diagram of the best-pruned tree. The tree has just one split and two leaf nodes. The values in the boxes are the predicted balance for customers that belong to each node. The tree shows that if a customer's income is less than \$74,000, then the predicted balance is \$2,942; otherwise, the predicted balance is $9,421. This suggests that high-income earners tend to have higher account balances. Next, we will evaluate the performance of the pruned tree using the validation data set.

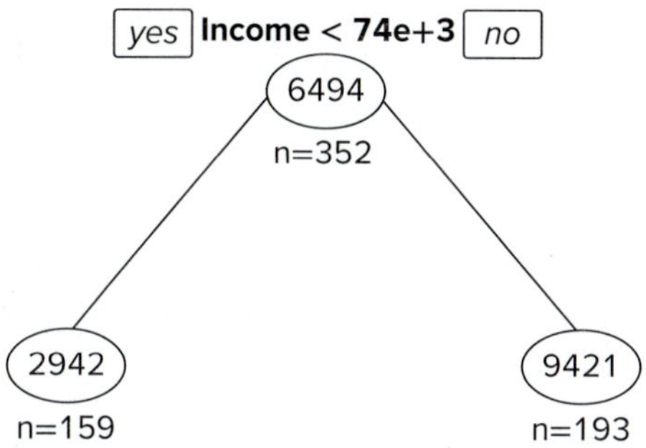

FIGURE 10.24 R's best-pruned tree

i. We predict the average balances of the observations in the validation data set using the predict function. Enter:

```
>predicted_value <- predict(pruned_tree, validationSet)
```

j. To evaluate the performance of our regression tree, we compute the performance measures for prediction using the **accuracy** function. The **accuracy** function requires two arguments: predicted values and actual values. Enter:

```
>accuracy(predicted_value, validationSet$Balance)
```

Various performance measures are produced, as shown in Figure 10.25.

FIGURE 10.25 R's performance measures

```
                 ME       RMSE        MAE        MPE       MAPE
Test set   27.64637   6818.736   4383.283   -305.334   334.4715
```

k. Finally, to score the 20 new cases, we import the data from the Balance_Score worksheet of the ***Balance*** data file into a data frame (table) called myScoreData and use the **predict** function to produce the predicted average checking account balance (called predicted_value_score) for the new cases using our regression tree. Enter:

```
>predicted_value_score <- predict(pruned_tree, myScoreData)
>predicted_value_score
```

The scoring results are summarized in Table 10.12. As you can see, the annual balances predicted by the regression tree constructed in R are somewhat different from those predicted by the regression tree produced in Analytic Solver. This is due to the different training data sets randomly selected in the two software products. However, as in the case of Analytic Solver, the pruned regression tree suggests that while Income plays a crucial role, Age and Sex have no impact on predicting Balance.

TABLE 10.12 R's Scoring Results

Record ID	Prediction: Balance	Age	Sex	Income
Record 1	2941.94	35	Female	65000
Record 2	9421.17	56	Male	160000
⋮	⋮	⋮	⋮	⋮
Record 20	9421.17	52	Female	155000

EXERCISES 10.3

Note: **AS** and **R** indicate that the exercise problems must be solved using Analytic Solver and R, respectively. For Analytic Solver, partition data sets into training, 30% validation, and 20% and use 12345 as the default random seed. For R, partition data sets into 70% and 30% validation. Use the statement set.seed(1) to specify the random seed of 1 for both data partitioning and cross-validation. Some data files have two worksheets (for example, Exercise_10.28_Data and Exercise_10.28_Score worksheets) for model development and scoring new records. If the predictor variable values are in the character format, then treat the predictor variable as a categorical variable. Otherwise, treat the predictor variable as a numerical variable.

Mechanics

23. **FILE** ***Exercise_10.23.*** The accompanying data set contains two predictor variables, x_1 and x_2, and one numerical target variable, y. A regression tree will be constructed using the data set.
    a. List the possible split values for x_1 in ascending order.
    b. List the possible split values for x_2 in ascending order.
    c. Compute the MSE of the partition $x_1 = 131$.
    d. Compute the MSE of the partition $x_2 = 105$.
    e. Compare and interpret the results from parts c and d.

24. **FILE** ***Exercise_10.24.*** The accompanying data set contains three predictor variables, x_1, x_2, and x_3, and one numerical target variable, y. A regression tree will be constructed using the data set.
    a. List the possible split values for x_1 in ascending order.
    b. List the possible split values for x_2 in ascending order.
    c. List the possible split values for x_3 in ascending order.
    d. Compute the MSE of the partition $x_1 = 252$.
    e. Compute the MSE of the partition $x_2 = 92.5$.
    f. Compute the MSE of the partition $x_3 = 14.25$.
    g. Compare and interpret the results from parts d, e, and f.

25. **FILE** ***Exercise_10.25.*** The accompanying data set contains two predictor variables, x_1 and x_2, and one numerical target variable, y. A regression tree will be constructed using the data set.
    a. Which split on x_1 will generate the smallest MSE?
    b. Which split on x_2 will generate the smallest MSE?
    c. Which variable and split value should be used to create the root node if a regression tree is constructed using the accompanying data set?
    d. State the rules generated from this split.

26. **FILE** ***Exercise_10.26.*** The accompanying data set contains three predictor variables, x_1, x_2, and x_3, and one numerical target variable, y. A regression tree will be constructed using the data set.
    a. Which split on x_1 will generate the smallest MSE?
    b. Which split on x_2 will generate the smallest MSE?
    c. Which split on x_3 will generate the smallest MSE?
    d. Which variable and split value should be used to create the root node if a regression tree is constructed using the accompanying data set?
    e. State the rules generated from this split.

27. The regression tree below relates credit score to number of defaults (*NUM DEF*), revolving balance (*REV BAL*), and years of credit history (*YRS HIST*). Predict the credit score of each of the following individuals.

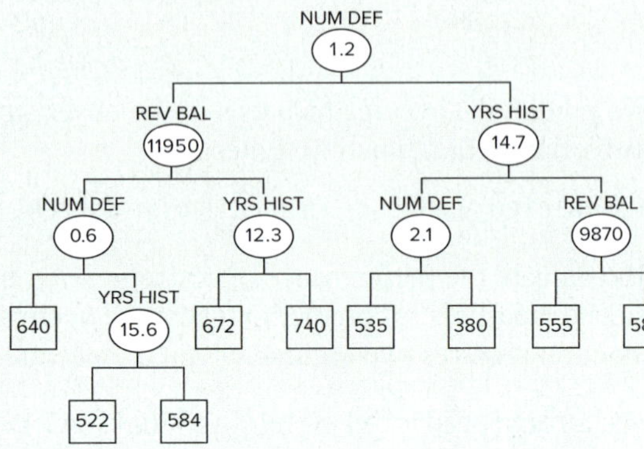

    a. An individual with no defaults, $4,200 revolving balance, and 12 years of credit history.
    b. An individual with two defaults, $6,500 revolving balance, and seven years of credit history.
    c. An individual with one default, $12,700 revolving balance, and 25 years of credit history.
    d. An individual with two defaults, $8,100 revolving balance, and 16 years of credit history.

28. **FILE** ***Exercise_10.28.*** **AS** Create a regression tree using the accompanying data set in Exercise_10.28_Data worksheet (predictor variables: x_1 to x_5; target: y). Select the best-pruned tree for scoring and display the full-grown, best-pruned, and minimum error trees.
    a. What is the minimum validation MSE in the prune log? How many decision nodes are associated with the minimum error?
    b. How many leaf nodes are in the best-pruned and minimum error trees?
    c. Display the best-pruned tree. What are the predictor variable and split value for the first split (root node) of the best-pruned tree? What are the rules that can be derived from the root node?
    d. What are the RMSE and MAD of the best-pruned tree on the test data?
    e. Score the new observations in the Exericse_10.28_Score worksheet using the best-pruned tree. What is the predicted value of y for the first observation?
    f. What are the minimum, maximum, and average values of predicted y?

29. FILE *Exercise_10.29.* AS Create a regression tree using the accompanying data set (predictor variables: x_1 to x_4; target: y). Select the best-pruned tree for scoring and display the full-grown, best-pruned and minimum error trees.

a. What is the minimum validation MSE in the prune log? How many decision nodes are associated with the minimum error?

b. How many leaf nodes are in the best-pruned and minimum error trees?

c. Display the best-pruned tree. What are the predictor variable and split value for the first split (root node) of the best-pruned tree? What are the rules that can be derived from the root node?

d. What are the RMSE and MAD of the best-pruned tree on the test data?

e. According to the best-pruned tree, what is the predicted y for a new observation with the following values: $x_1 = 20$; $x_2 = 40$; $x_3 = 36$; $x_4 = 8.3$?

30. FILE *Exercise_10.30.* R Create a regression tree using the accompanying data set in the Exercise_10.30_Data worksheet (predictor variables: x_1 to x_4; target: y).

a. Use the **rpart** function to build a default regression tree. Display the default regression tree. How many leaf nodes are in the default regression tree?

b. What are the predictor variable and split value for the first split (root node) of the default regression tree? What are the rules that can be derived from the root node?

c. Use the **rpart** function to build a fully-grown regression tree. Display the cp table. Which tree has the lowest cross-validation error? How many splits are in the minimum error tree?

d. Is there a simpler tree with a cross-validation error that is within one standard error of the minimum cross-validation error? What is the cp value associated with the best-pruned tree?

e. Prune the full tree to the best-pruned tree or minimum error tree if the answer to part c is "No." Display the pruned tree. How many leaf nodes are in the pruned tree?

f. What are the ME, RMSE, MAE, MPE and MAPE measures of the pruned tree on the validation data?

g. Score the new observations in the Exercise_10.30_Score worksheet. What is the predicted value of y for the first observation? What are the minimum, maximum, and average values of predicted y?

31. FILE *Exercise_10.31.* R Create a regression tree using the accompanying data set in the Exercise_10.31 worksheet (predictor variables: x_1 to x_4; target: y).

a. Use the **rpart** function to build a default regression tree. Display the default regression tree. How many leaf nodes are in the default regression tree? What are the predictor variable and split value for the first split of the default regression tree?

b. Use the **rpart** function to build a fully-grown regression tree. What is the cp value that is associated with the lowest cross-validation error? How many splits are in the minimum error tree?

c. Is there a simpler tree with a cross-validation error that is within one standard error of the minimum cross-validation error? What is the cp value associated with the best-pruned tree? How many splits are in the best-pruned tree?

d. Prune the full tree to the best-pruned tree or minimum error tree if the answer to part c is "No." Display the pruned tree. What are the ME, RMSE, MAE, MPE, and MAPE measures of the pruned tree on the validation data?

e. Comment on the performance of the pruned regression tree.

32. FILE *Exercise_10.32.* AS Create a regression tree using the accompanying data set (predictor variables: x_1 to x_4; target: y). Select the best-pruned tree for scoring and display the full-grown, best-pruned, and minimum error trees.

a. What is the minimum validation MSE in the prune log? How many decision nodes are associated with the minimum error?

b. Display the best-pruned tree. How many leaf nodes are in the best-pruned and minimum error trees?

c. What are the predictor variable and split value for the first split (root node) of the best-pruned tree? What are the rules that can be derived from the root node?

d. What are the RMSE and MAD of the best-pruned tree?

33. FILE *Exercise_10.33.* R Create a regression tree using the accompanying data set (predictor variables: x_1 to x_4; target: y).

a. Use the **rpart** function to build a default regression tree. Display the tree using the **prp** function. How many leaf nodes are in the default regression tree?

b. What are the predictor variable and split value for the first split (root node) of the default regression tree? What are the rules that can be derived from the root node?

c. Use the **rpart** function to build a fully grown regression tree. Display the cp table. Which tree has the lowest cross-validation error? Which cp value is associated with the minimum error tree?

d. Is there a simpler tree with a cross-validation error that is within one standard error of the minimum error? If there is, then which cp value is associated with the best-pruned tree?

e. Use the **prune** function to prune the full tree to the best-pruned tree or the minimum error tree if the answer to part d is "No." Display the pruned tree using the **prp** function. What are the ME, RMSE, MAE, MPE, and MAPE measures of the pruned tree on the validation data?

Applications

34. **FILE** ***Travel.*** **AS** Jerry Stevenson is the manager of a travel agency. He wants to build a model that can predict customers' annual spending on travel products. He has compiled a data set that contains the following variables: whether the individual has a college degree (College), whether the individual has credit card debt (CreditCard), annual household spending on food (FoodSpend), annual income (Income), and annual household spending on travel products (TravelSpend). A portion of the Travel_Data worksheet is shown in the accompanying table. Create a regression tree model for predicting the customer's annual household spending on travel products (TravelSpend). Select the best-pruned tree for scoring and display the full-grown, best-pruned, and minimum error trees.

College	CreditCard	FoodSpend	Income	TravelSpend
Yes	Yes	5472.43	49150	827.4
No	Yes	9130.73	47806	863.55
⋮	⋮	⋮	⋮	⋮
Yes	Yes	5584	53504	1748.1

a. How many leaf nodes are in the best-pruned tree and the minimum error tree? What are the rules that can be derived from the root node of the best-pruned tree?

b. What are the RMSE and MAD of the best-pruned tree on the test data?

c. Score the two new customers in the Travel_Score worksheet using the best-pruned tree. What are their predicted annual spending amounts on travel products?

35. **FILE** ***Travel.*** **R** Refer to the previous exercise for a description of the data set. Build a default regression tree to predict the customer's annual household spending on travel products (TravelSpend). Display the regression tree.

a. How many leaf nodes are in the default tree? What are the predictor variable and split value for the first split of the default regression tree?

b. Build a full-grown tree. Which cp value is associated with the lowest cross-validation error? How many splits are in the minimum-error tree? What is the minimum cross-validation error?

c. Is there a simpler tree with a cross-validation error that is within one standard error of the minimum error? If there is, then which cp value is associated with the best-pruned tree?

d. Prune the full tree to the best-pruned tree or the minimum error tree if the answer to part c is "No." Display the tree. How many leaf nodes are in the pruned tree?

e. What are the ME, RMSE, MAE, MPE, and MAPE of the pruned tree on the validation data?

f. Score the two new customers in the Travel_Score worksheet using the pruned tree. What are their predicted annual spending amounts on travel products?

36. **FILE** ***Houses.*** **R** Melissa Hill is a real estate agent in Berkeley, California. She wants to build a predictive model that can help her price a house more accurately. Melissa has compiled a data set in the House_Data worksheet that contains the information about the houses sold in the past year. The data set contains the following variables: number of bedrooms (BM), number of bathrooms (Bath), square footage of the property (SQFT), lot size (Lot_Size), type of property (Type), age of the property (Age), and price sold (Price). A portion of the data set is shown in the accompanying table. Build a default regression tree to predict house prices (Price). Display the regression tree.

BM	Bath	SQFT	Lot_Size	Type	Age	Price
4	2	1520	4050	Single Family	110	500000
3	2	1251	3200	Single Family	112	775000
⋮	⋮	⋮	⋮	⋮	⋮	⋮
4	4	4314	7056	Single Family	78	2635000

a. What are the predictor variable and split value for the first split of the default regression tree? What are the rules that can be derived from the root node?

b. Build a full-grown tree. Which cp value is associated with the lowest cross-validation error? How many splits are in the minimum-error tree?

c. Is there a simpler tree with a cross-validation error that is within one standard error of the minimum error? If there is, then which cp value is associated with the best-pruned tree?

d. Prune the full tree to the best-pruned tree or the minimum error tree if the answer to part c is "No." Display the tree. How many leaf nodes are in the pruned tree?

e. What are the ME, RMSE, MAE, MPE, and MAPE of the pruned tree on the validation data? On average, does the regression tree over- or under-predict prices of houses? Is the regression tree model effective in predicting prices of houses?

f. Score the two new houses on the market in the Houses_Score worksheet using the pruned tree. What are their predicted prices?

37. **FILE** ***Houses.*** **AS** Refer to the previous exercise for a description of the data set. Create a regression tree model for predicting house prices (Price). Select the best-pruned tree for scoring and display the full-grown, best-pruned, and minimum error trees.

a. Display the best-pruned tree. How many leaf nodes are in the best-pruned tree? What are the predictor variable and split value of the root node of the best-pruned tree?

b. What are the RMSE and MAD of the best-pruned tree on the test data? On average, does the regression tree over- or under-predict prices of houses? Is the regression tree model effective in predicting prices of houses?

c. Score the two new houses on the market in the Houses_Score worksheet using the best-pruned tree. What are their predicted prices according to your model?

38. **FILE** ***E_Retailer.*** **AS** An online retail company is trying to predict customer spending in the first three months of the year. Brian Duffy, the marketing analyst of the company, has compiled a data set on 200 existing customers that includes sex (Female: 1 = Female, 0 otherwise), annual income in 1,000s (Income), age (Age, in years), and total spending in the first three months of the year (Spending). A portion of the E-Retailer_Data worksheet is shown in the accompanying table. Create a regression tree model for predicting customer spending during the first three months of the year (Spending). Select the best-pruned tree for scoring and display the full-grown, best-pruned, and minimum error trees.

Female	Income	Age	Spending
0	87.5	52	156.88
1	66.5	43	275.16
⋮	⋮	⋮	⋮
0	51.9	61	159.51

a. Display the best-pruned tree. How many leaf nodes are in the best-pruned tree?

b. What are the RMSE and MAD of the best-pruned tree on the test data?

c. Score the 10 new customers in the E-Retailer_Score worksheet using the best-pruned tree. What are the mean and median values of the predicted spending amounts according to your model?

39. **FILE** ***E_Retailer.*** **R** Refer to the previous exercise for a description of the data set. Build a default regression tree to predict the customer's spending during the first three months of the year (Spending). Display the regression tree.

a. What are the rules that can be derived from the default regression tree?

b. Build a full-grown tree. Which cp value is associated with the lowest cross-validation error? How many leaf nodes are in the minimum-error tree?

c. Is there a simpler tree with a cross-validation error that is within one standard error of the minimum error? If there is, then which cp value is associated with the best-pruned tree?

d. Prune the full tree to the best-pruned tree or the minimum error tree if the answer to part c is "No." Display the tree. How many leaf nodes are in the pruned tree?

e. What are the ME, RMSE, MAE, MPE, and MAPE of the pruned tree on the validation data?

f. Score the 10 new customers in the E-Retailer_Score worksheet using the pruned tree. What are the mean and median values of the predicted spending amounts during the first three months?

40. **FILE** ***Electricity.*** **R** Kyle Robson, an energy researcher for the U.S. Energy Information Administration, is trying to build a model for predicting annual electricity retail sales for states. Kyle has compiled a data set for the 50 states and the District of Columbia that contains average electricity retail price (Price in cents/kWh), per capita electricity generation (Generation), median household income (Income), and per capita electricity retail sales (Price in MWh). A portion of the data set is shown in the accompanying table. Build a default regression tree to predict per capita electricity retail sales (Sales). Display the regression tree.

State	Price	Generation	Income	Sales
Alabama	9.56	29.12	$44,765	18.05
Alaska	17.93	8.58	$73,355	8.3
⋮	⋮	⋮	⋮	⋮
Wyoming	8.19	81.32	$60,214	28.86

a. What are the predictor variable and split value for the first split of the default regression tree? What are the rules that can be derived from the default regression tree?

b. Build a full-grown tree. Which cp value is associated with the lowest cross-validation error? How many leaf nodes are in the minimum-error tree?

c. Is there a simpler tree with a cross-validation error that is within one standard error of the minimum error? If there is, then which cp value is associated with the best-pruned tree?

d. Prune the full tree to the best-pruned tree or the minimum error tree if the answer to part c is "No." Display the tree. How many leaf nodes are in the pruned tree?

e. What are the ME, RMSE, MAE, MPE, and MAPE of the pruned tree on the validation data?

f. What is the predicted per capita electricity retail sales for a state with the following values: Price = 11, Generation = 25, and Income = 65,000?

41. **FILE** ***Electricity.*** **AS** Refer to the previous exercise for a description of the data set. Create a regression tree model for predicting per capita electricity retail sales (Sales). Select the best-pruned tree for scoring and display the full-grown, best-pruned, and minimum error trees.

a. How many leaf nodes are in the best-pruned tree and minimum error tree?

b. What are the predictor variable and split value for the first split of the best-pruned tree? What are the rules that can be derived from the root node?

c. What are the RMSE and MAD of the best-pruned tree on the test data?

d. What is the predicted per capita electricity retail sales for a state with the following values: Price = 11, Generation = 25, and Income = 65,000?

42. FILE ***NBA.*** **AS** Merrick Stevens is a sports analyst working for ACE Sports Management, a sports agency that represents over 200 athletes. He is interested in understanding the relationship between an NBA player's salary and his physicality and performance statistics. Merrick has constructed a data set that contains information on 30 competing NBA teams and 445 players. A portion of the NBA_Data worksheet is shown in the table below. A detailed description of each field in the data set can be found in NBA Information.docx. Create a regression tree model for predicting an NBA player's salary (salary). Select the best-pruned tree for scoring and display the full-grown, best-pruned, and minimum error trees.

player_number	salary	age	...	points
1	947276	36	...	13.5
2	25000000	37	...	17.6
⋮		⋮	⋮	⋮
445	525093	23	...	1.2

a. How many leaf nodes are in the best-pruned tree and minimum error tree?

b. Display the best-pruned tree. What are the predictor variable and split value for the first split of the best-pruned tree?

c. What are the RMSE and MAD of the best-pruned tree on the test data?

d. Score the three NBA players Merrick is trying to sign as ACE Sports Management clients in the NBA_Score worksheet using the pruned tree. What is the average predicted salary of the three players?

43. FILE ***NBA.*** **R** Refer to the previous exercise for a description of the data set. Build a default regression tree to predict an NBA player's salary (salary). Display the regression tree.

a. What are the predictor variable and split value for the first split of the default regression tree?

b. Build a full-grown tree. Which cp value is associated with the lowest cross-validation error? How many leaf nodes are in the minimum-error tree?

c. Is there a simpler tree with a cross-validation error that is within one standard error of the minimum error? If there is, then which cp value is associated with the best-pruned tree?

d. Prune the full tree to the best-pruned tree or the minimum error tree if the answer to part c is "No." Display the tree. What are the rules that can be derived from the pruned tree?

e. What are the ME, RMSE, MAE, MPE, and MAPE of the pruned tree on the validation data?

f. Score the three NBA players Merrick is trying to sign as ACE Sports Management clients in the NBA_Score worksheet using the pruned tree. What is the average predicted salary of the three players?

LO 10.3

Apply ensemble tree models to classify new records.

10.4 ENSEMBLE TREE MODELS

While decision trees are a highly popular classification and prediction technique, they are sensitive to changes in the data. Even small changes in the data may render drastically different trees and results. Moreover, a single tree model tends to overfit, meaning that it fits the current data well but fails to generalize to unseen data sets. One solution to these problems is to use **ensemble tree models**, which combine multiple single-tree models into an ensemble model. Ensemble trees have gained increasing popularity and have been proven to produce better and more stable predictive performance than a single-tree model in many situations.

The principle behind the ensemble trees is that the outcomes of a collection of single trees are combined into a single classification or prediction model. In other words, a group of relatively weak single-tree models (often called weak learners) are combined to form a stronger ensemble tree model to reduce the variation in prediction error. For classification, we use the majority rule where the most frequently predicted class from all the single-tree models is chosen as the final classification. For prediction, we use the average of the predictions from all the single-tree models. Sometimes, more sophisticated techniques such as weighted majority vote or weighted average can be used by giving more weight to better-performing trees and may produce more accurate predictions. Unlike a single tree, an ensemble tree model cannot be displayed visually using a tree diagram as multiple trees are combined to construct the ensemble model.

Three common strategies are used when creating ensemble models: *bagging, boosting,* and *random forest.* **Bagging** uses the bootstrap aggregation technique to create multiple training data sets by repeatedly sampling the original data with replacement. Each training set is then used to construct a single decision tree. Bagging helps improve the stability of the tree model by combining the results from single-tree models produced by different training data.

The second ensemble strategy is called **boosting**. The boosting strategy also uses repeated sampling with replacement to generate multiple single-tree models. However, it is an iterative and sequential process that pays more attention to cases that are misclassified or have large prediction errors. In each iteration, cases that are misclassified or have large prediction errors from the previous round are given a higher probability (or more weight) of being included in the next sample. As a result, the individual single-tree models that initially have high classification or prediction error rates will eventually adjust to make better classifications or predictions on these difficult cases, and therefore the model performance will improve over multiple iterations.

The key difference between the bagging and boosting strategies is that, with bagging, every case has an equal probability of being included in the sample, but with boosting, the probability of inclusion increases for cases that have been previously misclassified or have large prediction errors. The advantage of the boosting strategy is that it forces the modeling process to place emphasis on the most difficult cases, but at the same time, it is more prone to overfitting.

Random forest, also called random trees, is an extension of the bagging strategy. With the bagging strategy, the single trees are created from the same pool of predictor variables in the training set and, therefore, tend to be very similar to each other. As a result, single trees generated from the bagging method and their predictions may be highly correlated to each other. Averaging predictions from highly correlated trees may not result in a substantial decrease in the variance of prediction errors. To overcome this issue, the random forest strategy implements not only repeated sampling of the training data, but also a random selection of a subset of predictor variables, called features, to construct each tree.

The random forest technique is particularly useful if the predictor variables are highly correlated. This approach results in a greater diversity and less-correlated single-tree models, which can substantially reduce the variance in the prediction errors. As a guideline, the square root of the total number of predictor variables is used as the number of random features to select for each tree. For example, if there are 16 predictor variables in the data, each tree would randomly select $\sqrt{16} = 4$ features to be included in the tree. The feature importance information allows you to decide which predictor variables should be excluded from future analyses as they do not contribute much to the classification or prediction process.

ENSEMBLE TREE MODELS

Ensemble tree models combine multiple single-tree models to reduce the variation in prediction error. For classification, majority rule is often used, where the most frequently predicted class from all the single-tree models is chosen as the final classification. For prediction, the average of the predictions from all the single-tree models is often used. Common ensemble tree strategies include bagging, boosting, and random forest.

- Bagging is an ensemble modeling strategy that uses the bootstrap aggregation technique to create multiple training data sets by repeatedly sampling the original data with replacement.
- Boosting is an ensemble modeling strategy that forces the model to pay more attention to cases that are misclassified or have large prediction errors in previous trees through a weighted sampling process.
- Random forest is an ensemble modeling strategy that creates a collection of trees by repeatedly sampling the original data with replacement and randomly selecting a subset of predictor variables, called features, to construct each tree.

In summary, bagging is easy to implement, and trees can be developed in parallel. Boosting focuses on cases that are difficult to classify or predict. However, boosting cannot develop trees in parallel (weights depend on prior trees); thus, it is more computationally expensive and may lead to overfitting. Random forest provides the simplicity and computational efficiency of bagging and adds more diversity to the process. Finally, because multiple single-tree models are generated, pruning is usually not necessary for the ensemble model. As such, we only need to partition the data into training and validation sets. Without the need for a test data set, this approach increases the amount of data available for sampling and training the model. Unfortunately, ensemble trees cannot be displayed graphically using the tree diagram; therefore, they are more difficult to interpret than single trees. Whether or not ensemble tree models perform better than single-tree models will depend on the data, the predictor variables, and other factors unique to each problem. In most cases, ensemble models lead to more accurate and reliable predictions. In Example 10.8, we demonstrate how to use Analytic Solver and R to develop ensemble classification tree models; ensemble prediction tree models can be developed similarly.

Using Analytic Solver and R to Develop Ensemble Classification Tree Models

FILE
HELOC

EXAMPLE 10.8

Use Analytic Solver and R to develop ensemble classification tree models using the ***HELOC*** data set used in Example 10.5. Compare the model performance of the ensemble tree model with the single-tree model developed in Example 10.5.

SOLUTION: We will first provide detailed instructions for the bagging technique. The necessary adjustments to develop the boosting and the random forest models are given at the end of the example.

Using Analytic Solver

a. Open the HELOC_Data worksheet of the ***HELOC*** data file.
b. Choose **Data Mining > Partition** (under the *Data Mining* group) **> Standard Partition**.
c. In the *Standard Data Partition* dialog box, we select the data range \$A\$1:\$D\$501 and move Age, Sex, Income, and HELOC to the *Selected Variables* box. As the ensemble tree modeling process does not involve pruning, only the train and validation data sets are needed for constructing the model and evaluating the model's performance. Select *Pick up rows randomly* and check the *Set seed* checkbox to use the default random seed of 12345. Select *Specify percentages* to allocate 60% and 40% of the data to training and validation sets, respectively. Click *OK*.
d. With the STDPartition worksheet active, choose **Classify > Ensemble > Bagging**. In the **Data** tab, move the predictor variables Age and Income to the *Selected Variables* box and Sex to the *Categorical Variables* box. Select and move HELOC to the *Output Variable* box. Accept other defaults. Click *Next*.
e. In the **Parameters** tab, select *Decision Tree* from the pull-down menu for *Weak Learner*. Accept other defaults and click *Next*. Analytic Solver will construct 10 decision trees as the weak learners and uses the bagging technique for the ensemble tree model.
f. In the **Scoring** tab, check the *Summary Report* boxes for *Score Training Data* and *Score Validation Data*. Also check the *Lift Charts* box for *Score*

Validation Data. Check the *In Worksheet* check box under the *Score New Data* section. Under the **New Data (WS)** tab, select HELOC_Score in the *Worksheet* box. These 20 records of new bank customers in *Data Range* $A$1:$C$21 will be scored by the ensemble tree model. Make sure the *First Row Contains Headers* box is checked and click the *Match By Name* button. Accept other defaults and click *Finish*. You will notice that it takes slightly longer for Analytic Solver to return the output of the ensemble tree model as it needs to create 10 single classification trees before constructing the final ensemble tree model.

To assess model performance, we turn to Validation: Classification Summary in the CBagging_validationScore worksheet shown in Figure 10.26. The performance measures show that the ensemble model yields an overall misclassification rate of 21.5%, sensitivity of 0.6735, and specificity of 0.8212. Recall that the single classification tree in Example 10.5 has a misclassification rate of 23%, sensitivity of 0.5385, and specificity of 0.8514. The current ensemble tree model has slightly better overall predictive performance, a higher sensitivity rate, and performs better at correctly identifying Class 1 cases (customers who respond to the HELOC offer) than the single-classification tree model.

FIGURE 10.26 Analytic Solver's summary measures

Confusion Matrix

Actual\Predicted	0	1
0	124	27
1	16	33

Error Report

Class	# Cases	# Errors	% Error
0	151	27	17.88079
1	49	16	32.65306
Overall	200	43	21.5

Metrics

Metric	Value
Accuracy (#correct)	157
Accuracy (%correct)	78.5
Specificity	0.821192
Sensitivity (Recall)	0.673469
Precision	0.55
F1 score	0.605505
Success Class	1
Success Probability	0.5

Source: Microsoft Excel

Recall that the performance measures in Figure 10.26 are based on the cutoff value of 0.5. Lowering the cutoff value will classify more cases into the target class, resulting in different performance measurement values. Therefore, in order to evaluate model performance, it is recommended that we inspect the cumulative lift chart, the decile-wise lift chart, and the ROC curve because they are independent of the cutoff value.

Figure 10.27a shows the cumulative lift chart. Because the blue line lies well above the red diagonal line, the ensemble tree performs considerably better in terms of predicting whether or not a potential customer will respond to the HELOC offer, compared to the baseline model. For example, if we send HELOC offers to 100 bank customers (half of the validation data sample size) who have the highest predicted probability of responding to the offer, we will be able to reach 42 out of 49 (85.71%) customers who actually respond to the offer. Alternately, if we send the offer to 100 randomly chosen customers, we would reach only 50% of the customers who actually responded to the offer.

Figure 10.27b shows the decile-wise lift chart. The first 10% of potential customers selected by the ensemble tree, for example, include 1.84 times as many customers who would respond to the HELOC offer, compared to a random selection of 10% of potential customers.

Finally, the ROC curve (see Figure 10.27c) shows that the ensemble tree performs much better than the baseline model in terms of sensitivity and specificity across all cutoff values. The area under the curve (AUC) is 0.8008, which is closer to the optimum classifier (AUC = 1) as compared to the random classifier (AUC = 0.5). Overall, the ensemble model demonstrates slightly better predictive performance than that of the single-tree classification model produced in Analytic Solver; refer to Example 10.5 for comparing measures such as sensitivity, specificity, and AUC.

FIGURE 10.27 Analytic Solver's performance charts

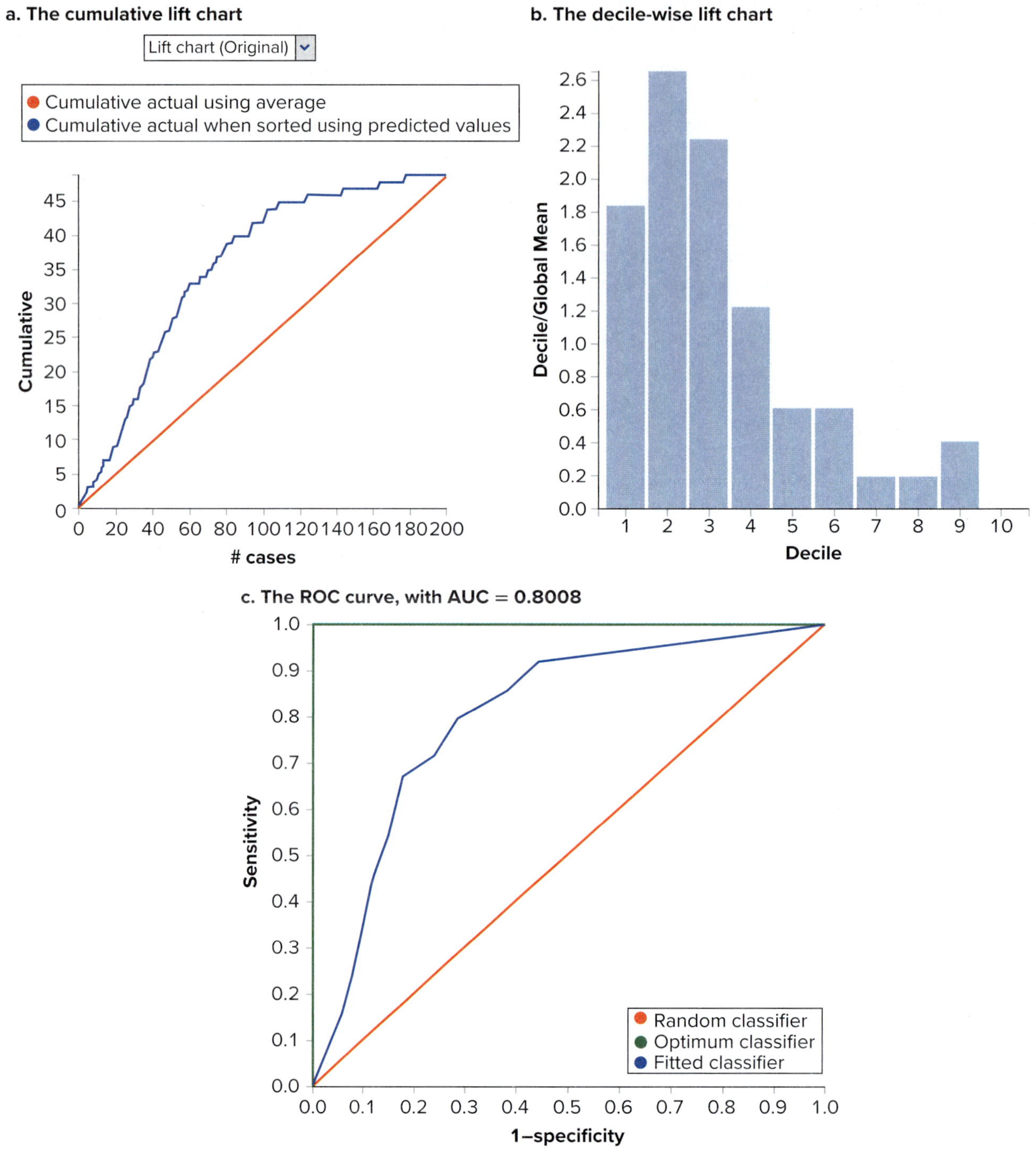

In the CBagging_NewScore worksheet, the 20 new bank customers are scored, and the results are summarized in Table 10.13. The Prediction: HELOC column displays the classification result for each of the 20 records. The first potential customer on the list is classified as not likely to respond to the HELOC offer, while the second potential customer is likely to respond. The PostProb:0 and PostProb:1 columns provide the predicted probabilities of the customer belonging to Class 0 and Class 1, respectively.

TABLE 10.13 Analytic Solver's Scoring Results

Record ID	Prediction: HELOC	PostProb: 0	PostProb: 1	Age	Sex	Income
Record 1	0	1	0	25	Female	45000
Record 2	1	0.6	0.4	23	Male	22000
⋮	⋮	⋮	⋮	⋮	⋮	⋮
Record 20	1	0.1	0.9	51	Male	43000

To create an ensemble tree model using the boosting strategy, repeat the previous procedure while choosing **Classify > Ensemble > Boosting** in step d. In the **Parameters** tab, Analytic Solver offers three variants of the AdaBoost algorithm that differ based on how training record weights are updated. Accept all default settings. In this case, the boosting ensemble model has slightly worse predictive performance than the bagging ensemble model and the single classification tree in Example 10.5, with an overall misclassification rate of 27.5%, sensitivity of 0.3469, and specificity of 0.8477. The cumulative lift chart, decile-wise lift chart, and ROC curve suggest the same information. The AUC value for the boosting ensemble tree is only 0.7590.

To create an ensemble tree model using the random forest strategy, repeat the previous procedure while choosing **Classify > Ensemble > Random Trees** in step d. In the **Parameters** tab, the default number two for the *Number of Randomly Selected Features* indicates that two predictor variables will be randomly selected to construct each tree. Check the box next to *Show Feature Importance*. Accept all other default settings. The performance measures and charts show that the random forest model performs almost the same as the bagging tree model with an overall misclassification rate of 21%, sensitivity of 0.6939, and specificity of 0.8212. The AUC value for the random forest ensemble model is 0.8100. The feature importance table shown in Table 10.14 indicates that Age is the most important predictor of whether a bank customer will respond to a HELOC offer, followed by Income.

You probably have noticed that this result contradicts with the single-tree model developed in Example 10.5, which finds Sex to be the most important variable to distinguish responders from nonresponders. The reason for the discrepancy is that the student edition of Analytic Solver only allows you to create 10 weak learners, each of which randomly selects only two predictor variables to construct the tree. The predictor variable Sex may not have been sufficiently represented in the very limited number of weak learners, resulting in a biased feature importance assessment. As we will see in the R example, by constructing an ensemble tree model with 100 weak learners, we will be able to conduct a more reliable feature importance analysis.

TABLE 10.14 Analytic Solver's Feature Importance Table

Feature	Importance
Age	3.048356023
Income	1.874119349
Sex	0.285117909

Using R

a. Import the data from the HELOC_Data worksheet of the ***HELOC*** data file into a data frame (table) and label it myData.

b. Install and load the *caret*, *gains*, *pROC*, and *randomForest* packages. Enter:

```
>install.packages("caret", dependencies = c("Depends", "Suggests"))
>install.packages("gains")
>install.packages("pROC")
>install.packages("randomForest")
>library(caret)
>library(gains)
>library(pROC)
>library(randomForest)
```

c. Because the *randomForest* package requires that all categorical variables be declared as factor variables explicitly, we use the **as.factor** function to convert the categorical target variable, HELOC, and categorical predictor variable, Sex, into factor variables. Enter:

```
>myData$HELOC <- as.factor(myData$HELOC)
>myData$Sex <- as.factor(myData$Sex)
```

d. We partition the data into training (60%) and validation (40%) data sets. By setting the random seed to 1, you will generate the same partitions as shown in this example. Enter:

```
>set.seed(1)
>myIndex <- createDataPartition(myData$HELOC, p=0.6, list = FALSE)
>trainSet <- myData[myIndex,]
>validationSet <- myData[-myIndex,]
```

e. We first use the **randomForest** function to construct the ensemble tree model using the bagging strategy. We set the *ntree* option equal to 100, which tells the function to build 100 single-tree models. As there are three predictor variables in the data, we set the *mtry* option equal to 3, which uses all three predictor variables in each single-tree model; this also indicates that we are using the bagging strategy. We set the *importance* option equal to TRUE to produce the feature importance information. Again, by setting the random seed to 1, you will get the same results as in this example. Enter:

```
>set.seed(1)
>bagging_tree <- randomForest(HELOC ~ ., data=trainSet, ntree=
100, mtry = 3, importance = TRUE)
```

f. To display the feature importance information, use the **varImpPlot** function to display feature importance graphically. We set the *type* option equal to 1 to show the feature importance in terms of the average decrease (or mean decrease) in overall accuracy. Alternately, if we set the *type* option equal to 2, then R uses the average decrease in the Gini impurity index to compare the feature importance. As Figure 10.28 shows, the most important predictor variable is Sex as the model suffers the most decrease in classification accuracy if the predictor variable is dropped. The second most important predictor variable is Age.

```
>varImpPlot(bagging_tree, type=1)
```

g. The following commands create the confusion matrix by comparing the predicted class memberships and actual class memberships of the validation data set. Enter:

```
>predicted_class <- predict(bagging_tree, validationSet)
>confusionMatrix(predicted_class, validationSet$HELOC,
positive = "1")
```

The confusion matrix is displayed in Figure 10.29. The performance measures show that the bagging ensemble tree model has an overall accuracy rate of 80% on the validation data. As shown earlier, the model is much better at classifying Class 0 cases correctly (specificity = 0.8851) than at classifying Class 1 cases correctly (sensitivity = 0.5577).

FIGURE 10.28 R's feature importance plot

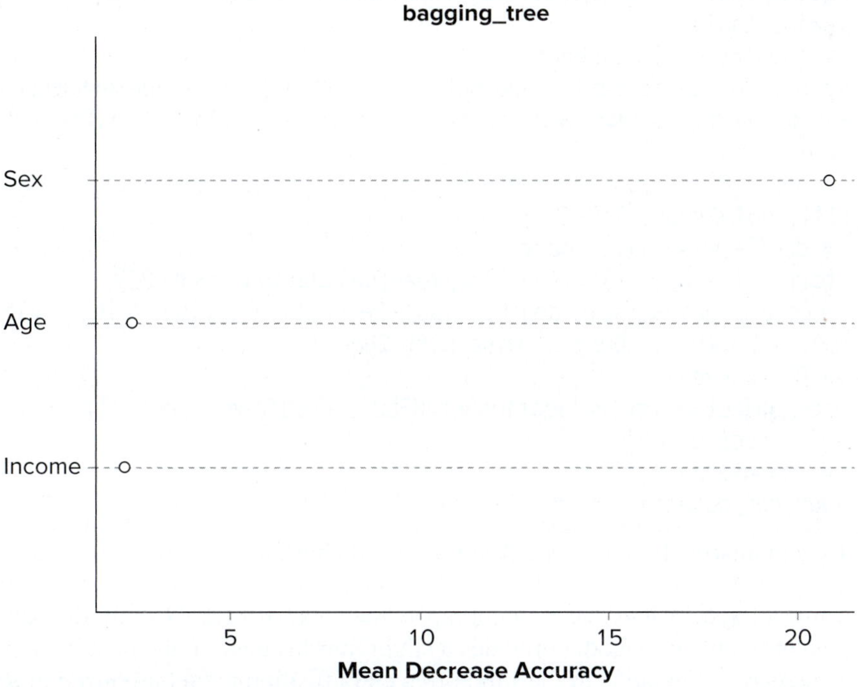

FIGURE 10.29 R's summary measures

```
Confusion Matrix and Statistics

            Reference
Prediction    0   1
          0 131  23
          1  17  29

               Accuracy : 0.8
                 95% CI : (0.7378, 0.8531)
    NO Information Rate : 0.74
    P-Value [ACC > NIR] : 0.02937

                  Kappa : 0.46

 Mcnemar's Test P-Value : 0.42920

            Sensitivity : 0.5577
            Specificity : 0.8851
         Pos Pred Value : 0.6304
         Neg Pred Value : 0.8506
             Prevalence : 0.2600
         Detection Rate : 0.1450
   Detection Prevalence : 0.2300
      Balanced Accuracy : 0.7214

       'Positive' class : 1
```

h. The following commands create the cumulative lift chart, the decile-wise lift chart, and the ROC curve. As the syntax for creating these graphs has been discussed in previous sections, we will not repeat it here. Enter:

```
>predicted_prob<- predict(bagging_tree, validationSet, type="prob")
>validationSet$HELOC <- as.numeric(as.character(validationSet$
HELOC))
>gains_table <- gains(validationSet$HELOC, predicted_prob[,2])
>gains_table
># cumulative lift chart
>plot(c(0, gains_table$cume.pct.of.total*sum(validationSet$HELOC))
~ c(0, gains_table$cume.obs),xlab = "# cases", ylab="Cumulative",
type ="l")
>lines(c(0, sum(validationSet$HELOC)) ~ c(0, dim(validationSet)
[1]), col="red", lty=2)
># decile-wise lift chart
>barplot(gains_table$mean.resp/mean(validationSet$HELOC),
names.arg=gains_table$depth, xlab="Percentile", ylab="Lift", ylim=
c(0, 3), main = "Decile- Wise Lift Chart")
># ROC curve
>roc_object<- roc(validationSet$HELOC, predicted_prob[,2])
>plot.roc(roc_object)
># compute auc
>auc(roc_object)
```

The cumulative lift chart, the decile-wise lift chart, and the ROC curve are displayed in Figure 10.30. Because the findings are comparable to those found using Analytic Solver, we will not repeat the analysis here. Overall, the bagging ensemble tree model provides a slight improvement in the predictive performance as compared to the single-tree classification model produced in R in Example 10.5.

i. Finally, to score the 20 new cases, we import the data from the HELOC_Score worksheet of the ***HELOC*** data file into a data frame (table) called myScoreData and use the **predict** function to produce the predicted class memberships and probabilities for the new cases using the bagging ensemble tree. We first convert the categorical predictor variable, Sex, to a factor variable so that it is consistent with the Sex variable in the bagging tree model created in step e. Enter:

```
>myScoreData$Sex <- as.factor(myScoreData$Sex)
>predicted_class_score <- predict(bagging_tree, myScoreData,
type="class")
>predicted_class_score
>predicted_class_prob <- predict(bagging_tree, myScoreData,
type="prob")
>predicted_class_prob
```

The scoring results are summarized in Table 10.15. As before, the probabilities predicted by the bagging ensemble tree constructed in R and Analytic Solver differ due to the different built-in algorithms used in the two software products.

TABLE 10.15 R's Scoring Results

Record ID	Prediction: HELOC	PostProb: 0	PostProb: 1	Age	Sex	Income
Record 1	0	1	0	25	Female	45000
Record 2	0	0.72	0.28	23	Male	22000
⋮	⋮	⋮	⋮	⋮	⋮	⋮
Record 20	1	0.39	0.61	51	Male	43000

To create an ensemble tree model using the random forest strategy, simply replace the R commands in step e with the following commands:

```
>set.seed(1)
>randomforest_tree <- randomForest(HELOC ~ ., data=trainSet,
ntree= 100, mtry = 2, importance = TRUE)
```

FIGURE 10.30 R's performance charts

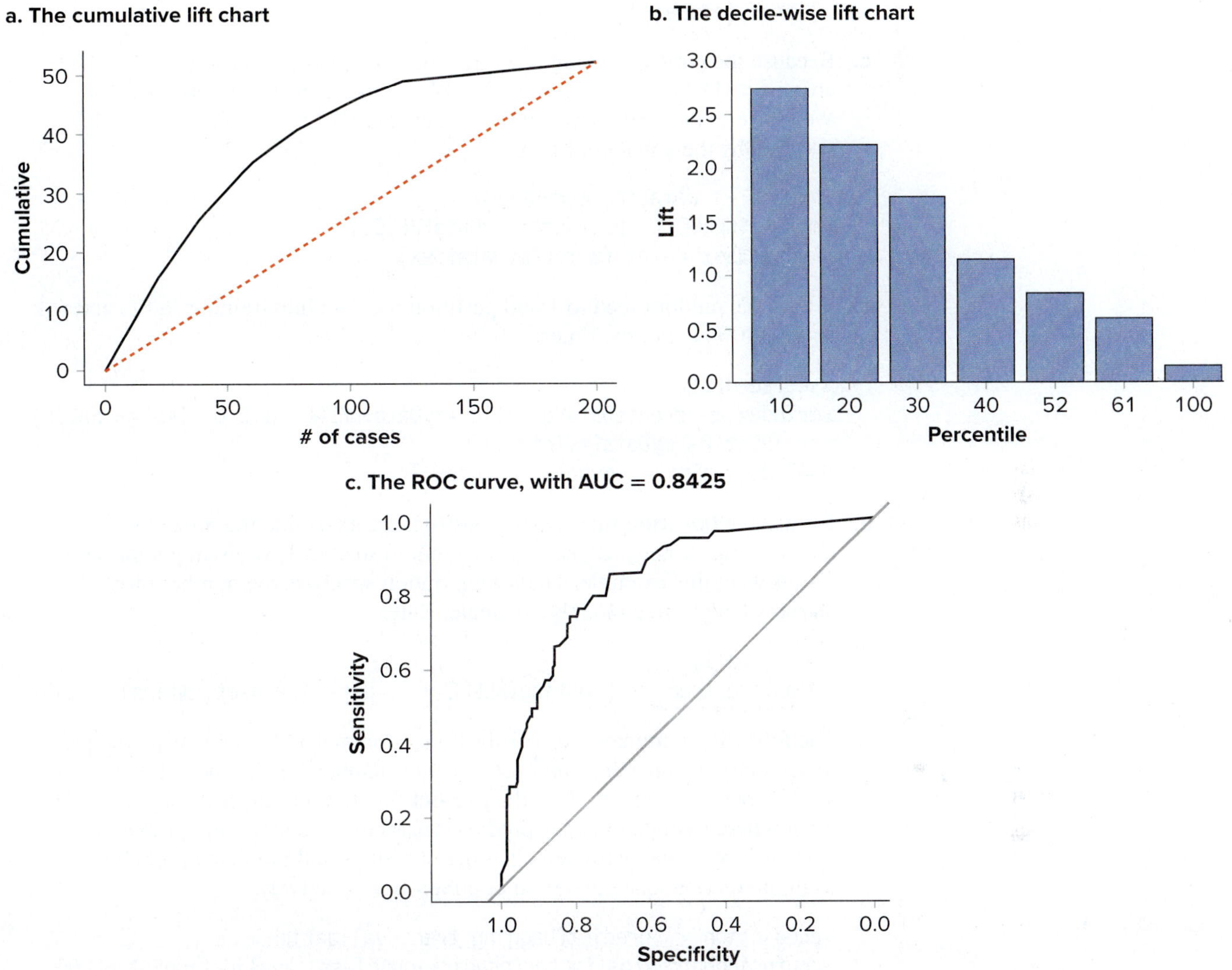

As you can see, the only difference between the commands for bagging and random forest is the number you specify for the *mtry* option in the **randomForest** function. Because random forest selects a subset of the predictor variables for building each single-tree model, we specify the number of predictor variables to include in the subset. In this case, we ask the function to randomly select two predictor variables for building individual single-tree models.

R uses the **boosting** function of the *adabag* package to create ensemble tree models that implement the boosting strategy. Due to the technical requirements of the *adabag* package, we create the boosting tree model slightly differently as shown in the example below:

a. Import the data from the HELOC_Data worksheet of the ***HELOC*** data file into a data frame (table) and label it myData.

b. Install and load the caret, gains, pROC, and adabag packages. Enter:

```
>install.packages("caret", dependencies = c("Depends", "Suggests"))
>install.packages("gains")
>install.packages("pROC")
>install.packages("adabag")
>library(caret)
>library(gains)
>library(pROC)
>library(adabag)
```

c. Because the *adabag* package requires the use of data frame class objects, we convert myData to a data frame class object using the **data.frame** function. We convert categorical variables (i.e, Sex and HELOC) to factor variables as required by the software. Enter:

```
>myData <- data.frame(myData)
>myData$HELOC <- as.factor(myData$HELOC)
>myData$Sex <- as.factor(myData$Sex)
```

d. We set the random seed to 1 and partition the data into training (60%) and validation (40%) data sets. Enter:

```
>set.seed(1)
>myIndex <- createDataPartition(myData$HELOC, p=0.6, list = FALSE)
>trainSet <- myData[myIndex,]
>validationSet <- myData[-myIndex,]
```

e. We use the **boosting** function to construct the ensemble tree model using the boosting strategy. By setting the random seed to 1, you will get the same results as in this example. The *mfinal* option specifies the number of weak learners (single-tree models) to create. Enter:

```
>set.seed(1)
>boosting_tree <- boosting(HELOC ~ ., data=trainset, mfinal = 100)
```

f. The following commands create the confusion matrix by comparing the predicted class memberships and actual class memberships of the validation data set. For boosting tree models, the **predict** function produces a list (named prediction here), which includes predicted class memberships and probabilities. You can access the predicted class memberships and predicted probabilities using prediction$class and prediction$prob, respectively.

```
>prediction <- predict(bagging_tree, validationSet)
>confusionMatrix(as.factor(prediction$class), validationSet$HELOC,
positive = "1")
```

Verify that the accuracy rate, sensitivity, and specificity are 0.8, 0.5577, and 0.8851, respectively. Using the default cutoff value of 0.5, the boosting ensemble tree shows the same predictive performance as the bagging ensemble tree does.

g. The following commands create the cumulative lift chart, the decile-wise lift chart, and the ROC curve. As the syntax for creating these graphs has been discussed in previous sections, we will not repeat it here. Note that we access the predicted probability of a validation case belonging the Class 1 (target class) using prediction$prob[, 2] because the Class 1 probabilities are listed in the second column of the object. Enter:

```
>validationSet$HELOC <- as.numeric(as.character(validationSet$HELOC))
>gains_table <- gains(validationSet$HELOC, prediction$prob[,2])
```

```
>gains_table
>#cumulative lift chart
>plot(c(0, gains_table$cume.pct.of.total*sum(validationSet$HELOC))
~ c(0, gains_table$cume.obs),xlab = "# cases", ylab="Cumulative",
type ="l")
>lines(c(0, sum(validationSet$HELOC)) ~ c(0, dim(validationSet)
[1]), col="red", lty=2)
># decile-wise lift chart
>barplot(gains_table$mean.resp/mean(validationSet$HELOC), names.
arg=gains_table$depth, xlab="Percentile", ylab="Lift", ylim= c(0,
3), main = "Decile-Wise Lift Chart")
># ROC curve
>roc_object<- roc(validationSet$HELOC, prediction$prob[,2])
>plot.roc(roc_object)
># compute auc
>auc(roc_object)
```

Verify that the AUC value of the ROC curve is 0.8209, which is slightly lower than the AUC value of the ROC curve derived from the bagging ensemble tree.

h. Finally, to score the 20 new cases, we import the data from the HELOC_Score worksheet of the ***HELOC*** data file into a data frame (table) and label it myScoreData. Convert myScoreData to a data frame class object and predictor variable Sex to a factor variable as required by the software. Enter:

```
>myScoreData <- data.frame(myScoreData)
>myScoreData$Sex <- as.factor(myScoreData$Sex)
>predicted_class_score <- predict(boosting_tree, myScoreData)
>predicted_class_score$class
>predicted_class_score$prob
```

The scoring results of the boosting ensemble model are slightly different from those of the bagging ensemble model; the 20th case is classified as a Class 0 case by the boosting model, whereas it is classified as a Class 1 case by the bagging model. As discussed before, unlike the bagging and random forest models, the boosting model does not provide variable importance information.

EXERCISES 10.4

Note: These exercises can be solved using Analytic Solver and/or R. The answers, however, will depend on the software package used. For Analytic Solver, partition data sets into 60% training and 40% validation, and use 12345 as the default random seed. Create 10 weak learners when constructing the ensemble model. For R, partition data sets into 60% training and 40% validation, and use the statement set.seed(1) to specify the random seed for data partitioning and constructing the ensemble tree models. Create 100 weak learners when constructing the ensemble model. If the predictor variable values are in the character format, then treat the predictor variable as a categorical variable. Otherwise, treat the predictor variable as a numerical variable.

Mechanics

44. **FILE** ***Exercise_10.44.*** Create a bagging ensemble classification tree model using the accompanying data set (predictor variables: x_1 to x_4; target: y).
    a. What are the overall accuracy rate, sensitivity, and specificity of the model on the validation data?

b. What is the AUC value of the model?
c. Score a new record with the following values: $x_1 = 3.45$, $x_2 = 1$, $x_3 = 18$, $x_4 = 5.80$. How would the record be classified using the bagging ensemble tree model? What is the probability of the record belonging to Class 1?

45. FILE ***Exercise_10.45.*** Create a boosting ensemble classification tree model using the accompanying data set (predictor variables: x_1 to x_4; target: y).
    a. What are the overall accuracy rate, sensitivity, and specificity of the model on the validation data?
    b. What is the AUC value of the model?
    c. Score a new record with the following values: $x_1 = 3.45$, $x_2 = 1$, $x_3 = 18$, $x_4 = 5.80$. How would the record be classified using the boosting ensemble tree model? What is the probability of the record belonging to Class 1?

46. FILE ***Exercise_10.46.*** Create a random forest ensemble classification tree model using the accompanying data set (predictor variables: x_1 to x_4; target: y). Select two predictor variables randomly to construct each weak learner.
    a. What are the overall accuracy rate, sensitivity, and specificity of the model on the validation data?
    b. What is the AUC value of the model?
    c. Which is the most important predictor variable?
    d. Score a new record with the following values: $x_1 = 3.45$, $x_2 = 1$, $x_3 = 18$, $x_4 = 5.80$. How would the record be classified using the random forest ensemble model? What is the probability of the record belonging to Class 1?

47. FILE ***Exercise_10.47.*** Create a bagging ensemble classification tree model using the accompanying data set (predictor variables: x_1 to x_5; target: y).
    a. What are the overall accuracy rate, sensitivity, and specificity of the model on the validation data?
    b. What is the lift value of the leftmost bar of the decile-wise lift chart?
    c. Score a new record with the following values: $x_1 = 52.8$, $x_2 = 230.50$, $x_3 = 1$, $x_4 = 144$, $x_5 = 6.23$. How would the record be classified using the bagging ensemble tree model? What is the probability of the record belonging to Class 1?

48. FILE ***Exercise_10.48.*** Create a boosting ensemble classification tree model using the accompanying data set (predictor variables: x_1 to x_5; target: y).
    a. What are the overall accuracy rate, sensitivity, and specificity of the model on the validation data?
    b. What is the lift value of the leftmost bar of the decile-wise lift chart?
    c. Score a new record with the following values: $x_1 = 52.8$, $x_2 = 230.50$, $x_3 = 1$, $x_4 = 144$, $x_5 = 6.23$. How would the record be classified using the boosting ensemble tree model? What is the probability of the record belonging to Class 1?

49. FILE ***Exercise_10.49.*** Create a random forest ensemble classification tree model using the accompanying data set (predictor variables: x_1 to x_5; target: y). Select two predictor variables randomly to construct each weak learner.
    a. What are the overall accuracy rate, sensitivity, and specificity of the model on the validation data?
    b. What is the lift value of the leftmost bar of the decile-wise lift chart?
    c. Which is the most important predictor variable?
    d. Score a new record with the following values: $x_1 = 52.8$, $x_2 = 230.50$, $x_3 = 1$, $x_4 = 144$, $x_5 = 6.23$. How would the record be classified using the random forest ensemble model? What is the probability of the record belonging to Class 1?

Applications

50. FILE ***Spam.*** Mateo Derby works as a cyber security analyst at a private equity firm. His colleagues at the firm have been inundated by a large number of spam e-mails. Mateo has been asked to implement a spam detection system on the company's e-mail server. He reviewed a sample of 500 spam and legitimate e-mails with relevant variables: spam (1 if spam, 0 otherwise), the number of recipients, the number of hyperlinks, and the number of characters in the message. A portion of the Spam_Data worksheet is shown in the accompanying table.

Spam	Recipients	Hyperlinks	Characters
0	19	1	47
0	15	1	58
⋮	⋮	⋮	⋮
1	13	2	32

    a. Create a bagging ensemble classification tree model to determine whether a future e-mail is spam. What are the overall accuracy rate, sensitivity, and specificity of the model on the validation data? What is the AUC value of the model?
    b. Create a random forest ensemble classification tree model. Select two predictor variables randomly to construct each weak learner. What are the overall accuracy rate, sensitivity, and specificity of the model on the validation data? What is the AUC value of the model? Which is the most important predictor variable?
    c. Score the new cases in the Spam_Score worksheet using the bagging ensemble classification tree model. What percentage of the e-mails is spam?

51. FILE ***HR.*** Daniella Lara, a human resources manager at a large tech consulting firm, has been reading about using analytics to predict the success of new employees. With the fast-changing nature of the tech industry, some employees have had difficulties staying current in their field and have

missed the opportunity to be promoted into a management position. Daniella is particularly interested in whether or not a new employee is likely to be promoted into a management role after 10 years with the company. She gathers information on current employees who have worked for the firm for at least 10 years. The information is based on the job application that the employees provided when they originally applied for a job at the firm. For each employee, the following variables are listed: Promoted (1 if promoted within 10 years, 0 otherwise), GPA (college GPA at graduation), Sports (number of athletic activities during college), and Leadership (number of leadership roles in student organizations). A portion of the HR_Data worksheet is shown in the accompanying table.

Promoted	GPA	Sports	Leadership
0	3.28	0	2
1	3.93	6	3
⋮	⋮	⋮	⋮
0	3.54	5	0

a. Create a bagging ensemble classification tree model to determine whether a new employee is likely to be promoted into a management role after 10 years with the company. What are the overall accuracy rate, sensitivity, and specificity of the model on the validation data? What is the AUC value of the model?
b. Create a random forest ensemble classification tree model. Select two predictor variables randomly to construct each weak learner. What are the overall accuracy rate, sensitivity, and specificity of the model on the validation data? What is the AUC value of the model? Which is the most important predictor variable?
c. Score the new cases in the HR_Score worksheet using the random forest ensemble classification tree model. What is the probability of the first new employee being promoted within 10 years? How many new employees in the data set will likely be promoted within 10 years based on a cutoff probability value of 0.5?

52. **FILE** ***Heart.*** In recent years, medical research has incorporated the use of data analytics to find new ways to detect heart disease in its early stage. Medical doctors are particularly interested in accurately identifying high-risk patients so that preventive care and intervention can be administered in a timely manner. A set of information is available regarding a patient's age (Age), blood pressure (BP Systolic and BP Diastolic), and BMI, along with an indicator of whether or not the patient has heart disease (Disease = 1 if heart disease, 0 otherwise). A portion of the data set is provided in the accompanying table.

Disease	Age	BP Systolic	BP Diastolic	BMI
0	44	112	111	17
1	55	128	90	27
⋮	⋮	⋮	⋮	⋮
0	29	144	85	32

a. Create a bagging ensemble classification tree model to determine whether a patient has heart disease. What are the overall accuracy rate, sensitivity, and specificity of the model on the validation data?
b. Create a boosting ensemble classification tree model. What are the overall accuracy rate, sensitivity, and specificity of the model on the validation data?
c. Compare the two ensemble models. Which model shows more robust performance according to the AUC value?

53. **FILE** ***Solar.*** New Age Solar sells and installs solar panels for residential homes. The company's sales representatives contact and pay a personal visit to potential customers to present the benefits of installing solar panels. This high-touch approach works well as the customers feel that they receive personal services that meet their individual needs, but it is more expensive than other, mass-marketing approaches. The company wants to be very strategic about visiting potential customers who are more likely to install solar panels. The company has compiled a data set of past home visits by sales reps. The data include the age (Age in years) and annual income (Income, in $1,000s) of the potential customer and whether or not the customer purchases the solar panels (Install: Y/N). A portion of the Solar_Data worksheet is shown in the accompanying table.

Income	Age	Install
115	45	N
68	31	Y
⋮	⋮	⋮
73	34	N

a. Create a bagging ensemble classification tree model to determine whether a customer purchases the solar panels. What are the overall accuracy rate, sensitivity, and specificity of the model on the validation data?
b. Create a boosting ensemble classification tree model. What are the overall accuracy rate, sensitivity, and specificity of the model on the validation data?
c. Compare the two ensemble models. Which model shows more robust performance according to the lift value of the leftmost bar of the decile-wise lift chart?
d. Score the new cases in the Solar_Score worksheet using the bagging ensemble classification tree model. What percentage of the potential customers are likely to purchase the solar panels based on a cutoff probability value of 0.5?

54. **FILE** ***MedSchool.*** Admission to medical school in the United States is highly competitive. The acceptance rate to the top medical schools could be as low as 2% or 3%.

With such a low acceptance rate, medical school admissions consulting has become a growing business in many cities. In order to better serve his clients, Paul Foster, a medical school admissions consultant, wants to build a data-driven model to predict whether or not a new applicant is likely to get accepted into one of the top 10 medical schools. He collected a database of 1,992 past applicants to the top 10 medical schools with the following information: Sex (F = female, M = male), CollegeParent (1 if parents with college degrees, 0 otherwise), GPA (1 if undergraduate GPA of 3.50 or higher, 0 otherwise), and Med (1 if accepted to a top 10 medical school, 0 otherwise). A portion of the data set is shown in the accompanying table.

Sex	CollegeParent	GPA	Med
F	1	1	1
M	1	0	1
⋮	⋮	⋮	⋮
M	0	0	0

a. Create a bagging ensemble classification tree model to determine whether a new applicant is likely to get accepted into one of the top 10 medical schools. What are the overall accuracy rate, sensitivity, and specificity of the model on the validation data? What is the AUC value of the model?

b. Create a random forest ensemble classification tree model. Select two predictor variables randomly to construct each weak learner. What are the overall accuracy rate, sensitivity, and specificity of the model on the validation data? Which is the most important predictor variable?

c. Compare the two ensemble models. Which model shows more robust performance according to the AUC value?

55. **FILE** ***Fraud.*** Credit card fraud is becoming a serious problem for the financial industry and can pose a considerable cost to banks, credit card issuers, and consumers. Fraud detection using data mining techniques has become an indispensable tool for banks and credit card companies to combat fraudulent transactions. A sample credit card data set contains the following variables: Fraud (1 if fraudulent activities, 0 otherwise), Amount (1 if low, 2 if medium, 3 if high), Online (1 if online transactions, 0 otherwise), and Prior (1 if products that the card holder previously purchased, 0 otherwise). A portion of the data set is shown in the accompanying table.

Fraud	Amount	Online	Prior
0	2	0	1
0	3	0	0
⋮	⋮	⋮	⋮
0	2	0	1

a. Create a bagging ensemble classification tree model to determine whether a transaction is fraudulent. What are the overall accuracy rate, sensitivity, and specificity of the model on the validation data? What is the AUC value of the model?

b. Create a random forest ensemble classification tree model. Select two predictor variables randomly to construct each weak learner. What are the overall accuracy rate, sensitivity, and specificity of the model on the validation data? What is the AUC value of the model? Which is the most important predictor variable?

c. Compare the two ensemble models. Which model shows more robust performance according to the lift value of the leftmost bar of the decile-wise lift chart?

56. **FILE** ***Travel_Plan.*** Refer to Exercise 11 for a description of the data set. Partition the data into 60% training and 40% validation data. For Analytic Solver, use 12345 as the random seed and create 10 weak learners. For R, use one as the random seed and create 100 weak learners.

a. Create a bagging ensemble classification tree model to determine whether a customer will travel within the next year. What are the overall accuracy rate, sensitivity, and specificity of the model on the validation data? What is the AUC value of the model?

b. Compare the performance of the bagging ensemble model to that of the single-tree model created in Exercise 11 (for Analytic Solver) or Exercise 12 (for R). Which model shows more robust performance? Explain.

c. Score the two new customers in the Travel_Plan_Score worksheet using the bagging ensemble classification tree model. What is the probability of the first customer having plans to travel within the next year? What is the probability for the second customer?

57. **FILE** ***Continue_Edu.*** Refer to Exercise 13 for a description of the data set.

a. Create a boosting ensemble classification tree model. What are the overall accuracy rate, sensitivity, and specificity of the model on the validation data? What is the AUC value of the model?

b. Compare the performance of the boosting ensemble model to that of the single-tree model created in Exercise 13 (for R) or Exercise 14 (for Analytic Solver). Which model shows more robust performance? Explain.

c. Score the two new cases in the Continue_Edu_Score worksheet using the boosting ensemble classification tree model. What is the probability of the first person enrolling in continuing education classes? What is the probability for the second person?

58. **FILE** ***Church.*** Refer to Exercise 15 for a description of the data set.

a. Create a random forest ensemble classification tree model. Select two predictor variables randomly to construct each weak learner. What are the overall accuracy rate, sensitivity, and specificity of the model on the validation data? What is the AUC value of the model? Which is the most important predictor variable?

b. Compare the performance of the random forest ensemble model to that of the single-tree model created in Exercise 15 (for Analytic Solver) or Exercise 16 (for R). Which model shows more robust performance? Explain.

c. Score the new cases in the *Church_Score* worksheet using the random forest ensemble classification tree model. What percentage of the individuals in the score data set are likely to go to church based on a cutoff probability value of 0.5?

59. **FILE** ***Graduate.*** Refer to Exercise 19 for a description of the data set.

a. Create a random forest ensemble classification tree model. Select three predictor variables randomly to construct each weak learner. What are the overall accuracy rate, sensitivity, and specificity of the model on the validation data? What is the AUC value of the model? Which is the most important predictor variable?

b. Compare the performance of the random forest ensemble model to that of the single-tree model created in Exercise 19 (for R) or Exercise 20 (for Analytic Solver). Which model shows more robust performance? Explain.

c. Score the new cases in the Graduate_Score worksheet using the random forest ensemble classification tree model. What is the probability of the first student graduating within four years? What is the probability for the second and third students?

60. **FILE** ***In_App_Pur.*** Refer to Exercise 21 for a description of the data set.

a. Create a boosting ensemble classification tree model. What are the overall accuracy rate, sensitivity, and specificity of the model on the validation data? What is the AUC value of the model?

b. Compare the performance of the boosting ensemble model to that of the single-tree model created in Exercise 21 (for Analytic Solver) or Exercise 22 (for R). Which model shows more robust performance? Explain.

c. Score the new cases in the In_App_Pur_Score worksheet using the boosting ensemble classification tree model. What is the probability of the first gamer making in-app purchases? What is the probability for the second gamer?

10.5 WRITING WITH BIG DATA

Case Study

As millions of people in the U.S. are crippled by student loan debt and high unemployment, policymakers are raising the question of whether college is even a good investment. Richard Clancy, a sociology graduate student, is interested in developing a model for predicting an individual's income for his master's thesis. He found a rich data set maintained by the U.S. Bureau of Labor Statistics, called the National Longitudinal Surveys (NLS), that follows over 12,000 individuals in the United States over time. The data set focuses on labor force activities of these individuals, but also includes information on a wide range of variables, such as income, education, sex, race, personality trait, health, and marital history.

FILE ***NLS***

Sample Report—Predicting Personal Income

Rawpixel.com/Shutterstock

According to the U.S. Bureau of the Census, the median personal income in 2000 was $29,998. Because an individual's personal income is determined by a large number of factors, it would be useful to build a model that helps predict whether an individual will earn an income that is at or above the median personal income. Based on the literature concerning personal income and data available from the U.S. Bureau of Labor Statistics, the following predictor variables are used to explain an individual's personal income:

- Years of education
- Mother's years of education
- Father's years of education
- Urban (equals 1 if the individual lived in an urban area at the age of 14, 0 otherwise)
- Black (equals 1 if the individual is black, 0 otherwise)
- Hispanic (equals 1 if the individual is Hispanic, 0 otherwise)
- White (equals 1 if the individual is white, 0 otherwise)
- Male (equals 1 if the individual is male, 0 otherwise)
- Self-Esteem (the individual's self-esteem using the Rosenberg Self-Esteem Scale; a higher score indicates a higher self-esteem.)
- Outgoing kid (equals 1 if the individual was outgoing at the age of six, 0 otherwise)
- Outgoing adult (equals 1 if the individual is outgoing as an adult, 0 otherwise)

As the objective is to determine whether an individual has an income that is at or above the median personal income rather than an individual's actual income, the target variable income is converted into a categorical variable that assumes the value one if income is greater than or equal to $29,998 and 0 otherwise. The final data set includes 5,821 observations, after observations with missing values were removed from the analysis.

To build a predictive model and assess the model's performance, the data are partitioned into training (60%) and validation (40%) sets. As the predictor variables include both numerical and categorical data types, the decision tree methodology is a suitable technique to build a classification model for this application. Figure 10.31 shows the best-pruned classification tree with eight decision nodes and nine leaf nodes. A number of conclusions can be drawn from the classification tree that shows that personal income level can be predicted using an individual's

FIGURE 10.31 Best-pruned classification tree

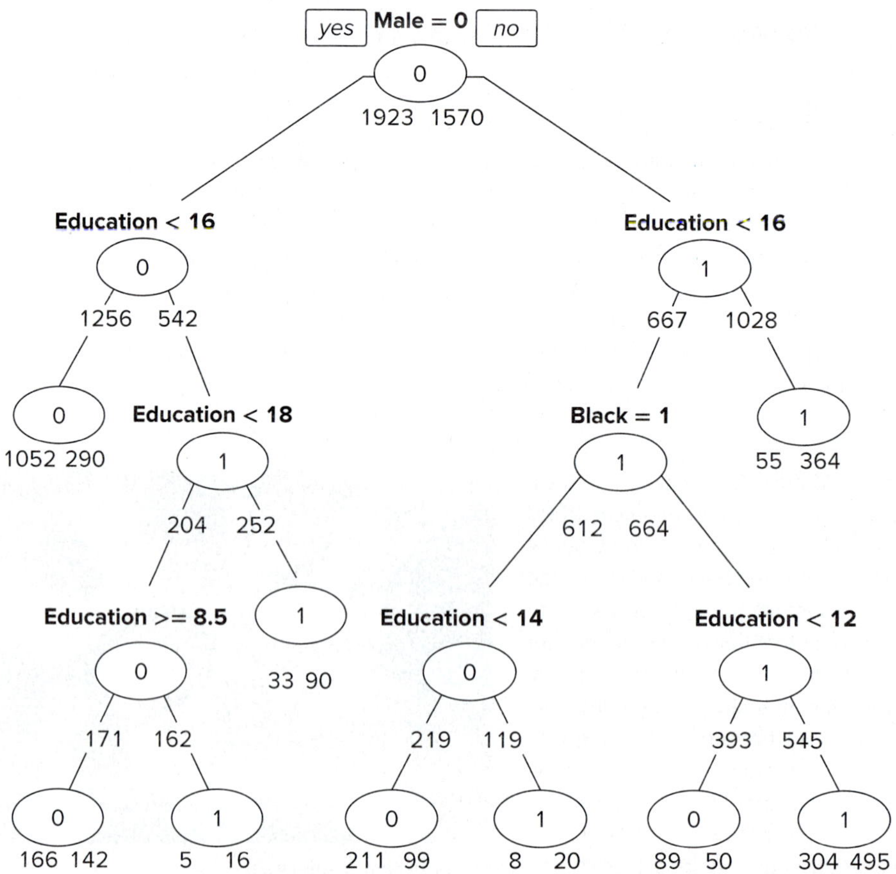

sex, education, race, and mother's education. For example, if an individual is male and had more than 16 years of education, he has a high probability of earning an income that is at or above the U.S. median income. If a person is female and has less than 16 years of education, she has a high probability of earning an income that is below the U.S. median income.

The performance of the classification tree is evaluated based on how accurately the model classifies cases in the validation data. The results from the confusion matrix, shown in Table 10.16, can be used to calculate an overall accuracy rate of 69.5%, sensitivity of 0.5994, specificity of 0.7730, and precision of 0.6830. Overall, the model demonstrates reasonably good performance in predicting an individual's income level.

TABLE 10.16 Confusion Matrix

	Predicted Class	
Actual Class	Class 1	Class 0
Class 1	627	291
Class 0	419	991

In an attempt to improve the predictive performance, a random forest ensemble model is also developed. The ensemble model shows an accuracy rate of 69.72%, sensitivity of 0.6138, specificity of 0.7652, and precision of 0.6808, which represents only a slight improvement over the single-tree model. Because the single-tree classification model is easier to interpret than the ensemble model, a single decision tree model is used as the final predictive model.

The conclusions drawn from the classification tree in Figure 10.31 are not surprising. For example, it has been well documented that higher education leads to a higher income. Similarly, while the salary difference based on sex and race has shrunk over the years, it still persists. According to a Pew Research Center analysis, women earned 85% of what men earned in 2018 and households headed by a black person earned, on average, little more than half of what the average white household earned.

What is surprising, however, is that an individual's self-esteem level and whether a person is outgoing as a kid or adult do not impact an individual's income level. Perhaps these psychological factors are related to multiple indicators of later-year academic achievement. Therefore, an individual with high self-esteem may go for higher education, which in turn impacts the individual's income.

The classification model developed in this report offers important and actionable insights for policymakers. The model highlights that sex and racial gaps continue to exist. Males and non-black people are more likely to earn an above-median income than females and black people do. Special attention should be given to groups identified by the model as likely to earn below-median income when developing equitable policies for improving economic prospects.

Suggested Case Studies

Decision trees are considered to be one of the most transparent and easiest to interpret supervised data mining techniques. They can be applied to many situations and different data sets. Here are some suggestions using the big data that accompany this text.

Report 10.1 FILE ***Car_Crash.*** Subset the data to include only the accidents that occurred in one city or during one month. Develop a decision tree model that predicts whether an automobile accident results in fatal or severe injuries using predictor variables, such as traffic violation category, weather condition, type of collision, location of the accident, and lighting condition. Note: Many of the predictor variables are categorical; therefore, you will need to convert them to the appropriate data form prior to the analysis.

Report 10.2 FILE ***Longitudinal_Survey.*** Subset the data to include only those individuals who lived in an urban area. Develop a decision tree model to predict an individual's body mass index (BMI) or whether an individual is going to be overweight or not using predictor variables, such as sex, number of years of education, parents' years of education, self-esteem scale, and whether the person is outgoing as a kid and/or adult. Note: The Centers for Disease Control and Prevention (CDC) defines overweight as someone whose BMI is equal to or greater than 25.

Report 10.3 **FILE** ***TechSales_Reps.*** Subset the data to include only college-educated sales professionals in the software product group. Develop a decision tree model to predict whether or not the sales professional will receive a high (9 or 10) net promoter score (NPS), using predictor variables, such as age, sex, tenure with the company, number of professional certificates acquired, annual evaluation score, and personality type. Note: You may need to perform data transformation in order to meet the requirements of the analytics technique.

Report 10.4 **FILE** ***College_Admissions.*** Subset the data to include only one of the three colleges. Develop a series of decision tree models to predict which college is most likely to accept a given university applicant based on the applicant's sex, race, high school GPA, SAT/ACT score, and parents' years of education. Note: You will construct a decision tree model for each college. The college whose model produces the highest probability of acceptance is the one that is most likely to accept the applicant.

Report 10.5 **FILE** ***House_Price.*** Develop a decision tree model to predict the sale price of a house by using predictor variables, such as number of bedrooms, number of bathrooms, home square footage, lot square footage, and age of the house. Note: As real estate values can differ dramatically from region to region, you may want to develop a model for each geographic location in the data set. Compare the performance of the decision tree model with predictive models that use other supervised learning techniques discussed in Chapter 9.

11 Unsupervised Data Mining

LEARNING OBJECTIVES

After reading this chapter, you should be able to:

LO **11.1** **Conduct hierarchical cluster analysis.**

LO **11.2** **Conduct *k*-means cluster analysis.**

LO **11.3** **Conduct association rule analysis.**

As discussed in earlier chapters, data mining is a process of applying analytical techniques to find hidden structures, patterns, and relationships among data. It is categorized as supervised (or predictive or directed) or unsupervised (or descriptive or undirected) data mining. An overview of data mining concepts including topics such as distance measures between observations (or records) and principal component analysis for dimension reduction was provided in Chapter 8. The focus of Chapters 9 and 10 was on supervised data mining. In this chapter, we turn our attention to unsupervised data mining.

We explore two popular unsupervised data mining techniques: cluster analysis and association rule analysis. Cluster analysis finds similarities among data and groups them into clusters of observations that share similar characteristics. Clusters are formed in such a way that objects are similar within a group but dissimilar across groups. This analysis is valuable, for example, to marketers who identify distinct segments in their customer bases and then use this knowledge to develop targeted marketing programs. Association rule analysis (or market basket analysis) identifies hidden relationships and common occurrences among data. This analysis is valuable, for example, to e-commerce companies that identify associations to make product recommendations to customers based on their previous purchases.

©Lissandra Melo/Shutterstock

INTRODUCTORY CASE

Nutritional Facts of Candy Bars

Aliyah Williams is an honors student at a prestigious business school in Southern California. She is also a fledgling entrepreneur and owns a vending machine business. Most of her vending machines are located on campus and in the downtown area, and they are stocked with a variety of snacks, including a large selection of candy bars. Aliyah is aware that California consumers are becoming increasingly health conscious when it comes to food purchase. She has learned from her consumer research class that the U.S. Department of Agriculture (USDA) maintains a website with a database of nutritional facts about food products, including candy bars.

Aliyah wants to come up with a better selection of candy bars and strategically group and display them in her vending machines. She also wants to feature certain products more prominently in different locations based on the type of consumers that tend to frequent these locations. Table 11.1 shows a portion of the data that Aliyah has downloaded from the USDA website. Listed for each candy bar are the calories per serving (Calories), total fat (Fat in grams), protein (Protein in grams), and carbohydrates (Carb in grams).

TABLE 11.1 Candy Bar Nutritional Facts

Brands	Calories	Fat	Protein	Carb
Peanut Butter Twix	311.0	18.5	5.3	31.4
Baby Ruth	275.0	13.0	3.2	39.0
⋮	⋮	⋮	⋮	⋮
Twizzlers Cherry Nibs	139.0	1.1	1.0	31.7

FILE
Candy_Bars

Aliyah wants to use the information in Table 11.1 to:

1. Analyze the nutritional fact data and group candy products according to their nutritional content.
2. Select a variety of candy bars from each group to better meet the taste of today's consumers.
3. Select and display the candy bars in her vending machines according to the grouping and the locations of the vending machines.

A synopsis of this introductory case is presented at the end of Section 11.2.

11.1 HIERARCHICAL CLUSTER ANALYSIS

Data mining uses many kinds of machine learning algorithms to identify patterns in data. These algorithms are classified into supervised (or predictive or directed) and unsupervised (or descriptive or undirected) data mining, depending on the way they "learn" about data to make predictions. Supervised data mining, also called supervised learning, is the more commonly used methodology for developing predictive models. The two primary types of supervised data mining applications, classification and prediction, were discussed in Chapters 6, 7, 9, and 10. These models are used to predict the outcome of an output (response or target) variable based on several input (predictor) variables. In some supervised techniques such as regression, a mathematical model that relates the outcome of the response variable (commonly referred to as y) to one or more predictor variables (commonly referred to as $x_1, x_2, \ldots, x_k$) is estimated. A regression model, for example, is therefore "trained" or "supervised" because the known values of the response variable are used to build a model in the training set. In addition, the performance of the model can be evaluated based on the extent to which the predicted values deviate from the actual values of the response variable in the validation set.

In this chapter, we focus on unsupervised data mining, also referred to as unsupervised learning, that requires no knowledge of the response variable. It is called unsupervised because, unlike supervised learning, the algorithms allow the computer to identify complex processes and patterns without any specific guidance from the analyst. Unsupervised learning is an important part of exploratory data analysis because it makes no distinction between the response variable y and the predictor variable x; in this chapter, we represent all k variables as $x_1, x_2, \ldots, x_k$. Several machine learning algorithms are readily available to implement two core unsupervised data mining techniques: cluster analysis and association rule analysis.

In Chapter 8, we explored several similarity measures to gauge whether a group of observations (or records) are similar or dissimilar to one another. In particular, we used Euclidian and Manhattan distance measures for numerical variables, which were often first standardized or normalized to make them independent of scale. In addition, matching and Jaccard's coefficients were used to measure similarity for categorical variables. These measures are necessary for both supervised and unsupervised data mining techniques. For example, in cluster analysis, similarity measures are used to form clusters in such a way that objects are similar within a group but dissimilar across groups.

LO 11.1

Conduct hierarchical cluster analysis.

Hierarchical Cluster Analysis

Grouping objects into categories that share some similar characteristic or trait is an important task that, as humans, we do almost every day. We all have the ability to recognize patterns or common characteristics among objects and classify them into groups or clusters. Because grouping is such an important function in our everyday lives, **cluster analysis** is one of the most widely used unsupervised data mining techniques. It groups observations (records) in a data set such that observations are similar within a cluster and dissimilar across clusters, using similarity measures discussed in Section 8.2.

Cluster analysis is often considered part of descriptive analytics because it performs useful exploratory analysis by summarizing a large number of observations in a data set into a small number of homogeneous clusters. The cluster characteristics or profiles help us understand and describe the different groups of observations that exist in the data.

While cluster analysis can be performed on its own, it is sometimes performed prior to supervised learning techniques to help separate observations that display very different patterns. For example, pricing luxury or collectible vehicles may require a very different model from the one that is used to price economy vehicles. Therefore, it is reasonable to cluster different types of vehicles into different groups and develop pricing models for each group separately to achieve better predictive performance.

CLUSTER ANALYSIS

Cluster analysis is an unsupervised data mining technique that groups data into categories that share some similar characteristic or trait.

A popular application of cluster analysis is called customer or market segmentation, where companies analyze a large amount of customer-related demographic and behavioral data and group the customers into different market segments. For example, a credit card company might group customers into those who pay off their account balance every month versus those who carry a monthly balance, and, within these two customer segments, group them further according to their spending habits. The company would likely target each of the customer segments with different promotion and advertising campaigns or design different financial products for each group.

Cluster analysis allows us to form groups of people, products, business transactions, and many other types of observations into internally homogenous groups where each group has unique characteristics and can be treated differently from other groups. Similarly, insurance companies might want to group motor insurance policy holders based on their characteristics such as age, annual miles driven, and average claim cost, thus allowing them to set optimal insurance premiums.

Two common clustering techniques are hierarchical clustering and k-means clustering. We discuss hierarchical clustering in this section and k-means clustering in the next section. **Hierarchical clustering** is a technique that uses an iterative process to group data into a hierarchy of clusters. Common strategies of hierarchical clustering usually follow one of two methods: **agglomerative clustering** (or agglomerative nesting or AGNES) or **divisive clustering** (or divisive analysis or DIANA). AGNES starts with each observation being its own cluster, with the algorithm iteratively merging clusters that are similar to each other as one moves up the hierarchy; it is loosely referred to as "the bottom-up" approach. Conversely, DIANA starts by assigning all observations to one cluster, with the algorithms iteratively separating the most dissimilar observations as one moves down the hierarchy; it is loosely referred to as a "top-down" approach.

HIERARCHICAL CLUSTERING

Hierarchical clustering is a technique that uses an iterative process to group data into a hierarchy of clusters. Common strategies of hierarchical clustering usually follow one of two methods: agglomerative clustering or divisive clustering.

- Agglomerative clustering is a "bottom-up" approach that starts with each observation being its own cluster, with the algorithm iteratively merging clusters that are similar to each other as one moves up the hierarchy.
- Divisive clustering is a "top-down" approach that starts by assigning all observations to one cluster, with the algorithms iteratively separating the most dissimilar observations as one moves down the hierarchy.

In this text, we focus on agglomerative clustering, which is the more commonly used approach between the two methods for hierarchical clustering; the computer applications for agglomerative clustering can easily be modified to implement divisive clustering. We first create agglomerative clusters with data on variables that are either numerical or categorical. We then extend the analysis to include mixed data, which combines data from both numerical and categorical variables.

Agglomerative Clustering with Numerical or Categorical Variables

As mentioned earlier, in AGNES, each observation in the data initially forms its own cluster. The algorithm then successively merges these clusters into larger clusters based on their similarity until all observations are merged into one final cluster, referred to as a root. We measure the (dis)similarity of observations using the Euclidean distance or Manhattan distance measures for numerical variables and matching or Jaccard's coefficient for categorical variables. Here, we use the z-score standardization to make the data on numerical variables independent of scale. Distance measures and z-score standardization were discussed in Section 8.2.

During the iterative process to merge clusters, the AGNES algorithm uses one of several linkage methods to evaluate (dis)similarity between clusters.

- **The single linkage method** uses the nearest distance between a pair of observations that do not belong to the same cluster.
- **The complete linkage method** uses the farthest distance between a pair of observations that do not belong to the same cluster.
- **The centroid method** uses the centroid distance between clusters, where the mean values for individual variables in the cluster collectively represent the "center" or centroid of the cluster.
- **The average linkage method** uses the average distance between all pairs of observations that do not belong to the same cluster.
- **Ward's method**, developed by Joe H. Ward in 1963, uses a slightly different algorithm to minimize the dissimilarity within clusters. Specifically, it uses the "error sum of squares (ESS)" to measure the loss of information that occurs when observations are clustered, where ESS is defined as the squared difference between individual observations and the cluster mean. Ward's method is widely implemented in many clustering analysis software applications including Analytic Solver and R.

For illustration of the first three linkage methods, consider Figure 11.1 with two potential clusters. The blue line shows the single linkage distance, and the green line represents the complete linkage distance. The centroid distance is presented as a red dotted line. The average linkage distance (not displayed in the figure) is the average distance of all nine possible pairs between the two clusters. Ward's method (not displayed in the figure) involves computing the error sum of squares to measure the loss of information when observations are clustered.

FIGURE 11.1 Linkage distance for hierarchical clustering

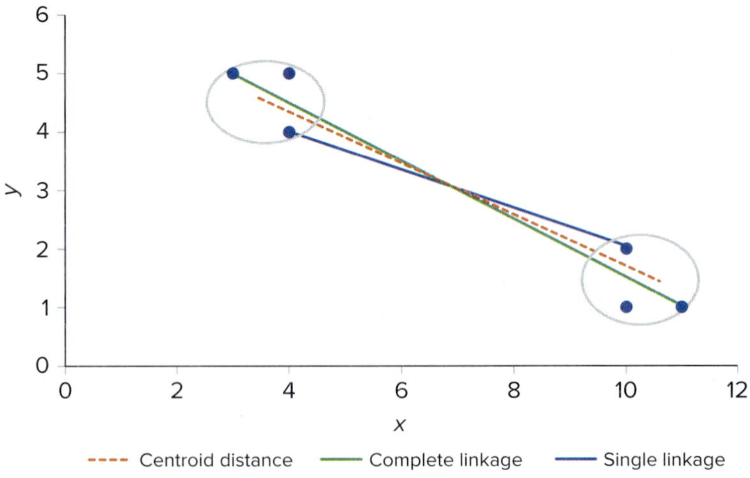

Dendrogram

Once the AGNES algorithm completes its clustering process, data are usually represented in a treelike structure where each observation can be thought of as a "leaf" on the tree. The treelike structure is called a **dendrogram**. It allows users to visually inspect the clustering result and determine the appropriate number of clusters in the data. Determining the right number of clusters is somewhat subjective, but we can visually inspect a dendrogram to help guide our decision. Figure 11.2 shows an example of a dendrogram.

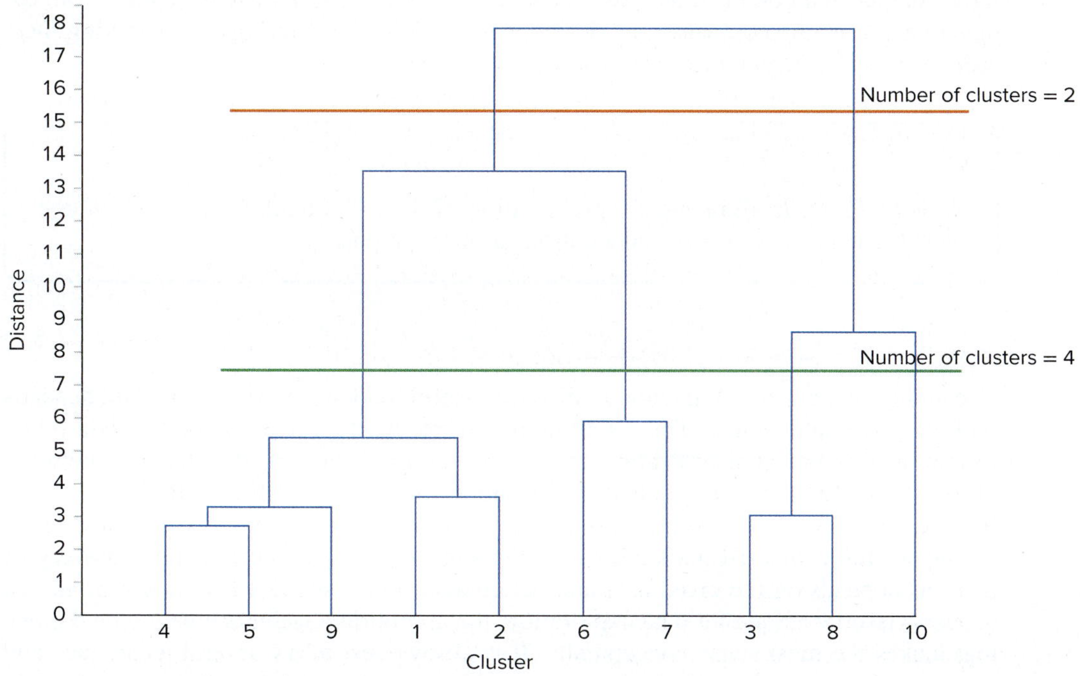

FIGURE 11.2
Dendrogram

Viewing from the top of the dendrogram, we can see two main branches. Each branch represents a possible cluster of observations. Collectively, the two branches consist of 10 sub-branches or sub-clusters, labeled by the values below the horizontal axis. The smaller branch on the right-hand side includes three sub-branches or sub-clusters numbered 3, 8, and 10. The height of each branch (cluster) or sub-branch (sub-cluster) indicates the distance, or how dissimilar it is from the other branches or sub-branches with which it is merged. The greater the height, the more distinctive the cluster is from the other cluster. For example, sub-clusters 4 and 5 are very similar to each other and therefore connect at a lower height. As a result, we can often determine an appropriate number of clusters by visually inspecting the dendrogram. For the dendrogram in Figure 11.2, we might decide that the observations should be grouped into two clusters. As such, we may "cut the dendrogram tree" horizontally to obtain the two main branches (two clusters), as shown by the red line.

Relying solely on the height of a dendrogram tree branch may lead to statistically distinctive clusters that have little or no practical meaning. Therefore, we often take into account both quantitative measures (such as a dendrogram) and practical considerations to determine an appropriate number of clusters. For example, suppose the dendrogram in Figure 11.2 represents the process of clustering customers into groups that are internally homogenous. If a firm wants to target particular groups for one of the four different products that it produces, then settling on four clusters seems appropriate in this scenario; that is, in Figure 11.2 the tree would be cut at the green line, rather than the red line.

We should also review the profile of each cluster using descriptive statistics. For example, if age, sex, income, educational attainment, and number of hours online per week are the variables used in the cluster analysis to group customers, each resulting cluster can be described with respect to its most defining characteristics. One cluster may include predominantly high-income, highly educated female customers between the ages of 35 and 45, and another cluster may include predominantly customers between the ages of 18 and 25 who spend over 20 hours online weekly. We can label the first group as "middle-age female professionals" and the second group as "young Internet surfers."

Another common approach to profile clusters is to incorporate variables that were not used in clustering but of interest to the decision maker. For example, we may find that a large percentage of the customers in the first cluster have purchased our products at least five times during the past year, while the majority of the customers in the second cluster have not placed an order in the last six months. Based on these insights gained from the cluster analysis, the company may design different product offerings or marketing messages to target different customer groups.

A DENDROGRAM

A dendrogram is a graphical representation of data as a treelike structure, where each branch can be considered a cluster of observations.

A Note on the Choice of the Hierarchical Approach

The ability of a clustering method to discover useful hidden patterns of the data depends on how it is implemented. The resulting clustering structure depends on the data transformation (z-score standardization or min-max normalization), the distance between observations (Euclidian or Manhattan), the algorithm used (AGNES or DIANA), and the linkage between clusters (single, complete, average, centroid, or Ward's method). There are no well-documented guidelines for selecting a technique because the discovery of patterns depends on the given data and the context. Because clustering is essentially an unsupervised technique for data exploration, the appropriate technique would be the one that makes the most sense conceptually. It is always best to try several techniques and select the cluster structure that allows us to generate some insight.

Using Analytic Solver and R to Perform Agglomerative Clustering

In Example 11.1 we demonstrate how to use Analytic Solver and R to perform agglomerative hierarchical clustering. We should note that cluster analysis is sensitive to the specific algorithms implemented in different software packages. The algorithms used in Analytic Solver differ from the algorithms used in R, and, thus, the clustering results may differ.

EXAMPLE 11.1

FILE
Cities

Table 11.2 shows a portion of data relating to the crime rate (crimes per 100,000 residents), the poverty rate (in %), and the median income (in $1,000s) for 41 cities in the United States. Use Analytic Solver and R to perform agglomerative hierarchical clustering. Interpret the results.

TABLE 11.2 Demographic Data for 41 Cities in the U.S.

City	Crime	Poverty	Income
Barnstable	710.6	3.8	58.422
Boston	1317.7	16.7	48.729
⋮	⋮	⋮	⋮
Warwick	139.7	3.9	59.445

SOLUTION:

Using Analytic Solver

a. Open the ***Cities*** data file.

b. From the menu, choose **Data Mining > Cluster > Hierarchical Clustering**.

c. See Figure 11.3. Click on the ellipsis button next to the *Data range* and select cells \$A\$1:\$D\$42. Make sure that the box *First Row Contains Headers* is checked. The *Variables in Input Data* box will populate. Select and move variables Crime, Poverty, and Income to the *Selected Variables* box. Accept other defaults and click *Next.*

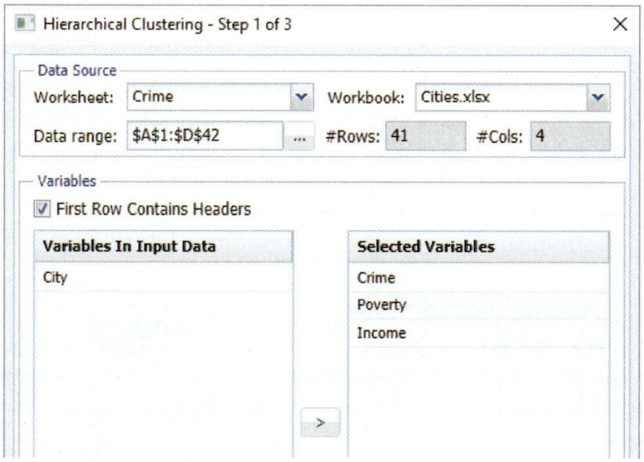

Source: Microsoft Excel

FIGURE 11.3 Hierarchical Clustering dialog boxi n Analytic Solver

d. In the next dialog box, select *Normalize input data.* As explained in Section 8.2, variables with a large scale (the crime rate in this case) can dominate the results. Note that Analytic Solver uses the input "Normalize" for a *z*-score standardization. For *Similarity Measure*, we choose *Euclidean distance* because all the input variables are numerical. For *Clustering Method*, we choose to use *Ward's Method* in this example. Click *Next.*

e. In the final dialog box, under *Output Options* select *Draw Dendrogram* and *Show Cluster Membership.* Set the *Maximum Number of Leaves* at 10 and the *Number of Clusters* at 3. Click *Finish.*

Next to the Cities worksheet, Analytic Solver will insert three new worksheets: HC_Output, HC_Clusters, and HC_Dendrogram. The HC_Output worksheet simply provides a summary of the input parameters that we have entered. The HC_Clusters worksheet lists each observation, its assigned cluster, and its sub-cluster. What is of most interest to us at the moment is the HC_Dendrogram worksheet. If you select this worksheet, the dendrogram appears as a pop-up, and other information appears in the accompanying worksheet.

The top half of Figure 11.4 shows the dendrogram and the bottom half shows each observation's cluster assignment. Visual inspection of the dendrogram shows that the observations in the data belong to three distinct clusters. We can cut the dendrogram (e.g., where the *y*-axis value is 8) to obtain these clusters where, for instance, the first cluster consists of sub-clusters 1, 5, and 10. This cluster includes observations 1 (from sub-cluster 1); 7, 9, 16, 20, 21, 29, 32, and 41 (from sub-cluster 5); and 35 and 37 (from sub-cluster 10).

The height of each of the three branches is tall, indicating a good clustering structure because the distances between the clusters are large. This confirms that our decision to specify three clusters in step e yields a reasonably good outcome. To add the cluster membership to the original data in the Cities worksheet, we can go to the HC_Clusters worksheet and copy and paste the cluster numbers onto the Cities worksheet. Table 11.3 shows a portion of the updated Cities worksheet.

FIGURE 11.4 Analytic Solver's ***HC_Dendrogram*** worksheet

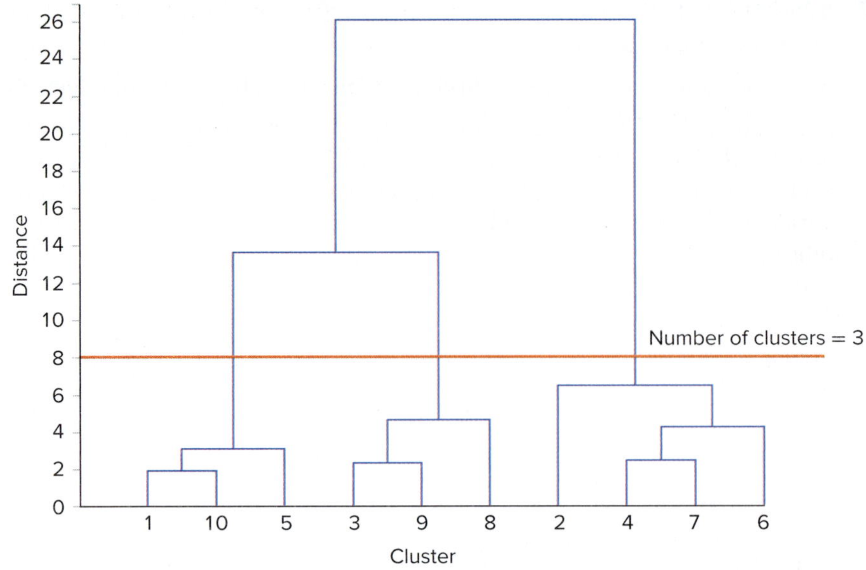

Cluster Legend (Numbers show the record sequence relative to the original data)									
Sub-Cluster 1	Sub-Cluster 2	Sub-Cluster 3	Sub-Cluster 4	Sub-Cluster 5	Sub-Cluster 6	Sub-Cluster 7	Sub-Cluster 8	Sub-Cluster 9	Sub-Cluster 10
1	2	4	5	7	8	15	23	25	35
	3	13	11	9	30		24	27	37
	6	17	12	16	40		26	34	
	10	19	28	20			38	36	
	14	22	33	21			39		
	18	31		29					
				32					
				41					

TABLE 11.3 Updated ***Cities*** Data using Analytic Solver for Example 11.1

City	Crime	Poverty	Income	Record ID	Cluster	Sub-Cluster
Barnstable	710.6	3.8	58.422	Record 1	1	1
Boston	1317.7	16.7	48.729	Record 2	2	2
⋮	⋮	⋮	⋮	⋮	⋮	⋮
Warwick	139.7	3.9	59.445	Record 41	1	5

We can now compute summary statistics for each cluster to review the cluster characteristics. Table 11.4 shows these summary statistics, with the average crime rate, poverty rate, and income for each cluster. We identify Cluster 1 as a group of 11 cities with the lowest crime rate, the lowest poverty rate, and the highest median income among the three clusters. On the other hand, Cluster 2 represents a group of 15 cities with the highest crime rate, highest poverty rate, and lowest median income among the three clusters. Cluster 3 has a crime rate closer to Cluster 1, a medium poverty rate, and a median income closer to Cluster 2. Policymakers may find this type of information useful when they make funding decisions or try to understand the varying effect of an economic policy on different cities.

TABLE 11.4 Hierarchical Clustering Results using Analytic Solver for Example 11.1

Cluster	Crime	Poverty	Income
1 (N = 11)	235.90	5.51	61.39
2 (N = 15)	1,096.20	18.45	40.33
3 (N = 15)	362.03	11.61	44.61

Compared to other clustering methods, the Ward's method in this case yields a clustering structure where each cluster has a reasonable number of observations. Had we used the single linkage or centroid clustering method, the analysis would have resulted in several clusters that have only one observation, which usually is not a desirable outcome. Students are encouraged to experiment with different clustering methods and examine the different outcomes.

Using R

a. Import the ***Cities*** data into a data frame (table) and label it myData.

b. Install and load the *cluster* package. Enter:

```
> install.packages("cluster")
> library(cluster)
```

c. We exclude the City variable from the analysis; standardize the Crime, Poverty, and Income variables; and store their standardized values in a data frame called `myData1`. We use the **scale** function to standardize the values of the three variables. Enter:

```
> myData1 <- scale(myData[ , 2:4])
```

If no standardization is needed, we simply select the three numerical variables and our R code would be `> myData1 <- myData[ , 2:4]`.

d. We use the **dist** function to determine similarity among observations, and store the distance values in a new variable called d. For options within the **dist** function, we use *method* to specify the distance calculation. Options for the distance calculation include "euclidean", "manhattan", "binary" (for Jaccard's coefficient), "maximum", and "minkowski". [The last two options are beyond the scope of this text.] We specify "euclidean" to use the Euclidean distance as the similarity measure. Enter:

```
> d <- dist(myData1, method = "euclidean")
```

e. We use the **agnes** function to perform agglomerative clustering and label the results as aResult. For options within the **agnes** function, we use *method* to specify the clustering method. Options for the clustering method include "single" (single linkage), "complete" (complete linkage), "average", "ward" (Ward's method), "weighted", and "flexible". We specify "ward". The *diss* option (meaning dissimilarity) is set equal to TRUE to indicate that variable d contains a distance matrix instead of the original variables. Enter "aResult" to obtain the clustering results including an agglomerative coefficient, which measures the strength of the clustering structure and whether or not there is a natural clustering structure in the data. Generally, a coefficient value of 0.75 or greater is indicative of the existence of a good and natural clustering structure. Enter:

```
> aResult <- agnes(d, diss = TRUE, method = "ward")
> aResult
```

R reports the following portion of results:

```
Call: agnes(x = myData, method = "ward")
Agglomerative coefficient: 0.942097
```

The agglomerative coefficient (0.942097) suggests that a good and natural clustering exists in the data.

f. We use the **plot** function to produce the dendrogram as well as a banner plot. Enter:

```
> plot(aResult)
Hit <Return> to see next plot:
```

You will be prompted to press <Return> (the "Enter" key) to display the plots. If you press <Return> once, the banner plot appears.

Figure 11.5(a) shows the banner plot. A banner plot is an alternative to the dendrogram. The red bars in the banner plot represent observations, and each empty gap between the red bars represents potential clusters. As with the dendrogram, we can cut the banner to obtain a desired number of clusters. In this example, if we cut the banner where the Height value = 7 (shown as a blue line), we will obtain a result with three clusters.

If you press <Return> again, then the dendrogram appears. Figure 11.5(b) shows the dendrogram; the results are consistent with those obtained using Analytic Solver.

FIGURE 11.5 R's banner plot and dendrogram plot

(a) The banner plot

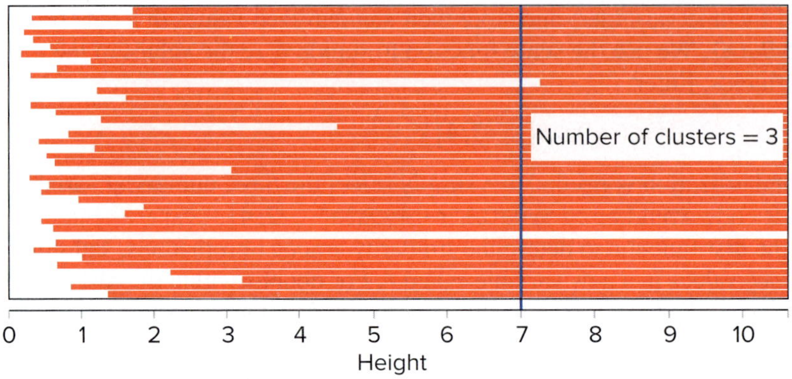

Agglomerative Coefficient = 0.94

(b) The dendrogram plot. Observations 1 through 41 are labeled on the x axis.

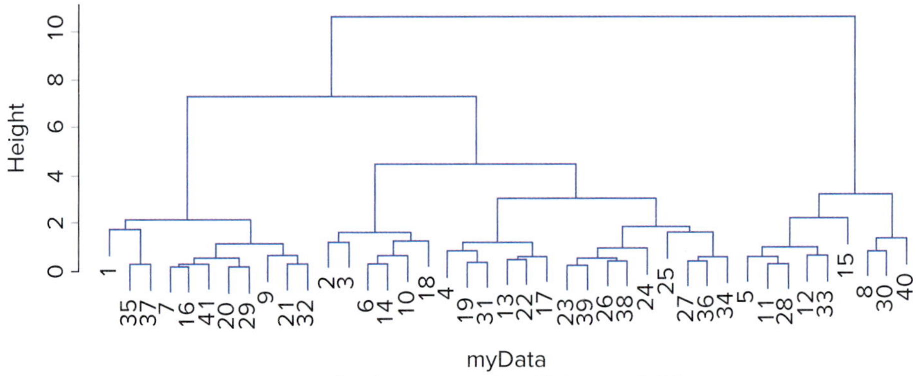

Agglomerative Coefficient = 0.94

g. Based on inspection of the banner plot and the dendrogram, we can determine the number of clusters. We use the **cutree** function to create three distinct clusters. Enter:

```
> aClusters <- cutree(aResult, k = 3)
```

h. We can append the cluster membership to the original data frame, myData, using the **data.frame** function. We then use the **View** function to inspect the updated myData data frame. Enter:

```
> myData <- data.frame(myData, aClusters)
> View(myData)
```

Table 11.5 shows a portion of the updated Cities data frame.

TABLE 11.5 Updated Cities Data Using R for Example 11.1

City	Crime	Poverty	Income	aClusters
Barnstable	710.6	3.8	58.422	1
Boston	1317.7	16.7	48.729	2
⋮	⋮	⋮	⋮	⋮
Warwick	139.7	3.9	59.445	1

i. We use the **summary** function to obtain summary statistics for the three clusters. Enter:

```
> summary(subset(myData, aClusters==1))
> summary(subset(myData, aClusters==2))
> summary(subset(myData, aClusters==3))
```

j. To find out the number of observations in each cluster, we use the **as.factor** function to convert aCluster to categorical data and then use the **summary** function to find out the number of observations in each cluster. Enter:

```
> summary(as.factor(aClusters))
```

Table 11.6 shows average values for the crime rate, the poverty rate, and median income for each of the three clusters. The results do differ from those obtained by Analytic Solver, but they are consistent. Cluster 1 is still a group of 11 cities with the lowest crime rate, the lowest poverty rate, and the highest median income among the three clusters. However, only nine cities fall in Cluster 3, with the highest crime rate, the highest poverty rate, and the lowest median income—Analytic Solver clustered 15 cities in this category. R also groups 21 cities falling somewhere in the middle, whereas Analytic Solver grouped 15 in this category.

TABLE 11.6 Hierarchical Clustering Results using R for Example 11.1

Cluster	Crime	Poverty	Income
1 (N = 11)	235.90	5.51	61.39
2 (N = 21)	544.2	12.28	45.64
3 (N = 9)	1,160.5	21.46	35.06

Agglomerative Clustering with Mixed Data

So far, we have discussed clustering with data on numerical variables. We will now extend the analysis with data consisting of both numerical and categorical variables, which is also referred to as mixed data. Mixed data are quite often of interest in business applications. For example, a firm may want to cluster the observations based on numerical variables such as income and age along with categorical variables such as sex and race.

In order to measure the distance between two observations with mixed data, it is common to use the distance measure, referred to as Gower's coefficient, proposed by John C. Gower. Gower's coefficient computes the distance for each variable, converts it into a [0, 1] scale, and calculates a weighted average of the scaled distances as a measure of similarity between two observations. The conceptual detail of the Gower's similarity coefficient is beyond the scope of this text.

The current version of Analytic Solver does not calculate Gower's similarity coefficient; therefore, we will use only R for agglomerative clustering with mixed data. Consider the following example.

FILE
Subscribers

EXAMPLE 11.2

A national phone carrier conducted a socio-demographic study of their current mobile phone subscribers. Subscribers were asked to fill out survey questions about their current annual salaries (Salary), whether or not they live in a city (City equals 1 if living in a city, 0 otherwise), and socio-demographic information such as marital status (Married equals 1 if married, 0 otherwise), sex (Sex equals 1 if male, 0 otherwise), and whether or not they have completed a college degree (College equals 1 if college degree, 0 otherwise). Table 11.7 shows a portion of the survey data collected from 196 subscribers.

TABLE 11.7 Mobile Phone Subscribers

Salary	Sex	Married	College	City
61643	1	1	1	0
91095	1	1	1	1
⋮	⋮	⋮	⋮	⋮
54638	1	1	1	1

Perform agglomerative hierarchical clustering using Gower's similarity measure. Interpret the results.

SOLUTION:

We use R to perform agglomerative cluster analysis with the Gower's coefficients using many of the same steps that we used in Example 11.1. For this reason, in some steps, we are brief.

Using R

a. Import the ***Subscribers*** data into a data frame (table) and label it myData. Install and load the *cluster* package, if you have not already done so. Enter:

```
> install.packages("cluster")
> library(cluster)
```

b. The first variable in the data set contains the mobile subscriber identification numbers and will not be used in the cluster analysis. We use the **daisy** function to determine similarity among observations and label the results as d. For options within the **daisy** function, we use *metric* to specify the distance calculation. Options for distance calculation include "euclidean", "manhattan", and "gower". We specify "gower". Enter:

```
> d <- daisy(myData[ , 2:6], metric = "gower")
```

If you enter `d` again, R reports all "dissimilarity" measures for all possible pairs of observations. Verify that the dissimilarity measure for observations 1 and 2 is `2.277405e-01`. This is simply 1 minus the Gower coefficient.

c. We use the **agnes** function with Ward's method to perform agglomerative clustering and label the results as mResult. Enter:

```
> mResult <- agnes(d, method = "ward")
> myResult
```

R reports an Agglomerative coefficient of 0.9972604.

d. We use the **plot** function to obtain the banner plot and the dendrogram. Enter:

```
> plot(mResult)
```

Follow the prompts to view the banner plot and the dendrogram. Figure 11.6 shows the dendrogram.

FIGURE 11.6 R's dendrogram for Example 11.2

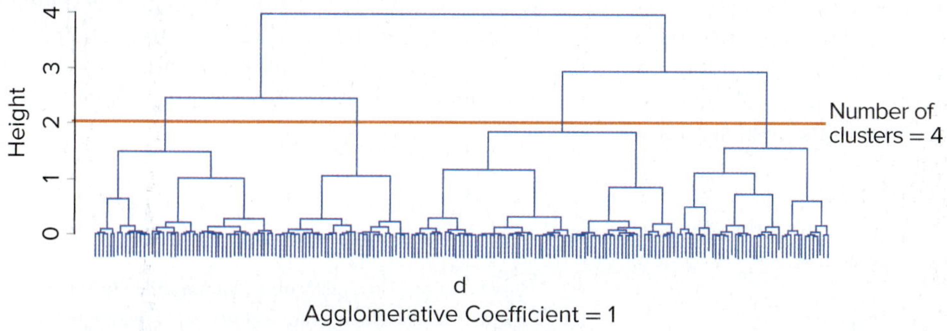

e. We use the **cutree** function to obtain four clusters, and then add the cluster membership information to the myData data frame. We use the **summary** function to obtain summary statistics for each cluster. Table 11.8 provides mean values for each cluster.

```
> mClusters <- cutree(mResult, k = 4)
> myData <- data.frame(myData, mClusters)
> summary(subset(myData, mClusters==1))
> summary(subset(myData, mClusters==2))
> summary(subset(myData, mClusters==3))
> summary(subset(myData, mClusters==4))
```

f. To find out the number of observations in each cluster, we use the **as.factor** function to convert mCluster to categorical data and then use the **summary** function to find out the number of observations in each cluster. Enter:

```
> summary(as.factor(mClusters))
```

TABLE 11.8 Hierarchical Clustering Results for Example 11.2

Cluster	Salary	Sex	Married	College	City
1 (N = 48)	96158	1	1	0.3958	0.6875
2 (N = 71)	94392	0.3803	0	0	0.3944
3 (N = 36)	97176	0	1	0	0.6111
4 (N = 41)	106586	0.3171	0.2195	1	0.5366

Based on these results, we can make the following observations about each of the four clusters.

- All subscribers in Cluster 1 are married males, most of whom live in a city. Only about 40% of them completed a college degree.
- All subscribers in Cluster 2, the largest of the four clusters, are not married and did not complete a college degree. About 40% of these subscribers are male. Most subscribers in this group live outside a city.
- All subscribers in Cluster 3 are married females who did not complete a college degree. Most of them live in a city.
- All subscribers in Cluster 4 completed a college degree and, on average, earn the highest salary among the four groups. They tend to be unmarried, and most of them are female.

The main appeal of hierarchical clustering is that it does not require the pre-specification of the number of clusters and, therefore, is purely data driven. It is also easy to understand and interpret. Note that because hierarchical clustering evaluates individual observations in order to merge or split them in each iteration, it is inherently slow and does not scale efficiently to a large data set. This poses a major challenge when dealing with Big Data. The method is also not stable in that the interpretation may change with even a small change in the sample data. To overcome these limitations, practitioners often combine hierarchical clustering with other, more efficient, clustering techniques. This is discussed in the next section.

EXERCISES 11.1

Mechanics

Notes: **AS** and **R** indicate that the exercise must be solved using Analytic Solver or R, respectively. If it is not specified, then the exercise can be solved using Analytic Solver and/or R. The answers, however, will depend on the software package used. Please note that Analytics Solver uses the input "Normalize" for z-score standardization.

1. FILE ***Exercise_11.1.*** Perform agglomerative clustering on the accompanying data set.
   a. Include all five variables, first standardized to z-scores, for the analysis. Choose Euclidean for the distance between observations and single linkage for the distance between clusters. Plot and inspect the dendrogram. How many clusters are generated if the minimum distance between clusters is 5?
   b. Repeat part a but choose the complete linkage clustering method.
   c. Repeat part a but choose Ward's clustering method.
2. FILE ***Exercise_11.2.*** Perform agglomerative clustering on the accompanying data set. Include all seven variables, first standardized to z-scores, for the analysis. Choose Euclidean for the distance between observations and Ward's method for the distance between clusters. Plot and inspect the dendrogram. How many clusters are generated if the minimum distance between clusters is 5? How many clusters are generated if the minimum distance between clusters is 3?
3. FILE ***Exercise_11.3.*** Perform agglomerative clustering on the accompanying data set. Include all seven variables, first standardized to z-scores, for the analysis. Choose Euclidean for the distance between observations and complete linkage for the distance between clusters. Plot and inspect the dendrogram. How many clusters are generated if the minimum distance between clusters is 5? How many observations are in the largest cluster? What is the average value of x_1 of the largest cluster?
4. FILE ***Exercise_11.4.*** Perform agglomerative clustering on the accompanying data set.
   a. Include all five variables, first standardized to z-scores. Use the Euclidean distance for similarity and single linkage for the clustering method to cluster the data into three clusters. How many observations are in the largest cluster? What is the average value of x_4 of the largest cluster?
   b. Repeat part a but choose the complete linkage clustering method.
   c. Repeat part a but choose Ward's clustering method.
5. FILE ***Exercise_11.5.*** Perform agglomerative clustering on the accompanying data set. Use the first five variables, x_1, x_2, x_3, x_4, and x_5, in the analysis. Do not standardize the variables. Note: For R, use the method = "binary" option in the **dist** function.
   a. Use Jaccard's coefficients for the similarity measure and average linkage for the clustering method to cluster the data into four clusters. How many 1s are in x_1 of the largest cluster?
   b. Use Jaccard's coefficients for the similarity measure and single linkage for the clustering method to cluster the data into six clusters. How many 1s are in x_1 of the largest cluster?
6. FILE ***Exercise_11.6.*** Perform agglomerative clustering on the accompanying data set, using all 11 binary variables. Use Jaccard's coefficients for the similarity measure and average linkage for the clustering method. Inspect the dendrogram. How many clusters are generated if the minimum distance between clusters is 0.8? Note: For R, use the method = "binary" option in the **dist** function.
7. FILE ***Exercise_11.7.*** Perform agglomerative clustering on the accompanying data set, using all 11 binary variables. Use Jaccard's coefficients for the similarity measure and complete linkage for the clustering method to cluster the data into 5 clusters. How many observations are in the largest cluster? How many 1s are in x_1 of the largest cluster? Note: For R, use the method = "binary" option in the **dist** function.
8. FILE ***Exercise_11.8.*** **R** Perform agglomerative clustering on the accompanying data consisting of both numerical and categorical variables. Use Gower's coefficient for the distance between observations and Ward's clustering method. Plot and inspect the dendrogram. How many clusters are generated if the minimum distance between clusters is 0.8? What is the average value of x_5 of the largest cluster?

Applications

9. **FILE** ***Colleges.*** Peter Lara, an aspiring college student, met with his high school college advisor to discuss potential colleges to which he might apply. He was advised to consult with the College Scorecard information on the Department of Education website. After talking to his family, he downloaded a list of 116 colleges and information on annual post-college earnings (Earnings in $), the average annual cost (Cost in $), the graduation rate (Grad in %), the percentage of students paying down debt (Debt in %), and whether or not a college is located in a city (1 denotes a city location, 0 otherwise). Peter and his family want to group these colleges based on the available information to help narrow down their choices. The accompanying table shows a portion of the data.

School	Earnings	Cost	Grad	Debt	City
St. Ambrose Univ.	44800	22920	62	88	1
Albion College	45100	23429	73	92	0
⋮	⋮	⋮	⋮	⋮	⋮
Wittenburg Univ.	42700	26616	64	90	1

a. Perform agglomerative clustering based on the earnings, cost, graduation rate, and debt information, all standardized to *z*-scores. Use the Euclidean distance and Ward clustering method to determine appropriate cluster membership for the 116 colleges. How many clusters are generated if the minimum distance between clusters is 15?

b. Separate the colleges based on whether or not they are located in the city into two different data sets. Group the colleges that are located in the city into clusters based on the earnings, cost, graduation rate, and debt information using the Euclidean distance and Ward's clustering method. Inspect the dendrogram. How many clusters are generated if the minimum distance between clusters is 10?

c. Repeat the analysis for the colleges not located in the city. Inspect the dendrogram. How many clusters are generated if the minimum distance between clusters is 10?

10. **FILE** ***Student_Body.*** Anne Cutberth has just started her new job as an academic adviser at a small liberal arts college in Colorado. She is going through a list of students in an academic department and wants to gain a better understanding about the student body in the department. The accompanying table shows a portion of the data that she has collected on 100 students. Note that all variables are categorical with a value 1 implying that the given student is a transfer student, was on the Dean's list last semester, is currently receiving financial aid, or is female, respectively. Note: For R, use the method = "binary" option in the **dist** function.

Transfer	Dean's list	Financial aid	Female
0	1	1	1
1	0	1	0
⋮	⋮	⋮	⋮
1	0	0	1

a. Perform agglomerative clustering to group the students in Anne's data set. Use Jaccard's coefficients for the similarity measure and the complete linkage clustering method. Inspect the dendrogram. How many clusters are generated if the minimum distance between clusters is 0.8? How many transfer students are in the largest cluster?

b. Repeat part a but choose average linkage clustering method. How many students are on the Dean's list in the largest cluster?

11. **FILE** ***Football_Players.*** Denise Lau is an avid football fan and religiously follows every college football game. During the current season, she meticulously keeps a record of how each quarterback has played throughout the season. Denise is making a presentation at a local college football fan club about these quarterbacks. The accompanying table shows a portion of the data that she has recorded. Variables include the player number (Player), completed passes (Comp), attempted passes (Att), completion percentage (Pct), total yards thrown (Yds), average yards per attempt (Avg), yards thrown per game (Yds/G), number of touchdowns (TD), and number of interceptions (Int).

Player	Comp	Att	. . .	Int
1	107	166	. . .	4
2	238	353	. . .	4
⋮	⋮	⋮	⋮	⋮
43	184	294	. . .	3

a. Perform agglomerative clustering to group the quarterbacks according to their performance to help Denise prepare for this presentation. Standardize the variables and use the Euclidean distance and the Ward clustering method. Cluster the data into three clusters. How many players are in the largest cluster? What is the average number of touchdowns of the largest cluster?

b. Select only the quarterbacks with at least 150 attempted passes and repeat the cluster analysis performed in part a. Cluster the data into two clusters. How many players are in the larger cluster? What is the average number of touchdowns of the larger cluster? Note: For Analytic Solver, use the Filter option in Excel to select the observations. Copy the observations to a new worksheet. Do not alter the order of the observations.

12. **FILE** ***Baseball_Players.*** **R** Ben Derby is a highly paid scout for a professional baseball team. He attends at least five or six Major League Baseball games a week and watches as many recorded games as he can in order to evaluate potential players for his team. He also keeps detailed records about each perspective player. His team is now seeking to add another hitter to its roster next season. Luckily, Ben has information on 144 hitters in the league who have played at least 100 games during the last season. The accompanying table shows a portion of the data. Variables include the player number (Player), the number of games played (G), at bats (AB),

runs (R), hits (H), homeruns (HR), runs batted in (RBI), batting average (AVG), on base percentage (OBP), and slugging percentage (SLG).

Player	G	AB	. . .	SLG
1	140	558	. . .	0.497
2	127	405	. . .	0.451
⋮	⋮	⋮	⋮	⋮
144	129	471	. . .	0.516

Use agglomerative clustering to group the 144 players into three clusters using all variables except Player. Standardize the variables and use the Euclidean distance and single linkage clustering method. How many players are in each cluster? Describe the characteristics of each cluster using the average values of the variables.

13. **FILE** ***Internet_Addiction.*** Internet addiction has been found to be a widespread problem among university students. A small liberal arts college in Colorado conducted a survey of Internet addiction among its students using the Internet Addiction Test (IAT) developed by Dr. Kimberly Young. The IAT contains 20 questions that measure three underlying psychometric factors. Questions 1 through 9 measure emotional/psychological conflicts, which refer to the degree to which the individual uses the Internet as a means to avoid interactions with friends and family. Questions 10 through 14 measure time management issues, which refer to the degree to which the individual chooses to spend time online at the expense of other responsibilities. Finally, Questions 15 through 20 measure mood modification, which refers to the degree to which the individual's Internet dependence is motivated by the need for mood improvement. The accompanying table shows a portion of the responses from 350 students. Students respond on a scale of 1 to 5, where higher values are indicative of possible problematic Internet use.

Record	IAT1	IAT2	. . .	IAT20
1	2	2	. . .	1
2	2	3	. . .	1
⋮	⋮	⋮	⋮	⋮
350	1	2	. . .	1

a. The scores for the three psychometric factors (i.e., emotional/psychological conflicts, time management issues, and mood modification) can be calculated by averaging the scores for the questions that are designed to measure them. First, find the average score for each psychometric factor for each student. Then, perform agglomerative clustering to group the 350 university students into five clusters based on the three underlying psychometric factors. Use Euclidean distance and the single linkage clustering method. Do not standardize the variables. How many students are in the largest cluster?

b. What are the average scores for emotional/psychological conflicts, time management issues, and mood modification for students in the largest cluster?

14. **FILE** ***Health_Population2.*** The accompanying data set contains country-level health and population measures for 38 countries from the World Bank's 2000 Health Nutrition and Population Statistics database. For each country, the measures include death rate per 1,000 people (Death Rate, in %), health expenditure per capita (Health Expend, in US$), life expectancy at birth (Life Exp, in years), male adult mortality rate per 1,000 male adults (Male Mortality), female adult mortality rate per 1,000 female adults (Female Mortality), annual population growth (Population Growth, in %), female population (Female Pop, in %), male population (Male Pop, in %), total population (Total Pop), size of labor force (Labor Force), births per woman (Fertility Rate), birth rate per 1,000 people (Birth Rate), and gross national income per capita (GNI, in US$). The accompanying table shows a portion of the data.

Country	Death Rate	Health Expend	. . .	GNI
Argentina	7.8	706.9	. . .	7440
Austria	9.6	2415.78	. . .	26790
⋮	⋮	⋮	⋮	⋮
Switzerland	8.7	3540.86	. . .	43460

a. Perform agglomerative clustering to group the 38 countries according to their health measures (i.e., Death Rate, Health Expend, Life Exp, Male Mortality, and Female Mortality) only. Use the Euclidean distance and the average linkage clustering method to cluster the data into three clusters. Is data standardization necessary in this case?

b. Describe the characteristics of each cluster. Compare the average GNI per capita (US$) of each group and report your findings.

15. **FILE** ***Health_Population2.*** Refer to the previous exercise for a description of the data set.

a. Perform agglomerative hierarchical clustering to group the 38 countries according to their population measures (i.e., Population Growth, Female Pop, Male Pop, Total Pop, Labor Force, Fertility Rate, and Birth Rate) only. Use the Euclidean distance and the average linkage clustering method to cluster the data into three clusters. Is data standardization necessary in this case?

b. Report the size and average GNI per capita (US$) of the largest cluster of countries.

c. Compare your findings with those from the previous exercise. Discuss the differences in cluster membership and characteristics.

16. **FILE** ***Pizza_Customers.*** **AS** A local pizza store wants to get a better sense of who its customers are. The accompanying table shows a portion of data that it collected on

30 randomly selected customers. Variables include age, female (1 if female, 0 otherwise), annual income, married (1 if married, 0 otherwise), own (1 if own residence, 0 otherwise), college (1 if completed college degree, 0 otherwise), household size (Size), and annual store spending (Spending).

Record	Age	Female	...	Spending
1	25	0	...	288
2	27	0	...	474
⋮	⋮	⋮	⋮	⋮
30	41	1	...	1401

a. Perform agglomerative clustering to group the customers based on the numerical variables only. Use the Euclidean distance and Ward's clustering method to cluster the customers into two clusters. Describe each cluster of customers based on the cluster characteristics.

b. Use agglomerative clustering to group the customers based on the categorical variables only. Use matching coefficients and the complete linkage clustering method to cluster the customers into two clusters. Describe each cluster of customers based on the cluster characteristics.

17. **FILE** ***Pizza_Customers.*** **R** Refer to the previous exercise for a description of the data set.

a. Perform agglomerative clustering on the accompanying data consisting of both numerical and categorical variables. Use Gower's coefficient for the distance between observations and Ward's clustering method. How many clusters can be generated if the minimum distance between clusters is 1?

b. How many customers are in the largest cluster? What is the average income of the customers in the largest cluster?

18. **FILE** ***Temperature.*** The accompanying table shows a portion of data consisting of the January, April, July, and October average temperatures of 50 selected U.S. cities.

City	Jan	April	July	Oct
Albuquerque, N.M.	35.7	55.6	78.5	57.3
Anchorage, Alaska	15.8	36.3	58.4	34.1
⋮	⋮	⋮	⋮	⋮
Washington, D.C.	34.9	56.1	79.2	58.8

a. Perform agglomerative hierarchical clustering to group the cities based on their January, April, July, and October average temperatures. Standardize the variables and use the Euclidean distance and the Ward's clustering method to cluster the cities into three clusters. How many cities are in the largest cluster?

b. What are the average January, April, July, and October average temperatures for the largest cluster of cities?

19. **FILE** ***MLB.*** The accompanying table lists a portion of Major League Baseball's pitchers, their earned run average (ERA), and their salary (in millions of $).

Player	ERA	Salary
1	2.53	17
2	2.54	4
⋮	⋮	⋮
10	3.09	0.5

a. Perform agglomerative clustering to group the players based on ERA and Salary. Standardize the variables and choose the Euclidean distance and the single linkage clustering method to cluster the players into four clusters. How many players are in the largest cluster?

b. What are the average ERA and salary for the largest cluster of players?

20. **FILE** ***Chicago_CA.*** Sanjay Johnson is working on a research paper that studies the relationship between the education level and the median income of a community. The accompanying table shows a portion of the data that he has collected on the educational attainment and the median income for 77 areas in the city of Chicago. Sanjay plans to cluster the areas using the educational attainment data and compare the average median incomes of the clusters. For each community area, the measures include total number of residents 25 years and over (25 or Over), number of residents with less than high school education (Less than HS), number of residents with high school education (HS), number of residents with some college (SC), number of residents with bachelor's degree or higher (Bachelor), and median household income (Income).

Community	25 or Over	Less than HS	...	Income
Albany Park	32541	11347	...	46198
Archer Heights	7327	2669	...	42571
⋮	⋮	⋮	⋮	⋮
Woodlawn	15267	2738	...	27413

a. Should Sanjay standardize the data before cluster analysis? Explain.

b. Perform agglomerative clustering to group the community areas based on the standardized variables related to the education attainment of the population (i.e., Less than HS, HS, SC, and Bachelor). Use the Euclidean distance and the Ward clustering method. Inspect the dendrogram. How many clusters are generated if the minimum distance between clusters is 10?

c. What are the size and average median household income of the largest cluster of community areas?

21. FILE ***Internet_Addiction2.*** R Internet addiction has been found to be a widespread problem among university students. A small liberal arts college in Colorado conducted a survey of Internet addiction among its students using the Internet Addiction Test (IAT) developed by Dr. Kimberly Young. The IAT measures three underlying psychometric factors: emotional/psychological conflicts (Factor1), time management issues (Factor2), and mood modification (Factor3). Individuals who score high on the IAT are more likely to have problematic Internet use. The accompanying table shows a portion of the scores for the three psychometric factors for 350 students. The respondents also provided a couple of pieces of demographic data including sex (equals 1 if female, 0 otherwise) and level of study (equals 1 if graduate study, 0 otherwise).

Record	Factor1	Factor2	...	Graduate
1	1.44	2.40	⋮	1
2	2.44	2.80	⋮	0
⋮	⋮	⋮	⋮	⋮
350	1.33	2.20	⋮	0

a. Perform hierarchical clustering to group the 350 university students using the three psychometric factors as well as the other demographic variables. Use Gower's coefficient for the distance between observations and Ward's clustering method to cluster the students into three clusters. How many students are in the largest cluster?

b. What are the average scores for emotional/psychological conflicts, time management issues, and mood modification for students in the largest cluster?

22. FILE ***Longitudinal_Partial.*** R The accompanying table contains a portion of data from the National Longitudinal Survey (NLS), which follows over 12,000 individuals in the United States over time. Variables in this analysis include Urban (1 if lives in urban area, 0 otherwise), Siblings (number of siblings), White (1 if white, 0 otherwise), Christian (1 if Christian, 0 otherwise), FamilySize, Height, Weight (in pounds), and Income (in $).

Urban	Siblings	White	...	Income
1	8	1	...	0
1	1	1	...	40000
⋮	⋮	⋮	⋮	⋮
1	2	1	...	43000

a. Use hierarchical clustering to group the respondents. Use Gower's coefficient for the distance between observations and Ward's clustering method to cluster the individuals into four clusters. How many individuals are in the largest cluster?

b. Describe the characteristics of the clusters.

LO 11.2

11.2 *k*-MEANS CLUSTER ANALYSIS

Conduct *k*-means cluster analysis.

Unlike hierarchical clustering, discussed in the previous section, in ***k*-means clustering**, we need to specify the number of clusters, *k*, prior to performing the analysis. The objective is to divide the sample into a prespecified number *k* of nonoverlapping clusters so that each of these *k* clusters is as homogenous as possible. In practice, we may experiment with different values of *k* until we obtain a desired result, or use hierarchical clustering methods to help determine the appropriate *k*. In addition, we may have prior knowledge or theories about the subjects under study and can determine the appropriate number of clusters based on domain knowledge. For example, if we were to sort through a stack of books, we might unconsciously group them into fiction and nonfiction categories. Or while organizing a pile of shoes, we might naturally place them into casual, athletic, or dress shoe categories.

Once the number of clusters *k* is determined, the *k*-means algorithm is based on the choice of the initial cluster centers. There are several ways to find initial cluster centers. A popular approach is to initiate the algorithm by randomly selecting *k* observations from the data to serve as initial cluster centers. Each remaining observation is then assigned to the nearest cluster center, forming *k* clusters. Cluster centroids for the *k* clusters are calculated to be used as the updated cluster centers. The algorithm then reassigns each observation to its nearest cluster center and recalculates the cluster centroids.

The reassignment of observations and recalculation of cluster centroids are repeated, with the goal of minimizing the dispersion within clusters, where dispersion is defined as the sum of Euclidean distances of observations from their respective cluster centroid. The cluster assignment and centroid update steps are iteratively repeated until convergence is achieved and cluster dispersion can no longer be improved. Because it uses only the Euclidean distance as a similarity measure, the *k*-means algorithm can only handle data with numerical variables. In other words, it cannot analyze categorical variables unless they are transformed to numerical variables prior to the cluster analysis.

> **THE *k*-MEANS CLUSTERING METHOD**
>
> The *k*-means clustering method assigns each observation to a cluster, such that the observations assigned to the same cluster are as similar as possible. The number of clusters *k* is determined prior to estimation. The *k*-means clustering method can only be applied to data with numerical variables. The general process of the *k*-means clustering algorithm can be summarized as follows:
>
> 1. Specify the *k* value.
> 2. Randomly assign *k* observations as cluster centers.
> 3. Assign each observation to its nearest cluster center.
> 4. Calculate cluster centroids.
> 5. Reassign each observation to a cluster with the nearest centroid.
> 6. Recalculate the cluster centroids and repeat step 5.
> 7. Stop when reassigning observations can no longer improve within-cluster dispersion.

Compared to the hierarchical clustering methods, the *k*-means clustering method is more computationally efficient, especially when dealing with large data sets. This is because hierarchical clustering requires computation of distances between each possible pair of observations while *k*-means clustering only requires computation of distances between each observation and the cluster centroids during each iteration. For example, with a relatively small data set that contains 100 observations, hierarchical clustering would need to compute the distances of 4,950 possible observation pairs in order to form clusters. At the same time, for the same data set and a pre-determined number of clusters (*k*) of 4, *k*-means clustering only needs to compute 400 distance measures during each iteration. Therefore, it is customary to cluster large data sets using the *k*-means clustering method instead of the hierarchical clustering methods.

Using Analytic Solver and R to Perform *k*-Means Clustering

Results from *k*-means clustering are highly sensitive to the random process for finding the initial cluster centers as well as implementing specific algorithms. The initial cluster centers and the algorithms used in Analytic Solver and R are not the same, and, therefore, their outputs will differ. As mentioned earlier, because clustering is essentially an unsupervised technique for data exploration, the appropriate approach is the one that produces a clustering structure that makes the most sense conceptually.

In the following example, we demonstrate how to perform *k*-means clustering using Analytic Solver and R.

EXAMPLE 11.3

FILE
CandyBars

Recall that the objective outlined in the introductory case is to help Aliyah Williams group candy bars into meaningful clusters and improve product selection and display for her vending machines. Perform *k*-means clustering on the data assuming four clusters. Interpret the results.

SOLUTION:

Using Analytic Solver

a. Open the ***CandyBars*** data file.

b. From the menu, choose **Data Mining > Cluster > K-means Clustering.**

c. See Figure 11.7. Click on the ellipsis button next to the *Data range* and select cells \$A\$1:\$E\$38. Make sure that the box *First Row Contains Headers* is checked. The *Variables in Input Data* box will populate. Select and move variables Calories, Fat, Protein, and Carb to the *Selected Variables* box. Click *Next.*

FIGURE 11.7 Analytic Solver's *k*-Means Clustering dialog box

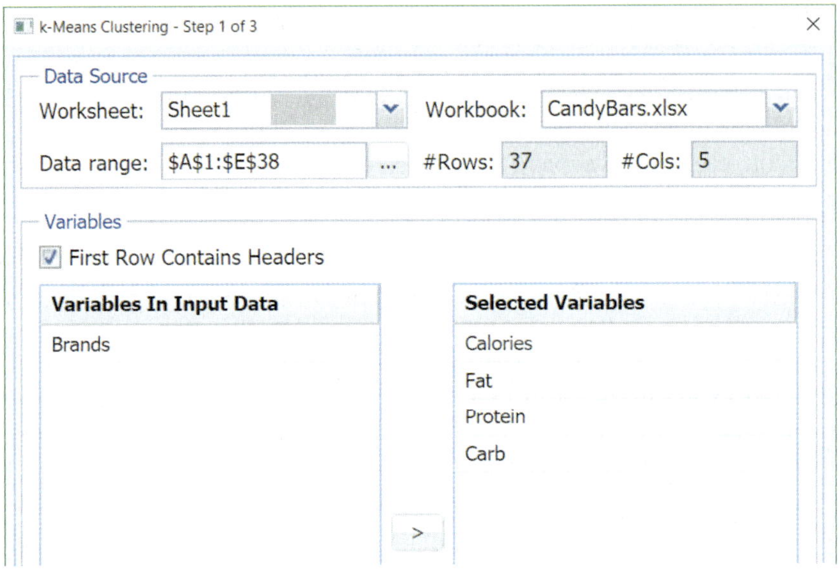

Source: Microsoft Excel

d. In the next dialog box, select *Normalize input data.* Set *# Clusters* to 4. Accept other defaults and click *Next.*

Note: Analytic Solver uses the term "Normalize" for *z*-score standardization. Also, *k*-means clustering is a random process for finding the initial cluster centers and implementing specific algorithms. Analytic Solver allows you to control the *k*-means algorithm by changing the random seed and the maximum number of iterations. For simplicity, we will use the defaults: 10 iterations, fixed start, and random seed of 12345.

e. In the final dialog box, select *Show data summary* and *Show distances from each cluster center.* Click *Finish.*

Next to the CandyBars worksheet, Analytic Solver will insert two new worksheets: KMC_Output and KMC_Clusters. The KMC_Output worksheet contains three tables. See Figure 11.8. The Cluster Centers table displays *z*-score values of calories, fat, protein, and carbohydrate levels for each cluster centroid. For example, Cluster 1 includes three candy bars with a relatively high amount of carbohydrates (*z*-score of 2.5591) and a low amount of fat (*z*-score of −1.8673), while Cluster 2 includes six candy bars that are relatively low in calories (*z*-score of −1.4164) and in fat (*z*-score of −1.2567). The Inter-Cluster Distances table shows the distance between the four clusters. The Cluster Summary table shows the number of candy bars in each cluster as well as the average distance within each cluster, also referred to as intra-cluster distances. We want the inter-cluster distance to be greater than the intra-cluster distance.

FIGURE 11.8 Analytic Solver's KMC_Output worksheet for Example 11.3

Cluster Centers

Cluster	Calories	Fat	Protein	Carb
Cluster 1	0.4344022	−1.867295284	−1.335739	2.559095
Cluster 2	−1.416441	−1.256703059	−0.948871	0.069739
Cluster 3	0.7383751	0.599335558	1.0200085	−0.106252
Cluster 4	−0.224415	0.339386171	−0.32712	−0.472013

Inter-Cluster Distances

Cluster	Cluster 1	Cluster 2	Cluster 3	Cluster 4
Cluster 1	0	3.1851222	4.3393882	3.93807215
Cluster 2	3.1851222	0	3.46346242	2.156037299
Cluster 3	4.3393882	3.4634624	0	1.715538953
Cluster 4	3.9380722	2.1560373	1.71553895	0

Cluster Summary

Cluster	Size	Average Distance
Cluster 1	3	1.118793392
Cluster 2	6	0.963186733
Cluster 3	14	1.254417684
Cluster 4	14	0.799549588
Total	37	1.024082227

Source: Microsoft Excel

Figure 11.9 shows a portion of the results from the KMC_Clusters worksheet. Analytic Solver displays each observation, the cluster to which it is assigned, and distances to the cluster centroids. For example, the first record is closest to the centroid of Cluster 3 (a distance value of 2.0269, compared to the distance from the other three clusters: 5.6182, 5.3371, and 3.3590), and, therefore, it is assigned to Cluster 3. Similarly, records 2 through 5 are also assigned to Cluster 3 due to their proximity to the centroid of Cluster 3. Record 6 is closest to the centroid of Cluster 1 (a distance value of 1.6274, compared to the distance from the other three clusters) and is assigned to Cluster 1.

FIGURE 11.9 A portion of the Analytic Solver's KMC_Clusters worksheet

Cluster Labels

Record ID	Cluster	Dist.Cluster-1	Dist.Cluster-2	Dist.Cluster-3	Dist.Cluster-4
Record 1	3	5.618157641	5.337090046	2.026926879	3.358950069
Record 2	3	3.477183815	3.492883427	1.400265669	1.984001764
Record 3	3	3.67685852	3.709306476	1.755223667	2.109681512
Record 4	3	3.689441762	3.848690031	1.271978137	2.439509931
Record 5	3	4.266657463	3.810589213	0.667135497	2.019485176
Record 6	1	1.627385194	4.48149861	4.970912002	5.059541297

Source: Microsoft Excel

Using R

a. Import the ***CandyBars*** data into a data frame (table) and label it myData. Install and load the *cluster* package. Enter:

```
> install.packages("cluster")
> library(cluster)
```

b. We exclude the Brand variable from the analysis and standardize the other variables using the **scale** function. The new data frame is called myData1. Enter:

```
> myData1 <- scale(myData[ , 2:5])
```

c. We use the **set.seed** function to set the random seed and the **pam** function to perform the *k*-means clustering. Within the **pam** function, we set the option *k* to 4 because we have preselected 4 clusters. We store the clustering results in a variable called kResult. We use the **summary** function to view the results. Enter:

```
> set.seed(1)
> kResult <- pam(myData1, k = 4)
> summary(kResult)
```

Table 11.9 shows a portion of the R results that we have rearranged for presentation purposes. Despite the fact that the results are quite different than the ones that we obtained with Analytic Solver, there are some similarities. For example, Cluster 2 in R, like Cluster 1 in Analytic Solver, includes three candy bars with a relatively high amount of carbohydrates (z-score of 2.0860) and a low amount of fat (z-score of −1.9482). Similarly, Cluster 4 in R is like Cluster 2 in Analytic Solver and Cluster 1 in R is like Cluster 3 in Analytic Solver.

TABLE 11.9 R's clustering results with z-scores

Cluster	Calories	Fat	Protein	Carb
1 (N = 14)	0.8081	0.5993	0.7920	−0.2614
2 (N = 3)	0.1355	−1.9482	−1.8193	2.0860
3 (N = 16)	−0.1547	0.2354	−0.3686	−0.3160
4 (N = 4)	−2.0275	−1.5842	−0.9489	0.1207

e. In order to visually show the clusters and their members, we use the **plot** function. Enter:

```
> plot(kResult)
```

Follow the prompts to view the cluster and silhouette plots (Figure 11.10) that R produces. The cluster plot in Figure 11.10(a) incorporates principal component analysis (PCA) to summarize information from the four variables (Calories, Fat,

FIGURE 11.10 R's cluster plot and silhouette plot for Example 11.3

(a) The cluster plot

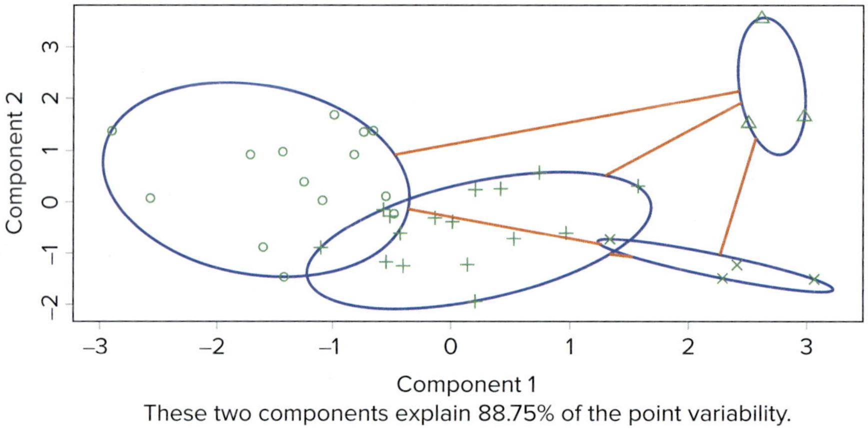

(b) The silhouette plot

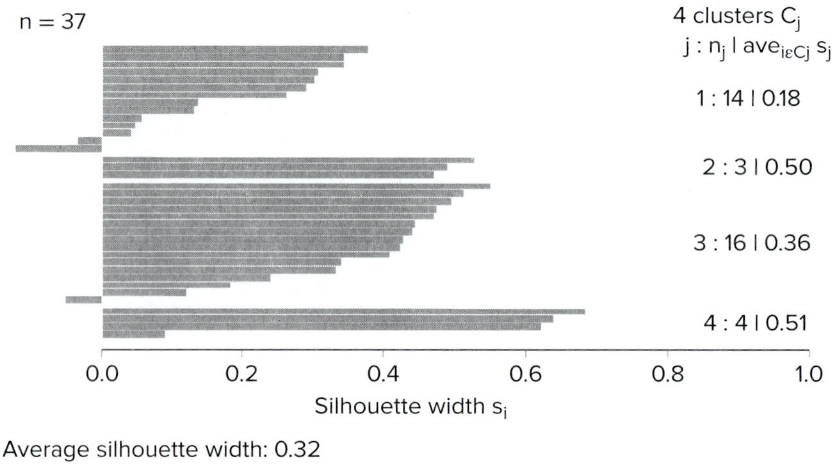

Protein, and Carb). Because we cannot plot a four-dimensional graph based on the four variables, we use PCA in order to plot the clusters onto a two-dimensional graph with the first two principal components as the x- and y-axes. Recall from Chapter 8 that these principal components explain the highest degree of variability in the data. In this case, the first two principal components explain 88.75% of the variability. Each blue oval represents a cluster, and the observations in each cluster are displayed using a different marker.

The silhouette plot in Figure 11.10(b) shows how close each observation in one cluster is to observations in the other clusters. It also allows us to visually determine the appropriate number of clusters. The silhouette width for each observation, s_i, ranges from -1 to $+1$, where a value closer to $+1$ indicates that the observation is well matched to its own cluster and poorly matched to neighboring clusters. If most observations have values close to $+1$, then the clustering configuration is appropriate. If many points have a low or negative value, then the clustering configuration may have too many or too few clusters. The results in Figure 11.10(b) seem to suggest that the results are good, but not great. Clusters 2 and 4 seem well-configured. Two of the observations in Cluster 1 and one observation in Cluster 3 have silhouette widths that are negative. The average silhouette width is 0.32 suggesting a reasonable clustering configuration overall. It is not clear if a different configuration would necessarily improve the results.

SYNOPSIS OF INTRODUCTORY CASE

Aliyah Williams is a fledgling entrepreneur who owns a vending machine business. In order to strategically group and display candy bars in her vending machines, she chooses four clusters to perform *k*-means clustering. Aliyah observes a certain theme in the grouping of candy bars. For example, Three Musketeers, 100 Grand, Raisinets, York Peppermint Pattie, After Eight Mints, and Twizzlers Cherry Nibs are grouped in a cluster that is relatively low in calories, fat, and protein. In addition, fruit-flavored candies like Skittles, Starburst, and Twizzlers, with a relatively low amount of fat and protein but high in carbohydrates, are also assigned into a cluster.

Steve Degenhardt/Shutterstock

The defining characteristics of the two remaining groups are less obvious. However, Aliyah observes that one of the remaining two clusters includes candy bars, such as Reese's Pieces, that have a high content of protein and calories. Finally, the last cluster tends to include candy bars that contain a moderate amount of the four nutrients.

Given the increase in health-conscious consumers in the market, Aliyah feels that her vending machines would best meet customer needs by increasing the proportion of candy bars that are low in calories and fat, found in the first two clusters. These candy bars would likely attract customers who crave for something sweet but at the same time do not want to add too much calories and fat to their diet. The fruit-flavored candies would likely cater to customers who are on a low-fat, high-carb diet. She will also place the healthier candy bars in a more prominent place in her vending machines located close to healthcare and fitness facilities and display a sign listing the nutritional facts of each candy bar.

Aliyah also decides to increase the number of selected candy bars from the third cluster for customers who are looking to consume a little more protein in their diet. Finally, to maintain product variety, she will also choose an assortment of popular candy bars from the remaining cluster to include in her vending machines.

EXERCISES 11.2

Notes: **AS** and **R** indicate that the exercise must be solved using Analytic Solver and R, respectively. If it is not specified, then the exercise can be solved using Analytic Solver and/or R. The answers, however, will depend on the software package used. Use the following defaults in Analytic Solver: 10 iterations, fixed start, and random seed of 12345. For R, use the **set.seed(1)** statement to set the random seed.

Mechanics

23. FILE ***Exercise_11.23.*** Perform *k*-means clustering on the accompanying data set.
    a. Use all variables in the analysis. Do not standardize the variables. Set the number of clusters to 3. What are the size and average distance for the largest cluster?
    b. Specify the same settings as in part a, but standardize the variables. What are the size and average distance for the largest cluster?

24. FILE ***Exercise_11.24.*** Perform *k*-means clustering on both variables in the accompanying data set. Standardize the variables. Experiment with the *k* values of 2, 3, and 4. Compare the number of observations and distance statistics of the largest cluster for each *k* value.

25. FILE ***Exercise_11.25.*** Perform *k*-means clustering on the accompanying data set.
    a. Use variables x_1, x_2, and x_3 in the analysis. Standardize the data. Specify the *k* value as 2. What are the cluster center values for the larger cluster?
    b. Specify the *k* value as 3. What are the cluster center values for the smallest cluster?

26. FILE ***Exercise_11.26.*** R Perform *k*-means clustering on the accompanying data set. Use variables x_4, x_5, x_6, and x_7, standardized to *z*-scores, in the analysis.
    a. Specify the *k* value as 2 and plot the cluster membership using the cluster and silhouette plots. What is the average silhouette width?
    b. Specify the *k* value as 3 and plot the cluster membership using the cluster and silhouette plots. What is the average silhouette width?
    c. Specify the *k* value as 4 and plot the cluster membership using the cluster and silhouette plots. What is the average silhouette width?

27. FILE ***Exercise_11.27.*** Perform *k*-means clustering on the accompanying data set. Use variables x_1, x_3, and x_5 in the analysis. Do not standardize the variables.
    a. Set the number of clusters to 3. What are the size and cluster center values for the largest cluster?
    b. Perform the same analysis as in part a, but with variables standardized to *z*-scores. What are the size and cluster center values for the largest cluster?

28. FILE ***Exercise_11.28.*** R Perform *k*-means clustering on all the variables in the accompanying data set. Do not standardize the variables.
    a. Specify the *k* value as 2 and plot the cluster membership using the cluster and silhouette plots.
    b. Specify the *k* value as 3 and plot the cluster membership using the cluster and silhouette plots.
    c. Specify the *k* value as 4 and plot the cluster membership using the cluster and silhouette plots.

29. FILE ***Exercise_11.29.*** Perform *k*-means clustering on the accompanying data set.
    a. Use variables x_1, x_3, and x_5 in the analysis. Do not standardize the variables. Set the number of clusters to 4. What are the size and cluster center values for the largest cluster?
    b. Perform the same analysis as in part a, but with variables standardized to *z*-scores. What are the size and cluster center values for the largest cluster?

30. FILE ***Exercise_11.30.*** R Perform *k*-means clustering on all the variables in the accompanying data set.
    a. Standardize the data. Specify the *k* value as 2 and plot the cluster membership using the cluster and silhouette plots. What is the average silhouette width?
    b. Specify the *k* value as 3 and plot the cluster membership using the cluster and silhouette plots. What is the average silhouette width?
    c. Specify the *k* value as 4 and plot the cluster membership using the cluster and silhouette plots. What is the average silhouette width?

Applications

31. FILE ***Iris.*** British biologist Ronald Fisher studied iris flowers and classified them according to the width and length of the flower's petals and sepals (a small, green leafy part below the petal). The accompanying table shows a portion of the data that Fisher used in his study.

Sepal length	Sepal width	Petal length	Petal width
5.2	3.5	1.4	0.2
4.9	3.0	1.4	0.2
⋮	⋮	⋮	⋮
5.9	3.0	5.1	1.8

    a. Perform *k*-means clustering using $k = 4$. What are the size and cluster center values of the largest cluster?
    b. Experiment with $k = 3$ and $k = 5$. What are the size and cluster center values of the largest cluster in each case?

32. FILE ***Football_Players.*** Denise Lau is an avid football fan and religiously follows every college football game. During the

current season, she meticulously keeps a record of how each quarterback has played throughout the season. Denise is making a presentation at the local college football fan club about these quarterbacks. The accompanying table shows a portion of the data that Denise has recorded, with the following variables: the player number (Player), completed passes (Comp), attempted passes (Att), completion percentage (Pct), total yards thrown (Yds), average yards per attempt (Avg), yards thrown per game (Yds/G), number of touchdowns (TD), and number of interceptions (Int).

Player	Comp	Att	...	Int
1	107	166	...	4
2	238	353	...	4
⋮	⋮	⋮	⋮	⋮
43	184	294	...	3

a. Perform k-means clustering using $k = 3$ on all variables except the player number. Standardize the variables. What are the size and cluster center values of the largest cluster?

b. Select only the quarterbacks with at least 150 attempted passes and repeat part a. Note: For Analytic Solver, use the Filter option in Excel to select the observations. Copy the observations to a new worksheet. Do not alter the order of the observations.

c. Comment on the differences in the clustering results of parts a and b.

33. **FILE** ***Napa.*** Jennifer Gomez is moving to a small town in Napa Valley, California, and has been house hunting for her new home. Her Realtor has given her a list of 35 homes with at least 2 bedrooms that were recently sold. Jennifer wants to see if she can group them in some meaningful ways to help her narrow down her options. A portion of the data is shown in the accompanying table with the following variables: the sale price of a home (Price, in $), the number of bedrooms (Beds), the number of bathrooms (Baths), and the square footage (Sqft).

Price	Beds	Baths	Sqft
799,000	4	3	2,689
795,680	4	2.5	2,507
⋮	⋮	⋮	⋮
327,900	3	1	1,459

a. Perform k-means clustering on the list of 35 homes using $k = 3$. Standardize the variables. What are the size and cluster center values of the largest cluster?

b. Perform k-means clustering on the standardized data using $k = 4$. What are the size and cluster center values of the largest cluster?

34. **FILE** ***Baseball_Players.*** Ben Derby is a highly paid scout for a professional baseball team. He attends at least five or six Major League Baseball games a week and watches as many recorded games as he can in order to evaluate potential players for his team to recruit at the end of the season. He also keeps detailed records about each perspective player. His team is now seeking to add another hitter to its roster next season. Luckily Ben has information on 144 hitters in the league who have played at least 100 games during the last season. A portion of the data is shown in the accompanying table with the following variables: the player number (Player), the number of games played (G), at bats (AB), runs (R), hits (H), homeruns (HR), runs batted in (RBI), batting average (AVG), on base percentage (OBP), and slugging percentage (SLG).

Player	G	AB	...	SLG
1	140	558	...	0.497
2	127	405	...	0.451
⋮	⋮	⋮	⋮	⋮
144	129	471	...	0.516

a. Perform k-means clustering to group the 144 players into three clusters. Standardize and include all the variables except the player number in the analysis. What is the size of the largest cluster? Which cluster has the highest average number of homeruns?

b. Select only the players with at least 500 at bats ($AB \geq 500$). Perform k-means clustering with $k = 3$. What is the size of the largest cluster? Which cluster has the highest average number of homeruns? Note: For Analytic Solver, use the Filter option in Excel to select the observations. Copy the observations to a new worksheet. Do not alter the order of the observations.

35. **FILE** ***Health_Population2.*** **AS** The accompanying data set contains country-level health and population measures for 38 countries from the World Bank's 2000 Health Nutrition and Population Statistics database. For each country, the measures include death rate per 1,000 people (Death Rate, in %), health expenditure per capita (Health Expend, in US$), life expectancy at birth (Life Exp, in years), male adult mortality rate per 1,000 male adults (Male Mortality), female adult mortality rate per 1,000 female adults (Female Mortality), annual population growth (Population Growth, in %), female population (Female Pop, in %), male population (Male Pop, in %), total population (Total Pop), size of labor force (Labor Force), births per woman (Fertility Rate), birth rate per 1,000 people (Birth Rate), and gross national income per capita (GNI, in US$). The accompanying table shows a portion of the data.

Country Name	Death Rate	Health Expend	...	GNI
Argentina	7.8	706.9	...	7440
Austria	9.6	2415.78	...	26790
⋮	⋮	⋮	⋮	⋮
Switzerland	8.7	3540.86	...	43460

a. Perform k-means clustering to group the 38 countries into four clusters according to their health measures (i.e., Death Rate, Health Expend, Life Exp, Male Mortality, and Female Mortality) only. Is data standardization necessary in this case?

b. What are the size and the average GNI per capita for the largest cluster of countries?

36. **FILE** ***Health_Population2.*** **AS** Refer to the previous exercise for a description of the data set.

a. Perform k-means clustering to group the 38 countries into four clusters according to their population measures (i.e., Population Growth, Female Pop, Male Pop, Total Pop, Labor Force, Fertility Rate, and Birth Rate) only. Is data standardization necessary in this case?

b. Describe the characteristics of each cluster. Compare the average GNI per capita of each group and report your findings.

37. **FILE** ***Chicago_CA.*** **R** Sanjay Johnson is working on a research paper that studies the relationship between the education level and the median income of a community. The accompanying table shows a portion of the data that he has collected on the educational attainment and the median income for 77 areas in the city of Chicago. Sanjay plans to cluster the areas using the educational attainment data and compare the average median incomes of the clusters. For each community area, the measures include total number of residents 25 years and over (25 or Over), number of residents with less than a high school education (Less than HS), number of residents with a high school education (HS), number of residents with some college (SC), number of residents with a Bachelor's degree or higher (Bachelor), and median household income (Income, in $). The accompanying table shows a portion of the data.

Community Area	25 or Over	Less than HS	. . .	Income
Albany Park	32541	11347	. . .	46198
Archer Heights	7327	2669		42571
⋮	⋮	⋮	⋮	⋮
Woodlawn	15267	2738	. . .	27413

a. Does Sanjay need to standardize the data before performing cluster analysis? Explain.

b. Perform k-means clustering to group the community areas into three clusters based on the variables related to educational attainment of the population (i.e., Less than HS, HS, SC, and Bachelor). Plot the three clusters using the cluster and silhouette plots. What is the average silhouette width? What are the size and cluster center values of the largest cluster? Which cluster of community areas has the highest average median household income?

38. **FILE** ***Nutritional_Facts.*** **AS** The accompanying data set contains the nutrition facts on 30 common food items; a portion of the data is shown. The values are based on 100 grams of the food items. Perform k-means clustering using $k = 3$ on the nutritional facts of the food items. Standardize the variables. Describe the characteristics of each cluster.

Name	Calories	Total fat	. . .	Protein
Banana	89	0.3	. . .	1.1
Egg	155	11	. . .	13
⋮	⋮	⋮	⋮	⋮
Tuna	184	6	. . .	30

39. **FILE** ***Websites.*** **R** Jake Duffy is the e-commerce manager of a major electronics retailer. He is researching his company's e-commerce competitors and wants to group the competitors based on their performance data. He has compiled a data set that contains the following four performance measures of the major competitors' e-commerce operations: Annual Revenue (Revenue, in $), Growth Rate (in %), Monthly Visits (Visits), and Conversion Rate (in %). In order to avoid any personal bias in grouping these competitors, he decided to replace the names of the competitors with a code. A portion of the data set is shown in the accompanying table.

Website	Revenue	Growth Rate	Visits	Conversion Rate
1	3276000	13.6	78047136	1.928
2	2485716	9.6	28000000	4
⋮	⋮	⋮	⋮	⋮
32	484720000	23.44	872000	4.72

a. Perform k-means clustering to group the competitors into five clusters using all four performance measures. Does the data set need to be standardized prior to cluster analysis?

b. Plot the cluster membership using the cluster and silhouette plots. What is the average silhouette width? Describe the characteristics of each cluster. What are the size and cluster center values of the largest cluster of competitors?

40. **FILE** ***Development.*** **AS** The accompanying data set contains economic development indicators for 11 African countries collected by the World Bank in 2015. The economic development indicators include annual % growth in agriculture (Agriculture), annual % growth in exports (Exports), annual % growth in final consumption (Final consumption), annual % growth in GDP (GDP), and annual % growth in GDP per capita

(GDP Per Capita). A portion of the data set is shown in the accompanying table.

Country	Agriculture	Exports	. . .	GDP Per Capita
Burkina Faso	−3.476123489	1.382199926	. . .	0.884822306
Burundi	−2.982607113	−9.90	. . .	−6.81765662
⋮	⋮	⋮	⋮	⋮
Mali	6.924199557	4.671865704	. . .	2.898828067

a. Perform *k*-means clustering to group the countries into three clusters using all the development indicators. Is data standardization necessary in this case?
b. What is the size of the largest cluster? Which cluster has the highest average growth in GDP per capita?
c. Compare the cluster membership between parts a and b.

41. FILE ***SAT_NYC.*** AS The accompanying data set contains the school level average SAT critical reading (CR), math (M), and writing (W) scores for the graduating seniors from 100 high schools in New York City. The data set also records the number of SAT test takers (Test Takers) from each school.

School Name	Test Takers	CR	M	W
A. Philip Randolph Campus High School	228	430	456	423
Abraham Lincoln High School	475	396	437	393
⋮	⋮	⋮	⋮	⋮
Williamsburg Preparatory School	113	397	410	380

a. Perform *k*-means clustering to group the 100 high schools into four clusters on the critical reading, math, and writing scores. Is data standardization necessary in this case? What are the size and cluster center values of the largest cluster? Which cluster has the fewest average number of test takers?
b. Select only the schools with at least 200 SAT test takers and repeat the cluster analysis performed in part a. What are the size and cluster center values of the largest cluster? Note: Use the Filter option in Excel to select the observations. Copy the observations to a new worksheet. Do not alter the order of the observations.

42. FILE ***Telecom.*** A telecommunications company wants to identify customers who are likely to unsubscribe to the telephone service. The company collects the following information from 100 customers: customer ID (ID), age (Age), annual income (Income), monthly usage (Usage, in minutes), tenure (Tenure, in months), and whether the customer has unsubscribed to the telephone service (Unsubscribe). A portion of the data set is shown in the accompanying table.

ID	Age	Income	Usage	Tenure	Unsubscribe
1	33	49156	154	43	1
2	35	23538	107	12	1
⋮	⋮	⋮	⋮	⋮	⋮
100	46	44018	192	23	1

a. Perform *k*-means clustering to group the 100 customers into four clusters based on age, income, monthly usage, and tenure. Describe the characteristics of each cluster.
b. Compute the percent of customers that have unsubscribed to the telephone service from each cluster. Which cluster has the highest percent of customers who have unsubscribed to the telephone service?

43. FILE ***Information_Technology.*** A country's information technology use has been linked to economic and societal development. A non-profit organization collects data that measure the use and impact of information technology in over 100 countries annually. The accompanying table shows a portion of the data collected, with the following variables: country number (Country), hardware industry (Hw), software industry (Sw), telecommunications industry (Tele), individual usage (IU), business usage (BU), government usage (GU), diffusion of e-business (EB), and diffusion of e-payment (EP). Each value in the table represents the score a country has achieved for a given category. The range of the score is from 1 (lowest) to 7 (highest).

Country	Hw	Sw	. . .	EP
1	4.2	4.6	. . .	3.9
2	4.0	4.3	. . .	2.6
⋮	⋮	⋮	⋮	⋮
139	2.4	3.7	. . .	3.1

a. Perform *k*-means clustering to group the countries into three clusters using the following variables: individual usage, business usage, and government usage. Is data standardization necessary in this case?
b. What are the size and cluster center values of the largest cluster? Which cluster has the highest average diffusion of e-business? Which cluster has the highest average diffusion of e-payment?
c. Use *k*-means clustering to group the countries using all the variables except the country number into the same number of clusters as in part a. What are the size and cluster center values of the largest cluster?

LO 11.3

11.3 ASSOCIATION RULE ANALYSIS

Conduct association rule analysis.

Association rule analysis, also referred to as affinity analysis or market basket analysis, is another widely used unsupervised data mining technique. It is essentially a "what goes with what" study designed to identify events that tend to occur together. In a classic application of association rule analysis, retail companies seek to identify products that consumers tend to purchase together. This type of information is useful to retail store managers when they display products next to each other on the shelf or when they develop promotional campaigns to cross-sell (encourage a customer to purchase complementary products or services) or up-sell (encourage a customer to purchase higher-end products or services).

In addition to the brick-and-mortar retailers, other companies also use association rule analysis to improve sales and customer services. For example, after purchasing a smartphone on a retail website, a customer is likely to receive a recommendation to purchase other related products, such as a smartphone case or a screen protector. Or after subscribing to a movie streaming service, a customer is likely to see a list of recommended movies or TV shows based on the information obtained from other subscribers with similar viewing habits. In health care, association rule analysis can help doctors diagnose illnesses based on different symptoms that tend to occur together.

The simplest way to understand an association rule is to think of it as an If-Then statement. Association rules rely on If-Then logic to discover hidden relationships among transactions (or observations or records) in a data set.

ASSOCIATION RULES ANALYSIS

Association rule analysis is a series of If-Then logical statements that represent relationships among different items or item sets. The analysis is designed to identify hidden patterns and co-occurring events in data.

Consider an example where an online retailer wants to know how often customers simultaneously purchase the following three seemingly unrelated products: smartwatches, LED lightbulbs, and books on meditation. After extracting a data set with the 10,000 most recent transactions, the retailer observes that 1,200 of the 10,000 transactions include smartwatches and LED lightbulbs, and out of these 1,200 transactions, 750 of them include meditation books. Based on this scenario, we might suggest an association rule that if a transaction includes smartwatches and LED light bulbs, then a meditation book is likely to be purchased as well. This association rule can also be expressed as {smartwatch, LED lightbulb} => {meditation book}. With this information, the retailer might discover later that these three products are often purchased together by health-conscious consumers who tend to purchase eco-friendly products (the LED lightbulbs) as well as products that help improve their physical and mental health (the smartwatches and meditation books).

The If portion of this statement is called the **antecedent**, and the Then portion is called the **consequent**. Antecedents and consequents can comprise a single product or a combination of products. For the {smartwatch, LED lightbulb} => {meditation book} example, the antecedent consists of two products, while the consequent has only one product. In association rule analysis, we refer to such product or a combination of products as an **item** or **item set**.

ANTECEDENT AND CONSEQUENT

In an If-Then logical statement, the item or item set in the If portion of the statement is called the antecedent, and the item or item set in the Then portion of the statement is called the consequent.

One inherent problem with searching for hidden relationships between items or item sets is dealing with the extremely large number of possible combinations. For example, the three items mentioned in the previous example would result in 12 possible combinations that need to be examined. These combinations include {smartwatch} => {LED lightbulb}, {smartwatch} => {meditation book}, {smartwatch} => {LED lightbulb, meditation book}, and so on. Four items would result in 50 possible combinations. As you can see, the number of possible combinations is exponential to the number of items, and it can be estimated using the following formula:

$$\text{Number of combinations} = 3^n - 2^{(n+1)} + 1,$$

where n is the number of items. Even a small convenience store with a modest number of items, say 100, would lead to 5.15378E+47 possible combinations. With the number of items often in thousands or even tens of thousands in many cases, the search problem becomes extremely computationally intensive and time-consuming.

There are several algorithms that can be used to perform association rule analysis in a more efficient manner. They all focus on the frequency of item sets. One of the most widely used methods is called the **Apriori algorithm**. The Apriori algorithm is designed to recursively generate item sets that exceed a predetermined frequency threshold; the term **support of the item or item set** is often used synonymously with the frequency of the item or item set. The Apriori method allows us to set a minimum support value, below which an item or item set is excluded, thus making the analysis more computationally feasible. For example, if it is found that smartwatches are included in 2,000 of the 10,000 transactions, then the support of smartwatches is calculated as 2,000/10,000 = 0.20. The Apriori method eliminates infrequent items that are below a predetermined frequency threshold, and makes it easier to analyze relevant information in a large data set with thousands of items and millions of transactions.

THE APRIORI ALGORITHM

The Apriori algorithm eliminates items or item sets that do not meet a predetermined frequency threshold in order to reduce the computational intensity of the association rule analysis.

With enough data, we can propose many of these If-Then association rules. However, we need a way to evaluate the effectiveness of these rules; this is the strength of association among products. Only the strong associations that occur frequently have the potential to reappear consistently in the future and lead to financially rewarding strategies. The **support of the association rule** is a ratio of the number of transactions that include all the items mentioned in the If-Then statement to the total number of transactions. In other words, we examine the probability of the If-Then statement in the data set. The support of the association rule is calculated as:

$$\text{Support} = \frac{\text{Number of transactions including both antecedent and consequent}}{\text{Total number of transactions}}$$

In the {smartwatch, LED lightbulb} => {meditation book} example, 750 of the 10,000 transactions included smartwatches, LED lightbulbs, and meditation books, and, therefore, the support of the {smartwatch, LED lightbulb} => {meditation book} association rule is 750/10,000 = 0.075.

The **confidence of the association rule** is another measure that is interpreted as a conditional probability of the consequent occurring, given that the antecedent occurs. The confidence of the association rule is calculated as:

$$\text{Confidence} = \frac{\text{Number of transactions including both antecedent and consequent}}{\text{Number of transactions including antecedent}}$$

In the {smartwatch, LED lightbulb} => {meditation book} example, smartwatches and LED lightbulbs are the products in the antecedent, and 1,200 of the 10,000 transactions included both smartwatches and LED lightbulbs. Therefore, the {smartwatch, LED lightbulb} => {meditation book} association rule has a confidence of 750/1,200 = 0.625. This is the conditional probability that a customer would purchase a meditation book, given that a smartwatch and an LED lightbulb are included in the transaction. Naturally, a retailer would look for an association rule that has high support and confidence values as they suggest strong associations that occur frequently.

However, sometimes, simply looking at support and confidence to determine the strength of association can be misleading. For example, suppose a store in town offers the lowest prices on broccoli and milk, which attracts many customers to the store to purchase these two items. As a result, you will get high support and confidence values for the {broccoli} => {milk} association simply because a large percent of customers purchase these two items. In this case, there is not necessarily a relationship between the two items. In order to avoid this common trap in association rules, we often turn to the **lift ratio** to evaluate the strength of the association. The lift ratio explicitly compares the confidence with a benchmark value called "expected confidence." It is calculated as:

$$\text{Lift ratio} = \frac{\text{Confidence}}{\text{Expected confidence}},$$

where

$$\text{Expected Confidence} = \frac{\text{Number of transactions including consequent}}{\text{Total number of transactions}}.$$

In the {smartwatch, LED lightbulb} => {meditation book} example, the expected confidence is simply an overall, unconditional probability of a meditation book purchase, regardless of other products. The lift ratio is a useful measure that compares the confidence of the association rule with the overall unconditional probability. A lift ratio of 1 suggests that the level of association between the antecedent and the consequent is just as likely as if there was no rule at all.

A strong and positive association rule should demonstrate a better outcome (i.e., confidence) than the overall probability (i.e., expected confidence), and, therefore, we should expect a lift ratio to be greater than 1 if a strong and positive association exists. The higher the lift ratio, the stronger the association between the antecedent and consequent. Conversely, a lift ratio between 0 and 1 indicates a negative association. The closer the lift ratio is to 0, the stronger the negative association between the antecedent and consequent is. If we assume that the number of transactions that include a meditation book is 1,000, the expected confidence would be 1,000/10,000 = 0.10. The lift ratio would be 0.625/0.10 = 6.25, suggesting a strong positive association between {smartwatch, LED lightbulb} and {meditation book} item sets. In practice, a common approach used in association rule analysis is to sort all the rules by lift ratio in descending order and focus on strong associations only.

ASSESSING AN ASSOCIATION RULE

An association rule can be evaluated using quantitative measures such as the support of the association rule, the confidence of the association rule, and the lift ratio.

The support of an association rule is calculated as:

$$\text{Support} = \frac{\text{Number of transactions including both antecedent and consequent}}{\text{Total number of transactions}}.$$

Support values that are closer to one are preferred to values closer to 0 because they suggest high occurrence frequency of the association rule.

The confidence of an association rule is calculated as:

$$\text{Confidence} = \frac{\text{Number of transactions including both antecedent and consequent}}{\text{Number of transactions including antecedent}}.$$

Confidence values that are closer to one are preferred to values closer to 0 because they suggest strong associations.

The lift ratio compares the confidence with a benchmark value called expected confidence. It is calculated as:

$$\text{Lift ratio} = \frac{\text{Confidence}}{\text{Expected confidence}},$$

where

$$\text{Expected Confidence} = \frac{\text{Number of transactions including consequent}}{\text{Total number of transactions}}.$$

A lift ratio greater than 1 implies a strong and positive association. A lift ratio between 0 and 1 indicates a negative relationship.

EXAMPLE 11.4

Consider the 10 retail transactions of cosmetics in Table 11.10. For example, the first transaction includes a lipstick, mascara, and an eye liner, while the second transaction includes an eye shadow and a mascara.

TABLE 11.10 Retail Transactions of Cosmetics

Transaction	Items
001	lipstick, mascara, eye liner
002	eye shadow, mascara
003	primer, concealer, lip gloss
004	face brush, concealer, primer
005	mascara, lipstick, eye liner
006	mascara, eye liner, eye shadow
007	lip gloss, eye liner, mascara
008	mascara, eye shadow, lip gloss
009	face brush, mascara, primer, eye liner
010	eye liner, lipstick, primer

a. Construct a frequency distribution that summarizes the number of purchases for each cosmetic product. Based on the frequency distribution, develop an association rule.

b. Compute and interpret the support, the confidence, and the lift ratio of the association rule developed in part a.

SOLUTION:

a. Table 11.11 shows the frequency distribution. This helps us gauge the support for each product. Seven of the 10 transactions include mascara (support = 7/10 = 0.7). The next most frequently purchased product is eye liner (support = 6/10 = 0.6). Thus, it seems reasonable to learn how often customers purchase mascara and eye liner together. The corresponding association rule can be written as {mascara} => {eye liner}. Both antecedent (mascara) and consequent (eye liner) of the association rule have only one item.

TABLE 11.11 Frequency Distribution for Cosmetics

lipstick	mascara	eye liner	eye shadow	primer	concealer	lip gloss	face brush
3	7	6	3	4	2	3	2

b. To assess the quality of this association rule, we first calculate the support of the association rule. We find the proportion of the transactions that include both mascara and eyeliner. Of the 10 transactions, mascara and eye liner are purchased in five transactions.

$$\text{Support} = \frac{\text{Number of transactions including both antecedent and consequent}}{\text{Total number of transactions}} = \frac{5}{10} = 0.50.$$

We then calculate the confidence of the association rule. Here, we find the probability that the transaction includes eyeliner, given that the transaction includes mascara. Of the seven transactions that include mascara, five of them include both mascara and eyeliner.

$$\text{Confidence} = \frac{\text{Number of transactions including both antecedent and consequent}}{\text{Number of transactions including antecedent}} = \frac{5}{7} = 0.71.$$

Finally, we calculate the lift ratio, which entails first calculating the expected confidence, or, equivalently, the probability that a transaction includes eye liner. Of the 10 transactions, there are six transactions with eye liner. So, the expected confidence is:

$$\text{Expected confidence} = \frac{\text{Number of transactions including consequent}}{\text{Total number of transactions}} = \frac{6}{10} = 0.60.$$

The lift ratio is calculated as:

$$\text{Lift ratio} = \frac{\text{Confidence}}{\text{Expected confidence}} = \frac{0.71}{0.60} = 1.19$$

Thus, with a lift ratio greater than one, a strong and positive association between the purchase of mascara and eye liner appears to exist, relative to having no rule at all. The lift ratio of 1.19 implies that identifying a customer who purchased a mascara as one who also purchased an eyeliner is 19% better than just guessing that a random customer purchased an eyeliner.

Using Analytic Solver and R to Perform Association Rule Analysis

With a small data set, it is relatively easy to manually describe and assess association rules with one item in the antecedent and consequent. Discovering more complex associations with multiple items in the antecedents and/or consequents in a larger data set will require computer applications. The following example demonstrates how to use association rule analysis in Analytic Solver and R.

Note: Association rule algorithms in Analytic Solver and R use comma-separated data as an input.

EXAMPLE 11.5

FILE *Transaction*

The store manager at an electronics store collects data on the last 100 transactions. Five possible products were purchased: a keyboard, an SD card, a mouse, a USB drive, and/or a headphone. Table 11.12 shows a portion of the data. For example, transaction 1 shows that the customer purchased a keyboard, a mouse, and a headphone. This type of data is called a "basket" of products, which is often used in a market basket analysis.

TABLE 11.12 Sample of Transactions at Electronics Store

Transaction 1	keyboard, mouse, headphone
Transaction 2	keyboard, SD card, mouse
⋮	⋮
Transaction 100	mouse, headphone

Conduct association rule analysis to help the store manager understand the relationships among these products. How might the store manager use this information?

SOLUTION:

Using Analytic Solver

a. Open the ***Transaction*** data file. [Note: The data are already in a comma separated format.]

b. From the menu, choose **Data Mining > Associate > Association Rules.**

c. See Figure 11.11. Click on the ellipsis button ... next to the *Data range* option and highlight cells $A$1:$E$100. Make sure that the box *First Row Contains Headers* is unchecked. Accept other defaults and click **OK**.

FIGURE 11.11 Association Rules dialog box in Analytic Solver

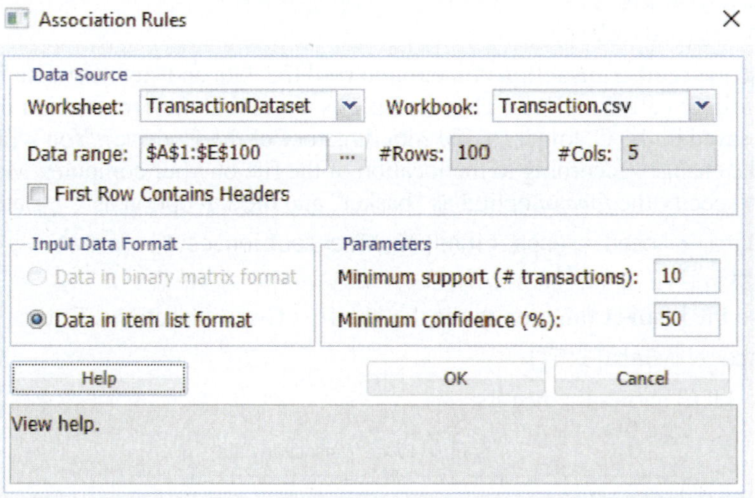

Source: Microsoft Excel

d. Next to the Transaction worksheet, Analytic Solver will insert two new worksheets: AR_Output and AR_PMMLModel. The two worksheets contain the same output information, but in a different format. We will focus on the Rules table from the AR_Output worksheet that is shown in Figure 11.12. The Rules table lists all the rules that meet the 10 minimum transactions and 50% minimum confidence specified in the default option in step c. Figure 11.12 shows the rules sorted by the lift ratio. Of the nine rules in the output, rules 2, 3, 6, 7, 8, and 9 have lift ratios greater than 1 and relatively high confidence values.

FIGURE 11.12 Association rules results from Analytic Solver

Rules

Rule ID	A-Support	C-Support	Support	Confidence	Lift-Ratio	Antecedent	Consequent
Rule 2	67	62	55	82.08955224	1.324025036	[keyboard]	[SDcard]
Rule 3	62	67	55	88.70967742	1.324025036	[SDcard]	[keyboard]
Rule 7	26	67	23	88.46153846	1.32032147	[mouse,SDcard]	[keyboard]
Rule 6	29	62	23	79.31034483	1.27919911	[keyboard,mouse]	[SDcard]
Rule 8	14	62	11	78.57142857	1.267281106	[keyboard,headphone]	[SDcard]
Rule 9	14	67	11	78.57142857	1.172707889	[headphone,SDcard]	[keyboard]
Rule 1	49	67	29	59.18367347	0.88333841	[mouse]	[keyboard]
Rule 4	19	67	11	57.89473684	0.86410055	[USBdrive]	[keyboard]
Rule 5	49	62	26	53.06122449	0.855826201	[mouse]	[SDcard]

Source: Microsoft Excel

We find that rule 2, {keyboard} => {SDcard}, and rule 3, {SDcard} => {keyboard}, have the highest lift ratios, suggesting the strongest associations. One recommendation for the store manager might be to place these two products next to each other.

Now let's assess the effectiveness of rule 2: {keyboard} => {SDcard}. The support frequency of 55 implies that 55 of the 100 transactions included both a keyboard and an SD card. The confidence for rule 2 implies that there is an 82.09% chance that a transaction includes an SD card, given that the transaction includes a keyboard. Interestingly, rule 3, {SDcard} => {keyboard}, has higher confidence because SDcard has a lower support value than keyboard has. And, finally, the lift ratio of 1.32 means that identifying a customer who purchased a keyboard as one who also purchased an SD card is 32% better than just guessing that a random customer purchased an SD card.

Using R

a. Install and load the *arules* and the *arulesViz* packages. Enter:

```
> install.packages("arules")
> install.packages("arulesViz")
> library(arules)
> library(arulesViz)
```

b. We use the **read.transactions** function to read the data and store the data in a new variable called myData. This example assumes that the ***Transaction*** data file is saved in the C: folder (or the root directory of the C: drive). You will need to make changes according to the location of the file on your computer. Make sure to specify the *format* option as "basket" and the *sep* option as ",". Enter:

```
> myData <- read.transactions("C:/Transaction.csv", format =
"basket", sep = ",")
```

c. We use the **inspect** function to display the first five transactions. Enter:

```
> inspect(myData[1:5])
```

Figure 11.13 shows the results.

FIGURE 11.13 A sample of the transaction data

```
items
[1] {headphone,keyboard,mouse}
[2] {keyboard,mouse,SDcard}
[3] {headphone}
[4] {keyboard}
[5] {keyboard,mouse,SDcard,USBdrive}
```

d. We use the **itemFrequency** and the **itemFrequencyPlot** functions to check the frequency of the items. Enter:

```
> itemFrequency(myData)
> itemFrequencyPlot(myData)
```

Figure 11.14 shows the item frequency table and plot. The results indicate that headphones appear in 32% of the transactions (support of {headphone} = 0.32), while USB drives appear in only 19% of the transactions (support of {USB drive} = 0.19).

FIGURE 11.14 R's item frequency table and item frequency plot

headphone	keyboard	mouse	SDcard	USBdrive
0.32	0.67	0.49	0.62	0.19

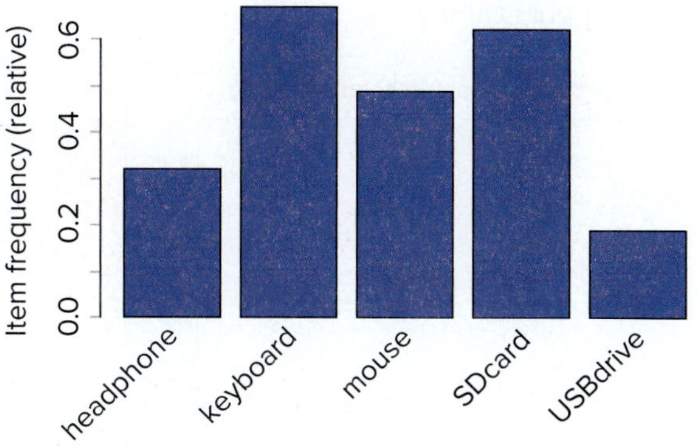

e. We use the **apriori** function to conduct association rule analysis. We set minimum values of *supp* (support) and *conf* (confidence) at 0.1 and 0.5, respectively. Practitioners usually experiment with different support and confidence thresholds to see whether or not interesting results might emerge. Inspecting the lift ratios (see step f below) can also help determine these thresholds. [If you do not specify any *parameter* values, the default minimum support and confidence values will be set at 0.1 and 0.8, respectively.] We also set the *minlen* option to 2 to prevent R from displaying association rules without an antecedent. Enter:

```
> rules <- apriori(myData, parameter = list(minlen = 2,
supp=0.1, conf=0.5))
```

f. To view the rules sorted by their lift ratios, we use the **sort** function to sort the rules. We use the *by* and *decreasing* options to sort by the lift ratio in descending order. Enter:

```
> srules <- sort(rules, by = 'lift', decreasing = TRUE)
> inspect(srules)
```

Figure 11.15 shows the results. As expected, the association rules generated by R are identical to those generated by Analytic Solver, and, thus, the conclusions are the same as those outlined in the Analytic Solver section.

g. If we have a larger data set and the **apriori** function produces many association rules, we can visually inspect the rules using the **plot** function. The scatterplot makes it easy to identify the rules with high lift ratios, confidence values, and support values. Enter:

```
> plot(rules)
```

FIGURE 11.15 Association rules generated by R

	lhs		rhs	support	confidence	lift	count
[1]	{keyboard}	⇒	{SDcard}	0.55	0.8208955	1.3240250	55
[2]	{SDcard}	⇒	{keyboard}	0.55	0.8870968	1.3240250	55
[3]	{mouse, SDcard}	⇒	{keyboard}	0.23	0.8846154	1.3203215	23
[4]	{keyboard, mouse}	⇒	{SDcard}	0.23	0.7931034	1.2791991	23
[5]	{headphone, keyboard}	⇒	{SDcard}	0.11	0.7857143	1.2672811	11
[6]	{headphone, SDcard}	⇒	{keyboard}	0.11	0.7857143	1.1727079	11
[7]	{mouse}	⇒	{keyboard}	0.29	0.5918367	0.8833384	29
[8]	{USBdrive}	⇒	{keyboard}	0.11	0.5789474	0.8641005	11
[9]	{mouse}	⇒	{SDcard}	0.26	0.5306122	0.8558262	26

Figure 11.16 shows the results. The rules with higher lift ratios are displayed in a more intense color. As the plot shows, two rules have high lift ratios, confidence values, and support values.

FIGURE 11.16 R's scatterplot for the rules

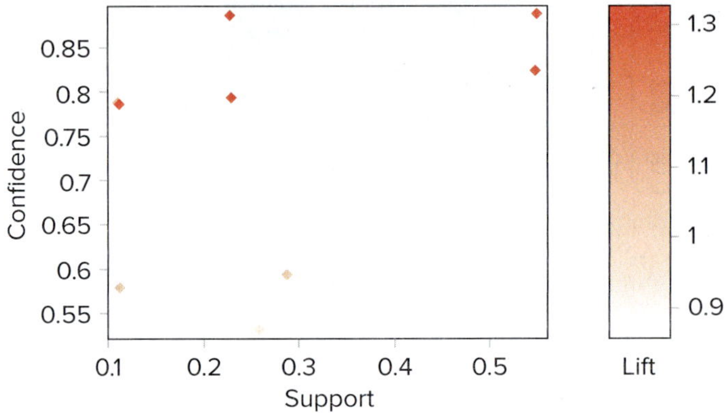

EXERCISES 11.3

Notes: All data for these exercises are already in a comma-separated (csv) format. **AS** and **R** indicate that the exercises must be solved using Analytic Solver and R, respectively. When asked to identify the top association rule, select the rule with the highest lift ratio. If multiple rules have the same lift ratio, select the rule with the highest confidence value as the top rule.

Mechanics

44. **FILE** ***Exercise_11.44.csv*** **AS** Consider the following portion of data consisting of 25 transactions.

Transaction 1	a, i, j, k
Transaction 2	c, g, i, k
⋮	⋮
Transaction 25	a, e, f, j

a. Generate association rules with a minimum support of 10 transactions and minimum confidence of 75%. Sort the rules by lift ratio. What is the lift ratio for the top rule?

b. Interpret the support count of the top rule.

c. Generate association rules with a minimum support of 5 transactions and minimum confidence of 50%. What is the lift ratio for the top rule?

d. Interpret the confidence of the top rule.

45. **FILE** ***Exercise_11.45.csv*** **R** The data are the same as in the preceding exercise. Read the data file into R using the **readtransactions** function and perform the following tasks.

a. Produce an item frequency plot and a frequency table. Which item is the most frequent item?

b. Generate association rules with a minimum support of 0.25 and minimum confidence of 0.75. Sort the rules by lift ratio. What is the lift ratio for the top rule?

c. Interpret the support proportion of the rule with the largest lift ratio in part b.

d. Generate association rules with a minimum support of 0.15 and minimum confidence of 0.60. Sort the rules by lift ratio. What is the lift ratio for the top rule?

e. Interpret the confidence of the rule with the largest lift ratio in part d.

f. Generate and interpret the scatterplot for the rules generated in part d.

46. **FILE** ***Exercise_11.46.csv*** **R** Consider the following portion of data consisting of 40 transactions. Read the data file into R using the **readtransactions** function and perform the following tasks.

Transaction 1	a, d
Transaction 2	a, b
⋮	⋮
Transaction 40	b, d, f

a. Produce an item frequency plot and frequency table. Which item is the least frequent item?

b. Generate association rules with a minimum support of 0.25 and minimum confidence of 0.50. Sort the rules by lift ratio. What is the lift ratio for the top rule?

c. Generate association rules with a minimum support of 0.10 and minimum confidence of 0.50. Sort the rules by lift ratio. What is the lift ratio for the top rule?

47. **FILE** ***Exercise_11.47.csv*** **AS** The data are the same as in the previous exercise. Perform association rule analysis using the following settings.

a. Generate association rules with a minimum support of 10 transactions and minimum confidence of 75%. How many rules are generated?

b. Generate association rules with a minimum support of 5 transactions and minimum confidence of 50%. How many rules are generated? Sort the rules by lift ratio. What is the lift ratio for the top rule?

48. **FILE** ***Exercise_11.48.csv*** **AS** Consider the following portion of data consisting of 100 transactions.

Transaction 1	a, c, d
Transaction 2	c, e, g
⋮	⋮
Transaction 100	c, d, e, g

a. Generate association rules with minimum support of 10 transactions and minimum confidence of 50%. How many rules are generated? Sort the rules by lift ratio. Which is the top rule? What is the lift ratio for the top rule?

b. Generate association rules with minimum support of 20 transactions and minimum confidence of 80%. How many rules are generated? Sort the rules by lift ratio. Which is the top rule? What is the lift ratio for the top rule?

49. **FILE** ***Exercise_11.49.csv*** **R** The data are the same as in the previous exercise. Read the data file using the **readtransactions** function and perform the following tasks.

a. Produce an item frequency plot and frequency table. Which item is the most frequent item?

b. Generate association rules with a minimum support of 0.1 and minimum confidence of 0.75. Sort the rules by the lift ratio. Report and interpret the lift ratio for the top rule.

c. Generate association rules with a minimum support of 0.25 and minimum confidence of 0.75. Sort the rules by the lift ratio. Report and interpret the lift ratio for the top rule.

d. Generate a scatterplot to display the rules obtained in part c.

50. **FILE** ***Exercise_11.50.csv*** **R** Consider the following portion of data consisting of 41 transactions. Read the data file using the **readtransactions** function and perform the following tasks.

Transaction 1	a, b, c, e, f
Transaction 2	a, b, c, d, e
⋮	⋮
Transaction 41	a, b, c, e, f, g

a. Produce an item frequency plot and frequency table. Which item is the least frequent item?

b. Generate association rules with a minimum support of 0.25 and minimum confidence of 0.7. Sort the rules by lift ratio. Report and interpret the lift ratio for the top rule.

c. Generate a scatterplot comparing the rules obtained in part b.

51. **FILE** ***Exercise_11.51.csv*** **AS** The data are the same as in the previous exercise. Perform association rule analysis using the following settings.

a. Generate association rules with a minimum support of 10 transactions and minimum confidence of 50%. Sort the rules by lift ratio. Report and interpret the lift ratio for the top rule.

b. Generate association rules with a minimum of 10 transactions and minimum confidence of 70%. How many rules are generated? Sort the rules by lift ratio. Report and interpret the lift ratio and confidence for the top rule.

Applications

52. **FILE** ***Movies.csv*** **AS** An online movie streaming company conducts a consumer study to find out the movie genres that its customers watch. Eighty-eight households volunteered to

participate in the study and allow the company to track the genres of movies they watch over a one-week period. A portion of the data is shown in the accompanying table. Record 1 shows that members of that household watched action, romance, and drama movies during the week, while the second household watched only action movies during the same week.

Record 1	action, romance, drama
Record 2	action
⋮	⋮
Record 88	romance, drama

Perform association rule analysis using the following settings.

a. Specify a minimum support of 9 and a minimum confidence of 50%. Sort the rules by lift ratio. What is the top rule? Report and interpret the lift ratio for the top rule.

b. Specify a minimum support of 5 and a minimum confidence of 25%. Sort the rules by lift ratio. What is the top rule? Report and interpret the lift ratio for the top rule.

53. **FILE** ***Movies.csv*** **R** Use the movie data set from the previous exercise and R to perform association rule analysis. Make sure to read the data file using the **readtransactions** function first.

a. Explore the data using an item frequency plot and a frequency table. Which genre of movie is the most frequently watched?

b. Generate association rules with a minimum support of 0.1 and minimum confidence of 0.5. How many rules are generated?

c. Sort the rules by lift ratio. What's the lift ratio of the top rule? What does it mean?

54. **FILE** ***Fruits.csv*** **AS** A local grocery store keeps track of individual products that customers purchase. Natalie Jackson, the manager in charge of the fresh fruits and produce section, wants to learn more about the customer purchasing patterns of apples, bananas, cherries, oranges, and watermelons, the five most frequently purchased fruit items in the store. She gathers data on the last 50 transactions, a portion of which is shown in the accompanying table. Transaction 1 shows that the customer purchased apples, bananas, and watermelon, while the second customer purchased bananas, cherries, and oranges. Find association rules for this consumer study. Use 10 as the minimum support and 50% as the confidence values. Report and interpret the lift ratio of the top three rules.

Transaction 1	apple, banana, watermelon
Transaction 2	banana, cherry, orange
⋮	⋮
Transaction 50	apple, banana, watermelon, orange

55. **FILE** ***Beatles_Songs.csv.*** **AS** An online music streaming service wants to find out which popular Beatles songs are frequently downloaded together by its users. The service collects the download logs for 100 users over the past month, where the download logs show which songs were downloaded during the same session. A portion of the data is shown in the accompanying table.

User 1	Yesterday, All You Need Is Love . . . Here Comes the Sun
User 2	Hey Jude, Come Together . . . Here Comes the Sun
⋮	⋮
User 100	Hey Jude, Come Together . . . Here Comes the Sun

Perform association rule analysis using the following settings.

a. Use a minimum support of 20 and a minimum confidence value of 60%. Sort the rules by lift ratio. Report and interpret the lift ratio of the top rule.

b. Use a minimum support of 15 and a minimum confidence value of 50%. Sort the rules by lift ratio. Report and interpret the lift ratio of the top rule.

56. **FILE** ***Beatles_Songs.csv.*** **R** Use the online music data set from the previous exercise to perform association rule analysis. Make sure to read the data file into R using the **readtransactions** function first.

a. Explore the data using an item frequency plot and a frequency table. What is the most frequently downloaded song?

b. Generate association rules with a minimum support of 0.1 and minimum confidence of 0.5. Sort the rules by lift ratio. Report and interpret the lift ratio of the top rule.

c. Display a scatterplot comparing the rules obtained in part b. How many rules have at least 0.75 confidence, 0.15 support, and 1.2 lift ratio?

57. **FILE** ***Condition_Symptoms.csv*** **R** Allen Chu is a first-year medical student. He is interested in finding out which symptoms of medical conditions tend to appear together in his research. He compiles a data set for 36 patients where the first entry lists the medical condition and the remaining entries are common symptoms associated with the medical condition. A portion of the data is shown in the accompanying table.

Patient 1	Acute Sinusitis, Fever . . . Decreased smell
Patient 2	Alcohol Intoxication, Abnormal gait (walking) . . . Stool leaking (incontinence)
⋮	⋮
Patient 36	West Nile Virus, Chills . . . Confusion, Fever

Make sure to read the data file into R using the **readtransactions** function first.

a. Generate association rules with a minimum support of 0.1 and minimum confidence of 0.5. Sort the rules by lift ratio. Report and interpret the lift ratio of the top three association rules.

b. Display a scatterplot comparing the rules obtained in part a. How many rules have at least 0.75 confidence, 0.15 support, and 1.2 lift ratio?

58. **FILE** ***Crime_Analysis.csv*** **AS** Assistant police chief Todd Beck wants to analyze the city's historic crime data in order to better allocate police resources in the future. He collects data over the past two years. Each record in the data shows the type of crime reported and the location of the crime. Todd is interested in answering the following question: Which types of crimes are often associated with which locations?

Record 1	NARCOTICS, STREET
Record 2	ASSAULT, RESIDENCE
⋮	⋮
Record 2,500	NARCOTICS, SIDEWALK

a. Generate association rules with a minimum support of 50 records and minimum confidence of 30%. How many rules are generated?

b. Based on the rules, which type of crime is most likely to be committed in a department store? Which type of crime is most likely to be committed on the sidewalk? Which type of crime is most likely to be committed in apartments?

59. **FILE** ***Crime_Analysis.csv*** **R** Use the crime data from the previous exercise to perform association rule analysis. Make sure to read the data file using the **readtransactions** function first.

a. Explore the data using an item frequency plot and a frequency table. What type of crime occurred most frequently? What location is associated with crimes most frequently?

b. Generate association rules with a minimum support of 0.02 and minimum confidence of 0.30. How many rules are generated?

c. Based on the rules, which type of crime is most likely to be committed in a department store? Which type of crime is most likely to be committed on the sidewalk? Which type of crime is most likely to be committed in apartments?

60. **FILE** ***Social_Media.csv*** **AS** Adrian Brown is a researcher studying social media usage patterns. In his research, he noticed that people tend to use multiple social media applications, and he wants to find out which popular social media applications are often used together by the same user. He surveyed 100 users about which social media applications they use on a regular basis. A sample of the data set is shown in the accompanying table.

User 1	Facebook, Snapchat, LinkedIn
User 2	Facebook, Snapchat, Instagram, Pinterest, LinkedIn, Twitter
⋮	⋮
User 100	Instagram, Tumbler, LinkedIn

a. Generate association rules with a minimum support of 20 and minimum confidence of 60%. How many rules are generated?

b. Sort the rules by lift ratio. What is the top rule? Report and interpret the lift ratio of the top rule.

61. **FILE** ***Business_Licenses.csv*** **R** Claire Williams is an intern working for the city government of New York City (NYC). She is given an assignment to find out which types of business are most likely to open in which area of NYC. She located a data file that contains the business license types and location of over 70,000 NYC businesses. A portion of the data is shown in the accompanying table. Make sure to read the data file into R using the **readtransactions** function first.

License 1	Electronics Store,BROOKLYN
License 2	Home Improvement Salesperson,CORONA
⋮	⋮
License 76,705	Secondhand Dealer - General,NEW YORK

Source: New York City Open Data, https://opendata.cityofnewyork.us/.

a. Generate association rules with a minimum support of 0.01 and minimum confidence of 0.25. How many rules are generated?

b. Sort the rules by lift ratio. What is the top rule? Report and interpret the lift ratio of the top rule.

62. **FILE** ***Bank_Accounts.csv*** **AS** Beau Crew is the branch manager of a major bank. He is interested in understanding which types of accounts a customer tends to have simultaneously so that he can offer additional financial services to his clients. He has compiled a list of customers and the accounts they have. A portion of the data is shown in the accompanying table. Find association rules for Beau's study. Use 10 as the minimum support and 50% as the minimum confidence values. How many rules are generated. Report and interpret the lift ratio of the top rule.

Customer 1	HELOC,IRA,Checking
Customer 2	Mortgage,CD,Checking,CD
⋮	⋮
Customer 81	Checking,Savings

63. FILE ***Bank_Accounts.csv*** R Use the bank account data set from the previous exercise to perform association rule analysis. Make sure to read the data file into R using the **readtransactions** function first.

a. Explore the data using an item frequency plot and a frequency table. Which account type is the most frequent item?

b. Generate association rules with a minimum support of 0.1 and minimum confidence of 50%. Sort the rules by lift ratio. How many rules are generated? Report and interpret the lift ratio of the top rule.

11.4 WRITING WITH BIG DATA

As explained earlier in this chapter, sometimes we need to convert the data into a format that is appropriate for the analysis. With big data, it is impractical to transform the data manually. In order to replicate the results for the big data case in this section and complete the accompanying exercises, you will need to consult Chapter 2 on the topic related to the transformation of categorical variables into binary variables.

Case Study

FILE ***Car_Crash.*** Ramona Kim is a California Highway Patrol (CHP) officer who works in the city of San Diego. Having lost her own uncle in a car accident, she is particularly interested in educating local drivers about driver safety. After discussing this idea with her commanding officer, she learns that since 2005 the CHP headquarters receives traffic-related collision information from local and state agencies and makes them publicly available on its website. Her commanding officer recommends that she focus on car accidents that result in deaths and severe injuries and encourages Officer Kim to share her findings with her colleagues as well as make presentations at local community meetings to raise awareness about car accidents among local drivers.

Sample Report— Severe Car Crashes in San Diego, CA

Many factors contribute to car accidents. Bad weather, reckless driving, distracted driving, lack of visibility at night, and failure to observe traffic laws can all lead to car accidents. In 2013, there were 3,000 deaths caused by motor-vehicle-related accidents in California. That is almost 10 motor-vehicle-related deaths per day. Conventional wisdom tells us that to stay safe, one should be careful in severe weather or while driving at night, refrain from driving under the influence, and always observe traffic laws. Beyond these conventional safety rules, it is critical to gain a better understanding of the different circumstances under which car accidents result in fatalities and severe injuries.

John Panella/Alamy Stock Photo

Relevant San Diego traffic-accident data are extracted from the Statewide Integrated Traffic Records System database from January 1, 2013, through February 28, 2013. It is the rainy season in California during this time period; thus, drivers often have to travel in heavy rain and other bad weather conditions. Table 11.13 shows a portion of the data from the 785 accidents

TABLE 11.13 San Diego Traffic-Accident Data, January–February 2013

Accident	WEEKEND	CRASHSEV	WEATHER	HIGHWAY	LIGHTING
1	0	1	0	0	0
2	1	1	1	0	1
⋮	⋮	⋮	⋮	⋮	⋮
785	1	0	1	0	1

that occurred in the city of San Diego over this time period. The five variables of interest for the analysis include the day of the week (WEEKEND =1 if weekend, 0 otherwise), crash severity (CRASHSEV =1 if severe injury or fatality, 0 otherwise), whether or not there was inclement weather (WEATHER = 1 if inclement, 0 otherwise), whether or not the accident occurred on a highway (HIGHWAY = 1 if highway, 0 otherwise), and whether or not there was daylight (LIGHTING = 1 if daylight, 0 otherwise). For example, the first observation represents an accident that occurred on a weekday that resulted in a severe injury or fatality. At the time of the accident, the weather was not inclement, but there was no daylight. And finally, the accident did not occur on a highway.

Agglomerative clustering analysis is performed using the matching coefficients as the distance measure and average linkage for the clustering method. Because the values of 0 and 1 (e.g., for the WEEKEND variable, 0 = weekdays, and 1 = weekends) are equally important in this analysis, the matching coefficients distance measure is appropriate. Figure 11.17 shows the resulting dendrogram plot.

FIGURE 11.17 Dendrogram for traffic-accident data

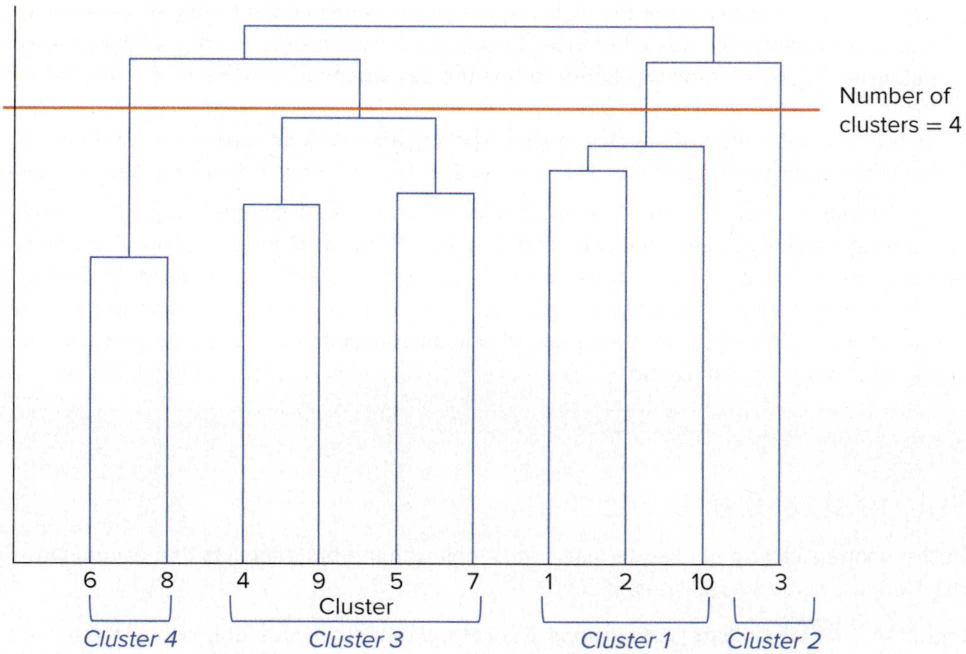

A careful inspection of the dendrogram suggests that the 785 observations should be grouped into four clusters, as shown in Figure 11.17. Each cluster forms a meaningful group of observations that are distinctive from one another. The cluster membership is assigned to each observation. In order to gain a better understanding of these clusters, the average value of each variable is calculated for each cluster. These averages are shown in Table 11.14. The last column shows the number of cases in each cluster.

TABLE 11.14 Clustering Results for Traffic Accidents in San Diego

Cluster	WEEKEND	CRASHSEV	WEATHER	HIGHWAY	LIGHTING	# of Cases
1	0.3207	1.00000	0.0755	0.2076	0.5660	53
2	0.2500	1.00000	1.0000	0.6250	0.0000	8
3	0.1599	0.0000	0.2297	0.2951	0.6003	688
4	1.0000	0.0000	0.3889	1.0000	0.5000	36

Based on these results, the following observations can be made.

1. All of the accidents that resulted in fatalities or severe injuries are grouped into Cluster 1 (53 cases) and Cluster 2 (8 cases).
2. An overwhelming majority of fatal and severe-injury cases in Cluster 1 occurred when the weather conditions were clear.
3. Surprisingly, most fatal and severe-injury cases occurred on a weekday; only 32.1% of cases in Cluster 1 and 25% of cases in Cluster 2 occurred over the weekend. A possible explanation is that there are more weekdays than weekends in a week and, therefore, weekdays would naturally have a larger portion of the total fatal or severe-injury cases.
4. Cluster 2 consists of eight cases that involved fatalities or severe injuries. All eight cases happened during bad weather conditions and after dark, and the majority of them occurred on the highway.
5. The vast majority of the accidents are grouped into Cluster 3. These accidents tended to happen during the weekdays on nonhighway roads when the weather condition was not inclement. None of them resulted in fatalities or severe injuries.
6. All the accidents in Cluster 4 happened on the highway. However, none of them resulted in fatality or severe injuries. Comparing Cluster 4 to Cluster 2, where the majority of the accidents also happened on the highway, but all cases resulted in fatality or severe injuries, we notice that the key differences between the two clusters are that all the accidents in Cluster 2 happened on weekends during the day when the weather was not inclement. While none of the variables may be a strong indicator for fatal or severe-injury cases on its own, a combination of traveling on the highway after dark on weekdays during bad weather seems to increase the chance of an accident resulting in fatality or severe injuries.

The key finding from the cluster analysis is that many fatal and severe-injury accidents occur on weekdays when the weather condition is clear. Perhaps, when the weather condition is favorable, drivers tend to speed, causing severe injuries or fatalities in an accident. During the weekdays, drivers might also be in a rush to get home or to get to work, adding to the severity of a car accident. This study can be used to design an educational campaign to raise awareness among local drivers in San Diego.

Suggested Case Studies

Cluster analysis can be applied to many situations with the big data sets that accompany this text. Here are some suggestions.

Report 11.1 FILE ***College_Admissions.*** Subset the data to include only one of the three colleges. Group college applicants into clusters based on categorical variables of your choice (e.g., sex, parent's education). Determine the appropriate number of clusters. Report the characteristics of each cluster and explain how they are different from each other. Note: You will need to transform the categorical values into binary variables in order to perform cluster analysis. See Chapter 2 for procedures used to transform categorical variables.

Report 11.2 FILE ***College_Admissions.*** Subset the data to include only one of the three colleges. Find a combination of numerical and categorical variables to include in cluster analysis. Determine the appropriate number of clusters and write a report to explain your decision and describe how each cluster is different from other clusters. Note: Cluster analysis with mixed data can only be performed in R.

Report 11.3 **FILE** ***TechSales_Reps.*** Subset the data set to include only sales professionals in one of the two product groups. Cluster the sales professionals based on numerical variables of your choice (e.g., age, salary). Determine the appropriate number of clusters. Describe each cluster and compare the average net promoter scores of the clusters.

Report 11.4 **FILE** ***NBA.*** Group NBA players into clusters based on either their career performance or performance statistics from a particular season (e.g., 2013–2014). Determine an appropriate number of clusters, and write a report based on the clustering results.

Report 11.5 **FILE** ***Longitudinal_Survey.*** Subset the data set to include only those individuals who lived in an urban area. Cluster the individuals using a combination of numerical and categorical variables. Determine the appropriate number of clusters and write a report to describe the differences between clusters. Note: Cluster analysis with mixed data can only be performed in R.

12 Forecasting with Time Series Data

LEARNING OBJECTIVES

After reading this chapter, you should be able to:

- LO **12.1** **Describe the time series forecasting process.**
- LO **12.2** **Use smoothing techniques to make forecasts.**
- LO **12.3** **Use linear regression models to make forecasts.**
- LO **12.4** **Use nonlinear regression models to make forecasts.**
- LO **12.5** **Apply cross-validation techniques for model selection.**
- LO **12.6** **Use advanced smoothing methods to make forecasts.**

Observations of any variable recorded over time in sequential order are considered a time series. Forecasting with time series is an important aspect of analytics, providing guidance for decisions in all areas of business. In fact, the success of any business depends on the ability to accurately forecast vital variables. Sound forecasts not only improve the quality of business plans, but also help identify and evaluate potential risks. Examples include forecasting product sales, product defects, the inflation rate, cyber attacks, or a company's cash flows.

In this chapter, we focus on the trend, the seasonal, and the random components of a time series. Several models are introduced that capture one or more of these components. In particular, we use simple smoothing techniques for making forecasts when short-term fluctuations in the data represent random departures from the overall pattern with no discernible trend or seasonal fluctuations. Forecasting models based on regression and advanced smoothing are introduced when trend and seasonal fluctuations are present in the time series. Because it is highly unlikely to know *a priori* which of the competing models is likely to provide the best forecast, we apply in-sample and out-of-sample criteria to select the preferred model for forecasting.

©icon Stocker/Shutterstock

INTRODUCTORY CASE

Apple Revenue Forecast

On August 2, 2018, Apple Inc. reported its fourth consecutive quarter of record revenue and became the first publicly traded American company to surpass $1 trillion in market value. Its explosive growth has played a big role in the technology industry's ascent to the forefront of the global market economy (*The Wall Street Journal*, Aug. 2, 2018). Although the company designs, develops, and sells consumer electronics, computer software, and online services, the iPhones segment continues to be the company's core source of revenue.

Cadence Johnson, a research analyst at a small investment firm, is evaluating Apple's performance by analyzing the firm's revenue. She is aware that Apple could be seeing some resistance to its newly revamped and high-priced line of iPhones, stoking fears among investors that demand for iPhones is waning. Cadence hopes that Apple's past performance will aid in predicting its future performance. She collects quarterly data on Apple's revenue for the fiscal years 2010 through 2018, with the fiscal year concluding at the end of September. A portion of the data is shown in Table 12.1.

TABLE 12.1 Quarterly Revenue for Apple Inc. (in $ millions)

Year	Quarter	Revenue
2010	1	15,683
2010	2	13,499
⋮	⋮	⋮
2018	4	62,900

FILE *Revenue_Apple*

Cadence would like to use the information in Table 12.1 to

1. Explore models that capture the trend and seasonal components of Apple's revenue.
2. Forecast Apple's revenue for fiscal year 2019.

A synopsis of this case is provided at the end of Section 12.4.

LO 12.1

12.1 THE FORECASTING PROCESS FOR TIME SERIES

Describe the time series forecasting process.

In this chapter, we focus our attention on time series data. Observations of any variable recorded over time in sequential order are considered a time series. The time period can be expressed in terms of a year, a quarter, a month, a week, a day, an hour, or even a second. Examples of time series include the *hourly* volume of stocks traded on the New York Stock Exchange (NYSE) on five consecutive trading days; the *daily* number of loan applications over the months of June and July; the *monthly* sales for a retailer over a five-year period; and the *annual* growth rate of a country over the past 30 years.

Let $y_1, y_2, \ldots, y_T$ represent a sample of T observations of a variable y with y_t denoting the value of y at time t. With time series data, it is customary to use the notation T, instead of n, to represent the number of sample observations and to use a subscript t to identify time. For instance, if the number of daily loan applications over five days are 100, 94, 98, 110, 102, then $y_1 = 100, y_2 = 94, \ldots, y_5 = 102$.

Time series consist of the trend, the seasonal, the cyclical, and the random components. The **trend** component represents long-term upward or downward movements of the series. For example, product sales or a firm's stock price may go up (or go down) over a certain time period. The **seasonal** component typically represents repetitions over a one-year period. For example, every year, sales of retail goods increase during the holiday season, and the number of vacation packages sold goes up during the summer. The **cyclical** component represents wavelike fluctuations or business cycles, often caused by expansion and contraction of the economy. The main distinction between seasonal and cyclical patterns is that seasonal patterns tend to repeat within periods of one year or less, whereas cyclical patterns last for one to several years—plus, the duration of a cycle differs from one cycle to the next. In addition, the magnitude of the up-and-down swings of the time series are more predictable with seasonal patterns as opposed to cyclical patterns. The **random** component is difficult to identify as it captures the unexplained movements of the time series. For example, there may be an increase or decrease in customers at a retail store for no apparent reason. In this text, we will focus on the trend, the seasonal, and the random components of a time series when making forecasts.

TIME SERIES

A time series is a set of sequential observations of a variable over time. It is generally characterized by the trend, the seasonal, the cyclical, and the random components.

FILE *Revenue_Apple*

In the introductory case, we considered Apple's quarterly revenue from 2010 through 2018, with the fiscal year concluding at the end of September. Figure 12.1 is a scatterplot of the series, with the dots connected, where we have relabeled the nine years of quarterly observations from 1 to 36.

FIGURE 12.1 Scatterplot of Apple's quarterly revenue (in $ millions)

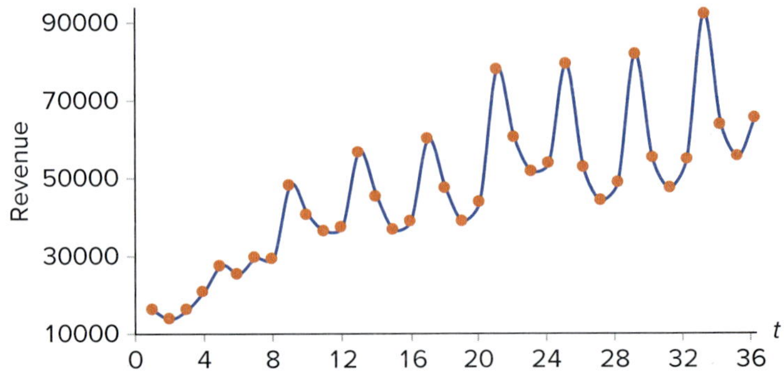

The graph highlights some important characteristics of Apple's revenue. First, there is a persistent upward movement with the series plateauing near the end of the observation period. Second, a seasonal pattern repeats itself year after year. For instance, revenue is consistently higher in the first quarter as compared to the other quarters. Note that given Apple's fiscal calendar, the first quarter, ending in December, encompasses the holiday period with usual strong sales.

Forecasting Methods

Forecasting methods are broadly classified as quantitative or qualitative. **Qualitative forecasting** methods are based on the judgment of the forecaster, who uses prior experience and expertise to make forecasts. On the other hand, **quantitative forecasting** methods use a formal model along with historical data for the variable of interest.

Qualitative forecasting is especially attractive when historical data are not available. For instance, a manager may use qualitative forecasts when she attempts to project sales for a new product. Similarly, we rely on qualitative forecasts when future results are suspected to depart markedly from results in prior periods, and, therefore, cannot be based on historical data. For example, major changes in market conditions or government policies will render the analysis from historical data misleading.

Although attractive in certain scenarios, qualitative forecasts are often criticized on the grounds that they are prone to some well-documented biases such as optimism and overconfidence. Decisions based on the judgment of an overly optimistic manager may prove costly to the business. Furthermore, qualitative forecasting is difficult to document, and its quality is totally dependent on the judgment and skill of the forecaster. Two people with access to similar information may offer different qualitative forecasts.

Formal quantitative models have been used extensively to forecast variables, such as product sales, product defects, house prices, inflation, stock prices, and cash flows.

FORECASTING METHODS

Forecasting methods are broadly classified as quantitative or qualitative. Qualitative methods are based on the judgment of the forecaster, whereas quantitative methods use a formal model to project historical data.

In this chapter, we focus on quantitative models to project historical data, where each model is specially designed to capture one or more components of a time series.

Model Selection Criteria

Numerous models can be used to make a forecast, with each model well-suited to capture a particular feature of the time series. It would be easy to choose the right model if we knew for certain which feature describes the given series. Unfortunately, such certainty rarely exists in the business world. Because we do not know which of the competing models is likely to provide the best forecast, it is common to consider several models. Model selection is one of the most important steps in forecasting. Therefore, it is important to understand model selection criteria before we even introduce any of the formal models.

We can assess competing forecasting models, using what is referred to as in-sample criteria, where the same sample period is used for both the estimation of the model and its assessment. In-sample criteria do not help us assess how well an estimated model will predict in an unseen sample. In Chapters 7–10, we used cross-validation techniques to evaluate competing models by partitioning the sample into a training set to build (train) the model and a validation set to assess (validate) it. Because it is possible for a model to perform well in the training set but poorly in the validation set, an independent assessment of the model performance is achieved in the validation set, using what is often referred to as out-of-sample criteria.

Both in-sample and out-of-sample criteria are based on the forecast error $e_t = y_t - \hat{y}_t$, where y_t denotes the value of the series at time t and $\hat{y}_t$ denotes its forecast. Commonly used performance measures for the comparison of competing forecasting models are the familiar mean square error (*MSE*), the mean absolute deviation (*MAD*), and the mean absolute percentage error (*MAPE*). These performance measures were also discussed in Chapter 8; recall that *MAD* is also referred to as the mean absolute error (*MAE*). The preferred model will have the lowest *MSE*, *MAD*, or *MAPE* values. Because there is no 'primary' model selection criterion, multiple performance measures are used for model selection. The formulas for *MSE*, *MAD*, and *MAPE* are shown in the following definition box.

PERFORMANCE MEASURES

In-sample and out-of-sample criteria are based on the forecast error $e_t = y_t - \hat{y}_t$, where y_t denotes the value of the series at time t and $\hat{y}_t$ denotes its forecast. We use e_t to compute the mean square error (*MSE*), the mean absolute deviation (*MAD*), and the mean absolute percentage error (*MAPE*) as

$$MSE = \frac{1}{n}\sum e_t^2,$$

$$MAD = \frac{1}{n}\sum |e_t|, \text{ and}$$

$$MAPE = \frac{1}{n}\left(\sum \left|\frac{e_t}{y_t}\right|\right) \times 100$$

where n is the number of observations used in the computation. We choose the model with the lowest *MSE, MAD*, or *MAPE* values. Because there is no 'primary' performance measure, multiple measures are used for model selection.

Recall from Chapter 8 that for any given model, there is no universal "good" value for the above performance measures; therefore, these are best used as model selection criteria. *MSE* heavily penalizes models with large forecast errors and, therefore, is preferred if relatively large forecast errors are particularly undesirable. Another popular measure is the root mean square error (*RMSE*), which is simply the square root of *MSE*. A large *RMSE* relative to *MAD* is indicative of relatively large errors in the forecast. The main attraction of using *MAPE* is that it shows the error as a percentage of the actual value, giving a sense of the magnitude of the errors.

As mentioned earlier, in-sample and out-of-sample criteria give rise to two important questions: How well does a model explain in-sample forecasts in the training set? And how well does a model make out-of-sample forecasts in the validation set? Ideally, the chosen model is best in terms of in-sample and out-of-sample criteria. We focus on in-sample criteria in Sections 12.2 through 12.4; we extend the discussion to include out-of-sample criteria in Sections 12.5 and 12.6.

LO 12.2

Use smoothing techniques to make forecasts.

12.2 SIMPLE SMOOTHING TECHNIQUES

As mentioned earlier, a time series is a sequence of observations that are ordered in time. Inherently, any data collected over time is likely to exhibit some form of random variation. For instance, the checkout time at a campus bookstore or weekly sales at a convenience store encounter random variations for no apparent reason. In this section we focus on applications where the time series is described primarily by random variations around an unknown level. In other words, there are no variations due to trend and/or seasonality.

A simple plot of the time series provides insights into its components. A jagged appearance, caused by abrupt changes in the series, indicates random variations.

Smoothing techniques are employed to reduce the effect of random fluctuations. These techniques can also be used to provide forecasts if short-term fluctuations represent random departures from the structure, with no discernible patterns. These techniques are especially attractive when forecasts of multiple variables need to be updated frequently. For example, consider a manager of a convenience store who has to update the inventories of numerous items on a weekly basis. It is not practical in such situations to develop complex forecasting models for each item. We discuss two distinct smoothing techniques: the moving average technique and the simple exponential smoothing technique.

The Moving Average Technique

Due to its simplicity, the **moving average technique** ranks among the most popular techniques for processing time series. The method is based on computing the average from a fixed number m of the most recent observations. For instance, a 3-period moving average is formed by averaging the three most recent observations. The term "moving" is used because as a new observation becomes available, the average is updated by including the newest observation and dropping the oldest observation.

CALCULATING A MOVING AVERAGE

An m-period moving average is computed as

$$\text{Moving Average} = \frac{\text{Sum of the } m \text{ most recent observations}}{m}.$$

EXAMPLE 12.1

In preparation for staffing during the upcoming summer months, an online retailer reviews the number of customer service calls received over the past three weeks (21 days). Table 12.2 shows a portion of the time series.

a. Construct a 3-period moving average series for the data.

b. Plot the time series and its corresponding 3-period moving average, and comment on any differences.

c. Using the 3-period moving average series, forecast the number of customer service calls for the 22nd day.

d. Calculate *MSE*, *MAD*, and *MAPE*.

TABLE 12.2 Daily Customer Service Calls

Day	Calls
1	309
2	292
3	284
4	294
5	292
⋮	⋮
19	326
20	327
21	309

FILE *Service_Calls*

SOLUTION:

a. We would like to point out that the calculations are based on unrounded values even though we show rounded values in the text. For notational simplicity, let Calls be denoted by y_t and the corresponding moving average be denoted by $\bar{y}_t$. We form a 3-period moving average series by averaging all sets of three consecutive values of the original series. The first value of a 3-period moving average is calculated as

$$\bar{y}_2 = \frac{y_1 + y_2 + y_3}{3} = \frac{309 + 292 + 284}{3} = 295.$$

We designate this value $\bar{y}_2$ because it represents the average in days 1 through 3. The next moving average, representing the average in days 2 through 4, is

$$\bar{y}_3 = \frac{y_2 + y_3 + y_4}{3} = \frac{292 + 284 + 294}{3} = 290.$$

Other values of $\bar{y}_t$ are calculated similarly and are presented in column 3 of Table 12.3. Note that we lose one observation at the beginning and one observation at the end of the 3-period moving average series $\bar{y}_t$. (If it were a 5-period moving average, we would lose two observations at the beginning and two at the end.)

TABLE 12.3 3-Period Moving Averages, Forecasts, and Errors

Day (1)	y (2)	$\bar{y}$ (3)	$\hat{y}$ (4)	$e = y - \hat{y}$ (5)
1	309	—	—	—
2	292	295	—	—
3	284	290	—	—
4	294	290	295	−1
5	292	290.33	290	2
⋮	⋮	⋮	⋮	⋮
19	326	320.67	304	22
20	327	320.67	309	18
21	309	—	320.67	−11.67

b. In Figure 12.2, we plot the time series and its corresponding 3-period moving average against days. Note that the original time series has a jagged appearance, suggesting the presence of an important random component of the series. The series of moving averages, on the other hand, presents a much smoother picture.

FIGURE 12.2 Number of customer service calls and 3-period moving average

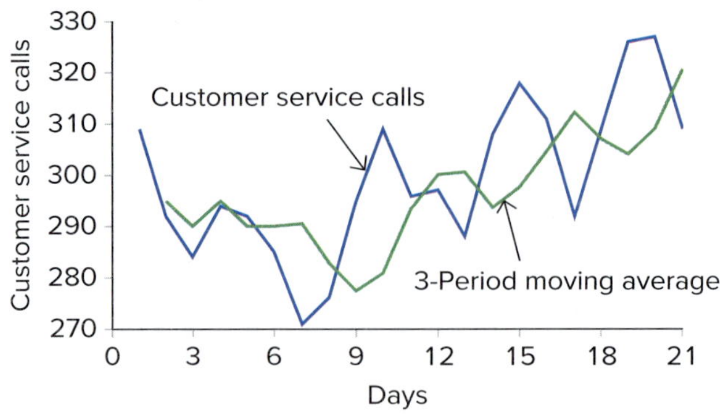

c. As mentioned earlier, if the series exhibits primarily random variations, we can use moving averages to generate forecasts. Because $\bar{y}_2$ represents the average for days 1 through 3, it is the most updated estimate of the series prior to period 4. Therefore, we use $\hat{y}_4 = \bar{y}_2$ where $\hat{y}_4$ is the in-sample forecast for period 4. Similarly, $\hat{y}_5 = \bar{y}_3$ is the forecast for period 5, where $\hat{y}_3$ is the average for days 2 through 4, and so on. These forecasts, derived as $\hat{y}_t = \frac{y_{t-3} + y_{t-2} + y_{t-1}}{3}$, are shown in column 4 of Table 12.3. Following this simple process, we compute the out-of-sample forecast for day 22 as

$$\hat{y}_{22} = \bar{y}_{20} = \frac{y_{19} + y_{20} + y_{21}}{3} = \frac{326 + 327 + 309}{3} = 320.67.$$

Therefore, the forecast for the number of customer service calls for the 22nd day is 321 calls. One potential weakness when using the moving average technique is that all future forecasts take on the same value as the first out-of-sample forecast; that is, the forecast for the 23rd day is also 321 calls.

d. To calculate *MSE*, *MAD*, and *MAPE*, we first compute the forecast error, $e_t = y_t - \hat{y}_t$, as shown in column 5 of Table 12.3.

$$MSE = \frac{1}{n}\sum e_t^2 = \frac{(-1)^2 + (2)^2 + \cdots + (-11.67)^2}{18} = 208.90,$$

$$MAD = \frac{1}{n}\sum |e_t| = \frac{|-1| + |2| + \cdots + |-11.67|}{18} = 11.85, \text{ and}$$

$$MAPE = \frac{1}{n}\left(\sum\left|\frac{e_t}{y_t}\right|\right) \times 100 = \frac{1}{18}\left(\left|\frac{-1}{294}\right| + \left|\frac{2}{292}\right| + \cdots + \left|\frac{-11.67}{309}\right|\right) \times 100 = 3.92.$$

These performance measures will prove useful when comparing alternative models.

The Simple Exponential Smoothing Technique

Although the moving average approach is popular, it has some shortcomings. First, the choice of the order m is arbitrary, although we can use trial and error to choose the value of m that results in the smallest *MSE*, *MAD*, or *MAPE*. Second, it may not be appropriate to give equal weight to all recent m observations. Whereas the moving average technique weighs all recent observations equally, the method called **simple exponential smoothing** assigns exponentially decreasing weights as the observations get older. As in the case of moving averages, exponential smoothing is a procedure for continually revising a forecast in light of more recent observations.

Let L_t denote the estimated level of the series at time t, where L_t is defined as

$$L_t = \alpha y_t + \alpha(1-\alpha)y_{t-1} + \alpha(1-\alpha)^2 y_{t-2} + \alpha(1-\alpha)^3 y_{t-3} + \cdots, \text{ where } 0 < \alpha < 1.$$

That is, L_t is simply a weighted average of exponentially declining weights, with α dictating the speed of decline. For example, with $\alpha = 0.8$,

$$L_t = 0.8y_t + 0.16y_{t-1} + 0.032y_{t-2} + 0.0064y_{t-3} + \cdots.$$

Similarly, with $\alpha = 0.2$,

$$L_t = 0.2y_t + 0.16y_{t-1} + 0.128y_{t-2} + 0.1024y_{t-3} + \cdots.$$

Note that the speed of decline is higher when $\alpha = 0.8$ as compared to when $\alpha = 0.2$.

Using algebra, it can be shown that the initial equation simplifies to

$$L_t = \alpha y_t + (1 - \alpha)L_{t-1}.$$

We use this representation to define the formula for exponential smoothing. Because L_t represents the most updated level at time t, we can use it to make a one-period-ahead forecast as $\hat{y}_{t+1} = L_t$. This equation shows that the forecast $\hat{y}_{t+1} = L_t$ depends on the current value, y_t, and its earlier forecast, $\hat{y}_t = L_{t-1}$. In other words, we continually revise the forecast in the light of more recent observations.

CALCULATING A SIMPLE EXPONENTIALLY SMOOTHED SERIES

The simple exponential smoothing technique continually updates the level of the series as

$$L_t = \alpha y_t + (1 - \alpha)L_{t-1},$$

where α represents the speed of decline. Forecasts are made as $\hat{y}_{t+1} = L_t$.

In order to implement this method, we need to determine α and the initial value of the series, L_1. Typically, the initial value is set equal to the first value of the time series, that is, $L_1 = y_1$; the choice of the initial value is less important if the number of observations is large. The optimal value for α is determined by a trial-and-error method. We evaluate various values of α and choose the one that results in the smallest *MSE*, *MAD*, *MAPE*, or some other selection criteria. In Section 12.6, we show how to use Analytic Solver and R for simple as well as advanced exponential smoothing methods. Both software packages allow user-supplied and computer-generated values for the smoothing parameters, including α.

EXAMPLE 12.2

Revisit the ***Service_Calls*** data from Example 12.1.

a. Construct the simple exponentially smoothed series with $\alpha = 0.20$ and $L_1 = y_1$.

b. Plot time series and its corresponding exponentially smoothed series against days. Comment on any differences.

c. Using the exponentially smoothed series, forecast the number of customer service calls for the 22nd day.

d. Calculate *MSE*, *MAD*, and *MAPE*. Compare these values with those obtained using the 3-period moving average technique in Example 12.1.

SOLUTION: Again, the calculations are based on unrounded values even though we show rounded values in the text.

a. In Column 3 of Table 12.4, we present sequential estimates of L_t with the initial value $L_1 = y_1 = 309$. We use $L_t = \alpha y_t + (1 - \alpha)L_{t-1}$ to continuously update the level with $\alpha = 0.2$. For instance, for periods 2 and 3 we calculate

$$L_2 = 0.20 \times 292 + 0.80 \times 309 = 305.60, \text{ and}$$
$$L_3 = 0.20 \times 284 + 0.80 \times 305.60 = 301.28.$$

All other estimates of L_t are found in a like manner.

b. In Figure 12.3, we plot the original time series and its corresponding exponentially smoothed series against days. As mentioned earlier, while the original time series has the jagged appearance, the exponentially smoothed series removes most of the sharp points and, like the moving average series, presents a much smoother picture.

TABLE 12.4 Exponentially Smoothed Series with $\alpha = 0.20$, Forecasts, and Errors

Day (1)	y (2)	L_t (3)	$\hat{y}$ (4)	$e = y - \hat{y}$ (5)
1	309	309.00	—	—
2	292	305.60	309.00	−17.00
3	284	301.28	305.60	−21.60
⋮	⋮	⋮	⋮	⋮
20	327	310.95	306.93	20.07
21	309	310.56	310.95	−1.95

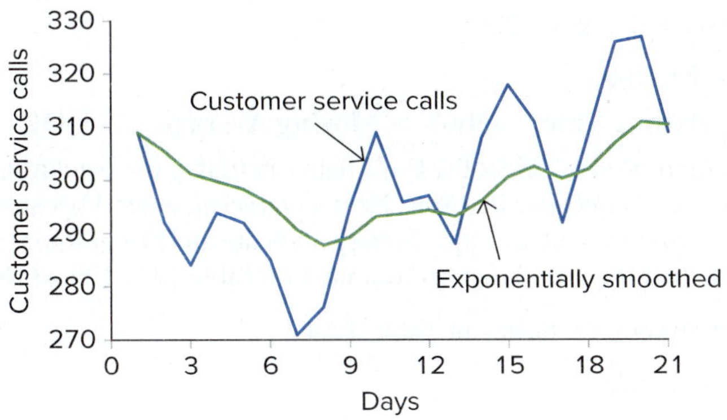

FIGURE 12.3 Number of customer service calls and exponentially smoothed series

c. Forecasts, given by $\hat{y}_{t+1} = L_t$, are presented in column 4 of Table 12.4. For instance, for period 2, $\hat{y}_2 = L_1 = 309$. Similarly, $L_2 = 305.60$ is the forecast for $\hat{y}_3$. Therefore, the forecast for the 22nd day is computed as $\hat{y}_{22} = L_{21} = 0.20 \times 309 + 0.80 \times 310.95 = 310.56$, or 311 customer service calls. As with the moving average technique, any further out-of-sample forecasts also assume this same value; for instance, $\hat{y}_{23} = 311$ customer service calls.

To calculate *MSE*, *MAD*, and *MAPE*, we first compute the forecast error, $e_t = y_t - \hat{y}_t$, as shown in column 5 of Table 12.4.

$$MSE = \frac{1}{n}\sum e_t^2 = \frac{(-17.00)^2 + (-21.60)^2 + \cdots + (-1.95)^2}{20} = 217.16,$$

$$MAD = \frac{1}{n}\sum |e_t| = \frac{|-17.00| + |-21.60| + \cdots + |-1.95|}{20} = 12.91, \text{ and}$$

$$MAPE = \frac{1}{n}\left(\sum\left|\frac{e_t}{y_t}\right|\right) \times 100 = \frac{1}{20}\left(\left|\frac{-17.00}{292}\right| + \left|\frac{-21.60}{284}\right| + \cdots + \left|\frac{-1.95}{309}\right|\right) \times 100 = 4.32.$$

There is nothing special about $\alpha = 0.2$; we used this value primarily to illustrate the exponential smoothing technique. As we noted earlier, it is common to evaluate various values of α and choose the one that produces the smallest *MSE*, *MAD*, or *MAPE* values. In order to illustrate how α is chosen, we generate *MSE*, *MAD*, and *MAPE* with α values ranging from 0.1 to 0.9 with increments of 0.1. The results are summarized in Table 12.5.

Here, the choice of α depends on whether we employ *MSE*, *MAD*, or *MAPE* for model comparison. In this example, it may be appropriate to select $\alpha = 0.5$ because it leads to the smallest value for two out of three performance measures (*MAD* and *MAPE*). This model (with $\alpha = 0.5$) also outperforms the moving average model as measured by lower *MSE*, *MAD*, and *MAPE* values.

TABLE 12.5 Various Values of α and the Resulting *MSE*, *MAD*, and *MAPE*

α	0.1	0.2	0.3	0.4	0.5	0.6	0.7	0.8	0.9
MSE	257.20	217.16	192.44	180.42	175.40	173.61	172.82	171.79	169.97
MAD	13.60	12.91	12.18	11.42	11.10	11.11	11.25	11.41	11.43
MAPE	4.57	4.32	4.07	3.81	3.70	3.70	3.75	3.81	3.82

Using Excel for Moving Averages and Exponential Smoothing

FILE *Service_Calls*

Obtaining the Moving Averages in Table 12.3

A. Open the ***Service_Calls*** data file.

B. From the menu, choose **Data > Data Analysis > Moving Average**. Click **OK**.

C. Click on the box next to *Input Range*, select the Calls data (including the heading), and then check the box in front of *Labels in First Row*. Next to *Interval*, enter 3 because we want to generate a 3-period moving average. Finally, indicate an *Output Range*; we enter D3, thus replicating the forecasts shown in column 4 of Table 12.3. Click **OK**.

Obtaining the Exponentially Smoothed Series in Table 12.4

A. Open the ***Service_Calls*** data file.

B. From the menu, choose **Data > Data Analysis > Exponential Smoothing**. Click **OK**.

C. Click on the box next to *Input Range*, select the Calls data (including the heading), and then check the box in front of *Labels*. Select the box next to *Damping Factor*. If we want to construct an exponentially smoothed series with $\alpha = 0.2$, then for *Damping Factor* we enter $1 - \alpha = 0.8$. Finally, indicate an *Output Range*; we enter D2, thus replicating the forecasts shown in column 4 of Table 12.4. Click **OK**.

Note: In Section 12.6, we will show how to use Analytic Solver and R for simple as well as advanced exponential smoothing techniques. Both software packages allow user-supplied and computer-generated values for the smoothing parameters, including α.

EXERCISES 12.2

Applications

1. FILE ***Convenience_Store.*** The owner of a convenience store near Salt Lake City in Utah has been tabulating weekly sales at the store, excluding gas. The accompanying table shows a portion of the sales for 30 weeks.

Week	Sales
1	5387
2	5522
⋮	⋮
30	5206

a. Use the 3-period moving average to forecast sales for the 31st week.

b. Use simple exponential smoothing with $\alpha = 0.3$ to forecast sales for the 31st week.

c. Which is the preferred technique for making the forecast based on *MSE*, *MAD*, and *MAPE*?

2. FILE ***Spotify.*** Spotify is a music streaming platform that gives access to songs from artists all over the world. On February 28, 2018, Spotify filed for an initial public offering (IPO) on the New York Stock Exchange. The accompanying table shows a portion of the adjusted monthly stock price of Spotify from April 1, 2018, to February 1, 2019.

Date	Stock Price
Apr-18	161.67
May-18	157.71
⋮	⋮
Feb-19	134.71

a. Use the 3-period moving average to forecast Spotify's stock price for March 2019.

b. Use simple exponential smoothing with $\alpha = 0.2$ to forecast Spotify's stock price for March 2019.

c. Which is the preferred technique for making the forecast based on *MSE*, *MAD*, and *MAPE*?

3. **FILE** ***FoodTruck.*** Food trucks have become a common sight on American campuses. They serve scores of hungry students strolling through campus and looking for trendy food served fast. The owner of a food truck collects data on the number of students he serves on weekdays on a small campus in California. A portion of the data is shown in the accompanying table.

Weekday	Students
1	84
2	66
⋮	⋮
40	166

a. Use the 3-period moving average to make a forecast for Weekday 41.

b. Use the 5-period moving average to make a forecast for Weekday 41.

c. Which is the preferred technique for making the forecast based on *MSE*, *MAD*, and *MAPE*?

4. ***Exchange_Rate.*** Consider the exchange rate of the $ (USD) with € (Euro) and $ (USD) with £ (Pound). The accompanying table shows a portion of the exchange rates from January 2017 to January 2019.

Date	Euro	Pound
Jan-17	1.0635	1.2367
Feb-17	1.0650	1.2495
⋮	⋮	⋮
Jan-19	1.1414	1.2845

a. Find the 3-period and the 5-period moving averages for Euro. Based on *MSE*, *MAD*, and *MAPE*, use the preferred model to forecast Euro for February 2019.

b. Find the simple exponential smoothing series for Pound with possible α values of 0.2, 0.4, 0.6. Based on *MSE*, *MAD*, and *MAPE*, use the preferred model to forecast Pound for February 2019.

5. **FILE** ***Downtown_Cafe.*** The manager of a trendy downtown café in Columbus, Ohio, collects weekly data on the number of customers it serves. A portion of the data is shown in the accompanying table.

Week	Customers
1	944
2	997
⋮	⋮
52	1365

a. Use the simple exponential smoothing technique with $\alpha = 0.2$ to make a forecast for Week 53.

b. Use the simple exponential smoothing technique with $\alpha = 0.4$ to make a forecast for Week 53.

c. Which is the preferred technique for making the forecast based on *MSE*, *MAD*, and *MAPE*?

6. **FILE** ***Gas_Prices.*** It is difficult to predict gas prices given a multitude of factors affecting them. Consider 22 weeks of the average weekly regular gasoline price ($ per gallon) in New England and the West Coast.

Date	New England	West Coast
9/3/2018	2.855	3.329
9/10/2018	2.864	3.336
⋮	⋮	⋮
1/28/2019	2.346	2.928

c. Find the 3-period and the 5-period moving averages for gas prices in New England. Based on *MSE*, *MAD*, and *MAPE*, use the preferred model to forecast gas prices for the first week of February 2019.

d. Find the simple exponential smoothing series with possible α values of 0.2, 0.4, 0.6 for gas prices on the West Coast. Based on *MSE*, *MAD*, and *MAPE*, use the preferred model to forecast gas prices for the first week of February 2019.

12.3 LINEAR REGRESSION MODELS FOR TREND AND SEASONALITY

LO 12.3

Use linear regression models to make forecasts.

The smoothing techniques discussed in Section 12.2 are used when the time series represent random fluctuations with no discernible trend or seasonal fluctuations. When trend and seasonal variations are present, we need to use special models for the analysis. In this section, we first focus on trend analysis, which extracts long-term upward or downward movements of the series. We then incorporate seasonal dummy variables that extract the repetitive movement of the series within a one-year period.

The Linear Trend Model

We estimate a **linear trend model** using the regression techniques described in earlier chapters. Let y_t be the value of the response variable at time t. Here we use t as the predictor variable corresponding to consecutive time periods, such as 1, 2, 3, and so on.

> **THE LINEAR TREND MODEL**
>
> The linear trend model is used for a time series that is expected to grow by a fixed amount each time period. It is specified as $y_t = \beta_0 + \beta_1 t + \varepsilon_t$, where y_t is the value of the time series at time t. The estimated model is used to make forecasts as $\hat{y}_t = b_0 + b_1 t$, where b_0 and b_1 are the coefficient estimates.

Example 12.3 provides an application of the linear trend model for making forecasts.

EXAMPLE 12.3

A local organic food store carries several food products for health-conscious consumers. The store has witnessed a steady growth in the sale of chef-designed meals, which are especially popular with college-educated millennials. For planning purposes, the manager of the store would like to extract useful information from the weekly sales of chef-designed meals for the past year, a portion of which is shown in Table 12.6.

FILE
Organic

Table 12.6 Weekly Sales (in $) at Organic Food Store

Week	Sales
1	1925
2	2978
⋮	⋮
52	6281

a. Visually inspect the time series to confirm the existence of a trend.

b. Estimate and interpret the linear trend model for the sale of chef-designed meals.

c. Forecast the sale of chef-designed meals for the next four weeks.

SOLUTION:

a. As a first step, it is advisable to visually inspect the time series. Figure 12.4 is a scatterplot of the weekly sales of chef-designed meals for the past year with a superimposed linear trend line. We see an upward movement of the series over this time period.

FIGURE 12.4 Scatterplot of weekly sales of chef-designed meals

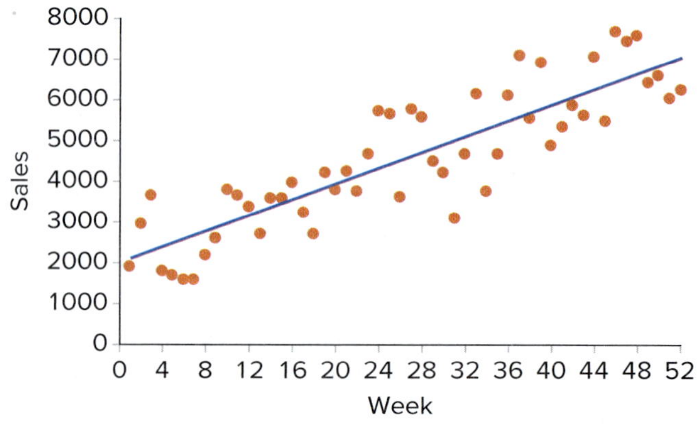

b. The linear trend model is specified as Sales $= \beta_0 + \beta_1$ Week $+ \varepsilon$. The estimated linear trend equation is $\widehat{\text{Sales}} = 1998.2285 + 96.8383$ Week, implying that every week, sales increase by about \$96.84. The estimated $R^2 = 0.7538$ suggests that about 75.38% of the sample variations in sales are explained by the sample trend line.

Note: Please refer to Chapter 6 for Excel and R instructions on how to estimate the linear model.

c. We use Week = 53 to forecast sales for the next week as $\widehat{\text{Sales}} = 1998.2285 + 96.8383 \times 53 = \$7{,}130.66$. Similarly, we use Week = 54, 55, and 56 to forecast sales for the subsequent three weeks as \$7,227.49, \$7,324.33, \$7,421.17, respectively.

Trend forecasting models, like the model used in Example 12.3, extract long-term upward or downward movements of a time series. These models are appropriate when the time series does not exhibit seasonal variations or has been stripped of its seasonal variation; that is, it has been deseasonalized. We now move our attention to making forecasts that extract both trend and seasonal variations.

The Linear Trend Model with Seasonality

With seasonal data, we estimate a linear trend model that also includes dummy variables to capture the seasonal variations. Recall that a dummy variable is commonly used to describe a categorical variable with two categories. Here, we use dummy variables to describe seasons. For quarterly data, we need to define only three dummy variables representing three quarters, using the fourth quarter as reference.

LINEAR TREND MODEL WITH SEASONAL DUMMY VARIABLES

With quarterly data, a linear trend model with seasonal dummy variables can be specified as

$$y = \beta_0 + \beta_1 d_1 + \beta_2 d_2 + \beta_3 d_3 + \beta_4 t + \varepsilon,$$

where d_1, d_2, and d_3 are the dummy variables representing the first three quarters. Forecasts based on the estimated model are made as follows:

$$\text{Quarter 1 } (d_1 = 1, d_2 = 0, d_3 = 0): \hat{y} = (b_0 + b_1) + b_4 t$$
$$\text{Quarter 2 } (d_1 = 0, d_2 = 1, d_3 = 0): \hat{y} = (b_0 + b_2) + b_4 t$$
$$\text{Quarter 3 } (d_1 = 0, d_2 = 0, d_3 = 1): \hat{y} = (b_0 + b_3) + b_4 t$$
$$\text{Quarter 4 } (d_1 = 0, d_2 = 0, d_3 = 0): \hat{y} = b_0 + b_4 t$$

Here, $b_0, b_1, \ldots b_4$ are the coefficient estimates.

Note that the above forecasting equations can easily be modified if a different quarter is used as reference. Also, the model for the quarterly data can be modified to make forecasts with monthly or other forms of seasonal data. Example 12.4 provides an application with quarterly data.

EXAMPLE 12.4

With Amazon.com at the lead, e-commerce retail sales have increased substantially over the last decade. Consider quarterly data on e-commerce retail sales in the U.S. from the first quarter of 2010 to the first quarter of 2019, a portion of which is shown in Table 12.7.

FILE
ECommerce

Table 12.7 Quarterly e-Commerce Retail Sales (in $ millions)

Year	Quarter	Sales
2010	1	37059
2010	2	38467
⋮	⋮	⋮
2019	1	127265

a. Visually inspect the data to confirm the existence of trend and seasonality.

b. Estimate and interpret the linear trend model with seasonal dummy variables for e-commerce retail sales.

c. Forecast e-commerce retail sales for the last three quarters of 2019.

SOLUTION: Given quarterly data, we have to first construct relevant variables for the linear trend models with seasonal dummy variables. Table 12.8 presents a portion of the constructed data for sales, seasonal dummy variables d_1, d_2, and d_3 representing the first three quarters (using the fourth quarter as reference), and the trend variable t representing the 37 quarters of data. (Shortly, we will provide R instructions for replicating the results.)

Table 12.8 Constructing Variables for Example 12.4

Year	Quarter	Sales	d_1	d_2	d_3	t
2010	1	37059	1	0	0	1
2010	2	38467	0	1	0	2
2010	3	40075	0	0	1	3
2010	4	54320	0	0	0	4
⋮	⋮	⋮	⋮	⋮	⋮	⋮
2018	4	158548	0	0	0	36
2019	1	127265	1	0	0	37

a. Figure 12.5 is a scatterplot of quarterly sales, with the dots connected, and the quarterly data relabeled from 1 to 37. The graph highlights some important characteristics of e-commerce retail sales. First, there is a persistent upward movement in sales. Second, a seasonal pattern repeats itself year after year. For instance, sales are consistently higher in the fourth quarter as compared to the other quarters. The graph makes a strong case for a model that captures both seasonality and trend.

FIGURE 12.5 Scatterplot of e-commerce retail sales (in $ millions)

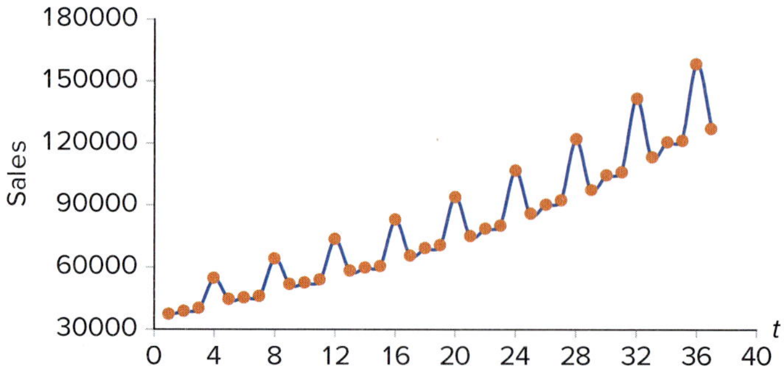

b. The estimated linear trend model with seasonal dummy variables is: $\widehat{Sales} = 46{,}682.6508 - 21{,}611.6437d_1 - 21{,}295.7984d_2 - 22{,}594.1214d_3 + 2{,}649.8786t$

The coefficients for the seasonal dummy variables indicate that, relative to the 4th quarter, e-commerce sales are about \$22,000 lower in the other three quarters. The estimated coefficient for the trend variable suggests that the predicted quarterly sales increase by about \$2,650 million every quarter, in addition to the seasonal variations.

c. For the 2nd quarter of 2019, we use $d_1 = 0$, $d_2 = 1$, $d_3 = 0$, and $t = 38$ to forecast $\widehat{Sales} = 46{,}682.6508 - 21{,}295.7984 + 2{,}649.8786 \times 38 =$ \$126,082 million. Similarly, we use $d_1 = 0$, $d_2 = 0$, $d_3 = 1$, and $t = 39$ for the 3rd quarter and $d_1 = 0$, $d_2 = 0$, $d_3 = 0$, $t = 40$ for the 4th quarter to forecast sales as \$127,434 and \$152,678 million, respectively.

Estimating a Linear Trend Model with Seasonality with R

FILE *ECommerce*

In order to replicate the results in Example 12.4, we follow these steps.

A. Import the ***ECommerce*** data into a data frame (table) and label it myData.

B. Install and load the *forecast* package. Enter:

```
> install.packages("forecast")
> library(forecast)
```

C. We use the **ts** function to create a time series object and call it newData. Within **ts**, we specify the *start* and *end* periods as well as *frequency*, denoting the number of seasons in a year. Enter:

```
> newData <- ts(myData$Sales, start = c(2010,1), end = c(2019,1),
frequency=4)
```

D. We use the **tslm** function to estimate the model and the **summary** function to view the regression output. Enter:

```
> TSReg <- tslm(newData ~ trend + season)
> summary(TSReg)
```

Note that by default R uses the first quarter as the reference season, which explains why the intercept and the coefficient estimates differ from those reported in Example 12.4. The forecasts, however, are not influenced by the choice of the reference dummy variable.

E. Use the **forecast** function where *h* denotes the number of forecasts. Enter:

```
> forecast(TSReg, h=3)
```

A Note on Causal Models for Forecasting

So far, we have discussed noncausal, or purely time series, models that capture trend and seasonality for making forecasts. These models do not offer any explanation of the mechanism generating the target variable and simply provide a method for projecting historical data. Causal models, on the other hand, are standard regression models that exploit the relationship between the target and the predictor variables for making forecasts. For example, we can use causal models to forecast product sales using predictor variables such as the firm's advertising budget and its pricing strategy. The regression framework also allows us the flexibility to combine causal with time series effects. In other words, the list of predictor variables may include k causal variables $x_1, x_2, \ldots x_k$ along with the trend variable t and seasonal dummy variables $d_1, d_2, \ldots d_{p-1}$ for p seasons.

For example, consider quarterly data for developing a forecasting model for product sales y. Let the predictor variables include the firm's advertising budget x, the trend variable t, and seasonal dummy variables, d_1, d_2, d_3, representing the first three quarters. We can easily estimate the regression model to make forecasts as:

$$\hat{y} = \hat{b}_0 + \hat{b}_1 d_1 + \hat{b}_2 d_2 + \hat{b}_3 d_3 + \hat{b}_4 t + \hat{b}_5 x$$

Note that in addition to the known future values of t, d_1, d_2, and d_3, this approach will work only if we also know, or can predict, the future value of the variable x. In other words, we cannot forecast product sales if the advertising budget in the future is not known. Sometimes, we can justify the use of lagged values of causal variables for making forecasts. In the product sales example, the relationship between advertising budget and sales may not be contemporaneous. Therefore, we can specify a model where product sales is related to the trend term, seasonal dummy variables, and the value of the advertising budget in the previous period. Further discussion of lagged regression models is beyond the scope of this text.

EXERCISES 12.3

Applications

7. FILE ***Inquiries*** Morgan Bank has been encouraging its customers to use its new mobile banking app. While this may be good for business, the bank has to deal with a number of inquiries it receives about the new app. The following table contains a portion of weekly inquiries the bank has received over the past 30 weeks.

Week	Inquiries
1	286
2	331
⋮	⋮
30	219

Estimate the linear trend model to forecast the number of inquiries over the next two weeks.

8. FILE ***Apple_Price.*** Apple Inc. has performed extremely well in the last decade. After its stock price dropped to below 90 in May 2016, it made a tremendous comeback to reach about 146 by May 2017 (SeekingAlpha.com, May 1, 2017). An investor seeking to gain from the positive momentum of Apple's stock price analyzes 53 weeks of stock price data from 5/30/16 to 5/26/17. A portion of the data is shown in the accompanying table.

Date	Price
5/30/2016	97.92
6/6/2016	98.83
⋮	⋮
5/26/2017	153.57

a. Estimate and interpret the linear trend model (no seasonality).

b. Make a forecast for the next week (54th week).

9. FILE ***Tax_Revenue.*** In Colorado, sales of medical marijuana began in November 2012; however, the Department of Revenue did not report tax collection data until February of 2014. The accompanying table shows a portion of the monthly revenue from medical and retail marijuana tax and fee collections as posted in the Colorado state accounting system.

Date	Revenue
Feb-14	3,519,756
Mar-14	4,092,575
⋮	⋮
Oct-18	22,589,679

Use the linear trend model (no seasonality) to forecast the tax revenue for November and December of 2018.

10. FILE ***Revenue_Lowes.*** Lowe's Companies, Inc., is a home improvement company offering a range of products for maintenance, repair, remodeling, and decorating. During the recovery phase since the financial crisis of 2008, Lowe's has enjoyed a steady growth in revenue. The following table contains a portion of quarterly data on Lowe's revenue (in $ millions) with its fiscal year concluding at the end of January.

Year	Quarter	Revenue
2010	1	12,388
2010	2	14,361
⋮	⋮	⋮
2018	3	17,415

a. Estimate and interpret the linear trend model with seasonal dummy variables.

b. Use the estimated model to forecast Lowe's revenue for the fourth quarter of 2018.

11. FILE ***Vacation*** Vacation destinations often run on a seasonal basis, depending on the primary activities in that location. Amanda Wang is the owner of a travel agency in Cincinnati, Ohio. She has built a database of the number of vacation packages (Vacation) that she has sold over the last twelve years. The following table contains a portion of quarterly data on the number of vacation packages sold.

Year	Quarter	Vacation
2008	1	500
2008	2	147
⋮	⋮	⋮
2019	4	923

a. Estimate the linear regression models using seasonal dummy variables with and without the trend term.

b. Determine the preferred model and use it to forecast the quarterly number of vacation packages sold in the first two quarters of 2020.

12. FILE ***Consumer_Sentiment.*** The following table lists a portion of the University of Michigan's Consumer Sentiment index. This index is normalized to have a value of 100 in 1966 and is used to record changes in consumer morale.

Date	Consumer Sentiment
Jan-10	74.4
Feb-10	73.6
⋮	⋮
Nov-18	97.5

a. Estimate and interpret the linear trend model with seasonal dummy variables.

b. Use the estimated model to make a consumer sentiment index forecast for December 2018.

13. FILE ***UsedCars*** Used car dealerships generally have sales quotas that they strive to hit each month, quarter, and calendar year. Consequently, buying a used car toward the end of those periods presents a great opportunity to get a good deal on the car. A local dealership has compiled monthly sales data for used cars (Cars) from 2014-2019, a portion of which is shown in the accompanying table.

Date	Cars
Jan-2014	138
Feb-2014	179
⋮	⋮
Dec-2019	195

a. Estimate the linear regression models using seasonal dummy variables with and without the trend term.

b. Determine the preferred model and use it to forecast used cars sales in the first two months of 2020.

12.4 NONLINEAR REGRESSION MODELS FOR TREND AND SEASONALITY

LO 12.4

Use nonlinear regression models to make forecasts.

Although the linear relationship assumed in Section 12.3 can be adequate, there are many cases in which a nonlinear functional form is more suitable. In this section, we discuss the exponential, the quadratic, and the cubic trend models with and without seasonal dummy variables.

The Exponential Trend Model

A linear trend model uses a straight line to capture the trend, thus implying that for each period, the value of the series is expected to change by a fixed amount, given by the estimated coefficient b_1. The **exponential trend model** is attractive when the expected increase in the series gets larger over time. It is not uncommon for some variables to exhibit exponential growth over time. For example, in recent years, technology firms such as Amazon, Netflix, Spotify, Airbnb, and Paypal have exhibited exponential growth for which the linear trend model would clearly be inadequate.

FIGURE 12.6 Scatterplot with superimposed linear and exponential trend lines

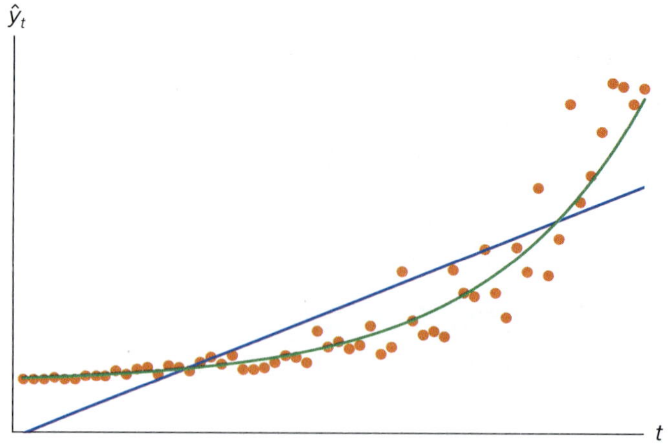

Figure 12.6 presents a scatterplot of a time series with superimposed linear and exponential trend lines. While both trend lines capture positive growth, the exponential trend line (green) correctly allows the values to grow by an increasing amount over time. Here, the linear trend line (blue) would under-forecast future values.

Recall from Chapter 7 that we specify an exponential model as $\ln(y_t) = \beta_0 + \beta_1 t + \varepsilon_t$. In order to estimate this model, we first generate the series in natural logs, $\ln(y_t)$, and then run a regression of $\ln(y_t)$ on t. Because, in the exponential model, the response variable is measured in logs, we make forecasts in regular units as $\hat{y}_t = \exp(b_0 + b_1 t + s_e^2/2)$, where s_e is the standard error of the estimate.

THE EXPONENTIAL TREND MODEL

The exponential trend model is appropriate for a time series that is expected to grow by an increasing amount each time period. It is specified as $\ln(y_t) = \beta_0 + \beta_1 t + \varepsilon_t$, where $\ln(y_t)$ is the natural log of y_t. The estimated model is used to make forecasts as $\hat{y}_t = \exp(b_0 + b_1 t + s_e^2/2)$, where b_0 and b_1 are the coefficient estimates and s_e is the standard error of the estimate.

Note: It is advisable to use unrounded values for making forecasts in an exponential model because even a small difference, when exponentiated, can make a big difference in the forecast. Example 12.5 provides an application of the linear and the exponential trend models for making forecasts.

EXAMPLE 12.5

According to data compiled by the World Bank, the world population has increased from 3.03 billion in 1960 to 7.53 billion in 2017. This rapid increase concerns environmentalists, who believe that our natural resources may not be able to support the ever-increasing population. Additionally, most of the rapid population growth has been in 34 low-income countries, many of which are located in Africa. Consider the population data, in millions, for low-income countries from 1960 to 2017, a portion of which is shown in Table 12.9.

FILE *Population_LowInc*

TABLE 12.9 Population in Low-Income Countries

Year	Population
1960	166.5028
1961	170.2108
⋮	⋮
2017	732.4486

a. Estimate and interpret the linear and the exponential trend models.

b. Use *MSE*, *MAD*, and *MAPE* to select the appropriate model.

c. Forecast the population in low-income countries for 2018.

SOLUTION: As a first step, it is advisable to inspect the data visually. Figure 12.7 is a scatterplot of the population in low-income countries from 1960 through 2017. We relabel the 58 years of annual observations from 1 to 58 and superimpose the linear and exponential trends to the data.

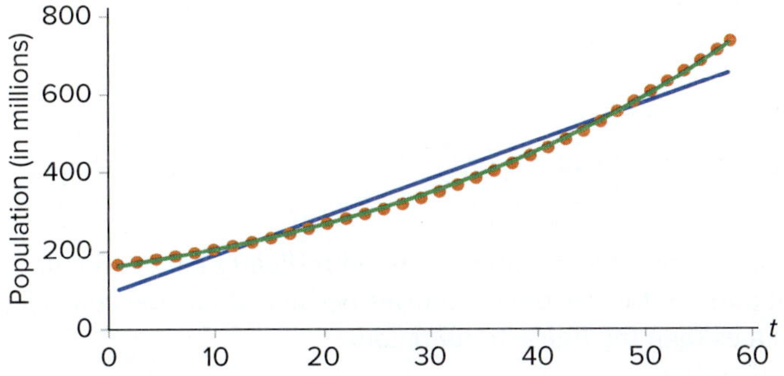

FIGURE 12.7 Population in low-income countries with superimposed trends

The scatterplot makes a strong case for an exponential growth in the population in low-income countries.

a. We estimate the linear and the exponential trend models, where the linear model is used for comparison with the visually preferred exponential model. To estimate the exponential trend model, we first transform the population series to natural logs. Table 12.10 shows a portion of the log-transformed population along with the predictor variable t, relabeled from 1 to 58.

TABLE 12.10 Constructing Variables for Example 12.5

Year	Population	t	ln(Population)
1960	166.5028	1	5.1150
1961	170.2108	2	5.1370
⋮	⋮	⋮	⋮
2017	732.4486	58	6.5964

The estimated trend models, where y denotes population, are:

Linear: $\hat{y}_t = 92.9213 + 9.6799t$

Exponential: $\hat{y}_t = \exp\left(5.0614 + 0.0264t + \frac{0.0104^2}{2}\right)$

Note: Please refer to Chapter 7 for the Excel and R instructions for estimating the exponential model.

The slope coefficient of the linear trend model implies that the population in low-income countries has grown, on average, by approximately 9.6799 million each year. The slope coefficient of the exponential trend model implies that the population in low-income countries has grown, on average, by approximately 2.64% (= 0.0264 × 100). The exact growth rate can be calculated as 2.68% (= (exp(0.0264) − 1) × 100).

b. In Table 12.11, we present a portion of the series y_t along with $\hat{y}_t$ for both models using unrounded values for the estimates. As discussed in Section 12.2, we use the forecast error, $e_t = y_t - \hat{y}_t$ to compute *MSE*, *MAD*, and *MAPE*. These performance measures are used to find the preferred model for forecasting. The *MSE*,

MAD, and *MAPE* values for the linear and the exponential models are shown in the last two rows of Table 12.11.

TABLE 12.11 Analysis of Linear and Exponential Trend Models for Example 12.5

t	y	$\hat{y}$ (Linear)	$\hat{y}$ (Exponential)
1	166.5028	102.6011	162.0398
2	170.2108	112.2810	166.3719
⋮	⋮	⋮	⋮
58	732.4486	654.3529	729.0290
	MSE	1,176.74	12.28
	MAD	29.58	2.87
	MAPE	9.36	0.82

Consistent with the scatterplot, the exponential trend is clearly better suited to describe the population in low-income countries because it has lower *MSE*, *MAD*, and *MAPE* values than the linear trend model.

c. For 2018 ($t = 59$), we use unrounded values of the estimates to forecast the population in low-income countries as $\hat{y}_{59} = \exp\left(5.0614 + 0.0264 \times 59 + \frac{0.0104^2}{2}\right) =$ 748.52 million.

The Polynomial Trend Model

Sometimes a time series reverses direction, due to any number of circumstances. A common polynomial function that allows for curvature in the series is the **quadratic trend model**. The quadratic regression model was first introduced in Chapter 7. This quadratic trend model allows one change in the direction of a series and is estimated as

$$\hat{y}_t = \beta_0 + \beta_1 t + \beta_2 t^2 + \varepsilon_t.$$

The coefficient β_2 determines whether the trend is U-shaped or inverted U-shaped.

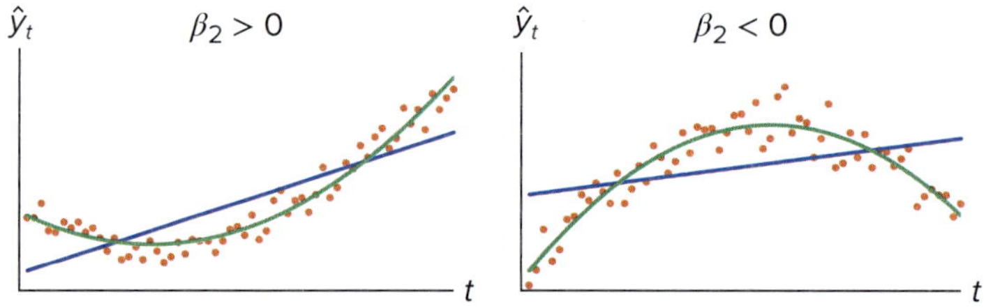

FIGURE 12.8 Scatterplots with superimposed linear and quadratic trend lines

Figure 12.8 presents a scatterplot of a time series with superimposed linear (blue) and quadratic (green) trend lines. Here, the linear trend line would under-forecast future values when $\beta_2 > 0$ and over-forecast future values when $\beta_2 < 0$.

In order to estimate the quadratic trend model, we generate t^2, which is simply the square of t. Then we run a multiple regression model that uses y as the response variable and both t and t^2 as the predictor variables. The estimated model is used to make forecasts as

$$\hat{y}_t = b_0 + b_1 t + b_2 t^2.$$

Higher-order polynomial functions can be estimated similarly. For instance, the **cubic trend model** is specified as

$$y_t = \beta_0 + \beta_1 t + \beta_2 t^2 + \beta_3 t^3 + \varepsilon_t.$$

The cubic trend model allows for two changes in the direction of a series. In the cubic trend model, we basically generate two additional variables, t^2 and t^3, for the regression. A multiple regression model is run that uses y as the response variable and t, t^2, and t^3 as the predictor variables. The estimated model is used to make forecasts as $\hat{y}_t = b_0 + b_1t + b_2t^2 + b_3t^3$.

We cannot use *MSE*, *MAD*, and *MAPE* to compare polynomial trend models because these values decrease as the order of the polynomial increases. The problem is similar to that of the coefficient of determination R^2 discussed in earlier chapters where R^2 increases as the number of predictor variables increases. When comparing polynomial trend models, we use adjusted R^2, which imposes a penalty for over-parameterization.

THE POLYNOMIAL TREND MODEL

The polynomial trend model of order q is estimated as

$$y_t = \beta_0 + \beta_1 t + \beta_2 t^2 + \beta_3 t^3 + \cdots + \beta_q t^q + \varepsilon_t.$$

This model specializes to a linear trend model, quadratic trend model, and cubic trend model for $q = 1, 2$, and 3, respectively. The estimated model is used to make forecasts as $\hat{y}_t = b_0 + b_1t + b_2t^2 + b_3t^3 + \cdots + b_qt^q$, where $b_0, b_1, \ldots, b_q$ are the coefficient estimates. We use adjusted R^2 to compare polynomial trend models with different orders.

It is important to be mindful of overfitting when using higher-level polynomials. Recall that overfitting occurs when an estimated model begins to describe the quirks of the data rather than the real relationships between variables. By making the model conform too closely to the given data, the model's predictive power is compromised. Although adjusted R^2 imposes a penalty for additional predictor variables, the measure still suffers from the fact that the same data are used for both estimation and assessment. In Section 12.5, we discuss cross-validation techniques to assess forecasting models.

The Nonlinear Trend Models with Seasonality

In Section 12.3, we developed linear forecasting models for trend and seasonality; here we extend the analysis to include nonlinear models. With quarterly data, the exponential, and the quadratic, trend models with seasonal dummy variables are summarized in the following definition boxes. These models can be easily modified to forecast with monthly or other forms of seasonal data.

EXPONENTIAL TREND MODEL WITH SEASONAL DUMMY VARIABLES

With quarterly data, an exponential trend model with seasonal dummy variables is specified as

$$\ln(y) = \beta_0 + \beta_1 d_1 + \beta_2 d_2 + \beta_3 d_3 + \beta_4 t + \varepsilon.$$

Forecasts based on the estimated model are as follows:

Quarter 1 ($d_1 = 1, d_2 = 0, d_3 = 0$): $\hat{y}_t = \exp((b_0 + b_1) + b_4t + s_e^2/2)$

Quarter 2 ($d_1 = 0, d_2 = 1, d_3 = 0$): $\hat{y}_t = \exp((b_0 + b_2) + b_4t + s_e^2/2)$

Quarter 3 ($d_1 = 0, d_2 = 0, d_3 = 1$): $\hat{y}_t = \exp((b_0 + b_3) + b_4t + s_e^2/2)$

Quarter 4 ($d_1 = 0, d_2 = 0, d_3 = 0$): $\hat{y}_t = \exp(b_0 + b_4t + s_e^2/2)$

Here, $b_0, b_1, \ldots b_4$ are the coefficient estimates and s_e is the standard error of the estimate.

Note that for the exponential model, we compute $\hat{y}_t$ in regular units and not in natural logs. The resulting $\hat{y}_t$ also enables us to compare the linear and the exponential models in terms of their *MSE*, *MAD*, and *MAPE*.

QUADRATIC TREND MODEL WITH SEASONAL DUMMY VARIABLES

With quarterly data, a quadratic trend model with seasonal dummy variables is specified as

$$y = \beta_0 + \beta_1 d_1 + \beta_2 d_2 + \beta_3 d_3 + \beta_4 t + \beta_5 t^2 + \varepsilon.$$

Forecasts based on the estimated model are as follows:

Quarter 1 ($d_1 = 1, d_2 = 0, d_3 = 0$): $\hat{y} = (b_0 + b_1) + b_4 t + b_5 t^2$

Quarter 2 ($d_1 = 0, d_2 = 1, d_3 = 0$): $\hat{y} = (b_0 + b_2) + b_4 t + b_5 t^2$

Quarter 3 ($d_1 = 0, d_2 = 0, d_3 = 1$): $\hat{y} = (b_0 + b_3) + b_4 t + b_5 t^2$

Quarter 4 ($d_1 = 0, d_2 = 0, d_3 = 0$): $\hat{y} = (b_0 + b_4 t + b_5 t^2$

Here, $b_0, b_1, \ldots b_4$ are the coefficient estimates.

We simply use adjusted R^2 to compare the linear and the quadratic models. Example 12.6 provides an application of the quadratic trend model with seasonal dummy variables.

EXAMPLE 12.6

FILE *Revenue_Apple*

The objective outlined in the introductory case is to forecast Apple's quarterly revenue, in \$ millions, from 2010 to 2018. Use the data in Table 12.1 to

a. Estimate the linear and the quadratic trend models with seasonal dummy variables for Apple's revenue.

b. Determine the preferred model and use it to forecast Apple's revenue for fiscal year 2019.

SOLUTION: In Section 12.1, we used Figure 12.1 to highlight important characteristics of Apple's revenue. First, there is a persistent upward movement with the series plateauing near the end of the observation period, which is suggestive of a quadratic trend model. Second, a seasonal pattern repeats itself year after year. For instance, revenue is consistently higher in the first quarter (September–December), as compared to the other quarters.

a. Given quarterly data, we first construct relevant variables for the linear and the quadratic trend models with seasonal dummy variables. Table 12.12 presents a portion of the constructed data representing the revenue variable y; three seasonal dummy variables d_1, d_2, and d_3 representing the first three quarters (using the fourth quarter as reference); and the trend variable t and its square t^2.

TABLE 12.12 Constructing Variables for Example 12.6

Year	Quarter	y	d_1	d_2	d_3	t	t^2
2010	1	15,683	1	0	0	1	1
2010	2	13,499	0	1	0	2	4
2010	3	15,700	0	0	1	3	9
2010	4	20,343	0	0	0	4	16
⋮	⋮	⋮	⋮	⋮	⋮	⋮	⋮
2018	3	53,265	0	0	1	35	1225
2018	4	62,900	0	0	0	36	1296

The estimated trend models are:

Linear: $\hat{y}_t = 13{,}969.3750 + 19{,}757.1382d_1 + 4{,}047.0181d_2 - 2{,}522.9910d_3 + 1{,}401.5646t$; Adjusted $R^2 = 0.8324$

Quadratic: $\hat{y}_t = 4{,}668.5985 + 19{,}757.1382d_1 + 3{,}967.2971d_2 - 2{,}602.7119d_3 + 2{,}876.4020t - 39.8605t^2$; Adjusted $R^2 = 0.8824$

The coefficients for the seasonal dummy variables indicate that the revenue is about \$19,757 million, or \$19.76 billion, higher in the first quarter as compared to the fourth quarter. The results also suggest that compared to the fourth quarter, the revenue is somewhat higher in the second quarter and lower in the third quarter. The positive coefficient for the trend variable t in the linear model indicates an upward movement of the revenue. The positive coefficient for t along with a negative coefficient for t^2 in the quadratic model captures the inverted U-shape of the series. Given the coefficients, holding seasonality constant, the revenue reaches its maximum at $t = 36.08\left(= \frac{2{,}876.4020}{2 \times 39.8605}\right)$, which suggests that Apple's revenues reached their maximum in the fourth quarter of 2018.

b. The quadratic trend model with seasonal dummy variables is preferred for making forecasts because of a higher adjusted R^2 value ($0.8824 > 0.8324$). Therefore, the revenue forecasts for fiscal year 2019 are:

$\hat{y}_{2019:01}(d_1 = 1, d_2 = 0, d_3 = 0, t = 37, t^2 = 1{,}369) = \$76{,}283.63$ million

$\hat{y}_{2019:02}(d_1 = 0, d_2 = 1, d_3 = 0, t = 38, t^2 = 1{,}444) = \$60{,}380.65$ million

$\hat{y}_{2019:03}(d_1 = 0, d_2 = 0, d_3 = 1, t = 39, t^2 = 1{,}521) = \$53{,}617.79$ million

$\hat{y}_{2019:04}(d_1 = 0, d_2 = 0, d_3 = 0, t = 40, t^2 = 1{,}600) = \$55{,}947.93$ million

The quarterly forecasts result in a sum of \$246,230 million in revenue for fiscal year 2019.

SYNOPSIS OF INTRODUCTORY CASE

Pavel L Photo and Video/Shutterstock

Apple Inc. is an American multinational technology company headquartered in Cupertino, California. It designs, manufactures, and markets mobile communication and media devices, personal computers, and portable digital music players. It also sells a range of related software, streaming services, accessories, networking solutions, and third-party digital content and applications.

For several years, Apple's smartphone segment has been the company's core source of revenue, resulting in record revenue. A scatterplot of Apple's quarterly revenue for the fiscal years 2010 through 2018 highlights some important characteristics. First, there is a persistent upward movement with the revenue plateauing near the end of the observation period. Second, a seasonal pattern repeats itself. For each year, the revenue is the highest in the first quarter (October–December) followed by the second (January–March), fourth (July–September), and third (April–June) quarters.

The coefficients of the estimated quadratic trend model with seasonal dummy variables suggest that the revenue is about \$20 billion higher in the first quarter as compared to the fourth quarter. This is not surprising because given Apple's fiscal calendar, the first quarter encompasses the holiday period with usual strong sales. The positive coefficient for the trend variable t along with a negative coefficient for t^2 captures the plateauing of the series. In fact, given the coefficients, holding seasonality constant, the revenue reaches its maximum in the fourth quarter of 2018. This finding is consistent with the concern that while Apple is clearly doing well for now, its future growth may be murky partly because, in terms of the smartphone market, it only sells on the somewhat saturated mid-to-high-end range market. The quarterly revenue forecasts for 2019 are \$76.28, \$60.38, \$53.62, and \$55.95 billion, respectively, resulting in a whopping \$246 billion in revenue for fiscal year 2019.

EXERCISES 12.4

Applications

14. **FILE** ***Whites.*** In 2016, demographers reported that deaths outnumbered births among white Americans in more than half the states in the U.S. (*The New York Times*, June 20, 2018). Consider the white American population, in millions, from 2005 through 2017; a portion of the data is shown in accompanying table.

Year	Whites
2005	215.33
2006	221.33
⋮	⋮
2017	235.51

   a. Use the scatterplot to explore linear and quadratic trends; the cubic trend is not considered. Which trend model do you think describes the data better?
   b. Validate your intuition by comparing adjusted R^2 of the two models. Use the preferred model to forecast the white population in 2018 and 2019.

15. **FILE** ***TrueCar.*** Investors are always reviewing past pricing history and using it to influence their future investment decisions. On May 16, 2014, online car buying system TrueCar launched its initial public offering (IPO), raising $70 million in the stock offering. An investor, looking for a promising return, analyzes the monthly stock price data of TrueCar from June 2014 to May 2017. A portion of the data is shown in the accompanying table.

Date	Price
Jun-14	14.78
Jul-14	13.57
⋮	⋮
May-17	17.51

   a. Estimate the linear, the quadratic, and the cubic trend models.
   b. Determine the preferred model and use it to make a forecast for June 2017.

16. **FILE** ***Miles_Traveled.*** The number of cars sold in the United States in 2016 reached a record high for the seventh year in a row (CNNMoney, January 4, 2017). Consider monthly total miles traveled (in billions) in the United States from January 2010 to December 2016. A portion of the data is shown in the accompanying table.

Date	Miles
Jan-10	2953.305
Feb-10	2946.689
⋮	⋮
Dec-16	3169.501

   a. Estimate the quadratic and the cubic trend models.
   b. Determine the preferred model and use it to make a forecast for Miles in January 2017.

17. **FILE** ***Café_Sales.*** With a new chef and a creative menu, Café Venetian has witnessed a huge surge in sales. The following data show a portion of daily sales (in $) at Café Venetian in the first 100 days after the changes.

Day	Sales
1	263
2	215
⋮	⋮
100	2020

Estimate the exponential trend model to forecast sales for the 101st day.

18. **FILE** ***Population_Japan.*** For several years, Japan's declining population has led experts and lawmakers to consider its economic and social repercussions (*NPR*, December 21, 2018). Consider the population data, in millions, for Japan from 1960 to 2017; a portion of the data is shown in the accompanying table.

Year	Population
1960	92.50
1961	94.94
⋮	⋮
2017	126.79

   a. Use a scatterplot of the series to suggest the appropriate polynomial trend model and follow it up with a formal model selection measure.
   b. Use the preferred model to forecast the population in Japan for 2018 and 2019.

19. **FILE** ***Case_Shiller.*** The S&P's Case-Shiller home price index measures repeat-sales house price indices for the United States. The index, normalized to have a value of 100 in January 2000, captures price movements of the same homes relative to January 2000. Consider the seasonally adjusted monthly series from January 2016 to November 2018; a portion of the data is shown in the accompanying table.

Date	Case Shiller
Jan-16	177.412
Feb-16	177.828
⋮	⋮
Nov-18	206.263

a. Estimate the linear and the exponential trend models and calculate their *MSE*, *MAD*, and *MAPE*.

b. Use the preferred model to forecast the Case-Shiller index for December 2018.

20. **FILE** ***Expenses.*** The controller of a small construction company is attempting to forecast expenses for the next year. He collects quarterly data on expenses (in $1,000s) over the past five years, a portion of which is shown in the accompanying table.

Year	Quarter	Expenses
2008	1	96.50
2008	2	54.00
⋮	⋮	⋮
2017	4	22335.30

a. Estimate and interpret the exponential trend model with seasonal dummy variables.

b. Use the estimated model to forecast expenses for the first two quarters of 2018.

21. **FILE** ***Treasury_Securities.*** Treasury securities are bonds issued by the U.S. government. Consider a portion of quarterly data on treasury securities, measured in millions of U.S. dollars.

Year	Quarter	Securities
2010	1	927527
2010	2	1038881
⋮	⋮	⋮
2018	3	2284572

Estimate the exponential trend model with seasonal dummy variables to make a forecast for the fourth quarter of 2018.

22. **FILE** ***House_Price.*** The West Census region for the U.S. includes Montana, Wyoming, Colorado, New Mexico, Idaho, Utah, Arizona, Nevada, California, Oregon, and Washington. Consider the median house prices in the West Census region from 2010:01 through 2018:03, a portion of which is shown in the accompanying table.

Year	Quarter	Price
2010	1	263600
2010	2	264100
⋮	⋮	⋮
2018	3	404300

a. Estimate and interpret the quadratic trend model with seasonal dummy variables.

b. Use the estimated model to forecast the median house price in the West Census region for the fourth quarter of 2018.

23. **FILE** ***Vehicle_Miles.*** The United States economy picked up speed in 2012 as businesses substantially built up their inventories and consumers increased their spending. This also led to an increase in domestic travel. Consider the vehicle miles traveled in the U.S. (in millions) from January 2012 through September 2018, a portion of which is shown in the accompanying table.

Date	Vehicle Miles
Jan-12	227527
Feb-12	218196
⋮	⋮
Sep-18	260555

a. Estimate the linear and the exponential trend models with seasonal dummy variables for vehicle miles and calculate their *MSE*, *MAD*, and *MAPE*.

b. Use the preferred model to forecast vehicle miles for the last three months of 2018.

24. **FILE** ***Housing_Starts.*** Housing starts are the number of new residential construction projects that have begun during any given month. It is considered to be a leading indicator of economic strength. The following table contains a portion of monthly data on housing starts (in 1,000s) in the U.S. from Jan-11 to Nov-18.

Date	Housing Starts
Jan-11	40.2
Feb-11	35.4
⋮	⋮
Nov-18	95.9

a. Estimate and interpret the exponential seasonal trend model.

b. Use the estimated model to forecast housing starts for December 2018.

25. **FILE** ***Weekly_Earnings.*** Data on weekly earnings are collected as part of the Current Population Survey, a nationwide sample survey of households in which respondents are asked how much each worker usually earns. The following table contains a portion of quarterly data on weekly earnings (Earnings, adjusted for inflation) in the U.S. from 2010–2017.

Year	Quarter	Earnings
2010	1	347
2010	2	340
⋮	⋮	⋮
2017	4	347

a. Estimate the linear and the quadratic trend models with seasonal dummy variables.

b. Determine the preferred model and use it to forecast earnings for the first two quarters of 2018.

LO 12.5

Apply cross-validation techniques for model selection.

12.5 DATA PARTITIONING AND MODEL SELECTION

So far, we have assessed competing forecasting models on the basis of in-sample criteria where the predictability of a model is assessed in the sample period that was also used to build the model. Unfortunately, these measures do not help us gauge how well an estimated model will predict in an unseen sample period.

As in Chapters 7–10, we will apply cross-validation techniques to assess forecasting models. Using the holdout method, we partition the series into a training set to build (train) the model, and a validation set to assess (validate) it. As discussed in Section 12.1, out-of-sample criteria are based on the forecast error $e_t = y_t - \hat{y}_t$, where y_t and $\hat{y}_t$ denote the value of the series and its forecast, respectively, at time t in the validation period. We use performance measures *MSE*, *MAD*, and *MAPE* in the validation period to determine the preferred model for forecasting.

It is important to note key differences between cross-validation techniques applied to cross-sectional data and time series data. First, unlike random partitioning used for cross-sectional data, we use sequential partitioning for time series data. Here, the series is split into early and later periods, representing the training and the validation sets, respectively. Because all forecasting models exploit intrinsic patterns in time series, random partitioning would create unnecessary holes in the data. It is common to split the series so that the validation period consists of about 20% of the total sample data; however, this value depends on the series length. Sometimes, the series is not sufficiently long for meaningful partitioning and, therefore, for accurate estimation and assessment. For example, if we have only 20 observations, an 80/20% split leaves only 16 observations for training and 4 for validation. Here, it might be better to assess competing forecasting models in terms of the in-sample criteria discussed earlier.

We always use the entire data, that combines training and validation sets, for estimating the preferred model for making forecasts. There are several reasons for doing so. First, by combining the training and validation sets, we create a bigger sample needed for accurate estimation. Second, and more importantly, the validation set contains the most recent information on the series, which is useful for projecting into the future; otherwise you will be introducing unnecessary noise by using the training period to project past the validation period.

CROSS-VALIDATION WITH TIME SERIES

Cross-validation with time series involves the following steps.

A. Split the series into early and later periods, representing the training and the validation sets, respectively.

B. Explore suitable forecasting models for the training set and use the forecast errors in the validation set to compute *MSE*, *MAD*, and *MAPE*. Choose the model with the lowest *MSE*, *MAD*, or *MAPE*.

C. Use the entire data set, one that combines the training and the validation sets, to reestimate the preferred model for making forecasts.

In Examples 12.7 and 12.8, we use cross-validation to find the appropriate models for trend, and trend with seasonality, respectively.

EXAMPLE 12.7

Revisit the population data (in millions) for low-income countries from 1960 to 2017. These data were earlier used in Example 12.5. Let the training and the validation sets comprise the periods from 1960 to 2000 and 2001 to 2017, respectively.

FILE *Population_LowInc*

a. Use the training set to estimate the linear and the exponential trend models and compute the resulting *MSE*, *MAD*, and *MAPE* for the validation set.

b. Determine the preferred model and reestimate it with the entire data set to forecast the population in low-income countries for 2018.

SOLUTION: As in Example 12.5, the trend variable t is relabeled from 1 to 58 denoting the period between 1960 and 2017. For the exponential trend model, we first transform the population series into natural logs.

a. The estimated trend models with the training set, where y denotes population, are:

Linear: $\hat{y}_t = 133.2689 + 7.3168t$

Exponential: $\hat{y}_t = \exp\left(5.0711 + 0.0258t + \frac{0.0086^2}{2}\right)$

The derivations for the resulting *MSE, MAD*, and *MAPE* in the validation set are:

TABLE 12.13 Cross-Validation for Example 12.7

Year	t	y	$\hat{y}$ (Linear)	$\hat{y}$ (Exponential)
2001	42	478.4780	440.5724	470.7753
2002	43	491.7650	447.8892	483.0757
⋮	⋮	⋮	⋮	⋮
2017	58	732.4486	557.6404	711.2759
MSE			11,809.76	276.15
MAD			100.18	16.00
MAPE			16.08	2.62

b. Consistent with the in-sample criteria used in Example 12.5, the exponential model is preferred because it has lower *MSE*, *MAD*, and *MAPE* values. We reestimate the exponential model with the entire data set from 1960 through 2017, as in Example 12.5. For 2018 ($t = 59$), the population forecast is $\hat{y}_{59} = \exp\left(5.0614 + 0.0264 \times 59 + \frac{0.0104^2}{2}\right) = 748.52$ million.

EXAMPLE 12.8

Revisit Apple's quarterly revenue data (in $ millions) from 2010 to 2018. This data set was outlined in the introductory case and used in Example 12.6. Let the training and the validation sets comprise the periods from 2010 to 2016 and 2017 to 2018, respectively.

FILE *Revenue_Apple*

a. Use the training set to estimate the linear and the quadratic trend models with seasonal dummy variables and compute the resulting *MSE*, *MAD*, and *MAPE* for the validation set.

b. Determine the preferred model and reestimate it with the entire data set to forecast Apple's revenue for fiscal year 2019.

SOLUTION: As in Example 12.6, the trend variable t is relabeled from 1 to 36 denoting the quarterly period between 2000 and 2018. In addition to t and its square t^2, we also compute three seasonal dummy variables d_1, d_2, and d_3 representing the first three quarters, using the fourth quarter as reference. (Shortly, we will provide R instructions for replicating the results.)

a. The estimated trend models with the training set, where y denotes revenue, are:

Linear: $\hat{y}_t = 11{,}487.3929 + 17{,}564.8013d_1 + 5{,}057.9152d_2 - 1{,}018.9710d_3 + 1626.0290t$

Quadratic: $\hat{y}_t = 1{,}086.5768 + 17{,}564.8013d_1 + 4{,}913.4594d_2 - 1{,}163.4268d_3 + 3{,}720.6378t - 72.2279t^2$

The derivations for the resulting *MSE*, *MAD*, and *MAPE* in the validation set are:

TABLE 12.14 Cross-Validation for Example 12.8

Year	t	y	$\hat{y}$ (Linear)	$\hat{y}$ (Quadratic)
2017:01	29	78,351	76,207	65,806
2017:02	30	52,896	65,326	52,614
⋮	⋮	⋮	⋮	⋮
2018:04	36	62,900	70,024	41,422
MSE			114,191,876	199,075,964
MAD			9,812	11,298
MAPE			17.84	16.79

b. The linear model is preferred over the quadratic model because it has markedly lower *MSE* and *MAD* and only a slightly higher *MAPE*. We reestimate the linear model with the entire data set from 2010–2017 as $\hat{y} = 13{,}969.3750 + 19{,}757.1382d_1 + 4{,}047.0181d_2 - 2{,}522.9910d_3 + 1{,}401.5646t$ to make forecasts for fiscal year 2019.

$$\hat{y}_{2019:01}(d_1 = 1, d_2 = 0, d_3 = 0, t = 37) = \$85{,}584.40 \text{ million}$$
$$\hat{y}_{2019:02}(d_1 = 0, d_2 = 1, d_3 = 0, t = 38) = \$71{,}275.85 \text{ million}$$
$$\hat{y}_{2019:03}(d_1 = 0, d_2 = 0, d_3 = 1, t = 39) = \$66{,}107.40 \text{ million}$$
$$\hat{y}_{2019:04}(d_1 = 0, d_2 = 0, d_3 = 0, t = 40) = \$70{,}031.96 \text{ million}$$

The quarterly forecasts result in a sum of \$292,999.61 million in revenue for fiscal year 2019.

Note that the results based on out-of-sample criteria are not consistent with those based on in-sample criteria used in Example 12.6, where the quadratic model was preferred. So, which model should we use for making forecasts? Unfortunately, there is no definitive answer for this question. Arguably, out-of-sample criteria are more important because forecasting is essentially an out-of-sample exercise and it also avoids overfitting. In this example, however, we have a small sample of 36 observations that is further split into training and validation sets. Furthermore, the plateauing of the revenue is most evident in 2017 and 2018, a period not included in the training set. Therefore, the estimates in the training set, and the resulting *MSE*, *MAD*, and *MAPE* in the validation set may not have been accurate. In such conflicting situations, we sometimes rely on the experience of the forecaster for making the right decision.

Cross-validation of Regression Models with R

FILE *Revenue_Apple*

In order to replicate the results in Example 12.8, we follow these steps.

A. Import the ***Revenue _Apple*** data into a data frame (table) and label it myData.

B. Install and load the *forecast* package. Enter:

```
> install.packages("forecast")
> library(forecast)
```

C. We use the **ts** function to create a time series object and call it newData. Within **ts**, we specify the *start* and *end* periods as well as *frequency*, denoting the number of seasons in a year. Enter:

```
> newData <- ts(myData$Revenue, start = c(2010,1), end = c(2018,4),
frequency=4)
```

D. We use the **window** function to partition the series into training and validation sets, labeled TData and VData, respectively. Enter:

```
> TData <- window(newData, end = c(2016, 4))
> VData <- window(newData, start = c(2017, 1))
```

E. We use the **tslm** function to estimate seasonal linear and quadratic models. Enter:

```
> Reg1 <- tslm(TData ~ trend + season)
> Reg2 <- tslm(TData ~ trend + I(trend^2) + season)
```

F. We use the **length** function to find the number of observations in the validation set, the **forecast** function to make *h* number of forecasts for the validation set, and the **accuracy** function to view the resulting performance measures. Note that R denotes validation set as test set and MAD as MAE and MSE is found by squaring the reported RMSE. Enter:

```
> nV <- length(VData)
> fReg1 <-forecast(Reg1, h=nV)
> fReg2 <-forecast(Reg2, h=nV)
> accuracy(fReg1,VData)
> accuracy(fReg2,VData)
```

G. We use the entire data, that combines the training and the validation sets, to re-estimate the preferred linear model for forecasting Apple's revenue for fiscal year 2019. Enter:

```
> RegFin <- tslm(newData ~ trend + season)
> forecast(RegFin, h=4)
```

EXERCISES 12.5

Applications

26. FILE ***Population_Japan.*** The accompanying data file contains annual population data (in millions) for Japan from 1960 to 2017. For cross-validation, let the training and the validation sets comprise the periods from 1960 to 2005 and 2006 to 2017, respectively.
    a. Use the training set to estimate the linear, the quadratic, and the cubic trend models and compute the resulting *MSE*, *MAD*, and *MAPE* for the validation set.
    b. Determine the preferred model and reestimate it with the entire data set to forecast the population in Japan for 2018.

27. FILE ***Tax_Revenue.*** The accompanying data file contains 57 months of tax revenue from medical and retail marijuana tax and fee collections. For cross-validation, let the training and the validation sets comprise the first 45 months and the last 12 months, respectively.

a. Use the training set to estimate the linear, the quadratic, and the cubic trend models and compute the resulting *MSE*, *MAD*, and *MAPE* for the validation set.
b. Determine the preferred model and reestimate it with the entire data set to forecast tax revenue for the 58th month.

28. **FILE** ***Cafe_Sales.*** The accompanying data file contains daily sales (in $) at Café Venetian for 100 days. For cross-validation, let the training and the validation sets comprise the first 80 days and the last 20 days, respectively.
    a. Use the training set to estimate the linear and the exponential trend models and compute the resulting *MSE*, *MAD*, and *MAPE* for the validation set.
    b. Determine the preferred model and reestimate it with the entire data set to forecast sale for the 101st day.

29. **FILE** ***Apple_Price.*** The accompanying data file contains 53 weeks of Apple's stock price data. For cross-validation, let the training and the validation sets comprise the first 40 weeks and the last 13 weeks, respectively.
    a. Use the training set to estimate the linear and the exponential trend models and compute the resulting *MSE*, *MAD*, and *MAPE* for the validation set.
    b. Determine the preferred model and reestimate it with the entire data set to forecast Apple's stock price for the 54th week.

30. **FILE** ***Expenses.*** The accompanying data file contains quarterly data on expenses (in $1,000s) over five years. For cross-validation, let the training and the validation sets comprise the periods from 2008:01 to 2015:04 and 2016:01 to 2017:04, respectively.
    a. Use the training set to estimate the linear and the exponential trend models with seasonal dummy variables and compute the resulting *MSE*, *MAD*, and *MAPE* for the validation set.
    b. Determine the preferred model and reestimate it with the entire data set to forecast expenses for the first quarter of 2018.

31. **FILE** ***House_Price.*** The accompanying data file lists quarterly data on median house prices in the West Census region. For cross-validation, let the training and the validation sets comprise the periods from 2010:01 to 2016:04 and 2017:01 to 2018:03, respectively.
    a. Use the training set to estimate the linear and the quadratic trend models with seasonal dummy variables and compute the resulting *MSE*, *MAD*, and *MAPE* for the validation set.
    b. Determine the preferred model and reestimate it with the entire data set to forecast house price for the fourth quarter of 2018.

32. **FILE** ***Vehicle_Miles.*** The accompanying data file lists monthly data on vehicle miles traveled in the U.S. (in millions). For cross-validation, let the training and the validation sets comprise the periods from Jan-12 to Dec-16 and Jan-17 to Sep-18, respectively.
    a. Use the training set to estimate the linear and the exponential trend models with seasonal dummy variables and compute the resulting *MSE*, *MAD*, and *MAPE* for the validation set.
    b. Determine the preferred model and reestimate it with the entire data set to forecast vehicle miles for October 2018.

33. **FILE** ***Weekly_Earnings.*** The accompanying data file contains quarterly data on weekly earnings (Earnings, adjusted for inflation) in the U.S. For cross-validation, let the training and the validation sets comprise the periods from 2010:01 to 2015:04 and 2016:01 to 2017:04, respectively.
    a. Use the training set to estimate the linear and the quadratic trend models with seasonal dummy variables and compute the resulting *MSE*, *MAD*, and *MAPE* for the validation set.
    b. Determine the preferred model and reestimate it with the entire data set to forecast earnings for the first quarter of 2018.

34. **FILE** ***Housing_Starts.*** The accompanying data file contains monthly data on housing starts (in 1,000s) in the U.S. For cross-validation, let the training and the validation sets comprise the period from Jan-11 to Dec-16 and Jan-17 to Nov-18, respectively.
    a. Use the training set to estimate the linear and the exponential trend models with seasonal dummy variables and compute the resulting *MSE*, *MAD*, and *MAPE* for the validation set.
    b. Determine the preferred model and reestimate it with the entire data set to forecast housing starts for December of 2018.

LO 12.6

Use advanced smoothing methods to make forecasts.

12.6 ADVANCED EXPONENTIAL SMOOTHING METHODS

In Section 12.2, we used the simple exponential smoothing method to forecast a series $y_1, y_2, \ldots, y_T$ described by random variations around an unknown level. Given no trend and/or seasonality, we employed the recursive equation $L_t = \alpha y_t + (1 - \alpha)L_{t-1}$ to continually update the level. We then used the most current level of the series at time T to forecast for the next period as $\hat{y}_{T+1} = L_T$. Because there are no trend and/or seasonal variations, the level cannot be updated and, therefore, the s-step ahead forecasts are also made as $\hat{y}_{T+s} = L_T$.

As discussed earlier, smoothing is a procedure for continually revising the forecast in the light of more recent observations. In the case of simple exponential smoothing, forecasts are weighted averages of past observations, with the weights decaying exponentially as the observations get older. Recall that the smoothing parameter α, representing the speed of decline, is the key to the analysis. With larger values of α, we pay attention mainly to the most recent observations, whereas with smaller values, greater emphasis is placed on past observations.

In this section, we extend the analysis to include variations due to trend and/or seasonality and implement it with Analytic Solver and R. These software packages allow implementation with user-supplied as well as computer-generated smoothing parameters. It is important to note that the results may differ not only between Analytic Solver and R but also between the different versions of the software packages used. This is due to the choice of initial values used in the recursive equations as well as the performance measures used to obtain optimal smoothing parameters. The differences are negligible when the sample size is large.

The Holt Exponential Smoothing Method

The Holt exponential smoothing method, also referred to as the double exponential smoothing method, incorporates long-term upward or downward movements of a time series. It is appropriate when the time series does not exhibit seasonal variations or the series has been deseasonalized.

The Holt exponential smoothing method uses two recursive equations to smooth the series for level, L, as well as trend, T. (A formal discussion of these equations is beyond the scope of this text.) The recursive equations depend on initial values L_1 and T_1 as well as the values of the smoothing parameters α and β, for level and trend, respectively. Recall that the smoothing parameters indicate the speed of decline. The parameter values can be user-supplied or computer-generated by minimizing MSE, or some other performance measure. Computer-generated values are prone to over-fitting where the selected model does well in the sample period but not so well in the future. Intuition and prior experience, as well as cross-validation, dictate the approach used. Common user-supplied values are $\alpha = 0.20$ and $\beta = 0.15$.

THE HOLT EXPONENTIAL SMOOTHING METHOD

The Holt exponential smoothing method is an extension of the simple exponential smoothing method in that the level L_t as well as the trend T_t adapt over time. It is appropriate when the time series exhibits trend but no seasonality (or has been deseasonalized).

In Example 12.9, we will use Analytic Solver and R to implement the Holt exponential smoothing method. As noted earlier, results may differ between the software packages and their different versions.

EXAMPLE 12.9

Revisit the population data (in millions) for low-income countries from 1960 to 2017. As in Example 12.7, let the training and the validation sets comprise the periods from 1960 to 2000 and 2001 to 2017, respectively. Use the training set to implement the Holt exponential smoothing model with user-supplied parameters ($\alpha = 0.20$ and $\beta = 0.15$), as well as computer-generated smoothing parameters, and

FILE
Population_LowInc

compute the resulting *MSE*, *MAD*, and *MAPE* for the validation set. Determine the preferred model and reimplement it with the entire data set to forecast the population in low-income countries for 2018.

SOLUTION:

Using Analytic Solver

a. Open the ***Population_LowInc*** data file.

b. From the menu, choose **Data Mining > Time Series > Partition**. Specify the data range by highlighting cells A1:B59 and check *First Row Contains Headers.* Select and move Year to *Time Variable* and Population to *Variables in the Partition Data.* For both *Specify Partitioning Options* and *Specify # Records for Partitioning,* choose *Specify # records* and input 41 in *Training Set,* which automatically creates 17 observations in the *validation set.* Click **OK**.

c. From the TSPartition worksheet, choose **Time Series > Smoothing > Double Exponential**. Select and move Population to *Selected Variable.* Check *Optimize* for computer-generated parameters or input user-supplied parameters, $\alpha = 0.20$ and $\beta = 0.15$. We will do both, one at a time. Check *Produce forecast on validation.* Click **OK**.

As expected, the forecasts are a lot closer to the actual values for the training set than for the validation set. The DoubleExpo worksheet contains a lot of other useful information. In Table 12.15, we present the smoothing parameters and the *MSE*, *MAD*, and *MAPE* values found under the heading 'Error Measures: Validation'.

TABLE 12.15 Example 12.9 Results with Analytic Solver

Values	User-supplied	Computer-generated
α	0.20	0.9137
β	0.15	0.4158
MSE	2,563.58	1,086.32
MAD	44.07	26.44
MAPE	6.94	4.06

Here, computer-generated smoothing parameters are preferred as they result in lower *MSE*, *MAD*, and *MAPE* values. (We would like to point out that for simple exponential smoothing, discussed in Section 12.2, we choose **Time Series > Smoothing > Exponential**.)

d. We now use the entire data, which combine the training and the validation sets to reimplement the preferred model for making forecasts. From the original data worksheet, choose **Time Series > Smoothing > Double Exponential**. Specify the Data range by highlighting cells A1:B59. Select and move Year to *Time variable* and Population to *Selected Variable.* Check *Optimize* and *Produce forecast* and input 1 in the *# Forecasts* box. This generates a one-year-ahead forecast of 750.08 million for 2018.

Using R

a. Import the ***Population_LowInc*** data into a data frame (table) and label it myData.

b. Install and load the *forecast* package. Enter:

```
> install.packages("forecast")
> library(forecast)
```

c. We use the **ts** function to create a time series object and call it newData. Within **ts**, we specify the *start* and *end* periods as well as *frequency*, denoting the number of seasons in a year. Enter:

```
> newData <- ts(myData$Population, start = c(1960), end = c(2017),
frequency=1)
```

d. We use the **window** function to partition the series into training and validation sets, labeled TData and VData, respectively. Enter:

```
> TData <- window(newData, end = c(2000))
> VData <- window(newData, start = c(2001))
```

e. We use the **ets** function, denoting error, trend, and seasonality, respectively. Within **ets**, we use a three-letter string in *model*, where the first letter represents the error type (A, M, or Z), the second letter represents the trend type (N, A, M, or Z), and the third letter represents the season type (N, A, M, or Z); N, A, M, and Z stand for none, additive, multiplicative, and automatically selected, respectively. In this text, we will always use the additive level for the error type as well as trend. For example, for the Holt method, we specify A for error, A for trend, and N for seasonality. The **ets** function allows both user-supplied and computer-generated smoothing parameters. Finally, we use the **summary** function to view the results. Enter:

```
> HUser <- ets(TData, model = "AAN", alpha=0.2, beta=0.15)
> HCmp <- ets(TData, model = "AAN")
> summary(HUser)
> summary(HCmp)
```

Here, HUser and HCmp implement the Holt exponential smoothing model with user-supplied and computer-generated smoothing parameters, respectively. (We would like to point out that for the simple exponential smoothing model, discussed in Section 12.2, we would set *model* = "ANN".)

f. We use the **length** function to find the number of observations in the validation set, the **forecast** function to make *h* number of forecasts for the validation set, and the **accuracy** function to view the resulting performance measures. Enter:

```
> nV <- length(VData)
> fUser <-forecast(HUser, h=nV)
> fCmp <-forecast(HCmp, h=nV)
> accuracy(fUser,VData)
> accuracy(fCmp,VData)
```

In Table 12.16, we present the smoothing parameters and the resulting *MSE*, *MAD*, and *MAPE* values found by the **summary** and **accuracy** functions. Recall that R denotes validation set as test set and *MAD* as *MAE*. *MSE* is found by squaring the reported *RMSE*.

TABLE 12.16 Example 12.9 Results with R

Values	*User-supplied*	*Computer-generated*
α	0.20	0.9999
β	0.15	0.9999
MSE	988.34	801.62
MAD	25.12	22.27
MAPE	3.86	3.40

Again, computer-generated smoothing parameters are preferred as they result in lower *MSE*, *MAD*, and *MAPE* values.

g. We use the entire data, which combine the training and the validation sets, to reimplement the preferred model for making forecasts. Enter:

```
> HFinal <- ets(newData, model = "AAN")
> forecast(HFinal, h=1)
```

This generates a one-year-ahead forecast of 750.87 million for 2018.

Summary:

The results reported in Tables 12.15 and 12.16 differ because of the algorithms used. Here, the algorithm used in R produces lower *MSE*, *MAD*, and *MAPE* values. Fortunately, the one-year-ahead forecasts for 2018 are almost the same (750.87 versus 750.08 million), suggesting that the differences between software packages are negligible when the sample size is large. Furthermore, with both software packages, the Holt exponential smoothing method is inferior to the exponential trend model estimated in Example 12.7 with *MSE*, *MAD*, and *MAPE* values of 276.15, 16.00, and 2.62, respectively (see Table 12.13). This result is not surprising as the scatterplot in Figure 12.6 suggested an exponential trend. The Holt exponential smoothing method with a multiplicative trend might have produced better results; however, we do not discuss it in this text.

The Holt-Winters Exponential Smoothing Method

We will now extend the Holt exponential smoothing method to include seasonality. This method is often referred to as the Holt-Winters exponential smoothing method or the triple exponential smoothing method. It incorporates the long-term upward or downward movements of the time series as well as seasonality.

The Holt-Winters exponential smoothing method uses three recursive equations to smooth the series for level, L; trend, T; and seasonality, S. The recursive equations depend on initial values L_1, T_1, and S_1 as well as the values of three smoothing parameters α, β, and γ. Recall that the values of the smoothing parameters indicate the speed of decline.

The Holt-Winters exponential smoothing method is further divided into additive and multiplicative structures depending on the type of seasonality exhibited by the series. The additive method is preferred when the seasonal variations are roughly constant through the series, while the multiplicative method is preferred when the seasonal variations are proportional to the level of the series.

THE HOLT-WINTERS EXPONENTIAL SMOOTHING METHOD

The Holt-Winters exponential smoothing method is an extension of the Holt exponential smoothing method in that the seasonality S_t along with the level L_t and the trend T_t adapt over time. It is appropriate when the time series exhibits trend and seasonality.

In Example 12.10, we will use Analytic Solver and R for the Holt-Winters exponential smoothing method using computer-generated smoothing parameters. As noted earlier, results may differ between the software packages and their different versions.

EXAMPLE 12.10

Revisit Apple's quarterly revenue data (in $ millions) from 2010 to 2018. As in Example 12.8, let the training and the validation sets comprise the periods from 2010 to 2016 and 2017 to 2018, respectively. Use the training set to implement the Holt-Winters smoothing method with additive and multiplicative seasonality and compute the resulting *MSE*, *MAD*, and *MAPE* for the validation set. Determine the preferred model and reimplement it with the entire data set to forecast Apple's revenue for fiscal year 2019.

FILE
Revenue_Apple

SOLUTION: Here, the instructions for Analytic Solver and R are brief because the general implementation is similar to the Holt exponential smoothing method that was outlined in Example 12.9.

Using Analytic Solver

a. Open the ***Revenue_Apple*** data file.

b. Prior to using Analytic Solver, enter the column heading Time in cell D1. Populate cells D2:D37 with values 1, 2, . . . 36 that correspond to the nine years of quarterly observations. These non-repetitive values in column D will be used for partitioning the series.

c. From the menu, choose **Data Mining > Time Series > Partition**. Specify the Data range by highlighting cells A1:D37 and check *First Row Contains Headers.* Select and move Time to *Time Variable* and Revenue to *Variables in the Partition Data.* For both *Specify Partitioning Options* and *Specify # Records for Partitioning,* choose *Specify # records* and input 28 in *Training Set,* creating 8 observations in the *validation set.* Click **OK**.

d. From the TSPartition worksheet, choose **Time Series > Smoothing > Holt-Winters > Additive**. Select and move Revenue to *Selected Variable.* Input 4 in the *Period* box, denoting the number of seasons. Check *Optimize* and *Produce forecast on validation.* Click **OK**. Repeat the process, replacing **Additive** with **Multiplicative**. In Table 12.17, we present the relevant information for additive and multiplicative seasonality.

TABLE 12.17 Example 12.10 Results with Analytic Solver

Values	Additive	Multiplicative
α	0.4202	0.6746
β	0.0323	0.0321
γ	0.9155	0.9156
MSE	10,837,599	15,529,454
MAD	2,583.34	3,017.45
MAPE	3.88	4.36

The additive method with lower *MSE*, *MAD*, and *MAPE* values is preferred.

e. From the original data worksheet, choose **Time Series > Smoothing > Holt-Winters > Additive**. Select and move Revenue to *Selected Variable.* Input 4 in the *Period* box and check *Optimize.* Also, check *Produce forecast* and input 4 in the *# Forecasts* box. The revenue forecasts (in $ millions) are $95,206.29 for quarter 1, $67,774.63 for quarter 2, $60,275.86 for quarter 3, and $69,155,45 for quarter 4. The quarterly forecasts result in a sum of $292,412.23 million in Apple's revenue for fiscal year 2019.

Using R

a. Import the ***Revenue_Apple*** data into a data frame (table) and label it myData.

b. Install and load the *forecast* package if you have not done so already.

c. We use the **ts** function to create a time series object and call it newData. Within **ts**, we specify the *start* and *end* periods as well as *frequency*, denoting the number of seasons in a year. Enter:

```
> newData <- ts(myData$Revenue, start = c(2010,1), end = c(2018,4), frequency=4)
```

d. We use the **window** function to partition the series into training and validation sets, labeled TData and VData, respectively. Enter:

```
> TData <- window(newData, end = c(2016, 4))
> VData <- window(newData, start = c(2017, 1))
```

e. We use the **ets** function, with *model* inputs "AAA" for additive seasonality and "AAM" for multiplicative seasonality. Also, we enter FALSE in *restrict*; sometimes the default setting of TRUE results in an error. Finally, we use the **summary** function to view the results. Enter:

```
> WAdd <- ets(TData, model = "AAA", restrict = FALSE)
> WMlt <- ets(TData, model = "AAM", restrict = FALSE)
> summary(WAdd)
> summary(WMlt)
```

f. We use the **length** function to find the number of observations in the validation set, the **forecast** function to make *h* number of forecasts for the validation set, and the **accuracy** function to view the resulting performance measures. Enter:

```
> nV <- length(VData)
> fAdd <-forecast(WAdd, h=nV)
> fMlt <-forecast(WMlt, h=nV)
> accuracy(fAdd,VData)
> accuracy(fMlt,VData)
```

In Table 12.18, we present the relevant information for additive and multiplicative seasonality; note that R denotes validation set as test set and *MAD* as *MAE*. *MSE* is found by squaring the reported *RMSE*.

TABLE 12.18 Example 12.10 Results with R

Values	Additive	Multiplicative
α	0.3967	0.9995
β	0.0001	0.0857
γ	0.6033	0.0005
MSE	60,955,870	32,459,808
MAD	6,560	4,589
MAPE	10.02	6.81

Here, the multiplicative method with lower *MSE*, *MAD*, and *MAPE* values is preferred.

g. We use the entire data, which combine the training and the validation sets, to reimplement the preferred model for forecasting Apple's revenue for fiscal year 2019. Enter:

```
> WFinal <- ets(newData, model = "AAM", restrict = FALSE)
> forecast(WFinal, h=4)
```

The revenue forecasts, in millions, are $98,643.87 for quarter 1, $70,144.73 for quarter 2, $61,848.01 for quarter 3, and $69,723.77 for quarter 4. The quarterly forecasts result in a sum of about $300,360 million in Apple's revenue for fiscal year 2019.

SUMMARY:

Again, the Analytic Solver and R results in Tables 12.17 and 12.18 differ because of the algorithms used. The resulting *MSE*, *MAD*, and *MAPE* suggest that the Holt-Winters model outperforms the trend model with seasonal dummy variables that was estimated in Example 12.8.

EXERCISES 12.6

Applications

Note: These exercises can be solved using Analytic Solver and/or R. The answers, however, will depend on the software package used. In R, use AAN for the Holt method, and use AAA and AAM for the Holt-Winters method with additive and multiplicative seasonality, respectively.

35. FILE ***Population_Japan.*** The accompanying data file contains annual population data (in millions) for Japan from 1960 to 2017. For cross-validation, let the training and the validation sets comprise the periods from 1960 to 2005 and 2006 to 2017, respectively.
    a. Use the training set to implement the Holt exponential smoothing method with user-supplied ($\alpha = 0.20$ and $\beta = 0.15$), as well as the computer-generated, smoothing parameters and compute the resulting *MSE*, *MAD*, and *MAPE* for the validation set.
    b. Determine the preferred model and reimplement it with the entire data set to forecast the population in Japan for 2018.

36. FILE ***Tax_Revenue.*** The accompanying data file contains 57 months of tax revenue from medical and retail marijuana tax and fee collections. For cross-validation, let the training and the validation sets comprise the first 45 months and the last 12 months, respectively.
    a. Use the training set to implement the Holt exponential smoothing method with user-supplied ($\alpha = 0.30$ and $\beta = 0.20$), as well as the computer-generated, smoothing parameters and compute the resulting *MSE*, *MAD*, and *MAPE* for the validation set.
    b. Determine the preferred model and reimplement it with the entire data set to forecast tax revenue for the 58th month.

37. FILE ***Cafe_Sales.*** The accompanying data file contains daily sales (in $) at Café Venetian for 100 days. For cross-validation, let the training and the validation sets comprise the first 80 days and the last 20 days, respectively.
    a. Use the training set to implement the Holt exponential smoothing method with two sets of user-supplied smoothing parameters, $\alpha = 0.20$ and $\beta = 0.10$ and $\alpha = 0.30$ and $\beta = 0.20$. Compute the resulting *MSE*, *MAD*, and *MAPE* for the validation set.
    b. Determine the preferred model and reimplement it with the entire data set to forecast sales for the 101st day.

38. FILE ***Apple_Price.*** The accompanying data file contains 53 weeks of Apple's stock price data. For cross-validation, let the training and the validation sets comprise the first 40 weeks and the last 13 weeks, respectively.
    a. Use the training set to implement the Holt exponential smoothing method with user-supplied ($\alpha = 0.20$ and $\beta = 0.10$), as well as the computer-generated, smoothing parameters and compute the resulting *MSE*, *MAD*, and *MAPE* for the validation set.
    b. Determine the preferred model and reimplement it with the entire data set to forecast Apple's stock price for the 54th week.

39. FILE ***Expenses.*** The accompanying data file contains quarterly data on expenses (in $1,000s) over five years. For cross-validation, let the training and the validation sets comprise the periods from 2008:01 to 2015:04 and 2016:01 to 2017:04, respectively.
    a. Use the training set to implement the Holt-Winters exponential smoothing method with additive and multiplicative seasonality and compute the resulting *MSE*, *MAD*, and *MAPE* for the validation set.
    b. Determine the preferred model and reimplement it with the entire data set to forecast expenses for the first quarter of 2018.

40. FILE ***House_Price.*** The accompanying data file lists quarterly data on median house prices in the West Census region. For cross-validation, let the training and the validation sets comprise the periods from 2010:01 to 2016:04 and 2017:01 to 2018:03, respectively.
    a. Use the training set to implement the Holt-Winters exponential smoothing method with additive and multiplicative seasonality and compute the resulting *MSE*, *MAD*, and *MAPE* for the validation set.
    b. Determine the preferred model and reimplement it with the entire data set to forecast house price for the fourth quarter of 2018.

41. **FILE** ***Vehicle_Miles.*** The accompanying data file lists monthly data on vehicle miles traveled in the U.S. (in millions). For cross-validation, let the training and the validation sets comprise the periods from Jan-12 to Dec-16 and Jan-17 to Sep-18, respectively.

a. Use the training set to implement the Holt-Winters exponential smoothing method with additive and multiplicative seasonality and compute the resulting *MSE*, *MAD*, and *MAPE* for the validation set.

b. Determine the preferred model and reimplement it with the entire data set to forecast vehicle miles for the last three months of 2018.

42. **FILE** ***Housing_Starts.*** The accompanying data file contains monthly data on housing starts (in 1,000s) in the U.S. For cross-validation, let the training and the validation sets comprise the period from Jan-11 to Dec-16 and Jan-17 to Nov-18, respectively.

a. Use the training set to implement the Holt-Winters exponential smoothing method with additive and multiplicative seasonality and compute the resulting *MSE*, *MAD*, and *MAPE* for the validation set.

b. Determine the preferred model and reimplement it with the entire data set to forecast housing starts for December of 2018.

12.7 WRITING WITH DATA

Case Study

feverpitched/123RF

Leading economic indicators, such as the stock market or the housing market, often change prior to large economic adjustments. For example, a rise in stock prices often means that investors are more confident of future growth in the economy. Or, a fall in building permits is likely a signal that the housing market is weakening – which is often a sign that other sectors of the economy are on the downturn.

Consider what happened prior to the 2008 recession. As early as October 2006, building permits for new homes were down 28% from October 2005. Analysts use economic indicators to predict future trends and gauge where the economy is heading. The information provided by economic indicators helps firms implement or alter business strategies.

Pooja Nanda is an analyst for a large investment firm in Chicago. She covers the construction industry and has been given the challenging task of forecasting housing starts for June 2019. She has access to seasonally adjusted monthly housing starts in the United States from January 2016 to May 2019. A portion of the data is shown in Table 12.19.

FILE *Starts*

TABLE 12.19 Monthly Housing Starts (in 1,000s)

Date	Housing Starts
Jan-16	1114
Feb-16	1208
⋮	⋮
May-19	1269

Pooja would like to use the sample information to identify the best-fitting model to forecast housing starts for June 2019.

Sample Report—Forecasting Monthly Housing Starts

Leading economic indicators are often used to gauge where the economy is heading. The housing market is one of the most important indicators because it is a significant component of the economy. When this sector weakens, just about everyone and everything feels it – from homeowners and construction workers to government municipalities that rely on property taxes to operate. Given the importance of the housing market, this report will forecast next month's housing starts using historical data.

A scatterplot of housing starts from January 2016 to May 2019 is shown in Figure 12.9. A casual observation of the scatterplot suggests quite a bit of random variation and possibly a slight upward trend. There is no concern for seasonality as the housing starts data represent seasonally adjusted annual rates.

FIGURE 12.9 Scatterplot of housing starts (in 1,000s)

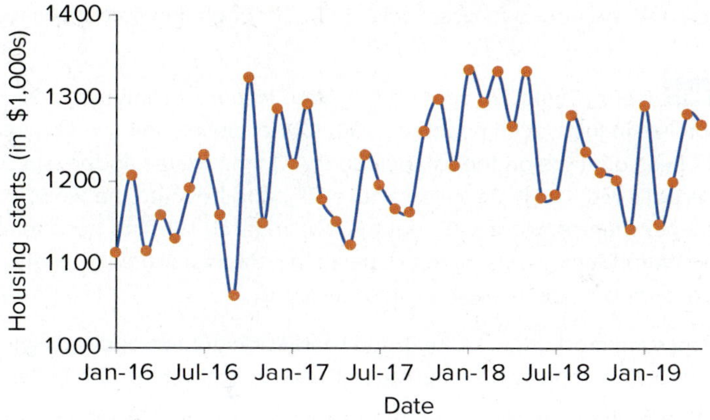

Given the findings from Figure 12.9, three trend models are estimated.

1. The three-period moving average model.
2. The simple exponential smoothed model with various values for the speed of decline α.
3. The simple linear trend model, $y_t = \beta_0 + \beta_1 Time_t + \varepsilon_t$, where y_t represents housing starts.

Three performance measures are used for model selection: mean square error (*MSE*), mean absolute deviation (*MAD*), and the mean absolute percentage error (*MAPE*). The preferred model will have the lowest *MSE*, *MAD*, or *MAPE*. Table 12.20 shows the values of these three performance measures for the models.

Table 12.20 Performance Measures of Competing Models

	3-period Moving Average	Exponential Smoothed ($\alpha = 0.20$)*	Linear Regression Model
MSE	5,069.50	4,798.44	4,091.72
MAD	60.55	57.13	54.24
MAPE	4.96	4.65	4.46

*For the exponential smoothing model, $\alpha = 02$ provides the lowest values for *MSE*, *MAD*, and *MAPE*.

The linear trend model provides the best sample fit, as it has the lowest values for *MSE*, *MAD*, and *MAPE*. Therefore, the estimated linear trend model is used to derive the forecast for June 2019 as

$$\hat{y}_{42} = 1{,}170.2524 + 2.1413 \times 42 = 1{,}260.19.$$

Housing starts plays a key role in determining the health of the economy and is, therefore, always under scrutiny. The U.S. housing market seems to be on solid ground even though there has been slowdown from its peak in early 2018. In this report, we employ simple time series models to project historical data on housing starts.

Suggested Case Studies

Report 12.1 **FILE** ***Fried_Dough.*** Fried dough is a popular North American food associated with outdoor food stands at carnivals, amusement parks, fairs, festivals, and so on. Usually dusted with powdered sugar and drenched in oil, it is not particularly healthy, but it sure is tasty! Jose Sanchez owns a small stall at Boston Commons in Boston, Massachusetts, where he sells fried dough and soft drinks. Although business is good, he is apprehensive about the variation in sales for no apparent reason. The accompanying data file contains information on the number of plates of fried dough and soft drinks that he sold over the last 30 days. In a report, use the sample information to

- Explore forecasting models, including moving averages and the simple exponential method, to smooth the time series for fried dough and soft drinks.
- Use the preferred method to forecast sales of fried dough and soft drinks for the 31st day.

Report 12.2 **FILE** ***India_China.*** According to United Nations estimates, more than half of the world population live in just seven countries, with China, closely followed by India, leading the pack. The other five countries on the list include the United States, Indonesia, Brazil, Pakistan, and Nigeria. It is believed that India will overtake China to become the world's most populous nation much sooner than previously thought (*CNN*, June 2019). The accompanying data file, compiled by the World Bank, contains the population data, in millions, for India and China from 1960 to 2017. In a report, use the sample information to

- Explore forecasting models, including trend regression models and the Holt exponential smoothing model, to capture the population trend for both China and India.
- Use the preferred model to forecast the population of China and India from 2018–2020.

Report 12.3 **FILE** ***Revenue_Amazon.*** Amazon.com, Inc., was a money-losing company when it went public on May 15, 1997, with an IPO valued at a modest $438 million. Amazon has since had an epic 20-year run as a public company, worth about $460 billion in 2017. Many analysts attribute the success of the company to its dynamic leader, Jeff Bezos, who, according to the Bloomberg Billionaires Index, is the richest man in modern history (*CNBC*, July 2018). An important question for investors and other stakeholders is if Amazon's growth is sustainable. The accompanying data file contains quarterly data on Amazon's revenue for the fiscal years 2010 through 2018, with the fiscal year concluding at the end of December. In a report, use the sample information to

- Explore forecasting models, including trend regression models with seasonal dummy variables and the Holt-Winters exponential smoothing model, to capture the trend and seasonality of Amazon's revenue.
- Use the preferred model to forecast Amazon's revenue for fiscal year 2019.

13 Introduction to Prescriptive Analytics

LEARNING OBJECTIVES

After reading this chapter, you should be able to:

LO **13.1** **Generate values for random variables.**

LO **13.2** **Develop and apply Monte Carlo simulation models.**

LO **13.3** **Formulate a linear programming model.**

LO **13.4** **Solve and interpret a linear programming model.**

LO **13.5** **Formulate and solve a linear integer programming model.**

In the previous chapters, we focused on descriptive and predictive analytics to extract value from data. Descriptive techniques were used to explore the data, and predictive methods were implemented to classify or predict new records. In this chapter, we introduce prescriptive analytics, which is the third and final stage of business analytics where analytical models are developed, and the results are analyzed to improve decision making. In particular, prescriptive analytics uses simulation and optimization algorithms to quantify the effect of different possible actions of a decision maker to make a more informed decision.

For simulation, we use random variables to represent the risks and uncertainties that are encountered in many day-to-day, real-life events. We learn how to generate values for various random variables. We then focus on a technique called the Monte Carlo simulation method, which is widely used by many practitioners and researchers. Finally, we demonstrate how to use the linear and integer programming techniques to develop optimization models under constraints.

INTRODUCTORY CASE

FashionTech: Operation and Staffing Strategy

FashionTech is an online apparel retailer that specializes in activewear for both men and women with an active and outdoors lifestyle. FashionTech's best-selling item is a red pullover jacket for women. Abigail Kwan, the company's operations manager, is looking for a better, more data-driven strategy for production and staffing for this product.

The selling price of each pullover jacket is $50. Abigail also obtains the weekly demand and production data from the corporate data warehouse. She believes that the weekly demand for the pullover follows a normal distribution with an average of 139 units and a standard deviation of 14.61 units. The material-per-unit cost of a pullover is also normally distributed with a mean of $12 and a standard deviation of $1.37. The weekly production rate for each tailor varies between 31 and 41 units and follows a discrete uniform distribution. FashionTech usually pays each tailor $700 per week. The overhead cost allocated to the pullover jacket production is approximately $800 per week.

Although the production process for the pullover is partly automated, many important steps are done manually by skilled tailors. Abigail wants to get a better estimate of the demand of the pullover and determine how many tailors she needs to hire. In addition, she is considering increasing the level of automation in the manufacturing process. While the added automation will incur a one-time installation and training cost as well as raise the overhead cost to $900 per week, it will allow FashionTech to use less-skilled tailors at a lower weekly wage of $550, and the weekly production rate will likely have less variability. Based on the data from other manufacturers, Abigail believes that with increased automation, the weekly production rate will be uniformly distributed with lower and upper limits of 36 and 41 units, respectively. Abigail wants to analyze her data, and based on the results, confirm her plan to send out a request for proposals from automation vendors for the possible installation and training cost.

Abigail would like to use the information described above to accomplish the following tasks.

1. Develop a simulation to examine the profit at each staffing level as well as evaluate the plan to increase the automation level in the production process.
2. Examine the profit variability given the uncertainty of the demand and the production rate.

A synopsis of this case is provided in Section 13.2.

13.1 OVERVIEW OF PRESCRIPTIVE ANALYTICS

Prescriptive analytics is a process of using analysis tools to improve decision making. In many cases, prescriptive analytics can help a decision maker determine the best course of action among different alternatives. Some people regard prescriptive analytics as a very broad term that encompasses all analytics techniques with an overall goal of improving business decision making. However, most people prefer making a distinction between descriptive, predictive, and prescriptive analytics, where prescriptive analytics uses simulation and optimization algorithms to quantify the effect of different possible actions by a decision maker to help make a more informed decision.

Recall from Chapter 1 that these three types of analytics techniques—descriptive, predictive, and prescriptive—are used to extract value from data and make better business decisions. Descriptive analytics refers to gathering, organizing, tabulating, and visualizing data to summarize "*what has happened.*" Predictive analytics refers to using historical data to determine "*what could happen in the future.*" Prescriptive analytics, our focus here, refers to using simulation and optimization algorithms to advise on "*what businesses should do.*" Simulation is an attempt to imitate a real-world process that produces several business scenarios, whereas optimization is an attempt to find an optimal way to achieve a business objective under constraints, such as limited capacities, financial resources, and competing priorities.

PRESCRIPTIVE ANALYTICS

An analytics process of using decision analysis tools such as simulation and optimization to improve decision making. Simulation is an attempt to imitate a real-world process to demonstrate the outcome from different scenarios. identified by decision makers, whereas optimization is an attempt to find an optimal way to achieve a business objective under given constraints.

Section 13.2 discusses a specific type of simulation—Monte Carlo simulation. Sections 13.3 and 13.4 explore two optimization techniques: linear and integer programming.

13.2 MONTE CARLO SIMULATION

To imitate real-world business scenarios, simulations are often performed using computer software with relevant variables and relationships among those variables. The usefulness of a computer simulation largely depends on how we select variables and construct the simulation to adequately and accurately reflect the real world. Once a computer simulation is developed, we can study how changes in certain variables might impact the overall result.

Simulation has been extensively used in a wide variety of business settings to explore alternative solutions or improve business processes. Companies may use it in engineering and manufacturing to experiment with different product designs, changes in production lines, and streamlining a supply chain. Financial institutions often use simulation to explore different investment decisions in various market scenarios. Retail stores, restaurants, commercial airlines, hospitals, and many other service providers use simulation to study the fluctuation of consumer demand to design a better work schedule of their employees as well as manage their inventory in order to meet the demand. A computer simulation also allows us to quickly experiment with different values and parameters of the variables without disrupting the actual business process and operation.

In business analytics, computer simulation is often synonymous with the Monte Carlo method, which is a family of computer algorithms used to model the risk or uncertainty of a real-world process or system. Stanislaw Ulam and John von Neumann are often credited for inventing the *Monte Carlo simulation*, named after the Monte Carlo Casino in Monaco. The technique was used to study nuclear fission by Ulam and von Neumann, who worked on the Manhattan Project at Los Alamos National Laboratory during World War II. Because the technique relies on random sampling to mimic the odds of all possible outcomes, Monte Carlo simulation is also called probabilistic or stochastic simulation, as opposed to a deterministic process that can be accurately described by a formula and whose outcome can be precisely estimated.

> **MONTE CARLO SIMULATION**
>
> A statistical technique used to model probabilistic (stochastic) processes. By recreating a real-world process, Monte Carlo simulation is used to understand the impact of the risk and uncertainty in a wide variety of business settings.

To understand the probabilistic nature of Monte Carlo simulation, let's first consider a deterministic scenario where a simulation may not be needed. For example, if we deposit $1,000 in a savings account that yields a 2% annual return, we would certainly end up with $1,020 in our bank account at the end of the year. In this deterministic case, repeating the same scenario (i.e., investing $1,000 in the same savings account) would yield the exact same outcome (i.e., $1,020 in our bank account) every time, and no simulation is needed to predict the outcome. However, most real-life situations are much more complicated. An investment of the same $1,000 in the stock market would involve a much higher risk and uncertainty. In a good year, the return may be in double digits, whereas in a bad year the return may be negative. Here, a stock investor needs to make an investment decision when the actual return on the investment is not known with certainty. Similarly, a retailer has to determine the inventory level in the store when the precise demand for each product is unknown. In all these cases, we can use a Monte Carlo simulation with relevant variables to capture the inherently probabilistic nature of the real-world financial and economic markets to make better-informed decisions.

Here, one might ask why we cannot simply consider the average values such as the average return on the stock investment or the average customer demand for a product to help make a decision for the stock investor or the retailer. This is because the actual outcome (i.e., actual return on the investment or the actual customer demand) can wildly fluctuate and deviate significantly from the averages. Many real-life events serve as a cautionary tale that relying solely on average values could lead to a negative, and sometimes disastrous, consequence. In 1994, the government of Orange County in California made an investment decision based on an average value of the then-very-low interest rate, instead of considering a range of possible outcomes and the uncertainty of the future interest rate. In the end, the investment decision resulted in a loss of almost $2 billion, and Orange County became the largest municipality in the U.S. forced to declare bankruptcy (Source: *The Flaw of Averages* by Sam. L. Savage).

Even outside of the financial market, the pitfalls of relying on averages have long been well known and documented. Back in the 1950s, the U.S. Air Force set out to design a better cockpit in a fighter jet by measuring more than 100 body parts of over 4,000 pilots, including the size of their chest, neck, torso, hip, and thighs as well as the distance between their eyes and ears. The main objective of the project was to build a better-fitting cockpit to reduce the number of accidents and plane crashes. However, an early attempt to build a cockpit to fit an "average" pilot turned out to be a mistake, as one researcher on the project quickly realized that none of the thousands of pilots would comfortably fit within the overall average specifications. A pilot with an average height might have a longer-than-average arm length or a shorter-than-average torso. A pilot with some average measurements often turned out to be an outlier on many other body dimensions. Had the Air Force built a cockpit for an "average" pilot, the cockpit would have fit no one! (Source: *The "Average Man"* by Gilbert S. Daniels.)

Instead of relying solely on the average value, Monte Carlo simulation is useful because it considers all possible values using a random variable to capture the risk and uncertainty. From Chapter 4, recall that a random variable is a function that assigns numerical values to the outcomes of an experiment. A discrete random variable assumes a countable number of distinct values. A continuous random variable, on the other hand, is characterized by uncountable values in an interval. Examples of discrete random variables include the number of students receiving the grade A in a class or the number of firms filing for bankruptcy in a given month. Similarly, the return on an investment or the height of an individual are examples of continuous random variables because they are both associated with uncountable outcomes. The following subsections use Monte Carlo methods to model the risk and uncertainty using random variables based on discrete and continuous probability distributions.

LO 13.1

Generate values for random variables.

Modeling Risk and Uncertainty

We generally rely on random variables to capture the risk and uncertainty in the real world. Monte Carlo simulations are based on both discrete and continuous probability distributions of random variables. Students are advised to review the discussion of these probability distributions in Chapter 4.

Two of the most relevant discrete probability distributions for Monte Carlo simulation are binomial and Poisson distributions. Recall from Chapter 4 that a binomial random variable must first satisfy the conditions of a Bernoulli process. A binomial random variable is defined as the number of successes achieved in the n trials of a Bernoulli process. Examples include the number of customers, in a sample of 100, whose loan application will be approved by a bank and the number of customers, in a sample of 20, who will return a purchased product.

The Poisson distribution is particularly useful for modeling when we are interested in finding the number of occurrences (successes) of a certain event over a given interval of time or space. Examples include the number of customers arriving at a retail store between 10 am and noon on a weekday, the number of bankruptcies that are filed in a month, and the number of defects in a 50-yard roll of fabric.

The discrete uniform distribution, which was not discussed in Chapter 4, is another important probability distribution for conducting Monte Carlo simulation. A discrete uniform random variable has a finite number of specified values, with each value being equally likely. When rolling a fair six-sided die, the number rolled is an example of a discrete uniform random variable. The distribution is symmetric. To generate random observations from these probability distributions, we can use computer software such as Excel and R.

Using Excel and R to Generate Random Observations from a Discrete Probability Distribution

In Example 13.1, we show how to use Excel and R to generate random observations based on the binomial probability distribution. We also modify the instructions to accommodate Poisson and discrete uniform distributions.

EXAMPLE 13.1

In the United States, about 30% of adults have four-year college degrees (*U.S. Census*, July 31, 2018). In Example 4.10, we demonstrated how to calculate probabilities based on this application of the binomial distribution. Here, we use a similar scenario to demonstrate how to generate random observations that represent the number of four-year college degree holders in a randomly selected group of 10 individuals in the U.S. Use Excel and R to simulate random observations based on 100 selections of 10 individuals.

SOLUTION: Recall from Chapter 4 that this example satisfies the conditions for a Bernoulli process and the binomial probability distribution. Moreover, the mean and the standard deviation of a binomial probability distribution are $\mu = np$ and $\sigma = \sqrt{np(1-p)}$, respectively, where n represents the number of trials and p represents the probability of success on each trial. In this example, we randomly select 10 individuals where each individual has a 30% chance of holding a college degree, so $n = 10$ and $p = 0.30$. Thus, the mean and the standard deviation of this binomial probability distribution are 3 (= 10 × 0.30) and 1.4491 ($= \sqrt{10 \times 0.30 \times (1 - 0.30)}$), respectively. The process of selecting 10 individuals will be repeated 100 times where, for each random selection, the number of college-degree holders will vary between 0 to 10. This variation represents the uncertainty in the process.

Using Excel

a. To model the uncertainty, we use the **RAND** and the **BINOM.INV** functions. The RAND function generates a random value between 0 and 1. The BINOM.INV(n, p, α) function returns the smallest value for which the cumulative binomial distribution is greater than or equal to a criterion value denoted as α. Here, we open a new Excel workbook and enter =BINOM.INV(10, 0.30, RAND()) in cell A1. Whenever the F9 key is pressed, Excel redraws a new observation, and the output changes. The output can potentially vary from 0 to 10 but most values will be clustered around the mean of 3.

b. To repeat the random selection 100 times, we copy and paste the formula in step a to cells A2 through A100. We can calculate the average number of college degree holders from the 100 random observations using the =AVERAGE(A1:A100) function in cell B1. As expected, the average value is approximately 3. We calculate the sample standard deviation from the 100 random observations using the =STDEV.S(A1:A100) function in cell B2. The answer should be close to 1.4491.

Excel can also generate random observations based on other discrete probability distributions. For the discrete uniform distribution, we use =RANDBETWEEN(a, b) to generate random values between a and b, inclusive. For example, if we enter =RANDBETWEEN(2, 5) in a cell, then Excel will generate 2, 3, 4, or 5. There is no built-in Excel function to generate random observations for the Poisson probability distribution.

When using built-in functions in Excel to generate random observations, we cannot set a random seed, and, therefore, the random observations we obtain will vary each time. To store random numbers obtained from the built-in function, we can use the Paste Values feature in Excel to copy and paste only the values into other blank cells (e.g., C1 through C100). Excel's Analysis ToolPak, discussed in earlier chapters, allows us to set a random seed so we can obtain consistent outputs each time. Excel's Analysis ToolPak also allows us to generate random observations for a Poisson random variable.

Using Excel's Analysis ToolPak

a. Choose **Data > Data Analysis > Random Number Generation** from the menu. (Note: If you do not see the **Data Analysis** option under **Data**, you must add in the **Analysis Toolpak** option. From the menu, choose **File > Options > Add-Ins** and choose **Go** at the bottom of the dialog box. Select

Analysis Toolpak and then click **OK**. If you have installed this option properly, you should now see **Data Analysis** under **Data**.)

b. See Figure 13.1. In this example, we set *Number of Variables* to 1 and *Number of Random Numbers* to 100. For *Distribution* we select Binomial, and for *Parameters* we set *p Value* (probability) equal to 0.3 and the *Number of trials* equal to 10. For consistency of results, we set *Random Seed* equal to 1. We choose to place the output starting in cell A1. Click **OK**.

FIGURE 13.1 Excel's Random Number Generation dialog box

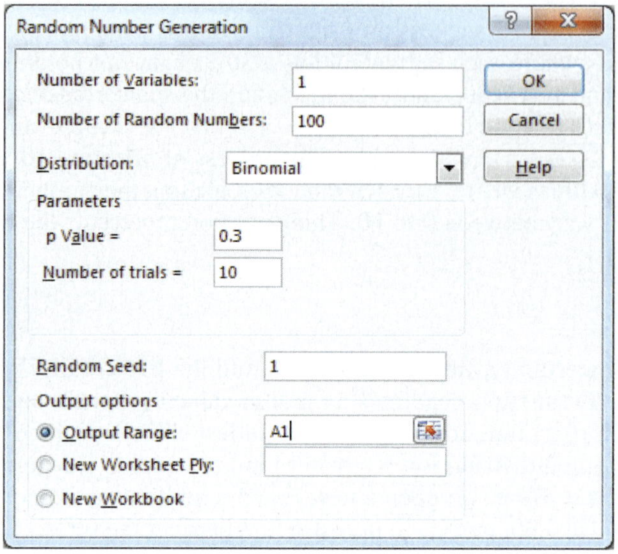

Source: Microsoft Excel

c. Excel will generate 100 random observations in cells A1 through A100. For the 100 random observations that we generated, we use the AVERAGE and STDEV.S functions and find that the mean and the standard deviation are 2.95 and 1.3734, respectively. As expected, the values are close to the population mean of 3 and the population standard deviation of 1.4491 of the binomial probability distribution.

To generate random observations from other probability distributions, we can choose other options in the *Distribution* box in Figure 13.1 and specify appropriate parameter values. For example, in order to generate random observations from the Poisson distribution, we select Poisson in the *Distribution* box and specify the value of lambda (λ), where λ is the mean and variance for the Poisson distribution. In Chapter 4, we used the Greek letter μ in place of λ.

Using R

a. In order to ensure consistency of the output, we use the **set.seed** function. Enter:

```
> set.seed(1)
```

b. We use the **rbinom** function to generate random observations for a binomial random variable. We enter rbinom(*numobs, n, p*) where *numobs* denotes the number of observations that R will generate for a binomial process with *n* trials and a probability *p* of success on each trial. We store the random observations in an object called output and retype output to display the random observations. Enter:

```
> output <- rbinom(100,10,0.3)
> output
```

c. In order to calculate the mean and standard deviation of the 100 random observations, we use the **mean** and the **sd** functions. Enter:

```
> mean(output)
> sd(output)
```

The mean and the standard deviation for the 100 random observations are 3.08 and 1.3156, respectively. As expected, the values are close to the population mean of 3 and the population standard deviation of 1.4491 of the binomial probability distribution.

R can also generate random observations based on other probability distributions. For the discrete uniform and the Poisson distributions, instead of the **rbinom** function, we use the **sample** and **rpois** functions, respectively. For example, if we enter sample(2:5, 100, replace = TRUE), then R generates 100 random observations between the values of 2 and 5 (inclusive) using a sampling method with replacement. If we enter rpois(100, 3), then R generates 100 random observations from a Poisson distribution with a mean of 3. Make sure to use the **set.seed** function before generating each set of random observations to ensure consistency of the output.

So far, we have generated random observations from discrete probability distributions. We will now turn our attention to simulating random observations for continuous random variables. The normal, the continuous uniform, and the exponential distributions are among the most widely used probability distributions for the Monte Carlo method.

As discussed extensively in Chapters 3 and 4, the normal distribution is bell-shaped and symmetric around its mean. It is the most extensively used probability distribution for statistical work and analytical modeling and accurately describes numerous random variables of interest. Examples include the amount of rainfall during a planting season, students' exam scores, or monthly usage of cell phones among consumers.

Other important distributions, not discussed in Chapter 4, include the continuous uniform and the exponential distributions. The continuous uniform distribution is also referred to as the rectangular distribution as it represents a constant probability within a specified range. Examples include the delivery time of an appliance, the arrival time of an elevator in a building, or the scheduled flight time between destinations. Unlike the normal and the continuous uniform distributions, the exponential distribution is appropriate when the data are believed to be generated from a nonsymmetric distribution.

The exponential distribution is also related to the Poisson distribution. While a Poisson random variable counts the number of occurrences of an event over a given interval of time or space, an exponential random variable captures the time that elapses between such occurrences. Examples include the time between text messages or between customer purchases. The exponential distribution is also used in modeling failure times such as the life of an appliance or a person. It has a noted "memoryless" feature that implies a constant failure rate. It assumes, for example, that the probability of an electric bulb burning out on a given day is independent of whether the bulb has lasted for 10, 100, or 1,000 hours. It is common to define the exponential probability distribution in terms of its rate parameter λ, which is the inverse of its mean.

Using Excel and R to Generate Random Observations from a Continuous Probability Distribution

In Example 13.2, we show how to use Excel and R to generate random observations based on the normal distribution. We also modify the instructions to accommodate the continuous uniform and the exponential distributions.

EXAMPLE 13.2

From the introductory case, the material cost of a red pullover jacket sold by FashionTech is normally distributed with a mean of \$12 per unit and a standard deviation of \$1.37. Generate the material cost for 100 randomly selected jackets.

SOLUTION: Similar to Example 13.1, we can use Excel or R to generate the material cost of 100 randomly selected jackets. Based on the 100 observations, we should expect the average value to be approximately \$12 with a standard deviation of approximately \$1.37; however, the exact cost of individual jackets may vary.

Using Excel

a. We use the **RAND** and the **NORM.INV** functions. As in Example 13.1, the RAND function generates random observations between 0 and 1. The NORM.INV(α, μ, σ) function returns the smallest value for which the cumulative normal distribution is greater than or equal to a criterion value denoted as α. Here, we open a new Excel workbook and enter =NORM.INV(RAND(), 12, 1.37) in cell A1. Whenever the F9 key is pressed, Excel redraws a new observation, and the output changes.

b. To repeat the random selection, we copy and paste the formula in cell A1 to cells A2 through A100. We can use the AVERAGE and STDEV.S functions to find the mean and the standard deviation of the 100 random observations.

We can use Excel to generate random observations from other continuous probability distributions. For the continuous uniform distribution with a lower limit of a and an upper limit of b, we enter $=a + (b - a)$ * RAND () to generate random observations between a and b, inclusive. In order to generate random observations from the exponential distribution with a rate parameter of λ, we use $(-1/\lambda)$ * ln(1 – RAND()). Recall that $1/\lambda$ is the mean of the exponential distribution.

Using Excel's Analysis ToolPak

a. Similar to Example 13.1, from the menu we choose **Data > Data Analysis > Random Number Generation**.

b. In this example, we set *Number of Variables* to 1 and *Number of Random Numbers* to 100. For *Distribution* we select *Normal*, and for *Parameters*, we set *Mean* equal to 12 and *Standard Deviation* equal to 1.37. For consistency of the output, we set *Random Seed* equal to 1. We choose to place the output starting in cell A1. Click **OK**.

c. We can use the AVERAGE and STDEV.S functions to find that the mean and the standard deviation of the 100 observations as 11.9628 and 1.5055, respectively. To generate random observations from the continuous uniform distribution, for *Distribution* we select *Uniform* and specify the values for the lower and upper limits of the distribution. The exponential distribution is not one of the options in Excel's Analysis ToolPak, but we can simulate an exponential random variable, y, from a continuous uniform variable, x, using the following transformation, $y = (-1/\lambda) * \ln(1 - x)$, where $1/\lambda$ is the mean of the exponential distribution. For example, to generate an exponential random variable whose λ is 3, start by selecting the uniform distribution, specify [0, 1] for the lower and upper limits, and place the random numbers in cells A1:A100. In cell B1, enter =(–1/3) * ln(1 – A1) and copy and paste the formula to cells B2:B100.

Using R

a. Again, we use the set.seed(1) statement to ensure consistent results. We use the **rnorm** function to generate random observations for a normal random variable. We enter rnorm(*numobs*, μ, σ), where *numobs* denotes the number of observations that R will generate for a normal process with mean μ and standard deviation σ. We store the random observations in an object called output and retype output to display the random observations. Enter:

```
> set.seed(1)
> output <- rnorm(100, 12, 1.37)
> output
```

b. We use the **mean** and **sd** functions to find the mean and the standard deviation of the 100 random observations. Enter:

```
> mean(output)
> sd(output)
```

For the 100 observations generated in step b, the mean and standard deviation are 12.1492 and 1.2305, respectively.

For the continuous uniform distribution, we use runif(100, 20, 21) to generate 100 random observations with values between 20 and 21, inclusive. To generate 100 observations from the exponential distribution with $\lambda = 3$, we use rexp(100, 3).

So far, we have demonstrated how to model uncertainty based on theoretical probability distributions. In many real-world settings, an appropriate distribution is not known in advance. Sometimes, we may be able to plot the data and inspect the histogram for distinctive shapes corresponding to these theoretical distributions. For instance, if the histogram displays data that are evenly distributed, we might assume a continuous uniform distribution. If the histogram displays data that are symmetrically clustered around the middle with decreasing probabilities in the tails, we might assume a normal distribution. Formal methods, including the chi-square goodness of fit test, are used to determine which theoretical probability distribution is appropriate. Distribution fitting functions can also be found in many software applications. In this chapter, we focus on developing simulation models based on known theoretical distributions.

Formulating and Developing a Monte Carlo Simulation

LO 13.2

Develop and apply Monte Carlo simulation models.

In any business setting, when the probability distributions are known for all relevant random variables, we can easily formulate and develop a Monte Carlo simulation. The next crucial step is to construct a quantitative model that represents the relationship among relevant variables. In the introductory case, Abigail wants to examine the profit at each staffing level for the production of a red pullover jacket for women. A quantitative formulation that relates the random variables, constants, and the profit can be constructed based on basic accounting principles, as shown in the following equation:

$$\text{Profit} = \text{Revenue} - \text{Cost} = RQ_s - (F + VQ_p),$$

where R = the selling price per jacket; Q_s = the number of jackets sold; F = the fixed overhead cost; V = the variable cost per jacket consisting of the material cost and weekly wages of the tailors; and Q_p = the number of jackets produced.

Of course, for other scenarios, the quantitative formulation would be different. Regardless of the context or underlying situations, the Monte Carlo formulation needs to capture the uncertainty with random variables, in relation to the outcome. Based on the quantitative formulation, we can repeat the simulation and generate possible outcomes of interest.

If the simulation process is repeated many times, relevant information such as average values, best and worst cases, and a range of outcome values can be gathered to inform decision makers about the appropriate course of actions. For example, in the introductory case, Abigail wants to examine the demand and production rate of the pullover jacket to see how they affect the profit. A Monte Carlo simulation can be used to estimate the average profit or a range of best- and worst-case scenarios at different staffing levels. More importantly, we can easily change the parameter values in the simulation to help FashionTech make a decision regarding the appropriate staffing level and whether or not to automate the manufacturing process. This is shown in Example 13.3.

EXAMPLE 13.3

From the introductory case, Abigail wants to develop an analytical model to analyze the demand and production information for a red pullover jacket for women, the top-selling product for FashionTech. She obtains relevant demand and cost information from her corporate database, which is summarized in Table 13.1. Create a Monte Carlo simulation to help Abigail examine the profit at each staffing level. Also, use the simulation results to determine whether or not FashionTech should consider increasing the automation in its production process.

TABLE 13.1 Summary of FashionTech's Demand and Cost Data

Description	Data
Weekly demand	Normal distribution with μ = 139 units and σ = 14.61 units
Weekly production rate per tailor	Uniform distribution between 31 and 41 units
Selling price per jacket	\$50
Material cost per jacket	Normal distribution with μ = \$12 and σ = \$1.37
Weekly wage per tailor	\$700
Overhead cost per week	\$800

SOLUTION: We develop a Monte Carlo simulation based on the profit equation presented earlier. In Example 13.2, we generated random observations of the material cost for the red pullover jacket. We use the same technique to generate random observations for the weekly demand and production rate. Because the number of jackets should be an integer, we will generate random numbers and convert them into whole numbers. For the material cost, we will use two decimal places.

Using Excel

FILE *Jacket*

There are many ways to develop a Monte Carl simulation in Excel; however, for consistency, we recommend that students use a template provided in the ***Jacket*** worksheet for this example. Also, to obtain consistent results, we use the random number generation feature in Excel's Analysis ToolPak and set the random seed equal to 1. We will repeat the simulation for 100 iterations and summarize the results on the ***Jacket*** worksheet.

a. Open the ***Jacket*** worksheet. Use **Data > Data Analysis > Random Number Generation** to generate 100 random numbers for the weekly demand in cells L11:L110, the production rate in cells M11:M110, and the material cost in cells N11: N110. Figure 13.2 shows the Random Number Generation options for the three random variables; note that the random seed is set equal to 1 in all simulations.

FIGURE 13.2 Random number generations for Demand, Production Rate, and Material Cost

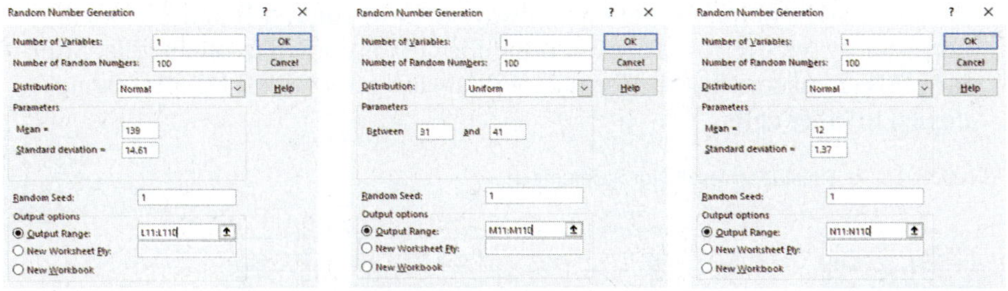

Source: Microsoft Excel

b. We convert the random numbers for the weekly demand and production rate into integers and use two decimal places for the material cost using Excel's ROUND function. In cells B11, C11, and D11, enter the formulas =ROUND(L11, 0), =ROUND(M11, 0), and =ROUND(N11, 2), respectively. Copy and paste the formulas to cells B12:D110. Figure 13.3 shows a portion of the random numbers.

FIGURE 13.3 A portion of the ***Jacket*** worksheet for FashionTech

	A	B	C	D	E	F	G	H	I	J	K	L	M	N
1	**Input parameters:**			**Simulation results:**	Summary of weekly profit at each staffing level									
2	Selling price	$ 50			1	2	3	4	5	6				
3	Overhead cost	$ 800		Average										
4	Tailor's wage	$ 700		Std Dev										
5				Best case										
6				Worst case										
7														
8														
9		Rounded values of random numbers			Weekly profit at each staffing level (1 through 6 tailors)							Random numbers		
10	Simulation number	Demand	Production rate per tailor	Material cost	1	2	3	4	5	6		Demand	Production rate	Material cost
11	1	95	31	7.86								94.8338	31.0125	7.8585
12	2	141	37	12.22								141.3386	36.6359	12.2193
13	3	126	33	10.81								126.3509	32.9330	10.8139

Source: Microsoft Excel

c. Enter the selling price, $50, in cell B2; weekly overhead cost, $800, in cell B3; and the tailor's weekly wage, $700, in cell B4. Label these input parameters, as shown in Figure 13.3. Recall that Abigail wants to examine the possibility of increasing the automation in her production process. Storing the input parameters in their own cells will allow us to later change these values and obtain results from different scenarios.

d. Recall that the profit is calculated as revenue minus cost. To compute the revenue, we multiply the selling price by the number of jackets sold. Note that the number of jackets sold is the lower value between the demand and the number of jackets produced, and we use the MIN function in Excel to determine the number of jackets sold. The total cost is an aggregate of the overhead cost, the tailors' wages, and the material cost. To calculate the weekly profit for hiring one tailor in cell E11, we enter the following formula.

Number of jackets produced by 1 tailor
Demand
Selling price

= $B$2*MIN($B11,$C11*E$10)-$B$3-($B$4*E$10)-($D11*E$10*$C11)

Overhead cost
Wage for 1 tailor
Material cost used by 1 tailor

To calculate the profit for other cells and different staffing levels, copy and paste the formula to the remaining cells in the E11:J110 range. Figure 13.4 shows a portion of the profit values.

It is important to pay close attention to the dollar signs ($) in the above profit formula. A column name or row number with a preceding dollar sign will not change even if the formula is copied elsewhere on the worksheet. For example, \$B11 in the formula will always refer to column B and E\$10 will consistently refer to row 10, even if the formula is copied to other cells. Similarly, \$B\$2 ensures that the formula will always refer to cell B2 after being copied to other cells.

FIGURE 13.4 Simulation results for FashionTech

	A	B	C	D	E	F	G	H	I	J	K	L	M	N
1	Input parameters:			Simulation results:	Summary of weekly profit at each staffing level									
2	Selling price	$ 50			1	2	3	4	5	6				
3	Overhead cost	$ 800		Average	-$135.50	$529.00	$1,193.50	$1,560.99	$436.49	-$678.01				
4	Tailor's wage	$ 700		Std Dev	$59.42	$118.84	$178.26	$399.88	$373.44	$290.04				
5				Best case	-$37.94	$724.12	$1,486.18	$2,248.24	$1,726.50	$341.80				
6				Worst case	-$237.92	$324.16	$886.24	$175.36	-$768.30	-$1,711.96				
7														
8														
9		Rounded values of random numbers			Weekly profit at each staffing level (1 through 6 tailors)							Random numbers		
10	Simulation number	Demand	Production rate per tailor	Material cost	1	2	3	4	5	6		Demand	Production rate	Material cost
11	1	95	31	7.86	-193.66	412.66	1019.02	175.36	-768.30	-1711.96		94.8338	31.0125	7.8585
12	2	141	37	12.22	-102.14	595.72	1293.58	1641.44	489.30	-662.84		141.3386	36.6339	12.2193
13	3	126	33	10.81	-206.73	386.54	979.81	1273.08	216.35	-840.38		126.3509	32.9330	10.8139

Source: Microsoft Excel

e. We now use the *Simulation results* section on the ***Jacket*** worksheet to calculate relevant statistics for each staffing level. Enter the following formula in cells E3 through E6, respectively: =AVERAGE(E11:E110), =STDEV.S(E11:E110), =MAX(E11:E110), and =MIN(E11:E110). Copy and paste the formula from cells E3:E6 to cells F3:J6. Additional statistical information can also be obtained by using other Excel functions; see Chapter 3 for a review. The ***Jacket*** worksheet and the simulation results should now look similar to Figure 13.4. Figure 13.5 displays a scatterplot of the profits from the 100 simulations for the scenarios with three and four tailors (cells G11:G110 and H11:H110). Figures 13.4 and 13.5 show that hiring four tailors generates the highest profit, but variability of the profit levels is also much greater than in other scenarios (i.e., a higher risk as indicated by a larger standard deviation). Alternately, hiring three tailors generates the second-highest profit but presents a much lower risk than hiring four tailors.

FIGURE 13.5 Profit distribution for FashionTech

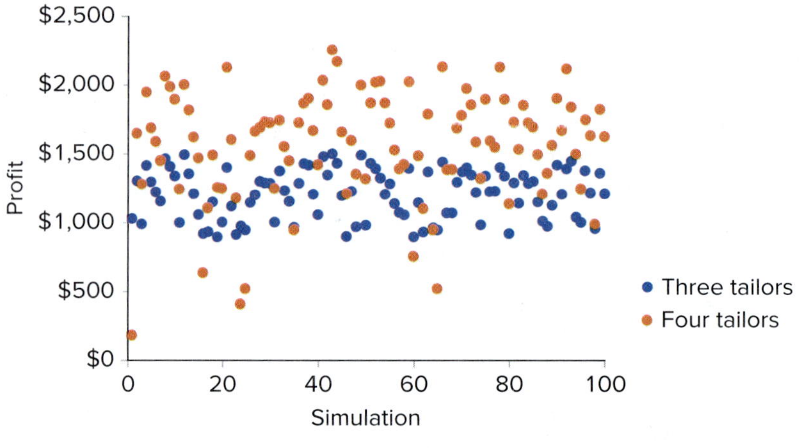

f. To evaluate the possibility of increasing automation in the production process, change the weekly overhead cost and the tailor's wage in cells B3 and B4 to 900 and 550, respectively. Also, generate new random numbers in column M by specifying a uniform distribution with values between 36 and 41. The ***Jacket*** worksheet will repeat the 100 simulations for the new scenario and recalculate the simulation results as shown in Figure 13.6. In this new scenario, hiring 4 tailors remains the most profitable option and poses the highest risk. However, the expected profit from hiring 3 tailors is now much closer to the 4-tailor scenario, but at a much lower risk. Further discussion of the results is included in the synopsis of the introductory case.

FIGURE 13.6 Simulation results with updated input parameters

Simulation results:	Summary of weekly profit at each staffing level					
	1	2	3	4	5	6
Average	$11.59	$923.17	$1,820.26	$1,950.85	$966.94	-$45.48
Std Dev	$19.45	$38.90	$77.49	$448.41	$431.67	$357.94
Best case	$67.04	$1,034.08	$1,918.80	$2,748.24	$2,376.50	$1,141.80
Worst case	-$84.70	$730.60	$1,351.12	$518.16	-$314.80	-$1,147.76

As mentioned earlier, alternative spreadsheet designs can be used to achieve similar Monte Carlo simulation results, as well as to add more complexity and gain additional insights. For example, one might consider treating the production rate for each tailor as a separate random variable (e.g., six random variables for the six tailors), or separating the demand for various jacket sizes (i.e., S, M, and L) into different random variables or simulation templates.

Using R

a. To ensure that we obtain consistent results, use the **set.seed** function. Enter:

```
> set.seed(1)
```

b. Generate 100 random observations for the demand, the production rate, and the material cost variables using the designated distributions. Then use the **round** function to convert the random numbers for the weekly demand and production rate into integers and use two decimal places for the material cost. Enter:

```
> demand <- rnorm(100, 139, 14.61)
> demand <- round(demand, digits = 0)
> productionRate <- sample(31:41, 100, replace = TRUE)
> productionRate<-round(productionRate, digits = 0)
> materialCost <- rnorm(100, 12, 1.37)
> materialCost<-round(materialCost, digits = 2)
```

c. Assign the per-unit price, the overhead cost, and the tailor's weekly wage to the corresponding variables. Enter:

```
> price <- 50
> overheadCost <- 800
> wageCost <- 700
```

d. Create a function called profitCalc that includes the formula for computing the profit value. Enter:

```
> profitCalc <- function(staffLvl, priceLvl, overhead, wage,
demandLvl, productionLvl, material)
{priceLvl * pmin(demandLvl, productionLvl * staffLvl) - overhead -
(wage * staffLvl) - (productionLvl * staffLvl * material)}
```

In the **function** statement, we list all the necessary arguments (staffLvl for staffing level, priceLvL for the selling price, and so forth) within the parentheses and define the profit formula within the curly brackets ({ }). Recall that the profit is calculated as revenue minus cost. To compute the revenue, we multiply the selling price by the number of jackets sold. Note that the number of jackets sold is the lower value between the demand and the number of jackets produced, and we use the **pmin** function to determine the number of jackets sold. The total cost is an aggregate of the overhead cost, the tailors' wages, and the material cost.

e. The **sapply** function applies the profitCalc formula defined in step d for each of the staffing levels (i.e., hiring 1–6 tailors) using each of the random observations for the demand, production rate, and material cost. The output is stored in the profitResults data frame. Enter:

```
> profitResults <- sapply(1:6, profitCalc, price, overheadCost,
wageCost, demand, productionRate, materialCost)
```

The first argument (1:6) in the **sapply** function represents the six scenarios for hiring one to six tailors. The second argument in the **sapply** function recalls the **profitCalc** function defined in step d. The remaining arguments apply the selling price, overhead and wage costs, product demand, production rate, and material cost to the **profitCalc** function based on the corresponding variables defined in steps b and c. Note that we list these arguments in the same order as the corresponding variables defined in step d. If we were to evaluate staffing levels between three and eight tailors, we would change the R statement to `profitResults <- sapply(3:8, profitCalc, price, overheadCost, wageCost, demand, productionRate, materialCost)`

f. To calculate and view the average profit and identify the minimum and maximum profits for each staffing level, use the **summary** function. Enter:

```
> summary(profitResults)
```

As shown in Figure 13.7, hiring 3 and 4 tailors are likely to generate the highest profit, with an average of $1,110.50 and $1,396.50, respectively. However, the range of profit values is larger in the four-tailor scenario.

FIGURE 13.7 Summary statistics

```
       V1                V2                V3               V4                V5                 V6
Min.     :-410.0   Min.   : -20.08   Min.   : 369.9   Min.   :-416.4   Min.   :-1658.0   Min.   :-2899.66
1st Qu.:-261.6     1st Qu.: 276.77   1st Qu.: 815.2   1st Qu.:1090.9   1st Qu.:  116.2   1st Qu.:-1020.04
Median :-181.9     Median : 436.20   Median :1041.2   Median :1418.6   Median :  551.9   Median : -562.78
Mean   :-160.5     Mean   : 479.01   Mean   :1110.5   Mean   :1396.5   Mean   :  598.0   Mean   : -516.98
3rd Qu.: -69.7     3rd Qu.: 660.60   3rd Qu.:1370.0   3rd Qu.:1678.3   3rd Qu.: 1179.2   3rd Qu.:   83.84
Max.   : 137.9     Max.   :1075.90   Max.   :2013.8   Max.   :2596.3   Max.   : 2281.4   Max.   : 1257.52
```

g. To calculate the standard deviation for the profits at each staffing level, we use the **sd** function. The following commands compute the standard deviation for the scenarios with 3 and 4 tailors; the standard deviations for the other staffing levels can be computed similarly. Enter:

```
> sd(profitResults[,3])
> sd(profitResults[,4])
```

The standard deviation for the three-tailor scenario is 380.7242, and the standard deviation for four tailors is 507.4703. This is consistent with our observation in step f that hiring four tailors yields a higher average profit but is also riskier than hiring three tailors.

h. To evaluate the possibility of increasing automation, we start by changing the overhead cost to $900 and the weekly wage of each tailor to $550. We also redraw random observations for the production rate variable using a uniform distribution between 36 and 41. Enter:

```
> set.seed(1)
> overheadCost <- 900
> wageCost <- 550
> productionRate <- sample(36:41, 100, replace = TRUE)
> productionRate<-round(productionRate, digits = 0)
```

i. Recalculate the profits using the **sapply** function and store the new output in the profitResultsAutomation data frame. Also, calculate the summary statistics by using the **summary** and **sd** functions. Enter:

```
> profitResultsAutomation <- sapply(1:6, profitCalc, price,
overheadCost, wageCost, demand, productionRate, materialCost)
> summary(profitResultsAutomation)
> sd(profitResultsAutomation[,3])
> sd(profitResultsAutomation[,4])
```

Figure 13.8 shows the new output from the summary function. In addition, the standard deviations for hiring three and four tailors are 255.2004 and 646.9132, respectively.

FIGURE 13.8 Summary statistics for increasing automation

```
       V1               V2               V3              V4               V5               V6
Min.   :-205.12   Min.   : 489.8   Min.   : 1185   Min.   : 242.1   Min.   : -809.9   Min.   :-1861.88
1st Qu.: -31.99   1st Qu.: 836.0   1st Qu.: 1704   1st Qu.: 1548.1   1st Qu.: 529.1   1st Qu.: -507.67
Median :  14.10   Median : 928.2   Median : 1842   Median : 2044.5   Median : 1021.0   Median :  -21.06
Mean   :  15.34   Mean   : 930.7   Mean   : 1842   Mean   : 2024.4   Mean   : 1059.2   Mean   :   45.06
3rd Qu.:  74.30   3rd Qu.: 1048.6   3rd Qu.: 2023   3rd Qu.: 2590.5   3rd Qu.: 1626.7   3rd Qu.:  640.75
Max.   : 228.40   Max.   : 1356.8   Max.   : 2485   Max.   : 3255.2   Max.   : 2753.4   Max.   : 1884.08
```

Additional discussion of the results is presented in the synopsis of the introductory case.

SYNOPSIS OF INTRODUCTORY CASE

Izf/Shutterstock

Abigail Kwan develops an analytical model to analyze the demand and production information for a red pullover jacket for women, the top-selling product for FashionTech. She obtains relevant demand and cost information from her corporate database. After reviewing the Monte Carlo simulation results, Abigail determines that hiring three or four tailors per week would likely be the best scenarios for FashionTech to generate a higher average weekly profit for the pullover jacket than at other staffing levels. On average, hiring four tailors would generate the highest profit, but it also poses a higher risk than hiring fewer tailors. With hiring three tailors per week, the average profit is slightly lower, but it is less risky with a narrower range of possible profits and a smaller standard deviation.

Abigail also evaluates the simulation results where additional automation is implemented. Being able to hire less-skilled tailors would reduce the labor cost, and the added automation would help decrease the variability in the production rate. With these potential benefits, the three-tailor scenario becomes much more viable as the average profit is now much closer to the average profit in the four-tailor scenario, but with much less variability. However, this plan would also incur a one-time installation and training cost for the added automation, which will be determined through a request for proposals (RFP) from potential vendors. At her next meeting with the company owner, Abigail plans to recommend that FashionTech move forward with the RFP process.

EXERCISES 13.2

For exercises in this section, set the random seed at 1 for the *Random Number Generation* feature in Excel's Analysis ToolPak. In R, use the statement **set.seed(1).** This ensures consistency of the results.

Mechanics

1. Use Excel's Analysis ToolPak or R, both with a seed of 1, to simulate 25 random observations based on a binomial distribution with five trials and $p = 0.2$. What are the mean and standard deviation of the 25 observations?

2. Use Excel's Analysis ToolPak or R, both with a seed of 1, to simulate 50 random observations based on a continuous uniform distribution over the interval [23, 37]. What is the range of simulated observations?
3. Use Excel's Analysis ToolPak or R, both with a seed of 1, to simulate 200 random observations based on a Poisson distribution with $\lambda = 2$. What are the mean and standard deviation of the 200 observations?
4. Use Excel's Analysis ToolPak or R, both with a seed of 1, to simulate 120 random observations of a continuous uniform random variable over the interval [10, 75]. What are the mean, the standard deviation, and the range of the 120 observations? How many observations are greater than 65?
5. Use Excel's Analysis ToolPak or R, both with a seed of 1, to simulate 1,000 random observations of a normally distributed random variable with $\mu = 9.23$ and $\sigma = 0.87$. Report the mean and standard deviation of the 1,000 observations. How many of the 1,000 observations have a value less than 8?

Applications

6. A manager at a local grocery store learns that 75% of her customers will use a credit card when making a purchase. Use Excel's Analysis ToolPak or R, both with a seed of 1, to simulate a sample of 12 customers waiting in line at the grocery store to make a purchase and repeat the simulation 500 times. Based on the 500 simulations, report the average number of customers who use a credit card to make a purchase. What is the range of the number of customers using a credit card?
7. On a given day, about 85% of Internet users in the U.S. visit a social media site. Use Analysis ToolPak or R, both with a seed of 1, to generate 100 simulations of a sample of 10 Internet users and report the mean and the standard deviation of the number of users in the sample who visit a social media site.
8. At a highly selective 4-year college, only 25% of transfer students go on to graduate on time. Use Analysis ToolPak or R, both with a seed of 1, to generate 400 simulations where each simulation contains a group of 10 transfer students. Report the mean, the standard deviation, and the range of the number of transfer students with on-time graduation.
9. A local grocery store observes that on average 4 customers enter the store every 5 minutes during the hour between 5:30 pm and 6:30 pm each day. Use Analysis ToolPak or R, both with a seed of 1, to generate a simulation for a period of 50 days. Report the mean and the standard deviation from the 50 simulations.
10. Monthly demand for a 60" TV at a local appliance store is normally distributed with a mean of 11 units and standard deviation of 4.17 units. Use Analysis ToolPak or R, both with a seed of 1, to develop a simulation for 300 months and report the mean and the range of the demand for the TV.
11. Peter plans to invest $25,000 in a mutual fund whose annual returns are normally distributed with a mean of 7.4% and standard deviation of 2.65%. Use Analysis ToolPak or R, both with a seed of 1, to generate 100 trials to estimate the return on Peter's investment after one year. What are the mean and the range of the investment returns?
12. Every Saturday morning between 9:00 am and 10:00 am, customers, on average, arrive at a local coffee shop every 1.2 minutes, and the customer arrival follows an exponential distribution. Use Analysis ToolPak or R, both with a seed of 1, to generate 500 trials to simulate the time between customer arrivals and report the sample mean and the standard deviation. Repeat the simulation with 1,000 trials and compare the new sample mean and the standard deviation with the theoretical values.
13. On average, a smartphone battery lasts about 6.5 hours with normal usage. The smartphone battery life follows an exponential distribution. Use Analysis ToolPak or R, both with a seed of 1, to generate 50 smartphone battery life simulations, and report the sample mean and the standard deviation. If the number of simulations is increased to 500, compare the sample mean and the standard deviation to the theoretical values.
14. A manufacturer of a smartphone battery estimates that monthly demand follows a normal distribution with a mean of 400 units and standard deviation of 26. Material cost is uniformly distributed between $7.00 and $8.50. Fixed costs are $2,700 per month, regardless of the production rate. The selling price is $15 per unit.
    a. Use Analysis ToolPak or R, both with a seed of 1, to simulate 1,000 trials to estimate the expected monthly profit and standard deviation. Demand values need to be rounded to integers, and use two decimal places for the material cost.
    b. What are the best and worst profit scenarios for the company?
15. Peter has $30,000 to invest in a mutual fund whose annual returns are normally distributed with a mean of 5% and standard deviation of 4.2%.
    a. Use Analysis ToolPak or R, both with a seed of 1, to simulate 5,000 trials to estimate the mean balance after one year.
    b. What is the probability of a balance of $32,000 or more?
    c. Compare your results to another investment option at a fixed annual return of 3% per year.
16. Each week, a grocery store purchases eggs from a local ranch for $1.99 for each 12-egg carton and sells it for $3.89. Any cartons not sold within a week will be on "manager's special" sales or sold to a low-cost outlet for $1.25. If the eggs sell out before the end of the week, an estimated opportunity cost of not meeting demand is $1.75 per carton. The demand distribution is normally distributed with a mean of 75 cartons and a standard deviation of 12.5 cartons. Use Analysis ToolPak or R, both with a seed of 1, to develop a Monte Carlo simulation for 500 weeks to answer parts a and b.

a. If the store has been ordering exactly 75 cartons per week from the rancher, what are the likelihood and opportunity cost of not meeting the weekly demand?
b. If the store increases the weekly order to 85 cartons, what is the estimated cost of having too many eggs in store?

17. A local coffee shop observes that, on average, four customers enter the store every 5 minutes during the rush hour between 6:30 am and 7:30 am each day. The number of customers arriving at the coffee shop follows a Poisson distribution. Each barista can serve 2 or 3 customers every 8 minutes, a pattern that follows a uniform distribution. The shop owner staffs her coffee shop with two baristas. During the rush hour in the morning, customers are in a hurry to get to work or school and will balk when there is a line. The opportunity cost when a customer balks is \$4.25 per customer. The profit generated from each customer is normally distributed with a mean of \$6.50 and standard deviation of \$2.37. Each barista is paid \$20 per hour.
    a. Use Analysis ToolPak or R, both with a seed of 1, to develop a Monte Carlo simulation with 500 trials to examine the current staffing level and report the average profit or loss during the rush hour.
    b. If the owner hires a third barista, what is the impact of the new hire on the profit?

18. Hoping to increase its sales, a pizzeria wants to start a new marketing campaign promising its customers that if their order does not get delivered within an hour, the pizzas are free. Historically, the probability of on-time pizza delivery follows a binomial distribution with $n = 50$ and $p = 0.88$. The order amount follows a normal distribution with a mean of \$35 and a standard deviation of \$11.
    a. Use Analysis ToolPak or R, both with a seed of 1, to simulate 1,000 pizza orders. What is the average loss of revenue based on the 1,000 simulations?
    b. In order to break even, how many new orders does the marketing campaign need to generate?

19. An investor wants to invest \$300,000 in a portfolio of three mutual funds. The annual fund returns are normally distributed with a mean of 2.00% and standard deviation of 0.30% for the short-term investment fund, a mean of 5.00% and standard deviation of 2.50% for the intermediate-term fund, and a mean of 6.25% and standard deviation of 5.50% for the long-term fund. An initial plan for the investment allocation is 45% in the short-term fund, 35% in the intermediate-term fund, and 20% in the long-term fund.
    a. Use Analysis ToolPak or R, both with a seed of 1, to simulate 100 trials to estimate the mean ending balance after the first year and assess the risk of this investment.
    b. If the allocation is changed to 30% short-term, 55% intermediate-term, and 15% long-term, estimate the ending balance after the first year and the risk of the investment.

20. At a local appliance store, weekly demand for a large screen TV during the week prior to the Super Bowl is normally distributed with a mean of 35 units and standard deviation of 12 units. The store usually keeps 40 units in its inventory. Use Analysis ToolPak or R, both with a seed of 1, to simulate 500 trials to estimate the likelihood of overstocking and understocking.

21. Following an exponential distribution, the average lifespan of a smartphone battery is 2.3 years. The battery manufacturer wants to offer a warranty for its customers to receive a free replacement if the battery fails during the first year. Each battery generates a profit of \$10.85, and the replacement cost is \$6.35. Develop a Monte Carlo simulation using Analysis ToolPak or R, both with a seed of 1, for 100 battery units sold.
    a. What is the expected total cost of this warranty program?
    b. In order to cover the cost of the warranty program, how many additional battery units does the company need to sell?

22. An amusement park has a roller coaster that can accommodate up to 45 park goers per ride, and each ride lasts about 20 minutes. For each hour, the park gives out 200 tickets for the ride, and on average, only 60% of the ticket holders come to ride on the roller coaster. The number of roller coaster riders follows a normal distribution with a mean of 120 riders per hour and standard deviation of 35 riders. Develop a Monte Carlo simulation using Analysis ToolPak or R, both with a seed of 1, of 400 trials. What is the average number of riders unable to get on the roller coaster?

13.3 OPTIMIZATION WITH LINEAR PROGRAMMING

LO 13.3

Formulate a linear programming model.

Optimization is a family of quantitative techniques where an objective function is maximized or minimized for obtaining optimal solutions to complex business problems. We usually start by clearly defining a business objective. For example, the objective may be to maximize profits or to minimize costs subject to resource constraints, such as a fixed amount of available materials, limited financial resources, and a finite amount of time.

Linear programming (LP), a subset of the optimization techniques, is one of the simplest ways to perform optimization. By making a few simplifying assumptions, such as linear relationships among relevant variables, it helps in solving some very complex optimization problems. The LP technique is widely used, and common LP applications include developing a mix of financial investment options, choosing a combination of products to manufacture, and minimizing the delivery cost for shipping products and packages.

This section discusses a class of LP problems where optimal solutions can take on fractional values. Section 13.4 discusses the linear integer programming technique where optimal solutions are integers. Other optimization techniques where nonlinear relationships exist among relevant variables are beyond the scope of this text.

> **OPTIMIZATION AND LINEAR PROGRAMMING**
>
> Optimization: A family of quantitative techniques for obtaining optimal solutions to complex problems with resource constraints.
>
> Linear programming (LP): A simple way to perform optimization by assuming linear relationships among relevant variables.

The first step in performing LP is to formulate a problem into a series of mathematical expressions. Naturally, different applications require different formulations, but regardless of the context, the mathematical representation of most LP problems has four essential components: an objective function, decision variables, constraints, and parameters.

In any optimization problem, a single objective with a mathematical representation is referred to as the **objective function**. In LP, the objective function is assumed to be linear. Two general types of an objective function are a maximization function (e.g., for profit, revenue, or the return on investment) or a minimization function (e.g., for manufacturing cost, the amount of time to complete a project, or the distance traveled to complete a delivery).

Decision variables refer to the different choices or alternatives from which a decision maker has to choose, in order to maximize or minimize the value of the objective function. For example, an investor might choose from several stocks or bonds to maximize the potential return on investment. Similarly, a manager might choose from several production inputs to minimize manufacturing cost.

An LP optimization problem includes a number of **constraints** or limitations within which a decision maker needs to operate. These constraints represent the limited resources available to the decision maker. Examples of constraints include a fixed amount of money an investor contributes toward retirement, a limited amount of raw materials a manufacturer can procure each month, or a certain number of hours a delivery truck driver is available to work.

Sometimes, a constraint also reflects the knowledge gained from historical data or human expertise. For example, a retail store owner might learn from experience that there is a limit to the demand for certain products in the local market and maintains the quantity of products in the retail store accordingly. Other constraints are based on intuitive assumptions about the nature of the LP problem. When a manufacturer decides how many units of products to produce or when an investor decides how much money to invest in each financial asset, the units to produce and the amount of investment are assumed to be non-negative.

Finally, **parameters** (or input parameters) are numerical values associated with the objective function, decision variables, and constraints. For example, a delivery truck driver in the United States can only work up to 14 consecutive hours within a 24-hour period, and, therefore, the value 14 is the parameter value for the working hour constraint. For other LP problems, parameter values might be derived from historical data (e.g., the amount of time and raw materials needed to manufacture a product might be obtained from the manufacturing data from the previous month). The input parameters usually remain constant and do not change when the solution to the LP problem is implemented, unless there are significant changes to the external factors surrounding the LP problem (e.g., changes in the manufacturing process).

FOUR COMPONENTS OF LINEAR PROGRAMMING

Objective function: A mathematical representation of an objective, usually expressed as a maximization or minimization function of a single variable such as profit or cost.

Decision variables: Choices or alternatives available for a decision maker to choose, in order to maximize or minimize the value of the objective function.

Constraints: Limitations within which a decision maker needs to operate that usually represent the limited resources available to the decision makers.

Parameters: Numerical values in the LP mathematical expression associated with the objective function, the decision variables, and the constraints.

Formulating a Linear Programming Model

In Example 13.4 and Example 13.5 we show how to specify a maximization function and a minimization function, respectively, given various constraints.

EXAMPLE 13.4

Gordana Sermek/ Shutterstock

After obtaining useful results and actionable insights from the Monte Carlo simulation, Abigail Kwan wants to continue using prescriptive analytics to solve other business problems for FashionTech. One of the difficult decisions that she has to make every winter season is deciding how many parkas and winter jackets for women to produce. Both products use the same materials and require very similar sewing and stitching skills and manufacturing steps, and, therefore, compete for the same resources. The main difference between the two products is the length—jackets are generally shorter and end at the waist or just below, while parkas are longer fitting, and therefore offer more warmth. Due to their length, parkas have a higher manufacturing cost, but also have a higher selling price and generate a greater profit per unit.

Jackets and parkas come in different sizes, but the most popular ones are the medium size. Abigail will start by focusing on analyzing data for the medium-sized jackets and parkas. Based on her records, the per-unit profits for a winter jacket and parka are \$9 and \$12.50, respectively. Also, a medium-sized jacket requires approximately 8.5 feet of fabric, while a medium-sized parka requires about 12.5 feet of the same fabric. The amount of machine time needed to produce a jacket and a parka are 1.5 hours and 2 hours, respectively. A tailor usually spends about 2 hours on sewing and stitching for a winter jacket and about 3 hours for a parka.

FashionTech has a monthly contract with its supplier to procure 4,000 feet of the required fabric. The amount of machine time allocated to producing the two products is 650 hours per month, and each month a number of skilled tailors are assigned to these products for approximately 900 hours. Historically, FashionTech has never sold more than 150 parkas or 400 jackets in a month, and, therefore, Abigail wants to make sure that the monthly production rates of parkas and winter jackets are no more than these historical limits. Use the information provided to help Abigail formulate this problem into an LP model.

SOLUTION: The objective of this analysis is to find a solution that maximizes the profit contribution from producing and selling the medium-sized jackets and parkas. The two decision variables are the number of winter jackets and parkas to produce. The objective function for this LP model can be formulated as follows.

$$\textit{Maximize:} \qquad \textit{Profit} = 9x_1 + 12.5x_2,$$

where x_1 and x_2 are the decision variables that represent the number of jackets and parkas produced, respectively. For tractability, we assume that the quantity produced and the quantity sold are the same. Note that the per-unit profits, \$9 and \$12.50, are the parameter values. The parameter values in the objective function are also referred to as the objective function coefficients.

Furthermore, FashionTech needs to operate within the five constraints mentioned in the problem description: the amount of fabric available from the supplier, the limited machine time, the number of hours the skilled tailors are assigned to the two products, and the historical demand for parkas and winter jackets. The five constraints and their corresponding parameters can be formulated as follows.

$$\begin{array}{ll} \textit{Fabric:} & 8.5x_1 + 12.5x_2 \le 4{,}000 \\ \textit{Machine time:} & 1.5x_1 + 2x_2 \le 650 \\ \textit{Labor:} & 2x_1 + 3x_2 \le 900 \\ \textit{Demand for jackets:} & x_1 \le 400 \\ \textit{Demand for parkas:} & x_2 \le 150 \end{array}$$

A maximization LP model usually has at least one constraint with the $\le$ sign, which reflects the fact that a decision maker needs to operate within these limitations. In addition to the five constraints, the number of winter jackets and parkas are non-negative. Consequently, we add the last constraint to the LP formulation.

$$\textit{Non-negativity:} \qquad x_1, x_2 \ge 0$$

As mentioned earlier, another type of linear programming problem is to minimize the value of the objective function. In these cases, the objective function would be formulated in a similar fashion as in Example 13.4, but we would instead aim to minimize its value. In addition, the constraints in the minimization problem are usually formulated to describe minimum requirements that need to be met. For example, a shipping company may want to minimize the total delivery cost of packages (i.e., the objective function) while making sure that at least a certain number of customers will receive their packages on a given day (e.g., each delivery truck driver must deliver at least 35 packages a day). As such, a minimization LP model usually has at least one constraint with the $\ge$ sign. Example 13.5 demonstrates how to formulate a minimization LP problem.

EXAMPLE 13.5

Yerba Buena Tea is a manufacturer and wholesaler of high-quality tea products. Spiced chai is becoming increasingly popular among younger consumers, and Yerba Buena offers two chai products: spiced chai powder mix and spiced chai tea concentrate. An older production facility costs \$190 per hour to operate and, for each hour of operation, can produce 295 ounces of the powder mix and 260 ounces of the tea concentrate.

JulijaDmitrijeva/Shutterstock

Because of its age, the old facility cannot operate longer than 8 consecutive hours at a time. A newer facility costs $260 per hour to operate and produces 385 ounces of the powder mix and 375 ounces of the tea concentrate per hour. Yerba Buena also owns a small, single-purpose facility that costs $150 per hour to operate and produces 350 ounces of the powder mix per hour. Several coffee shops have placed orders for a total of 5,500 ounces of the chai powder mix and 4,000 ounces of the tea concentrate.

Anika Patel, the general manager at Yerba Buena, has none of the two products left in inventory and needs to decide how many hours to operate each facility to fulfill the orders while minimizing the production cost. Formulate this problem into an LP model for Yerba Buena.

SOLUTION: The objective for Yerba Buena is to minimize the production cost while being able to fulfill the orders. The objective function represents the total cost of operating the three production facilities and can be formulated as follows.

Minimize: *Production cost* $= 190x_1 + 260x_2 + 150x_3$

Subject to:

Orders for powder mix:	$295x_1 + 385x_2 + 350x_3 \geq 5{,}500$
Orders for tea concentrate:	$260x_1 + 375x_2 \geq 4{,}000$
Old facility operating hours:	$x_1 \leq 8$
Non-negativity:	$x_1, x_2, x_3 \geq 0$,

where x_1, x_2 and x_3 represent the number of hours to operate the three facilities, which are the decision variables. The first two constraints in the LP formulation represent the order amounts for the chai powder mix and tea concentrate with the corresponding parameters. The third constraint indicates that the old facility cannot operate longer than 8 hours. Following a similar assumption in Example 13.4, we include the last three non-negativity constraints in the LP formulation.

In the next subsection, we demonstrate how to solve the LP model and obtain the optimal solution to help a decision maker, such as Abigail Kwan at FashionTech or Anika Patel at Yerba Buena Tea, make an informed business decision.

Solving a Linear Programming Problem

LO 13.4

Solve and interpret a linear programming model.

In this chapter, we solve linear programming problems using Excel and R. However, to gain an understanding of a linear programming technique, we first demonstrate how to solve an LP problem with two decision variables through graphical representation. Given the linearity of the objective function as well as the constraints, we can plot the mathematical expressions in a line chart and identify possible solutions that satisfy the constraints. Consider the FashionTech example where Abigail Kwan tries to decide how many winter jackets and parkas to produce. The mathematical expression for the objective function and constraints can all be presented graphically in a line chart. To find an optimal solution to the LP model, we identify the values of the decision variables, in this case x_1 and x_2, that maximize the profit while satisfying all of the constraints. In the Yerba Buena case, we find the values of the decision variables, x_1, x_2, and x_3, that minimize the production cost subject to the constraints.

We will illustrate the graphical approach with the FashionTech example. We start by plotting the machine time and the two demand constraints. Recall that x_1 and x_2 denote the number of jackets and parkas produced, respectively. The orange line in Figure 13.9 represents the machine time constraint, $1.5x_1 + 2x_2 \leq 650$. Note that x_1

reaches a maximum value of 433.33 (= 650/1.5) when $x_2 = 0$, and x_2 reaches a maximum value of 325.00 (= 650/2) when $x_1 = 0$. These values provide the coordinates for the line representing the machine time constraint. Furthermore, because the machine time constraint is an inequality with the ≤ sign, the area under the orange line represents the values of x_1 and x_2 that satisfy this constraint. We also plot the demand limits for x_1 and x_2 as two dotted purple lines. Similar to the machine time constraint, the two demand constraints, $x_1 \leq 400$ and $x_2 \leq 150$ have the ≤ sign, and, therefore, the area to the left of the vertical dotted line and the area under the horizontal dotted line represent the values of x_1 and x_2 that satisfy the constraints. Recall also that x_1 and x_2 must be non-negative, and, therefore, we only consider the first quadrant of x_1 and x_2. The shaded area in Figure 13.9 represents the values of x_1 and x_2 that satisfy the machine time constraint and the two demand constraints.

FIGURE 13.9 Graphical representation of the machine time constraint for FashionTech

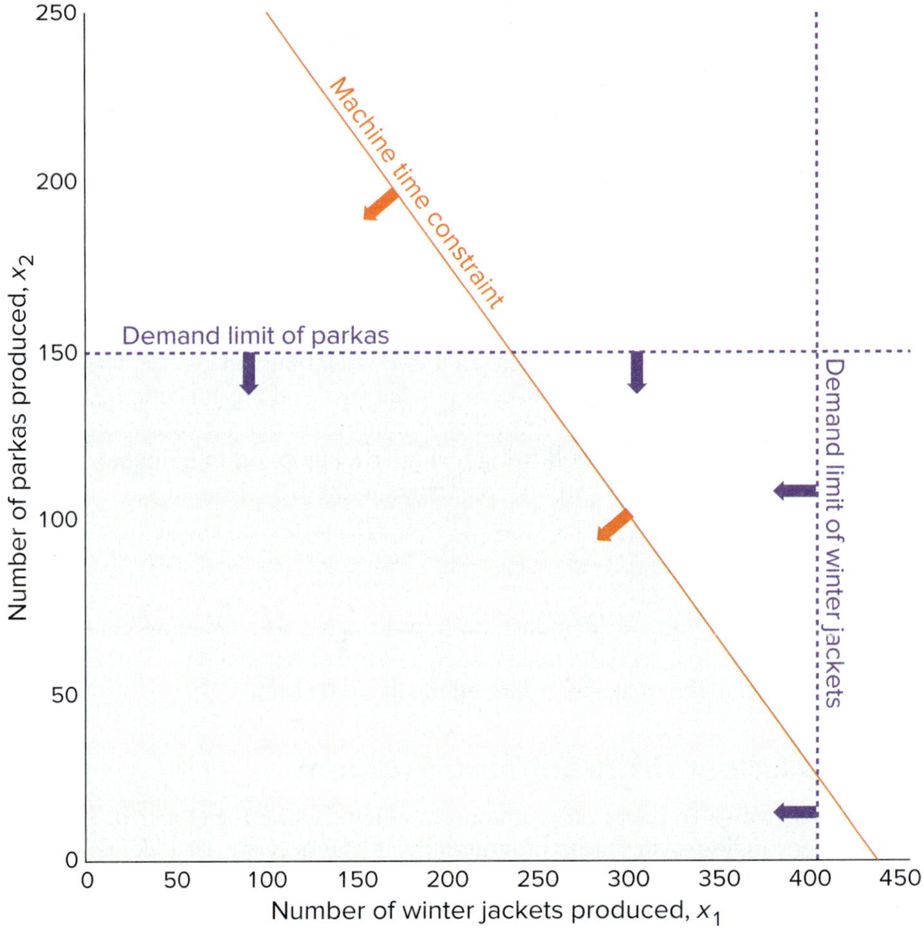

The other two constraints for fabric and labor as well as the objective function can also be plotted in a similar fashion. Figure 13.10 shows a line chart, and the resulting shaded area represents the values of x_1 and x_2 that satisfy all five constraints. This shaded area is referred to as the feasibility region of the LP model. Because we do not yet know the maximum profit we can achieve, we start by superimposing three black solid lines representing the objective function at a profit value of \$500, \$1,500, and \$2,500. As we increase the profit, the line shifts further to the right-hand side of the chart. Note that at a profit value of \$2,500, part of the profit line already falls outside of the feasibility region. The values of x_1 and x_2 outside of the feasibility region cannot be considered in the LP solution as they violate at least one of the constraints (e.g., the number of parkas cannot exceed 150). Conversely, any part of the profit line that stays within the feasibility region satisfies all of the constraints, and the corresponding values of x_1 and x_2 are possible candidates for a solution to the LP problem.

In order to maximize the profit while satisfying all the constraints, we continue to increase the profit as long as part of the profit line remains within the feasibility region. Normally, an optimal solution to an LP model can be found at the boundary or at a corner of the feasibility region. In this example, if we continue to shift the profit line further to the right-hand side of the chart, we will find that an optimal solution is where $x_1 = 300$ and $x_2 = 100$ (see the dotted black lines in Figure 13.10). At these optimal values, we calculate the maximum profit as \$3,950 (= 9 × 300 + 12.5 × 100), as shown in black dotted lines.

FIGURE 13.10 Graphical representation of the LP model for FashionTech

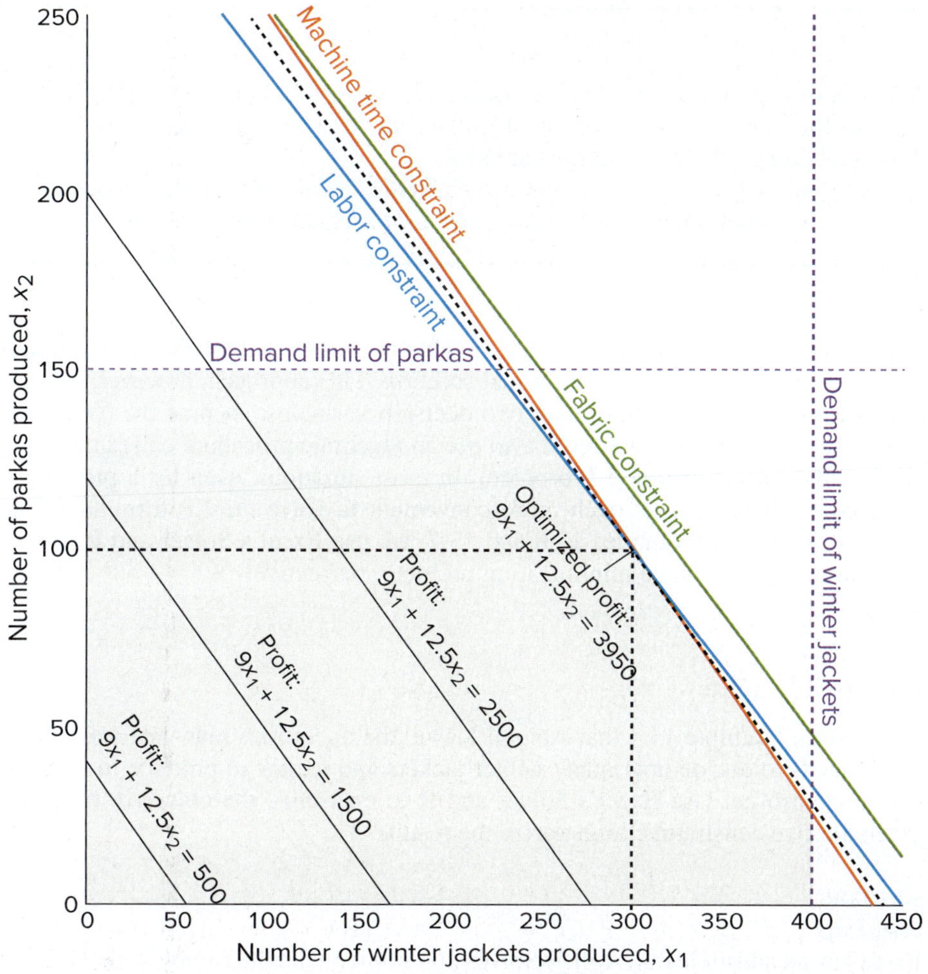

Note that at the optimal solution of 300 winter jackets and 100 parkas, FashionTech would have used only 3,800 (= 8.5 × 300 + 12.5 × 100) of the 4,000 feet of fabric available from the supplier. The remaining 200 feet of fabric is called "slack," indicating an excess supply that can be used for other products; FashionTech could also renegotiate with its supplier to order less fabric per month. For a minimization problem, this would be called "surplus," instead of slack.

Constraints with slack or surplus in the LP solution are called **nonbinding** constraints. Adding or reducing the nonbinding constraint value by one unit (i.e., increasing the amount of available fabric to 4,001 feet) will not change the LP solution. At the optimized values, however, FashionTech will have used all of the allotted machine time (650 hours) and labor (900 hours), so there is no slack in these two resources. As a result, the machine time and labor are called **binding** constraints. Increasing or decreasing the available resource of a binding constraint will impact the LP solution and, in most cases, the optimized value of the objective function.

Another important concept related to LP is that of a **shadow price**, also referred to as a **dual price**, of a constraint. It indicates the change in the optimized value of an objective function due to a 1-unit change in a binding constraint, holding the other parameters constant. In the FashionTech example, it can be shown that reducing the available machine time by one hour (i.e., from 650 to 649 hours) would cause the optimized profit to decrease from \$3,950 to \$3,946, making the shadow price of the machine time \$4. Note that the optimized value of an objective function will not change due to a 1-unit change in a nonbinding constraint.

CONSTRAINTS IN A LINEAR PROGRAMMING PROBLEM

A constraint in an LP problem is considered to be binding if changing it also changes the optimized value of the objective function. Nonbinding constraints are those that do not affect the optimized value.

The shadow price of a constraint measures the change in the optimized value of the objective function when a binding constraint is changed by one unit.

With only two decision variables, we are able to plot the LP formulation onto a two-dimensional line chart and find an optimal solution. This approach, however, is not suitable for LP problems with more than two decision variables, such as the Yerba Buena Tea example. Conceptually, we could also use an algebraic procedure called the Simplex method to manually solve the LP problem. In most situations, even for a problem with two decision variables, it is much more convenient to solve the LP formulation using computer software. In Examples 13.6 and 13.7, we use Excel's Solver and R to solve a maximization problem and a minimization problem, respectively.

EXAMPLE 13.6

Recall from Example 13.4 that Abigail Kwan, the operations manager at FashionTech, needs to decide how many winter jackets and parkas to produce in order to maximize profits. Use Excel's Solver and R to maximize the objective function, given the five constraints. Summarize the results.

SOLUTION:

Using Excel

FILE
Parkas

Excel has an add-in feature called Solver that implements the Simplex method and performs necessary computations to solve LP problems. There are many ways to structure an Excel spreadsheet for an LP problem. For consistency, we will use the ***Parkas*** worksheet as a template to demonstrate how to use Solver. Similar to the Monte Carlo simulation example, creating an Excel worksheet with input parameters in separate cells, as in the ***Parkas*** worksheet, will allow us to easily change the parameter values in the LP model and evaluate alternative scenarios.

a. Open the ***Parkas*** worksheet and make sure *Solver* is activated by going to **File > Options > Add-ins > Go** (next to Manage Excel Add-ins). Check the *Solver* checkbox and click **OK**. Verify that a button labeled **Solver** is in the **Analyze** group under the **Data** tab.

b. Navigate to the Parameters section of the ***Parkas*** worksheet and, in cells B5 through B8, enter the values 8.5, 1.5, 2, and 9, which correspond to the amount of fabric, the machine time, the amount of labor, and the per-unit profit that are associated with the production of one winter jacket. In cells C5 through C8, enter the corresponding values for the production of one parka.

c. Enter the amount of fabric available to FashionTech each month (4,000 feet) in cell D14 and enter the remaining applicable information in cells D15 through D19. Your ***Parkas*** worksheet should look similar to Figure 13.11.

FIGURE 13.11 Excel template for Example 13.6

	A	B	C	D	E
1	**FashionTech**				
2					
3		Products			Objective function (profit maximization):
4	Parameters:	Jackets	Parkas		
5	Fabric (feet/unit)	8.5	12.5		
6	Machine time (hours/unit)	1.5	2		
7	Labor (hours/unit)	2	3		
8	Per-unit profit	$9.00	$ 12.50		
9					
10		Jackets	Parkas		
11	Decision variables (units to produce):				
12					
13	Constraints:	Quantity used		Quantity available	
14	Fabric (feet)		<=	4000	
15	Machine time (hours)		<=	650	
16	Labor (hours)		<=	900	
17		Units produced		Demand	
18	Number of jackets		<=	400	
19	Number of parkas		<=	150	

Source: Microsoft Excel

d. We use cell E4 to represent the objective function and cells B11 and C11 to represent the two decision variables: the number of winter jackets and parkas that FashionTech should produce. To formulate the objective function from Example 13.4, enter =SUMPRODUCT(B8:C8, B11:C11) in cell E4. Note that the SUMPRODUCT formula is equivalent to inputting =B8*B11+C8*C11. Verify that the profit calculation is correct by entering 1 in cells B11 and C11. Cell E4 should display a profit of \$21.50 $(= 9 \times 1 + 12.50 \times 1)$.

e. Enter =SUMPRODUCT(B5:C5, B11:C11) in cell B14 to calculate the amount of fabric used; =SUMPRODUCT(B6:C6, B11:C11) in cell B15 for the total machine time; and =SUMPRODUCT(B7:C7, B11:C11) in cell B16 for the total number of hours the tailors will spend making the jackets and parkas each month.

f. Enter =B11 and =C11 in cells B18 and B19, respectively, to replicate the numbers of winter jackets and parkas to be produced. Your ***Parkas*** worksheet should now look similar to Figure 13.12.

FIGURE 13.12 Completed Excel template for Example 13.6

	A	B	C	D	E
1	**FashionTech**				
2					
3		Products			Objective function (profit maximization):
4	Parameters:	Jackets	Parkas		**$21.50**
5	Fabric (feet/unit)	8.5	12.5		
6	Machine time (hours/unit)	1.5	2		
7	Labor (hours/unit)	2	3		
8	Per-unit profit	$9.00	$ 12.50		
9					
10		Jackets	Parkas		
11	Decision variables (units to produce):	1	1		
12					
13	Constraints:	Quantity used		Quantity available	
14	Machine time (hours)	3.5	<=	650	
15	Labor (hours)	5	<=	900	
16	Fabric (feet)	21	<=	4000	
17		Units produced		Demand	
18	Number of jackets	1	<=	400	
19	Number of parkas	1	<=	150	

Source: Microsoft Excel

g. Launch Solver by navigating to the **Data** tab and click the **Solver** button in the Analyze group.

h. In the Solver Parameters dialog box, enter E4 for the *Set Objective* box. Make sure to choose the *Max* option to maximize the profit value in cell E4.

i. Enter B11:C11 in the *By Changing Variable Cells* box. Recall that these two cells represent the decision variables.

j. Click the *Add* button to add the constraints for the amount of fabric, total machine time, and labor available to FashionTech. In the *Change Constraint* dialog box, enter B14:B16 for *Cell Reference,* choose <= from the drop-down list of operators, and enter D14:D16 for the *Constraint* option; see Figure 13.13. Click *Add.*

FIGURE 13.13 Adding the constraints in Excel's Solver

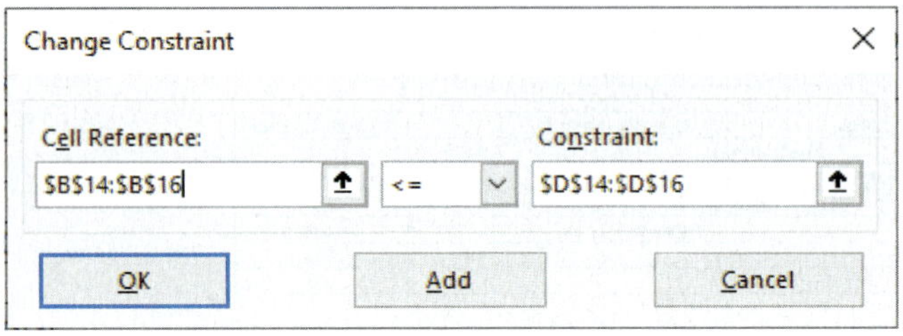

Source: Microsoft Excel

k. Click the *Add* button again, and in the next *Change Constraint* dialog box, enter B18:B19 in the *Cell Reference* box for the demand constraints, choose the <= option, and enter "D18:D19" for the *Constraint* option. Click **OK**.

l. Make sure the option *Make Unconstrained Variables Non-Negative* is checked to enforce the non-negativity constraints. For the *Select a Solving Method* option, choose *Simplex LP.* Your Solver dialog box should look similar to Figure 13.14. Click *Solve.*

FIGURE 13.14 Solver Parameters

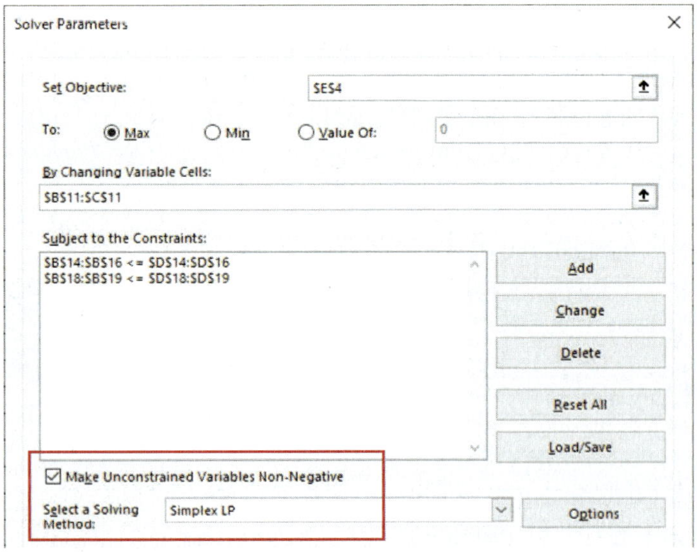

Source: Microsoft Excel

m. In the *Solver Results* dialog box, click the *Answer* and *Sensitivity* options under the *Reports* section and then click *OK.* The solution to the LP model is shown in Figure 13.15. Solver will also create two new worksheets labeled Answer Report 1 and Sensitivity Report 1. [The actual worksheet number might be different.]

FIGURE 13.15 Solver optimal LP solution

	A	B	C	D	E
1	**FashionTech**				
2					
3		Products			Objective function (profit maximization):
4	Parameters:	Jackets	Parkas		**$3,950.00**
5	Fabric (feet/unit)	8.5	12.5		
6	Machine time (hours/unit)	1.5	2		
7	Labor (hours/unit)	2	3		
8	Per-unit profit	$9.00	$ 12.50		
9					
10		Jackets	Parkas		
11	Decision variables (units to produce):	300	100		
12					
13	Constraints:	Quantity used		Quantity available	
14	Machine time (hours)	650	<=	650	
15	Labor (hours)	900	<=	900	
16	Fabric (feet)	3800	<=	4000	
17		Units produced		Demand	
18	Number of jackets	300	<=	400	
19	Number of parkas	100	<=	150	

Source: Microsoft Excel

As shown in Figure 13.15, Solver indicates in cells B11 and C11 on the ***Parkas*** worksheet that FashionTech should produce 300 winter jackets and 100 parkas, well within the two demand constraints of 400 winter jackets and 150 parkas. Recall that this is the same solution found on the line chart in Figure 13.10. The maximum profit from this optimal solution is $3,950 as calculated in cell E4. It is important to note that for other LP problems, there may be multiple optimal solutions that maximize the objective function value.

Figure 13.16 shows a relevant portion of the Answer Report worksheet produced by Solver. As noted earlier, the amount of fabric is a nonbinding constraint because only 3,800 of the 4,000 feet of fabric are used, resulting in a slack of 200 feet. The machine time and labor are binding constraints because all of the allotted machine time (650 hours) and labor (900 hours) are used at the optimal values.

FIGURE 13.16 Excel's Solver Answer Report

Constraints

Cell	Name	Cell Value	Formula	Status	Slack
$B$14	Machine time (hours) Quantity used	650	$B$14<=$D$14	Binding	0
$B$15	Labor (hours) Quantity used	900	$B$15<=$D$15	Binding	0
$B$16	Fabric (feet) Quantity used	3800	$B$16<=$D$16	Not Binding	200
$B$18	Number of jackets Units produced	300	$B$18<=$D$18	Not Binding	100
$B$19	Number of parkas Units produced	100	$B$19<=$D$19	Not Binding	50

Source: Microsoft Excel

Relevant information from the *Sensitivity Report* worksheet is shown in Figure 13.17. The Variable Cells section describes the optimal LP solution where 300 jackets and 100 parkas are produced and sold at the per-unit profit of $9 and $12.50. Recall that the per-unit profits are called objective function coefficients. A change in these coefficients beyond the allowable increase or decrease (the last two columns in Figure 13.17) will cause the optimal LP solution to change. For example, if the per-unit profit of the winter jacket decreases by more than $0.6667, we would need to solve the LP model again to obtain a new solution; that is, producing 300 jackets and 100 parkas would no longer generate the maximum profit. Likewise, if the per-unit profit of a jacket increases by more than $0.3750, we will need to find a new LP solution. In such scenarios, we will need to replace the per-unit profits with the new values on the ***Parkas*** worksheet and rerun Solver to obtain a new solution. Any other changes smaller than the allowable amount would not alter the optimal solution, even though the actual profit amount will change. In other words, as long as the per-unit profit of the jackets falls between \$8.3333 and \$9.375 (or \$9 – \$0.6667 and \$9 + \$0.375), it will be optimal for FashionTech to continue to produce 300 jackets and 100 parkas per month, but the total profit will change depending on the per-unit value. This range of values between the allowable increase and decrease is referred to as the range of optimality; the optimal solution will remain the same as long as the objective function coefficient stays within this range. The range of optimality for the per-unit profit of the parkas is between \$12 and \$13.5 (or \$12.5 – \$0.5 and \$12.5 + \$1). The range of optimality is useful for business managers like Abigail Kwan at FashionTech who regularly make decisions about product discounts, sales, and marketing campaigns in relation to their manufacturing plan.

FIGURE 13.17 Solver's Sensitivity Report

Variable Cells

Cell	Name	Final Value	Reduced Cost	Objective Coefficient	Allowable Increase	Allowable Decrease
\$B\$11	Decision variables (units to produce): Jackets	300	0	9	0.375	0.666666667
\$C\$11	Decision variables (units to produce): Parkas	100	0	12.5	1	0.5

Constraints

Cell	Name	Final Value	Shadow Price	Constraint R.H. Side	Allowable Increase	Allowable Decrease
\$B\$14	Machine time (hours) Quantity used	650	4	650	16.66666667	12.5
\$B\$15	Labor (hours) Quantity used	900	1.5	900	16.66666667	25
\$B\$16	Fabric (feet) Quantity used	3800	0	4000	1E+30	200
\$B\$18	Number of jackets Units produced	300	0	400	1E+30	100
\$B\$19	Number of parkas Units produced	100	0	150	1E+30	50

Source: Microsoft Excel

The *Constraints* section of Figure 13.17 also shows the allowable increase and decrease for each constraint. Because the Fabric constraint is nonbinding, increasing the amount of fabric in the production process would not have any impact on the LP solution (the 1E+30 value implies that even an infinite increase in the amount of fabric would not alter the LP solution). The allowable decrease is simply the slack value, or the difference between the amount of Fabric available (4,000 feet) and the amount used (3,800 feet). Decreasing the amount of fabric below 3,800 feet per month will alter the LP solution. This is also the case for the two demand constraints at the bottom of Figure 13.17.

The shadow price column in Figure 13.17 is the change in the profit for each unitary change in the binding constraint within the allowable increase and decrease. For example, the shadow price of the machine time is \$4. This means that reducing the available machine time by one hour (from 650 to 649 hours) would cause the total profit to decrease from \$3,950 to \$3,946. In other words, a \$4 decrease in profit is the "price" the company will have to pay for not allocating the one hour of machine time to the production of jackets and parkas. We can verify this by entering 649 for the available machine time in cell D15 in the ***Parkas*** worksheet. Rerunning Solver would yield a new optimal solution of 294 winter jackets and 104 parkas in the decision variables (cells B11 and C11), and the new profit of \$3,946 in cell E4. Likewise, allocating one additional hour of machine time (i.e., from 650 to 651 hours) would increase the profit from \$3,950 to \$3,954 by producing 306 jackets and 96 parkas.

The shadow price remains constant only within the allowable increase and decrease. For the machine time, the shadow price stays at \$4 as long as the available machine time is between 637.5 (i.e., 650 – 12.5) and 666.67 (i.e., 650 + 16.67) hours. This range is called the range of feasibility, over which the shadow price remains unchanged. The labor constraint has a shadow price of \$1.50 with a range of feasibility between 875 and 916.67 hours.

In certain situations, the shadow price of a binding constraint could also be zero. The zero value of the shadow price of a binding constraint simply means that changing the available amount of resources within the allowable range will cause the LP solution to change, but the optimized objective function value (e.g., profit) will remain the same. The shadow price information is particularly useful for business managers like Abigail Kwan at FashionTech who have to regularly decide where to allocate additional resources. Intuitively, allocating additional resources to the constraint with the highest shadow price would yield the greatest financial return.

Using R

We use the *lpSolve* package in R to find an optional solution for the FashionTech example. Like Excel's Solver and many other linear programming software, the *lpSolve* package also implements the Simplex method. The optimal solution found by Excel's Solver and R for the LP examples in this chapter are identical. The answers may differ when an LP model has multiple optimal solutions, which we will not pursue in this chapter.

a. Install and load the *lpSolve* package. Enter:

```
> install.packages("lpSolve")
> library(lpSolve)
```

b. Specify the two objective function coefficients for the per-unit profits of winter jackets ($9) and parkas ($12.5). Enter:

```
> lp.objective <- c(9, 12.5)
```

c. Store the parameters from the left-hand side of the five constraints in a matrix using the **matrix** command. Each constraint has two left-hand side parameters, which are specified in pairs. Enter:

```
> lp.constraints <- matrix(c(8.5, 12.5, 1.5, 2, 2, 3, 1, 0, 0, 1),
nrow=5, byrow=TRUE)
```

Recall that the first pair of parameters, 8.5 and 12.5, are the amount of fabric required to produce one winter jacket and one parka; the second pair, 1.5 and 2, are the amounts of machine time needed for one winter jacket and one parka, and so forth. It is important to note that the *lpSolve* package requires that we specify the parameter values for all of the decision variables (x_1 and x_2 in this case), even for decision variables that may not appear in a constraint. For example, for the demand constraint for jackets ($x_1 \leq 400$), even though x_2 does not appear in this constraint, we need to specify that its parameter is zero. As a result, the parameter values of x_1 and x_2 for the jacket demand constraint are 1 and 0, respectively. Likewise, for the demand constraint for parkas ($x_2 \leq 100$), the parameter values for x_1 and x_2 are 0 and 1. This is why the last four parameters for the two demand constraints appear as 1, 0, 0, 1.

d. Specify the $\leq$ sign for each of the five constraints. Enter:

```
> lp.directions <- c("<=", "<=", "<=", "<=", "<=")
```

e. Specify the available amount of fabric, machine time, and labor as well as the two demand limitations (i.e., the values on the right-hand side of the five constraints). Enter:

```
> lp.rhs <- c(4000, 650, 900, 400, 150)
```

f. By default, the *lpSolve* package imposes non-negativity constraints on all decision variables, and, therefore, we do not need to explicitly specify these constraints. We use the **lp** function to maximize the objective function given the constraints and store the results in an object called lp.output.

To display the maximum profit and LP solution, we retype lp.output as well as lp.output$solution. Enter:

```
> lp.output <- lp("max", lp.objective, lp.constraints,
lp.directions, lp.rhs, compute.sens = TRUE)
> lp.output
> lp.output$solution
```

R reports that the maximum profit is $3,950, and the LP solution is for FashionTech to produce 300 winter jackets and 100 parkas. These are the same results that we obtained graphically as well as with Excel Solver.

g. To display the range of optimality for the two objective function coefficients (the per-unit profit of the jackets and parkas), enter:

```
> lp.output$sens.coef.from
> lp.output$sens.coef.to
```

The range of optimality for the per-unit profit of a winter jacket is between $8.333 and $9.375, while the range for the per-unit profit of parkas is between $12.000 and $13.500. The optimal number of jackets and parkas to be produced will remain at 300 and 100 units as long as the objective function coefficients stay within these ranges.

h. To display the shadow price for the constraints (called the dual price in the *lpSolve* package) and the range of feasibility, enter:

```
> lp.output$duals
> lp.output$duals.from
> lp.output$duals.to
```

For the two binding constraints, machine time and labor, the shadow prices are $4 and $1.5, respectively. The ranges of feasibility for the two resources are between 637.50 and 666.67 hours and between 875 and 916.67 hours, respectively. As mentioned earlier, the optimal solution found by Excel's Solver and R for the LP examples in this chapter are identical. For further discussion of the range of optimality, the shadow price, and the range of feasibility, refer to the discussion of the Excel results.

EXAMPLE 13.7

Recall from Example 13.5 that Anika Patel, the general manager at Yerba Buena Tea, needs to decide how many hours to operate each of the three production facilities. This decision must be made to ensure that all orders for the spiced chai powder mix and the chai tea concentrate are filled, while the production cost is kept at minimum. Use Excel's Solver and R to minimize the objective function given the four constraints. Summarize the results.

SOLUTION:

Using Excel

FILE *Chai*

In this example, we use a template in the ***Chai*** worksheet for consistency. If you have not already done so, activate the Solver software by launching Excel and go to **File > Options > Add-ins > Go**. Check the Solver checkbox and click **OK**. Because many of the steps are analogous to those that we outlined in Example 13.6, we are brief. Because Excel and R produce identical results, we summarize the results after the R instructions.

a. Open the ***Chai*** worksheet and enter the parameter values from Example 13.5 in cells B5:D7 and cells D13:D14 and D16. See Figure 13.18.

b. Enter =SUMPRODUCT(B5:D5, B10:D10) in cell B13, =SUMPRODUCT(B6:D6, B10:D10) in cell B14, and =B10 in cell B16.

c. Enter =SUMPRODUCT(B7:D7, B10:D10) in cell F4. Cell F4 represents the value of the objective function (i.e., the total production cost). Remember that our objective is to minimize the production cost.

d. Verify the Excel formula by entering 1 in cells B10, C10, and D10. We use these three cells to store the number of hours to operate the three production facilities (i.e., the decision variables). Your worksheet should look similar to Figure 13.18.

FIGURE 13.18 Excel template for minimization problems

	A	B	C	D	E	F
1	**Yerba Buena Tea**					
2						
3		Production facilities				Objective function (cost minimization):
4	Parameters:	Older	Newer	Special		$600.00
5	Powder mix (ounces/hr)	295	385	350		
6	Tea concentrate (ounces/hr)	260	375	0		
7	Cost per hour	$190	$260	$150		
8						
9		Older	Newer	Special		
10	Decision variables (hours to operate):	1.00	1.00	1.00		
11						
12	Constraints:	Quantity produced		Quantity needed		
13	Powder mix (ounces)	1030	>=	5500		
14	Tea concentrate (ounces)	635	>=	4000		
15		Operating hours		Limit		
16	Operating hours of the older facility	1	<=	8		

Source: Microsoft Excel

e. Go to **Data > Solver**. Enter the options and constraints as shown in Figure 13.19 and click Solve. Note that we choose the *Min* option for the minimization problem and use the ≥ sign in the first two constraints.

FIGURE 13.19 Excel's Solver Parameters dialog box for Example 13.7

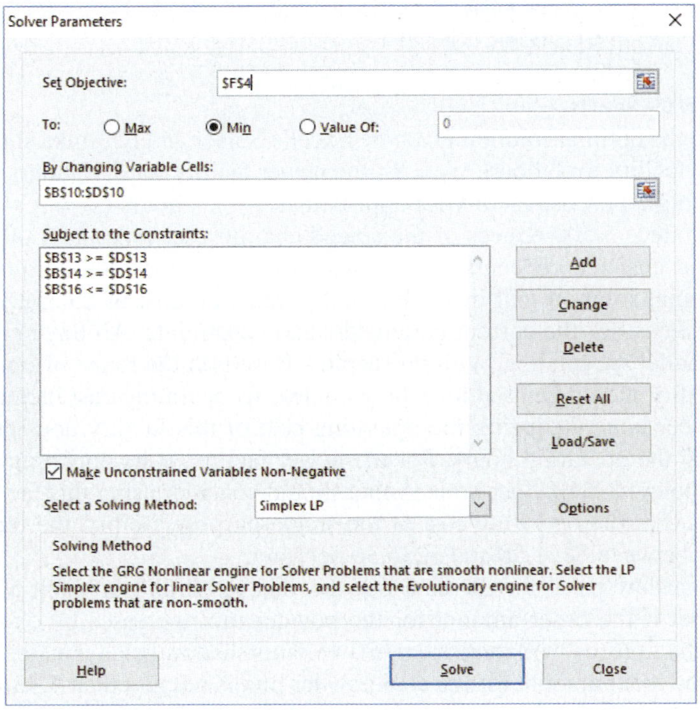

Source: Microsoft Excel

f. In the Solver Results dialog box, click the *Answer* and *Sensitivity* reports. Then click **OK**.

Using R

Because many of the steps are analogous to those that we outlined in Example 13.6, we are brief.

a. If you have not already done so, install and load the *lpSolve* package.

b. We specify the three objective function coefficients, the parameters in the three constraints, the ≥ and ≤ signs, and the amounts on the right-hand side of the three constraints. Note that the constraint for the order amount for the tea concentrate ($260x_1 + 375x_2 \geq 4{,}000$) only has two decision variables, so the parameter value for x_3 is specified as 0. Similarly, the limit on the operating hours for the old facility ($x_1 \leq 8$) has only one decision variable, so the parameter values for x_2 and x_3 are both 0. As a result, the last four parameters in the **matrix** function are 0, 1, 0, 0. Enter:

```
> lp.objective <- c(190, 260, 150)
> lp.constraints <- matrix(c(295, 385, 350, 260, 375, 0, 1, 0, 0),
nrow=3, byrow=TRUE)
> lp.directions <- c(">=", ">=", "<=")
> lp.rhs <- c(5500, 4000, 8)
```

c. In order to solve the LP minimization model, we use the **lp** function with the min option. Enter:

```
> lp.output <- lp ("min", lp.objective, lp.constraints,
lp.directions, lp.rhs, compute.sens = TRUE)
```

d. In order to display the LP solution and relevant output, enter:

```
> lp.output
> lp.output$solution
> lp.output$sens.coef.from
> lp.output$sens.coef.to
> lp.output$duals
> lp.output$duals.from
> lp.output$duals.to
```

Summary of the Results

Based on the optimal solution given by Excel's Solver and R, Anika should operate the older facility for 8 hours ($x_1 = 8$), the newer facility for 5.12 hours ($x_2 = 5.12$), and the single-purpose facility for approximately 3.34 hours ($x_3 = 3.34$). This plan would produce 5,500 ounces of the spiced chai powder mix and 4,000 ounces of the spiced chai tea concentrate, which are precisely the total amounts ordered. This optimal solution will incur the total production cost of $3,352.11, which is the lowest cost for the current parameters and constraints. All three constraints in the LP model are binding, with no surplus. Based on the range of optimality, the older facility should be used for 8 hours unless its operating cost increases beyond $192.30 per hour. Reducing the operating cost of this facility does not have any impact on the operating hours. For the newer facility, if its operating cost can be reduced below $256.69 per hour, Anika should consider using this facility for longer hours. For the operating cost of the single-purpose facility, the range of optimality is between $121.38 and $236.36 per hour.

The shadow price for the chai powder mix constraint is about $0.43, which means that if the order amount for the powder mix increases by one ounce, the total production cost will increase by $0.43. This shadow price remains the same as long as the order amount for the chai powder mix is not less than 4,331.20 ounces. The shadow price for the tea concentrate is about $0.25, which indicates that if the order amount for the tea concentrate increases by one ounce, the total production cost will increase by $0.25. The range of feasibility for this shadow price is between 2,080.00 ounces and 5,138.44 ounces.

The shadow price for the constraint on the operating hours of the older facility is about −\$2.30. Recall that unlike the other constraints in the LP problem, this constraint ($x_1 \leq 8$) has a $\leq$ sign. The negative shadow price means that if Anika is able to use the older facility for one additional hour of operation, the total production cost will decrease by \$2.30. This shadow price remains unchanged as long as the facility does not operate longer than 15.38 hours. To decide whether or not to operate the older facility longer than normal, Anika would need to take into account the potential cost saving along with the risk of manufacturing equipment breaking down from extended operation.

EXERCISES 13.3

Mechanics

23. Consider the following LP problem.

Maximize	$z = 3x_1 + 2x_2$

Subject to:

Constraint 1	$2x_1 + 3x_2 \leq 40,$
Constraint 2	$3x_1 + x_2 \leq 30,$
Constraint 3	$x_1, x_2 \geq 0,$

where x_1 and x_2 represent the decision variables. Solve the LP problem to answer the following questions.

a. What are the values of x_1 and x_2 at the optimal solution? What is the maximum value of z?
b. Identify the binding and nonbinding constraints and report the slack value, as applicable.
c. Report the shadow price and range of feasibility of each binding constraint.
d. What is the range of optimality for the two objective function coefficients?

24. Consider the following LP problem.

Maximize	$z = 2x_1 + 3x_2$

Subject to:

Constraint 1	$4x_1 + 7x_2 \leq 115,$
Constraint 2	$3x_1 + 2x_2 \leq 70,$
Constraint 3	$x_1, x_2 \geq 0,$

where x_1 and x_2 represent the decision variables. Solve the LP problem to answer the following questions.

a. What are the values of x_1 and x_2 at the optimal solution? What is the maximum value of z?
b. Identify the binding and nonbinding constraints and report the slack value, as applicable.
c. Report the shadow price and the range of feasibility of each binding constraint. Interpret the results.
d. What is the range of optimality for the two objective function coefficients? Interpret the results.

25. Consider the following LP problem.

Minimize	$z = 9x_1 + 6x_2$

Subject to:

Constraint 1:	$5x_1 + 3x_2 \geq 30,$
Constraint 2:	$2x_1 + 5x_2 \geq 33,$
Constraint 3:	$x_1, x_2 \geq 0,$

where x_1 and x_2 represent the decision variables. Solve the LP problem to answer the following questions.

a. What are the values of x_1 and x_2 at the optimal solution? What is the minimum value of z?
b. Identify the binding and nonbinding constraints and report the surplus value, as applicable.
c. Report the shadow price and range of feasibility of each binding constraint.
d. What is the range of optimality for the two objective function coefficients?

26. Consider the following LP problem.

Minimize	$z = 12x_1 + 10x_2$

Subject to:

Constraint 1:	$8x_1 + 6x_2 \geq 70,$
Constraint 2:	$4x_1 + 10x_2 \geq 80,$
Constraint 3:	$x_1, x_2 \geq 0,$

where x_1 and x_2 represents the decision variables. Solve the LP problem to answer the following questions.

a. What are the values of x_1 and x_2 at the optimal solution? What is the minimum value of z?
b. Identify the binding and nonbinding constraints and report the surplus value, as applicable.
c. Report the shadow price and the range of feasibility of each binding constraint(s). Interpret the results.
d. What is the range of optimality for the two objective function coefficients? Interpret the results.

27. Consider the following LP problem.

Maximize	$z = 5x_1 + 8x_2 + 6x_3$

Subject to:

Constraint 1	$5x_1 + 10x_2 + 5x_3 \leq 80,$
Constraint 2	$6x_1 + 9x_2 + 8x_3 \leq 90,$
Constraint 3	$x_1 \leq 15,$
Constraint 4	$x_1, x_2, x_3 \geq 0,$

where x_1, x_2, and x_3 represent the decision variables. Solve the LP problem to answer the following questions.

a. What are the values of x_1, x_2, and x_3 at the optimal solution? What is the maximum value of z?

b. Identify the binding and nonbinding constraints and report the slack value, as appropriate.

c. Report the shadow price and range of feasibility of each binding constraint. Interpret the results.

d. What is the range of optimality for the three objective function coefficients? Interpret the results.

28. Consider the following LP problem.

Minimize	$z = 7x_1 + 7x_2 + 6x_3$

Subject to:

Constraint 1:	$7x_1 + 6x_2 + 4x_3 \geq 50,$
Constraint 2:	$10x_1 + 13x_2 + 14x_3 \geq 150,$
Constraint 3:	$x_1, x_2, x_3 \geq 0,$

where x_1, x_2, and x_3 represent the decision variables. Solve the LP problem to answer the following questions.

a. What are the values of x_1, x_2, and x_3 at the optimal solution? What is the minimum value of z?

b. Identify the binding and nonbinding constraints and report the surplus value, as appropriate.

c. Report the values and ranges of feasibility of the shadow price of each binding constraint. Interpret the results.

d. What is the range of optimality for the three objective function coefficients? Interpret the results.

Applications

29. Big Sur Taffy Company makes two types of candies: salt water taffy and special home-recipe taffy. Big Sur wants to use a more quantitative approach to decide how much salt water and special taffy to make each day. Molasses, honey, and butter are the main ingredients that Big Sur uses to make taffy candies. For a pound of salt water taffy, Big Sur uses 8 cups of molasses, 4 cups of honey, and 0.7 cup of butter, and the selling price is \$7.50/lb. For a pound of special taffy, Big Sur uses 6 cups of molasses, 6 cups of honey, and 0.3 cup of butter, and the selling price is \$9.25/lb. Taffy candies are made fresh at dawn each morning, and Big Sur uses ingredients from a very exclusive supplier who delivers 400 cups of molasses, 300 cups of honey, and 32 cups of butter once a day before sunrise.

a. Formulate and solve the LP model that maximizes revenue given the constraints. What is the maximum revenue that Big Sur can generate? How much salt water and special taffy does Big Sur make each day?

b. Identify the binding and nonbinding constraints and report the slack value, as appropriate.

c. Report the shadow price and the range of feasibility of each binding constraint.

d. What is the range of optimality for the objective function coefficients?

30. A French vineyard in the Chablis region uses Chardonnay grapes to make Chardonnay wine and Blanc de Blancs blended champagne. To produce 1 liter of wine, the vineyard uses about 8 kilograms of Chardonnay grapes, and the winemakers usually spend about 2.5 hours in the winemaking process, including pressing, blending, and processing. To produce 1 liter of Blanc de Blancs champagne, about 6 kilograms of Chardonnay grapes are used, with the pressing, blending, and processing time of 3 hours. A liter of Chardonnay from the vineyard is usually sold at \$55, and each liter of champagne is sold at \$45. Each week, 400 kilograms of Chardonnay grapes and 150 hours for pressing, blending, and processing are available.

a. Formulate and solve the LP model that maximizes revenue given the constraints. What is the maximum revenue that the vineyard can make from selling Chardonnay wine and champagne? How many liters of Chardonnay wine and champagne should the vineyard make each week?

b. If the amount of Chardonnay grapes available to the vineyard increases to 500 kilograms per week, how much wine and champagne should be made? Explain.

c. If the price of champagne drops to \$30 per liter, how much wine and champagne should the vineyard make? Explain and discuss your answer.

31. A consumer product company makes two types of dishwasher detergents: regular and concentrate. The company has two manufacturing facilities for making detergent products. The first facility has an operating cost of \$120 an hour and can produce 300 ounces of regular detergent products per hour and 220 ounces of concentrate detergent per hour. The second facility has an hourly operating cost of \$220 and produces 350 ounces of regular detergent and 450 ounces of concentrate detergent per hour. The company received wholesale orders totaling 4,500 ounces of regular detergent and 5,200 ounces of concentrate detergent.

a. Formulate and solve the LP model that minimizes costs given the constraints. How many hours should the company operate each facility in order to fulfill the orders and minimize the operating cost?

b. Identify each binding constraint and report the shadow price and the range of feasibility.

c. If the hourly operating cost of the second facility is reduced to $200, how many hours should the company operate each facility? What is the minimum operating cost in this scenario?

32. Calcium and vitamin D are some of the most essential nutrients for bone health. According to the Institute of Medicine, an average adult should have in his or her daily diet 1,000 mg of calcium and 600 IU of vitamin D. These two nutrients are found in milk and cold cereal, which many people eat for breakfast. One cup of whole milk has 270 mg of calcium and 124 IU of vitamin D. A cup of a popular whole grain cereal brand contains 150 mg of calcium and 120 IU of vitamin D. One gallon of whole milk contains about 16 cups and costs $4.89. A box of the popular cereal also contains about 16 cups and costs $3.19. Suppose an adult relies on getting these two nutrients only from breakfast. Formulate and solve the LP model that minimizes the cost of milk and cereal but satisfies the daily requirement of calcium and vitamin D. How much milk and cereal should an adult consume? What is the minimum cost?

33. A renowned chocolatier, Francesco Schröeder, makes three kinds of chocolate confectionery: artisanal truffles, handcrafted chocolate nuggets, and premium gourmet chocolate bars. He uses the highest quality of cacao butter, dairy cream, and honey as the main ingredients. Francesco makes his chocolates each morning, and they are usually sold out by the early afternoon. For a pound of artisanal truffles, Francesco uses 1 cup of cacao butter, 1 cup of honey, and ½ cup of cream. The handcrafted nuggets are milk chocolate and take ½ cup of cacao, ⅔ cup of honey, and 2/3 cup of cream for each pound. Each pound of the chocolate bars uses 1 cup of cacao butter, ½ cup of honey, and ½ cup of cream. One pound of truffles, nuggets, and chocolate bars can be purchased for $35, $25, and $20, respectively. A local store places a daily order of 10 pounds of chocolate nuggets, which means that Francesco needs to make at least 10 pounds of the chocolate nuggets each day. Before sunrise each day, Francesco receives a delivery of 50 cups of cocao butter, 50 cups of honey, and 30 cups of dairy cream.

a. Formulate and solve the LP model that maximizes revenue given the constraints. How much of each chocolate product should Francesco make each morning? What is the maximum daily revenue that he can make?

b. Report the shadow price and the range of feasibility of each binding constraint.

c. If the local store increases the daily order to 25 pounds of chocolate nuggets, how much of each product should Francesco make?

34. CaseInPoint is a start-up company that makes ultra-slim, protective cases in stylish bold colors for a highly popular smartphone with two models: a large MÒR model and a compact BEAG model. CaseInPoint uses thermoplastic polyurethane, or TPU, to make all of its phone cases. The MÒR case is larger but is mostly solid color in design. To produce a MÒR case, 30 grams of TPU are used with 35 minutes of manufacturing time. The BEAG model is smaller but more elaborate in design and requires 22 grams of TPU and 53 minutes of manufacturing time. For each production period, 700 grams of TPU and 1,500 minutes of machine time are available. The profits from the MÒR and BEAG cases are $9 and $7.50, respectively.

a. Formulate and solve the LP model that maximizes revenue given the constraints. How many MÒR and BEAG cases should CaseInPoint make for each production period?

b. If the amount of TPU available increases to 1,000 grams for each production period, report the new LP solution and discuss your answer.

35. Many vitamin C products are made from ascorbic acid, which is derived from corn. A small dietary supplement company makes two types of vitamin C supplements: capsules and chewable tablets. To produce 1 kilogram of vitamin C capsules, 30 kilograms of corn, 2.3 hours of manufacturing time, and 2 hours of packaging time are required. To produce 1 kilogram of vitamin C tablets, 40 kilograms of corn, 4.2 hours of manufacturing time, and 1 hour of packaging time are required. Each week, the company has 2,000 kilograms of corn from its suppliers and allocates 180 hours of equipment time for manufacturing and 110 hours of packaging equipment time for vitamin C supplements. One kilogram of vitamin C capsules generates a profit of $9.50, and one kilogram of chewable tablets generates a profit of $12.

a. Formulate and solve an LP model to maximize the profit contribution from the two vitamin C products. How many kilograms of vitamin C capsules and tablets should the company produce each week? What is the maximum profit the company can make?

b. If the per-kilogram profits of vitamin C capsules and tablets increase to $11.50 and $16, respectively, how much of each product should the company make? What is the corresponding profit amount?

36. A rancher has a six-year old pony that weighs about 180 pounds. A pony of this age and size needs about 6.2 Mcal of digestible energy, 260 grams of protein, and 9,700 IU of vitamin A in her daily diet. EquineHealth and PonyEssentials are two popular brands of horse feed. One serving of the EquineHealth feed costs $10.50 and provides 1.5 Mcal, 52 grams of protein, and 1,800 IU of vitamin A. One serving of the PonyEssentials feed costs $12 and provides 1.8 Mcal, 58 grams of protein, and 2,200 IU of vitamin A. If the rancher were to blend the two feed products to make horse feed for his pony, how much of each brand should he use each week to minimize the cost? Explain and discuss your answer.

LO 13.5

13.4 OPTIMIZATION WITH INTEGER PROGRAMMING

Formulate and solve a linear integer programming model.

Linear programming (LP) discussed in Section 13.3 finds an optimal solution where the values of the decision variables are fractional. In many cases, the assumption of fractional decision variables is realistic. In Example 3.5, it was realistic for Yerba Buena Tea to operate the older facility for 8 hours, the newer facility for 5.12 hours, and the single-purpose facility for 3.34 hours. Similarly, it is realistic to produce products in fractional quantities such as 20.5 gallons of wine, 15.8 pounds of chocolate, etc.

In some other situations, it is critical that decision variables are integers. Consider a capital budgeting problem where a pharmaceutical company has to decide which of the several new drug development projects it should fund. Here, each decision variable represents whether or not the company should fund a certain project; it takes a value of 1 if the company decides to fund the project and 0 otherwise. The LP framework might find an unrealistic value, such as 0.3, for a decision variable. In such situations, we use linear integer programming, or simply integer programming (IP), to provide integer solutions for the decision variables.

We would like to point out that in certain situations we could possibly use LP where we round optimal fractional values to the nearest integer. In general, rounding optimal values to the nearest integer leads to a suboptimal solution. However, if the objective function coefficients are relatively small, and the values of the decision variables are relatively large, rounding the decision variables to the nearest integer would not have a significant impact on the underlying business decision.

In this section, we discuss two common types of IP problems: (1) a capital-budgeting problem for selection of investment projects and (2) a transportation problem for selection of supply locations for product delivery.

Capital Budgeting

In a typical capital-budgeting problem, a decision maker tries to choose from a number of potential projects. Examples include choosing among possible manufacturing plant locations or among new drug development projects. In these situations, it does not make sense to partially fund individual projects. There are no real benefits from building just 45% of a manufacturing plant or partially developing a new drug. In Example 13.8, we demonstrate how to mathematically formulate a capital budgeting problem as an IP model and use Excel's Solver and R to find an optimal solution.

EXAMPLE 13.8

North Star Biotech is exploring six new drug development projects. Each project has a five-year cash investment estimate and an expected return on investment as shown in Table 13.2. For example, to develop Drug 1, North Star has to make a cash investment of $2 million in Year 1 and $1 million in Years 2, 3, and 4, and no cash investment is needed in Year 5. Once completed, the company expects a return of $12.5 million. To develop Drug 2, the company needs to make a $2 million cash investment in Years 1 and 2, and $1 million in Years 3, 4, and 5, and expects a return of $13.5 million.

Even though each drug development project has a positive return, after accounting for the cash investment, North Star Biotech cannot possibly fund all six projects because of financial constraints. The amount of cash available to North Star Biotech is $10 million in Year 1, $8 million in Year 2, $7 million in Year 3, $5 million in Year 4, and $3 million in Year 5. Develop an integer programming model to help North Star Biotech decide which of the six projects to fund in order to maximize its total expected return.

TABLE 13.2 North Star Biotech's New Drug Development Projects

Cash Investment (in $ millions)	Drug 1	Drug 2	Drug 3	Drug 4	Drug 5	Drug 6
Year 1	2	2	1	4	2	4
Year 2	1	2	2	3	0	1
Year 3	1	1	1	2	4	1
Year 4	1	1	2	1	1	1
Year 5	0	1	0	0	0	1
Expected return (in $ million)	12.5	13.5	13	14.5	15	15.5

SOLUTION:

Integer Programming Formulation

North Star needs to decide whether or not to fund each project; therefore, each decision variable x_i, where $i = 1, 2, \ldots, 6$, has binary values. For example, $x_1 = 1$ if North Star invests in developing Drug 1, and 0 otherwise. We also define c_i as the expected return on investment for Drug i. For example, the expected return for Drug 1 is $12.5 million. For brevity, we show the financial amounts in millions of dollars, and, hence, $c_1 = 12.5$. We formulate the objective function as follows.

$$\textit{Maximize:} \qquad \textit{Expected Return} = \sum_{i=1}^{6} c_i x_i$$

In addition, each project requires an annual cash investment over a five-year period. We define a_{ij} as the cash investment required for Drug i in Year j, where $j = 1, 2, \ldots, 5$. For example, the annual cash investments, in $ millions, for Drug 1 are $a_{11} = 2$ for Year 1, $a_{12} = 1$ for Year 2, $a_{13} = 1$ for Year 3, $a_{14} = 1$ for Year 4, and $a_{15} = 0$ for Year 5. The cash investments for other projects are defined similarly. The constraints for the integer programming formulation can be written as follows.

$$\textit{Year 1:} \qquad \sum_{i=1}^{6} a_{i1} x_i \leq 10$$

$$\textit{Year 2:} \qquad \sum_{i=1}^{6} a_{i2} x_i \leq 8$$

$$\textit{Year 3:} \qquad \sum_{i=1}^{6} a_{i3} x_i \leq 7$$

$$\textit{Year 4:} \qquad \sum_{i=1}^{6} a_{i4} x_i \leq 5$$

$$\textit{Year 5:} \qquad \sum_{i=1}^{6} a_{i5} x_i \leq 3$$

The right-hand side of these constraints represent the amount of cash North Star Biotech has available in each of the five years. Finally, we specify that the decision variables must be binary.

$$x_i = 0 \text{ or } 1, \text{ where } i = 1, 2, \ldots, 6$$

We now show how to use Excel Solver and R to solve the integer programming problem.

Using Excel Solver

a. Open the ***Biotech*** worksheet and make sure the *Solver* add-in is activated. Note that cells B10:G10 represent the decision variables that will have a value of either 0 or 1 (i.e., whether or not each drug development project is funded). To help verify our Excel formula, we initially have 1 in cell B10 and 0 elsewhere.

FILE *Biotech*

b. Cells B2:G6 store the annual cash investments required for each project. To calculate the total cash investment spent in Year 1, enter =SUMPRODUCT(B2:G2, B$10:G$10) in cell H2. Verify that the value in cell H2 is 2. Copy and paste the formula to cells H3:H6.

c. Cells B8:G8 contain the expected returns from the six projects. To calculate the total return, enter =SUMPRODUCT(B8:G8, B10:G10) in cell I8 (the objective function for the IP problem). Verify that the result in cell I8 is 12.5.

d. Navigate to the **Data** tab and click on **Solver**. Enter cell I8 in the *Set Objective* box. Make sure to choose the *Max* option to maximize the total return value in cell I8. See Figure 13.20 for all solver parameters.

FIGURE 13.20 Solver parameters for Example 13.8

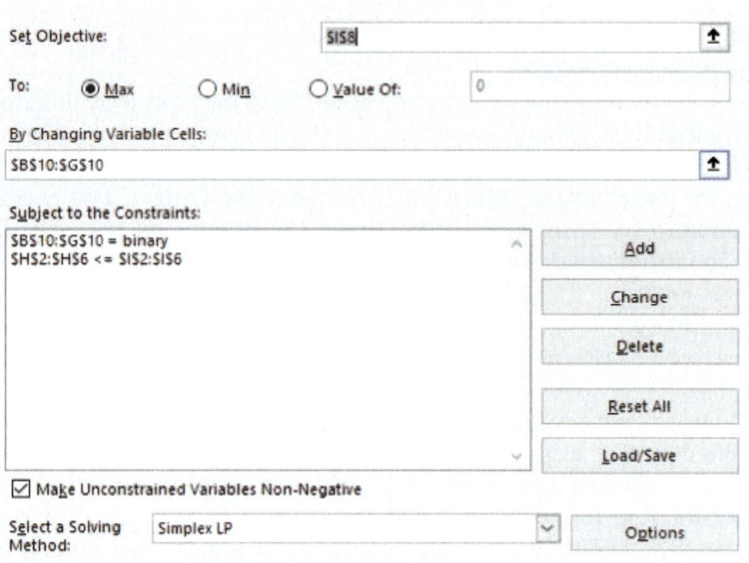

Source: Microsoft Excel

e. Enter B10:G10 in the *By Changing Variable Cells* box. Recall that these cells represent the binary decision variables.

f. Click the *Add* button to add the constraints for the amount of cash available. In the *Add Constraint* dialog box, enter H2:H6 for *Cell Reference*, choose <= from the drop-down list of operators, and enter I2:I6 for the *Constraint* option. Click *Add*.

g. In the next *Add Constraint* dialog box, enter B10:G10 in the *Cell Reference* box and choose the *bin* option from the drop-down list of operators to indicate that cells B10:G10 must have binary values. Click **OK**.

h. Choose *Simplex LP* in the *Select a Solving Method* box. Click *Solve*. Verify that your results are similar to Figure 13.21.

FIGURE 13.21 Results for the North Star Biotech problem

	A	B	C	D	E	F	G	H	I
1	Cash Investment (in $ millions)	Drug 1	Drug 2	Drug 3	Drug 4	Drug 5	Drug 6	Cash Spent	Cash Available
2	Year 1	2	2	1	4	2	4	9	10
3	Year 2	1	2	2	3	0	1	5	8
4	Year 3	1	1	1	2	4	1	7	7
5	Year 4	1	1	2	1	1	1	5	5
6	Year 5	0	1	0	0	0	1	2	3
7									
8	Expected Return (in $ millions)	12.5	13.5	13	14.5	15	15.5	Total Return:	57
9									
10	Funding: (1 = Yes, 0 = No)	0	1	1	0	1	1		

Source: Microsoft Excel

Using R

a. If you have not already done so, install and load the *lpSolve* package.

b. As in the previous examples, we specify the five objective function coefficients, the parameters in the constraints, the ≤ signs, and the available annual cash amounts on the right-hand side of the constraints. Enter:

```
> lp.objective <- c(12.5, 13.5, 13, 14.5, 15, 15.5)
> lp.constraints <- matrix(c(2, 2, 1, 4, 2, 4,
                     1, 2, 2, 3, 0, 1,
                     1, 1, 1, 2, 4, 1,
                     1, 1, 2, 1, 1, 1,
                     0, 1, 0, 0, 0, 1),
                     nrow=5, byrow=TRUE)
> lp.directions <- c("<=", "<=", "<=", "<=", "<=")
> lp.rhs <- c(10, 8, 7, 5, 3)
```

c. We use the **lp** function with the *max* option. We also add the *all.bin = TRUE* parameter to specify that the decision variables are binary. (For other types of problems where the decision variables can take on any integer values, we would use the *all.int = TRUE* parameter instead.) Enter:

```
> lp.output <- lp("max", lp.objective, lp.constraints,
lp.directions, lp.rhs, all.bin = TRUE)
```

d. Display the integer programming solution. Enter:

```
> lp.output
> lp.output$solution
```

Summary of the Results

Both the Excel Solver and R outputs indicate that North Star Biotech should invest in Projects 2, 3, 5, and 6, and not in Projects 1 and 4. Therefore, the company would make the annual cash investments of \$9, \$5, \$7, \$5, and \$2 million over the five-year period. This investment plan results in \$1 million of excess cash in Year 1, \$3 million in Year 2, and \$1 million in Year 5. Recall that for a maximization problem, these are called slack in the linear and integer programing constraints. Based on this recommendation, North Star Biotech would maximize its expected total return at \$57 million.

Transportation Problem

A classic example of a transportation problem involves a manager who needs to decide which of the warehouses to use in order to deliver products to retail stores or customers. The manager's goal (or the objective function) is usually to minimize the overall shipment cost while meeting the demand at each retail store or from individual customers. Intuitively, a transportation problem is feasible only when the total supply (i.e., the combined capacity of all warehouses) is at least equal to the total demand (i.e., the total amount being ordered).

In many situations, the transportation model deals with a large bundle of goods, such as a pallet of 1,600 bottles of water or a bundle of 300 2 × 4 wood planks. As such, it is impractical to transport these bundles of goods in fractional units, and we use the IP technique to solve a transportation model to obtain integer solutions, instead of using the LP technique and rounding the solutions to the nearest integers. Example 13.9 demonstrates how to formulate an IP model for a simple transportation problem and use Excel's Solver and R to find an optimal solution.

EXAMPLE 13.9

Rainier Spring Water has two warehouses that service three retail stores. Per week, the first warehouse can supply up to 160 pallets of bottled water and the second warehouse can supply up to 155 pallets. The manager at Rainier Spring Water receives a weekly order from the three retail stores for 85, 125, and 100 pallets, respectively. Note that the combined capacity of the two warehouses is larger than the total number of pallets of bottled water ordered by the three stores, a required condition for a feasible solution. The shipping cost for each pallet varies among the warehouses and retail stores, depending on the distance, traffic, and road conditions. As shown in Table 13.3, to ship one pallet of bottled water from Warehouse 1 to the three stores, it would cost \$4.15, \$5.95, and \$6.25, respectively. Likewise, to ship one pallet from Warehouse 2 to the three stores, it would cost \$3.75, \$4.25, and \$8.25, respectively.

TABLE 13.3 Shipping Cost per Pallet of Bottled Water

	Store 1	Store 2	Store 3
Warehouse 1	\$4.15	\$5.95	\$6.25
Warehouse 2	\$3.75	\$4.25	\$8.25

Develop an integer programming model to help the manager decide how many pallets of bottled water to ship from each warehouse to individual stores in order to fulfill the orders while minimizing the total shipping cost.

SOLUTION:

Integer Programming Formulation

We require that the number of pallets that Rainier Spring Water ships from its warehouse be an integer value. We define our decision variables x_{ij} as the number of pallets to be shipped from warehouse i to retail store j, where $i = 1$ and 2, and $j = 1$, 2, and 3. We assume x_{ij} to be non-negative integers. The per-pallet shipping cost c_{ij} is defined as the cost of shipping one pallet of bottled water from warehouse i to retail store j. For example, as shown in Table 13.3, the values of c_{11}, c_{12}, and c_{13} are \$4.15, \$5.95, and \$6.25, respectively. We formulate the objective function as follows.

$$\textit{Minimize:} \qquad \textit{Total shipping cost} = \sum_{i=1}^{2} \sum_{j=1}^{3} c_{ij}x_{ij}$$

The constraints in the transportation problem reflect the demand for bottled water from each store and the capacity of each of the two warehouses. The first three constraints below specify that the total number of pallets shipped to each retail store must at least meet the order amount. Alternatively, we can use an equal sign (=) to specify that the number of pallets shipped to the store must be exactly the same as the amount ordered. The next two constraints indicate that the number of pallets shipped from each warehouse cannot exceed its capacity.

Demand from retail store 1	$\sum_{i=1}^{2} x_{i1} \geq 85$
Demand from retail store 2	$\sum_{i=1}^{2} x_{i2} \geq 125$
Demand from retail store 3	$\sum_{i=1}^{2} x_{i3} \geq 100$
Capacity of warehouse 1	$\sum_{j=1}^{3} x_{1j} \leq 160$
Capacity of warehouse 2	$\sum_{j=1}^{3} x_{2j} \leq 155$

We now show how to use Excel Solver and R to solve the transportation problem.

FILE
Rainier

Using Excel Solver

a. Open the Rainier worksheet and make sure the *Solver* add-in is activated. Note that cells B5:D6 represent the decision variables and will have only integer values (i.e., the number of pallets of bottled water to ship from a warehouse to a retail store). Initially these cells are blank.

b. We use cells E5 and E6 to show the total number of pallets shipped from the two warehouses, respectively. Enter =SUM(B5:D5) in cell E5. Copy and paste the formula to cell E6.

c. We use cells B7:D7 to show the total number of pallets shipped to the three stores, respectively. Enter =SUM(B5:B6) in cell B7, and copy and paste it to cells C7 and D7.

d. We use cell F13 to calculate the total shipping cost (the objective function), based on the per-unit cost in cells B13:D14 and the number of units shipped in cells B5:D6. Enter =SUMPRODUCT(B13:D14, B5:D6) in cell F13.

e. Navigate to the **Data** tab and click on **Solver**. Enter cell F13 in the *Set Objective* box. Make sure to choose the *Min* option to minimize the total shipping cost. See Figure 13.22 for all solver parameters.

FIGURE 13.22 Solver parameters for Example 13.9

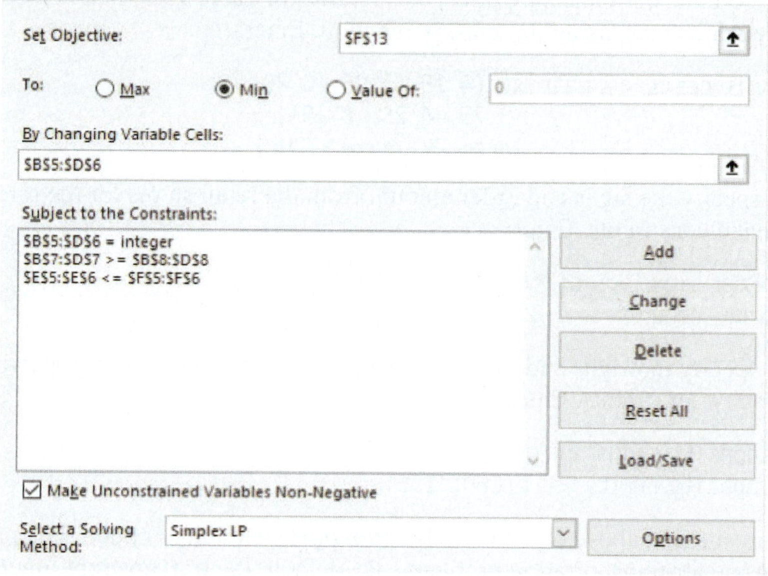

Source: Microsoft Excel

f. Enter B5:D6 in the *By Changing Variable Cells* box. Recall that these cells represent the integer decision variables.

g. Click the *Add* button to add the integer constraints for the decision variables. In the *Add Constraint* dialog box, enter B5:D6 in the *Cell Reference* box and choose the *int* option from the drop-down list of operators to indicate that cells B5:D6 must have integer values. Click *Add.*

h. In the next *Add Constraint* dialog box, enter E5:E6 for *Cell Reference*, choose <= from the drop-down list of operators, and enter F5:F6 for the *Constraint* option. This is to ensure that the number of pallets shipped from each warehouse does not exceed the capacity of each warehouse. Click *Add.*

i. In the next *Add Constraint* dialog box, enter B7:D7 for *Cell Reference*, choose >= from the drop-down list of operators, and enter B8:D8 for the *Constraint* option. This is to ensure that each retail store receives at least the ordered amount. Click **OK**.

j. Choose *Simplex LP* in the *Select a Solving Method* box. Click the *Option* button and make sure that the *Ignore Integer Constraints* box is unchecked. Click **OK**.

k. Click *Solve* and verify that your results are similar to Figure 13.23.

FIGURE 13.23 Results for the Rainier Spring Water problem

Rainier Spring Water Shipment

Shipment Plan

From\To	Store 1	Store 2	Store 3	Units shipped from warehouses	Units available at warehouses
Warehouse 1	55	0	100	155	160
Warehouse 2	30	125	0	155	155
Units shipped to stores	85	125	100		
Units ordered	85	125	100		

Per-unit Shipping Costs

From\To	Store 1	Store 2	Store 3
Warehouse 1	$4.15	$5.95	$6.25
Warehouse 2	$3.75	$4.25	$8.25

Total shipment cost
$1,497.00

Source: Microsoft Excel

Using R

a. If you have not already done so, install and load the *lpSolve* package. The *lpSolve* package includes the **lp.transport** function developed especially for solving transportation problems.

b. We store the per-pallet shipping costs (shown in Table 13.3) in an object called unit.costs, using the **matrix** function. Enter:

```
> unit.costs <- matrix(c(4.15, 5.95, 6.25,
                         3.75, 4.25, 8.25),
                         nrow=2, byrow=TRUE)
```

c. We specify the signs and order amount from the retail stores for the three demand constraints. Enter:

```
> order.signs <- c(">=", ">=", ">=")
> order.amount <- c(85, 125, 100)
```

d. We specify the signs and the capacity of the two warehouses for the two capacity constraints. Enter:

```
> capacity.signs <- c("<=", "<=")
> capacity.limits <- c(160, 155)
```

e. As mentioned above, we use the **lp.transport** function to obtain the optimal solution for transportation problems. By default, the **lp.transport** function assumes that all decision variables are integers. We use the *min* option to minimize the total shipping cost and include the shipping cost matrix and all the constraints. Enter:

```
> lp.output <- lp.transport(unit.costs, "min", capacity.signs,
capacity.limits, order.signs, order.amount)
```

f. To display the optimal shipping cost and solution to the transportation model, we use the following statements. Enter:

```
> lp.output
> lp.output$solution
```

Summary of the Results

The Excel Solver and R outputs indicate that from Warehouse 1, the manager at Rainier Spring Water should ship 55 pallets of bottled water to Retail Store 1 and 100 pallets to Retail Store 3. From Warehouse 2, the manager should ship 30 pallets to Retail Store 1 and 125 pallets to Retail Store 2. This shipment schedule would fulfill the orders from all three stores. Warehouse 1 would deliver 155 out of the 160 pallets available in its weekly inventory, whereas Warehouse 2 would use up all of its weekly bottled water inventory. The five remaining pallets in Warehouse 1 are available for shipping to other stores. Recall that in a minimization problem, the excess quantity at Warehouse 1 is called a surplus. With this shipment plan, Rainier Spring Water will incur the minimum overall shipment cost of $1,497 per week.

EXERCISES 13.4

Mechanics

37. Consider the following IP problem.

Maximize $z = \sum_{i=1}^{3} c_i x_i$, where $c_1 = 15, c_2 = 13,$ and $c_3 = 12$

Subject to:

Constraint 1 $5x_1 + 3x_2 + 6x_3 \leq 10,$

Constraint 2 $3x_1 + 4x_2 + 2x_3 \leq 8,$

Constraint 3 $3x_1 + 3x_2 + 2x_3 \leq 6,$

Constraint 4 $x_1, x_2, x_3 = 0$ or 1,

where x_1, x_2, and x_3 represent the decision variables. Solve the IP problem to answer the following questions.

a. What are the values of x_1, x_2, and x_3 at the optimal solution?

b. What is the maximum value of z?

38. Consider the following IP problem.

Minimize $z = \sum_{i=1}^{2} \sum_{j=1}^{2} c_{ij} x_{ij}$, where $c_{11} = 2, c_{12} = 1,$ $c_{21} = 1$, and $c_{22} = 3$.

Subject to:

Constraint 1 $\sum_{i=1}^{2} x_{i1} \geq 50$

Constraint 2 $\sum_{i=1}^{2} x_{i2} \geq 60$

Constraint 3 $\sum_{j=1}^{2} x_{ij} \leq 65$

Constraint 4 $\sum_{j=1}^{2} x_{2j} \leq 45$

Constraint 5 x_{ij} = non-negative integer

where x_{ij} represent the decision variables. Solve the IP problem to answer the following questions.

a. What are the values of x_{ij} at the optimal solution?

b. What is the minimum value of z?

Applications

39. An online apparel retailer runs regular marketing campaigns on social media channels. The retailer is considering four social media marketing campaigns on Facebook, Instagram, Pinterest, and Twitter for the four weeks prior to the December holiday season. However, due to its limited marketing budget, the retailer cannot run all four proposed campaigns. The following table describes the weekly cost (in $1,000s) and the expected numbers of consumers each campaign will reach (in 1,000s).

Marketing Cost	Facebook	Instagram	Pinterest	Twitter	Weekly Budget
Week 1	4.5	3.5	3	4	15
Week 2	5	4	4	3	12
Week 3	4	3	5	3	10
Week 4	4.5	4	5.5	2	12
Consumers Reached	34	28	32	25	

a. Formulate and solve the IP model to determine which of the four marketing campaigns the retailer should run in order to maximize the number of consumers reached, without going over its budget. What is the maximum number of consumers that the retailer can reach?

b. Which social media channels should the retailer use in order to maximize the number of consumers reached?

c. Will the retailer use up all of its marketing budget each week?

40. Akkadian Capital, a real estate investment firm, owns five apartment buildings around a four-year college campus. The five buildings need significant repairs and renovation, and each renovation project will take about three months to complete. The company expects each renovated apartment building to generate a substantial rental income from college students. However, Akkadian Capital has a limited budget during the next three months and cannot repair and remodel all five buildings. The remodeling cost and the expected annual income after expenses from each apartment are shown in the following table. Also included in the table is Akkadian's budget for the next three months.

Cost (in $1,000s)	Kirkland Apartment	Hillside Residence	La Jolla Manor	Park Views	Campus Hamlet	Monthly Budget
Month 1	44	25	17	33	20	130
Month 2	32	30	42	51	25	100
Month 3	19	29	26	35	19	85
Income (in $1,000s)	315	246	240	387	193	

a. Formulate and solve an IP model to help Akkadian determine which apartment buildings to renovate in order to maximize its rental income, while staying within its budget. What is the maximum amount of rental income that Akkadian can generate?

b. Which apartment buildings should Akkadian remodel? Why?

c. Will Akkadian use up all of its budget in each month?

41. A microbrewery company in Portland, Oregon, operates two breweries that supply its popular craft beer to five local restaurants. The first brewery can produce 56 barrels of craft beer per week, and the second brewery can produce 72 barrels per week. The delivery cost per barrel and the average weekly order from each of the five restaurants are summarized in the following table.

Delivery Cost	Restaurant 1	Restaurant 2	Restaurant 3	Restaurant 4	Restaurant 5
Brewery 1	$1.05	$1.50	$1.55	$1.10	$1.40
Brewery 2	$1.25	$1.45	$1.39	$1.00	$1.50
Weekly Order	20	29	31	21	27

a. Formulate and solve an IP model to determine the number of barrels of craft beer to be shipped from each brewery to the restaurants. What is the lowest delivery cost that the microbrewery would incur?

b. How many barrels of craft beer should the microbrewery ship from each brewery to each of the five restaurants in order to minimize the total delivery cost?

42. An electric car company owns two facilities that manufacture and supply high-capacity lithium-ion batteries to three vehicle assembly plants. The first battery facility can produce and ship up to 10,000 lithium-ion batteries per month, and the second facility can produce and ship up to 8,000 batteries per month. The per-unit shipping cost and the battery demand from the three assembly plants are provided in the following table.

Shipment Cost per Battery	Plant 1	Plant 2	Plant 3
Manufacturer 1	$15.67	$12.30	$13.55
Manufacturer 2	$13.75	$13.90	$14.00
Monthly Demand	5,000	6,600	6,400

a. Formulate and solve an IP model to determine the number of batteries to be shipped from each manufacturer to the three assembly plants. What is the lowest shipping cost that the electric car company would incur?

b. How many batteries should the company ship from each manufacturer to each of the three assembly plants in order to minimize the shipping cost?

13.5 WRITING WITH DATA

Case Study

FamVeld/Shutterstock

Demand for organic food has grown steadily over the years. Organic strawberry farming is one of the segments in the food and agriculture industry that is projected to continue expanding in the foreseeable future. Estuary Organic, a fruit farming company on the coast of California, struggles to reduce its production cost while staying true to its mission of offering fully certified organic produce to its customers.

To address the cost issue, Estuary Organic hires Professor Tom Richards as a consultant to review different types of organic fertilizers that the company has used. His task is to find a combination of organic fertilizers that can meet the three primary nutrient requirements in the soil, nitrogen (N), phosphate (P_2O_5), and potassium (K_2O). At the same time, Professor Richards needs to take into consideration the cost of certified organic fertilizers in his analysis.

For each strawberry planting season, growers need to have the right combination of nitrogen, phosphate, and potassium in the soil. Adding too much or too little of these nutrients is detrimental to the plant growth and its ability to bear fruit. This combination of N, P_2O_5, and K_2O nutrients is often called the NPK value. Generally, the minimum amount of NPK per acre is 100 lbs, 50 lbs, and 50 lbs, respectively.

Based on the current soil condition and soil testing results, Professor Richards also determines that the maximum amount of NPK per acre is 125 lbs, 55 lbs, and 55 lbs, respectively. Some of the fertilizers commonly used in the local area and by Estuary Organic include alfalfa meal (typically made from fermented alfalfa), soybean meal, fish meal (typically pollock, mackerel, and/or anchovies), and compost made from animal manure. The cost and NPK composition of each fertilizer is listed in Table 13.4.

TABLE 13.4 Organic Fertilizers, Their Cost, and Nutrient Contents

Organic fertilizers	Cost per 50 lbs	N	P_2O_5	K_2O
Alfalfa meal	$14.00	3.0%	2.0%	2.5%
Soybean meal	23.00	5.0	2.0	1.0
Fish meal	32.00	5.0	3.0	2.0
Animal manure compost	6.50	1.5	1.0	1.0

The goal of this consulting engagement is to provide Estuary Organic a recommended combination of fertilizers that meet the NPK requirements at a minimal cost. After analyzing relevant information, Professor Richards submits the following report to the Estuary Organic owner.

Sample Report—Organic Strawberry Farm

In this report, we consider the cost and NPK information provided by Estuary Organic Farm and develop an optimization model that represents the relationship among the cost and NPK values of each type of organic fertilizer as well as the NPK requirements for each acre of land. We use a linear programming technique and develop the following formulation.

Minimize: *Fertilization cost* $= 0.28x_1 + 0.46x_2 + 0.64x_3 + 0.13x_4$

Subject to:

Minimum amount of nitrogen: $0.030x_1 + 0.050x_2 + 0.050x_3 + 0.015x_4 \geq 100$
Minimum amount of phosphate: $0.020x_1 + 0.020x_2 + 0.030x_3 + 0.010x_4 \geq 50$
Minimum amount of potassium: $0.025x_1 + 0.010x_2 + 0.020x_3 + 0.010x_4 \geq 50$
Maximum amount of nitrogen: $0.030x_1 + 0.050x_2 + 0.050x_3 + 0.015x_4 \leq 105$
Maximum amount of phosphate: $0.020x_1 + 0.020x_2 + 0.030x_3 + 0.010x_4 \leq 55$
Maximum amount of potassium: $0.025x_1 + 0.010x_2 + 0.020x_3 + 0.010x_4 \leq 55$
Non-negativity: $x_1, x_2, x_3, x_4 \geq 0$

The four decision variables, x_1, x_2, x_3, and x_4, represent the amount of alfalfa meal, soybean meal, fish meal, and compost (in pounds) to be mixed into the fertilizer compound. We also convert the cost of each fertilizer into a per-pound basis (e.g., $0.28 per pound for the alfalfa meal, $0.46 per pound for the soybean meal, and so on). The cost-per-pound values are used as the objective function coefficients.

Based on the results obtained from the linear programming formulation, we recommend the mix of organic fertilizers for each acre of land as shown in Table 13.5.

TABLE 13.5 Recommended Mix of Fertilizers per Acre

Organic Fertilizers	Recommended Amount (lbs)	Cost
Alfalfa meal	750	$210.00
Soybean meal	875	$402.50
Fish meal	0	$ 0.00
Animal manure compost	2,250	$292.50
Total cost:		$905.00
Total NPK amount (in lbs): 100-55-50		

The optimal combination provides 100 pounds of nitrogen, 55 pounds of phosphate, and 50 pounds of potassium per acre. The base for the fertilizer compound is the animal manure compost, which is the most inexpensive fertilizer but has the least NPK values among the four fertilizer choices. We then supplement the compost with alfalfa and soybean meals to reach the required amount of nitrogen and potassium. Because we do not use any fish meal, the most expensive of the four fertilizers, in the recommended fertilizer mix, we are able to keep the cost per acre to a minimal amount of $905.

We also examine the impact of possible changes in the cost of fertilizers. For example, if the cost of animal compost increases from $6.50 to $7.00 per 50 pounds, we will have to reformulate our fertilizer mix. In such a scenario, one possible option is to use only alfalfa and soybean meals to achieve the NPK requirements while keeping the cost reasonably low. Based on our initial analysis, we would recommend using 1,578.95 pounds of alfalfa meal and 1,052.63 pounds of soybean meal, which will result in a total cost of $926.31 per acre.

Another scenario that we consider in our analysis is if the cost of alfalfa meal drops from $14 to $13 per 50 pounds (while the cost of compost remains at $6.50 per 50 pounds). With its well-balanced NPK value, we could use a much higher amount of alfalfa meal while keeping the total cost low. Specifically, one possible fertilizer mix in this scenario would be to use 1,750 pounds of alfalfa meal, 875 pounds of soybean meal, and only 250 pounds of animal manure compost. This would result in a total cost of $890 per acre.

Suggested Case Studies

Prescriptive analytics can be applied to many situations. Here are some suggestions and examples of Monte Carlo simulations and linear programming problems.

Report 13.1. A grocery store manager wants to analyze customer spending data by product categories: fresh baked goods, meat and dairy, produce, and frozen food. For each shopping trip, about 30% of shoppers purchase baked good items, and the spending in this category tends to follow a continuous uniform distribution between $3 and $19. For the meat and dairy products, 70% of shoppers make regular purchases from this category, and their spending is normally distributed with a mean of $21 and standard deviation of $5.27. Eighty percent of the shoppers spend an average of $15 on produce, and their spending follows a normal distribution with a standard deviation of $2.31. Sixty-five percent of shoppers purchase at least an item from the frozen food aisles; the spending amount in this category follows a uniform distribution between $7.25 and $28.50. On average, approximately 220 customers make a trip to the grocery store each day. Develop a Monte Carlo simulation to analyze the customer spending and the fluctuation in daily revenue.

Report 13.2. An oil and gas company has two refineries that produce light and heavy crude oil. The first refinery can produce 500 barrels of light crude oil and 300 barrels of heavy crude oil per day, and the second refinery can produce 600 barrels of light crude oil and 450 barrels of heavy crude oil per day. The daily operating cost of each refinery is $15,000 and $20,000, respectively. The company has to fulfill production orders totaling 3,200 barrels of light crude oil and 2,100 barrels of heavy crude oil. Analyze the information and recommend an appropriate production plan.

Report 13.3. South Bay Candles makes two types of scented candles: 10-inch pillars and 2-inch decorative gel. The production requirements for each product and available resources are shown in Table 13.6. The sales price for each pillar and gel candle is $2.15 and $3.55, respectively. Analyze the data provided and create a report to recommend how many pillar and gel candles South Bay should make.

TABLE 13.6 Product Information for South Bay Candles

		Required Materials for Each Candle Type	
Materials/Resources	**Amount Available**	**Pillar**	**Gel**
Cotton wick (ft.)	12,000	0.580	0.800
Beeswax (lb.)	7,000	0.500	0.325
Essential oils	3,200	0.240	0.130
Manufacturing time (min.)	120,000	5.320	9.460

APPENDIX A

Big Data Sets: Variable Description and Data Dictionary

A distinctive feature of the text is the access to select big data sets with relevance to numerous applications to which students can relate. Although the data sets represent a highly simplified (modified) portion of the actual data, they still retain several features of big data. Throughout the text, we use these big data sets to help introduce problems, formulate possible solutions, and communicate the findings, based on the concepts introduced in the chapters. Data dictionaries for the six big data sets used in the text are described below.

FILE *Car_Crash*

Data 1: Car Crash Data

The ***Car_Crash*** data are extracted from the Statewide Integrated Traffic Records System database that serves as a means to collect and process data gathered from a collision scene in California (http://www.chp.ca.gov). The data are based on the information provided to the California Highway Patrol (CHP) from both local and government agencies. CHP collected data regarding the actual collision, the parties involved, as well as information on the victims. The data set represents a highly simplified/modified sample of about 113,000 collisions within the span of a single calendar year.

Table A.1 Data Dictionary for Car Crash Data

Variable Name	Description or Possible Values
ID	A modified ID for each motor vehicle accident
County	Actual county name
City	Actual city name
Weekday	1 – Monday 2 – Tuesday 3 – Wednesday 4 – Thursday 5 – Friday 6 – Saturday 7 – Sunday
Severity	1 – Fatal or severe injury 0 – Others
ViolCat	01 – Driving or Bicycling Under the Influence of Alcohol or Drug 02 – Unsafe Speed 03 – Following Too Closely 04 – Improper Passing 05 – Unsafe Lane Change 06 – Improper Turning 07 – Automobile Right of Way 08 – Pedestrian Right of Way 09 – Pedestrian Violation 10 – Traffic Signals and Signs 11 – Fell Asleep
ClearWeather	1 – Clear weather 0 – Not clear weather

Table A.1 *(Continued)*

Variable Name	Description or Possible Values
Month	1 – January 2 – February 3 – March 4 – April 5 – May 6 – June 7 – July 8 – August 9 – September 10 – October 11 – November 12 – December
CrashType	A – Head-On B – Sideswipe C – Rear End D – Broadside E – Hit Object F – Overturned G – Vehicle/Pedestrian
Highway	1 – Highway 0 – Not highway
Daylight	1 – Daylight 0 – Not daylight

Data 2: College Admissions Data

FILE
College_Admissions

The ***College_Admissions*** data contain important college admission and enrollment information related to a selective four-year university in North America. The data shed light on admission and enrollment decisions made by the admissions office and the applicants. Based on the admissions dashboard, there are about 18,000 applicants for fall admissions in three colleges within the university. Also included in the data is the college GPA of enrolled applicants. The data represent a highly simplified/modified sample of anonymized applicants.

Table A.2 Data Dictionary for College Admissions Data

<table>
<tr><th>Variable Name</th><th>Description or Possible Values</th></tr>
<tr><td>Applicant</td><td>A modified ID for each applicant</td></tr>
<tr><td>Edu_Parent1</td><td rowspan="2">1 – No High School
2 – Some High School
3 – High School Graduate
4 – Some College
6 – 4-Year College Graduate
7 – Postgraduate</td></tr>
<tr><td>Edu_Parent2</td></tr>
<tr><td>Gender</td><td>M – Male
F – Female</td></tr>
<tr><td>White</td><td>1 – White
0 – Not White</td></tr>
<tr><td>Asian</td><td>1 – Asian
0 – Not Asian</td></tr>
<tr><td>HSGPA</td><td>High school weighted GPA, ranging from 0 to 5.</td></tr>
</table>

Continued

Table A.2 *(Continued)*

Variable Name	Description or Possible Values
SAT/ACT	The higher of the SAT/ACT score, where the ACT score is first converted into the equivalent SAT score for English and Math
College	Arts & Letters Business & Economics Math & Science
Admitted	1 – Admitted by College 0 – Not Admitted by College
Enrolled	1 – Applicant enrolled 0 – Applicant not enrolled
College_GPA	College GPA, ranging from 0 to 4, four years after enrollment; blanks for those who did not enroll

FILE
House_Price

Data 3: House Price Data

Investment in college town real estate is attractive because students offer a steady stream of rental demand as cash-strapped public universities are unable to house their students beyond freshman year. Data on about 11,000 homes sold in a single year are extracted from Zillow for 50 campus towns in the U.S. (https://www.zillow.com). The ***House_Price*** data represent a highly simplified/modified sample of anonymized homes, excluding homes with observations that seem erroneous and/or not pertaining to sales.

Table A.3 Data Dictionary for House Price Data

Variable Name	Description or Possible Values
Record	A modified ID for each house
Sale_amount	Sale price of the house in U.S. dollars
Sale_date	Sale date of the house
Beds	Number of bedrooms in the house
Baths	Number of bathrooms in the house
Sqft_home	Square footage of the house
Sqft_lot	Square footage of the lot
Type	Multiple Family Multiple Occupancy Single Family
Build_year	Year the house was built
Town	Name of the campus town
University	Name of the university

FILE
Longitudinal_Survey

Data 4: Longitudinal Survey Data

The National Longitudinal Survey (NLS) follows over 12,000 individuals in the United States. Starting in 1979, individuals were surveyed annually up until 1994; thereafter, surveys were conducted every other year. When first surveyed in 1979, individuals ranged in age from 14 to 21 years old. Survey questions focused on "labor force activity;" however, the survey also covered a large variety of subjects including, "educational attainment, training investments, income and assets, health conditions, workplace injuries, insurance coverage, alcohol and substance abuse, sexual activity, and marital and fertility histories." The ***Longitudinal_Survey*** data represent a highly simplified/modified sample of anonymized respondents.

Table A.4 Data Dictionary for Longitudinal Survey Data

Variable Name	Description or Possible Values
ID	A modified ID for each respondent
Age	Age, as of 1979
Urban	At the age of 14, respondent lived in: 1 – Urban area 0 – Non-urban area
Mother_ Edu	Number of years of mother's education
Father_ Edu	Number of years of father's education
Siblings	Number of siblings in 1979
Black	1 – Black 0 – Non-Black
Hispanic	1 – Hispanic 0 – Non-Hispanic
White	1 – White 0 – Non-White
Christian	As of 1979, 1 – Christian 0 – Non-Christian
WomenPlace	Opinion on: "A woman's place is in the home, not in the office or shop." 1 – Agree 0 – Disagree
Male	1 – Male 0 – Female
FamilySize	Family size in 1979
Self_Esteem	The Rosenberg Self-Esteem Scale measures individuals' self-evaluation. The overall score can range between zero and 30 points, where higher scores indicate higher self-esteem. Actual scores in 1980.
Height	Height in inches in 1981
Weight	Weight in pounds in 1981
Outgoing_Kid	At the age of 6, the respondent was: 1 – Outgoing 0 – Shy
Outgoing_Adult	In adulthood, the respondent was: 1 – Outgoing 0 – Shy
HealthPlan	Covered by health insurance/health care plan in 2000: 1 – Yes 0 – No
Income	Income in 2000
Marital_Status	Marital status in 2000: 0 – Never Married 1 – Married 2 – Separated 3 – Divorced 4 – Remarried 5 – Widowed
Education	Number of years of education as of 2000
WeeksEmployed	Number of weeks employed in past calendar year in 2000
NumberSpouses	Number of spouses/partners reported in 2000

FILE *NBA*

Data 5: NBA Data

In this text, we use a highly simplified/modified sample of the National Basketball Association (NBA) data collected for 2016. This information is valuable to sports enthusiasts who use data on players' statistics and other sports-related information to inform decisions. The data represent a highly simplified/modified sample of 30 competing teams and 457 players. The player statistics are for several seasons as well as for their career. The ***NBA*** data were collected from the following sources:

- http://stats.nba.com/help/glossary/
- http://www.basketball-tips-and-training.com/basketball-statistics.html
- http://www.sportingcharts.com/NBA/dictionary/
- http://espn.go.com/nba/dailyleaders

Table A.5 Data Dictionary for NBA Data

Variable Name	Description or Possible Values
Player	A unique ID for each NBA player
Name	Player's name
Position	C – Center PF – Power Forward SF – Small Forward PG – Point Guard SG – Shooting Guard
Age	Player's age in 2015–2016
Height	Player's height in inches as of 2015–2016
Weight	Player's weight in pounds as of 2015–2016
Salary	Player's annual salary in 2015–2016
Season	1999–2000 to 2015–2016
Postseason	TRUE – Playoff FALSE – Regular season
Team	Player's team in 2015–2016
Games_played	Total number of games played
Games_started	Number of games played as a starter
Minutes	Average minutes per game
FG_made	Total number of baskets made
FG_attempted	Total number of baskets attempted
FG_percent	Field goal percentage
3P_made	Total number of 3 pointers made
3P_attempted	Total number of 3 pointers attempted
3P_percent	Three pointer percentage
FT_made	Free throws made
FT_attempted	Free throws attempted
FT_percent	Free throw percentage
Rebounds_off	Total times player caught basketball after missed shot when playing offense
Rebounds_def	Total times player caught basketball after missed shot when playing defense
Assists	Total times player passed to another player who then scored a basket
Blocks	Total times player stopped the opponent from taking a shot (the ball must "be on its way up" to count)

Table A.5 *(Continued)*

Variable Name	Description or Possible Values
Steals	Total times player gained legal control of the basketball from opponent
Fouls	Total times player made illegal physical contact with an opponent
Turnovers	Total times player lost possession of basketball to opponent
Points	Average points per game

Data 6: Tech Sales Reps Data

FILE
TechSales_Reps

Analytics can help managers and organizations make well-informed decisions about their workforce. Instead of making personnel decisions based on perception and instinct, managers can use data to help identify, attract, and retain employees. The ***TechSales_Reps*** data contain records on 21,990 sales representatives from the hardware and software product groups of a high-tech company. For each employee, the data include socio-demographic and education information, salary, sales performance, and a personality indicator. Also included in the data is the net promoter score, which is an indicator of customer satisfaction with each sales rep. In this text, the ***TechSales_Reps*** data represent a highly simplified/modified sample.

Table A.6 Data Dictionary for Tech Sales Reps Data

Variable Name	Description or Possible Values
Rep	A unique ID for each sales representative
Business	One of the two product groups: Hardware and Software
Age	Employee's actual age
Female	1 – female 0 – otherwise
Years	The number of years the employee has been employed at the company
College	Whether or not the employee has a four-year college degree (Yes/No)
Personality	Analyst: This personality type exemplifies rationality. Analysts tend to be open-minded and strong-willed. They like to work independently and usually approach things from a very practical perspective. Diplomat: Diplomats care about people and tend to have a lot of empathy toward others. They exemplify cooperation and diplomacy. Explorer: Explorers are highly practical and can think on their feet. They tend to be very good at making quick, rational decisions in difficult situations. Sentinel: Sentinels are cooperative and practical. They like stability, order, and security. People with this personality type tend to be hardworking and meticulous.
Certificates	The number of relevant professional certifications each employee has earned
Feedback	The average feedback score that each employee receives from his or her peers and supervisor on the 360-degree annual evaluation. The possible scores range from 0 (lowest) to 4 (highest).
Salary	Annual base salary of each employee
NPS	The net promoter score (NPS) is a key indicator of customer satisfaction and loyalty.

APPENDIX B

Getting Started with Excel and Excel Add-Ins

Microsoft Excel

Microsoft Excel is arguably the most widely used computer application among business professionals. Accountants, economists, financial analysts, marketers, HR managers, and many others use Excel spreadsheets for everyday business tasks. Oftentimes, these tasks involve entering, editing, and formatting data as well as performing data analysis. We rely heavily on Excel and Excel add-ins in virtually every chapter of this text. Analytic Solver is the most relevant Excel add-in that offers a powerful tool for business analytics. In this appendix, we summarize Excel formulas, references, and functions that are commonly used for calculations and data analysis. We also show how to build a simple spreadsheet model for solving a business problem. Finally, we provide a brief description of Analytic Solver and other add-ins at the end of the appendix; detailed instructions on the use of these add-ins are included in the relevant chapters of the text.

Formulas

In Excel, we use formulas to perform basic calculations. When we enter a formula in a cell, Excel carries out the specified calculation and returns the result in the same cell. We also use formulas to manipulate the cell content such as rounding a number. A formula in Excel always starts with an equal sign (=) and usually includes cell addresses. A cell address or cell reference consists of a column name and a row number. For example, cell reference A1 refers to the top and leftmost cell in column A and row 1. Basic calculations can be performed using arithmetic operations such as addition (+), subtraction (–), multiplication (*), division (/), and exponentiation (^). For example, we select an empty cell and use the formula =A1+B1+C1 to add values from cells A1, B1, and C1, and the formula =A1^2 to square the value in cell A1.

Relative, Absolute, and Mixed References

There are three types of cell references: relative, absolute, and mixed. The three cell reference types behave differently when copied elsewhere on the worksheet. By default, cell addresses in a formula, such as =B1+C1, are relative references and will change when a formula is copied to another cell. For example, if we enter the formula =B1+C1 in cell A1 and copy it to cell D4, the formula in cell D4 will appear as =E4+F4. In other words, references to cells B1 and C1 are relative to where the formula is placed on the worksheet. We use relative references when we want to repeat similar calculations while allowing column names and row numbers to change.

Absolute references allow us to maintain the original cell references when a formula is copied elsewhere. We specify absolute references by adding a dollar sign ($) in front of the column name and row number (e.g., $B$1). From the previous example, if we enter the formula =$B$1+$C$1 in cell A1 and copy it to cell D4, the formula in cell D4 will remain =$B$1+$C$1. Unlike relative references, absolute references remain unchanged when copied elsewhere on the worksheet.

We use mixed references by adding a dollar sign ($) in front of either the column name or the row number (e.g., $B1 or B$1), but not both. This will keep the reference to the specific column name or the row number constant. From the previous example, if we enter the formula =$B1+$C1 in cell A1 and copy it to cell D4, the formula in cell D4 will become =$B4+$C4. Similarly, if we enter the formula =B$1+C$1 in cell A1 and copy it to cell D4, the formula in cell D4 will become =E$1+F$1.

In Table B.1, we summarize the different results when using relative, absolute, and mixed references with the same formula.

Table B.1 Relative, Absolute, and Mixed References

Reference	Formula in Cell A1	Formula in Cell A1 Copied to Cell D4
Relative	=B1+C1	=E4+F4
Absolute	=$B$1+$C$1	=$B$1+$C$1
Mixed	=$B1+$C1	=$B4+$C4
Mixed	=B$1+C$1	=E$1+F$1

Functions

Functions in Excel are predefined formulas. Like a formula, a function always begins with an equal sign (=) and must be written with the correct syntax enclosed within parentheses. Most functions require at least one argument. Arguments are the values that Excel uses to perform calculations. For example, the COUNT function is used to count the number of cells that contain numerical values and has the syntax =COUNT(A1:A10), where A1:A10 is the argument indicating the array of cells to be counted. Table B.2 provides a summary of some of the most basic descriptive functions in Excel. The notation array in the function's argument in the table specifies the range of cell addresses to be included in the calculation.

Important: Due to different fonts and type settings, copying and pasting formulas and functions from this text directly into Excel may cause errors. When such errors occur, you may need to replace special characters such as quotation marks and parentheses or delete extra spaces in the functions.

Table B.2 Basic Descriptive Functions in Excel

Function and Syntax	Description	Example
=COUNT(array)	Returns the number of cells in the array with numerical values.	=COUNT(A1:A10)
=COUNTA(array)	Returns the number of cells in the array that are not blank.	=COUNTA(A1:A10)
=COUNTBLANK(array)	Returns the number of cells in the array that are blank.	=COUNTBLANK(A1:A10)
=COUNTIF(array, criteria)	Returns the number of cells in the array that meet a specific selection criterion.	=COUNTIF(A1:A10, ">10")
=IF(logical statement, result if the statement is true, result if the statement is false)	Returns a result based on the outcome of the logical statement.	=IF(A1="Yes", 1, 0). If A1 = "Yes", returns a 1. If not, returns a 0. See also Example B.1
=SUM(array)	Adds and returns the sum of the numbers in the array.	=SUM(A1:A10)
=VLOOKUP(lookup value, reference table, column number in the reference table containing results)	Searches and retrieves information from a specified column in a reference table.	See Example B.1

Table B.3 provides a summary of some basic date and time functions in Excel.

Table B.3 Basic Date and Time Functions in Excel

Function and Syntax	Description	Example
=DAY(date value)	Returns the day of the month as a number between 1 and 31 given the date value in the argument.	=DAY("3/15/2019") Excel returns 15.
=MONTH(date value)	Returns the month of the year as a number between 1 and 12 given the date value in the argument.	=MONTH("3/15/2019") Excel returns 3.
=NOW()	Returns the current date and time. The NOW function does not require any argument.	=NOW()
=TODAY()	Returns the current date. The TODAY function does not require any argument.	=TODAY()
=WEEKDAY(date value)	Returns the day of the week as a number between 1 (Sunday) and 7 (Saturday) given the date value in the argument.	=WEEKDAY("3/15/2019") Excel returns 6, meaning that March 15, 2019, was a Friday.
=YEAR(date value)	Returns the year portion of the data value in the argument.	=YEAR("3/15/2019") Excel returns 2019.

Table B.4 provides a summary of some basic statistical functions in Excel. Other functions are introduced and discussed in the relevant chapters of the text.

Table B.4 Basic Statistical functions

Function and Syntax	Description	Example
=AVERAGE(array)	Returns the arithmetic mean of the array.	=AVERAGE(A1:A10)
=MAX(array)	Returns the largest number in the array.	=MAX(A1:A10)
=MEDIAN(array)	Returns the median of the array.	=MEDIAN(A1:A10)
=MIN(array)	Returns the smallest number in the array.	=MIN(A1:A10)
=RAND()	Returns a uniformly distributed random number that is greater than or equal to 0 and less than 1.	=RAND()
=RANDBETWEEN(lowest value, highest value)	Returns a uniformly distributed random number between the specified lowest and highest values, inclusive.	=RANDBETWEEN(1,10) Excel returns a random number between 1 and 10.
=ROUND(value, decimal digit)	Rounds the numerical value to the specified decimal digit.	=ROUND(2.6589,2) Excel returns 2.66.
=STDEV.S(array)	Estimates and returns the sample standard deviation of the array.	=STDEV.S(A1:A10)

Developing a Spreadsheet Model

While using formulas, references, and functions involves an understanding of Excel syntax, crafting a well-structured spreadsheet requires critical thinking and creativity. We usually build a spreadsheet model to represent simplified reality with the goals of solving a business problem, performing data analysis, and gaining insightful information. Ideally, a spreadsheet model should allow users to easily experiment with different assumptions, evaluate and compare different scenarios, and, more importantly, improve decision making. Spreadsheet modeling is more an art than a science, and it takes experience to hone the craft. A good spreadsheet model empowers both model developers and model users with the knowledge to improve its effectiveness.

In this appendix, we offer a few general guidelines for developing a spreadsheet model. Students are encouraged to find additional resources on spreadsheet modeling and to design their own spreadsheet whenever possible. When constructing a spreadsheet model, we consider the following general principles.

- The spreadsheet model should be well-organized. Similar information should be grouped together, be clearly labeled, and use the same format.
- The spreadsheet model should allow users to experiment with different scenarios based on input parameters, which are stored in individual cells and separately from the data.
- When entering a formula, careful consideration should be given to the choice of absolute, relative, and mixed references so that the formula can be copied to other cells that require a similar calculation.
- Output, including charts, should be clearly labeled and appropriately formatted. Users should be able to easily identify and understand the results.

Example B.1 demonstrates how to construct a simple spreadsheet model that follows these guidelines. In Chapter 13, we follow these guidelines to implement Monte Carlo simulations and linear programming analysis in Excel.

EXAMPLE B.1

FILE
Consulting

Sarah Washington, a manager at Iniesta Consulting Group, oversees a team of business consultants. Each of her team members has a highly specialized expertise that is crucial to the success of her consulting group. Sarah wants to examine the after-tax earnings of her team members to ensure that their salary remains competitive compared to the salaries offered by competing firms. Iniesta offers each employee medical benefits, but each employee is required to pay a co-premium (a portion of the medical insurance cost). The annual co-premium amount differs between a management employee ($1,800) and a non-management employee ($1,250). Even though Iniesta's medical benefits are much better than those offered by other employers, the co-premium reduces an employee's net earnings. Sarah collects the salary information of her team members and income tax rates in an Excel spreadsheet, shown in Figure B.1. She includes her own information in the table in order to verify the accuracy of her results. Develop a spreadsheet model to help Sarah analyze the salary, income tax, co-premium, and net earnings of each employee.

Developing a Spreadsheet Model in Excel

Sarah's spreadsheet organizes the five employees into a table with each column containing similar information. Each row is a simplified model representing an employee. All columns are clearly labeled with column headings and appropriately formatted (e.g., a dollar sign and no decimal places for the salary column). In addition, the input parameters, such as the medical co-premium and income tax rates, are stored in separate cells below the data. This way, if Sarah wants to experiment with different scenarios (e.g., reducing the medical co-premium cost for non-management employees), she can simply change the value in these individual cells.

FIGURE B.1 Salary and Tax Information of Employees

	A	B	C	D	E
1	**Iniesta Consulting Group**				
2					
3	**Employee ID**	**First name**	**Last name**	**Job classification**	**Salary**
4	1001	Kim	Clovis	Management	$ 89,046
5	1023	Florence	Anderson	Non-Management	$ 76,521
6	2544	Jack	Chen	Non-Management	$ 80,250
7	2135	Sarah	Washington	Management	$ 102,735
8	3327	Tim	Liu	Management	$ 98,623
9					
10	**Assumptions:**				
11		Management	Non-management		
12	Co-premium	$1,800	$1,250		
13					
14	Income tax				
15	Salaries	Tax rate			
16	$ 60,000	19%			
17	$ 70,000	22%			
18	$ 80,000	24%			
19	$ 90,000	26%			
20	$ 100,000	27%			

Source: Microsoft Excel

In order to perform relevant calculations for the spreadsheet model, we follow these steps.

A. Enter column headings Co-premium in cell F3, Tax amount in cell G3, Net earnings in cell H3, and Net earnings as percent of salary in cell I3. Format the column headings and cells in these columns similar to the first five columns. We will use columns F, G, H, and I to perform calculations and display analysis results.

B. Enter the formula =IF(D4=”Management”, B$12, C$12) in cell F4. We use the IF statement to evaluate whether the employee has a management-level position. If true, the co-premium is $1,800 (from cell B12), otherwise the co-premium is $1,250 (from cell C12). Verify that the output in cell F4 is $1,800.00.

   Copy and paste the formula to cells F5 through F8. In the formula entered in cell F4, we used a relative reference (without dollar signs) for cell D4 and mixed references for cell B12 and C12 with a dollar sign in front of the row numbers. The job classification varies from one employee to another, and therefore we use the relative reference for cell D4. When we copy the IF function to cells F5 through F8, the relative reference in the formula changes from D4 to D5 through D8, respectively. The co-premium amounts for management and non-management positions in cells B12 and C12 are applicable to all employees, and, therefore, we use mixed references to ensure that the two cell addresses remain unchanged for all formulas in column F. In other words, all formulas in column F refer to cells B12 and C12. It is important to note that absolute references (e.g., $B$12 and $C$12) would yield the correct result in the current example. This, however, is not necessary because we are not changing columns when copying and pasting the IF statement.

C. Enter the formula =VLOOKUP(E4,A$16:B$20,2,TRUE)*E4 in cell G4 to retrieve the tax rate for the first employee. The VLOOKUP function in the formula includes three required arguments and one optional argument:

   1. The lookup value (i.e., the salary in cell E4 in this case),
   2. A lookup or reference table (ranges of salaries and corresponding tax rates in cells A16:B20, without the column headings),
   3. A column number in the reference table that contains the output (in the current example, the tax rates are in the second column in the reference table), and
   4. Whether we want to look up a value within a range (TRUE) or find an exact match (FALSE). The last parameter is optional; if omitted, the default value is TRUE.

   In the reference table, if the salary is at least $60,000 and less than $70,000, the tax rate is 19%. If the salary is at least $70,000 and less than $80,000, the tax rate is 22%, and so forth. For a salary of $100,000 and above, the tax rate is 27%. These criteria in the reference table are applicable to all five employees. Verify that the tax amount for the first employee is $21,371.04 (= 24% × 89,046).

Copy and paste the formula to cells G5 through G8. Because we use mixed references for the reference table in cells A$16 through B$20, these cell addresses remain unchanged when copied from cell G4 to cells G5 through G8.

D. Enter the formula =E4-G4-F4 in cell H4. Copy and paste the formula to cells H5 through H8. Because we use relative references for these three cells, when we copy the formula from cell H4 to cells H5 through H8, the three cell addresses change to the corresponding row number. For example, the formulas in cell H5 and H8 should appear as =E5-G5-F5 and =E8-G8-F8, respectively. Format cells H4 through F8 with the Accounting Number format by highlighting the cells and clicking on the Accounting Number format button (with a dollar sign icon) in the Number group on the Home tab. Verify that the net earnings of the first employee is $65,874.96.

E. Enter the formula =H4/E4 in cell I4. Again, we use relative references here for the same reason as in step D. Format the value in cell I4 as a percentage by clicking the Percent (or Percentage) Style button in the Number group on the Home tab. Copy and paste the formula from cell I4 to cells I5 through I8. Verify that the net earnings as a percent of salary for the first employee is 73.98%.

F. We calculate the average net earnings of the five employees by using the AVERAGE function. Enter =AVERAGE(I4:I8) in cell I9. Format cell I9 as a percentage. Verify that the average net earnings is 73.64%. Enter Average in cell H9 as a label. Your completed spreadsheet should look similar to Figure B.2.

FIGURE B.2 Spreadsheet Model for Iniesta Consulting Group

	A	B	C	D	E	F	G	H	I
1	**Iniesta Consulting Group**								
2									
3	**Employee ID**	**First name**	**Last name**	**Job classification**	**Salary**	**Co-premium**	**Tax amount**	**Net earnings**	**Net earnings as percent of salary**
4	1001	Kim	Clovis	Management	$ 89,046	$ 1,800.00	$ 21,371.04	$ 65,874.96	73.98%
5	1023	Florence	Anderson	Non-Management	$ 76,521	$ 1,250.00	$ 16,834.62	$ 58,436.38	76.37%
6	2544	Jack	Chen	Non-Management	$ 80,250	$ 1,250.00	$ 19,260.00	$ 59,740.00	74.44%
7	2135	Sarah	Washington	Management	$ 102,735	$ 1,800.00	$ 27,738.45	$ 73,196.55	71.25%
8	3327	Tim	Liu	Management	$ 98,623	$ 1,800.00	$ 25,641.98	$ 71,181.02	72.17%
9								Average	73.64%
10	**Assumptions:**								
11		Management	Non-management						
12	Co-premium	$1,800	$1,250						
13									
14	Income tax								
15	Salaries	Tax rate							
16	$ 60,000	19%							
17	$ 70,000	22%							
18	$ 80,000	24%							
19	$ 90,000	26%							
20	$ 100,000	27%							

Source: Microsoft Excel

In the spreadsheet model in Figure B.2, Sarah can easily experiment with a different co-premium amount by changing the values in cells B12 and C12, and the results in columns F through I will be updated without requiring modifications to the formulas in those columns. And because the formulas do not need to be rewritten, there will be fewer chances of Sarah making mistakes when evaluating different scenarios.

Moreover, recall that we have to write the formulas only for the first employee in row 4 and simply copy them to other cells in rows 5 through 8. This is possible because we carefully use mixed and relative references. This way, formulas are used uniformly for cells that require a similar calculation, resulting in fewer potential mistakes and errors.

We also show the calculation results in columns F through I separately from the data in columns A through E. Sarah can easily see the net earnings of each employee in column H. By using the AVERAGE function to summarize the results, she can also conclude that, on average, the consultants in her group take home approximately three-quarters (i.e., 73.64%) of their salary.

Analytic Solver

Analytic Solver (formerly known as XLMiner) is an add-in software that runs on Microsoft Excel. It offers a comprehensive suite of statistics and data mining tools, including data wrangling, data partitioning, and supervised and unsupervised data mining methods.

The Interface

Once Analytic Solver is installed, launch Excel and verify that you can see the Analytic Solver, Data Mining, and Solver Home tabs. In this text, we focus primarily on the features in the Data Mining tab. Figure B.3 shows the features on the Data Mining tab. Examples and exercise problems in this text are developed based on Analytic Solver 2019. Other versions of Analytic Solver may have a different user interface and display the output in a different format.

FIGURE B.3 Data Mining Tab in Analytic Solver 2019 for Excel

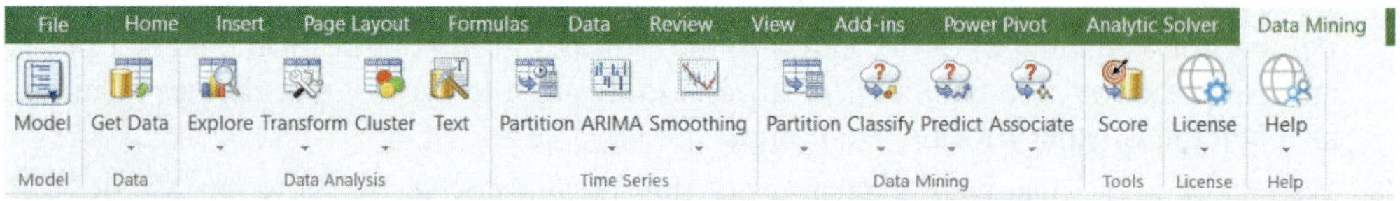

Source: Microsoft Excel

As shown in Figure B.3, there are six groups of features in the Data Mining tab. The Data Analysis and Data Mining groups are used extensively throughout this text. In the Data Analysis group, the Transform feature contains functions for handling missing data and transforming continuous and categorical data (see Chapter 2). The Transform feature also performs principal component analysis (or PCA), a widely used technique for data reduction (see Section 8.3). Under the Cluster feature, *k*-means and hierarchical clustering functions are part of the unsupervised data mining techniques (see Chapter 11).

In the Data Mining group, we use the Partition, Classify, and Predict features when we examine supervised data mining techniques (see Chapters 8, 9, and 10). We also use the Associate feature when we discuss Association Rules (see Section 11.3). Detailed instructions and examples on how to use these functions in Analytic Solver are presented in the relevant chapters throughout the text.

Other Excel Add-Ins

In addition to Analytic Solver, there are many other add-in software in Excel. In this text, we use two additional add-ins that come preinstalled with Excel. The Analysis ToolPak add-in is used for statistical analysis in Chapters 3 through 7 and for random number generation in Chapter 13. The Solver Add-In, developed by the same company that offers Analytic Solver, is used for linear and integer programming discussed in Chapter 13. The following instructions activate these two Excel add-ins.

Activating Analysis ToolPak and Solver Add-Ins

A. In Excel, go to **File** > **Options** > **Add-Ins**.

B. In the Manage Excel Add-ins section (toward the bottom of the screen), click **Go** . . . .

C. On the Add-ins dialog box, check the Analysis ToolPak and Solver Add-In boxes and click **OK**. Note: Analytic Solver should already have been checked by default.

D. In Excel, go to the **Data** tab and verify that the Data Analysis and Solver command buttons appear in the Analyze (or Analysis) group.

Getting Started with R

What is R?

R is a powerful computer language that merges the convenience of statistical packages with the power of coding. It is open source as well as cross-platform compatible. This means that there is zero cost to download R, and it can be run on Windows, macOS, or Linux. In this appendix, we will introduce you to some fundamental features of R and provide instructions on how to obtain solutions for many of the exercises in the text.

What is RStudio?

RStudio is a program that makes R easier to use. On its own, R acts like a programming language and, as such, comes with a minimal user interface. As standalone software, R shows a single prompt for you to enter commands; this is called the Console. While everything we will ever need from R can be done by combining Console commands with other programs, things can quickly get messy. To make coding in R easier, we use an integrated development environment (IDE). IDEs are programs that combine in one place many common features needed in programming and give them a graphical user interface.[1] In this text, we use an open source version of an IDE called RStudio, which is very popular among students, professionals, and researchers who use R.

Installation

Installation of both R and RStudio is straightforward and requires no special modifications to your system. However, it should be noted that RStudio does not come with R; *therefore, both pieces of software need to be installed separately.* Also, all R code in the text and its accompanying output are based on **R version 3.5.3 on Microsoft Windows**. Even though there will be newer versions of R when you prepare to download it, we suggest that you download **R version 3.5.3**. Newer versions of R may not be compatible with certain R packages, especially those packages that we use in later chapters of this text. All versions of R for Windows can be found at the following website: https://cran.r-project.org/bin/windows/base/old/. We discuss R packages at the end of this Appendix.

Installing R for Windows

A. Navigate to https://cran.r-project.org/bin/windows/base/old/.

B. Select *R 3.5.3 (March 2019).*

C. Select *Download R 3.5.3 for Windows.*

D. Locate the downloaded file and double-click.

E. Select *Yes* when asked about verifying the software publisher, and then select the language that you prefer. We select *English.*

F. Follow the instructions in the R Setup window.

For Mac and Linux, follow the instructions at https://cran.r-project.org/bin/macosx/ and https://cran.r-project.org/bin/linux/, respectively, and choose the appropriate link for your operating system and version.

[1]More formally, this is called a "graphical user interface," or a GUI. In practice, this means that charts, graphs, and buttons can be seen and used.

Installing RStudio

A. Navigate to https://www.rstudio.com/products/rstudio/.

B. Select *RStudio Desktop,* then select *Download RStudio Desktop.*

C. Scroll down to the *Installers for Supported Platforms* section, select the link that corresponds to your operating system, and then select *Open* or *Run.*

D. Select *Yes* when asked about verifying the software publisher.

E. Follow the instructions in the RStudio Setup window.

The Interface

Installation should now be complete. You can close all windows and then double-click on the RStudio icon.

The RStudio interface consists of several panes. By default, three panes are visible. We will refer to these by the names of the default tab shown in each: Console, Environment, and Help. We will also briefly discuss the Source pane, which is hidden until you open it. Figure C.1 shows what you should see when you open RStudio for the first time.

FIGURE C.1 The Console, Environment, and Help Panes

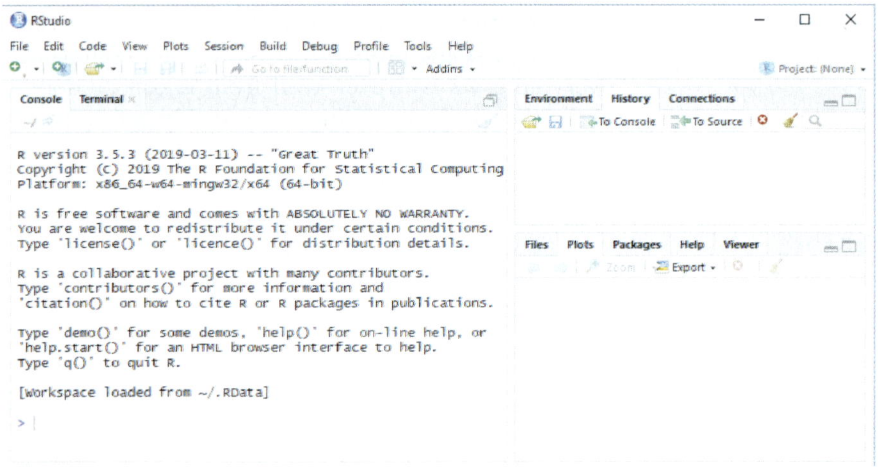

Source: R Studio

- **Console pane:** The Console pane is the primary way that you interact with R. It is here that you input commands (at the > prompt) and then view most of your output.
- **Environment pane:** Two relevant tabs in the Environment pane are: Environment and History. A common feature between them is the broom icon, which clears the content of each tab. The Environment tab shows the data, objects, and variables in the current R session. The History tab provides a list of all console commands issued in the session.
- **Help pane (or Files pane):** The help section has five tabs. We discuss two of these here: Help and Plots.
  - The Help tab is where you can view R documentation (help files). For example, to learn about the **print** function, select the Help tab and then enter `print` next to the magnifying glass icon. (You can also view R documentation by entering a question mark followed immediately by the topic of interest in the Console pane; so, for this example, you would enter `?print` after the prompt.)
  - The Plots tab is where you can see all graphs and charts. Any graph or chart can be cleared with the broom icon.
- **The Source pane:** The Source pane is hidden by default in R. This is where you can write your own scripts. As you will see, most of what we do in this text can be accomplished by importing a data set and then using a single command in the Console. Nonetheless, here is an example of how you would write a simple script:

  A. From the menu, select **File > New File > R Script**

  B. In the new window, enter the following:

```
print("This is my first script.")
print("This is easy!")
```

Save the script with **File > Save As.** Name your script `Script1`. Figure C.2 shows what you should see in the Source pane.

Important: Due to different fonts and type settings, copying and pasting formulas and functions from this text directly into Excel may cause errors. When such errors occur, you may need to replace special characters such as quotation marks and parentheses or delete extra spaces in the functions.

FIGURE C.2 The Source Pane After Writing First Script

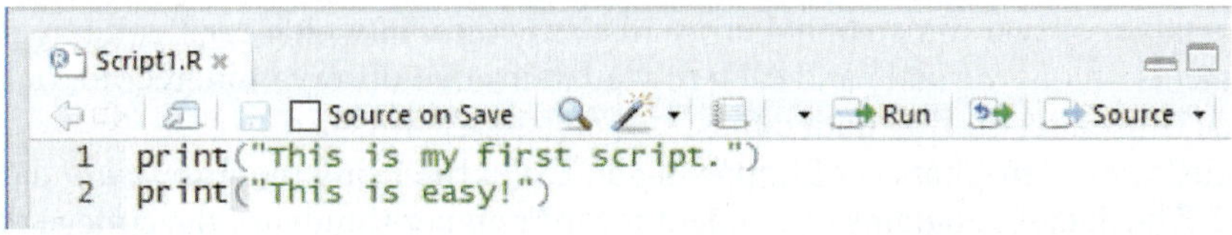

Source: R Studio

C. Again refer to Figure C.2. Click the Source button from the menu on the Source pane; this tells R to read and execute the script. Figure C.3 shows what you should see in the Console pane after executing your first script.

FIGURE C.3 The Console Pane After Executing First Script

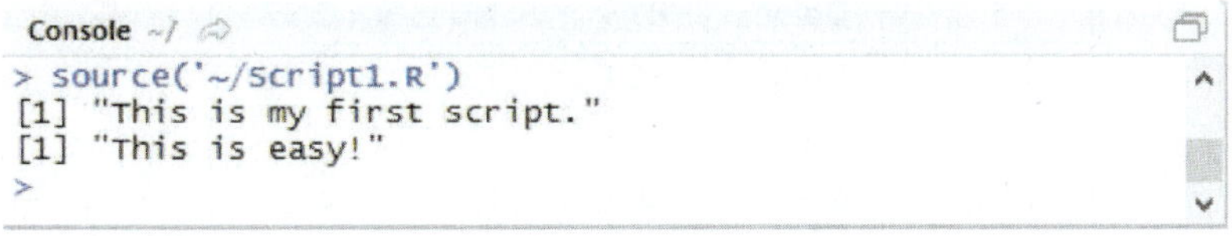

Source: R Studio

R executes complete statements in the order that they appear. Unique to RStudio, there is also a way to run specific sections of scripts. This is done by highlighting the desired section of the script in RStudio and selecting the Run button from the menu on the Source pane.

Entering Data and Using Functions

Throughout this text, our goal is to provide the simplest way to obtain the relevant output. Seasoned users of R might argue that there are "better" approaches than the ones we suggest, but we feel that they may distract from learning the important concepts.

Like Excel and other statistical packages, R has many built-in formulas or functions. In the text, we denote all function names in **boldface.** Within each function, R also provides various options, such as labeling the axes of a graph, inserting colors in a chart, and so on. We will not use every option within a function; rather, we use those that we feel are most useful and least cumbersome. We denote all option names in *italics*.

Most of the time we will be importing data files, as we explain in the next section. However, suppose we want to use R to perform a simple calculation. Suppose we want to calculate the mean given the following data: −4, 0, 6, 1, −3, −4. In order to input these values into R, we use the **c** function, which combines the values to form a list; or, perhaps more mathematically precise, the **c** function combines the values to form a vector. We label this data as Example_1 and use the expression "<-" which is equivalent to the equal sign. We enter:

```
Example_1 <- c(-4, 0, 6, 1, -3, -4)
```

You should see Example_1 listed in the Environment pane. You can view the data in the Console pane by entering Example_1 after the prompt. Additionally, you can use the **View** function and the data will appear in the Source pane. (Note that R is case sensitive.) We enter:

```
View(Example_1)
```

Another common function is the **mean** function which we discuss in more detail in Chapter 3. In order to calculate the mean of the data, we enter:

```
> mean(Example_1)
```

And R returns: −0.6666667.

FILE
Admission

Importing Data and Using Functions

All the data for *Business Analytics—Communicating with Numbers* have been stored in Excel spreadsheets. We will assume that you have stored all the relevant spreadsheets in a Data folder. When we import a spreadsheet into R, it is referred to as a data frame. A data frame is a table, or two-dimensional array-like structure, in which each column contains measurements on one variable and each row contains one observation, record, or case. A data frame is used for storing data tables.

We illustrate the mechanics of importing an Excel file using the ***Admission*** data from Chapter 2. The data set contains the student record number (Student), the college decision on acceptance (Decision = Admit or Deny), the student's SAT score, whether the student is female or male (Female = yes or no), and the student's high school GPA (HSGPA). Table C.1 shows a portion of the ***Admission*** data.

TABLE C.1 Portion of the Admission Data

Student	Decision	SAT	Female	HSGPA
1	Deny	873	No	2.57
2	Deny	861	Yes	2.65
⋮	⋮	⋮	⋮	⋮
1230	Admit	1410	No	4.28

In order to import this data file into R, we select **File > Import Dataset > From Excel,** as shown in Figure C.4.[2] (The first time you import data, R might prompt you to add updates. Simply follow the steps to add the relevant updates.)

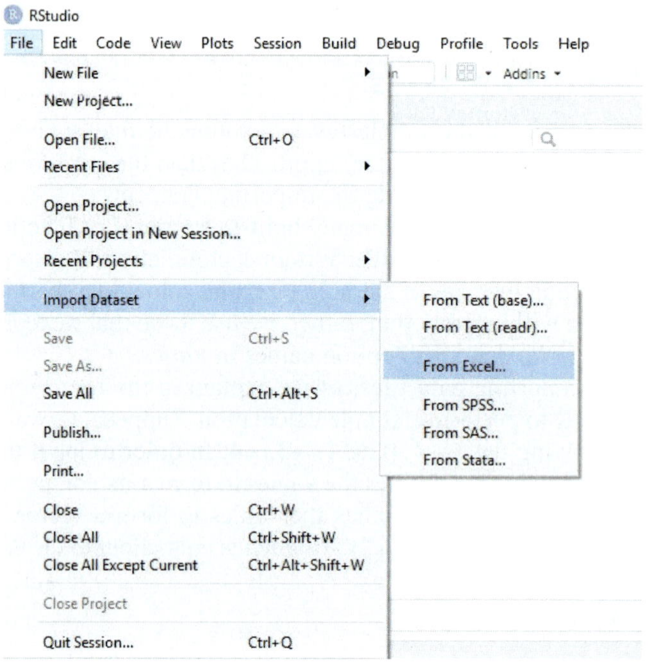

Source: R Studio

FIGURE C.4 Importing the Admission Data into R

[2]Note that you can also import a comma- or tab-delimited text file by selecting **File > Import Dataset > From Text (base)** or **File > Import Dataset >From Text (readr),** respectively.

See Figure C.5. We select the Browse button and then navigate to the ***Admission*** data in the Data folder. Once we select the ***Admission*** data, we should see the data in the *Data Preview* dialog box. In the R instructions in this text, we label all data files as myData for simplicity and consistency. Because of this, in the *Import Options* dialog box, replace Admission with myData. Once you select the Import button (see the bottom of Figure C.5), you have successfully imported the data. You can verify this in a number of ways. For instance, you should now see myData in the Environment pane under Data, or you can enter `View(myData)` in the Console pane and a portion of the data will appear in the Source pane.

FIGURE C.5 Viewing the Admission Data Prior to Importing Source: R Studio

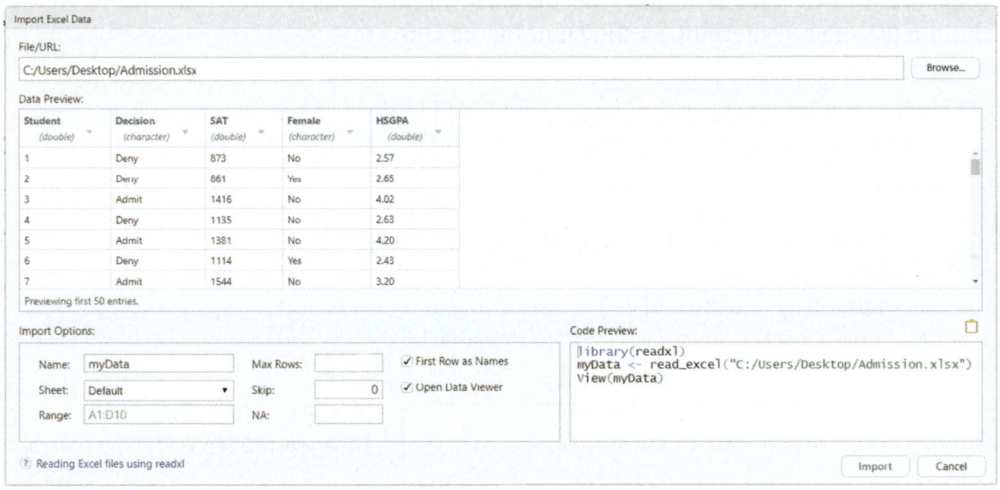

Note: For an Excel file with multiple worksheets, select the appropriate worksheet from the *Sheet* drop-down option.

Suppose we want to calculate the mean SAT score in myData. In order to select a variable from a data frame, we attach the expression $VariableName to the name of the data frame. Here, we enter:

```
> mean(myData$SAT)
```

And R returns: 1197.348.

If the variable name in the data frame is more than one word or numeric (such as year), then it is necessary to enclose the variable name with single quotation marks. For instance, if the variable name was SAT score instead of SAT, then we would have entered mean(myData$'SAT score').

Another function that we discuss in Chapter 3 is the **summary** function. This function provides various summary measures for all variables in a data frame. We could enter `summary(myData)` and R would return summary measures for all the variables in the myData data frame, including the categorical variables. Suppose we would like summary measures only on SAT and HSGPA. In this case, we attach square brackets to the name of the data frame, and within the brackets we indicate the columns that should be included in the calculations using the **c** function. In order to obtain summary measures for SAT (third variable) and HSGPA (fifth variable), we enter:

```
> summary(myData[,c(3,5)])
```

Notice in the above command that we enter a comma directly after the left square bracket. This implies that we are including all 1,230 observations (all 1,230 rows) in the calculations. If for some reason we only wanted to include the first 100 observations in the calculations, we would have entered `summary(myData[1:100,c(3,5)])`.

Finally, suppose we want to delete the myData data frame. We use the **rm** function and enter:

```
> rm(myData)
```

You will find that myData no longer appears under *Data* in the Environment pane.

A Note on Line Breaks

The commands that we have outlined here have been relatively short. There are some instances, however, when the commands get long and become difficult to read. To mitigate this, we can break up a command into parts. R will prompt you to finish the command with plus + symbols in lines following the first line. For example, in Chapter 3 we discuss a scatterplot. Suppose we want to construct a scatterplot of SAT against HSGPA for the first 20 observations using R's **plot** function. In addition to constructing the scatterplot, we use the *ylab* and *xlab* options to add titles on the *y*-axis and the *x*-axis. Two entries for constructing a scatterplot are shown below. Entry 1 uses a single line in R (even though two lines are shown on the page). Entry 2 uses three lines. Both entries result in the same scatterplot, as shown in Figure C.6.

Entry 1:

```
> plot(myData$SAT[1:20] ~ myData$HSGPA[1:20],
  ylab="SAT Score", xlab="High School GPA")
```

Entry 2:

```
> plot(myData$SAT[1:20] ~ myData$HSGPA[1:20],
  + ylab="SAT Score",
  + xlab="High School GPA")
```

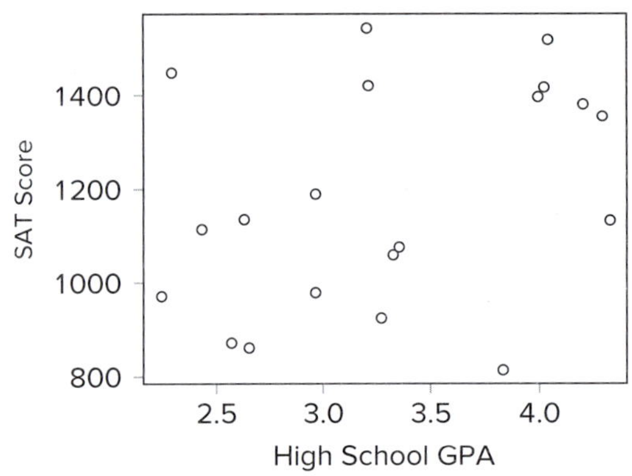

FIGURE C.6 Scatterplot of SAT against HSGPA

Packages

Part of what makes R so powerful is its large collection of packages, or collections of objects not included in the base version. Packages greatly expand what can be done with R by adding custom functions and data structures. As mentioned earlier in this Appendix, we use these packages in conjunction with **R version 3.5.3.** Compatibility issues may arise if you use another version of R.

To use a package, you must install it and then load it. We use the *caret* package, which stands for Classification and Regression Training, to demonstrate how this is done:

```
> install.packages("caret")
> library(caret)
```

The **install.packages** function connects to the official R servers (CRAN), downloads the specified package(s) and those it depends on, and installs it. This must be done with each package only once on each computer used. The **library** function loads the installed package(s). Suppose you want to install multiple packages, such as *caret, gains,* and *pROC.* Instead of installing each package separately, you can use the following command:

```
> install.packages(c("caret","gains","pROC"))
```

However, you still need to use the **library** function separately for each package as follows:

```
> library(caret)
> library(gains)
> library(pROC)
```

Sometimes, R may prompt you to install additional packages. If this is the case, follow the steps outlined here to download and install these additional packages.

Note that each package only needs to be loaded once per R session. Once the package is downloaded and loaded, documentation for commands it contains can be viewed in R using the help feature discussed earlier. Documentation files for an entire package can be viewed online. All information associated with available packages can be found at https://cran.r-project.org/web/packages/.

Statistical Tables

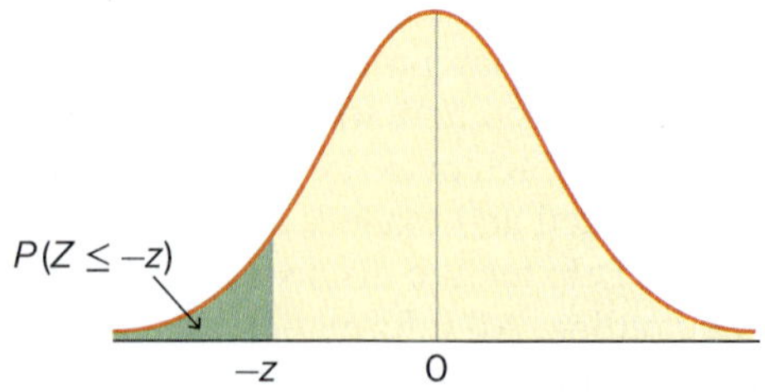

TABLE D.1 Standard Normal Curve Areas

Entries in this table provide cumulative probabilities, that is, the area under the curve to the left of $-z$. For example, $P(Z \leq -1.52) = 0.0643$.

z	0.00	0.01	0.02	0.03	0.04	0.05	0.06	0.07	0.08	0.09
−3.9	0.0000	0.0000	0.0000	0.0000	0.0000	0.0000	0.0000	0.0000	0.0000	0.0000
−3.8	0.0001	0.0001	0.0001	0.0001	0.0001	0.0001	0.0001	0.0001	0.0001	0.0001
−3.7	0.0001	0.0001	0.0001	0.0001	0.0001	0.0001	0.0001	0.0001	0.0001	0.0001
−3.6	0.0002	0.0002	0.0001	0.0001	0.0001	0.0001	0.0001	0.0001	0.0001	0.0001
−3.5	0.0002	0.0002	0.0002	0.0002	0.0002	0.0002	0.0002	0.0002	0.0002	0.0002
−3.4	0.0003	0.0003	0.0003	0.0003	0.0003	0.0003	0.0003	0.0003	0.0003	0.0002
−3.3	0.0005	0.0005	0.0005	0.0004	0.0004	0.0004	0.0004	0.0004	0.0004	0.0003
−3.2	0.0007	0.0007	0.0006	0.0006	0.0006	0.0006	0.0006	0.0005	0.0005	0.0005
−3.1	0.0010	0.0009	0.0009	0.0009	0.0008	0.0008	0.0008	0.0008	0.0007	0.0007
−3.0	0.0013	0.0013	0.0013	0.0012	0.0012	0.0011	0.0011	0.0011	0.0010	0.0010
−2.9	0.0019	0.0018	0.0018	0.0017	0.0016	0.0016	0.0015	0.0015	0.0014	0.0014
−2.8	0.0026	0.0025	0.0024	0.0023	0.0023	0.0022	0.0021	0.0021	0.0020	0.0019
−2.7	0.0035	0.0034	0.0033	0.0032	0.0031	0.0030	0.0029	0.0028	0.0027	0.0026
−2.6	0.0047	0.0045	0.0044	0.0043	0.0041	0.0040	0.0039	0.0038	0.0037	0.0036
−2.5	0.0062	0.0060	0.0059	0.0057	0.0055	0.0054	0.0052	0.0051	0.0049	0.0048
−2.4	0.0082	0.0080	0.0078	0.0075	0.0073	0.0071	0.0069	0.0068	0.0066	0.0064
−2.3	0.0107	0.0104	0.0102	0.0099	0.0096	0.0094	0.0091	0.0089	0.0087	0.0084
−2.2	0.0139	0.0136	0.0132	0.0129	0.0125	0.0122	0.0119	0.0116	0.0113	0.0110
−2.1	0.0179	0.0174	0.0170	0.0166	0.0162	0.0158	0.0154	0.0150	0.0146	0.0143
−2.0	0.0228	0.0222	0.0217	0.0212	0.0207	0.0202	0.0197	0.0192	0.0188	0.0183
−1.9	0.0287	0.0281	0.0274	0.0268	0.0262	0.0256	0.0250	0.0244	0.0239	0.0233
−1.8	0.0359	0.0351	0.0344	0.0336	0.0329	0.0322	0.0314	0.0307	0.0301	0.0294
−1.7	0.0446	0.0436	0.0427	0.0418	0.0409	0.0401	0.0392	0.0384	0.0375	0.0367
−1.6	0.0548	0.0537	0.0526	0.0516	0.0505	0.0495	0.0485	0.0475	0.0465	0.0455
−1.5	0.0668	0.0655	0.0643	0.0630	0.0618	0.0606	0.0594	0.0582	0.0571	0.0559
−1.4	0.0808	0.0793	0.0778	0.0764	0.0749	0.0735	0.0721	0.0708	0.0694	0.0681
−1.3	0.0968	0.0951	0.0934	0.0918	0.0901	0.0885	0.0869	0.0853	0.0838	0.0823
−1.2	0.1151	0.1131	0.1112	0.1093	0.1075	0.1056	0.1038	0.1020	0.1003	0.0985
−1.1	0.1357	0.1335	0.1314	0.1292	0.1271	0.1251	0.1230	0.1210	0.1190	0.1170
−1.0	0.1587	0.1562	0.1539	0.1515	0.1492	0.1469	0.1446	0.1423	0.1401	0.1379
−0.9	0.1841	0.1814	0.1788	0.1762	0.1736	0.1711	0.1685	0.1660	0.1635	0.1611
−0.8	0.2119	0.2090	0.2061	0.2033	0.2005	0.1977	0.1949	0.1922	0.1894	0.1867
−0.7	0.2420	0.2389	0.2358	0.2327	0.2296	0.2266	0.2236	0.2206	0.2177	0.2148
−0.6	0.2743	0.2709	0.2676	0.2643	0.2611	0.2578	0.2546	0.2514	0.2483	0.2451
−0.5	0.3085	0.3050	0.3015	0.2981	0.2946	0.2912	0.2877	0.2843	0.2810	0.2776
−0.4	0.3446	0.3409	0.3372	0.3336	0.3300	0.3264	0.3228	0.3192	0.3156	0.3121
−0.3	0.3821	0.3783	0.3745	0.3707	0.3669	0.3632	0.3594	0.3557	0.3520	0.3483
−0.2	0.4207	0.4168	0.4129	0.4090	0.4052	0.4013	0.3974	0.3936	0.3897	0.3859
−0.1	0.4602	0.4562	0.4522	0.4483	0.4443	0.4404	0.4364	0.4325	0.4286	0.4247
−0.0	0.5000	0.4960	0.4920	0.4880	0.4840	0.4801	0.4761	0.4721	0.4681	0.4641

Source: Probabilities calculated with Excel.

TABLE D.1 *(Continued)*

Entries in this table provide cumulative probabilities, that is, the area under the curve to the left of z. For example, $P(Z \leq 1.52) = 0.9357$.

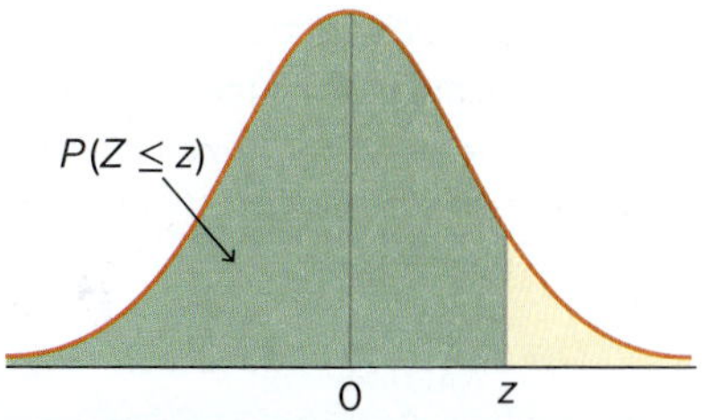

z	0.00	0.01	0.02	0.03	0.04	0.05	0.06	0.07	0.08	0.09
0.0	0.5000	0.5040	0.5080	0.5120	0.5160	0.5199	0.5239	0.5279	0.5319	0.5359
0.1	0.5398	0.5438	0.5478	0.5517	0.5557	0.5596	0.5636	0.5675	0.5714	0.5753
0.2	0.5793	0.5832	0.5871	0.5910	0.5948	0.5987	0.6026	0.6064	0.6103	0.6141
0.3	0.6179	0.6217	0.6255	0.6293	0.6331	0.6368	0.6406	0.6443	0.6480	0.6517
0.4	0.6554	0.6591	0.6628	0.6664	0.6700	0.6736	0.6772	0.6808	0.6844	0.6879
0.5	0.6915	0.6950	0.6985	0.7019	0.7054	0.7088	0.7123	0.7157	0.7190	0.7224
0.6	0.7257	0.7291	0.7324	0.7357	0.7389	0.7422	0.7454	0.7486	0.7517	0.7549
0.7	0.7580	0.7611	0.7642	0.7673	0.7704	0.7734	0.7764	0.7794	0.7823	0.7852
0.8	0.7881	0.7910	0.7939	0.7967	0.7995	0.8023	0.8051	0.8078	0.8106	0.8133
0.9	0.8159	0.8186	0.8212	0.8238	0.8264	0.8289	0.8315	0.8340	0.8365	0.8389
1.0	0.8413	0.8438	0.8461	0.8485	0.8508	0.8531	0.8554	0.8577	0.8599	0.8621
1.1	0.8643	0.8665	0.8686	0.8708	0.8729	0.8749	0.8770	0.8790	0.8810	0.8830
1.2	0.8849	0.8869	0.8888	0.8907	0.8925	0.8944	0.8962	0.8980	0.8997	0.9015
1.3	0.9032	0.9049	0.9066	0.9082	0.9099	0.9115	0.9131	0.9147	0.9162	0.9177
1.4	0.9192	0.9207	0.9222	0.9236	0.9251	0.9265	0.9279	0.9292	0.9306	0.9319
1.5	0.9332	0.9345	0.9357	0.9370	0.9382	0.9394	0.9406	0.9418	0.9429	0.9441
1.6	0.9452	0.9463	0.9474	0.9484	0.9495	0.9505	0.9515	0.9525	0.9535	0.9545
1.7	0.9554	0.9564	0.9573	0.9582	0.9591	0.9599	0.9608	0.9616	0.9625	0.9633
1.8	0.9641	0.9649	0.9656	0.9664	0.9671	0.9678	0.9686	0.9693	0.9699	0.9706
1.9	0.9713	0.9719	0.9726	0.9732	0.9738	0.9744	0.9750	0.9756	0.9761	0.9767
2.0	0.9772	0.9778	0.9783	0.9788	0.9793	0.9798	0.9803	0.9808	0.9812	0.9817
2.1	0.9821	0.9826	0.9830	0.9834	0.9838	0.9842	0.9846	0.9850	0.9854	0.9857
2.2	0.9861	0.9864	0.9868	0.9871	0.9875	0.9878	0.9881	0.9884	0.9887	0.9890
2.3	0.9893	0.9896	0.9898	0.9901	0.9904	0.9906	0.9909	0.9911	0.9913	0.9916
2.4	0.9918	0.9920	0.9922	0.9925	0.9927	0.9929	0.9931	0.9932	0.9934	0.9936
2.5	0.9938	0.9940	0.9941	0.9943	0.9945	0.9946	0.9948	0.9949	0.9951	0.9952
2.6	0.9953	0.9955	0.9956	0.9957	0.9959	0.9960	0.9961	0.9962	0.9963	0.9964
2.7	0.9965	0.9966	0.9967	0.9968	0.9969	0.9970	0.9971	0.9972	0.9973	0.9974
2.8	0.9974	0.9975	0.9976	0.9977	0.9977	0.9978	0.9979	0.9979	0.9980	0.9981
2.9	0.9981	0.9982	0.9982	0.9983	0.9984	0.9984	0.9985	0.9985	0.9986	0.9986
3.0	0.9987	0.9987	0.9987	0.9988	0.9988	0.9989	0.9989	0.9989	0.9990	0.9990
3.1	0.9990	0.9991	0.9991	0.9991	0.9992	0.9992	0.9992	0.9992	0.9993	0.9993
3.2	0.9993	0.9993	0.9994	0.9994	0.9994	0.9994	0.9994	0.9995	0.9995	0.9995
3.3	0.9995	0.9995	0.9995	0.9996	0.9996	0.9996	0.9996	0.9996	0.9996	0.9997
3.4	0.9997	0.9997	0.9997	0.9997	0.9997	0.9997	0.9997	0.9997	0.9997	0.9998
3.5	0.9998	0.9998	0.9998	0.9998	0.9998	0.9998	0.9998	0.9998	0.9998	0.9998
3.6	0.9998	0.9998	0.9999	0.9999	0.9999	0.9999	0.9999	0.9999	0.9999	0.9999
3.7	0.9999	0.9999	0.9999	0.9999	0.9999	0.9999	0.9999	0.9999	0.9999	0.9999
3.8	0.9999	0.9999	0.9999	0.9999	0.9999	0.9999	0.9999	0.9999	0.9999	0.9999
3.9	1.0000	1.0000	1.0000	1.0000	1.0000	1.0000	1.0000	1.0000	1.0000	1.0000

Source: Probabilities calculated with Excel.

TABLE D.2 Student's *t* Distribution

Entries in this table provide the values of $t_{\alpha,df}$ that correspond to a given upper-tail area α and a specified number of degrees of freedom df. For example, for $\alpha = 0.05$ and $df = 10$, $P(T_{10} \geq 1.812) = 0.05$.

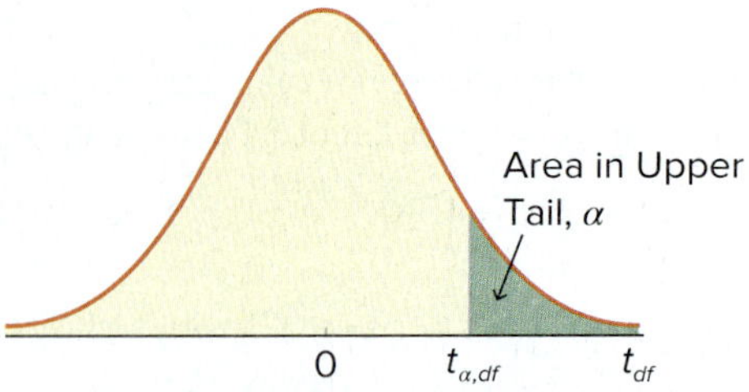

df	α 0.20	0.10	0.05	0.025	0.01	0.005
1	1.376	3.078	6.314	12.706	31.821	63.657
2	1.061	1.886	2.920	4.303	6.965	9.925
3	0.978	1.638	2.353	3.182	4.541	5.841
4	0.941	1.533	2.132	2.776	3.747	4.604
5	0.920	1.476	2.015	2.571	3.365	4.032
6	0.906	1.440	1.943	2.447	3.143	3.707
7	0.896	1.415	1.895	2.365	2.998	3.499
8	0.889	1.397	1.860	2.306	2.896	3.355
9	0.883	1.383	1.833	2.262	2.821	3.250
10	0.879	1.372	1.812	2.228	2.764	3.169
11	0.876	1.363	1.796	2.201	2.718	3.106
12	0.873	1.356	1.782	2.179	2.681	3.055
13	0.870	1.350	1.771	2.160	2.650	3.012
14	0.868	1.345	1.761	2.145	2.624	2.977
15	0.866	1.341	1.753	2.131	2.602	2.947
16	0.865	1.337	1.746	2.120	2.583	2.921
17	0.863	1.333	1.740	2.110	2.567	2.898
18	0.862	1.330	1.734	2.101	2.552	2.878
19	0.861	1.328	1.729	2.093	2.539	2.861
20	0.860	1.325	1.725	2.086	2.528	2.845
21	0.859	1.323	1.721	2.080	2.518	2.831
22	0.858	1.321	1.717	2.074	2.508	2.819
23	0.858	1.319	1.714	2.069	2.500	2.807
24	0.857	1.318	1.711	2.064	2.492	2.797
25	0.856	1.316	1.708	2.060	2.485	2.787
26	0.856	1.315	1.706	2.056	2.479	2.779
27	0.855	1.314	1.703	2.052	2.473	2.771
28	0.855	1.313	1.701	2.048	2.467	2.763
29	0.854	1.311	1.699	2.045	2.462	2.756
30	0.854	1.310	1.697	2.042	2.457	2.750

TABLE D.2 (*Continued*)

	α					
df	0.20	0.10	0.05	0.025	0.01	0.005
31	0.853	1.309	1.696	2.040	2.453	2.744
32	0.853	1.309	1.694	2.037	2.449	2.738
33	0.853	1.308	1.692	2.035	2.445	2.733
34	0.852	1.307	1.691	2.032	2.441	2.728
35	0.852	1.306	1.690	2.030	2.438	2.724
36	0.852	1.306	1.688	2.028	2.434	2.719
37	0.851	1.305	1.687	2.026	2.431	2.715
38	0.851	1.304	1.686	2.024	2.429	2.712
39	0.851	1.304	1.685	2.023	2.426	2.708
40	0.851	1.303	1.684	2.021	2.423	2.704
41	0.850	1.303	1.683	2.020	2.421	2.701
42	0.850	1.302	1.682	2.018	2.418	2.698
43	0.850	1.302	1.681	2.017	2.416	2.695
44	0.850	1.301	1.680	2.015	2.414	2.692
45	0.850	1.301	1.679	2.014	2.412	2.690
46	0.850	1.300	1.679	2.013	2.410	2.687
47	0.849	1.300	1.678	2.012	2.408	2.685
48	0.849	1.299	1.677	2.011	2.407	2.682
49	0.849	1.299	1.677	2.010	2.405	2.680
50	0.849	1.299	1.676	2.009	2.403	2.678
51	0.849	1.298	1.675	2.008	2.402	2.676
52	0.849	1.298	1.675	2.007	2.400	2.674
53	0.848	1.298	1.674	2.006	2.399	2.672
54	0.848	1.297	1.674	2.005	2.397	2.670
55	0.848	1.297	1.673	2.004	2.396	2.668
56	0.848	1.297	1.673	2.003	2.395	2.667
57	0.848	1.297	1.672	2.002	2.394	2.665
58	0.848	1.296	1.672	2.002	2.392	2.663
59	0.848	1.296	1.671	2.001	2.391	2.662
60	0.848	1.296	1.671	2.000	2.390	2.660
80	0.846	1.292	1.664	1.990	2.374	2.639
100	0.845	1.290	1.660	1.984	2.364	2.626
150	0.844	1.287	1.655	1.976	2.351	2.609
200	0.843	1.286	1.653	1.972	2.345	2.601
500	0.842	1.283	1.648	1.965	2.334	2.586
1000	0.842	1.282	1.646	1.962	2.330	2.581
∞	0.842	1.282	1.645	1.960	2.326	2.576

Source: *t* values calculated with Excel.

APPENDIX E

Answers to Selected Exercises

Chapter 1

1.2 35 is likely the estimated average age of the population. It would be impossible to reach all video game players.

1.4 a. The population consists of all recent college graduates with an engineering degree.

b. No, the average salary was likely computed from a sample in order to save time and money.

1.6 Answers will vary depending on when data are retrieved. The data are cross-sectional data.

1.8 The data on the front page of *The New York Times* are likely to be unstructured in that they do not conform to a predefined row-column format.

1.10 Answers will vary depending on when data are retrieved. The data are time series data.

1.12 Structured; cross-sectional data.

1.20 a. Nominal

b. Interval

c. Ratio

1.24 a. Country Happiness GDP

Finland 7.769 45670

Denmark 7.600 57533

Norway 7.544 75295

Iceland 7.494 73060

Netherlands 7.488 48754

b. Country,Happiness,GDP

Finland,7.769,45670

Denmark,7.600,57533

Norway,7.544,75295

Iceland,7.494,73060

Netherlands,7.488,48754

Chapter 2

2.4 Choice c is the correct definition of a foreign key.

2.6 Choices b, c, and d correctly describe SQL. Choice a describes NoSQL.

2.12 a. 1 of the 10 highest income earners is married and always exercises.

b. 9 individuals are married, exercise often, and earn more than $110,000 per year.

c. 5 values are missing for Exercise, 2 for Marriage, and 3 for Income.

d. 281 individuals are married, and 134 are not.

e. 69 married individuals always exercise, and 74 unmarried individuals never exercise.

2.18 a. There are no missing values in x_2, x_3, and x_4.

b. The remaining data set has 35 observations. The average values for x_3 and x_4 are 170.6571 and 21.2286 respectively.

2.24 a. Variables x_1, x_3, x_4, and x_5 all have at least one missing value.

b. Observations 15, 24, 33, 34, 43, 63, 66, 78, and 95 have missing values.

c. There are 9 missing values in the data set.

d. 2 missing values of x_2 were replaced.

e. After replacing missing values of x_3, x_4, and x_5, their means and median in the new data set are 3.8832, 1260, and 3.1330 respectively.

f. There are 43 observations remain in the dataset.

2.26 a. There are missing values in the variable Travel Plan. All other variables are complete.

b. 300 observations were removed.

2.28 a. There are 3 missing values in the data set. In the Yards variable, the missing value is for observation 25. In the Attempts variable, the missing value is for observation 28. In the Interceptions variable, the missing value is for observation 30. All other variables and observations are complete.

b. Using the omission strategy, 3 observations were removed.

2.32 a. All variables other than Name and Market Cap have missing values. Observation 20 is missing for the variable Price; observation 173 is missing for variable Dividend; observations 38 is missing for the variable PE; observation 26 is missing for variable EPS, observation 98 is missing for the variable Book Value; observation 26, and 154 are missing for the variable 52 week low, observation 46 is missing for the variable 52 week high, and observation 51 is missing for variable the EBITDA. There are 9 missing values in the data set.

b. 8 observations were removed.

c. Missing values for variable PE, EPS, and EBITDA were replaced with 21.915, 3.255, and 1.845, respectively. There were no missing values for Market Cap, whose median value is 21.17.

2.34 a. Observation 26 has missing values for the Siblings variable, observation 13 is missing for the variable Height, observation 47 is missing for the variable Weight, and observations 17 and 51 have missing values for the Income variable. All other variables are complete. In the data set, there are 5 missing values.

b. 3 observations were removed.

c. Observation 13 has a missing value for the Height variable, and observation 47 has a missing value for the Weight variable. The missing value for Height was replaced with its mean, 67.3088, and the missing value for Weight was replaced with its mean, 150.8971. The missing value for Siblings was replaced with its median, 2, and the missing values for Income were replaced with its median, 33,361. There were no missing values for FamilySize, whose median is 4.

2.38 a. There are 41 observations in the data set. After binning, 4 of the five bins should have 8 observations, and the remaining bin should have 9 observations.
b. The number of observations with a score of 431 is: 0. The number of observations with a score of 222 is: 2.

2.40 a. The average of Difference is −1.91.
b. The average PercentDifference is 0.2273.
c. The average of Log is 12.84.

2.42 a. The average difference in year is 29.01.
b. The average month value is 6.
c. Group 3 has the highest number of observations.

2.46 a. Number of customers assigned to Group 4 is 26.
b. Number of customers assigned to Group 3 is 21.
c. Number of customers assigned to Group 2 is 36.
d. The average difference is 124.7.
e. The average percentage difference is 0.5642.
f. The average age of the players is 28.70 years.
g. September is the most frequent birth month.

2.50 a. There are 23 observations in the "Other" category.
b. The average category score for x_2 is 3.6200.
c. Three dummy variables should be created.

2.52 a. 15 observations have a category score of 3.
b. There are 3 observations in the "Other" category.
c. Four dummy variables should be created.

2.54 a. The variables LoanType, PropertyType, and Purpose are nominal data because they do not have naturally ordered categories.
b. Conventional is the most frequent category for LoanType. Multi-family is the most frequent category for PropertyType. Refinancing is the most frequent category for Purpose.
c. Three dummy variables should be created. Conventional should be the reference category of LoanType. Multi-family should be the reference category of PropertyType. Refinancing should be the reference category of Purpose.

2.56 a. One dummy variable should be created.
b. The average damage score of the cell towers is 0.7959.

Chapter 3

3.2 a. The proportion of the sales for medium-sized shirts was 0.302.
b. Sales of large-sized shirts had the highest frequency and sales of small-sized shirts had the lowest frequency.

3.4 a. 19.3% of people in the Midwest are living below the poverty level.
b. The South has the highest relative frequency as compared to the other three regions, which are roughly equal.

3.6 a. A rating of 5 has the highest frequency
b. The higher ratings have the higher frequencies.

3.8 a. Not Religious is the most common response.
b. About 35% responded "Not Religious" which is consistent with the Pew Research survey.

3.10 a. 125 stocks had returns of at least 10% but less than 20%.
b. The distribution is symmetric.

3.14 a. No. The distribution is not symmetric. It is positively skewed.
b. Over this time period, the stock price was between \$50 and \$250.
c. The \$100 up to \$150 interval has the highest relative frequency, which is about 0.44.

3.16 a. 14 customers spent between \$700 and \$999.
b. 52 customers spent \$1,300 or less; 48 customers spent more than \$1,300.

3.18 a. The DJIA was more than 26,000 on 44 days in the first half of 2019.
b. The distribution is not symmetric; it is negatively skewed.

3.20 It does not; by using a relatively high value as an upper limit on the vertical axis (\$500), the rise in stock price appears dampened.

3.22 a. 202 of the customers were male; 60 of the customers drank wine.
b. 142/202 = 0.7030; 38/68 = 0.5588.
c. Beer is the popular drink at this bar, followed by wine, and then soft drinks. Both men and women are more likely to choose beer over the other two options.

3.24 a. 5 components from shift 1 were defective; 94 components from shift 2 were not defective.
b. 6/24 = 0.2500; 13/24 = 0.5417; components constructed during shift 3 seem to be defective at a higher rate.
c. No, defective rates are not consistent over the shifts.

3.26 a. 120 students are business majors; 68 students study hard.
b. 20/120 = 0.1667; 48/150 = 0.3200; the data suggest that nonbusiness majors are more likely to study hard, which supports the report.
c. The majority of both business and nonbusiness students do not study hard, but nonbusiness students are more likely to study hard.

3.28 Negative relationship between obesity and life expectancy.

3.30 No relationship between the returns of A and B, so investing in both would diversify risk.

3.32 a. Negative relationship between the price of a car and its age.
b. Negative relationship between the price of a car and its mileage.

3.34 Both countries have an upward trend, but China's begins to stall slightly around 2000.

3.36 a. Age is negatively correlated with price and positively correlated with mileage. Price is negatively correlated with mileage.
b. Seven cars have mileage greater than 50,000.
c. The negative relationship between age and price is consistent for cars of both mileage categories.

3.38 a. There are 511 cases of a burglary in a residence.
b. Theft on the street is the most common crime, followed by narcotics on a sidewalk, then motor vehicle theft on the street.

3.40 a. HD $\bar{x} = 79{,}231$; median = 77,349
Lowe's $\bar{x} = 52{,}754$; median = 50,208
HD had a higher average revenue.
b. HD $s^2 = 106{,}175{,}095$; $s = 10{,}304$
Lowe's $s^2 = 56{,}414{,}505$; $s = 7{,}511$
HD had a higher dispersion.

3.42 a. mean = 2.3122; median = 2.18
b. Q1 = 2.01; 25% of the states had gas prices below $2.01.
Q3 = 2.55; 75% of the states had gas prices less than $2.55.
c. $s^2 = 0.1482$; $s = 0.3849$

3.44 a. Monthly rent is positively skewed, with tails longer than that of a normal distribution.
b. Square footage is positively skewed, with tails longer than that of a normal distribution.

3.46 a. Firm A: $\bar{x} = 75.39$; $s^2 = 52.02$; $s = 7.21$
Walmart $\bar{x} = 73.51$; $s^2 = 319.21$; $s = 17.87$
b. Firm B had the higher average stock price.
c. Firm B had a higher dispersion in stock price.

3.48 a. The Latin America fund is positively skewed, with tails shorter than that of normal distribution.
b. The Canada fund is negatively skewed, with tails longer than that of a normal distribution.

3.50 $\gamma_{\text{Final,Midterm}} = 0.5518$; positive and moderate linear relationship.

3.56 a. Approximately 25% of the observations have values that are less than 200; Approximately 75% of the observations have values that are less than 550.
b. IQR = 350; Limit: 1.5 × IQR = 525. Q1 – Min = 75 < 525 and Max – Q3 = 750 > 525; thus, there is at least one outlier on the right side of the distribution.
c. The distribution appears positively skewed because the median falls left of center in the interquartile range and the right whisker is longer than the left whisker.

3.58 a. About 68% of the scores are in the interval [84, 116].
b. About 95% of the scores are in the interval [68, 132]. About 2.5% of the scores are less than 68.
c. About 16% of the scores are more than 116.

3.60 a. About 95% of the games will last between 2.2 and 3.8 hours.
b. About 16% of the games are longer than 3.4 hours.
c. About 2.5% of the games are shorter than 2.2 hours.

3.62 a. The boxplot suggests that there are no outliers for the Debt variable.
b. $\bar{x} = 983.4615$; $s = 124.6086$. The smallest and the largest observations for the Debt variable are 763 and 1,285, respectively.
The z-score for the smallest observation is
$$z = \frac{763 - 983.4615}{124.6086} = -1.7692$$
The z-score for the largest observation is
$$z = \frac{1{,}285 - 983.4615}{124.6086} = 2.4199$$
Since the absolute value of both z-scores is less than 3, we conclude that there are no outliers for the Debt variable. This is consistent with the boxplot, which showed no outliers.

3.64 a. The Technology boxplot suggests that there are outliers in the upper part of the distribution.
b. $\bar{x}_{\text{Tech}} = 17.6992$; $s_{\text{Tech}} = 36.5637$. The smallest and the largest observations in the data set are −51.09 and 131.75, respectively.
The z-score for the smallest observation is
$$z = \frac{-51.09 - 17.6992}{36.5637} = -1.8814$$
The z-score for the largest observation is
$$z = \frac{131.75 - 17.6992}{36.5637} = 3.11924$$
Since the z-score for the largest observation is greater than 3, we conclude that there are outliers for Technology. This is consistent with the boxplot, which showed outliers in the upper part of the distribution.
c. The Energy boxplot suggests that there is an outlier in the lower part of the distribution.
d. $\bar{x}_{\text{Energy}} = 10.0314$; $s_{\text{Energy}} = 22.9492$. The smallest and the largest observations in the data set are −54.00 and 52.02, respectively.
The z-score for the smallest observation is
$$z = \frac{-54.00 - 10.0314}{22.9492} = -2.4402$$
The z-score for the largest observation is
$$z = \frac{52.02 - 10.0314}{22.9492} = 2.1796$$
Since the absolute value of both z-scores is less than 3, we conclude that there are no outliers for Energy. This is not consistent with the boxplot, which showed an outlier in the lower part of the distribution. Since the boxplot indicates that Energy is not symmetric, we are better served identifying outliers in this case with a boxplot.
e. $\bar{x}_{\text{Tech}} = 12.3666$; $\bar{x}_{\text{Energy}} = 11.8100$

Chapter 4

4.2 a. Not exhaustive because you may not get any offer.
b. Not mutually exclusive because you may get both offers.

4.4 Let event *A* correspond to "Firm raising an alarm", and event *F* to "Fraudulent Transaction". We have $P(A) = 0.05$, $P(A|F) = 0.80$, and $P(F) = 0.01$.
$P(A^c \cap F) = 0.002$, and therefore, $P(F|A^c) = 0.0021$

4.6 a. $P(A) = 0.70$, $P(A^c) = 0.30$, $P(B) = 0.50$
b. Not mutually exclusive
c. $A \cap B$

4.10 Let event A_i be "the *i*-th selected member is in favor of the bonus".
a. $P(A_1 \cap A_2) = 0.4286$
b. $P(A_1^c \cap A_2^c) = 0.0952$

4.12 Let event *A* correspond to "Asians", *B* to "black", *W* to "white", *H* to "Hispanic", and *T* to "both parents at home". We have $P(T|A) = 0.85$, $P(T|W) = 0.78$, $P(T|H) = 0.70$, and $P(T|B) = 0.38$
a. $P(A \cap B) = 0$; mutually exclusive
$P(A) + P(B) < 1$; not exhaustive
b. $P(W^c) = 0.44$
c. $P(W \cap T) = 0.4368$
d. $P(A \cap T^c) = 0.015$

4.14 Let event *C* correspond to "Using own car daily", and event *U* to "Under 35". We have $P(C) = 0.62$, $P(C|U) = 0.38$, and $P(U) = 0.43$.

a. $P(C \cap U) = 0.1634$

b. $P(U|C) = 0.2635$

4.16 Let event D be "Experience a decline", and event N be "Ratio is negative". We have $P(D) = 0.20$, $P(N|D) = 0.70$, and $P(N|D^c) = 0.15$.

$P(N) = 0.26$, and therefore, $P(D|N) = 0.54$

4.18 Let event O correspond to "obese", W to "white", B to "black", H to "Hispanic", and A to "Asian". We have $P(O|W) = 0.33$, $P(O|B) = 0.496$, $P(O|H) = 0.43$, $P(O|A) = 0.089$, $P(W) = 0.48$, $P(B) = 0.19$, $P(H) = 0.26$, and $P(A) = 0.07$.

a. $P(O) = 0.3707$

b. $P(W|O) = 0.4273$

c. $P(B|O) = 0.2542$

d. $P(A|O) = 0.0168$

4.20 Let F = "Player is fully fit to play", S = "Player is somewhat fit to play", N = "Player is not able to play", and W = "The Lakers win the game". We have $P(F) = 0.40$, $P(S) = 0.30$, $P(N) = 0.30$, $P(W|F) = 0.80$, $P(W|S) = 0.60$, and $P(W|N) = 0.40$.

a. $P(W) = 0.62$

b. $P(F|W) = 0.52$

4.22 Let event R correspond to "Republican", D to "Democrat", I to "Independent", and S to "Support marijuana legalization". We have $P(R) = 0.27$, $P(D) = 0.30$, $P(I) = 0.43$, $P(S|R) = 0.41$, $P(S|D) = 0.66$, and $P(S|I) = 0.63$.

a. $P(S \cap R) = 0.1107$

b. $P(S \cap D) = 0.1980$

c. $P(S \cap I) = 0.2709$

d. $P(S) = 0.5796$

e. $P(R|S) = 0.1910$

4.26 Let X be the amount spent on a warranty and Y be the revenue earned by the store.

$E(X) = \$30$

$E(Y) = \$3{,}600$

4.32 a. $P(X < 2) = 0.6517$

b. $P(X < 2) = 0.4580$

4.34 a. $E(X) = 905$; $SD(X) = 27.22$

b. $E(X) = 1430$; $SD(X) = 31.95$

4.36 a. $P(X > 2) = 0.5276$

b. $P(X > 2) = 0.1362$

4.38 Let X be the number of designers who show the acceptable design.

a. $P(X \geq 1) = 0.4375 < 0.50$; statement is not correct

b. $P(X \geq 1) = 0.5781 > 0.50$; statement is correct

4.40 Let X be the number of attendees whom the manager contacts.

a. $P(X = 10) = 0.1171$

b. $P(X \leq 10) = 0.8725$

c. $P(X \geq 15) = 0.0016$

4.42 a. $P(X \leq 4) = 0.8153$

b. $P(X \geq 3) = 0.5768$

4.44 a. $\mu_1 = 6$; $P(X = 2) = 0.0446$

b. $\mu_1 = 6$; $P(X \geq 2) = 0.9826$

c. $\mu_{10} = 60$; $P(X = 40) = 0.001$

4.46 a. $\mu_1 = 2$; $P(X > 2) = 0.3233$

b. $\mu_5 = 10$; $P(X = 6) = 0.0631$

c. $\mu_{180} = 360$

4.50 a. $\mu = 304$; $P(X > 320) = 0.1717$

b. $\mu = 2128$; $P(X > 2200) = 0.0586$

4.52 Let X equal points scored in a game.

a. $P(85 < X < 125) = 0.9544$

b. $P(X > 125) = 0.0228$; approximately 2 games ($82 \times 0.0228 = 1.87$)

4.54 Let X represent the mpg rating of passenger cars.

a. $P(X \geq 40) = 0.0384$

b. $P(30 \leq X \leq 35) = 0.4952$

c. $x = 33.8 + 2.326(3.5) = 41.94$

4.56 Let X represent the return on a portfolio.

$P(X > 16) = 0.2514 \neq 0.15$; not normal.

4.62 Let X equal the length of time of a football game.

a. $P(X < 2.5) = 0.1056$

b. $P(X < 2.5) + P(X > 3.5) = 0.2112$

c. $x = 3 - 2.326(0.4) = 2.07$

Chapter 5

5.4 a. $P(\overline{X} \geq 18) = P(Z \geq 1.85) = 0.0322$

b. $P(\overline{X} \geq 17.5) = P(Z \geq 2.03) = 0.0212$

c. Janice; her findings are more likely if a representative sample is used.

5.6 a. $P(\overline{X} > 25{,}000) = P(Z > -1.04) = 0.8508$

b. $P(\overline{X} > 30{,}000) = P(Z > 0.39) = 0.3483$

5.8 a. $P(X > 1{,}000{,}000) = P(Z > 0.80) = 0.2119$

b. $P(\overline{X} > 1{,}000{,}000) = P(Z > 1.60) = 0.0548$

5.10 a. $P(X < 90) = P(Z < -0.63) = 0.2643$

b. $P(\overline{X} < 90) = P(Z < -1.25) = 0.1056$

c. $(P(X < 90))^4 = (0.2643)^4 = 0.0049$

5.12 a. $E(\overline{P}) = 0.33$ and $se(\overline{P}) = 0.047$; the normal approximation conditions are met because $np = 33 > 5$ and $n(1 - p) = 67 > 5$.

b. $P(\overline{P} < 0.30) = P(Z < -0.64) = 0.2611$

c. $P(0.31 \leq \overline{P} \leq 0.35) = P(-0.43 \leq Z \leq 0.43) = 0.3328$

5.14 For $n = 50$, $P(\overline{P} > 0.70) = P(Z > 1.44) = 0.0749$

For $n = 100$, $P(\overline{P} > 0.70) = P(Z > 2.04) = 0.0207$

You would choose 50 balls because with larger sample sizes the standard deviation of $\overline{P}$ is *reduced*. The probability of getting 70% green balls is slightly higher with a smaller sample because of the increased standard deviation.

5.16 a. $2.11\frac{9.2}{\sqrt{18}} = 4.58$

b. 12.5 ± 4.58 or $[7.92, 17.08]$

c. To reduce the margin of error of a 95% confidence level, the program should increase its sample size.

5.18 a. $2.724\frac{10}{\sqrt{36}} = 4.54$

b. 100 ± 4.54 or $[95.46, 104.54]$

5.20 a. 17.25 ± 7.36 or $[9.89, 24.61]$

b. The population is normally distributed.

5.24 $1{,}080 \pm 89.30$ or $[990.70, 1{,}169.30]$

The manager is wrong with the new strategy, since 1,200 is not within the 95% confidence interval.

5.26 a. microeconomics: [68.74, 74.91]; macroeconomics: [66.16, 74.64]

b. The widths are different because the sample standard deviations for microeconomics and macroeconomics are different.

5.28 a. For research expenditure: [231.44, 373.49]

b. For duration: [18.40, 22.60]

5.30 a. 0.37 ± 0.011 or [0.359, 0.381]

b. 0.37 ± 0.017 or [0.353, 0.387]

c. The margin of error in part b is greater because it uses a higher confidence level.

5.32 a. 0.47 ± 0.025 or [0.445, 0.495].

b. 0.025

c. 0.038

5.34 a. 0.275 ± 0.037 or [0.238, 0.312]

b. No, because the value 0.30 falls in the interval.

5.38 a. Type I error; the new software is purchased even though it does not reduce assembly costs.

b. Type II error; the new software is not purchased even though it reduces assembly costs.

5.40 a. H_0: $\mu \leq 5$; H_A: $\mu > 5$

b. $t_6 = 0.643$; p-value $= 0.272$. It is necessary to assume that the population is normally distributed.

c. Because $0.272 > 0.10$, do not reject H_0. The average waiting time is not more than 5 minutes at the 10% level.

5.42 H_0: $\mu \leq 6.6$; H_A: $\mu > 6.6$; $t_{35} = 2.7$; p-value $= 0.0053$. Because $0.0053 < 0.05$, reject H_0. At the 5% significance level, he can conclude that the mean increase in home prices in the West is greater than the increase in the Midwest.

5.44 a. H_0: $\mu = 50$; H_A: $\mu \neq 50$

b. $t_{49} = -2.324$; p-value $= 0.024$

c. Because $0.024 < 0.05$, reject H_0 At the 5% significance level, we conclude that the average differs from 50.

5.46 a. H_0: $\mu \leq 65$; H_A: $\mu > 65$

b. $t_{39} = 2.105$; p-value $= 0.021$.

c. Because $0.021 > 0.01$, do not reject H_0. At 1% significance level, we cannot conclude that the average speed is greater than the stated speed limit of 65mph.

5.52 H_0: $p \leq 0.60$; H_A: $p > 0.60$; $z = 1.04$; p-value $=$ 0.1492. Because $0.1492 > 0.01$, do not reject H_0. At the 1% significance level, we cannot conclude that more than 60% of seniors have made serious adjustments to their lifestyle.

Chapter 6

6.2 a. The positive sign for the Poverty coefficient is as expected; the slope coefficient for Income is not as expected.

b. $\widehat{\text{Crime}} = -301.62 + 53.16(20) + 4.95(50) =$ 1,009.08

6.4 a. Female employees

b. Female employees without an MBA

c. No

6.6 a. $\widehat{\text{GPA}} = 0.4256 + 0.0041\text{GRE}$

b. 3.34

6.8 a. $\widehat{\text{Consumption}} = 2{,}365.67 + 0.8465$ Disposable Income

b. As disposable income increases by \$1, consumption is predicted to increase by \$0.8465.

c. \$31,993.17

6.12 a. Assuming electricity is used for cooling (but not for heating), we expect electricity cost to be higher in months with a higher average outdoor temperature, higher in months with more working days, and higher in months in which more tons of product are produced.

b. $\widehat{\text{Cost}} = 14{,}039.19 + 92.78$ Ave Temp $+$ 446.14 Work Days $-$ 27.00 Tons Produced

c. \$28,279.11.

6.14 a. $\widehat{\text{Net Profit}} = -0.2091 + 0.0875$ Counter Sales $+$ 0.1123 Drivethrough Sales

b. For every additional \$1,000,000 in drive-through sales, net profits are predicted to increase by \$112,300, holding counter sales constant.

c. 0.7467; or net profits are predicted to be \$746,700 when counter sales are \$6,000,000 and drive-through sales are \$4,000,000.

6.16 a. $\widehat{\text{Startups}} = 0{,}4190 + 0.0087$ Research $+$ 0.0517 Patents $-$ 0.0194 Duration

b. 1.49 startups

c. A \$1 million increase in research expenditure results in a predicted increase in the number of startups by 0.0087, holding everything else constant. Approximately \$114.94 million $\left(\frac{1}{0.0087} = \$114.94\right)$ in additional research expenditures would be needed to have 1 additional predicted startup, everything else being the same. Note that $\$114.94 \times 0.0087$ equals (approximately) 1.

6.18 a. $R^2 = 0.8299$

b. 0.1701

6.22 Model 2 is a better fit since it has a smaller standard error and a higher adjusted R^2. We cannot use R^2 for comparison because the models have different numbers of predictor variables.

6.24 a. $s_e = 0.2144$.

b. 0.7573; 75.73% of the variability in net profits is explained by the model.

c. Adjusted $R^2 = 1 - (1 - 0.7573)\left(\frac{100 - 1}{100 - 2 - 1}\right) =$ 0.7523

6.32 a. $\widehat{\text{Return}} = -12.0243 + 0.1459\text{P/E} + 5.4417\text{P/S}$

b. H_0: $\beta_1 = \beta_2 = 0$; H_A: At least one $\beta_j \neq 0$; $F_{(2,27)} =$ 2.817 with p-value $= 0.077$. Because $0.077 <$ 0.10, reject H_0. At the 10% significance level, the two explanatory variables are jointly significant.

c. H_0: $\beta_1 = 0$; H_A: $\beta_1 \neq 0$; p-value $= 0.738$. Because $0.738 > 0.10$, do not reject H_0. At the 10% significance level, P/E is not significant in explaining Return.

$H_0 : \beta_2 = 0$; H_A: $\beta_2 \neq 0$; p-value $= 0.025$. Because $0.025 < 0.10$, reject H_0. At the 10% significance level, P/S is significant in explaining Return.

6.34 a. $\widehat{\text{Watches}} = 35.9090 - 0.0261$ Time

b. H_0: $\beta_1 \geq -0.02$; H_A: $\beta_1 < -0.02$; $t_{18} =$ $\frac{-0.0261 - (-0.02)}{0.0022} = -2.773$; p-value $= 0.006$.

Because 0.006 < 0.05, reject H_0. At the 5% significance level, an extra second of Time decreases Watches by more than 0.02.

6.36 a. $\widehat{Cost}$ = 14,039.1873 + 92.7827 Temp + 446.1406 Days − 27.0033 Tons

b. H_0: $\beta_1 = \beta_2 = \beta_3 = 0$; H_A: At least one $\beta_j \neq 0$; because 0.026 < 0.10, reject H_0. At the 10% significance level, the predictor variables are jointly significant in explaining the electricity costs.

c. At the 10% significance level, the average temperature is significant in explaining the electricity costs, the number of work days is not significant, and the tons produced is not significant.

6.42 a. $\widehat{Salary}$ = 62.3383 − 0.9605 BMI + 4.4855 White; at the 5% significance level, BMI influences salary.

b. White college-educated man: 38.01; non-white college-educated man: 33.52.

6.44 a. $\widehat{Time}$ = 0.0357 + 0.0079 Machine Parts + 0.6465 Manual Parts

b. 14.1322 minutes

c. 85.30%

d. At the 5% significance level, the predictor variables are jointly significant. At the 5% significance level, each predictor variable is individually significant.

6.46 a. $\widehat{Vehicles}$ = 135.3913 + 23.5056 Garage Bays + 0.5955 Population + 84.5998 Access + 77.4646 Winter

b. As the number of bays increases by 1 bay the number of vehicles served per month is predicted to increase by 23.5056, holding other variables constant; as the population in a 5-mile radius increases by 1,000 people, the number of vehicles served per month is predicted to increase by 0.5955, holding other variables constant. When changing to convenient interstate access, the number of vehicles served per month is predicted to increase by 84.5998, holding other variables constant. When changing to the winter, the number of vehicles served per month is predicted to increase by 77.4646, holding other variables constant.

c. At the 5% (and 10%) significance level, the predictor variables are jointly significant in explaining the number of vehicles served per month. At the 5% significance level, Access and Winter are significant, but Garage Bays and Population are not significant. At the 10% significance level, Access, Winter, and Garage Bays are significant, but Population is not significant.

d. 0.8739

e. 361.34 vehicles

6.48 a. $\widehat{Sales}$ = 47,095.6859 + 65.0548 GNP + 108765.2580d_1 − 30486.2947d_2 − 48805.0461d_3

b. $1,057,485.47

c. At the 5% significance level, all the quarters are significantly different from the fourth quarter.

d. At the 5% significance level, we cannot conclude that the sales differ between quarters 2 and 3.

6.50 Create dummy variables for White, Black, Asian, and Hispanic students using the Ethnicity variable.

a. $\widehat{SAT}$ = 1388.8919 + 201.1447 White − 31.4544 Black + 264.8581 Asian

Asian student: 1654; Hispanic student: 1389

b. At the 5% significance level, Asian students score differently on the SAT than Hispanic students.

c. At the 5% significance level, white students score lower than Asian students.

6.52 a. The residuals fan out when plotted against x.

b. Constant variability; with changing variability, the estimators are unbiased, but not efficient. Another problem is that the t tests and F test are not valid. It is common to use robust standard errors for conducting significance tests.

6.54 The scatterplot shows that a simple linear regression model is not appropriate as GPA is positively related to Hours at lower levels, but negatively related at higher levels of Hours.

6.56 a. Perfect multicollinearity, because Study + Sleep + Leisure = 24. The proposed model cannot be estimated.

b. Drop the Sleep variable.

6.58 a. Experienced (older) employees are likely to have more variability in salaries because not all employees reach the same level of success over time.

b. The residuals fan out when plotted against experience, confirming the changing variability problem.

6.60 There does not appear to be an issue with correlated observations, as the residuals do not show any pattern around the horizontal axis.

6.62 a. $\widehat{Sales}$ = −1,730.0915 + 302.9945 Temp + 505.5782 Advertising + 202.2232 Discount: The predictor variables are jointly significant. At the 5% significance level, Advertising is significant, but Temp and Discount are not significant.

b. The correlation matrix reveals excessive correlation among the predictor variables which suggests multicollinearity. It might be best to do nothing about multicollinearity because none of the predictor variables appears to be redundant. Also, although Temp and Discount are found to be individually insignificant, the estimated model has high explanatory power.

c. The residuals appear to be (reasonably) randomly dispersed across the domains of each predictor variable. Changing variability does not seem to be serious.

Chapter 7

7.8 a. $\widehat{\text{Majority Male}}$ = 88.5714 − 8.5714 Female − 6.2185 Minority Male − 18.7815 (Female × Minority Male); predictor variables are jointly and individually significant at the 5% level.

b. 80% (Just Woman); 55% (Woman and Hispanic Man)

7.10 a. $\widehat{Usage}$ = 14.9236 + 0.9808 Income − 42.3267 Rural + 20.4745 College + 49.8701 (Rural × College); predictor variables are jointly and, except for College, individually significant at the 5% level.

b. 160.64 (Rural); 153.10 (Urban)

7.12 a. $\widehat{\text{Errors}} = 37.9305 - 1.2814\text{ Exper} - 7.4241\text{ Train}$
$\widehat{\text{Errors}} = 42.7765 - 1.6991\text{ Exper} - 23.1111\text{ Train} + 0.9785\text{ (Exper} \times \text{Train)}$
b. The model with the interaction term is preferred because it has a higher adjusted R^2 and the interaction variable is significant at the 10% level.
c. 12.46 (10 years); 8.79 (20 years)
d. Less experienced employees benefit more from the training program (reduced pick errors) than more experienced employees.

7.14 a. $\widehat{\text{Comp}} = 2677.1892 + 10.3154\text{ Profit} + 1227.6866\text{ Years} + 36655.1363\text{ Grad} - 0.5227\text{ (Profit} \times \text{Grad)} - 193.1612\text{ (Years} \times \text{Grad)}$
b. Predictor variables are jointly significant at the 5% level.
c. Profit, Years, and Grad are individually significant at the 5% level, but the interaction variables are not.
d. $101,855

7.16 a. $\widehat{\text{College GPA}} = -6.8195 + .0063\text{ SAT} + 1.9401\text{ HSGPA} + 1.6688\text{ White} - 0.0011\text{ (SAT} \times \text{HSGPA)} - 0.0010\text{ (SAT} \times \text{White)}$; predictor variables are jointly and, except for the second interaction term, individually significant at the 5% level.
b. White: 3.23 (SAT = 1200); 3.41 (SAT = 1300); 3.59 (SAT = 1400)
Non-White: 2.81 (SAT = 1200); 3.10 (SAT = 1300); 3.38 (SAT = 1400)

7.18 a. $\widehat{\text{Earnings}} = 34169.6282 - 0.7398\text{ Cost} - 319.0062\text{ Grad} + 219.1327\text{ Debt} + 2643.2320\text{ City} + 0.0185\text{ (Cost} \times \text{Grad)}$; the partial effect of Cost increases with Grad and the partial effect of Grad increases with Cost.
b. $42,666 (Cost = $20,000); $46,398 (Cost = $30,000); $50,130 (Cost = $40,000)
c. $43,706 (Cost = $20,000); $51,148 (Cost = $30,000); $58,589 (Cost = $40,000)

7.26 a. $\widehat{\text{Salary}} = -5609.3722 + 3.7938\text{ BA} + 81.9459\text{ RBI} + 897.2709\text{ Experience} - 22.5490\text{ Experience}^2$. The negative coefficient of the quadratic term implies an inverted U-shape influence of Experience on salary.
b. 19.90 years

7.28 a. $\widehat{\text{Time}} = 14.4886 + 0.7502\text{ Parts}$ (Linear);
$\widehat{\text{Time}} = -6.7165 + 0.4476\text{ Parts} + 0.0025\text{ Parts}^2$ (Quadratic)
b. Higher Adjusted R^2 for the quadratic model.
c. 20.53

7.30 a. $\widehat{\text{Watches}} = 32.1839 - 0.0232\text{ Time} + 5.9820\text{ Male}$
For every 50 second increase in the time, there is a decrease of about one watch.
$\widehat{\text{Watches}} = 25.43$ (Male), 19.45 (Female)
b. $\widehat{\text{Watches}} = 117.2733 - 15.5293\ \ln(\text{Time}) + 5.7493\text{ Male}$
For every 10% increase in the time, there is a decrease of about 1.55 watches.
$\widehat{\text{Watches}} = 25.03$ (Male); 19.28 (Female)
c. Logarithmic Model because of its higher R^2 (0.6437 > 0.6335)

7.32 a. $\widehat{\text{Cost}} = 16776.04 + 475.75(23) + 147.78(65) - 271.95(76) = \$16,655.57$
b. $\widehat{\text{Cost}} = \exp\left(9.7378 + 0.0301(23) + 0.0093(65) - 0.0181(76) + \frac{0.2029^2}{2}\right) = \$15,912.73$
c. Exponential Model because of its higher R^2 (0.7099 > 0.6935).

7.34 a. $\widehat{\text{Savings}} = -40.8632 + 0.0041(10,500) = 2.6364$
$\widehat{\text{Savings}} = \exp\left(-112.0910 + 12.2033(10,500) + \frac{0.2446^2}{2}\right) = 2.5380$
b. Linear Model because of its higher R^2(0.7001 > 0.6498)

7.48 a. $\widehat{\text{Crime}} = \frac{\exp(9.0293 - 0.3454x_1 + 1.2729x_2)}{1 + \exp(9.0293 - 0.3454x_1 + 1.2729x_2)}$
b. At the 10% level, Age is significant, but Gender is not; neither is significant at the 5% level.
c. 0.8412 (Male); 0.5973 (Female)

7.52 a. $\widehat{\text{Pass}} = -0.9002 + 0.2981(3.8) + 0.0404(5) = 0.4343$
b. $\widehat{\text{Pass}} = \frac{\exp(-6.9321 + 1.4918(3.8) + 0.1948(5))}{1 + \exp(-6.9321 + 1.4918(3.8) + 0.1948(5))} = 0.4282$

7.54 a. Linear: $\widehat{\text{Acceptable}} = 0.9900 - 0.0037\text{ Age} - 0.2019\text{ Religious}$
Logistic: $\widehat{\text{Acceptable}} = \frac{\exp(2.5028 - 0.0209\text{ Age} - 1.0396\text{ Religious})}{1 + \exp(2.5028 - 0.0209\text{ Age} - 1.0396\text{ Religious})}$
Both variables are significant at the 5% significance level.
b. 74% (linear); 74.5% (logistic)
c. 0.6516 (Religious); 0.8410 (Not religious)

7.60 a. Choose Model 2 because its RMSE is slightly lower (37.2535 < 37.7394).
b. Choose Model 2 because its average RMSE is lower (38.5315 < 39.8582).

7.64 a. Choose Model 2 because its RMSE is lower (273.2006 < 305.1602).
b. Choose Model 1 because its average RMSE is lower (362.9936 < 365.2085)

7.66 a. Choose Model 1 because its RMSE is lower (7.3696 < 7.8195).
b. Choose Model 2 because its average RMSE is lower (6.7026 < 6.9891).

7.70 a. Both models have the same accuracy rate of 68%; so, choose any.
b. Choose Model 2 because its average accuracy rate is higher (75% > 74%).

Chapter 8

8.2 a. The Euclidean distance between observations 1 and 2 = 421.0001
b. The Manhattan distance between observations 1 and 2 = 421.3300

c. $\bar{x}_1 = 5130.10$; $\bar{x}_2 = 3.1790$; $\bar{x}_3 = 0.2330$; $s_1 = 2369.6638$; $s_2 = 0.3958$; $s_3 = 0.2211$.

The normalized Euclidean distance between observation 1 and 2 = 0.7902

d. x_1 min = 1346, x_2 min = 2.67, x_3 min = 0.01, $Range_1 = 7587$, $Range_2 = 1.16$, $Range_3 = 0.61$.

The min-max standardized Euclidean distance between observations 1 and 2 = 0.269.

8.6 a. The Euclidean distance between observation 1 and 2 = 0.469

The Euclidean distance between observation 1 and 3 = 0.8307

The Euclidean distance between observation 2 and 3 = 1.1705

$\bar{x}_1 = 5.0333$; $\bar{x}_2 = 3.3167$; $\bar{x}_3 = 1.4333$; $s_1 = 0.4774$; $s_2 = 0.2368$; $s_3 = 0.3114$.

The normalized Euclidean distance between observation 1 and 2 = 1.5533

The normalized Euclidean distance between observation 1 and 3 = 1.8437

The normalized Euclidean distance between observation 2 and 3 = 2.8573

b. The Manhattan distance between observations 1 and 2 = 0.8

The Manhattan distance between observations 1 and 3 = 1.1000

The Manhattan distance between observations 2 and 3 = 1.5000

x_1 min. = 4.3; x_2 min = 2.9; x_3 min = 0.9; $Range_1 = 1.9$; $Range_2 = 0.8$; $Range_3 = 1.0$

The min-max standardized Manhattan distance between observations 1 and 2 = 0.7329

The min-max standardized Manhattan distance between observations 1 and 3 = 0.7461

The min-max standardized Manhattan distance between observations 2 and 3 = 1.0789

8.8 a. Matching coefficients:

Observations 1 and 2 = 1/4
Observations 1 and 3 = 0/4
Observations 1 and 4 = 3/4
Observations 2 and 3 = 2/4
Observations 2 and 4 = 0/4
Observations 3 and 4 = 1/4

b. Most similar: Observations 1 and 4 have matching coefficients of 3/4.

Least similar: Observations 1 and 3, and 2 and 4 have matching coefficients of 0/4

8.12 a. Matching coefficients:

Observations 1 and 2 = 0/3
Observations 1 and 3 = 1/3
Observations 1 and 4 = 1/3
Observations 1 and 5 = 1/3
Observations 2 and 3 = 2/3
Observations 2 and 4 = 2/3
Observations 2 and 5 = 2/3
Observations 3 and 4 = 1/3
Observations 3 and 5 = 1/3
Observations 4 and 5 = 1/3

b. Most similar: Vehicles 2 and 3, 2 and 4, and 2 and 5 have a matching coefficient of 2/3. Vehicles 2 and 3 are both sedans without all-wheel drive while 2 and 4 are both manual without all-wheel drive, and 2 and 5 are both manual sedans.

Least similar: Vehicles 1 and 2 have a matching coefficient of 0/3. Vehicle 1 is an SUV with all-wheel drive, and automatic transition; vehicle 2 is a sedan without all-wheel drive, with a manual transition.

8.14 a. Matching coefficients:

Students 1 and 2 = 1/4
Students 1 and 3 = 0/4
Students 1 and 4 = 1/4
Students 1 and 5 = 2/4
Students 2 and 3 = 3/4
Students 2 and 4 = 2/4
Students 2 and 5 = 1/4
Students 3 and 4 = 3/4
Students 3 and 5 = 2/4
Students 4 and 5 = 3/4

b. Most similar: Students 2 and 3 and Student 4 and 5 have a matching coefficient of 3/4. Student 2 and 3 are both male undergraduate students who are not statistic minors. Student 2 is a math major, while Student 3 is not. Student 4 and 4 are both female non-math majors and non-statistic minors. Student 4 is an undergraduate student while Student 5 is a graduate student.

Least similar: Students 3 and 1 have a matching coefficient of 0/4. Student 3 is a male undergraduate non-math major, non-statistic minor; Student 1 is a female graduate math major, statistics minor.

8.16 a. Matching coefficients:

Observations 1 and 2 = 2/4
Observations 1 and 3 = 0/4
Observations 1 and 4 = 2/4
Observations 1 and 5 = 2/4
Observations 2 and 3 = 2/4
Observations 2 and 4 = 2/4
Observations 2 and 5 = 0/4
Observations 3 and 4 = 2/4
Observations 3 and 5 = 2/4
Observations 4 and 5 = 2/4

b. Jaccard's coefficients:

Observations 1 and 2 = 2/4
Observations 1 and 3 = 0/4
Observations 1 and 4 = 2/4
Observations 1 and 5 = 1/3
Observations 2 and 3 = 1/3

Observations 2 and 4 = 2/4
Observations 2 and 5 = 0/4
Observations 3 and 4 = 1/3
Observations 3 and 5 = 0/3
Observations 4 and 5 = 1/3

c. Most similar: The pairs of observations 1 and 2, 1 and 4, and 2 and 4 each have a matching coefficient of 2/4 and Jaccard's coefficients of 2/4.

Least similar: The pairs of observations 1 and 3, and 2 and 5 have matching coefficients of 0, and Jaccard's coefficients of 0.

Comparing Matching and Jaccard's coefficients: Jaccard's coefficients are all less than or equal to their corresponding matching coefficients.

8.18

Actual Class	Predicted Class 1	Predicted Class 0
Class 1	3	2
Class 0	2	3

8.22 Misclassification rate = 0.02
Accuracy rate = 0.98
Sensitivity = 0.9820
Precision = 0.9750
Specificity = 0.9782

8.24 a. Lift (1:5) = 0.8571
b. Lift (1:8) = 1.0714

8.32 a. At cutoff value = 0.25

Actual Class	Predicted Class 1	Predicted Class 0
Class 1	18	1
Class 0	45	36

At cutoff value = 0.5

Actual Class	Predicted Class 1	Predicted Class 0
Class 1	14	5
Class 0	12	69

At cutoff value = 0.75

Actual Class	Predicted Class 1	Predicted Class 0
Class 1	7	12
Class 0	2	79

b. At cutoff value = 0.25
Misclassification rate = 0.46
Accuracy rate = 0.54
Sensitivity = 0.9474
Precision = 0.2857
Specificity = 0.4444

At cutoff value = 0.5
Misclassification rate = 0.17
Accuracy rate = 0.83
Sensitivity = 0.7368
Precision = 0.5385
Specificity = 0.8519

At cutoff value = 0.75
Misclassification rate = 0.14
Accuracy rate = 0.86
Sensitivity = 0.3684
Precision = 0.7778
Specificity = 0.9753

c.

c. Cumulative lift chart

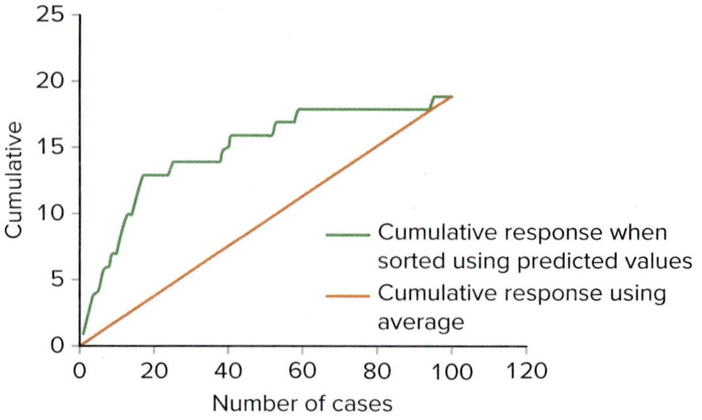

Decile wise lift chart

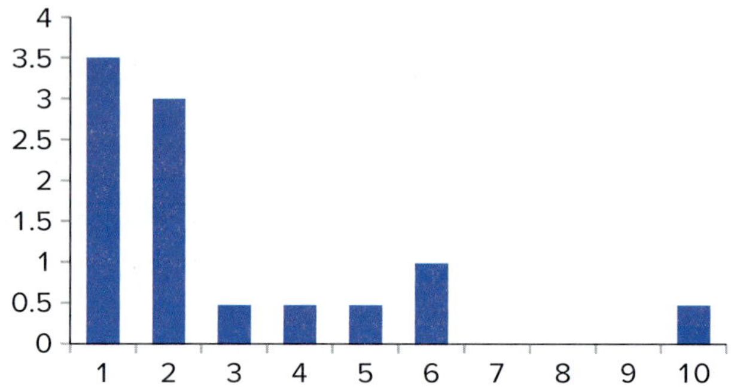

d. Lift (1:20) = 3.4211
e. Lift (1:50) = 1.6842

8.36 a. Using the covariance matrix, the weights for the first principal component scores are: $w_1 = -0.8074$, $w_2 = -0.5900$. The first principal component accounts for 86.1636% of the total variability of the data.

b. Using the correlation matrix, the weights for the first principal component scores are: $w_1 = -0.7071$, $w_2 = 0.7071$. The first principal component accounts for 85.3173% of the total variability of the data.

c. The numbers are different because the raw data are on slightly different scales. Hence, when we use the covalence matrix, the scale of the data influences its weight when calculating the principal components. When we use the correlation matrix, we remove the effects of scales on the calculated weights.

8.42 a. $z_{11} = 0.45$, $z_{21} = 0.2684$, $z_{12} = 0.5$, and $z_{22} = 0.1132$

b. The first principal component score of the first observation, $PC_{1,1} = -0.5227$

c. The second principal component score of the second observation, $PC_{2,2} = 0.1251$

8.46 a. There are 9 variables in the original data set.

b. The third principal component accounts for 13.16% of the variance in the data.

c. We need to retain 3 principal components to accounts for at least 85% of the total variance in the data.

Chapter 9

9.2 Analytic Solver:

a. Optimal value of k: 5

b. Accuracy = 50%; Specificity = 0.3846; Sensitivity = 0.6667; Precision = 0.4286.

c. The model is not effective due to low overall predictive accuracy and low AUC value (0.5085).

R:

a. Optimal value of k: 4

b. Accuracy = 0.5814; Specificity = 0.6190; Sensitivity = 0.5455; Precision = 0.6.

c. The model is not effective due to low overall predictive accuracy and low AUC value (0.5411).

9.4 Analytic Solver:

a. Optimal value of k: 9

b. Misclassification rate: 18.33%

c. Accuracy = 67.5%; Specificity = 0.8438; Sensitivity = 0; Precision = 0.

d. Accuracy = 77.5%; Specificity = 0.9375; Sensitivity = 0.125; Precision = 0.333.

e. The model is only slightly effective due to relatively low overall predictive accuracy and AUC value (0.5313).

R:

a. Optimal value of k: 6

b. Misclassification rate: 0.2163

c. Accuracy = 0.75; Specificity = 0.9375; Sensitivity = 0; Precision = 0.

d. Accuracy = 0.6; Specificity = 0.625; Sensitivity = 0.5; Precision = 0.25.

e. The model is only slightly effective due to relatively low overall predictive accuracy and AUC value (0.6406).

9.6 Analytic Solver:

a. Optimal value of k: 9

b. Accuracy = 91.5%; Specificity = 0.9564; Sensitivity = 0.4545; Precision = 0.4839; AUC = 0.8839.

c. The KNN classifier is better at classifying non-target class cases than classifying target class cases.

d. The plots show that the KNN classifier performs better than the baseline model. Both the lift curve and ROC curve lie above the diagonal line. The AUC value is 0.8839 suggesting an effective model.

R:

a. Optimal value of k: 10

b. Accuracy = 0.9036; Specificity = 0.9623; Sensitivity = 0.3902; Precision = 0.5424; AUC = 0.9118.

c. The KNN classifier is better at classifying non-target class cases than classifying target class cases.

d. The plots show that the KNN classifier performs better than the baseline model. Both the lift curve and ROC curve lie above the diagonal line. The AUC value is 0.9118 suggesting an effective model.

9.8 Analytic Solver:

a. Optimal value of k: 9

b. Accuracy = 79.17%; Specificity = 0.8889; Sensitivity = 0.7333; Precision = 0.9167.

c. AUC = 0.8037; The predictive performance measures and graphs suggest that the KNN classifier is effective in classifying the data.

d. Predicted admission outcome for the first new applicant: 1(Admit)

R:

a. Optimal value of k: 7

b. Accuracy = 0.8298; Specificity = 0.8421; Sensitivity = 0.8214; Precision = 0.8846.

c. AUC = 0.828; The predictive performance measures and graphs suggest that the KNN classifier is effective in classifying the data.

d. Predicted admission outcome for the first new applicant: 1(Admit)

9.10 Analytic Solver:

a. Optimal value of k: 3

b. Accuracy = 56.14%; Specificity = 0.625; Sensitivity = 0.48; Precision = 0.5.

c. AUC = 0.6031; The predictive performance measures and graphs suggest that the KNN classifier is slightly effective in classifying the data.

d. Predicted outcome for the first new consumer: 0 (Do not respond)

e. Accuracy = 54.39%; Specificity = 0.5313; Sensitivity = 0.56; Precision = 0.4828.

R:

a. Optimal value of k: 6

b. Accuracy = 0.6814; Specificity = 0.7681; Sensitivity = 0.5455; Precision = 0.6.

c. AUC = 0.7085; The predictive performance measures and graphs suggest that the KNN classifier is moderately effective in classifying the data.

d. Predicted outcome for the first new consumer: 0 (Do not respond)

e. Accuracy = 0.6106; Specificity = 0.4203; Sensitivity = 0.9091; Precision = 0.5.

9.12 Analytic Solver:

a. Optimal value of k: 3

b. Misclassification rate: 33.33%

c. Accuracy = 58.33%; Specificity = 0.2857; Sensitivity = 0.8438; Precision = 0.5745.

d. No. Part of the lift curve lies below the baseline.

e. Lift value of the leftmost bar of the decile-wise lift chart: 1.25

f. AUC = 0.6908

g. The predictive performance measures and graphs suggest that the KNN classifier is slightly effective in classifying the data.

R:

a. Optimal value of k: 9
b. Misclassification rate: 0.3072
c. Accuracy = 0.6167; Specificity = 0.6154; Sensitivity = 0.6176; Precision = 0.6774.
d. Yes. The entire lift curve lies above the baseline.
e. Lift value of the leftmost bar of the decile-wise lift chart: 1.5
f. AUC = 0.7216
g. The predictive performance measures and graphs suggest that the KNN classifier is moderately effective in classifying the data.

9.14 Analytic Solver:

a. Optimal value of k: 9
b. Misclassification rate: 27.78%
c. Accuracy = 63.89%; Specificity = 0.6154; Sensitivity = 0.6522; Precision = 0.75.
d. The plots show that the KNN classifier performs better than the baseline model. Both the lift curve and ROC curve lie above the diagonal line. The AUC value is 0.7508.
e. The predictive performance measures and graphs suggest that the KNN classifier is moderately effective in classifying the data.

R:

a. Optimal value of k: 9
b. Misclassification rate: 0.2459
c. Accuracy = 0.7042; Specificity = 0.5862; Sensitivity = 0.7857; Precision = 0.7333.
d. The plots show that the KNN classifier performs better than the baseline model. Both the lift curve and ROC curve lie above the diagonal line. The AUC value is 0.7697.
e. The predictive performance measures and graphs suggest that the KNN classifier is moderately effective in classifying the data.

9.16 Analytic Solver:

a. Optimal value of k: 7; Predicted outcome for the first new consumer: N (Do not install solar panels)
b. Misclassification rate: 36.55%
c. Accuracy = 66.30%; Specificity = 0.7371; Sensitivity = 0.5548; Precision = 0.5912.
d. The plots show that the KNN classifier performs better than the baseline model. Both the lift curve and ROC curve lie above the diagonal line. The AUC value is 0.6929.
e. The predictive performance measures and graphs suggest that the KNN classifier is moderately effective in classifying the data.

R:

a. Optimal value of k: 8; Predicted outcome for the first new consumer: Y (Install solar panels)
b. Misclassification rate: 0.3818
c. Accuracy = 0.6569; Specificity = 0.7535; Sensitivity = 0.5088; Precision = 0.5737.
d. The plots show that the KNN classifier performs better than the baseline model. Both the lift curve and ROC curve lie above the diagonal line. The AUC value is 0.7022.
e. The predictive performance measures and graphs suggest that the KNN classifier is moderately effective in classifying the data.

9.18 Analytic Solver:

a. Accuracy = 75%; Specificity = 0.7; Sensitivity = 0.7917; Precision = 0.76.
b. Lift value of the leftmost bar of the decile-wise lift chart: 0.9167; This implies that by selecting the top 10% of the validation cases with the highest predicted probability of belonging to the target class, the naïve Bayes model would identify 0.9167 times as many target class cases as if the cases are randomly selected.
c. AUC = 0.725
d. Predicted outcome for the first three new observations: Yes, No, Yes

R:

a. Accuracy = 0.7674; Specificity = 0.6; Sensitivity = 0.913; Precision = 0.7241.
b. Lift value of the leftmost bar of the decile-wise lift chart: 1.17; This implies that by selecting the top 19% of the validation cases with the highest predicted probability of belonging to the target class, the naïve Bayes model would identify 1.17 times as many target class cases as if the cases are randomly selected.
c. AUC = 0.7196
d. Predicted outcome for the first three new observations: Yes, No, Yes

9.20 Analytic Solver:

a. Accuracy = 69.23%; Specificity = 0.25; Sensitivity = 0.8889; Precision = 0.7273.
b. No, the lift curve does not lie above the baseline entirely.
c. AUC = 0.5417
d. Predicted outcome of the five new observations: 1, 0, 0, 1, 1
e. Accuracy = 46.15%; Specificity = 0.25; Sensitivity = 0.5556; Precision = 0.625; No, the lift curve does not lie above the baseline entirely; AUC = 0.4236; The naïve Bayes model that uses all four predictors performs better.

R:

a. Accuracy = 0.5; Specificity = 0.1; Sensitivity = 0.75; Precision = 0.5714.
b. No, the lift curve does not lie above the baseline entirely.
c. AUC = 0.6188
d. Predicted outcome of the five new observations: 1, 1, 1, 0, 1
e. Accuracy = 0.6154; Specificity = 0.1; Sensitivity = 0.9375; Precision = 0.625; No, the lift curve does not lie above the baseline entirely; AUC = 0.6344; The naïve Bayes model that uses only x_1 and x_2 performs better.

9.22 Analytic Solver:

a. Accuracy = 67.09%; Specificity = 0.7143; Sensitivity = 0.6; Precision = 0.5625.
b. Yes, the entire lift curve lies above the baseline.
c. AUC = 0.8051

d. The predictive performance measures and graphs suggest that the naïve Bayes classifier is effective in classifying the data.

R:

a. Accuracy = 0.7051; Specificity = 0.7273; Sensitivity = 0.6765; Precision = 0.6571.

b. Yes, the entire lift curve lies above the baseline.

c. AUC = 0.7871

d. The predictive performance measures and graphs suggest that the naïve Bayes classifier is moderately effective in classifying the data.

9.24 Analytic Solver:

a. Observation 1: $x_1 = 1, x_2 = 2, x_3 = 1$; Observation 2: $x_1 = 1, x_2 = 2, x_3 = 1$.

b. Accuracy = 68.75%; Specificity = 0.7826; Sensitivity = 0.4444; Precision = 0.4444.

c. AUC = 0.6787

d. Accuracy = 37.5%; Specificity = 0.1304; Sensitivity = 1; Precision = 0.3103.

R:

a. Observation 1: $x_1 = 1, x_2 = 2, x_3 = 1$; Observation 2: $x_1 = 1, x_2 = 2, x_3 = 1$.

b. Accuracy = 0.6774; Specificity = 0.8571; Sensitivity = 0.3; Precision = 0.5.

c. AUC = 0.4548

d. Accuracy = 0.2903; Specificity = 0.1429; Sensitivity = 0.6; Precision = 0.25.

9.26 Analytic Solver:

a. Observation 1: $x_1 = 1, x_2 = 1, x_3 = 2$; Observation 2: $x_1 = 1, x_2 = 1, x_3 = 1$.

b. Accuracy = 48.57%; Specificity = 0.8421; Sensitivity = 0.0625; Precision = 0.25.

c. AUC = 0.3664

d. Accuracy = 41.43%; Specificity = 0.1316; Sensitivity = 0.75; Precision = 0.4211.

R:

a. Observation 1: $x_1 = 1, x_2 = 1, x_3 = 2$; Observation 2: $x_1 = 1, x_2 = 1, x_3 = 1$.

b. Accuracy = 0.5797; Specificity = 1; Sensitivity = 0; Precision = NaN.

c. AUC = 0.5384

d. Accuracy = 0.5507; Specificity = 0.4750; Sensitivity = 0.6552; Precision = 0.4750.

9.28 Analytic Solver:

a. Accuracy = 75%; Specificity = 0.5263; Sensitivity = 0.92; Precision = 0.7188.

b. AUC = 0.8189

c. The predictive performance measures and graphs suggest that the naïve Bayes classifier is effective in classifying the data.

R:

a. Accuracy = 0.7907; Specificity = 0.5882; Sensitivity = 0.9231; Precision = 0.7742.

b. AUC = 0.759

c. The predictive performance measures and graphs suggest that the naïve Bayes classifier is moderately effective in classifying the data.

9.30 Analytic Solver:

a. Accuracy = 70.39%; Specificity = 0.1639; Sensitivity = 0.9421; Precision = 0.7186.

b. Lift value of the leftmost bar of the decile-wise lift chart: 1.22. This implies that by selecting the top 10% of the validation cases with the highest predicted probability of belonging to the target class, the naïve Bayes model would identify 1.22 times as many target class cases as if the cases are randomly selected.

c. AUC = 0.6223

d. The predictive performance measures and graphs suggest that the naïve Bayes classifier is only slightly effective in classifying the data.

R:

a. Accuracy = 69.35%; Specificity = 0; Sensitivity = 1; Precision = 0.6935.

b. Lift value of the leftmost bar of the decile-wise lift chart: 1.20. This implies that by selecting the top 11% of the validation cases with the highest predicted probability of belonging to the target class, the naïve Bayes model would identify 1.20 times as many target class cases as if the cases are randomly selected.

c. AUC = 0.6549

d. The predictive performance measures and graphs suggest that the naïve Bayes classifier is only slightly effective in classifying the data.

9.32 Analytic Solver:

a. Accuracy = 81.4%; Specificity = 0.9551; Sensitivity = 0.6593; Precision = 0.9305.

b. Lift value of the leftmost bar of the decile-wise lift chart: 1.92; AUC = 0.8298.

c. Predicted outcome for the first three individuals: 0 (Do not volunteer), 0, 1 (Volunteer)

R:

a. Accuracy = 0.8184; Specificity = 0.9712; Sensitivity = 0.6517; Precision = 0.9541.

b. Lift value of the leftmost bar of the decile-wise lift chart: 1.98; AUC = 0.8481.

c. Predicted outcome for the first three individuals: 0 (Do not volunteer), 0, 1 (Volunteer)

9.34 Analytic Solver:

a. Observation 1: Age = 1, Hours = 2; Observation 2: Age = 1, Hours = 1.

b. Accuracy = 48.75%; Specificity = 0.4079; Sensitivity = 0.5595; Precision = 0.5109.

c. AUC = 0.4865

d. The predictive performance measures and graphs suggest that the naïve Bayes classifier is not effective in classifying the data.

R:

a. Observation 1: Age = 1, Hours = 2; Observation 2: Age = 1, Hours = 1.

b. Accuracy = 0.566; Specificity = 0.28; Sensitivity = 0.8214; Precision = 0.5610.

c. AUC = 0.5562

d. The predictive performance measures and graphs suggest that the naïve Bayes classifier is not effective in classifying the data.

9.36 Analytic Solver:

a. Accuracy = 66.25%; Specificity = 0.375; Sensitivity = 0.95; Precision = 0.6032.

b. Yes, the entire lift curve lies above the baseline.

c. AUC = 0.8009

d. The predictive performance measures and graphs suggest that the naïve Bayes classifier is effective in classifying the data.

R:

a. Accuracy = 0.6835; Specificity = 0.6944; Sensitivity = 0.6744; Precision = 0.725.

b. Yes, the entire lift curve lies above the baseline.

c. AUC = 0.7565

d. The predictive performance measures and graphs suggest that the naïve Bayes classifier is moderately effective in classifying the data.

9.38 Analytic Solver:

a. Accuracy = 71.25%; Specificity = 0.75; Sensitivity = 0.6923; Precision = 0.8372.

b. The plots show that the naïve Bayes classifier performs better than the baseline model. Both the lift curve and ROC curve lie above the diagonal line.

c. AUC = 0.8310

d. The predictive performance measures and graphs suggest that the naïve Bayes classifier is effective in classifying the data.

R:

a. Accuracy = 0.7975; Specificity = 0.5667; Sensitivity = 0.9388; Precision = 0.7797.

b. The plots show that the naïve Bayes classifier performs better than the baseline model. Both the lift curve and ROC curve lie above the diagonal line.

c. AUC = 0.802

d. The predictive performance measures and graphs suggest that the naïve Bayes classifier is effective in classifying the data.

9.40 Analytic Solver:

a. Observation 1: Age = 2, Education = 2, Hours = 1; Observation 2: Age = 2, Education = 1, Hours = 1.

b. Accuracy = 87.5%; Specificity = 0.854; Sensitivity = 0.8929; Precision = 0.8772.

c. AUC = 0.8531

d. The predictive performance measures and graphs suggest that the naïve Bayes classifier is effective in classifying the data.

R:

a. Observation 1: Age = 2, Education = 2, Hours = 1; Observation 2: Age = 2, Education = 1, Hours = 1.

b. Accuracy = 0.7864; Specificity = 0.7556; Sensitivity = 0.8103; Precision = 0.8103.

c. AUC = 0.7395

d. The predictive performance measures and graphs suggest that the naïve Bayes classifier is moderately effective in classifying the data.

Chapter 10

10.2 a. Possible split points for days: {191, 208.5, 217.5, 229, 249.5, 287.5}

b. Possible split points for precipitation: {24.9, 35.55, 38, 40.95, 48.25, 58.2}

10.4 a. Gini index for root node: 0.2888

b. Gini index for age < 45.5: 0.1958

c. Gini index for age ≥ 45.4: 0.3648

d. Gini index for the split: 0.2803

e. Rules generate from this split: If age < 45.5, then the probability of a diabetes diagnosis is 11%. If age ≥ 45.5, then the probability of a diabetes diagnosis is 24%.

10.6 a. C

b. B

c. A

10.8 a. Minimum error: 0.1917; Number of decision nodes: 2.

b. Number of leaf nodes in the best-pruned tree: 3; Number of leaf nodes in the minimum error tree: 3.

c. Predictor variable: x_2; Split value: 63.5.

d. Accuracy = 83.75%; Sensitivity = 0.9762; Specificity = 0.6842; Precision = 0.7736.

e. Yes. The entire lift curve lies above the baseline.

f. AUC = 0.8365

g. Predicted response values of the new observations: 1, 1, 0, 1, 1; Class 1 probability of the first observation: 0.7887.

10.10 a. Number of leaf nodes: 8; Predictor variable: x_2; Split value: 62

b. cp value = 0.0075188; Number of decision nodes: 2

c. No

d. Number of leaf nodes: 3

e. Accuracy = 0.8235; Sensitivity = 1; Specificity = 0.625; Precision = 0.75

f. Lift value of the leftmost bar of the decile-wise lift chart: 1.42. This implies that by selecting the top 71% of the validation cases with the highest predicted probability of belonging to the target class, the model would identify 1.42 times as many target class cases as if the cases are randomly selected.

g. AUC = 0.8125

h. Predicted response values of the new observations: 1, 1, 0, 1, 1; Class 1 probability of the first observation: 0.7604

10.12 a. Number of leaf nodes: 6; Predictor variable: CreditCard; Split value: "Yes" (whether or not the customer has credit card debt).

b. cp value = 0.0357143; Number of splits: 2.

c. No

d. Number of leaf nodes: 3

e. Accuracy = 0.7119; Sensitivity = 0.8696; Specificity = 0.6111; Precision = 0.5882.

f. The model is moderately effective because 1) the lift value of the leftmost bar of the decile-wise lift chart = 1.51, 2) the lift curve lies above the diagonal line, and 3) AUC = 0.7506

g. Probability of the first new customer: 0.0714; Probability of the second new customer: 0.2593

10.14 a. Number of leaf nodes of the best-pruned tree: 3; Predictive variable: Income; Split value: 135,000; Number of leaf nodes of the minimum error tree: 5.

b. Accuracy = 97.25%; Sensitivity = 0.8182; Specificity = 0.9864.

c. The model is effective because 1) the lift value of the leftmost bar of the decile-wise lift chart = 8.18, 2) the lift curve lies above the diagonal line, and 3) AUC = 0.9352.

d. Probability of the first community member: 0.016; Probability of the second community member: 0.9589.

10.16 a. Number of leaf nodes: 3; Predictor variable: Age; Split value: 35; Rule: If Age is at least 35, then the individual is more likely to go to church.

b. cp value = 0.00233508; Number of splits: 27; Number of leaf nodes: 28.

c. Yes; Number of splits: 18; cp value = 0.00291886.

d. Accuracy = 0.5317; Sensitivity = 0.4482; Specificity = 0.6118; Precision = 0.5256.

e. AUC = 0.5467; The model is not effective because 1) the lift value of the leftmost bar of the decile-wise lift chart = 1.05, 2) the lift curve lies only slightly above the diagonal line, and 3) AUC = 0.5467.

f. 50%

10.18 a. Number of leaf nodes: 14; Rule: If the individual is 44 or older with an income of less than 15000, the individual is likely to download the mobile banking app.

b. cp value = 0.0085714; Number of splits: 4.

c. No

d. Accuracy = 0.5503; Sensitivity = 0.68; Specificity = 0.4189; Precision = 0.5426.

e. Lift value of the leftmost bar of the decile-wise lift chart: 1.02. This implies that by selecting the top 30% of the validation cases with the highest predicted probability of belonging to the target class, the model would identify 1.02 times as many target class cases as if the cases are randomly selected.

f. AUC = 0.5359

g. Number of new customers who are likely to download: 12; Probability of the first customer downloading: 0.6125.

10.20 a. Number of leaf nodes in the best-pruned tree: 2; Number of leaf nodes in the minimum error tree: 2; Rules: If GPA is less than 2.65, then the student is not likely to graduate within 4 years. If GPA is at least 2.65, then the student is likely to graduate within 4 years.

b. Accuracy = 90.25%; Sensitivity = 1; Specificity = 0.7045; Precision = 0.8730.

c. The lift curve lies above the baseline.

d. AUC = 0.8523

e. Students 2 and 3

10.22 a. Predictor variable: Income; Split value: 64.

b. cp value = 0.0122180; Number of splits: 2.

c. No

d. Accuracy = 0.8151; Sensitivity = 1; Specificity = 0.6071; Precision = 0.7412.

e. The model is effective because 1) the lift value of the leftmost bar of the decile-wise lift chart = 1.4, 2) the lift curve lies above the diagonal line, and 3) AUC = 0.8036.

f. Probability of the first gamer: 0.7725; Probability of the second gamer: 0.0714.

10.24 a. Possible split values for x_1: {179.5, 252, 289}

b. Possible split values for x_2: {66, 92.5, 105.5}

c. Possible split values for x_3: {6.25, 9.75, 14.25}

d. MSE of the partition $x_1 = 252$:

$MSE_{x_1 < 252} = (1/2) \times [(14 - 19)^2 + (24 - 19)^2] = 25$

$MSE_{x_1 \geq 252} = (1/2) \times [(15 - 23.5)^2 + (32 - 23.5)^2] = 72.25$

$MSE_{split(x_1 = 252)} = (2/4) \times 25 + (2/4) \times 72.25 = 48.625$

e. MSE of the partition $x_2 = 92.5$:

$MSE_{x_2 < 92.5} = (1/2) \times [(14 - 23)^2 + (32 - 23)^2] = 81$

$MSE_{x_2 \geq 92.5} = (1/2) \times [(15 - 19.5)^2 + (24 - 19.5)^2] = 20.25$

$MSE_{split(x_2 = 92.5)} = (2/4) \times 81 + (2/4) \times 20.25 = 50.625$

f. MSE of the partition $x_3 = 14.25$:

$MSE_{x_3 < 14.25} = (1/3) \times [(15 - 20.3333)^2 + (14 - 20.3333)^2 + (32 - 20.3333)^2] = 68.2222$

$MSE_{x_3 \geq 14.25} = (1/1) \times (24 - 24)^2 = 0$

$MSE_{split(x_3 = 14.25)} = (3/4) \times 68.2222 + (1/4) \times 0 = 51.1667$

g. Because split $x_1 = 252$ generates the lowest MSE, the best split is on x_1, and the best split point is $x_1 = 252$.

10.26 a. The split $x_1 = 7.5$ will generate the least MSE:

$MSE_{split(x_1 = 4)} = (2/3) \times (1/2) \times [(74 - 49.5)^2 + (25 - 49.5)^2] + (1/3) \times (86 - 86)^2 = 400.1667$

b. The split $x_2 = 22.5$ will generate the least MSE:

$MSE_{split(x_2 = 22.5)} = (1/3) \times (25 - 25)^2 + (2/3) \times (1/2) \times [(86 - 80)^2 + (74 - 80)^2] = 24$

c. The split $x_3 = 15$ will generate the least MSE:

$MSE_{split(x_3 = 15)} = (2/3) \times (1/2) \times [(74 - 49.5)^2 + (25 - 49.5)^2] + (1/3) \times (86 - 86)^2 = 400.1667$

d. Because the split $x_2 = 22.5$ has the lowest MSE, the best split is on x_2, and the best split value is 22.5.

e. Rules: If $x_2 < 22.5$, then $y = 25$; if $x_2 \geq 22.5$, then $y = 49.5$.

10.28 a. Minimum MSE: 27.8093; Number of decision nodes: 2

b. Number of leaf nodes in the best-pruned tree: 3; Number of leaf nodes in the minimum error tree: 3.

c. Predictor variable: x_5; Split value: 7.58; Rules: If $x_5 < 7.58$, then y = 36.13; If $x_5 \geq 7.58$, then y = 19.57.

d. RMSE = 5.8746; MAD = 4.5801.

e. Predicted value of the first observation: 15.47

f. Minimum = 15.47; Maximum = 36.1267; Average = 21.15.

10.30 a. Number of leaf nodes: 8

b. Predictor variable: x_5; Split value: 11; Rules: If $x_5 < 11$, then $y = 32$; If $x_5 \geq 11$, then $y = 19$.

c. Tree with the lowest cross-validation error: 21st tree; Number of splits: 28.

d. Yes; cp value = 0.027056.

e. Number of leaf nodes: 7

f. ME = −0.0074; RMSE = 5.6235; MAE = 3.9277; MPE = −3.9765; MAPE = 18.8877.

g. Minimum = 13.47; Maximum = 27.25; Average = 18.90.

10.32 a. Minimum MSE: 46.1824; Number of decision nodes: 2.

b. Number of leaf nodes of the best-pruned tree: 2; Number of leaf nodes of the minimum error tree: 3

c. Predictor variable: x_3; Split value: 102.53; Rules: If $x_3 < 102.53$, then $y = 299.18$; If $x_3 \geq 102.53$, then $y = 312.81$.

d. RMSE = 7.9182; MAD = 6.7371.

10.34 a. Number of leaf nodes of the best-pruned tree: 7; Number of leaf nodes of the minimum error tree: 7; Rules: If CreditCard = No, then TravelSpend = 2764.35; If CreditCard = Yes, then TravelSpend = 1502.48.

b. RMSE = 1011.3150; MAD = 740.4973

c. Predicted annual travel spending of the first customer: $1,747.83; Predicted annual travel spending of the second customer: $2,128.47

10.36 a. Predictor variable: SQFT; Split value: 2221; Rules: If SQFT < 2221, then Price = 970,000; If SQFT ≥ 2221, then Price = 1,700,000.

b. cp value = 0.01878; Number of splits: 9.

c. Yes; cp value = 0.023827.

d. Number of leaf nodes: 6

e. ME = −51189.13; RMSE = 467558.6; MAE = 332553; MPE = −34.90362; MAPE = 53.6871; Over-Predict because of the negative ME; The model is not very effective due to the large prediction errors.

f. Predicted price of the first house: $829, 762.6; Predicted price of the second house: $1,190,534.5.

10.38 a. Number of leaf nodes: 4

b. RMSE = 27.2155; MAD = 21.4680.

c. Mean = 221.947; Median = 234.857.

10.40 a. Predictor variable: Generation; Split value: 17; Rules: If Generation < 17, Price ≥ 12, then Sales = 7.7; If Generation < 17, Price < 12, the Sales = 13; If Generation ≥ 17, then Sales = 18.

b. cp value = 0.018209; Minimum validation error = 0.27671; Number of leaf nodes: 5.

c. Yes; cp value = 0.019442.

d. Number of leaf nodes: 4

e. ME = 0.0523; RMSE = 3.1054; MAE = 2.4323; MPE = −4.4364; MAPE = 17.9348.

f. Predicted per capita electricity sales: 16.6075

10.42 a. Number of leaf nodes in the best-pruned tree: 11; Number of leaf nodes in the minimum error tree: 11.

b. Predictor variable: games_started; Split value: 186.

c. RMSE = 4,636,301.156; MAD = 2,856,216.137.

d. Average predicted salary = 8,174,731.90

10.44 Analytic Solver:

a. Accuracy = 84.375%; Sensitivity = 1; Specificity = 0.8214.

b. AUC = 0.9375

c. Predicted value: 1; Class 1 probability: 0.5.

R:

a. Accuracy = 0.7742; Sensitivity = 0.5; Specificity = 0.84.

b. AUC = 0.87

c. Predicted value: 1; Class 1 probability: 0.56.

10.46 Analytic Solver:

a. Accuracy = 84.375%; Sensitivity = 1; Specificity = 0.8214.

b. AUC = 0.9241

c. Most important predictor: x_1

d. Predicted value: 1; Class 1 probability: 0.5.

R:

a. Accuracy = 0.8387; Sensitivity = 0.5; Specificity = 0.92.

b. AUC = 0.9

c. Most important predictor: x_4

d. Predicted value: 0; Class 1 probability: 0.43.

10.48 Analytic Solver:

a. Accuracy = 73.75%; Sensitivity = 0.7674; Specificity = 0.7072.

b. Lift value of the leftmost bar of the decile-wise lift chart: 1.8605

c. Predicted value: 1; Class 1 probability: 1.

R:

a. Accuracy = 0.8608; Sensitivity = 0.8250; Specificity = 0.8974.

b. Lift value of the leftmost bar of the decile-wise lift chart: 1.98

c. Predicted value: 1; Class 1 probability: 1.

10.50 Analytic Solver:

a. Accuracy = 84.50%; Sensitivity = 0.8144; Specificity = 0.8738; AUC = 0.8864.

b. Accuracy = 83%; Sensitivity = 0.8351; Specificity = 0.8252; AUC = 0.8865; Most important predictor: Characters.

c. 53.85% of the cases are predicted as spams.

R:

a. Accuracy = 0.8291; Sensitivity = 0.7864; Specificity = 0.8750; AUC = 0.8924.

b. Accuracy = 0.8442; Sensitivity = 0.8252; Specificity = 0.8646; AUC = 0.8912; Most important predictor: Hyperlinks.

c. 53.85% of the cases are predicted as spams.

10.52 Analytic Solver:

a. Accuracy = 66.67%; Sensitivity = 0.6341; Specificity = 0.7097.

b. Accuracy = 62.50%; Sensitivity = 0.6098; Specificity = 0.6452.

c. The bagging tree shows more robust performance because of higher AUC value (0.7352 vs. 0.6943).

R:

a. Accuracy = 0.7324; Sensitivity = 0.7857; Specificity = 0.6552.

b. Accuracy = 0.7042; Sensitivity = 0.8095; Specificity = 0.5517.

c. The bagging tree shows more robust performance because of higher AUC value (0.7878 vs. 0.757).

10.54 Analytic Solver:

a. Accuracy = 70.39%; Sensitivity = 0.9421; Specificity = 0.1639; AUC = 0.5560.

b. Accuracy = 70.39%; Sensitivity = 0.9421; Specificity = 0.1639; AUC = 0.5560; Most important predictor: CollegeParent.

c. Both models have the same performance.

R:

a. Accuracy = 0.7186; Sensitivity = 0.9402; Specificity = 0.2172; AUC = 0.5968.

b. Accuracy = 0.7186; Sensitivity = 0.9402; Specificity = 0.2172; AUC = 0.5968; Most important predictor: GPA.

c. Both models have the same performance.

10.56 Analytic Solver:

a. Accuracy = 71.25%; Sensitivity = 0.6562; Specificity = 0.75; AUC = 0.6911.

b. The single-tree model is more robust due to higher accuracy, sensitivity, and AUC values.

c. Probability of the first customer having plans to travel: 0.1; Probability of the second customer having plans to travel: 0.

R:

a. Accuracy = 0.7215; Sensitivity = 0.5806; Specificity = 0.8125; AUC = 0.7547.

b. The bagging ensemble model is more robust due to higher accuracy, specificity, and AUC values.

c. Probability of the first customer having plans to travel: 0.01; Probability of the second customer having plans to travel: 0.14.

10.58 Analytic Solver:

a. Accuracy = 54.95%; Sensitivity = 0.7996; Specificity = 0.3078; AUC = 0.5613; Most important predictor: Income.

b. The random trees ensemble mode is slightly more robust due to higher accuracy, sensitivity, and AUC values.

c. 100% of the individuals in the data set are likely to go to church.

R:

a. Accuracy = 0.5223; Sensitivity = 0.4632; Specificity = 0.5788; AUC = 0.5382; Most important predictor: Age.

b. The random trees ensemble mode is slightly more robust due to higher accuracy, sensitivity, specificity, and AUC values.

c. 33.33% of the individuals in the data set are likely to go to church.

10.60 Analytic Solver:

a. Accuracy = 84.38%; Sensitivity = 0.8523; Specificity = 0.8333; AUC = 0.9123.

b. The boosting ensemble model is more robust due to higher AUC value.

c. Probability of the first gamer making in-app purchases: 0.3945; Probability of the second gamer making in-app purchases: 0.2082.

R:

a. Accuracy = 0.8428; Sensitivity = 0.8571; Specificity = 0.8267; AUC = 0.9135.

b. The boosting ensemble model is more robust due to higher accuracy, specificity, and AUC values.

c. Probability of the first gamer making in-app purchases: 0.4908; Probability of the second gamer making in-app purchases: 0.4199.

Chapter 11

11.2 Analytic Solver: At most 6 clusters if the minimum distance between clusters is 5; At most 10 clusters if the minimum distance between clusters is 3.

R: At most 6 clusters if the minimum distance between clusters is 5; At most 10 clusters if the minimum distance between clusters is 3.

11.4 Analytic Solver:

a. Number of observations in the largest cluster (Cluster 1): 42; Average value of x_4 of the largest cluster (Cluster 1): 141.1191.

b. Number of observations in the largest cluster (Cluster 2): 22; Average value of x_4 of the largest cluster (Cluster 1): 157.3636.

c. Number of observations in the largest cluster (Cluster 2): 21; Average value of x_4 of the largest cluster (Cluster 1): 158.1905.

R:

a. Number of observations in the largest cluster (Cluster 1): 42; Average value of x_4 of the largest cluster (Cluster 1): 141.1191.

b. Number of observations in the largest cluster (Cluster 2): 22; Average value of x_4 of the largest cluster (Cluster 1): 157.3636.

c. Number of observations in the largest cluster (Cluster 2): 21; Average value of x_4 of the largest cluster (Cluster 1): 158.1905.

11.6 Analytic Solver: At most 3 clusters if the minimum distance between clusters is 0.8.

R: At most 3 clusters if the minimum distance between clusters is 0.8.

11.8 At most 3 clusters if the minimum distance between clusters is 0.8. The average value of x_5 is 13.14.

11.10 Analytic Solver:

a. At most 10 clusters if the minimum distance between clusters is 0.8; Number of transfers in the largest cluster (Cluster 1): 30.

b. At most 10 clusters if the minimum distance between clusters is 0.8; Number of students on the Dean's list in the largest cluster (Cluster 1): 35.

R:

a. At most 5 clusters if the minimum distance between clusters is 0.8; Number of transfers in the largest cluster (Cluster 3): 12.

b. At most 3 clusters if the minimum distance between clusters is 0.8; Number of students on the Dean's list in the largest cluster (Cluster 1): 31.

11.12 Cluster 1: 142 players; Cluster 2: 1 player; Cluster 3: 1 player.

11.14 Analytic Solver:

a. Yes. Variables are measured using different scales.

b. Cluster 1, which includes 31 countries, has the highest average GNI per capita (19439.6774), Cluster 3, which includes 3 countries, has the 2nd highest average GNI per capita (1106.6667), and Cluster 2, which includes 4 countries, has the lowest average GNI per capita (392.5).

R:

a. Yes. Variables are measured using different scales.

b. Cluster 1, which includes 31 countries, has the highest average GNI per capita (19439.6774), Cluster 3, which includes 3 countries, has the 2nd highest average GNI per capita (1106.6667), and Cluster 2, which includes 4 countries, has the lowest average GNI per capita (392.5).

11.16 a. Compared to Cluster 1, customers in Cluster 2 tend to be older (average age of 41.4706 vs. 24.5385), have higher income (average income of 73117.6471 vs. 28307.6923), have larger families (household size of 3.8824 vs. 2.0769), and spend more on pizzas annually (average spending of 1011.5882 vs. 290.4615).

b. Compared to Cluster 1, Customers in Cluster 2 are more likely to be married (15 vs. 6) and own houses (15 vs. 0).

11.18 Analytic Solver:

a. Number of cities in the largest cluster (Cluster 1): 28.

b. Average January average temperature: 31.6286; Average April average temperature: 51.7429; Average July average temperature: 73.8357; Average October average temperature: 55.1821

R:

a. Number of cities in the largest cluster (Cluster 1): 33.

b. Average January average temperature: 33.1455; Average April average temperature: 53.1030; Average July average temperature: 74.7727; Average October average temperature: 56.3939.

11.20 Analytic Solver:

a. Yes. Variables are measured using different scales.

b. At most five clusters are generated if the minimum distance between clusters is 10.

c. Number of community areas in the largest cluster: 33; Average median household income of the largest cluster (Cluster 2): 45228.0606.

R:

a. Yes. Variables are measured using different scales.

b. At most two clusters are generated if the minimum distance between clusters is 10.

c. Number of community areas in the largest cluster: 43; Average median household income of the largest cluster (Cluster 2): 45449.44.

11.22 a. Number of individuals in the largest cluster (Cluster 1): 28.

b. Cluster 1: low weight, low income; Cluster 2: non-Christian; Cluster 3: high income; Cluster 4: non-white, large family.

11.24 Analytic Solver:

- With $k = 2$, size of the larger cluster (Cluster 1): 23; Average distance for the larger cluster (Cluster 1): 0.7895.
- With $k = 3$, size of the largest cluster (Cluster 3): 24; Average distance for the largest cluster (Cluster 3): 0.8002.
- With $k = 4$, size of the largest cluster (Cluster 4): 21; Average distance for the largest cluster (Cluster 4): 0.6147.

R:

- With $k = 2$, size of the larger cluster (Cluster 2): 27; Average distance for the larger cluster (Cluster 2): 0.8629.
- With $k = 3$, size of the largest cluster (Cluster 3): 19; Average distance for the largest cluster (Cluster 3): 0.5980.
- With $k = 2$, size of the largest cluster (Cluster 3): 16; Average distance for the largest cluster (Cluster 4): 0.5807.

11.26 a. Average silhouette width: 0.54

b. Average silhouette width: 0.34

c. Average silhouette width: 0.33

11.28 a. Average silhouette width: 0.66

b. Average silhouette width: 0.54

c. Average silhouette width: 0.58

11.30 a. Average silhouette width: 0.26

b. Average silhouette width: 0.39

c. Average silhouette width: 0.46

11.32 Analytic Solver:

a. Size of the largest cluster (Cluster 2): 27; Cluster center values of the largest cluster: Comp = 0.6922, Att = 0.7019, Pct = 0.3269, Yds = 0.6784, Avg = 0.2571, Yds/G = 0.3333, TD = 0.5974, Int = 0.4804.

b. Size of the largest cluster (Cluster 1): 14; Cluster center values of the largest cluster: Comp = 0.6531, Att = 0.5442, Pct = 0.7095, Yds = 0.8063, Avg = 0.9606, Yds/G = 0.8719, TD = 0.8139, Int = −0.2428.

c. The clustering structures are similar for players in both data sets. The largest clusters in the two clustering structures contain better performing players with more touchdowns.

R:

a. Size of the largest cluster (Cluster 1): 16; Cluster center values of the largest cluster: Comp = −1.3499, Att = −1.3296, Pct = −1.1689, Yds = −1.3121, Avg = −0.7293, Yds/G = −0.9251, TD = −1.1840, Int = −0.8474.

b. Size of the largest cluster (Cluster 3): 13; Cluster center values of the largest cluster: Comp = 0.3080, Att = 0.3344, Pct = 0.1511, Yds = 0.1018, Avg = −0.3667, Yds/G = −0.6465, TD = 0.2621, Int = 0.6625.

c. The clustering structures are similar for players in both data sets. The first cluster includes the lowest performing quarterbacks, the second cluster includes the highest performing quarterbacks, and the third cluster includes the medium performing quarterbacks.

11.34 Analytic Solver:

a. Size of the largest cluster (Cluster 2): 56; Cluster with the highest number of homeruns: Cluster 3.

b. Size of the largest cluster (Cluster 1): 30; Cluster with the highest number of homeruns: Cluster 3.

R:

a. Size of the largest cluster (Cluster 1): 63; Cluster with the highest number of homeruns: Cluster 1.

b. Size of the largest cluster (Cluster 2): 22; Cluster with the highest number of homeruns: Cluster 1.

11.36 a. Yes. Variables are measured using different scales.

b. Cluster characteristics and GNI:

- Cluster 1: High population growth, low % of female population, high % of male population. GNI = 17930.
- Cluster 2: Relatively high population growth, high fertility rate, high birth rate. GNI = 270.
- Cluster 3: Medium on all indicators. GNI = 18663.2258.
- Cluster 4: Low population growth, high % of female population, low % of male population, low fertility rate, how birth rate. GNI = 4975.

11.38 Cluster characteristics:

- Cluster 1: Food items that are high in calories, total fat, potassium, carbohydrate, dietary fiber.
- Cluster 2: Food items that are high in saturated fat, cholesterol, sodium, and protein, but low in carbohydrate, dietary fiber, and sugar.
- Cluster 3: Food items that are high in sugar but low in calories, total fat, saturated fat, potassium, and protein.

11.40 a. No. All measures are percentage growth.

b. Size of the largest cluster (Cluster 1): 6; The cluster that has the highest average growth in GDP per capita: Cluster 2.

11.42 Analytic Solver:

a. Cluster characteristics:

- Cluster 1: Medium on all indicators.
- Cluster 2: Youngest, lowest income, lowest usage, and shortest tenure.
- Cluster 3: Older, medium income, high usage, and medium tenure.
- Cluster 4: Medium age, high income, high usage, and longer tenure.

b. Percent of unsubscribers: Cluster 1 (43.90%), Cluster 2 (93.94%), Cluster 3 (0%), Cluster 4 (0%); Cluster with the highest percent of unsubscribers: Cluster 2.

R:

a. Cluster characteristics:

- Cluster 1: Relatively younger, lower income, lower usage, and shorter tenure.
- Cluster 2: Youngest, lowest income, lowest usage, and shortest tenure.
- Cluster 3: Oldest, highest income, highest usage, and longest tenure.
- Cluster 4: Relatively older, higher income, higher usage, and longer tenure.

b. Percent of unsubscribers: Cluster 1 (46.15%), Cluster 2 (93.94%), Cluster 3 (0%), Cluster 4 (0%); Cluster with the highest percent of unsubscribers: Cluster 2.

11.44 a. Lift ratio of the top rule ({b} => {c}): 1.2277

b. The support count of 11 implies that 11 of the transactions include both {b} and {c}.

c. Lift ratio of the top rule ({g,e} => {f}): 2.5

d. The confidence of 100 implies that 100% of the transactions that include {g, e} also include {f}.

11.46 a. The least frequent item: d

b. Lift ratio of the top rule ({e} => {c}): 1.3333

c. Lift ratio of the top rule ({c,d}=>{e}: 2.6667

11.48. a. Number of rules generated: 10; Top rule: {c,g} => {e}; Lift ratio of the top rule: 2.3602

b. Number of rules generated: 2; Top rule: {e} => {c}; Lift ratio of the top rule: 1.5633

11.50 a. The least frequent item: e

b. Lift ratio of the top rule ({e} => {c}): 1.4006; The lift ratio implies that identifying a transaction with item set {e} as one which also contains item set {c} is 40.06% better than just guessing that a random transaction contains {c}.

11.52 a. Lift ratio of the top rule ({horror} => {action}): 1.6369; The lift ratio implies that identifying someone who watches a horror movie as one who also is going to watch an action movie is 63.69% better than just guessing that a random individual is going to watch an action movie.

b. Lift ratio of the top rule ({drama, horror} => {action, comedy}: 2.6190; The lift ratio implies that identifying someone who watches drama and horror movies as one who also is going to watch action and comedy movies is 161.90% better than just guessing that a random individual is going to watch action and comedy movies.

11.54

- Lift ratio of the top rule ({watermelon} => {cherry}): 1.3285; The lift ratio implies that identifying someone who purchases watermelon as one who also is going to purchase cherry is 32.85% better than just guessing that a random individual is going to purchase cherry.
- Lift ratio of the 2nd top rule ({watermelon} => {banana}): 1.1752; The lift ratio implies that identifying someone who purchases watermelon as one who also is going to purchase banana is 17.52% better than just guessing that a random individual is going to purchase banana.
- Lift ratio of the third top rule ({orange} => {apple}): 1.0417; The lift ratio implies that identifying someone who purchases orange as one who also is going to purchase apple is 4.17% better than just guessing that a random individual is going to purchase apple.

11.56 a. Most frequently downloaded song: *Here Comes the Sun*

b. Lift ratio of the top rule ({All You Need Is Love, Here Comes the Sun, Yellow Submarine} =>

({A Day in the Life}): 1.7730; The lift ratio implies that identifying someone who downloads *All You Need Is Love, Here Comes the Sun*, and *Yellow Submarine* as one who also is going to download *A Day in the Life* is 77.30% better than just guessing that a random individual is going to download *A Day in the Life*.

11.58 a. Number of rules generated: 11

b. Crime most likely to be committed in the department store: Theft; Crime most likely to be committed on the sidewalk: Narcotics; Crime most likely to be committed in apartments: Battery.

11.60 a. Number of rules generated: 8

b. Lift ratio of the top rule ({horror} => {action}): 1.2766; The lift ratio implies that identifying someone who uses Snapchat as one who also uses Instagram is 27.66% better than just guessing that a random individual uses Instagram.

11.62 a. Number of rules: 4

b. Lift ratio of the top rule ({HELOC} => {Checking}): 1.2214; The lift ratio implies that identifying someone who has a HELOC account as one who also has a checking account is 22.14% better than just guessing that a random individual has a checking account.

Chapter 12

12.2 a. 127.8867

b. 146.0634

c. The exponential smoothing model is preferred because it leads to the smallest value for *MSE* (551.54 < 649.95), *MAD* (19.94 < 20.40), and *MAPE* (14.03 < 14.46).

12.4 a. The 3-period moving average model is preferred because it leads to the smallest values for $MSE = 0.0009$, $MAD = 0.0244$, and $MAPE = 2.0832\%$; $\hat{y}_{26} = 1.1386$

b. The $\alpha = 0.6$ model is preferred because it leads to the smallest values for $MSE = 0.0007$, $MAD = 0.0213$, and $MAPE = 1.6115\%$; $\hat{y}_{26} = 1.2819$

12.8 a. $\hat{y}_t = 90.4938 + 1.1124t$; positive trend.

b. $\hat{y}_{54} = 150.56$

12.10 a. $\hat{y}_t = 9324.1892 + 1655.6701d_1 + 4094.4722d_2 + 1124.83d_3 + 189.4201t$; positive trend; the revenue consistently higher in the first three quarters, especially the 2nd quarter.

b. $\hat{y}_{2018:04} = 16{,}143.31$

12.12 a. $\hat{y}_t = 66.9930 + 1.4226d_1 + 1.7334d_2 + 0.2330d_3 + 0.0549d_4 + 1.3323d_5 + 0.5542d_6 - 2.5573d_7 - 3.6466d_8 - 3.6025d_9 - 3.2695d_{10} - 1.9032d_{11} + 0.3337t$; positive trend; consumer sentiment consistently higher in the first six months of the year.

b. $\hat{y}_{2018:12} = 103.03$

12.14 a. The quadratic trend seems to fit the data well.

b. Linear: $\hat{y}_t = 219.31 + 1.437802t$

Quadratic: $\hat{y}_t = 213.7527 + 3.6607t - 0.1588t^2$

The quadratic model is preferred because it has the higher adjusted R^2 (0.9550 > 0.8349)

$\hat{y}_{2018} = 233.88$; $\hat{y}_{2019} = 232.94$

12.16 a. Quadratic: $\hat{y}_t = 2975.811 - 2.3423t + 0.0552t^2$

Cubic: $\hat{y}_t = 2953.7899 + 0.6775t - 0.0331t^2 + 0.0007t^3$

b. The cubic model is preferred because it has the higher adjusted R^2 (0.9886 > 0.9741); $\hat{y}_{Jan\text{-}17} = 3{,}197.89$

12.20 a. $\hat{y}_t = \exp(4.0278 + 0.4087d_1 + 0.2025d_2 - 0.3273d_3 + 0.1552t + \frac{(0.4481)^2}{2})$

b. $\hat{y}_{2018:1} = 54{,}080.47$; $\hat{y}_{2018:2} = 51{,}387.09$

12.22 a. $\hat{y}_t = 241332.1180 - 4024.3036d_1 - 512.1212d_2 - 10589.2436d_3 + 4219.4278t + 27.9857t^2$

b. $\hat{y}_{2018:4} = 429{,}501.04$

12.26 a. Linear: $\hat{y}_t = 96.4907 + 0.8013t$

Quadratic: $\hat{y}_t = 90.0719 + 1.6036t - 0.0171t^2$

Cubic: $\hat{y}_t = 90.9063 + 1.4014t - 0.0064t^2 - 0.0002t^3$

b. The quadratic trend model is preferred because it leads to the smallest value for *MSE*, *MAD*, and *MAPE*; $\hat{y}_{2018} = 90.2568 + 1.5766 \times 59 - 0.0164 \times 59^2 = 126.07$

12.28 a. Linear: $\hat{y}_t = 154.4222 + 14.0343t$

Exponential: $\hat{y}_t = \exp(5.5922 + 0.0211t + \frac{(0.2182)^2}{2})$

b. The exponential trend model is preferred because it leads to the smaller value for *MSE*, *MAD*, and *MAPE*; $\hat{y}_{101} = \exp(5.6127 + 0.0204 \times 101 + \frac{(0.2085)^2}{2}) = 2201.59$

12.30 a. Linear: $\hat{y}_t = -1983.3665 + 664.5257d_1 + 924.0796d_2 - 671.7664d_3 + 229.3586t$

Exponential: $\hat{y}_t = \exp(3.9912 + 0.4799d_1 + 0.1781d_2 - 0.4081d_3 + 0.1583t + \frac{(0.4721)^2}{2})$

b. The exponential trend model is preferred because it leads to the smallest value for *MSE*, *MAD*, and *MAPE*;

$\hat{y}_{2018:1} = \exp(4.0278 + 0.4087 + 0.1552 \times 41 + \frac{(0.4481)^2}{2}) = 54080.47$

12.32 a. Linear: $\hat{y}_t = 238314.5250 - 16013.7660d_1 - 30045.4236d_2 + 9114.5188d_3 + 9731.0611d_4 + 19083.6035d_5 + 17153.7458d_6 + 22072.4882d_7 + 20695.8306d_8 - 959.0271d_9 + 13745.7153d_{10} - 5750.7424d_{11} + 360.2576t$

Exponential: $\hat{y}_t = \exp(12.3832 - 0.0669d_1 - 0.1291d_2 + 0.0363d_3 + 0.0385d_4 + 0.0742d_5 + 0.0668d_6 + 0.0848d_7 + 0.0801d_8 - 0.0037d_9 + 0.0537d_{10} - 0.0227d_{11} + 0.0014t + \frac{(0.0134)^2}{2})$

b. The exponential trend model is preferred because it leads to the smallest value for *MSE*, *MAD*, and *MAPE*;

$\hat{y}_{2018:10} = \exp(12.3884 + 0.0526 + 0.0013 \times 82 + \frac{(0.0124)^2}{2}) = 281{,}707.66$

12.36 The computer-generated model is preferred.

Analytic Solver: $\hat{y}_{58} = 23{,}867{,}993.50$

R: $\hat{y}_{58} = 23{,}354{,}173.31$

12.38 The computer-generated model is preferred.

Analytic Solver: $\hat{y}_{54} = 154.53$

R: $\hat{y}_{54} = 154.76$

12.40 The multiplicative model is preferred.

Analytic Solver: $\hat{y}_{36} = 427{,}119.82$

R: $\hat{y}_{36} = 428{,}075.17$

12.42 The additive model is preferred.

Analytic Solver: $\hat{y}_{96} = 93.06$

R: $\hat{y}_{96} = 90.73$

Chapter 13

13.2 Excel: The range of simulated observations is 13.8218.

R: The range of simulated observations is 13.69922.

13.6 Excel: Mean = 8.9700, Standard deviation = 1.3961, Maximum = 12, Minimum = 4

R: Mean = 8.9980, Standard deviation = 1.4609, Maximum = 12, Minimum = 5

13.10 Excel: Average demand = 11.0259 units, Standard deviation = 4.2025

R: Average demand = 11.1400 units, Standard deviation = 4.0186

13.16 Excel:

a. The likelihood of not meeting a weekly demand is 50.2000%. On average, the opportunity cost is \$8.5890 per week.

b. On average, the cost of having too many eggs is \$8.5958 per week.

R:

a. The likelihood of not meeting a weekly demand is 46.60%. On average, the opportunity cost is \$8.9915 per week.

b. On average, the cost of having too many eggs is \$8.39456 per week.

13.20 Excel: The likelihood of overstocking is 66.20% (331 out of 500 simulations), and the likelihood of understocking is 33.80% (169 out of 500 simulations).

R: The likelihood of overstocking is 65.40% (327 out of 500 simulations), and the likelihood of understocking is 34.60% (173 out of 500 simulations).

13.22 Excel: The average number of riders unable to get on the roller coaster is 7.06.

R: The average number of riders unable to get on the roller coaster is 7.755.

13.24 a. Optimal solution: $x_1 = 20$, $x_2 = 5$, and $z = 55$

b. Both constraints are binding, and there is no slack.

c. Constraint 1: Shadow price = 0.3846, Range of feasibility = 93.3333 to 245.0000

Constraint 2: Shadow price = 0.1538, Range of feasibility = 32.8571 to 86.2500

d. Range of optimality: x_1 = 1.7143 to 4.5000, x_2 = 1.3333 to 3.5000

13.26 a. Optimal solution: $x_1 = 3.9290$, $x_2 = 6.4286$, and $z = 111.4286$

b. Both constraints are binding, and there is no surplus.

c. Constraint 1: Shadow price = 1.4286, Range of feasibility = 48 to 160

Constraint 2: Shadow price = 0.14286, Range of feasibility = 35.0000 to 116.6667

d. Range of optimality: x_1 = 4.0000 to 13.3333, x_2 = 9 to 30.

13.30 a. Maximum revenue = \$2,833.3333 by making 33.3333 liters of Chardonnay wine and 22.2222 liters of Blanc de Blancs champagne.

b. Both grapes and processing time constraints are binding.

c. Grapes constraint: Shadow price = \$5.8333, Range of feasibility = 300 to 480 kgs

Processing time constraint: Shadow price = \$3.3333, Range of feasibility = 125 to 200 hours

d. Range of optimality: Chardonnay wine = \$37.50 to \$60.00, Blanc de Blancs champagne = \$41.25 to \$66.00.

13.32 Consuming 2.1739 cups of milk and 2.7536 cups of cereal will meet the daily requirements of calcium and vitamin D, at a minimum cost of \$1.2134.

13.38 a. $x_{11} = 5$, $x_{12} = 60$, $x_{21} = 45$, $x_{22} = 0$

b. $z = 115$.

13.42 a. The lowest shipping cost is \$238,000.

b. Manufacturer 1 should ship 6,600 batteries to Plant 2 and 3,400 batteries to Plant 3. Manufacturer 2 should ship 5,000 batteries to Plant 1 and 3,000 batteries to Plant 3.

INDEX

D

E

F

G

H

I

J

K

L

M

N

O

P

Q

R

S

T

U

V

W

Y

Z